A Critical History

of

WESTERN

PHILOSOPHY

EDITED BY

D. J. O'Connor, *University of Exeter*

 THE FREE PRESS
A Division of Macmillan, Inc.
New York

The Free Press
A Division of Macmillan, Inc.
866 Third Avenue, New York, N. Y. 10022

Collier Macmillan Canada, Inc.

First Free Press Paperback Edition 1985

Printed in the United States of America

printing number

2 3 4 5 6 7 8 9 10

Library of Congress Cataloging in Publication Data
Main entry under title:

A Critical history of Western philosophy.

   Bibliography: p.
   Includes index.
   1. Philosophy—History—Addresses, essays, lectures.
I. O'Connor, D.J. (Daniel John)
B73.C75   1985   190   85-10300
ISBN 0-02-923840-4 (pbk.)

Contents

Contents

A Critical History of Western Philosophy, which was first published in 1964, has been reprinted seven times since then and issued in a seven-volume Spanish translation. This paperback edition is designed to introduce the book to a wider public. The text and notes have not been altered except to correct minor mistakes and misprints, but the bibliography has been simplified and updated to meet the needs of present-day students and the general reader.

D. J. O'CONNOR

THERE ARE MANY HISTORIES OF PHILOSOPHY, and those who offer a new one to the public may fairly be asked how theirs differs from the rest. This is a history of western philosophy from the time of the early Greeks until the present day. It is designed for the use of undergraduate students of philosophy and for the intelligent general reader.

The writers have tried to do two things: (1) to explain the principal philosophical concepts and theories in the order in which they were developed; and (2) to evaluate and criticize them in the light of contemporary knowledge and to bring out whatever may be in them that is of permanent philosophical interest. A history of philosophy may be expected also to trace and estimate the historical influences of earlier thinkers on their successors. But philosophical analysis and criticism is a discipline very different from the history of ideas. Though each has its place as an intellectual enterprise, for the student of philosophy the first is vastly more important than the second. We have, accordingly, given space to exposition and criticism at the expense of purely historical questions. These have not been entirely neglected, but the discussion of them has been kept to a useful minimum.

It is naturally impossible, in the space of one volume, to give a critical account of all the important philosophers of the last twenty-five centuries. We have had, therefore, to be selective both in our choice of philosophers and in our treatment of their doctrines. In the chapters relating to those periods in the history of philosophy which are usually studied in British and American universities — the chapters on the philosophies of ancient Greece and of Europe and Great Britain during the seventeenth and eighteenth centuries — no major names have been omitted. But in dealing with the Middle Ages and with recent times, we have had to be more selective. Not everyone will be satisfied with all our choices, and a different editor with different contributors would no doubt have chosen otherwise. Where it has not been possible, for reasons of space, to discuss all of a philosopher's theories, we have tended to deal with questions of metaphysics and theory of knowledge at the expense of ethics and political theory. We have, for example, given more attention to Plato's important and influential theory of knowledge than to his fanciful, authoritarian politics — although these have not been ignored.

This selectivity has had two advantages which may be claimed as the main features of the book. The space saved by omitting discussion of minor figures and historical influences has been used (1) to give space to more philosophical criticism, and (2) to give a much more detailed treatment to important phases of thought than is usual in histories of this size. Accounts of major figures like Aquinas, Hume, Kant, Mill, and Hegel are much fuller than those ordinarily found in books of this scope.

We hope that the variety of the contributors will be a stimulus to the reader. They represent many different points of view, and they have been asked to treat their subjects just as they please, subject only to the needs of their readers. Simplicity and directness have been aimed at throughout, though naturally some philosophers are far more difficult to read and to explain than others. We have tried to avoid a common failing of books written for students of philosophy — simplifying to the point of caricature. But we hope that even the more difficult chapters will be found as lucid as the complexity of their subject matter allows.

D. J. O'CONNOR

I am glad to acknowledge the help and advice I have had from colleagues in editing this book. My principal thanks go to Professor Paul Edwards, the general editor of the Free Press philosophy series. He has given so much of his time and skill that he ought really to be named as co-editor. Sandra Litt, Margaret Miner and Donald Levy did most useful work in preparing the bibliographies. Marilyn Goldin undertook the task, a formidable one in a book of this size, of making the index. Their help has been invaluable.

Acknowledgment is gratefully made of the permissions granted by publishers and copyright holders to reprint material included in this volume. Specifically, acknowledgment is due the following:

George Allen & Unwin Ltd., for material from *The Correspondence of Spinoza*, edited by A. Wolf; and from *Human Knowledge* and *My Philosophical Development*, by Bertrand Russell.

Belknap Press of Harvard University Press, for material from *The Collected Papers of Charles Sanders Peirce*, vols. 1–6, edited by C. Hartshorn and P. Weiss.

Burns & Oates Ltd., for material from *History of Philosophy*, by F. C. Copleston. Doubleday & Company, Inc., for material from *The Will to Live*, edited by Richard Taylor.

Gerald Duckworth & Co. Ltd., for material from *Spinoza's Ethics*, translated by W. Hale White and A. H. Stirling.

Carl Hanser Verlag, for material from *Friedrich Nietzsche, Werke in drei Bänden*, edited by Karl Schlechta.

Harvard University Press, for material from *The Collected Papers of Charles Sanders Peirce*, vols. 7–8, edited by A. W. Burks.

The Library of Living Philosophers, for material from *The Philosophy of Bertrand Russell*, edited by P. A. Schilpp.

Thomas Nelson and Sons Ltd., for material from *Descartes: Philosophical Writings*, translated and edited by Elizabeth Anscombe and Peter Thomas Geach.

The Newman Press, for material from *History of Philosophy*, by F. C. Copleston.

Simon and Schuster, Inc., for material from *Human Knowledge* and *My Philosophical Development*, by Bertrand Russell.

D. J. O'C.

Early Greek Philosophy

A. P. CAVENDISH

EVIDENCE ON THE LIVES of the early Greek philosophers is scanty and inconclusive. Even their life dates, in most cases, are not exactly known. The dates cited below will place the chief philosophers mentioned in approximately the right chronological order. Where no dates of birth and death are given, "fl." indicates the time when the philosopher was active. All dates are, of course, B.C.

THALES	*about* 624 *to* 546
ANAXIMANDER	*about* 610 *to* 546
ANAXIMENES	*about* 585 *to* 528
PYTHAGORAS	*about* 571 *to* 497
XENOPHANES	*fl.* 540
HERACLITUS	*fl.* 504
PARMENIDES	*fl.* 501 *to* 492
ZENO OF ELEA	*fl.* 464
ANAXAGORAS	*about* 500 *to* 428
EMPEDOCLES	*about* 484 *to* 424
DEMOCRITUS	*about* 460 to 371
GORGIAS	*fl.* 444
PROTAGORAS	*about* 483 *to* 414

THE CITY OF ATHENS was the heart of Greek civilization, and from the time of Socrates, who died at the end of the fifth century before Christ, philosophy was centered there. But philosophy before Socrates had grown up elsewhere, principally in two places that had been developed as colonies from the Greek mainland. The Ionian cities of Asia Minor, in particular Miletus, were the home of Thales and the other Ionian cosmologists, of Anaxagoras, and of the Atomists Leucippus and Democritus. The Pythagoreans, Parmenides and his school, and Empedocles came from the south of Italy and Sicily. Although some of these early philosophers visited Athens, and Anaxagoras did much of his work there, Asia Minor and southern Italy were the cradles of Greek thought.

The history of early Greek philosophy is quite unlike that of later thought. There are special difficulties in the way of finding out what these early thinkers said and in deciding what they meant. We are dealing with a period of thought when no clear distinction had been drawn between questions of philosophy, science, and religion, or between scientific methods and magical procedures, or between history and myth. It is part of the achievement of the early Greek thinkers that their work did begin to draw the lines between these different fields and did raise questions about nature and man that could be approached by rational methods. Their achievement lies not so much in any specific doctrines as in creating an intellectual atmosphere conducive to the disinterested use of reason. This is why the pre-Socratic philosophers are rightly regarded as the ancestors of philosophy and of science also. However strange and far fetched their views may often appear to us in the twentieth century, the story of Western philosophy starts with the speculations of these Greek colonists in Asia Minor and southern Italy in the fifth and sixth centuries before Christ. We cannot understand Socrates, Plato, and Aristotle unless we know what went before them and provided the stimulus for their work.

Part of the difficulty in studying Greek thought before the fourth century is that first-hand documentary evidence is very scanty. Such of it as has come down to us has survived in quotations in later writers, the earliest of whom was Plato, who wrote in the fourth century before Christ. But many of our quotations are from much later sources. Indeed, one of the most valuable witnesses for our knowledge of early Greek philosophy is the philosopher Simplicius, who wrote in the sixth century of the Christian era, a thousand years after the writers with whom we are concerned. Apart from direct quotations, we have a good deal of comment and criticism by later writers on the views of these early philosophers. This, too, starts in the writings of Plato, and continues in the works of Aristotle and Theophrastus later in the same century. And much of this information is later still. Most of it, moreover,

is vitiated by the fact that the commentators were concerned not so much with giving disinterested historical accounts of their early predecessors as with refuting them in the interests of their own philosophical opinions. This is especially the case with Aristotle, who, in the first book of his *Metaphysics*, gives us a useful but very tendentious account of Greek thought up to his time. We have, therefore, to piece together the views of the early Greek philosophers from scanty and selective quotations and biased comments and criticism. The suspect nature of our sources must be borne constantly in mind, and in this first chapter of the history of Western philosophy we shall be concerned less than we shall be later with criticism of our material. The thought is hardly developed enough to bear the weight of serious criticism, and in any case, we know the opinions of these writers only in very rough outline.

How, then, do the problems of these early Greeks arise? The three great events of human life — birth, maturation, and death — have always occupied the imaginations of men. In every society, from the simplest to the most complex, these crises are embedded in a system of ritual and belief, the function of which, often unavowed, is to canalize and ultimately to dissipate the powerful and disturbing emotions of joy and sorrow, hope and fear. But sometimes, for whatever reason, there remains in the mind a kind of residual emotion, a sense of the mystery of life, which is the curiosity or wonder in which Plato and Aristotle saw the beginning of philosophy. And this sense of wonder is something very different from the everyday need for information of immediate use in the practical conduct of life.

The sense of the mystery of birth and death is capable of detachment and generalization from its original objects. On the one hand, we find in philosophy a preoccupation with the phenomena of change in general, with the visible impermanence of things, and with the supposed origin and possible destruction of the physical universe. On the other hand, there is a felt need to understand man's station in the world, his relationship with supernatural beings, and his prospects of happiness and of life after death. These interests are not a distinguishing mark of philosophy, for they are also the subjects of poetic myth and religious faith. The difference is often expressed by saying that in philosophy we have a *rational* attempt to understand the origin of things, and the nature and destiny of man.

The Ionians

THE MILESIAN COSMOLOGISTS

The earliest philosophical speculations were attempts to explain the origin and structure of the physical world. Thales of Miletus is named by

Aristotle as "the founder of this kind of philosophy," Anaximander and Anaximenes developed his materialist account of the origins of the universe. These thinkers held in common, first that there must be some entity from which all other things come into being, and second that this entity is some kind of material. They differed on the nature of the material.

Thales named water as the original material from which everything else is produced. Aristotle[1] suggested that Thales may have been led to his conclusion by the following considerations: (1) The nutriment of all things is moist, heat is generated from the moist and kept alive by it, the seeds of all things have a moist nature, and water is the origin of the nature of moist things. (2) Primitive and ancient notions were that Ocean and Tethys are the parents of creation and that the oath of the gods is by the water of the Styx. It seems that Aristotle did not, in fact, know how Thales arrived at his principle, and that no direct information was available to him. Thales said that "all things are full of gods" and that the magnet is alive because it can move iron.[2]

Anaximander differed from Thales in that he held that the origin of all things is not water but the *apeiron* (*apeiron* is usually rendered "indefinite", "infinite", or "unlimited".[3]) The *apeiron* is deathless, imperishable, everlasting, and ageless. Except that Anaximander applied these divine attributes to the *apeiron*, what he conceived its nature to be remains obscure to us. We do, however, have some information on his conception of the processes whereby other things were generated. A few remarks will suffice to convey the general character of the theory. The *apeiron* is the initial state of things, and in the beginning "that which could generate hot and cold" separated off from it in consequence of "the eternal motion." A kind of nucleus was formed, which separated into flame (hot and dry) and air (cold and wet). The flame formed a spherical sheath around the cold and wet. Then this cold wet core separated into air and a kind of mud, and the flame dried the mud. We thus have earth (cold and dry) in the center, water (cold and wet) partly covering the earth, air (warm and wet) surrounding the earth and water, and fire (hot and dry) enclosing the whole. Anaximander also explains the origin of the heavenly bodies and of living organisms. The former are rings of fire enclosed in tubes of mist. Formed through the disturbance of the fire caused by the expansion of the heated air, the latter arose from the mist when it was evaporated by the sun. The world order so formed is not permanent. Simplicius tells us that the *apeiron* is the source of existing things and then goes on to repeat what appear to be Anaximander's own words: "that from which things have their birth (*genesis*) is also that to which they return at death (*phthora*), according to necessity; for they give justice and pay the penalty to one another for their injustice."[4] Anaximander is also said by Theo-phrastus to have believed that there are innumerable other worlds besides this one in the *apeiron*.

Anaximenes proposed that air is the origin of all things. Other things are formed from air through the processes of condensation and rarefaction. The earth itself was formed through the condensation ("felting") of air; the earth is flat and floats on the air "like a leaf." Anaximenes explained various meteorological phenomena such as hail, rain, snow, thunder, and lightning. Worlds come into being and pass away in the course of "cycles of time." One sentence of Anaximenes' survives: "As our soul, being air, holds us together, so do breath and air surround the whole universe."[5] Anaximenes is said to have held that air is always in motion.

The fantastic speculations of the Milesians have been regarded by many as marking a revolution in human thought. Thales has been viewed as one who introduced the calm light of divine reason to a world governed by blind instinct and savage superstition. The early Ionians have been repeatedly hailed as the first "scientists"; the word "scientist" may well have some special sense in this connection, but its use can scarcely be other than misleading if we take into account its present-day connotation. For the fact is that these thinkers were not scientists. That is to say, they did not generalize cautiously from careful observation and experiment. On the contrary, they immediately proceeded by tenuous analogy to the most extensive generalization, thus exhibiting a characteristic of magical rather than of scientific thinking. A thoroughgoing appreciation of any kind of speculation must rest on the answers to three questions, namely: (1) What is the object of the speculation and what questions are asked? (2) What methods are employed to answer those questions? (3) What sort of answers are given? We may analyze the thought of the Milesian philosophers from this point of view.

According to Aristotle, the object of the Milesians' speculation was to find out what sort of material the world was made of. But Aristotle seems to have been mistaken on this occasion, for the evidence we have available does not suggest that this was its aim. On the contrary, they seem to have assumed that the world is made from such and such a material, and their chief aim appears rather to have been to give an explanation of *how* the world came to be, and how the things in it come into existence. That is to say, the question they tried to answer was not "What is the world made of?" but "How did the world and the things in it come into existence?" And of course asking such a question does rest on the assumption that the world had a beginning. There was, at that period, no evidence whatever to support such an assumption. Thus, the questions that the Milesians set out to answer were scientific questions only in the vaguest sense of the term.

Long before the sixth century people had asked these same questions and had answered them with tales that seemed plausible. From the very earliest times and in all countries men have been fascinated by the phenomena of birth and death and of the coming into being and passing away of things and by the transitory nature of the world. The Milesians exhibited no originality in their choice of questions, nor were they original in their methods of enquiry, so far as we can see. But they gave a new kind of answer. For various reasons, pre-philosophical myths about origin generally involve the postulation of the activities of semianthropomorphic deities; the creation of the world is often the outcome of such deities' sexual congress or of the pronouncement of a magic word. This is the feature, and the only feature, that is present in myths of creation and absent in Milesian cosmology. In myths the great mystery is explained by analogy with, and using the terminology of, biological processes, and the actors are anthropomorphic monsters. In Milesian cosmology these biological processes are replaced by *manufacturing processes* ("separating off" and "felting"), and the gods are replaced by a *material*. It is not "more rational" to prefer manufacturing processes to gods, unless you have good evidence in your favor. But though they were not scientists, they show a common-sense and unmystical attitude which is a part of the scientific temper.

HERACLITUS

The next philosopher to command our attention is Heraclitus of Ephesus. Although he was profoundly interested in the phenomena of *genesis* and *phthora*, of coming into being and passing away, of creation and destruction, he did not attempt a cosmology in the manner of his Milesian predecessors. Over a hundred fragments from his writings survive, enough for us to form a first-hand impression of his views. He wrote in an obscure, oracular style, full of puns and oblique allusions.

The fragments may be divided rather roughly into two kinds: (1) cosmic fragments, dealing with the processes of creation, and (2) anthropocentric fragments, dealing with the nature of the soul, of good and evil, and of justice and injustice. Aristotle said that for Heraclitus fire was the origin or material cause of things. This is supported by a few of the fragments:

> This ordered universe (*cosmos*) which is the same for all, was not created by any one of the gods or of mankind, but it was ever and is and shall be ever-living Fire, kindled in measure and quenched in measure.
>   Fire lives the death of earth, and air lives the death of fire; water lives the death of air, earth that of water. [6]

Evidently Heraclitus does not attempt to give an account of the creation of the cosmos, which he believes to be uncreated; he attempts to account only for the creation of the things within the cosmos. There is nothing permanent in the world: everything is changing forever. But these changes are governed by laws which Heraclitus, like Anaximander, conceives of in social terms. Strife and tension are fundamental features of existence. Many of the fragments of Heraclitus' writings are obscure, and it does not seem possible to assimilate them all into a single consistent whole.

The anthropocentric fragments are of much more interest, and give us some insight into Heraclitus' real intentions. It is clear enough from these that he does not suppose himself to be imparting theoretical knowledge: his tone is not that of disinterested science or academic philosophy. He has an urgent message. What seems to strike him most strongly is mankind's ignorance and lack of understanding. In particular, man does not understand "the purpose which steers all things through all things," and lack of understanding on this score engenders arrogance and lack of moderation, which are the greatest of sins. To get this understanding, one most "follow what is common," and what is common is the *logos*.

The word *logos* is a very important one in Heraclitus and in Greek philosophy in general. In Homer, it simply means "word" or "speech"; much later on it came to mean "law." Homer, as well as most primitive thinkers, often describes thinking as "speaking" and words as breaths. Poets and prophets are inspired through breathing in words, and therefore knowledge, from a divine source. Perception generally seems to be thought of as "breathing in." There is, of course, a universal tendency in primitive thought to identify the soul with air or breath. The sense in which Heraclitus used "*logos*" is uncertain. The traditional account says he taught that we breathe in the *logos*, that in sleep our minds lose contact with the *logos* except for the part of the mind preserved as a kind of root in breathing, and that "on awakening, it leans out again through the passages of the senses as if through windows, and making contact with that which surrounds us, it assumes the power of the *logos*." [7]

The *logos* is explicitly mentioned in seven fragments, in which Heraclitus states that (1) all things come into being according to the *logos*, (2) the *logos* is common, (3) though men are closely connected with it, and hear it, yet they are separated from it, and do not understand it, (4) the wise, having heard the *logos*, agree that all things are one, and (5) the psyche has a *logos* that is deep and increases itself. Men's lack of understanding (which is relieved by contact with the *logos*) is described as follows: men are unaware of what they are doing after they awake, the majority live as if they had understanding peculiar to themselves, they seem to themselves to understand but do not, they know only what seems, they do not see the meaning of things. Ignorance consists in not grasping certain unities, for example, those of "that which is wise," "all things," "day and night," "the straight and crooked way," and "up and down." The wisdom of the gods is superior to that of man. Understanding consists of greater awareness and wakefulness, which in turn is connected, rather unexpectedly, to dryness. Wisdom is, chiefly, understanding the purpose that governs things; its practical results are self-control, moderation and lack of presumption.

So far as our information takes us, it appears that Heraclitus introduced a new element into Ionian philosophy. This element is not his well-known doctrine that all things change, but much more the notion that the object of philosophical speculation is the acquisition of wisdom and understanding, rather than simply of factual or quasi-factual knowledge. The fruits of this wisdom are moderation and modesty, the two traditional Greek virtues. It is also evident that for Heraclitus the way to wisdom was not anything that we would call a rational process. Indeed, if we read our authorities literally, wisdom came about through "inspiration" or "breathing in the *logos*." He may have supposed that his puzzling way of speaking served to initiate the process in his audience. If so, he was by no means the last philosopher to entertain some such idea.

The Pythagoreans

PHILOSOPHICAL speculation existed at an early period in the Greek colonies of southern Italy. It may have been carried there by refugees from Ionia, but if it was, on arrival it suffered a profound change. While questions about the origin of the world and the processes of change were still important, the answers proposed to these questions were totally different in character from the Ionian ones. Moreover, a new interest, the interest in personal salvation, was made an object of philosophy. All this was marked by the incorporation into philosophy of religious conceptions quite foreign to the speculations of early Ionia.

Pythagoras of Samos was the first philosopher of this new type. He is said to have been born in Samos, an island off the coast of Ionia. However, he settled in the Greek colony of Croton in southern Italy. He left no writings (at least none are extant), nor did his immediate followers. The first written account of his thought was made by Philolaos of Tarentum in about 430 B.C., and a few fragments of Philolaos' work survive. Apart from this, we have summaries and accounts by early authors, notably Aristotle. Aristotle wrote a book on the Pythagoreans, but it has not survived. The revival of Pythagoreanism in the early Christian period is more fully documented, but the documents cannot be taken as giving an accurate account of the early doctrines. It is impossible to separate the opinions and discoveries of Pythagoras from those of his followers because the latter had a pious habit of attributing

everything to their leader. We may, of course, form conjectures, but they remain conjectures.

Three things are reasonably certain: (1) Pythagoras made important discoveries in what we now call pure mathematics; (2) he constructed a cosmology, in which "numbers" and certain numerical ideas play an essential part; and (3) he formed a community or brotherhood practising a "way of life" that distinguished its members from the rest of mankind — members of this brotherhood held certain religious and political views. The mathematical, the cosmological, and the religious were somehow united in the Pythagorean philosophy. In order to gain some understanding of this complex system, we must first consider some general features of the religion and mathematics of the time.

RELIGIOUS VIEWS

In order to study early religious beliefs, it is essential to clear the mind of preconceptions derived from Christianity. Christianity is not a typical religion: there are many religions that lack its chief features — its ethics and its dogmatism — and that appear not merely to embody different beliefs but to have quite different aims. It is true that one widespread, though not universal, characteristic of most religions is a belief in gods — that is, in nonhuman powers endowed with some kind of "personality." Religions having this feature may be classified rather roughly into two kinds by means of the two distinct attitudes that may be adopted towards gods. One attitude is that there is an unbridgeable gulf between gods and men, and that the greatest crime on the part of human beings is the attempt to ape the gods or in any way steal their power and prerogatives. The other attitude is that there is a very close relationship between gods and men, and that the chief aim of religious exercises is to acquire divinity, or at least to achieve some kind of union with the god. The former attitude is characteristic of Homer and the Pentateuch; the latter is found in Buddhism and in the so-called "mystery" religions. It is evident that the two attitudes are diametrically opposed.

Early Greek religion was of the former type. It was anthropomorphic: the relations between gods and men were really modeled on the relations between the aristocratic and servile classes in human society. The gods showed little concern for the private morality of their worshippers, but responded swiftly to conduct that might prejudice their own status. There was no reward and punishment after death except in very special circumstances, and the life after death was conceived of in negative and gloomy terms. Life in this world was conceived of as good, and death or life in the afterworld as bad and undesirable. The gods could be influenced in one's favor by prayer and sacrificial gifts; the help of the gods could bring success in worldly affairs.

The other type of religion became more prominent in Greece in the seventh century B.C. The new religion was not predominantly anthropomorphic, and the relations between gods and men were not conceived of in terms of social class. The central concept was that of salvation by purification, a purification that was usually ritual rather than moral, although the notion of ascetic abstention was often present. This purification secured for the initiate a better lot after death. Life was thought of as a bad thing, and this world as one of suffering; the aim was to escape from it to something better. Death did not secure this escape, because unless one had been saved, one was reborn to suffer again. The doctrine of reincarnation, or metempsychosis, was a prominent feature of this religion, and for obvious reasons. In Orphism, a typical religion of this type, initiation was said to spare souls from the cycle of birth and death. The Orphics called themselves descendants of the gods, and salvation was attained by ritual purification.

Even during antiquity there was heated debate as to what Pythagoras' religious doctrines were; but what persists is that (1) he believed in the transmigration of souls, (2) he proposed a way of life that included certain taboos or rules of abstention, and (3) he believed in the divine character of the human soul. If we believe that the well-known passages by Plato are representations of the Pythagorean view, he believed that the soul becomes divine by "copying the order of the *kosmos*." The religious life is the pursuit of truth, and salvation consists in the acquisition of a special kind of knowledge. The aim of philosophy is the achievement of immortality.

MATHEMATICS

I observed that mathematical knowledge was much pursued by the Pythagoreans, and I must now try to elucidate this. We can make real distinction between practical calculation and mensuration, on the one hand, and arithmetic (in the sense of theory of numbers) and geometry, on the other. The Rhind Papyrus (1700 B.C.) from Egypt exemplifies the former, and the *Elements* of Euclid (300 B.C.), the latter. The essential difference between the two does not seem to lie in the fact that one is practical and the other theoretical. For the Rhind Papyrus gives examples of various calculations some of which are of considerable complexity and not all of which have obvious practical importance. It calls itself a "guide for calculation, a means of ascertaining everything, of elucidating all obscurities, all mysteries, all difficulties." The methods used for solving the problems are not usually made explicit but have to be inferred from the examples. The so-called "proofs" consist simply in what we should call checking the answer. There is never any proof that the method used must always provide the correct answer in all cases. The most striking features of Euclid's work are (1) the summing up of a method of solution in

the form of a general proposition, and (2) the proof of this proposition by deductive steps from axioms. These features are absent from the Rhind Papyrus. It is said that Euclid was indifferent, if not opposed, to practical applications of his science. But it is to be noticed that this indifference to practice, and the associated notion that mathematics has an importance over and above practical uses, is already hinted at in the Rhind Papyrus.

It is not likely that Pythagoras discovered the axiomatic method of proof; probably it was developed by late Pythagoreans. But, according to Proclus, a fifth-century commentator of the Christian era, Pythagoras transformed the study of geometry into a liberal education, "examining the principles of the science from the beginning and proving the theorems in an immaterial and intellectual manner." Proclus also ascribes to the Pythagoreans the view that "the geometry which is deserving of study is that which, at each new theorem, sets up a platform to ascend by, and lifts the soul on high instead of allowing it to go down among sensible objects and so become subservient to the common needs of this mortal life."

COSMOGONY

The surviving material on the Pythagorean account of the origin of the universe hardly admits of any intelligible interpretation. It is almost as if we had before us a fragmentary communication in cipher, the key to which has been lost. Aristotle himself, to whom we are indebted for most of our reliable information, was evidently not acquainted with any clear and articulate statement of the theory. Furthermore, Aristotle's treatise on the Pythagoreans has not survived, and we have to rely on summary statements made by him in other connections.

According to Aristotle,[8] the chief elements of Pythagorean cosmogony were (1) numbers and (2) the ten principles. He says, "they supposed the elements of numbers to be the elements of all things, and the whole heaven to be a musical scale and a number." The ten principles are arranged by Aristotle in the following Table of Opposites: Limit and unlimited, odd and even, one and plurality, right and left, male and female, resting and moving, straight and curved, light and darkness, good and bad, square and oblong. These contraries are "the principles of things." Numbers, as "the element of things," are connected with the first two pairs of contraries as can be seen by the following remark: "the elements of number are the even and the odd, and of these the former is unlimited, and the latter limited." Objects of sense are formed out of number, as is the whole heaven. These numbers are conceived of as aggregates of units having spatial magnitude.

The conception of numbers as aggregates of units,

together with the Pythagorean habit of representing numbers by geometrical arrangements of dots, suggests some form of atomism. But there are several features of Pythagorean thought that cannot be reconciled with atomism. One of these is the account given of the process of cosmic generation. Aristotle reports that according to the Pythagoreans generation began with the "one" or "unit," which was constructed in an unspecified way. Then, when this "one" had been constructed, "the nearest part of the unlimited began to be drawn in and limited by the limit." This process is also described as follows: "from the unlimited there are drawn into it time, breath, and the void that constantly distinguishes the places of the various classes of things." The first things to be so distinguished are numbers. We know nothing of subsequent stages of creation.

The Pythagorean account of the structure of the cosmos is chiefly remarkable for two features: (1) The earth is not the center: the center is a fire that is not to be identified with the sun; and (2) the motion of the stars produces a musical harmony; the sounds the stars make are in harmony with one another. We have already seen that the Pythagoreans regarded "the whole heaven as a musical scale and a number." The soul was also said to be "a harmony," although this is explained by Aristotle in non-musical terms. Plato notes that the Pythagoreans regarded music and astronomy as two sister sciences.

The cosmological doctrines of the Pythagoreans have an affinity with views of which traces survive in many parts of the world. Thus, in China a system of musical sounds is related to the order of the universe and with the orderly sequence of the seasons. In India the sound OM is the creative principle of the universe; the Vedic chants maintain cosmic stability and compel even the gods. In Babylonia the creative deities were identified with musical instruments or with the sounds produced by them. Primitive peoples sometimes think of the sounds of nature as the voices of spirits who dwell in natural objects. Similarly, the Pythagoreans are said to have believed that the sound of a beaten gong was the voice of a demon imprisoned in the bronze.

It seems possible, therefore, that the Pythagorean identification of things with numbers may have been preceded by or associated with their identification of the essences of things with musical tones or chords. The Pythagoreans certainly saw the numerical relations involved in the tuning of stringed instruments and attempted to associate numerical relations with the natural sequence of sounds in a musical scale. Aristotle's lack of interest in music is much to be regretted, since it leaves us without good evidence on this matter. The nature of instrumental scales together with the imperfect discrimination of the ear lead us (and led the Pythagoreans) to view the audible continuum as composed of a sequence of distinct pure tones.

The Eleatic School

THE philosophers included here are Xenophanes, Parmenides and Zeno. Members of the school are characterized as holding two opinions: (1) There is in reality no such thing as change, and (2) existence or being is a unity. Xenophanes is the only member of the group to whom the first of these opinions cannot be attributed. He is also distinguished from the others by the fact that he did not attempt to support his views by reasoning. But Aristotle mentions Xenophanes together with Parmenides, and says that he "was the originator of this attempt to reduce all things to a One,"[9] and it is convenient to accept this classification.

XENOPHANES

Fragments of a poem are all that have survived of Xenophanes' work. These fragments indicate that he had interests and opinions somewhat at variance with those attributed to him by later writers. The most striking features of the views presented in the fragments are (1) a rejection of Homeric anthropomorphism; and (2) a skepticism with regard to the possibility of human knowledge. Later writers tried to attribute to him a cosmogony, but the variety of accounts produced shows that they were unable to extract a consistent scheme from his works. It is now impossible to determine the nature and purpose of Xenophanes' cosmological observations, but we may reasonably conjecture that his purpose was not to produce a plausible system in the Ionian manner.

It is clear from the fragments that Xenophanes engaged in a passionate denunciation of Homeric anthropomorphism. "Both Homer and Hesiod," he says, "have attributed to the gods all things that are shameful and a reproach among mankind: theft, adultery, and mutual deception."[10] This indicates some development of the moral consciousness, for the manners and customs of the gods of the Iliad accurately reflect those of the savage Greek warlords in whose honor the epic seems to have been composed. Xenophanes also remarks that men create gods in their own images: "Ethiopians have gods with snub noses and black hair, Thracians have gods with grey eyes and red hair," and horses and oxen would create gods in their own image if they could. In place of the Homeric pantheon, Xenophanes postulates the existence of one god who is "not at all like mortals in body or in mind," and who "moves all things by the thought of his mind." This god is absolutely motionless, and if there are other gods they are subservient to him. These positive pronouncements are moderated by skepticism. There has not been, nor will there ever be, "a man who knows about the gods and about all the things I mention." Statements on these subjects are merely conjectural; mortals can perceive or know only the appearances of things, not, presumably, their reality.

Xenophanes explicitly denies the possibility of knowledge by divine revelation.

PARMENIDES

Parmenides also expressed his opinions in a poem, and a substantial part of his poem has been preserved. It is divided into three parts: Prologue, Way of Truth, and Way of Seeming. In the Prologue, Parmenides claims to have received his knowledge from a goddess; the body of the poem is purportedly her address to him. This Prologue is something more than a literary device: the central thought is that knowledge can be acquired by divine revelation, and it is made clear that such knowledge is something wholly distinct from what common sense regards as knowledge.

The goddess tells Parmenides that there are "only two ways of seeking that can be thought of," and that it is possible to follow only one of these.

The first [way], *namely that* it is, *and that it is impossible for it not to be, is the way of belief, for truth is its companion. The other, namely, that* it is not, *and that it must needs not be, — that, I tell thee, is a path that none can learn at all. For thou canst not know what is not — that is impossible — nor utter it.*

It needs must be that what can be spoken and thought is; *for it is possible for it to be, and it is not possible for what is nothing to be.*

One path only is left for us to speak of, namely, that it is. *In this path are very many tokens that what is is uncreated and indestructible; for it is complete, immovable, and without end. Nor was it ever, nor will it be; for now it is all at once, a continuous one. For what kind of origin for it wilt thou look for?*[11]

It is not at all clear what the subject of these observations is, but it is something which is "uncreated and indestructible, complete, immovable, and without end." Later on we are informed that the entity in question is continuous, indivisible, finite, spherical. All these characteristics are established through arguments, which must be examined in due course. But there is another point we must consider first.

Parmenides constantly asserts that we cannot know or even think or assert what is not, and that what can be spoken or thought must be. This seems not so much paradoxical or incomprehensible as simply false. Yet he does not argue the point, and so we must conclude that what he means must be plainly and obviously true, must need only clear and forthright assertion in order to be accepted. Now the obvious interpretation of "knowing what is not" is "knowing that certain things do not exist." For example we know, perhaps, that unicorns do not exist, and we can think, believe, and say this, too.

Evidently, then, this is not what Parmenides means. There is, however, another sense of "know" which is appropriate in this context, and in which we *cannot* be said to know something that does not exist. This is the sense in which we are said to know a person, the sense of "being acquainted with." We may suppose that this is the sort of knowledge Parmenides has in mind. It is impossible to be acquainted with, to be in contact with, or to possess what is not. Similar considerations apply, less strongly, to "thinking of" and "saying": there is a sense in which you cannot contemplate what is not and cannot have a sign of something that does not exist.

We now proceed to Parmenides' arguments to prove that becoming and destruction are "mere names" and "not to be heard of." The arguments are as follows:

1. What is is uncreated and imperishable, for it is entire, immovable, and without end.
2. It was not in the past, nor shall it be, since it is now, all at once, one, continuous.

The second of these arguments is much more difficult to understand than the first, and it is not easy to see how the two conclusions can be made compatible. Nevertheless it does seem that Parmenides did regard them as compatible, and that what he wished to prove is most clearly stated in the first argument. If "it is entire, immovable, and without end" it does indeed follow that "it is imperishable", if not that "it is uncreated." Now the conclusion that "it is uncreated" is the subject of further argument:

3. For what creation wilt thou seek for it? How and whence did it grow? Nor shall I allow thee to say or to think, "from that which is not"; for it is not to be said or thought that it is not.
4. And what need would have driven it on to grow, starting from nothing, at a later time rather than an earlier? Thus it must either completely be or be not.

The argument of (3) is that it cannot be said or thought that what is is created from what is not, that there is nothing else for what is to be created from (this premise is suppressed), and therefore that what is is uncreated. The premise of (4) does not seem to be related to the conclusion "it must either completely be or be not." It does, however, provide another reason for denying an origin to what is. The reasoning would be (a) there is no need for it to begin at one time rather than another, (b) if it began it began at a particular time, (c) if it began at a particular time there must have been some need for it to do so. Hence it cannot have begun at any time.

There are two further arguments:

5. Nor will the force of true belief allow that, beside what is, there could also arise anything from what is not; wherefore Justice looseth not

her fetters to allow it to come into being or perish, but holdeth it fast. . . .

6. How could what *is* thereafter perish? and how could it come into being? For if it came into being, it is not, nor if it is going to be in the future.[12]

Concerning (5), we note that the statement "Justice looseth not her fetters" is very different in character from what has gone before. It is impossible to assess (6); on the face of it, it is an invalid argument.

The conclusion from these arguments, with the possible exception of (2), is that "coming into being is extinguished and perishing unimaginable," and the premises used are as follows:

a. What is is entire, immovable, endless.
b. It is now, all at once, one continuous.
c. It cannot be thought to come from what is not.
d. No need would have made it become at any particular time.
e. If it came into being or is about to be, it is not.

It is not clear whether Parmenides thought these statements could be deduced from an axiomatic "it is and cannot not be."

Two further arguments survive:

7. . . . Strong Necessity holds it firm within the bonds of the limit that keeps it back on every side, because it is not lawful that what is should be unlimited; for it is not in need — if it were, it would need all.
8. But since there is a furthest limit, it is bounded on every side, like the bulk of a well-rounded sphere, from the centre equally balanced in every direction; for it needs must not be somewhat more here or somewhat less there.
8a. For neither is there that which is not, which might stop it from meeting its like, nor can what is be more here and less there than what is, since it is all inviolate; for being equal to itself on every side, it rests uniformly within its limits.[13]

Argument (7) is purportedly proof that what is is limited on every side; (8) that it is spherical; (8a) that it is continuous. They may be analyzed as follows:

7. a. If it were in need it would need all.
b. It does not need all (suppressed).
Therefore: c. It is not in need.
d. If it were lawful that it should be unlimited, it would be in need.
Therefore: e. It is not lawful that it should be unlimited.
Therefore: f. It is limited.

8. a. It cannot be more here, less there.
Therefore: b. It is spherical.

8a. a. If that which is were discontinuous there must be something interposed between the discontinuous parts.
b. This could only be what is not.
c. What is not cannot be.
Therefore: d. What is must be continuous.
e. What is is inviolate.
Therefore: f. It cannot be more here, less there.
Therefore: g. It is evenly distributed.

It is evident from these arguments, especially (8) and (8a), that the mysterious unchangeable entity, which is the subject of Parmenides' discourse, is conceived of by him in spatial terms. It is also clear that some parts of the premises used in arguments (1) to (6), notably parts of premises (a), (b) and (c), are proved in arguments (7), (8), and (8a). Thus we can distinguish roughly two lines of argument: first, those that proceed from (c), (d), and (f), and are related to the principle that what is not cannot be, and cannot be thought, and second, that which proceeds from the principle that "what is is not in need", and introduces the figure of Justice or Necessity or Fate which holds what is in bonds or fetters. Both lines of argument lead independently to the denial of coming into being and destruction. Only the first line leads to the conclusions of (8a) that what is is continuous and evenly distributed. Only the second line of argument leads to the conclusion that what is is limited.

ZENO OF ELEA

Zeno of Elea was a pupil of Parmenides, and supported the latter's views as to the impossibility of motion and the impossibility of plurality. Zeno's work seems to have consisted of an aggregation of short, independent *reductio ad absurdum* arguments that he called "Attacks." It is therefore likely that, as well as supporting Parmenides, he was attacking the views of some other philosophers, and it is most likely that these were the Pythagoreans. According to Proclus, Zeno produced about forty arguments, or "Paradoxes" as they are commonly called, of which perhaps eight survive. Of these, two arguments against plurality and four against motion are the most important.

The arguments as they have been reported to us[14] are very difficult to understand, but the main gist of the two most important may be explained as follows:

1. Take any continuum — a segment of time, such as an hour, or a segment of space, such as a yard. It can clearly be subdivided into shorter segments — halves, quarters, eighths, and so on. Now, either this process of subdivision can go on *ad infinitum* or it cannot. In the first case, we have an infinite number of unextended pieces of space (or time) making up a finite extended segment. In the second, we have a segment of

space (or time) that is indivisible. And both of these alternatives seem impossible to accept. How *can* there be a piece of space that cannot in principle be subdivided? And how is it possible for an infinite number of unextended points to be put together into a finite extended continuum?

2. Consider a race between Achilles and a tortoise. They race over a 100-yard course, and the tortoise is given a start of 50 yards. Then Achilles can never catch the tortoise and pass him. For by the time Achilles has reached P_1 where the tortoise started, the tortoise has reached P_2, a little farther on. And by the time Achilles reaches P_2, the tortoise has moved on to P_3, and so on. Whenever Achilles reaches P_n, where his rival was a short time before, the tortoise will always have moved on to P_{n+1}. This will *always* happen, and though the distance between P_n and P_{n+1} will get smaller and smaller *ad infinitum*, it will never vanish.

The second argument is designed to show that motion is impossible. Of course, in practice Achilles *does* overtake the tortoise. Thus we have a clear conflict between logic and experience. We can resolve the conflict by pointing out the flaw in the logic or by deciding that experience is illusory. The first course seems the obvious one to follow but it is in fact extremely difficult to show just where the fallacy lies. Philosophers in recent years have been debating the point without arriving at a clear cut decision. Zeno, of course, wanted to draw the second conclusion in order to support Parmenides' general position.

Empedocles and Anaxagoras

EMPEDOCLES

Empedocles was a native of Acragas in Sicily. He had both of the two interests that dominated early speculation — an interest in the origin and fate of the physical world and an interest in the origin and fate of the individual soul. He wrote a poem on each of these topics and seems to have kept them quite separate. Only a few fragments from his poems have survived.

His poem "On Nature" shows the direct influence of Parmenides. Empedocles denies the possibility of creation and destruction, but his reasons for this conclusion have not come down to us. Unlike Parmenides, he allows the existence of some forms of change and motion, and his denial of creation and destruction is really a form of the conservation principle. In other words, the basic materials, of which Empedocles names four — earth, air, fire, and water — cannot be created or destroyed, but individual objects may be created or destroyed by a rearrangement of these materials. He calls the process of change "coming together," "scattering" or "being

borne apart," "interchange of place," and "mixing." He does not refer to "separation" as the opposite of "mixing" in the extant fragments, although Simplicius ascribes this view to him. Change is initiated and maintained by two opposing powers, Love and Strife.

The following picture emerges from Empedocles' remarks. The process of universal change is a cyclic one, so we cannot speak of an absolute beginning. A complete cycle is as follows:

1. The four "elements" are completely separate from one another, held apart by Strife.
2. Love enters in, and the process of mixing occurs as Love gains ascendancy. Individual objects are formed.
3. Everything is mixed together in a uniform homogenous sphere, held together by Love.
4. Strife once more prevails and the elements are gradually driven apart.

Thus there are two terminal states, the Rule of Love and the Rule of Strife, and two processes in which both Love and Strife operate with increasingly unequal effect.

The generation of mortal beings takes place in four stages:

1. The production of separate parts of plants and animals, not joined together.
2. The coming together of these parts — arms, legs, and the like — to form a multitude of monsters.
3. The chance formation, among these monsters, of viable forms.
4. The persistence of these viable forms by reproduction.

The poem called "Purifications" describes the fate of the human soul in terms that suggest analogies with the cosmic cycle. It is not easy to render the fragments of this poem consistent. First, a kind of Golden Age is described, in which no gods were worshipped, but only a goddess, "Cypris the queen." Blood sacrifice and meat eating were regarded as the greatest abominations. The present age is marked by the prevalence of these evil practices. It is plain that Empedocles supposed the age of Cypris to be one of universal happiness and innocence, and the present to be a time of misery and sin. The cause and process of man's downfall was probably described, but this part of the poem has not been preserved. Cypris is, of course, Aphrodite, the goddess of love.

Another set of fragments describes the fall from a godlike state of Empedocles himself. The cause of his fall is either his having shed blood or having "sworn a false oath." He is doomed to wander for 30,000 seasons far from the blessed, and to be born and reborn in many forms. But his term has nearly expired. He is now a prophet or a bard, and after his present life will be reborn no more and will return to the abode of the blest.

ANAXAGORAS

Although we have a good deal of information on Anaxagoras' work, the interpretation of this material is unusually difficult. Anaxagoras' main interest was certainly the same as that of earlier Ionian thinkers: he, too, undertook to give an account of the origins of the cosmos and of living beings. A central feature of this account is his denial of coming into being and perishing: "for," he says, "nothing comes into being nor perishes, but is rather compounded or dissolved from things that are. So they [the Greeks] would be right to call coming into being composition and perishing dissolution."[15] Such remarks have been taken, probably rightly, as evidence of Parmenidean influence. But our first problem is what Anaxagoras meant by this denial. It is not likely that he was simply denying the possibility of creation *ex nihilo* ("out of nothing"), or of destruction in the sense of complete annihilation, for no Greek philosophers, with the very doubtful exception of the Pythagoreans, ever asserted either of these things.

What Anaxagoras seems to have been denying is the possibility of producing some new material, or rather the possibility of producing something having properties not previously observed together in any material. For example, in chemical manufacturing processes, a new material seems to be produced from other materials that do not have the same appearance or properties as the product. In the time of Anaxagoras, the production of iron from iron ore and other metallurgical processes would perhaps have been the most familiar processes by which something new seems to be produced. Another process of this type would no doubt be the transformation of food into bodily tissue, although this process is by no means so obvious. Both metals and bodily tissues were mentioned as examples, either by Anaxagoras himself or by commentators. If what he meant to say was that new materials cannot be formed from the combination or transformation of existing materials, he differed essentially from earlier Ionian thinkers. It was usual to postulate the existence of one or of a small number of materials out of which everything else was made. The consequence for Anaxagoras was that all materials, all metals, and all bodily tissues were always in existence.

He goes on to state that (presumably before the formation of the cosmos) "All things were together, infinite in respect of both number and smallness; for the small too was infinite."[16] This remark, together with what follows it, has been the subject of much discussion. Air and ether are named as the greatest ingredients in the mixture "both in number and in size." There are also said to be in the mixture innumerable *seeds* "in no respect like one another." Also specifically mentioned as present are "the hot and the cold, the moist and the dry, the bright and the dark; and earth." It is not clear how, if at all, the other materials present are related to the "seeds." In this primeval chaos individual materials cannot be discriminated. Two reasons are given for this: (1) The great preponderance of air and ether, which overwhelms all the other things, and (2) the supposed intimacy of the mixture.

Apart from such a mixture of all materials, and not included in it, there is another entity, Mind (*nous*), the function of which is to set the mixture in motion and thus initiate formation of the cosmos. Mind is omniscient. It controls all living things and also initiates and controls a rotary motion in the mixture which causes a separation of "the dense from the rare, the hot from the cold, the bright from the dark, and the dry from the moist." The process of separation is clearly stated to be partial and incomplete. It was caused by the rotary motion, by what has always been supposed to be a centrifugal effect. However, it is the lighter that is separated from the heavier by this means, and this suggests, not a centrifugal force, but rather some process analogous to panning for gold dust in river sand.

In all this, the nature of the "seeds" remains unclear. Perhaps the defects of our sources prevent us from knowing exactly what Anaxagoras meant, or it may be that he himself was unclear about the implications of his doctrine. He states that the separation of materials is never complete: "There is a portion of everything in everything." By this he seems to mean that you can get relatively pure materials, as when you smelt iron ore, but never absolutely pure material. It is not clear why he should have held this view unless it is based on some empirical observation that no material, naturally occurring or manufactured, is ever pure. It must be remarked that purification, or rather separation, would for Anaxagoras cover every sort of chemical or physical transformation. It has been usual in interpreting Anaxagoras (and the interpretation is a natural and obvious one) to view the "seeds" as atomic particles of pure material. Any material aggregate, a lump of gold for example, would consist largely of gold particles or seeds mixed with relatively small quantities of other seeds. But if there *are* pure particles of gold or of anything else, then it is untrue that "there is a portion of everything in everything." It is not possible to combine an atomic theory of matter with a proposition that implies that matter is indefinitely divisible. Modern students of Anaxagoras have devoted much discussion to this problem without finally resolving it. This is one of the reasons why "no Presocratic philosopher has given rise to more dispute, or been more variously interpreted, than has Anaxagoras."[17]

The Atomists

LEUCIPPUS

Leucippus is said to have been the founder of

Atomism. No part of his writing survives, and our knowledge of his views rests entirely on secondary sources. He postulated the existence of atoms and a void, identifying the former with the Eleatic "being" and the latter with "not-being." His object seems to have been to explain the phenomenon of change whilst preserving the essential unchangeability of being. The atoms of Leucippus were indivisible (*atomos*, in Greek, means "uncut" or "indivisible"), infinite in number, and of many different shapes. They also differed in size, although, according to Aristotle, all were invisibly minute. A material object was an aggregation of atoms, and the creation or destruction of such an object consisted simply in the coming together or removing apart of the component atoms. It is then clear that the atoms themselves could not be created or destroyed. Leucippus also gave an account of the origin and destruction of worlds: it consists largely of the transposition of Milesian notions onto an atomic base. He is reputed to have denied the possibility of chance events and to have asserted that everything happens "according to necessity," but it would be an anachronism to regard him as a mechanist.

Democritus is often mentioned with Leucippus as having held the same, or similar, views concerning atoms and the void. He wrote a great deal, and a substantial number of fragments from his writings survive. It seems likely that his was one of the greatest and most comprehensive intellects of antiquity. He worked out not only an atomic theory of change but also theories of knowledge and morals, of which the former, at least, is based on Atomism. Nearly all the surviving fragments are ethical in content.

The chief feature of Atomistic cosmology is the postulation of the formation of a whirl or vortex in the chaos of atoms, by means of which the cosmos was formed. The ordering principle invoked by Democritus was the principle that "like seeks like." An important part of his work consisted of detailed explanations of various natural phenomena like thunder, lightning, winds, earthquakes, and the saltness of the sea. His explanations were purely speculative and were not inferred from observation, but they excluded appeal to supernatural causation. Biological phenomena also received attention, and although observation played some part here, explanations were largely speculative.

One of the most important parts of the theory concerns the soul, sense perception, and knowledge. The soul is made of spherical atoms akin to atoms of fire, and is contained in the body in much the same way that a gas or fluid is held in a container. Death is the separation of soul and body, and the soul is scattered when it leaves the body, there being nothing to hold the atoms together. All perception is touch, that is, contact between atoms. For example, visual perception is effected through a giving off by material objects of images that affect the air in some way, and consequently the eye.

There are two kinds of knowledge, genuine and obscure. The latter is acquired by sense perception, the former by some other, presumably intellectual, process. Perceptual knowledge is inferior because it is knowledge of appearances and of secondary qualities that do not exist in reality. The world of atoms is not susceptible to direct perception, and knowledge of it is attained by another route. Nevertheless, if beliefs acquired by intellectual insight contradict those of sense perception, the former must be rejected. So far as we can ascertain, knowledge of the atomic constitution of the world is not gained by any kind of rational argument, but rather it is derived through direct intuition.

The ethical doctrines of Democritus, which were very influential in ancient times, are what might be expected from his general tendency to eliminate the supernatural. The private aim of conduct, and of philosophical enquiry, is the attainment of a state variously described as well-being, cheerfulness, and tranquillity. The social aim is the maintenance of friendly cooperation with one's fellow men. There is no question of a divine origin of moral rules, or of supernatural reward and punishment either in the present life or after death. The gods exist, but are indifferent to the conduct of men. The soul is not immortal, and so cannot incur eternal reward or punishment. If we judge by his remark that "Some men, not knowing about the dissolution of mortal nature, but acting on knowledge of the suffering in life, afflict the period of life with anxieties and fears, inventing false rules about the period after the end of life," and by the opinions of later Atomists, one of the chief objects of Atomism is to free people of such fears.

The Sophists

XENOPHON, an essayist and historian of the fourth century B.C., describes the Sophists as "those who offer wisdom for sale in return for money to all comers." That is to say, they were professional educators, and in the fifth century B.C. there was evidently a substantial demand for their services. In earlier ages there was no such class, and Greek education did not subsist on a commercial basis. The training of a youth for public life was left in the hands of members of his family, or of a powerful friend or protector to whom he attached himself. Changes in the structure of Greek society seem to have impaired the efficiency of this system and to have led to a demand for paid teachers.

The wisdom imparted by the Sophists varied in content, but they all claimed to teach people the art of success in the conduct of life. Such a claim naturally involves some theory or assumption about what constitutes a successful life, about what the proper end of human endeavor is. Two kinds of theory on this point had already been adumbrated, one by the Atomists, the other by the Pythagoreans and by Empedocles. The theory of the former was that the proper end of conduct is worldly success, construed in a broad sense to include not only the acquisition of material goods but also the peaceful enjoyment of them, bodily and mental health, and the respect and friendship of one's fellow men. The other kind of theory is that the proper end of conduct is not any of these things, but rather the approval of some divine being, mystical communion, or post mortem translation to a state of bliss. These two theories are not, on the face of it, altogether incompatible, but they are usually made incompatible because people who hold the second theory suggest also that concern for worldly success is not merely irrelevant but actually inimical to what they conceive to be the true end of human endeavor.

The Sophists adopted the first theory, and were later to be attacked on this score by Socrates and Plato. That is to say, the Sophists believed the proper aim of human endeavor to be worldly success, construed usually in a broad and humane sense. Such an attitude is almost invariably associated with three philosophical opinions: (1) Skepticism, concerning the gods or the relations between gods and men, (2) human as opposed to a supernatural theory of morals, and (3) a contractual theory of the State. We find all these exemplified in the teachings of the Sophists.

Protagoras, the first and greatest of the Sophists, said, concerning the gods, that he could not know "Whether they exist or not, nor what they are like in form; for the factors preventing knowledge are many: the obscurity of the subject, and the shortness of human life." This skeptical attitude tends always to be transformed into a negative one: either the gods are placed at such a great distance from mankind that their existence ceases to be relevant, or else their existence is denied. Prodicus of Ceos attempted to trace the belief in gods to a natural interest in accounting for beneficial phenomena, and his approach was followed and developed by many later writers. Prodicus may have been directly influenced by Democritus, and he seems to have denied the immortality of the soul. Thrasymachus of Chalcedon said that "the gods do not see the affairs of men." Critias of Athens, although not a typical Sophist, nevertheless claimed that the story of the gods' concern for human conduct was invented by a wise and clever man to prevent secret crimes.

Protagoras said that "man is the measure of all things, of the things that are, that they are, of the things that are not, that they are not." This is usually taken to mean that all opinions are equally true and equally worthy of consideration. Plato, at least, understood it in this way, though it hardly seems to be a principle that would have commended itself to an able man like Protagoras. But in the absence of evidence, it is not profitable to speculate about Protagoras' meaning. His ideals of conduct were those of Democritus. Lycophron put forward the view that law is a social contract or covenant and, again according to Plato, Thrasymachus maintained that justice is the advantage of the stronger. Our knowledge of Sophistic teaching consists of disconnected dicta of this kind. We get a vague general impression of the tenor of their doctrines rather than any coherent outline of them.

The other obvious feature of Sophistic teaching is their insistence on the power and importance of words. Success in life was to be gained by mastery of the arts of rhetoric and of forensic oratory. The Sophists laid stress on persuasion rather than knowledge as the end of argument. Such a view would be a consistent concomitant of a thoroughgoing skepticism and would understandably lead to the reproaches in intellectual superficiality and cynicism that their teachings incurred. But their interest in persuasion led, too, to an interest in linguistic analysis and in the confusions that may occur in common speech. Thus, Prodicus spent much time on the analysis of minute differences in usage, and Antiphon seems to have developed a verbal therapeutic technique. Such developments may perhaps have been early anticipations of some of the practices of twentieth-century philosophy that will be discussed in the final chapter of this book.

However, conjectures about the meanings of the Sophists' doctrines are unrewarding in the absence of their works, which have not survived. Such evidence we have about them comes from suspect sources. Plato, for example, was bitterly critical of the Sophists and can hardly be supposed to have done them justice. But we may fairly see them as representatives and, to some extent, as pioneers of a major change of philosophical interest. This change of interest from the problems of nature to the problems of man is best shown to us in the work of Socrates. To this we may now turn.

2

Socrates and Plato

PAMELA M. HUBY

SOCRATES (470–399 B.C.) was a native Athenian and had a wife and three children. He was comparatively poor, at least later in life, but as a young man he was able to study the fashionable physical philosophy. When the Delphic oracle declared that no man was wiser than Socrates, he conceived it his mission to show up the ignorance of those of his fellow-citizens who thought themselves wise. To do so he developed a technique of asking awkward questions about fundamental problems of ethics and politics; his use of this technique made him unpopular with politicians of all parties, although it attracted to him a circle of young men, including Alcibiades, and later Plato. He was finally tried and put to death on the charge of corrupting young people and not believing in the gods of the city. He was courageous both as a soldier and as a citizen who carried out his public duties, and he claimed to be guided by an inner voice that checked him when he intended to do something wrong.

He left no writings, and our knowledge of him comes from the dialogues of Plato, the works of Xenophon, and a comedy by Aristophanes, "The Clouds." This evidence is not consistent, and interpretations of it vary widely.

PLATO (427–347 B.C.) was a member of one of the leading families of Athens, and was expected to become a politician. But he came under the spell of Socrates and was deeply shocked by his execution. He abandoned practical politics in order to carry out Socrates' reforming mission in his own way. In about 385 he set up the Academy in Athens to provide a higher education for young men who would be the future rulers or leaders of the Greek cities. In old age he unwillingly undertook to educate the young and ignorant ruler of Syracuse, Dionysius II, to fit him to be the leader of the Sicilian Greeks; but, as he had feared he would, he failed completely.

There are a large number of dialogues bearing his name, and a few letters. The majority of both are genuine.

IN THE MIDDLE of the fifth century B.C., under the leadership of Pericles, the Athenians were at the height of their glory, and prominent men from all parts of Greece came to visit their city. Among these were many intellectuals, including both philosophers like Anaxagoras, and Sophists, men who were prepared for a fee to take pupils and teach them a variety of newly-developed subjects. Most of these subjects, especially the art of rhetoric or public speaking, were thought to be useful in attaining political power or for winning cases in the law courts. Much of what the Sophists taught was sound and valuable, but much was meretricious, and the Sophists aroused hostility not only among the more conservative Athenians but also in Socrates and, after him, in his follower, Plato.

The Sophists were important historically because they brought home to thinkers even more vividly than Parmenides and Zeno what can and cannot be done with words and argument. Many of them concentrated on the art of verbal trickery in order to win their points at all costs. Their style is well brought out by a story told of the Sophist Protagoras: He sued a pupil for nonpayment of fees, saying that the pupil had promised to pay if he won his first law-suit. If the judgment was for Protagoras, the pupil must pay; if the pupil won, by the terms of the agreement he still ought to pay. (It would not escape an intelligent man that the pupil could reverse the argument and claim that he was released from obligation if he lost the suit.) On the whole, Protagoras had a good reputation, but many Sophists traded only in paradoxes and quibbles, and their activities tended to bring the whole process of reasoning by logical argument into disrepute. It seemed that anything and everything could be proved by such means. The virtue of Socrates and of Plato was that they retained faith in the powers of reasoning and started to tackle the immense problem of what forms of argument are valid and what are not. However, it would be a mistake to suppose that they singled out logic as a separate subject for study — in Plato's dialogues logical problems are mingled with ethical, political, and metaphysical ones, and advances are made on many fronts at once.

Socrates: the Search for Definitions

IT is impossible to distinguish sharply between the contributions of Socrates and those of Plato. It is probable that Plato's earliest dialogues give a fair impression of Socrates' methods and the subjects he chose to discuss, though it is not likely that the dialogues themselves are reports of actual conversations. From them we may conclude that Socrates believed that knowledge was the key to virtue and happiness, and that it was to be obtained by means of a search for definitions. The correct definition of a word would give an exact account of the essential nature of the object to which it referred. Thus, he would ask his comrades to say what justice or courage or beauty really was, and would try, seldom successfully, to guide them to an adequate definition. If they could once achieve this, their conduct, he believed, would improve in the light of the knowledge so gained.

Socrates gave no formal rules for making definitions; rather, he tested suggested definitions in a number of ways. He would not accept a list — of just actions, for example, as a definition of justice. He supposed that because all members of the list were called "just," there must be something they had in common, apart from the name, and it was this that was to be defined. Further, he would not accept as a definition a phrase that itself contained, either explicitly or tacitly, the word to be defined. This is illustrated by his criticism[1] of Theaetetus' definition of knowledge as geometry, the craft of shoemaking, and carpentry. According to Socrates, such a definition is unacceptable both because it is a mere list and because the craft of shoemaking may be defined as "knowing how to make shoes." Other suggestions fail on the grounds of vagueness or ambiguity or because they can easily be shown to be too narrow or too broad.

If a suggestion did not fail on any of these grounds, it was then tested by reasoning. Socrates took the definition as one of the premises of an argument, and the remaining premises were agreed on, some explicitly and many tacitly, between himself and his interlocutor. Deductions were then made from this set of premises, and the result might be unsatisfactory either because a contradiction was reached or because a conclusion could be drawn which was in conflict with the obvious facts. In either case, it followed that there was something wrong with the premises. As the rest of these had been agreed upon, it had to be the definition itself that was faulty; it therefore had to be rejected.

Here is a much abridged example. In the *Gorgias*,[2] Socrates considers Callicles' view that "good" means "pleasant." First, Callicles is induced to agree that a man cannot be both well off and badly off with regard to the same thing at the same time, and to agree that he can feel both pleasure and pain at the same time, as does a thirsty man at the moment when he begins to drink. But if "good" and "pleasant" are the same, it would not be possible for both agreed-upon statements to be true. Again, Callicles identifies good men with brave men and bad men with cowards, and says that good men are good in virtue of being filled with good things, and bad men bad because they are filled with evil things. So we would expect good men to feel only pleasure, which is good, and bad men only pain, which is evil. But in fact we find that brave men, who on Callicles' showing are good, and cowards, who are bad, seem to feel pleasure and pain to a roughly equal extent. The consequences of the proposed definition are therefore

15

clearly in conflict with the facts, and the definition cannot be accepted.

Socrates did not discuss the nature of a definition as such, but it is clear from his activities that he was seeking what are called "real" definitions. Various things may be aimed at by definition. A man may say in what sense he proposes to use a word himself or how he recommends that others use it; or, again, he may try, as does a dictionary, to show how the word is in fact used in speaking and writing. In either case he is giving a *nominal* definition — he is showing how the word is, or in his view, should be, used; he is not, except indirectly, concerned with the thing to which the word refers. Such a procedure is of no direct help to knowledge, except philological knowledge. Definitions can only directly give us knowledge, and be true or false, if they state something about the thing and not merely about the word. Socrates took it for granted that this could be done, and that when, for instance, he asked what virtue was, the correct answer would define the thing "virtue."

Various points are involved here.

1. Socrates assumes that when a man uses a word he does so because he recognizes the presence of, or has in mind, the thing or quality or whatever it may be for which the word stands. But at the same time he assumes that the man does not fully know what the thing is until he has given an adequate definition.

2. Socrates seems to have two rather different ideas of what a definition may do. Sometimes he seems to be satisfied if it indicates a distinguishing mark, i.e. some feature by which we may with certainty recognize the presence of the thing defined; thus, in the *Meno*[3] he defines figure as "that which alone of all things invariably accompanies color." But sometimes he wants more. He wants a statement of what in later terminology would be called the essence of the thing. By "essence" seems to be meant something which is peculiarly central to the thing, stated so that we have in a nutshell enough information to feel that now at last we really know what it is. Once we have this information, not only can we always recognize the presence of the thing defined, but we can also deduce from the definition a great deal more information about it.

Much of all this is mistaken. To indicate what we are to define we must start with a word, and words, particularly abstract ones, are usually vague and may easily be applied to a number of cases having little in common. Socrates himself recognized this fact in practice, as when he says in the *Laches*[4], that it is wrong to call unwise persistence "courage," though at first this had seemed the right thing to do. But he still felt that by some kind of higher insight we may be able to sort out the "real" meaning of the word from the confusion of subordinate usages. The belief in this one "real" meaning dies hard, but it seems to have no justification. Words have the meanings they have only because people use them in the ways that they do, and we cannot get beyond actual or proposed usage.

In spite of this, Socrates' search for definitions was not totally misguided and useless. Finding an adequate definition can clearly be a help in understanding the facts and not just an elucidation of verbal usage. We may put the point another way by saying that some nominal definitions are better than others just because they are better adapted to our need to use words in talking and thinking about the world. A good definition helps us to organize our thoughts in a useful way. An analysis of a complex into its parts — for example, the definition of "loam" as "a soil of clay, sand, and animal and vegetable matter" — can be extremely illuminating, as can a biological definition that places a plant or animal in an understood system of genera and species. These examples, however, are of cases where we can have a pretty accurate understanding of the application of our terms; after a little experience, we can usually recognize a polecat or a patch of loam if we meet one. Socrates' problem was more difficult because he was dealing with abstract terms whose application was not so clear, and he went wrong because he still believed that they must ultimately have some single, clear application. But the difference between "loam" and "justice" remains one of degree and not of kind: on the one hand, we cannot in every case say of a patch of soil that it definitely is or is not loam; and on the other hand, there are some actions that we would not hesitate to call "just" or "unjust," even though we might be uncertain about many others. Starting from this point we can have a fruitful discussion; and even if all the proposed definitions are rejected, they may still help in clarifying our ideas. So far as they achieved this, Socrates' methods were of extreme value. And an excellent example of this type of approach will be found later in Plato's *Theaetetus*.

Plato's Works

IN order to understand how Plato carried on Socrates' work we must be clear about the chronology of his writings. Few of the dialogues can be dated directly, but a study of the development of his style and language has enabled scholars to reach substantial agreement on a relative system of dating, and the order so achieved gives a consistent picture of Plato's philosophical development. The following rough grouping is suggested:

1. *Laches, Charmides, Lysis, Crito, Euthyphro, Apology.*

2. *Protagoras*, *Gorgias*, *Meno*.
3. *Symposium* and *Phaedo*.
4. *Republic* and *Phaedrus*.
5. *Theaetetus* (about 367), *Parmenides*, *Timaeus*.
6. *Sophist* and *Statesman*.
7. *Philebus* and *Laws*.

The position of the *Cratylus* is uncertain. The *Letters*, most of which are now believed to be genuine, belong to the period after 360. The earliest dialogues were written perhaps soon after Socrates' death in 399, and the latest dialogue, the *Laws*, was left unfinished when Plato died in 347. The titles are mostly taken from the names of speakers in the dialogues.

In most of the works, Socrates is the chief speaker, but many points of view are expressed by other characters, nearly all of whom bear the names, and are probably portraits, of Socrates' contemporaries. In general, these characters use arguments that would have appealed to the speakers, but we must sometimes attend carefully to the general tone of a passage to decide if Plato himself took the arguments seriously. Not even all that Socrates says is meant seriously; sometimes he seems to use obvious and deliberate tricks, and sometimes he makes a series of tentative approaches to a problem. On the other hand, it is often reasonable to suppose that the chief speaker in each of the later dialogues, whether Socrates or another, represents Plato's own views.

An exposition of Plato's philosophy is complicated by two other points. He says several times that the written word cannot convey philosophical teaching adequately, and we must therefore regard the dialogues as popular works in which much is omitted or simplified. His views were expressed fully only in oral teaching at the Academy, and of this teaching we know very little. Attempts to reconstruct it differ considerably, and it has even been denied that there *was* any such teaching. But this difficulty is of minor importance because the dialogues themselves are of profound philosophical value.

The other difficulty is that in many dialogues Plato introduces picturesque passages, generally known as "myths," in which he seems to be trying to express thoughts that he cannot put in a more straightforward form. Interpretation of them is not easy, but they cannot be ignored. In short, the dialogues are very far from being textbooks, and an account of Plato's philosophy must depend on interpreting and placing together passages from many different works.

It is convenient to divide this study into two parts. In the first, which covers the dialogues through the *Republic*, Plato is developing a consistent theory or interwoven group of theories. After writing the *Republic*, he wrote, perhaps as the result of discussions in the Academy, a series of "critical" dialogues which are far more technical and less dramatic than his earlier works. Most of these we shall study separately.

Plato's Earlier Philosophy

THE EARLIER THEORY OF FORMS

At the heart of Plato's philosophy lay his belief that the ordinary world that we know with our five senses cannot be fully real. He felt that it is, as Heraclitus and Parmenides in their different ways had shown, unstable and imperfect, shot through with change and decay. Knowledge, on the other hand, being certain and not open to error, must, Plato thought, be of something stable and perfect. Hence, unless we are to believe that knowledge is utterly unobtainable, there must be a world of stable and perfect objects behind the fleeting objects of sense. And the ultimate task of the philosopher is to explore this world. Many aspects of Plato's thought are connected with this quest.

The first aspect comes from Socrates and his interest in definitions. In his earliest dialogues Plato probably followed Socrates closely: these dialogues are mainly concerned with ethical questions like "What is courage?". But the method used, centering on the finding of definitions, led Plato on into other fields. It is never questioned in these dialogues that there really is something, justice, courage, or virtue, which we are seeking to define, and that it is only our own inadequacy that prevents us from reaching our goal. It was not a long step for Plato to become interested in the problem of knowledge and its objects in its own right. Socrates' line of thought could easily be extended far beyond the sphere of ethics. We can ask for a definition of anything we care to mention. Wherever a word is applied to a number of different things or situations, as when we say that Penelope and Helen are both women, or that this pencil is equal to that pencil and this stick equal to that stick, we may assume that there is something shared by these things or situations, and that it is this that we are to define when we define "woman" or "equal."

The extension of the search for definitions was not, however, the limit of Plato's thought. He not only wanted to deal with questions of the "What is X?" type, which can be answered by a definition of X, but also to ask, "Why is this X what it is?" when "this X" refers to a particular object or action — e.g. "Why is this beautiful statue beautiful?" This may seem a curious kind of question, but it is in line with the general trend of Greek philosophy. The question "Why is what is what it is?" was in the minds of most of the earlier, physical philosophers, and Plato is asking the same kind of question; but as he himself fully realized, he is finding a new kind of answer. In the *Phaedo*[5] he makes Socrates contrast two types of causal explanation, the physical or mechanical explanation, which was all that even Anaxagoras had been able to achieve, and an explanation in terms of purpose, which he himself was seeking. Anaxagoras and those like him wanted to reduce all causation to the kind found when, for example, one billiard ball hits another; Socrates, on the other hand, found the only satisfying form of causation in the activity of the mind, in particular in the situation where a man decides to pursue a certain end *because it is good*. Plato, in his turn, wanted all causal explanation, all explanation of why things are as they are, to be of this one type, with the idea of purpose extended far beyond the sphere of human mental events.

And so, to the question "Why is this X X ?" Plato answered, 'This X is X because it partakes of Xness," e.g. "This white flower is white because it partakes of whiteness," or "This just deed is just because it shares in justice." In so doing he treated words like "justice" and "whiteness" as the names of objects, but objects of a different order from those referred to by "this white flower" or "this just deed."

Plato concludes, then, that objects like justice and whiteness exist. But if so, we may go on to ask questions, and try to give answers, not merely about justice and whiteness but about the class of objects to which they belong. And what Plato has to say about this is generally known as his "theory of forms or ideas." This "theory" is not set out in full anywhere in the dialogues, and on many points the dialogues are uninformative or inconsistent. But the theory may be reconstructed in its essentials without much difficulty. The forms were universals, but not merely universals; they were unchanging objects existing apart from this world and more real than it, knowable by the mind as opposed to the senses, and the source of the existence of particular things in this world. Such is the theory in outline, and we shall have to take each part of it separately.

First, however, a word must be said about Plato's terminology. He was never given to a strict use of a technical vocabulary, but tended to use whatever way of speaking would make his points most clear. However, as soon as we try to use ordinary language to speak of extraordinary objects, as a philosopher tends to do, words begin to acquire a technical meaning. Further, the words we use tend at the same time to retain at least something of their common meaning and usage, and so very subtly to influence the form of the theory we are developing. As Sellars says,

> The creation of the Theory of Ideas was identical with the creation of the language of the Theory of Ideas. The differences between the philosophical and the everyday meanings of the words, as well as the awareness of these differences, was the slowly ripening fruit of philosophical argumentation about the Ideas, and of catch-as-catch-can wrestling with the perplexities they were introduced to resolve.[6]

It is therefore worth our while to make a survey of the terminology Plato used. First, he spoke of ideas or forms ("*idea*" or "*eidos*"). These two words

originally meant something like "shape," and in Plato's time "idea" had no reference to thoughts in the mind. Secondly, in speaking of an individual form he used either the standard abstract noun when one existed — e.g., "justice" ("*dikaiosyne*") — or else an expression of the type "the X itself" ("*auto to . . .* "), where "X" stands for an adjective in the neuter gender — e.g., "the just itself." Sometimes this is shortened to "the just" or "the holy." He was always ready to rely on the context to make clear what he meant.

This second way of speaking was probably influenced by another line of thought, which also led to a belief in the forms. This concept may be summed up as *the inferiority of particulars*; it took a number of forms.

1. In geometry we become familiar with the notion of perfect triangles and circles, and we distinguish these from the diagrams we draw on paper and the actual triangular or circular shapes of some tables, postage-stamps, or shawls. The diagrams and the tables are only approximately triangular, and if we measure them carefully enough we shall find out their flaws. The triangles that are the subject of our theorems, however, are necessarily perfect. If these exist, then, they must be very different from the things we see and touch. And to Plato it would have seemed absurd to suggest, as later philosophers might, that things about which we can reason so clearly and surely did not exist.

2. Particulars may be imperfect in other ways. Even the most beautiful woman or statue is not flawless, and we can conceive of something more beautiful still. We can, Plato believed, think of absolute beauty, but this too cannot exist in the world of sense.

3. Finally, there is the puzzling fact that particulars are able to be the subject of contrary predicates. Peter, for instance, may be tall when compared with James, but short by the side of John. But all the time he is one man, Peter. But if you can say two contrary things of the same man at the same time, it looks as if he is somehow imperfect and not fully real. That which was truly tall would surely never in any way be short.

By arguments like these, Plato was led to suppose that there existed, somehow, somewhere, those perfect objects which the things we know strive so unsuccessfully to emulate. Here again he had come back to the forms.

A final line of thought is illustrated most strikingly in the *Meno*[7]. Socrates questions an ignorant young slave about a geometrical problem, drawing a diagram for him to follow. By asking appropriate questions he leads the boy on to the correct answer without actually telling him anything at all. He thus shows that the boy has a knowledge of geometry that he did not know he possessed. He had never been taught geometry in this life, and must therefore, it is suggested, have acquired the knowledge before birth. Socrates concludes that men must have existed before birth, and at that time had full knowledge, which they lost in the process of being born and could now recall only with difficulty. This knowledge was of the forms, and that we had it accounts for our ability in favorable circumstances to reason out mathematical problems untaught and also to understand the meaning of expressions like "a perfectly straight line" and "perfect beauty" although we never meet examples of them in this world. On seeing imperfect examples, however, we are reminded of their perfect originals.

This is an outline of how Plato came to develop the theory of forms. Once he had adopted it he devoted his life to working out its consequences in all fields — political, moral, religious, educational, artistic, and scientific. He held that we are to regard the world we know with our senses as a world of change and imperfection that reflects dimly the eternal, perfect, and changeless forms, the only true objects of knowledge. Man is a compound of soul and body: his body belongs to this world, but his soul has affinity with the forms and is likely to be itself eternal, existing both before birth and after death.

There are many gaps and difficulties in this theory, and in the arguments on which it is based. Many of them were at least partially seen and considered by Plato himself in later life, and we shall leave criticism of them until we come to the relevant dialogues. But a number of points may be dealt with here.

Of the arguments from the imperfection of particulars the weakest is the last. The example given, that a man may be both tall and short, overlooks an important distinction, that between simple predicative terms and relational terms. Words like "tall" and "short" or "heavy" and "light" have no absolute meaning, but always imply reference to some standard of comparison. A man is tall either by comparison with some other man or by comparison with the average height of all men. Without such reference the term is empty of meaning. This implies that nothing is simply both tall and short, or both heavy and light. An object can only be so in relation to different things, and there is no ground for saying that Peter, for instance, is both tall and short in an absolute sense and thus the subject of genuinely contrary predicates and not fully real.

The other two arguments, about geometrical perfection and something like absolute beauty, are more subtle. But two points must be proved fully before we can conclude that anything like Plato's forms exist. We must be satisfied both that all the particulars of whatever kind with which we are acquainted fall short of perfection, and that the knowledge of perfection which Plato says we have can only be derived from the forms.

It may be that no material object is ever perfectly circular or has absolutely straight edges, and that if one examined such an object carefully enough, with a microscope, for example, one would find small irregularities in its outlines. But this has no bearing on the fact that many edges appear straight, or, to put it another way, that the appearance to me is of a straight-sided object. And if this is so, it is enough to give me the idea of straightness without going beyond the evidence of my senses. Even if this were not so, I might still attain an idea of straightness by comparing things that were less and less curved or crooked in outline, and so reach the notion of something that was not curved or crooked at all — i.e. perfectly straight. The idea of perfect beauty, however, is more complex. We might again say that we recognize that one thing is more beautiful than another and so form the idea of something so beautiful that nothing can be more beautiful than it. This does not mean, however, that we have an intuitive idea of absolute beauty or a mental picture of what an absolutely beautiful thing would be like; it means only that we can understand the expression "something so beautiful that nothing can be more beautiful than it." If this is all there is to it, then again we need have no recourse to the forms.

It seems, then, that the arguments from the inferiority of particulars do not go far toward establishing the existence of the forms. We may deal in a similar way with the slave boy's knowledge of geometry. It is undoubtedly true that suitably gifted people are able to work out mathematical problems in this way, but Plato's conclusion does not follow. Mathematics is a form of knowledge that is independent of experience in a way that history and botany, for example, are not. But for that very reason we do not need to postulate antenatal experience to explain how the slave acquired it. All that is needed is an understanding of the meanings of the terms used, such as "straight line," "triangle," or the words for numbers, together with certain assumptions about them which, in the case of Euclidean geometry, are derived from our experience of the world about us. They remain assumptions, however, and we, in effect, argue only that if they are true, certain theorems resulting from them are also true. If a geometrical system is set out formally, some of these assumptions will be treated as axioms, and the special terms used will be defined carefully. It then becomes clear that all we need for a knowledge of geometry is the ability to understand these axioms and definitions plus the ability to draw deductive conclusions. This is the ability used when I take the two statements that John is unmarried and that John has a brother-in-law, and conclude that John has a married sister. Plato's argument proves only that men naturally have this kind of reasoning ability and not that men existed before birth.

It is not clear whether Plato was aware that his example was a peculiar one and that similar cases could not easily be found. If the boy had shown knowledge of events in Greek history that had happened before he was born and of which he had never been told, or if he had produced, for instance, certain medical knowledge that he had never been taught, the case would be very different. The first would suggest that he had lived in Greece at a previous time, and would be evidence for the kind of reincarnation suggested by Pythagoras; the second would probably be nearer to what Plato wanted — evidence for some kind of scientific knowledge of principles, not of events, that might well be derived from acquaintance with the forms. But as such cases are not known to occur, it would have been implausible to use them as examples.

These criticisms should show that Plato was worried about a number of points of great philosophical importance; and although his treatment of them was unsatisfactory, at least he showed where the problems lay.

KNOWLEDGE AND BELIEF

So far we have been interested mainly in the proofs of the existence of the forms, but we must now go on to consider Plato's concept of how they were known and his general treatment of the nature of knowledge and belief. This is extremely complicated because he attempted to do justice not only to his own theoretical standpoint but also to the views enshrined in the common-sense way of using these terms. As a result, different aspects of the problem are dominant in different passages, and it is difficult to put them together in a satisfactory way. In a book of this kind, however, that is of little importance, for we are less interested in making a thoroughgoing but mistaken synthesis than in analyzing the various points concerned.

A basic distinction made by Plato is that between two different cognitive states which we may not too misleadingly call "knowledge" and "belief" (or "opinion"). What we know must be true, but what we believe may be true or false. In his earlier works, Plato paid little attention to false belief and concentrated mainly on the similarities and differences between knowledge and true belief. In the *Meno*,[8] both are treated in a common-sense way. A man may be said to *know* the way to Larissa if he has traveled there along it; he may have a *correct opinion* about how to get there even if he has never been there but has been told the route by someone else. The two men will be alike in that both can tell another, or themselves find, the way to Larissa. But the knowledge of the man who has been there is more firmly based and less likely to be distorted or lost than is the belief of the man who has not. Knowledge and true belief are here treated as similar in their immediate effectiveness, although they differ in their psychological foundations. Both are connected with the same kinds of objects, in this case ordinary, everyday facts. Plato suggests that belief can be turned into knowledge "by reasoning about

principles," which, in his passage on the young slave and his geometry, he identified with *anamnēsis*, the recall of the knowledge acquired before birth.

Such reasoning can hardly be applied to cases like the one using the example of the road to Larissa; but it can to studies like geometry. Plato probably had in mind the fact that in geometry — as in many other school subjects — there is a difference between learning parrot-fashion and learning with real insight. The slave, having had to reason things out for himself, necessarily acquired real insight; and indeed Socrates' whole method, in the moral as well as the mathematical sphere, would lead toward this end. Most people learn moral principles unthinkingly from their parents and teachers; and if the teaching is sound, they have true beliefs about morals. But it is only by thinking things out for themselves, as Socrates urged them to do, that they can attain real knowledge.

So far we have brought into the open no difficulties in connection with Plato's theory of knowledge and belief; but the account in the *Republic*[9] goes far deeper and inevitably raises awkward questions. Here, belief (*doxa*) and knowledge (*epistēmē*) are explicitly distinguished, both as being separate states of mind and as having different objects, knowledge of the invisible, intangible forms, opinion of the world of sense. What Plato had in mind was this: Knowledge and belief are separate faculties, just as sight and hearing are separate senses, and therefore, they must have different objects. With sight we see colors and shapes, and with hearing we hear sounds. Similarly, knowledge and belief must have different objects. The difficulty is that whereas sight and hearing are on a level and are closely related because both are ways of apprehending material objects, knowledge and opinion are of different worth and standing, and their objects, as given by Plato, are so different that they are in danger of becoming entirely unrelated. In this way, we may reach an unacceptable position similar to those discussed by Plato later in the *Parmenides*.

However, Plato always had some feeling for common sense, and he tried to adapt his theories to what was obviously the case. He therefore accepted the natural view that knowledge and opinion are closely connected, and had to develop a very complex theory to accommodate every point he wished to make. A link between the two faculties can be found by means of a link between their objects, and this approach is set out in the masterly series of illustrations known as "The Sun," "The Divided Line," and "The Cave" in *Republic*, vi–vii. At the same time, these are only illustrations and not fully logical arguments, which suggests that Plato did not have a fully reasoned grasp of the matter.

The illustrations are included in an outline of the education to be given to the future rulers of the ideal state that Plato has been sketching. The aim of this education is to bring students to a complete understanding of the realm of forms, which they are to apply to practical matters when their turn comes to govern.

For an understanding of Plato's epistemology the most important of the three illustrations is "The Divided Line."

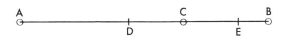

Take a line *AB* and divide it unequally at *C*. Then divide *AC* and *CB* in the same ratio at *D* and *E* respectively. We now have $BC : CA = BE : EC = CD : DA$. These ratios are to indicate the relations among various cognitive activities and also among the objects of those activities. As with so many of Plato's examples, we cannot give a completely consistent interpretation of all the details, and it is unlikely that he meant us to press our questionings too far. The essential features of the line are these: the whole section *BC* stands for the world of sense and our ways of perceiving it, and the whole section *CA* for the realm of forms and the mental activities by which we know them. To understand how these stand to each other, we must look at the subdivisions of *BC*, which serve to illustrate the rest. Here, the larger part, *EC*, stands for material objects like horses and beds and trees, and the smaller, *BE*, for copies of these in the form of mirror-images, shadows, reflections, and the like. Plato makes two important points here: (1) We may study how the copies are related to their originals, noting that they are somehow less real than the originals and dependent on them for their existence; (2) We may also compare the state of mind of a man looking at a reflection or a shadow with that of one who looks at the real thing. There are two ways of doing this: he may either look at the copy for its own sake, as a painter may study reflections in a- stream, or he may look at it *as a copy* and try to learn from it something of the original.

The relationship between copies and their originals in the sensible world is like that between the sensible world as a whole, known by *doxa* (*BC*), and the forms, known by reason or thought (*noēsis*) (*CA*). Material objects are copies, and inferior copies, of their originals. Like shadows and reflections, it is possible to take them as they stand, and not seek to pass beyond them. But the world of sense is fleeting and full of contradictions, and by reflecting on these a man will realize that he cannot gain true knowledge from that world, and will seek to know the forms from which it is derived. *Doxa*, then, is different from knowledge because it concerns different objects, and these are such that we cannot have true knowledge of them. But there is still some connection between the two realms, expressed by the metaphor of imitation; and if we can obtain knowledge of the forms, we shall at the same time win greater understanding of the world of sense.

Doxa comes naturally in the course of our daily living, by contact with the world around us. But how do we obtain knowledge? In the Divided Line passage, Plato concentrates on mathematics as a bridge between the two worlds. In geometry, for instance, we draw rough diagrams on paper, but our arguments are about, not these imperfect figures, but rather perfect squares, circles, and triangles, which cannot be drawn. In this way, we are led from appearances to a reality behind them, to objects about which true knowledge is possible. But mathematics is not the highest form of knowledge. It belongs in the line to *CD*, the lower section of the upper part. When, by its means, we have been made aware of the world of forms, we may pass to the upper division *DA*, where by "Dialectic" we study the forms in and for themselves. Mathematics is inferior because it must start with hypotheses and draw conclusions from them; the hypotheses themselves are unexamined. But in dialectic, we go up from hypotheses, which are uncertain, to something that is not hypothetical and which is a sure and unquestionable starting-point for deduction. Once this has been achieved, we can justify our earlier hypotheses by deriving them from our starting-point.

Plato hoped, then, that at the end of his mental training some object of knowledge that was completely certain would be reached. What this was we may discover in rather greater detail from the similes of "The Sun" and "The Cave." In the former, we are told that the sun in the visible world is like the form of the good in the mental. And as the sun is the source of light, and hence of sight and also of life, so the form of the good is the source of knowledge and of existence for all things. The Cave passage illustrates how educational advancement may be made. Prisoners are held in a cave, where they see only shadows cast on the wall by a fire behind them. When set free, they are led out of the cave and see things in the outside world, and they realize the futility of their former life. Finally, as their eyes grow stronger they are able to look at the sun itself, which here, too, stands for the form of the good. Knowledge of the form of the good is the culminating point of a man's education and enables him to understand everything else, but how knowledge of the form of the good leads to the understanding of everything we do not know from what Plato says. The most hopeful clue is to be found in the *Phaedo*[10], where Socrates says that only one kind of explanation will satisfy him, that which shows that things are as they are because it is best that way. If things are derived from the form of the good, they must be good themselves, and if we can grasp the form of the good we shall understand through it everything else as well.

We must now look at various parts of this great synthesis more critically. The meaning of the word for knowledge, in Greek as well as in English, is a very complex one. On the objective side, it implies that if we know a fact, that fact must be true. We cannot know what is not the case. But this is not all. We also distinguish, on the subjective side, between knowing, which involves being absolutely certain about something, and less certain states like believing or thinking that something is so. Because of this duality of subjective and objective, no simple account of knowledge is possible. In fact, analysis must go further and point out that not only are there these two aspects, but that they are entirely independent. Many things are as they are without our knowing it, and we may easily be in a state of complete certainty about something which is, in fact, not so. The will-o'-the-wisp of philosophers has been to describe a state where the two are necessarily connected, and where if I am certain about a thing, it must be so and cannot be otherwise.

Plato fully recognized the duality of knowledge. He considered the psychological side in the example of "The Road to Larissa," bringing out the points that one can only be said to know something if one has very good grounds for holding it to be the case, and that knowledge is usually more stable than belief. When he turns to the objective side, he is perhaps less successful: he recognizes that what is known must be true, but draws unsound conclusions from this. It will help us to understand Plato's distinctions here if we remember that while we normally speak of knowing facts, which are expressible in words — e.g., knowing that it is raining or that grass is green — we also sometimes speak of another kind of knowing, which appears to be more direct and which is more suited to Plato's thought. This is the kind of knowledge we have in sensation. When I look at a lawn, I am directly aware of its greenness. This is more than knowing *that* it is green. There is a direct and unquestionable visual relationship between me and the green patch I am now seeing. And it is because of this relationship that I can go on to say that I know that this particular lawn is green. Another point to note is that this type of awareness has grades of clearness. There is a difference between looking at a lawn on a sunny day and glimpsing a distant figure through a fog. In both cases there is a direct visual experience, but the interpretation of the latter is uncertain, whereas that of the former is not.

Plato wanted to find something similar to the direct awareness of greenness that would apply to the whole range of knowledge. He believed that our mental experiences, like our visual ones, can be graded for clarity and certainty, although uncertainty concerning mental experiences is due, not, as with the fog, to an impeding medium, but to the fact that the objects of which we are aware lack full reality. The analogue for the type of uncertainty involved in mental experiences is not the fully real man or tree seen in a fog, but the shadow or reflection, which Plato himself uses as an illustration. Plato's ideal, on the other hand, is a clear mental state in which the object is directly known. But only a fully real object can be known in this way. Thus, for Plato, truth on the objective side and certainty on the subjective are not independent.

The question remains, whether the analysis of knowing which I have suggested (where the two aspects are independent), is sufficient, or whether it applies to only one form of knowledge, that of material objects known with the aid of the senses. Undoubtedly many people have believed in and sought for some higher form of knowledge such as Plato had in mind. But those who are most likely to have succeeded, the mystics, are generally agreed that the knowledge so achieved can hardly be put into words. They are in the position of a man who sees the greenness of the grass but cannot say that it is green; and this was not at all what Plato wanted. He believed that knowledge once achieved was expressible and usable, as it would be by the rulers of his ideal state, in everyday life. The only limitation he foresaw was that it could not be taught as in a textbook, but only by a close partnership between master and pupil. And this is no more than we believe of any university subject today. In fact, in his earlier works, Plato seems to have worried very little about how knowledge was to be expressed; but, as we shall see, he later paid considerable attention to problems of language and of how language and knowledge are related.

THE IMMORTALITY OF THE SOUL

Most of Plato's arguments for the immortality of the soul are found in the *Phaedo*, which tells of the last hours of Socrates. But there are others in the *Republic*, the *Phaedrus*, and the *Laws*, and we shall consider them altogether.

They fall into two groups. In the arguments in the larger group, the distinction between body and soul is taken for granted, and attention is concentrated on proving that the soul is of such a nature as to be imperishable. In the *Phaedo*, however, in response to objections from his friends, Socrates does discuss a rival theory that would make the soul nothing but an aspect of the body. We shall begin with that.[11]

The question is raised by the Pythagorean Simmias and seems to have a medical origin. He suggests that the soul is to the body as the fact of being in tune is to the lyre. If the strings are in a certain relationship (of which the Pythagoreans could give a mathematical account), the lyre is in tune; when the strings are broken no such attunement can exist. Similarly what we call the soul is no more than a certain relationship between the elements of the body and cannot survive the dissolution of the body. This comes very close to the view that man is a machine, or to the very recent doctrine that there is great similarity between the mental activities of human beings and the behavior of "mechanical brains." On any such theory, the only *thing* is the body or machine. There is nothing else that may survive its destruction.

Socrates answers by pointing out certain important differences between a man and a lyre. The relationship between the notes produced by the strings of a lyre, whether they are in tune or not, is determined entirely by the strings. That is, the relationship is an entirely passive one. But it may be argued that the soul is not entirely passive. For instance, it may oppose the body's urges. Sometimes, when a man feels thirsty and desires to drink, he does not do so because he may think it unwise. A possible interpretation of this situation is that the body wants to drink and the soul says "no" and stops it. If this is so, the soul is something active and must be to some extent independent of the body.

Now this is clearly not enough to prove Socrates' point. It certainly shows that a man is more complicated than a lyre, where no string can affect any other string, but the possibility still remains open that one part of the body may oppose or control the action of another part, without any intervening soul. Nowadays machines are common in which one part controls the behavior of many other parts, although these still have their own "drives." So we can conclude only that the body is at least more complicated than a lyre.

The other arguments start by assuming that there is a separate thing called the "soul". The first returns to the argument from *anamnēsis*, which we have already met. A man may know geometry without having been taught it — i.e., he may have knowledge that he has not acquired in this world. He must therefore have had a previous existence in which this knowledge was obtained. If so, the state before birth was one in which the soul existed, apart from the body, and it is reasonable to conclude that just as we pass from sleep to waking and then to sleep again, so we may exist out of the body, then in it, and then again out of it in death. We have seen, however, that the proof of *anamnēsis* is unsatisfactory, and so we need not consider the rest of this argument.

Other arguments are that the soul is akin to the forms, therefore, like them, immortal, and that it is the master of the body and more divine than it. And since the body, when embalmed, can last indefinitely, the soul must be capable of enduring even longer. These arguments need not detain us.

The next argument is at first sight more important. First, we must recognize a difference between the accidental and the essential characteristics of an object, the former it can lose without losing its identity, but not the latter. Thus, Socrates can cease to be short and become tall without ceasing to be Socrates, but fire cannot cease to be hot, or the number three cease to be odd, without their ceasing to be fire and three, respectively.

What are the essential characteristics of the soul? The soul is essentially *living*, so that when it is present in a body, life is present. And if life is a necessary characteristic, the soul cannot admit the presence of death if it is to remain soul. Now there are other things that cannot admit death, such as God and the form of life, and these are in fact indestructible. It is likely, then, that the soul is indestructible too, and goes elsewhere in good order when death comes to the body.

Plato's argument so presented must seem implausible, and it is fair to add that many trimmings have been stripped away and Plato's attempt to set it out in the terminology of the forms abandoned. But the skeleton is given above, and its shortcomings are clear.

The most interesting point raised is the discussion of essential characteristics. The notion that some characteristics are essential and others accidental is a plausible one and has had a long history. But like the notion of real definition, with which it is connected, it becomes less plausible when we examine it more closely. If there were real definitions, we could say that an essential characteristic is one that forms part of a definition or that can be deduced by accepted methods from the definition. But we have seen that, in fact, definitions are to some extent arbitrary, and that we cannot find one single real definition for each object. Hence, according to one definition, characteristic *A* would be essential and, according to another, characteristic *B*.

On the other hand, we may sometimes describe a characteristic as essential because of its causal importance. For instance, you cannot destroy the heat of a fire without destroying the fire itself, and for that reason we, like Plato, may regard heat as essential to the existence of fire. But one can still conceive of a fire that was, say, bright and destructive, yet not hot to sensation. We might still be prepared to describe it as fire, and heat would not then be essential. What characteristics are in fact causally connected in this way can only be found out by experience, and even this may often be mistaken. So we can never be sure that a given characteristic is essential even in this sense. At best, then, Plato's argument contains two links that cannot be more than probable: the view that life is essential to soul, and the inductive proof that many things to which life is essential are indestructible.

The question is taken up again in the *Phaedrus* with an argument elaborated later in the *Laws*.[12] This begins with the fact of movement, and divides all movement into two classes: the communicated, like that of a thrown ball, and the spontaneous, which originates in the moving thing itself. All communicated motion must arise from spontaneous motion. And the only source of spontaneous motion known to us is the soul. In fact, when we see something that moves by itself, we say it has a soul. This amounts to saying that the soul is essentially self-moving. Plato concludes from this that the soul's motion cannot cease and that the soul must therefore be immortal. His detailed argument is interesting, even if we cannot accept it: That which is the source of its own motion cannot have received its original impetus from any other source, and must therefore be uncreated; and that which is uncreated is also eternal. Again, unless all movement, change, and generation in the universe are to cease, the originator of motion, the soul, must be in endless motion and must therefore be immortal.

The big assumption that Plato is making here is that nothing new can come into existence at a point of time, and the corollary that nothing can totally cease to be at a point of time, however much movement and change there may be. Many philosophers have either believed these assumptions to be certainly true or have taken them for granted in their arguments. It is, however, conceivable that they should not be true — i.e., they are not logical truths and could hardly be proved empirically. We must conclude that Plato has failed to make out his case.

Plato's Later Philosophy

THE LATER THEORY OF FORMS

There are many questions about the early theory of forms that cannot easily be answered. It is probable that after the founding of the Academy, Plato's colleagues and pupils began to raise them and force Plato to face them. We cannot here give a detailed account of these criticisms, for the evidence is extremely fragmentary. But we can get some impression of them from Plato's attempts to answer them.

In the *Parmenides*, probably written when Plato was in his sixties, Socrates as a very young man meets the venerable Parmenides and puts to him the theory of forms as a way to overcome the difficulties of the one and the many. Parmenides reduces him to despair with a number of awkward questions, but suggests that with greater experience of logic and reasoning, Socrates may be able to retrieve his position.

The difficulties are these:

A. *Are there forms of everything?* We have seen that the lines of thought that led to the theory of forms are various and hang uneasily together. On the one hand, the forms are based on similarity: where two things are similar, we want to say that they share a common form. We might then conclude that there are as many forms as there are common names or class-words — like "man" and "green" and "equal." Here forms have the same functions as the "universals" discussed in later philosophy. But for Plato, forms are also perfect beings that things in this world aspire to imitate, although they continually fail in their aspiration. This applies well enough to ethical concepts like justice and courage, to mathematical concepts like equality, and to a few others like beauty. But it begins to look odd in cases where the imperfection of particulars is not so clearly marked.

Parmenides takes four classes of objects, and asks if there are forms for each of these. Of the first class, likeness, unity, and plurality, Socrates is absolutely certain, and also of the second, justice, beauty and goodness. But his doubts begin with the next group, man, fire, and water, and he cannot, finally, admit that there are forms of things like mud and hair and dirt. The reasons for his doubts are not explained, but they may have been due to an obscure feeling that individual men and individual flames are all equally men and fire, just as we read in the *Phaedo*[13] that all souls are equally souls. Hence there is no scale of perfection of which the form is the culminating point. Again, it seems ridiculous to contemplate perfect hair or mud. And so we find revealed a chink between form as universal and form as ideal.

B. *How are forms and particulars related?* Hitherto Plato has been content to use metaphorical terms like "imitate" and "participate" for this relationship. But now he sees that a more detailed account is needed. If forms exist apart from particulars and are yet somehow the source of the being of particulars, how are the two connected? In this dialogue, a particularly crude interpretation which may really have been held in the Academy by the astronomer Eudoxus, is put on the word "participate": If each particular contains a part of the form, the form will be divided into parts, and will no longer be a unity; further, in some cases, the parts will be inadequate to their role. For instance, if each equal thing contains a portion of equality that is less than real equality, it will not, by that portion, be equal (but, rather, less than equal), to something else. This argument may seem absurd and very far from what was really meant by the theory of forms, but it is valuable because it emphasizes the point that philosophical terminology must not be taken for granted. The sense in which each word is used must be understood clearly, and if it has, for good reasons, a sense of its own peculiar to this context, we must make that point clear.

Later the "imitating" metaphor is explored. Particulars are to forms as copies — e.g., mirror images — are to their originals. But we immediately come up against a difficulty that is not merely due to the metaphor, but needs separate treatment on its own merits. This has come to be known as the "Third Man" argument, and challenges the whole basis of the theory of forms.

We suppose that forms exist because, for example, we suppose that all large things are alike in being large, and postulate a form of largeness as the source of this resemblance. But, Plato supposes, largeness must itself be large, and in this way must resemble other large things. We now have a new group of large things, the old ones plus the form of largeness. So a further form of largeness must exist, which is the source of this new set of resemblances. And this process can be repeated again and again, each time introducing a new form of largeness. But this is absurd.

The argument again brings out the incompatibility of the two aspects of the forms, as universals and as ideals. If we regard the form of largeness merely as a universal, as that which all large things have in common, there is no reason why it should itself be large, any more than, e.g., manhood should be human. But if we regard this very same thing, largeness, as ideal, then it must be large; the regress at once arises.

c. *Are forms thoughts in the mind?* In view of Plato's habit of emphasizing the objectivity of the forms, this point is curious. Socrates suggests that forms do not exist independently but are only thoughts in the mind. It is quite likely that this suggestion was made in the Academy. Taken seriously, it amounts to the view that classifying Socrates, Plato, and Parmenides together as men is a useful but arbitrary mental activity, and that the form is nothing but our thought of all these men taken together. To this Parmenides rightly objects that thoughts are always of something real; or, put differently, when we group Socrates, Plato, and Parmenides together and call them all men, we do so because they already resemble each other objectively, quite apart from our mental activities.

d. *Are the forms cut off from the world?* Forms are relative to forms, and particulars to particulars. Thus mastership is relative to slavery, but an individual owner is master of an individual slave. This in itself might be unimportant, but it follows that knowledge must be of reality alone, and the knowledge possessed by this or that man must be confined to things in this world. He cannot therefore know the forms. On the other hand, God must surely have knowledge itself, and by that can know the forms only, and not the affairs of men.

One point here is the problem of knowledge, at which Plato made another attempt in the *Theaetetus*, to be discussed later. But the statement of the difficulty here again brings out the duality of the forms. If they were bare universals, God's knowledge would be a particular just like the knowledge of any individual man, however much wider in scope it might be. But because for Plato the form is also something more perfect than any particular, it seems appropriate that the form alone should belong to God.

No direct answer to any of the difficulties raised is given in the *Parmenides*, but Socrates' perplexities are attributed to his inexperience; and this suggests that Plato did not regard them as insurmountable. Certainly he did not abandon the forms at once, though he seems to have modified his views on them considerably as time went on. His optimism here is not really surprising; as an opponent of the Sophists, he was familiar *ad nauseam* with the paradoxes to which arguments can lead, and may well have hoped to solve in due course these particular

puzzles raised by himself or his pupils. A likely account of his development is that after the *Parmenides*, he dropped the similarity metaphor, believing that the Third Man arguments could not be met, but continued to speak of "participation." He was certainly still aware of the problems of participation in the very late *Philebus*.[14]

The second part of the *Parmenides* has been interpreted in widely different ways. It was once fashionable to treat it as a ponderous joke, but most modern writers believe that it has a serious purpose. Plato himself says that it is a sample of the kind of dialectical exercise by which Socrates will learn to become a true philosopher. The argument has eight parts, all variations on the theme, "Unity Exists." In each there is a chain of deduction from the premise that unity does, or does not, exist, showing what can be said on this hypothesis about unity and about everything else. The conclusion is that everything can be stated and everything denied, both about unity and about everything else, whether unity exists or not. The arguments as a whole are tedious, and many of the details unconvincing.

What is the purpose of this exhibition? We should perhaps look back to a question that has frequently been mentioned by Socrates in the first half of the dialogue. How can one form be many? Or, in more modern terms, how is it possible to make statements about forms? We may say that "This statue is beautiful" means that the statue partakes of the form of beauty. But if we say, as for instance Plato does in the *Symposium*[15], that the form of beauty is "eternally existing and neither begotten nor perishable, neither increasing nor decaying," we seem to be meaning that it is the form of beauty that partakes of the form of eternity and the rest. And this seems to mean that the forms themselves intercommunicate and, in a sense, that "each is many" or has many predicates. The problem of reconciling this with the essential unity of the forms is clearly faced in the *Sophist*, and seems to be touched on and played with in the *Parmenides*. There the conclusion is entirely negative; we reach a complete, eightfold *reductio ad absurdum*. Yet in the course of it many interesting points are made, and it is possible that here, as elsewhere, Plato was inculcating a number of lessons at the same time. However, because of the difficulty of the whole matter, I shall mention only one or two of these points.

There may be a general lesson that by arguments of this type, not closely examined, we can prove anything and everything. Further progress must, therefore, depend on a careful examination of our methods and presuppositions in each case.

As an example, we may take a distinction that is made in the course of the arguments. In the first hypothesis we treat the premise as equivalent to "Unity is a unit — and nothing else besides." But this leads to purely negative conclusions, and we start again with the different interpretation "Unity exists." This also turns out to be unsatisfactory, but a step forward has been taken because two distinct meanings of the original, ambiguous Greek sentence have now been discovered.

THE THEAETETUS

The *Theaetetus* can be dated fairly accurately. Its opening scene tells of the death of Theaetetus, a member of the Academy, and this must have taken place on a military expedition against Corinth in 369. It is very probable that the dialogue was written shortly afterward as a memorial to him. Unfortunately, there is no way of deciding whether the *Parmenides* or the *Theaetetus* is the earlier work, but they must be near in time.

The declared purpose of the *Theaetetus* is to define knowledge. Most philosophers would agree with Cornford that there is also a concealed purpose to show that knowledge is impossible without the forms. The forms are, in fact, scarcely mentioned in it, but their very absence makes them conspicuous, and the totally negative conclusion reached makes it clear that we need some way of solving our difficulties different from those explored there.

It may seem odd that this dialogue has been regarded by many modern philosophers as Plato's greatest contribution to philosophy. But if we believe that the theory of forms was only a magnificent failure, which raises a host of problems but solves none, it is reasonable to see this more analytical work as Plato's most permanent achievement. The range of theories it covers is extremely wide. It begins with the simple view that knowledge is sensation, but this is soon linked with two other ideas. The first, attributed to Protagoras, is a theory about truth, and says that all that a man believes, whether on the basis of direct sensation or not, is true. The second view, based on Heraclitus, is about the nature of things and dismisses the apparent permanence of most material objects as illusory; all that really exists, it maintains, is a number of motions. These views are eventually abandoned and a new start is made which attempts to equate knowledge with true belief. Although it also fails, a number of advances are made. We must now look at the theories in detail.

Knowledge is perception or sensation ("*aisthē-sis*").* Here for the first time Plato tries to take sense experience seriously. In examining the view that knowledge is equivalent to seeing, hearing, and so on, he touches on many of the peculiarities of perception that are still discussed in this connection:

1. The same "things" — e.g., a breeze — may seem warm to one man and cold to another. Is it then warm or cold or both or neither?
2. Dreams seem to present us with a real world

* In the Greek at Plato's disposal, there was no simple distinction between the concepts of perception and sensation.

different from the one we know when we are awake. But we do not believe in it when we are awake. Why is this?
3. What tastes sweet to a man when he is healthy may seem bitter to him when he is sick. Is it really sweet or bitter?

All these problems turn on the point that we do not, in all cases, accept what our senses tell us as correct, and do not, therefore, believe in a simple equation between sensation and knowledge. If the equation is valid, it remains a paradox. The first man to treat it as true, according to Plato, was Protagoras with his doctrine that "Man is the measure of all things." Plato now examines this view, giving his own interpretation of the words. It is a wider theory than the simple one that knowledge is sensation; it implies, at least in Plato's hands, that whatever a man believes, whether on the basis of sensation or reasoning or anything else, is true. But some remarks that apply to it apply also to the simpler theory.

It may be said that if we accept a view of this kind, certain changes in our ways of speaking and thinking are necessary, and at least two courses are possible. We may — e.g., in the first example — say that the wind is both hot and cold and deny that there is any logical difficulty in applying contrary adjectives to the same subject at the same time. But this would lead to great difficulties in formal reasoning, and Plato does not consider this alternative. Instead, he adopts a form of relativism: We may no longer say simply, "This is hot" or "This is cold," but must always say, "This is hot relative to that person" or even "to that person in that state." Then we may say, without awkward logical consequences, "The wind is hot for this man and cold for that." But we cannot make any simple statement about the wind. And the next step, as Plato sees, could be to try to do without the wind, or any other object, altogether. He takes this step by bringing in a complicated theory of motions derived from Heraclitus. This reduces both the man who perceives and the environment that he perceives into sets of slow motions. Perception takes place when, for example, the motion of my eye interacts with some external motion, thus producing a more rapid motion. This may be regarded on the one hand as the sensation of color I have (in my eye), and on the other as that color which we normally believe to be in, or on the surface of, an external object. Plato tantalizingly extends this analysis beyond the senses to cover pleasures and pains, desires and fears. But no details are given, and it is doubtful if he had fully worked out how this could be done.

Basically, this is a form of what is known as "neutral monism." That is, it supposes the world to consist ultimately of certain units, the motions, which are neither mental nor physical. When perception occurs, the common-sense interpretation is that there is a mental event, connected with the eyes and brain, which is seeing, and a permanent object outside the observer, which is seen. But according to this theory, that is not true; all that really exists are groups of the basic units. For Heraclitus, these are motions; many modern writers have treated sense-data as basic. On any such view, every perception is equally valid; but the way in which we normally interpret perception is gravely at fault.

When the theory has been stated, Socrates raises a number of objections that bear mainly on the theory of truth attributed to Protagoras.

1. It would seem to be implied that the pig's or baboon's view of the world is just as good as that of a man.
2. More seriously, the views of one man will be no better than those of another, and, in particular, we shall have no reason for believing that Protagoras is more correct than anyone else. "Man is the measure of all things" may be true for Protagoras, but it will be false for Socrates and Plato if they do not believe in it.

However, Plato says, these difficulties may be overcome. He does not say how, but perhaps we can fill in the gap ourselves. The first objection is not serious if we are willing to admit that the pig's view, as far as it goes, is as good as that of a man. Why not? The second difficulty is still serious, but as Plato now returns to a discussion of the view that knowledge is perception, he may have realized that Protagoras' theory was a much wider one and that the objection raised is one that applies to theoretical beliefs, which are far more complicated than bare sensations. If we interpret Protagoras with reference solely to sensations and not to theories, his view may perhaps still stand.

We now have a series of detailed objections to the simple view that knowledge is sensation.

1. Consider a man who hears a language that he does not understand being spoken. He certainly has sensations of hearing, but he still does not know what is being said. However, this is not serious. We must distinguish, says Plato, between knowledge of the sounds of the syllables, which he has, and knowledge of the meaning of those sounds, which he has not. But a point still remains, which Plato does not cover here: how does one come to know this meaning? We shall see that this question occupied him very much in later life.
2. A man who has seen something may shut his eyes and remember what he has seen. With this short example, Plato makes the immensely important point that memory, which is not directly connected with the senses, has as good claims to be treated as knowledge as has sensation.

However, these points are not now followed up, and Plato returns to the wider views of Protagoras and Heraclitus. What answer would Protagoras give to the critic who said that on his own showing his views were no more true than those of any other man? Perhaps we can still maintain both that each thing is for each man as it seems to him *and* that there are wise men whose views must be heeded and less wise men whose views may be disregarded. The wise man is one who can change appearances both for others and for himself. Thus, it is neither the sick nor the healthy man who is wise, but the doctor who knows how to give the sick man better sensations, like those of the healthy man; or, again, it is the teacher who gives his pupils sound judgments, and the statesman who makes good things seem just to the people. In this way Protagoras tries to shift the fundamental distinction between men's views from true or false to good or bad.

Socrates has little difficulty in showing that one cannot dispose of truth and falsity so easily.

1. It is commonly believed, at the very least, that the reason why one man is wise is that he has true beliefs, and another is foolish because he has false beliefs. But if I believe this, my belief must, according to Protagoras himself, be true, and there must in fact exist true and false beliefs. But as Protagoras has also declared that all beliefs are true, there cannot also be false beliefs, and he is involved in a contradiction.
2. People may, like some Sophists, believe that what is just is merely a matter of convention and that nothing is really just or unjust in itself; but no one holds this about what is healthy or useful. We believe that some things really are health-giving or useful, or, in other words, that it can be *true* that A is health-giving or B is harmful. What this amounts to is that people persist in using the notions of true and false in such cases. This is an appeal to psychological facts, and as such might not have carried much weight with Protagoras.
3. The third argument is similar: Let us distinguish between beliefs about the present, to which Protagoras' arguments mostly apply, and beliefs about the future. Again, all men would agree that with regard to the future, the expert's estimation of what will happen is better than the layman's. The same holds true for the doctor's regarding prognosis and the cook's about how a dish will taste. Here again the truth or falsity of an opinion is important.

Protagoras has now been shown to be in danger of self-contradiction and also in conflict with many accepted beliefs. We may still feel that he has not had a full run for his money, but Plato probably thought that he had done enough to expose the difficulties inherent in the theory and that it was now up to its supporters, if they were so inclined, to show in detail how his arguments were to be met. This would probably involve even more extreme changes in ways of speech and arguing than had yet been suggested, and their views might still turn out to be untenable in the end.

Plato's next criticism is aimed at the view that everything is, as Heraclitus said, in a state of "becoming" or motion, and that nothing stable exists at all. The common-sense view is that we are surrounded by more or less permanent objects like tables and horses that may indeed change to some extent, either by moving (change of place) or by qualitative alteration (change of state), but in which there is always something permanent that persists through such changes. Heraclitus denies this permanence, and leaves only the change.

Plato's criticism of this is that if it were true, our normal use of language would be impossible. We can only name something if there is some permanent thing to be named. Otherwise, even while we are speaking, that which we have named has vanished and there exists nothing to which we are referring by the name. Again, our sensations themselves will be continually changing, and so we have no more right to speak of seeing and hearing than of not-seeing and not-hearing. But if perception is knowledge, this is fatal to our hopes of being able to say what knowledge is, for knowledge itself will be changing all the time. Thus any definition of knowledge we may give will apply equally to not-knowledge.

With this compressed argument we reach the end of the discussion of whether knowledge is perception. Plato claims to have shown that this definition is true if Protagoras' theory is true, and that it, in turn, leads on to the view about the nature of reality attributed to Heraclitus. But on this theory it is impossible to give a stable meaning to words, and so any definition whatsoever must be abandoned. Theories of truth, or reality, and of language are here mixed up in such a way that only a very lengthy analysis could disentangle them; and that is beyond our present scope. We can, however, agree that on a number of grounds the proposed definition is unsatisfactory, and that a new attempt must be made to say what knowledge is.

Before a new suggestion is made, however, Plato tries to say something positive about how knowledge and sensation are connected. Socrates distinguishes between the activities of the senses — seeing with the eyes or hearing with the ears — and thinking, which is an activity of the mind. The mind uses the organs of sense as its tools, but can go far beyond them by comparing and contrasting their deliverances. In this way, certain characteristics are discovered which cannot be known by the senses, such as reality or being, number, sameness, difference, and good and bad. These are known by reflection, which is, therefore, one of the sources of knowledge.

Plato has here put his finger on, or near, a number of important points. The first is that the evidence of the senses must be coordinated; unless we can link what we see with our eyes with what we hear with our ears or feel with our fingers, we can have no proper understanding of the world around us. This linkage cannot be the work of any one, or indeed of all, the senses. It must be the function of something else, which it may be convenient to call "the mind." But, for Plato, the mind does more than this. Once it has coordinated the senses, it can reflect upon the external world presented to it and make use of a number of concepts of very general application. These are not directly connected with sensible experience, as, for example, color concepts are. They are, therefore, particularly good examples of nonsensible components of thought. We shall see in the *Sophist* how deeply concerned about them Plato was.

We conclude, then, that the senses are not enough. A new suggestion, that knowledge is equivalent to true belief (*doxa*), is now made. Here Plato is abandoning another of his former views — that knowledge and belief are irrevocably different. *Doxa* now covers the whole activity of the intellect in thinking and is no longer sharply opposed to knowledge (*epistēmē*). However, there may still be either true or false belief, and if knowledge is true belief, we must be able to say something about false belief that will mark the difference. How indeed is false belief possible?

This leads Plato into psychology. True and false belief are for him subjectively indistinguishable and differ only in their relations to the object. He brings in a simile that emphasizes these points: The memory is like a wax tablet on which impressions can be made with a signet ring; such impressions are made by our sensible experience, and they vary in clearness of definition and in the length of time they remain undistorted. That is to say, our memories of past events are often vague and become even vaguer with the passage of time. In an act of recognition, a man attends to his sensations and tries to link them up with the impressions on his tablet of memory. If he makes a mistake here and links the man he now sees with his memory image of Socrates when that man is, in fact, not Socrates, a false judgment is made.

However, Plato continues, false judgments do not occur only when a present sensation is misinterpreted by memory. We can, for instance, make mistakes when thinking without sensations — e.g., if we think that seven plus five equals eleven. A more complicated theory is therefore needed, which we may approach by means of a new analogy. Think of an aviary in which a man keeps some birds. He may be said to "possess" the birds as long as they are in the aviary, but he may also "have and hold" one more closely if he actually has it in his hand. The aviary is the mind; all the items of knowledge we possess, even when we are not thinking of them, are the birds; when we are actually thinking of something we are holding a bird in our hands. And if we have somehow caught the wrong bird, we are making a false judgment. But here the analogy breaks down. For we have already made a mistake in capturing the wrong bird. And this is a mistake on a different level — i.e., one not due to holding a bird at all, which itself needs explanation.

This analogy has again suggested a psychological account of memory and, by implication, of belief. It shows well that we must distinguish two kinds of memory-knowledge, the first when we are capable of recalling a fact — e.g., what we had for breakfast this morning — and the second when we are actually recalling it. And it points out again that some mistaken judgments occur by confusion of memories. But it takes us nowhere in our attempt to distinguish knowledge from belief because it is so purely psychological.

That something more is needed is shown by the next point, which gives a case where true belief is clearly distinguishable from knowledge: A jury may be led to a correct verdict solely by the power of brilliant advocacy. It will not then have knowledge, as it would if it had actually seen the crime committed, but only a correct belief. Here we seem to be back again at the road to Larissa of the *Meno*. Plato is again emphasizing the importance of the origins of the psychological state.

But an example is not enough, and a third definition of knowledge is suggested, that it is "true judgment with an account." Unfortunately, the word here translated "account," *logos*, is one of the most ambiguous in the Greek language, and the suggestion therefore requires considerable clarification.

First, *logos* may be taken as equivalent to "analysis into elements." We can, Socrates says, distinguish between complex wholes and the elements of which they are composed — e.g., between syllables and the letters that form them. We might then say that we have knowledge of the syllable "so" if we can say that it is made up of "s" and "o". But we cannot do the same for the letters, because they have no such elements. This is one difficulty that Socrates finds here. The other is that we still need to be able to say exactly how "so" is related to its elements. Is it just "s" and "o" in that order, or a fresh unit of a higher type? If the former, it is odd that we can know "so" but not "s" and "o"; if the latter, "so" is itself an element of a new kind, and as such not analyzable and not an object of knowledge.

This attempt to "atomize" knowledge is an interesting one, and brings out some important points. First, if knowledge involves analysis, the elements into which an object is analyzed may or may not themselves be analyzable; and, if they are not, they will be either unknowable or, as some later writers would claim, knowable in a different way. To say that they are unknowable seems paradoxical, but to say

that they are knowable in a different way foils our hope of having given a full definition of knowledge. As long as he hoped for a single definition, this way was barred to Plato.

Secondly, it raises the question of what a complex whole is. Plato had already touched on this problem in the obscure second part of the *Parmenides*, and it is one on which it is fatally easy to become confused. We may be content with the view that a whole is just the sum of its parts in a certain order, or we may say that, on such an analysis, something is omitted. Difficulties begin as soon as we try to say what this extra something is. It must be, as Plato saw, something entirely different from the already enumerated parts. It cannot therefore be analyzed, and it seems almost as difficult to describe it verbally in any other way. The problem can, in fact, be dealt with satisfactorily only by an entirely new approach, by examining the kinds of occasions when we speak of wholes and seeing what is characteristic of them. Otherwise, an unnecessary sense of mystery tends to surround the question.

Plato now looks at various meanings of the word "*logos*."

1. It may mean simply the use of language, spoken or written. But both true opinion and knowledge may be expressed in speech, so that cannot mark the difference between them.

2. It may mean the enumeration of the parts of a thing, as one might list the parts of a wagon if one really knew what a wagon was. But we are back at the problem of analysis. We would not be sure that a man knew what a particular complex whole was unless he also knew, in some sense, the parts well enough to recognize them in a different context. So a man who could spell "Theaetetus" correctly, and therefore seemed to know the syllable "the," might make a mistake in spelling it as part of "Theodorus," and would therefore not be said to know "Theaetetus" properly either. So a mere enumeration of parts, even if full and accurate, is not enough to prove knowledge.

3. Perhaps the meaning we are seeking of "*logos*" is that which indicates the differentia of a thing — i.e., the mark or characteristic that distinguishes it from every other thing. Here Plato is approaching the theory of definition which he later developed in the *Sophist*, but he dismisses it here because if we are to have even a true belief about Theaetetus, for example, we must already be able to mark him off from everything else. Knowledge involves something more.

Plato is perhaps being unfair to his own suggestion here by the example he takes. In the *Sophist*, he is concerned with the problem of scientific definition and by the fact that a very important part is played by the ability to find characteristics suitable to mark off one species from another, for example. But marking off individuals like Theaetetus is another matter. However, he may have been well aware of this, and have used the example to show indirectly that if knowledge of this kind is possible, it cannot be of individuals but must be of something else — i.e., the forms.

The dialogue now ends in complete skepticism. No proposed definition has stood up to criticism; every proposed definition has either led to a contradiction or has not been in accord with normal usage. Throughout, we have been concerned with a "common-sense" view of knowledge, and the moral seems to be that it, in itself, is insufficient and needs to be completed by bringing in the forms.

THE SOPHIST

The *Sophist* is linked dramatically with the *Theaetetus*, and supplements it with a more positive teaching. Plato's new method of division is set out in the first and last parts of the dialogue, whereas the central part, probably written later, contains a discussion of the intercommunication of forms and the possibility of negative judgment, which leads to a general theory of predication.

1. Division (*diairesis*) was probably invented by Plato, and he was clearly extremely proud of it. Most modern writers think little of it, but it is worth our while to ask why Plato himself valued it so much. It is used by him chiefly as a way of reaching a definition, and this was for him an essential part of the process of obtaining knowledge. Division is mentioned first in the *Phaedrus* (which was written probably between the *Republic* and the *Sophist*), and is there linked with the prior activity of collection. To obtain a definition we must first run over in our minds a number of scattered types of things and bring them together under a single form in virtue of a common underlying resemblance. This is collection. We are then to divide this form up into a number of subordinate forms, under one of which comes the object we are trying to define. This second form is again divided, and we continue in this way until, after a number of steps, we reach the lowest possible form, the species, under which our object comes. Then we arrive at the definition by taking together the names of all the forms through which we have passed. Thus, in the *Sophist*[16], Plato tells us that to obtain the definition of "Sophist" we survey a number of operations like filtering, sifting, and winnowing, and by collection get the idea of a technique of separating that is common to all these. Then we start the division: a type of separation is purification, and one kind of purification is ridding the soul of evil. This evil may be wickedness or ignorance, and the division goes on until we get what we want, a definition of "Sophist" as "one who practices the art of purifying the soul of a false belief in its own wisdom by education." Many of the other examples of division given are frivolous,

but that must not make us underestimate the value of the method for Plato. It was the first time a systematic way of reaching a definition had been discovered, and as such it was a great advance on Socrates' method of trial and error. Socrates depended on suggestions made out of the blue, but now Plato could give formal rules for definition, even if they still needed common sense and judgment in their application. That is, collection must cover the right things to get the correct *summum genus* (highest genus), and the division must be carried out along natural lines of cleavage, for which no rules can be given. But the *form* of the definition is laid down, and this form is, in effect, an expansion of the definition *per genus et differentiam* (by genus and difference) familiar to us from the works of Aristotle.

Why did Plato think this type of definition particularly satisfactory? He had now developed the theory of forms beyond its original scope; he believed that the forms were related among themselves in a number of ways, one of which is like a pyramid. One higher form embraces a number of subordinate ones as "animal" embraces "man," "dog," "horse," and so on. A definition then serves to map out the world of forms and shows exactly the place in it of the form being defined. Such a procedure still has its place in biology, and Plato's pioneer work here should not be minimized, even though his method has not the supreme importance he attached to it.

2. The problem of *negation* is also connected with the interrelation of forms, which was first mentioned in the *Parmenides*, and was treated from one point of view in the discussion of the method of division. The problem has two main parts: "What do negative statements mean" and "How is a false statement, negative or positive, meaningful but false?" Greek philosophers had already explored to the full the extremist view that negation is just impossible. Their explanations had culminated in the complicated philosophy of Parmenides and the utter skepticism of Gorgias. The argument that negation is impossible runs something like this: To say a name is to mention *something* — i.e., something that *is*. Therefore, a statement of the form "*X* is not," where *X* is a name, is impossible. Again, any statement must be about something that is named in it and therefore *is*, and hence false statement is impossible. Plato had himself sketched such arguments in the *Euthydemus* and the *Cratylus*.[17] Now he tries to find a more constructive approach, which involves him in an even more general problem, that of predication and the meaning of "is" used as a copula. The expounding of this problem is traditionally ascribed* to Antisthenes, the friend of Socrates. Antisthenes is said to have adopted the extreme view that you could say nothing about *X* except *X* "is *X*." You can say "Man is man," but not "Man is white."

Plato was perfectly satisfied that these views were unsound, and that our normal uses of language were

* But the sources are very imprecise and scanty.

fully meaningful. His only problem, therefore, was to show how it is possible to use language in the normal way in spite of the arguments given above. His solution amounts to pointing out that the verb "to be" in Greek, as in most other languages, has a number of separate meanings, and that when these have been distinguished, no problem remains.

His exposition is complicated, however, by the fact that he is still concerned with the intercommunication of forms and realizes that the pyramidal relationship used in his theory of definition is not the only one. There are, he thinks, a number of forms at the highest level of generality, which are not *summa genera* but of which practically everything partakes. These include "being," "motion," "rest," and "goodness." A single object may, we know, at the same time exist, be at rest, and be good; or, to put it another way, "being," "rest," and "goodness" combine or communicate with each other in that object. It is clear, therefore, that the forms are related among themselves in the sense that some, at least, combine with, or do not exclude, others; further study will give us knowledge of which form can combine with which.

There are, however, two different points here. One is the question of how one particular can have many "names" or predicates. The other is how a form itself can have predicates. That is, how can we say, on the one hand, "That man is tall," using the words "man" and "tall" of the same object, and, on the other, "Unity exists," where the object of which we are speaking is the form "unity." The simplest explanation of Plato's treatment of these topics is that he was himself confused about them. But fortunately what he says is still of great philosophical importance.

First he takes Parmenides' difficulty that not-being cannot be spoken of. We may take "not-being" as equivalent to "that which in no sense is" — a phrase that puts the point as clearly as possible. Plato now recognizes firmly what many Greeks were reluctant to admit, that an expression which is perfectly good grammatically might yet have no real sense. We can say the words, but they have no meaning. It is therefore more valuable to consider "what is not" in some different sense, to find the clue to our troubles.

Statements that describe *what is not* are falsehoods; they involve "thinking things contrary to the things that are" or "thinking things that are not," and, further, thinking that things that are not in some sense are, or thinking that things that certainly are, are not in any way at all. We are back at the problems of the *Theaetetus*. But before we settle these, we must look at the general question of predication and negation. Take the statement, "Motion is not rest," which all agree to be true. This does not deny that motion exists, as some have thought; here "is not" merely means "is different from," and can be used without any implications about existence. We must distinguish, then, between the existential meaning of the verb "to be" and that meaning which links concepts in various ways. With the latter, negative statements are perfectly legitimate.

We can now return to falsehoods. Plato begins by analyzing speech and, in particular, statements. Statements are not just strings of words; they consist basically of two kinds of words in conjunction, nouns and verbs. Only through such words in conjunction do we get a statement, as distinct from a mere naming or reference. A statement is about its subject, as "Theaetetus is sitting" is about Theaetetus, and it may be true or false. "Theaetetus is flying", for instance, is about Theaetetus and is false. A true statement states things as they are, and a false one states things different from the things that are.

Plato's account is concise and leaves many questions unanswered. There is a sudden switch from a discussion of forms to a discussion of language, and the place of the forms in falsehoods is not made clear. But all this does not affect the main point, that for the first time a philosopher has faced the paradoxes of negation and given some convincing, if not fully worked-out, answers. Much more work on the various meanings of "is" remains to be done, but the vital first step of making at least one distinction has been taken.

PLATO'S FURTHER THEORIES OF LANGUAGE

Plato also discusses language at some length in two other places, the *Cratylus*, which I would like to place as certainly later than the *Republic*, and the *Seventh Letter*, written 353/2, which is very late indeed. The genuineness of the relevant part of the latter has been doubted, but on insufficient grounds.

In the *Cratylus* the original question raised is whether language is natural or conventional, or, to put it more crudely, whether there is one right name for each thing or whether any name by which men have agreed to call it is equally good as any other. Plato even discusses the more extreme possibility that each man may have his own private language and give names to things at his own wish.

In the course of the argument, two main views of the nature of names and words in general may be distinguished, the imitative and the functional. If there is a single correct word for each thing, or even a limited number of correct words, it is reasonable to find this correctness in the fact that the words imitate adequately the nature of that thing and so enable us to learn what it is. Socrates considers two ways in which this can be done. With compound words and names we may look at the meaning of their elements and see if they provide a good description of the thing or person named — for example, Astyanax means "lord of the city," and is an appropriate name if the holder is indeed lord of the city. But with simple words this analysis cannot be performed, and we are reduced to imitation by means of letters and sounds. For instance, the letter "r" indicates movement, and "l" smoothness. But it soon becomes clear that this approach is unsatisfactory for two reasons: it cannot be carried out empirically on existing languages, and, more important, it ignores the fact that words have a function.

The function of words, according to Plato, is to give information and make distinctions; or, again, to convey to you the thoughts I have in my mind. For this, it does not matter much whether the word is a good or poor imitation; what is important is that you know what the word means. That you get from knowing its usage, which again comes ultimately from convention — i.e., from the way in which men are agreed in using the word.

Perhaps the most important point is that Plato demolishes thoroughly the belief that knowledge of words can be prior to, and more important than, knowledge of things. This is an ancient superstition, but, as Plato shows, it is unlikely that indirect knowledge through words would ever be better than direct knowledge of things. This is taken up again in the *Seventh Letter*,[18] where Plato distinguishes three tools for gaining knowledge of reality, the word, the definition, and the image. Examples are the case of a circle, the word "circle," the definition given in words, and the circular outline drawn or turned on a lathe. Words are entirely conventional and so cannot give us knowledge; definitions, made up of words, are no better off. The image, the drawn circle, is also imperfect and therefore useless for our purpose; knowledge may come as the result of long study using words, definitions and images, but it does not come *through* them. It comes through some kind of direct insight into the essence of a thing.

In fact, in this late letter Plato seems to return to his earlier views. After the detailed epistemological and linguistic studies of his later dialogues, he shows that he has kept his basic tenets unchanged. There is, however, evidence that in his last years, he was developing the theory of forms in a complicated and perhaps fantastic way, in which numbers played a large part, as it did with the Pythagoreans. It may have contained points of interest, but the subject is obscure and its philosophical value doubtful, so I do not propose to say anything more about it.

Socrates' and Plato's Ethical Theories

ALTHOUGH we have so far concentrated on other aspects of his philosophy, Socrates' main interest was in questions of morals. Indeed, his whole life's work had a practical purpose — to make men better. That purpose was shared by Plato, whose experience of contemporary politics sharpened his concern; though his scope was much wider and he touched on philosophy in all its branches, his final goal was still the same, the improvement of mankind. As a result of this practical aim, both men's approaches to ethics were very different from that of most modern philosophers. The latter are content to leave exhortation to the preachers and reformers, but both Socrates and Plato were reformers and theoretical philosophers in one. Their preaching had two parts, to prove to men that they ought to be good, and to show them how to become good.

Attempts to prove that men ought to be good have been frowned on by some later philosophers. Such proofs may be criticized on two different grounds:

1. It may be said that the statement "Men ought to be good" is a tautology, necessarily true but uninformative. To this, Socrates and Plato could reply that their proof must be linked with their analysis of the nature of goodness, which *was* informative.

2. The more serious criticism is that proofs of the kind found, for instance, in the *Republic*, strike at the foundations of morality by trying to show that men will profit from being virtuous. True virtue, it is said, seeks no rewards, and men who behave well for ulterior motives are not genuinely good. We shall have to discuss this point at greater length in connection with the *Republic*. Here I need only say that Socrates and Plato would not have been much troubled by this point. They did indeed quarrel with the Greek man in the street, who believed that virtue was desirable only because it enabled men to live at peace with their neighbours and to avoid being punished after death; but they saw nothing wrong in trying to show that it brought rewards of a greater kind, in the form of complete personal happiness.

Before such proof could be reached, however, a good deal of preliminary spadework was necessary, and much of this we can attribute with reasonable certainty to Socrates. He aimed at bringing home to individuals their ignorance of what virtue is and at proving to them that if they knew what it was they would inevitably seek and find it. His teaching may be summed up in three sentences: No man does wrong willingly. Virtue is knowledge. All virtues are ultimately one. These are more closely connected than might at first appear, and the arguments that led up to them can be reconstructed from Plato's dialogues thus:

1. All men desire only what is good.
   Therefore no man desires what is evil.
   To do wrong is to act in a way that will bring about evil.
   Therefore no man desires to do wrong.
   Therefore when a man does wrong he does so unwillingly.

2. All men desire only what is good.
   Therefore all men would bring about what is good if they could do so.
   If they cannot do so, it is because they do not know how to bring about what is good.
   Virtue is the bringing about of what is good.
   Therefore virtue is knowledge (of what is good).
3. Each separate virtue aims at what is good in particular circumstances.
   All men desire what is good in all circumstances.
   If they fail to obtain it, it is because they do not know what is good.
   Therefore a man can only be virtuous in any way if he knows what is good.
   Therefore all virtues depend on one thing — knowledge of what is good.
   Therefore all virtues are ultimately one.

Much of this is easily acceptable, but there are also several controversial points:

a. In argument (1), there is a vagueness about the statement that to do wrong is to act in a way that will bring about evil. On a common-sense level, it seems clear that to do wrong is usually to bring about evil for another but possibly good for oneself, and it would not then follow that no man desires to do wrong. In fact, as we shall see, Plato devoted much attention to showing that doing wrong was harmful to the wrong-doer.
b. In argument (2), the controversial point is the claim that if men cannot bring about what is good it is because, and only because, they do not know how to do so. This intellectualist view was criticized as early as Aristotle on the ground that it did not do justice to the psychological state of the man who in some sense has knowledge of what is good but from weakness of will cannot bring himself to seek it. A great deal depends, of course, on what one means by "knowledge" in this situation, and it is unlikely that Socrates himself ever gave a detailed account of what he meant. It is not unreasonable to see in some of Plato's dialogues an attempt to work out the implications of Socrates' unanalyzed claim.
c. The view that all virtues are ultimately one has the awkward consequence that it is correct if a man cannot in particular be brave without being also just, pious, and self-controlled, in fact having all other virtues. This seems contrary to the facts of common experience, and Plato treats the problem at length in the *Laches* and the *Protagoras*. It happens that we are already puzzled in everyday life about courage. Should we praise more the man who does a heroic deed without feeling fear or the man who does it although he is afraid? What Plato does is to recommend one way out of this dilemma. He suggests that the only man who is brave in the

true sense is the one who, knowing what good and evil are, for that reason feels no fear when the situation calls for courageous action, and for that reason is also just, pious, and self-controlled.

Socrates, then, left a number of problems for Plato. One big question was "What is this knowledge that is virtue?" Plato's first attempt to answer it, in the *Protagoras*, is a straightforward one, a form of psychological hedonism. The knowledge men lack when they do wrong, he suggests, is knowledge of how to calculate the future balance of pleasures and pains that will result from a contemplated action. Pleasure and avoidance of pain are the agreed goals; it is only in working out how to reach them that a man may go wrong. Significantly, it is assumed that only a man's own pleasures and pains are to be taken into account; we are not presented with the utilitarianism of Bentham and Mill.*

However, this crude theory did not satisfy Plato for long. In the *Gorgias*, probably a little later than the *Protagoras*, he departed from the view that pleasure is necessarily good and is in fact the only good for man. He analyzed the concept of pleasure and showed that some pleasures are "mixed" — i.e., that they involve pain as a necessary counterpart to pleasure. For instance, he claimed that a man gets pleasure from drinking only as long as he is thirsty. The pain of depletion must be there for the pleasure of repletion to be felt. Hence, since it depends on pain, a pleasure of this kind cannot be good, and it would seem to follow that the kind of knowledge needed for virtue must be something other than the ability to calculate pleasures and pains. This does, of course, ignore the possibility that there are some pure pleasures that do not involve pain, and, as we shall see, Plato developed his views further in the very late *Philebus*. But we must now turn to other difficulties arising from Socrates' paradoxes, which may have helped Plato reach his mature theories.

1. If virtue is knowledge, we would expect there to be practitioners and teachers of virtue, just as there are skills like shoemaking, navigation, and medicine. Where are these practitioners? The views that they are leading politicians or Sophists are dismissed. Perhaps all the citizens of a state are teachers of virtue and pass it on to their sons. But this, too, seems unsatisfactory. Is the true teacher of virtue yet to be found in the unhonoured philosopher?
2. If virtue is knowledge it must have some subject-matter, as other forms of knowledge do. In fact, it seems at first that each virtue has some subject-matter — e.g., justice is concerned with making treaties and keeping things safe. But

* On the other hand, Plato's theory that punishment is justified, not as retribution, but only as a means of reforming the criminal or as a deterrent to others is pure utilitarianism.

then there is a paradox: A man who is skilled at keeping things safe will also be good at stealing them, and the just man will be a good thief. In general, the good man — and the Greek notion of virtue involves goodness in fact and not merely goodness of intention — is one who knows how to achieve his purpose, whether that purpose be good or ill. That there is a paradox here was obvious to Socrates, but it is not certain if he ever saw how to deal with it. The answer Plato gave was that the knowledge needed by a virtuous man was knowledge of good and evil, and that this was extremely difficult to achieve.

His fullest treatment of the problem is to be found in the *Republic*. Here the ethical problem is set against a grand political and metaphysical background. In the light of the theory of forms, Plato has come to believe that knowledge of good and evil must be knowledge of the form of the good, which can be achieved by very few, and then only at the end of a long and difficult education. Exactly what this knowledge is is obscure, but it seems to involve an understanding of how man ought to live in order to be in harmony with the universe. (This statement must be taken without reference to later theories of what it is to be in harmony with the universe.) Those who attain such knowledge are to be leaders of their fellow men and are to organize their lives for them in a society devised for this purpose.

We have here a considerable shift in Plato's notion of virtue. Socrates had been concerned almost solely with individuals, but Plato had come to believe that the problem must be seen in a far wider context. In the *Republic*, the discussion centers on the virtue of justice (*dikaiosynē*), which for the Greeks had both a wide and a narrow meaning. In its wider sense it was practically equivalent to the whole of virtue and could perhaps have been called "righteousness," whereas in its narrower sense it was much like our word "justice." Justice in the individual involves a correct relationship of the three parts of the soul, which Plato here distinguishes as reason, the appetites, and an intermediate that we may perhaps call "sense of honor." If reason controls the appetites with the aid of the sense of honor, the individual will be just. In fact, Plato thinks that very few are capable of reaching this state by themselves, but in the ideal state, the few who can do so are able to control the other members of their society and to direct *their* appetites according to the dictates of reason. And so the whole community becomes virtuous.

We are now at the heart of the proof that men ought to be good. Plato has taken justice to be a correct balance of the parts of the soul — a form of mental health. He now adds that it is only by being mentally healthy that a man can be happy, and so justice is necessary for happiness.

It may seem just an unfortunate complication that he has also proved that justice is in effect only attainable in a community. Or, more seriously, it may seem that in the efficiently working community that Plato depicts, virtue, as we know it, has been elbowed out. Many modern writers have been horrified by the illiberal elements in the *Republic*, seeing Plato's community as a forerunner of modern totalitarian systems. But this is to misunderstand Plato's whole outlook and purpose. Modern thought, under the influence of Christianity, emphasizes the importance of individual freedom, by which each man may work out his own salvation. Further, freedom to *be* good is largely freedom to *do* good, and this involves, as often as not, the sacrifice of one's own interests to those of other people. Plato's outlook was different. It may be regarded as a form of utopianism. The modern idea of virtue is closely connected with the shortcomings of human existence. We must be charitable because others need our help. We must be humble because we are lowly creatures before God. But if all were strong, healthy, and free from want, such virtues would be unnecessary. In a perfect society men could aim at presenting themselves to their fellows as perfect works of art, beautiful and intelligent as well as brave and kind. And that is the aim embodied in the Greek notion of virtue. Their word *aretē* did indeed include moral virtue in our sense, but it also covered gifts of mind and body that Christian thought would exclude. As an example, the *aretē* of a carpenter is skill in carpentry, and a man's *aretē* is to conduct well the whole of a man's activities. Hence, in some ways the word "excellence" is a closer equivalent, extending as it does far beyond the sphere of morals.

The antithesis between the Greek and the modern outlooks on virtue must not, however, be pressed too far. It may be due to a paradox at the heart of our notions of morality. Certainly neither the Greek nor the modern view is free from inconsistencies. For instance, Plato and Aristotle were much troubled by the problem of whether a good man suffering the extremes of misery could still be happy. Plato dared to say that he would, but recognized that his claim was paradoxical; Aristotle denied it, but only with some shilly-shallying. Yet if virtue was enough for happiness, there would be no problem. Again, the Greek fear of *hybris*, the overweening pride that calls down vengeance from the Gods, accords ill with the elements of utopianism that are brought out by Plato's treatment of virtue. Similarly, in modern times we find a difficulty over whether virtue is rewarded: we feel, on the one hand, that a good deed is truly good only if it is done with no hope of reward; but on the other, moralists and preachers still strive to show that virtue *is* rewarded, probably on earth but certainly in heaven.

The difficulties discussed here derive from the question of whether virtue *guarantees* happiness. The lesser claim that virtue is necessary, whether or not it is sufficient, for happiness is more easily accepted. Plato has little difficulty in showing that the tyrant — for the Greeks the typical successful wrongdoer — is mentally sick and therefore unhappy, and that injustice necessarily harms the doer more than the sufferer.

The gap that remains to be filled is the connection between justice-as-mental-health and justice-as-the-doing-of-just-actions. Plato was here at one with those modern thinkers who believe that all crime is due to mental disturbance of some kind. A man with his desires properly under the control of reason would feel no temptation to do wrong or injure his fellows. Exactly how this was to be accomplished is obscure, presumably because it was only in the light of knowledge of the form of the good that a man would be fully aware of how he ought to live. But the high point of the *Republic*, and of Plato's own life, was the hope that somehow after much seeking, virtue could be brought by the philosopher to dwell among men.

At the end of the *Republic*[20] and in the tortuous *Philebus* are what may best be described as "some thoughts on pleasure." The *Philebus*, possibly Plato's last work except for the *Laws*, may have been written as a contribution to an argument going on in the Academy on the question "What is the good for man?" The astronomer Eudoxus said that it was pleasure; Speusippus believed it to be thought. Plato claimed neither would do because the good must be something which a man who knew it would choose before anything else, and by which he would be completely satisfied. But neither a life of pleasure without thought nor a life of thought without pleasure would be entirely satisfying to man, although beasts and gods might be different; rather, both pleasure and thought find a place in the good for man. But we have already seen in the *Gorgias* that not all pleasures are good, and that leads us into a complicated and difficult discussion of pleasure. From it and from the passage in the *Republic* a number of points emerge: There are pleasures of the body and pleasures of the soul; some pleasures are pure, but many are "mixed" and necessarily bound up with pain. Scratching an itch is an example of a bodily pleasure accompanied by

a bodily pain; drinking when thirsty is pleasant, but as shown in the *Gorgias*, must be accompanied by pain. Desire is a state of bodily disturbance in which the soul remembers past disturbances and how they were corrected, and so has an image of what will now be satisfying. After pain, a neutral state between pleasure and pain seems pleasant, but is not really so. There are pleasures of anticipation which are purely mental, but they frequently anticipate mixed bodily pleasures and so are mixed themselves. Another mixed mental pleasure is malicious joy at the discomfiture of our friends. Among pure pleasures are seeing beautiful shapes and colors, hearing beautiful notes, and smelling pleasant scents; these are preceded by no felt want and are therefore free from pain. Last of all, for the few, are the pleasures of learning.

From all this, it is concluded that many pleasures, being linked with pain, cannot be good. Further, it is likely that intense pleasures are not good, for they are found in diseased states — for example, the pleasure a feverish man gets from quenching his thirst. But the pure pleasures and those others that are necessary to a normal life are to be admitted into the good life.

On this moderate note Plato ends his contribution to personal moral theory. But his growing interest in the part played by pleasure and pain in influencing moral action finds final expression in the *Laws*, a grand, complex, and illiberal work that here can only be mentioned. There is also no space for a number of other theories for which Plato is renowned: the *Republic* is a classic work on political theory and education, and the treatment of love in the *Symposium* has had immense influence on later thought. Full justice would be done to Plato only by including all these and much more. Here we have studied him as a metaphysician, epistemologist, logician, and moralist. His metaphysical structure, the theory of forms, was attacked even by Aristotle, and in its original form it can hardly be defended. But much of value can be salvaged from the ruins, and his studies in logic and theory of knowledge provided an excellent starting point for Aristotle's work. In breadth of interests he has never been surpassed.

3

Aristotle

D. J. O'CONNOR

ARISTOTLE WAS BORN in 384 B.C. at Stagira in northern Greece. His father was Nicomachus, physician to the Macedonian court and its king, Amyntas II. At the age of eighteen, Aristotle left Macedonia to study in Athens. For the next eighteen years, until Plato's death in 347, he studied in the Academy. After Plato's death, he appears to have found himself out of sympathy with the mathematical interests of Plato's nephew, Speusippus, who succeeded Plato as head of the Academy. He traveled to Assos in Asia Minor, where the local ruler, Hermias, welcomed the formation of a small philosophical and scientific school. For the next five years he worked at philosophy and biology. (The details of his biological work make it probable that most of his specimens came from this area.) He spent three years at Assos and married Hermias' daughter there. He then moved to Mitylene in Lesbos, where he spent two more years on his biological studies.

He was then invited to return to Macedonia to be tutor to the heir to the Macedonian throne. The boy, later Alexander the Great, was then thirteen years old. Alexander spent three or four years under Aristotle's tutelage. It is difficult to trace any of the philosopher's influence in Alexander's later career. In 335, Aristotle left the Macedonian court to return to Athens. He there set up a philosophical school at the Lyceum or Peripatos. (The name of "Peripatetic", later given to the Aristotelian school, was taken from this word.) He taught there for twelve years, until the death of Alexander the Great in 323. The anti-Macedonian reaction at Athens consequent on Alexander's death brought some unpopularity and even danger to Aristotle, and on being indicted for "impiety" he left the city for Chalcis. It is said that he did so to prevent the Athenians from sinning again against philosophy as they had done in the case of Socrates. He died at Chalcis in the following year at the age of sixty-two.

ARISTOTLE IS ONE of the two or three most influential philosophers in the history of Western thought. He is also one of the most difficult. It may help us to understand him if we first make clear to ourselves the questions we want to ask about his philosophy and then look briefly at some of the reasons why people find him difficult to understand. We must notice, to begin with, that the causes of a philospher's influencing later thinking are not necessarily connected with the philosophical value of what he has to say. All sorts of accidental historical factors may result in the fact that one philosopher's writings affect men's ways of thought for generations while another's are neglected. In the case of the philosophers of the ancient world, the most important of these accidents was undoubtedly the extent to which their writings survived into medieval and modern times. Plato and, to a lesser extent, Aristotle, were fortunate in this. But Democritus and Chrysippus, for example, though probably their equals in philosophical genius, are shadowy figures to us. Their doctrines have to be conjectured uncertainly from the reports of obscure and sometimes unfriendly commentators and from the scanty surviving fragments of what they wrote. In literature, as in life, survival is the first condition of success.

The study of the various causes that make a philosopher influential in the history of thought is very complicated. Happily, it is comparatively unimportant for the student of philosophy; it is of interest only to the historian of ideas. For us, as students of philosophy, the question, "Why were Aristotle's doctrines so influential?" is a historical side issue with which we need not be concerned (although I shall refer to it briefly at the end of this chapter). We are interested in very different questions: What were his doctrines? Were they true? Or if, regrettably, it seems odd to contemporary ears to talk of philosophical doctrines as being *true* or *false*, we can at least ask: Are his doctrines defensible by reason? It may indeed sometimes happen that a doctrine survives and is influential because it is true or rationally defensible. But the intellectual history of mankind does not lead us to suppose that this has happened very often in philosophy. It is fortunate that in some fields, notably in the natural sciences, truth has a greater survival value.

But before we try to answer the question "Are Aristotle's doctrines true?" we have first to determine what those doctrines were. In saying above that Aristotle is one of the most difficult philosophers to understand, I have implied that it is not always easy to determine just what he did mean. There are two main reasons for this. The first is the nature of the intellectual background of his time; the second is the character of his writings as they have come down to us.

1. It is not always easy to understand a philosopher of our own day and our own society who writes in our own language. Philosophical concepts and arguments are often abstruse, subtle, complex, or in other ways unobvious and difficult to grasp. When they are expressed in a language different from our own, they have to be seen either through the distorting glass of a translation or through our necessarily imperfect knowledge of the language in which they are written. And when they are expressed, as Aristotle's are, in a dead language that is the vehicle of a culture quite alien to our own, our difficulties are greatly increased. The moral, religious, and, above all, scientific outlook of Greek civilization was quite different from that of our modern Western society. The much-talked of affinity between the civilizations of ancient Greece and modern Europe has been much exaggerated by old-fashioned propagandists for a classical education. In so far as it can be established at all, this affinity amounts to no more than the tenuous and fitful, but somehow tenacious, respect for the free exercise of human reason which is manifest in the best products of both Greece and modern Europe. This respect is indeed very clearly at work in much of Aristotle's writings. But in all other ways, the presuppositions of Aristotle's philosophy, and of Greek philosophy in general, seem strange and alien to us. This strangeness must somehow be discounted if we are to understand Aristotle. I shall, therefore, try to make these background beliefs explicit at those points where they seem to be specially relevant.

2. Substantial parts of the works of Aristotle have come down to us. In the standard English translation,[1] they amount to twelve volumes. But what we have is by no means all of what he wrote. He was the author of popular works and a number of dialogues in the manner of Plato, which seem to have been much more readable than any that have survived. Good judges in antiquity* spoke highly of their literary style, but such a compliment can hardly be paid to what *we* know of Aristotle's writing. The popular works have all perished, along with a collection of scientific notes and materials. We know of their existence and their contents only through references to them by later authors. With one exception,† what has survived is a collection of his serious philosophical and scientific treatises, much of it in a rather rough and unedited form. The style, for the most part, is terse, even cryptic, and full of puzzling discontinuities, although some parts seem to have been much more carefully written than others. At its best, the style has an austere beauty of its own. It is, however, far removed from the

* e.g. Cicero and Quintilian.
† *The Constitution of Athens.* This belongs to the second group of writings. The complete text was recovered only in 1891.

mannered elegance of Plato, who is, perhaps unfortunately, regarded as the model of ancient philosophical writing. Much devoted scholarship has been exercised in elucidating the difficulties of Aristotelian texts and in determining their genuineness and the order in which they were written. But the difficulties remain for the ordinary philosophical reader.

These two obstacles to understanding Aristotle, the unfamiliarity of his intellectual background and the difficulty of the text, have resulted in an enormous mass of writing by ancient, medieval, and modern commentators devoted to elucidating his theories. And we cannot say even now that the outcome is clear and settled. Any detailed interpretation that is given of his philosophy is likely to be controversial. However, the main outlines are pretty clear. And that is all we are now concerned with.

Modern writers on Aristotle have one big advantage over their predecessors: They are able to see which parts of his work have retained their importance in the face of considerable modern developments in formal logic and in natural science. A brief verdict in the light of modern knowledge would be something like this: As a formal logician, Aristotle has never stood higher. He is one of the half-dozen really great logicians that the world has seen. As a moral philosopher, too, his work has stood up well to the test of time. The *Nicomachaean Ethics* is still, at least in some of its parts, a very influential book. Echoes of its doctrines can be found in a good deal of present-day ethics. The rest of his philosophy, however, is vitiated by a fatal flaw. It is very closely tied up with an entirely false scientific picture of the world. And it is not at all easy in evaluating his philosophical ideas to disinfect them of this discredited science.

It is easy for us nowadays to make a fairly sharp distinction between science and philosophy. Scientific questions are those which can be decided by the evidence of our senses strengthened and directed by various instruments (microscopes, telescopes, etc.) and by devices of method (measurement, experimental procedures, and so on). It is by such means that men have found out the distances and constitutions of the heavenly bodies, the laws of mechanics, the number and nature of the elements, the ways plants and animals are nourished, the laws of heredity, and countless other facts of this sort. We are not able to decide by such means whether or not there is a god, whether Plato's theory of forms is true or false, and whether we should prefer the Christian code of ethics to that of Nietzsche. The scientific revolution of the last three hundred years has given us a standard by which we can judge human knowledge and human problems. Some problems yield to scientific methods and give us scientific knowledge; others do not. Even when we meet unsolved and intractable problems, we know at least if they are problems of science. We know, for example, that the

problem of the cause, prevention, and cure of cancer is a scientific problem (or, rather, a cluster of such problems). But this distinction, so obvious and useful to us, was by no means obvious to Aristotle and his contemporaries. They made no clear distinction between scientific and other problems. The same thinker might occupy himself with questions of empirical science, mathematics, and philosophy, as did Aristotle himself. He is a considerable figure in the early history of science. But his great intellectual versatility and his deep interest in scientific questions blinded him to the essential differences between science and philosophy. This results in much of his work being a very intimate mixture of false science and philosophical doctrines; the latter are impossible to evaluate until we have distinguished them clearly from the scientific matrix in which they developed.

Perhaps the best way for us to make this essential distinction is to sketch Aristotle's scientific picture of the world before we go on to discuss his philosophical doctrines. We shall, of course, be making a distinction which Aristotle did not himself recognize. But it will help us to understand what his doctrines were and to judge them more fairly. It is most important in the study of both ancient and medieval philosophy not to allow false and absurd scientific theories to devalue philosophical ideas which may have no more than a fortuitous association with them. But it is equally important to recognize false science for what it is.

I shall first of all give a brief sketch of Aristotle's greatest achievement, his formal logic. I shall then outline the scientific background of his philosophy. After this, we shall be in a position to look more fairly at his specifically philosophical doctrines.

Formal Logic

ALTHOUGH logic was not for Aristotle, any more than it is for us today, a part of philosophy, it is very closely bound up with certain philosophical questions. A particular view of logic may easily influence the philosophical outlook of the man who holds it. Aristotle rightly regarded logic as providing the method or technique of philosophical progress. His logical works were, in fact, given the title of *organon* (instrument) by one of his ancient commentators. Of the six works so classified, only one, the *Prior Analytics*, expounds formal logic, as Aristotle himself understood the subject. Of the rest, the *Topics* and *Sophistical Refutations* deal with types of reasoning that fail to meet Aristotle's standards of scientific thinking. They do not deal with "informal logic," for there can be no such subject. But they contain, as recent research has shown,[2] a good deal of logic imperfectly formulated. The *Posterior Analytics* deals largely with questions that would today be classified as "a theory of knowledge." And the

Categories and *De Interpretatione* discuss topics that nowadays fall under the headings of philosophical logic and semantics. We shall be discussing some of these questions later.

Formal logic can roughly be described as the science of deductive proof. It is a characteristic of such proof that if the information from which we start (the *premises*) are true, the *conclusion* inferred from these premises must also be true. A complete formal logic would anatomize and classify all the different types of proof and show how they are related. Aristotle's formal logic was very far from complete. He studied only one very restricted type of argument and did not succeed, as we shall see, in perfecting his study of that. His achievement lies in inventing certain concepts and techniques which subsequent research has shown to be essential to the development of the subject. He also explored very thoroughly the varieties of one important type of argument and the connections between these varieties. The details of Aristotle's logical writings make it clear that he was acquainted with logical rules other than those he formulated explicitly in the *Prior Analytics*. But he seems never to have realized their importance or to have given them conscious attention.[3]

In his work on formal logic, Aristotle restricts his attention almost entirely to the so-called "classical" or "Aristotelian" syllogism.* His definition of "syllogism" in the *Prior Analytics* is "discourse in which certain things being stated, something other than what is stated follows of necessity from their being so."[4] This is a very wide definition which covers any valid deductive argument. Any theorem of Euclid's geometry, for example, along with the propositions from which it is validly derived, would satisfy it. What Aristotle means by "syllogism" in the specialized technical sense of his formal logic may be illustrated simply, though somewhat inaccurately, by an argument of the following kind familiar from the traditional "Aristotelian" logic:

A. All theories based on empirical evidence deserve
       rational consideration.
     All psychological theories are based on empirical
       evidence.
     Therefore: All psychological theories deserve
       rational consideration.

This is, of course, not an example taken from Aristotle's own writings. As Lukasiewicz has shown, it differs from a genuine Aristotelian syllogism in certain important respects.[5] But to look at the differences between this familar type of traditional syllogism and the genuine Aristotelian variety is a good way of introducing some of Aristotle's basic logical

doctrines. The example just given resembles a valid Aristotelian syllogism in having two premises ("All theories based on empirical evidence deserve rational consideration" and "All psychological theories are based on empirical evidence"), and a conclusion ("All psychological theories deserve rational consideration") that follows necessarily from the premises. It is also Aristotelian in that it concerns three and only three "terms" ("theories based on empirical evidence," "theories deserving rational consideration," and "psychological theories"). Moreover, the three terms differ in their relative "width" or extension. Clearly the relations of extension control in some fashion the way in which the conclusion follows from the premises. The term "theories deserving rational consideration" is widest in scope and the term "psychological theories" is narrowest. And the extension of the term that occurs in both premises, "theories based on empirical evidence," falls between the two. We can express this relationship and illustrate the validity of the syllogism by a diagram thus:

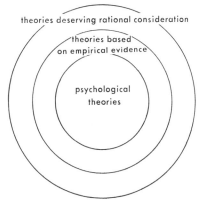

Aristotle did not himself use diagrams to show the relative extension of terms in a syllogism,* but he puts the same point in a general way by saying, "Whenever three terms are so related to one another that the last is contained in the middle as in a whole and the middle is either contained in or excluded from the first as in or from a whole, the extremes must be related by a perfect syllogism. "And he adds,[6] "I call that term 'middle' which is itself contained in another and that in which another is contained."† The other two terms, which Aristotle here calls "extremes," he elsewhere calls "major" and "minor," respectively. In our example, "psychological theories" is the minor and "theories deserving rational consideration" the major term. "I call that term the major in which the middle is contained and that term the minor which comes under the middle."[8] This terminology of major, minor, and middle terms has persisted in logic until the present day. In these

---

* In what follows, the discussion will be confined to the so-called assertoric syllogism. The *modal* syllogism containing premises of the type "*S* is necessarily *P*" or "*S* is possibly *P*" is a complex and difficult part of Aristotle's logic whose problems have not yet been fully resolved.

* Diagrams of this sort were introduced by the German mathematician Euler (1707–1783).
† This is faulty, as Lukasiewicz has shown. But for our present purpose we may ignore this.

respects, then, the example we have taken conforms to Aristotle's doctrine of the syllogism. But in two very important respects it differs from it.

First, Aristotle very rarely gives concrete specific examples of syllogistic arguments in explaining his theory. (A) is an argument consisting of three logically related statements about certain kinds of theories. But clearly the logical force of an argument of this kind in no way depends on what the argument is *about*. If we were to substitute for the major, minor, and middle terms occurring in our example terms that actually do occur in this function in Aristotle's writings[9] we get another valid argument with a totally different subject matter but the same structure (or "logical form," as it is nowadays called):

B.   All broad-leaved plants are deciduous.
     All vines are broad-leaved plants.
     Therefore: All vines are deciduous.

This brings out the very important fact exemplified, though not explicitly stated, in Aristotle's writings that *the subject matter of formal deductive arguments is quite irrelevant to their validity.* And this vital fact can be elucidated far better by substituting arbitrary *symbols* for the concrete descriptive terms. This is just what Aristotle does in explaining the rules of his formal logic. He uses letters of the alphabet for the major, minor, and middle terms. If we amend our illustrative syllogism in this way and use "M" for the middle term, and "P" and "S" respectively for the major and minor,* we have:

C.   All M is P.
     All S is M.
     Therefore: All S is P.

This formulation brings out the essential structure of the argument. Whatever terms we may care to put in place of M, P, and S will yield a concrete instance of a valid argument. Now, this replacement of concrete terms by arbitrary symbols is an innovation of the very first importance — the introduction of *variables* into logic. In (C), the letters M, P, and S can stand for any terms we please, and we can obtain a correct argument by making an appropriate substitution, as for example, in (A) and (B). Aristotle does not, himself, comment on this very important innovation, perhaps because, as Lukasiewicz says,[10] he "regarded his invention as entirely plain and requiring no explanation." It is probable, of course, that the idea is an extension of the practice of contemporary geometers of using arbitrary letters to name points. The step from an arbitrary name to a variable in mathematical and logical contexts is a short one. The point to notice, however, is this: the introduction of variables into logic made it possible to develop the subject as *a science* instead of

a collection of examples. For it is one of the essential characteristics of a science that it aims at formulating general laws — for example, "all arguments of such-and-such a structure are valid."

However, we have still not got a proper Aristotelian syllogism when we express our arguments as *argument-forms* with variables for terms, as in (C). Indeed, if we look carefully at (C), we realize that, so far from being a true statement, it is in fact meaningless. For (C) affirms the truth of "All M is P" and of "All S is M" and, in consequence, the truth of the conclusion "All S is P." But these cannot possibly be either true or false nor can they even be sensibly affirmed. For they are not statements. They are statement-forms, which become true or false when we replace the variables "S," "M," and "P" with suitable terms as in (A) and (B). There is a big difference between an *inference* or *argument* in which we affirm certain premises as true and then draw certain conclusions from them as in (A) and (B) above, and an *implication* or *entailment* which says only that *if* certain premises are true, then a certain conclusion necessarily follows. The implication corresponding to (A) is:

D.   If all theories based on empirical evidence deserve rational consideration, and if all psychological theories are based on empirical evidence, then all psychological theories deserve rational consideration.

And the implication corresponding to (C) is:

E.   If all M is P and all S is M, then all S is P.

Now, this is not only a true statement [unlike (C)], but is, apart from a minor difference of phrasing,* a genuine Aristotelian syllogism. Such syllogisms are all implications, not inferences, and are expressed with variables in place of concrete terms.

The questions we have now to consider are:

1.   How many kinds of valid syllogisms are there?

2.   How do we distinguish valid from invalid syllogisms?

3.   How are the valid syllogisms related to one another?

We first ask how many different kinds of premises there are and in how many different ways they may be combined into syllogisms. We then have to find some systematic way of distinguishing the valid instances from the invalid. And Aristotle's own method of doing this provides, as we shall see, an answer to (3).

He divides the statements that can constitute the premises and conclusions of a syllogism into four different types. For his premises, he considers only sentences in what is now called "the subject-predicate

---

* Following the conventions of the traditional logic where "S" and "P" stand respectively for the *subject* and *predicate* of the conclusion of the syllogism.

* Instead of "All A is B," Aristotle says, "B belongs (*hyparchei*) to all A" or "B is predicated of (*katēgoreitai*) all A."

form," sentences — in Aristotle's own phrase, "affirming or denying one thing of another."[11] These may be either universal — of the type "All *S* is *P*", or "No *S* is *P*" — or particular — of the form "Some *S* is *P*" or "Some *S* is not *P*." (A third category of "indefinite" statements — lacking the quantifiers "all" or "some" — is mentioned by Aristotle, but he does not use it in developing his logical theory.) We have, thus, the four kinds of premises recognized by the traditional logic — universal affirmative, universal negative, particular affirmative, and particular negative. In the terminology of that logic, they are conveniently symbolized *SaP*, *SeP*, *SiP*, and *SoP*, respectively. But it should be noted that this terminology is medieval in origin and is not found in Aristotle. We use it here for convenience.

These four types of premise are one source of variety in syllogisms. Another is the order in which the terms may occur in the premises. Plainly there are four possible arrangements:

$$\text{(a) } M - P \quad \text{(b) } P - M \quad \text{(c) } M - P \quad \text{(d) } P - M$$
$$S - M \qquad\quad S - M \qquad\quad M - S \qquad\quad M - S$$
$$S - P \qquad\quad S - P \qquad\quad S - P \qquad\quad S - P$$

Aristotle calls these arrangements "figures" (*schē-mata*). Of the four possibilities, he confines his attention to the first three and treats the fourth as a variant of (a).* If now we combine the four types of premise with the four figures, we have 4×4^3 or 256 possible varieties of syllogistic argument. The great majority of these are invalid forms and Aristotle restricts his attention to fourteen valid forms ("moods" as they are called in the traditional logic) of the first three figures: in (a), *aaa*, *eae*, *aii*, *eio*; in (b), *eae*, *aee*, *eio*, *aoo*; in (c), *aai*, *iai*, *aii*, *eao*, *oao*, *eio*. These he establishes one by one in the first book of the *Prior Analytics*. In addition, he notes as valid variants of first figure syllogisms the five valid moods of the traditional "fourth figure," *aai*, *aee*, *iai*, *eao*, *eio*.

But what criteria does he use in distinguishing valid from invalid forms? He points out in the first chapter of the *Posterior Analytics*[13] that "not all knowledge is demonstrative; on the contrary, knowledge of the immediate premises is independent of demonstration." He explains that there must be indemonstrable starting points to any chain of argument. If there were not, we should have to prove *A* by *B*, *B* by *C*, *C* by *D*, and so on *ad infinitum*, or else end the regress by proving, say, *D* by *A*, and so argue in a circle. We shall return later to this point in discussing his theory of knowledge. For the present, we may admit that it sounds like good sense (at least if we distinguish between *indemonstrable* and *undemonstrated* starting points to argument). But

how are we to select our indemonstrable starting points? The answer to this question has been given only in recent years by the modern theory of axiom systems. Aristotle, indeed, is on debatable ground in giving his own answer. He makes a distinction in the first chapter of the *Prior Analytics*[14] between *perfect* and *imperfect* syllogisms. "I call that a perfect syllogism which needs nothing other than what has been stated to make plain what necessarily follows." In what he calls "imperfect" syllogisms, on the other hand, certain additional propositions are required to make plain the logical necessity linking premises and conclusion. Aristotle makes clear what he means in working out the details of his logic. What he does is to take as basic and unproved two of the four moods of the first figure. One of these, known to the medievals as *Barbara*, is given in (E). The other, known to the medievals as *Celarent*, is given in (G). Aristotle then uses various logical devices to "reduce" (*anagein*) the imperfect syllogisms to one of these two.

The idea underlying this is very important. It is nothing less than the idea of an axiomatic system in which theorems (the imperfect syllogisms) are derived from unproved assumptions (the perfect syllogisms). The usual process of derivation from axioms is here reversed to a process of reduction to axioms. The notion of an axiomatic system was not unknown to mathematicians contemporary with Aristotle. Euclid's famous synthesis of geometrical knowledge was made public only a few years after Aristotle's death. But Aristotle must have the credit for seeing its relevance to a scientific logic. We may take as an example of the method the second figure syllogism, *Camestres*:

F. If all *P* is *M*, and no *S* is *M*, then no *S* is *P*.

This becomes *Celarent* in the first figure:

G. If no *M* is *S*, and all *P* is *M*, then no *P* is *S*.

The reduction is done by interchanging the order of the premises and "converting" the first premise and the conclusion by transposing subject and predicate.[15] Other reductions need more elaborate logical maneuvers, which we need not consider here.[16]

Some points must be noticed in criticism. In the first place, the theory of the syllogism, as Aristotle states it, is not complete and self-contained. For in order to perform the reductions of imperfect to perfect syllogisms, he has to assume logical rules which, though he uses them intuitively, he never states formally. And these logical rules are not always themselves part of syllogistic logic. Many of them belong to the logic of propositions. This is a more basic and primitive part of logic than the logic of the syllogism, but it was one that Aristotle himself did not investigate. It was studied by the Stoics some years afterward and considerable progress was made. But the discoveries of the Stoics were largely neglected by later philosophers. In spite of more pioneer

---

* A separate fourth figure was introduced very late in antiquity by an unknown writer. The usual attribution, in traditional text-books, of the fourth figure to Galen (second century A.D.) has been shown by Lukasiewicz[12] to be mistaken.

work by medieval logicians, it was left to nine-teenth-century workers to re-establish the logic of propositions as a fundamental branch of logic. Thus, Aristotle's logical system is fragmentary and un-finished. Secondly, his distinction between perfect and imperfect syllogisms, important as it is as a first attempt at a logical axiom system, depends on a dubious criterion for distinguishing the perfect from the imperfect. He does not say explicitly that first-figure syllogisms are self-evident and those in other figures are not: but this is the natural way of understanding what he says, and he has been so in-terpreted by ancient and modern commentators. The notion of self-evidence, as we shall see, is basic to his theory of knowledge. But whether or not a given statement is self-evident is a psychological question and not a logical one. It depends on the innate mental capacities and the previous training of the person who considers the statement.

Moreover, it is certainly not essential to a logical or a mathematical system that the axioms from which it starts should be intuitively obvious. We have only to ask, "Obvious to whom?" to see the absurdity of such a suggestion. There are indeed conditions to which a set of axioms should conform. (They must, for example, be consistent). But how obvious or un-obvious they are is of no consequence for logic.

It must also be said in criticism that Aristotle seems to have thought that the logic of the syllogism was the whole of logic, in that every demonstration must be capable of being broken down into a set of syllogisms of standard type.[17] He also supposed as a corollary of this that every proposition forming a premise or a conclusion of an argument must be in the so-called subject-predicate form. "Every pre-mise states that something is or must be or may be the attribute of something else."[18] It is surprising that his own considerable competence in mathe-matics did not at once bring counter-examples to his attention. There are countless arguments in the geometry known to the Greeks whose premises and conclusions were not in subject-predicate form and which were not syllogisms. This was a mistake in logic which had far-reaching effects on the philoso-phical views of those who accepted it — including, of course, Aristotle himself.

However, these are small criticisms of so consider-able an achievement as Aristotle's formal logic. The introduction of variables into logic and the systematization of an important part of it turned the subject from a collection of rules of thumb to a vigorously growing science. That the later history of logic failed to match this brilliant beginning was not the fault of Aristotle. As matters turned out, subsequent developments in antiquity and in the Middle Ages did not meet the understanding and appreciation they deserved, and Aristotle's own work was misinterpreted to a grotesque degree. But the rise of a genuinely scientific logic over the past hundred years has put us in a position to make a true estimate of the merits and defects of the work of the man who founded the science.

The Scientific Background

IT has already been noted that neither Aristotle nor any other Greek made a clear distinction between scientific and philosophical speculation. It may therefore seem to do violence to Aristotle's philoso-phy to try to dissect out the scientific background of his thinking and set it aside before discussing what we in the twentieth century regard as the properly philosophical parts of his system. However, we are forced to do this if we are to evaluate the philoso-phical ideas. For much of his science was simply wrong. And we must discount these mistakes and their influence if we are to judge his system fairly.

Aristotle's scientific speculations covered a wide field. He was a competent but unoriginal mathemati-cian. He speculated shrewdly though mistakenly in chemistry, cosmology, and mechanics;* and he was a first-rate biologist. In biology, indeed, he is one of the great figures in the history of science. His work in this field was greatly admired by Darwin. It is very noticeable, however, that his achievements were those of a skilled and patient *observer* rather than those of an *experimenter*. Experiment, roughly speaking, is observation under conditions controlled and varied by the observer himself. Thus, there is no sharp and clear-cut distinction between experiment-ing and merely observing. Nor is it true that the Greeks never experimented. But the realization of the immense fecundity of the experimental method and its consequent adoption as a systematic policy is partly cause and partly consequence of the modern scienti-fic age — the last 300 years. And it is a fact of nature that while a good deal of elementary biology can be learned by accurate and careful observation, the laws of physics and chemistry cannot be dis-covered in this way. Fairly sophisticated experimental methods allied to accurate techniques of measure-ment are needed before progress can be made.

Unfortunately, the most successful part of Aris-totle's science, his biological discoveries, were of particular facts that could make little impact on his philosophy. What was carried over from his biology was a certain point of view, the teleological attitude. Teleology is the doctrine that the structure and workings of nature are to be explained in terms of the purposes which they serve. So many biological phenomena seem to be clearly purposeful or func-tional that biologists tend naturally to interpret their material in terms of concepts like *purpose*, *function*, and *aim*. Since Darwin, they have come to realize that this natural tendency is very misleading, but in ancient times there was little to check it. Aristotle was a very thoroughgoing teleologist who

* Though by no means all of his theories in mechanics were abortive.[19]

interpreted not only the behavior of living matter but all the workings of nature as the outcome of purposefully directed processes. That nature does nothing in vain or haphazardly is a recurring theme in his writings.[20] He did not mean, as we shall see, that these directed processes were the outcome of some conscious planning by a superhuman intelligence. Purpose was for him, as it were, immanent or inherent in all natural processes, whether organic or merely physical. "If therefore purpose is present in art," he says in the *Physics*,[21] "it is present also in nature."

Today, by contrast, we tend to explain all phenomena mechanically as far as we can. We resort to teleological explanations only as a last resort, if at all. We do this because we have found that mechanical modes of explanation tend to be successful even in cases where common sense might suppose purpose of some kind to be at work. Let us take a simple example of this. It is a matter of common observation that some parts of plants (for example, the growing shoots) tend to turn toward the light. To say that the growing shoots of young plants were *seeking* the light would not be a mere metaphor for an Aristotelian. This would be for him a genuinely explanatory statement. But a modern botanist tries to find the *mechanism* by which these movements take place. He may show, for example, that when a shoot bends towards the right, it is because the cells on the left-hand side of the shoot are growing faster than the corresponding cells on the right-hand side, thus warping the shoot to the right. He may show further that certain chemicals (auxins) that stimulate the growth of cells tend to collect in the stem on the side furthest from the light. And so on. Such explanations are not, of course, logically incompatible with Aristotelian explanations in terms of purpose and "natural movement." But by tracing the chemical and physical processes underlying these phenomena, they remove the necessity of trying to explain them teleologically. The Aristotelian "explanation" becomes superfluous because it adds nothing to the scientific one. We shall be considering later on some examples of Aristotle's use of teleology. What we have to remember is that it is often an illegitimate extension of a biological way of thinking into nonbiological contexts. Even within biology, teleological explanations are now found to be of very doubtful value. Outside it, they merely divert our attention from more useful approaches. It is interesting to note that Aristotle's own pupil, Theophrastus, made some trenchant criticisms of his teleology. Unhappily for the subsequent history of science, these criticisms were less highly regarded than the theory to which they were directed.

The science of chemistry is the product of the last two hundred years. It can hardly be said to have existed in ancient times. But it will have been seen in Chapter 1 of this book that the Greeks had ideas on the nature and constitution of matter. In particular, Empedocles' theory of the four basic elements, fire, earth, air, and water, was taken over by Aristotle. Modern chemists believe in the existence of ninety-two naturally occurring elements out of which every substance in the universe is made. Water consists of hydrogen and oxygen in the proportion of two atoms to one; sugars consist of carbon, hydrogen, and oxygen in various proportions (6:12:6 for glucose, for example); common salt consists of chlorine and sodium in equal proportions; and so on, indefinitely. For Aristotle, everything in the universe, with one important exception (to be discussed below), consisted of fire, earth, air, and water in varying proportions. He does not, however, state or even conjecture on the proportions in which these basic elements combine to form the different materials of the world around us. And indeed, without some kind of atomic theory he could not have done so. For although he believed that these basic substances were elements in the sense that they could not be resolved into more primary substances, he had no satisfactory theory of *how* they combined to form rocks, wood, leaves, flesh, bones, and so on. He rejected, though for no good reason, the brilliant atomic theory of Democritus and Leucippus. He was, therefore, unable to adapt it to his own purposes and talk of "atoms" or smallest particles of the four elements. He never explained satisfactorily how it is possible for, say, my body to be a mixture of the four elements without there being separate particles of the elements existing side by side in the mixture. The modern chemist recognizes that even in chemical compounds having much more intimate associations of particles than a mere mechanical mixture, the atoms of the constituent elements exist side by side in some regular pattern.

However, Aristotle's theory was not a mere superstition. It was based on a rough kind of empirical evidence. The words we translate as "earth," "air," "water," and "fire" had for Greek philosophers a much wider meaning. They can be understood as referring to four different phases of matter — solid, liquid, gaseous, and the hot, luminous gas that we call flame. Common observation supports the theory that matter can adopt one or another of these disguises in differing circumstances. Ice becomes water and then steam. Wood burns to vapor and flame, leaving a little residual ash; the phenomenon of the silting up of rivers can be interpreted as water turning to earth; water condenses from vapor when dew falls; and so on. That the true interpretation of such phenomena is very different must not prevent us from appreciating that the doctrine of the four elements is at least in harmony with much of our unreflective observation of nature. It is unclear to what extent Aristotle was influenced to adopt this theory by its consonance with experience. At any rate, he certainly affirms, against Empedocles, that the elements change into each other and are not immutable.[22]

Moreover, he follows tradition in "explaining" the four elements as combining in pairs the four elementary qualities of hot, cold, wet, and dry. Fire is hot and dry, water cold and wet, and so on. And he finds in these elements the source of movement in the sublunary world. Each of the four elements has a "natural place" towards which it tends to go — earth and water down, toward the center of the earth, fire and air up, away from the earth's center. But earth is heavier than water, and fire is lighter than air; that is, they tend to go further in their natural directions. Fire, says Aristotle, has no weight, nor has earth any lightness.[23] (It will be seen from this that both weight and direction for him are *absolute*, not *relative*, concepts. A body's weight [or lightness] is something it possesses in itself without any relation to other bodies.)

Bodies compounded of the four elements tend to move in the natural direction of the element predominating in the compound.[24] And he gives arguments, though very poor ones, to show that every piece of matter occurring naturally in the world must contain all the four elements.[25] Indeed, it is difficult to know if he believes that we ever could meet with any one of the elements in a pure state. On his principles, it seems improbable that this would happen. The fatal theoretical objection to this theory (an objection that should have been obvious to him without the help of reliable chemical knowledge) is that he cannot explain how one element can be said to preponderate in a compound. He does seem to have been aware that it was necessary to suppose that different materials were compounded of the four elements in some kind of arithmetical proportion. (In the first book of the *de Anima*, he approves a statement of Empedocles to this effect.) But what kind of proportion? By weight or by volume or what? He has no satisfactory answer to this, and without the atomic theory that he had rejected he could hardly give one.

He does, however, try to explain the fact that the four elements do not finally precipitate out of the mixture and settle permanently in their natural place — earth at the center, surrounded in concentric shells by water, air, and fire. The sun in its eternal circular path periodically approaches and recedes from various regions of the earth in turn. This motion produces, in a way that Aristotle leaves very unclear, both the transmutation of one element into another and the various processes of growth and decay, change and destruction on the face of the earth.[26]

We must now consider briefly Aristotle's cosmology — his account of the structure of the universe and the relative places and movements of the earth and the planets, the sun, the moon, and the fixed stars. Astronomy was a science in which the Greeks were brilliantly successful. They did as much as could be expected of anyone working without optical instruments and with only the simplest

mathematics. But it was a field heavily infected with religious superstition and, therefore, difficult to view with the detached eye of science. The heavenly bodies were in some sense divine. Their behavior, therefore, tended to be looked at and interpreted in very different ways from that of earthly bodies. Aristotle's cosmology is a remarkable compromise between the rational and the superstitious approach to celestial phenomena.

The earth is spherical and is at rest at the center of the universe. The heavenly bodies revolve round the earth and their various paths have to be accounted for in any rational account of the workings of the cosmos. In his attempt to find an explanation for the movements of the heavenly bodies in his earth-centered universe, Aristotle relies largely on the work of Eudoxus, a mathematician who, like Aristotle himself, had been a pupil of Plato. Eudoxus had pictured the universe as a set of concentric spheres with the earth as their common center. Each sphere revolved at a constant velocity and in a constant direction. But the velocities and directions could be different for different spheres, and each sphere revolved on its own axis. This complicated system was necessary in order to account for the apparent movements of the sun, moon, planets, and fixed stars. The outermost sphere, that of the fixed stars, made one revolution every 24 hours. But the apparent motions of the sun and moon, and especially of the planets, were not simple periodic revolutions. The planets in particular followed an irregular path, for which reason the Greeks gave them the name of *planētes* ("wanderers"). Eudoxus found that he could adapt his system of concentric revolving spheres to account for the apparent irregularities in the observed movements of the heavenly bodies. The principle of this system can be illustrated simply, though the details are complex.[27]

Suppose two spheres are related as follows:

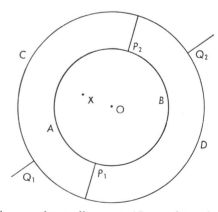

The inner sphere, diameter AB, revolves about its axis P_1P_2 at its own speed. The outer sphere, diameter CD, revolves about its own axis Q_1Q_2. We suppose, of course, that the axis of the inner sphere, P_1P_2, is attached to fixed points on the outer sphere. Its movement is therefore the resultant of two motions, the spinning of the outer sphere *CD* and its own rotation as axis of *AB*. Now suppose there is an observer at *O*, the common center of the two spheres, looking at the apparent path traced by a point, say, *X* on the surface of the inner sphere *AB*. The motion of *X* as it appears from *O* will be a complex curve that results from the combination of the motions of the two spheres. And it is easy to see that by combining a sufficient number of spheres related in this way with suitably chosen axes and speeds of revolution, we could get a model of any observed motion of a point on any of the spheres. In fact, Eudoxus found that by assigning three spheres each to the moon and the sun and four to each of the five planets known to the Greeks — Mercury, Venus, Mars, Jupiter, and Saturn — and by suitably adjusting the speeds of revolution of the spheres and the positions of their axes, he could account satisfactorily for all the movements of the heavenly bodies as they appeared to an observer on earth. This required a total of twenty-seven spheres in Eudoxus' system if we add the outermost sphere of all, that of the fixed stars. A subsequent revision of Eudoxus' model to remedy some inaccuracies was made by Callippus. This increased the number of spheres to thirty-three. The work of Eudoxus was a great achievement of the Greek mathematical genius.

Our present interest in the theory is that it was adopted by Aristotle and modified by him. The details, both in Aristotle's own writings[28] and in those of his commentators, are very obscure. It appears, however, that Eudoxus and Callippus did not think of their hypothetical spheres as real material entities. They were simply geometrical devices to account for the facts of observation, mere hypothetical surfaces of revolution. But when Aristotle adopted the system, he mistakenly supposed the spheres to be real material parts of the universe. And since the heavenly bodies were eternal and not subject to change like the things of the sublunary world, he supposed that they must be composed of a fifth element, *aithēr*. This he thought of as a transparent material, changeless and indestructible and having as its "natural" movement not the upward or downward tendency of the four sublunary elements but an eternal circular motion. He has various arguments, none of them very plausible, to show that circular motion is the only kind of motion possible for heavenly bodies. Important among these "arguments" is the affirmation that the circle is the "perfect" figure[29] and so somehow an appropriate path for heavenly bodies. This curious introduction of a value concept into philosophical argument is not uncommon in Aristotle (nor indeed in the medievals who were his disciples). We often find him affirming that such-and-such must be the case because it is "more noble" or "more honorable" than it should be.

Having committed himself to the notion that the spheres of Eudoxus were material spheres composed of a fifth element, Aristotle was faced at once with a difficulty. According to his physical system, as we shall see, a void or space empty of all matter could not exist. There could thus be no empty space between the spheres and they must therefore be in contact with each other. But if this were so, the movement of any one of them would interfere with the movement of the sphere next to it. The nature of this interference is left obscure, but presumably Aristotle had frictional forces in mind. The system of Eudoxus would thus fail to work. Aristotle therefore postulated the existence of "counteracting" spheres. By spinning in the opposite direction to their neighbors, these are supposed to neutralize the movements of the "starless" spheres, those that do not actually carry the heavenly bodies. This raises the total number of spheres (or "heavens," as they are sometimes called) to fifty-five. This clumsy misinterpretation of the astronomers' elegant mathematical fiction must fail, in fact, to do the task Aristotle assigns to it. For if there are no empty spaces anywhere between the spheres, the extra ones postulated to insulate the star-carrying spheres from the inconvenient influence of their neighbors must presumably themselves be subject to the same forces whose effect they were designed to neutralize. But the whole theory is too obscure and confused to permit of rational criticism.

Finally, we must consider Aristotle's mechanics. This part of his scientific theory has been greatly maligned by historians. It was, of course, mistaken. And due to Aristotle's great prestige in the middle ages and the accidental association of his philosophy with sacrosanct theological dogmas, his scientific ideas became a barrier to the development of physics. But his theories about force and motion were not arbitrary or *a priori*. On the contrary, they were closely related to the facts of experience and about as sensible a doctrine as unaided common-sense observation could have yielded. Aristotle failed simply because intelligent theorizing based on everyday experience is not enough in matters of this kind. But it has taken the genius of Galileo, Newton, and their successors to make us realize this.

Nature (*physis*) for Aristotle is the sum total of those things that have sources of motion internal to themselves.[30] It is this realm, organic and inorganic, that provides the subject-matter for the Aristotelian science of physics. A flower, a dog, a stone, and a man are parts of nature. An artifact like a table or a ship is not. That is to say, it is not a part of nature in its capacity of table or ship. But the wood of which it is composed *is* a part of nature. Aristotle tries to combine this belief in a world of natural objects having motive forces internal to themselves with the doctrine that the primary and original source of all motion in the universe is God who directly moves the "outer heaven," the sphere of the fixed stars. But the nature of the connection between these two sources of motion is never made clear. Nor does the distinction between "nature" and artifact stand up to scrutiny. Modern developments in biology and in engineering have eroded the borderline between the self-moving and the things moved by external forces.

Movement (*kinēsis*) was a much wider concept for Aristotle than it is for us. It meant *any kind of change*, whether of quality, size, or place. (It even covers, in some contexts, generation and destruction.) The fall of an apple was an event of a kind basically similar to its growth or its ripening. In talking of Aristotle's mechanics, we may confine our attention to local movement (*phora*). (He does, in some parts of his writings, recognize this as the basic sense of the word *kinēsis*.) Like any other kind of change, it is of two kinds: "natural," or springing from the nature of the moving thing itself, and "forced," brought about by influences external to the moving body. The fall of a stone or the flying upwards of a spark are instances of "natural" movement of bodies. Also natural are the purposive movements of plants and animals. Movements contrary to nature are those that result from external forces being applied to a body. The flight of an arrow, for example, is a combination of its natural motion taking it toward the earth's center, and the "unnatural" motion resulting from the impulse given it by the bow string.

In modern language the principles of Aristotle's mechanics may be put briefly as follows: The speed of a body is directly proportional to the force propelling it and inversely proportional to the resistance of the medium through which it moves. In the case of "natural" movements like the falling of heavy bodies, the motion is due to the natural tendency (*rhopē*) of the body overcoming the resistance of the medium through which it falls.* The more of this tendency a body has (that is, in the case of a falling body, the larger and heavier it is) the faster it will fall. And the thicker and more resistant the medium, the slower it will fall.[32] The doctrine of the resisting medium seems, of course, to be in agreement with observation. Bodies fall faster through air than through water; and faster through water than through treacle. And in a resistant medium, large and heavy bodies fall faster than small and light ones.

From these supposed laws of motion, Aristotle deduces his strongest argument against the possibility of a vacuum.† Since the speed of a falling body is inversely proportional to the resistance of the medium, a body falling in a void would move with infinite speed. Since this is clearly impossible, there can be no void.[33] There are one or two places in his scientific writings where Aristotle comes near to seeing some of the truth about moving bodies. He recognizes the existence of inertia in the admission

that even bodies at rest offer resistance.[34] And in one part of his argument against the possibility of the void, he actually states (but only to reject it) something very like Newton's first law of motion. If a void existed, a moving body subject to no external forces would move for ever. But since this is impossible, the void cannot exist.[35] This is a sad example of one false scientific belief reinforcing another.

THE DIVISIONS OF PHILOSOPHY

The word *philosophia* had, for Aristotle and for the Greeks in general, a much wider meaning than the word "philosophy" has for us. We have already seen that Aristotle did not himself draw the clear line that we nowadays (perhaps too confidently) draw between scientific questions and philosophical ones. Philosophy for Aristotle consisted of the whole body of organized knowledge in so far as this was the outcome of disinterested human reason. Philosophy, so understood, is divided into various branches. For the details of this division, we have to rely as much on Aristotle's ancient commentators as on his own writings, though the hints he gives there bear out pretty well what his interpreters have to say. Philosophy is divided into two main branches, the theoretical and the practical. The theoretical sciences are three: (1) first philosophy or theology (later called "metaphysics," though this is not an Aristotelian term); (2) mathematics; (3) physics. Physics concerns itself with "nature" (*physis*), those parts of the universe that are material and possess a source of motion internal to themselves. Mathematics deals with the embodied but immobile aspects of the universe. This is Aristotle's quaint (and inaccurate) way of referring to geometry and arithmetic. "First philosophy" is concerned with what is both unmoved and separate from matter.[36] The meaning of this overly neat and strange-sounding classification will become clearer when we have looked at some of the features of Aristotle's metaphysics. He has a good deal to say on (1) and (3), though much of his teaching on physics is the mistaken science that we have looked at already. His mathematical teaching is incidental to his philosophical and scientific writing.[37] Practical knowledge, knowledge for the sake of action, seems not to have been formally subdivided in this way. Aristotle discussed it under the headings of *politics* and its subsidiary, *ethics*. The aim of politics was the right organization of society. Ethics dealt with individual morality, which in Aristotle's view depended largely on the nature of society and of man as a social animal.

THE NATURE OF KNOWLEDGE

Any survey of Aristotle's account of knowledge must begin with some reference to the influence of Plato. Aristotle spent many years of his life as a

---

* The only other factor affecting the speed of fall is the shape of the falling body.[31]

† Aristotle has a large number of arguments to prove the impossibility of a vacuum. None has any value.

student in the Academy, and he is known as the most distinguished of Plato's disciples. We may therefore expect to find many signs of Plato's influence in his writings. These influences can indeed be seen. But more important are the differences, not only of detail, but of method and outlook between Plato and Aristotle. Where Plato is rationalistic, dogmatic, and contemptuous of the world of the senses, Aristotle is empirical, cautious, and anxious to consult all relevant facts and opinions before making up his mind. This seems to have been a temperamental difference between the two philosophers, but it is an important one. The history of human knowledge since their time has shown decisively that *a priori* dogmatizing gives no lasting results in the search for truth, and that cautious empiricism does in the end give genuine insight into the nature of things. That Aristotle failed to get nearer the truth than he did must be put down to the victory of his Platonic training over his scientific spirit.

Associated with this difference in intellectual attitude is a difference of approach and emphasis. Roughly speaking, Plato tried to deduce the nature of the universe from what he thought to be the nature of human knowledge. Aristotle started with the facts of nature as he saw them, and reduced them to a system. He then found a place for human knowledge, as one natural phenomenon among others, in his system. This contrast is oversimplified, but it brings out an important difference between them. Unfortunately, as we shall see, Aristotle's view of human knowledge was not entirely consistent. He inherited too much from Plato to enable him to view knowledge as just one more aspect of nature.

Plato had believed that only those things that were universal, permanent, and changeless, could be genuine objects of knowledge. What was particular, mutable, and contingent might be the object of mere belief or guesswork but it could not, properly speaking, be *known*. Aristotle was sufficiently influenced by Plato to agree with this view. But as we shall see, he interpreted it in his own way. In particular, he rejects the Platonic theory of forms. At some places in his writings, indeed, he seems inclined to allow some value to the theory. But in general he rejects it decisively. His criticisms are scattered through his writings and are nowhere neatly and clearly summarized.[38] Some of his points are trivial and some are very difficult to understand. The most important of them amount to the following:

1. Plato nowhere explained the relation of forms to the concrete individual things of the sensible world. He used merely metaphorical terms like "participation" (*methexis*) and "imitation" (*mimēsis*) to describe this relationship. These do not explain in any way how form and thing are connected. They are, as Aristotle himself says,[39] "mere empty phrases and poetic metaphors."

2. The hypothesis of the existence of forms does not account for the multiplicity of things in the world, nor for the coming into existence of these things or the ways in which they change. In short, the theory adds nothing to our knowledge.

3. The theory is, in any case, open to serious logical objections. Aristotle details these. They all stem from trying to separate the essential characters of things from the things themselves.

It has sometimes been suggested that many of Aristotle's criticisms of Plato are unfair and that the theory he attacked is only a caricature of Plato's real views. This may be so. But Aristotle was a pupil of Plato for many years and we may reasonably suppose him to have been better acquainted with Plato's meaning than any scholar of today. The upshot of his critique is this: Plato was correct in supposing that the only possible objects of genuine knowledge must be general or universal. But these objects cannot exist apart from the concrete individual things or facts in which they are found in human experience. What this means and how much truth there is in it we shall see in due course.

Aristotle's account of human knowledge is in two parts. The nature and conditions of truly scientific knowledge are discussed in the *Posterior Analytics*. This is a work that shows well marked signs of Plato's influence, and at least the first half of it seems to have been written early in Aristotle's career. Knowledge obtained through the senses is dealt with chiefly in the *De Anima* and some associated shorter works. This is a part of his philosophy falling under the general head of *physics*, the study of nature. Its details are worked out in characteristically Aristotelian terms. The life of the senses is a natural phenomenon to be accounted for on the same general principles as any other part of nature. This divided attitude to the problems of knowledge leaves us in some doubt as to the connections between sense and reason, a doubt that Aristotle leaves unresolved.

The view that a philosopher takes about the nature of knowing naturally depends on the *examples* of knowledge that he has available to examine and criticize. Thus a philosophical theory about knowing will depend on the extent of human knowledge at the time the theory is made. Every age has a standard of knowledge constructed on the basis of whatever is thought at the time to be reliable and authentic instances of knowing. Thus, natural science is the paradigm of knowledge for the present century. For some medievals, the supposed revealed truths of theology provided the model. For the Greeks of Aristotle's day, the single example of certain and reliable knowledge was mathematics—geometry and arithmetic. And when Aristotle talks of scientific knowledge (*epistēmē*), he means knowledge that is certain and necessarily true. He believed, of course, that the scope of such knowledge was much wider than logic and mathematics. And in this belief he was certainly mistaken. But it is impossible to understand his account of scientific knowledge unless we bear this mistaken belief in mind.

A science, for Aristotle, is a body of true statements about a particular subject matter — geometry, astronomy, or botany, for example. The statements must tell us that certain facts *are* so and also *why* they are so. But more is required than that the scientific statements should be true. They must be *necessarily* and *demonstrably* true. Aristotle is drawing attention here to a distinction between types of statement, which has become of great importance in modern philosophy. Most statements are true or false by virtue of observable matters of fact. Their truth has thus to be checked by the evidence of our senses. Some statements, however, are true or false in some way independent of experience. I say "in some way" because it is a matter of philosophical debate exactly how this comes about. But we can all recognize the difference between (1) "It is now raining" and (2) "Either it is now raining or it is not." We know that (2) is true without making any observations on the state of the weather. (1) has to be checked by observation. We may call statements like (1) *contingent* or *empirical* and those of type (2) *necessary* or *analytic*.

Aristotle did not make this perhaps overly sharp distinction which has become so familiar in recent philosophy. His views on this differed from those of most modern philosophers in at least two respects:

1. He believed that all the propositions of any science must be necessarily true. Modern philosophers tend to confine the scope of necessary statements to the provinces of logic and mathematics. No physicist, for example, would nowadays regard a particular law of physics as a necessarily true statement expressing a law of nature *which could not be other than it is*. But Aristotle believed mistakenly that all scientific propositions were of this nature. His mistake is due to taking mathematics, the only well-developed science of his day, as a model for all the other sciences.
2. As a natural corollary of his belief that all scientific propositions were necessarily true, Aristotle held also that they were all *universally* true, that is, admitted no exceptions. In this he shows the marks of his Platonic training. (For Plato, of course, universality was an essential mark of genuine knowledge.) Here again Aristotle is at variance with present-day opinion in science and philosophy. Here again he is mistaken, and for the same reason. Most of the propositions of natural science are now regarded (and with good reason) as well-established statements of probability ("Nearly all *A*'s are *B*'s") rather than universal and necessary ("All *A*'s must be *B*'s").

Let us now return to Aristotle's argument. If a statement S_1 is both necessarily true and demonstrably so, we must be able to prove it from prior premises, S_2 and S_3, say, which are themselves necessarily true. For no statement can be necessarily true if it is proved from premises that are not themselves so. Now what of S_2 and S_3 themselves? If they are to be demonstrated too, there must be further necessary statements, $S_4 \ldots S_k$ from which they are deducible. It is clear, as Aristotle points out, that such a process of proof cannot go on *ad infinitum*. Sooner or later we must come to a starting point in a set of statements $S_m \ldots S_n$ which, though true and necessarily so, are not themselves demonstrable and do not contain any of the statements $S_1 \ldots S_{m-1}$ which they are used to prove. (If they did, the argument would be circular.) In Euclid's *Elements of Geometry*, for example, if we take any particular theorem, we can trace its logical ancestry back, step by step, to earlier theorems, until we arrive at last at the axioms and definitions with which Euclid's system of geometry begins.

But if the basic premises of scientific knowledge cannot be demonstrated, how can they be known? Aristotle deals with this question in the last chapter of the *Posterior Analytics*. His discussion, though very obscure, is important. Not only does he here answer the question "How do we know basic scientific principles?" but he also sketches his answer to the problem of universals whose Platonic solution he had rejected so decisively. That is to say, he discusses here both universal *principles* and universal *concepts*.* Unfortunately, his explanation of how we come to know universals is by no means clear. Sense-experience gives us the materials for this kind of knowledge but cannot of itself provide knowledge of general cases. For this we need repeated sense experiences, which, in virtue of memory, leave a coherent residue of experience within the mind. This experience (*empeiria*) Aristotle calls, with an obscure literary flourish reminiscent of Plato,[40] "the universal now stabilized in its entirety within the soul." However, the universal, principle or concept, is recognized for what it is not by sensation or memory but by intellectual intuition (*nous*). Universal knowledge is thus acquired by induction (*epagōgē*) from sense experience but apprehended and justified by intuition. The sort of instance which best exemplifies what Aristotle seems to have in mind occurs in mathematics, where we may make intelligent guesses at the general principle exemplified by particular cases. For example, we see that $1+3 = 4$, $1+3+5 = 9$, $1+3+5+7 = 16$ and hazard the conjecture that the sum of the first n odd numbers is n^2.

But if this is "intuition" it certainly does not do the

---

* He starts to discuss how we come to know the "primary immediate premises" of science. Later in his argument, he explains how we acquire universal concepts like "man". The process is the same in each case.

work that Aristotle demands of it. The sum of the first *n* odd numbers is, in fact, *n²*. But we have to give a general proof of this before we can rank it as knowledge. Intuition of supposedly self-evident propositions cannot guarantee their truth. What appears self-evident to us will depend upon our intelligence, our interests, and our training. Thus *A* may accept as self-evidently true what *B* will reject as false or doubtful. The history of mathematics has in fact shown that the axioms at the basis of a mathematical system do not have it be "true", still less, "self-evident." They have merely to be *consistent*. "True" is not an appropriate predicate for such propositions.

This notion of intellectual intuition as a direct source of knowledge has been a persistent one in philosophy. It seems to have been conceived as a sort of nonphysical "seeing,"* an immaterial analogue of sense perception. Aristotle took it over from Plato and transmitted it to his successors. In the seventeenth century, it lay at the basis of Descartes' theory of knowledge and it is one of the sources of inconsistency in John Locke's empiricism. It was not finally discredited until the work of C. S. Peirce became generally known to philosophers in recent years.[41]

There is thus an important part of Aristotle's theory of knowledge which turns out to be very similar to Plato's. Though universals are immanent in facts, and not, as for Plato, separated from them, they are after all the only real objects of knowledge. And though sense-perception, memory, and finally, induction are necessary for a knowledge of universals, they are not sufficient. An unexplained faculty of intuition is invoked to account for knowledge. This has led a modern critic of Aristotle to complain, not unjustly, that "he seems either to be an empiricist or a Platonist according as you choose to remember one-half of his statement or the other."[42] Moreover, he has so far left unexplained how universals are embedded in physical facts. We shall see later, in looking at a less Platonic phase of his thinking, how he tries to explain this.

SUBSTANCE AND CAUSE

For Plato, the ultimately real features of the universe were the forms. For Aristotle, they were the individual things that make up the world — people, animals, plants, stones, stars, and so on. The central concept of Aristotle's metaphysics (or theory of being) is substance, the concrete individual thing. His detailed account of substance is very difficult to understand. He treats it from several different points of view and seems at times to say inconsistent things about it. But the rough outlines of his doctrine

can be discerned, and the rest of his philosophy develops naturally from his view of substance.

In the *Categories** he talks about substance from the point of view of language and of logic. It is "that which is neither predicable of a subject nor present in a subject; for instance, the individual man or horse."[43] The world is divided into (1) logical subjects of discourse that can be talked about, and (2) qualities and relations that can be affirmed or denied of logical subjects. Aristotle goes on to make a list (the Aristotelian "categories") of nine types of predicate which can be attributed truly or falsely, to logical subjects. The doctrine is not a defensible one and owes a great deal to the accidental peculiarities of the Greek language. In other parts of his writings, chiefly in his *Physics* and *Metaphysics*, we find a more understandable approach. It can be condensed briefly but not too misleadingly as follows. The concrete individual thing — man, horse, tree, stone, and the like — may be viewed by the philosopher from two different points of view. (1) He may look at it as a permanent static feature of the world with a fixed nature. A nature (or *essence*) is thought of by Aristotle as a core or kernel of properties of which three things can be said: (a) they are essential to a thing of that particular kind, so that anything which lacks them does not belong to that natural type; (b) they can be grasped by intellectual intuition (*nous*); (c) they can be expressed in language as a definition. (2) We may also look at substances as centers of change. We then ask, simply, "What happens when something changes?"

The belief in intellectual intuition (1b), has been dealt with above and we need not discuss it further now. And (1a) and (1c) belong together. The belief that things in the world are hallmarked by the possession of sets of essential properties and are neatly pigeonholed by nature into distinguishable species seems superficially plausible. Aristotle held it strongly and his belief on this point affects his account of definition. He supposed that to define *X* was merely to express in language the essence apprehended by *nous*; and that the essence of a thing was a fixed and definite group of properties. Thus, to define something was to say something important (indeed, literally, *essential*) about the nature of the thing.

The possibility of giving this kind of definition clearly depends on the properties of a given thing falling into two classes, the necessary properties belonging to the essential core of the thing and their accidental concomitants. A dog, for example, must have a backbone, a heart, a brain, and a certain type of teeth in order to rank as a dog at all. But he can be black or white or brown, with long hair or short, large or small, and so on without losing his canine status. The one group of properties seems

---

* As the derivations of words like "intuition," "*Anschauung*" show. The chief Greek verb for "know" is derived from an Indo-European root meaning "see".

* There is some doubt if the text of the *Categories* was written by Aristotle, but no doubt about the expressed views being genuinely Aristotelian.

essential, the other not. Why may we not give up our belief in intuition (1*b*), and retain the assumptions made by (1*a*) and (1*c*)? After all, do not classificatory biologists deal with plants and animals on just this assumption? The answer is that taxonomy, the systematic sorting out of organisms into genera and species, *may* proceed on this assumption; but it need not. Once it did; but since the revolution in biology brought about by the theory of evolution and modern genetics, the assumption has been shown to be false. There are no invariable essences to be discovered in nature. Naturally occurring properties are not *invariably* associated in standard groups. Their concurrence is merely a matter of probability. Definitions are now recognized as being, not *descriptions* of naturally occurring types, but *prescriptions* of what things shall count as individuals belonging to species *A*, *B*, *C*. . . . A definition in science is usually a statement of qualifications to be read as saying: If anything has qualities *p*, *q*, *r* . . . it shall rank as a specimen of type *A*. In other words, both "essences" and definitions are determined, not by nature, but by human knowledge, needs, and interests. And as our knowledge, needs, and interests change, our definitions change too.

In considering (2), substance as a center of change, we seem to be on more familiar ground. To ask "What happens when *X* changes?" is a recognizable type of scientific question, which can be answered once we put the name of some specific substance for *X*. A chemical change can be explained by describing the re-assembling of atoms, a physical change in terms of transformations and discharges of energy, a biological change by talk of nerve functions or enzyme actions or the like. But for Aristotle, this was not a scientific question in our sense of the phrase. No modern scientist would attempt to answer the question "What happens when something changes?" He would reply that he could not answer until you told him what particular "something" you were talking about and exactly what kind of a change you were referring to. But Aristotle did attempt to answer just this question.

For what he tried to do in this part of his philosophy was to explain why the world and the things in it are as they are and how they came to be so. And he was looking for an answer to a *general* question, "Why are things as they are in general?" and *not* the more manageable type of question, "How did this or that *particular* thing come to be in its present state?" His answer to this highly general question is contained in three closely linked parts of his philosophy — his doctrines of matter and form, potentiality and actuality, and causality. These doctrines have traditionally been regarded as the very heart of the Aristotelian philosophy. Today, they are of chiefly historical interest. We shall consider the reasons for this depreciation in status.

At the beginnings of both the *Metaphysics* and the *Physics*, Aristotle reviews the opinions of his predecessors about causality and the "first principles of nature." He comes to the conclusion that nearly all the points of his own theory have been recognized by one or another of them but that no one has previously joined them into one coherent account. If we consider any object, natural or artificial, we can distinguish in it two factors: the stuff of which it is made and the shape or organization that art or nature has impressed upon it. Two bowls may both be of silver but differ in their design. Or they may share an identical design but one may be moulded in silver and one in gold. This contrast of stuff and shape, material and organization, or, to use Aristotle's terms, matter (*hylē*) and form (*eidos*, *morphē*), can be traced throughout nature. But it is not for Aristotle just a common-sense contrast between what a thing is made of and how it is constructed. He very characteristically extends and generalizes the notion in three ways:

1. Matter and form are correlative notions that can be distinguished anywhere in nature. A silver bowl may be analyzed into its matter — silver — and its form — the structure given to the silver by the craftsman who made the bowl. But a piece of unworked silver provides the same distinction. It has an observable character, different, for example, from an otherwise similar piece of gold or copper. This is its form. And its matter, for Aristotle, consists of the elements out of which the silver must ultimately be composed — fire, earth, air, and water. The *proportions* of the elements present in the silver are, of course, part of the form. For it is to these proportions that Aristotle must trace the difference between silver and other substances. But what of the basic elements of fire, earth, air, and water themselves? They, too, are composed of form and matter. Two pairs of contrary qualities, hot–cold, dry–wet, are, as we have seen, combined in pairs to make the four elements.[44] Thus, the form of fire is the hot and the dry, that of earth, the cold and the dry, and so on. But the matter of the elements is what Aristotle calls "prime matter." This is distinguished from matter at higher levels in that it is never found apart from its form.[45] It is entirely featureless and structureless.

2. The second way in which he generalizes his concept of matter and form is that form is the *knowable* element in things. It is what we can describe, define, classify, communicate, and be aware of. Matter is the unknowable structureless residue of things that mind cannot assimilate or deal with. We shall see in discussing Aristotle's theory of body and mind what use he makes of this notion.

3. Lastly, matter is the source of plurality and individuality in things.[46] If the form in two or more things of the same species is identical, those things can be distinguished only by their matter.

Consider, for example, pennies minted at the same time. Aristotle seems to have been too ready to assume that the forms of two things of the same species were identical. Later philosophers, notably Leibniz, have more plausibly attributed the individuality of things to their possession of a unique set of *properties.* It is indeed very difficult to see what Aristotle means by the individuating function of matter. It was a point much debated by his medieval followers.

Matter and form are the outcome of Aristotle's analysis of things regarded as static and unchanging. But things in nature do change. They grow, decay, shed some qualities and assume others, move, and so on. And he develops the concepts of matter and form to account for the fact of change. Consider a simple case of change, say, the change of color in an apple as it ripens. We have here the replacement of one form by another. Matter may here be regarded as a substratum in which change takes place. And in order for a given substratum, *X*, to be the site of a change from property *A* to property *B* (in order, let us say, for an apple to become yellow from being green), it must have the capacity or *potentiality* for the change. Nature works in a certain order and within certain limits. Only those changes can take place in a thing for which the potentiality exists there. Apples become red or yellow but not blue or white. Tadpoles develop into frogs and not into crocodiles. Stones fall downward and not upward. The form that supersedes another in a process of change is called the actuality (*energeia*) of the previous potency (*dynamis*). Thus matter and form regarded as factors in a process of change become potentiality and actuality (or potency and act).[47]

In spite of its fame in the history of philosophy, this is a curiously unexplanatory doctrine. Aristotle does not just mean that whenever there is a change from *A* to *B*, the change must have been possible. This would be a simple tautology. He clearly means that this *particular* change from *A* to *B* (green leaf to yellow leaf, caterpillar to butterfly, or whatever it may be) has to be grounded in some way *in the nature of the changing thing.* But for this statement to be more than a bare tautology we have to investigate each type of change *empirically,* and show how it comes about. In other words, *we have to do science and not metaphysics.* To take one example, a modern botanist does not explain the development of an oak from an acorn by saying that an acorn has the potentiality of being actualized as an oak. He explains, in terms of genetics and biochemistry, how certain molecules in the nucleus of the acorn's cells carry information stored in chemical form, which control the development of the plant along certain lines. Certainly, he has not yet a complete explanation in these terms. But what he does say (even if it later turns out to be false) is at least explanatory. Aris-

totle's talk of *dynamis* and *energeia* is not and never could be explanatory. And it is important to see why this is so. Scientific explanations are specific and detailed and therefore capable of being confirmed *or refuted* by observed facts. Metaphysical explanations are overly general and consistent with any observed states of affairs. No facts count as refuting them, nor, consequently, as confirming them either.

The last of the three associated theories by which Aristotle tries to explain how things come to be as they are is his famous account of causality. In looking at his theory, we have to remember to understand the meanings of the words he uses for "cause" (*aition, aitia*) and to forget as far as we can the associations of the English word. The overtones of the Greek words are legal and moral. Instead of asking "What is the cause of *X*?" we get nearer to the Greek notion by asking "To what factors can we assign responsibility, credit, or blame for *X*?" This is easier to understand if we remember that primitive thinking about causes tends to be *animistic.* It attributes to conscious agencies what more developed thought attributes to the unconscious operations of natural laws. Thunder and lightning, tempests, earthquakes, and other impressive natural phenomena are interpreted as expressing divine disapproval. There are gods of the sea, the wind, and the forest, and their moods and wishes are evinced in the face of nature. Civilized man emancipates himself only gradually from these ways of interpreting natural events. Much of Greek popular thinking was still at this level. We have seen too that even the philosophers and scientists, at least in their attitudes to the heavenly bodies, tended to think in this way.

Aristotle's account of causality is certainly in some ways an advance on those of his predecessors. He tries to do justice to previous theories, but is more careful and systematic than the earlier philosophers. But even he has not freed himself from animistic ways of thinking. The moral overtones of the terms *aitia* and *aition* must not be taken by themselves as evidence that Aristotle held an animistic view of cause. The word *aitia* occurs in the writings of early materialists like Anaximander, and even Democritus, who tried consciously to explain the world on a materialistic hypothesis, uses the word in the sense of "cause." Obviously Aristotle had to make use of the current Greek vocabulary to explain his theories. But there are, as we shall see, other traces of animism in his account of cause.

In his main discussion of this question,[48] Aristotle distinguishes four factors that are each necessary, and together sufficient, to account for a thing being in a certain state. The first of these factors is the existence of material in which the change takes place, "such as, for example, the bronze of the statue, the silver of the bowl." This is the *material* cause of a thing. Secondly, we have the law, formula, or definition of the thing giving the *principles* according to which it is constructed. This is the *formal* cause. Thirdly, we have the source of movement or change. This is the *efficient* cause. And lastly, there is the *final* cause, the *end* or *purpose* of the thing. Aristotle's specific examples given to illustrate his theory are not very satisfactory. Perhaps we can most easily see what he has in mind by expanding his example of house-building. The bricks, mortar, glass, tiles, and so on which go to make a house are its material cause. The craftsmen who put this material together are the efficient cause. The formal cause lies in the plans of the architect, and the final cause is the purpose for which the house was built, that of providing comfort and shelter.

It is easy to agree that these four factors are all required if we are to give a full explanation of an artifact like a house or a ship. But the analysis seems much less appropriate if we consider other kinds of change — from a seed to a plant, for example, or a chemical change, or a movement of a particle under external forces. But we have to remember that, as in his theory of knowledge, his treatment is deeply influenced by what he takes to be the *paradigms* or standard cases of what he is trying to explain. To a modern philosopher, the paradigm causes of causality are simple mechanical instances like one billiard ball hitting another or the flight of a projectile or the path of a planet in the sun's gravitational field. To Aristotle, the paradigms were those cases where the influence of a final cause seemed most clearly at work — human artifacts and biological processes. To us, of course, these are far too complex to be suitable subjects for causal analysis. It seems not unfair to attribute Aristotle's liking for explanation in terms of final causes and his reading of purpose into nature as an unexorcized residue of the magical animistic thinking with which Greek philosophy was infected.

In fact, the concept of the four causes in a straightforward sense is not really applicable to any process other than the construction by human beings of a planned artifact like a house or a machine. Once we turn to causes where no conscious foresight is involved, we have to stretch the notion of final cause from "that for the sake of which something is done" to the much vaguer notions of "unconscious purpose" or function. In the end, the final cause of *X* comes to be no more than the *last stage* of the process of *X*'s development. The Greek word *telos*, like the English word "end," carried the two meanings of "an end in view" and "an end in time." Thus, the final cause of a biological change like the growth of a plant came to be equated with the developed plant itself.* In fact, Aristotle admits that the efficient, formal, and final causes "often coincide,"[50] so that

his account of causality is one aspect of his doctrines of matter and form. The material cause is matter; the formal, efficient, and final causes together constitute the form.

MIND AND BODY

Plato had supposed that soul and body were essentially different and that the individual human being was an immaterial immortal soul in a temporary association with a corruptible material body. This view has been reinforced by various religious and philosophical doctrines from Plato's day to the present and is still very influential in popular religious thinking. For Aristotle, on the contrary, a human being, like any other individual substance, was a genuine unit. Soul and body were distinguishable, but not separable, parts of the individual. Man was regarded by Aristotle as a part of nature. His properties and his activities were to be explained in the same terms as those of any other part of nature, that is, in terms of his key concepts of matter and form, potentiality and actuality. This common-sense sober approach to the problems of mind and body makes the doctrine of the *de Anima* one of the most plausible parts of his philosophy. It suffers, however, like other parts of his thinking, from a conflict between his own common-sense scientific approach and the traces of his Platonic training. But although he does not keep consistently to the point of view from which he starts, his insistence on the fundamental unity of soul and body excuses him from having to explain, like the followers of Plato or Descartes, how two such dissimilar substances can ever come to interact.

Aristotle's *de Anima* is a book about *psychē*. This Greek word is sometimes very misleadingly translated as "soul" and sometimes, much more appropriately, as "life principle." It occurs in Plato with the theological overtones of the English word "soul," but in Aristotle it is much better understood in the sense of "life principle." "What has soul (*psychē*) in it differs from what has not in that the former displays life."[51] Thus, not only men, but plants and animals as well possess *psychē*. The *psychē* of any organism is evinced in its organization and functions. Thus, the "souls" of plants are manifest in their powers of nutrition and reproduction; those of animals in the powers of sensation in addition to those of the "nutritive" souls of plants. The sensitive stage of *psychē* is shown in the functions of sense perception (at least at the primitive level of touch), instinctive desire, and, in some animals at least, locomotion. Lastly, we have, at the human level, intelligence (*nous*). This supervenes on various lower mental powers like memory and imagination (*phantasia*), some of which are seen in other animals. Thus, Aristotle has what has sometimes been called an "evolutionary" view of nature. He sees the world of living matter as organized in levels of ascending

---

* We find a similar stretching of the notion of material cause. "The letters are the causes of the syllables."[49] Here again there is a verbal confusion between the two senses of a Greek word — *stoicheion*, which can mean both "element" and "letter of the alphabet".

complexity, from the most primitive to the most advanced. The "higher" organisms have all the functions of the lower and others in addition. Man, the highest of all, has not only the vegetative functions of nutrition and reproduction and the animal functions of sensation, desire, and movement but also the specifically human powers. And as these various powers and functions are the counterparts of the structure and organization of the individual, the level of *psychē* in an organism will be a measure of its form. There is *more to know* in a man than in a dog, in a dog than in a worm, in a worm than in a plant, and in a plant than in a stone. Aristotle's famous *scala naturae* (ladder of nature) is a ladder in which the higher rungs show, so to speak, a higher ratio of form to matter than the lower. There is therefore some reason for calling Aristotle's view of nature evolutionary. He sees the whole of nature as hierarchically organized in levels of increasing complexity. But the resemblances between Aristotelian and modern biology do not go deep. He did not believe that higher types developed from lower. Species were fixed and eternal.

The soul of man is therefore the form of his body — its nature, organization, and manner of working. "Suppose that the eye were an animal — sight would have been its soul," he explains in a striking metaphor. At first glance, this seems like a straightforward account of the relation of mind and body. The mind (or "soul") is the body in action, and its various modes of consciousness — sensing, desiring, thinking, and the rest — are just byproducts of the body's working. Many passages in Aristotle's writings support this interpretation of his theory of mind and body. He certainly defends the opinion that the soul cannot exist without a body,[53] and rejects the view of Plato and his followers who seemed to him to suppose that any soul and any body could be put into an arbitrary conjunction. "We can," he says, "wholly dismiss as unnecessary the question whether the body and soul are one: it is as meaningless as to ask whether the wax and the shape given to it by the stamp are one."[54] Moreover, the soul is a unity in spite of its different powers or faculties. And although Aristotle sometimes talks metaphorically of the soul having "parts," he holds that it is mistaken to believe, as Plato did, that one part of the soul thinks and another desires.[55] But the outlines of this firmly scientific account of mind are blurred when Aristotle comes to work out its details. Indeed, in an early chapter of the *de Anima*[56] where he is outlining this account, he qualifies it: "From this it indubitably follows that the soul is inseparable from its body or at any rate that certain parts of it are (if it has parts) — for the actuality of some of them is nothing but the actualities of their bodily parts. Yet some may be separable because they are not the actualities of any body at all." It becomes obvious, as we shall see, that he had freed himself less completely than

he supposed from the Platonic superstitions of his early education.

We need not examine the details of this account. It will be sufficient to look at his views on sense perception and on thought and reason. In sense perception, we receive the forms of things without their matter "in the way in which a piece of wax takes on the impress of a signet-ring without the iron or gold."[57] This metaphorical explanation is not made any easier to understand by his assurance that the sense-organ actually takes on the qualities of the thing that is being sensed.[58] He means, for example, that if I am looking at the blue sky, my eye actually *becomes blue.* Clearly, in the straightforward sense of these assertions they are simply false. But Aristotle leaves unclear what nonliteral sense, if any, we are to put upon his remarks. Moreover, they involve a most important development in his doctrine of matter and form. Form is now no longer simply an integral part of a substance, its shape, qualities, and organization. It is somehow detachable from the object whose form it is. Moreover, it can be present simultaneously in many places. If you and I both look at a rose, the red of the rose, along with its other sensed qualities, is, at the same time *and in the same sense,* in the rose and in my eyes and in yours. It is clear than in spite of his rejection of Plato's theory of forms, Aristotle is here still under its spell.

He recognizes, in addition to the senses of touch, taste, smell, hearing, and sight, a "common sense" whose sense organ is the heart.* He gives several reasons for postulating this additional "sense." The most important are: (1) Some qualities are perceptible to sense but are not peculiar to any one sense, as color is to sight or sound to hearing. Such qualities are movement, shape, number, and size. (These "common sense-qualities" or "common sensibles" reappear in seventeenth-century philosophy as "primary qualities.") (2) We must suppose a common sense to provide a single forum of consciousness or a common sensory field. I not only see, but I am aware *that* I am seeing. And I am aware that I am *both* seeing *and* hearing. I am also able to discriminate between and compare the findings of different senses. A stick in water, for example, *looks* bent but *feels* straight. This kind of awareness cannot be attributed to any of the special senses. What Aristotle attributes to "sense" here, we would more naturally regard as a kind of thinking. But this is unimportant and largely a matter of terminology.† He is pointing to important facts of consciousness

---

* Aristotle believed that the heart and not the brain was the organic center of conscious activity. The brain was merely an organ for cooling the blood. This unfortunate doctrine retarded the advance of physiology. The truth had been known to some of his predecessors and even to Plato.
† Aristotle specifically denies that there is a *sixth* sense, and talks of "a general sensibility which enables us to perceive them [sc, the common sense properties] directly."[59] He uses the phrase "common sense" [*koinē aisthēsis*] rather rarely.

which have somehow to be accounted for in any theory of the working of the mind.

Thinking, reasoning, and understanding depend on prior sense-experience and the residue of such experience stored in memory and imagination. But they concern *universals* rather than particular sense qualities and particular objects.[60] Mind or reason (*nous*) acts as matter to the form of the essences and universal truths in the way that the sense organs act as matter to the form of sense qualities. In order to be able to do this, it must have no specific form of its own. It has to be able to receive the form of anything knowable. It must for this reason be independent of the body.[61] All this is very difficult to understand. It seems at variance with Aristotle's earlier account of the *psyche* as the form of the body. He talks as if (1) there is in each individual man a kind of surplus of form not taken up in the bodily organization, and (2) this can itself serve as matter to the impress of intelligible forms. Again we have the suggestion that *form*, which was originally explained as a concept correlative to matter and an intrinsic aspect of the concrete individual, is capable of existing on its own without its material partner. This is a fundamental difficulty in understanding what Aristotle means by his doctrine of form and matter. We shall return to it when we look at his account of God.

The same divorce of form from matter is made in the last book of the *de Anima*, where Aristotle introduces the famous distinction between active and passive reason. The crucial passage runs as follows:[62]

> Mind as we have described it is what it is by virtue of becoming all things, while there is another which is what it is by virtue of making all things: this is a sort of positive state like light; for in a sense light makes potential colors into actual colors. Mind in this sense of it is separable, impassable, unmixed. . . . When mind is set free from its present conditions it appears as just what it is and nothing more: this alone is immortal and eternal (we do not, however, remember its former activity, because while mind in this sense is impassable, mind as passive is destructible), and without it nothing thinks.

It is fair to say that no one knows what this means. Even the translation of the last phrase is in doubt owing to an ambiguity in the Greek text. There have been two main interpretations of it. St. Thomas Aquinas and his followers identified the active intellect with the Christian "immortal soul." Alexander of Aphrodisias, a famous commentator of the second century A.D., identified the active intellect with God and held that it was identical in all men. This view was developed by Averroës, a Moslem philosopher of the twelfth century, who maintained the fundamental unity of all minds and, in consequence, the impossibility of attributing any thinking to any individual. (*Mind thinks in me* instead of *I*

think.) This view, strangely enough, had some followers among the Christian Aristotelians of the thirteenth century, and Aquinas wrote a famous pamphlet against them. There is no warrant in Aristotle's text for any of these interpretations.

Presumably Aristotle is trying to explain the distinction between mind as merely receptive of knowledge and mind as active and productive. But the suggestion that this active intellect is separable from the body and that by virtue of it we even have a strange kind of immortality (without memory) seems quite at variance with his account of soul as the form of the body. However we understand it, it is, as a modern writer has said, "the most startling of all the clashes between the naturalistic and the spiritualistic strains in Aristotle's philosophy."[63] His philosophy may not unfairly be regarded as a battleground between Plato and science. And on this point at least, Plato triumphed in the end.

GOD

God serves two roles in Aristotle's philosophy. He is the source of motion and change in the universe, and he rounds off Aristotle's pseudo-evolutionary view of the cosmos by providing an example of pure form or actuality existing out of any relation to matter. As usual, we must notice some differences of meaning between Greek and English terms. The Greek word *theos*, which is usually translated "god," did not have anything like the sense of "creator and providence" which Christianity has given to the English word. Aristotle's universe was eternal and required no creator; nor did his god concern himself with human affairs. His theology is set out in Books VII and VIII of the Physics and Book XII of the Metaphysics. It can be summarized in the answers to two questions: (1) Why must we postulate the existence of God? (2) What can we know about God?

In answer to (1), Aristotle develops one argument,* the argument from the existence of change or motion. His statement is very complex, but its main outlines can be indicated as follows: (a) There exists an eternal circular motion, namely the movement of the sphere of the fixed stars. (b) Everything that is moved is moved by something else. (c) Therefore, there must be either an infinite series of causes or a cause of motion that is itself unmoved. (d) An infinite series of causes and effects is impossible. Therefore, (e) there is an unmoved cause of motion, and this is God. We need not take this argument very seriously, since we have no reason for accepting most of the premises. (a) is incompatible with the second law of thermodynamics and (b) with Newton's first law of motion. And if (b) is false, we are not forced to accept (c). Aristotle gives no satisfactory proof for (d), and though it may conceivably be true, there

* This is the only argument that he works out. Others are hinted at in other parts of his writing but not developed.

seems no good reason to believe it. Indeed, it is surprising that so dubious an argument has had so long a history. It was, however, canonized by Aquinas as one of his "five ways," and is still seriously propounded in neo-scholastic textbooks of natural theology.

Aristotle's reply to (2) runs as follows: Since God is an unmoved mover he must be changeless. He cannot therefore be composed like other substances of potentiality and actuality. He must accordingly be all form, all actuality, and so completely *immaterial*. He moves the outermost sphere of the fixed stars, and this motion is transmitted to the inner spheres by ordinary mechanical processes. But God himself does not move the outer heaven mechanically. Indeed, he could not do so, since he is immaterial and not in space.[64] Instead, he moves it in a nonphysical way—by being an object of attraction or desire.[65] God is thus efficient cause by being a final cause. His own activity, being that of a purely immaterial being, must be an activity of thought which has itself for its object. Any lesser object would be a degradation of his divinity, and a changeable object of thought would entail a change in the thinker. "Its thinking," Aristotle concludes mysteriously, "is a thinking on thinking."

These doctrines not unnaturally have exercised the ingenuity of commentators for over 2,000 years. It is hardly possible to elucidate them, but a few critical comments can be made.

1. If God is literally an object of desire to the outermost sphere of the heavens, the desire must presumably be conscious in some way. (And there are passages to support this view.[66]) But it is left unexplained why a perpetual desire for God should leave the unsatisfied lover forever spinning on its axis. And if God is not literally desired, how does his causality operate?

2. Nor does Aristotle explain how God, as the first author of movement in the world is related to nature (*physis*). For nature has been defined, as we have seen, as that which has a source of motion internal to itself.

3. We meet once again the motion of form divested of matter. And it cannot be affirmed too strongly that the whole plausibility of Aristotle's doctrine of form and matter is that these concepts are explained as *correlatives* like parent and offspring, cause and effect, or owner and property. One cannot have parents, causes, or owners without offspring, effects, or property, respectively. Such concepts live in pairs and take their meanings from each other. Aristotle is cheating his readers if, having introduced and made intelligible his key concept, *form*, as a correlative of *matter*, he then uses it in a totally different sense. (The same applies, of course, to talk of "prime matter." But Aristotle uses this concept without affirming the

actual existence of prime matter.) Clearly the original Aristotelian notion of form has degenerated in these contexts to something very reminiscent of the Platonic *eidos* which Aristotle has repudiated. Once again the influence of Plato has overcome Aristotle's natural good sense.

Moral Philosophy

THE *Nicomachaean Ethics* is one of the great books of moral philosophy. But for the twentieth-century reader it seems a curious mixture. There is much acute philosophical analysis and some pioneer work in the psychology of moral action. In addition, there is a good deal of description (of interest only to social historians) of the various virtues appreciated by the Greeks in Aristotle's day. This culminates in what must charitably be regarded as a ponderous joke—Aristotle's account of the "great-souled" man[67] who seems by any reasonable moral standards a pompous and ridiculous prig. Fortunately, it is not difficult to sort out the valuable parts of the *Ethics* from the less important.

We have to recognize at once that Greek attitudes to conduct, as to so many other things, were very different from our own. Modern Western attitudes to moral questions have been deeply affected, for better or worse, by Christianity. In many of its forms, Christianity has set up external standards of morality. The good man is the man who conforms not to his own desires or to his own nature but to the will of God. This will may be thought of as embodied in some revealed code of conduct like the Ten Commandments, or in the teaching of some authoritative church believed by its adherents to be divinely commissioned. But however it is conceived, the moral law is something external to human nature, which is itself pictured as flawed or corrupted by original sin. For the Greeks, on the contrary, the good man was usually thought of as following or developing his own human nature. To do wrong was somehow to fail to develop one's natural human functions. This is not an easy notion to make sense of, and we shall have to ask how far Aristotle succeeded in working out what was the most explicit version of this Greek belief.

Secondly, the Greeks did not make a sharp distinction, as we are apt to do, between the individual and his community. The modern liberal believes that the individual man or woman is the valuable unit in society and that the various communities of men are merely devices to ensure the individual's development and welfare. But this is a notion that has developed slowly, fostered partly by the ideals of Protestant Christianity and partly by the growth of political democracy. It was, however, a strange notion to the Greeks. When it does appear in Greek literature (as in Sophocles' *Antigone*) it seems a striking and prophetic idea. Aristotle certainly has little use for it. He accepts with what seems to us a monstrous complacency that men are basically unequal not only in gifts and capacities (as they obviously are) but also in their rights and in their worth as human beings. Slavery is accepted as part of the order of nature, and artisans are excluded from citizenship on the ground that "the life of a mechanic is incompatible with the practice of virtue."[68] His idea of the good life for man was limited by his very restricted and parochial notions of the ideal society, which he identifies with the Greek city-state. Ethics is for him a branch of politics, for it is the science of politics which is ultimately concerned with human good.[69]

It will be remembered that Aristotle has divided human knowledge into theoretical and practical. But practical knowledge is not moral philosophy in our modern sense — that is, it is not the reflective analysis of moral concepts and the relations between them. It is rather the art of living in the good sense of that ambiguous phrase. (It cannot be too often emphasized that "knowledge" [epistēmē] for a Greek meant "knowing how," practical grasp of techniques, as often as it meant the abstract understanding of facts and principles.) The Nicomachaean Ethics does, in fact, contain a good deal of ethics or moral philosophy in the contemporary sense of these phrases. This is difficult to fit into Aristotle's classification of human knowledge, but it is what gives his ethical writings their lasting value. But he believes his work to have much more than a merely theoretical interest. He wants to make himself and his audience better men. "For we are enquiring not in order to know what virtue is but in order to become good since otherwise our enquiry would have been of no use."[70]

At the beginning of his book,[71] he is careful to warn his readers that the subject that he is going to discuss does not yield clear-cut proofs and indubitable conclusions. He adds that it is a sign of an educated man that he looks for only that amount of certainty and exactness in the conclusions of his study that the subject matter makes possible. It is not clear what Aristotle conceives to be the source of this inexactness in ethics. But it seems probable that he would have attributed it more to the extreme complexity of the facts of human behavior than to the difficulty of understanding and verifying ethical judgments. It is, however, this second problem that has chiefly exercised moral philosophers in recent years. Aristotle does not go on to specify what degree of certainty or what kind of proof we should properly look for in ethics. We have to gather this from his subsequent argument. He does not, however, hesitate to lay down general conclusions about the nature of virtue and its relation to human nature and to happiness. And it is difficult to understand what sort of doubt, if any, Aristotle means his readers to entertain about them. Perhaps

his remarks should be interpreted as no more than a warning against dogmatism in our moral judgments.

The opening sentences of the Ethics indicate very clearly the main theme of Aristotle's moral philosophy. Like his metaphysics and his philosophy of nature, it is a teleological theory concerned in relating concepts like nature, function, and purpose to the notion of the good life. "Every art and every enquiry and similarly every action and pursuit is thought to aim at some good; and for this reason the good has rightly been declared to be that at which all things aim."[72] His argument develops this theme. Every human activity has its own aim or object. These objects in turn are means to yet other ends, and so on. To take mundane examples: A boy may study Latin in order to pass an examination. This examination may qualify him to enter a university to study law. This further study may lead to his qualifying as a lawyer. This qualification may give him a position in his father's law firm, where he can earn his living. It may well be that the boy would not choose any of these things for themselves alone. He may dislike studying Latin or law. He may take no pleasure in practising as a lawyer. But he may wish to please his father or simply to have the means of earning a large income. And the ends that he does accept for themselves afford the motive for striving for the intermediate ends that are merely necessary stages in his progress toward his final aim. But equally, to revert to the first step in the process, he may study Latin simply because he finds it enjoyable. Or he may find it enjoyable and recognize that it is a step toward something else that he finds desirable in itself. But however long or short this chain of activities may be, there must be at the end of it something that is sought after for itself alone and not as a means to anything else.

So far most people would agree. But Aristotle assumes further that there is one supreme or final good to which all human activities ultimately tend or toward which they are finally directed. Everyone agrees, he says, on what to call this ultimate good. In Greek, its name is eudaimonia, a word often translated as "happiness" and, more suitably, as "well-being." But this verbal agreement on the final good conceals profound disagreement as to its nature. Some men identify it with pleasure, others with the honors of political life, still others with the life of theōria, reflective contemplation. Aristotle briefly reviews arguments refuting the first two of these three suggestions and defers the third, which is his own preferred interpretation of eudaimonia, for later examination. This threefold division of human goods was almost a platitude in Greek ethics, though a modern critic would want to question both its clarity and its completeness.

We may naturally ask why Aristotle assumes that there is only one final good to which all other activities are directed. The answer is that eudaimonia is the only thing that is (1) always desirable for itself and never for the sake of something else and (2) self-sufficient.[73] Since we have not yet been given a definition or description of *eudaimonia*, how can we know this about it? The answer seems to be partly that Aristotle is here anticipating later discussion and partly that this is how the word is used. He often (and properly) consults common usage to determine the meaning of a phrase or the range of a concept.

He now proceeds to give a more specific account of human well-being.[74] We shall be better able to do this, he thinks, if we can first identify the *ergon* of man, that is, his work or function. Specific kinds of men — flute players, artists, carpenters, and so on — have their own specific works or functions. So do all the parts or organs of man — his eyes, his hands, his feet, and the rest. It would seem odd, then, if man himself *qua* human being did not have his own special task or function. But how are we to find out what it is? We do this by looking for what is peculiar to man as distinct from everything else in the world. Aristotle refers here to his own "evolutionary" biology discussed above. The specifically human function cannot lie merely in the life of nutrition, growth, and reproduction which we share with plants; nor again with the life of the senses and the power of self-movement which we share with the animals. It must therefore lie in the life of rational activity peculiar to man.

Clearly this is a feeble argument. It does not follow that because I have a special function in my social role of teacher or doctor or whatever it may be, that I must also have a special function in my biological status as a human being. Social roles do entail functions simply because they are the product, in origin at least, of purposeful activity. But to try to assimilate a biological status to a special role as Aristotle does is simply to beg one of the questions here at issue: Does man, in his capacity as a human being, have any function at all? Nor does it follow that because parts of an organism, for example, the leaves of a plant or its stamens, have specific biological jobs to do, that therefore the whole plant has a specific job to do. So there is no reason whatever to take this argument seriously. However, let us grant, for the sake of the argument, that *eudaimonia* does, in some way still to be specified, consist in an activity of reason. Two obvious questions arise at once: First, what *kind* of rational activity? Second, what, in any case, is the connection between *eudaimonia* so defined and the morally good life? The second question is particularly important. It would, after all, be contrary to fact, or at least contrary to appearances, to claim that bad men are never happy or that they never indulge in rational activity. Aristotle's answer to the first question is developed gradually in the course of the *Ethics* and is made quite explicit only in the concluding sections; he never asks himself the second question. But had it been put to him, it is not too difficult to see what his answer would have been. It is clearly implicit in what

he does say. The good for man, *eudaimonia*, consists in a certain kind of rational activity practised throughout a complete life (for, as Aristotle explains, we do not call a man *eudaimōn* if he is so only occasionally). And it must be an activity "in accordance with virtue and if there are more than one virtue, in accordance with the best and most complete."[75] Virtue (*aretē*) is not a sufficient condition for the good life, since Aristotle admits that a man may be virtuous without being happy.[76] But it is apparently a necessary condition; a man cannot be happy without being virtuous.

We seem to have been led round in a circle. Aristotle started to talk about *eudaimonia* in order to elucidate the concept of a good life. But in analyzing the notion of *eudaimonia*, he has introduced this unexplained concept of "virtue." And this is, to us nowadays, simply a rather archaic synonym for "moral goodness," the very concept that we are expecting Aristotle, as a moral philosopher, to elucidate. We must follow the argument further to see if this criticism is justified. Before we do so, however, it must be noted that *aretē*, traditionally but unfortunately translated "virtue," stands for a peculiarly Greek concept. The word has a far wider meaning than the narrow one of "human moral goodness." It refers to those qualities which make a thing good of its kind. Greek philosophical writers speak of the *aretē* of horses or of hunting dogs,* creatures to which they certainly denied moral virtues. When it is applied to human beings, the word connotes that constellation of qualities which make a man excel as a human being.[78] These qualities are not only what we would call "moral virtues," though in moral contexts, as in the *Nicomachaean Ethics*, they are certainly included.

Aristotle continues: "Since happiness (*eudaimonia*) is an activity of soul in accordance with perfect virtue, we must consider the nature of virtue; for perhaps we shall thus see better the nature of happiness."[79] Human virtues are of two kinds, intellectual and moral, relating respectively to the rational and irrational "parts" of the soul. The irrational part is also the source of desires or drives to action. So that one faculty (*dynamis*) or part of the soul formulates rules for action; the other sets goals for action and, at least to some degree, is controlled by the rules set by reason. Intellectual virtue is acquired through being taught, whereas moral virtues are the result of habit.

Aristotle discusses the moral virtues first. They are not natural to man in the sense of being inborn, but like any other skill, are acquired and improved by exercise. (Like Plato, Aristotle draws frequent and very misleading analogies between moral habits and techniques or skills.) "For the things we have to learn before we can do them, we learn by doing them — e.g., men become builders by building and lyre-players

---

*Aristotle does so himself,[77] and the usage is very common in Plato's dialogues.

by playing the lyre, so too we become just by doing just acts, temperate by doing temperate acts, brave by doing brave acts."[80] Thus, education and even legislation are important in providing the conditions and environment for acquiring correct moral habits. In saying that we become good by doing good acts, Aristotle means, as he explains,[81] that it is not sufficient evidence that a man is good merely that he does good acts. He must know that the acts in question are good and he must choose them for that reason. "And thirdly, his action must proceed from a firm and unchangeable character." A man who has constantly to struggle against temptation is a worse man, even though he struggles successfully, than a man who does good acts with ease and pleasure. To Aristotle, our moral struggles are a sign that though we are on the road to virtue, we have not yet arrived.

That good character is a stable disposition learned or established through practice is a sensible piece of moral psychology with which most people would agree. No one becomes a good man overnight. However, Aristotle has not yet told us what it is that distinguishes good actions from bad. There are two parts to his account of the nature of virtue. The first is the famous "doctrine of the mean"; the second is the part played by intellectual virtue in forming virtues of character. Virtues (and, indeed, vices too) are states of character which are evinced in action. But the distinction between virtue and vice is that in virtuous action we aim at a mid-point between excess and defect, to take a typical case, between overindulging a particular natural tendency (hunger, sex, anger, etc.) and repressing it too far. This is another notion that may seem curious to us today, especially if we have been exposed to those kinds of Christianity which commend asceticism. But it is again a characteristically Greek idea. Mēden agan, "nothing too much," was a proverb attributed to one of the traditional sages of Greece. A famous medical theory attributed to a sixth-century physician, Alcmaeon of Croton, represented health in the body as due to a balance of forces and disease as the triumph of one of these over the rest. This theory was variously elaborated by later writers as a balance of elements or of "humors." Aristotle's medical training made him very familiar with these notions, and many of his commentators, following a hint given by Aristotle himself,[82] have seen the doctrine of the mean as an account of moral health framed by analogy with Alcmaeon's theory.

Aristotle's final account of virtue[83] is that it is a habit of choosing courses of action that lie midway between indulging and repressing natural tendencies. Further, this mid-point has to be chosen in relation to the person making the choice, and the choice itself must be controlled by a rational principle (logos) such as would be determined by a man of practical wisdom — that is, by the phronimos who possesses intellectual virtue. We have seen what Aristotle intends by calling virtue a habit and by saying that it is a mean between extremes. But we have not considered his account of choice nor what he means by "the mean relative to us" nor yet how the intellectual virtues are related to the moral virtues we are discussing. Let us look at these points in turn.

Aristotle's account of choice is not by any means an attempt to solve the so-called problem of free will. This was not a problem with which the Greeks were much concerned. Its prominence in later philosophical discussion has been largely a consequence of two factors, Christian doctrines of divine foreknowledge, omnipotence, and grace, and the modern scientific world-picture. Aristotle is concerned simply with the conditions under which we assign responsibility for actions or, in his own words, "praise and blame." He contrasts such actions with those which we pardon or even pity on the ground that they are involuntary. If an action is involuntary, it does not qualify for assessment as moral or immoral. And it is involuntary if it is due either to compulsion or to ignorance. An action is compulsory if its source is external to the agent. This is not a very satisfactory criterion, as the morally crucial cases are just those in which we find it difficult to say if the cause of the action is external to the agent or not. Suppose, for example, a resistance worker gives away secrets under torture or a bank clerk hands over money at the point of a gun. Are such actions voluntary by this test or not? Aristotle himself is uncertain about such cases and says, unhelpfully, that "it may be debated whether such actions are voluntary or involuntary."[84] (He adds, however, that they are more like voluntary acts.) He realizes, of course, that most temptations and spurs to action are external to the agent. But this, of itself, does not make the action involuntary. Otherwise, he says, all acts would be reckoned so. And as to the second cause of involuntary action, it is not any kind of ignorance leading to action that exempts us from praise or blame. For example, ignorance of right and wrong does not excuse. But ignorance of the relevant circumstances in which we have to act may excuse us if the ignorance itself was unavoidable. Suppose, for example, that I start my car not knowing that a child had crawled under it in play and so cause an accident.

Any action which is not for one or both of these reasons involuntary is voluntary. But not all voluntary actions involve choice (proairesis) of the kind Aristotle has specified in his account of virtue. Many voluntary acts, even of rational moral creatures, may be spontaneous or impulsive. These are voluntary but not chosen. Under this heading would fall any actions "of which the moving principle is in the agent himself, he being aware of the particular circumstances of the action,"[85] such actions being like those of small children and the higher animals. Choice involves deliberation; and we do not deliberate about the ultimate ends of our actions but only about the means by which we may achieve them.

The objects of our actions may be (1) determined by our desiring nature (*orexis*), or (2) decided upon after deliberation as a means to (1). Once decided upon, they too must be sought by further intermediate means until deliberation shows me something which is both here and now in my power and a step to by ultimate goal. I desire *X*. *A* is known to be a means to *X* and *B* is a means to *A*. *C* is a means to *B* and *D* is a means to *C*. Now *D* is something that I can do here and now. I therefore choose to do it.

This account of choice is perhaps an accurate description, so far as it goes, of how a perfectly rational man would behave. But, to say the least, only a small minority of human beings are perfectly rational men. And it takes no account of those spontaneous or impulsive actions that often *are* the objects of moral praise or censure — unreflective generosity or meanness, bravery or cowardice, and so on. Moreover, it is important that a theory of virtue should take account of the fact that many of our actions are done through weakness of will. We may know quite clearly the action that our accepted moral standards prescribe. Nevertheless, we fail to do it. Our desire for what we believe to be wrong is somehow "stronger than" our desire for what we believe to be right. And not all such acts are done impulsively. It is notorious that we sometimes seem to follow the worse course even after deliberation and reflection. Can Aristotle account for this? He spends some time in Book VII of the *Ethics* in trying to explain these facts consistently with the theory of conduct he has expounded. The outcome of a long, tentative, and undogmatic discussion[86] is that the weak-willed man (*akratēs*) is not really fully aware of the circumstances in which he is acting. Part of Aristotle's solution is that when we act under the influence of passion, we are like "men asleep, drunk or mad" who know the moral principles and facts relevant to the situation but who are not in a position to make use of this knowledge. This is a quite unsatisfactory solution. If Aristotle is to be consistent with what he has already said, he must call such actions "involuntary." And not only is this at variance with common moral opinion, as he has already admitted, but it endorses the views of Socrates on virtue and knowledge which he has already rejected. Perhaps Aristotle could hardly have got to grips with this problem without concerning himself with the wider issues of free will and determinism. And, as I have said above, no Greek philosopher deals seriously with this problem.

So far, we have been concerned with Aristotle's account of moral virtue and with lapses from it. We still have to look at his very important doctrine of the intellectual virtues.[87] It has been seen that in his account of moral activity he insists that a good action consists of choosing a mean course between extremes and that the choice has to be made in accordance with a rule or rational principle. Aristotle's explanation refers back to his psychological doctrines. The soul has a rational part and an irrational one, the rational part being itself divided into two. One of these (*to epistēmonikon*) deals with the stable invariable world of necessary truth; the other (*to logistikon*), with the shifting world of contingent fact. It is this second "principle" which is concerned with the good life. One of its virtues is prudence (*phronēsis*), which enables us to choose the right means to good actions. And just as the man of scientific knowledge proves his conclusions by means of the demonstrative syllogism, so the man of practical wisdom (*ho phronimos*) "proves" the right course of action by means of a quasi-syllogistic type of argument, the so-called "practical syllogism."* The good man of well-formed character recognizes the good for man, and it is the work of practical reason to make a correct estimate of the means to achieve that good. Recognition of the good end corresponds to the major premise of the syllogism and recognition of the means to the minor. The conclusion consists in the actual choice. "*A* is good and *B* is the means to *A* — therefore I do *B*," is a crude condensation of this type of "practical argument." Its nature is very cursorily indicated by Aristotle himself.[88]

Moreover, it seems to be the work of *phronēsis* to make a correct estimation of the "mean" in which any particular instance of virtuous action consists. Aristotle does not explain how we do this. He illustrates his meaning by a reference to the training of athletes.[89] Here the correct amount of food or exercise cannot be estimated by any convenient formula which will give us the answer whenever we ask, "How much?" We have to judge the amounts in relation to the particular circumstances of the case under consideration. Perhaps a better illustration would be some skilled activity like playing tennis. The distance, direction, and force of each stroke has to be judged in relation to the positions of the player and his opponent and their respective powers. Skill at the game consists in being able to estimate and execute the stroke appropriate to the occasion. So it is with Aristotle's moral theory. The man of good judgment can make the correct estimation of the "mean" in a complex situation. This analogy is imperfect in that skill at tennis, though learned like *aretē*, does not depend on the intellectual apprehension of any abstract principles. However, common experience does suggest, contrary to Aristotle's moral theory, that we do learn to behave in very much the same way that we learn any other skilled activity.

The reader will have felt that the foregoing argument is extremely abstract. For all its promising talk about man's final good, it tells us little of what that consists in. To say that it is an activity of reason in accordance with virtue may sound impressive, but it is hardly informative. In the final chapters of the

---

*Aristotle does not use the Greek equivalent of this phrase. But it is a traditional way of referring to the "argument".

Ethics,[90] Aristotle tries to remedy this. The good for man consists in the exercise of his highest powers — that is to say, it consists in the contemplative activity of the philosopher. And because we cannot live continuously in a state of philosophic contemplation, Aristotle has to recognize that "in a secondary degree, the life in accordance with the other kind of virtue is happy; for the activities in accordance with this befit our human estate."[91] Ordinary moral virtue seems to play a double role. It is at once the means by which we reach the life of contemplation and a second-rate substitute for it.

How are we to criticize this curious but very influential view of human life? Its basic premise is a sound one that has been too much neglected by "other-worldly" moralities: *The good life for human beings must be an ideal firmly grounded in human nature*. What we ought to do is limited by what we are capable of doing; and that, in turn, depends on our nature. But "human nature" is an empirical concept. The sciences of biology, psychology, and sociology combine to show us what our nature is. We cannot expect to answer the question, "What is the nature of man?" without a great deal of experimental enquiry. And even twenty-three centuries after Aristotle, these enquiries are far from complete. Certainly, Aristotle's own naïve equation of man's specific nature with his rational capacities and his good with their exercise does not get us very far. Yet his belief that ethics must be somehow grounded in the nature of the moral agent is an important one. The notion is implicit in much of Greek moral thinking, but Aristotle must have the credit for the first determined attempt to work it out.

But against this we must set some serious defects. It will be sufficient to select two of the most important. In the first place, we may reasonably question Aristotle's assumption that there is one and only one ultimate good toward which all human activities are ultimately directed — *eudaimonia*, human happiness or well-being. Certainly it is true that if *A* is chosen as a means to *B*, *B* as a means to *C*, and so on, this chain must sooner or later conclude with something chosen for its own sake and not merely as a stepping-stone to some further good. But why must all such chains of action end with *the same* self-sufficient good? It is plain that experience of human behavior does not support Aristotle here. Different people choose all sorts of different things as ends in themselves. And the same person may choose, at different times, food, rest, exercise, conversation, or piano-playing, let us say, as self-sufficient ends of action. There are various sources of Aristotle's mistake. First, because all such self-sufficient activities are accompanied by happiness, it by no means follows that they are chosen *as a means to* happiness. That it is impossible to acquire happiness by pursuing it directly has been remarked so often as to be a platitude of common-sense psychology. Indeed, in his discussion of pleasure Aristotle comes close to

making this point himself.[92] Second, Aristotle seriously underestimates the immense variety of human nature and the diversity of men's talents and temperaments. His belief in essences led him to postulate a human nature common to all men. A more empirical approach to his material might have led him to doubt it. Finally, his mistake may be one of simple logic. It is easy, but mistaken, to argue from:

(1) For all *x* there is a *y* such that *x* is in relation *R* to *y* to (2), there is a *y* such that for all *x*, *x* is in relation *R* to *y*. To say that every rat has a tail is not the same as saying that there is one tail common to all rats. Similarly, to say that every action has a final end is not to say that there is one and the same end to all actions. This is a type of reasoning that lies beyond the reach of his own formal logic. He may, for this reason, have been more easily deceived by the fallacy.

Then, we may also ask how "good," in the sense of "that which is sought after or desired," is connected with "good" as a description of human action or character. Aristotle never shows clearly how, if at all, *eudaimonia*, the good for man, is connected with moral obligation. It is true that this is not the sort of question that would naturally occur to a Greek of Aristotle's day. Nevertheless, it is a question that more recent moral philosophers have shown to be crucial to any ethical theory that tries to argue from man's nature to man's duties. Virtue for Aristotle is both an element in and a way toward *eudaimonia*. But on his account of the matter it is unclear why we ought to try to be virtuous. And if we are told that it is silly to ask why I ought to do what I ought, at least it is not silly to point out that the mere fact that we have a natural bent to behave in a certain way cannot endow that course of action with any moral value. "Nature" is a treacherously ambiguous word in ethical discussion. It raises at once Hume's famous query about the propriety of arguing from matters of fact to conclusions of value. How are the *facts* of human nature related to the *values* of human conduct? Aristotle nowhere begins to make this clear. The very notion of moral obligation is a shadowy background concept in his *Ethics* and plays no part in its logical structure. Perhaps he was right to ignore it. But we would like to be shown the reason why he does so and how he proposes to argue from man's nature to his duties.

CONCLUSION

We have seen that parts of Aristotle's work, in particular, his formal logic and moral philosophy, have survived with credit not only centuries of critical scrutiny but also a profound change in the intellectual outlook of the Western world. Other parts, such as his natural science, his metaphysics, and his theory of knowledge, have been found wanting in one way or another. His general view of the universe is now just a part of the history of ideas. There are still other parts of his writings that we have not had space or occasion to examine here — his theories about literature, for example, and his political thought. All of these have been influential at one time or another. Indeed, the reason why Aristotle is so important in the history of philosophy is the degree to which he affected his successors — in particular, the philosophers of the Middle Ages and later, despite a conscious reaction against him, those of the seventeenth century.

The philosophy of the Middle Ages, whether Jewish, Moslem, or Christian, was designed as an intellectual background to the favored religious system. It is a proof of the fertility and adaptability of Aristotle's ideas that they could be used, more or less successfully, to give some rational color to the theological systems of Judaism, Islam, and the Catholic Church. Whether so chameleonlike a character is a virtue in a philosophical system may be debated, but its historical importance cannot be questioned. When the full range of Aristotle's writings became known to Europe in the thirteenth century, church authorities were alarmed by their pagan background and their preconceptions so alien to the world picture of Christianity. At times it was forbidden to teach Aristotelian doctrines in the leading universities of Europe. Yet the synthesis of Aristotelianism and Christianity so brilliantly worked out by Aquinas succeeded well enough to become an orthodoxy of its own. Contemporary Neo-Scholastics of the Thomist school still attempt to interpret the world view of the twentieth century in terms of Aristotle's philosophic principles.

These historical facts are the evidence of Aristotle's influence, but they have, of course, no bearing on the truth of his doctrines. We may therefore usefully end this discussion by asking what value his philosophy still has for us in the present day. Let us concede his great achievement in formal logic and a more limited success in ethics. Is there anything else? There is, I think, much to admire though little to believe. His theories may be mistaken, but the spirit of untiring rationalism which he brought to all of his vast range of problems must surely command our admiration. And at a time when many philosophers seem to deny that theirs is essentially a rational enterprise, it is salutary to remember that one of the greatest of European philosophers had a strong and persistent faith in the powers of human reason. Moreover, his rationalism was controlled by a genuine scientific temper and a respect for empirical fact. Where he fails, it is nearly always because the Platonist in him overcomes the scientist. In this, he shows himself to be the victim of his own education. But this is a fate that few of us can escape.

4

Greek Philosophy After Aristotle

D. W. HAMLYN

BIOGRAPHICAL DETAILS of the philosophers of this period are scanty and generally ill-authenticated. The following list gives the dates of the principal figures:

ARISTIPPUS	*about* 435 *to* 360 B.C.
DIOGENES	412 *to* 323 B.C.
PYRRHO	365 *to* 275 B.C.
EPICURUS	341 *to* 270 B.C.
ZENO	340 *to* 265 B.C.
ARCESILAUS	315 *to* 241 B.C.
CHRYSIPPUS	280 *to* 206 B.C.
CARNEADES	213 *to* 129 B.C.
PANAETIUS	180 *to* 110 B.C.
POSEIDONIUS	128 *to* 44 B.C.
LUCRETIUS	97 *to* 54 B.C.
SENECA	4 *to* 65 A.D.
EPICTETUS	*born about* 60 A.D.
SEXTUS EMPIRICUS	Second century A.D.
PLOTINUS	204 *to* 269 A.D.
PORPHYRY	233 *to* 304 A.D.
IAMBLICHUS	*died about* 330 A.D.
PROCLUS	410 *to* 485 A.D.

PHILOSOPHERS OFTEN BEHAVE as if Greek philosophy ended with Aristotle. There is some excuse for this point of view, however incorrect it may be, for after the death of Aristotle there came a change in the character of Greek philosophy. Its aim became, for some time, more practical in the sense that a main aim of philosophers was to indicate the way toward attaining some kind of salvation. Festugière[1] claims that the Stoic, Epicurean, and Skeptic schools all attempted to provide ways out of the fatalism which the Academy and the Lyceum were thought to have inculcated with their stress on the astral gods and divine necessity. However this may be, it is clear that there was in some ways a return, perhaps conscious, to Socrates (or to Socrates as they then saw him), and that there became established a cult of the wise man, with different recipes for attaining wisdom. Each philosophical school taught a view of the world with this aim in mind. The Hellenistic period was a time of political, social, and religious upheaval,* and it was for this reason that philosophy became of practical importance.

Although the Academy and the Lyceum continued in active existence, there were no big figures as heads of these schools, with the exception of a brief period in which the Academy benefited by the influence of Skepticism, which ended when there was a recrudescence of Platonism in the third century A.D. It is nevertheless noteworthy that there was an almost immediate perversion of the original doctrines of Plato and Aristotle after their deaths. Speusippus, the successor to Plato in the Academy, seems to have given up the forms, holding instead that to know something was to know how it was related to everything else — an anticipation of the views of the much later absolute idealists. With Xenocrates, Speusippus' successor, the perversions became more extreme. It is no surprise to find the Academy in its Skeptical period (under Arcesilaus and, a hundred years later, Carneades), apparently far from Plato.

In Aristotle's Lyceum, Theophrastus seems to have continued the trend, already apparent in Aristotle, toward empirical observation and a consequent lack of stress on teleology. His successor, Strato of Lampsacus, known as "The Physicist," embraced a completely mechanical account of things, together with an Atomic theory and perhaps with some gestures toward the use of experiment. But thereafter we know nothing of the Lyceum except its existence.

Before turning to the Stoic, Epicurean, and Skeptic schools, it will be well to note the existence before the death of Aristotle of movements that were influential in determining some trends in post-Aristotelian thought. The Cynics, originated by Diogenes (although the ancient world gave the credit to Plato's rival Antisthenes), and the Cyrenaics, originated by Aristippus, both thought of themselves as followers of Socrates. They both eschewed theory of every sort and stressed practice, the one proclaiming the virtues of austerity and self-sufficiency, the other those of pleasure. The Cynics made claims for the dignity of man independently of his ties to social conventions and laws (Diogenes was notorious for flouting even the most obvious conventions), and this led to a belief that men were citizens of the world, a belief that was to be emphasized strongly by the Stoics. As opposed to Diogenes, and despite what might be expected from his proclaimed views, Aristippus seems to have practiced and preached a sober way of life. He thought the pursuit of pleasure would lead to wisdom, and indeed be the only thing that could lead to it. Nevertheless (and in this respect he differed from Epicurus), he maintained that it was the pleasure of the moment that was to be pursued, pleasure that was not just the absence of pain. The wise man will practice virtue because and only because it will produce real pleasure. Diogenes Laertius quotes a saying of Aristippus to the effect that the advantage of philosophy lies in the fact that if all the laws were done away with "we should go on living in just the same way." However difficult it is to square such a dictum with the overt aims of the school, it is clear that the pursuit of pleasure was meant to lead to the observance of a definite morality.

The other movement which it is necessary to mention is that of the Megarians. This school stemmed from Eucleides, a citizen of the Greek town of Megara, who was a contemporary of Plato. The members of the school held to a version of Eleaticism: they considered the One to be the Good. Attempts to meet their views can be found in Aristotle. For present purposes their importance lies in their inquiries into logic, in which they had a profound influence upon the Stoa. They were the first to formulate the principles of a logic that, unlike Aristotle's, was propositional — that is, a logic the fundamental notion of which was the proposition rather than the term. The connection between their innovations in logic and their metaphysics is not altogether clear, but there is enough evidence to enable us to make guesses about it. One of the school, Stilpo, held the same view as the earlier Antisthenes, that predication was impossible, apparently because he held that the meaning of all expressions is their reference. It was inferred that to say that man is good is to say that one thing, denoted by the word "man," is the same as another thing, denoted by the word "good" — which is impossible, since being a man is not the same as being good. Thus, it may be noted, predicative statements are characterized as statements of identity. The same sort of premises underlie an argument used by Menedemus of the Eretrian school, an offshoot of the Megarian school. This argument[2] is to the effect that, given that two different

---

* It was also, incidentally, a time that saw the rise of Greek science, but this had little connection with philosophy.

things are different and that goodness and the conferring of benefits are two different things, goodness is not beneficial – or alternatively, depending on the textual reading, to confer benefits is not good.* The logical view that all statements are statements of identity is compatible with the metaphysical views either in that there is only one thing (for then there is nothing else to be identified with it) or that there are a number of disconnected things (for then no one of them can be identified with any other). The Megarian and Eretrian schools held to a form of Monism – that ultimately there is only one thing – and it is characteristic of Monists that they are interested in such a coherence between statements that the statements form a system applicable to that one thing. It may have been for some such reason that the Megarians evolved a propositional logic.

However that may be, such a logic was formulated, and it was taken up by the Stoa. Of the Megarians, Eubulides was interested in logical paradoxes. Most of those which he outlined are trivial, but two of them are of some importance: (1) The Liar, and (2) The Sorites or Heap. The first is that familiar to modern logicians – to give it in Cicero's words,[3] "If you say that you are lying and you tell the truth, you are lying; but you say that you are lying and you tell the truth: therefore you are lying." It is to be noted that this formulation gives the paradox as an argument of the *modus ponens* form (that is, if *p* then *q*; but *p*: therefore *q*), and it leads to a conclusion incompatible with one of the premises. But the paradox is given in other forms by other writers. Eubulides is not credited with a solution to the paradox, although Chrysippus of the Stoa may have held that for you to say that you are lying is meaningless (a view held by some logicians today). The second paradox depends upon the notion of a continuum. Fundamentally, it is founded on the question, "How many grains of corn make a heap?" Obviously, 1,000 grains, for example, do; but if I take away one grain at a time when does it cease to be a heap?

More important is the work of the Megarian logicians, Philo and Diodorus Cronos. It appears that they became involved in a dispute on two main issues — the analysis of hypothetical propositions and the analysis of modal concepts. Philo defended an analysis of hypothetical propositions in terms of what Russell in this century called "material implication". A hypothetical is true if and only if it does not have a true antecedent and a false consequent. Diodorus wanted stronger truth conditions, maintaining that a true hypothetical is one which neither was nor is capable of having a true antecedent and a false consequent. Sextus Empiricus, the head of the Skeptic school for a time in the second century, reports a saying to the effect that in Alexandria even the crows on the roof tops were

cawing over which hypothetical is true. In the case of modalities, Philo maintained that a proposition was possible only if it could be true by its intrinsic nature, and it was necessary only if by its very nature it could not be false. Diodorus maintained that a proposition was possible if and only if it is so or will be so, and it is necessary if and only if it is so and always will be so. In the latter connection, Diodorus employed what became known as the "master-argument" — an argument that gained some notoriety. He maintained (according to the late Stoic, Epictetus) that the following three propositions cannot all be true: (1) Everything that is past is necessarily so. (2) A proposition which is impossible cannot follow from one that is possible. (3) Something is possible which neither is nor will be so. In accordance with his theory about possibility, Diodorus therefore maintained that the third proposition should be denied. Other logicians attempted other solutions, but the fact of the incompatibility between the propositions did not seem to be questioned. Whatever the reason Diodorus held them to be incompatible, it must have had something to do with his belief in the necessity of things (indeed, Cicero discusses it in this context).[4] It is an interesting exercise to try to work out the reasons in this light.

So much, then, for the movements that influenced one or another of the main schools which started around 300 B.C. The Skeptics, originated by Pyrrho, did not, in all probability, constitute a formal school at first; but one arose later. The Stoa and the Epicurean school were teaching schools from the beginning, and Epicurus' school (known as the Garden because of its location, just as the Stoa received its name from its location) formed some kind of society for life. The Stoa was in many ways in direct contrast with Epicurus and was probably founded in conscious opposition to him.

Epicurus

EPICURUS claimed to be self-taught, and he was certainly critical and even abusive toward those philosophers from whom he might have been expected to have derived something (he even denied the existence of Leucippus, the father of Greek Atomism). He lived an austere life and showed great fortitude during his last very painful illness. The society which he founded in Athens seems to have lived frugally, and there was in it a great stress on friendship. (Indeed, it has been suggested that the Epicurean society was the prototype of the later Christian society.) Epicurus had one disciple of note, Metrodorus, but he died before Epicurus. Although Epicurus was a prolific writer, little of his work has survived, and apart from fragments, we are almost entirely indebted to the three letters and the maxims included in Diogenes Laertius' biography. In addi-

---

* There are points of affinity between this argument and that used in this century by G. E. Moore against the "naturalistic fallacy" in ethics.

tion, of course, there is the *De Rerum Natura*, written much later by the Roman poet Lucretius. Lucretius differs from Epicurus in one important respect: Lucretius' poem makes no reference to any ethical point of view, whereas this was the goal of Epicurus' philosophy. For this philosophy, like that of other contemporary philosophers, was meant to teach wisdom, and the metaphysical view that he provided of the world, the gods, and the human soul was meant to be put to that end. Epicurus was attempting to provide a new kind of remedy for people's ills by giving a new view of the world. The new view was meant to show that there was no reason to worry about things, and thus the goal of all wisdom was *ataraxia*, or freedom from care. In a parallel way, the Skeptics taught that the only correct attitude to the world and its problems was indifference, whereas the Stoics provided a new conception of man's place in the universe with the same aim as that of Epicurus. The latter's recipe for men's ills can be summed up in the "quadrupal remedy" given by Philodemus: The gods have no concern with us, death is nothing to us, pleasure is easy to obtain, pain does not last long.[5] But the only way to show this was to produce a metaphysical view of the world from which such conclusions could be derived. Hence Epicurus' system is a good example of a deductive metaphysics.

CANONICE

Epicurus had no interest in or knowledge of logic, but he prefaced his system with what he called *Canonice* — a theory of knowledge and methodology. In this he insisted upon the fact that all knowledge rests upon sensations (in common with other Greek philosophers, he failed to distinguish between sensation and perception). Sensations are the result of contact with a sense organ on the part of "*eidola*" — i.e., films of atoms given off by objects. Sensation is thus immediate and admits of no check (a fact on which he insisted). Hence it is useless to look for any other source of knowledge. He seems to have held that in some sense every sensation is true (although this has recently been disputed);[6] but by this he seems to have meant that no sensation is corrigible in itself. Even delusions and dreams are "true" in the sense that a man cannot be mistaken as to what they are *of*. Hence sensations were for Epicurus rather like the sense data which some modern philosophers have invoked; and also like some modern philosophers Epicurus thought that the primary use of words should correspond to these sensations. Nevertheless, he did hold that it was possible to distinguish between veridical and non-veridical presentations or appearances of objects, and indeed that we do in fact make mistakes in perception. He believed in fact that objects seen at close quarters produce clear and distinct presentations on which science must rely.

Knowledge, therefore, cannot consist only of sensations, even if it rests upon them. Epicurus makes clear that it also involves "preconceptions," a preconception being a sort of abstract idea built up in experience and stored in the mind in such a way as to be applicable to the objects of perception. Thus, on his view, perceiving consists both in the receiving of a sensation and its falling under a concept. Error arises in consequence from wrong expectations with regard to sensations. Cicero[7] held that Epicurus meant these "preconceptions" to be innate ideas, and this view has been supported recently by De Witt.[8] The arguments for this conclusion, however, are not good. It is true that Epicurus did distinguish between *primary* and *secondary* ideas; but this distinction does nothing to reinforce Cicero's point of view, for the primary ideas are those derived from perception, and the secondary ideas are those built up from the primary ones by processes of reasoning. Knowledge, then, depends upon sensations and "preconceptions," and although our sources sometimes mention feelings as a criterion of truth, it is clear that feelings were the concern of ethics and had nothing to do with the Epicurean theory of knowledge.

Because some things — for example, the stars — cannot be closely inspected, perception of them can never, in Epicurus' view, be clear and distinct; hence it is necessary for us to make inferences as to their nature and behavior from what we *can* closely inspect. But Epicurus is strangely tolerant about what he was prepared to count as a good inference in this respect. In the letter to Pythocles, and again in Lucretius, one finds catalogues of celestial phenomena with a variety of alternative explanations for each. Any hypothesis that seemed to be consistent with the phenomena was held to be possible, and Epicurus showed no inclination to speculate further. He clearly had no conception of any canons of scientific inference or inquiry, and thought that all that mattered was that a hypothesis should be consistent with sensation.

PHYSICS OR METAPHYSICS

Epicurus' tolerance with regard to detailed astronomical phenomena did not extend to his metaphysical principles. This has seemed puzzling to some people, but it is less puzzling when the difference between his views on metaphysics and his views on science is seen. It is clear that his metaphysical system depended upon a series of primary truths, for which he attempts to provide some rational justification. These truths are probably twelve in number (although it is difficult to distinguish them in the letter to Herodotus, given in Diogenes Laertius).

Epicurus started from the common pre-Socratic tenet that nothing comes into being out of nothing or disappears into nothing; but he supports this dogma with arguments to the effect that otherwise there would be no specific causal history for each thing. In other words, anything could have come about in any way whatever, and also, if things went out of existence everything would have perished long ago. A further corollary of this is that the sum total of things is constant. Next, he states that everything consists of bodies and the void (the existence of bodies is obvious, and the void, he thinks, is necessary for motion). Some bodies are compounds, some indivisible elements—i.e., the atoms. The latter are infinite in number, and the void is infinite in extent. The atoms are in continual motion, falling with equal velocity through the void. (Although they are of different weight, this makes no difference to the velocity of their fall, because the void offers no resistance. It is tempting, but perhaps not strictly accurate, to refer to this as an anticipation of Galileo.) There are two difficulties in this connection: First, in an infinite universe, as Aristotle saw, there is no "up" or "down" in an absolute sense; here Epicurus insists that the sense in which the atoms fall downward is that they fall in this direction *relative to ourselves*. Second, if the atoms fell with uniform velocity and direction there would be no collisions, and these are necessary if compounds are to form; hence Epicurus attributes to the atoms an arbitrary swerve, a notion that he introduces rather as a *deus ex machina*. Lucretius invokes the same notion to account also for the freedom of the will, and his position is in this respect rather like those who have invoked indeterminacy in modern physics as an explanation of free will. It is clearly the wrong kind of explanation, since whatever we mean by "freedom" in this connection, it is not "arbitrariness."

The atoms vary in size, although they are never visible and never infinitely small. To prove the last point Epicurus introduces a curious argument[9] to the effect that just as there is a *minimum visibile* in the case of perceptible things, so, by analogy, must there be limits to the divisibility of atoms even in principle. That is to say, the atoms are composed of minimal parts that are not capable of independent existence, and such parts are not capable of being divided even in principle, let alone in fact! The atoms also vary in shape, but not with infinite variety, for the shape of an atom depends upon the structure of the minimal parts. The third property of the atoms, that of weight, has already been remarked upon. It is responsible for the motion of the atoms but not for the velocity of that motion. Atoms possess no other properties, and all the other properties that ordinary things possess are secondary, produced by atoms in forming compounds. In this connection, Epicurus distinguishes between those properties which are permanent and those which are mere accidents. The latter conception is used in an interesting way in the case of time, which he calls an "accident of accidents" on the grounds that temporal extension is a property that happens to belong to processes like

feelings, which are movements that themselves happen to result from the behavior of bodies. Unfortunately, it is difficult to see how any movement could *not* take time, and it is therefore difficult to see the justification of calling time an "*accident* of accidents," unless it be that not all accidents of things are such that they involve, or are, processes.[10]

When the atoms collide they set up semistable systems within which the individual atoms rebound off each other, so setting up a state of vibration. (This seems to be the general view despite the occasional use of language, especially in Lucretius, which suggests that the atoms become hooked onto each other.) The compounds formed by such systems vary according to the density of the atoms—for example, in gases the atoms are dispersed, while in solids they are closely packed. It follows from this view that the identity of any object is given, not by the constituent parts (for these may change — atoms may leave the system and others may arrive), but by the *system* as a whole. Groups of objects form higher-order systems, the highest being a world, of which Epicurus thinks that there are an infinite number. Between the worlds, where the density of the atoms is least, are the gods, who preserve their identity, not because they are gods, but because, as systems of atoms themselves, they are least subject to buffeting there. They function only as patterns to which men may look. The worlds themselves are always liable to perish, and new ones are liable to come into existence.

The grandeur of this scheme of things is obvious. Everything comes about as a result of mechanical forces. There is no providence, nor is there fate in any sense that implies retribution for men's sins. In this way, Epicurus provides a general remedy for the fears of men. There is nothing to fear, he holds, for both we ourselves and the gods are part of the nature of things; we come into being and die, and that is all there is to it.

This conclusion is reinforced by his account of the soul. He maintains that it is a complex of atoms like everything else, but in this case of very fine atoms which permeate the body and are held together by it. The main constituents of the soul are "particles resembling breath and heat," to which the doxographer Aetius[11] adds air and a nameless element, the "fourth nature," which is responsible for sensation and other functions. Sense perception comes about when *eidola* (simulacra or images) come from things in succession and affect the sense organs and thereby the part of the soul that is in them. Epicurus gives a complicated account of the different forms of perception and the illusions to which we may be subject, but there is no space to discuss this account here. He maintains also that on occasion, individual simulacra may affect our minds without there being a succession of them to affect the sense organs, and this he adduces to explain figments of the imagination, dreams, and even visions of the gods. Nevertheless, the soul, being composed of atoms, is dispersed with the body when we die. Hence there is no possibility of life after death. Death, says Epicurus, is nothing to us; for after death there is no "us." Hence there is nothing in death to fear. This is the second aspect of his remedy for men's fears.

ETHICS

Epicurus' system of ethics is typical of those of the time, in that it is naturalistic in the special sense that he thought he could indicate what men ought to do by appealing to a view of nature in general and of human nature in particular.[12] The idea is that if it can be discovered what it is natural to do, then what one *ought* to do is thereby discovered. One feature of this belief is that the philosopher concerned is liable to write into his account of what is natural something of the ethical ideal that he wishes to advocate. That is to say, at a crucial stage in the account of what is natural, ethical notions are slipped in, whether intentionally or not.

Epicurus maintains that "pleasure is the beginning and end of the blessed life." This means that the attainment of pleasure is at least a necessary condition of the good life. This is true, as Epicurus stresses, even of the pleasures of the stomach. But is the attainment of pleasure a sufficient condition of the good life? The limit of pleasure, Epicurus thinks, is to be found in complete absence of pain, and it arises both from the satisfaction of desire and from the equilibrium subsequently attained. Because pleasure is a natural phenomenon it is in man's power to attain that limit; but it must be noted that pain must sometimes be endured in order for greater pleasure to result. For this reason, Epicurus says that the wise man will be happy even on the rack (although this view is given no other justification).

But at this point Epicurus begins to adjudicate on what sort of pleasure is to be pursued. He is not content merely to say that, the pursuit and attainment of pleasure being natural, the good life consists in its pursuit. For, apart from the general invalidity of the move from statements about what is natural to statements about what one ought to do, the view that we should pursue pleasure in general *because* it is natural would lead to ethical views other than those which Epicurus wishes to maintain. In other words, the attainment of pleasure is not in itself a sufficient condition of the good life. Not any pleasure is to be pursued. Epicurus maintains that pleasures may be natural and necessary, natural and not necessary, or neither natural nor necessary. The last kind of pleasure is to be eschewed and the first made the primary object of one's aims. Thus, although Epicurus has started from the premise that pleasure is a natural phenomenon, at the crucial point where the supposed ethical consequences are drawn, not all pleasures are allowed to be natural. It is clear that this last use of the word "natural" is at least partly normative, so that to say that Epicurus deduces what men ought to do from an account of human nature is not strictly true. To say that certain pleasures are natural is to say that they are at least permissible, not that it is human nature to pursue them.

It follows that the good life is not any life according to any view of nature, but the life according to the view that incorporates in its conception of what is natural the end to be sought. Epicurus' conception of the good life is a life of friendship without fear of what lies beyond. Nevertheless, in putting forward his view of morality, Epicurus was bold enough to set it against any conventional morality. One of his sayings is "I spit upon what is noble (i.e., what men call noble) and upon those who vainly admire it when it does not produce any pleasure." Whether or not pleasure is a sufficient condition of the good life, it is certainly for him a necessary condition. In a similar way he maintained that there is no such thing as absolute justice which has value apart from its conduciveness to the production of pleasure. Justice is the result of a sort of social contract, to which men adhere for the sake of expediency.

The Epicurean view of morality is not of the sort that is likely to have far-reaching social effects, and it is clear that, unlike Stoicism, Epicureanism had no widespread influence. It was a view meant to provide guidance and comfort for the individual or the group of individuals bound together by ties of friendship. The metaphysical view of nature, which is the essence of Epicureanism, was an austere one that possessed a certain grandeur, but not one that could provide an acceptable view of the world to ordinary men. In its approach to social affairs it was too negative. Nevertheless, it stands as a clear-cut example of a deductive metaphysical system with very explicit ends. The same will be seen to be true of Stoicism, to which it may be opposed. But the Stoa provided a conception of man's place in nature such that it was eventually capable of acceptance as a philosophical basis for Roman humanism.

The Stoa

THE Stoa was founded in Athens, perhaps in conscious opposition to Epicurus, about 300 B.C., by Zeno of Citium; the most important figure was Chrysippus, who became known as the "second founder" of the Stoa. The refounding of the Stoa by Chrysippus some sixty years after Zeno was necessary to meet the attacks of the Academy, which had by now become skeptical in its philosophical views. Chrysippus was a man of great catholicity and perhaps aridity of mind. He wrote a large number of works (705 in all), but stories were circulated in the ancient world about his fondness for quotations

— one to the effect that one of his books consisted of most of Euripides' *Medea*. He was perhaps most notable for his logic, and there was a saying that if the gods had any logic it would be Chrysippean.[13] After his death the Stoa came under fresh attacks from the Academy, and its doctrines were altered accordingly—so much so that about 80 B.C. there was some kind of amalgamation between it and the Academy and Lyceum (which had also altered in character). Despite the necessity for a modification of the orthodox doctrine after Chrysippus, there was never a *fixed* orthodoxy, but there were nevertheless breakaways; Ariston, for example, broke with the school on the significant point that according to him nature and reason were opposed to each other in the sense that there was a gulf between the ends of life fixed by nature and those discoverable by reason. That the orthodox view was that these ends were coincident illustrates the naturalistic ethical view that the school professed; in other words, it sought, like Epicurus, to indicate the nature of the wise and good life by appeal to a conception of nature. It also illustrates the fact that Stoicism was a compromise between Naturalism in a radical sense and Cynicism; it was, in effect, a Cynicism made to fit a certain view of the world. This accounts for the fact that it embraced certain Cynic doctrines — for example, that man is a citizen of the world and that the law established by the wise man is universal, for all men. These aspects of Stoicism in particular were passed into Roman thought and culture, and the school existed as some sort of entity until the death of the emperor Marcus Aurelius at the end of the second century A.D.

In their teaching, the Stoics divided philosophy into logic, physics, and ethics, each of which was thought of as interdependent with the others (a fact which they liked to illustrate by means of picturesque analogies). For them logic was a part of philosophy, not, as for Aristotle, merely an instrument for it. Their reason for this belief was that the wise man must know the principles of argument—i.e., he must know what reason is. Hence the Stoics were interested in logic as giving the principles of argument leading to conviction; they were not concerned with demonstration. The aim of logic, that is, is not to enable one to demonstrate necessary truths but to teach one how to be reasonable.

LOGIC

Logic, or dialectic, included grammar, the theory of signs, and the theory of knowledge, as well as logic proper. The Stoic treatment of grammar and the nature of signs is of little philosophical interest, although it may be pointed out that they were quite clear about the distinction between words and their use.

Their theory of knowledge has some similarity to that of Epicurus. Like Epicurus, they started from

sensations, believing that external things produce an impression on our souls (although Chrysippus was careful to stress that the word "impression" was not to be taken literally). As a result of this, we receive presentations (*phantasiai* or appearances — the word is the same as that used by Epicurus). Such presentations may be probable or improbable, and if probable, true or false; if true, literally, apprehensive (*kataleptike*, "gripping" — that is, clear and distinct) or the reverse.[14] If the presentations are apprehensive they are a criterion of truth—they bring certainty. For there to be apprehension, however, there has to be something else from the subject's side — assent. Zeno tried to illustrate the relation between a presentation and assent by means of an illustration with his hand — a presentation is like the open hand, assent like a slight contraction of the fingers, and apprehension like the closed fist. Except that the last point expresses the fact that an apprehensive presentation grips the soul, or *vice versa*, this illustration is not very helpful.

It is nevertheless clear that error was put down to erroneous assent, just as it was put down to erroneous anticipation by Epicurus and as it was later to be put down to judgment by Descartes. (There is, indeed, a great similarity between the position of the Stoics and that of Descartes in this respect, for Descartes, too, believed in clear and distinct ideas.) Chrysippus certainly also believed that assent is in our power, requiring a presentation only as a necessary condition (for he illustrated his views on free will by reference to this point). It seems, therefore, that the Stoics believed in the existence of presentations such that we cannot help, in some sense, giving our assent to them; for such is the nature of an intuition. Thus, in the long run, the Stoic theory of knowledge is based on intuition, and all other ideas are supposed to be derived from these intuitions by means of different kinds of mental operation. The Stoics thought that perception sometimes, though not always, consisted in having such intuitions; this is not always the case, since there are illusions that are not explicable entirely by reference to assent. Like Epicurus, the Stoics were ambivalent on this last point. It seems, however, that the whole view came under attack from the Academy, on the ground that it is impossible to tell from a presentation whether it is veridical or not. At any rate, later Stoics produced an amendment to the main view, maintaining that apprehensive presentations are incorrigible "provided that there is no obstacle" — i.e., unless other factors indicate that they are not. Thus the coherence of a presentation with others becomes of more importance, and with the emphasis on the notion of coherence there comes an increased emphasis on the notion of right reason.

The criteria of right reason are given by logic proper, this being concerned with the relations between propositions (which were distinguished from sentences and facts, and were, for reasons to be given later, called by the Stoics "incorporeal"). In their concern with propositions, and not terms or predicates, they differed from Aristotle. They thought of predicates as defective propositions, so agreeing with Frege and some other recent logicians that the basic form of discourse is the proposition. They classified propositions themselves into simple and complex and also produced subclassifications within these classes. It is impossible to go into great detail here, but it is sufficient to indicate that their analysis, like that of the Megarians and of the modern Russell-Whitehead logic, was truth-functional — i.e., it was in terms of relative truth and falsity alone, without regard to the content of the propositions.

For example, a conjunctive proposition of the form "*p* and *q*" was held to be true if and only if both *p* and *q* are true. In the case of disjunctive propositions of the form "*p* or *q*", the main view was that such a proposition is true if and only if one of the propositions is true and the other false. But it seems that the Stoics may have also distinguished another variety of disjunction, in which such a proposition is true if and only if at least one of the propositions *p* and *q* is true. This weaker form of disjunction is the one generally employed by modern logicians. It admits the possibility of both *p* and *q* being true.

The Stoics also carried on discussions of hypothetical propositions and modal concepts on lines already indicated by the Megarians. That is to say that a hypothetical "If *p*, then *q*" was held by some to be false only if it had a true antecedent and a false consequent. But another view insisted on the point that if a hypothetical was to be true the denial of the consequent must be *incompatible* with the antecedent. This is obviously a stronger view than the first. The example given by Diogenes Laertius is "If it is day it is light,"[16] where it is maintained that the denial of "It is light" is incompatible with the truth of "It is day." Unfortunately *this* incompatibility is not a logical incompatibility; for clearly there is no contradiction in asserting that it is day but not light. In consequence, it is not quite clear how strict this view was meant to be. Of their discussions of modal concepts we know little of the details other than that Chrysippus was interested in the matter.

The chief interest of the Stoic logic perhaps lies in the formulation and formalization of arguments and argument-schemata (*tropoi* or moods — arguments with symbols substituted for actual propositions). In a valid argument, they saw, it is impossible for a falsehood to follow from a truth or truths, but every other combination of premises and conclusion is possible. They saw too that to every valid argument there corresponds a true hypothetical proposition consisting of the premises as antecedent and the conclusion as consequent. For example, to the argument "If it is day, it is light; but it is day, so it is light" there corresponds the hypothetical "If it is true both that if it is day it is light and that it is day, then it is light." It was thus possible to conditionalize an argument so that a step in a general argument could consist of a hypothetical proposition summing up the foregoing argument. This use of the "principle of conditionalization," as logicians now call it, was important for their techniques in forming arguments. Valid arguments might be methodical or otherwise, the latter kind being distinguished from the former by being analogous to them but not in proper form by reason of containing metalogical words; for example, "It is false that it is both day and night; it is day, so it is not night" contains the metalogical phrase "it is false that," while the methodical argument, "It is not both day and night; it is day, so it is not night," is in proper form. Finally, they attempted to axiomatize their theory of argument-schemata by reference to five indemonstrable or undemonstrated argument-forms. Four of these have passed into traditional logic as the modes; for example, the *modus ponens* — "If *p* then *q*; but *p*, therefore *q*." The argument given above is in the form of another of these indemonstrable argument-forms. Other argument-forms were to be derived from these with the aid of certain auxiliary rules. But few examples of such derivations survive.

The Stoic logic is, therefore, a highly-developed formal system, similar to the Russell-Whitehead logic in being truth-functional, but unlike it and more like the so-called "natural logic" of Gentzen and some recent Polish logicians in being a theory of argument-schemata or inference-patterns rather than logical truths or theorems. Its direct successor was the medieval theory of "*consequentiae*," and a revival of interest today in both Stoic and medieval logic has produced further attempts to develop logic along these lines.

PHYSICS OR METAPHYSICS

The Stoic physics was a direct antithesis of Epicurean physics. In particular it maintained that the world was a rational entity, and that it was to be thought of as a continuum rather than as a jumble of atoms.

The Stoics defined a body as that which can act or be acted upon. This definition was taken very seriously and resulted in the position that the soul, for example, was called a body whereas propositions were called incorporeal. Incorporeal things play a rather indeterminate role in the Stoic scheme of things. To say that anything is a body or corporeal is to say, roughly, that it is real, and everything that is real must either act or be acted upon. It is form that is responsible for the activity and matter that is responsible for the passivity, the being acted upon, in the world. Matter and form are the first two of the Stoic categories, the latter being the main headings of the types of property, the attribution of which would exhaust the nature of a thing. (In this respect, they were different from the Aristotelian categories, and were rightly part of the Stoic physics or metaphysics, not their logic.) The other two categories were those of state and relation, these giving what is accidental to the thing in question while the first two give what is essential.

It is form which makes the world rational, and as the world consists essentially of the interaction between matter and form, it is thus rational throughout. Form was given many titles — for example, God and intelligence, but especially "the seminal reasons or principles" which act as the soul of the world (*pneuma*). The world was thus looked upon as living and organic, not merely mechanical. Indeed, the whole point of the Stoic view of the world was to exhibit it as living and intelligent. The Stoics were rather ambivalent as to whether God was the creator of the world or the rational principle or soul of that world, and there were definite complications as to what happened at the periodic conflagration of the world which they believed to take place. If the world was destroyed and God was the soul of the world, what happened to God? Chrysippus took the view that at this time everything became soul, but in the context it is difficult to see exactly what this means, or how it helps. Nevertheless, the rational nature of the world meant that there was room for providence, and a Stoic notion which became more prominent with the later Stoic Poseidonius was that of cosmic sympathy, an acting together of all the forces in the world.

Despite the determinist world view, Chrysippus, at any rate, believed strongly in free will. He sought to justify this belief by distinguishing between principal and auxiliary or proximate causes. Thus, in assenting to an apprehensive presentation, the existence of the presentation is a proximate cause of our assent; but the principal cause of the assent lies in ourselves. To illustrate this point, he appealed to a not altogether helpful analogy, maintaining that a stone cylinder, once pushed, will roll down a hill of itself. Its nature is the principal cause of its rolling down, but there are also proximate causes—for example, the slope of the hill. Correspondingly, in the case of human actions, the principal cause is the individual's decision, even if he is also subject to other, proximate, causes. Hence it is that people are to be blamed for their actions if they are bad. Given that there is a problem about the consistency of belief in free will with belief in determinism (which might well be disputed), it is not altogether clear that Chrysippus' distinction helps to deal with the problem. For it might be objected that Chrysippus is merely appealing to what we all know — to wit that we do make decisions — but that in doing so he forgets that those decisions may themselves be caused. Chrysippus' distinction does serve to point out that we do sometimes count our decisions as the causes of our actions in assessing responsibility (and

this is always worth pointing out, as Aristotle saw), but it is doubtful if this was all that he intended to show.

In the details of their world-picture, the Stoics were reactionary; for they identified reason with fire and in general harped back to Heraclitus, whom they interpreted according to their wishes. Hence the emphasis on the periodic conflagration of the world, out of which a new world was thought to be born. God survives this, the whole process being a victory for God in that everything becomes soul (soul being, of course, fire) — a victory of form over matter. They did, nevertheless, attempt to explain individual phenomena in an interesting way, in terms of continuous processes. Thus, they thought that vision was brought about, not by the impinging of atoms on the sense organs as Epicurus thought, but by the movement of a continuous medium which extends from the object of vision to the eye. Here again their position is similar to that of Descartes in his writings on optics. The antithesis between their approach to physics and that of Epicurus — the antithesis between continuity and atomicity — has its parallel in modern physical theory in the antithesis between field theories and particle theories.[17]

The Stoics thought of the individual soul as corporeal because it acts and is acted upon. It functions as the unifying principle of living creatures — animals as opposed to plants, on the one hand, and sticks and stones, on the other. It is to the physical body what the world soul is to the world, but *qua* individual soul it is perishable (although the souls of the good may survive until the conflagration). The Stoic psychology was extremely intellectual. According to it, the faculties are set under the controlling reason, and most aspects of the soul, including the passions, are therefore connected with kinds of judgment. Here again the effort to stress the rationality of everything becomes evident. Stoic physics is, in fact, the story of the working out of the principles of right reason in the world at large. It remains to be seen how this affects the individual, how it provides a way of life.

ETHICS AND POLITICS

The Stoic conception of the ideal life was the life which is in accordance with nature, and regardless of whether this means human nature or nature as a whole, it does involve a life in accordance with reason, since nature itself was thought to be rational. The first instinct of man, the Stoics held, is self-preservation (not, as Epicurus said, pleasure); but with the acquisition of reason, man aims at reason. In consequence, the supremely wise man will aim only at that which is consistent with reason. For him only what is ideal will be good and only what is vile will be bad ("*Nihil bonum est nisi honestum, nihil malum nisi turpe*"[18]). Everything else will be indifferent. It is somewhat difficult to see why if only what is ideal is good, only what is vile is bad. Certainly the one does not follow from the other. But this extreme view was one inherited from the Cynics, and it was perhaps taken over without much question. However that may be, the Stoics thought that virtue can be acquired, since, being a province of reason, it is a form of knowledge, and once attained it is never lost. This sense of virtue, however, is complete virtue, the possession of all the virtues; and at this level, all goods are equal and similarly all ends. For either you have virtue or you do not; there is no value in mere improvement.

This extreme view, inherited from Cynicism, was now given a naturalistic justification, in the view that such a life is according to nature. But even if it be maintained that nature as a whole is completely rational in some sense, it does not seem obvious that human nature is always rational, to say the least. The consequence is that there tended, in Stoic thought, to be a compromise between what was held appropriate to the wise man and what was held appropriate to the ordinary man. Hence it was maintained that among the things that were originally called "indifferent," some are preferable to others, perhaps because they were thought to be useful for the fulfillment of human nature in the ordinary sense. Thus Stoicism always tended toward a compromise between the extreme views inherited from Cynicism and their view of nature. Ariston left the Stoa on this very issue. Nevertheless, there was, in the early period at any rate, a harking after the cult of the supremely wise man as well as an ethical view appropriate to ordinary mortals, and in consequence there was produced a sort of double moral standard. This can be most clearly seen in their account of duties.

"Duty" is not quite the right word to use in this connection (Latin "*officia*"), for the notion is more closely connected with what is fitting. Nevertheless, it is perhaps the nearest that the Greeks got toward the notion of moral obligation. In general, an action was thought to be fitting when it was in accord with nature, but ordinary duties (*officia media*) may be distinguished from the perfect duties (*officia perfecta*), which are appropriate to the wise man in as much as they are in accordance with complete virtue. The point seems to be that the completely virtuous wise man, who lives in accordance with nature as a whole, and not merely in accordance with human nature as, at best, ordinary men do, does not have to ask on each occasion whether his action is good — i.e., whether it is justifiable in terms of some principle. The ordinary man may live in accordance with moral principles but without the knowledge and insight that the wise man possesses; and in consequence he will not have complete virtue. The ordinary man is good in so far as he does what is fitting, but only in so far as this, and not to the extent that he has what Kant called "a good will." To perform a perfect duty, therefore, it is necessary not only to do what is fitting but to do it with a good will; that

is to say, what is fitting must be done *because* it is so, and that it is so can be seen only by one with insight into the ends of life. The wise man who has this insight will be completely virtuous, and whatever he decides to do will be right by definition, even if, for example, it means committing suicide.

Emotions were thought to be irrational movements of the soul, which are contrary to its nature in the sense that they are contrary to reason. Nevertheless, something cannot have an emotion unless it is the sort of thing that can be rational. In this context, the Stoics tended to run together different things — desires, emotions, feelings, etc. — but there is much in their general point of view that rationality and the emotions are connected. Because of this connection an emotion involves some notion of the immediate end to be pursued (for instance, greed is the supposition that money is good) and thus *a fortiori* some form of judgment. Emotions, then, are judgments opposed to those arrived at by reason in their erroneous conception of the end to be pursued, and as such they are to be eschewed. This results in the Stoic ideal of "*apatheia*" — freedom from passions. Only by such freedom from passions can the wise man be completely rational, completely free from making irrational judgments about things.

The Stoic views on politics are corollaries of all that has been discussed already, and are once again antithetical to those of Epicurus. Society, the Stoics held, is a natural phenomenon based on natural fellow-feeling, and justice is a natural virtue, being to society what cosmic sympathy is to the universe at large. Zeno wrote a *Republic* which had similarities to that of Plato (he advocated, like the latter, community of women), but this was probably an early work revealing the influences of Cynicism. Generally speaking, in politics as elsewhere Stoicism was a compromise between Cynicism and the facts (or theories) of nature. In Stoic views on politics we meet with emphasis upon the royalty of the wise man, although with it goes the realization that existing states are by no means perfect. Nevertheless, the Cynic views on cosmopolity were given even greater emphasis by the Stoics, since it was argued that man, *qua* man, was part of nature, and as such could be viewed as subject to universal, and not merely local, law; hence he could be viewed as a citizen of the world. By the same token, the view that justice was a feature of nature led to the notion of natural law, and this became of importance when the Romans identified the *ius gentium*, the common law of nations, with the natural law. It was the Stoics too who handed down the notion of natural law and natural rights to the Middle Ages and later times.

All in all, the Stoic metaphysics presented a view of the world entirely different from that of Epicurus, and in the attempt to show that the universe was a rational being writ large, the Stoics provided a picture of man's place in that universe as able to be in community with it. As a faith, this could well provide consolation, and indeed it did so for many people in the early Roman Empire, especially under Nero. And even earlier than this, Cicero looked to Stoicism as providing the philosophical justification of the Roman Republic.

LATER DEVELOPMENTS

After Chrysippus, the Stoa came under fresh attacks from the Academy in the person of Carneades, and the next figures who were prominent in the school show his influence. There was a drift toward the views of Plato and Aristotle, or contemporary Academic interpretations of these. The Academy correspondingly became less skeptical, and the two schools came together; so a period of syncretism began. Antiochus of the Academy finally "brought the Stoa into the Academy" in the first century B.C., and Cicero could say that in his day all the schools differed only in words.

There were two major figures among the Stoa — Panaetius and Poseidonius — during the first century B.C. Neither was orthodox, and Panaetius showed skeptical leanings in his attitute to certain central Stoic doctrines, such as that of the world fire. He was a friend of Scipio Africanus, and it was from his work that Cicero's *De Officiis* was taken. His influence lay in the fact that he played down the Cynic aspects of Stoicism, especially the cult of the wise man; the resulting view was a humanism that made Stoicism acceptable to the Romans. Poseidonius was his disciple and was Cicero's teacher. He was a kind of universal mind, writing on a great variety of subjects (though none of his works survives). He stressed the doctrine of cosmic sympathy, and produced a scheme of things in which there were grades of being, with God at the top in Aristotelian fashion. Man was thought to be in an especially important position, being a bridge between the mortal and the immortal by reason of being a composite of body and soul. In this, his view of the soul is clearly unorthodox, and he did indeed go back to the Platonic account of it with its division into parts. This was important in that it made the passions part of us, not just irrational judgments that we can in principle do without, but something that has to be controlled. Hence the ideal of *apatheia* was in effect given up.

Thereafter, in the Roman Empire, Stoicism became more and more a philosophy of life; there was no room for the sort of political philosophy which Cicero had sought. Under Nero, Musonius Rufus and Seneca both used Stoicism as a sort of religion, a consolation for the evils of the time. But there is in Seneca a general sense of pessimism, and only lip service is paid to the Stoic ideals. At the end of the century, Stoicism received a new lease on life under Epictetus. Unlike Seneca and Musonius, Epictetus was a professional philosopher, but even he shows little interest in Stoicism as a metaphysical

point of view. He is more concerned with teaching a way of life, and maintains that true freedom lies in virtue (by achieving what you really want — that is, what your reason wants). All this is in accord with the notion that the universe is rational, but it adds little or nothing to the metaphysics. This is even more true of Marcus Aurelius in the second century A.D.; and after him Stoicism ceased to be a positive force.

Like Epicureanism, Stoicism is of interest by virtue of providing a model of a metaphysical theory of a deductive sort, which sets out a picture of the world and seeks to derive conclusions from it. The specific arguments used, where there are any, are of less importance than the general outline of the theory. This is true of much of the post-Aristotelian Greek philosophy, but it is less true of those who must be considered next. For both the Skeptics and the New Academy were critical in approach, and thus for them arguments were of great importance.

The Skeptics

PYRRHO, who founded the Greek Skeptic school, produced no overall picture of the world, and he was himself probably unsystematic. As the school grew, system grew too, and it came to be realized how little of a positive nature a Skeptic may say, if consistency is demanded. It was because this conclusion was reached that Hegel rightly looked at the Greek Skeptics as the *truly* skeptical philosophers, and perhaps the only ones. Pyrrho himself wrote nothing, although his immediate successor, Timon, wrote some satires. The source of nearly all our knowledge of Greek Skepticism comes from the last of the school, a doctor, Sextus Empiricus, who wrote in the second century A.D. (There was a definite connection between the Skeptics and medicine in the empiric school of medicine, whose practitioners refused to speculate about the causes of symptoms. Sextus himself claimed to be not a Skeptic or empiric in medicine, despite the name given to him, but a "methodist." Practitioners of this last school at least allowed that there might be methods or rules in diagnosing complaints, for there might be regular connections between the bodily manifestations of an illness.)

Pyrrho is perhaps the only certain case of a Greek philosopher who was at all influenced by oriental thought; he traveled to India and talked there with the "Magi and Gymnosophists." He was reported to have been consistent in applying his philosophy to his daily life, with the result that he feared "neither wagons, precipices, nor dogs"! In much of this he copied Socrates, as he saw him, and he was anxious, like the Stoics and Epicureans, to provide the recipe for the attainment of human happiness. To this end, he thought, we should consider (1) what things are like, (2) what attitude we should take toward things, and (3) what we should do about our attitude. His answer was that it is clear that sense experience is contradictory in what it tells us of the world. Hence, we should accept appearances, but suspend judgment about their causes. For it is speculation about these that produces anxiety. The goal of this refusal to speculate is freedom from fear, and its positive result, silence. It is clear that here also the recipe is designed to cure a disease caused by a rival philosophy; it consists in the refusal to be dogmatic.

But what are these contradictions in sense experience? The formulation of them in an explicit form was first provided by Aenesidemus in the first century B.C. He produced a list of ten *tropes* or arguments, some of which are forms of what has become known as the "argument from illusion." The arguments are of very unequal worth. They involve reference to

1. Differences in the way living things react to things
2. Differences in men's attitudes to things because of differences in men's natures
3. Differences in the appearances of things by reason of differences in the way our senses perceive them
4. Differences in appearances by reason of the conditions under which they occur
5. Differences in men's judgments about things owing to convention
6. Differences in appearances owing to context or their combination with each other
7. Differences in appearances due to their positions relative to the observer
8. Differences in the effects of things of varying quantity or quality
9. Differences in men's judgments about things because of familiarity or the lack of it
10. Differences in appearances due to their being relative (and since all things are relative to the mind at least, it follows that absolute knowledge is impossible).[19]

The general intention of the arguments presented is to stress the extent to which things present different appearances owing to varying factors, and the supposedly consequent impossibility of attaining certain knowledge of things. But it is clear also that the points raised constitute a rather mixed bag, and that they tend to stress not only differences between appearances but differences between things in general. Later Skeptics were to refine the list. Aenesidemus also brought forward arguments against the attempt to find the underlying causes of phenomena, along with a general criticism of the attempt to explain the seen by reference to the unseen. This is not a criticism of the invocation of unobservables in scientific theory (for no such notion was known in his time), but a criticism of metaphysical theories like that of Epicurus which postulated invisible atoms as the

underlying causes of phenomena. It is the "dogmatists" in this sense that the Skeptics were concerned with refuting.

The *tropes* of Aenesidemus were refined by Agrippa, who probably lived in the first century A.D. He produced five *tropes*, but these were of a different character from those of Aenesidemus, being, *not* classifications of differences in the appearances of things, but summaries of failures in reasoning to which dogmatists were liable. Such defects were inconsistency; liability to an infinite regress; the failure to take seriously the relativity of experience, when this implied that things are unknowable in themselves (cf. the tenth of the original ten *tropes*); resort to arbitrary hypotheses; and circularity in argument. Later Skeptics, perhaps in particular Menodotus, an empiric doctor who was a teacher of Sextus, are said to have reduced the list of *tropes* to two. But there is again a shift in the nature of what is meant. For what is now put forward is a dilemma to the effect that everything is known either through itself or through other things; but the first is impossible, as the inconsistency of the dogmatists shows (there is here an implicit appeal to the earlier *tropes*), and the second is impossible unless there is some fixed point of knowledge somewhere, which brings us back to the first horn of the dilemma. It is clear that the cogency of this argument depends upon whether it is thought that inconsistency on the part of the dogmatists has been demonstrated. Sextus Empiricus' lengthy writings are meant to show this in detail, at any rate with respect to existing theories. One point of interest here is that the Skeptics came to realize that in order to demonstrate the dubiousness of some view it is necessary to take one's stand upon some other point. Hence they insisted that it was on appearances alone that they took their stand; about the reality behind these they "determined nothing." Neither one view nor another about reality was to be accepted as true; judgment was to be suspended. Thus, in the end the only positive attitude to be taken toward the question of the nature of reality was silence, though much could be said about appearances. The Skeptic attitude toward any metaphysics was, therefore, essentially negative and critical; it was not designed to set up a rival view.

The difference between what may be said about appearances and what may *not* be said about reality is also explicit in their views on the nature of signs. For they distinguished between "recollective" signs, the recognition of which is the result of previous experience) and "indicative" signs, the recognition of which could not be the result of previous experience, inasmuch as they are of things outside experience). Epicurus had said that things on earth might be signs of astronomical events outside our vision. The Skeptics denied that we could have knowledge of such signs, any more than we could have knowledge of unseen causes. This, however, did not involve them in the denial that we might know that smoke is a sign of fire; for the recognition of such a sign could be the result of past experience. (In this, their views are very similar to those of Hume on the notion of cause.) Indicative signs are subject to all the objections that can be made against the use of inferences where one of the terms of the relation supposed to justify the inference is unknown. That is to say, we can have no justification in inferring one thing from another when there is no way of finding out how the two things are connected. To point this out was of the utmost importance.

It seems, therefore, that the Skeptics attempted to solve the problems that confronted Epicurus and the Stoa also, not by constructing a rival theory about the world, but by trying to show that any such theory involved inconsistencies. They were thus genuinely antimetaphysical in their aspirations, whatever their results, and in this they were unlike Kant and the Positivists in *their* attacks on metaphysics because the Skeptics produced no suggestion of a rival metaphysics. Thus, they run counter to Bradley's dictum that the man who sets out to refute metaphysics is "a brother metaphysician with a rival theory of first principles." There are points of affinity between their position and that of the later Wittgenstein, although there are profound differences also. For they had, in a sense, no positive philosophy at all; they were merely critical. Their approach was intended to be therapeutic in the sense that as a result of it a man might give up the attempt to speculate or philosophize at all and content himself with the acceptance of what things appear to be.

The New Academy

THE movement that went by the name of the "New Academy" contained two major figures — Arcesilaus and Carneades — who headed the Academy at the beginnings of the third and second centuries B.C., respectively. Under their leadership, the Academy could indeed be called "new" in that its outlook was profoundly different from that of Plato and his immediate successors. During this period, the Academy was in most respects skeptical. No explicit acknowledgment was made by it to Pyrrho and the Skeptic School as such, although there must have been influences. Probably, however, the conscious aim of the New Academy was to reinvoke the Socratic attitude; Socrates' attitude in the Platonic dialogues might *prima facie* appear skeptical in that he reaches no positive conclusions on many occasions. This is, in all probability, the truth of the matter, although Sextus Empiricus and others held that the skepticism was merely a prelude to dogmatism, since Arcesilaus used skeptical arguments against other metaphysical views with the intention of subsequently reinstating the views of Plato. The latter he was supposed to have done with the inner circle of disciples. It is likely, however, that this story was a later rationalization.

Arcesilaus' attack was directed explicitly against the Stoic doctrine of apprehensive presentations. He maintained on various grounds that there were no such presentations — no intuitions, that is. Anyone can *claim* to have intuitions, both the wise and the foolish, but there is no difference between their experiences other than that in one case the wise man has an experience and in the other, the fool. There is, therefore, nothing in any experience that guarantees the truth of what is accepted in it. One cannot tell from experience itself whether it is veridical — a telling point. And if this is so, Arcesilaus maintained, there is no basis for knowledge as the Stoics claimed was provided by apprehensive presentations. It should be noted that in this he shared with the Stoics the belief that the justification of claims to knowledge required the demonstration that some experience gives rise to certainty. Because he thought that there was no such experience he concluded that there was therefore no true knowledge. That there must be experiences which are indubitable if there is to be knowledge might well be, and should be, disputed, but it was a premise shared by all philosophers at this period.

While he maintained that theoretical knowledge was impossible, Arcesilaus added that if a man wishes to know how he should behave he should be told to behave in accordance with what is reasonable. We do not know exactly what he meant by this, but it was intended in any case to provide guidance for the conduct of life and it had no bearing upon epistemological views about the justification of claims to knowledge. For he held that there was no such justification. The Skeptics claimed that in this respect he was insufficiently skeptical in that he was here putting forward a positive point of view, and it is true that from their viewpoint they were right.

Carneades, who lived nearly a hundred years later, presented a more systematic and developed view of the same sort. But he was even more aggressive in his attacks, which confronted the Stoics at nearly every point. For example, he attacked their ethics and theology by reference to the plurality of standards that were in fact accepted in these fields — that is, he used a skeptical argument of the type that stresses the differences in men's beliefs. Carneades[20] says that he attacked not only the Stoics but all his predecessors. But his criticisms of the Stoa in particular were similar to those of Arcesilaus in his attacks on the Stoic apprehensive presentations. Like Arcesilaus, Carneades maintained that there was no distinguishing mark of the true presentation; there was nothing in the experience itself that could tell you whether it was veridical or the reverse. And because presentations offered no guarantee of truth in themselves, it was of no use to look elsewhere for this; for reason depends in the last resort on sense experience. Our judgments are always fallible, as witness the illusions and errors to which we are susceptible. Galen,[21] a Greek physician and logician of the second century A.D., says that he denied the self-evidence even of such mathematical truths as things equal to the same thing being equal to each other, although this may mean only that in experience we find that things that *seem* equal to the same thing are not always equal to each other.

Unlike Arcesilaus, however, Sextus Empiricus had a positive epistemological view to offer, although even here he asserts that his reasons for holding such a view were concerned with the conduct of life, as was the case with Arcesilaus. But Sextus may well be wrong in this. Carneades maintained that although no presentations or appearances were incorrigible, some might be probable—in other words, probably veridical—and that there were three degrees of probability: Ther merely probable; the probable and confirmed; and the probable, confirmed, and tested. It is clear that the acceptability of any given appearance increases with the degree of probability. If an appearance fits in with others of the same thing, it is confirmed; but it attains the highest degree of probability only if it is put to the test by the search for appearances that conflict with it—if, that is, it survives attempts to falsify it. Carneades' distinction between confirmability and testability is of some importance.* Indeed, one might say that Carneades was substituting for an epistemology aimed at the attainment of certainty something like a philosophy of science. In other words, instead of attempting to justify claims to knowledge by appeal to incorrigible sense data, he was giving an account of the criteria actually used in the acquisition of knowledge.

But the change of front was short-lived, and Philo, a successor in the Academy in the next century, returned toward epistemology as understood in the ordinary sense. For in pointing out that if something was to be known to be probable something must be known to be true, he in effect indicated that the general epistemological problem of whether anything at all can be said to be known is prior to the question of the criteria that we employ in assessing claims to knowledge in practice. In consequence, Philo maintained that the nature of things must be knowable in principle, even if there is no sure sign of the truth. This heralded a retreat from skepticism to a perverted version of Platonism, and it was Philo who maintained that Carneades' skepticism was merely a prolegomenon to Platoinsm. Antiochus, his disciple and subsequent rival, went further still, and it was he who held that there was no real difference between the Academy, the Lyceum, and the Stoa. This was true to the extent that the Stoa, influenced by the arguments of Carneades, had, in the persons of Panaetius and Poseidonius, moved nearer to the position at which the Academy had also now arrived.

The Eclectic Period

EXCEPT for the philosophers who held to one or another of the schools — to the Stoa or to Skepticism — the period from 100 B.C. to 200 A.D. was one of extreme eclecticism. Even Cicero shows signs of this tendency toward eclecticism. However, the position became far worse than that. During this period, clarity of thought was far less common than mysticism and mystery. Something indeed went wrong with philosophy, and the ideas that had been inherited from the previously existing philosophers were put to a variety of extraneous uses. It is the period when allegorical interpretations were continually being put upon the works of philosophers and others in the interest of producing some unanimity of view. It was the period of the Gnostics and the Hermetic movements — quasi-philosophical mystery religions — and indeed much of the philosophical thought of the time was devoted to the interest of some religious movement. Philo Judaeus applied a kind of Platonism to Judaism, producing an allegorical interpretation of the Jewish scriptures, and several of the early Christian writers also applied Greek philosophical ideas to similar purposes. In the second century A.D. there was also a revival of Pythagoreanism with some sort of connected cult, and the Platonism of the period (the so-called "Middle Platonism") served a similar purpose. Indeed, in many respects the Neo-Pythagoreans, typified by Numenius, and the Middle Platonists — Albinus and Plutarch — held similar views. Numenius, it might be noted in passing, was responsible for the remark, typical of the eclecticism of the period, "Plato was Moses talking Greek."

There is very little of philosophical interest in this very murky period, but one tendency must be noted as a background notion to Neo-Platonism, which arose in the third century. This is the tendency to find a threefold hierarchy of principles or minds to which the world is subject. Albinus distinguished first, the Supreme Mind, or One, of which the Platonic forms are thoughts and which was identified (absurdly) with Plato's *demiourgos*; then, the Second Mind, or God; and third, the world-soul of Plato's *Timaeus* (the stress on Plato's *Timaeus* is noticeable). Numenius differed from this by making the Supreme Mind *Nous* or Intellect, like Aristotle's first mover, and the Second Mind the *demiourgos*. Numenius held that matter was evil and Plutarch held that there was an evil soul immanent in matter. Albinus also made evil a result of embodiment in matter. He also used the *via negativa* as a way of specifying the One — that is to say, he held that the One was to be defined only by way of negations — and he appealed to Plato's *Parmenides* in support of this policy.

---

* The importance of falsifiability has been recognized in recent times, especially by Karl Popper, in connection with the philosophy of science.

A final point is that the Middle Platonists were divided on whether Plato was to be assimilated to Aristotle or to the Stoa. In consequence, there was a dispute as to whether Aristotle's logic was to be accepted. This dispute is reflected in Plotinus' criticisms of the Aristotelian and Stoic categories (in the 1st book of the 6th *Ennead*). But there was little interest in *formal* logic as such, a fact which is suggestive.

Plotinus and Neo-Platonism

PLOTINUS was born at Lyco in Egypt at the beginning of the third century A.D. He studied under a mystery figure, Ammonius Saccas (who wrote nothing and whose views can be guessed at only through the writings of pupils like Origen and Plotinus himself). After an abortive journey to the East with the Emperor Gordian at the age of 39, he went to Rome in 244 and founded some sort of school. The journey to the East was abortive because Gordian was killed in Mesopotamia and Plotinus got no further; there is certainly no evidence that he brought home any oriental ideas. Plotinus wrote nothing until he was about fifty, at which time he wrote the works that we now have in the form into which they were put by his chief disciple, Porphyry. Porphyry did not put them into chronological order, although we can gain some idea of what that order would be. Instead, he arranged them mainly by subject matter into six groups of nine books (hence the title *Ennead* — from the Greek word "*ennea*," meaning "nine").

Neo-Platonism became the dominant philo-sophical school and was even put forward by the Emperor Julian ("The Apostate") as a rival to Christianity. After Plotinus, the school split up to some extent, part of it continuing in Syria under Iamblichus and, later, another part in Athens under Proclus. After this, when Justinian closed the philosophical schools in 529 A.D., the remaining philosophers of the Neo-Platonic school, after a disastrous but temporary migration to Persia, settled down to writing commentaries on Aristotle. This tradition, preserved during the Byzantine period and then handed on to the Arabs, was the channel by which Aristotle was rediscovered in the West; for knowledge of Greek and Greek philosophy had all but ceased to exist in Western Europe during the early Middle Ages.

It is said that Plotinus had no taste for public controversy; he left that to his pupils. Certainly, the works we have show little enough in this direction, and indeed there is also little in the way of argument — except when he *has* to criticize, as when he is concerned with the categories, for example. And in such cases, the arguments do not add to his credit as a philosopher. In general, he *does* present us with a picture of the world, although of a type quite different from that of Epicurus and of the Stoa.

Again, the philosopher is promised some kind of salvation. Neo-Platonism was intimately involved in mysticism, even though Plotinus was not one who claimed that the mystical experience came readily or often. The world-picture presented is based on certain features of orthodox Platonism, but there is also much that is different.

The scheme of things is as follows: Reality is a continuum with a center from which, as it were, circles expand outward. There is reality throughout living, and it is based on a power that works from the center.* Secondary things are timelessly depend-ent upon what is prior in power; hence there is no temporal creation but a constant outgoing (*proodos*) from the center, whereby mind enters into matter. Higher things determine lower things without being affected themselves. But persons can reverse the outgoing process by identifying themselves with its source (compare Plato's *Republic* and the notion of the turning around of the eye of the soul and also the *Theaetetus* and the notion of becoming like God). At the circumference is the limiting case of reality and power — matter, pure indetermination, which is a phantasm of spatial extension though not extension itself, being definable only by negation.

In all this there are three stages (*hypostases*, as Plotinus calls them — substances or natures) the One, the intellect (which becomes plural in the shape of Platonic forms, which are themselves identified with the thinking mind), and the Soul (which becomes plural by instantiation in all things — a view that involves Plotinus in an extreme animism, which had been suggested, though not in fact accepted, by the Stoics). The relation between the *hypostases* is one of emanation (the outgoing process already referred to). Plotinus often talks as if there were a fourth principle, Nature, the world that the world-soul makes living and which is the bridge between that soul and bare matter. Nature is the province of practice, as opposed to contemplation; for, the latter is the responsibility of intellect, and nature is too weak for contemplation and so turns to practice, which Plotinus regards as a weak copy of contemplation. This is an extremely difficult notion, but Plotinus does little to explain it.

The One, though sometimes spoken of as God, is not a person. It is unknowable. The Intellect knows that there is a One, but not what it is like. Hence it too can be spoken of only by way of negation. But it is the goal of contemplation, and the aim of the mystic is identification with it. And on it the other *hypostases* depend.

The world of the Intellect is such that the sensible world is a complete copy of it, but it is stripped of

---

* In this notion of power, Plotinus reversed the Aristotelian conceptions of *dynamis* and *energeia*, or rather tried to square the distinction with Platonic views. The notion of *dynamis*, which Plotinus opposes in favor of that of *energeia*, is not the Aristotelian "potentiality" but the notion that Plato uses in the *Sophist*, where he talks of what is "real" as that which has power.

all imperfection, time, and extension. It follows that there are forms of individuals — a notion that Plato himself would not have accepted. The world of the Intellect is the world of eternity. We, *qua* Intellect, share in it and express the whole each after our manner. With the understanding (*dianoia*) we see the forms in separation from each other, but with the Intellect (*noēsis*) we could see them all together. Plotinus stresses the point that the division of the world of the Intellect into forms is not a spatial division; it is like the relation between a science and its propositions. But there is nevertheless a problem as to how it is divided not only into forms but also into individual minds that express the whole after their own manner, so that different minds have different powers. Presumably each individual mind is constituted by those forms of which it is actually aware; yet Plotinus emphasizes the point that it can be aware of the whole. Otherwise the upward ascent to the One would not be possible.

There is a similar problem with regard to Soul. Just as the Intellect is included in the One, so Soul is included in the Intellect. The world-soul is divided not only into all those things that instantiate it (in other words, everything) but also into individual souls, which again express it after their manner, in that they have different powers. We, on the other hand, are not just Soul, but partly Intellect. It is the latter which individuates us and by it we are linked to the world of forms. The world-soul as a whole orders the universe, not by conscious planning, for the Soul is below the stage where this is possible, but like a dancer dancing a dance. Soul is the source of time through movement. Thus if there were no soul there would be no time, but eternity alone. Like many other Greeks, Plotinus here tends to confuse the manner whereby we tell that time is passing, the necessary conditions of time, with what time itself is. In this particular view he influenced St. Augustine. But the latter equates Soul with the individual soul, and his conclusions — namely, that there would not be time without consciousness — are paradoxical. In Plotinus, however, given the system, the conclusion is more tenable in that without Soul there would be no world at all. For the sensible world is included in Soul.

Soul becomes united with matter (and hence each individual soul with each body) by its own will, despite the fact that matter is the source of evil. But matter is so only negatively, in that it consists in the privation of all form. (Hence Plotinus is one of those who hold that evil is only the lack of good, and in this again he influenced St. Augustine.) Plotinus equates matter with the "recipient" of Plato's *Timaeus*, and says that is known in the same way, although he also maintains that Plato's identification of matter with place is allegory.

In all this Plotinus uses certain aspects of Plato's philosophy to justify the view that his own philosophy is Platonic (and it is, of course, possible to see something of Neo-Platonism in parts of Plato's works). But Plotinus uses Aristotelian notions also, and there is an obvious attempt to make them fit in with the view of Plato which is being adopted. This is perhaps nowhere more clear than in the discussion of the Categories at the beginning of the 6th *Ennead*. This discussion is not, perhaps, of fundamental importance for the Neo-Platonic system as a whole, but it is of interest as one of the few places in the *Enneads* where arguments are employed extensively.

Plotinus' aim is to map the geography of the world of the Intellect, and there is something in common between his aim and that of Hegel. In the end he wishes to assert that the so-called Platonic "categories" of the *Sophist* — being, sameness, difference, motion, and rest — are the highest categories of the intellect and that the other forms can be "deduced" from them. But to achieve this end he has to show that the Aristotelian and Stoic categories (different from each other as they are) are inappropriate. He does this by leveling a series of criticisms against those categories; some are well-taken, but others are extremely dubious. The kind of general point made is that each of these categories is not a single category in fact, or alternatively that it is not independent of the others. (In this last respect it is worth noting that the Stoa had already subsumed several of the Aristotelian categories under that of relation.) As a positive view, on the other hand, he attempts to show that the Aristotelian notions of matter, form, the composite, and the categories of accidents are applicable to the sensible world only, whereas the Platonic "categories" are applicable to the world of the Intellect. Thus, for example, he maintains that to "being" in the world of the Intellect corresponds "matter" in the sensible world. The procedure adopted is very ingenious. It is a way of dealing with the more philosophical parts of the Aristotelian logic within a quasi-Platonic system, and it is Plotinus' answer to the dispute as to whether Aristotle was to be reconciled with the Academy.

But Neo-Platonism is in general a view that has to be accepted as a whole or not at all. It had a great influence, especially upon mystical thinkers, because it was the channel by which knowledge of Greek philosophy returned to the West after the Dark Ages. So great was its influence in this last respect that Plato and Neo-Platonism have perhaps been really distinguished only during the last century or two.

A few words about Plotinus' disciples remain to be said. His chief follower, Porphyry, was not an original thinker, although he became responsible for controversy with the early Christians — so much so that his books were condemned to be burned by the Council of Ephesus in 431 A.D. (He was even equated with the anti-Christ in some quarters.) His importance for philosophy lies in another direction — in his restoration of Aristotelian logic. His *Introduction to Aristotle's Categories* (the *Eisagoge*) set off the medieval dispute about universals because of a casual remark that philosophers had not dealt satisfactorily with the status of the species. He, too, was responsible, whether consciously or not, for a perversion of the Aristotelian doctrine of the predicables which passed into traditional logic — the adding of the species to the list of definition, genus, proprium, and accident, as if the list were a classification of terms applicable to *things* rather than of terms predicable of the species itself.

Iamblichus, the head of the Syrian school at the beginning of the fourth century A.D., though interested in the philosophy of mathematics from a rather mystical, Neo-Pythagorean point of view, was notable mainly for the development of theurgy, a kind of magical procedure for attaining identification with God. (Neo-Platonism was thus tending to swing from a philosophy toward a form of religion, and it was so adopted by the Emperor Julian in opposition to Christianity.)

Perhaps of more importance was Proclus, head of the Athenian branch of the school in the fifth century A.D. It was through him that Neo-Platonism was handed down. And he alone produced a systematic textbook of Neo-Platonism, the *Elements of Theology*. The book is extremely arid and complex. Only one or two aspects of it can be referred to here. First, Proclus continued a tendency that had been already observable in the school — that of postulating subordinate triads of hypostases. For example, Proclus divides the Intellect into being, life, and mind, each of which is subdivided into its own triad. The

appearance of this is extremely Hegelian, although its basis is somewhat different from that of Hegel. Proclus' aim in postulating these subordinate triads was to reconcile the Plotinian view of the three major *hypostases* with the view that reality is a continuum — to fill a gap, that is, in the Plotinian theory. The subordinate triads were meant to act as links producing continuity between the different levels of reality.* The second innovation was the doctrine of "henads." Plotinus had made the Intellect and Soul plural by differentiation into forms and individual souls respectively. Proclus thought that the plurality evident in the world should receive a justification at a higher level, and in consequence he differentiated the One into ones or henads, each of which is responsible for a hierarchy of subordinate entities extending downward to lower levels of reality. The complexity that this adds to the system is enormous, and it is extremely difficult to set out the scheme in detail.

It is clear that in all this, Neo-Platonism had become scholastic. After this time there are no major figures, and when Justinian closed the philosophical schools in 529 A.D., there was no fruitful philosophy to which to put a stop. The spirit of Greek philosophical thought, which, it is clear, had steadily become weaker during this period, had finally died.

---

* In the attempt to make a hierarchy of entities form a continuum, there is something in common between Proclus and Leibniz, as well as between Proclus and Hegel. Proclus may perhaps be regarded as Leibniz to Plotinus' Spinoza.

5

Augustine

R. A. MARKUS

AURELIUS AUGUSTINUS WAS BORN in the year 354 at Thagaste, in what is now Algeria. He completed his education in North Africa, finishing his higher studies at Carthage, the capital of Roman Africa. He was brought up along the lines of the established pattern current during late antiquity. His education was primarily literary and rhetorical. Soon after completing his studies he entered upon the career of a teacher, first in his native town, then as occupant of the chair of rhetoric at Carthage. After some years of teaching here he moved first to Rome, and, finally, to another municipal chair of rhetoric, that of Milan. This highly successful secular career was interrupted by his conversion to Christianity in 386.

Augustine's search for truth and wisdom had been aroused first by his reading Cicero's now lost *Hortensius*. In the Christianity professed by his mother, Monica, he could at this time find no satisfactory intellectual resting place, and he came to give his adhesion to the sect of Manichees, a popular and widespread form of dualistic gnosticism. His eventual dissatisfaction with the teaching of this sect became more and more acute, and led to Augustine's disillusionment with it. Within a few years of breaking with it, he met Ambrose, Bishop of Milan, and became acquainted with some works of Neo-Platonic philosophy and encountered the current Christian interpretation of Neo-Platonic doctrines. His mental turmoil was finally resolved with his decision to enter the Church and to renounce the world.

Returning to North Africa, he founded a kind of monastic community with a number of his friends; but within little more than two years his seclusion was abruptly ended by his ordination to the priesthood as a result of popular pressure. He now had to assist the aged Bishop of Hippo, Valerius, in his episcopal duties, and particularly in preaching. He eventually succeeded Valerius in the see of Hippo. He managed to combine with the duties of a busy see a life of monastic observance (he lived with his clergy in a community organized on a monastic pattern), continual traveling and preaching, and a far-flung correspondence, as well as a large output of works of a varied character. These include a number of early dialogues on philosophical subjects, works of doctrinal exposition of which the greatest is the *de Trinitate*, Scriptural commentaries, and works of theological controversy. The *de Civitate Dei*, his reply to those who blamed Christianity for the troubles of the Roman Empire since the desertion of the old gods, is a large-scale assessment of pagan culture and embodies his mature thought on history. The most important of his works, the *Confessions*, is an account of his spiritual pilgrimage and supplies the indispensable framework for any study of his thought.

Augustine died in the year 430, as the Vandals were closing in on his episcopal city, twenty years after Rome had fallen to the Visigoths under Alaric. He was a product of the Roman civilization of which his lifetime saw the final crumbling; his work did much to shape the civilization that was to emerge from the ruins.

Augustine and Philosophy

"CAN PAGANISM," Augustine asks in one of his controversial works, "produce any better philosophy than our Christian, the one true philosophy, in so much as we mean by this word the pursuit and love of wisdom?"[1] It is true that he does not often speak of a "Christian philosophy"; but the fact that he is able to do so even on occasion indicates to our modern ears a terminological oddity about his conception of *philosophia*. In modern usage, "philosophy," in whatever way we may wish to characterize this activity more closely, means an intellectual activity, an effort of understanding and analysis, a work of man's rational mind. To bring this into so close a relation with religion, with faith in a divine revelation and a whole manner of living as is suggested by the phrase "Christian philosophy" is possible only on one of two assumptions: either (1) Christianity is itself identifiable with a set of intellectual positions of a kind that we may, in some sense, call "philosophical," or (2) if Christianity cannot be so identified with intellectual activity, it has, at any rate, attached to it some special form of this intellectual activity, some special set of intellectual positions, of which it makes sense to speak of as "Christian philosophy." Now the first of these assumptions need not be considered since such an extreme form of Christian intellectualism has never been held. The difficulty with the second assumption is first an empirical, historical one: If there is such a "Christian philosophy," how can it have come about that Christian thinkers have managed to combine with their Christianity such widely varied philosophical standpoints as they have in fact done in the course of history? Further, few Christians would admit that their faith is compatible only with one particular philosophical position. In our modern sense of "philosophy," then, it does not make sense to speak of a "Christian philosophy," and we must inquire into what Augustine meant when he used the phrase, and what the underlying conception of "philosophy" is.

In the work from which the above passage has been quoted, Augustine refers his opponent to the lost dialogue of Cicero, the *Hortensius*. It was his reading of this work at the age of nineteen, as he tells us in his *Confessions*,[2] that was responsible for his mental upheaval and for the new direction given to his mind and desires. This "conversion" started Augustine on his long and tortuous quest for wisdom. This wisdom is not, however, purely theoretical. In common with his contemporaries, Augustine sees it as embracing all that is of ultimate concern to man. It deals not only with questions about the physical universe, about man's own nature and conduct, and about the gods or God, but it shows men the way to happiness. "Man has no reason for philosophizing except in order to attain happiness" (*ut beatus sit*).[3] According to Varro's manual, quoted by Augustine,[4] this had been the aim and purpose of all the different philosophic schools. All agreed on the ultimate end and purpose, but differed on the means by which it was to be obtained. Thus, Varro had distinguished 288 different philosophic positions — actual and possible — according to the various different answers given to the question of how happiness could be attained. The pursuit of happiness entailed the pursuit of knowledge, for in order to obtain happiness, one had to know not only in what happiness was to be found, but also how it was to be obtained. But this quest for knowledge is only one element in the quest for wisdom in *philosophia*, as understood by Augustine and his contemporaries. Thus, the reason, at bottom, Augustine came to reject the skepticism of the Second Academy (to which Cicero's work had introduced him) was precisely because to his mind it led to despair of attaining happiness. It claimed that the fundamental questions — on the answers to which the way to happiness depends — were unanswerable.

We are not here concerned with Augustine's intellectual development; we may, therefore, bypass the controverted question about its relation to his conversion to Christianity. After his conversion, Augustine accepted Christianity as the only way to happiness, and therefore, as the only true "philosophy." It is important to realize, however, that what makes this claim valid in Augustine's eyes is precisely what we should exclude from the realm of philosophy altogether. According to Augustine, what distinguishes Christianity from the teaching of philosophers known to him — above all of Neo-Platonists — is not a difference in their views about the world, about man, or even about God; Augustine is only too ready to read Christian views back into Neo-Platonic philosophy, and by and large he thinks of Neo-Platonism and Christianity as converging in so far as their respective *Weltanschauungen* were concerned — when, in his *Confessions*, he traces the stages of his passage from Neo-Platonism to

Christianity, he claims to have found in the works of Neo-Platonic philosophers, stated "in different and manifold ways," views about the world, about God (even about the Trinity), and about the human soul that are identical with Christian teaching. What he fails to find in the works of the philosophers, according to his own account, is any mention or hint of the Incarnation of Jesus Christ, or of his life, death, and resurrection — in short, of the events that constitute in his eyes, as in those of the Christian Church, the kernel of the Church's message about man's redemption.[5] It is in these events, and in the events associated with and leading up to them, that God has wrought his mighty works through which it pleases him to save men; and it is in these that the Church professes her faith, and it is upon these that Augustine takes his stand with his conversion.

This is both the essential kernel of Christian belief and the essential difference between the Church's teachings and those of philosophers. But the difference lies not in the dimension of theory, speculation, or reflection but in the dimension of history. As such, Augustine holds, these beliefs fall outside the realm of the abstract, general method of procedure appropriate to philosophic thought.[6] This is concerned with timeless truth, whereas such basic items of Christian faith as the Resurrection belong to a realm where philosophic enquiry is out of place: to the "course of changing things and the fabric of temporal history."[7] But what fell outside the scope of philosophy was nevertheless vital to "Christian philosophy." Though it shared what Augustine held to be the concern of all philosophy, the concern for blessedness,[8] "Christian philosophy" differed from other visions of the way to blessedness in stating that there was only one, that shown and given in Christ the Saviour.[9]

To summarize then, Augustine can speak of a "Christian philosophy" without any sense of the oddness of such a phrase to modern ears, because he sees in Christianity a way — a way unique in itself and admittedly very different from those canvassed by philosophers — to blessedness, the aim and object of all philosophic enquiry. We are now in a position to consider more precisely the manner in which Augustine conceived the relevance of what *we* should call philosophy to this "Christian philosophy."

In so much as Augustine considered beatitude to be the object of all philosophic activity, it might appear that after his conversion philosophic reflection as we know it had no place in his mental world. For in the Christian faith and its practice he had found the only, and a wholly sufficient, way to beatitude; so, we may ask, "what need was there for the further effort of human reflection and speculation?" Was there not rather a danger that continued interest in philosophical thinking — and for Augustine this meant thinking of a Neo-Platonic coloring in particular — would lead the mind astray from the one true way revealed by God? And even if it did not lead one astray — because, as Augustine was convinced, much of what was best in Greek philosophy had anticipated Christianity and therefore could not run counter to its teaching — even so, was it not at best a superfluous luxury for which a Christian has no need?

Augustine, at any rate, would have answered "no" to such questions. Neo-Platonism had served him as a preparation for the Gospel by liberating him from his previous materialism, and throughout his life he continued to utilize modes of thought he had learned from Neo-Platonic (and other) sources. Sometimes he deepened and developed these in ways peculiar to himself which we shall have to consider later. What did reflection of this kind have to contribute to "Christian philosophy," and how was it related to the faith at the center of this "philosophy"?

Possession of a rational mind is what distinguishes man from beasts;[10] the activities distinctive of mind are therefore distinctively and essentially human. Observation, memory, language, ordered social life, technical skills, creative arts, the power of thought and reasoning, these are some of the most characteristic modes of the mind's functioning.[11] The highest of these is the power of thought and judgment, because this regulates the exercise of all other distinctively human functions. Now while all human drives and impulses seek their satisfaction, beatitude consists in their balanced satisfaction according to the order of reason.[12] In the state of blessedness all man's faculties are thus satisfied, but blessedness consists above all in the complete satisfaction of man's rational faculties. His quest for knowledge and understanding is here fulfilled; human wisdom is here completed in the vision of truth, which belongs to the stuff of blessedness.[13]

We are not at present concerned with Augustine's views on the volitional elements in the state of blessedness and in the process of its realization, and we need not, therefore, consider what he has to say about love as an element both in beatitude and in man's striving after it. All we need to note at this stage is his insistence on the radically intellectual character of that complete self-realization of man which he calls blessedness. In so much as this goal of human life is an intellectual self-fulfillment, so is progress toward that goal a progress in knowledge and understanding. The happy life lies in wisdom, and its quest is inevitably a quest of wisdom, *philosophia*, which embraces a growth of insight and understanding.

We cannot identify this quest of wisdom (*philosophia*) with "philosophy" as we understand the term. We have already pointed out that for Augustine, as for his contemporaries, *philosophia* was an activity with a much more practical purpose than we should give it: its concern was to enable men to find happiness. This remains true even though for

Augustine this happiness has itself a deeply intellectual quality, since its substance is the contemplation of truth face to face in the vision of God. We have noticed that a Christian *philosophia*, as conceived by Augustine, was even less a purely theoretical business than other kinds of *philosophia*, for the essential difference between it and all the various schools of ancient philosophy lay in its being based on what was accepted as a historical revelation of divine action. This revelation was seen primarily not as a body of teaching, but as a record of what God had done; the record of these deeds was contained in the Bible, and the Church's creeds contained a kind of summary of this record. We have seen that the contemporary notion of *philosophia* could easily accommodate this revelation within its scope, notwithstanding the gulf between the distinctive categories of Greek thought and of Christian faith. Within the terms of this notion of *philosophia* there was no foothold for the distinction we should wish to draw between what is of revelation, held on faith, and what is known by reason. As a consequence, Augustine's *philosophia* merges in its scope what we should call "philosophy" and "theology," respectively. Yet such was the intellectualist ideal of Augustine's teaching that reason had an indispensable part in the building up of this Christian *philosophia*.

The reason why, for Augustine, faith alone was not able to discharge the function of a "Christian philosophy" was due to the incompleteness and rudimentary character of faith. Believing, as Augustine defines it, is "to think with consent."[14] It is an assent to something without full rational clarity, lacking compelling evidence to make that assent fully intellectual. In this respect, belief is contrasted, for instance, with assent to the conclusion of a logical inference seen as entailed by its premises or to a descriptive statement as supported by visible and tangible evidence. Believing is assenting to something on the authority of someone else, on the grounds that that authority is antecedently accepted as competent in the relevant sphere. As such, believing lacks the rational clarity and coherence of statements made on evidence or by inference from other statements. This is especially true about the statements of the Christian faith, because there is no human method of establishing their truth independently of divine revelation nor an inherent rational cogency in them, and there is an opacity in the way they present their object to the mind: "For now we see as in a glass darkly."[15] Adhesion to the content of this faith leads the mind to the full and clear vision to be disclosed only in the life of blessedness.

The function of faith in Augustine's "Christian philosophy" is simply to serve as a beginning, to put one's feet, so to speak, on the right way in the quest for understanding. Faith is only the first step, that which turns the mind in the right direction and holds out to it the promised reward, that of full understanding, which is the goal. Hence, the monotonous insistence in all Augustine's work, from his conversion to Christianity to his death, on the need for faith before embarking on the quest of understanding. We may see in this insistence a theoretical formulation of his own personal drama. (This is true of much that is most characteristic of Augustine's thought.) Faith is, for him, always the necessary prerequisite for a correct understanding. It is the starting-point of all growth in understanding and the gateway to truth: "Understanding is the reward of faith. Seek therefore not to understand in order that you may believe, but to believe in order that you may understand."[16] This often reiterated injunction, based on the verse of Isaiah vii. 9 as he read it in the Latin version, *nisi credideritis non intelligetis*, is given its fullest formulation in his letter 120, to Consentius, where the mutual relations of faith and reason are perhaps more thoroughly and systematically analyzed than anywhere else in Augustine's work.

Thus, faith for Augustine is prior to reason in the sense that without faith, reason is powerless to attain its object, happiness. But it is also inferior to reason in so much as faith is a blind assent, whereas rational understanding is a kind of vision, an intellectual insight which penetrated the nature of its object in a manner denied to mere faith. Hence, to remain content with *mere* faith would, in Augustine's eyes, amount to a decisive mutilation of human rationality. Faith is itself an act of rationality, even though a rudimentary act; it must on no account serve as a barrier to the fullest exercise of reason, or as a pretext for repudiating reason.[17] On the contrary, faith requires the work of understanding in order to bring it to its fully human stature.

To bring about this process of intellectual growth, all the resources of the human mind are to be utilized in the work of attempting to understand that which is believed. In his work *De doctrina Christiana* Augustine sketches a program for a Christian culture in which all the various branches of science and learning are to be brought to bear on the data of the Christian faith as it is contained in the Scriptures. All human studies are laid under contribution to help the Christian understand what he believes. Much of this, as it is carried out by Augustine, is somewhat naive, and it is certainly circumscribed by the limitations of a literary, rhetorical culture which he shared with his contemporaries. But it does, in principle, enable Augustine to assert that philosophy plays an important part in the attempt to achieve deeper insight into the content of faith. It belongs, together with the other human disciplines, to the mental equipment with which we try to seize and penetrate into the truth revealed by God.

Now we should certainly not regard such an activity as philosophical. We may regard it as "theology," if we concede the legitimacy of using philosophical analyses and concepts within the setting of faith with a view to expanding mere faith into an intellectually elaborated system with their aid. But whatever our views may be on such "use" of philosophical thought, it is only in such a context and utilized for such a purpose that we can find "philosophy" in Augustine's writings. Augustine is not a "philosopher" in any sense approaching that of our modern understanding of this term. He is not interested in what *we* call philosophy for its own sake. He is through and through a theologian, concerned with understanding what he believes God has revealed. In the course of his quest for theological understanding, he makes use of the human disciplines that are relevant, and among these philosophy takes pride of place. Typical examples of the manner in which Augustine uses philosophical procedures in the course of his theological work are his recourse to Aristotle's *Categories* in his discussion of substance and relation in the context of trinitarian theology, his inquiries into human knowledge and psychology with a view to detecting in man an image of the triune God, or his analysis of time undertaken in order to avoid some of the contradictions to which the theology of creation can easily lead. All these examples show that Augustine's real interest and purpose is theological. To discuss his philosophy, it will therefore be necessary to separate from its context what is, for us, recognizably philosophical in his work. In doing so we shall inevitably be misrepresenting Augustine's real concerns, laying stress on what he would have regarded as belonging to the sphere of means and techniques and leaving out of account the purpose for which he utilized these.

Augustine's originality lay primarily in the way in which he put inherited philosophical techniques — primarily Platonic in inspiration — to use in his theological work. The focus of his interests and the center of gravity of his work lies in the field of theology. This may account for the fact that often he fails to question the philosophical equipment he uses quite as radically as might be expected. As we shall see, one is often left with the impression that, ultimately, the philosophical views he holds are often accepted by him without serious scrutiny, without adequate reasons, usually simply because of their Platonic character. He was more interested in the insights into the scriptural revelation which they made possible than in the question of their being themselves supported by evidence and reflection. But his philosophical equipment — though Platonic in inspiration — is not simply that of Plato or of any Neo-Platonist. It has undergone modification, sometimes extensively, at his own hands, and much of it is the product of his own reflection. It is therefore worth separating Augustine's philosophical equipment from its context and examining at least some of its salient features in isolation from the theology which it always serves in his work.

Human Knowledge

AUGUSTINE's reflection on knowledge starts from his attempt to meet the challenge of philosophers whom he understood to deny its possibility, those whom he calls the "Academics." His earliest writings are full of this preoccupation, and his views put forward in them remain permanently established in his reflection. We cannot survey here his arguments in reply to this challenge in any detail. They assert, basically, that there are certain immediate certainties which no amount of doubt can impugn. Thus, however we may be deceived in what we think, we certainly know that we are alive,[18] that we think,[19] that we are.[20] All these arguments appear to be very similar to Descartes' famous *Cogito ergo sum*; but unlike Descartes, Augustine was not concerned with finding a firm foothold in the midst of doubt in order to advance stepwise to further certain truths. For Augustine these are merely more than usually compelling examples of the possibility of indubitable knowledge, amounting to a justification for rejecting skepticism. He does not, in fact, stop at these indubitable certainties. He regards them as the center of indefinitely widening circles of knowledge that decrease in certainty, perhaps, as the distance from the center of the circles become greater; nevertheless, they are not radically different from these indubitable certainties, and hence he sees them all as having a good claim to *prima facie* truth at least. All that we are immediately aware of is certain. This immediate awareness includes our sensory awareness at any particular moment, which cannot be false except in so far as we read more into it than it really contains. To the objector, for instance, who argues that one might even be deceived about the existence of a "world" at all, to which we may or may not be right to refer the content of what we perceive, Augustine is content to reply that he calls it "the world" that is disclosed in awareness.[21] And though we may be mistaken in our judgments prompted by our sensory awareness, for instance into asserting that the oar we see as bent is in fact bent, there are many judgments which we cannot doubt, that are necessarily true. We shall consider these later. Augustine regarded sense-awareness in general as reliable, since its data are always open to critical assessment by the mind.[22]

Augustine's vindication of the possibility of reliable knowledge proceeds along two fronts, according to the fundamental distinction he makes between two kinds of objects and their corresponding two kinds of knowledge: "There are two classes of things known: one is of those which the mind perceives through the bodily senses, the other of those it perceives through itself."[23] The first embraces the objects of the five senses, that is, the material world. The second is the intelligible world, known by the mind independently of sense-experience. Among the objects of this second mode of

knowledge is included the mind itself, which Augustine thought was known to itself without the intermediary of any sense-experience. Augustine's
discussion of self-knowledge embodies some of his
most original and most penetrating insights, but it
would take us too far afield even to summarize it
here. Its main features are well presented in his
de Trinitate, Books IX, X, and XIV;[24] and the
Confessions as a whole are an exercise in achieving
the self-knowledge that he describes[25] as the mind's
discovery of itself in the very process of seeking
itself, not as an object it comes across (for the mind,
like the eye, is "never within its own field of vision"[26]
but is nevertheless "wholly present to itself"[27]) but
as the subject and agent in its intellectual quest.
Apart from what will be said about self-knowledge
incidentally when we come to describe Augustine's
views about what he calls *memoria*, we shall have
to by-pass this topic here, and turn straight away
to his accounts of the two main modes of knowledge
he distinguishes.

SENSE-AWARENESS AND IMAGINATION

All knowledge, for Augustine, is the work of the
soul. This he defines as a "substance endowed with
reason and fitted to rule a body."[28] It is noteworthy
that notwithstanding the characteristically Platonic
dualism of his view of man, Augustine lays as much
stress on the substantial unity of man as he can
within the framework of this view. Man is, for him,
composed of body and soul, and would not be man
without either of these constituents.[29] But although
man is composed of these two constituents, he is yet
one, though Augustine confesses that it is not easy
to see how two substantial constituents can combine
to form one single substantial whole. While professing himself unable to solve this problem, Augustine
defines man in a way which seeks to escape this
difficulty. In effect he identifies man with one, the
dominant constituent, but imports into the definition
of this a reference to the other, the inferior constituent: "Man is, as far as we can see, a rational
soul making use of a mortal and material body."[30]
Both here and in his definition of the soul, Augustine
imports a reference to the body: although the body
is a separate substance, the human soul is of its
nature turned toward it and is incomplete without
it. Though its being is independent from the body,
the soul is essentially regulative in relation to its
body. The underlying scheme is Platonic, complicated by the fact that as a Christian Augustine could
not accept the full Platonic picture of the soul as
being exiled from its true home and held in captivity
within a material and temporal body.

The difficulties of this view make themselves
strongly felt in Augustine's account of the lowest
kind of knowledge, sense-knowledge. This, in
common with all kinds of knowledge, is a function
of the soul.[31] That much is taken for granted at the
outset of the sustained discussion of sense-knowledge
in the *De Quantitate Animae*.[32] But Augustine's
treatment of the body as an instrument *used* by the
mind leads him into describing sense-knowledge as
involving two acts. Using the analogy of the work of
a craftsman and the function of his tool, he distinguishes between the act of the mind and that of the
bodily organism used by the mind in sense-knowledge. Thus, he suggests[33] as a preliminary definition
that "sensation consists in the mind's being aware
of the body's experience" (*non latere animam quod
patitur corpus*).* What this formula draws attention
to in the first place is the indubitable fact that sense-
knowledge depends on the encounter of bodily
sense-organ with the object perceived. Whether the
definition is a felicitous statement of this truth is,
however, doubtful; and Augustine himself raises the
obvious difficulty. In assimilating sense-experience
to the category of passivity (*passio*), we are allowing
a metaphysical schema to obscure the facts of the
case. Augustine is well aware of this. What, he asks,
do the eyes "suffer"† in seeing an object? The only
possible answer is: vision itself, the physical modification of the sense-organ. This answer is forced
upon us if we insist on treating seeing on the model of
feeling, say feeling a pain. Now the eye can certainly
suffer a pain, but we should not call this seeing.
So, Augustine concludes, it is not the case that
everything felt by the eye is vision.[35]

But this does not exhaust the difficulties of this
account of seeing. For even if we say that not everything felt by the eye is seeing, we are nevertheless
committed to holding that what the eye does see it
feels or "suffers." So we are led to the paradoxical
conclusion that for instance in seeing somebody
else, we feel or "suffer" him. But this is absurd, as
Augustine points out, because feeling or "suffering"
requires the physical contiguity of the perceiving and
perceived bodies. I cannot feel the pain of a stab-
wound unless the knife has penetrated my flesh.
(Even so, I can scarcely be said to "feel" the knife,
except in a sense different from that in which I can
be said to "feel" the pain of the wound caused by it;
but Augustine does not raise this further difficulty.)
The absence of physical contiguity between eye and
object seen is enough to enforce the critique to
which he wants to subject this theory of sense-
perception. For this theory requires that in order to
see you, I should be where you are, since I can only
be said to feel or suffer something in the place where
it is. If this theory were true, it would follow that
the eyes could see only themselves.[36] But manifestly
what the eyes see are not modifications of their own

---

* This definition is preliminary, and a revised version is
offered by Augustine further in this work.[34] This revision is
intended to exclude from the scope of sensation knowledge
which may have been inferred from sense experience but is
not directly given by it.
† To bring out Augustine's point, I shall use this expression,
odd as it sounds in English, as the least misleading rendering
of "*pati*."

states, nor do we infer from the awareness of such modifications the existence and character of their causes. What we see is "out there."[37] The way in which Augustine proposes to solve this difficulty is by saying that in seeing, it is not the eyes but vision itself that feels. Thinking in terms of the contemporary physical account of vision, which conceived sight in terms of an emission of rays from the eyes, he likens seeing to using a stick for exploring a surface at some distance from the hand. "Just as when I touch you with a stick, it is I that touch you and I who feel that I am touching you, without myself being at the place where I touch you; so in like manner when I am said to see you by means of sight, though I am not in the same place as the object I see, this does not entail that it is not I who see."[38]

There are two valuable insights in this use of the analogy of exploring a surface with a stick. First, Augustine noticed that when we use a stick as a probe we are not handling it as an object external to ourselves, but as an extension, so to speak, of our body. We assimilate it to ourselves, and our awareness of it as separate from us is subsidiary to the awareness of the object which it helps us to explore. There is an important difference here to which Augustine is drawing our attention: that between focal and subsidiary awareness. It is rather like our use of words to describe objects, which are, unless we are specially attending to them as words, transparent, our attention being focused on the objects mentioned by them. It is only when we mention the words themselves (by placing them in quotation marks) that they become the object of our focal awareness. Similar accounts could be given of using tools in general. Secondly, Augustine appreciated the fact that when we see an object, it is the object on which our awareness is focused, and not the modification of the sense-organ (the eyes), which forms, at the most, an object of subsidiary awareness. This far the analogy of using a stick helps us to understand seeing. But by introducing the contemporary scientific account of the process of seeing, according to which this took place in virtue of an effusion from the eyes, Augustine was enabled to escape the difficulty of reconciling the manifest facts of the experience of sight with his definition of sensation in general. For this account made it possible for him to treat sight on the analogy of touch, and thereby enabled him to by-pass a closer scrutiny of his definition of sensation as awareness of feeling.

Thus, this definition, while it does justice to the case of touch, fails to give a satisfactory answer in the case of sight. We shall not discuss any of the other senses here specifically,[39] but shall turn to consider a general difficulty raised by Augustine's definition. This arises from the fact that it is axiomatic for Augustine that body cannot act on soul. The reason for this is not, as might be expected, the

ever-recurrent problem of how to render intelligible the interaction of mind and body once they have been decisively separated. This does not seem to have worried Augustine, for he always insists that mind does act on body. It is, however, by nature nobler than body and matter, and cannot in any way be affected or acted upon by the body. Hence the difficulty of understanding how a modification in the mind can arise from a bodily modification resulting from the encounter of sense-organ and object.[40]

Augustine began his theory of sense perception with the insistence that a mere modification of a sense-organ is not sufficient to constitute sense-experience unless this modification is somehow noticed by the mind. He has now to account for the possibility of the mind taking notice of such bodily disturbance. He does this by returning to his general view of the soul's function in the body: this consists in vivifying its body, pervading it with its presence in all its parts. In sentient creatures this spiritual presence includes awareness of what is going on in the body and what it suffers from external agencies as well as its internal modifications.[41] There is no question here of the bodily organ acting on the mind: it is a case of the mind watching, attending to bodily states. Augustine is quite uncompromising in his insistence that sense-perception is the work of the mind.[42] He is in a good position, as a result, to do full justice to the multifarious ways in which thought enters the content of sense-perception: it supplements the fragmentary data of sense, it places them within a context, an organized field, it interprets or distorts. If all perception is from the start the mind's awareness, as Augustine's account makes it, there is no difficulty in accounting for such "mental" activity within sense-experience. Augustine treats this at length in his discussion in Book VI of *de Musica* of hearing spoken words and sentences. His account does, however, make it necessary to treat all sense-experience on the model of touch and organic sensation of bodily states. We have already noted both the difficulties of a theory that is forced to do this, and the manner in which Augustine could nevertheless hold it.

We cannot here give a complete account of Augustine's views of imagination. However, since they are closely relevant and indeed arise from his views on sense-perception, we must mention them in passing. They will also help to throw light on his theory of sensory awareness. It is in Book XII of his commentary *De Genesi ad litteram* that Augustine considers this question in detail. He does this in terms of a distinction between three kinds of "sight". We are at present concerned only with the first two, which he calls "corporeal" and "spiritual" sight, respectively. The first is the name for seeing with the eyes. This seeing, in so far as the mind takes notice of it (and unless it does, it is not "seeing"), is accompanied by a mental process that can also occur in the absence of "corporeal" seeing. When it does so occur, or when he wants to focus attention to it in its own right, Augustine calls this "spiritual" sight.

"Spiritual" seeing is, however, not caused by the bodily seeing since matter cannot act on mind. Indeed, there is nothing to prevent it from taking place spontaneously in the absence of bodily seeing, as happens in dreams, visions, hallucinations, or the visualizing of remembered or imaginatively constructed objects. According to this account, there is, in fact, no difference between what goes on in the mind in the case of ordinary sight, and in imagining or "seeing things." In both cases, as Augustine insists, it is the mind itself which forms the image which it sees out of its own substance.[43] What is before the mind, in other words, is the likeness of objects, not objects themselves;[44] what is seen is of the same nature in the absence as in the presence of the external object.[45] Hence it is easy to be uncertain whether one is really seeing something or "seeing things": for instance, we only recognize that our dreams have had no real counterparts when waking up.[46] In general, Augustine holds the position that the difference lies in our awareness of the concurrent bodily modification in the one case, and its absence in the other. This awareness may be impaired either by physiological lesion, thus impairing the reception or transmission of sensory awareness, or by exclusive concentration of attention to what goes on in the mind, or by the withholding of attention from the bodily senses. This may happen in sleep when we dream, in ecstasy, or in other "abstraction" of the mind, such that it contemplates its own images without adverting to the accompanying bodily states.[47] The manner in which attention is focused is thus vital to perception. Attention is the voluntary directing of the mind to some specified part of the field before it. Thus, in mere imagination, the visualized object exhausts the mind's attention, whereas in sensory awareness there is, in addition, the awareness of being subjected to outside agency.[48]

The role of the will is thus central to Augustine's description of sensory awareness. A withholding of attention from bodily affection and its fastening upon the images in the mind is sufficient to make an experience an instance of "spiritual sight." Its turning to the bodily senses, thus checking the free play of imagery in the mind, converts the experience into one of "corporeal sight," without, of course, thereby changing the nature of what is before the mind. In his *De Trinitate* Augustine, stressing the function of the will, speaks simply of two kinds of sight, the sight of one who perceives (*sentientis*) or of one who is thinking (*cogitantis*), according to whether the will fastens the mind's attention on what comes from without or on what is within.[49] The feeling of the externality of what we perceive distinguishes sense-perception from imagination. For this reason Augustine feels entitled to speak of the physical processes involved in sense-awareness as conveying

"messages" to the mind, of "corporeal" sight as the messenger to the superior "spiritual" sight.[50] The third and highest kind of sight, which he calls "intellectual," interprets, judges, and corrects the "messages" received: it refers the images in the mind to external objects or refuses to refer them, and corrects possible distortions by selectively referring to the object only those features of the image that belong to it, and so on. Thus, for instance, the bend in a stick seen half-submerged in water belongs to the image only, and it would be erroneous to ascribe it to the stick.[51]

Clearly, an account of sense-awareness like this has many difficulties, some of which we have already mentioned. To summarize, it seems difficult to maintain — though Bishop Berkeley seems also to have thought so — that the only difference between imagining and seeing is that in the second case what we see is accompanied by a feeling of being acted upon; seeing just isn't like imagining under compulsion. Nor is it satisfactory to identify seeing with either of the constituent elements suggested by Augustine. When we see houses and people we just do not see mental images, nor, alternatively, do we undergo feelings of being subjected to house-shaped or people-shaped impacts on our sense-organs. Augustine, as we noticed, was aware of this last kind of difficulty, and tried to avoid it by a suggestion which depended for its efficacy on a scientific picture we can no longer accept.

Augustine tried to construct an adequate account of sense-awareness within the framework of a theory of mind and body of Platonic inspiration, but he failed to overcome the difficulties of this task. The Platonic framework is equally behind his account of rational thinking and understanding, to which we must now turn.

REASON AND TRUTH: THE MIND AND ILLUMINATION

Augustine's theory of sense-perception was prompted, in part, by a desire to defend it against skeptical attacks that would have disputed its claim of giving us any kind of access to truth. The manner in which he modified current Neo-Platonic views of the soul, too, helped to make it possible for him to ascribe greater value to sense-knowledge than many of his contemporaries would have been willing to do. And yet, Augustine shares with them the view that truth is really approached only in the knowledge to which the mind has access of itself, without the intermediary of the bodily senses, and that here alone is complete certainty possible. As Plato had taught, there are two worlds, the intelligible world "where truth itself dwells" and the sensible, which "impinges on us in sight and touch." Of these, the first is "itself true, the second is like truth and made in its image."[52]

We have discussed the way in which Augustine vindicates sense-knowledge against skeptical onslaught; we turn now to his views on knowledge not derived from sense. He first opposes skeptical arguments by pointing out that there are at any rate certain minimal truths that cannot be doubted. Among these are the indubitable truths of mathematics and of logic.[53] Augustine adds further examples of truths which appeared to him to be beyond doubt, like elementary value-judgments; to simplify our discussion, however, we shall leave these more debatable examples on one side for the present. We may readily agree with Augustine that logical and mathematical truth, at any rate, does possess complete universality, necessity, and immutability. These characteristics, Augustine argues, cannot belong to sense-knowledge. Knowledge derived from experience, he holds, cannot account for our holding certain mathematical propositions to be true and others false; for we hold these notwithstanding any apparent contradictions with which our experience may supply us. On the contrary, we use mathematics in our interpretation of experience as regulative.[54] If we find that by adding one rabbit to another the sum is three or more, we do not doubt our mathematics but conclude that one rabbit was a male and the other a female. Neither number nor mathematical operations are of empirical origin, and under no circumstances should we regard any empirical state of affairs as capable of producing evidence against their validity. The notion of unity, which Augustine holds is involved in the conception of number, is a particularly illuminating example of what we might call the "categorical" nature of mathematical concepts. He points out that unity is never an empirical datum: objects we experience are always made up of parts, and endlessly divisible into parts. In so far as we treat them as single wholes, we are relying on a decision of our own, on a line we draw round what we regard as "one." Empirical considerations are, admittedly, relevant to our decision as to what we decide to count as "one" in any given case. But they are not the complete and exhaustive grounds of our decision. This depends on other factors as well, such as the nature of our interest in the unity in question and our purpose in isolating it. The notion of unity, on which all counting rests, is thus not an empirical datum, but a category in terms of which we interpret the contents of our experience. Augustine extends this kind of treatment to mathematical concepts and operations in general.[55]

At any rate, most modern logicians would agree with some more or less sophisticated version of such an account of the formal truths of mathematics and logic. Where they would part company with Augustine is with regard to the conclusion to be drawn from this argument. The universal validity and certainty of these propositions, which struck Augustine very forcibly, suggested to him that this was due not to

the nature of the operations involved, but to their having objects, as empirical knowledge has objects, differing from these sense-objects only in being very much superior to them and capable of being known with much greater clarity and certainty. He says, in one of his philosophical dialogues,

> You will remember our earlier treatment of knowledge through the bodily senses. We noted that the public objects of our senses, the things we can all see and hear, colors and sounds, which you and I see simultaneously or hear simultaneously, belong not to the nature of our eyes or ears but are common to us precisely as the objects of our senses. Similarly, we must not say that the things which you and I both perceive mentally belong to the nature of our minds. For what the eyes of two persons see simultaneously cannot be identified with something belonging to the eyes of either one or the other, but must be some third thing to which the sight of both is directed.[56]

Augustine has pressed the analogy of mathematical and similar types of knowledge with empirical knowledge to its limits. Like his predecessors and contemporaries, Augustine had, of course, no conception of the radical distinction between empirical knowledge on the one hand and the sort of knowledge, on the other, which Kant was to call *a priori* and many modern logicians would call "formal." What he has done, in effect, is to deny that there is any radical difference in logical status between the two kinds of knowledge. In a very real sense he has made knowledge of "eternal" truths a kind of empirical knowledge, superior to that derived from sense-experience only in that it is derived from a superior kind of experience, one accessible to the mind without the intermediary of the body, and not subject to the uncertainties and relativities to which sense-experience is subject.

Augustine thought of the nature of this experience as analogous to bodily sight. He often treats it simply as a kind of seeing: "Understanding is the same thing for the mind as seeing is for the bodily senses";[57] "reason is the mind's sight, whereby it perceives truth through itself, without the intermediary of the body."[58] It is difficult to say whether it was his view of all knowledge as essentially a kind of seeing which prompted the theory that mathematical and logical knowledge had to have objects just as sight has to have something to see, or the other way round: that the theory of "eternal truths" existing in their own right as independent objects of intellectual knowledge suggested that the way they are known is somehow analogous to the way that the independently existing objects of sight are seen. The question is difficult to decide because there are hints in Augustine's work of both approaches. It is more likely that under Platonic inspiration the two views took shape in his mind together, and were developed by him step by step into the characteristic

Augustinian view of knowledge based on the "theory of illumination."

Thinking and reasoning, according to this view, discover their objects and do not create them.[59] Augustine held this to be universally true. He draws no fundamental distinction between the propositions of logic and mathematics and the basic certainties of moral judgment; they are equally clear and inescapable in his eyes. And thus he expands the realm of these indubitable truths in order to include all that he calls "wisdom" — that is to say, all that which is contained in the object we seek to know in philosophizing.[60] Augustine has here borrowed the certainty which is characteristic of the formal propositions of logic and mathematics and has transferred it to the certainly not formal propositions asserting judgments of value or fact. The result of this widening of the realm of "eternal truths" is that they merge in an inclusive world of intelligible reality, wholly transparent to understanding, at any rate in principle — wholly certain and completely real. This intelligible world became identified for Augustine with the divine mind as known to itself timelessly in its own rich fullness, and containing the archetypal ideas of all created things. This was further identified by him with God's creative Wisdom, the Word (*logos*) of God.

We have already noticed that Augustine speaks of our knowledge of this intelligible world as a mental vision. This analogy between seeing and understanding is deeply embedded in his thought, as indeed in all theories cast in a Platonic mold. Plato had used the analogy of light extensively in his account of the relation of knowledge to opinion, and of their respective objects, the forms and the perceptible objects of the material world. For Plato, it will be remembered, the intellectual "light" pervading the world of forms is the analogue of the light which renders material things visible to the eye. The intellectual light emanates from the supreme form, that of the good, and illuminates both the inferior forms, thus rendering them intelligible; and the mind that understands them — like the sun, itself supremely visible — makes other things visible by illuminating them. For Augustine (here following already established precedents), the forms are within the divine mind, and the intellectual light which renders them intelligible is a divine illumination within the human mind. Augustine speaks of this illumination in a number of different ways, as the mind's participation in the Word of God, as God's interior presence to the mind, as Christ dwelling in the human soul and teaching the mind from within, and so forth. With these substitutions, all Plato's essential similes are taken up by Augustine.[61]

For Augustine as for Plato, knowledge of the intelligible world was acquired independently of experience. Plato had accounted for our knowledge of the forms, of mathematical truth, and so forth, in terms of his theory of "reminiscence": cast in the language of myth, this theory represented our *a priori* knowledge as left in the mind in a kind of memory of another pre- and supra-mundane life when it was at home among the forms and beheld them directly. Augustine was attracted by this theory, but gradually came to reject it, since he saw that to assert the pre-existence of the human soul before this life would raise theological difficulties. But even after rejecting it, he held on to the philosophical content embodied in the myth: that this kind of knowledge enters the mind not from the outside, but is, in some way, present in the mind from the start. "The intellectual soul is by nature such, that being inserted by the Creator into the natural order of intelligible realities, it is capable of seeing these in a certain non-corporeal light akin to it in nature, just as the corporeal eye can see the things which surround it in this corporeal light."[62] Knowledge of the forms, divine ideas, eternal truths — it doesn't matter what we call them — is not, then, for Augustine, produced by the mind remembering something deposited in it previously, but is continually discovered in the light which is perpetually present in the mind. How close — in spite of the apparent divergence — this is to the Platonic theory we will see even more clearly when we consider Augustine's view of what he calls *memoria*.

The precise manner in which this divine light produces knowledge in the human mind is not made clear, and several views have been held with regard to this question by different writers. To begin with, we may rule out one view, according to which what the mind knows when it achieves true knowledge is the mind of God. This interpretation cannot be maintained in the face of statements in which Augustine insists that we cannot know the content of God's mind in this way; nor would he have thought it necessary to undertake a laborious demonstration of God's existence precisely from our knowledge of eternal truths taken as the premise of the argument if he had thought that the divine mind was directly known. There is much in Augustine's work, however, to support both the remaining chief types of view: that according to which the divine light imprints on our minds the ideas and concepts that it contains, and that according to which is supplies the mind with the standards for its judgments.

Augustine certainly held that one of the functions of divine illumination in the human mind was to provide it with rules for judgment. He did not, however, distinguish between the making of judgments and the formation of concepts as sharply as do many of his critics and interpreters. Hence, his view that illumination regulates judgment is not incompatible with a view — and we shall see to what an extent it was actually held by Augustine — that illumination also implants concepts in the mind. He certainly thought that the reason why different minds could agree on the truth of universal and necessary judgments was that under divine illumination the mind perceived the necessary and universal truth of these judgments. Illumination, for instance, in the extended discussion in the second half of the *de Magistro*, provides the absolute standard against which the judgments of individual minds — themselves temporal and changeable — about individual and changeable objects are measured, from which they derive their universal validity and necessity. But it is impossible to draw any clear line between this "regulative" function of illumination and its function as a source of ideas and concepts. We have already mentioned Augustine's account of our ideas of unity and number, and found that he regarded these as present *a priori* in the mind in such a way that we could not see them exemplified in the objects of our experience unless we already knew what unity is, what number is, and so on. Augustine extends the same treatment to truth and goodness. After enumerating a long list of things on which most of us would agree as good, he remarks: "In all these good things which I have enumerated, or any others you may discover or think of, we could not say that one was better than another when we make a true judgment about them, unless there was imprinted upon us a concept of good itself (*nisi esset nobis impressa notio ipsius boni*), according to which we approve things and prefer some to others."[63] This *notio impressa* is the *a priori* standard of our valuations — it is on the borderline of a rule against which we measure our judgments and of a concept into which we fit things. This impossibility of drawing any line between idea and judgment appears very clearly, for instance, in what Augustine says about our knowledge of the human mind. We each know our own minds, and each differs from all the others. Yet, in the light of the eternal truth, we can say certain things universally true about the mind as such. We do not get such a general idea of the mind by generalizing from our experience of individual minds, but "we perceive the inviolable truth, whence we define perfectly — as far as we are able — not what this or that man's mind is like, but what it ought to be in the light of the eternal truth (*sempiternis rationibus*)."[64] The general idea is the standard of our judgments on individual instances.

Augustine held this to be the case in spheres as diverse as geometry and ethics. In the case of the former, the judgments we make about visible shapes are dictated by our knowledge of their perfect and ideal exemplars. Similarly, our actions and judgments about them are measured against the absolute standard of human conduct seen in the light of divine illumination. The moral concern behind the whole theory of illumination is, however, dominant. He often speaks of judgment on the data of our experience in quasi-moral terms, almost, sometimes, in eschatological terms, alluding to the final divine judgment on all human things, as I have shown elsewhere.[65] Images and concepts in the mind are the material of judgments made under illumination

by the divine light. The language of this description of the process of knowledge makes it easy for Augustine to assert very much more than a theory of knowledge. He sometimes speaks of judgment made in the light of the eternal truth as a kind of echo of the divine judgment on all human concerns, involving a whole vision of man and his world in the sight of God: "In this eternal truth, which is the origin of all temporal things, we behold by a perception of the mind (*visu mentis*) the pattern which governs our being and our activities, whether in ourselves or in regard to other things, according to the rule of truth and right reason."[66]

Nothing, perhaps, is more characteristic of Augustine's procedure than this way of placing a philosophical view — of Platonic inspiration, at bottom, as often as not — into his general religious perspective and exploiting it in its service. We must now return to another, though closely connected, aspect of this version of what, as we have seen, is basically the Platonic theory of reminiscence. The mind, according to this view, perceives the truth, universality, and necessity of its judgments under illumination. Augustine does not appear to have held that we have any direct awareness of this process taking place in our minds. The *notiones impressae* in terms of which we make judgments, involving number or value for instance, are in the nature of mental dispositions to recognize instances of number or of value in their light. The *notio* is not itself arrived at by generalizing about all the things in which we have seen it displayed; it had to be present from the start for us to be able to recognize them as instances of it in the first place. We come to know the *notio* explicitly when we reflect on our judgments made in its light. In this respect, our *a priori* ideas are in the same position as much of the content of our minds: we can be said to know a good deal that we do not, at any particular moment, even think of. It is in one sense in the mind, and can be recalled, but is not in the mind in another sense, since it has to be "brought to mind," and may even be lost, forgotten. The name that Augustine gives to what is part of what is in the mind, but nevertheless not immediately before it, is *memoria*.[67]

Memoria includes what we should call "memory": Augustine conceives this as a kind of storehouse in which are deposited some sort of traces of our past experiences, which can be recalled at will or with some effort unless they have been forgotten. (We cannot pause here to discuss the appropriateness of this description of remembering.) But though *memoria* includes "memory," it is very much wider than this in its scope. It includes within it "the multitude of principles and rules of numbers and dimensions, none of them derived from any sense impression ... true, they have been perceived by the bodily senses in the objects we count; but those numbers *by* which we count are not the same numbers, nor their images, but are more real."[68] The *a priori* contents of the mind are here presented as included in the *memoria*, though they can scarcely be said to be "remembered"; and Augustine extends the scope of *memoria* so as to include all that we are capable of getting to know explicitly that does not come to us through sense-experience. This includes, for Augustine, knowledge of self, of the truths of reason, of moral and other values, of God.[69] Hence *memoria* loses its reference to the past, except in the case of knowledge derived from sense-experience, since the content of this is only in the mind if the experience has in fact occurred at some previous time; otherwise, *memoria* is not confined to past experience but embraces all that is latent and *present* as such in the mind.[70] *Memoria*, as Augustine says in a famous passage, is "a power of my soul, and belongs to my nature; yet I myself cannot grasp all that I am. Thus the mind is not large enough to contain itself."[71]

In this picture of the mind as not wholly contained within itself, as always capable of transcending itself by penetrating further into the obscurer depths of memory (*abstrusior profunditas memoriae*),[72] and thus disclosing to itself more of the truth unsuspected but nevertheless accessible to it, we are near the center of Augustine's views on knowledge, as well as on many other topics. All the *a priori* ideas of our knowledge, all the *notiones impressae* exercised in judgment, are contained in *memoria*, as we have seen; and, for Augustine, God himself is present in it, and capable of becoming known to us when we turn to him. His presence to the human mind is the ultimate ground of Augustine's theory of knowledge through divine illumination. God is intimately present to everything, thus also to our minds.

He is wholly everywhere; whence it is in him that [the mind] lives and moves and has its being, and hence it can remember him. Not that it remembers him as something experienced in the past . . . ; but it remembers in turning to its Lord, as to that light by which it had been touched in some measure even while turned away from it. Hence the faithless, too, can think of eternity and make true judgments of approval and disapproval about human conduct . . . Nor do they see these rules of judgment in their own natures; for although undoubtedly it is by the mind that these things are seen, it is equally clear that the mind is changeable. But whoever perceives in his mind these rules as the standard of conduct sees them to be unchangeable. Nor is it in any disposition (*habitu*) of their minds, since these rules are rules of righteousness, whereas their minds are, *ex hypothesi*, unjust. Where, then, are they written, unless it be in the book of that light which we call truth? It is there that all the rules of righteousness are inscribed, and from there that they pass into the soul of the just man, not by bodily transfer, but as though leaving their imprint on him.[73]

It is this presence of God in the mind, nonetheless real for being unconscious or unacknowledged, which is the real source of the illumination in which man knows the truth. To turn to the source of the light is to "remember" God, to be *with* him as he is with the mind. But his presence to the mind does not depend on the mind's presence to him. He is there, radically and ever present, just as his presence pervades everything that exists. The human mind is privileged above other things only in being able freely to turn toward and acknowledge this presence, or to turn away and "forget" it. And on this presence of God in the mind is founded the perpetual access of his light to the mind. Just as God's presence in things in general holds them in being and is operative in their functioning, so his presence in the human mind is operative in its functioning, that is to say, its thinking and knowing.

This description of human knowledge is scarcely, in the usual sense, a "theory of knowledge." What it asserts, reduced to its bare essentials, is that things function in ways proper to them, in accordance with their natures; and that in the functioning of all things the presence of God is operative, and that this is as true of the mind as it is of other things. Do we, when we add to our description of the way things work that they work in virtue of God's operative presence, add anything to our description of their functioning? In general, certainly not; but in the case of the mind's functioning, Augustine has to introduce a specific operation of the divine presence, illumination, in order to fill in a vital gap in his account. The gap is the same as that which Plato filled with the myth of recollection; and this is a final reminder that both Plato and Augustine support their "theories of knowledge" within a far-reaching metaphysical structure, of which they are, indeed, a vital part.

Man's Will and Actions

SINCE for Augustine the aim of philosophy is the attainment of happiness, and since this is conditional upon man's conduct, concern with morality lies at the very center of his reflection. Nor is this concern a theoretical matter primarily; indeed, the moral life itself, for Augustine, belongs more intimately to the stuff of "philosophy" than does the discussion and analysis of the language of morals. The reason for this lies in the way he thought of what he calls *philosophia*, already sufficiently described at the beginning of this chapter. Understanding and action both belonged, in the terms of his picture of *philosophia*, to the "philosophic life." Much of Augustine's thinking on human conduct is conditioned by the theological context of divinely revealed law and commandments, of divine grace as enabling men to fulfill God's will, of sin as a rejection of this help, and, above all, by the New Testament's conception of love. These conceptions, vital though they are to any understanding of Augustine's moral teaching, must remain largely outside the scope of our discussion, although it will be necessary to touch on some aspects of his thought which lie scarcely within the limits of philosophy.

Man is God's creature, made with a view to enjoying happiness in the vision of God. In this vision and loving union man attains his definitive state of rest, all else is striving and tension, conscious or blind groping toward this fulfillment. "Thou hast made us, and in making us turned us toward thyself (*fecisti nos ad te*) and our hearts are restless until they rest in thee."[74] So runs a famous (and untranslatable) phrase at the beginning of the *Confessions*. Man's nature embraces a multitude of desires, impulses, and drives, some conscious and some not; all these are in fact, though we are not aware of it, implicitly desires for the fulfillment which is to be had in its entirety only in the beatific vision. Man's "godwardness" is thus inscribed in his very nature, in its deepest recesses. Augustine often exploits here the analogy of physical weight: just as, according to the commonly accepted cosmological picture of his time, the weight of an object was what tended to carry it toward the place assigned to it in the world — heavy things downward, light things upward — so man's natural urges and desires tend to carry him in the direction appropriate to his nature. Augustine calls these dynamic forces in human nature collectively "love," and he often speaks of man's love or loves as his weight: "My weight is my love; by it I am carried wheresoever I am carried."[75]

If this analogy of "love" with physical weight were unqualified, man would necessarily arrive at his destined fulfillment by merely following the natural inclinations implanted in him. This, however, is patently not the case, as Augustine holds for two reasons. The first is that the analogy with the weight of a physical object does not fit human activity completely. A stone will fall if the support on which it lies is removed, but it does not follow that a hungry man will eat even if acceptable food is placed in front of him. The stone is at the mercy of its nature; its "activity"* is entirely determined by the manner in which its nature is inserted into an environment. Human activity is not thus determined. In some obvious sense, a man can decide whether or not to yield to at least some of his desires and inclinations, whether to act in accordance with his natural urges or otherwise.[76]

There is a further complication about human "nature," which limits the applicability of the analogy with inanimate nature. Augustine was well aware of the manifold and often conflicting character

---

* This word is being stretched here. "Passivity" would in fact be more appropriate. This is an indication of the difference about to be described between the "activity" of physical object and human "activity".

of human emotions and desires, the ease with which we succumb to our baser instincts, and the frustration of one impulse involved in pursuing another, whether better or worse. He summed up all such indisputable facts of human experience by saying that human nature was in fact distorted — disordered in such a way that all human impulses and drives could not be harmoniously satisfied at once. The theological background of this statement does not concern us here, though it was one of Augustine's favorite topics of reflection, discussion, and preaching. Now, bearing in mind that human impulses and drives are not only complex but often also conflicting with each other, Augustine noticed that we may speak of them as "natural" in one of two senses: the impulse, for instance, for a hungry man to satisfy his hunger is certainly "natural"; to satisfy it by stealing instead of working for his living may be "natural," but is at any rate not "natural" in the same sense. In this sense it may indeed be preferable to say that it is *not* natural for man to satisfy his hunger by stealing; it is more natural, i.e., in accordance with the sort of being man is, to work for one's living and to resist the temptation to steal when one is hungry.[77] In other words, the adjective "natural" is applicable to human desires and actions on different levels. On one level, that is natural which just happens to be there, felt, experienced, and undergone. On another level, that of choice, it is a matter of deciding whether or not to give in to these "natural" impulses. On this level it may well be (in another sense of the word) "natural" to restrain, rather than to follow, the urges that are "natural" on the first level.

This duality of "nature" is peculiar to rational beings. These, and these only, are not completely at the mercy of their elementary impulses, but are capable of assessing them critically and of acting on the strength of this assessment. It is important to realize that to Augustine's mind this distinction between two levels on which we can speak of "nature" is not a simple contrast between what popular preachers and moralists often refer to as our "baser" or "lower," and our "nobler" or "higher," natures. If he had meant to draw attention to a contrast of this kind, it would still have been possible for him to think of man as entirely at the mercy of the two conflicting natures, as necessarily following the resultant of the forces, lower and higher, at conflict within him. But what he was feeling his way toward was another duality of "nature," a duality of what is elementary in the sense already described, and of what is of a second order — i.e., concerned to decide between, regulate, and order the elementary or first-order forces collectively referred to as "human nature." He insists, therefore, that when a man gives in to or follows any of the elementary impulses among which he has to choose, it is only he himself who can, "by his own will and free choice," subject himself to them.[78]

Augustine does not, however, normally speak of a

duality of "natures" in man. When he wants to distinguish between first-order, elementary urges and voluntary choice among these, he usually does so by distinguishing between different "loves" as operative on different levels. We shall return to this distinction shortly. When discussing "nature" in man, Augustine, in his normal usage, confines the word to the elementary, first-order impulses and desires and excludes the free, voluntary choice explicitly from the sphere of what is "natural." In this usage, "voluntary" is opposed to "natural" (= determined), and means simply that the choice is the mind's own, that it incurs moral praise or blame.[79] The same systematic ambiguity to which we have drawn attention in the notion of "nature" when applied to man also attaches to the notion of "love" in Augustine's view. This is a consequence of the fact that Augustine speaks of the whole complex of forces that "move" man as his "love" or "loves." The word thus covers, on the one hand, the first-order, elementary forces, passions, emotions, and inclinations of all kinds, and, on the other, the freely chosen inclinations and voluntary preferences that a man does not just happen to find in himself, but imposes upon himself. Thus Augustine thinks of the notions of duty and obligation on the model of desires or inclinations that differ from those understood in their normal sense only in being self-imposed and voluntarily chosen.

The conflicting desires and inclinations, passions, emotions, and urges — all the springs of action — are thus morally neutral. But man, being a rational creature, is — at least to some extent — his own master; he is required to assess his natural impulses critically and to choose among them. He has to commit himself in voluntary action to one or another of what are often a bewildering complex of incompatible desires, where the satisfaction of one often involves the frustration of others. This self-commital in choice may take the form of abandoning oneself to the natural forces within one, taking the line of least resistance, and, in fact, surrendering the mind's freedom of choice and judgment. Augustine calls this "estrangement" (alienatio), and describes it as a voluntary surrender to impulses that solicit the mind's consent, which may, he thinks, in the long run lead to an involuntary captivity.[80] This, however, is only one of the possible types of situation. Indeed, the choice may well lie, not between "duty" and "inclination," but between alternative inclinations. The following example may illustrate the relation of desire and will, of first-order to higher-order desire.[81] A don who is about to go into dinner in Hall receives a telephone call. Knowing who is calling and how long it is likely to take, he says to himself, "I can get this over in two minutes. It's rather a bore, but I'll only be slightly late for dinner, so it doesn't really matter." In a clear sense his desire to go into Hall and dine is stronger than his "desire" to answer the telephone but he doesn't fatally go into Hall

following his strongest inclination. He can, in fact, work out a way of satisfying both desires. This is an exercise of will. If we suppose the call to be about a theater-ticket, it is easy to see that the conflict need not necessarily be between duty and desire, but between various desires. Praise or blame attaches only to what a man has chosen to do, or to his actions and state of disposition in so far as they are ultimately the result of his own decision.

Love, taken as an elementary passion or emotion, is thus morally neutral. Augustine expresses this by saying that there are loves that are to be loved and loves that are not to be loved, that is to say, inclinations which ought to be endorsed in voluntary choice and inclinations to be resisted, disowned, and restrained.[82] It is only in so far as a "love" is endorsed by the will that it becomes praise- or blameworthy. "A right will is therefore right love, and a perverse will perverse love. Love aspiring to possess its object we call desire; love possessing and enjoying it, we call gladness; love seeking to avoid what is hurtful is fear; feeling its presence, if it come to pass, it is pain or sorrow. All these are evil if the love is evil, good if it is good."[83] Man's task is to so order his inclinations and impulses that those he endorses in voluntary decision are morally good; that is to say, he has to impose a rational order upon them. "Love itself is to be loved critically (ordinate), so that what ought to be loved is rightly loved; and thereby we achieve virtue to live well."[84] Hence Augustine's definition of virtue is "the order of love," or "rightly ordered love."[85]

Virtue, moral excellence, goodness in life and conduct, thus become a matter of establishing a right order, first in the value one sets upon things, and second, in one's living, by embodying and displaying these rightly ordered valuations in action and conduct. "A man lives righteously and in holiness in so far as he values things at their true worth (qui rerum integer aestimator est). He has ordered love, which prevents him from loving what is not to be loved or not loving what is to be loved, or from preferring what ought to be loved less, or from loving equally what is to be loved either less or more, or from loving either less or more what is to be loved equally."[86] To embody such order of value in the texture of one's conduct, knowledge of the order to be embodied is, of course, presupposed. This order, in so far as it provides men with a pattern to which they are required to conform themselves in acting, Augustine calls "law."

Under the scope of this notion, he includes the ordinances of civil legislation and of positive promulgated law in general, but he means very much more than this by the term. Human laws may, on occasion, be unjust; they are in any case not all-embracing, they do not deal with many aspects of human conduct; they vary from place to place and from time to time. Behind them stands a "law," which is the standard whereby we criticize the justice or injustice of particular, formulated human laws, an all-embracing law in terms of which we approve or condemn our conduct. This "law" leaves no field of action nor any individual act untouched, and is unchanging. Individual human laws are framed with the needs of a particular social and historical context in mind. They should seek to embody the unchanging, eternal law, as far as possible, in a form relevant to these temporal and changing needs.[87] The *lex temporalis* is ultimately grounded in the *lex aeterna*; and whereas a human law may not, on occasion, be binding on our conscience, the dictates of the eternal law are necessarily binding.

> This discipline is God's law itself, which, while always remaining in him fixed and unalterable, is transcribed into the souls of the wise, in such a manner that they know that their lives are the better and the more sublime in proportion to the degree of perfection of their contemplating it by their minds and keeping it in their lives. This discipline therefore requires those who wish to know it to follow its order under two aspects, one of which concerns living, the other understanding.[88]

The realization of this order, under its twofold aspect, is wisdom,[89] and its attainment is a work of the mind, ordering both itself and the whole human composite which it rules in accordance with the eternal law.[90]

This law is God's "sovereign reason"; the question of how Augustine thought it was known to man has already been implicitly answered in the course of our discussion of the accessibility of the "eternal truths" to the mind. The eternal law is identical with the eternal truths: it is these taken simply as regulative of conduct and of moral value judgments. Augustine has recourse to the same analogies to explain the manner of its being known to us as he does to account for our knowledge in the light of the eternal truths. Thus, he speaks of the contents of the "eternal law" being "transcribed" into the human mind,[91] or its "notion" being "impressed upon us."[92] The theory of illumination, as we have already noted, always carries strong moral overtones in Augustine's work, and it is precisely here, invoked to account for our moral knowledge, that it comes into its own. The problems raised by it in this context are identical with the general problems we have sufficiently discussed already.

The deliverances of conscience are thus simply what our minds know of the eternal law. They constitute the eternal law as present, participated, transcribed into the mind as a *lex intima, in ipso . . . corde conscripta*[93] ("inner law, inscribed on the heart itself"). Conscience is reason as regulative of conduct, and its authority is absolute because its judgment is a participation in God's creative knowledge.* "The

mind informs itself by the divine light through reason";[94] "reason makes valuations (*aestimat*) by the light of the truth that by right judgment (*judicio*) it may subordinate the lesser to the greater."[95] The rational awareness of such order and its realization within the manifold impulses of (disordered) human nature in the texture of living are what constitutes virtue. It is beyond the scope of this chapter to give an account of Augustine's views of the individual virtues, especially the four "cardinal" virtues, or of the principles he uses to establish this right order. The achievement of such "ordered love" establishes man in the order that is natural to him; it directs his impulses and desires in a harmonious satisfaction of all that falls within this rational order. This fulfillment is "happiness" (*beatitudo*), achieved at the term of all human striving and struggle in the vision of God. Human life is a series of moral struggles in which men grope for the right course. In molding their actions to the pattern discerned as the standard of right, men conform their will to the order into which it is inserted. They pursue the course appropriate to them as men: "And hence the chain of right choices of will is so to speak a path whereby they ascend to beatitude."[96]

God and the World

ORDER is the expression of rationality in action. In human action, rational order is both the goal and the standard for judging all that falls short of achieving it. In divine activity, which cannot fall short of achieving its goal, order is the expression of its inherent "rationality." The created world is wholly the product of divine action, and must therefore be permeated by an order that is in some sense "rational." The notion of order is thus central not only to Augustine's ethics but also to his thinking about the world in relation to God, and, above all, to his reflection on human society — but with this last topic we shall not be concerned here.

The order pervasive of all things, is, however, not like that of an organization where all parts are geared to the smooth discharge of a definite function. There is a variety of purposes, as well as large enclaves of disorder which must all find their place within the overall scheme. The reasons for the existence of these indisputable facts of pain and sorrow, of human sin and misery and natural evils of all kinds, and the way in which Augustine seeks to reconcile their existence with the complete goodness and unlimited power of the source of all order, God, form the subject matter of theological discussion beyond the scope of this chapter. The result of such frustrations of "order," so far as we are concerned, at any rate, is that we shall have to be satisfied with pockets of orderliness in the world, glimpsed here and there, with tracts of disorder or randomness interspersed. We know, Augustine held, that every-

---

* The problem of whether conscience may be erroneous and of what authority it has if it is, is too complicated to pursue here.

thing — not only the bits in which we can glimpse some sort of rationality at work but even what is most radically opposed to rationality — must fit into the mysterious plan of God's purposes. But how they fit, and what, in detail, these purposes are, must remain dark and mysterious to us. But none of this prevents us from recognizing occasional instances of rational order.[97]

Augustine certainly believed that such order in the world as we are capable of perceiving testifies to the presence and activity of the divine mind.[98] He does not, however, make this an argument for believing in God's existence, nor does he ever seek to meet such objections as were to be made to arguments of this kind by such philosophers as, for instance, Hume. Indeed, his purpose in seeking to perceive God in the order or beauty of created things is never to make these a premise for an argument to prove His existence; his concern is basically a moral or religious one. Things do not simply lie around, pointing to their maker. Augustine often speaks of their having to be put to the question before they will reveal their dependence on God. In the famous passage of the *Confessions*,[99] for instance, in which Augustine writes of interrogating things about God, it is very clear that he thought of the process of coming to perceive created beauty and order as the result of a moral discipline. The point for him was not to prove that if there is order and beauty, then there must be a God responsible for them; it was rather that since God had created all things, we must discipline ourselves so as to see them as His work, see Him behind them, and worship Him, not His handiwork. Thus, things will not answer all interrogators equally; the answer men receive depends on their power of judgment, on the value they put upon things in the light of the truth within them. It is not so much created things as the response which it is fitting for men to make to them that compels us to affirm God's existence. And so when Augustine actually undertakes to argue out the existence of God at length[100] — we shall not follow him — he does so precisely in terms of a loyalty the mind is compelled to acknowledge in its judgments to standards not of its own making. He comes to present this loyalty ultimately as the subjection of man's mind to God's under the illumination by the divine light.

All things depend on God's creative knowledge of them. Human knowledge seeks to understand its objects and is said to be true when it succeeds. Divine knowledge creates its objects and cannot be anything but "true." Things can be spoken of as "true" in so much as they are the embodiment of God's creative ideas[101] or, what comes to the same thing, they can be said to be "true" in so far as they *are*.[102] Thus, the human mind under its illumination, is *ipso facto* getting conformed to the divine mind in getting to know the world, but this way of putting it would be to put the cart before the horse, from Augustine's point of view. In either case, however, it is true to say that the ultimate objective of human knowledge is to be as perfectly conformed in its knowledge to God's creative knowledge as it can be.[103] God's knowledge of things is a creative act. It not only gives rise to the existence of things in the first place and is responsible for their being what they are, but is perpetually sustaining them in their being, functioning, and activity.[104] It is completely free and is not circumscribed by limitations of any kind. Unlike a human craftsman's, God's work is not restricted by the possibilities of a pre-existing material out of which things are made, since the material of which they are formed is itself created by God out of nothing.

Beyond this bare summary we shall bypass any discussion of Augustine's doctrine of creation. There are, however, two questions arising from his reflection on creation which are of some philosophical interest. We must consider them in turn: First, his treatment of time; and second, his account of the functioning of created things in general.

The problem of giving an account of time arose for Augustine as a direct result of his doctrine of creation out of nothing. If creation really is *ex nihilo*, it is an absolute beginning and there can be nothing before it. Augustine was here faced with the objection that if the world is not conceived as eternal, then one can always ask what was happening before it came into existence. If one conceives time as a kind of receptacle which may be empty or full, then it is difficult to see any answer to the question as to why God should have created the world at one time rather than another, or indeed, any meaning to the question. From this kind of argument his opponents concluded that there can have been no absolute beginning, since to speak of one leads one into such difficulties. His answer consisted essentially in rejecting the picture of time that underlies this objection. The picture that makes one ask questions about what happened "before time" regards time as the same kind of thing as particular events or series of events. If someone tells us a story about what happened, we can always ask, "What happened before that?" If the story is an account of something that really did happen, something else will always have happened before the beginning of the story; and there will be some answer to the question which will consist in an account of some other event or series of events. We can press questions like this as far as we like, but they are of logically a different kind from the question, "What happened before all the stories, before time?" In the first group of questions time is a relation between things that happen before, after, or at the same time as other events. In the second case, time is spoken of in the same language, as if it were itself an event or series of events; and this way of speaking leads to the question, "What happened before time?" which can be asked in the same way as we can ask, "What happened before 1492?" But the grammatical similarity of the two questions hides an important difference, and the first stage of Augustine's answer to the problem put to him by his Manichaean opponents lay just in pointing out that it makes sense to speak of something "before" any given set of events, but not of something before all events. He conceived time not as a kind of fluid in which things float, or a box in which they are contained, but as the field of all the relations of "before" and "after" of events. Time, in other words, became for him a relation of temporal things.[105] It came into being with temporal things, and one cannot speak of it except as elapsing between them.

This met the immediate difficulty of reconciling the doctrine of creation *ex nihilo* with the logic of our language about time. But it was only the beginning of Augustine's reflection on time, and we must briefly sketch the lines along which he continued it. If time was past, present, and future, it was difficult to understand in what sense time could be in any sense real. For the past of a thing no longer exists; in calling it "past" we say precisely that it "was," not that it "is." Similarly, the future is not yet, but will be, and there is only the present time left with any claim to reality. But what is the present? Is it this year, this month, this day? Even the present day has 24 hours, each of which divides not only into minutes and seconds but endlessly into instants as short as we like to make them. It seems, therefore, that we are compelled to say that the present also vanishes to the point at which the future becomes past.[106] And yet, Augustine observes, we are aware of periods of time of varying duration, and we can and do measure time; how is it that we can measure what is not yet or is no longer and has no extension when it is? Augustine's first attempt at an answer consists in suggesting that "we measure time in its passing, by our awareness."[107] In the mind's awareness, Augustine suggests, what is actually past has a present existence of a kind in so far as it is remembered, and the future in so far as it is anticipated or foreseen. But, as Augustine is careful to note, this does not mean that the past and the future are after all somehow real. It means that we can speak of the past and the future as being present to the mind, in memory and expectation.[108]

Duration, therefore, though it would seem that the fragmentariness of passing time leaves no room for the reality of such a notion, may exist in the mind. Before elaborating this conception of duration further, Augustine considers the suggestion that time can be identified with movement, and in particular, with the regular movement of the heavenly bodies. He rejects this for the very good reason that there is no *logical* inconsistency in holding that the sun might change its speed — i.e., move a greater or lesser distance in the same time, or even stand still, as it was supposed to have done in the story of Joshua, while Israel defeated the Amorites. Thus, we cannot simply define time as movement, such as that of the heavenly bodies, to measure duration, or *vice versa*: we may rely on our awareness of duration to estimate the duration of motion or rest. Even if all external motion were to cease in our surroundings, we should still be aware of the state of rest continuing for a greater or lesser duration.[109] Thus Augustine is brought back to his suggestion that the mind is aware of duration as such. In its awareness of passing time the mind is "stretched out," so to speak, between an expectation of what is to come and a memory of what has passed. Such "stretching" (*distentio*) of the mind backward and forward within its attention to the present is its awareness of time. This is Augustine's final solution to the puzzle about the reality of time, somewhat hesitantly adopted: "Time, it seems to me, is nothing else than extension (*distentio*), though I do not know extension of what: probably of the mind itself."[110]

It is not clear why, at this point, Augustine should not have been ready to admit the possibility of such a temporal *distentio* existing outside the mind in temporally extended things. It looks as if, in spite of his critique of the conception of time as an all-containing flow, he was still haunted by the imaginative picture attached to this notion. His only way of exorcising the hold it had on him was to deny, in the end, that temporal reality could be envisaged as existing without awareness in the mind.

The second question arising from Augustine's doctrine of creation, which must be touched on here, is that concerning the activity, functioning, and development of creatures. This question is forced on him by the apparent contradiction between the Scriptural statements to the effect that God created all things at the same time, in the beginning, and the patent fact that some things did not come into existence until later. A sequence of some kind is hinted at even in the creation story that appears in Genesis. How is sequence of this kind to be reconciled with belief in a divine creation of everything in the beginning? In essence, Augustine's solution lies in the suggestion that God did indeed create everything at the beginning, but created different beings in different conditions. Some were ready-made. Others were left latent; potentially they contained and were waiting for the appropriate time and environment for their actual appearance and full development. Things of this latter kind he thought of as analogous to seeds from which the adult plant eventually develops, given the appropriate nourishment and climatic conditions. Augustine called things created in this germinal condition *rationes seminales* or *causales*. That idea was by no means original. Indeed it was a philosophical commonplace in Augustine's time; it went back to the Stoics' *logoi spermatikoi*, "seminal reasons."

There has been a great deal of controversy about the precise function of these "seminal reasons" in Augustine's thought. Sometimes they have been thought to have been postulated by Augustine so that he could account for the emergence of novelty in the created universe. Others, on the contrary, have urged that far from accounting for novelty, this postulate enabled Augustine to deny the very existence of novelty by saying that everything apparently new was already latent from the beginning. Both these views have some justification, but both seem to me to place the emphasis in the wrong place. First of all, it must be borne in mind that the problem for Augustine was not primarily a problem arising from a scientific view of physical and organic processes: it was primarily an exegetical problem: How to make sense of the different utterances of Scripture about creation. But it is necessary to go further than this. We are here in fact faced with another example of Augustine's procedure in trying to understand Scriptural data with the aid of philosophical concepts. The conception of "seminal reasons" was above all useful to him in enabling him in some rudimentary way to speak of creaturely causal efficacy, of the inherent activity of created things according to their own natures, without thereby being forced to withdraw them from the scope of the divine creative activity. Just as we can say about a blade of grass that God created it even if it grew from a seed (which God had created), so, Augustine suggests, we can say about things brought about by the causal interaction of processes in the course of time that they have been created by God, because these processes themselves go back to divine creative origination and, indeed, depend on it for their causal efficacy. Their later results can therefore be said to have been created "causally," "potentially," "seminally," "invisibly," or "as things to be, not things that are."[111] The law of their own development and functioning is thus part of the created nature of things.[112]

> All the normal course of nature is subject to its own natural laws. According to this, all created living things have their determinate inclinations — which even a perverse will is limited by — and also the elements of nonliving physical things have their determinate forces and qualities in virtue of which they function as they do and develop as they do and not in some other way. From these "seminal reasons" as if from a primordial origin everything that comes about emerges in its own time in the due course of events, and having come to its end passes away, each according to its nature.[113]

To say that things unfold from their "seminal reasons" is thus to say that they function in accordance with the laws of nature.

Augustine uses the conception of "seminal reasons" to account for the genuine causal efficacy of created causes in their own order, subject to their own laws. He distinguishes this creaturely causality sharply from the creator's "causality," on which depends the whole complex of created causal efficacy.[114] He is feeling his way toward the later distinction between a "first cause" and "second" causes, according to which the word "cause" is being used in a different sense when applied to the dependence of creatures on their Creator from that in which it is used when applied to the dependence of a creaturely effect on created causes. For Augustine, too, the question why such-and-such happens is not satisfactorily answered by saying "God made it so." That is the answer to a different sort of question and is never a legitimate answer to a question that seeks an explanation in terms of causal efficacy and natural process. It is, at best, a confession of our failure to have found such an explanation.

God is present and active in all process and happenings. In the normal course of nature, the laws and order according to which events take place "are not only in God, but are inserted by him into created things, concreated with them."[115] But though God is omnipotent not by arbitrary power (*potentia temeraria*) but by the strength of wisdom (*sapientiae virtute*),[116] and though his action in the world is precisely to endow created things with their appropriate efficacy, He is not bound by the nature of His own creation. He cannot, of course, bring about anything self-contradictory. This is not a limitation on His power, since there is nothing He cannot bring about. To say that something is self-contradictory is to assert that it cannot be the description of any thing, event, or state of affairs, that it is a mistaken use of language. Anything that can be described without such breach of the meaningful use of language lies within God's power, even if it is not inscribed into the natures of the created things He utilizes to bring about his purposes. If a certain event is in accordance with the normal order of nature, we can always say both that it is caused by the various causal factors that account for it in terms of natural laws, and that it is caused — in another sense of "caused" — by God, working in and through these natural causes. If, however, God chooses to act outside the scope of the natural order of functioning of things at certain times and places, though He is still the "cause" of such events, we shall not be able to assign them a cause in terms of the laws and order of nature. Such events are, Augustine holds, miracles in the order of inanimate and organic nature, and grace in the case of rational beings.[117] Such events are beyond the potentialities with which things are endowed and are not governed by the laws of their normal functioning, and they are, in this sense, not "natural"; but, Augustine says, "such exceptional events, when they happen, are not against nature except in so far as our notion of 'nature' is derived from what normally happens; but they are not against nature from God's point of view, for whom that is 'nature' which He has made."[118] Augustine, it is true, tends to minimize the significance of normality in nature, and often speaks of miraculous occurrences as the most natural things in the world if only we are not too prejudiced by our views of what ought to happen because we expect things to follow their usual pattern. But nevertheless, he is feeling his way toward a distinction between what is, strictly speaking, "natural" and what is not. The sharpness of this distinction is sometimes blurred by his concern not to appear to limit the freedom of God's action in nature. Nevertheless, in general God respects the nature of his creation: "He governs all the things He has created in such a way that He allows them to function and to behave in the ways proper to them."[119]

At this point we must break off our survey of Augustine's reflection on the nature of the created world. It is, in any case, reflection, not indulged in for its own sake, but as a step in achieving that wisdom which Augustine labored for, which he called *philosophia*, the quest for which he summed up in his youth, when, in his *Soliloquies*,[120] he stated his program thus: "It is God and my soul I want to know. — Nothing else? — No; nothing whatever."

6

Thomas Aquinas

KNUT TRANØY

THOMAS AQUINAS WAS BORN in 1225 of a noble Italian family. His family was deeply involved in Italian politics, and as a child Thomas was sent to the Benedictine Abbey of Monte Cassino in order to further the family's political aims. In 1239 Thomas went to the University of Naples, and while a student there he entered the Dominican order. His family made energetic efforts to dissuade him, and for a while he was even imprisoned in the family castle. However, Thomas stuck to his decision, and on regaining his freedom he went to Paris where he studied philosophy and theology under Albertus Magnus, with whom he taught for four years (1248–1252) at the University of Cologne. From then on his life was rather uneventful; he spent his time studying, writing, and teaching. He died in 1274, when he was on his way to attend the Council of Lyons.

In spite of his rather short life, Thomas managed to write an impressive number of books on theology and philosophy. His main works are the two great *Summae* — the *Summa Contra Gentiles* and the *Summa Theologica*. Thomas never really finished the *Summa Theologica*; it seems that in December, 1273, he had some kind of ecstatic experience or vision which made him stop writing. Besides the *Summae*, Thomas also wrote commentaries on the works of Aristotle, and a great number of minor treatises.

Thomas Aquinas was canonized in 1323. His influence, which was considerable in the centuries following his death, reached a new peak in 1879 when Pope Leo XIII recommended the philosophy of Thomas Aquinas as a model for Catholic thought.

THOMAS AQUINAS HOLDS a safe place in the history of philosophy. It is not obvious that this prominence is philosophically merited. Is he not, above all, a theologian, and — in so far as he is a philosopher at all — the appointed philosopher of the Catholic Church? Very often we find him introduced as "the angelic doctor."* It can be argued, however, that Thomas deserves his place in the history of philosophy, not primarily as theologian-philosopher, but simply as a philosopher who thought with considerable clarity and rigor about important problems connected with man's religious life.

Thomas Aquinas' literary style is dry, even arid. There is meticulous and serious argumentation throughout and an almost complete absence of decorative phraseology or appeal to the reader's poetic imagination. There is an equally conspicuous absence of explicit "ego-involvement." In marked contrast to Augustine, for example, he never refers to himself or uses the first person singular. Nevertheless, there emerges from Aquinas' texts the portrait of a man of unusual qualities. Sincerity, modesty, openness, innocence, are attractive attributes taken one by one, and when combined in the same individual who has also unusual intellectual abilities they produce an appealing and impressive figure indeed. But however impressive he may be, it would be silly to consider him to be faultless or so nearly so as to be above and beyond *critical* study. Greatness is obscured if adulation takes the place of critical discernment. Therefore a student of Thomist thought who is not a religious partisan may have certain advantages. The critical acumen of Catholics sometimes seems to crumble under the burden of admiration and reverence. Protestants and other confessional antagonists often lose their power of fair appraisal for other, but related, reasons: the mind of Thomas Aquinas is so different and so alien even to that of Martin Luther. To be a nonpartisan here is, then, ideally to be free from prejudice — presumably, at least. On the other hand, this freedom from commitment is a real advantage only if certain other conditions are also fulfilled.

Understanding would be denied to one confirmed in the opinion that metaphysics is always nonsense and that religious ideas are not intelligible but can only be explained as psycho-social events. Here already, we have come to one of the central features in the thought of Thomas Aquinas. Aquinas believed that the universe is intelligible in a strict sense of the word, i.e., that its structure and laws can be grasped by the limited or finite human intellect, that in consequence of intellectual effort men can come to *understand* it. For him the universe had a supernatural as well as a natural aspect: God

* Many medieval philosophers were given honorific titles. Thomas was called *doctor angelicus*. Lately he has been more often referred to as *doctor communis*, "the common doctor" — common, that is, to all the Catholic church.

and creation, cause and effect. And he believed in a continuity or intelligible connection between these two aspects. Man — as an effect, as created — could achieve a certain (though far from complete) understanding of his own cause and creator — and ultimate destiny. This idea of a (partly) intelligible connection between God and the world, between supernatural cause and natural effect, is a fundamental feature of the system of Aquinas. It is at the root of his metaphysics, in its theological as well as its philosophical aspect, and it is a basic feature in his conception of man. This, then, I venture to see as one of the main ambitions of the philosophy of Aquinas: what is *said* in it is meant to be *intelligible*. It is not esoteric in the sense that the understanding of it is the privilege of those who share his faith. However, the truth and understanding which we may attain as human beings, our "natural" understanding, is not (unlike the revealed truth) given once and for all. Therefore, it is a foregone conclusion that in our study of Thomas we shall be free to criticize with a view to questioning that which appears doubtful or invalid.

Perhaps a further reservation should be added. It is possible that a study of Thomas will be rewarding only for those who share one aspect at least of his faith: a faith, however modest, in the powers of the human intellect to understand man and the universe. For in one sense, Aquinas' undertaking in philosophy can be described as a singularly persistent attempt to delimit — within a universe considered essentially intelligible — the functions and the reach of man's finite and limited rational powers in relation to the creator-saviour God of the Christian religion, conceived as an infinite, all-powerful mind.

Faith and Reason: Two Ways of Knowing

ONE of the patent facts about the Middle Ages is its formidable extension in time. By any accepted reckoning it covers at least a thousand years. Even granted that things moved more slowly then than now — in the world of ideas as well as in other fields — it is no longer possible to retain the idea of the Middle Ages as a stagnant, uninteresting period in the history of thought, a protracted reign of darkness which was not dispelled until finally, toward the year 1500, modern science and philosophy emerged.

A better grasp of the time perspective is one condition for an understanding of the philosophy of Aquinas. Born in 1225, he lived and taught rather toward the end of the period. The nature of his philosophy was to a great extent determined by what had been thought, believed, and doubted by philosophers and theologians before him and in his own time. His thinking, which in some respects does constitute a high point — and thus also a turning point — in the history of medieval philosophy, came to exert a powerful influence on the climate of opinion in the century immediately following his death in 1274, when things were beginning to move at greater speed. And certain events in the history of ideas in the thirteenth and fourteenth centuries have profoundly influenced the spiritual climate of our own times. It was then, one may say, that the basic opposition between a Catholic and a Protestant attitude of mind became explicit for the first time in a series of fairly well-defined theoretical problems.

It can be said, I think, that the fundamental ideological concern of the Middle Ages was the relationship between theology and philosophy, between faith and reason, or — less traditionally put — between the insights revealed to man by the grace of God and the insights he might achieve for himself.

To have faith — in this sense — is also to *know* something, but it is not the only kind of knowledge available to man. The problem is how man's supernatural knowledge, attained by revelation, is related to man's natural knowledge, attained through intellect and sense. Reason and faith can thus stand for two different sources of knowledge which can be compatible or incompatible with each other. But for the problem to arise in these terms — as a problem of the compatibility of different kinds of knowledge or insight — faith cannot be conceived as being primarily an emotional attitude or an essentially nonintellectual affair. An intellectual conception of faith was, it seems, common ground for very many philosophers in the Middle Ages.

Three different ways of dealing with the relationship between faith and reason, theology and philosophy, will be distinguished here as a background for an understanding of the fourth, that of Aquinas.

In the second century, Tertullian's attitude to the problem had been epitomized in the phrase "*Credo quia absurdum*" ("I believe because it is absurd," although this is not his own, exact wording). In his teaching the revealed insights of Christianity made any other kind of knowledge superfluous. "With our faith we desire no further belief. For this is our palmary faith, that there is nothing which we ought to believe besides."[1] In this tradition, philosophy is not even the handmaid of theology; the two are enemies. Philosophy was downright incompatible with the insights of revelation — and even harmful. We find similar views expressed throughout the Middle Ages. This is indeed an extreme position. But it would probably be unwise to underestimate the strength of the attitude even from a more theoretical point of view. It avoids certain problems by admitting one source of authority only. On this view there can be no real competition between philosophy and theology at all, since the insights of philosophy can be relevant for none of the purposes and aims connected with man's religious life — and

these purposes and aims are the only ones which can concern us. And what is the need for and function of faith, indeed, of Christ himself, if we could acquire the insight necessary for salvation by means of our natural cognitive powers?

However, there are at least two serious weaknesses in this position. If man has important "natural" concerns this side of the grave as well, or if the nonreligious aspects of our natural lives have any bearing at all on our supernatural destinies, then a natural knowledge may become relevant even in the perspective of purely religious concerns. A second weakness might be put thus: the Tertullian attitude implicitly assumes that there is no need to interpret the revealed truths. We can just go ahead and believe the Bible and the Gospels. But what are we to do if, on inspection, it turns out that we do not believe the same things even though we say that we share a common Faith, i.e., profess acceptance of the same words?

A second and probably more important tradition which also gives priority to faith over reason is connected with Augustine. This tradition recognizes the need for a certain rational endeavor and also admits that knowledge through reason is possible, given certain conditions. These conditions lie in the Christian faith itself and in the divine grace and assistance accorded to believers. *Credo ut intelligam** ("I believe that I may understand") is the formula usually applied to this view. Any kind of intellectual understanding, in religious as well as in nonreligious matters, is conditional upon possession of the Christian faith. This is the doctrine of the "divine illumination" of the human intellect. Man's "natural light" — his intellect or reason — must first be lit by God; then and only then can man use this faculty to throw light on that which he desires to understand. Therefore, faith in the dogmas of religion must come first; the credibility of Christianity is not dependent on rational proofs (which nevertheless this tradition produced in abundance), the proofs being intended to show that the dogmas are *also* logically necessary in themselves. Why, then, should intellectual understanding be desirable when it is not necessary for faith? This question asks for the rationale of the *credo ut intelligam* tradition. Revelation — the Scripture — is the *word* of God, and words are addressed to and properly received by the understanding. Now, the complete and perfect understanding of the word of God as the Truth can, at best, be attained in the state of beatitude after death. The beatific vision of God is a supersensual, purely intellectual vision. Indeed, Augustine himself describes the essence of blessedness as *gaudium de veritate*, joy at the possession of truth. But even here on earth man thirsts for beatitude — and whatever truth he can attain to here and now administers to this need. Thus, understanding of truth by the

* This phrase was coined by Anselm of Canterbury (1033–1109), an exponent of the position.

"natural light" in this life is a premonition and a sample of the joy awaiting the blessed in the next life.

It may perhaps be said that theology, properly speaking, originated within this tradition, if by "theology" we mean the effort to elaborate the tenets of faith into a logically coherent and intelligible structure. There could be no clear distinction between theology and philosophy within such a tradition. The two shared a common foundation — faith — and they were inextricably mixed in the development of the resulting system. But the primacy of faith over reason is perfectly clear in the order of logical dependence.

A third tradition must be mentioned, Arabian and Latin Aristotelianism. It is here only that we can speak of the primacy of reason over faith. The greater part of Aristotle's writings — and the most important part, philosophically speaking — was unknown in Christian Europe for several centuries. Aristotle had hibernated, so to speak, among the Arabians, where his natural philosophy and his metaphysics had been intensively studied since the ninth century. During the eleventh and twelfth centuries there arose on Arabic soil a school of Aristotelian commentators. Because Spain was at that time Arabic soil, European culture was able to renew its contact with Aristotle in the twelfth and thirteenth centuries. What interests us in this development is the problem created by the encounter between the Koran on the one hand and the Aristotelian writings on the other: the meeting on Islamic soil between religion and philosophy. Islamic religion was well established. Aristotle's philosophy, however, proved to be an intellectual attraction so powerful that some of the best minds found it irresistible. A mode of coexistence had to be found. And it so happened that the greatest of the Arabian philosophers, Averroës (1126–1198), represented a fairly outspoken rationalism with a frank antitheological bias. Considered as a verbal communication, the Koran is in any event in need of interpretation. The theologians do interpret it, but they do not have the proper training for such an exacting task. The professional philosophers, however, are trained to deliver logically necessary arguments and strict demonstrations. *They* alone fulfill the conditions required for a proper interpretation of the Koran. They alone are fit to serve as arbiters in conflicts which may arise between reason and revelation. The best course to follow is to establish a clear and complete separation between theology and theologians, on the one hand, and philosophy and philosophers, on the other. If, nevertheless, conflicts occur between philosophy and theology, the philosopher should have the right of way. The best to be hoped for is a coexistence of the nature of an armistice.

A large part of Spain — the home of Averroës — was Arabian territory in the twelfth century, and Averroism was not long in crossing the borders to Christian Europe. Latin, or Christian, Averroism made itself heard at the University of Paris early in the thirteenth century. Obviously this tradition, which stood squarely for the primacy of reason over faith, was bound to conflict with outlooks of the Augustinian-Anselmian type. One implication of Averroism would be to make philosophy, not the handmaid, but rather the mistress of theology, supported by the new-found authority of Aristotle. The problem of the functional relations between theology and philosophy — a settlement of the conflicting claims — became so pressing that it called for new solutions.

Aquinas was to provide one such solution.

Thomas is often said to be responsible for the finest synthesis in medieval thought. The word "synthesis" carries overtones of evaluation and approval which may contribute to persuasion rather than to understanding. We might just as well say that Thomas was the architect of the Great Compromise in medieval philosophy: a system of ideas which provided a possibility for the logical coexistence of Christian dogma with some of the main ideas of, above all, Aristotle and, next, Augustine and some of the Neo-Platonic ideas introduced into Christian thought by the early fathers of the Church. Thomas makes two decisive moves. In the first place, he introduces a fairly consistently maintained separation of philosophy from theology, of knowledge by faith and grace from knowledge by natural cognition. Secondly, sensation — sensory experience — is made the basis of *all* cognition and knowledge. (How literally this statement is to be understood will be seen below.) This, really, is an Aristotelian principle, and it is not original with Thomas. *His* contribution consists in the application he makes of this principle in defining the functional relations between theology and philosophy.

The distinction between philosophy and theology produces no dualism in the system of Aquinas. The underlying unity of the system is provided, one might say, by the *object* of knowledge, which is the same in philosophy and in theology. *All* knowledge is knowledge of God: "All conscious things implicitly know God in everything they know."[2] Revelation gives us knowledge of God from above, as it were, from the source itself. By revelation God is known as cause of himself and of all creation. In philosophy — the term is used here to encompass also what would today be called the sciences — we know God from below, by way of the created things, *per ea quae facta sunt*, as Thomas says[3] with a quotation from Romans I. By our natural cognitive powers we can make inferences about God by way of a knowledge of things He has created. To *describe* any piece of created nature is also to describe God in so far as a description of the effects of any *x* is also a description of *x*. And there is nothing which is not created by God. The difference, then, on which the distinction is based is primarily a difference in method and in the direction of the cognitive process.

Each of the two "ways" is in a sense (to be explained below) self-contained and independent of the other. In fact, in so far as there is a relationship of dependence between the two, it is the way of faith which is dependent on the way of natural cognition. Both ways, however, may be said to serve a common purpose. The ultimate goal of all human cognitive effort is to know God.*

It is clear, then, that Thomas does not share the view of Augustine and Anselm on the divine illumination of the human intellect. He makes a deliberate effort to distinguish philosophy and theology; the theory of illumination precludes any sharp distinction between the two. Thomas is, in fact, unusually explicit about the principles from which the distinction may be said to follow as a logical consequence. These principles are laid down in the definitions which Aquinas gives of *faith* and *scientific knowledge*. Faith (*fides*) implies the assent of the intellect to that which is believed. But the intellect can assent to something in two ways. First, because it is moved to do so by the object, which is either known in itself (intuitively) — such as is the case with the first principles that are immediately grasped by the intellect — or known through something else; this holds for conclusions of which we have scientific knowledge (*scientia*). Second, the intellect can give assent to something not because wholly and sufficiently moved to do so by the object itself, but moved by some act of the will which inclines the intellect more in one direction than in another. And if such assent occurs with doubt and fear regarding the other alternative, then it (the assent) is called "opinion," but if it occurs with certitude and without any fear, then it is faith. That is, if I assent to *p* without being sure that not *p* is false, then my assent is *faith*. The article (which deals with the problem of whether the object of faith can be something *seen* by sensory sight or intellectual insight) continues: "Now, *that* can be said to be seen which by itself alone moves our intellect or our senses to cognition of itself. Therefore it is evident that we can have neither faith (*fides*) nor opinion (*opinio*) concerning that which is seen, be it by sense or by intellect."[4]

What Aquinas does in this passage is to distinguish faith and scientific knowledge *as two different species under a common genus: the assent of the intellect.*

The intellect assents to propositions about an object of faith not because sufficiently determined to do so by the object itself: it is *also* inclined to give its assent because told by the will to do so. The will, in its turn, can then be subject, for example, to the influence of God. For "natural" scientific knowledge, no such additional condition is required. It is the known object which alone suffices to determine the intellect to assent to a given proposition. It would now seem to be clear that the separation of theology from philosophy follows from this distinction if we

say that theology deals with propositions accepted on faith, philosophy with propositions accepted by knowledge.

At the same time, however, theology as a science — sacred doctrine, as Thomas says — remains in a double sense an intellectual pursuit; first, because its conclusions are proposed for acceptance by intellectual assent; secondly because that specific assent of the intellect which is faith is the result of a double set of conditions — one necessary condition being an act of the will, the other being a certain intellectual effort. "Faith presupposes natural cognition," Thomas says in so many words in the *Summa Theologica*.[5]

We have seen that Thomas cannot be called an advocate of the primacy of reason over faith in the Averroistic sense. He certainly showed no inclination to replace the authority of the believing theologian by that of the secular philosopher in questions concerning the interpretation of the Bible. Nor can he be said to adopt the "*credo quia absurdum*" position of Tertullian; he is plainly an opponent of this variety of the primacy of faith over reason. He shares with the tradition of Anselm and Augustine the attitude that a certain intellectual grasp of the divinely revealed truths is desirable, important, and possible. But he goes beyond the Augustinian precedent in maintaining that a certain degree of intellectual development is a necessary condition for receiving into the mind, and thus for accepting, the revealed truths.*

An unprepared intellect — as in an infant or in an illiterate person lacking a certain command of language — cannot even *understand* the word of God, and consequently (of course) it can neither accept nor reject the message conveyed in revelation. For Thomas, the word of God is essentially an *intelligible* word. Furthermore, Aquinas differs significantly from the Augustinians in holding that the unaided intellect can come to know some of the revealed truths without belief in revelation. By our natural cognitive powers we can grasp some — though not all — of the truths necessary for salvation.

It follows that Thomas must make room for two different kinds of theology: a revealed (or supernatural) theology, and a not revealed (or natural) theology. Natural theology deals with and can even prove *some* of the truths necessary for salvation. The province of supernatural theology extends to *all* the truths thus necessary, including those that we can prove without recourse to the Bible. But supernatural theology has its very basis and foundation, its *sine qua non*, in revelation itself. Thus, in one way, natural theology is a part of supernatural theology only in so far as the former contains fewer truths than the latter. But the main difference is not one of extension or quantity. The essential distinction between them

---

* The final attainment of this goal can only be in the beatific vision (*visio beatifica*) in the afterlife.

* For Anselm it is also required that before we can believe we must at least verbally understand the message directed to us.

is that natural theology starts "from below," as it were, from our experience of the sensible world and the things in it, and proceeds "upward" toward God who is the source of all truth: *per ea quae facta sunt.* And it is our natural cognitive powers which enable us to make this assent. However, and obviously, from this basis and by these means we cannot go all the way. If we could, there would be no need for any revelation at all. Now, for Thomas such a need manifestly exists as the most urgent need of all, which is exactly why God has revealed to us the truths necessary for this purpose, for the salvation of man. Thus supernatural theology starts "from above," from the truths given in the word of God, and proceeds "downward" in the task of explaining and elucidating the truths thus given. And this "descent" is made possible essentially by the grace of God and not by any powers or efforts on our part.

It might appear then that God has revealed to man more than is strictly necessary. Thomas maintains that even those truths which are in principle provable in natural theology, still need to be revealed, since their provability alone is no sufficient guarantee that they will in fact be proved without error and become known by all who need to know them.*

We can thus say that according to Thomas there are two degrees of revelation: (1) Revealed and intelligible truths that are not provable; and (2) Revealed and intelligible truths that *are* provable by the unaided human intellect.

The following diagram may serve to illustrate the point:

(1)

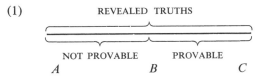

REVEALED TRUTHS

NOT PROVABLE   PROVABLE

A   *B*   *C*

The line *AC* represents the totality of revealed truths, while the segment *BC* covers those truths that are also naturally knowable — i.e., the area of natural theology.

If now we extend the line to cover *all* truths that can be known by man, the totality of possible human knowledge, the diagram will look like this:

(2)

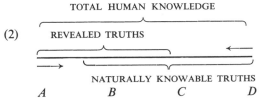

TOTAL HUMAN KNOWLEDGE

REVEALED TRUTHS

NATURALLY KNOWABLE TRUTHS

A   *B*   *C*   *D*

We should note that now the segment *BC* is of the nature of an overlap. In fact, this overlap, which

---

* The general point which Thomas wants to prove in the first article of the first question of the *Summa Theologica* is that it is necessary to have other doctrines, i.e., revelation, besides the disciplines of philosophy.

contains, for instance, the truths, both naturally provable *and* revealed about the existence of God and the immortality of the human soul, is a highly characteristic feature of the Thomist system of thought considered as a whole. It is the connecting link between supernatural and natural knowledge, between cognition by grace which proceeds from above and cognition by nature which proceeds from below (as indicated by the two arrows). But we should *also* note that the overlap *CB*, viewed from *C* to *B*, is logically dependent on the section *DC*, which covers truths which are naturally knowable but not revealed: the truths of secular philosophy and science. The section *CB* is a direct extension of the section *DC*. Viewed "from above," the section *BC* is an equally direct extension of the section *AB*, where we find, for example, the dogma of the Trinity[6] and the sacraments — in short, the Christian mysteries.

Thomas tries to determine as exactly as possible the precise location of point *B* by reducing the distance between points *A* and *C* as much as possible. (The position of point *C* is already given: the section *AC* extends as far as revelation itself can take us.) God's existence can be proved, as can a number of propositions about his nature and, in general, a substantial number of dogmas. But he is cautious of trying to prove them all. Some of them (briefly, the Christian mysteries) are not provable. Any attempt to prove them is bound to fail, and such failures are likely to harm the cause to which he and any other believing theologian is dedicated.

It is important to realize that when we use the terms "proof" and "provable" we refer, with Aquinas, to a proof or an argument which does not depend on theological premises drawn from revelation. Such proofs are, on the contrary, arguments that are based wholly on principles located within section *DC*, ultimately on sensory experience *and* the self-evident rational principles of philosophy (such as the principle of contradiction). When thinking as a theologian properly speaking, Aquinas proceeds in an analogous fashion. Then the basic dogmas of revelation function as something given and indubitable. The principles of natural reason are applied in thinking about and arguing from these data.[7] In this way we can also speak about proofs in supernatural theology — they are attempts to understand and explicate an essentially intelligible revelation. But it is important to see that these proofs are then of a very different nature and status from those produced in natural theology and in philosophy. They are at most rational reconstructions of articles of faith. Can conflicts arise within the section *BC* in the form of contradictions between the truths of revelation and truths proved in natural theology — i.e., can it not be the case that revelation affirms *p* while our philosophical proofs affirm its contradictory? In actual practice, *yes*; in ideal theory, *no*. For Aquinas, all truth is one in the sense that two truths cannot contradict each other if they are at all truths.* The world created by God is also in a certain sense His revelation — in so far, namely, as it is *intelligible*. It is not, however, a verbal revelation. But it can nevertheless be "read" and understood by man's natural cognitive powers, sense and intellect. Natural knowledge about the world is knowledge about God's work, about his effects: "We know God in all we know." However, human knowledge is fallible and inferior to the knowledge we acquire through the proper revelation of God who is infallible. Unless we are on our guard, therefore, our natural insights may lead us seriously astray. For it now follows that mistaken ideas about the world may produce mistaken ideas about God. "For error concerning created things will result in false knowledge of God and will lead men's minds away from God."[8]

It must now follow that when in actual practice conflicts arise between natural and revealed insights, the very fact of conflict is a sign that our natural cognition has gone wrong. The theory of the perfect internal consistency of all true knowledge in conjunction with the infallibility of God makes this conclusion inevitable. There can be only one reservation: *provided we have a correct understanding of the revealed truths.*

Aquinas' belief in the inherent intelligibility of God's works as well as his words marks a compromise and a half-way house in the history of Christian philosophy in the Middle Ages. Anselm represented one extreme with regard to the intelligibility and demonstrability of the Faith. Thomas is more moderate in this respect, since he holds that some of the articles of Faith — the Christian mysteries — cannot be proved. Indeed, although he would maintain that these dogmas — for example, the dogma of the Trinity — are also essentially intelligible (since they are understood by God's infinite intellect), yet he would not hold that they can be perfectly and properly understood by any finite human mind. The essential intelligibility of these truths is sometimes said to mean that they are "above," though not contrary to, human reason.[9] The one feature, however, that is so eminently characteristic of Thomas's position is what we might call the twofold intelligibility of those Christian tenets that fall within the section *BC* — the overlap in the schema on page 103. It is by virtue of this that his position can be said to be a mean between two extremes. The other extreme is the position of William of Ockham and other so-called nominalists in the thirteenth century (and later). According to them, we can have little or no knowledge, properly speaking, of God by our natural cognitive powers.

Aquinas and Aristotle

THE influence of Aristotelian philosophy on Aquinas is so marked that it takes closer reading to discover the differences. One major and obvious difference is, of course, that Thomas is a Christian. He is trying to be a good Aristotelian and a good Christian at the same time — and some rather difficult problems grow out of the effort to unite the two outlooks. However, partly through Thomas' training as a *Christian* philosopher, his philosophy also came to absorb elements of Platonic or Neo-Platonic origin. Thomas also had original ideas of his own. Nevertheless, it seems fair to say that his strength does not lie in originality of ideas. His greatness derives from the force, clarity, and persistence with which he tried to bring together into one coherent system elements of such different origins.

This impact of Aristotelian ideas on Thomas Aquinas is accounted for, partly at least, by a series of historical events. For several centuries, Christian Europe knew only Aristotle's logical works, while his books on metaphysics and natural philosophy were virtually unknown. These works, however, had been preserved in translations (which were not always very good) among the Arabs, and — as indicated above — toward the end of the twelfth century a new knowledge of Aristotle began to infiltrate into Christian Europe by way of Arabian philosophers like Avicenna and Averroës.[10] Gradually the whole of the *Corpus Aristotelicum* became available, and new and better translations from the Greek original texts were procured.

It must be very difficult for us today to understand the significance of this rediscovery of the major philosophical works of Aristotle — and to realize the impact it made on the thinkers of the thirteenth century. Until about the year 1200 the ideology of Christianity had been without any serious rival at all. Now, all of a sudden, here was a completely new set of ideas which (to some, at least) seemed to have at the same time three remarkable properties: (1) The philosophy of Aristotle was not the product of a Christian thinker, nor had it sprung from a Christian culture. (2) Some important ideas in this philosophy were in downright contradiction with important ideas in the prevailing Christian ideology; on other points the two were obviously not easily reconciled. (3) To some Christians who read and understood Aristotle, this new philosophy appeared to be *true*.

Unavoidably, then, the introduction of Aristotle in the West created a wholly new and problematic situation. Time and time again efforts were made to prohibit the reading and teaching of Aristotle in schools and universities.* On the whole, these efforts met with little or no success.

---

* This seems to follow from his definitions of *fides* and *scientia*. For if I should *believe* that *p* and *know* that not-*p*, then I should have to give intellectual assent to the contradictory proposition "*p* and not-*p*".

* Aristotle's works on natural philosophy were banned by the Council of Paris in 1210. Other bans were issued by various other ecclesiastical authorities in 1215, 1245, and 1263. A high point was reached in the great condemnation of

The historical importance of Thomas Aquinas derives to no small extent from the fact that his solution to this critical problem has become accepted in the Catholic church. The Thomistic solution consists, briefly, in accepting the philosophy of Aristotle wherever it is at all possible to do so without coming into manifest conflict with the doctrines of the church. On a few points Thomas has to reject or modify Aristotle. According to Aristotle, the world is eternal and uncreated. His "unmoved mover" is not a creator. It is not at all certain that Aristotelian philosophy makes room for the idea of an immortal individual human soul.

On points like these the doctrines of the Church allow for no compromise. But by and large, Thomas manages to preserve both the spirit and the ideas of Aristotelianism. His Aristotelian affinities and sympathies are clearly in evidence not only in his philosophy and his natural theology, but in his supernatural theology as well.

The Nature of Human Knowledge

I SUGGESTED above that the Thomist compromise or synthesis was primarily due to two factors: The fairly clearcut separation of philosophy from theology, and the empiricist basis which Thomas assumes for human knowledge. The importance of this empiricism will be realized when we recall some of Thomas' ideas concerning the relations between faith and natural knowledge: faith presupposes natural cognition.

What, then, does Thomas mean by natural cognition?

There are two kinds of natural cognition, sense cognition (*cognitio sensibilis*), and intellectual cognition (*cognitio intellectualis*).[11] What sensory cognition implies is probably clear enough for our purposes. It is the knowledge or acquaintance which we have of individual, material objects through sensory contact with them. It must be noted that any *judgment* concerning such objects belongs to the intellect, not to the senses. An example of intellectual cognition would be our understanding of the "first principles" — for example, the law of contradiction — and our use of this and other principles in drawing conclusions from given premises.

Thomas maintains emphatically that logically and generically, sensible cognition is prior to intellectual cognition. Thus it follows that sensory experience is a necessary condition of our knowledge of God in natural theology.

What we see at work here is simply a fairly consistent application of the Aristotelian principle:

There is nothing in the intellect which was not first in the senses ("*Nihil in intellectu quod prius non fuerit in sensu*"). It follows of necessity that man can have no innate ideas, not even of God or any aspect of him.

With a quotation from Aristotle, Thomas says that the intellect or mind of a newborn child is like a clean slate on which nothing is written ("*tabula rasa in qua nihil est scriptum*").[12]

The intellect is dependent upon sensory experience in two ways: for its very ability to operate, and for its contents. This means, in the first place, that the intellect has no possibility of knowing *anything* without the prior operation of the senses. Even self-consciousness, properly speaking, is impossible without sensation.[13] And that which is first presented to the mind, that of which we are first conscious, is sensible, physical particular things. Such particular objects are the only objects of which we have direct knowledge. All other knowledge is derivative and secondary in a sense to be explained below.*

Aquinas' epistemology would thus seem to entail a fairly outspoken empiricism, although one might not expect Thomas to see and accept the consequences. But he does. One can find statements by Thomas which have the ring of an empiricist's propaganda manifesto. The beginning or principle of every scientific enquiry lies in the senses, and all our intellectual apprehension is abstracted from their data.

So much for the *cognitio sensibilis*. What remains to be discussed is intellectual cognition, *cognitio intellectualis*.

"The operation of the intellect arises from sensation, but in the thing perceived by sense the intellect apprehends many aspects which the senses cannot perceive."[15] This is to say that from an epistemological point of view any physical particular presents two different aspects. We can know it, first, as something sensible, and secondly, as something intelligible. Qua sensible, a physical particular is something material which has (or is an aggregate of) sensible properties: colors, smells, weight, solidity, extension, shape, etc. These are all properties which we perceive by the senses.

Qua intelligible, the physical particular presents other aspects. Its sensible properties are not intelligible; they are directly given, as we usually say, in sense perception. Nor do I *understand* that a thing is red when I simply *see* (visually perceive) that it is red. But *given* certain sense perceptions and the ideas derived from these by abstraction, the intellect may proceed to certain acts of understanding. It is up to the intellect to decide whether the ideas which I have thus formed are *true* ideas. That is, the intellect alone decides whether there exists something outside

1277 by Etienne Tempier, bishop of Paris. To begin with it was Aristotle himself who was condemned. Later condemnations were directed to Averroistic and other heretical interpretations of Aristotle. In the end, the view prevailed that Aristotle was not contrary to faith.

* Thomas has a detailed and complicated theory to explain the dependence of the intellect on the senses. The senses present to the intellect some kind of image of the material object. From these "phantasmata" the intellect derives its ideas by a process of abstraction.[14]

of the mind itself corresponding to the ideas which I have formed. The properties of physical particulars are sensible. Their *existence* is not. Or again, it is not by sense perception alone that we decide whether our sensations are *veridical* or *illusory*. Such decisions presuppose intellectual acts of judgment.

To put this point in a language more germane to Thomism: An object of cognition is sensible in so far as it is a material individual; it is *intelligible* — "*inquantum est ens*" — in so far as it is in being or actually exists.

"*Inquantum est ens.*" This truly Thomist phrase cannot be properly understood without further explanations. It is the *existential* aspect of any individual thing that makes it intelligible. And judgments with existential import are not contained in that part of the cognitive process which is the act of sensation.

It is this notion of existence which needs to be explained. One thing must be made clear at once. There is not even the slightest similarity between the words "existence" and "existential" and their Latin equivalents as used by or of Thomas Aquinas, and these words as used by existentialists in our own day. Of course, historically speaking, the various notions of existence *are* related. But I think it may indeed be said — it probably even ought to be stressed — that the attempt to make an existentialist of Thomas is due to the misguided aspirations of some present-day Neo-Thomists to credit Thomas with all the seemingly acceptable thoughts that have ever been thought by anybody. If we try to understand the Thomist notion of existence in the light of modern existentialism, we are sure to go wrong.

The word "existence" (*existentia*) is hardly ever used by Thomas. His preferred word is "*esse*," which is also the infinitive of the Latin verb meaning *to be*. But Thomas uses it as a noun as well; and then we must translate it by *existence*. However, I shall also freely use Thomas' own word "*esse*," in order to avoid confusion with other notions of existence.

In the phrase "*inquantum ens*," however, the word "*esse*" does not appear. But it is contained, so to speak, in the word "*ens*," which is also the present participle of the Latin verb meaning *to be*. When used as a noun, it may be taken to mean *an individual which is in existence at present* — something that has actual existence and not only something that has possible existence or that has existed or will come to exist. An *ens* is something that is *real now*.

From the Thomist point of view, any actually existing individual — any real substance (*substantia*), as Thomas might also say — is composed of two "elements": (1) essence or nature (*essentia, natura, quidditas*), and (2) *esse*. These are not elements in the sense in which an aggregate or a class or a physical or chemical compound may be said to be composed of elements. Essence and *esse* are, rather, ontologically distinct aspects of an actually existing individual or substance. To say that they are onto-

logically distinct is to say that they can be distinguished logically; but it is also to say more than that. The two aspects belong to different categories of being. The distinction is not merely a logical distinction in the sense in which the inner and outer surface of a hollow sphere are logically distinct from each other. If we conceive a hollow sphere, we can distinguish these two surfaces logically or conceptually. But we cannot conceive of a hollow sphere that has an outer but no inner surface. Nor can there *be* such a sphere. The distinction between essence and *esse* is not in this sense like the distinction between the inner and the outer surface. For we can conceive of the essence of any substance (apart from God) without necessarily thinking at the same time that this essence has *esse* — i.e., without being logically forced to conclude that the substance whose essence we are conceiving also exists actually. I can very well know the essence or nature of a platypus or a mammoth and yet know nothing about whether it exists or not. And I may indeed know that such and such a thing exists ("there is a four-legged animal in my garden") without knowing *what* this thing really is — i.e., without knowing the essence or nature of this thing.

To put all this in Thomist language: The distinction between essence and existence or *esse* is not merely a logical distinction; it is also a *real* distinction. I may say that from the logical or epistemological point of view, the essence of a substance is the same as the *definition* of that substance. But a knowledge of definitions is without existential import (except if the definition involves a contradiction, because that which is logically impossible cannot exist). The Thomist *esse* is something that is added to the essence or nature of a substance to make the substance real or actual, to bring it into existence. It is that in virtue of which a substance becomes real, becomes *ens*: "*ipsum esse est quo substantia denominatur ens*" ("*Esse* itself is that by which a substance is characterized as a real thing").[16]

It is plain from what has just been said that the essence or nature of a substance is more than its definition. A definition is something conceptual that exists in men's minds, if anywhere. The essence or nature of a substance also has some kind of extramental existence even if the substance itself does not exist as an *ens*. To say that an essence receives *esse* is also to say that the *potential* existence of the substance becomes an *actual* existence. The notions of potentiality (or potency, *potentia*) and actuality (or act, *actus*) have important functions to perform in the conceptual scheme of Thomas. Just as the distinction between *esse* and *essentia* can be applied to all substances (save God), so also can the distinction between act and potency. But there are differences between act and *esse* on the one hand, and potency and essence on the other. Part of the difference is brought out if we say that a potency (potentiality) is a possibility that can be actualized. The actualization of a potentiality or a set of potentialities is a process of change, a movement, which, when completed, results in the substance becoming *ens*. An *ens* is a substance in act (*in actu*). This process of actualization is also a process of *perfection*. "Degree of perfection" will then mean "degree to which potentialities are actualized."

The notion of potentiality is in one sense more general than the notion of essence. An essence is a determinate set of potentialities. A potentiality in an essence is always a potentiality to become a determinate *this* rather than that — to become a man or a woman or a lion. Potentiality, *tout court*, entails little more than mere possibility, plus an inherent tendency (inclination, longing, urge) toward actualization.

God is a being in whom all — literally all — positive potentialities are actualized. This is also to say that he is *completely* in act, he is pure act (*actus purus*). It is furthermore to say that he is absolutely perfect, the most perfect being, because all imperfection implies the presence of unactualized potentiality.* Since a substance in act is the same as an *ens* to the extent that the essence of that substance has received *esse*, it then follows that no "part" of God's essence is without *esse*. Otherwise — since essence in itself would be unactualized potentiality — there would be unactualized potentialities in God, and then He could not be *actus purus*. From this "fullness of being" in God, all His other properties follow, as we shall see below.

It is a corollary of this that there is imperfection in *all* created substances. They represent an intermediate stage between absolute perfection and complete actualization (God) and, at the other extreme, that lack of perfection which is pure, unactualized potentiality. The concept of pure potentiality is a purely conceptual entity in Thomas; it can have no ontological correlate in the sense that nothing can exist which is pure potentiality. For existence (*esse*) involves actualization.

However, we can ask what this pure potentiality would be if it were possible for it to exist. Thomas answers that it would be identical with pure matter or prime matter (*materia prima*). And this introduces a third pair of concepts, *matter* and *form*. Now, in the first place, if pure potentiality is to be identified with prime matter, it follows that prime matter cannot exist (since pure potentiality cannot exist). Which is to say that matter always exists in conjunction with some form. This much we can infer without knowing anything else about form and matter. What else must be said about them?

In the first place, that they are a very tricky pair of concepts and not at all easy to understand.[17] In the second place, that they have been taken over from Aristotle. In the third place, that Thomas makes extensive and important use of them in his efforts to reconcile Aristotelian and Christian doctrines.

The usual analyses invoked to explain the concepts of form and matter are in part very misleading. We can talk about the wax and the signet, the matter and the form of a seal. But if we go out to plants and animals, it is entirely wrong to identify the form with a common or a uniform shape. And when we come to human beings there is nothing left of the initial analogy; for now it is said that the form of this substance is the rational soul, and the matter of this substance is the human body.

Substances are "composed" of matter and form, just as they are "composed" of essence and *esse*, potency and act. But the distinction between matter and form is *not* applicable to all substances. It is only applicable to corporeal substances. Since man is a corporeal substance, it is applicable to him.

In the realm of corporeal substances, the notion of matter is closely related to the notions of potency and essence, just as the notion of form is closely related to the notions of act and *esse*. As we have seen, matter is in a sense identical with potentiality. Whenever matter is formed, potentialities are actualized — i.e., an essence receives existence (and a substance becomes *ens*). Thus, when a human being is created, in the moment of conception God creates a soul to inform the incipient body. Matter is particularly important for Aquinas, since it represents also the principle of individuation. Human beings are numerically distinct because they have distinct bodies. As matter individuates, the form is the principle of "specification" — that is, it determines the species to which the individual is to belong. The form is that which is common to all individuals within a species, which makes them the *kind* of individuals they are. It follows that among incorporeal substances, angels for instance, there can only be one individual in each species. Since there is no matter, there is no principle of individuation except the form itself. Forms must then be distinguished in terms of their potencies and essences and degree of actualization. For even if something is pure form, it does not follow that it is free of potentiality, or perfect. Now it will also be seen that matter (i.e., the human body) is the principle of individuation of the human form — i.e., the rational (and immortal) human soul. Briefly, in Aquinas the *immortal* human soul is *individualized*, thanks to its association with matter, by the body. And without the individuation of the human soul, most of the central Christian doctrines would be nonsense. Consequently, the body is important in Aquinas' philosophy, in a positive sense. And he fully realizes this and accepts the consequences, in ethics as well as in epistemology.

The following diagram may be used to illustrate

---

* We must distinguish between two kinds of imperfection. (1) A substance S is imperfect if S has potentialities p_1–p_n and p_n is not actualized. (2) A substance S is imperfect if it has potentialities p_1–p_n even if all these potentialities are actualized provided that there is a further set of potentialities p_{n+1} etc. which S does not have at all. We can thus speak of relative and absolute perfection and imperfection. It will be seen that God alone is absolutely perfect.

what we have now said about essence and *esse*, potency and act, matter and form:

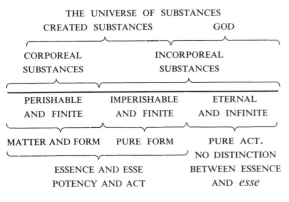

The diagram (note the arrow) also brings out the hierarchical structure of this universe. There is a scale of increasing degrees of perfection, from the perishable and finite up toward God. The notions of pure matter and pure potency would fall outside the diagram on the extreme left. Note also the distinction between *eternal* and *imperishable*. An imperishable substance need not be eternal, since it may be a created substance: there was a time when it did *not* exist.

We should now be in a better position to understand the distinction between sensible and intellectual cognition introduced above. In the first place, we need not find it surprising that the "angelic doctor" was not afraid of empiricism. The senses are bodily faculties, and Thomas recognizes the body as a necessary element in the scheme of things. It is not to the disadvantage of the soul to be joined to a material body, for in this earthly existence this union provides the soul with its only source of knowledge.

In the second place, we can now better understand the nature of intellectual cognition. We said above that an object of cognition is intelligible "*inquantum ens*, in so far as it is in being or actually exists." It will be seen now that the notion of intelligibility is intimately connected not only with the notion of *esse*, but also, and primarily, with the notions of *form* and *act*. Any created substance is intelligible in so far as it is *form* and *act*. A physical object is intelligible in so far as it is *form*. That is to say, a physical object is not intelligible qua individual (because its individuality is linked to its materiality) but in virtue of that which is *general* in it. "The proper object of the human intellect is the essence or nature existing in corporeal matter."[18] This point is connected with Aquinas' doctrine of universals, which will be outlined below. God, since he is pure act and pure *esse*, is then also supremely intelligible.

There is a general formula in Thomas which points up the connection between the existent and the intelligible: "*Ens et verum convertuntur*," "Being (= existing substance) and truth are interchangeable or equivalent." Truth and being (*ens*) are correlated aspects of the world. Truth is "in the mind."[19] Being is in the world. An intellectual judgment that can be true or false is always about that which is or is not. There is as much of possibly knowable truth in the world as there is of actual being in it. An intellectual judgment is true if there is an *ens* which corresponds to the *ens* assumed in the judgment.*

To understand the world, philosophically speaking, is to understand it in terms that account for its existence and the existence of the things in it — that is, to understand the world in terms of notions like matter and form, potency and act, and — eventually — essence and *esse*.

This is to point, also, to a difference between Aristotle (and the Greeks in general), on the one hand, and Thomas, on the other. The notion of *esse* is a Thomist notion not found in Aristotle. Thomas links this notion of *esse* with God as creator: to create is to give *esse* to. The notion of creation is absent in Aristotle. It might be said that the Greeks were primarily interested in *how* things are, in their essences or natures. *That* things are, that they exist, is given and obvious. Thomas cannot regard the existence of things as a matter of course (because he is a Christian, it might be added). His prime metaphysical question is rather, "Why are there things, why do things exist?" And the answer is that it is because they have received their existence from God. Aquinas' attitude on this point is rather akin to the attitude of Wittgenstein when he says, "Not *how* the world is, is the mystical, but *that* it is."[20]

Furthermore, since everything which is an *ens* has received its *esse* from God, directly or through intermediary causes, there is also a connection between God and truth. Formally, since *ens et verum convertuntur*, and since God is the supreme *ens*, we can infer that God is also the supreme truth. It is not altogether clear what such a statement means. But it contains the idea, at least, that all truth is connected with God, both in the sense that God is the creator and upholder of everything that is real (without which there could be no truth), and in the sense that God is the guarantor of all true judgments (that is, *if* a judgment is true, then there *is* something actual corresponding to it) and, thirdly, in the sense of the quotation already cited: We know God in everything we know.

Therefore, the world is God's "physical revelation." For the world is intelligible in so far as it has *esse*. And to the same extent, the intellect can "read" — understand and interpret — this "physical revelation," starting from the contact of the senses with material, physical objects.

---

* The theory of truth held by Thomas is a variety of the correspondence theory (to the extent at least that this appellation can be applied to Aristotle's theory of truth, which Thomas embraces). Thomas' theory has most of the advantages and disadvantages of any regular correspondence theory. His main work outside of the two *Summas* is *Quaestiones Disputatae de Veritate* (*On Truth*).

Ens, esse, act, potency, and all the other concepts, in terms of which we can obtain an intellectual understanding of the world, belong in the sphere of intellectual cognition. But they have been derived by abstraction from data given in our sensible cognition, which entails that the knowledge we can gain by means of such concepts is a derived and mediate knowledge. It is only in sensation that we have immediate and direct knowledge.

It now follows that in this life, as long as the intellect is dependent on the senses, we cannot have direct and immediate knowledge of anything intelligible — not of universals, not of incorporeal substances (the soul, angels), not of God.

Aquinas' position with regard to universals is again a halfway house between two extreme positions. (1) The extreme realists maintained, in the spirit of Plato, that universals exist *extra-mentally* prior to and in complete independence of the individual particulars (*universalia ante rem*, "concepts prior to objects"). (2) The nominalists maintained that universals have no extra-mental existence. Individuals resemble each other, and we summarize such traits of resemblance in terms used to denote properties common to several individuals. Universal notions like horse, man, wisdom, and goodness are formed on the basis of our knowledge of individuals; and they have *no* existence except as concepts in the mind of a knower (*universalia post rem*, "concepts subsequent to, i.e., derived from, objects").

With his so-called moderate realism, Aquinas assures for the universals both a mental and an extra-mental existence.[21] *Extra-mentally*, universals exist *in* individual substances as their form — i.e., that which is common to all the individuals in a species. All individuals belonging to one species *participate* in the same form, Thomas says, using a notion of participation which is of Neo-Platonic origin. But apart from this, universals have no extra-mental existence (save as ideas in the mind of God before creation). Forms are known in abstractive intellectual knowledge — indirectly, not immediately in sensation. The universal considered as a universal idea has existence only in the mind of a knower.

God

AQUINAS supplies five proofs for the existence of God. All five proofs begin by stating some observation — or, rather, by calling attention to some particular feature in the structure of the universe.* Thus, the first proof: "It is certain and sensation tells us that something is being moved in this world. But everything which is moved is moved by another." Since

---

* Thomas is not strictly consistent in his use of the terms *probare* (prove) and *demonstrare* (demonstrate). As we have pointed out, he does hold that supernatural theology is a strict science, which would entail that its proofs must be strict and necessary demonstrations. This they cannot be, since their premises are not evident.

---

to be moved is the same as to be carried from potency to act, and since actualization of an x can only take place through the agency of a y (which is in act prior to x, and which is *more in act*, that is, more perfect, than x), we are referred to an ascending series. The next step in the argument is to point out that the series of movers cannot go on to infinity "because in that case there would be no first mover, and consequently there would be nothing which moved another, for secondary movers do not move except in so far as they are moved by a first mover — Ergo, it is necessary to arrive at a first mover, which is moved by nothing, and this everybody understands to be God."[22]

Arguments of similar structure are also produced from the notion of efficient causation (that there cannot be an infinite series of efficient causes). This is the second proof. The third proof is perhaps the most interesting of the five. It is stated in terms of the notions of possibility, contingency, and necessity (applied to existing things), and argues, briefly, that if everything in the universe existed contingently, then nothing at all would exist. Consequently (since, as we see, something does exist), there must be something somewhere which exists of necessity; and this is God.[23] To this third proof we shall return later. The fourth proof argues, in similar manner, from the varying degrees of goodness and perfection found in the world, to the existence of a unique source of goodness and perfection. The fifth proof argues from the teleology and purposefulness which we can observe in the world to the existence of an intelligent being from whom all other things have received their ends and purposes.

Aquinas himself attached the greatest weight to the first proof, that from motion. Later times have been inclined to find the third proof the most interesting. However, there is hardly anybody today who would regard these proofs as proofs in any strict sense of the word.

In criticizing the proofs of Aquinas, we must take care not to commit anachronisms. Thus, it would not be fair to blame Aquinas for not having a proper understanding of the notion of infinity. It is probably safe to say that nobody at that time had such an understanding. Nevertheless, from the point of view of our own times, such criticism *is* relevant. For instance, in his *History of Philosophy*, Copleston seems to associate himself with Thomas in denying the possibility "of an infinite series in the ontological order of dependence." He seems to hold, with Aquinas, that if we assume such a series, the world will be "without any ultimate and adequate ontological explanation."[24] To this, one may say at least two things. In the first place, I may find it unpleasant and incredible that the world should have no "ultimate and adequate ontological explanation." Yet, for all that, it may be the case that there just is no such explanation. My dissatisfaction with such a state of affairs is in itself no evidence whatever for the existence of such an explanation. At most it may make me look for one. On the other hand, Copleston's position (which pretends to be that of Aquinas also) may turn out to involve a tautology. If an explanation is considered ontologically adequate, this is the case if and only if it avoids the infinite series in "the ontological order of dependence." But it seems perfectly possible to conceive of other concepts of ontological explanation — for instance, an explanation which explicitly relies on an infinite ontological series. It is not so hard to see that there are advantages in assuming the infinite regress. For one thing, it frees us from the onus of having to supply and describe a first mover or cause, for then there will be no "first," although there will always be a "prior to." Why, then, should we not say that the infinite series is the only adequate explanation?

It even seems that some such criticism can be leveled against the first proof of Aquinas without risk of committing an anachronism. Thomas says in the first proof that "secondary movers do not move except in so far as they are moved by a first mover."[25] It is not easy to see why "first mover" could not here be replaced by "prior mover" (unless *by definition* secondary or intermediate movers require a *first*, and not only a prior, mover). Then the argument would be that for any x, unless there is a mover y prior to x, then x will not move. But in an infinite series there will always be a y prior to any x.

Or again, with regard to the problem of "adequate ontological explanation," yet another solution is also possible. We retain the strict notion of explanation (whereby we do not have an adequate ontological explanation if we assume an infinite series). And then we argue that we *cannot prove* that there is an end or a first in the series which we begin to trace. This is the line of reasoning adopted by William of Ockham with regard to the argument from efficient causes. In this way, we get neither proof nor argument, strictly speaking, for the existence of God. But we make room for faith.

Criticism of the kind indicated above is serious criticism indeed, since it is directed at the heart of the argument itself. And this is not the only kind of criticism which it may be reasonable to prefer against Aquinas' arguments. Two more points will be mentioned.

Granted that each argument is in order as it stands, we then have five different series, each terminating in a "first" which is, respectively, a prime mover, a first efficient cause, a necessary being, a supreme perfection, and a designer or governor of the universe. In order to amount to a proof of the existence of God, it must then also be shown that (1) the five series converge in one and the same point (that prime mover = first efficient cause, etc.), and (2) that the point of convergence is identical with a being that has all the properties which the God of Christianity is said to have. And this Thomas does not show.

To prove or to produce evidence that a certain being, x, exists, is, one might say, to prove that a certain set of compossible properties is actualized. That is, we cannot prove or know that x exists without at the same time knowing something about the nature or essence of x.[26]

To prove the existence of God is, then, to show that the properties ascribed to the Christian God in the Bible are actualized in one and only one being. At least our proof must show that the property or set of properties is actualized from which all the other required properties necessarily follow.

Let us for the moment waive all objections against the logical validity of the five proofs. We then assume that they are valid — except for the final line in each of them: "And this all men call God." The five arguments then prove the existence of a first mover, a necessary being, etc. These are not, however, the properties ascribed to God in the Bible. The question then is, how are these properties (existing of itself necessarily, etc.) related to the properties of being good, wise, just, living, etc. — in short, the properties of the Christian God as we know him by revelation?

For clearly, our ideas of *what* God is, what his properties or his nature are, we derive from revelation. Before we can try to prove anything at all we must, of course, have some idea of the nature or properties of the being whose existence we want to prove. "Were there somebody who knew God in no way whatsoever, then he could not even name God, except in the way in which we use words whose meanings we do not know."[27]

As regards our knowledge and understanding of the nature of God, Aquinas proceeds in two different ways. One is to show how certain properties must necessarily be ascribed to God when God is conceived as the supreme necessary being. Or, in other words, given the conclusion of the third proof, we can deduce that God must also have a certain set of properties, such as being intelligent and having will, love, goodness, etc. But that is not all, for even granted that by these arguments certain predicates can be seen to apply to God, we have no assurance that words like "intelligent," "wise," "good," etc. have the same meaning when applied to God as they have when applied to things within the range of our natural experience. That is to say that although we may be entitled to use such words about God, we still have no assurance that we *understand* them when they are used about God. And if we do not in some measure understand the meaning of some of these divine predicates, then we have no knowledge of the nature of God.

The third proof issues in the conclusion that there is a supreme being that exists of necessity. This notion of a necessary being is explicated in various ways. It is said to mean that in this being there is no distinction between its essence and its existence or *esse*. It belongs to the nature of such a being to exist. It *is* its own existence. This attribute of the Supreme

Being — God — is summarized in saying that God is *ipsum esse subsistens*: His own self-subsisting existence.

One may be forgiven for finding this difficult to understand, since it seems to demand of us that we should understand what it is for existence itself to exist. However, we shall not here be concerned with these difficulties. It must suffice for us to note that according to these ideas, it is part and parcel of God's nature to exist.

From the concept of God as *ipsum esse subsistens*, Thomas deduces certain other properties which must belong to God. The precise logical structure of the series of deductions undertaken by Thomas[28] is very difficult to ascertain. It is a very complicated structure for one thing; and although it resembles a series of proofs for theorems in a calculus, this comparison is probably not fair. Thomas does nowhere systematically and exhaustively set out his equivalents of the definitions, axioms, and rules of inference of which he makes use. The order in which he proves his "theorems" is no order of strict logical dependence. Frequently he refers to principles and rules that are tacitly assumed as belonging to the Aristotelian *commune bonum* (the common stock of Aristotelian principles and ideas). The idea that the effect resembles its cause is frequently relied on as a matter of course. And clearly it would be unreasonable to criticize Aquinas for not maintaining a strict, logical order after the model of a logical calculus. Such criticism would involve an anachronism. Nor is it certain that he was absolutely clear in his own mind about the precise nature of his undertaking. Thus, when we say that Thomas tries to deduce the other properties of God from the notion of *ipsum esse subsistens*, this must be taken as a kind of reconstruction of his intentions. He nowhere says in so many words that this is what he is about to do. Nor is this his only premise; he also introduces premises drawn from the other proofs — for instance, the notion of God as *actus purus*. One may say, of course, that since *actus purus* and *ipsum esse subsistens* (and prime mover and all the other metaphysical "names of God") are applicable to one and only one substance, these terms are in a sense equivalent. Whether in fact these concepts are deducible from each other or whether they are logically independent is a question that we cannot enter into here. Even though in one sense they must be equivalent for Thomas, yet they are not synonymous. The term *ipsum esse subsistens* is more appropriate to God in some sense, than are the other terms.

We shall now, first, indicate superficially some of the lines of argument that Thomas makes use of to deduce the metaphysical properties of God. Next, we shall trace in some detail the deduction of some of his Christian properties, properly speaking.

Thomas proves the *infinitude* and *perfection* of God from the notion of *ipsum esse subsistens.*[29] God's *eternity* is proved[30] from the same notion and also by way of the notion of *immutability*, which is proved[31] by God's being simple, infinite, and *actus purus*: there can be no change or movement in God since there are no unactualized potentialities in him. That God is not body — i.e., is immaterial — is proved[32] as part of the proof of his simplicity. His immateriality can be said to be a consequence of his being pure act, i.e., without potentiality, i.e., without matter. (His immateriality is also said to follow from his infinity.)*

The above is meant to give an indication of how Thomas moves back and forth in his attempts to prove or deduce certain properties of God from certain other properties established in the five proofs. What interests us here, however, is that from these "metaphysical" properties of God, as I have called them (God as infinite, immutable, immaterial, pure act, etc.), Thomas now passes to the properties of the Christian God as he is revealed to us in the Scriptures. For instance, the Christian God is there supposed to be alive, omniscient, and loving. And now the presence in God of perfect knowledge (*quod in Deo perfectissime est scientia*) is proved[33] from his *immateriality*.

The order in which certain other properties of God are then proved is in itself highly interesting. That God is *living* is proved from his intelligence, truly in the spirit of Aristotle. Furthermore, the presence in God of perfect knowledge is used to show that God is also the *cause of things*: It is manifest, Thomas says,[34] that God causes things to be by his intellect "for his being (*esse*) is to understand (*intelligere*); therefore it is necessary that his knowledge is the cause of things." He adds, however, "according as he also has a will which joins in." (We shall comment on this additional clause in a moment.) The idea behind this argument is this: Anybody who wants to make or produce something must have an idea or a previous knowledge of what he wants to produce. And "the knowledge of God is related to all created things as the knowledge of an artisan is related to the artifact which he produces."[35]

The additional clause stipulated that the cooperation of the divine will is also necessary for the act of creative causation. This might make one think that this intellectualist view of God as prime cause is tempered by an element of voluntarism. A closer reading shows that this is not so. For in a subsequent question[36] Thomas explicitly says that the divine will is a consequence of the divine intellect: " . . . there is will in God just as there is intellect; for the presence of will follows upon the presence of intellect. . . . Therefore there is will in any being which has intellect. And thus there must be will in God as there is intellect in him." This statement is a very clear expression of a theologico-philosophical position sometimes designated as "the primacy of

---

* Cf. the reference in I.14 to I.7.1, which is the article in which God's infinity is proved.

the intellect over the will." As will be indicated later on, this problem — whether the will or the intellect should be regarded as the lord and governor of the soul — was one of the critical issues debated in medieval philosophy. There can be little doubt about the position of Aquinas. And it is easily seen that the choice thus made is consequential.

The derivation of the divine intellect from the divine will is one of the decisive steps in Thomas' reasoning concerning the nature and properties of God. It is hardly surprising now to find that God's love is viewed as a consequence of his will. Thomas asks whether there is love (amor) in God, and he answers: " . . . in whatever being there is will or appetite, there must also be love. . . . But it has been shown that there is will in God, therefore it is necessary to suppose that there is love also."[37] And to love is simply "to will some good for somebody."[38]

Thus, in sum, God's life, will, and love appear as necessarily following, or flowing from, his intellect. In simplified form, the structure of some of the derivations could be rendered as follows (the arrows stand for relationships of dependence and derivation):

esse subsistens / actus purus → immateriality / infinity (etc.) → intellect / knowledge → life / will → love

This illustration is, of course, designed to bring out the primacy of certain attributes over certain others. Now, it may be objected that this is unfair, for Thomas often stresses the view that in a sense all God's attributes coincide or are equivalent in reality. There is no distinction in *God's nature* between these properties, which are diverse only in relation to our very imperfect powers of understanding. And yet, the order in which Thomas sets out and deduces the properties is certainly not indifferent. The reactions of contemporary and later critics show very clearly that the pride of place accorded to the intellect in the Thomist description of the nature of God was considered a very important move.

There are other problems connected with the attempt to understand the nature and properties of God by means of our natural cognitive powers. Do terms such as living, intelligent, loving, good, etc. mean the same thing when applied to God as they do applied to men? If, in the two statements "God is good" and "This man is good," the term "good" has two entirely different meanings, then to use "good" about God is misleading, to say the least, for one who has only learned to use "good" in human contexts. Then he is either saying something inappropriate about God — that he is good just as humans are good — and implying that there is no difference between human and divine goodness, or he does not at all understand what it could mean to say that God is good.

Thomas argues that there are two ways in which we can approach a real understanding of God's nature, of *what* God is. One is called the *way of remotion* or the *negative* way, and is, in fact, a method of elimination. Given the proofs of God, we know that God exists as first mover, *esse subsistens*, etc. We can then also know that there are certain properties which he cannot possibly have — i.e., the properties that are inconsistent with the properties which he must necessarily have in his capacity of first mover, etc. The second, or *affirmative*, way is based on a principle of analogy between God, on the one hand, and the things created by God, on the other.

It seems important to realize that both the negative and the positive ways are attempts to understand God's nature and essence, means of understanding the predicates applied to God; they are not ways of proving that he exists. Both ways presuppose the proofs (or, at least, a knowledge that God exists). "We have shown that there exists a first being, whom we call God. We must, accordingly, now investigate the properties of this being. Now, in considering the divine substance, we should especially make use of the method of remotion. . . . For we know each thing more perfectly the more fully we see its difference from other things."[39]

If we make a list of properties thus ascribed to God, we find they are of two kinds. One kind of properties may be called negative: God is said to be immutable (without change), eternal (not in time), pure act (without potentiality), incorporeal, and simple (without composition), to mention some of the more important properties. The other kind of properties, however, cannot be said to be in this sense negative. They are properties like intelligence, living, having will, loving, goodness, etc. The first kind of properties can be understood to some extent because they immediately serve to set God apart from other things known to us. To the extent that these properties distinguish God from all other things known by us by ascribing to God a lack of properties found in other things, we can say that we approach a proper understanding of God by using the negative way.

The negative way, then, consists essentially in ascribing to God certain negative properties: immutability, etc. But this says that he cannot have certain positive properties that belong to all created things: mutability, finiteness, etc. It is clear, however, that if there is an infinite number of positive properties logically ascribable to any two objects A and B, then we say absolutely nothing about the nature of the object A if we maintain that it lacks certain properties which belong to B. But we do seem to say something about God when we say that he is immutable, infinite, etc. And there are other arguments besides to show that the way of remotion does not simply give us a series of pure negations. Indeed, the five proofs must necessarily give us *some* positive knowledge of God's nature on the argument that to prove that an object A exists is to prove that a certain set of properties is actualized. Thomas himself seems to be aware of this. "The understanding of negatives is always based on affirmatives. . . . Unless the human mind could make affirmations about God, it would be unable to deny anything about him."[40] Where, then, is this positive content?

One may argue as follows: To say that God is infinite (not finite), immutable (not changing), etc. is really to make use of a kind of double negation. In the Thomist system both "finiteness" and "mutability" — however positive in their verbal appearance — are names of imperfections or limitations. On this view the way of remotion is a way of denying that God has imperfections. And to say that God is perfect (that he possesses all perfections) is clearly not to ascribe to him a lack of positive properties. Again, we find in Thomas a full awareness of this. "God, therefore, who is his being — has being according to the whole power of being itself. Hence, he cannot lack any excellence that belongs to any given thing . . . just as every excellence and perfection is found in a thing according as that being *is* . . . all defect is absent from God. . . . No perfection, consequently, that is appropriate to this or that thing is lacking to him."[41]

The negative way really involves and throws us back upon the notions of *esse* and *perfection*. Now the positive way also operates, one may say, by means of the logic of these two terms. A thing is perfect to the extent that it has being or *esse*, to the extent that potentialities are actualized in it. But while the way of remotion brings out the differences between, say, God and man with regard to *esse* and perfections, the positive way stresses certain similarities between God and creation. God is pure *esse*; and to be created means to have received *esse* from God. Thus *esse* is something which, in a certain sense, God and creation have in common. This community or similarity makes it possible for us to argue by analogy from creatures to God. Because of the intimate tie-up between *esse* and perfection, to have being is the same as to have or partake in some perfection. Therefore, any term denoting a perfection can be used about created things and about God, and the meaning of the term will be at least partly the same in both instances of application.

Thomas distinguishes three different kinds of predication: univocal, equivocal, and analogical. A term is predicated *univocally* of two different objects, *A* and *B*, when it is used with exactly the same sense about both objects. Thus, the predicate "heavy" can be used univocally (to denote weight) about a man and a stone. A term is predicated *equivocally* about two different objects *A* and *B* when the literal sense of the term is completely different in the two instances of predication. Thus, the predicate "smiling" can be used equivocally about a person and a landscape. A term is predicated *analogically* of two objects *A* and *B* when it is used with partly the same sense about the two objects. One of Thomas' favorite examples

(drawn from Aristotle) is the term "healthy" applied to persons, medicines, food, urine, complexion, etc.[42] If I know what it is for a person to be healthy, then I can impart some knowledge by using "healthy" about food as well: it will be understood to mean, for instance, food that preserves the person in good health, or something like that.

Thomas' use of analogy is very far from clear. His theoretical treatment of it is certainly not satisfactory in the sense that it answers all reasonable questions. What precisely is the difference between analogical and metaphorical predication? In what sense does analogical predication give us an understanding which metaphorical predication does not? What are the precise conditions that must be fulfilled if we are to argue (infer) by analogy from a known object *B* to an unknown object *A*? Thomas discusses several kinds of analogical argument, and the relationships between the different kinds of analogy have been the topic of voluminous treatises. It would take us much too far afield if we were to go into these problems in detail.

We pointed out that the negative as well as the affirmative way — the latter being identical with analogical predication — both turn on the notions of *esse* and perfection. It might indeed be said that predication by analogy is simply the converse of predication by the way of remotion.

It seems fairly clear that there are certain definite conditions which must be fulfilled if analogical predication shall be made to work. It presupposes (1) a knowledge that God exists, (2) a knowledge that there is a certain resemblance, rooted in the notion of perfection, between God and the things we can observe and know directly by means of our natural cognitive powers, and (3) a certain general knowledge of his nature, namely, that he has all perfections. We might even add a fourth condition, implicit in the second, namely that God is the creator and first cause of the world and that there is a certain similarity between a cause and its effects.

That these conditions are necessary can be seen from the following arguments. Analogical predication always involves at least two objects, *A* and *B* (God and creation), which are in some sense to be compared. Of these two objects *B* alone is directly knowable by our natural cognitive powers; and this knowledge of the nature of *B* is to be the stepping-stone to an indirect or inferred knowledge of the nature of *A*. It would make no sense to attempt an argument from the nature of *B* to the nature of *A* unless the existence of *A* is granted; hence condition (1). Moreover, unless we know at the outset that there *are* points of similarity between *A* and *B*, we should never be able to go from *B* to *A*, since *A* is by definition not directly knowable; hence condition (2). (What would it mean to ask, "There exists an object *A* of an unknown nature and an object *B* whose nature we know; what can we infer about *A* on the basis of our knowledge of the nature of *B*?"

Clearly, on this basis alone, nothing at all.) Thirdly, a bare knowledge that an object A is in some unspecified respect similar to a known object B is not enough. We must have more information to begin with before we can even compare B and A, let alone make any inferences, since A is not open to inspection. Hence condition (3). (Compare: "There is an object x which is in certain respects similar to a bear. Describe x!" If the properties of a bear are very numerous — not to say infinite — this information cannot tell us much about x.)

Obviously such conditions seriously restrict the usefulness of predication by analogy from a known object to an object which is not directly knowable. It enables Thomas to say[43] about God that he is good, wise, just, etc. — i.e., to ascribe to him the perfections already found in man.* And even then there are restrictions, since these terms (good, wise, etc.) are not predicated *univocally* of God and man. In the first place, we *primarily* know these perfections from our acquaintance with mundane objects and human beings. But no perfection is perfectly realized in creation, which is to say that we cannot know what *perfect* wisdom, justice, etc. is. For *us* these words ("wisdom," "justice") signify "imperfect perfections"; in God these perfections are found realized in a "super-eminent manner."[45] If God were to use such words, *he* would have a perfect understanding of their real significance, an understanding which is denied to us. We can only approach this understanding by saying that God is wise, just, etc. — adding "but in a much more perfect manner than we."

To sum up, the negative way (the way of remotion) and the affirmative way (predication by analogy) are not so different as they might seem. They both turn on the notions of *esse* and perfection, and they presuppose a knowledge and an understanding of these concepts which are our basic tools, so to speak, in the attempt to understand the nature of God. Neither way gives us any *new* knowledge of God, strictly speaking; but they can serve to explicate and help us understand the meaning and contents of the proofs for the existence of God and both ways must presuppose these proofs. The difference between them is that the negative way contributes to such understanding of what God is by distinguishing God from created things; it underlines the differences. The affirmative way departs from and stresses the similarities. Therefore predication by analogy becomes involved in the problem of whether and to what extent the terms used to describe such similarities (names of perfections) have the same meaning when used about God and about man. The conclusion is that certain terms denoting perfections here on earth can also be used to describe the nature of God or, more properly, to approach such a descrip-

tion. From the point of view of philosophy, it seems to be a very open question what kind of understanding of God's nature we can attain by such approximate descriptions. To illustrate, by analogical reasoning we are enabled to affirm that God is wisdom. And let us keep in mind the qualifications which are necessary when we affirm this about God: that the term "wisdom" is not predicated univocally, with exactly the same sense, about God and men, that wisdom is found in God to an infinite degree, etc. Do we then really attain a degree of *positive* understanding of (an aspect of) God's nature — his wisdom — or do these qualifications simply amount to the negative rider: Wisdom — but not the way we know it. Father Copleston, who is a sympathetic interpreter of Thomas, finds this "a grave difficulty."[46] And he admits that in the nature of the case, the understanding attained by analogy cannot under any circumstances be perfect. "To demand that the content of analogical ideas should be perfectly clear and expressible, so that they could be understood perfectly in terms of human experience, would be to misunderstand the nature of analogy."[47]

Man and Morals

GOD created man in his own image. This is one of the presuppositions on which Thomas relies when giving an account of the nature of man. Thus, in order to understand Thomas' view of man we must recall his account of the nature of God.

The fact that man has a body is one of the facts that serve to set him apart from God, who is wholly spiritual and immaterial. The similarity must be found in the spiritual element of man, in his soul.[48] There is a certain similarity between the properties and structure of the human soul and the properties and structure of God, if such a way of speaking be permitted. The human intellect is related to human will and human love just as intellect, will, and love are related to each other in God. Without intellects men would have no will; without will, they would be without love. Thomas says: " ... in *whomever* there is intellect there is also will . . . ."[49] and "in *whomever* there is will or appetite, there must also be love."[50] The doctrine of the primacy of the intellect over the will is reflected in his theory of human nature also: man is indeed the *rational* animal.

It must be understood that by "soul" (*anima*) Thomas means more than just intellect and reason. Like his contemporaries, and in accordance with a tradition older than Aristotle, "soul" is used to mean the life-giving or animating principle. There was no quarrel among the thinkers of his time as to whether plants and animals also had souls. They did in so far as they were alive. But the (vegetative) soul of the plants was different from the (sensitive) soul of the animals. The specific mark of the human

---

* Thomas even says[44] that the name "God" is also used analogically. But this is really no more than a necessary consequence of his position.

soul is that it is a *rational* or intellective soul. The rational element is the noblest part of the soul, which also contains, however, two "lower" parts: the vegetative and the sensitive. The vegetative soul endows its possessor — plant or animal or human being — with powers of reproduction and nutrition. The sensitive soul — which must also contain a vegetative part — accounts for powers of sensation and locomotion, which we find in animals and in men, though not in plants. The specific ability with which man is privileged by virtue of his rational soul is the power of rational cognition. The structure of the human soul is thus hierarchical. And the operations of a higher power always presuppose the operations of a lower. This is a slightly more complex way of saying that the soul is dependent on the body, since it is to say that all our mental functions depend, directly or indirectly, on bodily functions. There is, of course, no such dependence in God.

Those features, then, which specifically characterize the human soul, stem from its intimate connection with and dependence on the body.

Man occupies an intermediate position between God (and the angels), on the one hand, and the animals, on the other. To say that the human soul is dependent on the body is to underline the kinship between man and the other animals. To view man as the only *rational* animal is to stress his privileged position as the only animal created in God's image. It is by virtue of this latter similarity, then, which is centered in the intellect, that man can become truly human. Not, of course, by the intellect alone, but in consequence of the cooperation of the intellect with our other *potentiae animae* or mental powers.

Besides the intellect, which for purposes of analysis Thomas divides into the theoretical and the practical,* the human soul "contains" at least three other (kinds of) mental powers: volition or the power of willing (the will), powers of sensation (sight, hearing, etc.), and sensuality or the sensitive appetite (*appetitus sensitivus*).

There is an analogy between reason and will on the one hand and sensation and sensuality on the other. Both will and sensuality are appetites; the former is called the rational appetite, the latter the sensitive appetite. This is to say that the objects (or ends) which these appetites desire or strive for have to be identified and pointed out for them by two different cognitive faculties. The will tends toward or strives for any object which practical reason (*ratio practica*) identifies as a good. Without the assistance of practical reason the will would not know *what* to will, so to speak. Similarly, the sensitive appetite in itself is "blind." Concrete objects of desire are supplied by the senses. Just as the will is, in one sense, a consequence of the intellect, so also sensuality (sensitive appetite) is a consequence of the power

of sensation. Intellect and sensory awareness are prior to and prerequisites for willing and desire.

It is in connection with the sensitive appetite that *passions* arise.[52] The term "passion" is used by Aquinas to signify what we would probably call emotions. A passion thus need not be a turbulent or stormy emotion. A passion is simply the motion which is called forth in the sensitive appetite upon apprehension of a proper object. Aquinas explicitly states that considered in themselves the passions are neither good nor bad.[53] In themselves, the passions are obviously necessary for human life, though from a moral point of view they are neutral. They become morally good or bad by virtue of their relationship to reason.

Aquinas' general attitude to the problem of the passions and to sensual pleasure in particular is strikingly illustrated in the question in which he discusses man in the state of innocence before the fall. He answers affirmatively — and against the teachings of certain "older doctors" — the question whether in the state of innocence there was generation by coitus — i.e., whether the children of Adam and Eve were conceived by sexual intercourse. Such intercourse, Thomas says, was natural to man because God had created him with the necessary prerequisites and organs, and "that which is natural to man, is neither taken from him nor given to him in consequence of sin."[54] The difference between our present state of sinfulness and the state of innocence is that in the latter "all the lower faculties of the soul were in every way under the dominion of reason."[55] Thus, he does not hesitate to draw the conclusion that before the fall, man's sensual delight in sexual intercourse was even greater than it is now "because his nature was purer and the body more sensitive."[56]

Passions are, so to speak, products of the interactions between body and soul. They have their origin in bodily functions; they are directed to material goods; this striving is registered as a conscious desire in the soul. The passions therefore definitely represent the less divine aspect of man. " . . . In God and in the angels there is no sensitive appetite, as there are no corporeal organs either in them; and therefore in them the good is not tied to the regulation of passions or bodily acts as it is in us."[57] The passions thus also represent something which is *specifically human*. The problem of morality is essentially a problem of how to handle the passions; and it is human reason which gives us the possibility of handling — i.e., controlling — the passions.

Because man is both body and soul, he is, metaphorically speaking, a citizen of two worlds. But this metaphor will mislead us if it invites us to believe that these two worlds are at war with each other and that man's body and soul carry on a kind of civil war within the human frame. There are, of course, Christian outlooks to which such views are not so

---

* Aquinas distinguishes *ratio* from *intellectus*. He explains[51] that they are not two faculties but two different functions of a single faculty.

alien. But it is not the view of Aquinas. For him, the term "man" designates the very union or unity of body and soul. He argues explicitly against "Plato and his followers" who hold that the term "man" does not designate a being composed of body and soul "but that the soul itself using the body *is* man, just as Peter is not a thing composed of man and clothes, but a man using clothes."[58] Thomas finds this completely unacceptable. "For animal and man are sensible and natural realities. But this would not be the case if the body and its parts were not of the essence of man and animal, rather the soul would be the entire essence of both, according to the aforesaid position; for the soul is neither a sensible nor a material thing."[59] He even argues that since the body is created not by an evil principle but by God, we ought to love the body in consequence of the love that we owe to God.

Just as there is a continuum, so to speak, from purely corporeal activities by way of sensation and the passions to purely intellectual activities and functions, so also there is a continuity between man as belonging to the natural and to the supernatural order. Of course, entrance to the supernatural order is by divine grace; and that is an act of God that man cannot influence at will. This divine grace — by which man attains to a state of perfection which he could not reach by himself alone — works by perfecting that natural human nature with which man is already endowed. "Grace does not destroy nature but completes it."[60] And morality has some of its main functions in helping to prepare human nature for perfection. In this sense, morals constitute a preamble to beatitude.

We recall that for Thomas *all* human knowledge is ultimately a knowledge of God. Now, however, since God is also the supreme end of man, whatever knowledge we may acquire is also in a sense a knowledge of this our supreme end. The more we come to know, the greater is our knowledge of God, and the better we understand and see the *perfection* of this supreme end. To the same extent, and in consequence of this knowledge, the human will (which is the rational appetite) is attracted and moved. We have already encountered the formula *ens et verum convertuntur* ("being and truth are interchangeable or equivalent"). But Thomas also says that *ens et bonum convertuntur* ("being and goodness are in the same sense equivalent"). Thus God, being *ens realissimum*, the highest being, is also perfect and infinite goodness. God as the final end of man must therefore attract the human will irresistibly.

Man's supreme goal is the vision of God in the next life — i.e., a purely intellectual and direct knowledge of God. This vision of God produces beatitude, the state of bliss whose essence, for Thomas as for Augustine, is joy at the possession of truth, *gaudium de veritate*.

It is to the achievement of this *finis ultimus*, this final end, that the moral life is also ultimately directed.

The teleological character of the ethics of Aquinas is a consequence of his view of the universe as a whole. Every action and event in the universe happens *because* there is some end toward which the event is directed or toward which the agent strives. That which gives to man his exceptional status is the fact that of all agents (apart from God and the angels), he is the only one with a conscious awareness of ends, and consequently, of means as well. Since the notions of end or goal (*finis*) and good (*bonum*) are closely related — *bonum habet rationem finis* ("the good has the nature of an end") — man is the only being who can be moved to action by *ideas* of goods and goodness, and consequently, as we shall see, of rightness.

But it does not follow that all human actions are directed by such ideas. Thomas distinguishes human actions (*actiones humanae*) from acts of man (*actiones hominis*) — a rough equivalent of the distinction between *action* and *event*. The former are the voluntary actions which, strictly speaking, alone are human. In Aquinas' account of voluntariness, which is largely Aristotelian, reason and will, the rational appetite, are ascribed different though complementary functions. In general, there are two necessary conditions of voluntariness: an internal principle of movement in the agent, and a knowledge or a cognitive awareness of the goal that the agent is seeking.[61] The will supplies the former, and reason the latter by providing the will with an object which is judged good or not good, desirable or not desirable. Being, truth, and goodness are interchangeable or equivalent notions: *ens et verum et bonum convertuntur*. Any given thing is intelligible, i.e., subject to true or false judgment (by theoretical reason), in so far as it is in being. Similarly, any given thing is subject to judgments of desirability (by practical reason), in so far as it is in being. To this point we shall return.

In this way the Thomist principle of the primacy of the intellect over the will finds expression in his ethics also. The will has or is a natural tendency to strive for the good. But this striving of the will would be completely chaotic without the intervention of reason. It is reason and reason alone that identifies objects as being good or bad, and by so doing, reason enables the will to perform determinate acts of volition.[62]

To say that the good is the object of the will is to say that any object will move the will in so far as it is apprehended as good. There is one and only one object that is good absolutely and unconditionally and in every respect: God. This is to say, there is only one object that moves the will with necessity: God. The goals which man can reach here on earth can at most be subordinate goals or means to the supreme goal. These secondary goals are not good from every point of view; they partake of the imperfections which attend upon everything human. The very fact of these imperfections makes room for the Thomist conception of human freedom of the will. The will, Thomas says, "can be free to do different things because reason can have different conceptions of the good."[63] Notice how in this way moral freedom is connected with the ideas of goods and goodness with which the intellect may move the will.

In relation to God, who is perfect goodness, the will of man is bound by laws of necessity: "It is only the perfect good (*bonum perfectum*) which is so good that the will cannot not will (*quod voluntas non potest non velle*)."[64] But in relation to the less perfect goods (*particularia bona*) that occur in our earthly existence, the will is not necessarily bound. Therefore it may be said that — once the supreme end of man is given — the chief interest of ethics must be concentrated on particular earthly goods.

The formula *ens et bonum convertuntur* permits us to say that goodness is *the same as* being. Degree of goodness is the same as degree of being, or, again, any given thing (action or event or whatever it is) is good exactly to the extent that it has *esse*.[65] Something has *esse* to the extent that it represents an actualization of potentialities. Since God is pure act (meaning that there is in Him no unactualized potentiality), He must also necessarily be perfect goodness. The notion of goodness thus presupposes the notions of potency and act.

Naturally, there will be an analogous notion of badness or evil (*malum*). Something is bad or evil to the extent that it is not in existence, or has a lack of being. This lack of being, this existential deficiency, is the same as unactualized potentialities.

There are two ways in which a human being can "have" unactualized potentialities. In the first place, there are certain potentialities which are not actualized in man simply because he does not possess these potentialities to begin with. No man can ever learn to fly like the birds because he does not have the required potentialities in him at all. But this is to say that man is *necessarily* imperfect when compared to the angels and to God. Such imperfections are irreparable, in the sense that it is impossible for man to overcome such deficiencies except by the gratuitous intervention of God. As an example, in this life all human cognition is dependent on the operations of the senses. In the state of beatitude the soul is enabled to know by immediate intellectual cognition. This is also to say that these unavoidable imperfections are not ethically relevant, except in so far as they state an absolute limit beyond which no human effort can take us.

However, it also happens that, by neglect or misfortune, man fails to actualize the potentialities that are in him. Deficiencies which arise in this manner are reparable, in principle at least. The possibility of a moral life is identical with the possibility of proceeding toward a maximum of fullness of being (*plenitudo essendi*) by actualizing the potentialities that we have in us. Thus it is that

Aquinas' general term for badness or evil is "*defectus*" or "*privatio*," deficiency or privation.

Human potentialities are actualized in human *action*. Thomas speaks not only of "*actiones humanae*" ("human actions") but also of "*actus humani vel morales*" ("human or moral actions"),[66] and the two expressions are very nearly synonymous. Keeping in mind also the contrast between action and passion, we can say that in the strict sense of the word any human action must represent an actualization of human potentialities. The potentialities which must be considered in the first place are those that are connected with human *potentiae animae* — mental powers or faculties. For it is by virtue of such potentialities that man stands out from the other animals and resembles God.

In this sense, then, we can say that any human action is good in so far as it is truly an action. For in so far as an action is a process of actualization, it also represents an existential growth or increase; and a thing has as much of goodness as it has of being (*esse*). But then it is also clear that this notion of goodness is not yet a fully *moral* notion. For human powers or faculties — intellect and will, say — can certainly be used both for good and for evil. Thomas is aware of this. Nevertheless, the groundwork of his moral theory is to be found in this basic notion of goodness — *ontological goodness*, as I shall call it. This ontological goodness can be regarded as a necessary but insufficient condition of moral goodness proper.

It would take us too far if we were to follow in detail the arguments by which Thomas develops his theory of moral goodness.[67] His general position is fairly clear and intelligible, as may be seen from the following quotation which sums up parts of the argument,

> Thus in the human action there may be said to be a fourfold goodness. The first is *generic* goodness [according to the genus] which it has in so far as it is an action. For it will have as much of goodness as it has of [true] action and being, as was said above. The second is *specific* goodness which the action receives from a fitting object. The third is *circumstantial* goodness (from the circumstances of the action) as from some accidental property. And the fourth is the *goodness deriving from the end* of the action as from its relationship to the cause of goodness. — And the action is not *good absolutely* unless all kinds of goodness are present in it.[68]

What we now have may be regarded as certain formal or abstract determinations of a concept of moral goodness as applicable to human actions. They amount to four conditions which are separately necessary and jointly sufficient. But before this schema can be applied to any given action, there are further questions which must be answered. Take the notion of specific goodness. We can do nothing about this as long as we do not know how to determine what is a "fitting object." Similar arguments can be applied to the other three conditions. That is, we have not yet been told how we can decide whether the four kinds of goodness are present or not in a given human action.

Thomas replies to such questions in a general way: That is good for man which is in accordance with reason.[69]

Such an answer appears either trivial or very controversial. It certainly explains nothing. Of course, everything now depends on what in fact it *is* to be in accordance with reason. And the concrete answer to this question will be postponed until we come to deal with Thomas' treatise on law. But there are a few things worth noting even about the purely formal schema we have so far outlined.

In the first place, Thomas' fourfold concept of goodness contains a certain insurance against oversimplification. For any action there are four distinct aspects of goodness with regard to which it must be measured or judged. Let us construct an example (none of this kind is supplied by Aquinas) by which we can show this. Take a case of theft. We do not know *enough* about an action to judge its moral quality simply by being told that it was an instance of theft. Even though theft should be considered always wrong, there is *certainly* room for degrees and distinctions that should not be obscured. Let us try to describe an instance of theft in such a way that the four criteria can be applied: (1) Deliberately and with great cunning, (2) *X* stole *Y*'s money, (3) although *Y* was poor, (4) in order to help a friend in need. In this example, the first point has reference to the generic or ontological aspect of goodness, because in acting deliberately and cunningly, *X* uses and actualizes human potentialities. Clearly, the kind of goodness here involved is ethically neutral, so to speak. The *moral* qualities of the action are derived from the following three points. Point (2) relates the (external) action to an object, money possessed by another, and *specifies* it as theft. (It should be easy to see that the external action can be "specified" in different ways depending on the object that it "is about" or manipulates. If I take my own money to help a friend in need, it is a gift and not theft. And so on.) Point (3) indicates the circumstances of the action. Although not necessarily related either to the object or to the end of the action, it is clear that such circumstances may influence the moral quality of the action as a whole. Finally, point (4) states the end or purpose of the action. All four aspects of the action are readily seen to influence its moral value, positively or negatively. The character of the end — to help a friend in need — may have some tendency to reflect morally on the other three factors. But the first three factors do not serve to determine the moral status of the end itself. We shall return to this problem below when discussing the notion of law.

Thomas' account of the fourfold goodness that can be found in human actions is the kind of account common sense is likely to consider reasonable and intelligible. Its purpose is perhaps more practical than theoretical: it may serve to remind us of questions which it may be useful to ask (and which lawyers regularly do ask) when trying to assess a given human action. It is characteristic of that aspect of Aquinas' ethics which may well be called realistic or down-to-earth: the desire to attend to the complexities of human life in its concrete details.

What is good for man is to be in accordance with reason, "*bonum hominis est secundum rationem esse.*" This summary statement of the general position of Aquinas does not say what it means to be in accordance with reason. Reason is a potentiality which can be actualized. And in Thomas' view *the law is reason actualized.* His definition of law is perfectly general. The definition contains four parts. The law is (1) *an ordinance of reason*, (2) *directed to the common good*, (3) *given by him who has care of the whole community*, and (4) *promulgated.*[70] We may regard these four parts of the definition as stating four separately necessary and jointly sufficient conditions. If we have a precept or dictate for which any one of these conditions is not fulfilled, then the fulfilment of the remaining three is not enough to give the precept the status of law.

There are three different types of wholes or communities which are in this sense regulated by laws: the universe (*communitas universi*), the state, and the individual person. Obviously it is God who is responsible for the "community of the universe," and the law by which He governs the universe is called the eternal or the divine law (*lex aeterna, lex divina*). The law regulating the political communities of men is called the human law (*lex humana*). The third community is a bit more problematic. An individual person may well be called a whole. But a person can only be called a community in an analogical sense. In order to accept a human individual as a community, we must regard the various organs, members, and faculties of that person as the individuals that make up the community. The law which is to regulate this particular community is called the natural law (*lex naturalis*). This natural law does not originate in the reason of man. It is, rather, a sort of image of the eternal law which God has projected into man. It is by virtue of the ability to read, interpret, and understand this natural law that human reason ought to be the ruler of the individual person.

We can now conclude that *everything* in the universe is governed by laws, and these laws are all of the same kind. This is apparent from the fact that Thomas gives one and only one definition of law, and further, from the analogies by which both the universe as a whole and the individual person are spoken of as communities. The basis of the analogy is the political community of men, governed by the rational dictates of an intelligent ruler.

In the first place, this means that Aquinas' notion of law is that of a prescriptive or juridical law, in contradistinction to a descriptive or, as we might now say, a scientific law of nature. Not even the eternal law which holds for all the inanimate and nonrational things in the universe — for planets, stones, rivers, plants, and animals — is a law which serves to describe the states, motions, and changes in the world. It contains precepts for how things in the world *should* be. In essence it is like a command, albeit the command of a rational will. The attempt to apply the notion of a prescriptive or normative law to all things in the universe leads to characteristic difficulties which Thomas faces with an equally characteristic openness.

The law must be *promulgated*, brought to the knowledge or awareness of those who are to be subject to the law. For the *lex humana*, this creates no problem; such laws are made known to the citizens in various ways. Nevertheless, the promulgation is an important aspect of the law; for if a law were not at all promulgated, then it would be impossible to obey it except by sheer accident. Knowledge of the law is a presupposition of knowledge of right and wrong.

We can make sense of the notion of promulgation even for the *lex naturalis*. We are born with this law implanted in us — though not, indeed, as an innate idea; there are no such things for Thomas. Rational creatures "participate in the eternal reason from which they have received their natural inclinations to seek proper actions and ends. And this participation by rational creatures in the eternal law is called the natural law."[71] By rational endeavor, man may find out what his natural inclinations are and thus also the ends he ought to seek and the acts he ought to perform.

The real difficulty arises in connection with the promulgation of the *lex aeterna* to inanimate and nonrational substances. They cannot have a law promulgated to them in any but the most farfetched metaphorical sense. For this reason alone it would be absurd to speak of such substances obeying the law. If actions performed in obedience to a law must be in some sense voluntary actions, then nobody who is not capable of voluntary action can ever come under such a law in any genuine sense.

Aquinas did not have at hand the current distinction between a prescriptive law and a descriptive one. For him, the two notions are, so to speak, rolled into one. This becomes apparent when we consider how he deals with the problem of *disobedience*. It makes poor sense, both for us and for Aquinas, to speak of planets or stones disobeying laws. It *is* possible for man, however, in a genuine sense to disobey a command or a prescriptive law. And then we may ask: Those who *trespass* against the law, can the law be said *to hold* even for them? Or does their disobedience place them outside the reach and range of the law?

In juridical law, this contingency is taken care of by the institution of sanctions in the form of punishment for those who transgress.

We observe, however, that there is no mention of sanctions in Aquinas' definition of law. The reason seems to be that he makes no important distinction between the sanctions attached to the law, and the rest of the law — the commands and prohibitions proper. The latter are addressed to the ordinary citizen who can obey or disobey them. But the citizen cannot obey or disobey the rules stipulating sanctions. For they are addressed not to him but to judges and officers of the law — in case citizens do disobey those rules of the law that demand obedience of them.

We might perhaps put the point this way. For Thomas the important thing about a law is that it should be able to move those for whom it is given. In one place[72] he says: "Two things are essential to a law: that it is a rule for the actions of men, and secondly that it should have constraining power (*vim coactivam*)."* There are two classes of substances who have to be moved by this *vis coactiva* directly (and not by way of an understanding of the law) if they are to be moved by the law at all. They are, in the first place, those who *cannot* be moved voluntarily because they lack intelligence and will — i.e., the nonintelligent substances. Secondly, there are those who *refuse* to be voluntarily moved by the rules of the law, i.e., the intelligent but disobedient substances.

Aquinas *is* troubled by the fact that it appears artificial to say of nonintelligent substances that they come under a law as defined by him. At one point he admits outright that since a law is a "reason and rule of action" (*ratio et regula operandi*), it is really only for rational creatures that laws can properly be given, for they are the only ones who can know the nature of their own action.[73] "Therefore irrational creatures come under the eternal law (*subduntur legi aeternae*) in another way in so far as they are moved by the divine providence and not by an understanding of the divine precepts as is the case with rational creatures."[74]

The conclusion now seems inescapable that only the rational creatures are subject to law in the genuine and proper sense of the terms. The law itself is something rational: "Animals which lack reason do not participate rationally in the eternal law; therefore as far as they are concerned we can only speak of law in a figurative sense (*per similitudinem*)." And this figurative sense of law must be extended even to some of the rational creatures: to those, namely, who do not voluntarily obey the law.

Thomas thus comes to the conclusion that his notion of law as established in the original definition given above finds full and proper application only to a small fraction of the universe: to those among

---

* Thomas here speaks of the *lex humana*, but the point he makes seems to be intended as a general one.

rational creatures who are morally good so that they voluntarily conform to the dictates of the law. And yet the notion of law serves an important unifying function in Thomas: It is by this one notion of law, originating in God and applicable to everything else in the universe, that the universe is held together, physically as well as morally. This slightly puzzling result is explained by the fact that Aquinas' single concept of law is required to do the jobs which today we distribute among two very different notions of law — the prescriptive and the descriptive. What we should now identify as the sanctions of a prescriptive law is extended to account for all the regularities that would nowadays be covered by scientific laws of nature.

But at the same time, we may say that this somewhat strained extension of the notion of a normative law to cover absolutely all events in the universe was a price Thomas had to pay. He did not have at hand the distinction between two types of law that might have made his account less forced.

The most general insights of practical reason are general indeed. They seem to be what we would call tautologies — for instance, that one should seek the good and avoid evil. Such principles are indeed self-evident, but in practice they are not so very useful.

Thomas does give us a key to further insight when he decrees that the natural law "follows and is in accord with" our natural inclinations. *Any* inclination in whatever part of human nature belongs to the natural law to the extent that it is regulated by reason.[75] No exception is made for sensual or bodily "inclinations." The basis for the attempt to determine the contents of the *lex naturalis* is man as he actually is, not an idealized or spiritualized superman. Of course, a privileged position is accorded to that inclination in man which makes him strive for "that kind of good which is in accord with the nature of reason. Thus man has a natural urge to know the truth about God and to live in society with others. Therefore it is part of the natural law . . . for instance that man should avoid ignorance, that he should not harm others with whom he must associate, and so on."[76]

Such arguments as these show two things. In the first place, they exhibit Thomas as a proponent of that general tradition in the philosophy of law and morals which is referred to as the theory of natural right or natural law. This places him firmly within the confines of one of the major ethical traditions of the West. Equally interesting, it seems to me, is the characteristic and personal stamp which he puts on the formulation of some of the basic aims and objectives of law and morals. In the quotation just given, notice the negative phrasings: "avoid ignorance," "should not harm others." In general, it holds that the purpose of the law is to help men to perfect their natural inclinations in the proper way. In practice, the purpose of the laws is to *prevent evil*. Their chief aim is the rather modest one of preventing the

transgressors and those that are evil from harming the good and the law-abiding. Laws are *necessary*, he says, in order to prevent evil; they are *useful* in so far as they help us to seek the good. Primarily they are intended to insure against disaster and not as a guide to happiness.

This emphasis is one of the most consistent and striking traits in Thomas' whole treatise of law in *Summa Theologica*.[77] The law is a measure, he says, and any measure must be appropriate to that which is to be measured. (We don't use minutes and seconds when we answer questions like "How long were the Middle Ages?")

> But now it is not the case that the same things are possible for those that are virtuous and for those that are not. Nor are the same things possible for the boy and the grown-up man. Therefore we do not give the same law for boys and for men. Much is permitted to the boy for which the adult would be punished or blamed. In the same way we must permit many things to persons whose virtue is not perfect, which we would not tolerate from the virtuous. However, the human laws are given for the great multitude of men, and most of them are persons of imperfect virtue. That is the reason why the law does not prohibit all the vices from which the virtuous ones abstain. The law only forbids the graver vices from which it is possible for the majority to abstain. And above all it forbids that which would injure others and where the absence of a prohibition would make it impossible to preserve human society."[78]

Human nature is not only, for Thomas, in one sense the origin and source of legal precepts. He also realizes that, by the same token, fairly strict limits must be set to the demands that the laws can make upon men in general. For "it is said in Matthew [9.17] that 'if we pour new wine' — that is, precepts for the perfect life — 'into old leather bottles' — that is, imperfect human beings — 'then the bottles will burst, and the wine will be spilt' — that is, the precepts themselves will fall into disregard and in consequence of this men will become even more corrupted than before."[79]

Where the laws — which are given "for the multitude" — leave off, the moral life begins. The moral life is the concern of the individual person. It is not a matter for public policy, but for the personal moral virtues.* And it is the task of these virtues to "perfect us by making us follow our natural inclinations in the right manner."[81]

Morality thus represents an extrapolation of human nature, a fulfillment of promises present in it. It is part of a process of perfection which runs

---

* Thomas' account of the virtues[80] is largely Aristotelian, with the notable exception, of course, that he adds to the classical moral and intellectual virtues (courage, wisdom, etc.) the three religious or theological virtues — faith, hope, and charity.

through three stages. The laws of human society safeguard the first stage, which amounts to little more than securing the groundwork and preserving the possibilities for further growth by insuring against disaster. Morality takes care of the second stage, in which man's *natural* possibilities for perfection are developed within the limits of human existence. The third stage of perfection is attained — if at all — in the next life, and by the additional, gratuitous intervention of God. Grace notwithstanding, each of the two higher stages presupposes the attainment of (some) perfection in the stage below. And all three, beatitude not excepted, *presuppose* human nature, for perfection is the fulfilment and not the extinction of that nature.

Epilogue

THE system of Thomas Aquinas is often referred to as the finest synthesis achieved in the Middle Ages. I have already suggested that it may be equally fitting to talk about a great compromise. In any event, he brought together into one system theories, outlooks, and ideas of widely differing origin and import. The two major elements thus fused were, of course, Christianity and Aristotelianism. But we can identify elements stemming from sources other than these two. There are Neo-Platonic traits in his ethics; for instance, the idea that evil is a defect, a lack of being. In his proofs of God's existence he draws upon Jewish and Arabian philosophy. All the way through he has ample references to earlier church fathers — Augustine in the first place — although the whole tenor of Aquinas' outlook and thinking is radically different from that of Augustine. Such facts as these are no doubt among the intended references when the word "synthesis" is used. But if we speak in terms of compromise, there is something else we have in mind — primarily, at least. We are thinking of the problem that occupied us during the first parts of this chapter — that of the coexistence of faith and reason, of theology and philosophy. The philosophy of Aquinas constitutes, as it were, the honeymoon of philosophy and theology, a metaphor which may be found fitting in more ways than one.

Undoubtedly, this synthesis or compromise marks a high point in medieval philosophy. It was the ultimate synthesis in the sense that synthesis could be carried no further. The generous comprehensiveness and internal coherence of the system would seem to promise a really *peaceful* coexistence between the two potential rivals. And yet, within a couple of generations critical attacks are mounted against the system of Aquinas, attacks that are out to destroy the synthesis, to disrupt the attractive continuity which runs through it. The two major critics are John Duns Scotus (1265–1308) and William of Ockham (1285?–1349), both of them Franciscans

and both of them from the British Isles. Some have seen in their criticism a deplorable decline of medieval philosophy, almost a fall from grace. Others have hailed the new development as the birth of a new philosophy, a new theology, a new outlook on God, man, and the world. Such evaluations are likely to depend on one's prejudices and will vary as the prejudices vary. But in any event, it is possible to *understand* why the Thomist synthesis was so soon to be subjected to such radical and damaging criticism.

It may be argued that Thomas' own philosophy was a presupposition of the new developments which were, ultimately, to issue in the separation of Protestants from Catholics. For the Thomist philosophy may indeed be described as the systematic and consistent attempt to think out in great detail one particular and ideally desirable solution to the problem of the relationship between faith and reason. He specified a set of conditions necessary for their harmonious coexistence. And the ideas, concepts, and theories that make up this set of conditions were stated with a considerable degree of precision and clarity. It is this very precision and clarity which makes possible the subsequent criticism. Now one could really see and survey the presuppositions and principles required for this particular solution to the problem of coexistence — which is also to say that philosophers of a different temper and outlook could begin to resent and fear the consequences.

It may be worth noting that the revolution in Christian thought which Thomas effected was stimulated by one overriding external event: the discovery of Aristotle. The equally important changes which take place from the thirteenth to the fourteenth centuries do not occur under the pressure of external events. They are the results of internal immanent criticisms of the system of Aquinas.

The process by which rival alternatives to the Thomist synthesis were established was complex and involved. In the main — though not exclusively — it occurred among thinkers belonging to the Franciscan order. Two aspects of the process will be mentioned here.

One aspect is the trend toward a more radical empiricism in philosophy. With William of Ockham, in the fourteenth century, we arrive at an empiricism so radical that we have to go all the way up to David Hume in order to find something like it. And yet, just as Hume can be said to bring to fruition a program first formulated by John Locke, so also Ockham (or, in general, the fourteenth-century empiricists or nominalists, as they are often called) can be said to carry out a program implicit — or even explicit — in Aquinas. Recall his doctrine of sensible cognition (*cognitio sensibilis*): All human knowledge, all our ideas, all our intellectual functions are dependent on and begin with sensory experience of concrete particulars. In its roots, the doctrine is Aristotelian; and Aquinas uses language foreshadowing Locke in stating it — for instance when he talks about the mind as a *tabula rasa*. The distance from this Thomist doctrine (that we have immediate knowledge of particulars only) to the central thesis of Ockham's empiricism (that the only kind of things existing extra-mentally are individuals) is after all not so great. But the consequences are considerable.[82]

It is also important to realize that Ockham, too, knew his Aristotle. In fact, he claimed to know and understand Aristotle better than did Aquinas, and thus pretended to represent a truer Aristotelianism. In some respects, Ockham may have been right about this — for instance with regard to Aristotle's theory of the sciences and his use of the various kinds of demonstration and proof. Ockham used this deeper understanding of Aristotle to criticize various points in Aquinas' theology — for instance, the use of the notion of demonstration.[83] In theology no *demonstration* is possible in the strict sense of the term, for this would require the premises from which we argue to be *necessarily true* and *evident*. But the revealed truths are certainly not necessarily true and evident.

These are two avenues of attack which are purely philosophical. One is a more consistent development of the empiricism of Aquinas himself. The other is a more consistent application of some of the ideas of Aristotle. Together they make it necessary to revise Aquinas on points of general metaphysical and methodological importance.

One of the consequences of the purely philosophical criticism leveled at the system of Aquinas was a restriction of the area and range of natural theology. It became increasingly difficult to see how natural cognition could proceed beyond the knowledge of concretely existing individuals. In other words, the Ockhamist doctrine that only individuals exist extra-mentally created problems for a metaphysician who would proceed *per ea quae facta sunt* to that which is eternal and uncreated and beyond the range of natural cognition. At the same time the *sui generis* character of supernatural theology, which stays within the framework of divine revelation, was emphasized. The result was a much sharper distinction between natural and supernatural theology and eventually between philosophy, science, and theology. The continuity between theology and rationally established knowledge was weakened or even broken.

However, while one can certainly find philosophical reasons for the new developments in fourteenth-century thought, there were also strictly religious motives behind them.

One characteristic feature of the Thomist synthesis can be described as continuity. As we proceed through the hierarchy, we find that each higher stage presupposes the actualization of the potentialities of the lower stages. Of course, at each higher stage something *new* is introduced by which the higher stage transcends the stage immediately prior to it. This element of novelty comes from above, so to speak, and not from below. If this were not so, then *all* the requirements for the final development of the whole system would be contained in its very first stage. Obviously this is an idea which must be alien to any Christian thinker. The striking feature then is the systematic continuity of the system which makes it intelligible in a specific sense. For a necessary condition for understanding a higher stage is that we should already know and understand the lower stages. This even holds for the summit of the system — for God and our knowledge of him through analogies with created things. We might say this entails a certain kind of continuity not only within the world but between God and the world as well. Another presupposition of this whole conception is the idea of God as being primarily an intellect and secondarily will and love. Against a God so conceived it was objected that he was too far removed from the living and loving God of the Bible.

One of the important *religious* concerns of Duns Scotus and later critics of Aquinas was therefore to emphasize the distance between, on the one hand, the world, including man, and, on the other hand, God. There is no continuity. The world is out and out *contingent*, and if it had pleased Him, God could have created a world entirely different from the one we now have. While the existence of the world is contingent, God's existence is necessary. God therefore must primarily be an infinite, all powerful *will*, for nothing short of an infinite, unrestricted will could bridge the gap between the necessary and the contingent. And to bridge this gap is to create.

In other words, what we find at work here in problems of central theological importance is the doctrine of *the primacy of the will over the intellect*.

It is readily seen that this principle is rich in consequences.

We can no longer infer from the world to its creator with any degree of confidence. God, being all powerful and absolutely *free*, could have created an entirely different world, and there is no necessary chain which we can follow connecting the world with God. The tendency of this kind of reasoning obviously is to weaken natural theology and to throw man back on the Bible, on the revelation itself, as the *only* source of insight in religious matters. It would be wrong to say that for Thomas the world is a logical consequence of God's intellect. But it certainly is something like that: for the creation of the world is preceded by ideas in the infinite intellect of God, and these ideas are realized by way of God's infinite will because they are seen to be good by God's infinite intellect. The Scotists and the Ockhamists would have nothing like that, nothing that could make the relationship between God and the world even remotely resemble the relationship between a logician and his proofs.

The doctrine of the primacy of the will entails a different concept of the nature of God. Above all else, He is now will and love. If man is still created in God's image, the conception of man's essential nature must also change accordingly. To be created means, for Ockham, to be wholly and completely dependent on the will of God. What is now emphasized is man's helplessness, his utter dependence, his need for love, and God's infinite grace. It is probably correct to talk about a change of emphasis from Thomas to — for instance — Ockham. The basic dogmas of Christianity were accepted as true by both of them. What *we* underline here is that this change of emphasis, the importance of which should not be underrated, is tied to a different set of philosophical ideas in which the change is motivated or by which it can at least be defended and justified.

Perhaps the most radical instance of change is found in the sphere of ethics. Being all powerful, God could also have given commandments different from those he has in fact given. Moral laws and commandments derive their validity entirely from their connection with the will of God. This will of God must remain unknown to man except in so far as God chooses to make it known, which entails, of course, that man can have no knowledge of morals apart from the explicit commandments of God. The basic commandment is that man should *love* God; and to love God means to obey Him whatever He commands. There is no room for a doctrine of natural law within such a conception — another restriction on the range of the natural cognitive powers of man, another illustration of the utter dependence of man on God.

What this amounts to, in the end, is a rather different interpretation on a series of key points of truths accepted by revelation in the Christian religion. And it is not so difficult to recognize, in some of the ideas of Scotus and Ockham, features that were to become dominant with Luther and Protestantism.

The Thomist synthesis in which all truth, theological or philosophical, is in principle of one and the same kind could be described metaphorically as a ship with only one room. The advantages of such an arrangement are considerable. Everybody in it is a member of one and the same community, although at different stations. There may be quite some distance from one end of the ship to the other, but nevertheless it is in principle possible to communicate all the way. However, a ship of this type suffers from the serious disadvantage that if it starts leaking, no matter where, then the whole ship and everybody aboard it are imperiled. If, for some reason or other, the philosophical end of it (which was also that of the sciences) does not hold water, there is imminent danger that the theological and religious end may become uninhabitable too. To exploit the metaphor, the critics of Aquinas wanted to protect the ship against such dangers. For them, there was still one ship only, but they introduced a water-tight compartment by which the ship was divided into two sections. A ship of this kind will not so readily sink even if its philosophical section — frailer because more human — should take to leaking. But the vessel now suffers from another weakness. In rough seas, it may break in two, each section taking its own course. The separate sections may even begin to behave as separate ships, and their masters may quarrel and fight each other, each claiming to sail the better ship on the safer course.

It seems to me that this metaphor can be used to illustrate, in the first place, the ideal relationship between faith and reason which Thomas Aquinas tried to institute in his system — and, secondly, some of the reasons why his critics found the system unacceptable, its attractions notwithstanding.

7

William of Ockham

RUTH L. SAW

WILLIAM OF OCKHAM was born towards the end of the thirteenth century at the village of Ockham near Guildford, Surrey. His date of birth usually appears as "circa 1300," but a recently discovered document tells us that he was ordained subdeacon on February 26, 1306. He became a student at Oxford at an early age, and soon afterward entered the Franciscan order. He taught at Oxford from about 1315 to 1323 and was a *Baccalaureus Formatus* between the years 1319 and 1323. Though he fulfilled the requirements for the degree of *Magister Theologiae*, he never occupied an official chair of theology, so remaining an *Inceptor*. Later he became renowned as the *Venerabilis Inceptor*, not, as is sometimes thought, the "originator of the nominalist school," but simply one who has not become a Master.

At that time, it was the custom for teachers of philosophy to inaugurate their courses of lectures with a course on the *Four Books of Sentences*. This was a collection, compiled by Peter Lombard in about 1150, of opinions of the Fathers of the Church upon the principle topics of theology. The teachings of St. Augustine held the chief place in this collection, which was used as a textbook. Ockham's commentary was unorthodox in its empiricism and in its rejection of the traditional grounding of theological doctrines. In 1324 he was summoned to Avignon by the Pope to undergo an examination of his teachings. Judgment upon them was delayed, and in the meantime, Ockham was confined in the Franciscan house at Avignon. In 1326, a commission of six theologians pronounced fifty-one articles in his commentaries "heretical and pestilential." Ockham refused to retract them and, in 1328, further endangered his position. The Pope had condemned the doctrine of absolute apostolic poverty practiced by the Mendicants of the Franciscan order, but his condemnation had been resisted by the General of the Franciscan order, Michael of Cesena. Ockham now joined himself to Cesena, signing the protest which Cesena had drawn up against the Papal Bull.

On the night of May 24, Ockham and Cesena, accompanied by the brilliant Franciscan lawyer Bonogratia, succeeded in escaping from Avignon. They made their perilous way to Pisa, where Ockham placed himself under the protection of the Emperor, Louis of Bavaria. Louis had proclaimed the deposition of Pope John XXII in 1327 and set up an anti-Pope of his own choosing in Rome. By joining Louis, Ockham effectively cut himself off from the authority of the Pope, who thereupon excommunicated him.

The Emperor now returned to Munich and Ockham went in his train. Ockham, it is said, had undertaken to defend the Emperor with his pen, and he now devoted himself, in his monastery at Munich, to writing a series of pamphlets directed against the Pope. The most important of these pamphlets were the *Eight Questions Concerning the Power and Dignity of the Pope* and the *Dialogue between Master and Disciples upon the Power of Emperors and Popes*. These pamphlets advocated stricter discipline within the Church and, more daringly, the principle of political representation in Church and State. Not surprisingly, Ockham stressed the importance of the individual as against the corporate body, and placed the source of the "law of nature" in the moral decisions of individual citizens.

Meanwhile, the Emperor was shifting his position in relation to the Papacy. He entered into negotiations with Pope Benedict XII and endeavored to find excuses for his past actions, foreswearing in the process his former partisans, including Cesena and Ockham. Finally, in 1344, he agreed to the most humiliating conditions at the hands of Pope Clement VI. Added to the troubles of this period was the devastation by the Black Death, to which Ockham succumbed in 1349. He was buried in the old Franciscan Church in Munich. His tomb was moved from its place before the altar in 1802, and his remains were taken to a place which is still unknown.

THE SCHOLASTIC PHILOSOPHERS of the thirteenth and fourteenth centuries were primarily theologians and incidentally philosophers, dealing with epistemological and metaphysical problems as they presented themselves in connection with the existence and attributes of God, his relation to his creatures, and their knowledge of the world and its maker. Consequently, much medieval speculation on philosophical topics appears scattered in theological writings, and Ockham is no exception in this respect. He produced no systematic account of his philosophy, though he planned a complete treatise on science — *Philosophia Naturalis* — of which he wrote only the first part. His writings on logic form the most complete and systematic part of his work, comprising not only the *Summa Totius Logicae* but also expositions of Aristotle's doctrine of the Categories, the *De Interpretatione*, and Book IX of the *Topics*. He treated political problems in his pamphlets written against Pope John XXII. His position in all branches of philosophy and in his theology was remarkably consistent. He was a nominalist, insisting on the primacy of the individual both as being and as object of knowledge, and as the source of moral principles and of political power. His logical doctrines contained accounts of meaning and truth in accordance with his nominalism.

In his years at Oxford, science and mathematics were flourishing, and though like his celebrated predecessor, Roger Bacon, he accepted the Aristotelian account of science, he insisted that a true interpretation of Aristotelian doctrine needed no absolutes whatever. Particular moving bodies at particular times and places gave all that was needed, with no recourse to space, time, and motion. Moreover, everything that is and happens in this world is contingent, dependent for its existence and actions upon the free will of God. "Whatever God produces by means of secondary [i.e. created] causes, God can produce and conserve immediately and without their aid."[1] Hence, in order to acquire knowledge of created beings, it is necessary to find out what they actually are; for everything might be otherwise. This is the foundation of Ockham's empiricism.

Language, Logic and Meaning

NOT only is Ockham's logic the most completely developed part of his work; it is also central to it. It gives the account of meaning and truth implicit in his other works and supplies the method to be used in the pursuit of knowledge, the method of analysis. The doctrines of signification and supposition are thus the foundation both of his logic and of his thinking in general. It will therefore be suitable to make this our starting point.

Ockham distinguishes very carefully between kinds of signs. The general characteristic of all signs of whatever kind is that "when apprehended, they bring to knowledge something other than themselves."[2] A sign may be anything at all; a mental event, a word, a puff of smoke, the barrel hoop before an inn, all equally make known something other than themselves. An intuition may make known the existence of the thing intuited, a word the existence of the speaker, a hoop outside an inn the existence of wine within, and smoke the existence of fire. These are all "natural" signs and they share in common a further feature: No one of them can yield *primary* cognition of the thing they signify. We apprehend the sign, but it can make that which is signified known only if it is stored in the memory, i.e., *habitually* known.[3] The apprehension of the sign makes the thing signified actually known. Thus, if we have no habitual knowledge of fire and of the fact that it produces smoke, smoke cannot operate as a sign of fire. This has nothing to do with the possibility of inference, for so

125

far we have no propositions. We have two "things," smoke and fire, and primary knowledge of one cannot cause primary knowledge of the other, but only reinstate habitual knowledge.

"Word" appeared in the list of natural signs, but in this context it is a thing or an occurrence like any other. However, words are also conventional signs, and as such possess features of logical interest. Smoke naturally signifies fire, "smoke" naturally signifies a speaker and conventionally signifies that for which it stands (*supponit*), i.e., smoke. Conventional signs are sounds if they are spoken (*voces*) and marks if they are written; when they are combined, they form *orationes*. The spoken expression is "uttered with the mouth and is intended to be heard with the bodily ear"; the written is "in some medium and is seen or is able to be seen, with the bodily eye." They both mean, secondarily, what the mental expression means primarily: they do not mean the mental expression, but they all mean the same thing or state of affairs. Mental terms are described as "intentions or passions of the mind," naturally signifying what they stand for; and they are formed (*nata*) to be parts of mental propositions. They are in no language and cannot be uttered externally. Spoken and written words are unique among signs in that they are intended to mean what they stand for. Mental signs mean what they stand for naturally.

We may now look a little more closely at the relationship between written and spoken words, on the one hand, and mental terms on the other. Written and spoken words presuppose mental terms; for example, the words "the sun" in the sentence "the sun is shining" presuppose a mental term which is an element in a mental proposition, and which naturally stands for and means the particular bright object in the sky. "The sun" stands for and means that same object conventionally. If the mental term changes its meaning, then the conventional terms also change their meanings without the need for a new convention.[4] Mental terms change their meaning if and only if the objects they signify change their qualities. If Socrates ceases to be white, then the mental term Socrates which is an element in the mental proposition "Socrates is white" changes its meaning. "White" also changes its meaning but in a slightly more complicated manner which will be investigated later.

There is one obvious difficulty in this view of the relation between mental and spoken propositions; confronted with Socrates we might say "He is white," "That one is white," "Socrates is white," though presumably the mental proposition, since it is in no language, would be identical in the three cases. Ockham meets this and similar difficulties by limiting the elements in spoken language which have mental correlates. In general, only those distinctions arising from the necessity of meaning will presuppose a similar distinction in mental propositions.

Distinctions arising from "grace of language" or from some similar accidental cause belong to mental and written propositions only. The only distinctions necessitated by meaning among the elements of language are into nouns, verbs, adverbs, conjunctions, and prepositions. Pronouns, then, are among those words having no mental correlates, presumably because "he" — indicating Socrates — is synonymous with "Socrates." Synonymous terms, for instance, verbs and their participles, do not appear as separate and distinct elements in mental propositions. "Socrates runs" is the same proposition as "Socrates is running," unless the first proposition is intended to mean that Socrates is in the habit of running; but this is a real difference in meaning which could be expressed by an adverb and it would be a separate element in the mental proposition. There seems to be no reason for preferring nouns to pronouns, however. It is difficult to see what would be meant by preferring "Socrates" as a mental term to "he" in an intention of mind not expressible in words. It would be better to say that "he" and "Socrates" presuppose indifferently the same intention of the mind. The only possible reason for preferring "Socrates" is that it could be used in the absence of Socrates to revive habitual knowledge of Socrates, while "he" needs a context either of earlier remarks or of the actual presence of Socrates to ensure reference. This is true to a certain extent even of "Socrates," since more than one person may be called Socrates.

There is one important class of names which people have sometimes thought to be distinct from another class where the distinction is not necessitated by meaning. Some abstract names mean the same as concrete names, though men have thought that in the one case they were talking about a quality and in the other a substance. "*Equus*" ("horse") is synonymous with the abstract term "*equinitas*" ("horseness") formed from it, not in the narrow sense that everyone using the names thinks that he is referring to the same thing, but in the wider sense that nothing is expressible by the use of the one name which is not expressible by the use of the other. That this is so is indicated by the fact that we have not bothered to form abstract names from all names of substances. We know, for instance, that we can say all we want to say about oxen without forming the abstract name "oxness"; in the same way, we do not find it necessary to talk about "Socratesness," but only about Socrates. Whether we use the word "*equus*" or "*equinitas*" is determined by elegance of utterance, not by the necessity of meaning.

"*Deus*" and "*Deitas*," then, are synonyms in the second sense: anything we wish to say about God may be said by using either word. In the case of two words, such as "*homo*" and "*humanitas*," it might be objected that we can say "*Homo currit*," "man runs," but not "*Humanitas currit*," or "humanity runs." Ockham's reply is that the abstract term means the same as the concrete term, plus some such phrase as "as such." Wherever we can say "*Homo in quantum*," "man as such," we can substitute "humanitas." "Humanity is rational" means nothing more than "Man as such is rational." This is not to forsake Ockham's central position that an abstract noun does not always name a quality, for a proposition containing a phrase such as "as such" is an exponible proposition. The proposition "Socrates runs in so far as he is a man" is false because when expanded into its component propositions it is seen that they are not all true. It means the same as:

1. Socrates is a man.
2. Every man runs.
3. If something is a man, something runs.

On the other hand, "Socrates is rational in so far as he is a man" is true, for each of the three component propositions is true:

1. Socrates is a man.
2. Every man is rational.
3. If something is a man, something is rational.

Ockham holds, however, that some abstract and concrete names are not synonyms. For instance, such abstract names as "justice," which are not formed from the names of substances but from the name of a particular kind within the species, i.e., "just man" as opposed to "man," are not synonymous with their corresponding concrete names. Justice is a virtue, the just man is virtuous, but justice is not virtuous nor is the just man a virtue. Ockham's wider sense of "synonymous" might have been applied in this case, but it does not seem to have occurred to him to investigate the possibility of expanding "Justice is a virtue" into propositions concerning just men, their virtue, and their justice. In his investigation into what is required for the truth of different kinds of propositions, he does not deal with propositions such as "Justice is a virtue." What he means by "substance" is Aristotelian substance, so that "justice" is not the name of a substance. It would be in conformity with his general view to substitute an adverb for the adjective — "Socrates acts justly" for "Socrates is just," and "to act justly is to act virtuously" for "justice is a virtue."

Complexes of terms — *orationes*[5] — in a wide sense may be any combinations of words: a collection of names or adjectives is an *oratio*. In the narrow sense, only a "suitable" arrangement of words is an *oratio* and what is suitable is determined by grammar. Such a suitable arrangement of words is a sentence, and a sentence may be a wish, a prayer, a command, or a question, or it may convey information. The last is the only type of sentence of interest to logicians: sentences of this type may have truth and falsity predicated of them, and they alone are *propositiones* or *enuntiationes*. We may now formulate the rule according to which spoken and written signs do or do not presuppose a mental term. It is that

whatever changes the truth or falsity of a proposition has its corresponding part in the mental proposition,[6] so that every element in the mental proposition has a corresponding part in the spoken or written proposition, but not *vice versa*.[7] We are now also in a position to distinguish language signs from signs of all other kinds. Like all other signs, language signs bring to cognition something other than themselves, but unlike all other signs, this cognition may be primary in the case of words. It is easier to see this point in connection with mental signs. On being confronted with smoke for the first time, the mental term corresponding to the word "smoke" is a sign of smoke. If the mental term were to occur again, then the habitual knowledge of smoke would be revived, but it is not a condition of a mental sign's being a sign that it should always bring a secondary cognition to mind. Correspondingly, the word "smoke" uttered on the first occasion of seeing smoke would be on that occasion a sign of smoke. It is not clear, however, whether the mental sign and the word would be *used* as signs here. It may be that it is a condition of their *use* as signs, that they should have occurred with a primary cognition of the thing signified and then function by bringing the thing to secondary cognition. This would correspond with the condition of smoke's being a natural sign of fire that they should first have been perceived together.

We may now turn to the difficult question of the nature of mental terms. They are described by Ockham in the following phrases: *intentio animae, conceptus animae, passio animae, similitudo rei*, and, following Boethius, *intellectum*. He defines *intentio animae* thus: "*Intentio est quoddam in anima, quod est signum naturaliter significans aliquid pro quo potest supponere: vel quod potest pars propositionis mentalis.*"* He points out that there are three possible interpretations of the phrase "somewhat in the mind." It may mean that the "intention" is constructed by the mind, or that it is a certain subjective quality existing in the mind and distinct from the act of understanding, or it may mean that the "intention" is the act of understanding itself. This last view has in its favor the fact that there seems no point in postulating many things when we can do with fewer — "*Frustra fit per plura quod potest fieri per pauciora.*" Accordingly, Moody defines "intention" as "the act or habit of understanding what something is or what it can be."[8] "*Conceptus*" and "*intellectum*" are simply names for the "intention," but "*similitudo rei*" and "*passio animae*" are in a different category. *Passio* seems to imply that the mind is passive in forming concepts, which is the very view that Ockham seems anxious to avoid. *Similitudo rei* is also puzzling. If a *likeness* of the thing is formed in the mind, then again the use of mental signs is not an active process but an act

* "*Intentio* is something in the mind which is a sign naturally signifying something which it is capable of standing for."

distinct from the *intentio* and used by it. This last phrase lends some color to the mistaken view that Ockham's "universal" is a kind of composite image. The explanation of these anomalies is probably that Ockham was more concerned with the logic of signs than with their psychological accompaniments, and simply mentioned current ways of describing what takes place when we are said to know states of affairs.

This becomes clear when we look at what Ockham has to say about universals. He treats them entirely in a logical context, pointing out that "universal" is a term of second intention — that is to say, a term about terms and not about things. The form " . . . is a universal" requires the name of a name, not the name of a thing, for its subject. As opposed to universal, "singular" is also a term of second intention. "Singular" may be taken in two senses:

1. For that which is one and not many. In this sense, a universal is singular, since it is a certain quality or intention of the mind predicable of many things, or a single word common by convention and applicable to many things but as a single word is one and not many.

2. In the second sense, a singular is that which is one and not many, and is a sign of anything that is singular in the first sense. "Socrates" is a single word and is a sign of a single man, so that it is singular in both senses. In the second sense, no universal is singular, for it is intended to be a sign of many, or to be predicated of many. In the first sense, everything is singular, for the commonly accepted definition of "universal" as that which is many and not one applies to nothing. There are *signs* that stand for one thing and *signs* that stand for many things, but every existing thing must be one in number. Ockham offers several proofs that a universal cannot be an entity. If it were a single substance outside the mind, say "man," there would be no reason why it should be one man rather than another; Socrates, Plato, Aristotle, either, or all of them would be equally candidates for being "man." If it is not a single substance outside the mind, then it is many; but we could ask, "Many what?" If "man" is many men, then it is not a universal but a set of individuals. If many *universals*, then we have to ask the same question again, and so *ad infinitum*. Again. if "man" exists outside the mind, then no new man can come into existence nor can any man be annihilated, for this would be to change or destroy an already complete "manhood."[9]

"Universal," then, is a term of second intention, a name of signs and not of things. It means that a name is the name of many things, while "singular" means that a name is the name of an individual. "White is a universal" means that "white" names Socrates or Aristotle or . . . , and "universal" names

"white" or "man" or . . . ; "singular" names Socrates" or "Aristotle" or . . . . It must not be forgotten, however, that it is the mental term that primarily stands for what it names, so that universals are primarily concepts and secondarily spoken or written names that stand for the same thing for which the mental term stands. So far, we have been speaking about signification, but terms entering into propositions have "*suppositio*," standing for that which they name in a different sense. "*Homo*" signifies Socrates, or Plato, or . . . ; but in the proposition "*Omnis homo rationalis est*," the term "*omnis*" is syncategorematic — that is, it means nothing by itself but makes determinate the "supposition" of the term "*homo*." "*Omnis homo*" stands "confusedly and distributively" for all men. This must not be interpreted as meaning that a universal confusedly and distributively stands for all men, almost as if it were a composite image, but that in uttering the proposition, the speaker is prepared to run over in his mind the various instances. It is true that the universal proposition presupposes a mental proposition composed of terms, and that a mental term is evoked in the mind by acquaintance with an individual; but repeated occasions of acquaintance with similar individuals does not result in a composite image but in habitual knowledge — that is, a readiness to recall similar individuals on each new occasion. Ockham, in fact, is not interested in the psychological status of concepts; he is simply clear that to have a concept is to be mentally active, and that nothing but individuals and acts of mind are essential to the formation and use of concepts. Concepts do not represent an external reality, though this does not make them into fictions. They are the ways in which we conceive or know individuals.

In his account of "what is required for the truth of propositions," Ockham divides propositions into two classes: (1) singular, particular, and indefinite propositions; and (2) universal propositions. Of class (1), he says that it is sufficient and necessary for their truth if the subject and predicate stand for the same things. "That one (or Socrates) is a man" is true if and only if Socrates is indeed a man. Outside a proposition, "man" signifies Plato or Aristotle or . . . ; within the proposition, "Socrates" and "a man" stand for the same object, though "man" evokes the recognition of the similarity of Socrates and other individual men. The indefinite proposition "*Homo animale est*" is true if and only if everything indicated by the predicate is also indicated by the subject. It would be false if there were a single thing denoted by "man" which was not also denoted by "animal."

A necessary proposition is one that is true whenever it occurs. A mental proposition is necessary if it is true whenever it occurs in the mind; a spoken proposition, if it is true whenever it is uttered; and a written proposition, whenever it is written. A necessary proposition may be expressed as a hypothetical, so that there may be necessary statements about individuals if we know not only that every S is P, but also know the reason why it is P. "If anything is S it is P" is a necessary statement, although we may have to know the S's by experience. "This S is P" is contingent, since it refers to a particular occurrence.

Propositions in which there are fictitious terms are plainly false. "The chimaera is nonexistent" is false, not in the sense that the chimaera is *not* nonexistent, but in that there is nothing of which we can say that it is nonexistent. Ockham shows that such a proposition is exponible, and when it is stated in its full form it will consist of two propositions, one of which is false. "*Chimaera est non ens*" is equivalent to "*Chimaera est illud*" and "*Illud est non ens*," the first of which is false. We might also interpret "*illud*" ("that") as a variable, "somewhat," and the second proposition as saying of it that no argument for that variable is to be found.

Hypothetical propositions are generally understood by Ockham as compound propositions in which the components are joined by connectives. He lists the subclasses of hypothetical statements as the conditional, the copulative, the disjunctive, the temporal, and the causal, and adds that more might be adduced. In his account of inferential operations, he states the equivalences familiar in modern formal logic between these various forms, including the famous De Morgan law: The contradictory opposite of a copulative proposition is an affirmative, disjunctive proposition in which both parts of the former are denied.[10] The conditions for the truth of compound propositions are similarly "modern," as is the recognition of a relation similar to material implication. From an impossibility anything follows: "You are a donkey, therefore you are God." What is necessary follows from everything: "You are white, therefore God is triune." He adds, however: "But these consequences are not formal ones and they should not be used much, nor, indeed, are they used much."[11]

A causal proposition consists of at least two categorical propositions linked by the connective "because" or an equivalent. What is required for its truth is the truth of the component propositions, and it must also be true that the one contains the reason for the truth of the other. We may infer the simple conjunction of the two parts from a causal proposition but not *vice versa*. The denial of a causal proposition will be a disjunction of the denial of both parts, and a denial of the connection between the two parts. " . . . *ut contradictio istius:* '*Petrus dormit, quia Plato currit*' *aequivalet isti:* '*Petrus non dormit vel Plato non currit*' *vel haec non est vera:* '*Petrus dormit, propter hoc quod Plato currit*' " ("Thus either the denial of 'Peter sleeps because Plato runs' is equivalent to 'Either Peter does not sleep or Plato does not run' or the following statement is false: 'Peter sleeps on account of the fact that Plato runs' ").[12]

What the connection between the two parts consists in must be considered in relation to Ockham's account of science.

Ockham's description of the difference between rational science, that is to say, logic, and empirical science is that logic is about terms of second intention and science is about things. Universals are terms that stand for more than one thing, so that logic alone deals with universals. Science deals with individual things about which it makes statements which are universally true — that is to say, true in all instances. It has intuitive knowledge as its foundation, even in such a case as knowledge of the proposition that the whole is greater than the part. We assent to the truth of this statement as soon as we understand the meaning of the terms; but without experience, the statement would not be formulated nor should we understand its meaning. Intuitive knowledge may be of the existence of an individual thing or of its relationship to other things or of it as possessing qualities.

> . . . when some things are known, of which the one inheres in the other or is locally distant from the other or is related in some way to the other, the mind straightway knows, by virtue of that simple apprehension of those things, whether the thing inheres or does not inhere, whether it is distant or not, and so with other contingent truths. . . . And in general, every simple apprehension of a term or of terms, that is, of a thing or things, by means of which some contingent truths, especially concerning the present, can be known, is intuitive knowledge.[13]

Intuitive knowledge is immediate: "The thing itself is known immediately without any medium between itself and the act by which it is seen or apprehended."[14] Such knowledge leads directly to a contingent, but evident, proposition that a thing exists or is white or is near to another thing. It is not sensation, but the apprehension of an individual thing and its qualities and relationships. Not only do we know intuitively material things, we also know our own acts and can formulate propositions such as "there is an understanding," "there is a will."[15] We also know intuitively self-evident propositions (*nota in se*) and the truths of revelation.

Causal propositions were said to be those for which the antecedent gives the reason for the truth of the consequent, but when Ockham investigates the nature of the causal connection, it turns out to be something very like regular sequence among events. To give X as the reason for Y is to assert that when X is present Y follows and that when X is absent, whatever other factors may be present, Y does not follow.

> . . . it is proved that fire is the cause of heat, since when fire is there and all other things [that is all other possible causal factors] have been removed,

heat follows in a heatable object which has been brought near [the fire]. . . . [Similarly] it is proved that the object is the cause of intuitive knowledge, for when all other factors except the object have been removed, intuitive knowledge follows.[16]

A cause is that "on the positing of which another thing is posited and on the nonpositing of which that other thing is not posited."[17]

Ockham's position is simply that every created thing is separate and distinct from every other created thing. Intuitive knowledge of one thing cannot yield intuitive knowledge of another thing, so that no abstract reasoning can yield a causal proposition. There are regular sequences as a matter of fact, but no connection between two distinct things can be necessary except in the sense of "true in every instance." This is a contingent matter, dependent entirely on God's will; and although we may continually observe the connection between fire and heat, yet it might be otherwise. Ockham is anxious to preserve God's absolute freedom. Just as there are no "natures" or "essences" to be a model for God's creation, so there is no necessary connection between one thing and another. What has been brought about by secondary causes could have been caused directly by God, even though as a matter of fact the created world displays order. The order of the world is entirely dependent on God's choice, so that it could not be possible to deduce it *a priori*.

Ockham's treatment of relations generally is in keeping with his account of causality. The world is composed of separate and distinct entities and their qualities, each one of which depends upon God for its creation and preservation, and between which there are no entities named "relations." There is no "order" of the universe separate and distinct from the existent parts of the universe. There is no relation of paternity distinct and separate from fathers and their children. If there were, we should have the absurdity of supposing that God might bestow "paternity upon a man who had never generated a child, or similarity upon red and white. A man is called a 'father' when he has generated a child and there is no need to postulate a third entity, paternity, linking the two existents. A relation is not the *same as* that which is related, but it is an 'intention' in the mind, signifying several absolute things."[18] Relations can thus be analyzed into two absolute things so that the causal relation is analyzable into two separate and distinct entities, of which it is true to say that one invariably succeeds the other. This is discovered by experience and there is nothing further to be discovered.

In the account of intuitive knowledge, the presence of the object was described as the cause of our intuitive knowledge of it. In conformity with his definition of "cause," Ockham holds that in this case too the cause and effect are distinct and separate, each dependent on God but not dependent on one another. It follows, then, that God might produce intuitive knowledge in us in the absence of the object supposed to be apprehended. "Intuitive knowledge cannot be caused naturally unless the object is present at the right distance, but it could be caused supernaturally."[19] "There can be by the power of God intuitive knowledge concerning a nonexistent object."[20] But God cannot produce a contradiction, and to say that I have intuitive knowledge of a nonexistent object is a self-contradiction, since intuitive knowledge is "evident" knowledge. "God cannot cause in us knowledge such that by it a thing is seen evidently to be present although it is absent, for that involves a contradiction, because such evident knowledge means that it is thus in fact as is stated by the proposition to which assent is given."[21] The impossible state of affairs is thus the conjunction of absence of stars and "evident" knowledge in me of the presence of the stars, though it is possible that God might produce in me a psycho-physiological condition indistinguishable from intuitive knowledge of the stars, in the absence of stars. That is, "God can cause a 'creditive' act in me by which I believe that an absent is present." I should then assent to the false proposition that here are stars. This "creditive" idea will, however, be "abstractive", not intuitive. Ockham seems to mean by this that I am not involved in the contradiction "what is present is absent," and moreover, that I am not seriously deceived, since my state yields me "abstractive" knowledge of what it would be like to be in the position of seeing the stars, though no star is present. This becomes clear when Ockham goes on to say that it would be a contradiction to say that I intuitively apprehend a chimaera, but it is not a contradiction to say "that that which is seen is nothing in actuality outside the soul, so long as it can be an effect or was at some time an actual reality."[22] God could thus cause in me a vision of what has been or what will be, though there is still the assent to the false proposition "It is so, here now." It is true that Ockham distinguishes evidence, which is objective, from certitude, which is a psychological state. This, however, is to spoil his account of intuitive knowledge as "evident".

It must be remembered, however, that in this context Ockham is not talking of the natural course of events. God, as a matter of fact, does not act in this way; it is simply a truth of faith, not provable, that he is omnipotent and consequently could act in this way if he chose. In considering the actual course of events, the intuitive apprehension of nonexistent objects does not arise. Doubt as to the "evidence" of immediate apprehension is not a doubt about our natural knowledge of the actual world, but only a recognition of our absolute dependence as creatures on our Creator. This relation of dependence is no more a "real" entity than is any other relation. All that is needed is God, on the one hand, and creatures, on the other — though Ockham is careful to point out that he is willing to call the relation of a stone to God "real" rather than mental if all that is meant is that the stone's dependence upon God is not dependent upon our knowledge of it; but it is still not a separate entity.

One of Ockham's arguments against the reality of relations is noteworthy. If I move my finger, its position is changed in relation to all the other things in the universe. If there are real relations apart from the objects related, then "it would follow that at the movement of my finger the whole universe, that is, heaven and earth, would be at once filled with accidents,"[23] which is absurd. At a fresh movement of my finger, then the world would be at once peopled with a fresh set of accidents. Complete knowledge of any one part of the world is, then, a possibility, and there is no implication at all that things cannot be understood out of relationship to other things and to God. This is the true empirical spirit of Ockham's philosophy. If we wish to know the things in the world and their interconnections, there is no method but to examine things, to note their qualities and their usual accompaniments. We may note that certain qualities co-inhere in the one object, and that objects of a certain kind are followed by objects of another kind, and express our knowledge in universal propositions; but these will mean no more than the individual instances.

It does not follow, however, that there can be no causal inference. Ockham accepts the Aristotelian account of science and of the possibility of demonstration and of the existence of indemonstrable principles. The most complete account of what he understands by science, or natural philosophy, is given in the *Prologue to the Exposition of the viii Books of the Physics*. The main points that he is concerned about making are the following:*

1. Knowledge is a *habitus* ("disposition") or collection of *habitus* in the soul in the same sense in which a single act of knowledge is in the soul. (After many acts of thought, a person is more fit and more inclined to have similar acts of thought than he was before.)
2. Knowledge is certain cognition of something that is true, either taken on trust or arising from an immediate apprehension, in which case it could be of a contingent fact, or arising from the immediate apprehension of a necessary truth — i.e., a first principle, or finally, an evident cognition of a necessary truth caused by the cognition of necessary premises and a process of syllogistic reasoning.
3. The *habitus* constituting *scientia* issue in propositions, and a collection of such propositions is a science.
4. A science is not one in the sense that it is about the same subject. The propositions constituting

* It is to be noted that Ockham uses the term *scientia* both for "knowledge" and for "science."

a science are universal, having universal terms as their subjects; but each proposition is about individuals. Each proposition is *about* the individuals for which its subject term stands, so that the collection of propositions is about a collection of objects. Knowledge is of the fact which is expressed by the whole proposition, but it is about the objects designated by the subject term. When people talk about *the* subject of metaphysics, or of natural philosophy, they usually mean that there is one subject which is prior to all others. If there is such a subject in natural philosophy, it consists of sensible substances composed of matter and form. Propositions concerning the substances constitute a science, but the subject matter of the science is constituted by the simple terms of the propositions.

The propositions of natural science are composed of terms, not of things, so that properly speaking the science of nature is about the concepts "mutable thing" and "corruptible thing," not about mutable and corruptible things. Improperly and metaphorically speaking, we may say it is about mutable and corruptible things, since it is about the terms that stand for these things. This, says Ockham, is what Aristotle meant when he said that knowledge is not about singular things but universals which stand for individual things. This is the important respect in which logic differs from the other sciences and which leads some people to deny that logic is a science. It is constituted by propositions composed of terms which do not stand for things but for other terms. However, knowledge of these propositions is possible and they may be true or false.

Scientific Thinking

OCKHAM now proposes to consider the science of nature in detail and to determine what it deals with. He is not, of course, a scientist in the modern sense of the word; his project is to analyze the concepts employed in the systematic description of the physical world. His standpoint is clearly expressed in the following passage from the *Tractatus de Successivis*:

Nouns which are derived from verbs and also nouns which derive from adverbs, conjunctions, prepositions, and in general from syncategorematic terms . . . have been introduced only for the sake of brevity in speaking or as ornaments of speech; and many of them are equivalent in signification to propositions, when they do not stand for the terms from which they derive. . . . Of this kind are all nouns of the following kind: negation, privation, condition, perseity, contingency, universality, action, passion . . . change, motion, and in general all verbal nouns deriving from verbs which belong to the categories of *agere* and *pati*, and many others which cannot be treated now.

In the first part — the only part that was actually written — of *Philosophia Naturalis*, Ockham deals with the fundamental notions of motion, time, and place in accordance with his scheme and in the spirit of the above quotation. In his analysis, Ockham never lets go of the fundamental position that scientific propositions are made true and false by actual individual states of affairs, just as are the statements of everyday discourse. Science is not a superstructure of conventional concepts invented for the sake of the system: it presupposes the external, knowable physical world, and its statements are true and false in the same sense as singular statements of perception; that is, they are true if they correspond to the facts, and are otherwise false.

> And, therefore, the numerous distinctions by means of which it is distinguished that mobile or mutable things can be considered thus, or thus, and that in one mode they are mutable, and in another mode, immutable, and in one mode contingent, and in another necessary, effects nothing. . . . My consideration or yours has nothing to do with the fact that a thing is mutable or immutable. . . . To hold that that thing which is outside is, owing to one consideration of mine mutable, and owing to another consideration of mine, immutable, is simply false and asinine, just as if I wish to say that Sortes, because of one consideration of mine is white, and because of another, is black.[24]

His general position, then, is that the only absolutes are the two kinds of entity existing in the world, substances and qualities, and whatever is truly said about the world must be reducible to statements involving these two kinds of entity. Statements apparently about the absolutes, motion, time, and place are to be shown as equivalent to statements about actual moving objects, their successive states, and their positions in relation to one another.

The first step in the reduction is to make the distinction between absolute and connotative terms. There is, clearly, a gap between the verification of statements such as "Sortes is swimming" and "Time is composed of instants," and this gap must be bridged by noticing the difference between a term such as "time" and the term "Sortes." The verification of the latter statement must be possible, and the only verification is of particular statements of particular facts. Absolute terms are "those which do not signify one thing primarily, and another thing . . . secondarily: but whatever is signified through such a name is signified with equal primacy."[25] A connotative term is "that which signifies something primarily, and something else secondarily; and such a name properly has a nominal definition."[26] Absolute terms have real definitions, and it is by the

nature of the definition that absolute and connotative terms are precisely differentiated. When the elements of the definition of a term signify only the individual entities for which the defined term can stand, then the term is absolute. Thus, in the definition "Man is a rational animal," "man" signifies primarily and stands for precisely those entities denoted by the term. Equally, "rational animal" signifies and stands for precisely those entities denoted by "rational animal." When, on the other hand, the elements of a definition of a term do not all signify the same individual entities for which the definiens stands, then we have a nominal definition. "Shape," for example, is a connotative term, since its definition, "substance whose parts are arranged in a determinate spatial order," primarily means the thing which possesses the shape, and secondarily connotes or consignifies its determinate physical configuration.

Since the physical universe contains nothing but substances and their qualities, there are only two kinds of absolute term; terms under the category of substance — concrete absolute terms, and terms under the category of quality — abstract absolute terms. Only the "qualitative contraries" are designated by absolute abstract terms: these are the qualities permitting of gradual alteration, and such qualities as shape, size and colour are signified by terms that are reducible to absolute terms. Professor Moody writes:

> . . . all such terms [*i.e.*, terms other than absolute terms] are capable of analysis or definition, whereby their meaning is exhibited as a function of elements or principles signified by absolute terms. Where we are able to state both parts of the nominal definition of a connotative term determinately [*e.g.*, to define "the calefactible" not merely as "*something* in which heat can be present" but as "a *body* determinable with respect to heat"], we achieve . . . a complete analysis of the connotative term, through reduction to absolute terms.[27]

Shapiro suggests that this might be put in more modern language as follows:

> Terms belonging to categories *other than substance and quality* are to be analyzed as statement forms of the form: "x is greater than y"; "j is at place m, n, o before v is at place z"; "r is successively next to place p, q, n, l"; and so on. When one wishes to determine designata for these, *only names of the substances or qualities actually connoted by these designata are to be substituted for the unknowns.*[28]

In order to establish his position, Ockham proceeds to examine the arguments of his predecessors and contemporaries who maintained the existence of absolute motion, time, and place, as real entities. Their "false arguments and errors" he attributes to a naïve belief that "because there are distinct names, there are distinct things correspond-ing to them."[29] They are culpable in that they make a science of the physical world impossible by con-fusing it with metaphysics, and by requiring of its statements a truth other than the truth of corres-pondence with individual facts. He does not outline their arguments in detail, presumably because they were too well known for it to be necessary, but he speaks of the "common opinion," opposing it both by his own opinion and that of the ancients, with whom he feels himself in sympathy. The *"moderni"* have spoiled Aristotelianism by turning what was intended for logical doctrine into metaphysical doc-trine.

At each point in his argument, Ockham opposes the attempt to make motion, time, and place something apart from the moving body, the body moving in time and located in space. He deals first with "mutation", or change in general, which he calls "motion in the broad sense." It is distinguished from motion in the strict sense by embracing all changes — sudden or successive — operating within the scope of the four categories of substance, quan-tity, quality, and place. Motion in the strict sense refers only to the successive changes properly attributable to the three categories of quantity, quality, and place. His first task, then, is to show that sudden change (*mutatio subita*), which belongs to motion in the broad sense, is not "another thing distinct as regards itself as a whole" from the changed object.

He first sets out some absurd consequences of supposing that "mutation" is a thing. Since the time during which change is taking place is infinitely divisible, it would follow that an infinite number of "things" would have been generated and destroyed with the finite time of change. Secondly, if "muta-tion" were a thing, it ought to be possible to assign it to some category, but it is immediately obvious that it is neither substance, quantity, quality, nor relation. Nor can it be relegated to a category through reduc-tion, for a condition of such reduction is that the thing to be reduced must belong to some subject existing *per se* in that category. For example, matter is reductively in the category of substance, for it belongs to a subject which is itself in the category of substance; but it is clear that "mutation" considered as a thing belongs to no subject. Finally, Ockham invokes the principle of economy: in order to "save" the phenomena, we do not need any factor beyond form, matter, and agency. To explain any single instance of mutation, all we need is to observe that some "suddenly changed" subject has a form which it previously had not, and that the form was ac-quired in a nonsuccessive manner.

Ockham's positive doctrine, then, is that "muta-tion" always involves a "mutated" subject. For a sub-ject to be mutated

is nothing else than for the subject itself to have a

form which it previously had not, or to lose a form which it previously had. Not, however, part-by-part, but so that it does not have one part of the form prior to another, nor does it previously lose one part and then another; but the whole form is received or lost simultaneously.[30]

Ockham is not denying that the *subject* of substantial change comes to be what it is through temporal process, but he is saying that the "substantial form" comes to be in the subject instantaneously. Generation and corruption are thus examples of instantaneous change, whether it be of a substantial or an accidental form. A man comes into being by a temporal pro-cess, but receives the form of a human being in-stantaneously; and wood becomes hot — i.e., is moved in the narrow sense — but the *heat* that is generated is moved only in the large sense.

It was necessary for Ockham to demonstrate the distinction between the two senses of "motion," for the defenders of the absolute theory had thought that what was proved of mutation held also for motion. For instance, the "common saying" that "mutation is indivisible and unextended" is simply to affirm the distinction between the two senses and not to assign a property to motion. Ockham assents to the saying in this sense, but remarks that it merely means that mutation is non-successive, thus differing from motion proper. When it is added, further, that a permanent thing is temporal, Ockham again as-sents, but points out that it must not be deduced from this that "mutation," being indivisible and unextended, must be a thing which is separate and distinct from the permanent thing. Since "mutation is instantaneous" merely means that the thing "mutated" is not changed successively, nothing follows from putting this proposition with the pro-position that permanent things are temporal.

Another "common saying" of his adversaries is that mutation ceases when a thing ceases to be changed; but no permanent thing then ceases. This has to be dealt with rather differently, since it con-tains no reference either implicit or direct to the character of the change. He points out first that there are certain names which unlike "animal," "agent," and "patient," "do not properly stand for any things whatsoever . . . such as 'action,' 'passion,' 'motion,' and the like." Names such as the latter are derivative from several other parts of speech, and they either stand in a proposition for the words from which they derive or they are equivalent to propositions. For example, in the proposition "Mutation is the loss or acquisition of something," "mutation" is equivalent to "when something changes," and the abstract names "acquisition" and "loss" reduce to the verbs from which they derive, "acquires" and "loses." The statement then be-comes: "When something is changed, it acquires something or loses something." Similarly, "Muta-tion ceases" becomes "The mutable ceases to be changed." There is thus no *entity* about which we can assert or deny that it has ceased to be. Ockham now imagines his opponents making a final stand and saying "Either mutation is something or nothing: if nothing, then it does not refer to anything known; if something, then either it is a permanent thing, which does not seem consonant with the Philosopher's view, or it is other than a permanent."[31]

Ockham concedes the conclusion both for himself and for "the ancients"; mutation *is* something, but not an absolute. To say "mutation is something" is simply to say that when a mutable is changed, and it acquires something or loses something, it is something. He offers another interpretation, equally unsatisfactory to the absolutists.

If you take this proposition "mutation is something" in another way — namely that "mutation" stands for some determinate in the way in which in this proposition, "white is something," the subject stands for the subject of the whiteness and in this proposition, "man is an animal," "man" stands for this and that thing which is a man, then it is proper to say that it [mutation] may stand for some permanent thing. . . . If, however, you say that it does *not* stand for a permanent thing in the way in which "permanent thing" has been above denoted . . . I say that mutation is *not* something, because there *is* no such thing.[32]

To sum up, a proposition in which the term "mutation" appears implies a proposition in which some *subject* is said to lose or acquire form suddenly. "Mutation" stands neither for the change nor for the changed object taken alone, nor for an entity apart from either; it stands for both the change and the changed object taken together.

This treatment of mutation sets the pattern for Ockham's account of motion in the strict sense, time and place, for what is said of "mutation" applies *mutatis mutandis* to "motion," "time," "instant," "place," and other similar words. He examines, for example, the meaning of the word "flux" in the absolutist argument that since motion is "a certain flux," and since no permanent thing can be considered a "flux," then motion is an entity separate and distinct from things. The first possible meaning is that of his opponents: "Motion is a thing distinct from all permanent things, which flows from being to nonbeing, or conversely, so that one part is being continuously destroyed and another succeeds it continuously in the nature of things."[33] The second is Ockham's "reduced" version. "When *something is moved*, it flows continuously, that is, *it* continuously acquires or loses something — as when something is locally moved, *it flows* continuously from one place to another — not due to [the presence of] anything beyond a mobile and the place which it acquires, but because it is always in one place and then

another."[34] He deals similarly with the argument that motion is successive and therefore distinct from permanent things that have all their parts simultaneously. It is shown to be reducible to the harmless statement that when something moves, it does not acquire or lose anything simultaneously, but successively. There is, then, no successive "thing" to be distinguished from the permanent thing. The fact that we can speak of a fast or slow movement, but not of a fast or slow thing, can be dealt with in a similar manner, without postulating a distinct *entity* to be fast or slow. To say of a motion that it is fast is simply to say of a thing that it acquires or loses something quickly. In the case of local motion, for example, more "places" would be acquired by a quickly moving body than would be acquired in the same time by a slowly moving body.

We may take one more interesting example of Ockham's method in his treatment of the word "instant." He writes: "Concerning an instant, it is the opinion of many that an instant is a certain flowing thing [*res fluens*] which is steadily destroyed, or lost, so that it does not remain. Whence, they posit that there is continuously another and another instant, and that it is itself a certain thing which cannot possibly remain through time. Indeed, they say, it is distinguished from all permanent things."[35] This is unsatisfactory on many counts; it involves the existence of an infinite number of beings in any finite stretch of time, and since whatever brings the instants into being is presumably still in operation, how is it that moments are continually being destroyed? Again, it is impossible to assign moments to any category; they are neither substance nor quality, for if they were a quality, that which possesses them must be either divisible or indivisible. All the accidents of a divisible substance are themselves divisible, and an indivisible is not a substance. Finally, by the principle of economy, everything to be explained by what is hypostatized (*i.e.*, moments) can equally well be explained without it. "Everything which can be explained through such a thing [the absolute moment], can be explained through this; that the heavens, according to their parts, are in such a position."[36] Time, in short, is the measure by which we determine the duration of motion, rest, and of objects subject to generation and corruption. Time is "the measure of all things whose duration can be certified by the intellect by means of something else better known to it." "When someone does not know for how long something is moved, he can be rendered certain through some motion known to him; for by considering and applying the motion of the sun [which is] known to him, to that other motion, and noting that that other mobile is moved from such a point to such a point, he knows for how long it was moved."[37] Though the motion of the sun is sufficiently accurate for practical purposes, the fundamental reference is to the *primum mobile*, the sphere of the fixed stars, which is the standard for the entire universe. Time is thus a "passion of the first motion": "First motion is time," but Ockham is quick to point out that this means nothing but that the prime mobile is uniformly and swiftly moved, through which motion the intellect can ascertain of other things how long they endure, move, or rest. The true moment of time is "a translation into temporal terms of the spatial changes suffered by the sphere of the fixed stars. As such, the temporal moment does not differ substantially from the prime motion; but each motion is, rather, a predication of the prime mobile, providing the mode through which its spatial changes, with respect to its parts, are known and expressed."[38]

Being and God

HAVING dealt thus with motion, time, and place, it might be thought that Ockham has shown practically that there is no science of metaphysics. It might be thought that "being" would receive similar treatment and metaphysics resolve itself into logic or into the natural sciences. However, in the *Sentences* and in the *Quodlibeta*, Ockham deals with questions which are usually considered to be metaphysical. Metaphysics is declared to be a real science, the primary subject of which is being, if we mean "primacy of predication"; if we mean primacy of perfection, then God is the first subject of metaphysics. "Being" stands for beings, and there is no being as such in the universe outside the mind. Metaphysics, then, is concerned with the concept *being*, though since being stands for every existent thing, each one of which is conceived as *a* being, metaphysics is concerned with every existing thing, in so far as it falls under the concept being. The concept is formed from the direct apprehension of particular things, which may be known though the concept has not yet been formed. "I say that a particular being can be known, although those general concepts of being and unity are not known."[39] The spoken and written term "being" is univocal, apply equally to God and to creatures. "There is one concept common to God and creatures and predicable of them."[40] If this were not so, we could not conceive God. We have no intuitive cognition of God, nor can we have a simple "proper" concept of God; but we have a concept that is predicable of him as it is of all other existing beings. This does not mean that in attributing being to God univocally with being as attributed to creatures, we know some feature of the Divine Being which he shares in common with other existing beings, nor does it mean that we are assured of his existence; the existence of God is known in other ways. It simply means that we are able to form the concept of the being of God.

I admit that the simple knowledge of one creature in itself leads to the knowledge of another thing in a common concept. For example, by the simple knowledge of a whiteness which I have seen, I am led to the knowledge of another whiteness which I have never seen, in as much as from the first whiteness I abstract a concept of whiteness which refers indifferently to them both. In the same way from some accident which I have seen I abstract a concept of being which does not refer more to that accident than to substance, nor to the creature more than to God.[41]

Thus, seeing a white patch leads to our having an idea of whiteness which will be applicable to other white patches when we see them; it will not lead to an assurance of the *existence* of other white patches. In the same way, to form the concept of being is to have a concept applicable to all existents, but it is not to be assured of the existence of any other than those immediately known.

Ockham distinguishes three types of univocity. A univocal concept may be common to a number of things which are exactly alike; it may be a concept which is common to a number of things alike in some respect and unlike in others; finally, it may be common to a number of beings which are alike in no way whatever. It is in this final way that a concept may be common to God and to creatures; the univocity of "being" does not mean that God and creatures are in any sense alike, or on the same level; it simply means that the spoken or written word "being" is applied to God and to creatures. If we were to use the term "being" while we thought of the beings designated as falling under various concepts, we should be using the word equivocally, equivocity and univocity being of words, not mental terms. With this proviso, we do not need the notion of analogical predication; all predication, says Ockham, is either univocal, equivocal, or denominative. Since denominative or connotative predication is reducible to either equivocal or univocal predication, we can say that all predication is univocal or equivocal.

We can, then, conceive God in the above sense, and we can even form a complex concept "proper" to God, though not a simple one. From creatures we can abstract the being that belongs to all beings, and the notion of "first" that belongs to all creatures who are first in any respect. We can then form the notion of "first being" which is "proper" to God. It is one thing to form a concept and another thing to prove that there is a being to whom the concept applies, and Ockham was not satisfied with any of the traditional proofs of the existence of God. There is no natural intuition of the Divine Being, so that "God exists" cannot be a self-evident proposition for earthly beings. In the presence of Socrates, "Socrates exists" is a self-evident proposition, and for a being enjoying the beatific vision, "God exists" will be a self-evident statement. But the proposition uttered by such a being, though similar in verbal form, will be a different proposition from that uttered by an earthly being, since the concepts are different.

Given Ockham's account of cause, we shall not expect him to accept the proof of God's existence as the cause of the created world. We cannot demonstrate, but only learn by experience, that A is the cause of B, so that it is only by actually experiencing A followed by B that we can assert that A is the cause of B, though we can know that B has *a* cause. Similarly, we can know that the world has *a* cause, but we cannot know anything of the nature of that cause. If we accept a "first mover," we still cannot know anything of the nature of the first mover; it might, says Ockham, be an angel, or some being lesser than God. Although we must stop at a first efficient cause and not proceed to infinity, yet we know by experience the causal efficacy of the sun, and this might be the first efficient cause. In the *Quodlibeta*, Ockham gives his own version of a causal argument for the existence of God. It would be better, he says, to argue from the conserved to a first conserver than from the product to a first producer. There are two reasons for this: First, there is the difficulty of proving that there are any beings other than corruptible beings: "It is difficult or impossible to prove against the philosophers that there cannot be an infinite regress in causes of the same kind, of which one can exist without the other."[42] For example, Ockham does not think that it would be possible to prove that a man does not owe his existence to his parents and they to their parents, and so on indefinitely. If it were objected that even in a series of this kind, the series would itself depend for its existence on another being external to the series, Ockham answers that "it would be difficult to prove that the series would not be possible unless there were one permanent being, on which the whole infinite series depended."[43]

The second reason is that a first conserver is in a different position from a first producer, in that an infinite series in time is not an evident absurdity as in an *actual* infinite. If there were an infinite number of *conservers*, they would coexist, so that an infinite regress in this case would involve an actual infinite. Ockham is satisfied that the arguments against an actual infinite are "reasonable enough."

The argument for God as the final cause of the created world is no better than the argument for his existence as its efficient cause. It is impossible to prove that the universe is ordered to one end; indeed, it cannot even be proved that the individual beings making up the world act for one end in a way that would justify an inference to God as that end. In the case of things acting without knowledge and will, we are justified in saying only that they act by a natural necessity. It makes no sense to say of such beings that they are acting *for* an end.[44] If we say of inanimate beings that they act for an end determined by God, who created their natures, we are presup-

posing the existence of God, and cannot be supposed to be producing evidence for that existence. Finally, in the case of agents acting with intelligence and will, the reason for their acts is their own will, and it cannot be shown that there is an order within which each will is turned toward God as its end. There is no "order" of the universe separate and distinct from absolute natures themselves.

We are left, then, with God as the conserver of the created world. Under no other aspect is it possible to prove his existence. Even now, we have not achieved our end, for it cannot be proved that there is only one conserver. It can be shown that there is some ultimate conserving being of *this* world, but there is no way of demonstrating that there is no other world, or worlds each having its own conserving being. The uniqueness of God is known with certainty only by faith.

The answer to the question whether Ockham believed that it was possible to demonstrate the existence of God philosophically, is then, in one sense, yes, and in another, no. If we consider that to prove the existence of a first conserving cause of this world, with no knowledge of the nature of this cause, is to prove the existence of God, then the answer is yes. If we shall not be satisfied with less than a demonstration of the existence of the supreme, perfect, infinite, and unique being, then the answer is no. We can know that *this* being exists only by faith. The existence of the God of theology cannot be proved philosophically. It is for this reason that theology is not a science. It is not because its propositions are not informative, but because its premises are supplied by revelation and by faith, so that any conclusions demonstrated by these premises will fall within the same field.

If we give up the idea of proving the existence of God, can we nevertheless, granted the concept of the absolutely supreme being, prove that God, as this being, is infinite and omnipotent? Ockham's answer is that no property such as infinity, omnipotence, eternity, or the power to create can be demonstrated to belong to the divine essence. The reason in that in a syllogism having as its conclusion "God is omnipotent," omnipotence must have been attributed to some being or class of beings to which God has been said to belong. All X is omnipotent; God is X; therefore: God is omnipotent. But there is no middle term that could be substituted for X, since the supreme and perfect being is the only omnipotent being. If it were suggested that we prove that omnipotence or infinity or power to create is an attribute of God by using the definition of the attribute as the middle term, the answer is that such a demonstration is a begging of the question. For example: Everything capable of creating something out of nothing is capable of creating; but God is a being who can create something out of nothing; therefore: God is capable of creating. This begs the question in that it would be impossible to know that

God was capable of creating something out of nothing and at the same time to doubt whether he was capable of creating. It does not increase our knowledge, and so is not a genuine demonstration.

It is possible to prove that God has *some* attributes from his possession of others. We can demonstrate his goodness from his supremacy, since we have a genuine middle term to which we may attribute goodness. "Being" is a genuine middle term in that it is attributable to beings other than God. So we can say: All beings are good; God is a being; therefore: God is good. This would not constitute a demonstration if "good" were taken absolutely, as designating the same beings as were designated by "beings." It must be taken connotatively, as containing a reference to the will, if the syllogism is not to beg the question. What is to be demonstrated must be open to doubt if the demonstration is to be genuine.

Granted that we may know the nature of God in the sense described, what is the character of such knowledge? It is not intuitive knowledge, for God is not present to human beings in the required sense. It is not abstractive knowledge, for that presupposes intuitive knowledge. We do not have a proper simple concept of God, that is, a concept applicable to God alone, for "no thing can be known by us through our natural powers in a simple concept proper to itself, unless the thing is known in itself. For otherwise we could say that color can be known in a concept proper to colors in a man born blind."[45] We can form a concept of God by using connotative concepts and concepts common to God and human beings, like being and wisdom, but such a complex concept is not a concept of *what God is*. God is a simple being and his attributes are not distinct from one another, so that by no means can we form a proper concept of God. A connotative concept such as infinity connotes the finite negatively; i.e., it connotes a reality other than the subject of which it is predicated, and a common concept such as wisdom is predicable of other realities than the one of which it is in fact predicated. We can then have no concept that corresponds to the single reality.

In consequence, our knowledge of God is a knowledge of concepts, and though we can form a complex concept of God which is applicable to him alone, it is a mental construction that is not able to mirror the single simple reality. "Neither the divine essence ... nor anything intrinsic to God nor anything which is really God can be known by us without something other than God being involved as object." "We cannot know in themselves either the unity of God ... or His infinite power or the divine goodness or perfection: but what we know immediately are concepts, which are not really God but which we use in propositions to stand for God."[46] We know the divine nature, then, only through the medium of concepts, and we have no apprehension of the essence of God. This does not mean that the statements of theologians are not true and meaningful, but their reasoning is performed upon concepts and not upon the real being. Their analysis of concepts could be performed equally well by agnostics or atheists, and what gives certain knowledge of the truth of the statements of theology is revelation accepted by faith. This knowledge, then, is not "science," since it has no intuitive knowledge as its foundation. This is not to demonstrate the falsity of the statements of theology, nor even to question their truth; it is to exhibit their logical nature.

Since God is a simple being who has no internal distinctions except that of the three persons, to speak of the essence of God, his intellect, or his will is to use different ways of referring to the one simple reality. Ockham similarly rejects the traditional doctrine of the divine ideas as anthropomorphic. The divine ideas had been regarded as intermediate in creation between God and creatures, but this is an unnecessary hypothesis. All that is needed to explain creation is God and what he has created. The "ideas" are the things themselves known by God. If an idea is to function as a pattern, it is nothing but the whole creature, known by God through all eternity. Since every creature is individual, God's ideas are all of individual things; there are no universal ideas, or genera, but simply the individual things known to God. Since negation, privation, and evil are not distinct things, there are no ideas of them. It may be seen that although allowing himself to use the traditional term "idea," Ockham has purged the notion of every hint of Platonism. Ideas are not models for God's creations: if they were, there would be a limit to God's freedom. The sphere of God's ideas is not limited to the actual world — he has an infinite number of ideas beyond those things which have been, are, or will be. These ideas are still of individuals but of possible individuals.

Ockham is unwilling to speak of God's knowledge; it is, he says, entirely outside our own experience of cognition, so that it is not possible to assert anything of it. It cannot be proved that God knows everything, nor indeed, that he knows some things or no things. But we know by faith that he is omniscient. What he knows includes future events, even those that are contingent in depending on acts of will for their actuality. "I say ... that it must be held without any doubt that God knows all future contingent events with certainty and evidence. But it is impossible for any intellect in our present state to make evident either this fact or the manner in which God knows all future contingent events."[47] Aristotle would have said, says Ockham, that no statement that a future event depending on choice will or will not happen is true. It is true that either the event will happen or it will not, but the statement of either alternative is neither true nor false. If a statement is neither true nor false, then it cannot be known. "In spite of this reason, however, we must hold that God evidently knows all future contingents. But the way [in which God knows them] I cannot explain."[48] Since God knows them with certainty, they are true. Although he does not know how God knows these truths, Ockham commits himself to the statement that they are not "present" to God, nor does he know them by the medium of ideas: he also rejects the notion that God knows them to be true because he determines them to be so. "However, it must be held that He does [know them], though contingently.[49] By "contingently," Ockham means that God knows them as contingent, and that his knowledge does not make them necessary. He knows them, Ockham suggests, by his essence, which is "intuitive knowledge which is so perfect and so clear that it is itself evident knowledge of all past and future events, so that it knows which part of a contradiction will be true and which false.[50] It is not easy to see how this differs from the "presence" of the facts to God, except that "presence" is known to us only in our own immediate apprehension.

In insisting that a statement about the future is true or false, Ockham is preserving the principle of excluded middle as against some of his contemporaries, who maintained that the principle did not apply to statements about future contingent events, which were neither true nor false. Not only does God know what alternative is true; he can reveal *which* is true, as he did to the prophets. Just how this was done "I do not know, because it has not been revealed to me."

As was said above, God's essence is identical with his intellect and with his will. It is therefore no more suitable to speak of God's will as the cause of things than of his essence or of his intellect. God simply is the immediate cause of everything, in the sense that without God's causality, no effect would follow, even if the secondary cause were present. Moreover, God could bring the effect about without the secondary cause. This, however, cannot be proved philosophically. God's power is unlimited in the sense that he can do all that is possible. To say that God cannot do what is intrinsically impossible is not to place a limit on his power, for it makes no sense to speak of doing what is intrinsically impossible.

Though the divine omnipotence cannot be proved, once it is assumed as an article of faith, the created world is seen in a different light. All empirical causal relations are seen as contingent, not only in that they are to be discovered by experience, but also in that every cause is a secondary one. God can always bring about *B* without using *A* as a secondary cause. This is not to suppose the possibility of divine intervention — that was common ground to all medieval thinkers — but to remove the stability conferred upon nature by "natures" or essences. Ockham's view of the natural world was of a collection of "absolutes" whose only relations and connections were coexistence and sequence. This contingency is the expression of the absolute omnipotence of God, not proved, but taken on faith.

Man and Morality

THIS belief has an important bearing on Ockham's view of human beings and on morality. Just as the existence of the supreme and perfect being cannot be proved, the existence of an immaterial soul as the form of the body cannot be proved. We have intuitive and evident knowledge of separate and individual acts of understanding and will, but no experience that would lead us to attribute them to anything but the body. "Understanding by intellectual soul an immaterial and incorruptible form which is wholly in the whole and wholly in every part [of the body], it cannot be known evidently either by arguments or by experience that there is such a form in us, or that a soul of this kind is the form of the body. I do not care what Aristotle thought about this, for he seems to speak always in an ambiguous manner. But these three things we hold only by faith."[51] It is clear that the material body has a form, and it is equally clear that since the body is corruptible, it is not directly informed by an incorruptible form. "I say that one must postulate in man another form in addition to the intellectual soul, namely a sensitive form, on which a natural agent can act by way of corruption and production."[52] This sensitive soul is distinct from the intellectual soul and it perishes with the body. There is only one sensitive soul in an animal or a man, but it is extended in such a way that "one part of the sensitive soul perfects one part of matter, while another part of the same soul perfects another part of matter."[53] Thus, there is one part of the sensitive soul which perfects the eye and another the ear, so that these "powers" are distinct. It is clear that we can lose the power of sight without the power of hearing being affected. "Powers" are not forms; Ockham is merely referring to the empirical fact that the conditions for hearing are distinct from the conditions for seeing, though they are connected by belonging to the one sensitive organism. It cannot be proved that the sensitive soul of man is distinct from the intellectual soul, though it seems to be indicated by such a fact of experience as our desiring a thing with the sensitive appetite and turning from it with the rational will.

It is difficult to say how Ockham can maintain the unity of a given rational being, since the intellectual soul belongs to it almost as the Aristotelian "mover." However, that the intellectual soul was the form of the body was accepted by Ockham as an article of faith, and in his account of the human person, he insists on its essential unity. The person is a *suppositum intellectuale*, and this definition holds both for created and uncreated persons. A *suppositum* is a complete being, incapable of inhering in anything, and the human person is the total being, not the rational soul. For this reason, the human soul in separation from the body after death is not a person.

One of the principal characteristics of a rational

being is freedom. Freedom is the power "by which I can act indifferently and contingently produce an effect in such a way that I can cause or not cause that effect, without any difference in that power having been made."[54] That we possess this power cannot be proved by *a priori* reasoning, but "it can, however, be known evidently through experience, that is, through the fact that every man experiences that however much his reason dictates something, his will can will it or not will it."[55] Moreover, the fact that we praise and blame people shows that we attribute responsibility to them for their acts and so accept freedom as a fact. Men are free in the further sense that they may or may not will their own happiness. This is clear in regard to the last end considered concretely, namely, God. "No object other than God can satisfy the will, because no act which is directed to something other than God excludes all anxiety and sadness. For, whatever created object may be possessed, the will can desire something else with anxiety and sadness."[56] But it cannot be proved that the enjoyment of the Divine essence is possible to us — it is an article of faith. If we do not *know* that a thing is possible, we cannot will it. Even if we know by faith that it is possible, experience shows that it is possible to will or not to will it. Intellect may believe that perfect happiness is not possible for human beings and so dictate that we keep our intentions within reasonable bounds and will the small ends which are possible of achievement. Even then, the will may or may not conform to the judgments of the intellect. Our freedom to will anything whatever is absolute. If there were an end which is necessarily desired, then it would be difficult to see how human freedom could be preserved.

Another aspect of Ockham's ethical theory which makes him reluctant to postulate a necessary end of desire is his account of virtue as willing conformity to the will of God. A command that cannot be disobeyed is hardly a command. God can command anything he likes, and no matter what it is, it is virtuous to obey the command. A created free will is under the moral obligation to will what God commands it to will, so that moral obligation is founded in our dependence upon God as creature to creator. "Evil is nothing else than to do something when one is under an obligation to do the opposite. Obligation does not fall on God, since He is not under any obligation to do anything."[57]

God's absolute freedom is thus as clearly to be seen in the moral order as in the natural order. Just as every part of the created world is contingent and in merely empirical connection with other parts, so the content of the moral law is contingent, and wholly dependent upon, the will and power of God. There is no "essence" of man in conformity with which he was created, so there is no "natural" law embodied in his very make up. Ockham draws the logical consequences of this position. God concurs in any act of a human being,

even an act of hatred of himself. But since he can be the total cause of any state of affairs in which he concurs, he could cause, as total cause, an act of hatred of himself. "Thus He can be the total cause of an act of hatred of God, and that without any moral malice."[58] Since he is under no obligation, he cannot sin, and so without sin, he can cause an act in the human will which would be a sin if the man were responsible for it. As a matter of fact, God has forbidden adultery, stealing, hatred of God, and so on, but since he can command anything or do anything which does not involve a logical contradiction, he could command adultery, stealing, even hatred of himself. These acts would then become not only licit, but positively meritorious.

It seems then, that Ockham's ethical theory is wholly authoritarian; yet there is another strand in his ethical thinking which is at first sight inconsistent with authoritarianism. He constantly speaks of "right reason" and of the virtue of acting in conformity with right reason. Some commentators have interpreted this apparent inconsistency in terms of a "double" standard, a lay and a theological. If left to himself, that is, without revelation, men might have evolved an Aristotelian ethic, and it is significant that Ockham insists on the obligation to follow conscience, even though it may be an erring conscience. Having done all we can to establish what is our duty, we must carry it out. This, however, is paralleled by our duty as scientists to follow experience: though the natural order is completely contingent, depending on God's will, yet as a matter of fact there *is* a natural order, and we may discover its laws by noting co-existences and regular sequences. In the same way, we follow right reason, remembering always that its "rightness" is contingent and wholly dependent upon God's will. The actual moral order stands to God's will as does the actual order of the physical world.

There is a special difficulty about the possibility of God's commanding one act which is absolutely sinful, namely that one should hate him. To love God is the first virtue: "For this act is virtuous in such a way that it cannot be vicious, nor can this act be caused by a created will without being virtuous."[59] Yet God could command

> that He be not loved for a certain time, because He can command that the intellect be occupied with study and the will likewise, so that at this time it cannot think anything about God. I now assume that the will then performs an act of loving God; then this act is either virtuous — but that cannot be said, since it is performed against the divine command — or it is not virtuous, and then we have our intended thesis that an act of loving God above all is not virtuous.[60]

Ockham's answer is that though there is no logical contradiction in God's utterance of the command "Do not love me," it is impossible that in the case described the will should perform the act of loving God in defiance of God's command. An act of loving God would not be an act of loving God, since under the above conditions, loving God would issue in bending the will and the intellect to study. If we were to ask whether in general God could command that his creatures hate him, it is not a logical impossibility, but to carry it out would be a moral impossibility, since in obeying this command of God, we should be loving God.

As in the case of all other disciplines, the moral nature of men is to be studied empirically; we note that as a matter of fact, men may will what goes against their sensuous nature, though it is very difficult. We may take this as the keynote of his whole philosophy. His greatest achievement is in logic, and by a study of the nature of propositions and their terms, he has shown that there is no place in knowledge for speculation. We cannot know *a priori* how things must be or ought to be, but by experience, informed by reason, we can find out how, as a matter of fact, they are. At the same time, there is an overriding obligation to accept revelation, so that all our knowledge is contingent in a double sense; it is of how things happen to be; they might have been otherwise in the sense that we can discover no necessity in the natural order, and even unbroken regularities are contingent regularities. The order itself might have been otherwise. This is to delimit the spheres of natural and theological knowledge. Neither fetters the other; it is proper that we should formulate laws, it is proper that we should remember that all such laws are contingent upon the will of God. We have the field left free for a science of the natural world, for a science of human nature including man's moral nature, but we can discover nothing that could nullify the truths of revealed religion.

Francis Bacon

MARY B. HESSE

FRANCIS BACON, later Viscount St. Albans and Lord Chancellor, was born in 1561, the son of a Lord Keeper of the Great Seal to Elizabeth I, and spent most of his life at Court, actively engaged in the affairs and intrigues of two reigns. He entered Trinity College, Cambridge, at the age of thirteen, and while there conceived a dislike of Aristotelian philosophy which remained with him throughout his life. After some diplomatic missions to France, he made law his profession. He appears to have spent overmuch time in early life angling for the royal favor, but these activities are seen in a more favorable light when it is realized that he regarded himself as the prophet of a new science, for which he needed money and sympathetic collaboration. Not much of either was forthcoming, even from the scholar James I, whom Bacon cast in the role of royal patron of the new science, and to whom he dedicated his major work.

In 1621 Bacon was banished from the Court and from public life after being condemned on a charge of taking bribes (to which he pleaded guilty, but always maintained that he never allowed bribes to affect his judgments). He spent his last five years in retirement at Gorhambury near St. Albans, where for the first time he was able to concentrate on writing, but even then much work he intended to do on his scheme for the new science remained unfinished. He died in 1626. The story of his death is told by Aubrey: he alighted from his carriage in the snow in order to obtain a chicken for an experiment on the preservative effects of snow, and developed a cold and fever from which he died a week later. His tomb and monument are in St. Michael's Church at St. Albans.

BACON WROTE WIDELY on matters of history, law, politics, and morals, but it is his design for a new science which is best known and has remained most influential, especially as it is contained in his *Advancement of Learning* of 1605 (reissued in an enlarged Latin version, the *De Augmentis Scientiarum*, in 1623) and his *Novum Organum* of 1620. Much of equal philosophical interest is, however, to be found in the shorter, and in some cases fragmentary, works.

The principal philosophical works, in probable chronological order, are as follows:

1603	*Valerius Terminus* (published 1734).
1605	*The Advancement of Learning.*
1608 (?)	*Inquisitio Legitima de Motu* (published 1653).
(?)	*Cogitationes de Natura Rerum.*
1609	*De Sapientia Veterum.*
1612	*Descriptio Globi Intellectus*, and *Thema Coeli* (published 1653).
before 1620	*De Principiis atque Originibus* (published 1653).
1620	*Novum Organum*, and *Parasceve.*
1622	*Historia Naturalis et Experimentalis*, to include:
	Historia Ventorum.
	Abecadarium Naturae (fragment published 1679).
	Historia Densi et Rari (published 1658).
	Historia Sulphuris, Mercurii, et Salis (preface only).
	Historia Vitae et Mortis (published 1623).
1623	*De Augmentis Scientiarum.*
	Sylva Sylvarum (published 1627).

His projected life-work was the *Great Instauration*, which was to lay the foundations of the sciences entirely anew, sweeping away all received notions, returning to a fresh examination of particulars and proceeding from them by an infallible method to axioms of greater and greater generality, and then descending by deduction to new particulars and useful operations upon matter. The work was to correct on the one hand the excessive rationalism of the ancient philosophers, who leaped straight from particulars to ill-founded general axioms and then reasoned only by the syllogism, and on the other hand it was to correct the unregulated empiricism of the alchemists and natural magicians, who wasted their time in unfruitful experimenting, and lit upon true discoveries only by accident. Bacon, by his method of inducing general axioms, intends to establish "a true and lawful marriage between the empirical and the rational faculty."[1]

This statement of his aim, occurring as it does near the beginning of the *Novum Organum*, should put us on guard against a frequent misinterpretation of Bacon as a mere fact-collector. The impression that this is the case can be derived from a hasty glance at his works, for a large proportion of these is devoted to unordered accounts of experiments and observations of all kinds and all degrees of reliability. But Bacon did not intend that these should be more than the materials on which his method was to work. The *Instauration* was to consist of six parts, of which the collection of "Phenomena of the Universe; or a Natural and Experimental History" was only one, and of which three were hardly begun by Bacon at all. We may conjecture, however, that even had Bacon lived ten years longer, been less encumbered by affairs of state, and received more enthusiastic cooperation in his projects, we should not know much more of the way his method was intended to work than can now be gathered from his anticipatory examples.

The six parts of the *Instauration* were to be:

1. The Classification of the Sciences.
2. Directions concerning the Interpretation of Nature, that is, the new inductive logic.
3. The Phenomena of the Universe, or natural history.
4. The Ladder of the Intellect, that is, examples of the application of the method in climbing from phenomena up the ladder of axioms to the "summary law of nature."
5. Anticipations of the New Philosophy, that is, tentative generalizations which Bacon considers of sufficient interest and importance to justify him in leaping ahead of the inductive method. And,
6. The New Philosophy or Active Science, which will exhibit the whole result of induction in an ordered system of axioms. If men will apply themselves to his method, Bacon thinks that this system will be the result of only a few years' work, but for himself he confesses "the completion of this last part is a thing both above my strength and beyond my hopes."[2]

Classification of the Sciences: De Augmentis

THE Plan of the *Instauration* and its second part, the *Novum Organum*, were published in 1620, and for its first part, Bacon made do with a revised version of his *Advancement of Learning* put into Latin and published in 1623. The book contains much that relates to other parts of the *Instauration*, but all that need concern us at this point are Bacon's views on the proper scope of natural philosophy.[3]

The Third Book of *De Augmentis* opens with the familiar distinction between knowledge inspired by divine revelation and knowledge arising from the senses. The latter constitutes philosophy, which is again divided into that concerning God (natural theology), that concerning Nature, and that concerning Man, and common to all these is the *Philosophia Prima* to which belong general logical axioms such as "things which are equal to the same thing are equal to one another."

Natural theology is only a rudimentary knowledge of God derived from his creatures. It is sufficient to establish his existence, providence, goodness, and some other properties, but not the mysteries of faith, which are obtained from revelation alone. Nature, however, Bacon says elsewhere, bears the signatures of God, and it is these, the true forms of things, which are the goal of natural philosophy, and not the false images imposed on things by man's mind.[4]

Natural philosophy is divided into the speculative and the operative. Here appears one of Bacon's major themes: that the object of natural philosophy is not mere speculative argument but also production of useful works to restore to man that dominion over nature which he lost at the Fall. However, just as due balance must be preserved between the rational and the empirical in developing the inductive method, so here there must be balance between "light" and "fruit." Without "experiments of light" to enable true axioms to be induced, the deductive descent to new works will be limited and imperfect, and without the intention to produce "experiments of fruit" the axioms will not be true reflections of things.[5]

There are two branches of speculative philosophy, the physical and the metaphysical, and two corresponding branches of the operative philosophy, namely the applications of these, which Bacon calls mechanics and magic. He makes the distinction between physics and metaphysics in the language of the Aristotelian causes: physics handles the material and efficient, and metaphysics the formal and final causes; but these terms are not to be understood in their Aristotelian senses, for Bacon regards these as superficial and unprofitable. Matter, for Bacon, is not mere potentiality and formlessness, but has its own existence and primary nature,[6] and his material and efficient causes are connected with the natural history of processes rather than with their philosophy, that is, with the accidental ways in which things come into being or are brought about, rather than with their fundamental nature.[7] Form, again, is not to be understood either in the Platonic sense of an ultimately unknowable idea abstracted from matter, nor in the Aristotelian sense of a species which is often merely apparent and has been hastily distinguished from other phenomena. A form is rather a "true specific difference, or nature-engendering nature, or source of its emanation," the discovery of which for all phenomena is the chief end of knowledge.[8] We shall discuss Bacon's forms in more detail at a later stage. Final causes, although included in metaphysics in this classification, are in fact not part of Bacon's natural philosophy but of his natural theology. This is because to assign purposes to phenomena is comparatively easy, but it is

anthropocentric and distracts the mind from the search for physical causes, which is the true end of natural philosophy. For physical causes enable us to discover a system of axioms from which new works can be derived, and final causes produce no works: "the research into Final Causes, like a virgin dedicated to God, is barren and produces nothing." But the virgin *is* dedicated to God, that is to say, Bacon does not reject all research into final causes, for he holds that by reflection upon them some of the attributes of God may be discovered. But his elimination of final causes from natural philosophy marks a stage in the transformation of the idea of causal explanation in science: true explanation is not henceforward to be an answer to the question "What for?" however satisfying to the mind such an answer may be, but is rather to be given in terms of consequences of antecedent physical events or conditions.[9]

The real distinction between physics and metaphysics for Bacon is the distinction between the lower and higher axioms of the inductive ladder. Physics stands between phenomena and the primary forms, that is, between natural history and metaphysics, and is concerned with causes which are more closely tied to particular phenomena and therefore more specific and more variable. It therefore deals with the "common and ordinary course of nature," while metaphysics deals with "her eternal and fundamental laws."[10]

Finally in Bacon's classification come the sciences of man. Here only two points can be noticed as particularly relevant to his philosophy of nature. The first is his doctrine of the dual nature of the human soul, which he divides into the rational and the irrational or sensible. The distinction clearly stems from Aristotle, but for Bacon the division between higher and lower parts of the soul is more radical, for the rational soul is understood in theological terms as that breathed into man by God, knowledge of which is part of revealed theology, while the sensible soul or spirit which man shares with the beasts is a corporeal substance, a "breath," which is the instrument of the rational soul and the physical cause of the motion of the human body.[11] How far this commits Bacon to a mechanical theory of the "animal spirits" similar to that of Descartes, we shall consider when we come to Bacon's views on the primary virtues of matter. The second point about the sciences of man which should be noticed is that Bacon explicitly intends his inductive method to apply to them as well as to the sciences of nature: "I form a history and tables of discovery for anger, fear, shame, and the like; for matters political; and again for the mental operations of memory, composition and division, judgment and the rest; not less than for heat and cold, or light, or vegetation, or the like."[12] He fulfils his promise to some extent in regard to the history of these things, but, not surprisingly, not in regard to their inductive theory.

The Interpretation of Nature: Novum Organum

WE now come to what Bacon himself regarded as the key to the whole project — the new method of induction. He claims that his method will lead to indubitable conclusions "as if by machinery," and believes that the unfallen human mind would naturally work in this way if it were not corrupted by "Idols" or false images which cause men to see everything in relation to themselves instead of in true perspective in relation to the universe. The intellect is to be purged by the practice of true induction,* but the idols should also be pointed out explicitly, "for the doctrine of Idols is to the Interpretation of Nature what the doctrine of the refutation of Sophisms is to common Logic."[15]

The idols are of four kinds. Idols of the tribe are those arising from the nature of human understanding itself, which is prone to impress its own ideas of order, reality, and importance, and its own preferences, upon nature, and to look rather for confirmations than possible refutations of its opinions. Further, the understanding is hindered by deficiencies of the senses, which take more account of what appears striking, and cannot detect the subtler changes of nature: "For the sense by itself is a thing infirm and erring; neither can instruments for enlarging or sharpening the senses do much; but all the truer kind of interpretation of nature is effected by instances and experiments fit and apposite; wherein the sense judges the experiment only, and the experiment the nature and thing itself."[16] Secondly, the idols of the cave are those which are peculiar to each man, and arise from his particular interests and preoccupations. Aristotle, for example, saw everything as subsidiary to his logic, and Gilbert to his investigations of the magnet. Thirdly, the idols of the market-place are those imposed by the deceptions of words, so that abstract names are reified, and equivocations are allowed to mislead. Finally, the idols of the theatre are those imposed by the received philosophical systems, which are based on common notions or superficial experiments or superstition. All this, says Bacon, must be purged and swept away. The mind is to be made into, what Locke was later to say it is naturally, a "*tabula abrasa*."[17]

Thus, some of the idols which obstruct clear ideas of nature are due, not to wilful prejudice, but to the inevitable disabilities of human perception, and in order to overcome these and prepare an adequate

natural history of phenomena, the senses must be helped. Again, the natural history when collected must be so ordered that the understanding can deal with it. But Bacon postpones discussion of these "ministrations" to the senses and the reason until he has expounded the method of induction itself.[18] There follow the best-known passages of the *Novum Organum*, where Bacon illustrates his tables of presence, absence in proximity, and comparison by an investigation of the form of heat. The method of drawing up these tables depends on Bacon's view of forms: "The Form of a nature is such, that given the Form the nature infallibly follows. Therefore it is always present when the nature is present . . . absent when the nature is absent."[19] One must therefore first draw up a table of instances of presence of the nature under investigation, for example, heat. The natural and previously universal mistake at this point has been to make an induction by simple enumeration and jump immediately to the conclusion that the form of the nature is some other feature obviously present in all these instances, and henceforth to notice only such instances as confirm their co-presence, while overlooking instances in which the alleged form is present without the nature:

> And therefore it was a good answer that was made by one who when they showed him hanging in a temple a picture of those who had paid their vows as having escaped shipwreck, and would have him say whether he did not now acknowledge the power of the gods, — "Aye," asked he again, "but where are they painted that were drowned after their vows?" And such is the way of all superstition, whether in astrology, dreams, omens, divine judgments, or the like.[20]

It is essential therefore that the instances in the table of presence be otherwise as unlike each other as possible, so as to eliminate the largest possible number of natures which are not co-present, and also that one should deliberately look for *negative* as well as affirmative instances, that is, those in which the nature in question is absent. Since there is an endless number of these, the most important should be collected, and these are the ones which are most akin to the several instances of presence in all respects except the nature in question. In this way all those features which are present in both tables will be eliminated as possible forms of the nature. Bacon illustrates by comparing pairs of instances of presence and absence of heat, among which he lists:

Presence	Absence
Rays of the sun.	Rays of the moon and stars.
Flame.	Phosphorescence, electric sparks.
Boiling liquids.	Liquids in their natural state.

This method of pairing of instances suggests further investigations and experiments when the negative instances are not immediately obvious: thus,

---

* With regard to the sins of the intellect, Bacon is a Pelagian: the intellect is fallen, but by the exercise of Bacon's method it can recover itself, and Bacon himself performs for the senses "the office of a true priest."[13] "For man by the fall fell at the same time from his state of innocency and from his dominion over creation. Both of these losses, however, can even in this life be in some part repaired; the former by religion and faith, the latter by arts and sciences."[14]

experiments should not be made at random, but in accordance with the requirements of the tables. Finally, one may draw up a table of comparison of degrees of heat: "For since the Form of a thing is the very thing itself . . . it necessarily follows that no nature can be taken as the true form, unless it always decrease when the nature in question decreases, and in like manner always increase when the nature in question increases."[21]

The drawing up of the three tables is, however, only the beginning of the method: "After the rejection and exclusion has been duly made, there will remain at the bottom, all light opinions vanishing into smoke, a Form affirmative, solid and true and well defined. This is quickly said; but the way to come at it is winding and intricate. I will endeavour however not to overlook any of the points which may help us towards it."[22]

The first of these points is the "First Vintage" or first attempt at the interpretation of nature drawn from the tables. A brief survey of the tables for heat, for example, suggests as the form of heat "a motion, expansive, restrained and acting in its strife upon the smaller parts of bodies."[23] Bacon does not, however, make clear how this first vintage is to affect the subsequent steps of the enquiry. On the one hand, his whole position rests on a rejection of "anticipations" drawn too hastily from the data without due regard to the method of exclusions. On the other hand, he does intend to devote the fifth part of the *Instauration* to "The Forerunners; or Anticipations of the new philosophy," and in his unfinished investigations into "Winds," "Life and Death," and "Dense and Rare," he commits himself to some "provisional canons" or "imperfect axioms" which may be "useful, if not altogether true."[24] More surprisingly, in *De Augmentis*,[25] after quoting Plato's "whosoever seeks a thing, knows that which he seeks for in a general notion; else how shall he know it when he has found it?" Bacon adds "and therefore the fuller and more certain our anticipation is, the more direct and compendious is our search."* But he nowhere gives any indication in practice that he realized how far anticipation or hypothesis must be allowed to guide further enquiry. This is the most notable difference between his method and the practice of his seventeenth-century successors such as Boyle and Hooke who, while paying their respects to him, nevertheless use hypotheses with considerable freedom.

The second step in the interpretation of the tables is consideration of "prerogative instances,"[27] that is, those instances which are to be enquired into first as the most likely to hasten the process of induction. They include experiments to aid the senses in discerning subtle and hidden processes, aids to the intellect in making definite and speedy exclusions, and aids to practical operations. Among them occur the celebrated *Instantiae Crucis* (Instances of the Finger-Post),[28] which separate two natures otherwise found together with the nature in question, and which therefore decide which of the two is its form and which is separable from it. Thus, the prerogative instances, and other aids to the process of induction which Bacon mentions but does not expound, give suggestions for drawing up the tables in the most economical way. They allow the great mass of natural data to be reduced to a "Designed History": "Let them but remember this and they will find out for themselves the method in which the history should be composed. For the end rules the method," and "we can command our questions, though we cannot command the natures of things."[29] Bacon gives a place to the exercise of judgment at least in shortening the work, but it is to be judgment directed by the requirements of his method, not judgment which relies on inspired guesses at hypotheses. Once the method is learned, therefore, men's wits are leveled; anyone can do science.[30]

Bacon's faith in the infallibility of the method seems to rest on four assumptions:

1. It presupposes that nature is in some sense finite. Bacon remarks that whereas the number of particulars in the universe is very large and perhaps infinite, the number of species or abstract natures or forms of things is few. The same point is made by means of illustration in *Novum Organum* when gold is regarded as "a troop or collection of simple natures." It is yellow, has a certain weight, is malleable, not volatile, not inflammable, "and so on for the other natures which meet in gold." Hence, if anyone knows the forms of these natures and methods for inducing them in some body, that body will be transformed into gold. "For if a man can make a metal that hath all these properties, let men dispute whether it be gold or no."[31]

2. If it be granted that the number of "simple natures" involved in any body or process is finite, it is necessary, in order to draw conclusive inductions from the tables, that all the simple natures should be enumerated. If there appear to be, for example, several natures in common in the instances of presence of heat, any of which may be its form, the method of exclusions by negative instances presupposes that this list of common natures is exhaustive.

3. The method also presupposes that it is possible to eliminate all natures not involved in the form either by finding appropriate negative instances existing naturally, or by constructing experiments to demonstrate them. Hence Bacon insists on the importance of artificial experiment: nature must usually be put to the question, not allowed

---

* But it is significant that although Bacon allows this sentence from *The Advancement of Learning* to stand, he has inserted the words "and more certain."[26] He seems to become more and not less doubtful of the value of anticipations as his work proceeds.

to run her ordinary course.[32] But even so there can be no guarantee that the appropriate experiment will always be practically possible.

4. Bacon also assumes a one-to-one correspondence between the form and the nature under investigation: "the Form of a thing is the very thing itself, and the thing differs from the form no otherwise than as the apparent differs from the real or the external from the internal, or the thing in reference to man from the thing in reference to the universe." The form is *convertible* with the thing; hence when Bacon draws from his tables for heat the "form or true definition of heat," that "Heat is a motion, expansive, restrained, and acting in its strife upon the smaller parts of bodies," he means "not that heat generates motion or that motion generates heat . . . but that Heat itself, or the *quid ipsum* of Heat, is Motion and nothing else."[33]

If these four conditions are fulfilled, then what Bacon is describing is a purely deductive argument, based on experimental rejection of the consequents of all but one of a limited number of possibilities. Bacon claims originality for this part of the method only in the sense that no one had previously recommended or practiced the systematic investigation of negative instances, although Plato had remarked on its logical form.[34]

Forms and the Ladder of Axioms

BEFORE considering what may have led Bacon to assume with very little argument that the conditions presupposed by his method are satisfied in nature, it is necessary to look more closely at what he means by "Forms." We have seen that the word is not used in the Platonic or Aristotelian senses; indeed, Bacon apologizes for using it at all: "a name which I the rather adopt because it has grown into use and become familiar." His most explicit definition is as follows: "The true Form is such that it deduces the given nature from some source of being which is inherent in more natures, and prior in the natural order of things . . . to the Form itself. For a true and perfect axiom of knowledge then the direction and precept will be *that another nature be discovered which is convertible with the given nature, and yet is a limitation of a prior nature, as of a true and real genus.*"[35]

Bacon's clearest example of this process is the problem of finding the form of whiteness. This occurs in an early work, *Valerius Terminus*, but the result there arrived at is ratified in *Novum Organum* and *De Augmentis*.[36] In *Valerius Terminus* the stress is on the operations required to produce whiteness rather than upon the discovery of forms, and the terminology used is correspondingly different.

Nevertheless, when Bacon speaks of the "freeing of direction," that is, finding a recipe for whiteness which is independent of particular initial materials or means, he is clearly foreshadowing the search for forms as defined in the passage just quoted. From the observation of instances in which air and water mixed together produce whiteness (foam and snow), Bacon rises to greater generality by discarding at each step the particular accompaniments of air and water, such as colorlessness and transparency, and finally reaches, in the "sixth direction" (which he admits he has not fully proved by induction), the statement that "all bodies or parts of bodies which are unequal equally, that is in a simple proportion, do represent whiteness." He adds the further axioms that "absolute equality produceth transparence, inequality in simple order or proportion produceth all other colours, and absolute or orderless inequality produceth blackness."[37]

We may represent this ladder of axioms symbolically as follows. The most general nature from which the rest can be derived is the property of a body of having its small parts in a certain ratio of size. Let this property be represented by A. It is then asserted that A is the form of color (including transparency). Instances of A can be further specified in four ways: as having their small parts equal (Aa_1), in simple proportion (Aa_2), in complex proportion (Aa_3), and of random sizes (Aa_4). Then we have:

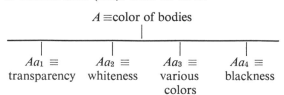

$A \equiv$ color of bodies

| $Aa_1 \equiv$ transparency | $Aa_2 \equiv$ whiteness | $Aa_3 \equiv$ various colors | $Aa_4 \equiv$ blackness |

From Aa_2 it is possible to descend the scale of axioms again to the original instances of whiteness by adding more specific determinations to Aa_2, until the particular recipe of mixing air and water is reached, and it is also possible to predict that any as yet unobserved instance which is a further specification of Aa_2 will also exhibit whiteness. Another way in which predictions may be made is by deduction from the relations between the four forms given. For example, it is clear that a mixture of two bodies which are separately instances of Aa_1, will fall under Aa_2, and hence will be white. Again, some instances of Aa_3 will approach Aa_1, since two numbers which are nearly equal are in complex proportion, but instances of Aa_2 and Aa_4 will never approach Aa_1, and hence Bacon concludes that of all colors, "whiteness and blackness are most incompatible with transparence." The ladder of axioms set out in this way therefore satisfies Bacon's demand that

> In establishing axioms by this kind of induction, we must also examine and try whether the axiom so established be framed to the measure of those particulars only from which it is derived,

or whether it be larger and wider. And if it be larger and wider, we must observe whether by indicating to us new particulars it confirm that wideness and largeness as by a collateral security; that we may not either stick fast in things already known, or loosely grasp at shadows and abstract forms; not at things solid and realized in matter."[38]

The ladder of axioms therefore appears to be constructed as follows: at each rung there is a convertible proposition which states that the form of a given nature is identical with a certain specification of a more general nature, and each of these propositions has been obtained by means of the inductive tables. We shall now consider some characteristics of the forms in more detail.

1. A form is not a cause in the sense of another nature merely found in constant conjunction with the given nature. Thus, Bacon's aim in using his inductive method is quite different from that of Mill, although Mill's methods of agreement and difference are based on the principles of Bacon's tables. But if Mill discovers from his methods that *A* causes *B*, for example that a certain fertilizer causes a good crop, this result is compatible with *A* having effects other than *B*, and with *B* being caused by something other than *A* in different circumstances. But if *A* is the *form* of *B*, then it *is* *B* under all circumstances, and its effects are simply *B*'s effects and no others.[39]

2. A form is not an abstract conception, but a physical property or "nature." This follows from the fact that the form has come up the ladder of axioms by appearing in tables of presence with the nature under investigation and not appearing in its tables of absence. A question arises here about "hidden" or practically unobservable forms, for example, subtle atomic processes. How are they to be elicited from tables of presence and absence? Bacon is fully aware that detailed knowledge of nature will involve hidden and subtle processes[40] and partly aware of the problem they present, for some of his prerogative instances direct attention to the need for "aids to the senses" such as microscopes and telescopes, and he also admits a certain amount of reasoning from observed to unobserved natures, as for example when the motion which is the form of heat is said to be motion of small (not directly observable) particles. The arguments by which he arrives at this specification of the form of heat are not inductive after his own recipe, but hypothetical and analogical; but it must be remembered that they are only arguments leading to the first vintage, and elsewhere Bacon warns against injudicious use of the method of analogy for eliciting "things not directly perceptible."[41] It cannot be said that he deals adequately with the difficulty inherent in explanations in terms of hidden natures, but given the presuppositions of his method it is impossible to see how he could have done better, for hidden natures demand hypothetical arguments.

3. A form is not a mere mathematical description of the phenomenal nature in question but must get behind this to its real cause. There are two outstanding examples of Bacon's application of this principle, in his discussions of astronomy and of optics. In criticizing both Ptolemy and Copernicus he remarks, "I am attempting a far greater work: for it is not merely calculations or predictions that I aim at, but philosophy: such a philosophy I mean as may inform the human understanding, not only of the motion of the heavenly bodies and the period of that motion, but likewise of their substance, various qualities, powers, and influences . . . what is found in nature herself, and is actually and really true."[42] And again with regard to the form of light: "Neither in perspective nor otherwise has any inquiry been made about Light which is of any value. The radiations of it are handled, not the origins. But it is the placing of perspective among the mathematics that has caused this defect . . . for thus a premature departure has been made from Physics."[43] In other words, Bacon would be satisfied with a wave or corpuscular theory of light, but not with mere geometrical optics.

His attitude to mathematics is not always so negative, but he considers that its proper place is not among the lower axioms, which should be concerned with concretes; it is, rather, an essential constituent of higher axioms which deal with generalities, for "of all natural forms . . . Quantity is the most abstracted and separable from matter." And the nearer an investigation approaches to simple natures "the easier and plainer will everything become. . . . And inquiries into nature have the best result, when they begin with physics and end in mathematics."[44] How quantity might enter the ladder of axioms and facilitate a descent to new particulars is indicated in the example of whiteness, but Bacon gives no further such examples of the use of mathematics in his later works.

4. The form of a given nature is not only to be a specification of a nature which is more general in the sense of being exhibited in more particulars; it is also to be prior, that is, to reflect the nature of things in relation to the universe and not in relation to man. In Bacon's comments on the direction for whiteness he sees this as a condition ensuring that the directions will actually enable the nature in question to be produced by operations: "To make a stone bright or to make it smooth it is a good direction to say, make it even; but to make a stone even it is no good direction to say, make it bright or make it smooth; for . . . evenness is the disposition of the stone in itself, but smooth is to the hand and bright to the eye."[45]

This is one of Bacon's clearest statements of a distinction between primary and secondary qualities, and of the view that forms must be found among the primary qualities. But his notion of a primary quality is here confused with that of a quality which can most easily be induced in a body by man. The two notions are certainly not identical, for it might be easier, for example, to heat a body by bringing it in contact with another hot body rather than by directly putting its small parts into motion, and in *Novum Organum* Bacon makes this distinction between the form of heat and the method of inducing heat. He does not, however, enlarge on his early distinction between primary and secondary qualities, and it must be assumed that he thought that they could only be identified as a result of the application of his method, and not as its starting point. It does at least follow from the requirements of the method that primary qualities have the property of relative independence of the accidental circumstances under which they are perceived. This is only a special case of the rule that the form of a given nature is to refer to another nature more general than that under investigation. Thus, Bacon distinguishes sensible heat from heat itself; the same tepid water may feel hot to the cold hand and cold to the hot hand, but these two instances do not appear in the tables of presence and absence of heat respectively, but in the table of degrees of heat. The form is elicited independently of them, and then used to explain them: they are due to "the effect of heat on the animal spirits."[46] Whatever else Bacon means by the primary qualities which are candidates for forms, they must at least be among the qualities of which the senses give most consistent reports. His robust realism is untroubled by doubts about the status of even these qualities.

5.   The character of Bacon's realism is further indicated by his references to forms as *laws*. It is not that forms or species have some existence apart from, or even embodied in, individuals, but that those individuals really act according to fixed laws: "For though in nature nothing really exists beside individual bodies, performing pure individual acts according to a fixed law, yet in philosophy this very law, and the investigation, discovery and explanation of it, is the foundation as well of knowledge as of operation. And it is this law, with its clauses, that I mean when I speak of *Forms*."[47] The word "law" does not here connote a "correlation" of phenomena, for, as we have seen, mere correlations do not express forms; it has rather the older association with order imposed by the civil power: "the first congregations of matter; which like a general assembly of estates, doth give law to all bodies." In regard to these laws, Bacon is a moderate determinist: "If a man knew the conditions, affections, and processes of matter, he would certainly comprehend the sum and general issue (for I do not say that his knowledge would extend to the parts and singularities) of all things, past, present, and to come." Two conceptions of the source of this order seem to be involved. If we could comprehend the configurations of matter clearly and truly, as they really are in nature, their laws of action would become apparent to us, but the resulting order is also (as we know by faith) due to divine power. Bacon sees no incompatibility between seeing things as reflections of divine purpose and seeking their natural causes, and leaves it an open question whether matter, once created with its original force, would in course of time have shaped itself into the existing configurations of things, even without specific design.[48]

6.   One further feature of forms which Bacon assumes, at least in his discussion of whiteness, appears to lead to a serious inconsistency between the demands of the inductive method and the construction of a ladder of axioms by means of forms. The notion of the ladder requires that a form be understood as relative to the state of development of the ladder at any given moment. Bacon remarks, for example, that the "direction for whiteness" which he gives in terms of relative sizes of particles, is not yet completely "free," since it is tied to bodies, whereas a more general direction would refer to the medium through which whiteness is conveyed to the eye and to the act of sense itself. In other words, he conceives of extending the ladder of axioms upward to account for all sensible appearances of whiteness by including a wider range of particulars relating to the medium and the conditions of sensation. Thus, there seems to be nothing to prevent unfinished portions of a ladder being incorporated in a more general structure, until we reach Bacon's ideal of the "summary law of nature," the "cone and vertical point," which "produces all the variety of nature."[49]

It therefore seems to be a reasonable interpretation of Bacon's intentions, and is indeed compatible with the subsequent development of science, that the forms identified with specific natures should change with every extension of the ladder of axioms based on instances of those natures. For if the ladder of axioms for color illustrated above were incorporated in a more general scale of which the summary form were B (where B might be wave-motion in the ether), then each axiom of the new ladder would show A identified with a certain specification of B, say Bb_1, and so the form of whiteness would now be Bb_1a_2. But remember how Bacon considers that the axiom "$Aa_2 \equiv$ whiteness" has been obtained. It is supposed to be derived deductively from the tables of discovery and this presupposes that Aa_2 is a simple nature, whereas it has now been found to be further analyzable as a specification of B. It seems that either the claim that induction is based on exhaustive enumeration of simple natures must be given up, and hence the claim to certainty of inductive conclusions, or no form can be discovered until the whole scheme of axioms is complete. To make matters worse, Bacon doubts whether the summary law of nature can ever be reached, and if this is so, the conditions of the method can never be fulfilled (Bacon admits that "no one can divide things truly who has not a full knowledge of their nature.")[50] The only way out of the dilemma would appear to be some kind of classification of natures into grades or types appropriate to each rung of the ladder of axioms, so that at each stage an exhaustive enumeration could be given. Bacon makes some mention of primary, secondary, tertiary, etc. qualities, and of "Forms of the first class,"[51] but it is not clear whether, or how, he meant to develop this classification, or even that he was aware of the dilemma to which it might have provided a solution in logic, although hardly in practice.

The notion of a ladder of axioms does not, however, depend on Bacon's untenable assumptions about his inductive method nor on his particular view of forms, and it is unfortunate that the greatest stress has been laid on these, and not on his vision of the deductive structure of the new science, in respect of which events have been kinder to him. In comparing his ladder of axioms with the subsequent hypothetico-deductive structure of theories, two points of similarity may be noticed. The first is the possibility of deducing new particulars, which depends, as we have seen, partly on logical or mathematical relations between the various forms. Bacon does not, however, develop this in detail, and he certainly underestimated the part that pure mathematical deduction would play in it. He is concerned not with the machinery of deduction, but with the identification of the forms with particular phenomena, and this is the second point of similarity with later theories. For, whatever may be the case more recently, it was certainly a requirement in the earlier stages of physics that theoretical explanations should be given in terms of models, initially mechanical models, and this involves identifying the properties of phenomena, for example heat, light, and sound, with a limited set of more general mechanical properties. Bacon's tables provide a systematic way of setting out the analogies which suggest the identification of heat with mechanical motion, and his "Consents and Dissents of Visibles and Audibles" suggest the comparison of the modes of transmission of light and of sound.[52] Where the tables proved scientifically useful, as in these two investigations, it was in virtue not of infallible inductions but of hypotheses suggested by the analogies they exhibited. It was a favorite pastime in the nineteenth century to criticize Bacon for not being a Galileo or a Newton, but this is somewhat beside the point, for neither Galileo nor Newton, in his *Principia*, was dealing with explanations of "secondary" phenomena in terms of mechanical models, and it is here if anywhere that Bacon's contribution lies.

Primary Matter and its Qualities

THE method of induction as Bacon presents it depends entirely on the possibility of identifying all the simple natures in a given instance: "Exclusion is evidently the rejection of simple natures: and if we do not yet possess sound and true notions of simple natures, how can the process of Exclusion be made accurate?" He promises to provide these sound and true notions by means of his aids to the understanding, but the prerogative instances are the first and only ones of these to be treated, and presumably Bacon intended to treat the important matter of simple natures later under the heading "*Limits of Investigation* or a Synopsis of all Natures in the Universe."[53]

There is no doubt that Bacon remained uncertain what simple natures should go into this list. He attacks the superficial division of things into species of animals, plants, and minerals, and also the theory of four elements and the Aristotelian classification of change. He gives several lists of qualities, variously described as cardinal and universal virtues, elementary qualities, and configurations of matter, which almost always begin with "Dense and Rare" (a title which is "so general, that if it were fully drawn out it would anticipate many of the succeeding titles"), and go on through "Heavy and Light," "Hot and Cold," "Tangible and Pneumatic," to such apparently complex natures as organization and animation.[54] It is never clear which, if any, of these natures are to be regarded as *simple*, and indeed, the term is in any case a misnomer, since, as we have seen according to the ladder of axioms, there can be only one, or at least only a few, irreducibly simple natures, namely those involved in the summary form of which all other natures are specifications. It is clear that if Bacon's method is to work at all there must be some way other than the method itself for anticipating, at least in general terms, what the simple natures or the summary forms are, since they are presupposed by the method. If the summary form is conceived, for example, in terms of Democritean atomism, the tables of presence and absence may be used to indicate what particular configurations and motions of atoms are co-present and co-absent with the given nature, as Bacon does in the cases of heat, "visibles and audibles," winds, and dense and rare. It is therefore important to consider the noninductive arguments which led Bacon to anticipate some form of mechanism as the summary law of nature.

Of all the ancient philosophers whose works he considers shallow and hopes to supersede, Bacon speaks most highly of Democritus.[55] But his views on the adequacy of atomism underwent considerable changes during the period of his philosophical writings; even in the early works he is by no means an orthodox atomist, and later he becomes convinced that atomism is false. It is convenient to take a work which apparently dates from his middle period, certainly before the *Novum Organum*, to indicate the progress of his views, since it is here that the most detailed arguments are to be found. The work is the *De Principiis et Originibus*, a revision of part of the *De Sapientia Veterum* of 1609, where

Bacon had adopted the popular device of interpreting the ancient myths of the gods as allegories of cosmological and philosophical theories.

In *De Principiis* he rewrites and expands the fable of Cupid as it appears in the earlier work.[56] He takes Cupid to be a representation of the nature and virtues of primary matter. In the myth Cupid is said to be without parents, to be naked, to be an infant, to be blind, and to shoot arrows. Each of these properties Bacon takes as representative of the characteristics of primary matter; first, it and its motions are without natural cause, that is, without parents; secondly, Cupid's nakedness provides Bacon with an allegory in terms of which he comments on five views of the nature and properties of primary matter; and (in *De Sapientia Veterum* only), the other three properties represent respectively the changelessness of matter, the "blind necessity of fate" inherent in the primary motions of matter, and the fact that if atoms are placed in a void they must necessarily act at a distance, or otherwise no motion would take place.

It is to the second property that Bacon devotes most attention.[57] In the myth Cupid is said to be a "person" with attributes, and this already contradicts the Aristotelian view of matter as mere potentiality and formlessness. But Cupid is represented as naked rather than clothed, and this Bacon takes as an allegory of atomism, whose adherents make "the principle of things one in substance, and that fixed and invariable; but deduce the diversity of beings from the different magnitudes, configurations, and positions of that same principle." There are other views which, as it were, represent Cupid as clothed; those of the monists, who assert that there is one principle and all things consist of its variations, of the pluralists, who set up many principles, and of those who set up an infinity of (or at least very many) specific principles and thus have no need for any device to account for the multiplicity of things. Of the monists Bacon mentions Thales, Anaximenes, and Heraclitus, who all attribute to primary matter a form which is "substantially homogeneous with the form of . . . the secondary essences." Bacon attacks this procedure on the following grounds: first, the monists pick out one nature which seems to them most excellent, and say that this is the only one which is what it seems, while all others are really the same as this although they appear to be different. But all natural things should be treated alike. Or if the monists mean to speak of an "ideal" water or air or fire, then they are guilty of equivocation and are no more intelligible than those who speak of abstract matter. Secondly, they do not describe how the variation of their principle occurs and produces "such armies of contraries in the world," for if it is really present in everything it must be received by the senses, and if it does not appear to be present, a reasonable explanation of the appearances must be given, "but you should by no means be required to

assent to those things whereof neither the being is manifest by the sense, nor the explanation probable by the reason." Thirdly, if there is only one principle, it ought to have a visible superiority, there ought to be nothing diametrically opposed to it, and it ought both to generate and to dissolve things indifferently. But none of this is the case with the principles suggested by the monists.

Bacon now turns to the pluralists, who, he says, have to be examined one by one, since they seem to have more strength on their side and certainly more prejudice.[58] The *De Principiis* is, however, incomplete, and closes here with a detailed attack on Telesius, who makes the first active entities to be heat and cold, whose textures are respectively rarity and density. In general Bacon has a good opinion of Telesius, whom he calls "the first of the moderns,"[59] but in the case of his active principles he is easily refuted by numerous instances of qualities more general than heat and cold and not arising from them, for example, impenetrability, cohesion, and heavy and light.

We may now return to the discussion of atomism. If Cupid's nakedness indicates that no form "homogeneous with the secondary essences" must be ascribed to the atom, and yet that it is not entirely abstract, then what form may be ascribed to it? Bacon's answers to this are not wholly consistent. In *De Principiis* he commends Democritus, who affirmed that atoms and their virtues "were unlike anything that could fall under the senses; but distinguished them as being of a perfectly dark and hidden nature," but complains that Democritus falls short of his own insight when he ascribes two particular primary motions to the atom: those of descent and of impact.[60] (It is unlikely that Democritus ascribed these motions to the atom, although Lucretius – Bacon's source – did so.) In motion as in substance the atom must be other than all larger bodies, and this would be discovered by the method of exclusions. But at this point Bacon realizes that insistence on the "heterogeneity" or otherness of the atom will result in the impossibility of saying anything at all about it, and continues with the remark that it is only in the case of God that "when his nature is inquired after by the sense, exclusions shall not end in affirmations." In the case of the atom something in the end can be affirmed after due use of the method of exclusions: "not only some notion . . . but a distinct and definite notion," and later the atom is said to be "a true being, having matter, form, dimension, place, resistance, appetite, motion and emanations; which . . . amid the destruction of all natural bodies, remains unshaken and eternal."[61] Why these properties are not subject to the same objections he brings against the monists and pluralists, Bacon does not explain.

There are other places, however, where Bacon does not adopt the Democritean view that atoms are "fixed and invariable" and have diverse shapes and sizes. In *Cogitationes de Natura Rerum* he commends Pythagoras for assuming a smaller number of primary properties of the atom, for he makes the atoms "equal," so that variety can be produced only by their different numbers and configurations. Thus, for Pythagoras "the world consists of numbers." Bacon thinks that Democritus' view that the atoms are diverse can be overthrown, for experiment tends to show that "all things can be made out of all things."[62] It was perhaps such experiments, together with the desire on theoretical grounds to minimize the number of fixed and primary properties of matter, which led Bacon by the time he published *Novum Organum* effectively to abandon atomism. There, in connection with the doctrine of atoms, we read that the presuppositions of the vacuum and the unchangeableness of matter are false.[63] All that is left of the principle of changelessness is the axiom that the quantity of matter in the universe is invariable. Bacon repeats this throughout his writings, and as far as natural philosophy is concerned, he regards it as an *a priori* principle of divine revelation, since nothing except God can create or destroy matter, and the activities of God are outside the scope of natural philosophy.[64]

A change in his views on void also contributed to the abandonment of atomism. In the earlier writings Bacon is prepared to consider its existence, and even in *Novum Organum*, in spite of the definite statement quoted above, he still vacillates, but in *Historia Densi et Rari* "There is no vacuum in nature" is given as a "provisional canon." There seem to be three main reasons for this hardening of view. First, Bacon becomes increasingly impressed with new empirical facts relating to gases which were then coming to light and which indicated the possible existence of subtle matter even in space void of air; secondly, he comes to think that Hero's theory of the interspersed vacuum is not necessary to explain expansion and contraction of bodies; and thirdly, he embraces a quasi-Aristotelian view that matter can "fold and unfold itself in space . . . without interposition of a vacuum," and comes to regard density and rarity as possibly the most fundamental properties of matter.[65]

This brings us to Bacon's views on the primary powers of matter. Here he is never an orthodox atomist, for according to orthodoxy the atoms move each other only when they come into contact, but Bacon never takes impenetrability and impact to be fundamental powers. Indeed, he usually speaks of the powers of matter in terms like "desire," "aversion," "instinct," or "force," as in his first account[66] of the fable of Cupid, where Love is "the appetite or instinct of primal matter; or to speak more plainly, *the natural motion of the atom*; which is indeed the original and unique force that constitutes and fashions all things out of matter." This is "the summary law of nature, that impulse of desire impressed by God upon the primary particles of matter which

makes them come together."* And when Bacon lists his primary motions it is clear that he is not using the word "motion" in the sense of local motion only, but in the general sense of "change," as in the Aristotelian *kinēsis*, and of the powers of bodies to produce change. In *Novum Organum*[68] the "principal kinds of motions or active virtues" are listed among "Prerogative Instances" as "Instances of Strife and Predominance," and include, as well as such purely local motions as expansion, motion of descent under gravity, and rotation; also such forces or qualities as those of impenetrability, cohesion, and excitation of new powers in a body, as when it is heated or magnetized.† And in his later works, Bacon speaks of bodies having "perceptions" when they are changed in some way in the presence of other bodies, although perception in inanimate bodies must be distinguished from sensation: "For though there are many kinds and varieties of pain in animals . . . it is yet most certain that all of them, as far as the motion is concerned, exist in inanimate substances; for example, in wood or stone, when it is burnt or frozen . . . though they do not enter the senses for want of the animal spirit."[70]

On the other hand, it is possible to reconcile this apparent animism with a mechanical view by noticing the pervasive powers which Bacon ascribes to "spirits" or pneumatic bodies. There is no doubt that he regards these as subtle material bodies, and that when he speaks of perceptions and influences passing between gross bodies, he usually conceives these as transmitted by spirits which, like the Stoic *pneumata*, are responsible for many of the qualities of bodies, and whose action may be in some sense mechanical.[71] This reconciliation of his apparently conflicting views may be correct as far as it goes, but it does not solve the problem of what exactly Bacon conceives these mechanical actions to be. He may not be committed to endowing bodies with all the animistic powers beloved of his sixteenth-century predecessors, but on the other hand, he is certainly not satisfied with atoms acting purely by impact, either in the case of gross bodies or of spirits. His reasons for this dissatisfaction are empirical, and are to be found, for example, in his discussions of cohesion and tenacity, or the "desire for continuity" of bodies, a nature which he thinks "will not easily be found out on enquiry" and which cannot be accounted for by spirits; also in his discussions of impenetrability and resistance to destruction, which he thinks must be accounted an "active virtue" of bodies, not a passive property; and, finally, he considers that certain actions at a distance, as of the

---

* Elsewhere, however, he repudiates sympathies and antipathies.[67]

† In *Inquisitio Legitima de Motu* and even in *De Augmentis* the primary motions are listed as if they were simple natures out of which the inductive tables are to be constructed, but in *Novum Organum* Bacon appears less sure of their fundamental nature, and dismisses them to mere helps in determining the relative strengths of the virtues of bodies.[69]

magnet, appear to imply virtue "subsisting for a certain time and in a certain space without a body" and this is impossible on the assumption of atomism.[72]

Bacon is unable to solve the problem which these facts present. The suggestions in his late fragmentary works are inconclusive and inconsistent. In *Historia Densi et Rari* he seems to be inclining to a continuum theory in which the most fundamental qualities are those of density and rarity; in *Historia Sulphuris, Mercurii, et Salis*, sulphur, the oily, fatty, inflammable principle, and mercury, the watery, crude, non-inflammable principle, are judged to be "the most primeval natures, the most original configurations of matter, and among the forms of the first class almost the principal."[73] The inconclusiveness is of course inevitable, for Bacon only claims to be trying to anticipate the results of induction. Nevertheless, his general conclusion in favor of some kind of mechanism or Pythagorean atomism is sufficient to account for the unshakeable faith in the simplicity of nature which underlies his method and convinces him that natural laws are there to be discovered.

To summarize, many things may be said in criticism of Bacon's method: he made little first-hand contribution to science by means of it, and his successors did not use it; he underestimated the place of hypothesis and of mathematics in scientific theories; he claimed a mechanical certainty for the method which is quite unjustified; and he failed to see the difficulties involved in introducing hidden entities and processes into science. On the other hand, it must be put to his credit that he encouraged detailed and methodical experimentation; he saw clearly the need to look for negative instances or refuting experiments in relation to all positive or confirmatory instances; he visualized a structure of scientific laws which is formally not unlike that of subsequent hypothetical-deductive systems; his tables of discovery constituted a method of systematic analogy which assisted the development of theoretical models; his influence in introducing mechanical hypotheses into seventeenth-century science can be compared with that of Descartes and Gassendi; and yet finally he did not allow the attractions of mechanism to blind him to the difficulties of pure atomism. On this last point some connection has been seen between Bacon's discussions and the basically similar, although more subtle and better informed, attacks upon atomism by Leibniz.[74]

9

Hobbes

A. G. N. FLEW

THOMAS HOBBES WAS BORN, prematurely, in 1588, the year of the Spanish Armada, the second son of the Vicar of Westport by Malmesbury in Gloucestershire, England. Educated at local schools, he made sufficient progress in classical studies to be able to render Euripides' *Medea* from the Greek into Latin iambics before he was fourteen. At the age of fifteen or thereabouts he went to Magdalen Hall, attached to Magdalen College, Oxford, staying there for five years, all at the expense of an uncle who came to the rescue when Hobbes' father had had to flee to escape the consequences of a brawl ("at the church doore," as Aubrey has it). On coming down from Oxford, Hobbes was appointed tutor companion to the eldest son of William Cavendish, who was later — in consideration of a payment of £10,000 to James I — created first Earl of Devonshire.

This was the beginning of a most happy lifelong connection with the Devonshire family. It introduced him to influential people, foreign travel, and a first-class library. But the only immediate literary issue of its first twenty years was a translation of Thucydides' *History of the Peloponnesian War*, published in 1629. In that year Hobbes had temporarily to transfer into the service of Sir Gervase Clinton. It was now, when he had already turned forty, that he first encountered Euclid; "This made him in love with Geometry." By 1630 Hobbes was back in the service of the Devonshires. He was on the Continent again from 1634 to 1636–7 with the next Earl. On this his third continental tour he became one of the intellectual circle of the Abbé Mersenne, which included Descartes, who was then working on the *Discours de la Méthode* and the other papers to be published in 1637. He also made in 1636 a pilgrimage to Italy to visit Galileo, whose *Dialogues* had appeared in 1632.

The England to which he returned was under the threat of civil war. He wrote, and in 1640 circulated manuscript copies of, his first essay in psychology and politics, *The Elements of Law*. A few months later he fled to France. In 1646 he began a short spell as mathematics tutor to the future Charles II. *Leviathan* was published in 1651. Later in the same year Hobbes returned to England. The *De Corpore* appeared in 1655, sparking off his protracted and misguided controversy with two of the leading mathematicians of his day. He continued writing, and publishing, right up till his death, at the age of ninety-one, in 1679. He is buried in the parish churchyard of Hault Hucknall in Derbyshire, across the park from the splendid Elizabethan Hardwick Hall, one of the seats of the Devonshires.

IT MAY HELP THE READER to have an annotated check list of Hobbes' main publications.

First, in 1629, is the translation of Thucydides.[1] Its main importance for us lies in the facts that the supremely tough-minded and detached Thucydides had, and still has, a claim to be "yet accounted the most politic historiographer that ever writ,"[2] and that Hobbes in his introduction summarized with obvious approval what he took to be the political preferences of Thucydides, who "least of all liked the democracy" and "best approved of the regal government."[3] These facts suggest that Hobbes formed early in his literary career, both an ideal of a detached but practically useful study of politics, and the personal political preferences which appear in all his later social writings. For Hobbes the study of Thucydides had to substitute for first-hand political experience. We quote the tribute of Thucydides' latest translator to his predecessor: "He, above all men, had an intellect equipped to understand and to enjoy the greatness of his original; nor is there anything in his style that is not exact, masculine and emphatic. There is no nonsense about Hobbes. His only defect is inaccuracy, a thing that was, to a large extent, unavoidable, considering the advances in textual criticism which have been made since his day . . . one cannot but express one's deference to a great philosopher, a great stylist, and one of the greatest of translators."[4]

Second, a group of short works. The most important of these is *A Short Tract on First Principles*. This was first published in 1889.[5] It was probably written in the early 1630's, after Hobbes had fallen in love with geometry and in the period of personal contacts with Descartes and Galileo. It attempts to account for *sensing* in terms of a general Galilean theory of motion. It has sometimes been referred to as *The Little Treatise*. This is a confusing usage, for Hobbes and hence some of his interpreters also use the same expression for a quite different work. There is also another short piece of the same sort written later and never published in full.[6] Both papers are of great importance for understanding the development of Hobbes' mechanical conception of nature.[7]

Third, the work now known as *The Elements of Law*. This was certainly completed in 1640, as in the *Considerations upon the Reputation, Loyalty, Manners and Religion of Thomas Hobbes*, which seems itself to have been written in 1662, the author makes clear:

> When the Parliament sat, that began in April 1640, and was dissolved in May following, and in which many points of the regal power, which were necessary for the peace of the kingdom, and the safety of his Majesty's person, were disputed and denied, Mr. Hobbes wrote a little treatise in English. . . . Of this treatise, though not printed, many gentlemen had copies, which occa-sioned much talk of the author; and had not his Majesty dissolved the Parliament, it had brought him into danger of his life.[8]

This has led some writers to call *this The Little Treatise*. Though circulated in 1640 only in manuscript, it was eventually printed in 1650, as two separate publications: *Human Nature, or the Fundamental Elements of Policy*; and *De Corpore Politico, or the Elements of Law, Moral and Politic*. Molesworth, the editor of the standard edition of Hobbes, presents these separately as the first two legs of *Hobbes' Tripos*. The third, with no obvious connection with these, is *Of Liberty and Necessity*.[9] This grouping and its general title seem to have been purely posthumous and to derive from an edition first issued in 1684. Tönnies presents the first two as one work and gives it the title, derived from the subtitle of the second component, *The Elements of Law*. He was certainly right in taking Hobbes to have intended the first as the psychological foundation of the second.

Fourth, on the assembly of the Long Parliament in November 1640 "Mr. Hobbes, doubting how they would use him, went over into France, the first of all that fled. . . . "[10] There Mersenne immediately asked him to write some Objections for Descartes' forthcoming *Meditations* (1641).[11] In the next few years he also wrote two or three papers on optics,[12] some of which he later incorporated into *De Homine*.[13]

Fifth, in 1642 Hobbes published *De Cive* (Concerning the Citizen) in Latin.[14] A second revised Latin edition followed in 1647, and an English translation — by the author — in 1651. A Preface explains:

> I was studying philosophy for my mind sake, and I had gathered together its first elements in all kinds: and having digested them into three sections by degrees, I thought to have written them, so as in the first I would have treated of body and its general properties; in the second of man and his special faculties and affections; in the third, of civil government and the duties of subjects. . . . Whilst I contrive, order, pensively and slowly compose these matters . . . it so happened in the interim, that my country, some few years before the civil wars did rage, was boiling hot with questions concerning the rights of dominion and the obedience due from subjects, the true forerunners of an approaching war; and was the cause which, all those other matters deferred, ripened and plucked from me this third part.[15]

The English version is given by Molesworth under its original title of *Philosophical Rudiments concerning Government and Society*. It is now usual to use the Latin title for both the Latin and the English.[16]

Sixth, in 1646 Hobbes wrote the pamphlet *Of Liberty and Necessity: A Treatise, wherein all con-

troversy concerning Predestination, Election, Free-will, Grace, Merits, Reprobation, etc. is fully decided and cleared, in reply to an essay on the same subject by John Bramhall, the Bishop of Derry. This was not intended for publication, but was pirated from a borrowed copy by John Davys of Kidwelly. So perhaps the sweeping subtitle, and certainly the epistle "To the Sober and Discreet Reader," are the work of Davys:

> Thus much, Reader, I have thought fit to acquaint you with, that thou mightest know what a jewel thou hast in thy hands, which thou must accordingly value, not by the bulk, but the preciousness. Thou hast here in a few sheets what might prove work enough for many thousand sermons and exercises . . . thou hast what will cast an eternal blemish on all the cornered caps of the priests and Jesuits, and all the black and white caps of the canting tribe.[17]

This furtive publication surprised Hobbes and angered Bramhall. Forthwith in 1655 Bramhall published his original rejoinder as *A Defence of True Liberty from Antecedent and Extrinsical Necessity*, explaining: "Here is all that passed between us upon this subject, without any addition, or the least variation from the original." In 1656 Hobbes replied with *The Questions concerning Liberty, Necessity, and Chance*.[18] In this he reprints the whole of Bramhall's book, commenting paragraph by paragraph. Bramhall came back in 1658 with *Castigations of Hobbes his Last Animadversions*, which Hobbes ignored, except that ten years later he wrote a reply to the personal attacks of the Appendix, which had been called "The Catching of Leviathan, the Great Whale." The reply was published only posthumously.[19]

Seventh, in 1651 came the notorious *Leviathan*, always the most read and most discussed of Hobbes' works, and the one upon which his general fame has mainly rested.[20]

Eighth, in 1655 in Latin,[21] is the first part, *De Corpore* (Concerning Body), of the long projected three-decker survey of the Elements of Philosophy. The English translation was revised but not written by Hobbes. It is in places seriously defective. In deference to the priority of the Latin text, it is usual with this first as with the earlier third part of the trilogy, to refer to both Latin and English versions by their Latin title.

Ninth, during the preparation of this English version Hobbes substantially rewrote Chapters XVIII and XX, made some minor alterations elsewhere, and added an appendix, "Six Lessons to the (Savilian) Professors of the Mathematics."[22] The chapters thus rewritten had been the first shots in a controversy with John Wallis and Seth Ward.[23] The controversy continued for nearly a quarter of a century; Hobbes' last blows having been delivered in the *Decameron Physiologicum*, published when he had already passed his ninetieth birthday.[24] At one stage Robert Boyle became involved, for Hobbes took *New Experiments touching the Spring of the Air* as a slight. His *Dialogus Physicus, sive de Natura Aeris*[25] was a rebuke to Boyle, urging that his experimental results — rightly interpreted — merely provided laborious but superfluous confirmation for Hobbes' own armchair discoveries. Before the end he was claiming not merely to square the circle, but to cube the sphere, and to duplicate the cube. Perhaps the kindest comment comes from Aubrey: "Twas pitty that Mr Hobbs had not begun the study of the mathematics sooner, els he would not have layn so open." But it must be added that Hobbes' incapacity in mathematics and his failure to appreciate the vital role of experiment in "natural philosophy" fully justified the Royal Society (chartered in 1662) in not electing him to membership.

Tenth, in 1657 Hobbes published in Latin[26] the second part of his trilogy on the Elements of Philosophy, *De Homine* (Concerning Man). This contains an account of optics, partly psychological and partly physiological, and a very condensed psychological introduction to politics on lines familiar from his previous works. With it the trilogy *De Corpore*, *De Homine*, and *De Cive* was at last completed. *De Homine* seems never to have been translated.

Eleventh, probably a few years after the Restoration (1660) Hobbes wrote a dialogue about the Civil War, *Behemoth*. There was no genuine edition in his lifetime.[27] A would-be historical essay, it has recently been described by the Regius Professor of Modern History in Hobbes' own university as "incorrigibly erroneous."[28] Probably in the same decade of his seventies, Hobbes worked on the unfinished *Dialogue between a Philosopher and a Student of the Common Laws of England*. This was part of his campaign against the common lawyers and in favor of statute law. Here and elsewhere Hobbes contributed substantially to the philosophy of law. It is perhaps significant that there are more references to him than to anyone else but Bentham in Austin's *The Province of Jurisprudence Determined*.

Twelfth, in his late eighties Hobbes, in swan song, translated the whole of Homer's *Odyssey* and *Iliad* into English verse.[29]

We have given a general survey of Hobbes' writings, both as a guide through the works and to provide perspective. We shall now present and comment upon some of his chief philosophical positions. We shall not attempt any further comprehensive review of his exceptionally wide-ranging and integrated thought. Instead, we select a few themes, trying to pick out those of the greatest historical interest, those most characteristic of Hobbes, and those of most relevance today. These three criteria can often be satisfied simultaneously. Inevitably, this method must involve that some themes will have disproportionate attention while others are neglected. But this is far preferable to the distant generality which would be the result of trying to cram in everything.

Matter, Motion, and Metaphysics

HOBBES is often thought of as primarily the founder of modern metaphysical materialism, insisting that stuff is all there is. This he certainly does. Thus, in a memorably liturgical passage of *Leviathan* he writes: "The Universe, that is the whole mass of things that are, is corporeal, that is to say body; and hath the dimensions of magnitude, namely, length, breadth, and depth. Also every part of body is likewise body, and hath the like dimensions. And, consequently, every part of the Universe is body, and that which is not body is no part of the Universe. And because the Universe is all, that which is no part of it is nothing, and, consequently nowhere."[30] This commitment he was prepared to follow right through to the end. While contemporaries like Descartes were careful to provide for incorporeal spiritual substances, exemplified in God and the human soul, Hobbes argues boldly that talk of incorporeal substances is simply self-contradictory. As for perceptual experience, it is an appearance of the reality of matter in motion: "All . . . qualities called sensible, are in the object that causeth them, but so many several motions of that matter by which it presseth our organs diversely. Neither in us that are pressed are they anything else but divers motions, for motion produceth nothing but motion."[31] Here and sometimes elsewhere be seems to be claiming that veridical and hallucinatory percepts in themselves *are* motions: "and in the brain itself nothing but tumult, proceeding either from the action of the objects or from the disorderly agitation of the organs of our sense."[32]

Again, Hobbes is thought of as the metaphysical spokesman of a mechanical conception of nature, urging that *everything* is some sort of machine. This too is correct. While Descartes saw reason to maintain only that all inanimate nature, animals, and the human body might be regarded as machines, Hobbes had no orthodox and Cartesian reservations about an unextended, non-mechanical, soul. "Man is a part of nature." (It is curious that in the face of Hobbes' remarkable boldness both in speculation and in publication his several autobiographical confessions of extreme constitutional timidity are so often taken *au pied de la lettre*.)

But though materialism and mechanism both have claims to be his key metaphysical ideas, motion has the best claim of all. Hobbes as a metaphysician might well be described in an adaptation of a phrase used of his younger contemporary and admirer Spinoza. Hobbes was the motion-intoxicated man. From the Galilean physics he caught a vision of a universe in motion. In the old Aristotelian

world-view, rest had been regarded as the natural state for bodies. Galileo turned the whole world upside down. Motion is the natural state; and, for good measure, the earth itself is moving. Hobbes took ideas from a revolution in physics and applied them metaphysically, as keys to an account of all there ultimately is. Where Galileo describes only the motions of bodies, Hobbes proclaims that really there is nothing else but the motions of bodies.

In his verse autobiography he tells us how he was haunted by the thought of motion.[33] His first essay in philosophy was an attempt to apply Galilean ideas to sensing. His whole psychology is permeated by them. He presents the human atoms of political society on the model of the restless spheres. "Continual success in obtaining those things which a man from time to time desireth . . . is that men call *felicity*. . . . For there is no such thing as perpetual tranquillity of mind, while we live here; because life itself is but motion, and can never be without desire, nor without fear, no more than without sense." Typically he will not forbear to point a moral for scholastic theology: "What kind of felicity God hath ordained to them that devoutly know him a man shall no sooner know than enjoy, being joys that are now as incomprehensible as the word of the schoolmen *beatifical vision* is unintelligible."[34] Again: "the felicity of this life consisteth not in the repose of a mind satisfied. For there is no such *finis ultimus* [utmost aim] nor *summum bonum* [greatest good] as is spoken of in the books of the old moral philosophers. . . . Felicity is a continual progress of the desire from one object to another, the attaining of the former being still but the way to the latter. . . . So that in the first place I put for a general inclination of all mankind a perpetual and restless desire of power after power, that ceaseth only in death."[35]

In this psychology, as in this Galilean world, the only sort of cause is a push: "A final cause has no place but in such things as have sense and will; and this also I shall prove hereafter to be an efficient cause."[36] Using the traditional puzzles about "seeing double," reflections in smooth surfaces, and after images, he argues to his conclusion, already quoted, about the subjectivity of the sensible qualities of things.* But it is part of this conclusion that these subjective appearances are caused by motions in the external world.

This is easily extended into an empiricist principle: "The original of them all is that which we call sense, for there is no conception in a man's mind which hath not at first, totally or by parts, been begotten upon the organs of sense. The rest are derived from that original."[38] From this we should not be surprised when we see Hobbes go on to display

* The rather more sophisticated doctrine that the "primary" qualities are in things while only the "secondary" are subjective is of course found in *Il Saggiatore*.[37]

other items of the traditional stock in trade of British empiricism — such as the assumption that thinking must always involve mental imagery, and the stress on the association of ideas. But again one must remark the immediate audacity with which Hobbes pushes principles to dangerous conclusions. No sooner has he laid down his empiricist principle than he is beginning[39] to probe its theological implications: "the name of God is used not to make us conceive him, for he is incomprehensible, and his greatness and power are unconceivable; but that we may honour him. Also because whatsoever ... we conceive has been perceived first by sense, either all at once or by parts, a man can have no thought representing any thing not subject to sense."*

Language and Its Abuses

THE chief sources are *Leviathan* and *De Corpore*.[40] There are also numerous passages scattered throughout the rest of the works in which ideas from this account are used polemically; not that polemical purposes are ever far out of mind even in the chief sources. As usual, the version in *Leviathan* is more vivid: "The invention of printing, though ingenious, compared with the invention of letters, is no great matter. ... But the most noble and profitable invention of all other, was that of speech, consisting of names or appellations, and their connection.... " The inventor of speech was, of course, God, who taught Adam to name the beasts. But these lessons did not go very far: " ... for I do not find any thing in the Scripture, out of which, directly or by consequence, can be gathered, that Adam was taught the names of all figures, numbers, measures, colours, sounds, fancies, relations; much less the names of words and speech, such as *general*, *special*, *affirmative*, *negative*, *interrogative*, *optative*, *infinitive*, all of which are useful and, least of all, of *entity*, *intentionality*, *quiddity*, and other insignificant words of the school."

From this pregnant and altogether typical beginning he proceeds to more systematic development:

The general use of speech is to transfer our mental discourse into verbal ... the train of our thoughts into a train of words. ... The manner how speech serveth ... consisteth in the imposing of names and the connection of them. Of names, some are *proper*, and singular to one only thing ... and some are *common* to many things, *man*, *horse*, *tree*; every one of which, though but one name, is nevertheless the name of divers particular things;

in respect of all which together, it is called an *universal*; there being nothing in the world universal but names; for the things named are every one of them individual and singular. One universal name is imposed on many things, for their similitude in some quality or other accident; and whereas a proper name bringeth to mind one thing only, universals recall any one of those many.

Only through the use of words is abstract or general reasoning possible. Significantly, the illustrations given are all mathematical, suggesting that science is to be derived from sound definitions: "So that in the right definition of names lies the first use of speech; which is the acquisition of science. ... " Hobbes notices: "The Greeks have but one word, *logos*, for both *speech* and *reason*: not that they thought that there was no speech without reason, but no reasoning without speech; and the act of reasoning they called *syllogism*, which signifieth summing up of the consequences of one saying to another." He proceeds to tabulate what seem to be four sorts of term: those which apply to material things; to qualities of things; to properties of our own bodies; and to sorts of term. "Fourthly, we bring into account, consider, and give names, to names themselves, and to speeches: for *general*, *universal*, *special*, *equivocal*, are names of names. And *affirmation*, *interrogation*, *commandment*, *narration*, *syllogism*, *sermon*, *oration*, and many other such, are names of speeches." This short list of four sorts is claimed exhaustive and turned forthwith to polemical account: "All other words are but insignificant sounds: and those of two sorts. One when they are new, and yet their meaning not explained by definition: whereof there have been abundance coined by schoolmen, and puzzled philosophers. Another, when men make a name of two names, whose significations are contradictory and inconsistent; as this name, an *incorporeal body*, or, which is all one, an *incorporeal substance* and a great number more." Again here the beloved paradigm reappears, leading him on: " ... whensoever any affirmation is false, the two names of which it is composed, put together and made one, signify nothing at all. For example, if it be a false affirmation to say *A quadrangle is round*, the word *round quadrangle* signifies nothing, but is a mere sound."[41] The chapter from which all these quotations are taken concludes with two or three observations of which he is going to make more later, particularly the politically important: "The names of such things as affect us, that is, which please and displease us, because all men be not alike affected with the same thing, nor the same man at all times, are in the common discourses of men of inconstant signification.... "

In the next chapter he develops the ideas that reasoning is a sort of calculation and that it may deviate from truth not only into error but also into senselessness. He lists seven causes of absurdity.

---

* Compare and contrast Part IV of the *Discourse on Method* in which Descartes, after correctly and carefully making a distinction between what we may conceive and what we may image, observes obliquely that the scholastic maxim *Nihil est in intellectu quod non prius fuerat in sensu* squares ill with the idea of positive theology.

The first is simply the failure to start from definitions. But the next five are types of what some modern philosophers label *type-fallacy*. The cause of the absurdity is the treatment of a word of one sort — which has been given one sort of meaning — as if it were a word of a radically different sort — had been given a quite different sort of meaning. Thus the fourth is that favorite enemy, "the giving of the names of bodies to names, or speeches, as they do that say that *There be things universal*." The seventh and last is "names that signify nothing; but are taken up, and learned by rote from the schools, as *hypostatical, transubstantiate, consubstantiate, eternal-now*, and the like canting of schoolmen."

Later in *Leviathan*[42] Hobbes puts some of this analysis to work.

> But to what purpose, may some man say, is such subtlety in a work of this nature, where I pretend to nothing but what is necessary to the doctrine of government and obedience? It is to this purpose, that men may no longer suffer themselves to be abused, by them, that by this doctrine of *separated essences*, built on the vain philosophy of Aristotle, would fright them from obeying the laws of their country, with empty names; as men fright birds from the corn with an empty doublet, a hat, and a crooked stick. For it is upon this ground, that when a man is dead and buried, they say his soul, that is his life, can walk separated from his body. . . . Upon the same ground they say, that the figure, and color, and taste of a piece of bread, has a being there, where they say that there is no bread.

He reiterates here a suggestion made perhaps rather better elsewhere in *Leviathan*[43]:

> The common sort of men seldom speak insignificantly, and are, therefore, by those other egregious persons counted idiots. But to be assured their words are without any thing correspondent to them in the mind, there would need some examples; which if any man require, let him take a Schoolman in his hands and see if he can translate any one chapter concerning any difficult point . . . into any of the modern tongues, so as to make the same intelligible; or into any tolerable Latin, such as they were acquainted withal, that lived when the Latin tongue was vulgar.

Here and elsewhere Hobbes advocates and employs this test of translation into the vernacular, but he never offers any further rationale for it. Even when Bramhall suggests that he is absurdly objecting to all technical terms as such, Hobbes makes no attempt to work out why in philosophy terms of art are peculiarly dangerous, or why generally the vernacular has a sort of logical priority over all technical discourse.[44]

Whereas in *Leviathan* observations on logic and language are introduced with an ulterior aim avowed, the more systematic and extended account in *De Corpore* has officially no such practical orientation. In fact, Hobbes employs the extra elbow room chiefly to spell out and underline points made in the earlier treatment, while still showing himself creditably undesirous and incapable of that studied narrowmindedness which ignores wider implications of special studies. Thus he begins by stressing again both the artificiality and the importance of language. The private use of words is logically prior to their employment in communication: "the nature of a name consists principally in this, that it is a mark taken for memory's sake; but it serves also by accident to signify and make known to others what we remember ourselves. . . . "[45] The original determination to employ one word and not another for any particular purpose is arbitrary: "A name is a word taken at pleasure to serve for a mark. . . . I suppose the original of names to be arbitrary, taking it a thing that may be assumed as unquestionable."[46] Hobbes then proceeds via a definition of *name* to a classification of sorts of "name"; not neglecting at the end to warn us against thinking that "the diversities of things themselves may be searched out through contradiction and determined in number by such distinctions as these. . . . "[47] Finally, after considering and classifying propositions and syllogisms, he presents a revised version of his table of the seven faults. The new list is more homogeneous and systematic than the old, for whereas there Hobbes started by distinguishing four categories of "name," and then listed four possible miscegenations of these (items 2–5) along with three other faults of a different kind (items 1, 6, and 7); here he simply runs through all the seven possible categorial mixtures methodically. But whereas the earlier table was offered as a list of causes of absurdity, the revision is presented as a schedule of sources of falsity, and all the illustrations provided are described as cases of falsehood: "The falsities of propositions in all these several manners, is to be discovered by the definitions of the copulated names."[48]

The *first* thing to observe in all this is the havoc wrought by Hobbes' infatuation with geometry. For, as our quotations show, it was this which led him so enormously to exaggerate the importance of definitions, and to think that all false propositions contain contradictions. In *De Corpore* he suggests that true propositions are all true by definition: "the first truths were arbitrarily made by those that first of all imposed names upon things. . . . For it is true . . . *man is a living creature*, but it is for this reason, that it pleased men to impose both names on the same thing."[49] As often, he gives the clue to his ideal paradigm by proceeding at once to a geometrical example. Yet however well such ideas may apply to geometry, they certainly cannot be applied universally. There is at least some plausibility in the contention that in geometry "primary propositions are nothing but definitions . . . truths constituted by the inventors of speech . . . "[50]; and false propositions in geometry do indeed involve contradictions. But to suggest that all truths are true by definition, and that all falsehood involves contradiction, is preposterous.

It is also of course entirely inconsistent with many other things which Hobbes himself very reasonably wants to say. It is inconsistent with his warning, quoted already, against any attempt to discover "the diversities of things" by considering the classification of "names." It is quite incompatible with any distinction, such as that which he makes forthwith, between contingent and necessary propositions: "A *necessary proposition* is when nothing can at any time be conceived or feigned, whereof the subject is the name, but the predicate also is the name of the same thing. . . . But in a *contingent proposition* this cannot be; for though this were true, *Every man is a liar*, yet because the word *liar* is no part of the compounded name equivalent to the name *man*, that proposition is not to be called necessary, but contingent, though it should happen to be true always."[51] Lacking though this account of the distinction may be in modern logical refinement it nevertheless clearly implies the possibility of contingent propositions which are false and yet not self-contradictory.

Again, though there is an element of choice about the creation of concepts it cannot be as arbitrary as Hobbes here suggests. Take his own first example: the proposition "Man is a living creature" is true by definition, in virtue of the way in which we elect to employ the words "man" and "is a living creature". But we are not free to falsify this proposition by a simple decision in future to give different employment to the words with which we now express it. Suppose we do change the use of these words. We do not thereby make what was formerly a necessary truth an untruth. We merely make it impossible to express the proposition "Man is a living creature" in the words which in the past we employed to express that still necessary truth. The choice which we do have — and it can often be not arbitrary but reasoned — is of what sounds to use as words, of what words to employ in what senses, and of what meanings to provide for in our vocabulary. None of this should be taken to imply that such choices are usually made deliberately "by one man or assembly of men." Typically they are a matter of natural growth and unexamined habit; "the order of numeral words is so appointed by the common consent of them who are of the same language with us (as it were by a certain contract necessary for society), that five shall be the name of so many unities as are contained in two and three taken together."[52]

Second, Hobbes writes always as if all words were names. We have already protested tacitly by putting the word "names" between warning quotes wherever it is used in our accounts of his views. Had Hobbes tried to develop his remarks on language more fully this would have led to serious trouble. For names are precisely those words which, qua names, do *not*

have meanings, whereas those words which have meanings are, as meaningful, not names. Thus, the apt response to Russell's assertion that "The relation of 'Scott' to Scott is that 'Scott' means Scott . . . "[53] would be: *either* "You have misspelt it; the word 'Scot' has only one 't' "; *or* "No, there is no use in looking that word up in your dictionary: it is a name." Fortunately Hobbes himself never presses the misleading suggestions of his abusage very far. Thus, to the exasperation of some interpreters, musclebound by their own inept terminology, he remarks: "One universal name is imposed on many things for their similitude in quality or other accident"; although this must make the word in question not a pure name but a descriptive, classificatory, term. Yet it does help to ensnare him into a gauche account of negative terms: "There be also other names, called negative, which are notes to signify that a word is not the name of the thing in question."[54]

Third, Hobbes is often thought to have held that all words are "names" not of things but of our conceptions of things. Such views certainly have been respectably held.* But their implications are most paradoxical. For if everyone's language consists entirely of terms defined by reference solely to his own "mental discourse," then surely everyone would have a different and logically private language, in the sense that all the terms in the language of each individual refer only to elements in his experience, which are presumably, like mental imagery, private by definition.[56] If this is indeed our human condition it is only by accident, if at all, that we succeed in using language to communicate.

The evidence that Hobbes actually did hold a clear-cut view of this sort is not strong. It consists first in his account of marks and signs — "marks by which we may remember our own thoughts and signs by which we may make our thoughts known to others" — and its rider that "names do both these offices, but they serve for marks before they be used for signs."[57] Next there is a passage which seems to say as much outright: "But seeing names ordered in speech . . . are signs of our conceptions it is manifest they are not signs of the things themselves, for that the sound of this word *stone* should be the sign of a stone cannot be understood in any sense but this, that he that hears it collects that he that pronounces it thinks of a stone."[58] Yet Hobbes continues, three sentences later, without any suggestion that it might be thought inconsistent: "a *man*, a *tree*, a *stone*, are the names of the things themselves, so the images of a man, of a tree, and of a stone . . . have their names also. . . . " And finally there is the account of understanding: "The imagination that is raised in

---

* See, for instance, Locke's *Essay concerning Human Understanding.*[55] The fact that Locke did hold this view is probably at least partly to be explained by the suggestion that in his furtive borrowings from Hobbes, Locke himself fell into precisely that misinterpretation which we proceed in the text to discuss.

man . . . by words or other voluntary signs is that we generally call understanding"[59]; and "When a man upon the hearing of any speech hath those thoughts which the words of that speech were ordained and constituted to signify, then he is said to understand it; *understanding* being nothing else but conception caused by speech."[60]

Take the second citation first. The context quoted suggests that the obvious — and usual — interpretation is perhaps not correct. Looking at the text again we notice that what Hobbes actually says is: that names are signs of our conceptions; not that they refer to or mean ideas in the mind of the speaker. So surely what, and all, he is maintaining is that my uttering the word "stone" can serve you as a sign that I am thinking about stone? This also squares with the definition he has just given of "sign".

Again, in the accounts of the uses of "names" as marks and signs Hobbes never says that they are all of, or mean, phantasms, ideas, or conceptions in the mind of the user. The nearest he does come to saying this is in his account of understanding. But this passage too seems to require a different interpretation — once we remember what has been said about "signs of," and hence presumably by implication about "signify." For surely what Hobbes is doing is offering a causal account of what happens when a man schooled in the appropriate association habits hears a train of words? No doubt he would have been inclined — had anyone ever confronted him with a distinction between logical questions about the meanings of words, and psychological questions about the effects of sounds — to deny the distinction and to equate the former with the latter. But to agree with this unverifiable speculation is not at all the same thing as to admit that he did in fact hold that all words are "names" of ideas in the mind of whoever is employing them. Perhaps in consistency with other views which he did hold, he should have held this. But he seems not to have done so. What he certainly does say is that "names" can be of things, of phantasms, of qualities, and of names.

Fourth, Hobbes argues: "there being nothing in the world universal but names, for the things named are every one of them individual and singular."[61] It is these claims which provide one ground to label him a nominalist. This may be a dangerous thing to do. This is not a term which he himself employs. Nor is it as unambiguously determinate in meaning as it is technical in sound. It may tempt us unfairly to insist that he is inconsistent when afterwards we find him saying things which a nominalist — in some other sense — is committed to deny. Nevertheless it is his nominalism — in this sense — combined with his materialism and his empiricism, as defined in the preceding section of this chapter, which generate a widely devastating, metaphysically deflationary, drive.

The first target and casualty is the putative class of "things universal" postulated as the entities of which general words might be the "names."* But the drive extends to all Aristotelian elaborations and amendments to the original Platonic doctrine, and to every other sort of construction and fiction which might seem to stand between us and the concrete, particular, individual, material, thing. Whenever Hobbes is confronted with talk suggesting the existence, or subsistence, of any extra entities he wants to know at once what its cash value amounts to in the only currency he is prepared to recognize. Thus, perhaps not surprisingly, it never even occurs to him that evaluative terms might refer to some special entities in another world of values: "But whatsoever is the object of any man's appetite or desire, that is it which he for his part calleth *good:* and the object of his hate or aversion, *evil. . . .*"[64] Again, possibly a more impressive example, he insists on analyzing the uses of the word "spirit" in Scripture to show that they can all be reduced to his terms. For they are all a matter either of "aerial substances," which are certainly corporeal, or of "those idols of the brain, which represent bodies to us," which here simply *are* "nothing but tumult in the brain itself"; or else they involve "metaphorical significations . . . as when . . . we say . . . for *sullenness, a dumb spirit . . .* for *inclination to godliness and God's service,* the *Spirit of God . . .* and *madmen* are said to be *possessed with a spirit.*" So much for "*substance incorporeal . . .* words, which when they are joined together, destroy one another, as if a man should say, an *incorporeal body.*"[65]

Perhaps the most important contributions which Hobbes made here were: to see the importance of language; to introduce this sort of discussion into the center of the philosophic stage; and to suggest a new sort of criticism. Language is important because without it all abstract reasoning and sophisticated communication is impossible. Elsewhere he defines the sense in which it is peculiar to men,[66] and this suggests a way in which greater point and precision might be given to the differentiation of man as the rational animal.[67] Later Locke, and after him Berkeley but not Hume, succeeded to Hobbes' interests in language. The new sort of criticism is the suggestion that even expressions which have obtained wide currency in philosophy may be strictly senseless; and that not because they embody a contradiction, but on account of some more esoteric conceptual malpractice. No doubt one could find many separate instances of such criticism earlier. But it is in Hobbes that it begins to become systematic and theory-guided. Of course his theory as a first venture was crude and rudimentary. Almost inevitably it was crippled by those

---

* For instance in Plato: "We have been in the habit . . . of positing a Form wherever we use the same name in many instances, one Form for each 'many.' "[62] Hobbes thought Plato "the best of the ancient philosophers."[63] We need scarcely add that there is much more to the forms doctrine than this.

perennial afflictions, the insistence on taking geometry as the paradigm of all true knowledge, and the suggestion that all words are, or are to be construed on the model of, names. Nevertheless this is one of the places where the work of Hobbes constitutes a landmark. It may strike us as quaint and awkward to rebuke "the giving of the names of accidents to names and speeches, as they do that say *The nature of a thing is its definition. . . .*"[68]. But there is nothing inept about recognizing the temptation to hypostatize definitions; to mistake whatever collections of characteristics we have found it convenient to prescribe as defining characteristics to have as such some sort of objective reality as the "real essences," "essential natures," or "metaphysical realities" of things. Again — though this is tied in with his theoretical schema very clumsily as an instance of the illegitimate coupling of "the name of a body" with "the name of a name" — Hobbes does spot as absurdities some of the mishandlings of the tricky concept "infinity": ". . . no number can be infinite, but only the word *number* is then called an indefinite name when there is no determined number answering to it in the mind."[69] This leads him to what is surely the essential key to the paradoxes of Zeno. These of course were to him peculiarly scandalous as a challenge to the universality of motion: " . . . the force of that famous argument of Zeno against motion, consisted in this proposition, *Whatsoever may be divided into parts, infinite in number, the same is infinite*, which . . . is false. For to be divided into infinite parts, is nothing else but to be divided into as many parts as any man will."[70]

Probably the character and the originality of this sort of criticism is seen best in Hobbes' repeated attacks on the peculiarly Roman Catholic doctrine of Transubstantiation. This was defined by the Council of Trent. Categorically rejecting any merely symbolic interpretation this Council proceeds to anathematize anyone who "shall say that in the most sacred sacrament of the Eucharist the substance of bread and wine remains . . . and shall deny that marvellous and singular conversion of the whole substance of the bread into the body and of the whole substance of the wine into the blood with the appearances of the bread and wine remaining, which conversion the Catholic Church most aptly calls transubstantiation."[71]

But this doctrine, Hobbes holds, "built on the vain philosophy of Aristotle," and involving that what is in no way whatever distinguishable from bread and wine is really something quite different, is not merely unneccessary for salvation; not merely unwarranted by Scripture; but strictly senseless. Hence it cannot aspire to the comparatively dignified positions of being unnecessary, unwarranted, or, even, untrue. "The Egyptian conjurers, that are said to have turned their rods to serpents, and the water into blood, are thought but to have deluded the spectators. by a false show of things. . . . But what should we

have thought of them, if there had appeared nothing like a serpent . . . nothing like blood, nor like anything else but water . . . ?"[72] "And therefore; if a man should talk to me of a *round quadrangle*, or *accidents of bread in cheese* . . . I should not say he were in error, but that his words were without meaning, that is to say, absurd."[73]

Liberty and Necessity

THE main sources are Hobbes' contributions to the controversy with Bramhall. But Hobbes gives the core of his position in a few paragraphs in *Leviathan*.[74]

> *Liberty*, or *freedom* signifieth, properly, the absence of opposition; by *opposition* I mean external impediments of motion. . . . And according to this proper, and generally received, meaning of the word, a free man is he that in those things which by his strength and wit he is able to do is not hindered to do what he has a will to do. But when the words *free*, and *liberty* are applied to anything but bodies, they are abused; for that which is not subject to motion is not subject to impediment . . . from the use of the word *free-will*, no liberty can be inferred of the will, desire, or inclination, but the liberty of the man. . . . Liberty and necessity are consistent: as in the water, that hath not only liberty but a necessity of descending by the channel; so likewise in the actions which men voluntarily do, which because they proceed from their will, proceed from liberty, and yet — because every act of man's will, and every desire and inclination, proceedeth from some cause, and that from another cause in a continual chain whose first link is in the hand of God the first of all causes — proceed from necessity.

The emphasis on motion and mechanics, and the suspicion of metaphorical or idiomatic uses of words, are characteristic of Hobbes. But the thesis that human freedom is not necessarily incompatible with complete universal causality had many earlier proponents — for instance among the Reformers from whom Hobbes quotes.[75] Later, it passes into the main stream of British secular philosophy through Locke* and Hume.

Neither Bramhall not Hobbes wished to confine themselves to this first question of compatibility or incompatibility. Together they traversed the further questions: whether the universe is in fact completely deterministic; and what would be the moral and theological consequences of their respective positions. Hobbes defends an interesting argument for

---

* Especially in view of Locke's reluctance to acknowledge the considerable debt which he owed to Hobbes, let us notice: "I think the question is not proper, *whether the will be free*, but *whether a man be free.*"[76]

determinism: "Let the case be put, for example, of the weather. *It is necessary that tomorrow it shall rain or not rain.* If therefore it be not necessary it shall rain, it is necessary it shall not rain, otherwise there is no necessity that the proposition, *It shall rain or not rain*, should be true."[77] This is a variant on the ancient Problem of the Sea Battle which Aristotle discusses in *De Interpretatione* IX. But neither Aristotle himself nor, so far as we know, any of the many others since who have ventured a fall with it* — save only Hobbes — have accepted the argument as a valid proof of determinism.

Certainly that *It will rain tomorrow or it will not rain tomorrow* is necessarily true, by the Law of the Excluded Middle. But from this is does not follow that: either *It will rain tomorrow* is necessarily true, or *It will not rain tomorrow* is necessarily true. The nature of Hobbes' mistake, or mistakes, becomes still clearer if we examine a further variant which he mentions but does not develop: "*A necessary act* is that the production whereof it is impossible to hinder ... this proposition, *What shall be, shall be*, is as necessary a proposition as this, *A man is a man.*" Certainly, as the song has it, "Whatever will be, will be," for, for all values of x, from "x will be" it follows necessarily that "x will be." But that is a very different thing from saying "Whatever will be (or occur), will be (or occur) necessarily and unavoidably"; for, for all values of x, from "x will occur" it by no means follows that "x will occur necessarily and unavoidably." The first mistake is to remove the adverb "necessarily" from its proper position modifying "it follows," and covertly to insinuate it into one of the propositions whose logical relations are under examination: for "*necessary, contingent* ... are not names of things, but of propositions."[80] The second mistake is then to interpret this "necessarily" as referring not to logical but to physical necessity: not as a matter of what is entailed by what, but as a matter of what is as a matter of contingent fact unavoidable. Of course, Hobbes, partly but only partly because he was misled by the fallacious arguments which we have just been considering, was committed to assimilating physical to logical necessity, although sometimes, not surprisingly, he overlooked implications of this ambitious enterprise.

In considering the consequences of his views here Hobbes insists on the distinction between, on the one hand, what the logical consequences are and what the ideally rational man would see them to be, and, on the other hand, what the actual consequences might be, if his views came to the attention of men who could not be relied on to be so rational. It was primarily because he was anxious about the

* There has been a burst of interest in recent years.[78] Perhaps a simple-minded attention to the basic errors of Hobbes' argument might have spared us elaborate attempts to "defend freedom" against this sort of attack in terms of a three-valued logic and/or the idea that contingent propositions about the future cannot be said either to be true or to be false.[79]

possible consequences in the second sense that he never consented to the publication of any of the exchanges with Bramhall until Davys forced his hand by his act of piracy: " ... the hurt I thought might proceed from a discourse of this nature. ... I never thought it could do hurt to a rational man but only to such men as cannot reason in those points which are of difficult contemplation."[81]

To all arguments that his determinism logically implied that praise or blame, reward or punishment, would be improper, "that counsels, arts, arms, instruments, books, study, medicines, and the like would be superfluous," he always replied with some variation on one simple theme: "If there be a necessity that an action shall be done, or that any effect shall be brought to pass, it does not therefore follow, that there is nothing necessarily requisite as a means to bring it to pass ... "[82]

About the logical implications for theology — and questions about these and about the Scriptural warrant for various views bulk very large in the whole debate — Hobbes is equally trenchant and uncompromising. Bramhall complains: "this opinion of absolute necessity destroys the truth of God, making him to command one thing openly, and to necessitate another privately. ... It destroys the justice of God, making him to punish the creatures for that which was his own act ... making him the true author of all the defects and evils which are in the world."[83] Entirely unabashed, Hobbes insists unrelentingly on facing without evasion what seem to him the manifest consequences of fundamental Christian doctrines. Repeatedly he quotes notorious hard sayings which underline the implications of omnipotence: "Therefore hath he mercy on whom he will have mercy, and whom he will he hardeneth. Thou wilt say then unto me, 'Why doth he yet find fault? For who hath resisted his will?' Nay, but, O man, who art thou that repliest against God? Shall the thing formed say to him that formed it, 'Why hast thou made me thus?' Hath not the potter power over the clay, of the same lump to make one vessel unto honour, and another unto dishonour?"[84] Contemptuously he sweeps aside scholastic laborings to show how God might be the cause of something without being the cause of "the sinfulness or irregularity of it." For, he says, "Such distinctions as these dazzle my understanding." It is as if someone were to suggest that "one man making a longer and a shorter garment, another can make the inequality that is between them."[85] Accepting, indeed insisting upon, the logical consequences of omnipotence, he urges that omnipotence is as such its own absolute justification. And, furthermore, that this is in fact the doctrine taught by Scripture. "When God afflicted Job, he did object no sin unto him, but justified his afflicting of him by telling him of his power. ... 'Hast thou,' saith God, 'an arm like mine? ... Where wert thou when I laid the foundations of the earth?' ... Power irresistible justifies all actions, really and properly, in whomsoever it be found; less power does not . . . "[86]

Political Anatomy

THE main sources in order of date are *The Elements of Law*, *De Cive*, and *Leviathan*. Of these the first may be regarded as a draft. The second is the political part of Hobbes' definitive trilogy of philosophical elements. The third presents his political ideas, and especially an extended treatment of the relations between religion and politics, along with an account, from which these ideas are derived, of human nature. Hobbes' political anatomy is presented as the fruit of an exercise in method. This method is supposed to be modelled on that of his friends Harvey and Galileo,[87] and Hobbes made no scruple about claiming his work as comparable with theirs. "Galileus . . . was the first that opened to us the gate of natural philosophy universal," while "the science of man's body . . . was first discovered . . . by our countryman Doctor Harvey." But "civil philosophy" is "no older . . . than my own book *De Cive*."[88] The method is explained in the Preface: "Concerning my method . . . everything is best understood by its constitutive causes. For as in a watch, or some such small engine, the matter, figure, and motion of the wheels cannot well be known, except it be taken insunder and viewed in parts; so to make a more curious search into the rights of states and duties of subjects, it is necessary (I say, not to take them in sunder, but yet that) they be so considered as if they were dissolved . . . "[89]

Hobbes therefore proceeds to consider what men are like, and, more particularly, what they would be like if all the restraints of law and society were removed. Unlike the social insects, men are not born adapted by nature for harmonious life together: "How, by what advice, men do meet will be best known by observing those things which they do when they are met."[90] Men have all sorts of occasions of conflict which these other creatures lack. "Among so many dangers therefore, as the natural lusts of men do daily threaten each other withal, to have a care of oneself is so far from being a matter scornfully to be looked upon, that one has neither the power nor wish to have done otherwise. For every man is desirous of what is good for him, and shuns what is evil, but chiefly the chiefest of natural evils, which is death; and this he doth by a certain impulsion of nature, no less than that whereby a stone moves downward."[91] Or, as *Leviathan* has it: "of the voluntary acts of every man the object is some good to himself."[92]

Without the constantly operating curb of social restraints such restless, contentious, grasping creatures would be in a perpetual state of war: "it cannot be denied but that the natural state of man, before they entered into society, was a mere war, and that

not simply, but a war of all men against all men."[93] In Hobbes this idea of a presocial state of nature is primarily a fiction of analysis, and is not to be taken, as in Locke,[94] as a would-be historical concept. He explains in *Leviathan*: "It may peradventure be thought there was never such a time nor condition of war as this; and I believe it was never generally so, over all the world." Then after references to "the savage people in many places of America" he insists on his crucial point, which is hypothetical: "Howsoever, it may be perceived what manner of life there would be, where there were no common power to fear, by the manner of life which men that have formerly lived under a peaceful government use to degenerate into in a civil war."[95] Essentially the Hobbist state of nature is not a matter of what has in fact occurred but of what would occur if government were to be removed: in this it is like the First Law of Motion in physics, which states not how bodies move, but how they would move if all impressed forces were withdrawn. The purpose of Hobbes' concept is, however, anatomical — to display the function of the state, by working out what would happen if there were no state. A further point is that its basic evil, and the source of all the others, is insecurity. This Hobbes is at pains to emphasize in the sentences immediately preceding that most famous and most quoted purple passage on the miseries of a state of nature. He does it through an elementary essay in conceptual analysis: "For as the nature of foul weather lieth not in a shower or two of rain, but in an inclination thereto of many days together; so the nature of war consisteth not in actual fighting, but in the known disposition thereto, during all the time there is no assurance to the contrary. . . . Whatsoever therefore is consequent to a time of war . . . the same is consequent to the time wherein men live without other security than what their own strength and their own invention shall furnish them withal."[96]

In this condition men live, or rather would live, subject only to the natural law or the law of nature. These were hallowed phrases, traditionally employed to refer to some set of moral principles, prior to and perhaps transcending any system of statute law or ethical revelation. Hobbes offers a very different concept: "*A Law of Nature* . . . is a precept or general rule, found out by reason, by which a man is forbidden, to do that which is destructive of his life or taketh away the means of preserving the same, and to omit that by which he thinketh it may be best preserved."[97] Now taking this definition in conjunction with the account of human nature given earlier, it becomes clear that it is a plain matter of fact that men always will obey Hobbist laws of nature — if only they have the wit to discern them as such, and the self-control to do what they thereby discern to be good for them. For every man, by a certain impulsion of nature, shuns chiefly the chiefest of natural evils. But a law of nature tells him to do just this, while specifying some general maxim which, in order to secure the objective, it is reasonable for him to follow. So whereas the traditional law of nature was thought to prescribe categorical obligations, the Hobbist substitute pretends rather to describe the hypothetical facts. It is a matter of what men would do, and do do, insofar as they appreciate what is good for them and act accordingly. It therefore is, and is intended to be, closely analogous to the conception of a law in natural science. It is a measure of the imaginative vision and intellectual audacity of Hobbes that he should be attempting to introduce concepts of the new science into psychology and politics even before they had consolidated their recent victories in physics and anatomy.

The conjunction of his concept of a law of nature with his conclusions about human psychology has another important consequence. It is nowadays a commonplace that the discovery of a scientific law always raises the logically additional questions of how, if at all, the knowledge thus epitomized can be applied: rightly, or expediently, or ideally both. But by Hobbes' view these questions have been settled in advance. For a law of nature, in his sense, is a maxim embodying a statement of what is in fact an effective means to a certain end.* It is equally a matter of fact, a natural law in the scientific sense, that precisely this end is what is chiefly dear to all men. Thus Hobbes is able to think of himself as at one and the same time both outlining a new science of society and providing knowledge which, once appreciated as such, cannot but be applied for good. "Those errors . . . inconsistent with the quiet of the commonweal, have crept into the minds of ignorant men, partly from the pulpit, partly from the daily discourses of men, who, by reason of little employment otherwise, do find leisure enough to study; and they got into these men's minds by the teachers of their youth in public schools."[98] In the "Conclusion" of *Leviathan* he writes of his own doctrine: "Therefore I think it may be profitably printed, and more properly taught in the Universities. . . ."† Later, in *De Corpore* he insists: "the cause of war is not that men are willing to have it; for the will has nothing for object but good, at least that which seemeth good. Nor is it from this, that men know not that the effects of war are evil. . . . The cause . . . is, that men know not the causes neither of war nor peace, there being but few in the world . . . that have learned the rules of civil life sufficiently."[101]

After the sketch of the fundamentals of psychology, the account of the state of nature, and the

introduction of this peculiar concept of a law of nature, Hobbes specifies the content of some of these laws. The first and fundamental, the law of self-preservation, is "that every man ought to endeavour peace, as far as he has hope of obtaining it, and, when he cannot obtain it, that he may seek and use all helps and advantages of war."[102] From which "is derived this second law, that a man may be willing, when others are so too (as far forth as for peace and defence of himself he shall think it necessary) to lay down this right to all things, and be contented with so much liberty against other men as he would allow other men against himself." Earlier in the same chapter "the right of nature" has been defined as "the liberty each man hath to use his power as he will himself"; and liberty as simply "the absence of external impediments." Might, or, less colorfully, the absence of any external physical impediment, is right — by definition.

How are such creatures, governed only by these and similar laws, all to be derived ultimately from the first, to be got out of a state of nature? "If a covenant be made wherein neither of the parties perform presently, but trust one another, in the condition of mere nature . . . it is void," for "he which performeth first does but betray himself to his enemy, contrary to the right he can never abandon, of defending his life and means of living." So we need some force to guarantee reciprocity: for "if there be a common power set over them both, with right and force to compel performance, it is not void."[103]

> The only way to enact such a common power, as may be able to defend them from the invasion of foreigners and the injuries of one another, and thereby to secure . . . they may nourish themselves and live contentedly, is to confer all their power and strength upon one man, or assembly of men . . . to bear their person; and every one to own, and acknowledge himself to be author of, whatsoever he that so beareth their person shall act, or cause to be acted. . . . This is the generation of the great LEVIATHAN or rather, to speak more reverently, of that mortal god to which we owe, under the immortal God, our peace and defence. . . . And he that carrieth this person is called *sovereign* and said to have *sovereign power*; and every one besides, his *subject*.[104]

Now what we might perhaps expect Hobbes to do at this stage in his theory construction is: first to introduce the notion of a constitutive *social contract*, giving it a logical status comparable to that of his state of nature; and then to say that the sovereign is established by a social contract, while the contract is validated by the supporting power of the sovereign. What Hobbes actually does is more complicated. He first distinguishes "commonwealths by institution" from "commonwealths by acquisi-

---

* It is thus interesting, as A. E. Taylor once suggested, to compare Hobbes' *laws of nature* with Kant's *hypothetical imperatives.*

† Compare what may be similar hints dropped by Plato in the *Republic*.[99] He offered a very different synthesis of fact and value in his Forms or Ideas and urged that it was only through knowledge of these that the welfare of a state might be secured. Hobbes himself compares *Leviathan* with *Republic*, favorably.[100]

tion." The former are those "instituted when a multitude of men do agree" to confer sovereign power on some one man or assembly of men. (Hobbes, by the way, is consistently careful to write "man, or assembly of men" in all such contexts, because he considered that his strong personal preference for absolute monarchy did not have the same status as his political science.) With these he proceeds as expected: "From this institution of a commonwealth are derived all the rights and faculties of him, or them, on whom sovereign power is conferred by the consent of the people assembled."[105] Although he is never so explicit in this case as in that of the state of nature, the whole course of the argument makes clear that the derivation here in question is not historical but logical. Thus he urges that the sovereign must have certain powers: "because the end of this institution is the peace and defence of them all, and whosoever has right to the end has right to the means"[106]; and not because these are the powers once detailed in some contract. The other sort of commonwealth is that "where the sovereign power is acquired by force." Yet here too there is a covenant, not this time among the subjects but between the sovereign and the subject.* It comes into force "when the victor hath trusted him with his corporal liberty."[108]

The powers of the sovereign are those which are necessary for the fulfillment of his function. He must be judge of what is needed "for the preserving of peace and security by prevention of discord at home and hostility from abroad." He must be judge of "what opinions and doctrines are averse, and what conducing, to peace; and, consequently, on what occasions, how far, and what men are to be trusted ... in speaking to multitudes of people, and who shall examine the doctrines of all books before they be published." He must have unrestricted power to make the law. He must control the judicature. He must have "the right of making war and peace with other nations ... and to levy money upon the subjects to defray the expenses thereof." He must have a monopoly of armed force. He must have the power to confer honors, and even to reward and to penalize although "there be no law made, according as he shall judge most to conduce to the encouraging of men to serve the commonwealth." These are the rights, he concludes,

which make the essence of sovereignty; and which are the marks whereby a man may discern in what man, or assembly of men, sovereign power is placed, and resideth. For these are incommunicable and inseparable. The power to coin money, to dispose of the estate and persons of infant heirs, to have preemption •in markets, and all

other statute prerogatives may be transferred by the sovereign; and yet the power to protect his subjects be retained. But if he transfer the *militia* [= control of armed forces], he retains the judicature in vain, for want of execution of the laws; or if he grant away the power of raising money, the *militia* is in vain; or if he give away the government of doctrines, men will be frighted into rebellion with the fear of spirits.

This account of sovereignty comes in Chapter 18 of *Leviathan*, "Of Commonwealth"; this is the second chapter of Part II. The rest of this Part elaborates these basic political ideas. Part I, "Of Man," laid the psychological foundations, and deployed the theoretical scheme. It is usual to ignore the remainder of *Leviathan*: Part III, "Of a Christian Commonwealth," and Part IV, "Of the Kingdom of Darkness." This is a mistake. For together they constitute nearly half the total length of the book. Even if we concluded that they were worthless we should still have to ask why Hobbes was so misguided as to put them in. In fact they are far from worthless. For instance, Part III marks an epoch in the history of biblical criticism: in it, for example, the internal evidence to disprove the Mosaic authorship of the Pentateuch is marshalled fully and unequivocally for the first time in print.[109] But what presently concerns us are political purposes. Hobbes in the epistle dedicatory apologizes for the "texts of Holy Scripture, alleged by me to other purposes than ordinarily they use to be by others." He explains: "I have done it ... in order to my subject, necessarily: for they are the outworks of the enemy, from whence they impugn the civil power." So in Part III he develops his biblical criticism to show that God in revelation endorses his concept of the government of doctrines by the civil sovereign, while in Part IV he assails the Church of Rome, primarily as enemy of this erastianism. The relevance of all this becomes quite obvious if we remember something of the historical context. The author of *Leviathan* lived through the periods of the Thirty Years War and the English Great Rebellion. He had grown up in the reign of Queen Elizabeth I, whose peace was menaced continually both at home and abroad by Vatican incitements and Catholic intrigues.[110]

But to return to the fundamental theory. Surely in all this purposeful redefinition and systematic deduction a vital part of the mechanism has been left out? *Quis custodiet ipsos custodes?*: who, or rather what interest, is to keep the sovereign dedicated to the welfare of his subjects? In Hobbist terms: the sovereign by institution is not himself a party to the contract[111]; and though the sovereign by acquisition is, this apparently makes no odds anyway.[112] This raises the radical difficulty of whether it would really accord with the Hobbist laws of nature to escape the state of nature on these terms. As Locke put it, penetratingly selecting arbitrariness

---

* It is often said that the Hobbist sovereign is never a party to the contract. This is not so: "seeing sovereignty by institution is by covenant of everyone to everyone, and sovereignty by acquisition by covenants of the vanquished to the victor."[107]

as the most obnoxious characteristic of the inconveniences of that state: "He being in a much worse condition that is exposed to the arbitrary power of one man who has the command of 100,000, than he that is exposed to the arbitrary power of 100,000 single men . . . "[113] Of course even the sovereign is subject to the law of nature; and ultimately no doubt to the judgment of God. But, as Hobbes has already argued in considering the state of nature, this law is inadequate directly to restrain the restless passions of men. Even in theory Leviathan escapes his Frankenstein.

Yet suppose we do allow that this constitutes a fatal flaw in the system as it was actually presented, that is by no means that. The importance of the enterprise lies not in what was achieved but in what was attempted. Hobbes appreciated what were the great and fertile intellectual achievements of his time: he took for his masters not Bacon and Descartes but Harvey and Galileo. From Thucydides he had learned how the detached study of history might supply experience to guide the calculations of a prudent politician. From *The Discourses on the First Ten Books of Titus Livy* and *The Prince* he might have learned how such experience could be crystallized into maxims of statecraft.* But what Thucydides and even Machiavelli had to offer was prudence only and not science. It was science, modelled on the work of Harvey and Galileo, which Hobbes set himself to supply. Prudence "is a presumption of the future, contracted from the experience of time past," and "being grounded only upon experience" it is necessarily uncertain. But science, in his view, formed on the paradigm of geometry, is demonstrative and hypothetical.[114] The Hobbist vision was of a politics based on a psychology, and of both giving the same sort of account of things as was being provided by the new natural sciences of physics and anatomy. Of course Hobbes failed. He could not succeed. His contribution lay precisely in his vision, in its inspiration and its challenge. If it is possible, we shall never know that it is unless we try it. If it is impossible, we shall never know that and why it is impossible except by meeting the challenge, and discovering in precisely what crucial respects the subject matter of psychology and politics differs from that of the natural sciences. Neither the inspiration nor the challenge of this audacious vision are even yet exhausted.

To realize this program Hobbes gave new values to such old terms as "social contract" and "law of nature." Unrelentingly he worked out consequences and, unabashed, accepted them. Only by the present power of the sovereign is the contract made valid. So if that power is destroyed, or effectively usurped, "there is no further protection of subjects in their

loyalty . . . and every man at liberty to protect himself by such courses as his own discretion shall suggest unto him."[115] Similarly: "If the sovereign banish his subject, during the banishment he is not subject."[116] It was against such consequences that loyal Clarendon in exile wrote, and dedicated to his King, the outstanding contemporary attack on *Leviathan.*[117]

Yet this total rejection of all sentiment and of all backward-looking ties, this abstract, geometrizing pursuit of the implications whatever they may be, have another aspect, less harsh and more humane. It is, for instance, a precept of the Hobbist natural law "that in revenge and punishments we must have our eye not at the evil past, but the future good," and on this he glosses, "that is, it is not lawful to inflict punishment for any other end but that the offender may be corrected, or that others warned by his punishment may become better" and "that revenge therefore which regards not the future proceeds from vain glory, and is therefore without reason."[118] Punishment must be for reform and for deterrence, never for retribution only.*

This forward-looking and enlightened doctrine meets a theological stumbling block. Whatever justification can it possibly allow for the unending punishments of Hell? Hobbes would not withdraw. Physically timorous he might be, but intellectually he never quailed. "Some resolve this objection by answering that God, whom no law restrains, refers all to his glory. . . . It is more rightly answered, that the institution of eternal punishment was before sin and had regard to this only, that men might dread to commit sin for the time to come."[119] This suggestion does infinitesimally little to reduce the moral scandal of divine frightfulness, while at the same time it insults the ingenuity of divine omnipotence. The alleged object of deterrence could have been attained far more efficiently, and that with merely finite penalties, if only these had been made more manifest, immediate, and obviously inescapable.

By the time he wrote *Leviathan* Hobbes had thought again more radically. Although ready always to insist that "the power of God alone without other helps is sufficient justification for any action he doth,"[120] Hobbes is disquieted. "It seemeth hard to say that God who is the father of mercies, that doth in heaven and earth all that he will, that hath the hearts of all men in his disposing, that worketh in men both to do and to will; and without whose free gift a man hath neither inclination to good nor repentance of evil, should punish men's transgressions without any end of time; and with all the extremity of torture that men can imagine, and more." So he sets to consider the relevant texts, observes

---

* I know of no evidence that Hobbes read Machiavelli for himself. But at the very least he could not have avoided considerable indirect contact. He had learned Italian on his first visit to Italy.

* Except of course in that artificial but important sense of "retribution" in which all punishment must involve retribution, inasmuch as it must — to be punishment at all — be supposed to be of offenders and on the ground that they have committed offences.

the oddity that "everlasting death" is ordinarily taken as the opposite of "everlasting life," but "interpreted *everlasting life in torments*," and concludes finally that though the Christian scriptures insist that hell is eternal they suggest that the miseries of each individual human victim end at last in "the second death."[122]

Another product of the same approach is Hobbes' egalitarianism. "The inequality that now is has been introduced by the laws civil. I know that Aristotle in the first book of his *Politics* for a foundation of his doctrine maketh men by nature, some more worthy to command (meaning the wiser sort, such as he thought himself to be for his philosophy), others to serve (meaning those that had strong bodies but were not philosophers as he)."[123] But for the foundation of his doctrine Hobbes needed something else. The human atoms of his mechanical society must differ relevantly only in position, never in quality. This was not the romantic protest of the Peasants' Rising:

> *When Adam delved and Eve span,*
> *Who was then the gentleman?*

Nor was it the passionate moral demand of the Leveller Colonel Rainboro: "I think the poorest he that is in England hath a life to live as the richest he."* It was a statement only of what Hobbes took to be the facts. Men just are sufficiently equal. "For as to the strength of body, the weakest has strength enough to kill the strongest; either by secret machination, or by confederacy with others that are in the same danger with himself."[124] As to the mind, he borrows a mischievous point from Descartes,[125] arguing that men are all equally wise: "For there is not ordinarily a greater sign of the equal distribution of any thing than that every man is contented with his share."[126]

Just as there was no place for sentiment, so the scientific analysis of the state could tolerate no reserves for mystery. There was scope here for the reductive, deflationary drive born of metaphysical materialism. Thus, as we have seen, value is rendered down to a matter of desire: "For these words of *good, evil, and contemptible*, are ever used with relation to the person that useth them; there being nothing simply and absolutely so, nor any common rule of good and evil to be taken from the nature of the objects themselves."[127] In the state of nature the reactions indicated are simply those of the individual using the term. In a commonwealth it is different. For "it belongs to the same chief power to make some common rules for all men . . . by which every man may know what may be called his, what another's, what just, what unjust, what honest, what dishonest, what good, what evil."[128]

It looks as if Hobbes is saying that value terms are now defined by and in terms of the prescriptions of the sovereign. Possibly he did not really want to go so far, but only to insist again on two favorite points: that all property rights derive from and depend on the arbitrary fiat of the sovereign — hence he has the right to requisition as he will;[129] and that the sovereign can never properly be accused of injustice to a subject — because every subject is "by this institution author of all the actions and judgments of the sovereign instituted,"[130] and *Volenti non fit iniuria* — no injury is done to one who consents to it. But whether it is all value words which are to be defined wholly in terms of the will of the sovereign or only some, Hobbes is quite definite that they must all get their meaning from some down-to-earth relationship to particular agents. They must involve no reference to any ethereal world of values.

Again, Hobbes will have no truck with any mystifications about groups. Talk about the doings of collectives has to be reducible to talk about the actual or possible activities of individuals: in the modern jargon, all groups are taken as logical constructions out of their members. Thus in a long note in *De Cive* he carefully distinguishes two senses of "multitude," and explains how a multitude may become one political person: "A multitude cannot promise, contract, require right, convey right, act, have, possess, and the like, unless it be every one apart and man by man. . . . Wherefore a multitude is no natural person. But if the same multitude do contract with one another that the will of one man, or the agreeing wills of the major part of them, shall be received for the will of all, then it becomes one person."[131]

There are too many other important things to be said about this richest part of Hobbes' thought. We must confine ourselves to two final remarks.

First, the total selfishness of the psychology became a scandal.* This is not, as Hobbes and others have mistaken it to be, a necessary feature of any truly scientific psychology. Certainly any action, to be an action at all, must in some sense be the outcome of the agent's own desires. But from this necessary truth it by no means follows that as a matter of contingent fact all actions are purely selfish, that "of the voluntary acts of every man the object is some good to himself." The temptation is to argue *a priori* that no action can be disinterested (in a new made-to-measure sense in which disinterested action is logically impossible), and then to misinterpret this dangerously dramatized tautology as the outrageous empirical falsehood that there are no disinterested actions (in the old narrower sense of "disinterested.")

Thus, it is argued, no action can be unmotivated. For it cannot properly be called an action at all unless it is voluntary, unless the agent in some (which is not the usual) sense wants to perform it.

---

* On October 25, 1647 at the Putney debates between representatives of the rank and file of the revolutionary New Model Army and its Grand Council of Officers.

* Which in the next century found in Bishop Butler its shrewdest critic.[132]

So the agent must have some interest in, some concern about, doing it; and hence it cannot be entirely disinterested (again in a new tailor-made sense). But all this has not the slightest tendency to show that no action can be disinterested (in the ordinary, narrower, reach-me-down, sense). From the premise that if I voluntarily do a kindness I must — at least in this new sense — want to do a kindness, it by no means follows that this act of kindness cannot be, in the old sense, disinterested. It could still perfectly well have been done without any ulterior selfish reason, such as gaining votes or winning applause, or even avoiding damnation and achieving the beatific vision. From the fact that an agent must want (new sense) to do what he does, if this is to rate as an action at all, it by no means follows that we cannot ever do what we do not want (old sense) to do. That in fact we can is shown every time anyone, because he realizes that he ought to do that uncongenial thing, does something he does not want to do.

The argument becomes even more deceptive, but no better, if its *a priori* base is laced with a little empirical material to show that many actions seeming disinterested are not. We must insist that if it is to be shown that men never in fact do act disinterestedly, this can only be by deploying appropriate and sufficient empirical evidence. A contingent empirical conclusion cannot be derived *a priori* from *a priori* premises, not even with the aid of a few disillusioning empirical illustrations.

Second, we must not be misled by the fact that Hobbes was personally a royalist to overlook the essentially radical character of his political thought. His concern with actual present functions rather than putative historical origins; his impatience with all mystery, mystification, and backward-looking sentiment; his insistence that all property and all law is the absolutely dependent creature of the sovereign power; his assumption that the state must be justified as the instrument of its subjects: all these explain the sympathy of utilitarians such as Bentham, Austin, Grote, and Molesworth. They even make intelligible the claim that Marx once hailed Hobbes as "the father of us all."*

Religion

HOBBES has been called "a complete atheist,"[133] both sympathetically and as an accusation. Of course he himself always hotly repudiated this description.[134] Yet some of his acknowledged doctrines, and still more perhaps the manner in which he expressed them, do give grounds for speculation. Certainly he never seems very wholeheartedly to go much beyond that unitarianism which has been defined as "belief in one God, at most." This is however primarily a

* Critics of Hobbes and Marx might press the analogy a little, suggesting that both were too apt from exaggerated features of their own times to generalize universally.

biographical question, and one on which the evidence available is and is likely to remain insufficient for any very definite decision. It is also secondarily a rather elusive question of another sort. Suppose we could settle the biographical question of which of his statements in this area Hobbes meant ingenuously and which of the corrosive implications of these he himself appreciated, and when. It would still perhaps be far from obvious whether the remaining hedged and qualified convictions were really sufficient to rate as a settled genuine belief in God. We can, however, say confidently that Hobbes shared with Hume a considerable interest in both the philosophy and the natural history of religion. But in Hobbes this always seems to have been subordinate to an overriding concern for civil peace.

We have already noticed trenchant remarks on transubstantiation — the alleged miracle of the Mass — and the short drastic Hobbist way with the Problem of Evil.* We have drawn attention also to the ventures in Biblical criticism in *Leviathan*. Nineteen years later in *Tractatus Theologico-Politicus*, Spinoza carried on from where Hobbes had left off. Spinoza was even more emancipated. He was in addition saturated in Hebrew idiom. Again we have seen how Hobbes was quick to probe the theological consequences of his radical empiricism. This probing issues in the characteristic doctrine that "in the attributes which we give to God we are not to consider the signification of philosophical truth, but the signification of pious intention, to do him the greatest honour we are able."[136] Hobbes has therefore no patience with attempts to determine the attributes of God by natural reason: "pretending to comprehend that which is incomprehensible."[137] For if we are to take seriously the things the theist theologians say about their God, how could anyone be in a position to make any positive assertions about such a being?

In *De Cive* Hobbes considers "what manner of worship of God natural reason doth assign us . . . first, it is manifest that existence is to be allowed him; for there can be no will to honour him, who, we think, hath no being." He proceeds to urge that "in attributes which signify greatness or power those which signify some finite or limited thing are not signs at all of an honouring mind. For we honour not God worthily, if we ascribe less power and greatness to him than possibly we can." So we must ascribe only

* It is instructive, though to the secular humanist nauseating, to follow the shifts to which the subtle Leibniz is forced in trying to avoid this brutal Gordian solution. He seeks in *Theodicy* "to banish from men the false ideas that represent God to them as an absolute prince employing despotic power, unfitted to be loved and unworthy of being loved" while yet insisting that "the work most worthy of God's wisdom involves among other things the sin of all men and the eternal damnation of the majority of men." Leibniz frequently expresses his shocked respect for Hobbes. But of course, as Leibniz himself makes clear, Hobbes' short way had been anticipated by many tough clear-headed eternity-serving theologians before him.

infinite attributes: "yet it follows not that we have any conception of an infinite thing. For when we say a thing is infinite we signify nothing really, but the impotency in our own mind. . . ." This idea is applied in detail: "When we therefore attribute a will to God it is not to be conceived like unto ours, which is called a rational desire (for if God desires, he wants, which for any man to say, is a contumely); but we must suppose some resemblance which we cannot conceive."[138]

In the face of this disembowelling of the idea of God's will it is difficult to follow those who regard as an expression of an integral element in Hobbes' political and metaphysical system his talk of laws of nature as commands of God.[139] His natural theology seems to be as empty of factual content as — short of explicit atheism — it could possibly become. Nevertheless, if we are to consider the biographical and associated questions, we must remember that both traditionalist exponents of the *via negativa* and fashionable contemporary Protestant theologians have sometimes said very similar things and have still remained in good standing with their churches. However the tone of voice has perhaps been rather different.

Even appeal to revelation can offer no help with the problem Hobbes broaches here. Revelation is at most a way of learning that something is true; this problem is one of understanding. It is logically prior to any question of how what is understood could be known to be true. Hobbes is willing when writing of another less basic subject — and one which does not, he thinks, raise these peculiar difficulties — to be disrespectful even about revelation: "there is no natural knowledge of man's estate after death," and revelation (though he does not use the word here) is "only a belief grounded on other men's saying that they know it supernaturally, or that they know those that know others that knew it supernaturally . . ."[140] Yet all his bold speculations and vivid, daring, sayings are subordinated explicitly to the arbitrament of the sovereign. He will argue that "it is with the mysteries of our religion, as with wholesome pills for the sick, which swallowed whole have the virtue to cure but chewed are for the most part cast up again without effect."[141] Yet, ever Erastian, he insists that he is maintaining nothing. He is instead simply "attending the end of that dispute of the sword, not yet amongst my countrymen decided concerning the authority by which all sorts of doctrine are to be approved or rejected, and whose commands . . . must by all men that mean to be protected be obeyed. For the points of doctrine concerning the kingdom of God have so great an influence on the kingdom of man as not to be determined but by them that, under God, have the sovereign power."[142]

10

Descartes

J. L. WATLING

RÉNÉ DESCARTES WAS BORN in 1596 near Poitiers. At the age of ten he was sent as a lay student to a college at La Flèche on the River Loire; this was one of the first of the Jesuit colleges. There were nine courses: four of grammar, one of humanity, one of rhetoric, two of philosophy, and one of moral theology; but in his last year at the college he studied mathematics. It is thought that when he left school he studied law at the University of Poitiers, taking his degree in 1616, when he was twenty. Then he entered the army, for the sole purpose, he wrote, of completing his education. Whilst in Holland, at the town of Breda, he first began to write: he wrote papers on mathematics and on the science of music, and he began to experiment on the refraction of light. At this time he had two dreams which he considered important; one was of the spirit of truth opening the treasures of the sciences to him. It was at this time that he first got the idea of applying algebra to geometry, and, in general, mathematics to all problems. He was present at the battle of Prague, one of the battles of the Thirty Years War, and had the idea of the method of universal doubt. Soon after this battle he left the army and travelled privately all over Europe, finally settling in Paris. During his travels he was interested for a time in the doctrines of the Order of Rosicrucians. In 1628 he left Paris to live in Holland, on account of the intellectual freedom enjoyed by the Dutch. At this time he wrote the *Rules for the Direction of the Mind* and began to study anatomy and physiology.

During the first part of his stay in Holland he wrote a comprehensive study of physics, but he suppressed it on learning that Galileo's *Massimi Sistemi* had been condemned by the Inquisition. Galileo's book was condemned because he set out to establish that the earth was not the stationary center of the solar system. In 1637 Descartes wrote the *Discourse on Method*, which was followed by essays on optics, physics, and geometry. In 1641 the *Meditations on First Philosophy* was published in Paris, and Descartes received the *Objections* from Hobbes and Gassendi. After the publication of the *Meditations* a long controversy took place between the disciples of Descartes and the supporters of the traditional philosophy of the time; the controversy ended in a legal decision against Descartes for writing defamatory letters, and the printed discussion of his philosophy was forbidden. Descartes' trust in the intellectual freedom of Holland was to some extent misplaced.

At about this time Descartes became friendly with the Princess Elizabeth of Bohemia and conducted a correspondence with her. The *Principles of Philosophy* was published in

1644. Descartes visited Paris several times in the following years. On one of these occasions he arrived in the middle of a revolution and was ignored for several months. He wrote that he longed once more for the "innocence of the desert." In 1649 he accepted an invitation from Queen Christina to live in Sweden and teach philosophy to her. In Stockholm he published the *Treatise on the Passions*. He died there in 1650.

D ESCARTES' PHILOSOPHY was an attempt to put the beliefs of his time on a sound basis, a basis that would make it possible to separate what was certain from what was probable, and what was probable from what was mere superstition: which would lead on to the discovery of new knowledge, and to the solution of new problems. His metaphysical argument had a practical purpose: it was intended to help in the solution of even such practical problems as those of medicine. By the application of his philosophical method, Descartes intended to replace the science of his time, which he saw as a mass of more or less justified beliefs, by a genuine science where every assertion would have its proof, and where no proof would reply on assumptions that were not simple and certain. He regarded his philosophical arguments as a fundamental part of science upon which the rest of science depended.

Descartes' Point of View

DESCARTES was himself a mathematician of very great ability. He discovered, for example, how to describe geometrical figures by means of algebraic equations and so solve problems in geometry by reasoning in algebra. And he made other important mathematical discoveries. Therefore he was impressed by the method by which truths are established in mathematics, and in particular by two features of this method, two features which he regarded as inseparably related.

First, the deductive method consists in accepting without proof a few propositions which appear to be unquestionable, and in arguing from these by steps which appear to be unquestionable. In this way it is possible to make only assumptions which are simple and obvious, to use only arguments which are simple and obvious, and yet to arrive at conclusions which are neither simple nor obvious. Descartes conceived the idea that this method, by which propositions in mathematics are proved, might be applied to the proof of propositions of every kind: propositions about God, about everyday life, and about causal connections between events.

Second, inference in mathematics does not depend upon making observations or upon carrying out experiments: the deductions of its deductive method can be seen to be valid or invalid by reason alone,

and they cannot be checked by empirical methods. And this is equally true of the fundamental assumptions of mathematics. Whether two and two make four or not is a question to which observation and experiment are irrelevant. Mathematics, and logic also, Descartes rightly held, depend solely on the reasoning faculties of man. Descartes believed that he could show that truths of every sort could be established without the aid of observation and experiment.

The first explanation of these ideas occurs in the *Rules for the Direction of the Mind*. In this work Descartes held that if only one had a complete understanding of a proposition then one knew whether it was true or false; and this method of coming to know whether a proposition was true or false he called *intuition*. Those propositions which one could come to understand completely would be self-evident, since one's knowledge about them would not depend upon knowledge of any other propositions; therefore they were suitable to stand as fundamental assumptions, to be the starting points from which other propositions could be deduced.

Descartes held also that if only one had a complete understanding of an inferential step, then one knew whether that step was valid or invalid: one knew, that is, whether or not it might possibly lead one to argue from a true proposition to a false. This knowledge he likewise called *intuition*. A difficulty arises here, for someone might hold that it is impossible to understand completely a step in an argument from one proposition to another, impossible to see all that taking that step involves, without understanding completely the proposition from which the step was made and the proposition to which it led. Now if this were so, then no step in an argument could be known by intuition to be valid unless one already understood, and hence knew by intuition, the conclusion of that step. But Descartes must have believed that one *could* understand an inferential step from one proposition to another without understanding each of these propositions, for he believed that one might come to know a proposition, which one did not know directly by intuition, by arguing to it from other propositions, themselves intuitively known, by means of inferences intuitively known to be valid. This method of coming to know whether or not a proposition was true, a method which depends entirely upon intuition, though not on intuition of the proposition itself, Descartes called *deduction*.

So, although Descartes recognizes no other way of coming to know anything except that of coming to understand completely, yet he implies that it is not necessary to come to understand completely the proposition which is the object of enquiry: it may be enough to understand some other propositions and some arguments from which the proposition, not itself understood, may be deduced. But although what Descartes says implies this, and although the recognition of these two methods of coming to know the truth of a proposition suits the mathematical method very well, yet in other places Descartes speaks as though he supposed that not only was coming to understand a proposition *enough* for knowing whether it was true or false, but *also that* it was *necessary* for knowing whether it was true or false. And this is very plausible, that a man who does not understand a proposition does not know whether it is true or false, since if you ask him what it is that he knows then he cannot tell you. But if Descartes accepted this, then he could not consistently have admitted deduction as a method of obtaining knowledge, for deduction is a method of coming to know the truth of a proposition without coming to a complete understanding of it. Now, in fact, in the *Rules for the Direction of the Mind* Descartes does not treat deduction as he defines it, as the method of coming to know a proposition by inferring it from other propositions, but rather as the method of coming to understand a proposition completely and *so* coming to know it. He treats deduction as a method of simplification rather than as a method of proof. This is the significance of the emphasis in the *Rules* on separating the parts of a problem, distinguishing the simple from the complex, and breaking down the complex into the simple. For example, Rule IV is, "There is need for a method of investigating the truth about things," and Rule V says, " . . . and we shall be observing this method exactly *if we reduce complex and obscure propositions step by step to simpler ones, and then, by retracing our steps, try to rise from intuition of all the simplest ones to knowledge of all the rest.*"[1] This makes it quite clear that Descartes regarded deduction as a method of enlarging intuition, not as a method of arguing from it. Descartes believed that it was inconceivable that a man should have a complete understanding of a proposition without knowing whether it was true or false, and inconceivable that he should know whether it was true or false without understanding it. This identification of knowledge with understanding characterizes Descartes as a rationalist philosopher, and I shall show how radically it determined his philosophy. In the *Rules for the Direction of the Mind* Descartes takes this identification as self-evident, but in his later works, for example in the *Meditations on First Philosophy*, he adopts another principle as more fundamental.

In fact, adopting this new principle as a definition of what it is for someone to know a proposition to be true, he attempts to derive the rationalist identification of knowledge with understanding. And in the *Meditations* it is this new principle which he uses to select his fundamental assumptions.

THE CONSEQUENCES OF RATIONALISM

The rationalist doctrine, that complete understanding of a proposition is not only necessary but also sufficient to enable a person to know whether the proposition is true or false, put forward by Descartes in the *Rules for the Direction of the Mind*, has important consequences, and many of these are inconsistent with Descartes' other philosophical views. Descartes attempted, but failed, to exhibit rationalism as a consistent theory of our knowledge.

A man who understands a proposition perfectly, as Descartes intended the word "understands," is one who can reason correctly with it, can see all that it entails and all that it denies. Therefore, understanding a proposition gives us a knowledge of its logic, of what inferences in which it is concerned are valid and what are invalid, but not of its truth. For example, a person who understands the proposition that there is a round pond in Kensington Gardens knows that if there is a round pond in Kensington Gardens then there is a pond in Kensington Gardens for which it is possible to find a point from which every point on its edge lies at an equal distance; but he does not know, just because he understands the proposition, whether or not there is a round pond in Kensington Gardens. Understanding, as Descartes intended it, teaches us the truth of propositions which are logically true and the falsity of those which are contradictory, but nothing more than this. Therefore, the view that understanding is sufficient for knowledge of all facts has the consequence that all facts are logical truths and all falsehoods are contradictions. It entails the view that the facts of science are of the same nature as the facts of logic and mathematics.

Leibniz, writing later in the seventeenth century, saw this consequence of rationalism and accepted it; his philosophical system is an attempt to maintain that all propositions are either logically true or contradictory. But Descartes never faced this consequence, and he argues as if rationalism were consistent with the existence of propositions which are neither logically true nor logically false.

Consider, for example, propositions about physical objects, such as tables and chairs. Understanding these propositions will be enough to teach us logical truths about these objects. It may teach us, for example, that if a thing is a table then it has a spatial position, a spatial extension, and a shape. Descartes says:

Before enquiring whether any such objects [material objects] exist outside me, I must consider the ideas of them, precisely as occurring in my consciousness, and see which of them are distinct and which are confused. I distinctly imagine quantity, the so-called continuous quantity of the philosophers; that is to say, the extension of the quantity, or rather of the quantified object, in length, breadth, and depth. I can enumerate different parts of it; to these parts I can assign at will size, shape, position and local motion; and to these motions I can assign any durations I choose. . . . The truth of these is obvious and so much in accord with my nature that my first discovery of them appears not as the learning of something new, but as the recollection of what I already knew — as the first occasion of my noticing things that had long been present to me, although I had never previously turned my mind's eye towards them.[2]

But understanding the proposition that there exists at least one table will not enable anyone to tell whether or not it is true.

Descartes, however, sets out to establish the proposition that at least one table exists by deducing it from propositions about ideas. Now, there is some justification for expressing the fact that the understanding can only teach us logical truths, by saying that the understanding teaches us propositions about ideas. The logical fact that if a thing is triangular, then it has three sides, might be said to be about the concept, or idea, of triangularity. But although logical truths are perhaps facts about ideas, yet it is not true that all facts about ideas are logical truths. For example, it is a fact about the proposition *cogito ergo sum* that Descartes once considered it. But this fact is not a logical fact, nor, therefore, one that the understanding alone can inform us of. Descartes employs premises about ideas which cannot be known by understanding alone. This mis-identification of "facts which the understanding alone can teach us" with "facts about ideas" arises because of a peculiar view which Descartes took of the nature of ideas, a view that was itself inconsistent with rationalism. I will deal with that presently.

Thus, Descartes in some places argues in this way: I have ideas of material objects, God is not deceitful, therefore the objects which these ideas represent must have produced these ideas in me. This is an argument from a fact about ideas, namely that Descartes had ideas of physical objects. But it is not an argument from logical truths, not an argument from a premise which it is sufficient to understand to know whether or not it is true. Descartes argues similarly for the *existence of* God. He establishes that he has an idea of a perfect being, that he understands what it is for a thing to be a perfect being. He then argues that this idea could only be produced in him by the action of something with at least as much reality as the thing which the idea represents. Therefore a perfect being must exist. The premise of this argument is likewise unsuitable to his purpose. The understanding could teach him logical truths about God but it could not teach him that he himself understood propositions about God.

And another of Descartes' arguments for the existence of material objects suffers from this same fault. This argument depends on the distinction between understanding what it is for a thing to have a certain property and imagining that something possesses that property. Descartes makes this distinction by pointing out that while one may both understand what it means to say that some figure is a triangle and imagine a triangular figure, yet though one can easily understand what it means to say that some figure has a thousand sides, one cannot imagine, that is, picture to oneself, a thousand-sided figure. Descartes suggests that it may be possible to explain this distinction by supposing that in understanding the mind is concerned only with its own ideas, while in imagining it is directed to some bodily picture in the brain and that the fact that the distinction exists means that some material body, in fact, the brain, exists. But, of course, even if this were the correct explanation of the distinction it would not require that some material body existed, but only that some material body might possibly exist. In order to reach the conclusion that some material body exists, it is necessary to know not only that imagination differs in a certain way from understanding but also that some act of imagination has actually taken place. Now whether any imagining has actually taken place cannot be decided by reasoning alone.

Another of Descartes' arguments for the existence of God is mistaken in a rather different way. He argues that reasoning alone shows him the truth of the proposition that a perfect being exists. He claims that it is logically true that a perfect being exists for, he argues, a being that did not exist would not be perfect. It is indeed a logical truth that if anything is perfect then it exists, but it does not follow from this that some being exists which is perfect, any more than from the logical truth that if anything is square then it has four sides, it follows that some square thing has four sides. The fallacy in this argument is that of taking the proposition "a perfect being exists" to mean "if a being is perfect then it exists" in order to argue that it is a logical truth and also taking it to mean "there is a perfect being" in order to argue that there exists something of the species "perfect being." In this argument for the existence of God, Descartes mistakenly argues that a proposition asserting that something exists is logically true. Descartes, in all these arguments except the last, confuses logical truths with truths about the mind.

But rationalism puts restrictions not only on the premises of Descartes' arguments but also on the conclusions. For the conclusions too must be propositions which may be known by being clearly understood, and so they too must be logically true. Now, of course, had Descartes really been able to prove these propositions from rationalist assumptions, he would have established that the propositions which were his conclusions, propositions asserting the existence of himself, of God, and of material objects, were indeed logically true. But he had not done this, and what is more, does not seem to suppose it necessary that he should have done it. He seems prepared to accept that propositions about God or about material objects are not propositions about ideas. Yet clearly, if the only conceivable propositions are those which to understand is to know true or false, then it is futile to try to establish the truth or falsehood of other sorts of propositions, e.g., those about material objects, by inference; for these other propositions cannot even exist. A consistent rationalist, as Leibniz was, must suppose that propositions about material objects are propositions about ideas, and are logically true, and then these inferential arguments in which Descartes engages are unnecessary.

DESCARTES' THEORY OF UNDERSTANDING

Amongst words it is possible to recognize two sorts: words which are proper names whose function is to refer to, or pick out, particular objects; and words whose function it is to describe objects, to ascribe properties to them. The name "Descartes" is an example of a word of the former sort; the description "is a philosopher" is an example of a phrase of the latter. A statement made with the help of a proper name cannot be known to be true or be known to be false without knowledge about the person whom the name picks out; we cannot know whether Descartes was a philosopher without being able to pick out Descartes from amongst all the other persons who have existed and investigate the person so picked out. Before we can begin to investigate the truth of a statement made with the help of a proper name we must pick out an existing object, in this example a person. Therefore, to know whether a statement made with the help of a proper name is true, it is not sufficient to understand the words used in making the statement; it is also necessary to have picked out an object or person. Any rationalist who believes that understanding a sentence is sufficient for coming to know whether it is true or whether it is false, must refuse to allow that any words are proper names. A rationalist, if he is to be consistent, must believe that no words are names, in contrast to an empiricist, who will most probably believe that all words are names. There is some plausibility in the view that one may understand and reason with the description "is a philosopher" without knowing any philosophers, or knowing whether there are any, and this is the position the rationalist takes; there is

no plausibility in the view that one may know whether a statement about an actual person is true without being able to pick out or identify that person, and this view Descartes correctly rejected.

Although Descartes avoided this trap, he did not avoid another which is in fact very similar to it. For he adopts a theory of what it is for someone to understand a describing phrase, such as "is a philosopher," which after all makes these phrases into names, albeit names of *mental* objects, objects which he called *ideas*. To understand what a circle is, to be able to recognize circles, and to be able to reason about circles, all this Descartes refers to as possessing, or as seeing clearly, the idea of a circle. And he speaks of these ideas on a visual analogy which strengthens the view that they are objects and that they exist in the mind. He speaks of inspecting ideas, and of ideas being, in a notorious phrase, clear and distinct. Just as physical objects are seen with our eyes, so ideas are seen with the mind's eye.

Descartes' use of this analogy has one trivial consequence. It makes it easy for his readers to suppose that when he spoke of an idea he meant an image, as Locke often did when he used the word "idea". For it is very natural to speak of inspecting a sensory image or a memory image and to speak of such an image as being clear and distinct. It is most important, though, in order to understand Descartes, to realize that when he used the word "idea" he hardly ever meant "image"; he meant "concept." Both empiricists and rationalists often expressed themselves by saying that words stood for ideas, but whereas, when they were speaking strictly, the empiricists meant "image," the rationalists meant "concept." Nevertheless, this ambiguity of the word "idea" helped both these sorts of philosopher to make their views more plausible than they would otherwise have been.

But the main objection to Descartes' speaking of understanding a describing word as possessing in one's mind a mental object, is that to do this is to treat describing words as proper names; it is inconsistent with rationalism to suppose that any words are names, whether they are supposed to be names of physical or of mental objects. Picking out and investigating objects in one's mind is as much an empirical study as picking out and investigating objects in one's garden: understanding and reasoning are insufficient for discovery of either sort of truth. Perhaps introspection, looking into one's own mind, seems at first sight like coming to understand concepts, but a little thought shows that it is not in reality like this at all. And, of course, since what rationalist philosophers believed to be true of all statements, that to understand them was sufficient to know whether they were true, does indeed appear to be true of the propositions of logic and mathematics, then the belief that understanding is inspecting ideas in one's mind, if taken strictly — and all philosophical theories must be taken strictly if we do not want our views to become a collection of vague and inconsistent principles — leads us to a false account of the nature of logic and mathematics. This account is that empirical science treats of physical objects, logic and mathematics of the objects of the mind. It is false because a true proposition of logic or mathematics could not conceivably be false, whereas a statement about a mental object, however mysterious a thing such an object may be, might conceivably be false. This account contains, in fact, two mistakes: that logic treats of the properties of a mysterious sort of object, and that this mysterious sort of object is mental.

Descartes' theory of understanding as the perception of ideas has important consequences for the development of his rationalist principles. If understanding arises from inspecting ideas, then all truths about ideas are truths that may be known by coming to understand them. Therefore Descartes could suppose that the question whether he had a certain idea, or whether he understood a certain concept, was a question of logic, and so could be decided just by coming to understand that question. So he was able to suppose, for example, that when he argued from the fact that he understood what it was to be an infinite being, then he argued from a premise which to understand was sufficient to know.

Second, the theory that understanding what it is for a thing to be circular is inspecting a mental object, allowed Descartes to think of concepts as objects which might represent other objects, and so to believe that propositions about ideas might be true if interpreted as propositions about objects outside the mind. This notion of concepts as representative of physical objects is ludicrous when one thinks of having a concept as understanding an idea. Considering concepts as objects, then, enabled Descartes to believe that concepts represented objects.

Third, this theory, by approximating logical and empirical truth, made it easier to accept that every proposition may be decided just by coming to understand it perfectly; for if propositions about whether Descartes had an idea of an infinite being could be so decided, then why should not all empirical propositions be so decided? In all these ways Descartes' theory of understanding softened the consequences of his strict rationalist principles.

THE METHOD OF DOUBT

I have described how in the *Rules for the Direction of the Mind* Descartes took as his starting point those propositions which were so simple that he could understand them completely, believing that this was sufficient for him to know for certain whether they were true or false. But in later works, the *Discourse on the Method of rightly directing one's Reason* and the *Meditations on First Philosophy*, he adopts a different method for selecting the proposi-

tions that are to serve as the basis for his reasoning. The new criterion provides a new definition of what knowledge is, and from the new definition he attempts to prove the earlier rationalist definition. He did not abandon the rationalist definition of knowledge, but ceased to regard it as fundamental.

This new method of selecting his fundamental assumptions was a thoroughgoing one. It has become famous as the method of universal doubt. He resolved to discard anything he believed if he could conceivably disbelieve it. In this way he would be left only with propositions which he could not conceivably disbelieve. He must have thought that he would be left only with propositions about which it was impossible for him to be mistaken. But this is not so. It is one thing to say of a proposition that Descartes could not conceivably disbelieve it and quite another to say that Descartes could not conceivably be mistaken about it: a proposition which Descartes could not doubt might be a false proposition, and if it were, then he would be mistaken about it. If Descartes' method of selecting his fundamental assumptions is to be successful it must be the method of discarding those propositions about which he could conceivably be mistaken, not the method of discarding those propositions which he could conceivably doubt.

It is important to realize that what Descartes asked about a proposition was not whether he could, being after all only human, actually bring himself to doubt it: he asked "Is it conceivable that I should doubt this proposition?" not "Is it psychologically possible that I should doubt this proposition?" For example, his experience with fire was probably so great that he could not in practice have brought himself to doubt that if he put his hand into a wood fire, then it would get burned. It was not psychologically possible for him to doubt this. But he could imagine himself not believing that fire would burn his hand; he could imagine himself as a child is who has not yet learned that fire burns. The question Descartes asked of every proposition was, "Can I even conceive myself doubting this proposition?" Descartes tried to find a proposition which it was not logically possible for him to doubt, and which it was not logically possible for him to be mistaken about.

There were two sorts of propositions which Descartes was tempted to accept as passing this test, when in fact they did not pass it. First, there were the simplest propositions of logic and arithmetic; and second, there were propositions about his own immediate experience of the world. But he avoided both temptations.

It is indeed impossible that two and two should not make four, and there are two reasons which might have led Descartes to conclude that he could not conceivably have been mistaken about whether two and two make four. The first is this: the fact that it is impossible that two and two should not make four is often expressed by saying that it is inconceivable that two and two should not make four. Now it might seem reasonable to argue that what is inconceivable is unbelievable: that if it is impossible to *conceive* that two and two make five, then it is impossible to *believe* that two and two make five. But however reasonable this may seem, it is not correct. People very often make mistakes in simple calculations and are led by these mistakes into holding false beliefs about simple arithmetical propositions; it is not conceivable that the figures in their sum should add up to the total they obtain, but nevertheless they believe that they do. Of course, in these problems careful calculation always produces a correct answer; but there are some arithmetical propositions, apparently simple enough, to which the answer is not known, but to which, although we cannot find it, a correct answer exists. Now whatever the correct answer is, no other answer could conceivably be correct. An example is the proposition, known as Goldbach's hypothesis, that every even number is the sum of two prime numbers. This generalization holds for every even number which has been tested, but of course not every number has been tested, and no proof or disproof of the theorem has ever been discovered. In the absence of such a proof it is quite possible to believe the theorem true, though perhaps it is inconceivable that it should be true; and it is quite possible to believe it false, though perhaps it is inconceivable that it should be false. This hypothesis had not been discovered in Descartes' time, but no doubt he was familiar with arithmetical hypotheses which he could not decide. These examples could, of course, be discounted by arguing that anyone who makes a mistake in checking an arithmetical proposition, or who cannot provide a proof of a proposition, does not understand it completely and does not, therefore, believe it. If this were so, then someone who says that he believes Goldbach's hypothesis, but who cannot provide a proof of it, would not be speaking the truth: he would not believe it because he would not understand it; and someone who asserted the result of a mistaken arithmetical calculation would not be making a mistake but speaking words which he did not properly understand. Descartes accepted this very strict condition for understanding, and he assumed it in the *Rules for the Direction of the Mind*; but in the *Meditations* he wished to *prove* that understanding was sufficient for knowledge, so he could not depend upon this principle in order to establish that it was impossible to be mistaken about the simple propositions of arithmetic. And except for this principle there is no reason at all for thinking that someone who is mistaken about a simple arithmetical sum must be someone who does not understand the numbers in it, or for thinking that because we cannot prove or disprove Goldbach's hypothesis, it must be that we do not understand what it means to say that every even number is the sum of two prime numbers.

The second reason which might have led Descartes to conclude that it was impossible for him to be mistaken about whether two and two make four, is that he might have confused the truth "It is impossible that a man should believe that two and two make four and be mistaken" with the falsehood "It is impossible that a man who believes that two and two make four should be mistaken." Descartes avoided this mistake, but perhaps this was because it did not occur to him, since he seems to have made this same confusion when he was discussing the proposition "I think."

The second kind of proposition which Descartes was tempted to accept, but which he did not accept, was that of propositions about his immediate experience of the world. He easily saw that it was possible to imagine himself mistaken about whether he was sitting in front of the fire in his dressing gown. For, he argued, it has often seemed to me that I was sitting in front of the fire when in truth I was in bed asleep. And other illusions where the senses deceived him pointed to the same conclusion.

This argument, although it is not invalid, cannot be regarded as convincing. It starts from the premise that he was sometimes mistaken in believing that he was sitting in front of the fire, and concludes that it is always possible for him to doubt whether he is sitting in front of the fire. The conclusion removes all reason for accepting the premise: if it is always possible to doubt whether or not he is sitting in front of the fire, then perhaps he was not wrong in the past. The argument is not a *reductio ad absurdum*, since it is not the premise itself which is disproved, but the reasons for accepting the premise. If, from the assumption of the premise, the premise had been disproved, then the argument would have been a perfectly respectable *reductio ad absurdum* argument leading to the final conclusion that the premise was false, and, moreover, logically false, since its falsity would have been entailed both by itself and by its negation. But the argument can easily be improved. For Descartes could have argued that there had been circumstances about which he had sometimes held one belief and at other times the contradictory of that belief. Therefore he must have been mistaken on at least one occasion; therefore it is always conceivable that he should be mistaken.

Descartes did not consider propositions such as the proposition that it *seemed* to him that he was sitting in front of the fire. It is possible to be mistaken about whether one is sitting by the fire in a way in which it is not possible to be mistaken about whether one seems to be sitting in front of the fire. Whether it is impossible to be mistaken about how things seem has been a very much disputed philosophical question; but whether or not Descartes ever considered the question, certainly he did not insist that it was impossible.

Now it is very difficult to conceive that one is deceived about such things as that two and two make four. In order to make this doubt plausible Descartes considered the possibility that the world was created and ruled, not by a benevolent God, but by an all-powerful malicious demon. Such a demon might, he supposed, wish to deceive him on every point. Since the demon would be all-powerful, then he would succeed in deceiving Descartes on nearly every point; if there were any propositions about which he could not deceive Descartes then these would be the propositions about which it was inconceivable that Descartes should be mistaken. Of course, Descartes did not really believe in the existence of such a demon, any more than he believed that fire would not burn him. He merely thought of the existence of such a demon as a possibility and argued that if this possibility were indeed the case, then he would be mistaken even about such simple and obvious matters as whether two and two make four, or whether he was sitting by the fire.

The supposition of a malicious demon brings out very clearly why it is conceivable that Descartes should doubt the simple propositions of mathematics and logic. The demon, of course, has no power over the truths of logic. Even he cannot contrive that the same statement should be both true and false; he cannot contrive that two and two do not make four; but he can contrive that Descartes should believe that two and two do not make four. It is necessary that two and two should make four, but it is not necessary that Descartes should believe that they do. If Descartes could find a proposition which it was not possible for him to be mistaken about, then he would escape the influence of the malicious demon. If he could find a proposition about which it was not possible for him to be mistaken, then he would have found what he wanted; if he found instead a proposition about which he could not possibly be correct, then he would not have found what he wanted. If there was a proposition about which he could not possibly be correct, then even an all-powerful and benevolent God could not free him from this error — though Descartes, illogically, attributed power over logical truths to God — for even an all-powerful and benevolent God can have no power to make true what is inconceivable. Of course the existence of a proposition about which it is impossible to be correct does not prove that there is no proposition about which it is impossible to be wrong. A proposition about which only error is possible would be of no use to Descartes as a foundation for science, but its existence would not prove that his search for such a foundation was hopeless.

COGITO ERGO SUM

"But I have convinced myself that nothing in the world exists — no sky, no earth, no minds, no bodies; so am not I likewise non-existent?" But if I did convince myself of anything, I must have existed. "But there is some deceiver, supremely powerful, supremely intelligent, who purposely always deceives me." If he deceives me, then again I undoubtedly exist; let him deceive me as much as he may, he will never bring it about that, at the time of thinking that I am something, I am in fact nothing. Thus I have now weighed all considerations enough and more than enough; and must at length conclude that this proposition "I am," "I exist," whenever I utter it or conceive it in my mind, is necessarily true.[3]

Descartes describes, both in the *Discourse on Method* and in the *Meditations*, how, whilst he was applying the method of doubt and rejecting one proposition after another as not being what he sought, he realized that in order to doubt anything he must exist. Therefore, he argued, here is a proposition about which it is impossible to be mistaken: the proposition that I exist. If I consider this proposition then it is true, so the belief that I exist cannot be mistaken. And the same argument held for the proposition "I think": since to doubt something is to think, then it is impossible to believe that one is thinking unless one is indeed thinking; it is impossible to believe that one is thinking and to be mistaken.

These two arguments are of exactly the same form. One depends upon the fact that believing entails existing, the other on the fact that believing entails thinking. "I believe that I exist" entails "I exist," because "I believe that . . . " entails "I exist" no matter what replaces the dots in "I believe that . . . " In exactly the same way, "I believe that I am thinking" entails "I am thinking," because "I believe that . . . " entails "I am thinking," no matter what replaces the dots in "I believe that . . . " The most obvious form of this argument would be that it is impossible to believe that one is holding a belief and be mistaken, since "I believe that I am holding a belief" entails "I am holding a belief." It was the validity of these inferences which Descartes intended to express by the statement "*cogito ergo sum*". He chose an unfortunate way of expressing it, because "I think, therefore I am" is not a statement at all, true or false: the word "therefore," or *ergo*, is a word used in conducting arguments, not in making statements, and someone who says the words "I think, therefore I am" asserts that he is thinking, and asserts that he exists, and displays the fact that he is arguing from the former to the latter; but he does not assert that this argument is valid, he does not assert that if he thinks then he exists. But evidently it was this that Descartes intended to assert; he used the words *cogito ergo sum* incorrectly, but his meaning is clear: he meant that the argument from "*cogito*" to "*sum*" was a valid argument.

The whole of the argument is this: first Descartes asserts that it is valid to argue from "I think that I exist" to "I exist." From this premise he argues that it is impossible for him to think that he exists and be mistaken; and from this he concludes that he has at last discovered a proposition which is beyond the power of the malignant demon, a proposition about which he cannot be mistaken, a proposition, therefore, which he certainly knows to be true.

His words at the end of the passage from the *Second Meditation*, "and must at length conclude that this proposition 'I am,' 'I exist,' whenever I utter it or conceive it in my mind, is necessarily true," might mislead someone into believing that Descartes thought that he had shown that the proposition "I exist," and likewise the proposition "I think," was necessarily true. If he had thought this then he would have been mistaken. It is a matter of fact, not logic, that Descartes existed and thought. Anyway, if this was what he had proved it would not have been enough, for it is necessary that two and two make four, yet Descartes agreed that he could conceivably have doubted it. Logical certainty is evidence for the reliability of an opinion, but not of the holder of that opinion: the fact that someone asserts a necessary proposition goes no way to show that he knows it to be true. Descartes intended these words to mean, not that it was necessarily true that he existed, but that it was necessarily true that when he considered whether he existed, he existed. He admitted that it was perfectly conceivable that he was not thinking, but he believed that it was not conceivable that he should be mistaken in believing that he was.

But in fact Descartes' argument is not valid, nor his conclusion true. It is true that he could not both believe that he was thinking and be mistaken about whether he was thinking; but it does not follow, nor is it true, that he could not be mistaken about whether he was thinking if he believed that he was thinking. He could quite easily be mistaken about this by believing that he was not thinking. From the fact that he believes that he is thinking it follows necessarily that he does not believe that he is not thinking, but it does not follow that it is necessary that he does not believe that he is not thinking. The fact that he is not mistaken does not make error impossible. It would be very strange for someone to believe that he himself was not thinking, but it is conceivable that someone should: the malicious demon could have contrived it.

Therefore the fact that Descartes could not believe that he was thinking and be mistaken does not entail that Descartes could not conceivably have been mistaken about whether he was thinking, even on those occasions when he believed that he was thinking. The proposition "I think" should have been rejected along with all the others as failing the test "Could Descartes conceivably have been mistaken about it?" Descartes had not found a proposition which satisfied his strict conditions for certainty: he had not found one which he could agree that he certainly knew to be true.

By itself, the fact that Descartes could not both believe that he was thinking and be mistaken, gives not the slightest reason for the conclusion that Descartes knew that he was thinking. For suppose that some person, tired of trying to decide whether he was thinking by rational means, allows his decision to rest on the toss of a coin, heads he is thinking, tails he is not. Suppose that the coin falls heads, so that he concludes that he is thinking. He has arrived at his conclusion by purely chance methods; therefore there is no justification at all for believing that he knows this conclusion to be true. Yet he cannot be mistaken in believing it, for if he believes it, then it is true. The same argument which Descartes used to prove that he himself knew that he was thinking would prove that this man who decides the matter by a toss of a coin knows that he is thinking.

It is important to notice that Descartes' argument, even if it had been valid, would have given no proof at all either that he existed, or that he thought. It proved only that if he believed that he existed, then he knew that he existed; that if he believed that he was thinking, then he knew that he was thinking. If the argument had been valid, then in taking the propositions "I exist" and "I think" as the fundamental assumptions of his philosophy Descartes would not have been assuming what he did not know.

Descartes nowhere gives more than a sketch of his argument concerning *cogito ergo sum*, so that it is not possible to decide with any certainty how he intended the argument to run. The account of it which I have given fits very well with the criterion for certainty provided by the method of doubt, for it shows how Descartes might have supposed that the propositions "I think" and "I exist" were such that it was contradictory to suppose that he himself was mistaken about them. But there are many other interpretations of the argument. I will mention two others, one because, though it is absurd, yet it is often put forward, the other because of its interest and plausibility.

In the absurd interpretation Descartes is said to have argued: "The proposition that I think follows both from the proposition that I believe that I think and from the proposition that I believe that I do not think. These are the only possibilities, therefore it must be true that I think. But 'I believe that I think' and 'I believe that I do not think' are not contradictories, and there is a third possibility 'I do not believe either that I think or that I do not think': the negation of 'I believe that I think' is 'It is not the case that I believe that I think,' and this does not entail 'I think.' "

The other interpretation is suggested by A. J. Ayer in *The Problem of Knowledge*,[4] and in a paper by N. Malcolm.[5] Ayer does not believe that the argument is cogent in this interpretation, but Malcolm believes that it is. Ayer says, "The sense in which I cannot doubt the statement that I think is just that my doubting it entails its truth: and in the same sense I cannot doubt that I exist." Ayer believes, that is, that Descartes supposed that a statement was indubitable if its truth followed from the fact that he doubted it. But I do not believe that this can be quite what Ayer means. For it does not follow from the fact that my doubting a statement entails that it is true, that it is a statement about which I am likely to be correct. Perhaps what Ayer means is that a statement is indubitable if it is *obvious* that if I doubt it then it is true. If this is obvious to me then I shall never wittingly disbelieve such a statement. Thus Descartes might have supposed that the fact that to argue from "I think that I exist" to "I exist" is to argue validly, shows quite clearly that it must be wrong for anyone to believe that he does not exist; and that no one who considers the argument from "I think that I exist" to "I exist," and sees that it is valid, can possibly arrive at a mistaken opinion about whether he exists. If this interpretation is correct then Descartes' conclusion is not the one I stated above, that anyone who believes that he himself exists, knows that he exists; but is rather that no one can see the validity of the argument from "I believe that I exist" to "I exist" and make the mistake of believing that he does not exist: no one can see the validity of this argument and fail to know that he exists.

It is quite possible that Descartes had some such argument as this in mind. But, in this interpretation, the proposition that he was thinking is not one about which Descartes could not conceivably have been mistaken, nor one which he could not have conceivably doubted. For he might have been misled over the validity of the argument from "I think that I exist" to "I exist." It is an obvious argument, but no more obvious than that from "there are two things here and two more things here" to "there are four things here," and Descartes agreed that he might be misled over this argument. Since this is so, Descartes might as well have accepted any very simple proposition as have accepted that he thought and that he existed, and the *cogito* argument would not have the unique position which Descartes gave to it.

But this second interpretation, though not fitting so well with Descartes' purposes, is a much more plausible argument. Malcolm believes that it is valid, and that anyone who sees that the argument from "I think that I exist" to "I exist" is valid, does indeed know that he exists. But Malcolm is mistaken. Consider an analogy. Suppose that someone is going to make a broadcast and is more concerned with avoiding error than with broadcasting something of importance, then he might attempt to broadcast the words "I am now broadcasting." If he succeeds in broadcasting these words then he does not make a false statement, and he tries to broadcast these words just because he sees this simple logical truth. But, of course, if we listened to the broadcast, knowing the man's plan and his reasons for it, and heard him broadcast these words, we should not say that he knew that he was broadcasting. He might be quite ignorant of whether he was broadcasting or not, not knowing, for example, whether the apparatus was in working order. A man who sees that he cannot broadcast that he is not broadcasting and be correct will never wittingly broadcast that he is not broadcasting; but this does not show that he knows that he is broadcasting since he may broadcast that he is not broadcasting unwittingly, because, perhaps, the apparatus has distorted his words. Nor do the words he broadcasts express his opinion about whether he is broadcasting; he tries to broadcast them, not because they express what he believes, but in order that he shall not broadcast words that express a false statement. Similarly with the man who chooses to believe that he exists because if he believes that he exists then he exists. Perceiving this logical truth will keep him from believing wittingly that he does not exist; but it will not keep him from believing this unwittingly, so that it will not keep him from falling into error unless he also knows whether or not he is believing that he does not exist. If he knows that he is holding a belief about whether he exists, then logic tells him what this belief ought to be, but without this piece of knowledge logic cannot help him. Nor, if a man chooses to believe that he exists because if he believes that he exists then he exists, is this choice really his opinion. It is one thing for a man to believe something, quite another for him to try to believe something because he sees that if he believes it then it will be true. A man's opinions are not to be identified with what he tries to believe in order to bring off a logical trick.

IDEAL KNOWLEDGE

The logical fact that if I believe that I exist, then I exist, does not entail that Descartes could not conceivably have been mistaken about whether he existed, nor that it was at all unlikely that he should have been mistaken about whether he existed. Nor does perceiving that he cannot both not exist and believe that he does exist, give a man knowledge that he exists, either certain or probable. The *cogito* argument does not prove what Descartes believed that it proved, and Descartes had not discovered in the propositions "I exist" and "I think" the certainty which he sought. This does not mean that Descartes was never certain that he existed or that he was thinking; it means, first, that he was never certain of these things in the sense that a mistake was logically impossible, and, second, the logical fact that *cogito ergo sum* was irrelevant to any certainty about existing or thinking that he might have.

But if these propositions are not beyond the power of the malicious demon, are there any which are beyond his power? Are there any propositions which Descartes could not conceivably have been mistaken about?

First, it seems that there cannot be any propositions which it is both inconceivable that Descartes should doubt, and inconceivable that he should be mistaken about. For if there were a proposition of this sort, then that it was true would entail that Descartes believed it, and that Descartes believed it would entail that it was true: the proposition would be identical with the proposition that Descartes believed it. For example, it seems plausible enough that a man could not conceivably be mistaken about whether he was in pain; but when we see that if this were so then the proposition that he was in pain would be identical with the proposition that he believed he was in pain, this plausibility vanishes.

It is not so obvious that it is impossible to find a proposition which Descartes might doubt but could not be mistaken about. If there were a proposition of this sort, then to say that Descartes believed it true would entail that it was true, and to say that Descartes believed it false would entail that it was false. The proposition "Descartes held a belief" fulfills the first condition but not the second. Now it does not seem possible that there should be any proposition for which the fact that Descartes believed it entails that it is true, except one which was entailed by "Descartes held a belief." But no proposition of this sort fulfills the second condition. Therefore it seems that there could not conceivably be propositions about which Descartes could not conceivably be mistaken. But though this seems so, it would be better to find some more rigorous proof of it.

Perhaps the question is not an important one, for even if there were propositions which Descartes could not conceivably be mistaken about, these would not be propositions which he knew to be true. For just as, in order that an event of one sort shall cause an event of another, it must be conceivable that an event of the first sort should happen without an event of the second sort happening, since if this is inconceivable then there are no longer two independent events; so, if a man's opinion is to count as knowledge, then it must be conceivable that it should be false; otherwise there are not two independent things, the fact and the man's opinion about the fact. For example, there is a sense in which a novelist's statements about his characters cannot be false; if the novelist says that one of his characters has a happy disposition, then that character has a happy disposition; but the novelist is not *describing* the characters in the way in which a historian describes people, and although it is in a way true that the novelist knows better than anyone else about his characters, yet he does not really know about them at all. Where there is no possibility of error there is no virtue in being correct.

What Descartes took to be the ideal of knowledge is not knowledge at all, and the method of doubt is a failure: for if he had applied it consistently Descartes would have discarded everything which he knew, and retained only what he did not know.

Existence of the Self

THE conclusion at which Descartes arrived in the *Second Meditation* was that he certainly knew that he existed and that he was thinking. Now apart from the question of whether this conclusion has been established, there arise serious difficulties over the two propositions "I exist" and "I think."

The fault with the proposition "I exist" is the same as that with any proposition which appears to assert that an individual thing or person exists. Every description must divide the individual things, or a certain class of them, into two sorts, those to which the description applies and those to which it does not; every description, that is, except logically true ones, such as "is either round or not round," and logically false ones, such as "is both round and not round." But the term "exists" does not divide the individual things: for there could not conceivably be an individual that did not exist. To say that an individual exists is either not to describe it at all, or else to assert a logical truth. The latter alternative would suit Descartes very well, for if it were correct, then all statements about the existence of individual things would be discoverable by the use of the understanding alone. But it is not correct; for every logical truth expresses the validity of some inference: for example, the logical truth that nothing is both red and not red expresses the validity of the inference from "This is red" to "It is not the case that this is not red." Now there is no inference whose validity is constituted by the fact that Descartes existed. Therefore the term "exists" which appears to be a description of an individual, is not a description at all. The assertion "I exist," if the word "I" is used merely to refer to a person, says nothing.

But the word "exist" does have a legitimate use. Evidently it is significant to say that starlings exist and phoenixes do not. Therefore the assertion that Descartes existed may, in order to make it significant, be interpreted to mean that a French philosopher existed, and the assertion "I exist" may be taken to mean, as Descartes took it to mean, that at least one thinking thing existed. The premise of the *cogito* could then be expressed as "It is impossible that someone should believe that at least one thinking thing exists and be mistaken."

This objection does not tell, of course, against the other conclusion of the *cogito*, that Descartes knew that he was thinking; and this conclusion is all that Descartes needed. This objection does not constitute a fundamental objection to Descartes' argument.

But there is one objection to "I exist" which applies equally to "I think": it is one which Descartes himself faced. These propositions tell nothing to anyone who is not acquainted with whatever it is that the word "I" is being used to denote. Some denoting words, such as "this" in the sentence "This is heavy," stand for physical objects which can be seen, touched, or pointed at; but Descartes believed that the word "I," in "I think," stood for a mind which could be neither seen, touched, nor pointed at. For he believed, as we shall see, that minds cannot conceivably have any properties that bodies can have, such as shape or weight. His mind, then, must have been something with which Descartes was acquainted, or he would not have understood the word "I" which denoted it, yet he could not have been acquainted with it in any way in which he was acquainted with physical objects: he could not see it or touch it or point at it. How was this to be explained?

Put differently the problem is: granted that a man may know many things about his mind, that it holds beliefs, makes decisions, and so on, yet it seems that he cannot possibly know what thing it is that has these properties. Is it of much use to know that *some* thing has a set of properties if we do not know *what* thing has them? The problem is one which a behaviorist might raise: what is the good of describing objects which can never be recognized by any sensory methods?

Descartes solves this problem not by exhibiting some way in which we can become acquainted with our own minds, perhaps by some inner sense with which we might perceive them, but by arguing that in fact sensory perception does not acquaint us even with physical objects. The argument he uses is the notorious one about the piece of wax.

This argument depends on considering how the same piece of wax takes on entirely different physical properties when it is heated, whilst remaining, of course, the very same piece of wax. Therefore all that the senses informed us about the wax was inessential to it. It seemed that in seeing a hard, cold, fragrant, easily handled object, we were seeing the wax, and seeing that it had these properties. But this, Descartes argued, was not so: for after it had been heated the wax remained, yet none of these qualities remained. The qualities which are alone essential to the piece of wax are, Descartes argued, those of being extended, flexible, and changeable, and these qualities can be perceived only by the mind.

Descartes is making two points, first, that sensory perception plays no part in our knowledge of the wax, a conclusion which he fails to establish, though he does establish that understanding is necessary as well as sensory perception; and second, that finding out what properties a thing has is all that is required for being acquainted with it. For example, he says, "For if I judge that wax exists from the fact that I see this wax, it is much clearer that I myself exist because of this same fact that I see it."[6] Perhaps the second conclusion is enough to make Descartes' point. For although one way of identifying an object is by having it pointed out to us, yet there is another perfectly good way, that of having it picked out by means of a description; and this way is a way in which a man can identify his own mind. But perhaps, on the other hand, this way of identifying

objects by describing them works only where there is the possibility of sensory acquaintance with them. Descartes' argument that the mind is no more mysterious a thing than the body is not entirely convincing.

It was from his certainty of the fact that he was a thinking being that Descartes derived his proof of the fundamental rationalist thesis, that in order to know whether a proposition is true or false, it is sufficient to understand it perfectly. He says, in the *Third Meditation*,

> I am certain that I am a conscious being. Surely then I also know what is required for my being certain about anything? In this primary knowledge all I need is a clear and distinct perception of what I assert; now this would not be enough to make me certain as to the truth of the matter if it could ever happen that something clearly and distinctly perceived in this way should be false; so it looks as though I could lay down the general rule: whatever I perceive very clearly and distinctly is true.[7]

This argument is invalid. Suppose that he had been certain that he was a conscious being, and suppose that having a clear and distinct understanding of this proposition had been sufficient to make him certain of it, then it would not follow that having a clear and distinct understanding of any proposition was sufficient for Descartes to be certain of it. For it might be that arriving at a clear and distinct understanding of a proposition was sometimes sufficient for coming to know whether it was true or false and sometimes not, depending upon what proposition was in question. Descartes, in fact, admitted that this was so, for he held that coming to a perfect understanding of the proposition that two and two make four does not lead to complete certainty, whilst coming to a perfect understanding of the proposition that I am thinking, does.

Nor is this the only mistake in this piece of argument. Descartes has not shown that it follows from the fact that I am certain of something, that I know what conditions are required for my being certain of it. Nor is this consequence true: animals know many things, but it is very doubtful whether they know what conditions must be fulfilled if they are to know something.

To avoid inconsistency Descartes modified his position: he admitted that perfect understanding would not yield certainty to anyone who did not know that the world was ruled by a benevolent god rather than by a malicious demon, but he argued that to someone who did know that the world was ruled by a benevolent god, a perfect understanding would yield certainty. Because of this he attempted to prove that a god existed, and his proofs of this stemmed, too, from the results of the *cogito*.

After this he was in a position to set about reinstating all the beliefs which he had put into doubt, and he did so by the arguments which I discussed when I was discussing rationalism. If his arguments had been valid then he would have ended by making it impossible for himself to doubt or to be mistaken about any propositions which he understood completely, explaining error as arising only from the rash acceptance of propositions which were imperfectly understood. But whether the arguments he employed were valid or invalid, there is something very strange about Descartes' philosophical position. For he must have held that whilst before he had carried out his enquiry he really did not know that physical objects existed, yet after his enquiry was finished he genuinely did know that they did. And the same is true of everyone else: before they read Descartes' work, or think of his arguments for themselves, they really do not know for certain that physical objects exist; only when they have followed his arguments do they know that they do. Probably G. E. Moore was chiefly responsible for making clear the absurdity of this position, and of any attempt to *prove* that physical objects exist or that the elementary propositions of mathematics are true. For what other beliefs are more certain than these, from which such proofs might start?

The Definition of Substance

DESCARTES defines "substance" by saying, "We mean by *substance* nothing other than a thing existing in such a manner that it has need of no other thing in order to exist."[8] But his doctrine of substance was in reality a doctrine of categories; when he spoke of "a substance" he did not mean "a thing" but "a kind of thing." He was able to treat the theory that there exist self-sufficient things as though it were identical with the quite different theory that there exist self-sufficient properties, or kinds of thing, because he believed that things had defining properties just as kinds of thing have. His definition of substance is an attempt to find a precise statement of the theory that there are in nature a number of fundamental kinds of thing, to one or other of which, but not to more than one, each individual thing must belong. But, in fact, Descartes' theory combines two quite separate theories about how nature divides into substances.

One sense in which one property has need of another in order to exist, is that in which one property presupposes another. Only integers, for example, are odd or even in number, so that both the property of being odd in number and the property of being even in number presupposes the property of being an integer. Again, the proposition "This is in the key of C" implies that a piece of music is in question, so that the property of being in the key of C presupposes the property of being a piece of music. The proposition "This is a democracy" implies that a community is under disscusion,

so that the property of being a democracy presupposes the property of being a community. Now although nearly every property which one can think of presupposes some other property, it may be that there are some properties which presuppose no other in particular, and this is one of the things Descartes means when he uses the words "has need of no other thing in order to exist." He says, "For example shape is not conceivable except in an extended thing, nor motion in an extended space; whereas imagination, sensation, and will are inconceivable except in a conscious being. But on the other hand extension is conceivable apart from shape or motion, and so is consciousness apart from imagination and sense, and so on; this is clear to anyone on reflection."[9] Descartes believed that the properties of being extended, and of being conscious, presupposed no other properties in particular; and he believed that every other property presupposed one or other of these.

If two properties are such that neither presupposes any other then they will satisfy a second condition which Descartes laid down for a substance: "Real distinction between two or more substances . . . is discovered from the fact that we can clearly and distinctly conceive one without the other."[10] For example, if neither being extended nor being conscious presupposes any other property in particular, then we can conceive of a thing which is extended but not conscious, and of a thing which is conscious but not extended. But this condition may be given another interpretation, that of Descartes' second theory, and in this other interpretation the fact that neither of two properties presuppose any other does not entail that the condition is satisfied.

One of Descartes' theories of substance, then, is this: every property that any thing might conceivably have presupposes one or the other of two fundamental properties, being extended or being conscious; but neither of these properties presupposes any other property in particular.

It is for this theory that Descartes is arguing when he maintains that he can conceive of a thing with the properties of a physical object without conceiving that it has any of the properties of a mind, and that he can conceive of a thing with the properties of a mind without conceiving that it has any of the properties of a physical object.

But although Descartes states his theory of substance in the way I have just explained, the theory he works with is a stricter one. He demands, for two properties to be substances, not only that it should be possible to conceive of one *without* the other, but also that it should be impossible to conceive of one *with* the other. Descartes believed not only that it was conceivable that something should be extended and not conscious, but also that it was inconceivable that one thing should be both extended and conscious. He may have supposed that the latter condition follows from the former, but in fact it does not.

We must add to the statement of the theory the condition that the two fundamental properties are incompatible with one another.

Descartes may have supposed that this theory provided an adequate statement of the doctrine that nature contains two fundamental, independent kinds of thing, the mental and the physical. But in fact this theory is inadequate. To see this inadequacy plainly, consider two properties which, though they are not substantial properties, since they each presuppose others, yet must belong to two different substances, since the properties presupposed by one are quite distinct from those presupposed by the other: the two properties are that of being a plumber, and that of being an average plumber. John Smith, for example, is a plumber, and the average British plumber is an average plumber. There are many properties which an average plumber can have which an individual plumber could not conceivably have: for example, the children of an average plumber can be $2\frac{5}{8}$ in number, but there would be literally no sense in the statement that the children of an individual plumber were $2\frac{5}{8}$ in number. Average plumbers are as fundamentally different from plumbers as minds are from bodies. This fact, however, would not convince many people that there exist in nature two fundamental sorts of thing, plumbers and average plumbers; though we talk as if average plumbers existed, and though if we talk in this way we must talk of them as being fundamentally different from individual plumbers, yet the truth is that this is no more than a way of talking, that we could say all that can be said without ever mentioning average plumbers, and that average plumbers do not exist at all. And just in the same way, we talk of minds whose properties could not conceivably be physical, yet perhaps there really are no minds at all.

Another two sorts of thing with fundamentally different properties are people and nations. Very many properties of people make no sense of nations, and very many properties of nations make no sense of people. Yet this fact does not force us to the conclusion that nations exist apart from the people that compose them.

Although the properties that average plumbers may have are quite different from those which individual plumbers may have, yet statements about average plumbers entail and are entailed by statements about particular plumbers. Although no individual plumber could have $2\frac{5}{8}$ children, yet the statement that the average plumber has $2\frac{5}{8}$ children is about individual plumbers: it is about individual plumbers in the very good sense that it can be translated into a statement which is incontestably about individual plumbers. And similarly, it is possible that, although the properties which minds have could not conceivably be those which bodies have, yet statements about minds can be translated into statements about bodies. It is because of this possibility that Descartes' theory that being physical

and being mental are two fundamental properties, which presuppose no other properties, one of which, but not both, is presupposed by every other property, and which are incompatible with one another, is not adequate to express the independence of mind and matter; it is possible that this theory is true and yet that all statements about minds are statements about bodies. To express the independence adequately we must demand that this translation should not be possible, that is, we must demand that no statement about a mind should follow logically from any statements that mention only bodies, and that no statement about a body should follow logically from any statements that mention only minds. We now have a definition of substance with which we can adequately represent the theory that mind and matter form two fundamental and independent kinds of thing. And this second theory is one which Descartes argues for, although he does not state it explicitly.

The argument in which he does so is an argument based on the *cogito*. He argues that by means of the *cogito* it is possible to prove that at least one thinking thing exists without giving any support whatsoever to the conclusion that a bodily thing exists. If it is possible to establish the former conclusion whilst doing nothing at all to establish the latter, then the former conclusion cannot entail the latter; that is, it must be possible for minds to exist without the existence of any bodies at all. Now this could only be possible if statements about minds were logically independent of statements about bodies. The argument itself is not a cogent one: for if a person were unaware that the existence of at least one body followed from the existence of at least one mind, then he might establish the existence of at least one mind without establishing, at least so far as he himself was concerned, the existence of any body at all. But Descartes' use of the argument indicates that he was aware of this second, and strongest, sense in which the mind might be independent of the body, and that he asserted its independence in this strongest sense. So the definition that a thing is a substance only if it has no need of any other thing in order to exist has a second interpretation; in this it states that a property is a substance only if it is conceivable that things with that property should exist and yet no things without that property exist. If mind is a substance then it must be conceivable that a mind should exist, but no body. If body is a substance then it must be conceivable that a body should exist, but no mind. This independence is logical; so far as this definition goes, substances may depend causally, but not logically, upon one another.

The question whether there are any substances, taking this word in the first of the two meanings which Descartes gave to it, is not an easy one to decide. I shall not attempt to do so, but I shall mention two difficulties. For one thing, the answer depends upon how strictly the word "property" is taken. If *any* disjunction of two properties is allowed itself to count as a property, then there is no property which does not presuppose another. For example, the property of being extended and the property of being conscious, would both presuppose the property of being either extended or conscious. Unless some way can be found of distinguishing properties which are merely disjunctions from genuine properties, then the question whether there are any substances is trivial, and the answer to it is "No." The problem is of some interest: are there genuine properties which, for example, both liquids and gases share, but no genuine properties which both minds and bodies share?

And there are some properties which make serious problems. Descartes' definition has the consequence that no thing belonging to one substance can share properties with a thing belonging to another. Yet there are some properties which even such diverse things as numbers, minds, and physical objects may all share. One example is the property of being describable, another the property of having been considered by Descartes. Ought we to conclude that there is only one substance, the property of being describable, since no thing could have any property at all without being describable? Probably we should not reach this conclusion, since "being describable" fails the same test that "existing" fails; that of asking whether it divides, or might conceivably divide, the things in the world into two classes. Nothing could conceivably not be describable, therefore "being describable" is not a property. The property of being describable is not a property presupposed by all others since it is not a property at all. But if this is correct, there remain difficulties over properties such as that of having been considered by Descartes. This property does not presuppose either being extended or being conscious, so it must belong to a third substance. But it cannot belong to a substance other than extension or consciousness, since it is compatible with both these properties. It is not the case, then, that every property that a thing may have presupposes one or other of a set of independent and incompatible properties.

It would be possible to avoid this difficulty if we could exclude relational properties, such as "was considered by Descartes," from consideration. But this is impossible, consistent with Descartes' theory, for the property of being extended, which he took to be the defining property of material substance, is a relational property.

MENTAL AND MATERIAL SUBSTANCE

The theory that minds and bodies belong to two fundamentally different kinds of thing, and that each human being is a union of two things, one of each kind, fits very closely to common sense. And there are many reasons which support it. Minds cannot, for example, have spatial properties. It makes no sense to say that the mind of one person is in a physical sense larger than that of another, nor to suggest to someone that someone should move his mind to a more convenient situation. Probably most people suppose that every mind is associated with a body which does have location, but this is not the same as supposing that every mind is itself located. Nor can minds sensibly be said to have any property that presupposes the property of being extended, such as color or density. Similarly, it makes little sense to discuss whether physical objects possess mental properties. Does it make sense to discuss whether or not an umbrella feels pain, or is thinking about its past life, or wishes that it had a different owner? But these considerations are scarcely conclusive: it is possible, if less plausible, to argue that physical objects can think and have sensations, and hence that thinking and sentient things can have mass and extension.

But do not arguments very similar to those which support Descartes' view that mind and body form two independent and incompatible substances, equally support the view that there are many other substances? It makes no sense to say that minds are extended, but equally it makes no sense to say that numbers are extended, or that governments are extended, or that songs are extended. And if it makes no sense to say that physical objects are conscious, then equally it makes no sense to say that numbers are conscious, or that songs are conscious, or that governments are conscious. Bodies and minds have no properties in common, but nor have governments and numbers. Neither numbers, nor songs, nor governments, belong to mental or to bodily substance. Therefore, if there are substances at all, there are more than two.

Probably Descartes did not consider that numbers and concepts constituted additional substances besides bodies and minds because he supposed that numbers and concepts were ideas, that they existed in the minds of people or of God, and that they belonged to mental substance. Had he strictly observed his own definition, though, he would have admitted that the properties of numbers are as independent of those of minds as are the properties of physical objects. The fact that minds reason about numbers does not entail that numbers are mental.

It is at this point, when we are wondering whether to admit the existence of a large number of different substances, that we remember that the definition of a substance as a property which presupposes no other, and which is incompatible with any properties which do not presuppose it, is not the most important sense of substance, and that substances which are independent in this weaker sense, as are individual plumbers and average plumbers, may be scarcely distinguishable in the stronger and more important sense. We remember that what is important is whether statements about minds can or can not be shown to be about physical objects, whether statements about numbers and statements about minds are logically independent. No one would want to say that mind, body, and number form independent substances if statements of the three sorts were translatable into one another. Of course the questions whether such translations can be carried out are very difficult questions, and they are questions with which contemporary philosophers have been very much concerned.

Whether in fact all statements about minds can be translated into statements about bodies, or all statements about bodies can be translated into statements about minds is too large a question to be discussed in this account of Descartes' philosophy. Some statements about minds seem to have such a translation, whilst others do not. For example, it seems reasonable to suppose that the statement that a man has a certain desire is settled by discovering how he would behave in various circumstances, particularly, that is, in those circumstances where he had the opportunity to fulfill this desire and knew that he had the opportunity. Even the man himself might be convinced by an account of his behavior that he did have a certain desire, without being at all convinced that he had ever felt that desire. An analysis of statements that people have certain desires into conditionals about how they would behave in certain circumstances makes clear how desires differ from mere feelings of dissatisfaction; it explains how desires can have objects. But this advantage of the behaviorist analysis can perhaps be secured by a nonbehaviorist analysis of a desire in terms of conditionals about what sort of feelings a man would have in various circumstances. On the other hand, some other statements about minds appear to have no plausible translation into statements about physical things. Statements that a person is in pain are certainly not translatable into statements about the disease of his body, nor can they be translated very convincingly into statements about tendencies to protect or withdraw a certain part of his body.

Besides asserting that there are only two substances, mind and body, Descartes attempts to say what the two fundamental properties are, the one presupposed by every physical property, so that every body must have it, the other by every mental property, so that every mind must have it. He identifies the former as the property of being extended, the latter as the property of being conscious. Could there conceivably be material objects which are not extended? Leibniz thought that there could be; he believed that it was possible for a material object to have a mass but no size. Indeed, he believed that the material world was entirely composed of such objects. Whether the concept of a mass which is situated at a point is acceptable or not, it does not seem very much less so than that of a physical object which has size but no mass. But the massive points would not be completely free from spatial properties, for they would have position, and it is certain that

nothing that did not have position could be called a physical object. Having spatial properties is necessary if an object is to be a physical object, but perhaps it is not sufficient; shadows, for example, have spatial properties, they fill volumes, but are not physical objects.

Is "being conscious" the defining property of minds? The work of Sigmund Freud has shown that there is not nearly so much reason for believing this as was supposed before. He showed that the ideas of unconscious belief, unconscious desire, and unconscious thought were not only perfectly respectable, but indispensable for understanding the mind properly: he did not show so convincingly that the concepts of unconscious sensation and unconscious pain were respectable. The belief that the mind always thinks, that is, is always conscious, which was always an uncomfortable consequence of Descartes' definition of the mind, became quite untenable after Freud's work. But what definition to put in the place of Descartes' is another question.

The Relation between the Mind and the Body

DESCARTES believed, then, that a living person was a very intimate union of two things; two things which were perfectly distinct but whose natures were as different as it was possible for two natures to be. One important thing about Descartes' theory is that it asserts the complete logical independence of every mind from its own body, so that it presents the relation between a mind and a body very much on the analogy of the relation between two physical objects; another is the account given of the fundamentally different nature of the mind from that of its body. These two features are important because of the bearing they have on the question of how Descartes supposed one person's mind and body to be related; on the question, that is, of the nature of the intimate union which he believed to exist between them. He could not, for example, explain this relation by saying that they were very very close together, for it makes no sense, he held, to suppose that the mind has a spatial position. For the same reason no other relation which might hold between physical objects could be used. He might have attempted an explanation in terms of a mental relation; for example, that the mind perceives its own body more clearly than it perceives any other material object. This relation could hold between the two, as no physical relation possibly could. In fact, Descartes held that the mind and its body were in intimate causal connection, so that occurrences in the mind, such as decisions, could cause effects in the body, and occurrences in the body, the decay of a tooth or the stimulation of the retina of the eye, could cause effects in the mind. Now Descartes himself perhaps, and certainly some of his disciples, believed that if minds and bodies belonged to two different substances, then they could not interact. Their reasons for believing this are not quite plain. They may have believed that the logical independence of statements about the mind from statements about the body meant that no causal interaction between the two was possible. For they may have confused logical necessity, which holds when if one statement is true a second could not conceivably be false, with causal necessity, which holds when if one statement is true a second could not as a matter of fact be false. If this was their reason, then it was a bad one, for the fact that statements about one object are logically independent of statements about another provides the best possible basis for a causal interaction between the objects. Or they may have believed that a change in the properties of a mind could not conceivably have produced a change in the properties of a body, just because these two properties were so fundamentally different. Perhaps this reason is more than a superstition, analogous to the superstition that cause and effect must somehow be alike, for there are some substantial differences which are accompanied by the impossibility of causal interaction: a change in the properties of a material object could not, for example, conceivably bring about a change in the properties of any number. But this example does not establish that the impossibility of interaction is due to the fundamentally different nature of numbers and physical objects. Presumably it *is* due to the nature of numbers; for they are immutable. Negative and positive integers are of the *same* fundamental kind, but there is equally no possibility that they should causally interact with one another; whilst in other examples of differing substances, where neither of the substances has a logical nature — for example, nations and people — causal interaction is possible. Descartes need not have feared that his belief that mind and body constituted two independent substances was inconsistent with his belief that minds and bodies acted causally upon one another.

The intimate union of a mind and its body was, then, a close causal connection. The body, Descartes believed, was nothing more than an apparatus for conveying information to the mind by means of signals, and for conveying orders from the mind in the same manner. It was a telegraph system which conveyed signals to and from a point in the brain, and the occurrences at this place directly affected, and were affected by, the mind. The motive for supposing that all messages were conveyed to and from one point, "the alleged seat of common sensibility," was presumably that if the mind were supposed to be in direct causal contact with the whole of the body, then the nerves would have no part to play as carriers of signals.

Although the thesis that the intimate union between a mind and its body is a causal one is consistent with the belief that mind and body form two independent substances, it did not provide Descartes with a satisfactory account of the nature of perception. Consistent with the casual thesis Descartes might have held that a mind perceives an object only when the object causes certain beliefs to arise in the mind. For example, he might have held that a mind perceives an apple tree only when an apple tree causes the mind to believe that an apple tree does stand in a certain place. This account ignores sensations and images, and it identifies perception with judgment; and none of this did Descartes wish to do. He says, though in a different connection, "Otherwise, when the body is hurt, I, who am simply a conscious being, would not feel pain on that account but would perceive the injury by a pure act of the understanding."[11] He could not escape this difficulty by supposing that the body acted causally upon the mind to produce sensations *in* it, since he did not suppose that the mind could contain sensations. Therefore he held that there was a second relation which existed between bodies and minds: this relation was that of a mind perceiving a body, sensation and imagination were species of it. In fact, he believed that the only body a mind could perceive was the brain to which it was united. The belief that minds could perceive bodies seems, in its turn, to be consistent with the thesis that mind and body form two independent substances.

Thus Descartes held that knowledge of objects was of two kinds: intellectual, in which a body caused beliefs to arise in a mind, and perceptual, in which a mind perceived a body directly; this happened in imagination and in sensations of pain and color. Part of Descartes' account of the relation between minds and bodies makes use of a relation which is not further explained, that of a mind perceiving a body; but perhaps it was better not to explain perception at all, than to explain it, as John Locke did, in terms of a mind perceiving its own sensations, and to leave this, in its turn, unexplained. Descartes failed to give a satisfactory account of the relations between bodies and minds, but then no satisfactory account has ever been given.

Spinoza

P. H. NIDDITCH

BARUCH BEN MICHAEL, better known by his Latin name of Benedictus de Spinoza, was born on November 24, 1632, in Amsterdam, his parents being Jewish refugees who went to Holland to escape the terrors of the Spanish Inquisition. His mother, the second wife of his father, died when he was only five. Spinoza's father, a successful business man, was an important figure in the Jewish community, for several different years being elected to the honored office of Warden of the Synagogue; he died in 1654. From an early age Spinoza was sent, like all the other Jewish boys, to the Rabbinical School. There he became fully literate in Hebrew and was immersed in the study of the Old Testament and the Talmud and the medieval commentaries on these. Later he also read Jewish medieval philosophy, especially the works of Maimonides, the Jewish Thomas Aquinas. (In view of Maimonides' priority that phrase could be inverted and Aquinas described as the Catholic Maimonides.) The principal philosophical work of Maimonides is *A Guide to the Perplexed*, in which he candidly and cogently formulates the various doubts and difficulties that could be prompted in the course of reflection on the foundations of Judaism and attempts, on the other side, to quell the doubts and solve the difficulties in a rational way. Perhaps Spinoza was more impressed by the grounds for perplexity than by Maimonides' answers thereto. Whatever the origins of Spinoza's dissent from Judaism — and they were sure to have been many, some of them subtle — they led ultimately to his being excommunicated from the community in 1656. Thenceforth he lived a rather lonely life as a paying-guest in various Dutch towns, earning a living by the grinding of lenses; this contributed to his tuberculosis, from which he died in 1677. He was offered a chair in philosophy at the University of Heidelberg in 1673 but refused it, preferring the safety of his solitude.

THE PRESENT AGE has delighted to honor the seventeenth century, which bears, as some have noted, certain remarkable affinities to our own, particularly in the spheres of politics, morality, and science. Perhaps we find in praising it a pleasant and not too immodest way of praising ourselves. Be that as it may, there is assuredly no denying that it was indeed a time abundant with greatness: Milton and Racine; Rembrandt, Vermeer, and Velasquez; Richelieu, Cromwell, and Peter the First; Galileo, Boyle, Harvey, Hooke, Huygens, and Fermat; Descartes, Pascal, Leibniz, and Newton. Yet even among such a splendid company as this, which forms in the skies of history a conspicuous part of the constellation Genius, the star of Spinoza is not outshone. His brilliant mind, his luminous power of systematization, the candor of his critical faculties, his ardent attachment to a lonely, intellectual ethic, and the fierce combustion of his energies in the determined pursuit of truth make him one of the most illustrious figures of the period.

Metaphysics is a species of literature; no one can actually be a metaphysician, any more than one can be a novelist, without the tools and techniques of writing that promote the expression on paper of thoughts and the development of thoughts. Of the origin of the species we know nothing — although, inversely, some believe it has been shown unfit to survive and are gladly witnessing what they take to be its current extinction. Metaphysics could not appear until scripts had been invented and writing materials manufactured. This is one reason why it is among the youngest of the arts. Another reason is its necessity for detachment. As long as the individual is dominated by mental habits engendered by social conventions, he is unable to apply his creative and critical powers of thought. Metaphysical thinking depends on the ability to arouse the dormant faculties that have been hypnotized in childhood and youth by traditions. The metaphysician must not be content with repeating recordlike the verbal forms of belief that were engrained into the plastic personality he had when he was young. The detachment needed involves the awakening and exercise of the conscious capacity to reflect. These conditions cannot be fulfilled unless the individual can see himself as distinct from the community. Once he perceives this distinctness he can transform himself from being a machine programed by social custom into being an independent observer, "a *spectator* of all time and all existence."

Spinoza was brought up as an Orthodox Jew amidst Orthodox Jews. That was his society. He was fed from birth on the religion of his ancestors, and throughout his early years he was continually assimilating this until it became a part of his nature. He underwent the traditional, unmitigated study of the Hebrew Bible and the Talmud, and of the Rabbinical Commentaries on these. This intense

Jewish education became a permanent deposit in his mind, and even afterwards, when later cultural strata had superseded it, it remained profoundly to affect the contours of his thought.

In classical Judaism everything is brought within the realm of morals and made subject to the rule of the Divine Legislator. The aim of Rabbinism was to cover all possible actions by prescribed regulations, these being produced by various devices of reason, wit, or fantasy from the raw material provided by the Words of God. Poring over for years the casuistical details and the sophisticated dialectic of the Rabbinical literature ensures the making of a moralist, prepared to criticize doctrines as well as deeds. So was Spinoza made. He wrote only one full-scale book presenting his metaphysical beliefs, and this, pertinently, was called the *Ethics*. Elsewhere, in the fragment entitled *A Treatise on the Correction of the Intellect*, the lasting impression made by his early Jewish instruction on the comprehensive importance of duty and salvation is readily apparent, being at this point still on the surface of his consciousness:

> After I had learned from experience that everything that repeatedly occurs in everyday life is futile and fruitless, and had seen that the things of which I was afraid were neither good nor bad intrinsically but only in so far as the mind is affected by them, I decided in the end to find out whether there was something that was really good and could convey itself as such and which could occupy the mind to the exclusion of all else; in other words, to find out whether there was something whose discovery and acquisition would enable me to enjoy continual, supreme, and everlasting happiness. I say "I decided in the end," for at first sight it seemed inadvisable to be willing to give up what was certain for the sake of something that was then uncertain. I was aware of the many advantages that come from fame and fortune and knew I would have to abstain from seeking them if I wanted seriously to pursue something new and different; and I recognized that if it should turn out that the highest happiness did reside in fame and fortune it would be bound to pass me by. On the other hand if it did not so reside and I devoted myself to them, then again I should fail to attain the highest happiness.[1]

This narration continues with an account of what are popularly the highest values — wealth, fame, and sensual pleasure — and of their defects. Spinoza's criticism comes to this, that the very gratification of pleasure necessarily leads to discomfort and the desires for wealth and fame are insatiable (and so cannot satisfy), for, like Dante's wolf, the more they are fed the more hungry they grow.

> After strenuous consideration I came to see that if only I could get to the heart of the matter, I

should be relinquishing what were surely evils for what was surely good. I realized that a supreme peril was confronting me, and so I forced myself to make a thorough search for a remedy, even an uncertain one; just as a sick man struggling with a deadly disease, who has the prospect of certain death before him unless a remedy be found, is forced to use all his powers in seeking one, however unreliable, for all his hopes depend upon it.[2]

But nothing in itself is either good or bad, perfect or imperfect,

especially when we come to know that everything that takes place does so in accordance with the eternal order and fixed laws of Nature. However, due to human weakness we cannot attain this order in our own thoughts. In the meantime man conceives a human nature much more stable than his own. When he then sees no obstacle to his acquiring such a nature, he is stirred to seek the means which will lead to this perfection and to regard everything as really good that can be a means to it. The supreme good is that he arrive, if possible with other individuals, at the enjoyment of such a nature. What that nature is I shall show in its proper place, namely that it is the knowledge of the union that the mind has with the whole of Nature. Thus this is the goal at which I aim: acquiring such a nature and trying to get many others to acquire it with me. . . . In order to bring this about it is necessary to understand as much of Nature as will suffice for the acquiring of such a nature; and in addition society must be arranged in such a way as is needed to enable the majority also to acquire it with certainty and ease. Further, attention must be paid to Moral Philosophy and to the Theory of Education. Since health is a not inconsiderable means to the attainment of our goal, the whole of Medicine must be included. And because much that is difficult is made easy by the use of technical skill, we must not at all look with contempt on Engineering, for this puts more time at our disposal and increases our comforts. But above all, and as far as possible to begin with, one must devise a means of purging and healing the intellect itself, in order that it may fruitfully understand things unerringly and in the best way. Therefore, as is apparent, I want to direct all the sciences to a single field and goal, this being the attainment of the supreme human perfection which we have described. Thus anything that belongs to the sciences and does not advance us toward our goal will have to be dismissed out of hand; for to put it in a word, all our thoughts and deeds have got to be directed to this one end.[3]

These passages make it clear that Spinoza's motive for tilling and planting his philosophic garden was solely to enable him to eat of the fruit of the Tree of Knowledge of Good and Evil.

God or Nature

THE four cardinal points of the Jewish theological compass are the existence of God, his unity and infinity, his causation and regulation of nature, and his assignment to man of happiness or misery in accordance with the fullness or the failure in man's love of God. In constructing his metaphysical map of the world Spinoza never doubted the accuracy of this compass, but on the contrary was constantly guided by it.

"*Deus necessario existit* — God necessarily exists."

The pattern of traditional instruction had been engraved with sufficient pressure on Spinoza's mind that for him, as for his many medieval predecessors, existence and perfection of God became psychologically and naturally indispensable, not contingent facts to be confirmed by the deliverances of faith or scripture.

More than 10,000 times when he was young Spinoza muttered in private devotion or in public prayer the biblical passage that begins "Hear, Israel, the Lord is our God, the Lord is one." The conditioned conviction remained that "*Deum esse unicum* — God is one." Like other Jews, Spinoza always despised those doctrines (such as the Christian doctrine of the Trinity) which seemed to involve dismemberment of the substance of the Deity; in his eyes theological anatomy was surgery. Again, Spinoza had been familiarized with the Rabbinic description of God as infinite and perfect, this description too, in common with that of his unity, occurring in the weekday and Sabbath liturgy. Even after Spinoza ceased to pray, and wrote Latin instead of Hebrew, this notion of God, so colored in childhood, was retained and kept as vivid as originally. "There is nothing of whose existence we can be more certain than of the existence of the perfect or absolutely infinite being, God."

Spinoza was a life-long student of the Hebrew Bible, in which God is envisaged as the maker and ruler of the cosmos. "In the beginning God made the Heavens and the Earth." "Praise him, supernal Heavens and the waters over the Heavens. Let them praise God's name, for he commanded and they were made. He has established them for the duration of the world, setting bounds that he will not transgress. . . . Let them praise God's name since his name and no other is sublime: he dominates Heaven and Earth." Analogously Spinoza says: "God is absolutely the first cause. . . .[4] From the supreme power of God or from his infinite nature infinite things in infinite ways — in short, all things — have necessarily emanated, or continually follow by the same necessity; just as it eternally follows from the nature of a triangle that its three angles are equal to two right angles."[5]

It is also Jewish doctrine that lasting felicity comes, and comes only, from the studious love of God. "Hear, Israel, the Lord is our God, the Lord is one. And you shall love the Lord your God with all your heart and with all your soul and with all your energy. And these words which I command you this day shall be kept in your heart. You shall get your children to memorize them, and you shall speak about them when you are sitting in your house or walking in the street, when you are lying down to sleep and when you are getting up." This last sentence was interpreted by the Rabbis, who were themselves, of course, intellectuals and scholars, as an injunction continually to learn and to analyze the traditions of Judaism. "It is well known and perfectly obvious that love of God cannot take deep root in man's heart unless it occupies his mind constantly so that nothing else whatever affects him except this love of God," says Rabbi Moshe ben Maimon (Maimonides), with whose writings Spinoza was familiar and whom he several times quotes in his *Tractatus Theologico-Politicus*. In the same passage the Rabbi also says: "God cannot be loved except through the knowledge by which he is known. The love is proportionate to the knowledge; the less knowledge the less love, the more knowledge the more love." Similarly, Spinoza affirms, "The highest good of the mind is the knowledge of God, and the highest virtue of the mind is to know God."[6] This kind of virtue consists in the progress toward the possession of adequate ideas of God and is called by Spinoza "the intellectual love of God." "The intellectual love of God is eternal . . . and from it arises the highest possible peace of mind."

It was remarked at the beginning that metaphysical thinking requires detachment. The metaphysician must cut the cords of convention with which he has been tied. But such self-release must await maturity, and by then the shape of growth has been permanently affected. Spinoza's break with Judaism occurred while he was still an adolescent, but he retained the form of Jewish culture: an ethical, theocentric intellectualism. The philosophical contents with which he proceeded to occupy his mind were certainly widely different from those detailed dogmas of Judaism that he had expunged. In Spinoza's converted conception of God the Deity has qualities of matter as well as those of mind; he is of the world, not apart from it; he is the impersonal, amoral All compelled by his own character, not a spirit who acts in freedom and justice, bestowing his unique guidance, love, and mercy on his separate creatures. Spinoza replaces the idea of dutiful, selfless love for God and man by one of contemplative pleasure. The terms he uses and his style persist from his Jewish background. A God he must have, salvation there must be; but his God is a new God, and his salvation a new salvation. His manner of discourse

must be magisterial and pointed, but practised in Latin, not in Hebrew, and in a secular framework of deduction, not in a Rabbinic context of debate and analytic argument. The voice is the voice of Jacob, but the hand is very much Spinoza's own.

The Preacher said long ago that there was nothing new under the sun. Almost every notion in Spinoza's philosophy, like that in every other philosophy, has been conceived and accepted before. In what respect can he then be properly described as a metaphysician, exercising original powers of critical and creative thought? The answer is provided by Spinoza's contemporary, Pascal, who defended Descartes (of whom he was no friend) against the charge of merely duplicating earlier conclusions:

I should like to ask the fair-minded if the principle that "Matter is naturally and insuperably unable to think" and the principle that "I think, therefore I am" are really the same in the mind of Descartes and in the mind of Saint Augustine, who said the same thing twelve hundred years before. I certainly am very far from holding that Descartes is not their true author, even if he had first become acquainted with them in reading the great saint; for I know what a difference there is between the incidental writing of a dictum, without reflecting any longer or more extensively upon it, and noticing in this dictum an impressive sequence of consequences which establishes the distinction between spiritual and material substances and makes out of this distinction a fixed and fundamental principle for the whole of Physics, as Descartes has tried to do. For without going into the question of whether he has in fact succeeded in his attempt, I take it for granted that he has and on that supposition I say that this doctrine in his writings is as different from the same doctrine in those of others as a man full of life and energy is different from a man who is dead. One person makes an isolated point without understanding its merits, while another will grasp a striking succession of its consequences; this leads us boldly to say that it is no longer the same doctrine and that he does not owe it to him from whom he learnt it any more than a towering tree belongs to him who, ignorantly and thoughtlessly, threw the seed into rich soil which thus profited through its own fertility. The same thoughts sometimes grow quite differently in another person than in their originator: sterile in their original field, fruitful when transplanted.

And in one of his *Pensées* Pascal returns to the same theme, though now his object is to defend himself, not Descartes: "Let no one say I have said nothing new: the presentation is new — *la disposition des matières est nouvelle*; in a game of tennis both players use the same ball but one places it better." Spinoza is original, not because each of his doctrines is new but because his arrangement and development of those doctrines is new.

There is originality also by virtue of his own powers having been used to erect and maintain the edifice of his thoughts. It does not matter in the least whether the bricks have been taken from the constructions of earlier thinkers, provided, as is the case, that Spinoza has made them his own by his working with them. It is on this ground that Montaigne says about an idea he shared with Plato: "*Ce n'est non plus selon Platon que selon moi* — it is no more Plato's than it is mine."

The Greek philosopher Parmenides had regarded the all as one, and the one as indivisible and perfect. And subsequently his disciple, the Eleatic Zeno, had attempted to confirm this conclusion by acute deductive dialectic. Spinoza was a fusion of Parmenides and Zeno: Parmenides, the poet, the man of speculative images; Zeno, the polemic, the man of rigid reasoning.

Thales and Anaximander held that all things are one, and historians of philosophy call them monists. They give the same name to Parmenides and Spinoza, although these denied the very existence of a distinct plurality. The monism of the earliest Greek thinkers is a monism of material substance: all things are derived from a single sort of stuff, they are homogeneous. The monism of Parmenides and Spinoza is a monism of structure: there is a unified organization of existence.

The first task of the metaphysician is to acquire appropriate speculative images. These are the bricks of metaphysical thought. The second task is to coordinate them, to build a system out of them. He must arrange them, connect them, not leave them as a jumble.

Spinoza's fundamental speculative image — the coping stone of his system — is of the all as one. He says in one of his letters,

Let us imagine, if you will, a worm living in the blood, this worm being able to distinguish by sight the blood corpuscles, the lymph and so on, and to observe how each part, on coming into contact with another part, is either repelled or communicates a part of its motion. That worm would be living in the blood as we live in one part of the universe, and it would consider each particle of blood as a whole and not as a part. It would be unable to know how all the parts are regulated by the general nature of the blood and are compelled by that nature to adapt themselves to one another so as to be mutually harmonized in conformity with a definite law. Were we to suppose that there is no space outside the blood and that there are no causes external to the blood which could communicate new motions to these parts, and that there are no other bodies to which the blood particles could transmit their motion, then it is inevitable that the blood would remain always in its original condition and that no other changes would affect its particles than those which can be inferred from a given relation of the blood's motion to the lymph, chyle and so on; in which case the blood would have to be considered as a whole and not as a part. But, since there is a large number of other causes which determine the laws governing the blood in a definite way and which in their turn depend on the blood, there arise in this liquid motions and changes which result not merely from the relation of the motion of its parts to one another, but also from the mutual relations between the blood and the external causes. Thus the blood has the character of a part and not of a whole. . . . Now, all the bodies of nature can and ought to be thought of in the same way as we have here thought of the blood; for all bodies are surrounded by others and are determined by them to exist and to act in a precise and definite way, while the total quantity of motion and rest in all bodies, that is in the whole universe, remains constant. Hence it follows that each body, in so far as its existence is subject to certain laws, has to be considered as a part of the whole universe, has to be in accord with the whole of it and to conform with it, and finally has to be connected with the other parts. [7]

For Spinoza, each object that appears as an individual in the world — be it a man, a house, a stone, or a star — is affiliated to others and both affects and is affected by the characteristics of others. None of these objects can lead an independent existence; in their origins they have not come from a process of self-creation but have been generated by other objects, and the manner of their continuance as objects is pervasively conditioned extrinsically as well as intrinsically. Consider, for example, a flower. This does not come from nothing. It develops from a bulb or seeds; and these in turn have their ancestry. And it cannot grow in empty space. It must be rooted in the soil and receive water and minerals and sunlight. The winds and the air affect the nature and direction of its growth. The frost makes it stiff and bent, the warm sunshine makes it bloom, erect. Bees may come and collect its pollen, insects eat its petals. Yet these external factors are themselves also influenced by others, and these by still others, these interactions being largely mutual. Nothing in the world endures completely severed from other members of the community of nature. "No man is an island," said Donne. Each man, each thing may indeed be an island; but all have arisen from the same foundation and are set in a single sea, whose currents ensure an ultimate common contact.

If Spinoza had lived another few years, how he would have welcomed the doctrines of Newton's *Principia* as providing direct confirmation of his own conviction of the general interrelatedness of things. If the Law of Gravitation is true, every two particles in the universe exert forces upon each other. So my writing these words affects the minutest insect crawling in Argentina, and the motion of your eyes in reading them affects the hugest stars whirling in the outermost galaxies.

Each abstracted event or thing — what Spinoza calls a "mode" — is affected by others both in its origins and in its duration; it is not self-explanatory. A complete comprehension of that mode which is a flower, of its presence, its structure, its properties, and the alterations it undergoes, depends on a precise and adequate knowledge of its parentage and heredity, of the varying environment and circumstances that support it and have in the past supported its ancestors, of the character and causes of evolution, of the origin of life on our planet, and of the birth and development of our planet itself. In turn, each of the factors contributing to the constitution of the flower derives its nature and existence from other factors. So, ultimately, a complete comprehension of the flower requires a complete comprehension of everything else; and conversely, a complete comprehension of the flower would bring with it a complete comprehension of everything. As Tennyson wrote:

> Flower in the crannied wall,
> I pluck you out of the crannies,
> I hold you here, root and all, in my hand,
> Little flower — but if I could understand
> What you are, root and all, and all in all,
> I should know what God and man is.

In the pursuit of the causes of things we are sent from one mode to another and to another. In Spinoza's speculative image of it, Nature is the totality to which these and all modes belong and which is self-sufficient. Such a totality must exist in order for there to be a closed, and so complete, system of causes. It is axiomatic that whatever exists is either an independent — self-sufficient — being or depends for its existence on something else. There must be an independent being, for otherwise there would be an infinite regress of dependence, this on that and that on something else and so on without end. Such an infinite regress is absurd since it involves the absence of any ultimate causes for observed effects. This argument is analogous to the argument of Aristotle, for the existence of an unmoved mover to account for the fact of motion. Aristotle tells us in his *Metaphysics* that "there is then something which is always moved with an unceasing motion, which is motion in a circle; and is plain not in theory only but in fact. Therefore, the first heaven must be eternal. There is therefore also something which moves it. And since that which is moved and moves is intermediate, there is something which moves without being moved, being eternal, substance and actuality."[8]

There is, on the one hand, "an order and interdependence of the universe as a whole," a thorough-going "connection of causes," and, on the other hand, an ultimate cause of this order, interdependence, and connection of causes. Spinoza's Nature is not simply the sum of the modes; that sum we may call the "universe." He conceives all things as forming a unity, that unity which is the universe; for if there is a "concatenation of causes," all things must be linked together into one. But this unity must itself have a cause. The cause is Nature.

All that is has a place on the scale of being: if, in thought, we climb up the rungs of that ladder, we shall find Nature at the top. It is the being than which nothing greater can be conceived, to use the phrase of St. Anselm in his so ingenious and elegant ontological argument; all other things are subordinate to it. Since it has the same properties as those essentially ascribed to God, Spinoza identifies God with Nature: "Of Nature all in all is predicated," he says in the *Short Treatise*, "and consequently Nature consists of infinite attributes each of which is perfect in its kind. And this is exactly equivalent to the definition usually given of God."

Affirmation implies negation. What is it that Spinoza wants to deny? He wants to deny that God is the Ruler of the Universe, the King of the World, as he was regarded in traditional Judaism. He wishes to destroy the belief that God is a pure spirit who designedly made the universe; that he is yet separate from the things of this world, sitting high on a throne of royal state far above the subjects of his realm; that he is the moral legislator and accountant (accounting in accordance with the legislation) who, when he closes an account, assigns an everlasting fate in proportion to the debts incurred and the credits obtained; that he is in the last resort unnamable, mysterious; and that our duty is, in the words of Pascal, to worship in humble silence the inscrutable sublimity of his secrets: "*Nous adorerons dans un humble silence la hauteur impénétrable de ses secrets.*" It was because of such antitheses of the traditional theism, forthrightly declared, that Spinoza was excommunicated from the Jewish community and was later in the wider world condemned as atheistical.

"No evil can happen to man except from external causes, that is, except in so far as he is a part of the whole of nature, whose laws human nature is compelled to obey — compelled also to adapt himself to this whole in almost infinitely many ways. It is impossible for a man not to be a part of nature or to follow her common order."[9] This "common order of nature" is the interconnected system of phenomena, what I have earlier called the "universe". It is not this that Spinoza calls "God or Nature — *Deus sive Natura*". God or Nature is the Supreme Being. It is the consummate, necessary condition for all concreteness and actuality. It is a universal rather than a particular, a species rather than an individual; and a universal and a species in the Aristotelian, rather than in the Platonic, sense. God is not external to nor separate from the objects of the universe. He is the ultimate totality of which these objects are the members; he is the ultimate cause of which these objects are the effects. "God is the immanent, not the transcendent, cause of all things."[10] He is an effective totality that is intrinsic to its members, much as a triangle is to its properties and the mind is to its ideas.

For Spinoza, as for most medieval philosophers, everything has an essence. The essence is the core of the thing, which distinguishes it from other things with other essences while also uniting it with all the things that have the same essence as it. All things belong by nature to types, each of which makes a unity — in the form of a group, totality, or species — out of multiplicity. The factor of unity is the possession of the same core of being. There are heartfelt qualities that affect all human beings, leading to laughter or tears or the adoption of sexual attitudes. These universal qualities are derived from our human essence. They are necessary consequences of being human, just as it is a necessary property of a Euclidean triangle that the sum of its interior angles is equal to two right angles. In this way the essence is an explanatory principle as well as a classificatory one. Why do you cry? Because you are human. Why does a figure have the sum of its interior angles equal to two right angles? Because it is a triangle. The properties of things follow from their essences, and so they account for why things have the properties they do have.

But in turn, all species belong to types. Taking biological species as examples, monkeys and men can be grouped together as primates; and the primates and other orders such as the carnivores and cetaceans can be grouped together within the class of mammals: this class can be grouped with other classes such as those of the birds and reptiles as tetrapods; tetrapods and fishes can be grouped together as vertebrates; and so on, higher and higher, until we rise to the kingdom that contains all the animals as members. Quite generally, both in the biological and in other spheres, any type, no matter what its order, is a principle both of classification and of explanation, for each type has its associated essence. It is because humans are vertebrate animals that they can be painters and ballet dancers and can admire or despise painters and ballet dancers; for having a backbone, with all that is attendant upon it, is a necessary condition for the conduct of these activities and the expression of these emotions. For Spinoza, God is the absolute supreme type: the highest principle of classification and explanation. And so God is everything and causes everything. He is everything just in the sense in which the species is (the totality of) its members, as a whole is to its parts. He causes everything just in the sense in which the essence associated with a species is the cause — what, in the Aristotelian philosophy, was given the name of the "formal cause" — of the particulars subsumable under that species. Thus Spinoza can say "Whatever is, is in God, and nothing can either be or be conceived without God."[11] And "from the supreme power of God, or from his infinite nature, infinite things in infinite ways, that is to say all things, have necessarily flowed, or continually follow by the same necessity, in the same way as it follows from the nature of a triangle, from eternity and to eternity, that its three angles are equal to two right angles."[12]

Spinoza has in mind, in the construction of his natural theology, the familiar situation in classical mathematics, where one learns, and can conclusively establish, a large number of the properties of triangles and circles and other mathematical concepts. The properties of triangles follow necessarily from their very nature as triangles: from their triangularity. And these properties of triangles are generated by triangularity quite irrespective of temporal conditions. The *fact* that the area of the square on the hypoteneuse of a right-angled triangle is equal to the sum of the areas of the squares on the other two sides of the triangle is an eternal truth, not a dated one. It is not a fact that was born and will die; it is not a fact that was created by Pythagoras and would be destroyed with the extinction of the human race. It is a truth that is true independently of all historical circumstances. And again, mathematical facts being eternal truths, none can be temporally prior to others; for none comes into being or ceases to be. The only priority possible is one of logic; an eternal truth is logically prior to another if and only if it implies without being implied by the other; in this sense, "the diagonals of a parallelogram are mutual bisectors" is prior to "the diagonals of a rectangle are mutual bisectors," and the latter is prior to "the diagonals of a square are mutual bisectors." Spinoza envisaged the world as a series of eternal truths proceeding logically from the all-embracing concrete concept of God. The things and events of the world are, ultimately and necessarily, derived from the essential nature of God, as the properties of the triangle are derived from the essential nature of the triangle.

In this way, Spinoza brings a systematic patterning among all the possible objects of experience. To the broadest extent he makes a unity out of the multiplicity of phenomena: where we see the paving stones, he sees the pavement. The unity is one not only of substance, but also of sequence. It serves as the universal principle of development within the common order of nature as well as the comprehensive dome of the hierarchical structure of species and genera pervading that common order. God (unlike Rome) unites to rule. The all is one.

What was Spinoza trying to do in his natural theology? He was trying to work out a consistent doctrine of deity in relation to the general idea of God that had been accepted in Judaism and in such Jewish heresies as Christianity. Spinoza believed that that general idea of God was self-contradictory as it stood. For example, according to it God is omnipotent; and yet is not omnipotent.

There are some who think that God is a free cause because he can, as they think, bring about that those things which we have said follow from his nature — that is, those things that are in his power — should not be, or should not be produced by him. But this is simply saying that God could bring about that it should not follow from the nature of a triangle that its three angles should be equal to two right angles, or that from a given cause an effect should not follow; which is absurd. But I shall show further on, without the help of this proposition (God acts from the laws of his own nature alone, and is compelled by no one), that neither intellect nor will pertain to the nature of God. I know indeed that there are many who think that they themselves can demonstrate that intellect of the highest order and freedom of will both pertain to the nature of God; for they say that they know nothing more perfect which they can attribute to him than that which is the chief perfection in ourselves. But although they conceive God as actually possessing the highest intellect, they nevertheless do not believe that he can bring about that all those things should exist which are actually in his intellect, for they think that by such a supposition they would destroy his power. If he had created, they say, all the things that are in his intellect, he could have created nothing more; and this, they believe, is not compatible with God's omnipotence. So then they prefer to consider God as indifferent to all things, and as creating nothing except that which he has decreed to create by a certain absolute will. But I think I have shown with sufficient clearness that from the supreme power of God, or from his infinite nature, infinite things in infinite ways, that is to say all things, have necessarily flowed, or continually follow by the same necessity, in the same way as it follows from the nature of a triangle, from eternity and to eternity, that its three angles are equal to two right angles. The omnipotence of God has therefore been actual from eternity, and in the same actuality will remain to eternity. In this way the omnipotence of God is, in my opinion, far more firmly established. My opponents indeed (if I may be allowed to speak plainly) seem to deny the omnipotence of God, inasmuch as they are forced to admit that he has in his mind an infinite number of things which might be created but which, nevertheless, he will never be able to create; for if he were to create all the things that he has in his mind he would, according to them, exhaust his omnipotence and make himself imperfect. Therefore, in order to make a perfect God, they are compelled to make him incapable of doing all those things to which his power extends, and anything more ab-

surd than this, or more opposed to God's omnipotence, I do not think can be imagined.[13]

Again, according to the general idea of God, he has created material substance. This creative aspect is incompatible with other aspects of that idea.

All men who have in any way looked into the divine nature deny that God is corporeal. That he cannot be so they conclusively prove by showing that by "body" we mean a certain quantity possessing length, breadth and depth, limited by some fixed form; and that to attribute these to God, a being absolutely infinite, is the greatest absurdity. But yet at the same time, from other arguments by which they try to confirm their proof, they clearly show that they completely remove corporeal or extended substance itself from the divine nature, affirming that it was created by God. However, by what divine power it could have been created they are completely ignorant; so it is obvious that they do not understand what they themselves are saying. But I have demonstrated, at least in my own opinion, that no substance can be produced or created by another entity.[14]

Spinoza's aim was to eliminate the self-contradictions in the received idea of God while retaining the functions of the original for the consistent, modified idea. Hence his insistent use of traditional descriptions of God for his own God. "God is one." "God is absolutely infinite." "All things are in God, and everywhich that happens does so only by the laws of the infinite nature of God." "In no way can it be asserted that God suffers from anything." "God's essence shuts out all imperfection and involves absolute perfection." "Things have been produced by God in the highest degree of perfection, since they have necessarily followed from the existence of a most perfect nature." "God is eternal." And, striving to be orthodox where he can, Spinoza recommends his version of deity by saying:

It remains for me now to show what service to our own lives a knowledge of this doctrine performs. . . . It is of service in so far as it teaches that we do everything by the will of God alone, and that we are partakers of the divine nature in proportion as our actions become more and more perfect and we understand God more and more. This doctrine, therefore, besides giving repose to the soul in every way, has also this advantage, that it teaches us in what our highest happiness or blessedness consists, namely, in the knowledge of God alone, by which we are drawn to do only those things that love and piety persuade.[15]

Spinoza's first speculative image is of the all as one. His second speculative image is of God as the ultimate, immanent, and comprehensive source of the universe. God, in this image, is the infinite and perfect being, the sovereign and uniquely self-dependent reality. "Since that which is moved and moves is a middle term, there must be an extreme which moves without being moved, which is eternal, substance, and actuality." These predicates of the Aristotelian prime mover are also predicates of Spinoza's God.

In one of his letters Spinoza says "That being only which possesses all perfections in itself I shall call God"; and in his next letter to the same recipient he repeats this definition: "A being that is absolutely unlimited and perfect I shall call God." For Spinoza the deity is that being which is absolutely unlimited, absolutely infinite: in all respects unbounded. The modal human intellect knows merely two attributes of deity, two essential expressions of the divine nature. These are thought and extension, mind and matter. But God being absolutely infinite, there must be infinitely many distinct and essential expressions of the divine nature. The myriad aspects of God's essence lie in the heavens beyond the reach of our most powerful intellectual or sensory telescopes; their character must forever be inaccessible to the few and tenuous sensibilities of humanity. Nevertheless, Spinoza cavalierly affirms, here charging directly with a pointed sentence against one of the fundamental convictions of accepted religious thought, that "The human mind possesses an adequate knowledge of the eternal and infinite essence of God," that, indeed, "the infinite essence and the eternity of God are known to all," for "each attribute expresses the eternal and infinite essence of God" and we know two attributes, thought and extension.

How is God the summit of perfections? Because he is absolutely infinite. There is nothing wanted to make him adequate, for he is the uniquely sufficient, self-sufficient, being. God, like the One of Parmenides, is the *plenum* of existence. Spinoza identifies perfection with completeness.

> Here I would have you note what I have just said with respect to the word "imperfection," namely, that this means that a thing lacks something which nevertheless belongs to its nature. For instance, extension can be said to be imperfect in respect of duration, position, or quantity: because it does not last longer, or does not retain its position, or is not greater. But it can never be said to be imperfect because it does not think, since nothing of that kind is required by its nature, which consists only in extension, that is in a certain kind of being. It is in respect of that alone that it can be said to be limited or unlimited, perfect or imperfect. And since the nature of God does not consist of a certain kind of being but of absolutely unlimited being, his nature also requires all that perfectly expresses being; otherwise his nature would be limited and deficient.[16]

Spinoza's identification of what is perfect with what is complete is one example, out of many, of the permanent influence of his reading of medieval

Hebrew literature, for that identification is often made there. Rabbi Shlomo ben Yitchak (Rashi) is generally esteemed as the greatest of the Biblical and Talmudic commentators of that period; ever since, every pupil of the Torah and Talmud has murmured his annotations when studying the sacred texts. Spinoza had been such a pupil. In Rashi's elucidation of Genesis, 1, 7 ("And God made the firmament and caused a division between the waters which were under the firmament and the waters which were *above the firmament*; and it was so. And God called the firmament Heaven. And it was evening and it was morning, a second day"), he says concerning the phrase I have italicized: "It does not say 'upon the firmament' but 'from above the firmament', because the waters were suspended in space. And why does it not say concerning the work of the second day 'that it was good'? Because the work concerning the waters was not completed until the third day, he only began it on the second; and anything that is not completed is not in its state of perfection and at its best."

So God is the summit of perfections because he is absolutely infinite, for absolute infinity involves conclusive fulfillment. But also, synonymously, because he is the supreme real being, for "By reality and perfection I mean the same thing." God is the consummation of existence.

Mind and Matter

THE third of Spinoza's speculative images is of the continuity of each attribute of divinity. Thinking cannot be divided. Thoughts are processes, not events, having no definite beginning or end, rising and mutually connected and merging like waves of the sea, a few crashing or lapping on the shores of human consciousness. Thought runs through all things without a break; all things always think. There can never be any lapse from cogitation even for the butterfly or the Sphinx. Again, and more paradoxically, extension cannot be divided. Corporeal substance has no parts: it is in itself elementary, simple. "Those who think," says Spinoza in a letter, "that extended substance consists of parts or of bodies really distinct from one another are talking foolishly, not to say madly. For this is just as if one endeavoured merely by adding together and accumulating many circles, to form a square, or a triangle, or something else different in its whole essence." And in the *Ethics* he offers an explanation of the popular belief in the divisibility of matter.

> If anyone should now ask why there is a natural tendence to consider quantity as capable of division, I reply that quantity is conceived by us in two ways: either abstractly or superficially, that is, as we imagine it; or else as substance, in which way it is conceived by the intellect alone.

If, therefore, we regard quantity (as we very often and easily do) as it exists in the imagination, we find it to be finite, divisible, and composed of parts; but if we regard it as it exists in the intellect, and conceive it in so far as it is substance, which is very difficult, then, as we have already sufficiently demonstrated, we find it to be infinite, one and indivisible. This will be plain enough to all who know how to distinguish between the imagination and the intellect, and more especially if we remember that matter is everywhere the same, and that, except in so far as we regard it as affected in different ways, parts are not distinguished in it; that is, they are distinguished with regard to mode but not with regard to reality. For example, we conceive water as being divided, in so far as it is water, and we conceive that its parts are separated from one another; but in so far as it is corporeal substance we cannot thus conceive it, for as such it is neither separated not divided. Moreover, water in so far as it is water is originated and destroyed; but in so far as it is substance it is neither originated nor destroyed.[17]

The doctrines of Epicurus had been aroused from the dead by the magical workings of the Renaissance mind, during the sixteenth century, and although the component theory of the atomic constitution of matter henceforth matured with ever increasing strength and vigor, it found little favor in Spinoza's eyes. Via Maimonides, he followed Aristotle who had rejected the original atomic theory of Leucippus and Democritus.

Not only are thought and extension continuous. All the attributes are continuous, the ones that we do not know along with those that we do know. And for this reason: that each attribute individually expresses the essence of the divine, and so each is the divine substance as conceived under a certain aspect. Therefore, if an attribute consisted of parts and was not continuous in its texture, there would be not one substance, but many; and this result is untenable, for it contradicts the simplicity and singularity of substance: there can be only one *summum genus*.

The fourth of Spinoza's speculative images is of the modal nature of what is effected by the first cause that is God. There are two kinds of mode: infinite modes and finite modes. In turn, infinite modes are of two sorts: immediate infinite modes and mediate infinite modes. Restricting attention to the attributes known to us, the attribute of thought issues in the immediate infinite mode of the Intellect; this is what Spinoza calls "the absolutely infinite understanding of God" or "the idea of God — *idea Dei*." The attribute of extension issues in the immediate infinite mode of Motion-and-Rest. For Spinoza, rest is not simply the absence of motion; it is something positive in itself. What I have called the "universe" forms a mediate infinite mode, described as being "the face of the whole universe — *facies totius universi*."

The immediate infinite modes are the active consequences of the corresponding attributes. "By 'attribute' I mean that which the [human] mind perceives of substance as if constituting its essence."[18] The attributes of the single substance God are our projections and distinctions. In the metaphysical conception of reality they are assigned a place on the side of principles, the explanation, the creation, rather than on the side of conclusions, the explained, the created. What Spinoza wishes to affirm is that these lateral distinctions created by the intellect are reflections of reality — metaphysics holds the mirror up to nature — in which they are so absorbed as to leave no differences between them. In the end, the species is nothing apart from its members; all that is potential is actual. "God is the *immanent* cause of all things." Since these distinctions must nevertheless be made, for the task of metaphysics is to explain and they are needed for the explanation, and since too in the last resort they must be transcended, we have to acknowledge on the one hand that the attributes are in themselves and by themselves indeterminate, in need of specific expression, and to acknowledge on the other hand that the particular entities of possible experience are in themselves and by themselves incomprehensible, in need of general derivation. The immediate infinite modes are the first consequences of the attributes, marking the first step toward everyday reality. They are the branches from which stem later the fruits of phenomena. The mediate infinite modes are the secondary consequences of the attributes, marking the second step toward everyday reality. They are the buds from which the fruits of phenomena come. More exactly, God as the first cause is the bare tree of being. Each immediate infinite mode is, as one aspect, the tree of being when it flowers. And the mediate infinite mode of the universe is the tree of being at the height of its fruit-bearing season: which never ends. The finite modes are the individual fruits of the tree of being. They are the final outcomes of the first cause. Since the finite modes are thus effected, the first cause must be, just to the extent that it can produce them, supremely active and actual.

The mediate infinite mode of the universe — *facies totius universi* — is for Spinoza like an individual within which there is change but which does not itself change. Things move within the universe but the universe does not itself move; things grow and decay within the universe but the universe does not itself grow or decay. He says:

Up to this point we have conceived an individual to be composed merely of bodies which are distinguished from one another solely by motion and rest, speed and slowness, that is to say, to be composed of the most simple bodies. If we now consider an individual of another kind, composed of many individuals of diverse natures, we shall discover that it may be affected in many other ways, its nature nevertheless being preserved. For since each of its parts is composed of a number of bodies, each part without any change of its nature can move more slowly or more quickly [by a thesis Spinoza puts forward as already established by him], and consequently can communicate its motion more quickly or more slowly to the remainder. If we now imagine a third kind of individual composed of these of the second kind, we shall discover that it can be affected in many other ways without any change of form. Thus, if we advance ad infinitum, we may easily conceive the whole of nature to be one individual whose parts, that is all bodies, differ in infinite ways without any change of the whole individual.[19]

The fifth of Spinoza's speculative images is of the mind as the mirror of the body.[20] Since God has the attributes of thought and extension, all individuals must be modes of thought and extension. "Hence it follows that man is composed of mind and body." But just as the attributes of thought and extension cannot be disjoined within the nature of God, so mind and body are inseparable within the nature of man: "The human mind is united to the body." What is a human mind? It is, abstractly, a part of the immediate infinite mode of thought. Concretely, it is the complex of ideas of the human body: "The object of the idea constituting the human mind is a body, or a certain mode of extension actually existing, and nothing else." All our ideas are "ideas of affections by which the body is affected." Our mind is simply the mirror that reflects the transactions of the body. We can have no direct knowledge of what lies outside the confines of the body; on the other hand, whatever occurs within those confines is directly known, the processes of knowledge corresponding to the physical processes: "The order and connection of ideas is the same as the order and connection of things." It must be stressed that the ideas are not the effects that follow from corporeal conditions as causes. They represent with respect to thought what the conditions are with respect to extension. The contents of mind and body are merely distinct expressions of the same reality: "A mode of extension and the idea of that mode are one and the same thing expressed in two different ways."

A consequence of the homologous character of mind and body is that the scope of knowledge is directly proportionate to the susceptibilities of the body: "In proportion as one body is better adapted than another for doing or suffering many things, so will the mind at the same time be better adapted for perceiving many things, and the more the actions of a body depend upon itself alone, the better adapted will the mind be for understanding distinctly. We can thus determine the superiority of one mind to another, and we can also see the reason why we have only a very confused knowledge of our own bodies."[21] namely, that "it is impossible for a man not to be a part of nature and to follow her common order"; hence, innumerable actions of the body do not depend upon the body alone.

If all our ideas only designate affections of the body, it may be asked how we are to escape from the narrow cell in which subjectivism would imprison us. The answer is that we have ideas, knowledge, of the bodies causing changes in our physical selves, in the ideas of these effected changes, for the conditions of our body that are caused by external objects must be reflected in our having ideas which involve the causative external objects, it being axiomatic that "The knowledge of an effect depends upon and involves a knowledge of the cause." Accordingly, the mind perceives modes of extension other than that one with which it is integrated. This perception is indirect and Spinoza does commit us to the prison of subjectivism insofar as he judges that "The ideas we have of external bodies indicate the constitution of our own body rather than the nature of external bodies." Yet the modern reader must not be too suspicious of Spinoza's consistency here, and should remember that Spinoza lived before academic discussions of the grounds of realist and idealist views of sensation became familiar. His sanity was strong enough to enable him to resist the infections of skepticism. Unlike Descartes, for example, he did not suffer from abnormal doubts. He would not have asked himself the question: if all my perceptions or conceptions are of my own body, how can I be certain that there are any other bodies at all? Indeed, he took multiplicity as fundamental. The world resolves itself into individuals. But these are not isolated from one another, not unrelated to one another. They have common ancestors — preceding causes — and they all stem from the single, ultimate ancestral cause that is God.

Spinoza's sixth speculative image is of each finite mode, whether of extension or thought or any other attribute, as striving for self-preservation. We may read in the book of sermons by Rabbi Saul Levi Monteira, one of Spinoza's teachers in his youth, that "Nature, mother of all created things, has implanted in them a will and impulse to strive for their self-preservation." This idea of the world as a field of endless battle between all things, in which each endeavors at all costs to survive, has indeed a long and ancient history. But Spinoza uses the idea more systematically than his predecessors. He offers general yet precise cosmological grounds for this universal self-love and striving — *conatus*. "*Conatus, quo unaquaeque res in suo esse perseverare conatur, nihil est praeter ipsius rei actualem essentiam* — the striving by which each thing strives to persevere in its being is nothing else than the actual essence of the thing itself."[22] The very core of being of each thing is the effort to persist in existence. And this effort is not a result of will or choice; it is automatic, instinctive. "From the given essence of anything certain things necessarily follow," just as from triangularity it follows that the sum of the interior angles of a triangle is equal to two right angles; "nor are things able to do anything else than what necessarily follows from their determinate nature," just as it is impossible for triangles to have any properties except those which they must have. "And therefore the power of a thing, or the effort by means of which it does anything or strives to do anything, either by itself or with others, that is to say, the power or effort by which it strives to persevere in its being, is nothing else than the given or actual essence of the thing itself." And so each thing has an innate tendency to endure, through its essential nature; indeed, this tendency is its essential nature. Material objects, that is objects conceived of under the attribute of extension, objects conceived of as extended, strive to persist without being aware of that striving. They unconsciously move or rest, change or remain, in the line of the greatest conservation of their energies. But, for Spinoza, such conservation is expression. There is no power but that which is made actual by determinate expression. Hence, physical objects are driven by their implanted natures to the maximum fulfillment of their potentialities. The mind too is similarly driven to the exercise of its capacities. But, unlike material modes, the mind is conscious of its self-love, its striving. Spinoza affirms:

> The mind, both insofar as it has clear and distinct ideas and insofar as it has confused ideas, strives to persevere in its being for an indefinite time, and is conscious of this effort . . . This effort, when it is related to the mind alone, is called will, but when it is related at the same time to both the mind and the body it is called appetite, which is, therefore, nothing but the very essence of man, from the nature of which necessarily follow those things that promote his preservation; and thus he is determined to do those things. Hence there is no difference between appetite and desire, except in this respect, that desire is generally related to men in so far as they are conscious of their appetites, and it may therefore be defined as appetite of which we are conscious. From what has been said it is plain, therefore, that we neither strive for, wish, seek nor desire anything because we judge it to be good, but on the contrary we judge a thing to be good because we strive for, wish, seek or desire it.[23]

Think of this analogy. The higher animals, we may suppose, breathe without being aware that they breathe. The breath is the life. And then conceive also of all the lower animals and the plants and physical objects as unconsciously respiring. Thus far we picture all these things as striving unconsciously to accomplish their capacities, to keep their roots in the soil of existence and bring their seed to fruit. Now consider man. In him also respiration is essential. But he can know that he breathes. And breathing is the sole physiological activity which is both automatic, continuing when he is asleep or in a faint or anesthetized as well as when he is awake, and consciously controllable. We can, in part, determine its rate and depth; we can improve it. But this determination, this improvement, is itself conditioned by the process — especially by the results of the previous functioning. We cannot work on our natures from outside. Self-help has to be practised in terms of one's whole nature as so far achieved. Thus we picture man as able consciously to strive toward self-determination through self-determination. And the active exercise of his power brings glory, for through that active exercise he realizes more perfectly the essence of God. "The power of God is his essence itself," and the power has to be manifested, declared, in the individuals of the world. The Kingdom of God is within you. In proportion as man succeeds in unfolding his own essence, to that extent he attains union with God. But it must not be forgotten that for Spinoza each thing can be considered as intellectual, under the attribute of thought. Hence each thing, in so far as it is a mode of thought, is striving with a greater or lesser degree of consciousness toward its own development and so through selfhood to Godhead.

Now it follows from Spinoza's view of the relation between the mind and the body that whatever increases, or decreases, the body's power of action also increases, or decreases, the mind's power of thought. We are said to act when we do something which, as an effect, can be comprehended from our nature alone, as cause: to understand why the deed was done, one need know only the agent. On the other hand, we are said to suffer when an event occurs in our history of which we are not thus the sufficient cause. We suffer when we are passive and not wholly active. How can we become wholly active and so become free from the constraining forces of the external world? Spinoza's answer is similar to that of Pythagoras and Socrates and Plato: by knowledge. "The actions of the mind arise only from adequate ideas, while the passions depend only on those that are inadequate." "An affect which is a passion stops being a passion as soon as we form a clear and distinct idea of it." Spinoza's conception of the free man — "homo liber" — is a conception of an intellectual man, a man who is reasonable, and reasonable actually, not merely potentially. "A free man, that is a man who lives in accordance with the dictates of reason alone, is not led by the fear of death but directly desires the good, that is to act, to live, and to preserve his being in accordance with the principle of seeking what is useful to himself."

> Our actions, that is those desires which are determined by man's power or reason, are always good, while the others can be both good and bad. It is therefore most useful in our lifetime to perfect the intellect or reason as much as we can, and in this

one thing consists man's highest happiness or blessedness; blessedness is certainly nothing but the peace of mind that arises from the intuitive knowledge of God, and to perfect the intellect is nothing but to understand God and God's attributes and actions which are consequences of the necessity of his nature. Therefore the ultimate goal of a man who is guided by reason, that is the principal desire by which he studies to govern all his other desires, is that by which he is led to the adequate conception of himself and of all things which can fall within his understanding.[24]

Good and Evil

THE seventh of Spinoza's speculative images is of man as the offspring of the world around him and as of no exceptional effectiveness in that world. He is little more than the shadow of a substance, than a vein in a single leaf of a multifoliate tree, than one blade of grass in a field that stretches on all sides on and on to the horizon. Here Spinoza firmly allied himself with the naturalism of the school of Democritus and Epicurus. Man's place is in the ordinary scheme of things, and the laws of nature are the laws of his nature. Only to man himself is man of particular significance in the universe. In reality he has no special power over his natural neighbors. The belief of biblical men in their dominion over the fish of the sea, over the fowl of the air, and over all the earth; the belief that we are physically, metaphysically, and morally at the center of the universe, dominating it; the belief that it has all been made for our peculiar benefit — these beliefs are manufactured by fancy, not by reason. With scarcely suppressed impatience with common stupidity, Spinoza furiously condemned and destroyed this anthropocentric standpoint. He attributes the origins of this standpoint to the fact that whatever we do is prompted by a conscious desire which is aimed at what is useful to ourselves. So we are interested in the uses of things; when we think we have discovered the uses — either by observation or by introspective reflection on actions of our own that are similar to the things we seek to understand — our curiosity is satisfied. Our explanations are by final and not by efficient causes. Our desires themselves are explained by the purposes motivating them, because, says Spinoza, we are conscious of our wishes and appetites but are ignorant of their efficient causes. Ignorance, ignorance of the causes of things, this is the reason why men think of themselves as forming a separate state from the surrounding state of nature.

Again, since we discover in ourselves and our environment many things which are useful to us — the eyes for seeing, the teeth for chewing, animals and plants for eating, the sun for warmth and light — we are inclined to suppose that everything is a means for obtaining what is advantageous to us. Being means, however, things cannot be considered as the outcome of necessity or chance; they must be the products of free and personal design. Accordingly, man postulates the existence of

some ruler or rulers of nature, endowed with human liberty, who have taken care of all things for men and have made all things for their use. Since men have heard nothing about the mind of these rulers, they have had to judge of it from their own. So they have established that the gods direct all things for men's use, in order that they may be bound to them and hold them in the highest honour. This is why each person has devised out of his own mind various ways of worshipping God, so that God might love him above the rest and direct the whole of nature for the use of his blind cupidity and insatiable avarice.[25]

In conformity with his naturalism Spinoza denies the objective existence of good and evil; they are for him not properties but relations. Whatever is, has to be: "In nature there is nothing contingent; on the contrary, everything is determined by the necessity of the divine nature to be and to operate in a certain way." Hence all that occurs occurs indifferently to the hopes and fears, and the judgments, of humanity. Facts in themselves are neither good nor bad; they have their natural properties, but no values. Values are relative to man's desires. Although nothing is good in itself, nevertheless something may appear as good to somebody insofar as it is advantageous to him, that is insofar as it assists his self-preservation and his self-fulfillment. "By good I mean that which we certainly know is useful to us." The moral philosopher has to distinguish between what is good for this or that person at this or that time and what is universally good; and his task — not necessarily his only task — is to propound what he takes to be this universal good, the *summum bonum*. The moral philosopher wants to form "a model of human nature"; then, that which serves as a sure means to the actual achievement of this ideal will be deemed to be good while what impedes the attainment of it will be regarded as objectionable. What is good and what is objectionable are clearly relative to the chosen ideal. The ideal to be chosen is, of course, that which will bring man the highest and most lasting happiness, bring him to a stable serenity.

To what is the term "good" as defined by Spinoza applicable? What do we certainly know is useful to us? "There is nothing that we certainly know to be good or bad except that which truly leads to understanding, or that which can impede us so that understanding is decreased." Although, however, the road to happiness which Spinoza delineates is essentially an intellectual, not to say intellectualist, one, still he does not require us to keep to the straight and narrow path of unrelaxed cogitation; far from it.

No deity nor anyone else, except an envious one, is pleased at my powerlessness and discomfort, or regards our tears, sighs, fear, and other such things — which are only signs of mental impotence — as virtues; but, on the contrary, the greater our joy, the greater the perfection to which we pass, that is the more do we necessarily participate in the divine nature. To make use of things, therefore, and, so far as possible, to get pleasure out of them (without indulging in them to the point of disgust — which is no pleasure), is what the wise man would do. I am maintaining that the wise man should refresh and restore himself with moderate and pleasant eating and drinking, with scents and the beauty of green plants, with ornamentation, music, sport, the theatre, and other such things, which can be practised by one person without its being at another person's cost. For the human body is composed of many parts that are of different natures which continually need new and varied nourishment, so that the whole body may be equally fit for everything which can result from its nature, and consequently that the mind too may be equally fit for understanding many things together.[26]

The eighth and last of Spinoza's speculative images that can here be referred to is of the adequacy of ideas and of the power of that adequacy. Spinoza puts the various members of the population of knowledge into classes, ranking these as a lower, middle, and upper class. First, there is the *profanum vulgus* of sensations and of unreasoned or irrationally held beliefs. These are at the bottom in the hierarchy of knowledge because they are so closely allied to ignorance and error: the slave class. (The Fourth Part of Spinoza's *Ethics*, in which he deals with the effects of ignorance and error, is called *De Servitute Humana — Of Human Bondage*.) Spinoza from his intellectual heights looks down with contempt on this lowly sort of knowledge, since it is so often mistaken, so easily misled, so quickly swayed and put in doubt.

The middle class of knowledge is through mediate deduction. This proceeds from premises that are either axiomatically true or validly derived, in the last resort, from axiomatic truths. Axiomatic truths are the primary truths about such fundamental concepts as mind and body, cause and motion, God and substance and freedom; they have common or simple notions for their subject-matter. An axiom is the clear and distinct conception of such a notion. Knowledge obtained by reasoning is necessarily true. From axiomatic truths only truth can be extracted, for those truths are the pure gold of intellect; no base metal of falsehood is contained in them. Falsehood is error, which arises from "putting together various confused ideas which belong to various things and operations in nature. . . . It consists solely in affirming, about anything, something which is not

contained in the concept we have formed of the thing . . . Falsehood consists in the privation of knowledge which inadequate, that is mutilated and confused, ideas involve." Spinoza denies the objective existence of falsehood, since this would be a blemish in the divine nature. "All things are in Him and so depend upon Him that without Him they can neither be nor be conceived." Therefore, if falsehood were real, it would exist inherently in God and he would be the cause of it, a conclusion repugnant to the orthodoxy in Spinoza's mind.

The third and highest kind of knowledge is called "*scientia intuitiva* — intuitive knowledge." "The third kind of knowledge proceeds from an adequate idea of certain attributes of God to an adequate knowledge of the essence of things." We have intuitive — the highest possible — knowledge of an individual when we clearly and distinctly understand how the essential characteristics of that individual are related to and conditioned by God's own essence. We have intuitive knowledge when we see God's hand at work, when we comprehend his nature realizing itself in action. The effort of the mind toward this comprehension is called, in a famous phrase, "*amor intellectualis Dei* — the intellectual love of God."

Spinoza believes that human misery and suffering, our tensions and contentions, are due to our lack of self-understanding, are due to our failure to achieve adequate ideas. Contentment is proportionate to genuine knowledge, to clear and distinct ideas. The final purpose of life, the *summum bonum*, is the permanent attainment of this contentment in the highest possible degree. Spinoza maintains[27] that all suffering results from having inadequate ideas. We must learn to be active, not passive. "Our mind acts at times and at times suffers: in so far as it has inadequate ideas, it necessarily suffers." Thus Spinoza links action to theoretical knowledge. The more we labor to understand, the more we strive toward the third kind of knowledge, the more we are occupied by the intellectual love of God, so much the greater is our action and our contentment. "From this third kind of knowledge arises the highest possible peace of mind."

By definition, "Love is joy attended by the idea of an external cause." The intellectual love of God is that intellectual enjoyment which is accompanied by the recognition of God as its cause. The search for knowledge is the essence of the mind. Accordingly, the satisfaction of that search brings with it the profound contentment that comes from the awareness of our action, from the fulfillment of our innermost urges.

It must not be forgotten that all our ideas are ideas of affections of our body. Therefore all our knowledge is of the affections of our body, and, indirectly, of the causes of those affections. Our search for knowledge must, then, primarily be a search for self-knowledge. Know thyself. Through an understanding of the particular modes that are our mind and body we can come to some understanding of the general substance that is God.

> The more we understand particular objects, the more we understand God. . . . He who clearly and distinctly understands himself and his affects loves God, and loves him better the better he understands himself and his affects. . . . This love towards God ought above all else to occupy the mind. . . . The highest effort of the mind and its highest virtue is to understand things by the third kind of knowledge. . . . The more objects the mind understands by the second and third kinds of knowledge, the less it suffers from those emotions that are evil and the less it fears death. . . . Blessedness is not the reward of virtue, but is virtue itself: nor do we delight in blessedness because we restrain our lusts, but, on the contrary, because we delight in it, therefore we are able to restrain them.

And, in the justly famous peroration to his *Ethics*, Spinoza concludes his lifework, so carefully and minutely conceived in the monastery of his mind, by saying:

> I have finished everything I wanted to explain about the power of the mind over its emotions and about its liberty. From what has been said we see in what the strength of the wise man consists and how much he surpasses the ignorant who is driven forward by lust alone. For the ignorant man is not only agitated in many ways by external causes and never enjoys true peace of soul, but also lives ignorant, as it were, both of God and of things, and as soon as he ceases to suffer ceases also to be. On the other hand, the wise man, in so far as he is considered as such, is scarcely ever moved in his mind, but being conscious by a certain eternal necessity of himself, of God and of things, never ceases to be and always enjoys true peace of soul. If the way which, as I have shown, leads to this seems very difficult, it can nevertheless be found. It must indeed be difficult since it is so seldom found. For if salvation lay ready to hand and could be discovered without great labour, how could almost everyone neglect it? *Sed omnia praeclara tam difficilia quam rara sunt* — but all excellent things are as difficult as they are rare.[28]

Because of such of Spinoza's propositions as "*Hic erga Deum amor mentem maxime occupare debet* — this love towards God ought above all to occupy the mind," "*Qui Deum amat, conari non potest, ut Deus ipsum contra amet* — whoever loves God cannot strive that God should love him in return," and "*Beatitudo non est virtutis praemium, sed ipsa virtus* — blessedness is not the reward of virtue but is virtue itself," he has from time to time been looked up to as a sort of Christian saint and mystic; and since these propositions are demonstrated like theorems, in a deductive system, it has been said of him that he "bound the spirit of Christ in the fetters of Euclid." But Spinoza was no saint or mystic, still less a Christian: he would have believed any of the Catholic Creeds to be illogical fiction, the product of imagination, not reason. Of course he was a saint — if every bachelor of frugal habits and ascetic turn of mind is a saint. And of course he was a mystic — if every intellectual who assigns the highest value to the search for the ultimate causes and essences of things is a mystic. ("He sometimes relaxed," says Colerus, one of his early biographers, "by smoking a pipe of tobacco; or, if he wanted to rest his mind rather longer, he sought out some spiders which he got to fight with one another, or some flies which he put into a spider's web, and then watched the battle with so much enjoyment that he sometimes burst out laughing." Such diversions are not what one has come to expect of a Christian saint or mystic; Spinoza was not a Francis of Assisi or John of the Cross.)

Spinoza was a rationalist for whom the most fundamental and sublime knowledge was to be obtained through intellectual processes of discovering and determining the innermost nature of things: through discovering true definitions, and of discovering true relations between individual essences and the divine essence (which is simply the *summum genus*). Spinoza's principal work, his world's classic, is *Ethica Ordine Geometrico Demonstrata — The Ethics Demonstrated in Geometrical Order*. The very title is a signature of his rationalism. He adopted the deductive method initiated by Euclid because he thought that metaphysical truth was precisely the same, epistemologically, as mathematical truth. The deductive exposition of geometry gave a model for metaphysics. In geometry there was certain knowledge. In metaphysics there could be the same. But deductive inference was not sufficient for the achievement of truth. The roots had to be sound if the fruits were to be whole. Why did the basis of geometry possess its certainty? Because the concepts involved could be clearly and distinctly understood: their essences could be grasped. A straight line, a right angle, a triangle, a circle — these could be adequately defined. Necessary and sufficient conditions could be precisely enunciated. Therefore, if the basis of metaphysics was similarly chosen so that the only fundamental concepts were those that were clearly and distinctly understood, metaphysics too would have a source of certain knowledge, from which an endless variety of further truths could logically be drawn.

There are, then, two requirements for a metaphysics aiming at the certainty of mathematics. In the first place, what one begins with must be sure, and that necessitates clarity and distinctness of conception: the ideas must be adequately (truly) thought of. In the second place, the propositions that one proceeds to affirm, as validated by what has gone before, must be sure, and that necessitates deduction, for only in this way can there be rational confidence in the correctness and justifiability of the conclusions. Accordingly, Spinoza has his definitions and axioms, and constructs these with the intention that they will possess the same desired characteristics as the definitions and axioms of geometry; he has, also, his propositions and demonstrations, and constructs these with similar intentions. (Nevertheless, in his "scholia" he launches devastating attacks, in the nature of Zeno, on his opponents, inveighing against them with his powerful and plentiful supplies of irony.)

Science is an ellipse of which theory and experience are the foci. In mathematics this ellipse is reduced to a circle, theory alone being the generating center. Mathematics can eliminate experience because its concepts need not have ordinarily existing objects to correspond to them and because its statements need not have ordinarily existing facts to correspond to them. Mathematical truths are conceptual truths, eternal truths; truths to be discovered and connected by the intellect. What Spinoza thus thought of mathematics, he thought also of philosophy. This gave him another reason for attempting to be the Euclid of metaphysics.

There was, finally, a third reason. He says over and over that all things follow from the nature of God with the same eternity and necessity as it follows from the nature of a triangle that its interior angles are equal to two right angles. He images the world as a body of conceptual truth; facts follow from causes as propositions follow from axioms and definitions. His metaphysical structure of deduction was meant to reflect the logical development in the tract of being, from the primordial nature of God to the consequent nature of men and his intellect and emotions.

One kind of criticism of a philosophy is to assert that the very type of philosophizing embodied in it is nonsensical or trivial or worthless. In particular, metaphysical systems are commonly dismissed as being in one way or another empty; like the primeval earth, they are waste and void. The question of the value of metaphysics has been passionately discussed in our time, very much the majority opinion among professional philosophers in reputed places in England and the United States being that metaphysics is refuse; it is the excretion of the intellect. Not long ago a favored theory in ethics of what it means to say that something is good was "I approve of it; do likewise." An adherent of the predominant view about metaphysics can be interpreted as saying "I disapprove of it; do likewise." Or this attitude can be regarded as the making of an unregretted announcement, by one philosopher, of the death of metaphysics — other philosophers please copy. (Saying is believing.) This is a not unexpected revolt of a new generation against the mysterious power of the Elders of the tribe.

Metaphysics' value is itself a philosophical question, and an important one; like all the important questions, it cannot be solved, or dissolved, simply. The more microscopically it is examined, the more complex and interwoven it becomes. One of the difficulties in talking about it is that the criterion, not to say the shifting criteria, of value accepted by a critic commonly remains unexpressed. If it is desirable for criteria, outside pure mathematics, to be plainly empirical, then a possible criterion is one of utility with respect to an increase of scientific knowledge. It might be suggested that a theoretical activity is publicly valuable if and only if it leads in the long run, directly or indirectly, to greater scientific knowledge than its absence promotes. (What exactly "leads," "long run," "directly," "promotes," and so on mean, if they mean anything *exactly*, cannot be determined here.) One would have to discover, not judge on a basis of ignorance, whether metaphysics is valuable on this criterion. To make the discovery, profound historical and psychological investigations are required, using, it may be suspected, techniques not yet devised. Because no suitable inquiries have been made in this connection, one can only, at this stage, project shivers of evidence and guess on which side of the neutral position there would be a preponderance if all the facts were known. These projections and guesses can be left to those who like them. I shall add, however, an argument that seems to be worth considering. Science needs an atmosphere of free thought for its secure perpetuation and success; and free thought that is of a highly intellectualized character. Like other pursuits, metaphysics can be done carefully and artfully or negligently. It might be urged that the existence in the background of a number of careful and artful metaphysical systems will encourage free and intellectual thought. The varied notions and theses that they contain might subtly assist the construction or development of scientific ones; it must be remembered that metaphysical ideas are intended to elucidate experience and will be partly grounded in that. They might also, on the other hand, by their very abstractness and their futility as guides to observable details of reality (to mention nothing of the mutual conflicts between the systems in which they are embedded), prevent the scientifically minded from being too engrossed in untestable speculations, stimulating them by way of revulsion from such speculations to follow their own more practical inclinations, more fully and confidently aware that a possible source of satisfying information has not been overlooked and knowing now that science is the only systematically fruitful method of research into the nature of things.

If metaphysics as a whole is condemned, then Spinoza's stands condemned too. But if no universal condemnation is made, the value of Spinoza's system can be considered as an individual case on its own merits and defects, the value assigned being dependent, of course, on the criterion adopted. Different judges will undoubtedly pass different verdicts if different codes are employed. All that the scholar and other persons of cultivated mind and taste can do is to hope for and endeavor to effect the formation of civilized codes and the sympathetic interpretation and implementation of them by those who take upon themselves responsibility for that.

If you must blow your own trumpet, at least vary the tune. And if you insist on being a philosophical writer, do not put all your eggs in one basket (probably a wastepaper basket anyway); the contents of the book of nature are too rich for a single transcription. The metaphysician has to speak from one standpoint; he needs that single-mindedness. That strength, is, however, also a weakness. He may see a world in a grain of sand, but even that tiny world cannot be adequately expressed except by a granary of "and's," a granary more plentiful than he can harvest. A few implications from a few premises will not suffice to cover the multitude of complex conjunctions in the cosmos.

12

Locke

D. J. O'CONNOR

JOHN LOCKE WAS BORN in Wrington in Somerset in 1632, ten years before the outbreak of the Civil War, and died in 1704 at the beginning of the reign of Queen Anne. His father was a west country lawyer who fought with the Parliamentarian army against Charles I. At the age of fourteen, Locke left Somerset for school at Westminster, where he stayed until his election to a junior studentship at Christ Church, Oxford. At the age of twenty-seven he was appointed to a senior studentship at the same college, an office then tenable for life. After some teaching in Greek and in moral philosophy, he became interested in medicine and after several years' study, obtained a license to practice from the university.

His medical skill brought him to the notice of Lord Ashley, later the first Earl of Shaftesbury, one of the ablest and most influential of the politicians who had to contend with the devious ambitions of Charles II. Locke entered Shaftesbury's service in 1667 and remained his friend and confidant until Shaftesbury, in serious danger of being impeached for treason, fled to Holland and died there in 1683. The political climate was dangerous for Shaftesbury's associates, and Locke too went into voluntary exile in Holland in the autumn of 1683. Here he remained until the final overthrow of the Stuart despotism in 1689. He used his leisure and freedom from office for writing. Most of his important works date from this period, including the *Essay concerning Human Understanding*, on which he had been working for some years.

In 1689 he returned to England after the expulsion of James II and the accession of William of Orange, with whose supporters he had been associated during his exile. He accepted a sinecure appointment in the Civil Service, but spent most of his time on the philosophical controversies that followed the publication of the *Essay* and the *Two Treatises on Civil Government*. The *Treatises* were influential political pamphlets intended by Locke as a vindication of the political principles of the "Glorious Revolution" of 1688. His health was very uncertain during the last few years of his life and he lived in retirement in the household of Sir Francis Masham at Oates in Essex. Lady Masham had long been an admirer of Locke and a frequent correspondent. He died at Oates in 1704.

Aim and Method

BOTH THE AIM and the method of the *Essay concerning Human Understanding* are clearly stated by Locke in his introductory chapter. He intends to "inquire into the original, certainty, and extent of *human knowledge,** together with the grounds and degrees of *belief, opinion* and *assent.*"[1] The terms of this inquiry pretty well cover those topics which comprise what is nowadays called "the theory of knowledge." The sources of our knowledge, its reliability, its varieties, and its scope are topics which can be treated in more than one way. Locke proposes to follow what he calls a "historical plain method," by which he meant a simple description of the facts relevant to the subject matter of his enquiry. This seems to imply that he thought of himself as engaged on a sort of natural history of the mind, a project of listing and classifying and relating the contents of human experience much as a naturalist might deal with the flora of a beechwood. Had it been possible for Locke to carry out such a project, he would have been doing psychology, though psychology of a rather primitive and naïve kind. In fact, it is doubtful if it is even possible in principle to make such an inventory of the contents of our mental life in the way in which we might list the furniture in a house. However, Locke does at least make his intentions clear.

He is equally explicit about the reasons for the inquiry. In the "Epistle to the Reader" which prefaces the *Essay*, Locke explains that a discussion with friends on "a subject very remote from this" led to the realization that "it was necessary to examine our own abilities and see what objects our understandings were and were not fitted to deal with." James Tyrrell, one of the participants, tells us that the discussion in question concerned "the principles of morality and revealed religion."[2] Thus, the difficulties raised in an examination of the problems of morals and theology led him to a general survey of the powers and limits of the human mind, and for a very practical reason. "If by this enquiry into the nature of the understanding, I can discover the powers thereof: how far they reach: to what things they are in any degree proportionate: and where they fail us, I suppose it may be of use to prevail with the busy mind of man to be more cautious in meddling with things exceeding its comprehension: to stop when it is at the utmost extent of its tether: and to sit down in a quiet ignorance of those things which, upon examination, are found to be beyond the reach of our capacities."[3]

Much of the philosophy with which Locke was familiar, in particular, much of the debased scholasticism which was current in his student days at Oxford, seemed to him to fail largely from want of this preliminary assessment of our mental powers. Neglect of this scrutiny leads either to an intolerant dogma-

*Italics in all quotes are Locke's unless otherwise noted.

tism, or to what was, in Locke's eyes, equally deplorable, a total skepticism. "Thus men, extending their enquiries beyond their capacities and letting their thoughts wander into those depths where they can find no sure footing, it is no wonder that they raise questions and multiply disputes, which, never coming to any clear resolution are proper only to continue and increase their doubts and confirm them at last in perfect scepticism."[4] The *Essay* was intended, then, to be a preliminary survey of the territory of human knowledge. And by roughly mapping this territory and its frontiers Locke hoped to save philosophy from the opposing but kindred evils of dogmatism and skepticism. His aims were modest: "It is ambition enough to be employed as an under-labourer in clearing the ground a little, and removing some of the rubbish which lies in the way to knowledge."[5] These impediments to knowledge were in Locke's view results of a wrong belief in the powers of human reason. This belief could be corrected only by a careful re-examination of the powers of the mind such as the *Essay* purported to offer.

Locke is usually described as an empiricist and, indeed, as the founder of the strong empirical tradition in English thought. There is some truth in these descriptions. Both Bacon and Hobbes in their very different ways had argued for the primacy of sense experience, but Locke does not seem to have been much influenced by their work. The nature of his empiricism will become clearer when we discuss the details of his theory of knowledge. Broadly speaking, it consists in a firm belief, for which the *Essay* argued the reasons, that all the materials of human knowledge are derived from experience, either of the external world through our senses or of our own mental life through introspection. "All those sublime thoughts which tower above the clouds, and reach as high as heaven itself, take their rise and footing here; in all that great extent wherein the mind wanders in those remote speculations it may seem to be elevated with, it stirs not one jot beyond those ideas which sense or reflection have offered for its contemplation."[6] We shall be enquiring later how successful Locke was in establishing this thesis.

For the present, however, it is important to notice that the word "empiricist" connotes to modern ears something more tough-minded and radical than the type of philosophy expounded in the *Essay concerning Human Understanding*. One feature of Locke's philosophy which is surprising if we are misled by the modern overtones of the word "empiricist" is his view of knowledge. He uses the words "know" and "knowledge" in a very strict and narrow sense which betrays not so much his empiricist ambitions as the strong influence on his thinking of the rationalism of Descartes. Locke refuses to admit that I *know* any proposition unless (a) I am quite certain of what I claim to know and (b) my certainty cannot be shown by further evidence to have been ungrounded. "What once we *know*, we are certain is so:

and we may be secure that there are no latent proofs undiscovered, which may overturn our knowledge or bring it in doubt."[7] This proposes a very severe criterion for the use of the word "know." And as we shall see, it raises important questions about the less reliable but more familiar forms of cognition which Locke calls "belief," "opinion," and "judgment," to which he paid less attention.

A second very characteristic feature of the *Essay* is less alien to Locke's proposed empirical foundations but is, nevertheless, not very closely tied to them. This is his doctrine of signs, explicitly mentioned as a seeming afterthought in the very last chapter but exploited throughout the book. This final chapter, entitled "Of the Division of the Sciences," divides the field of human knowledge into three sections: (1) natural philosophy, which studies the natures, properties, and ways of working of things, both material and immaterial; from Locke's description, "natural philosophy" comprises what we would nowadays call natural science, mathematics, and, surprisingly, those questions of theology which are decidable by reason rather than by revelation; (2) matters relating to the ends of human actions and to the means by which these ends can be attained; these matters would today comprise moral philosophy, the social sciences, and the various practical arts; (3) "the doctrine of signs"; this is the subject of the *Essay* and consists in the study of the ways in which the first two types of knowledge are attained and communicated.

Signs are of two kinds. In the primary sense of the word, a sign is an *idea*, something which *represents* to the mind whatever it is we are thinking of or are conscious of. "For since the things the mind contemplates are none of them, besides itself, present to the understanding, it is necessary that something else as a sign or representation of the thing it considers should be present to it: and these are *ideas*."[8] The second and derivative kind of sign is that which makes public the private world of ideas, that is, words. "Because the scene of ideas that makes one man's thoughts cannot be laid open to the immediate view of another . . . therefore to communicate our thoughts to one another, as well as record them for our own use signs of our ideas are also necessary."[9] Locke's doctrine of ideas is expounded chiefly in Book II of the *Essay* and his account of language in Book III.

The concept of "idea" is basic to Locke's empiricism and the origin of his notorious "representative" theory of knowledge. Locke himself apologizes to the reader in his Introduction[10] "for the frequent use of the word 'idea' which will be found in the following treatise." He goes on to explain that "idea" is the term "which, I think, serves best to stand for whatsoever is the *object* of the understanding when a man thinks." The term "idea" with the meaning that Locke here assigns to it is not his own invention. It was common enough in the philosophy of the

seventeenth century, and its currency was no doubt due in part to the prestige of Descartes, who had himself defined the term as "all that is in our mind when we conceive a thing in whatsoever manner we conceive it."[11] Locke uses the word in several senses. (1) "Idea" means the *immediate* objects of our sensory awareness, twinges of pain, noises, colored expanses, and so on. (These would nowadays be called *sense data* or *sensa*.) (2) In another sense, "idea" refers to sensory presentations of physical objects. I can have the idea of an apple, in this sense, when I see an apple *as an apple* and not, for example, as a peach or a tomato or a mere uninterpreted sense datum. (3) Images, occurring in memory or imagination (or presumably in dreams) are also called "ideas" by Locke. (4) What we should now call *concepts* or *abstract ideas* are also included under the term. Finally, (5) what Locke calls "ideas of reflection" are the concepts that we gain through introspection of our own mental operations.

It might be thought that a term used so ambiguously as Locke uses "idea" would be useless as a technical term in the theory of knowledge. However, this ambiguity matters less than might be expected. For though the entities to which the term is used to refer are various, Locke supposes them all to have *the same function*. They are all *signs* which represent to us the external world of physical objects and the inner world of consciousness. (They can even represent, he seems to suppose, a transcendental or supernatural world of God and spirits, though here the representation is somehow less direct.) There are, as we shall see, serious difficulties hidden in this notion of knowledge by representation. Of some of these, Locke was himself aware. Two of the principal difficulties may be noted here.

(1) Locke does not explain what it means to be "in the mind" or "present to the understanding." These are metaphorical expressions. It is imprudent to use such expressions in philosophical writings unless we can explain their meaning in plain descriptive terms. Locke nowhere succeeds in doing this. (2) What is worse, he nowhere gives a clear account of his concept of *sign*. He certainly uses the word in a sense far removed from that sanctioned by ordinary usage, for what that is worth. *A* ordinarily becomes a sign of *B* by being experienced in association with *B*. It is in this way that clouds become a sign of rain, bouts of fever signs of malarial infection, and words and phrases signs of the objects or situations to which they are taken to refer. Both the sign and what it signifies are themselves experienced. If they were not, one could not become a sign of the other. In Locke's view, however, ideas are all that we ever experience, and the realities of which they are said to be the signs lie forever beyond the reach of our senses and our powers of introspection. Since this is so, it is clear that (a) ideas are signs of things only in a very strained and novel sense of "sign" and (b) we can never know anything about the world as

it exists apart from the ideas through which its structure and its states are supposed to be conveyed to us. The ever-present curtain of ideas can never be pushed aside. Locke was well aware of this last difficulty and we shall see how he tried to meet it.

The Attack on Innate Ideas

THE first book of the *Essay* is a critical examination of a theory about the origins of human knowledge which was widely current in Locke's time. Proponents of this theory held that some kinds of human knowledge are not acquired in the ordinary course of experience but are innate in the sense of being part of the mind's initial equipment. To us nowadays such a doctrine seems fantastic enough and hardly worth rational consideration. It had, however, respectable antecedents in the history of philosophy. Plato and Augustine, for example, had relied on doctrines of this sort in their theories of knowledge. Locke had to take the theory seriously, not only because many of his contemporaries did so[12] but also because the doctrine offered an alternative to his own empiricism. It had therefore to be disposed of before Locke could give his own version of the origins of human knowledge.

He finds that the instances of allegedly innate knowledge fall into two classes: (1) self-evident logical principles; (2) moral rules. The main argument used by proponents of innate ideas was that these rules and principles are universally accepted as true. To this Locke replies that it is false that there are in fact any propositions which command universal assent. Principles of logic, however "self-evident" to trained minds, cannot be appreciated by small children or the feeble-minded. And as to moral rules, they were known even in the seventeenth century to vary widely in different times and places. "Any who have been but moderately conversant in the history of mankind and looked abroad beyond the smoke of their own chimneys"[13] will, Locke is confident, reject the suggestion that some moral principles are given universal assent. However, let us suppose that some propositions were generally accepted; would this make them innate? Locke replies that it would not unless it could also be established that the supposedly innate principles could not come to be known in any other way.

A weaker version of the doctrine suggested that innate principles were in the mind at birth but that men do not come to recognize them until they have attained a suitable level of mental development. Locke replied that this suggestion was ambiguous. It might mean that we have innate *capacities* for apprehending certain truths. This is true but beside the point, since on this standard any truth, however recondite, could be reckoned innate. Alternatively, it might be taken to mean that part of the mind's initial equipment was a set of innate principles

inscribed there *in an embryonic form*. Locke replies that we have no evidence of a truth being *in the mind* other than that it is actually understood. "If truths can be printed on the understanding without being perceived, I can see no difference there can be between any truths the mind is *capable* of knowing in respect of their original: they must all be innate or all adventitious: in vain shall a man go about to distinguish them."[14]

The Materials of Knowledge

HAVING disposed of the doctrine of innate ideas, Locke turned to the exposition of his own theories. "Let us suppose the mind to be, as we say, white paper, void of all characters, without any ideas; how comes it to be furnished? . . . Whence has it all the *materials* of reason and knowledge? To this I answer, in one word, from EXPERIENCE."[15] It is this answer and its elaboration which gives Locke the right to the title of empiricist. But the label means little until we see how he develops the answer. Experience, for Locke, consists of two parts, *sensation*, giving us information about the world outside us, and *reflection*, giving us what knowledge we have of the inner world of the mind. "Our sensation, employed either about external objects, or about the internal operations of our own minds, perceived and reflected on by ourselves, is that which supplies our understanding with all the *materials* of thinking. These are the two fountains of knowledge, from which all the ideas we have or can naturally have, do spring."[16]

Locke's view is, then, that sensation and reflection supply the mind with the raw materials of knowledge. We are not, however, just passive recipients of these materials. The mind has powers of analyzing and reassembling these raw materials, and in its final processed form human knowledge is very different from the fragments of sensory and reflective experience out of which it has grown. Locke says far too little about the ways in which the understanding works up the crude data of experience into the various kinds of knowledge. He notes that the materials supplied by sensation and reflection can be "with infinite variety compounded and enlarged by the understanding, as we shall see hereafter."[17] But in fact he pays little attention to all the important processes by which the bare deliverances of experience are interpreted and organized. The only part of the *Essay* in which he sets himself seriously to this task is the account of the origins of abstract ideas in the third book.

Perhaps it may be said that the study of these processes is a task for the psychologist rather than for the philosopher. This is true. But a clear distinction between the provinces of philosophy and psychology was not made until the rise of psychology as an independent experimental science in the late nineteenth century: and even today the borderline between is not perfectly delineated. Contemporary philosophers still indulge unawares in abortive psychology.* In any case, Locke himself made no such distinction. Indeed, as we have seen, he openly professed to use a descriptive method which should certainly have taken no less account of the workings of the mind than of its contents.

A second criticism that is sometimes made of Locke's account of the origins of knowledge is that he misdescribes the way in which our knowledge originates. He talks as if it were built up piecemeal like a pattern in mosaic, when the truth is that a baby is presented at birth with a confused welter of sensations which it has to learn to interpret and reduce to order. Sufficient has been established by psychologists about the ways in which perception grows out of bare sensation by processes of *learning* to put this beyond doubt. But Locke was more of a philosopher than he was a pioneer psychologist, and his account of the origins of knowledge need not be read merely as wrong-headed empirical description. A philosopher who studies the theory of knowledge is not concerned so much with the actual processes of thinking as with those features on which its reliability and validity depend. And these features are often masked by the fragmentary and incoherent character of those actual processes of thought which form part of the psychologist's data. In emphasizing that sensation and reflection are the only sources of knowledge, Locke is setting limits, though very rough limits, to the reach of our minds.

But the limits are not arbitrary. For if he is called on to justify the claim that sensation and reflection are the only sources of knowledge, he replies, first with an appeal to introspection, and secondly with a challenge to his opponents to produce an example of knowledge which cannot be traced to one or the other of these sources. "Let anyone examine his own thoughts, and thoroughly search into his understanding, and then let him tell me whether all the original ideas he has there are any other than of the objects of his senses, or of the operations of his mind considered as objects of his reflection; and how great a mass of knowledge soever he imagines to be lodged there, he will, upon taking a strict view, see that he has not any idea in his mind but what one of these two have imprinted."[18] In fact, he has some difficulty, as we shall see, in deriving all our concepts from sensation and reflection, though his difficulties are due less to the defects of his empiricist program than to a lack of resolution in carrying it out.

Locke says very little about sensation and reflection. In the case of sensation, this was probably wise. For anything that can usefully be said about sensation falls within the provinces of neurophysiology and experimental psychology, sciences unknown to the

seventeenth century. Locke believed, as we shall see, that ideas of sensation were effects in consciousness of physical stimuli acting on our sense organs, but he prudently declined to speculate on the details of the causal process. "I shall not at present meddle with the physical consideration of the mind; or trouble myself to examine wherein its essence consists; or by what motions of our spirits or alterations of our bodies we come to have any sensation by our organs or any *ideas* in our understandings."[19] He doubted, indeed, whether any knowledge of the physical processes of sensation could make conscious experience anything less of a mystery than he found it. "Impressions made on the retina by rays of light, I think I understand, and motions from thence continued to the brain may be conceived; and that these produce ideas in our minds I am persuaded but in a manner to me incomprehensible. This I can resolve only into the good pleasure of God whose ways are past finding out."[20]

The second source of our ideas Locke calls "reflection," which we should nowadays call "introspection." He defines reflection as "that notice which the mind takes of its own operations and the manner of them."[21] This, though Locke believes it to be sufficiently similar to sensation to merit the title of "internal sense," is yet different from it in two important ways: (1) it is not awakened to activity by stimuli external to ourselves; (2) it is secondary to other mental activities (and in particular, to sensation) and dependent upon them. Clearly, we cannot "take notice" of the operations of our minds unless there are operations to be taken notice of. Locke seems to think that this rather naïve account is a simple description of a basic mental activity common to all rational beings. In fact, however, he is begging important philosophical questions by two assumptions involved in this account. The assumptions are (1) that it makes sense to talk of mental activities or operations at all; (2) that even if we concede (1), we can assume without argument that such activities can properly be spoken of as open to observation. Both these points can plausibly be disputed and are, in fact, topics of controversy in philosophy at the present day.

He next proceeds to classify our ideas and to show how different kinds of idea are related. He first distinguishes *simple* from *complex* ideas. Though Locke intends it to be a key concept of the *Essay*, the notion of a simple idea is by no means clear. He gives at different places in the *Essay* two quite different tests for recognizing a simple idea. (1) Sensory experiences of one uniform character are said to be simple ideas. The coldness of a piece of ice and the whiteness of a lily are cited as examples.[22] (2) Alternatively, those ideas are simple in receipt of which "the understanding is merely passive."[23] Sometimes he uses the term of simple sense qualities like *hot* or *red*, sometimes of the smallest units of experience, sometimes again, of what is

* The most notorious example of this is Wittgenstein's *Philosophical Investigations*.

given in experience in contrast to what is interpreted or constructed out of it. And in discussing simple ideas of reflection, he is even vaguer. He appears to believe that there are two basic forms of mental activity of which reflection informs us. The first is *perception*, the second, *willing*. And these two are simple ideas which can take various different specific forms (which Locke discusses later under the heading of *modes*). Yet further simple ideas are said to "convey themselves into the mind by all the ways of sensation and reflection";[24] pleasure, pain, power, existence, and unity. Clearly, he is here in a hopeless muddle, assigning alleged simple ideas to correspond to the vaguest of abstract words. We need not try to unravel these complexities. It is sufficient if we understand simple ideas to be the bare uninterpreted data of sensation and introspection. Such "ideas" we do undoubtedly have, though it is only perhaps in early infancy and in a few other relatively uncommon circumstances, like recovering from a faint or an anesthetic, that we encounter them in their pristine "simplicity."

Locke's doctrine of complex ideas is made difficult by two seemingly incompatible accounts.[25] In the first edition of the *Essay*, complex ideas were classified according to the different sorts of object of which these ideas were the signs. He distinguishes *ideas of substances, modes,* and *relations*. Ideas of substances are ideas of things capable of independent existence. The straightforward instances of substances are ordinary physical objects, stones, chairs, animals, and the like. But the notion of substance, as we shall see, raises serious difficulties for Locke. Modes are ideas, other than simple ideas, of those features of reality which are not, like substances, capable of independent existence. Locke instances *space* and *time* as simple modes and *triangle* and *gratitude* as specimens of "mixed modes." Finally, relations are complex ideas which consist "in the consideration and comparing one idea with another."[26] In the fourth edition of the *Essay*, published in 1700, four years before his death, Locke added without amending his previous account, a second explanation based upon the activities of the understanding. By *combining* simple ideas together we obtain complex ideas, by *comparing* ideas we come by our ideas of relations, and by *abstracting* we attain to general ideas. This version distinguishes relations from complex ideas, an improvement on the doctrine of the first edition, and introduces the important topic of general ideas or universals, which Locke develops further in Book III. It is hardly possible to reconcile these incoherencies. We have to be content with the notion of a complex idea as any idea resulting from the operations of the understanding on the simple deliverances of sensation and reflection. That we have such ideas there can be no reasonable doubt. So far, then, we may accept Locke's main conclusions, even if we have to reject the details of his account as crude and inconsistent.

The Functions of Ideas: Perception

IF we may judge from the way Locke develops his argument in the later parts of the *Essay*, the varieties of ideas and their division into simple and complex are of less consequence for him than their function. It is the function of ideas to act as signs which represent the world to us. This world may be the external world of physical nature, the internal world of our own minds or, indeed, of the minds of others in so far as this can be made public and communicated through language and other signs. The representative character of knowing is the distinctive feature of Locke's theory of knowledge and the source of most of its difficulties. About some of these difficulties, Locke was himself uneasy.

The representative function of ideas is made clear chiefly in Locke's discussion of the problems of perception. The account of perception that we find in the *Essay* did not originate with Locke. Cruder versions of it can be found in ancient and in medieval thought. But the physical discoveries of the seventeenth century made it seem more acceptable by providing the beginnings of an account of the mechanism of perceiving. Both Galileo and Descartes had given this type of explanation of perception. Locke did little more than rephrase a widely held doctrine. The main point of the representative theory (and it is of course a "theory" which can take many different forms) is that sense perception cannot be explained by just the two elements of the process which are obvious to common sense, the mind of the perceiver and the object perceived. We have also to assume a third factor, the *idea of sensation*, in Locke's own phrase, or the *sense datum* or *sensum* as it is more usually called today.

> To discover the nature of our ideas the better and to discourse of them intelligibly, it will be convenient to distinguish them as they are ideas or perceptions in our minds and as they are modifications of matter in the bodies that cause such perceptions in us; that so we may not think (as perhaps usually is done) that they are exactly the images and resemblances of something inherent in the subject;* most of those of sensation being in the mind no more the likeness of something existing without us than the names that stand for them are the likenesses of our ideas, which yet upon hearing they are apt to excite in us.[27]

It is Locke's view that "ideas or perceptions in our minds," as he calls them, represent to us the physical objects which cause these ideas. Why should we accept such an account of perception?

It is not difficult to make a prima facie case for such a causal theory of perceiving, though Locke himself does not trouble to argue the case in any

---

* This is an archaic and misleading use of the word "subject." We should nowadays say "object."

detail. Perhaps he thought that the doctrine appeared, to educated common sense in the seventeenth century, too clearly true to need his advocacy. At any rate, he is more concerned, as we shall see, with drawing certain conclusions about the nature of the world which seemed to him to be established if the causal theory were true. Let us first ask, then, why a representative or causal account of perception can seem plausible.

Suppose that I am looking at a physical object, say, a penny. Its apparent size, shape, and color vary with its distance from my eyes, the angle from which I see its surface, the state of the light, and, indeed, the state of my eyes. From one point of view, it may seem larger than a chair, though from most others it will look much smaller. (It does not of course "seem larger than a chair" in the sense that we *take* it to be larger. It is merely that the part of our visual field taken up by the penny if we hold it close to our eye may well be larger than the part of the visual field occupied by a chair situated some feet away from us. But this fact raises the question: *What is it that is larger?*) Again, from angles more or less vertical to the surface, it will appear circular, while from most angles, it will appear more or less elliptical. Its color, too, will vary with the angle from which we view it. Common sense seems to tell us that we are looking all the time at the same surface of the same penny. But the surface and the physical object itself of which the surface is a part surely do not vary in shape, size, and color from one moment to another. Yet what we are immediately sensing does change in this way. We cannot therefore be perceiving the physical object or its surface. Let us then say, since obviously we are directly aware of *something*, that the object of this direct awareness is a *sense datum*, or, in Locke's terminology, an *idea of sensation*.

We can now call the sciences of physics and physiology to our aid. Our visual sense data of the penny can be understood to be *effects* in our consciousness of complex causes: (a) the physical events connected with the propagation of light, its reflection from the surface of the penny, and its entry into our eyes, and (b) the physiological events connected with the effect of this light upon the retinas of our eyes and the consequent electrical changes in the state of our optic nerves and brains. What we immediately experience is the effect. And though we have some knowledge from physics and physiology of these causes, we can of course never be directly aware of them. In particular, we can never be *directly* aware of the physical object which common sense assures us that we are seeing. All we can ever be directly aware of in perception is the "ideas of sensation" themselves. An argument of this type may be used in turn for each of the sensory modalities, sight, hearing, touch, and so on. The conclusion is similar in each case.

It was noted above that Locke does not set out this

argument in any detail, though clearly he accepts its conclusion. But the argument is very hard to state in a form that is immune to elementary objections.[28] Crudely stated, as it was above, it evokes obvious questions. If we can never know anything of the external world of physical objects but our own "ideas of sensation," how do we ever come by all this detailed knowledge about light rays, retinas, nerve cells, and how they work? These, after all, are themselves parts of the "external world." And if we cannot properly come by it, how can we use it to discredit the common-sense confidence that we place in the evidence of our senses? How, moreover, can we claim to know anything *at all* about physical objects, even that they cause our sensations, or, even worse still, that they exist? We shall consider Locke's answer to some of these points when we discuss his views on the nature of knowledge, set out in Book IV.

But to the question "What can we know of physical objects?" Locke replies with the celebrated doctrine of primary and secondary qualities. He first makes a distinction between *idea* and *quality*.

> Whatsoever the mind perceives in itself or is the immediate object of perception, thought or understanding, that I call *idea*; and the power to produce any idea in our mind, I call the *quality* of the subject wherein that power is. Thus a snowball having the power to produce in us the ideas of white, cold and round, the powers to produce these ideas in us as they are in the snowball I call qualities; and as they are sensations or perceptions in our understandings, I call them ideas.[29]

Qualities themselves are of three kinds: (1) The *primary* qualities of bodies are those qualities which are "utterly inseparable from the body in what state soever it be."[30] Such qualities are solidity, shape, motion, rest, and number. Our ideas of these primary qualities really resemble the qualities in question. (2) Secondary qualities "in truth are nothing in the objects themselves but powers to produce the various sensations in us by their primary qualities."[31] Colors, sounds, tastes, smells, touch sensations, and so on are all "ideas of secondary qualities" produced in us by "the operation of insensible particles on our senses."[32] Our ideas of secondary qualities do not resemble the qualities as they themselves exist in the external world. (3) In addition to secondary qualities, which are powers in material objects to produce certain changes in our consciousness, such objects have a third type of quality which Locke simply calls "powers". These qualities are the capacities which bodies have, in virtue of their primary qualities, "to make such a change in the bulk, figure, texture and motion of *another body* as to make it operate on our senses differently from what it did before."[33] Locke cites the power of fire to make lead fluid.

This doctrine is a rather indigestible mixture of

empirical science and *a priori* reasoning, and, in the form in which Locke states it, it is very easy to attack. It will be sufficient here to notice that his basic concept of *primary quality* is confused. (a) He fails to distinguish between *determinable* properties of size, shape, velocity, and so on and the *determinate* forms in which these general properties are manifested. A thing cannot have just shape or velocity in general. It must be some specific shape, spherical, cubical, or what not, and some specific velocity. (b) Once this necessary distinction has been made, the two marks which Locke assigns to primary qualities, (i) that they are "inseparable from the body in what state soever it be" and (ii) that they truly resemble our ideas of them, are seen to be either false or trivial. For it is certainly false that a given physical object has the same *determinate* shape or velocity "in what state soever it be." Changes of state are indeed precisely changes in the primary qualities of an object as it grows larger or smaller, alters its shape, or is accelerated. And it is equally false that our ideas of a thing's *determinate* primary qualities truly represent the quality itself. For as we saw in the case of the penny, its size and shape may *appear* to change from one moment to another. But if all that Locke is saying is that material objects must have some size or other, some velocity or other, and so on, and further that our ideas truly represent this fact to us, then he is saying very little indeed. For it is surely a defining property of a physical object that it has some "extension, figure, and mobility."[34] (c) He introduces a further confusion by distinguishing between sensible and "insensible" primary qualities. The second are the "bulk, figure, texture and motion" of the parts of a body which are too small to be perceived, that is, what we should nowadays call the atoms or molecules which make up the body. It is these which are responsible for the secondary qualities of a body and its "powers." Here, then, we have primary qualities which are not truly represented by our ideas.

Clearly all this is a great muddle. The doctrine of primary and secondary qualities is, in truth, nothing but some scientific truths dangerously elevated into a philosophical doctrine. Later discussions of the problem have shown how very difficult it is to use these scientific facts in philosophical arguments. The particular facts established by physics and physiology are as securely established as any other part of science. But they cannot easily be generalized into a theory of knowledge without confusion. It is one thing to offer a causal account of the mechanism of perceiving and quite another to meet the philosophical problems of perception with a causal analysis. Locke's representative theory of knowledge is one of the weak spots in his account of knowing. This does not mean, of course, that all representative theories of knowledge must fail. But if they are to be defensible, they need more careful treatment than Locke was able to give his own.

Things and Their Properties

COMMON sense makes a distinction between things and their qualities. An apple may be round, red, juicy, and sweet, or a piece of glass hard, smooth, and transparent. We can say of the one that *it* is round and red and of the other that *it* is hard and transparent. But what does the pronoun "it" refer to here? We naturally reply that it refers to the apple or to the piece of glass. But what *are* these things apart from their qualities? Suppose, for simplicity, that a certain thing, A, has five qualities only, Q_1, Q_2, Q_3, Q_4, Q_5. Then suppose we say "A is Q_5" (as we might say "The glass is transparent"). What would this mean? We seem to have two alternatives. Either A is just the collection of all its properties Q_{1-5} or it is (or includes) something additional to and distinct from its properties. Now the first alternative makes the statement "A is Q_5" a mere tautology. For it becomes "The set of properties Q_1, Q_2, Q_3, Q_4, Q_5 contains Q_5." And this would mean that no statement of the type "A has the property Q" could be other than analytically true. This suggestion is clearly false and moreover abolishes the distinction between logical and factual truth. But the second alternative, though not so clearly wrong, is almost equally difficult to accept. For A must then be something over and above the collection of its qualities, say $(Q_{1-5} + X)$ where X, not being a property, is something which cannot be described or referred to by descriptive words. For all our descriptive words are words that refer to properties. And since we cannot describe it, it is difficult to say how we can know anything about this hypothetical X except perhaps that it underlies its qualities and provides a sort of characterless nucleus in which the properties inhere. It is in some such way as this that the problem of substance presented itself to Locke.

This problem had been an important one in the philosophy of the Middle Ages because of its consequences in theology. Several important doctrines of the Roman church depended for their rational justification on a certain view of substance. And these theological associations were still active, as Locke was to discover, in the Anglican Christianity of seventeenth-century England. He discusses substance chiefly in Chapter 23 of the second book of the *Essay*. We find in the world groups of qualities which are always found together in a constant and uniform association. These qualities are accordingly "presumed to belong to one thing."[35] We therefore use one word, e.g., apple, to refer to the thing, and come to consider it as one simple idea, though it is, indeed, "a complication of many ideas together."[36] Moreover, "not imagining how these simple ideas *can* subsist by themselves, we accustom ourselves to suppose some *substratum* wherein they do subsist and from which they do result, which therefore we call *substance*."[37] It follows, therefore, that no one has any positive conception of substance "but only a supposition of he knows not what support of such qualities which are capable of producing simple ideas in us."[38] We naturally tend to ask, according to Locke, *what it is* in which qualities inhere. A piece of metal, for instance, may be gray and heavy. And if anyone is asked to say what the color or the weight inhere in, he will reply that they inhere in the solid extended parts of the thing. If asked further to explain what it is that solidity or extension inhere in, he would have nothing better to reply than that it inhered in "something, he knew not what."[39]

Locke admits, then, that we have no positive concept of substance, nothing more indeed than an "obscure and relative" notion of "the supposed, but unknown, support of those qualities we find existing, which we imagine cannot exist *sine re substante* without something to support them."[40] But he has claimed that all our concepts have an origin in experience, being derived from sensation and reflection. The idea of substance seems to offer an awkward counter-example to this claim. He was well aware of this, and already in his discussion of innate ideas in Book I he had touched upon this difficulty. "I confess there is another general idea which would be of considerable use for mankind to have, as it is of general talk as if they had it; and that is the idea of *substance* which we neither have nor can have by sensation or reflection."[41]

Had Locke been a consistent empiricist, he would at this point have rejected the notion of substance as nothing but a pseudo-concept, and the word itself as a word without meaning. Later philosophers, with principles similar to his, have in fact done this. But Locke, in spite of his principles, was too deeply committed to traditional ways of thinking to draw all the conclusions to which his premises entitled him. In the *Essay* itself, he leaves unresolved the conflict between his empiricism and his halfhearted acceptance of an admittedly incoherent idea. But on this point his critics were quick to challenge him. And in his reply to one of them, Dr. Stillingfleet, Bishop of Worcester, he tries (a) to explain why he was unable to dispense with the notion of substance and (b) to offer a rational justification of this notion. These letters to Stillingfleet have to be read with care. For though they provide a welcome amplification of some of the more puzzling parts of the *Essay*, they represent the cautious second thoughts of a man who was never eager to challenge religious orthodoxy too openly. Stillingfleet had accused him of having "almost discarded substance out of the reasonable part of the world," and Locke was anxious to evade the reputation among theologians of one addicted to dangerous thoughts. He professes himself unable to dispense with the concept of substance for the following reason: "The idea of these qualities and actions or powers are perceived by the mind to be inconsistent with existence . . . thence the mind perceives their necessary connection with inherence or being supported."[42] He is claiming here that it is patently self-

contradictory to suppose that the qualities of a body or the actions of a mind should exist on their own, unsupported by the mysterious and qualityless substratum whose existence Locke here postulates. Such appeals to allegedly self-evident propositions are notoriously ineffective, and a short answer can be given to this one. There are, *in fact*, causes of observable qualities which are not the qualities of any substance. Dreams and hallucinations provide endless examples. Or to take less bizarre instances, a visual after-image, the colored patch which floats in my field of vision after I had gazed at a bright light, is not inherent in any substance. It is just a colored patch detached from any physical object. (It is not, of course, inherent in my eye or in my visual field in the same sense of "inherent.") Thus Locke's argument for substance, such as it is, can be refuted by empirical counter-examples.

Locke was perhaps more worried by the necessity, as he saw it, of justifying the existence of a substratum to our ideas of reflection. It would have been much more damaging to traditional theology to destroy the foundation for belief in a *soul* or *self* than merely to criticize, however effectively, the notion of material substance. We must, he supposes, believe in "a substance wherein thinking, knowing, doubting and a power of moving, etc. do subsist."[43] Belief in such substances is indeed as vulnerable to argument from Locke's empirical premises as belief in a substratum for the qualities of physical objects. But we may usefully defer discussion of this point until the next section.

Having no reason to take seriously Locke's explanation of his inability to dispense with the concept of substance, we need not spend much time on his ingenious though fallacious attempt to justify the concept. Since we perceive according to Locke that there is a logical inconsistency between the nature of our ideas of sensation and reflection and their existing other than in some supporting medium, "the mind frames the correlative idea of a support."[44] "For I never denied," he adds, "that the mind could frame to itself ideas of relation but have showed quite the contrary in my chapters about relation." But he forgets that his account of our ideas of relation, though it is not very clear, is at least in conformity with his basic principles. And his account of the origin of our ideas of substance is not. We come by our ideas of relations like "larger than," "between," "after," and so on by comparing ideas *all of which are presented to us in experience*. But he is proposing here that we get the idea of a relation of *inherence* which holds between a quality presented in experience and a substance which *ex hypothesi* can never be experienced at all.

We must conclude, then, that Locke's attempt to defend the notion of substance fails. Indeed, in trying to defend it, he was arguing against the direction of his own thinking. For it was he, more than any other philosopher, who was responsible for the discredit into which the *substratum* view of substance has since fallen. Contemporary critics like Stillingfleet who were concerned at the implications of Locke's doctrine seem to have understood it better than Locke did himself. But it is important to notice that his failure to justify the notion of substance was not just a failure that might have been a success. The problem itself is a bogus one. It is always a meaningful question to ask of a set of *particular* properties "Why are they found in association?" For example, "Why are the properties of whiteness, salty taste, and crystallization in the cubic system found associated together in sodium chloride?" We may reasonably expect that discoveries in physical science could give us answers to such questions. But to generalize the question and ask why *any* property must be found conjoined with other properties is a question based on false assumptions. The substratum account of substance is an empty answer to an unnecessary question.

It is interesting to notice, however, that in Book IV of the *Essay*, where Locke is discussing other questions, he mentions in passing an entirely new approach to the problem of substance. One of the marks of substance in medieval philosophy had been that substances were those parts of the world which were capable of existing independently. This notion of substance which was developed by Descartes and Spinoza was never very satisfactorily assimilated to the more superficial *substratum* view. Locke remarks:

> We are wont to consider the substances we meet with, each of them, as an entire thing by itself, having all its qualities in itself, and independent of other things; overlooking for the most part, the operations of those invisible fluids they are encompassed with, and upon whose motions and operations depend the greatest part of those qualities which are taken notice of in them, and are made by us the inherent marks of distinction whereby we know and denominate them. Put a piece of gold anywhere by itself, separate from the reach and influence of all other bodies, it will immediately lose all its colour and weight, and perhaps malleableness too.... This is certain: things however absolute and entire they seem in themselves, are but retainers to other parts of nature for that which they are most taken notice of by us.[45]

Locke left this suggestion undeveloped. But had he followed it up, he would have been led to quite another view of substance. It is a fact of experience that capacity for independent existence is a property which different things possess in very different degrees. An animal is very vulnerable to changes in its environment, a stone less so, and an atom less so again. On this view, being a substance is a matter of degree. And the only fully substantial thing in the universe is the universe itself — a view to which Spinoza was led, to the scandal of all right-thinking men. Locke's undeveloped ideas are often more valuable than his cautious second thoughts.

The Nature of Mind

REFLECTION AND ITS OBJECTS

We have seen that Locke thought that "reflection" was one of the basic sources of human knowledge. While sensation gives us information about the external world of physical objects, reflection gives us ideas of our own mental operations. And just as all our knowledge of the external world is based upon our ideas of sensation, so all our knowledge of the mind is based upon our ideas of reflection. Locke believes that there is a very close analogy between these two sources of knowledge. He says of reflection: "This source of ideas every man has wholly in himself: and though it be not sense, as having nothing to do with external objects, yet it is very like it, and might properly enough be called *internal sense*.[46] The objects of this "internal sense" he lists as "*perception, thinking, doubting, believing, reasoning, knowing, willing*, and all the different actings of our own minds."[47] This rather naïve notion that introspection is a sort of searchlight which we can turn at will upon the inner world of our own mental activities has come in for a good deal of criticism from philosophers, especially in recent years. It has been held to be "entirely false, and false not in detail but in principle."[48] The claims of these present-day critics may well be exaggerated. Certainly they have not been established beyond argument. In any case we need not read any philosophical subtleties into Locke's statements. An important part of what he wants to maintain is that I can often be aware that I am seeing a tree, feeling annoyed, entertaining an argument, making a choice, and so on. Nobody can reasonably doubt this, though certainly we *can* doubt whether we would be debarred from such knowledge in the absence of a special power of "internal sense." We can at least agree with Locke that we do, from time to time, know how we are feeling, what we are thinking, and the like. What we can reasonably object to is his suggestion that "thinking, doubting, believing, reasoning, knowing, willing" and so on are *ideas* in the same sense as the objects of my perception are, in Locke's vocabulary, also ideas. But perhaps we should not interpret his rather misleading language too strictly. After all, he may want to say no more than that (a) what we know about the mind must be inferred from its operations and (b) those operations are observable only in introspection. If this is what his doctrine of introspection amounts to, we may accept (a) and reject (b). Our evidence for rejecting (b) is, in part, the development of a scientific psychology during the last hundred years. This has rested almost entirely on controlled observation of human and animal *behavior* and very little upon the private deliverances of introspection. Indeed, an acute observer might have anticipated the evidence of psychology here by noting that those who have the deepest understanding of men are not those who are given to intensive and careful introspection. They are those who are shrewd and experienced observers of human conduct.

PERSONAL IDENTITY

Locke believed, as we have seen, that we get our knowledge of the mind from ideas of reflection. If he had worked out an account of the nature of mind consistent with his empiricist program, he would have had to admit that our knowledge of the mental substances underlying our ideas of reflection is as meager as our knowledge of material substances. It would amount to a mere "something we know not what." But in this, as in other parts of his philosophy, he was not consistent. In the first place, he took over from medieval philosophy and Christian theology the idea that the human mind was something immaterial capable of existing in its own right independent of the body. Nothing in his own philosophical principles lends any support to this view, which nevertheless hovers uneasily in the background of his account of mind. On the other hand, he was prepared to admit, to the scandal of his critics, that it is not logically self-contradictory to suppose that "the first Eternal thinking Being or Omnipotent Spirit should, if he pleased, give to certain systems of created senseless matter, put together as he thinks fit, some degrees of sense, perception and thought."[49] In other words, the evidence of our ideas of reflection does not logically imply the existence of a substantial mind. Moreover, he is at one point prepared to abandon his representational theory of knowledge, so far at least as it concerns knowledge of our own minds. In the last chapter of the *Essay*, where he is discussing the ways in which ideas can serve as signs of things, he implies that the mind is known to us directly without the mediation of ideas. "The things the mind contemplates are none of them, besides itself, present to the understanding." This seems inconsistent with much that he says about ideas of reflection.

It is therefore difficult to find a clear and consistent account of the nature of mind in the *Essay*. He is hesitant, inexplicit, and conflicting save on one point — his famous doctrine of personal identity. The question "What makes me the *same person* that I was an hour, a month, or ten years ago?" is not, for Locke, merely a theoretical puzzle for philosophers. For he believes that practical matters of moral responsibility, reward and punishment turn upon the answer we make to this question. He approaches the problem by recognizing that adjectives such as "same" and "identical" have different senses in their application to different kinds of things, and he distinguishes a number of different senses of the word "identity." A simple material particle, for instance, has a different kind of identity from a compound material thing. In the first case, we trace its identity, when we have occasion to do so, by its position in space and time, and in the second by ensuring that all the particles making up the compound are identical in the former sense. In a living organism, on the other hand, or in a machine, identity does not consist in identity of material particles which may be joined to or separated from the organism without affecting its title to be *the same* organism. It consists, rather, in the organization or structure of the parts. When Locke comes to discuss identity in the case of human beings, he makes a sharp distinction between the identity of a *man* and that of a *person*. Identity of the same man consists in the same organization of the same living body. Human identity in this sense is not judged differently from that of an animal or a plant. Locke explicitly rejects the suggestion that identity of *soul* should be the criterion whether *A* is the same man as *B*, on the good empiricist ground that identity of soul cannot be tested and established.

Thus, when he comes to discuss personal identity he has repudiated the traditional orthodox view.[50] Personal identity consists for him in identity of *consciousness*.

> Since consciousness always accompanies thinking and is that that makes everyone to be what he calls self and thereby distinguishes him from all other thinking beings; in this alone consists personal identity, i.e., the sameness of a rational being; and as far as this consciousness can be extended backwards to any past action or thought, so far reaches the identity of that person: it is the same self now as it was then; and it is by the same self with this present one that now reflects on it, that that action was done.[51]

This statement is vague and open to some obvious objections. The continuity of my consciousness is interrupted by gaps from time to time, by dreamless sleep, for example, or by a faint. When I become conscious again, is my consciousness "the same" as it was in spite of the discontinuity? If it were not, I would no longer be the same person. Locke does not assert this absurd conclusion but claims instead that it is not continuity of duration that constitutes sameness of consciousness but continuity of *content*. I am the same person if I can remember my past experiences and only in so far as I can remember them. "As far as any intelligent being can repeat the idea of any past action with the same consciousness it had of it at first, and with the same consciousness it has of any present action; so far is it the same personal self."[52] His reason for this claim is that since I am now a person by being aware of my present state of consciousness, I can only be the person I was if I am aware of my past states.

Locke does not overlook the obvious objections.

I have forgotten many incidents of my last life and remember many others. Must I say that those I have forgotten did not happen *to the same person* as now remembers the others? Locke would answer "Yes." And if we object that this is an absurd consequence, he replies that we must distinguish between identity of the same *man* and of the same *person*. The incidents I have forgotten happened to the same man as now fails to remember them, but not to the same person.[53] He does not consider the odd consequences that follow from this view. What are we to say, for instance, of incidents of my past history which are at one time forgotten and at another remembered?

A further difficulty was pointed out by Bishop Butler in an appendix to the *Analogy of Religion*. My personal identity cannot consist in consciousness of my past experiences since it is presupposed by this consciousness. Locke says that I am the same person in so far as I can remember *my* past experiences. But what makes them *mine*? It cannot be the mere fact that I now *seem* to remember them. For I would not be genuinely recalling them had they not happened to *me*. And if they did happen to me, what account are we to give of the self to whom they happened? Clearly we cannot do so in Locke's terms.

Perhaps Locke could have elaborated his theory to meet this objection by using his distinction between "the same man" and "the same person." But even if the theory can be amended to meet Butler's criticism, there is another attack still to be met.[54] Locke's account is both too narrow and too wide. It excludes cases where everyone would want to say "*X* is the same person" and includes cases where few people would want to say this. In other words, Locke's account of personal identity diverges very widely from the established English usage of the phrase "same person." And since the meanings of words and phrases are constituted by the ways in which they are used, this is a serious objection. Unless it can be shown that the ordinary use of a word or phrase is confused and incoherent, there can hardly be a good case for supplanting it. Ordinary usage of terms like "self," "personal identity," and so on are, of course, confused in the sense that they are very vague, but they have not been shown to be inconsistent or radically misleading. And even if they were, it is doubtful if Locke's proposals have sufficient logical merit to make them worthy replacements.

Thinking and Language

LOCKE's object in the second book of the *Essay* was to examine the "instruments and materials of our knowledge," to list them and trace their origins. He had intended to go on immediately to discuss the ways in which ideas are combined and used in knowledge and belief. He then realized, as he explains, that the connection between language and thinking is so close that he could not talk at all about knowledge, the successful outcome of our thinking, without first looking at language. Book III is therefore devoted to examining some of the philosophical problems of language. It is, of course, no novelty today, to find a philosopher discussing the ways in which words work. But Locke seems to have been more conscious of the importance of these questions than most philosophers prior to the present century. In discussing the relationship between words, ideas, and things, he deals with three main questions: (a) the connection between language and thinking; (b) the way in which *general* words have meaning; (c) the nature of definition.

(a) Locke's account of the relation between language, thought, and what we think about is in accordance with his representational theory of knowledge. We can be *directly* aware of nothing but our ideas through which the world is represented to us. But these ideas are private and, of their nature, cannot be shared with another person. To communicate with others we need public signs to be what he calls "sensible marks of ideas." A language is a system of such signs. This view of the relation between language and thinking involves the totally false notion that there is no essential connection between thinking and using signs. Pure thinking is imagined as a private contemplation of a flow of "ideas" which can be translated on occasions into a public linguistic form. The ideas give the words their meaning but can exist without them. There cannot, on the other hand, be meaningful language without ideas to back it. Language is meaningful to the extent that it is backed with ideas, as currency is valuable to the extent that it is backed with goods. Locke is not the only philosopher who has endorsed this view, though few, other than William of Ockham, have expressed it quite so openly. It is indeed enshrined in much popular thinking on the subject of language, as when we talk of "expressing our thoughts in suitable language" and so on.

It would be silly to pretend that philosophers at the present day can answer, to the general satisfaction, questions like "What makes language meaningful?" or "How do we distinguish meaningful from meaningless discourse?" But they can at least give reasons for supposing that Locke's account is wrong. In the first place, if a stream of pure thinking accompanied all our speaking, writing, listening, reading, and all other uses of language, how could we fail to be aware of so important and universal an ingredient of our consciousness? Yet psychologists, using the most careful introspective methods, failed to agree in the famous controversy over the existence of "imageless thinking."[55] Secondly, it does not seem absurd to distinguish between meaningful and meaningless *thinking*. And if it is not, how is the distinction to be explained on Locke's view? Clearly, it cannot be accounted for in the way he distinguishes meaningful from meaningless *language*. Thirdly, what does Locke mean by "ideas" when he claims that words are signs of ideas? We saw that the word "idea" bears for him multiple and shifting senses. He can hardly mean "sense datum" or "image," and if he means "concept," what is a concept? Clearly, Locke depends on a satisfactory theory of concepts to make his account of meaning acceptable. We shall examine what he had to say about concepts in a moment.

Locke's mistake here seems to arise in the following way. We distinguish quite properly between the expression of a thought and the thought itself, just as we distinguish between the shape of a thing and the material it is made of. But it does not therefore follow that we can properly talk of the thought itself existing apart from *any* expression of it, any more than we can talk of the material of which a thing is made having no shape at all. But Locke was tempted to do this.

(b) Locke next discusses the nature of general concepts, the traditional problem of universals. His views on this were misunderstood by later philosophers, chiefly because they were caricatured by Berkeley in the Introduction to his *Principles of Human Knowledge*. Most of Locke's critics agree that there is no consistent theory of universals to be found in the *Essay*, but he makes in passing a good many useful points, particularly about the nature and functions of language. It is, moreover, at least possible to sketch the main points of his account. General words are essential to knowledge, since no language could possibly consist of proper names alone. The very possibility of communication depends on our use of general words. But everything that exists is a particular thing. How then can there come to be general words at all? In Locke's view, general words (and, in particular, the general ideas of which they are the signs) are not in any sense entities which exist in their own right. He will have nothing to do with the realism of Plato and his followers. The generality of these words lies in the way they work. The word "dog" is a general word, while "Fido" is a proper name used to refer to a particular dog. Now what does the general word "dog" refer to? Locke's answer is that it refers to a *general idea*. "Words become general by being made signs of general *ideas* and *ideas* become general by separating them from the circumstances of time and place and any other ideas that may determine them to this or that particular existence. By this way of abstraction they are made capable of representing more individuals than one; each of which having in it a conformity to that abstract *idea* (as we call it), of that sort."[56] A general idea, then, of a particular kind of thing, say a dog, is thought of as a complex idea containing the qualities common to all dogs but omitting those, such as size, shape, or color, in which they differ.

This notion of a general idea as a sort of highest common factor of the particular things it represents is a very unsatisfactory one. Are there any properties common to all dogs? And if there are, is it true that we cannot form the general idea until we know them? Further, what kind of an entity is this general idea supposed to be? Locke never answers this question explicitly, but he seems to have believed it to be a sort of composite image. Berkeley, at any rate, understood him thus and had no difficulty in showing the absurdity of such a notion. Let us suppose, however, that Locke could give satisfactory answers to these questions. His account would still not be an explanation of the way in which general words work. For he would be saying that general words function just like proper names. A proper name works by uniquely designating an individual thing, while a general word refers to an abstract idea. But one of the reasons why there is a philosophical problem about universals is precisely that general words seem to work very differently from proper names. Locke, like Plato before him, is simply transferring the problem from the word to the idea. No doubt he would say that the idea can stand for the thing because it *resembles* it, as, indeed, an image resembles its original. He hints at some such answer in the passage quoted above where he talks of the individual having "a conformity" to the abstract idea. But there is no reason whatever, even on Locke's own premises, to suppose that a sign cannot stand for what it signifies without resembling it. In fact, we may rarely find such representative images in our consciousness at all. And if we do find them, they are certainly not essential to our conceptual thinking. Here, as at so many other points in his theory of knowledge, his representative "ideas" turn out to be both useless and misleading. It is clear that this belief of Locke's is connected with his beliefs about the relations between language and thinking discussed above. If he had not believed that use of language had to be backed with a stream of ideas to be meaningful, he could have asked himself how general words work without invoking general ideas at all. This would have set him on the right road to answering the question, a road which Berkeley was afterwards to indicate to his successors.

(c) The most interesting and original part of Book III is the account of definition. It would be too much to say that this account of definition originated with Locke, for much of the view of language implicit in it can be found in the work of Hobbes. Locke acknowledged no debt to Hobbes and no doubt shrank from admitting the influence of so scandalous a master, but it seems very improbable that he had not read him. The traditional theory of definition (derived from Aristotle but oversimplified and distorted in the process) was that a definition expressed in words the *essence* or *nature* peculiar to the thing defined. A definition was a definition of something real, a part of nature and not just a word.

It thus expresses something true about the world and not just something about the speech habits of a particular community. When we give a definition of something, on this theory, we state both its *genus* and its specific difference from other members of that genus. Linnaeus' binomial system of classifying plants and animals, still current in biology, preserves the shadow of this once influential view. All buttercups, for example, are taken to belong to the genus *Ranunculus* in virtue of possessing a certain group of properties in common. And the members of this genus may differ among themselves in certain standard ways which are taken as determining the species to which a particular plant belongs. For example, the meadow buttercup (*Ranunculus acris*) has smooth stalks and upright sepals while the bulbous buttercup (*R. bulbosus*) has furrowed stalks and down-turned sepals.

Biologists recognize nowadays that this method of classifying their material, though convenient and practical, does not purport to assign every plant and animal encountered to a ready-made natural pigeonhole. Such classifications contain a large element of convention, and merely reflect a decision to apply a certain biological term to a certain range of material. Like most conventions, they have reasons supporting them; but if one biologist chooses to split one group into three different species while another lumps the three into one species, there is often no final way of adjudicating between them. Biologists do not now believe, as the Aristotelians seem to have done, that the plants, animals, and minerals making up the natural world have "real natures" which are fixed and clearly distinguishable, and that it is the aim of science to determine these natures. (Chemical elements and compounds fit this program more satisfactorily but even here there are difficulties.)

Against this notion of "real definitions" Locke argued that "a *definition* is nothing else but *the showing of the meaning of one* word by several other not synonymous terms."[57] Modern logicians would, almost without exception, agree that Locke was right. They will perhaps elaborate on this account by distinguishing *lexical definitions*, which record the way in which a particular term is used in a given speech community, from *stipulative definitions*, which record a determination or a recommendation to use a word (a new scientific term, for instance) in a particular way. But whatever modern glosses are made on Locke's account of definition, his main point, and it is a very important one, remains true. It is a view of definition which is so much taken for granted to-day that we are in danger of forgetting how valuable an innovation it was in the seventeenth century.

Knowledge and Belief

It has often happened in the history of philosophy that those parts of a philosopher's work which he himself regards as important turn out to be trivial or wrong. And conversely, other parts of his work which he had valued less highly or which perhaps were merely ancillary to his main purpose become the foundation of important developments. So it was with Locke's *Essay*. We can now see that Locke's important work in the theory of knowledge is to be found in the first three books. It will be remembered that the object of the *Essay* as set out in the Introduction had been "to inquire into the original, certainty and extent of *human knowledge* together with the grounds and degrees of *belief, opinion* and *assent*."[58] But of this program, Locke had covered only a small part by the end of the third book. He had discussed the origins of knowledge and, by implication at least, its possible limits, but the rest of his purpose remained to be completed. This was done in Book IV.

But Book IV is generally recognized to be the least successful and the least important part of the *Essay*. This is partly because of a radical inconsistency between Locke's account of knowledge in the first three books and that given in the last. But this inconsistency would have been less important had Locke's explanation of the nature of knowledge been at all plausible. In fact, however, not only was his account so restricted that we can scarcely be said, in Locke's sense of the word, to *know* anything at all of any consequence, but as we shall see he radically misconstrues the nature of some important ways of knowing.

The inconsistency between the first three books of the *Essay* and the last lies in this: Books I, II, and III expound an empiricist account of knowledge in which the sources of our knowledge and therefore its limits are restricted to the materials provided by sensation and reflection. Book IV gives a rationalist account of the way in which these raw materials are brought together and related in the mind. The standard case of knowing on which the first parts of the *Essay* rely is one provided by our everyday sense experience and by the observational sciences; the model of Book IV is pure mathematics. He talks there like Descartes, Spinoza, or Leibniz, but much less convincingly than they.

Of course, it may be said in Locke's defense that there is no *logical* inconsistency in giving one account of the way in which we come by the *materials* of knowledge and quite another of the way in which these materials are worked up into the finished product. Yet these two strands of thought fit very uncomfortably together, and the details of the argument of Book IV are unsatisfactory.

He defines "knowledge" as "nothing but the perception of the connexion of an agreement or disagreement and repugnancy of any of our ideas."[59] What he means is that we can intuitively "perceive" (in a metaphorical sense of this word) that there are certain relations either of necessary connection or of mutual incompatibility that hold between the ideas given to us in experience and that knowledge is just the intuitive perception of these relations. Such an account of knowledge is not informative without some detailed examples, and the examples Locke gives are not helpful. He lists four types of "agreement": (i) identity, (ii) relation, (iii) coexistence or necessary connection, and (iv) real existence. (i) can give us only tautologies. (Locke's examples are "blue is not yellow" and "a spirit is a spirit"!) By (ii) he seems to mean mathematical relations, for the example he gives is taken from geometry: "Two triangles on equal bases between two parallels are equal." His use of this example seems to imply that he thought that there can be necessary connections between mathematical concepts *taken by themselves* and independently of the axioms of the system in which they occur (in this instance, the system of Euclidean geometry). This is certainly false.

The third type, coexistence or necessary connection, is the relation between ideas found to occur uniformly together in our experience, which are, of course, reflections of properties occurring uniformly together in nature. Locke gives as an example the properties of gold, though immediately admitting, what is indeed obvious, that we cannot actually perceive the necessary connection between, for instance, the specific gravity of gold and its solubility in *aqua regia*. He seems to have thought that an improved knowledge of physical science will show us the necessary connections between the properties of things. Science has indeed advanced enormously since his time but we know of no more necessary connections between the properties of things today than he did in the seventeenth century. The reason for this is simply that there are *and can be* no necessary connections between matters of fact. The connections between the empirical properties of things are all contingent, and in a world ordered differently, with different laws of nature from those which hold in our world, might well be other than they are. Thus, Locke's account of scientific knowledge of this kind radically misrepresents it. If he were right, all natural science would be deducible *a priori* from the bare evidence of our senses, and scientists could dispense with hypotheses and experiments. But in any case, it is very doubtful if his account is even consistent with his own premises. For he admits that "there can be no idea in the mind which it does not presently,* by an intuitive knowledge, perceive to be what it is."[60] And if this is so, we could not fail to perceive the mutual relations of any two ideas "present to the mind." We would either know immediately or not at all.

The fourth type of "agreement or disagreement" is what Locke calls "real existence." His example is "God is" (that is, God exists). Here it is difficult to know exactly what he is claiming. He seems to be referring here only to the existence of God and not

* "Presently" here means, of course, "immediately."

generally to any statement of the form "*X* exists," as he discusses in a later chapter the existence of those things which are known to us through the senses. The most plausible interpretation seems to be that if we have "present to the mind" the two ideas "God" and "existence" we see that there is a necessary connection between the two. This would amount to a statement in a condensed form of the notorious "ontological argument" for the existence of God, which is invalid on a number of counts. A critic could fairly object here that existence is not an "idea" in Locke's sense, that is, as Hume and Kant were later to point out, it is not a genuine predicate at all. (Locke did, in fact, claim that existence was one of the ideas which "convey themselves into the mind by all the ways of sensation and reflection."[61])

I think it is clear that this account of knowledge is hopelessly misconceived. It fails even as an explanation of the *a priori* knowledge gained in formal logic and mathematics. For it is not between *ideas* but rather between *statements* or *propositions* that relations of necessary connection hold in those fields. Locke could indeed have turned a completely abortive account of knowledge into a correct (though partial) analysis if he had allowed propositions to rank as complex ideas. For example, he would have then had to admit that not only were "grass" and "green" ideas but that the proposition "Grass is green" is also an idea. For there are genuine relations of necessary connection and incompatibility that hold between propositions, and it is part of the work of the formal logician to trace and explain these relationships. But Locke had little regard for formal logic,[62] and indeed, the depressed state of the subject in his time offered little encouragement to anyone to look to it for philosophical enlightenment.

Were this all Locke had to say about knowledge, Book IV would indeed be of small philosophical interest. But he seems to be aware that his account is inadequate and tries to supplement it in three ways. (i) He raises and tries to answer the basic difficulty which has to be faced by the proponent of any representative theory of knowledge. (ii) He discusses further our knowledge of propositions of the form "*x* exists." (iii) He discusses the nature of "judgment" or "belief," those states of mind which lack that immediate and justified certainty which is the mark of genuine knowledge but which nevertheless are of much greater practical interest to us. After all, we very commonly *judge* or *believe* but very rarely *know*, in Locke's sense of these words.

The first two topics may be treated together, as Locke raises the question of knowing through ideas in the course of a discussion of knowledge by sensation. He admits that this kind of "knowledge" does not meet the strict definition that he has laid down. "There is, indeed, another perception of the mind, employed about *the particular existence of finite beings without us*; which going beyond bare probability and yet not reaching perfectly to either of the foregoing degrees of certainty, passes under the name of knowledge."[63] And in discussing this type of knowledge, Locke puts squarely the difficulty of his representational theory so far as it relates to sense perception. "For, the having of the idea of anything in our mind, no more proves the existence of that thing, than the picture of a man evidences his being in the world."[64] However, his treatment of the point is a stronger testimonial to his intellectual honesty than to his philosophical acumen. He thinks that there must be a real world corresponding to our ideas of sensation because (a) sense data are much livelier and more vivid than images and cannot be, as images can, brought into existence at will; (b) our different senses "bear witness to the truth of each other's reports concerning the existence of sensible things without us."[65] But it is clear that these facts are as compatible with a view of the world like Berkeley's which dispenses with material substances as they are with Locke's. They therefore do nothing to mitigate the difficulty of the "way of ideas."

Even Locke's hesitant admission of sense perception to the status of knowledge still leaves us knowing very little. And he concedes that "man would be at a great loss if he had nothing to direct him but what has the certainty of true knowledge."[66] However, we have also "judgment," the faculty which God has given to man to supply the want of clear and certain knowledge, in cases where that cannot be had."[67] When we *know* that A is B, we perceive intuitively the necessary connection linking the idea of A with the idea of B. If, however, we merely *judge* or *believe* that A is B, we presume that the connection holds without being able to verify by intuition that it does. Obviously Locke is right to admit that sometimes we believe propositions to be true on completely adequate evidence and sometimes, much more commonly, we merely presume their truth on admittedly imperfect evidence. But it is hard to see how he can reconcile this obvious fact with his own theory of knowledge. The reason is the same as that given above in criticism of our supposed knowledge of necessary connections between the properties of physical objects. "Let any idea be what it will, it can be no other but such as the mind perceives it to be."[68] If this is so, we must surely perceive the relations as soon as we consider the ideas. On what ground could we "presume" their existence?

Perhaps Locke had this point in mind, though he does not say so. At any rate, he admits that judgment is quite unlike knowledge in that "that which makes me believe is something *extraneous** to the thing I believe."[69] This extraneous evidence is of two kinds: (i) the extent to which a proposition conforms with my past experience; (ii) the testimony of others.

And he adds some sensible rules for estimating the value of the evidence of other people. He here opens a big question which he does not pursue. This is a pity, as Book IV would have been much more useful and influential had Locke spent more of his time analyzing the judgment or belief which is so common and of such practical consequence and less in discussing "knowledge," which, as he defines it, rarely occurs at all.

It is impossible to regard the last book of the *Essay* as a contribution to an empiricist theory of knowledge, for it is quite out of touch with those kinds of knowledge (in the common non-Lockean sense of that word) with which we are all acquainted. But a careful reading of Book IV will nevertheless reveal points of great philosophical importance scattered here and there as unregarded ancillaries to his main argument. For example, in introducing his discussion of our knowledge of existence, he makes by the way a point which has become a truism, though a very important one, in contemporary philosophy. "Universal propositions of whose truth and falsehood we can have certain knowledge, concern not existence; and further, that all particular affirmations . . . are only concerning existence; they declaring only the accidental union or separation of ideas in things existing which, in their abstract natures, have no known necessary union, or repugnancy."[70] These remarks show a much better insight into the problems of knowledge than his official doctrine reveals.

Again, in illustrating his account of knowing, meager though his illustrations are, he makes some attempt at a classification of logically distinct kinds of proposition. This again is an enterprise which in recent philosophy has become of paramount importance. Lastly, we find at the end of the book[71] an excellent discussion of the relations between reason and religious faith, so good indeed, and in his day so bold, that it is a landmark in the history of this thorny topic. These points, though incidental to Locke's main purpose, are of lasting importance and are the only parts of the last book of the *Essay* which give it any philosophical value. Apart from these, it is the first three books that have made a permanent impact on European thought and have more than justified Locke's own modest view of his own work. "It is ambition enough to be employed as an under-labourer in clearing the ground a little, and removing some of the rubbish which lies in the way to knowledge."[72] He did indeed clear the ground for his successors in the British empirical tradition. Without Locke's work, that of Berkeley, Hume, Mill, Russell, and Moore would have looked very different.

13

Leibniz

RUTH L. SAW

BORN ON JUNE 21ST, 1646, Leibniz was the son of the professor of moral philosophy at the University of Leipzig. At the age of fifteen, Leibniz entered the University, graduating in 1663 with a thesis entitled *Disputatio Metaphysica de Principio Individui*. This work contained many of the ideas of his later writings in embryo. From 1663 to 1666 he studied jurisprudence at Jena and published a paper on legal education. This paper recommended him to the notice of the Archbishop of Mainz, who thereupon took him into his service. Sent to Paris on a mission to Louis XIV, Leibniz did not succeed in seeing the king, but in a stay of four years he made the acquaintance of Malebranche, the French philosopher; Arnauld, the French Jansenist philosopher and theologian; Huyghens, the famous Dutch physicist; and Tschirnhaus, a German count of scientific tastes who was a correspondent of Spinoza's. Leibniz also invented a calculating machine which was an improvement upon Pascal's machine in that it could extract roots, multiply, and divide as well as add and subtract. One of the purposes of Leibniz's visit to Paris was to deflect the military ambitions of Louis XIV from Europe to Egypt. He had prepared a scheme for the invasion of Egypt which had interested Louis sufficiently to cause him to summon Leibniz to Paris to explain it. Though Leibniz never actually appeared at the French court, the plan remained in the archives, and it was so well conceived in every detail that historians have speculated, entirely upon internal evidence, whether it were not seen by Napoleon and taken as the basis for his own invasion of Egypt.

In 1673, Leibniz visited London, met the famous English chemist Boyle, and Oldenburg, a German who became secretary of the Royal Society and who was a friend and correspondent of Spinoza. In that year Leibniz demonstrated his calculating machine to the Royal Society, which thereupon elected him to membership. In 1676, the Archbishop of Mainz died, and in default of work more suited to his tastes and abilities, Leibniz became librarian to the Duke of Brunswick at Hanover. On his way to Hanover, Leibniz spent a month at Amsterdam, reading everything of Spinoza's which Spinoza could be persuaded to let out of his hands. Finally he was allowed to meet Spinoza, and he discussed with him those parts of his writings which he had been allowed to read. This was his last personal contact with fellow philosophers. From this time till his death he was at Hanover, traveling abroad only in connection with his work on a history of the House of Brunswick. He had to be content with the exchange of letters and articles with fellow philosophers and mathematicians.

In his later years, Leibniz was involved in a controversy with the friends of Newton as to the authorship of the infinitesimal calculus. There is no doubt that both Newton and Leibniz were working on the calculus during the same period. It also seems clear that there was nothing unlikely in its simultaneous and independent discovery. Many other mathematicians were working upon related ideas at that time. Further, there is no doubt that Leibniz's notation was more convenient than that of Newton: in fact, it is still in use.

Leibniz was similarly unfortunate in obtaining recognition for his original work in logic. In our day, he is largely valued for his original work on symbolic logic, but it was not until this century that it became known. His discoveries had to be made over again while his work lay buried in masses of manuscripts in the Royal Library at Hanover. Leibniz died in a similar state of neglect. George I had refused to allow him to come to England on the removal there of the court, telling him to attend to his duties as librarian. When Leibniz died in 1716, not a single member of the court of Hanover followed his body to the grave. The Academy of Berlin, of which Leibniz was founder and first President, ignored his death, as did the Royal Society of London. The studied neglect of 1716 has given place to the admiration of the twentieth century for a man of originality and insight, with great capacity for the detailed working out of large and new ideas.

LEIBNIZ WAS A FIRST-CLASS mathematician and scientist, sharing with Newton the honor of having discovered the infinitesimal calculus and contributing the concept of kinetic energy to mechanics. He was also an excellent philosopher whose metaphysical system is of peculiar interest to our generation in that it can be interpreted as a system of logical doctrines. Indeed, some commentators claim that its only validity lies in this interpretation, but Leibniz would not have accepted this view. He thought his metaphysical conclusions to be of great importance not only to theology and moral theory, but also to science. Moreover, his basic positions arose in the course of his scientific experimentation and as a result of the general overhaul of the concepts of space, time, motion, and matter necessitated by the "new science" of Galileo, Newton, Kepler, Descartes, and Huyghens. To a lesser degree, and to Leibniz alone among philosophers, the discoveries of biologists such as Swammerdam and Malpighi presented themselves as having important bearings upon the nature of the ultimate elements of the universe. Leibniz, then, as a philosopher, did not indulge in wild speculation, and his view of the constituents of the universe as nonextended, nonmaterial bearers of energy, engaging in no transactions with one another, was carefully and exactly related to his scientific work and shown to be demanded by mechanical principles, as well as by metaphysics and theology. He believed that his "new principle, pre-established harmony," was necessitated by and "proved" in all the disciplines with which he was concerned. Fellow scientists too, producing competing "world pictures," disputed with one another their relative merits on moral and theological as well as on scientific grounds. The famous Leibniz-Clarke correspondence originated typically, in a letter to Queen Caroline, in which

Leibniz attributed the decay of natural religion in England to the prevalence of the Newtonian philosophy. Queen Caroline wished the issue to be argued to a conclusion and Clarke undertook the defense of the Newtonian universe. Much of the dispute turned upon the reasonableness of the two universes and their consequent fittingness to be the creation of a wise and benevolent Deity. These considerations seemed to both disputants to be of equal importance with the scientific arguments about the meaning of force, velocity, mass, acceleration, and so on.

Metaphysics of Substance

IN formulating the laws of motion, a scientist has to determine what it is that can be most conveniently said to move, what is the agency, and what the movement is "in." If not an explicit part of his statement, there will be implicit in it views as to the nature of these fundamental entities. The possibilities are, first, that atoms of matter, extended yet indivisible, move through the void, and that motion is imparted to the atoms by contact with one another. Secondly, that nonextended elements may exert force on one another without contact and set up motion in the void. Thirdly, the Cartesian hypothesis, that material substance is essentially extended, material bodies being somehow engendered out of extension. Leibniz rejects all these possibilities, or rather, insists that they are not possibilities, in that they all contain manifest absurdities. He tells us that in his youth he was much attracted by the theory of atoms and the void, but that his scientific and metaphysical studies had convinced him that both these notions were absurdities, as is the notion of action at a distance. This was one of his chief objections to the Newtonian mechanics, but he gives no argument to demonstrate the impossibility of action at a distance. His fundamental objection to all these views is, however, that they all presuppose that motion is somehow imparted to an otherwise inert substance. Out of these objections emerges his own view of the ultimate entities as essentially active, nonextended, not *in* any sort of medium, not even in space, and as therefore passing through their changes entirely in terms of their own nature. The changes of these beings, though not causally interconnected, are correlated with one another in an orderly manner. In short, Leibniz assumes the existence of an external world, the *fact* of its existence revealed by sense perception, and its *nature* by the development of mathematical systems disclosing the nature of force, matter, space, time, and motion and their relation to the "real beings." Leibniz calls these real beings Monads, i.e. "simple substances without parts and without windows through which anything could come in or go out."[1]

ATOMS OF MATTER ARE ABSURDITIES

An atom of matter is presumably reached by a process of division. It is either the end of the process or not. If it is the end, it is the smallest possible particle of matter and it can be no further divided; but then it is not extended, and so *not* a particle of matter. If it is not the end, then it can be further divided, and so it is not the smallest particle of matter. The simple elements, then, cannot be described in spatial terms, and we must seek some other way of speaking of them. Even if atoms of matter were possible, they could not serve as the elements in the laws of motion. An atom whose only essential was extension could not resist impact. It would move endlessly before a moving force, and it would be no more difficult to move a large than a small body. But we know that motion is lost on impact and that more force is needed to move a large than a small body. The elements, then, must be such as to resist impact, that is to say, their essential property must be force, not extension. The elements must have at least inertia by which they persist in their own places, resisting equally forces which seek to move or to penetrate them.

THE VOID, OR EMPTY SPACE, AND EMPTY TIME, ARE ABSURDITIES

Leibniz always speaks as though atoms and the void are essentially connected, presumably because if atoms are to move they must move through a nonresisting medium. However, he opposes Newtonian absolute space with specific arguments, one frankly theological, the other directed toward the irrationality of supposing empty space and time, and so only indirectly theological. The first turns on Leibniz's conception of "metaphysical perfection"

and on his view that the more existence, the better. Metaphysical is contrasted with moral perfection. It is not morally better that a thing should be complete, or "perfect," but in a sense it is better that seeds should germinate and reach maturity. In that sense, it is better that all possibilities of existence should be fulfilled. If there were empty space, it would mean that a wise and benevolent being had missed the opportunity to "place" beings in it, which is absurd. (Whether this is a logical absurdity raises a difficult problem which must be discussed later.) The second argument invokes the principles of sufficient reason and the identity of indiscernibles. For every state of affairs, there is a sufficient reason why it is thus and not otherwise. Now suppose absolute space and a rational being deciding to place the material universe in it. To place it here rather than there, facing this way rather than that, is to contemplate states of affairs which are "indiscernible" and so identical. In choosing one of these pairs of alternatives, God would be acting without a reason. In fact, there is no choice. The same argument applies to empty time. In creating the universe earlier rather than later, God would again be acting without a reason. This argument occurs in Leibniz's third letter to Clarke. Clarke agrees that these several states of affairs are indiscernible, but maintains that God needs no reason for his acts other than his will. Leibniz is here extending the meaning of "sufficient reason"; it is not merely a cause, but a final cause, and moreover, a final cause which has the best as its end. Absolute space and time would not only make it impossible for the creation of the universe to be a rational act; it would challenge one who desires the best, immediately to fill it completely. We shall see later that it is not only in relation to the acts of God that Leibniz so interprets "sufficient reason." The only true cause in operation is final cause, and all Monads direct their activity toward the best.

The same arguments present a further objection to atoms. They too would be indiscernible, so that for them to change places would be no change, and the same must be said of extension. Either it is different in parts and then it is not simple extension, or it is homogeneous throughout, and then it offers no possibility of rational arrangement of its parts. However, the strongest objection which Leibniz feels to any theory of matter as extension or as made up of extended units is the impossibility of conceiving of the imparting of energy to a substance which is in itself inert. Gravitation he describes as a perpetual miracle, involving a metaphysical absurdity and a contradiction of the laws of motion. Finally, the principle of continuity makes it extremely unsatisfactory to think of the process of division as culminating in elements different in kind from that which is divided. Division of the extended cannot produce an entity which is essentially indivisible, nor could the essentially indivisible make up extension. Moreover, unity cannot belong to an extended body which is a mere aggregate of parts. Unity can belong only to an "entelechy," a center of activity, such as a mind. It is not too much to say that of all the beings we know, a mind in its unity and activity is most like a Monad.

Leibniz, then, is rejecting space, time, and matter as providing categories in terms of which the ultimate entities may be described. He does his job as a metaphysician properly, however, by relating these categories to the real properties of the Monads. Space, time, and matter are *phenomena bene fundata*, "phenomena" in that spatial and temporal categories are unsuitably applied to the Monads, "well founded" in that they may be systematically connected with properties of the Monads. It is suitable to speak of points, straight lines, and instants in some contexts, and also to speak of causal interaction among bodies in some contexts. But in the metaphysical context, it is suitable to speak of the Monads as differing only in the degree to which they possess the only essential property of Monads, namely, in the degree to which they possess energy. The Monads form a series in which no term can be interpolated between any two terms, each one differing from the terms next to it in an infinitely small degree. The compactness of the series of Monads — the *plenum* — is the real counterpart of the continuity of space, the infinite number of real beings constituting its infinite divisibility, or rather, its actual infinite division. Matter is not only infinitely divisible; it is infinitely divided. Its elements, however, are neither atoms nor mathematical points but actual entities. Points, atoms, instants are all "philosophers' myths." A mathematical point is a possible point of view. All points of view are actually occupied, but a possible point of view is a point of view abstractly considered. Leibniz, then, has managed to accommodate both continuity and divisibility in his system, and when we go on to consider the type of activity belonging to Monads, we shall see that continuity is reinforced.

The activity of Monads is "perception," that of more fully active Monads, whose perception is conscious, being called "apperception." Perception is not, in the ordinary sense, *of* external beings. It is an active process of unfolding its own nature in each Monad and it belongs to Monads of all grades of activity. This was not an entirely strange use of the word in the seventeenth century. The sunflower turning toward the sun, the iron moving toward the lodestone, were both described as cases of perception in the sense that they were both cases of orderly change in the neighborhood of the "perceived" body. This perceiving is directed toward the future, so that Monads are said also to possess "appetition." Again, in the case of highly active Monads, where appetition is conscious, we may speak of desire and purpose. The least active of the Monads, whose perception is dull and confused, differ from high

grade Monads only in degree. The difference in degree marks out three grades of Monad, "bare" Monads, souls, and spirits. Bare Monads would be inert matter if there were any such thing, and in aggregates, they constitute "inanimate" beings such as rocks and stones. We can dimly imagine what is their state of confused perception and appetition when we awaken from a deep, dreamless sleep or from a swoon. Animals, like men, can learn by experience and have a relatively high degree of clearness of perception. These are "souls," but men are "spirits," in that their memories are conscious and that they have knowledge by reason of the eternal truths. Malpighi and Swammerdam, who by the use of the improved microscope had discovered a world of ever smaller living beings, not only in living, but in what had hitherto been described as inanimate matter, spoke of the "living infinite," and described themselves as "almost swooning" before the vision. Leibniz took their discoveries as confirming his hypothesis of the whole universe as a vast concourse of living atoms. Swammerdam had further discovered that in an embryonic grub was its offspring in embryo, so that the notion of a living atom containing its future enfolded in itself seemed to be a fact as well as a metaphysical necessity.

No Monad is entirely without force, and no Monad is entirely without passivity, except the chief Monad, God. The essential passivity of every created Monad is "prime matter," "secondary matter," the "mass" of mechanics, belonging to aggregates of Monads. The Monads, being simple, can be destroyed only by annihilation and come into being only by creation, but aggregates of Monads are continually forming, being reinforced by the joining of other Monads to the aggregate, losing some Monads, and sometimes entirely disintegrating. These are the changes of bodies in the phenomenal world, and they are the appearances of the real changes within each Monad making up the aggregate. This must be so since change is a fact and the Monads cannot interact.

True unity belongs to each Monad, which is one in that it is a centre of activity, but a kind of unity is conferred upon aggregates by there being a dominant Monad in each aggregate. Organic unity is the most complete in that the dominant Monad is a soul or spirit more clearly mirroring in its own changes the changes of all the other Monads. It is dominant in the sense not that its changes *determine* the changes in the other Monads but that they *explain* these changes. The most complete example of such dominance is the relation of the human mind to its body. Changes of conscious perception are correlated with changes of sensitive organs and neural tissue, but since the mind is more active than the parts of its body, it is more suitable to speak of the mind as dominant.

We must now show how self-existent beings, each one of which is unfolding its changes according to its own inner principle, can be said to "mirror" the changes of other Monads. First, however, we must show why Leibniz thinks that the Monads do so mirror one another's changes. Put shortly, Leibniz assumes as "morally certain," though not provable, that we sensibly perceive the external world. But since he has shown that the Monads cannot interact, the *fact* of perception necessitates the harmonious unfolding of the states of each Monad with every other. This is his principle of pre-established harmony, and it gives the reason why we may safely speak of perceiving the world and at the same time believe that the Monads have no windows. Leibniz uses the analogy of two choirs singing from identical scores. In listening to one choir, we know what we should hear if we were listening to the other, though there is no interaction between them. Similarly, if there were two clocks, each keeping good time, that is to say, each unfolding its changes according to its own principle of uniform motion of its parts, we could read off the time registered by either from the other. Neither choir nor clock acts upon the other choir or clock, but each "mirrors" the changes of the other. The universe is such a system of parts in perfect mutual adaptation; granted perfect clearness of perception, the state of the whole universe could be read off from any one Monad. God alone possesses such clarity, and the whole universe mirrors His state. All the Monads mirror in their varying degrees the chief Monad, and the sole complete cause is God's purpose in creating this, the best of all possible universes. Built into it are the finite purposes of lesser beings and the adaptation to these purposes of the changes of less active beings.

Pre-established harmony thus solves the problem of the relation between thinking and extended substance, to speak in Cartesian terms. There is not the perpetual miracle of the action of one substance on another alien substance, but the eternal mutual mirroring of all substances. God's action upon the world, the relation of minds and bodies in perception and movement, are simply examples of the general mirroring. We are not confronted with a constant impossibility, the action of a substance whose whole essence consists in thinking upon a substance whose whole activity consists in extension, but with a relationship of mutual adaptation. Far from an irrationality, the relationship supplies the very condition of rational thinking about the world.

The principle of pre-established harmony also enables Leibniz to give an account of space in his own terms. Space is not only that in which bodies appear to move, the "well-ordered" appearance of togetherness of bodies; it is also that which gives rise to the appearance of togetherness. It is not the "real" vast expanse in which Newtonian particles absolutely move, but it is something which gives rise to this description of it. Space, says Leibniz, is "the order of possible co-existences."[2] Space "at an instant" is simply the fact of the vast concourse of Monads,

the state of each one in mutual adaptation to the state of every other. Just as we may abstract from the conceptual picture of Newton's universe a system of possible positions, so we may abstract from the metaphysical picture of the "real" universe of Monads the momentary togetherness of their states. The difference between the two pictures is that in the Newtonian, position is seen as *mere* position; in the Leibnizian, position, that is to say, phenomenal nearness and distance, must be seen as the appearance of mutual mirroring. "*Place* is that which we say is the same to A and to B, when the relation of the coexistence of B with C, E, F, G, etc. agrees perfectly with the relation of the coexistence which A had with the same C, E, F, G, etc., supposing there has been no cause of change in C, E, F, G, etc."[3] At first sight, this appears a perfectly ordinary account of change of position. A has moved away from C, E, F, and G, and B has moved into A's place. The only point which Leibniz seems to be making is the denial that "place" can be defined in absolute terms, apart from a relation to other bodies. Furthermore, it might be thought that in the phrase "supposing there has been no cause of change in C, E, F, G, etc." Leibniz is forgetting his own account of the Monads. It could not be true in the system of Monads that C, E, F, G, etc., remained unchanged while A and B changed places in relation to them. The above definition, however, stands at the level of scientific discourse: even at this level, it is not true that particles take up absolute positions, and at the level of metaphysical discourse, when we are speaking about the real beings, we must show the counterpart of the scientific definition. The position which A "had," and which B now has, cannot be an accident of A or of B. It is unthinkable that A should leave behind one of its accidents for B to assume. Change of position is the appearance of change taking place in the Monads. If A and B were Monads, then "A is near B and distant from C" means that A mirrors B more clearly than it mirrors C. If I take your place near the fire, we could make a diagram in which the abstract positions were noted. The concrete case is that I am now becoming warmer while you become cooler. Real beings cannot *merely* change places.

The notion that spatial relations may be the appearance of properties of the elements appearing to be in the spatial relations is not opposed to common sense. A very ordinary example is that of a crossword puzzle, which many people would describe as a rectangle constituted in a certain way. To take a very simple example: There is a word meaning "snake" whose first letter is the first letter of a word which is the name of a tree, the second letter of the first word being the first letter of a word meaning "ocean," and the second letter of the second word being the first letter of a word meaning "bishopric," and so on. How much simpler to stick to a diagram and number the words as follows:

```
(1) (2) (3)
 A   S   P    1 across — SNAKE        1 down TREE
(4)
 S   E   E    4 across — BISHOPRIC  2 down OCEAN
(5)
 H   A   G    5 across — UGLY OLD WOMAN
                                     3 down — PIN
```

The real properties of the interconnecting words is the interlocking of the letters, but there is a sense in which a square is the "well-founded" appearance of this set of related entities. It would fall naturally into no other shape.

We spoke above of "space at an instant" and said that it was an abstraction. The reality is the system of changing Monads considered from the point of view of their mutual adaptation. It is an abstraction in that a "state" of a Monad is passing continuously into its next state according to its own principle, and the mutual adaptation will hold among the whole series of states of every Monad. Time, again, is not that "in" which things happen, it is "the order of possibilities which are inconsistent but connected."[4] If state S of Monad A is succeeded by S', then time is the order of $S, S', S'' \ldots$, according to a principle. We might think of space as a kind of logical space, such as is engendered by thinking of the series of natural numbers as coexistent, and time as engendered by thinking of each of the natural numbers as the first term in another series, say, perhaps, of a series in geometrical progression. For the continuity of space and time, we have the compactness of the series, for their infinite divisibility, we have the separate and distinct existence of the members of the series. For the actual systems of Monads we have the further continuity of the overlapping points of view and their appetition, which holds together the successive states. The mathematical concepts of space, points, time, instants, are *entia rationis*, our own constructions based on the true *plenum* of the system of Monads.

A further feature of the system of Monads must be noticed. No more than in an arithmetical series may two members occupy the same position. To think of the possibility of there being two number sevens would be no more absurd than to think of the possibility of there being two Monads with the same point of view. The absurdity is the same in the two cases, since in both the number series and in the series of Monads the nature of the members of the series is determined by their position. This is expressed in Leibniz's famous principle of the identity of indiscernibles, according to which if two beings are exactly alike in quality, that is to say are "indiscernible" from one another, they are not two things but one. "To suppose two indiscernible things is to suppose the same thing under two names."[5] This is one of the consequences of the unreality of space. If things are two in number but identical in quality, it is easy to explain this by saying that they are in different places, but for Leibniz,

to be in a different place is to mirror the universe from a different point of view, that is, to be essentially different in quality. Leibniz is here making a determined attempt to solve the problem of individuation. Granted the essential connection of persons with a material body, and a public system of spatial relations, the problem is relatively easy. We may refer to individuals unambiguously by using uniquely referring expressions such as "this," together with gestures, or by a system of coordinates with reference to a common point of origin. An individual is then uniquely determined as occupying a uniquely determined position, either by reference to the person making the determination or to an agreed point. We assume that two bodies cannot be in the same place. If, then, A is at point P' and B at point P'', there is no question of their being identical with one another, however many features they share in common. It is logically possible that A and B have *all* their properties in common and remain distinct beings. Leibniz, too, says that it is abstractly possible that two beings have exactly similar properties and are separate beings, but it is instructive to see the difference in the meaning of "possible" in the two cases. The first meaning is that there would be no self-contradiction in stating that there were two beings, A and B, each completely described as possessing properties p, q, and r (p, q, and r being absolutely specific). In fact, it is being said that two such beings could exist in the same universe. When Leibniz says that it is abstractly possible that two such beings might exist, he means that we can form the concept of A as being p, q, r and B as being p, q, r. We could then go on to think of their coexistence. Our ignorance of the total state of affairs prevents us from seeing their incompatibility, as ignorance might prevent us from seeing the incompatibility of a figure's having five angles and those angles adding up to five right angles. In fact, A and B could not exist together. To complete the argument, Leibniz adds that a good and wise being would not make a universe in a manner so wasteful of the opportunities of variety.

It is often objected that this is to make the principle of the identity of indiscernibles a theological rather than a logical principle. We may grant that God has a complete concept of each Monad; while they remain concepts, identity of indiscernibles keeps its character as a logical principle. But then it is not about the actual world — it is a system of universals. If Leibniz is claiming that the Monads are particulars, then the reason that there are no two identical Monads is theological. We are now speaking about this actual world but at the cost of making the identity of indiscernibles a reason for God's act in creating this world. To pursue our earlier metaphor, the series of Monads is not like the number series but a number*ed* series. The number series is a conceptual system, the members of which are so defined that it would be absurd to suppose the possibility of two identical members. It would not be absurd to suppose that a number*ed* series might have two members with the same number, as when competitors tie in a race or are bracketed equal in a list of merit. To say *then* that there cannot be two indiscernible beings is to make a remark about God's purposes and their fulfillment in this actual world. In effect, it is being said that uniqueness of position or point of view can be guaranteed only in a spatial world and only of material entities. It is logically possible that there should be many occupants of a Leibnizian point of view, and it is a sheer matter of fact, if it is a fact, that there is only one such occupant. Leibniz might here invoke the principle of sufficient reason. If it were indeed possible to have many occupants of a point of view, there would be no sufficient reason why there should be two, three, four, or any number. If sufficient reason is a theological principle, it would not help Leibniz here, but it is, for Leibniz, the general condition not only for the nature of the world but a condition for our knowledge of it. The identity of indiscernibles makes it possible for sufficient reason to be applied. There is a sufficient reason why there should be one occupant of each point of view, namely that there should be the greatest amount of variety in the world. If there were two occupants, one of them would have been created without a sufficient reason, for its existence would not increase the amount of variety in the world.

Besides the arguments from the nature of force, Leibniz has another kind of argument leading to the conclusion that the real beings cannot interact, and that consequently their whole history is enfolded in each real being. In a letter to Arnauld, Leibniz says: "I expected that the argument drawn from the general nature of propositions would make some impression on your mind; but I confess also that few children are capable of appreciating such abstract truths, and that perhaps no one but you would have so easily perceived its truth." The argument from the general nature of propositions appears in the *Discourse on Metaphysics*, originally written in outline for Arnauld. It is generally believed that this logical argument constitutes the real grounds for Leibniz's metaphysical system, but it is more likely, in my opinion, that the metaphysico-scientific and the logical arguments were seen by Leibniz as reinforcing one another. In fact, Leibniz believed that the scientific discoveries of the seventeenth century, both his own and those of other people, all came together to "prove" his hypothesis of a vast concourse of Monads in pre-established harmony. The infinitesimal calculus itself is based on the possibility and usefulness of treating a finite amount as equivalent to the sum of an infinite number of infinitesimal amounts, and the continued improvement in the microscope led biologists to believe not only that minute differences among bodies are lost to large perception but that ever more minute differences were there to be revealed.

Logic, Language, and Metaphysics

THE abstract truths about the general nature of propositions were that every proposition is reducible to a proposition in which a property is attributed to a subject and that in every true proposition the subject contains its predicate. The first truth involves the denial that any proposition is ultimately relational in form; the second appears to deny that there are any contingently true propositions. But this problem must be left for fuller treatment in connection with the principle of contradiction. In considering the first truth, we must first examine the notion of a proposition's having a "true" or "ultimate" form. It is connected with a theory of meaning and truth which had hardly been disputed from the time of Aristotle. The theory of meaning, put shortly, is that the model of the meaning of words is naming, and that the ideal is "one name, one thing," to which Leibniz appears to add, "one thing, one name." The way the names are put together shows the way the things are put together, so that propositions "mean" by picturing the facts. Those propositions are true which picture actual states of affairs, or "correspond" to the facts, "or else" says Leibniz, "I do not know what truth means." There are simple names for simple things and complex names for complex things, and the complex names will show the structure of the things they name, as, for instance, H_2SO_4 shows the structure of sulphuric acid. The theory of simple and complex names belongs to Leibniz's search for a "universal characteristic" and will be examined later. It had to be mentioned here because put with the doctrine that every true proposition has a subject which contains its predicate, it implies that no true proposition can have a simple subject unless it is a statement of identity, A is A.

In everyday discourse, it is clear that many statements do not picture the facts in the sense described above. If the facts are such as to be pictured by statements attributing a predicate to a subject, then it is clear that most of our statements obscure the facts. All that the *facts* need is a statement to the effect that all or some things of a certain kind do or do not possess a given property, or that a given thing does or does not possess a given property. The required forms, then, are *All A is B, No A is B, Some A is B, Some A is not B, This A is B, This A is not B*. For emphasis or for rhetorical reasons, for elegance, we use devices such as inversion, phrases such as "none but," "only," "The *A*," "An *A*," when we mean "All *A*'s," and so on. And to "reduce to logical form" is to restate one such statement so that it simply shows what is being said, either that all or no *A*'s are *B*, and so on. Traditional logicians have accepted such a doctrine with minor criticisms, but contemporary logicians have disputed the whole doctrine, on the grounds that people mean what they say, and that if they say "None but the brave deserve the fair," that is what they meant to say, and not that "No nonbrave person is a deserver of the fair." They add, however, that there is no reason that we should not accept the restatement as yielding a "representative expression" for the purposes of the logical development of a symbolic system. The test whether or not it is a fair representation is supplied by a comparison of the logical powers of the two expressions. This position follows from a rejection of the doctrine of meaning and truth outlined above. The passage from the first position to the second is to be seen most interestingly in the development of Wittgenstein's account of meaning from the *Tractatus Logico-Philosophicus* to the *Philosophical Investigations*.

Whatever logicians may feel about this kind of reduction to logical form, there is no doubt whatever that with a few exceptions logicians reject the reduction of relational propositions to the subject-predicate form. Leibniz has a double reason for his insistence on the necessity for this reduction. On the one hand, there are no relationships among the real beings, so that a relational proposition could not picture the facts. On the other hand, he believes that the logical status of relations is so dubious that relational expressions cannot possibly be ultimate. He says:

> The ratio or proportion between two lines L and M may be conceived in three several ways: as a ratio of the greater L to the lesser M; as a ratio of the lesser M to the greater L; and lastly, as something abstracted from both, that is, as the ratio between L and M, without considering which is the antecedent, or which the consequent; which the subject, and which the object. . . . In the first way of considering them, L the greater is the subject, in the second, M the lesser is the subject of that accident which philosophers call *relation* or *ratio*. But which of them will be the subject, in the third way of considering them? It cannot be said that both of them, L and M together are the subject of such an accident; for if so, we should have an accident in two subjects, with one leg in one, and the other in the other; which is contrary to the notion of accidents. Therefore we must say that this relation, in this third way of considering it, is indeed *out of* the subjects; but being neither a substance nor an accident, it must be a mere ideal thing, the consideration of which is nevertheless useful.[6]

In short, relations must be treated either as properties of the "related" terms or as "mere ideal entities."

We have seen how Leibniz translated spatio-temporal relations into properties but he treats propositions of number as asserting "mere ideal" relationships. Propositions of number assert mere aggregates, the unity of which is conferred upon them by their being perceived together. To assert that there are twelve apostles is to assert that Peter is an apostle and Mark is an apostle and so on, and that we are considering the twelve men together in connection with their property of being apostles. This seems to leave the relation of coexistence as real at least, but coexistence alone among relationships seems to leave its terms unaffected and so not to fall under Leibniz's criticism. To be *one of the twelve apostles* is either different from being an apostle or it is not. If it is different, then the difference can be expressed in terms of properties of each apostle; if it is not different, then it can be regarded as conferred upon the group by joint perception and assertion. God certainly perceives the whole concourse of Monads as coexisting, and if he is not to perceive an illusion, coexistence must be a fact. But God also perceives the Monads as possessing the real properties which give rise to the appearance of all other relationships. He perceives each Monad as in harmony with every other, each with its history enfolded in it, and in this perception he is knowing the reality of the phenomenal system of spatio-temporal and interacting events.

Leibniz also gives examples of the reduction to the subject-predicate form of relational propositions in everyday discourse. "Paris loves Helen" is better expressed in the form "Paris is the lover of Helen," or better still, in the form "In so far as Helen is beloved, Paris is loving," since this expresses the correlation between "loving" and "beloved." Leibniz defines "love" as follows: "*A* loves *B* equals *A* rejoices in *B*'s welfare." "Rejoicing in *B*'s welfare" is then a property of *A*, and like any other property, but no more than any other property, demands adaptation in another object. If *A* is warm, then a warming agent is presupposed "at hand." If *A* loves *B*, then the following states are presupposed in *A* and *B*: *B* is happy, *A* is aware that *B* is happy and rejoices in that knowledge. This is not to leave a relation as ultimate. *A*'s awareness of *B*'s happiness is a state of *A* coexistent with a state of *B* and in pre-established harmony with it. If we ask whether *A* could mistakenly believe that *B* was happy, rejoice in his illusion, and still be loving *B*, the answer is that in mistakenly thinking that *B* was happy, he is in a state of confused perception, i.e., in a state of relative passivity, and could be truly said neither to know nor to love. The state of knowledge is itself a non-relational state, and so, literally, not knowledge *of*. With clear thinking, however, we have reached knowledge of the principle of pre-established harmony; we know when we have clear ideas, and we know that they are correlated with the true states of other beings. We know, therefore, and know that we know.

Leibniz's doctrine that propositions picture the facts, and that true propositions are such that the predicate is contained in the subject, leads to the belief that propositions in their proper form are transparently true and that false propositions are manifestly absurd. This is the foundation for his belief in the importance of discovering a "characteristic," a language which would be fitted to display the truth of true propositions. If we allow ourselves to use names which appear simple, and so cover up the complexity of the thing named, we shall be able to utter absurdities without knowing it. We could say, for example, without manifest absurdity, that sulphuric acid does not contain hydrogen; we could not say H_2SO_4 does not contain H. Conversely, we can see at a glance the truth, even the necessary truth, of the proposition "H_2SO_4 contains H." This view was connected with Leibniz's life-long search for a "universal characteristic" — a method of recording truths so that they would be accessible to scientists of any nationality. Leibniz was not only a scientist but a man with a passion for promoting the growth of knowledge. He was in correspondence with many of the rulers of Europe and hoped to induce them to establish centers of learning in their capitals, actually succeeding in getting an academy set up in Berlin. He was appalled by the spectacle of solitary scientists wasting time and energy working at problems already solved because the solutions had been stated in forms inaccessible to them. Moreover, scientists might work in a manner wasteful of their energies for want of a system of signs designed to make calculation easy. Leibniz himself had invented an extremely satisfactory notation for the infinitesimal calculus, a notation which is still in use. English scientists for some time used the much less efficient notation invented by Newton, and this was probably only one example of wasted energy. The first requirement of cooperation among scientists was, Leibniz considered, the compiling of an encyclopedia of all knowledge up to date, but here Leibniz fell into an indecision which lasted for the rest of his life. If we were to begin with the compiling of the encyclopedia without having first perfected our characteristic, we shall waste time — the job will have to be done over again. On the other hand, in the very act of perfecting our notation, we shall make further discoveries of implications hidden by the unsuitable language, so that the truths to be recorded will change while we perfect our method of recording them. Leibniz suffered from a similar indecision in working at his "universal characteristic" — in fact, he had inconsistent aims. His first attempts were at a symbolism which was completely formal, but he wished his method to be extended to moral and theological reasoning. In this connection he pointed out the dangers of "blind reasoning," that is to say, reasoning which might be carried out in a very efficient manner but hide from the reasoner the import of his conclusions. Just as we reach a mathematical conclusion with simple satisfaction in its validity and elegance, so we might reach a

moral conclusion with the same simple satisfaction. At this stage, Leibniz played with the notion of using iconic symbols, so that their very look would make an appeal to the will of the person using them. He corresponded with missionaries in many parts of the world, especially in China, and is given credit by Max Müller for having initiated the empirical study of languages. The difficulty with such symbols as the Chinese characters, or the word signs of ancient Egypt, is just that they do not lend themselves to symbolic development. The very quality of signs which leads to "blind reasoning" is the quality which fits them for calculation. To suggest that one kind of sign is suited to reasoning in science and another kind to reasoning in morals is to reject a position which Leibniz was very anxious to maintain, that calculation is the one sure method of reaching sound conclusions and that *any* truths may be so expressed as to lend themselves to calculation. He formulated a few moral definitions, and looked forward to the time when the science would be complete and men could say when faced with a moral problem: "Come, sit down and let us calculate."

Leibniz's attempts to invent a formal system of signs were based on the following assumptions:

1. All concepts are resolvable into simple concepts by a process analogous to finding the prime factors of numbers.
2. All complex concepts may be built up by taking the simples in order (the "combinatory art").
3. There are a small number of simple ideas, but they engender a multitude, thanks to the combinatory art.
4. Simple ideas are suitably represented by simple signs, complex by complex signs. The complex sign will be the definition of the complex concept.
5. Reasoning consists in uncovering all the relations in which the simples stand to one another.

His first idea was to let the simples be represented by the letters of the alphabet and their multiplication represent the composition of concepts. In this part of his work, he formulated many of the axioms of modern formal logic, but since his work on logic was not published till many years later, his discoveries had to be made over gain. He showed that the fundamental notions were common to algebra and a science of the combination of properties; for example, the axiom $a \times (b+c) = ab+ac$ is exemplified if a and b represent numbers or properties. His second plan was to let prime numbers represent simples and, again, multiplication their combinations. A true statement would then consist in an assertion that a number had certain factors. Leibniz uses the example of the statement "Man is a rational animal," without discussing whether "rational" and "animal" are simples or not. If 3 represents "rational" and 2 "animal," then "Man is a rational animal" would appear as $6 = 3 \times 2$. A false statement appears as the absurdity of asserting of a number that it does not contain one of its factors.

To this method of analysis, Leibniz added his "combinatory art," which he called a method of invention. This consists in a method for setting out all the possible combinations of the simples, so that if it were possible to compile a list of all the simple ideas, we should have set out in a table all the possible things there might be in the world. Suppose that there are five simple ideas, represented by *A*, *B*, *C*, *D*, *E*. This would be the table of all possible things:

A	*AB*	*ABC*	*ABCD*	*ABCDE*
	AC	*ACD*	*ABCE*	
	AD	*ADE*	*ABDE*	
	AE	*ABD*	*ACDE*	
		ACE		
		ABE		
B	*BC*	*BCD*	*BCDE*	
	BD	*BCE*		
	BE	*BDE*		
C	*CD*	*CDE*		
	CE			
D	*DE*			
E				

If we give names to the complexes which kept the names of the component simples, we could read off from the name of a thing all its properties. It is clear, too, that somewhere within the table will be found the definition of any concept exemplified in our experience and that the table might suggest the existence of things we have not yet met. Not only can we read from the table all possible predicates of a given subject; we can also read all possible subjects for a given predicate.

Leibniz pursued one further scheme for a universal language. This was to extract by logical analysis from already existing languages simple ideas and the manner of expressing them and their combinations. He intended to make a rational grammar by simplifying and regularizing a combination of actual grammars. The irreducible terms were simple words, accepted figures of speech and phrases the sense of which, consecrated by usage, could not be rendered by grammatical analysis, such as proverbs. Next came the study of syntax, the ways of combining the irreducible terms. Inflections and particles were to be reduced to a minimum, and each particle was to have a unique meaning. There were to be no irregularities and no exceptions. Since a language would be needed for fixing the rules, Leibniz proposed to adopt Latin for the time, a regularized Latin. Leibniz did quite a lot of work on the regularizing of Latin, though he never reached the next stage of inventing the language the rules of which had been

stated in the "rational" Latin. Some examples of the changes he proposed were the abolishing of moods and the reduction of oblique cases to one. *Ut* and *quod* show by their own difference that they express knowledge and will, that which is and that which one wishes were so. To have a different mood is to duplicate the expression of the difference. He considered whether to retain the accusative or the genitive case, and decided in favor of the genitive. For other reasons, "Paris loves Helen" is better expressed as "Paris is the lover of Helen." He next turned his attention to verbs and pointed out, as against Aristotle, that many other parts of speech besides verbs can show time. By forming participles from verbs we can make adjectives and even nouns which express time. The true distinction between noun and verb is that a noun signifies an idea, the verb a proposition. What he seems to have had in mind was that all the "matter" which we wish to assert could be collected into one grand term, or into two terms one of which contained the other, and the verb is simply the sign that the assertion has been made. "Man is a rational animal" in the universal language would be a sign for "man" showing its formation from "rational" and "animal" with a sign of assertion: Man (rational, animal) is. The "is" has no tense; if we want to say: "Peter will come," we shall say "Peter (about to come) is." In fact, says Leibniz, all we really need for our language is one noun, *ens*, one verb, *est*, and everything else could go into the predicate. Our dictionary would consist of a list of words each expressing a simple idea, and a list of endings to form derivatives, *am-o*, *am-atus*, *am-abilis*, etc. Particles would then be added to show the ways of combining sentences. Presumably, *ens* functions as a variable taking as its arguments any one of our possible combinations of simples, the predicate consisting of the actual combination of simples in question. When we recall Leibniz's insistence that every proposition is of the subject-predicate form, we begin to question whether "predicate" is a suitable word at all for what he has in mind. Our statements begin to look much more like the assertion of the coexistence of properties at a point of view.

A further problem is raised by Leibniz's account of propositions. The combinatory art presupposes that all simple properties are compatible with one another. Leibniz supplies a proof that all *perfections* are compatible among themselves, and his definition of a perfection leads one to the conclusion that we are as a matter of fact not acquainted with any simple properties. The definition is: "I call a *perfection* every simple quality which is positive and absolute, and expresses without any limits whatever it does express."[7] The proof is:

Let there be such a proposition as

A and B are incompatible

(understanding by A and B two such simple

forms or perfections — the same holds if several are assumed at once), it is obvious that this cannot be proved without a resolution of one or both of the terms A and B; for otherwise their nature would not enter into the reasoning, and the incompatibility of any other things could be shown just as well as theirs. But (by hypothesis) they are irresolvable. Therefore this proposition cannot be proved concerning them.

But it could be proved concerning them if it were true, for it is not true *per se*; but all necessarily true propositions are either demonstrable, or known *per se*. Therefore this proposition is not necessarily true. In other words, since it is not necessary that A and B should not be in the same subject, they can therefore be in the same subject; and since the reasoning is the same as regards any other assumed qualities of the same kind, therefore all perfections are compatible.

This proof occurs in Leibniz's demonstration that the notion of the perfect being is a possible concept. By "positive and absolute, expressing without any limits whatever it does express," Leibniz is ruling out all properties the attribution of which entails the denial of other properties of the same subject, such as properties of color and shape, and such properties as size and duration which cannot be attributed without limit. "Largest number," "greatest size" are self-contradictory expressions, but goodness and wisdom may be attributed in the highest degree. To attribute redness to a subject is to rule out green, blue, etc., so that these are not our simples. The difficulty is to imagine what properties could be simple in the required sense. Leibniz speaks of qualities of color and shape as *relatively* simple, in that they are "simple only in relation to us (because we have not the means of analysing them in order to reach the elementary perceptions of which they are composed), like hot, cold, yellow, green."[8] They will therefore have to be defined by "explaining their cause." If Leibniz is here referring to his doctrine of *petites perceptions*, he is using "simple" in a different sense. His favorite example of complex perception is of hearing the sound of the waves. In reality, we are hearing a multiplicity of minute sounds. Each particle of water in its changes is mirrored separately in each minute part of the hearing organism, so that once again, the "real" simple quality is that belonging to each Monad, and our perception is bound to be confused. We can never distinguish in the large sound of the waves each separate and minute change of each particle mirrored in each separate and minute element of our nervous system. It seems, then, that we cannot be acquainted with simple properties, and that in our thinking we use definitions *as if* the elements were simple, and that the combinatory art provides a model for the combination of elements, even if we can never exemplify the simples entering into the combinations in our experience. The other

possibility is that Leibniz looked forward to the account of sense perception in terms of movements of the elements of things with the corresponding movements in the elements of the perceiving organism.

Although Leibniz had appealed to Arnauld for agreement on the grounds of the logical nature of the proposition, Arnauld replied in terms of the metaphysical nature of the individual person. He drew the conclusion, and found it entirely obnoxious, that if the notion of an individual contains in itself all that the individual is to do or to become, then human freedom is impossible. The correspondence between Leibniz and Arnauld lasted over a period of four years, and human and divine freedom remained the chief issue. Neither succeeded in converting the other, Arnauld persistently replacing in his criticisms "Aristotelian individual" for "Leibnizian individual." Thus Arnauld says:

It seems to me that I ought to regard as involved in my individual concept only what is of such a nature that I would no longer be myself if it were not in me, while on the other hand, everything which is of such a nature that it might either happen to me or not happen to me without my ceasing to be myself, should not be considered as involved in my individual concept; (although by the ordinance of God's providence, which never changes the nature of things, it could never happen that that should be in me).

Arnauld, that is to say, regards himself as a rational animal essentially, who happens to have become a theologian and a celibate, though he might have chosen to be a physician and a married man. For Leibniz, the individual Arnauld had enfolded in his nature from his creation that he was to be a theologian and a celibate together with all the acts making up this condition including his acts of free choice. In creating Arnauld, God created all the other being involved in his actions with their states mutually adjusted. If it had been enfolded in Arnauld's nature, that is, if it had been included in his concept that he should choose to marry, then there would have been another being created in whose concept it was included that she would choose to marry Arnauld.

The individual, according to Arnauld, is a *specimen* of his kind, individuated by having his own piece of matter to be human in. Socrates is a specimen of humanity, doing the *kinds* of things which it is proper for a human being to do, in his own peculiar way. The actual things he does and says are his own ways of doing the human kinds of things, just as being snub-nosed is his own particular way of displaying the human characteristic of having a nose. There are general laws leading us to expect that Socrates will be able to learn to talk, to learn grammar, and to reason, but no laws which will lead us to expect him to say: "But is not the expression 'master of himself' a ridiculous one? For the man who is master of himself will also I presume, be the slave of himself, and the slave will be the master." But it is just this second kind of expectation which interests Leibniz. *His* Socrates is just the individual who says these and no other words, and God, who has a complete concept of each individual, can read off from the concept just this utterance, and moreover, has so adjusted things that the concept of some other individual contains the response to the utterance. Arnauld objects to this view that not only does it make human freedom impossible but it makes God's freedom impossible also. God in creating Adam has determined the whole course of events, which thereafter follow "with a more than fatal necessity." Leibniz rejects the word "fatal," and says that Arnauld is confusing hypothetical with absolute necessity. It is true that once God has chosen to create the actual Adam, that is, the Monad containing in itself the whole course of later events, including the offspring of Adam and their history, the actual history of the world is unfolded, not with "fatal" necessity but according to causes which "incline without necessitating." These are final causes, and the actual world fulfills the purpose of God, which is to create the best of all possible worlds. The necessity is hypothetical in that it is initially dependent upon God's choice and the whole course of events contains free choices which God had enfolded in the concepts of his creatures.

Leibniz's treatment of human and divine freedom raises the more general question of the relation of the principles of contradiction and sufficient reason in his system. At first sight, the distinction between the two principles is perfectly clear. The necessary truths of logic and mathematics are true according to the principle of contradiction, their opposites being self-contradictory. They are true of "all possible worlds," dependent on God's intellect and not on his will. God could not create a world in which the shortest distance between two points in a plane was not a straight line, but this is not a limitation to his freedom, but simply a recognition of the nature of his intellect. On the other hand, the principle of sufficient reason, though itself true of all possible worlds — of *any* world which God might have created it would be true to say that there was a reason why it should be thus and not otherwise — yet the *actual* truths for which there is a sufficient reason might not have been true. "There would be several Adams disjunctively possible . . . but what determines a certain Adam must involve absolutely all his predicates." That is to say, it is contingently true that Adam ate the apple and was turned out of Eden, since God might have created one of the other possible Adams, but granted that God created *this* Adam, "Adam did not eat the apple" is self-contradictory, since God created the Adam in whose concept was enfolded the free choice of eating the apple and all

the accompaniments of this act. Confusion arises if we describe this state of affairs in the statement: "Adam could not choose not to eat the apple." But we might equally say that it would be unsuitable to say of a straight line that it could not be other than the shortest distance between two points in a plane. It would be better to say that the proposition that a straight line is the shortest distance between two points is logically necessary and the proposition about Adam is hypothetically necessary, and leave out talk about what could or could not be the case.

Leibniz expressed the difference between the two principles by saying that they were corollaries, contradiction affirming that every analytic proposition is true, and sufficient reason that every true proposition is analytic. He pointed out, further, that the truths of mathematics do not need the principle of sufficient reason since they relate to possibles, and so they are true if possible, i.e., if analytic. Propositions about matters of fact, while analytic in exactly the same sense, are nevertheless genuinely contingent in that they are true of actual states of affairs only because God freely decreed that that state of affairs should become actual. Presumably, while they remain possibilities exactly what is said of the truths of mathematics must be said of them, except that they are infinitely more complicated in their interconnections than are the truths of mathematics. They are the objects of God's intellect, of his contemplation. God could no more choose that a certain set of properties should be compossible than he could choose that a certain set of mathematical properties should be compossible. God by his intellect recognizes that if two triangles are equilateral they are equiangular and that if Adam, defined by a complete concept, is tempted in a certain specific way, he will fall in a certain specific way. The distinction between what are called, in the ordinary sense, necessary and contingent truths, now appears to lie merely in that there are alternative sets of compossibilities making up possible worlds but there is only one possible set of mathematical truths. The one truly contingent truth would then be that God chose to create this actual world among all the possible worlds, though since God is perfectly good and wise, he will have a sufficient reason for his creation the desire to bring the best into existence, so that the proposition "God created an inferior world" is self-contradictory. Is this proposition logically impossible?

Leibniz says definitely in the *Monadology*, "Truths of reasoning are necessary and their opposite is impossible; truths of fact are contingent and their opposite is possible." But when we recall his doctrine that in a true proposition the subject contains its predicate, and remember, moreover, that the most satisfactory subject for a proposition is a complex sign containing the simple signs standing for the simples combined in the substance named, a contradiction appears. Suppose we know, for example, just three facts about Peter, that he was shock-headed, had long nails, and got in a rage. The proper name for Peter would be "Shock-headed, long-nailed, in-a-rage," and if we affirmed of the being so-named that he was shock-headed, we obviously have an analytic statement. Of course, many other things are true of Peter, and we might save the situation by claiming that any name we give must be inadequate and that true names are known only to God. But then the distinction between necessity and contingency would resolve itself into the distinction between complete and partial knowledge. This will not do for Leibniz, however; it is not a question of *apparent* contingency disappearing with more complete knowledge, nor is it a question of the contingency of states of affairs still in the future. He says: "Philosophers agree nowadays that the truth of future contingents is determined, i.e., that future contingents are future, or that they will be.... Thus the contingent, though future, is none the less contingent." [9] God, with his perfect knowledge, can read from the true names of individuals all that is true of them, past, present, and future, and all the true statements will be analytic, yet truly contingent. The clue lies in a consideration of what happens when we learn new facts about an individual. When we learn new facts about triangularity, we can see the essential connection between them and the facts we already know. When we learn new facts about an individual, there is a connection, certainly, between them and the facts we already know, but we do not see it as a necessary connection. If we add the new facts to the name of the individual, a statement asserting the new facts will be analytic, but the connection between the properties combined in the subject will be contingent, though according to a principle. Thus, to assert that Caesar did not cross the Rubicon is self-contradictory in that Caesar's true name contains the property "crossing the Rubicon," but not in the sense that it is logically impossible that the same subject could contain the two properties "not crossing the Rubicon" and "being assassinated by Brutus." The complete concept "Caesar" does not contain these two attributes, so any assertion having "Caesar" as its subject will be self-contradictory if these two attributes are jointly asserted of it. It will be an instance of "$ABCD$ is A and not B," just as "12 is not divisible by 3 and divisible by 2" is a case of "$ABCD$ is A and not-B." The two cases differ in the way the joint properties belong together. Being divisible by 2 and by 3 belong essentially to 12, but crossing the Rubicon and being assassinated belong together in virtue of final causes, which incline without necessitating. The successive events in the life history of a given Monad are connected by its appetition toward the good. But since the states of this Monad reflect the states of all other Monads, the complete system will reflect the final cause of God's intention of bringing into existence the greatest amount of good which can coexist.

God and Creation

WE may now look once more at [the] world. He has as the object of h[is] number of possible worlds each [with an] infinite number of possible be[ings] which are complete and all c[ompatible with one] another. To each member of o[ne he] adds existence, but the difficulty [is that existence can] not be a property, otherwise Go[d] the already complete concep[t] as we saw above, is a perfectio[n, a simple] quality which is positive and ab[solute. The exist-]ence of finite beings is differ[ent] existence is part of his essence, finite beings seems almost to them as the removal of a bar to activity. In his fragmentary Leibniz gives the following defi[nition of existence:] "The existent may be defined as that which is compatible with more things than is anything incompatible with itself." "The existent is what has being or possibility and something more." "I say therefore that the existent is the being which is compatible with most things, or the most possible being, so that all coexistent things are equally possible." We may say, then, of any actual being, not only that it exists, but also that it is a member of the fullest possible universe. In creating it, God added nothing to its concept, not even power to act, for a certain degree of activity is of the essence of any Monad; he simply allowed it to exert its power.

Although Leibniz does not regard the existence of finite beings as a property, when he comes to the proofs that God exists, God's existence is treated rather differently. Existence cannot be a property of finite beings, for if it were, it would be impossible for God to choose to create or not to create a given being. "Adam exists" does not assert a property of Adam; if it did, then existence would be contained in the concept "Adam" and he would necessarily exist. In his version of the ontological argument, Leibniz says that existence is a perfection, which is a simple quality which is positive and absolute. Leibniz criticizes the Cartesian version of the ontological argument on the grounds that Descartes had proved only that if the Divine Being is possible, he is actual, and has omitted to prove that the Divine Being is possible. He himself first proves that all perfections are compatible, then goes on: "Whence it follows also that He exists, for existence is among the number of the perfections." Now although Leibniz seems thus to be saying that God's existence is one of his attributes, when we look at the definitions of existence and of perfection together, it seems that this cannot be what he means. " ... a perfection expresses without any limits whatever it does express"; this is intelligible in connection with such properties as wisdom and goodness, since these may be possessed in varying degrees and there is no self-contradiction involved in ascribing them to God in the highest degree. But existence is not a property which finite beings possess, and certainly not in varying degrees. "Coexistent things are equally possible," not, it is true, "equally existing," for this is meaningless, but certainly, "possibility is not a matter of degree." God is not "possible in the highest degree," possibility as applied to God is the compatibility of perfections within his nature; and as applied to finite beings, it is the compossibility of the greatest number of beings combined with the greatest amount of variety. Nor does God exist in the highest degree. God's existence follows from the perfection of his own nature, and though Leibniz seems to be saying that this is an inference from the possession of all perfections, existence cannot be a perfection according to his own definition. If we remember that creation is a kind of removal of the bar to the exercise of power already possessed, it is unthinkable that God, who possesses all power in the highest degree and is completely active, should be hindered in the exercise of his power. " . . . as nothing can interfere with the possibility of that which involves no limits, no negation, and consequently no contradiction, this (His possibility) is sufficient of itself to make known the existence of God *a priori*."[10] However, Leibniz *says* that existence in the case of the Divine Being is a perfection, of simple quality, so that his version of the ontological proof is open to the Kantian criticism that existence is not a predicate.

Leibniz supplements this proof with an argument drawn from the existence of the eternal truths. God's intellect is the "place" of the eternal truths, the source of essences as well as of existences. There is no difficulty about the truth of contingent truths — they correspond to facts in the actual world, but there is nothing is this world to make the eternal truths true or necessary. Their truth, that is to say, the reality of essences or possibilities, is founded in the eternal and necessary being, without whom there would be nothing either possible or actual. Suppose I notice that a triangle has its angles equal to two right angles, and a quadrilateral to four right angles, and hastily assume that with an extra side the sum of the angles is doubled; I might then form the self-contradictory idea of a pentagon having its angles equal to eight right angles. The impossibility of the concept is demonstrated by exhibiting it as a self-contradiction. A pentagon having its angles together equal to eight right angles is identical with a set of three triangles, which set has its angles together equal to six right angles. The difference between the possible and the impossible idea of the pentagon lies in there being a counterpart of the one and not of the other in reality. They are both equally before a human mind, one when the mind is in a state of confusion, the other when it is thinking well, but to say that a statement of one is true and the other false would have no meaning if there were not the reality to correspond with the true statement.

There are, of course, other ways of "grounding" possibilities in the actual. We might hold, as some extreme empiricists have done, that mathematical statements are generalizations from experience of actual objects, and that our feeling of their peculiar certainty is only a feeling, arising from the fact that we never meet exceptions. The weakness of this position is that we do not look for exceptions but simply assume that they are not to be found. The more popular view is that necessary statements are certain simply because they are a human invention, and that they have been constructed to display just this characteristic. We define "square" as "four-sided, equal-angled . . . " and statements derived from the definition are certain because we have made them so. They are not true as matter-of-fact statements are true, but they are self-consistent.

Leibniz's version of the cosmological argument rests on the principle of sufficient reason, " . . . there can be no fact real or existing, no statement true, unless there be a sufficient reason why it should be so and not otherwise."[11] The cosmological argument is, Leibniz tells us, an *a posteriori* proof, since it needs the premise that something exists. Granted that something exists, then there must be a sufficient reason why it exists. The reason cannot lie in the existence of the finite beings themselves, i.e., their existence is contingent, so the reason must lie in something outside them, in something which will not suffer from the same disability, that is to say, in the necessary being. The difficulty here is that though we may admit the existence of finite beings as a fact, we may refuse to grant the second step, that there must be a reason for their existence. We may ask, as do some existentialists, "why anything rather than nothing?" and refuse any answer as satisfactory. Finite existence remains an absurdity — there *is* no reason why there should be anything. Leibniz's illegitimate passage from contingent to necessary existence consists in the confusion of our being obliged to grant as a fact what is a fact, with our granting it as necessary, i.e., following from a reason. "Why should there be anything?" "But there *is* something — you must admit that." "Yes, but that is not to admit that that something must be. It is, and remains, an absurdity."

Leibniz not only assumes that there must be a reason for that which undoubtedly is, but that the reason must be such as to explain all the minute particularity of what is. His principle of pre-established harmony is his version of the argument from design. From the mutual adaptation of all parts of the universe we infer something as to the nature of the Divine Being whose existence is necessarily involved in the existence of the finite world. He is infinitely wise and good; in fact, the necessary being is God. This is the last unjustified assumption of proofs of the existence of God. God is either the name of a real being, and as such, his existence can be known only by acquaintance, or it is the name of a concept, with those properties alone which we have shown to belong to it. We cannot *prove* the existence of the Person, God; if we can prove the existence of anything at all, it is that of the necessary being.

Moral Theory

LEIBNIZ cannot be described as a man of great moral insight, and there is very little that is new or of great interest in his moral theory. We may notice, however, his belief that the essential for good conduct, and therefore for happiness, is knowledge. We may notice, further, that his view of knowledge is the same in connection with moral truths as with scientific truths. In a letter to Arnauld, written when he was twenty-five years old, Leibniz outlines his achievements up to date and his projects for the future. He has, he says,[12] demonstrated that the essence of substance is activity and not extension, and has developed this demonstration into actual laws of motion and geometrical theorems concerning the infinitely little. His conception of substance will also enable him to throw light on the mysteries of religion, the Trinity, the Incarnation, and Transubstantiation. As an example, he shows Arnauld that Cartesian substance makes transubstantiation impossible, for if the essence of body is to be extended, it is a manifest absurdity to suppose that the same real body can be in many places. If, however, we distinguish between the reality and appearance of body, there is no reason why the same real body should be associated with a multiplicity of appearances. Leibniz seems really to have believed that people of varying creeds could be shown, in these ways, which of them was right, so that all their differences could be resolved by reasoning. Not only this, but with good definitions of the "*éléments d'esprit*," morality could be put on a firm foundation and serve as a basis for a much clearer and more certain science of right and equity. He looked forward to a time when people involved in a religious, moral, legal, or even aesthetic dispute would no longer argue but be in a position to say as in mathematical discussion: "Come, sit down and let us calculate."

The means by which this happy state of affairs was to be brought about were the same as in any other science: it was by resolving complex notions into their simple elements, so that a disputed statement would be seen either as analytic and therefore true, or as self-contradictory and therefore false. Leibniz gives some of the definitions relevant to moral disputes. *The permissible:* Everything possible to a good man. *The obligatory:* Everything necessary to a good man. *The good man:* He who loves everybody. *Love:* Pleasure in the well-being of another, sadness in his trouble. It follows from these definitions that to work for the welfare of others is an obligation, since it is necessary to the good man. If

we object that there is usually no dispute about general principles but about their application, Leibniz supplies rules for determining choice in a conflict of duties. The guiding principle is that in a conflict, we must choose so as to bring about the greatest amount of good, and this must be determined by calculation. Obligations, like probabilities, do not add; they multiply. If we have a choice of making a man of six degrees of goodness three times as powerful as he is, or a man of two degrees of goodness four times as powerful as he is, we ought to choose to benefit the first man by the smaller amount, since in this way we shall produce a greater amount of valuable properties. We evaluate persons by multiplying the amount of their various properties. If we ask how we reach our estimate of the properties, the answer is in terms of health, fortune, and intelligence. Leibniz assumes that on the whole people deserve their fortune. Health and happiness, on the whole, are signs of a good character and intelligence. This is another example of Leibniz's easy equating of moral with metaphysical perfection. A strong man of good fortune is one who will be active in the world, so of greater metaphysical goodness, so it will be safer to assume, also, of greater moral goodness. These principles come with a shock to modern ears, especially when we combine them with our moral calculations to conclude that we ought to choose to do good to the strong and the fortunate. I am not sure, though, that the shock does not lie rather in the enunciating than in the application of the principles. Leibniz states the connection between fortune and desert thus: "For happiness is to persons what perfection is to beings," and he makes a remark in passing, in *On the Ultimate Origination of Things*, that moral perfection is physical perfection in regard to spirits. Happiness is the passage of a spirit to a higher degree of activity, and sadness is the frustration of this passage. The passage to perfection is growth in clearness of perception and knowledge, so that intelligent beings are both morally and metaphysically better than the stupid, and consequently happier. Just as no movement in the physical world is lost, so no act of will is ever lost, each new act being a "harmonious composition of earlier acts of will." Pre-established harmony, in the moral sphere, shows itself as a delicate adaptation of merit to happiness, spirits being subjects of God's kingdom of grace.

This is the system within which we may see that it is reasonable to seek to acquire knowledge and to trust that it will lead us to behave better toward our fellows and to be more effective and so happier. With greater knowledge, we are able to see God's plans for the world. In fact, we are learning to see the blueprint of the universe, and the more clearly we see, the more we see that it is our duty and happiness to conform actively to God's will. Moreover, the contemplation of the workings of God's plan gives us the experience of beauty; aesthetic enjoyment is the perception of ordered variety, and though it is a pleasure of the intellect, it is not the same as the recognition of the detailed interconnection of the parts, for this would constitute reasoning. It is a pleasure of "confused" intellect, for we are willing to contemplate and not think. Works of art are pictures in miniature of the order of the universe, and we feel the same joy in their contemplation. This, then, is the best of all possible worlds, but we may note that the emphasis is on the word "possible." It is perfectly possible to imagine states of affairs better than the actual, but this world contains the largest number of good states of affairs that can coexist. Leibniz may be allowed one last word to those who find his optimism infuriating.

For it is to be observed that, as in a thoroughly well-constituted commonwealth care is taken, as far as may be, for the good of individuals, so the universe will not be sufficiently perfect unless the interests of individuals are attended to, while the universal harmony is preserved. And for this no better standard could be set up than the very law of justice which declares that each should participate in the perfection of the universe and in a happiness of his own in proportion to his own virtue and to the degree in which his will has regard to the common good; and by this is fulfilled that which we call charity and the love of God.[13]

14

Berkeley

J. F. THOMSON

GEORGE BERKELEY WAS BORN near Kilkenny in Ireland in 1685. He entered Trinity College, Dublin, at the age of fifteen, took his B.A. in 1704, and became a Fellow of the College in 1707. In that year and the year following he filled two notebooks with reflections suggested to him by his reading of Locke, Newton, Malebranche, and others. These notebooks, now called the *Philosophical Commentaries*, contain in germ almost all of his philosophy. Some of the ideas contained in them are worked out in the *Essay towards a New Theory of Vision*, which appeared in 1709, and in Berkeley's best-known work, *A Treatise Concerning the Principles of Human Knowledge*, which was published in 1710. The *Three Dialogues between Hylas and Philonous* (1713) restate and expand some of the main arguments and theses of the *Principles*. These are undoubtedly Berkeley's most important writings and it is from them that any discussion of his philosophy must start.

In 1724 Berkeley resigned his fellowship to become Dean of Derry. Much of the next period up to 1731 was spent in trying to found a college in Bermuda to educate native Indians and the sons of English planters. The attempt failed because the government support which had been promised was not provided. In 1734 Berkeley was appointed Bishop of Cloyne. In 1752 he settled in Oxford, where he died in 1753.

IT WILL NOT BE POSSIBLE in the space of this chapter to discuss more than a few central issues in Berkeley's philosophy. But there is something to be said for being clear about central issues before attempting to consider peripheral ones. I have therefore taken as a central question the meaning and importance of the principle *esse est percipi* — a principle which Berkeley himself certainly supposed to be his chief contribution to philosophy.

The "New Principle" and the Immaterialist World-Picture

THE central feature of Berkeley's philosophy is his principle that to exist is the same as to perceive or to be perceived. To understand his philosophy we need to see what this principle means, why and how Berkeley was led to assert it, and why he attached to it the importance that he did.

He discovered the principle as a young man of about twenty-two, and we find the discovery recorded in his notebooks (the *Philosophical Commentaries*). From what he says there it is clear that the discovery is intended to be a logical or conceptual one. To see that existence is the same thing as perceiving or being perceived we need only reflect, he thinks, on what we mean or could mean by "exists." And he thinks too that if we do do this we shall be liberated from a whole host of otherwise insoluble problems — in physics and mathematics, in theology, in almost every field of study. He sets down a memorandum,[1] "Diligently to set forth how that many of the Ancient philosophers run into so great absurdities as even to deny the existence of motion and those other things they perceived actually by their senses. This sprang from their not knowing what existence was and wherein it consisted. This the source of all their Folly. 'Tis on the discovering of the nature and meaning and import of Existence that I chiefly insist." Failing to ask what existence *was* was only one of an important set of such failures. "The Vast, Widespread, Universal Cause of our Mistakes is that we do not consider our own notions, I mean consider them in themselves, fix, settle and determine them."[2] For it is not that "our notions" or the words for them are inevitably perplexing. "I must not say the words thing, substance, etc., have been the cause of mistakes. But the not reflecting on their meaning. I will still be for retaining the words. I only desire that men would think before they speak and settle the meaning of their words."[3] But the failure to examine the idea of existence is the most important one. For bogus problems arise, Berkeley thinks, on the assumption that there exist things which neither perceive nor are perceived. People then worry about the nature and status of these alleged existents. His principle cuts off such problems and perplexities at their sources.

Acceptance of the principle leads to a certain world-view or world-picture, which Berkeley sometimes calls *immaterialism*. In this world-view there are, there exist, two and only two kinds of things — ideas and spirits. Spirits perceive ideas, or, as Berkeley sometimes says, "have them." The existence of an idea consists in its being perceived or had by some spirit. The existence of a spirit consists in its having ideas and in its exercising volitions. Only spirits perceive; only ideas are perceived; there cannot be any other kind of thing than these two.

Because they exercise volitions, spirits are causal agents. They and they alone initiate changes in the world. Ideas are passive, and owe their existence to spirits. There are two kinds of spirits. We (human being) are finite spirits. There is also at least one infinite spirit, which Berkeley calls God. For any given finite spirit, some of his ideas are caused by himself and some by God. The ideas caused by God tend to come in collections or bundles. These we call apples, chairs, houses, and so on, according to the kind of ideas that constitute them. When a finite spirit looks at the sun, he is perceiving or having ideas caused by God. When he thinks of or remembers the sun by night, he is having ideas of which he himself is the cause.

This, then, in sufficient outline, is immaterialism. Considering it simply as a picture of the world, one may be attracted by it or repelled. But its interest does not lie in its appeal or lack of appeal to the imagination. We must consider rather what claims they are that Berkeley makes on its behalf. He claims, first, that it is a picture the acceptance of which will rid us once and for all of all metaphysical problems, and make clear to us "the falseness and vanity of those barren speculations, which make the chief employment of learned men."[4] Secondly, he thinks that it is demonstrably the only world-picture that does not lead to metaphysical difficulties. Thirdly, and perhaps suprisingly, he thinks that it is the *natural* way of looking at the world, and that we all of us are, perhaps without realizing it, immaterialists, before we are seduced into confusion by false science and false philosophy; so that, in making immaterialism explicit, he is "recalling men to common sense."[5] These claims must now be considered.

In order to do this, let us begin by considering immaterialism quite naïvely, and without any preconceived ideas of how we ought to deal with a philosophical theory. What is conspicuously lacking from the picture is of course the notion of matter. Is Berkeley denying the existence of matter? And if he is, ought we to care?

"Matter"

THE *Three Dialogues* represent an extended discussion between Philonous, who is Berkeley's spokesman, and Hylas, a would-be common-sense man who has been led into error, though not incurably, by the materialism of Locke and Newton. The first dialogue begins with Hylas inquiring anxiously whether it is true that Philonous denies the existence of material substance. Philonous replies that he is seriously persuaded "that there is no such thing as what philosophers call material substance."[6] A little later[7] he says that he denies the existence of matter.

In the first quotation, Philonous means by "philosophers" the natural philosophers of his time, i.e., people whom we should now call physicists and chemists, and their apologists. Whether there is any such thing as what these people called material substance depends of course on what they said about it. For it is possible that their explanation of the term was confused or that they ascribed features to it which nothing could possibly have. But when in the second quotation Philonous says that he denies the existence of matter, we are entitled, at least provisionally, to take him (as Hylas does) to be denying the existence of what *we* call matter. What, then, do we call by this name? "Matter" comes from the Latin *materia*, which, like *hylē* in Greek, originally meant "wood." Now many things are made of wood and always have been, and many things which are now made of metal or plastics were once made of wood or not made at all. It is then easy to see how the word for wood came to be a general name for any kind of stuff from which artifacts could or might be made. This corresponds roughly to our present use of "material," as when we speak of material for a suit or for curtains. Now, many things are not artifacts; they are not literally made of anything for they are not, literally, made. But it is a natural extension to think of trees and stones and human bodies as made of different kinds of stuff in the sense of being composed of them or containing them. Thus we arrive at the idea of matter. "Matter" is a very general name for the various materials and stuffs of which things are made or composed. The various elements and their organic and inorganic compounds are then different kinds or varieties of matter. They are different material substances.

We should notice that because the notion of matter is a very general one it is for many purposes dispensable. We need quite often to speak of gold, linen, blood, cheese, and of material for something, but rarely of matter as such. The exception is in physics. Physicists are professionally concerned with the properties of matter, with properties that any piece of matter has just because it is a piece of matter. So the idea of matter may easily come to seem both unfamiliar and theoretical, and so fit to be philosophized about. But if we keep in mind how the idea of matter is related to that of, say, cheese, we shall see that there cannot be any serious doubt about the *existence* of matter in this, the ordinary, sense of the term. For if the existence of cheese entails the existence of matter, then the nonexistence

of matter entails the nonexistence of cheese. And to be committed to denying the existence of cheese because of some philosophical theory will seem certainly wrong.

In the *Second Dialogue*, Hylas says that "the reality of sensible things cannot be maintained without supposing the existence of matter."[8] We have just seen what the force of this remark is. It will help our enquiry to consider what Philonous says in reply.

> *Philonous.* My glove, for example?
> *Hylas.* That or any thing perceived by the senses.
> *Philonous.* But to fix on some particular thing; is it not a sufficient evidence to me of the existence of this glove, that I see it, and feel it, and wear it? Or if this will not do, how is it possible I should be assured of the reality of this thing, which I actually see in this place, by supposing that some unknown thing which I never did or can see, exists after an unknown manner, in an unknown place, or in no place at all? How can the supposed reality of that which is intangible, be a proof that anything tangible really exists? or of that which is invisible, that any visible thing . . . exists?

Two things now become plain. First, Philonous does not meet Hylas' point. Hylas should have said: That you can see and touch your glove does indeed show that it exists. But then it shows also that a material thing exists, a thing made of leather and so of matter. I did not mean that the supposition that there is matter is something which, if previously accepted, lends plausibility to the supposition that you are wearing a glove, but rather that anyone who maintains, as you do, that he is wearing a glove is thereby committed to maintaining the existence of matter.

But it is plain too that the conception of matter which Philonous is here rejecting is not the ordinary one. What is rejected under the title of matter is something which is "intangible, invisible, and which, if it exists, exists in an unknown manner, in an unknown place, or in no place at all." In this sense of "matter" it is indeed difficult to see that we have or could have any reason to believe in its existence. But this conception of matter is not the ordinary one; this sense is not the ordinary sense of the word.

We should then suspect that Hylas and Philonous are at cross-purposes; that what Hylas is concerned to defend is not what Philonous is concerned to attack: and thus, since Hylas as much as Philonous is a creature of Berkeley's imagination, that Berkeley did not understand what the ordinary conception of matter was. And this suspicion is confirmed by many passages in Berkeley's writings. Consider for example: "I do not argue against the existence of any one thing that we can apprehend, either by sense or by reflection. That the things I see with mine eyes and touch with my hands do exist, really exist, I make not the least question. The only thing whose existence we deny, is that which philosophers call matter, or corporeal substance. And in doing of this, there is no damage done to the rest of mankind, who, I dare say, will never miss it."[9] Here, then, Berkeley *intends* only to be denying the existence of what philosophers call "matter." Moreover, in saying that he does not deny the existence of things that he sees and touches he tacitly agrees that there *are* "material things," i.e., things made or composed of material substances. But now, how does this square with the thesis that there exist only ideas and spirits? Berkeley thinks that it is perfectly consistent. For what we ordinarily call "material things" are just combinations of sensible qualities, and sensible qualities are ideas. Further, he thinks that this is the ordinary conception of "material."

> It will be urged [i.e., against immaterialism] that thus much at least is true, to wit, that we take away all corporeal substances. To this my answer is, that if the word *substance* be taken in the vulgar sense, for a combination of sensible qualities, such as extension, solidity, weight, and the like: this we cannot be accused of taking away. But if it be taken in a philosophic sense, for the support of accidents or qualities without the mind; then indeed I acknowledge that we take it away, if one may be said to take away that which never had any existence, even in the imagination.[10]

We can now discern something of the character of Berkeley's theory. He recognizes only two possible conceptions of what a "material thing" is. There is the "philosophical" conception according to which the thing is held to be composed of some invisible and intangible something which underlies and supports its sensible qualities. And there is the conception of the thing as just a combination of sensible qualities. And since he thinks that these two conceptions are the only possible ones, he thinks, naturally enough, that to reject the former is to subscribe to the latter. To do this, to reject the "philosophical conception" and identify material things with combinations of sensible qualities, is to take the first step toward immaterialism. (We take the second when we identify sensible qualities with "ideas.") We have already seen reason to suspect that the dilemma from which Berkeley starts is a false one. If this is well-founded, we need not take the first step. But to understand its attraction for Berkeley, we must see more clearly what the "philosophical conception" of matter was, and how it arose.

LOCKE ON MATTER

For Berkeley, the official spokesman of this conception was Locke. We need not here be concerned to enquire exactly what Locke said. The following account will be sufficient for our purposes; we can certainly suppose that Berkeley thought that Locke and others had proposed something like it.

When we perceive (i.e., see or touch or hear or smell or taste) something, what essentially happens is that sensations are caused in us. These sensations are called "ideas", and are caused by or with the help of the material thing which is being perceived. So the material thing must have *powers* (must have the power to cause ideas). And its powers are what we ordinarily call its qualities. So when we ascribe a quality to something on the basis of having perceived it, we are saying that it has such and such a power. For example, a white piece of paper has the power to cause ideas of color in an observer when the conditions are suitable. If this happens, and then as a result the observer says or notices that the paper is white, he thereby ascribes to it the power to cause in him just those ideas he is having. It is thought to follow from this that ideas so caused are *of* sensible qualities.

But what are these powers and how are we to think of them? The official answer is that what powers a thing has depends on its physical structure, on the manner of the arrangement of the "minute parts" of which it is composed. For we wish to be economical in our hypotheses. We do not want to burden our theory with any features other than those which need to be mentioned in explaining the powers of things to cause sensations of certain kinds in us. But now it must be possible in principle to explain them in purely physical terms. So we find in this account that the features ascribed to material things are just those which seventeenth-century physicists had found interesting and important and useful. There now comes to be made a distinction between two kinds of features or qualities which a material thing may have. It must be supposed to have a size, a shape, a weight, and some degree of solidity. These are primary qualities. But it was thought that it need not be supposed to have *in the same way* a color or a smell. Everyone knows that a thing may look different colors — cause different ideas of color — in different lights. But we need not suppose that the physical structure of the illuminated object changes. Again, what ideas of color are caused in an observer may depend on his state of health; here we cannot suppose that there is a corresponding change in the object. From this it is concluded that things do not really have colors of their own — in their own right, so to speak. In their own right they have primary qualities, and, derivative from these and supposed to be explicable in terms of them, they have powers to cause ideas of color, of smell, of sound, and of hardness and softness — ideas of secondary qualities — in suitably placed observers. Locke puts this by saying that ideas of primary qualities are copies or resemblances of the thing, but that nothing in the thing corresponds to ideas of secondary qualities.

So far, although we have spoken of material

things, we have not had occasion to speak of matter or material substance. According to Locke, these notions come in, i.e., we need them, in the following way. Our ideas are of sensible qualities. But qualities must be of something; there must be something that has them, and this something cannot itself be a quality. Locke thinks that "matter" and "material substance" are names that we give to this something. Now if all our ideas are of sensible qualities, it follows that we have no idea of matter. Locke takes this to mean that we do not perceive matter and that we cannot know or say what it is really like in itself. We know what kinds of ideas may be caused in us, but we have no way of finding out anything about the intrinsic nature of their causes. And this ignorance is readily seen to be an inevitable one. For to know something about x is to be in a position to ascribe a quality to it. Whatever we discover about a material substance will only enable us to add an item to our list of sensible qualities, and what has the qualities cannot appear on the list.

This, then, is the conception of matter and of the material world that Berkeley is anxious to replace. In the course of arguing for his own account he offers many criticisms of Locke's. These criticisms are of great and even permanent importance. There is, however, one objection which he does not make, and is not in a position to make, and it is this objection which is really crucial, since it is aimed, not at one of the many objectionable consequences of the theory, but at what must be regarded as the central part of the theory itself.

To state the objection crudely: the theory confuses an empirical fact about perception with a thesis about what it is to ascribe a sensible quality to a material thing. Let us grant that a piece of paper has a power to excite ideas of color in us and that it is when it exercises this power that we are able to say, as a result of observation, what color it is. Why should we conclude from this that when we say what color it is — when we ascribe a color to it — we *mean* that it has that power? There is no reason why we should conclude this at all. Further, if we do, we are committed to saying that every statement ascribing a sensible quality to a thing is a statement about ideas. And this is what is most deeply objectionable about Locke's account.

To put the point another way: because, every time we see something, we have sensations, it does not follow that when we say what we see we mean anything about sensations. And in fact the statement "That piece of paper is white" is not about anyone's sensations at all.

The reason why Berkeley does not and cannot make this objection is that he too thinks that statements ascribing sensible qualities are about ideas. This makes an important point of contact between Berkeley and Locke. Roughly speaking, immaterialism is what you get if you start off with Locke's picture and replace matter by God.

THINGS AS BUNDLES OF QUALITIES

We must now try to see what is involved in saying that a thing or a substance is a bundle of sensible qualities.

Suppose that a scientist is given a piece of homogeneous stuff and asked to identify it. Eventually he says that it is gold. Then his reason for saying so will be, obviously, that the stuff has certain characteristics or qualities. And to tell that the stuff has these qualities he must be able to use his sense organs; he must look, see, weigh, and perhaps in other cases taste and smell. Perhaps he will use other things too — instruments, reagents, or whatever — but these are only adjuncts. Neither microscopes nor litmus paper are of use to the blind. Let us sum all this up by saying that what makes something a piece of gold are its sensible qualities.

There are, however, two things involved here. The first is that if someone gets to know for himself (i.e., as distinct from being told it by someone else) that something is gold or cheese, he will in fact do so by using his senses. Consider, however, the following case. Various things — coal, soap, cheese, platinum — are put one by one into a box which is hermetically sealed and entirely opaque. The box is then shown to someone who claims to have extrasensory powers. After looking at the box, he tells us what is inside. This happens not just once or twice but hundreds of times, and despite the most rigorous precautions against fraud and trickery. Could this happen? We are inclined to say, I think, that it could not. That it should happen is *incredible*. But in one sense of "could" it could happen. For if someone told us that it had happened, then, although we should not believe him, we should know what it was that he was saying had happened. Let us mark this by saying that the case, though incredible, is *conceivable*. And it is a case in which someone identifies gold or cheese or whatever without using his senses, or, at least, without using his senses in any ordinary way. It is then important to notice that if what is in the box is a piece of gold it is still determined to be gold by its having the sensible qualities that it has. For this story is relevant only if the clairvoyant's claim, to be able to identify things without using his senses, is successful. We test the claim, and so must he, by opening the box, and looking and seeing and touching and tasting and smelling. The clairvoyant's statement "There is gold in the box," though not made on the basis of the usual kinds of sense-experience, still has its usual meaning.

In saying, then, that the various material substances are determined to be the substances that they are by their sensible qualities, we are not only saying that we do in fact find out what substances they are by using our senses. We are saying also that the tests we carry out by using our senses are the primary or basic ones. They are the tests by which other tests are tested.

From this it is only a short step to saying "a material substance is just a collection of sensible qualities." We then come upon Locke's difficulty about "matter." For we wish also to say that, e.g., gold is something that has sensible qualities.

Let us speak of *detecting* sensible qualities, and let us agree to say that we detect *only* such qualities. Then, to identify a substance as gold, we shall need to detect hardness, yellowness, and so on. But gold is something that has these qualities. And we could not detect yellowness and hardness unless there were something that was yellow and hard. This something is not a sensible quality nor a combination of them. Then, since we have agreed to say that we detect only qualities, it follows that what possesses the qualities is undetectable.

If we do not like this conclusion, we have only to understand how we came to it. We are invited to say that we detect only sensible qualities, and (implicitly) to say that our knowledge of material things is "conversant about" such qualities. We can then either accept this invitation or we can reject it. If we accept it, we should do so clear-sightedly, and then not be surprised at the conclusion that "matter is unknowable." In opting to say that we know only about sensible qualities, and that something has those qualities, we were committing ourselves to saying that there was something that we cannot know about it. But this is not a real ignorance. It is a trivial consequence of our terminology. If, further, we choose to give the name "matter" to this something that has sensible qualities, then that is how we are using the word "matter." By this act of choice we choose to say that we know nothing about matter.

If on the other hand we do not like these consequences, we are at liberty to reject the terminology which has them. And it seems that we do in fact reject it most of the time. Even if we agree to say that we detect only the qualities of substance, it will not follow, without further agreement, that our knowledge is conversant only about such qualities. Indeed, we started by supposing that in detecting such and such qualities in something, the scientist came to know what it itself was. As we ordinarily speak, our knowledge is not conversant only about sensible qualities; it is conversant also about things which possess these qualities, and it could hardly be the one without being the other. To know that something in front of me has such and such qualities is necessarily to know something about it.

I have tried to describe and resolve the traditional problem about "material substance" in a deliberately simplified and schematic way. Historically, the problem was in fact more complicated (largely because of its being confused with other problems). But what is important for our purposes here is to notice that it is definitely wrong to seek to resolve Locke's difficulty by rejecting the idea of a material substrate and identifying what we ordinarily call the material substance with the sum of its sensible qualities. This is what Berkeley does. He says:

> For instance, in this proposition, a die is hard, extended, and square; they [i.e., philosophers] will have it that the word *die* denotes a subject or substance, distinct from the hardness, extension, and figure, which are predicated of it, and in which they exist. This I cannot comprehend: to me a die seems to be nothing distinct from those things which are termed its modes or accidents. And to say a die is hard, extended, and square, is not to attribute those qualities to a subject distinct from and supporting them, but only an explication of the word *die*.[11]

We may well agree that it is at least potentially mystifying to say that we ascribe the hardness and shape of the die to "a subject or substance which is distinct from and supports them." But the way to break down the mystery is to remark that what we ascribe these qualities to is simply the die itself. To say that the die is something distinct from its qualities can then be accepted as a misleading way of saying that the die is not a quality.

Confusion can be brought on here by using inappropriate metaphors, e.g., of undressing. "If you strip away the qualities, what do you have left, something or nothing? If nothing, Berkeley is right, and the thing just is a combination of qualities; if something, then something without qualities, and what would *that* be like?" But what operation is here envisaged under the title of *stripping away the qualities*?

We must notice, secondly, that Locke's difficulty is at least partly brought on by using "matter" as a kind of technical term while at the same time supposing it to have its ordinary use. The ordinary use of this word is certainly not to stand for something which is "unknowable" and lies "beneath" sensible qualities. But if we use it in this way, it is perhaps inevitable that we shall begin to think of matter in the ordinary sense as "unknowable." Berkeley's philosophy can be regarded as an implicit criticism of this procedure. His criticism consists in this: he insists, ruthlessly and consistently, on the word being taken throughout in its technical, specialized sense, and then rejects the notion altogether. Hence, as we saw, we take one step toward immaterialism. Immaterialism rejects material substance and allows only sensible qualities.

Now we saw also that a second step is necessary, the step which consists of identifying sensible qualities with ideas. But this step is in fact intimately connected with the first. For the notion of sensible qualities which are not sensible qualities of anything is a strange one. Berkeley, however, admits this. The qualities do, he thinks, belong to things. They belong to minds, to spirits. And he marks this by calling them ideas or sensations. This is a kind of pun. For the sense in which yellowness belongs to gold or to a lump of gold, and the sense in which a sensation belongs to the person who has it, are hardly the same. But by thus identifying sensible qualities with sensations Berkeley makes the rejection of matter appear quite naturally.

This identification is a main part of the force of the principle that to exist is either to perceive or be perceived.

"Immediate Perception"

LET us give the name "$E = P$" to the principle that for a sensible thing to exist is the same as for it to be perceived. In the *Three Dialogues* there are three main arguments for $E = P$. But before proposing any of them Philonous extracts an important concession from Hylas. $E = P$ is about sensible things, and these are defined as "those things which are perceived by the senses."[12] But now, Philonous asks, is it not the case that all the things perceived by the senses are perceived by them *immediately*.

The point of introducing this notion of immediate perception is to make a contrast between what we actually perceive and what we infer or take for granted on the basis of what we so perceive. Thus, to use one of Philonous' examples, if you *see* one part of the sky red and another part blue, it is reasonable to suppose that there is a cause of that phenomenon. But the cause is not itself something you *see*. Again, "when I hear a coach driving along the streets, immediately I perceive only the sound; but from the experience I have had that such a sound is connected with a coach, I am said to hear the coach." So far, perhaps, so good. But he goes on: "It is nevertheless evident, that in truth and strictness, nothing can be heard but sound; and the coach is not then properly perceived by sense, but suggested by experience."[13] And it turns out that the only things which we immediately perceive are those which we would think we perceived if *nothing* were suggested by experience. "In short, those things alone are actually and strictly perceived by any sense, which would have been perceived, in case that same sense had then been first conferred on us."[14] So we immediately perceive something only if in saying that we perceive it we should not be relying on any rule suggested to us by experience; if we should not be making any inference or taking anything for granted.

Now what does this come to? Because of the example of the coach, we may at first suppose that Berkeley is concerned with the distinction between someone who says there is a coach in the street outside because he hears the kind of sound a coach makes and takes the noise to be actually made by a coach and someone who says there is a coach there because he can actually see it. If, however, it is this distinction that is in question, Philonous would not be justified in saying that the first man does not perceive a coach but only a sound. Perhaps it would be incautious for this first man to say "I can hear a coach." But we must distinguish between the questions "Is it reasonable for him to say he hears a coach?" and "Is the sound in fact made by a coach?" The question whether he does hear a coach turns on the second of these and not on the first. But it seems quite clear that it is not this distinction that Philonous wants to make. For he would say that if we are to speak strictly the second man does not really perceive a coach either.

His suggestion is, rather, this: when we speak of ourselves hearing, seeing, or touching coaches — or apples or trees or houses — we are speaking in a loose and misleading way. For these just are not the *kind* of things that can be seen or touched or heard. The only things that we really see are light, colors, and figures; that we really hear sounds; that we really touch, tangible qualities.

Berkeley does not deny that we do sometimes see and hear material things, *in the sense that* such statements as "I hear a coach" are sometimes true. But he thinks that we are easily liable to be confused about what we mean when we make such statements. "I hear a coach" means, and can only mean, "I am having auditory ideas of sense which belong to a bundle of ideas of the kind to which we conventionally give the name *coach*." But we are liable to think it means "I am having ideas of sense which are caused in me by a chunk of matter." But reflection will show that this is absurd. For "I hear a coach" is about something sensible, and a chunk of matter is not something sensible.

So, negatively, the force of the suggestion "All perception is really immediate perception" is to point out that we do not perceive Lockean material substances. This is of the greatest importance for what follows in the discussion between Philonous and Hylas. With great literary and dialectical skill, Berkeley makes their discussion center on the question of which of them is really a skeptic about the sensible world. And if Hylas wishes to say that sensible things are made of material substances; and if these are not immediately perceived, and so, strictly speaking, not perceived at all; then he can be put in the absurd and skeptical position of holding that we do not perceive sensible things. But, positively, the force of the suggestion is virtually that of $E = P$. For Philonous certainly thinks that what we immediately perceive is always a sensation. "Make me to understand the difference between what is immediately perceived, and a sensation,"[15] Philonous asks; the implication being that there is no difference. (And elsewhere Berkeley asks "What do we perceive besides our own ideas of sensations?")[16] But now it would seem that, so far from its being the case that everything we perceive is a sensation, nothing is. We are *aware of* sensations. But Berkeley tacitly claims to be using "perceive" as a generic term to cover seeing, touching, hearing, and so on. And we do not see or touch or hear sensations. Why then does he speak consistently as if we do? The answer must be that this is a thesis which he unthinkingly accepts from Locke. And it is here, then, that we have the important point of contact which we mentioned above. Immaterialism represents an attempt to avoid the difficulties of Locke's account of the material world without rejecting one of Locke's fundamental premises.

At this point, however, Philonous does not make it clear that he intends to say that anything immediately perceived is a sensation. The thesis that strictly speaking all perception is immediate perception is accepted by Hylas without demur (although he later tries to go back on it), and Philonous proceeds to argue, for each sense in turn, that what is perceived is a sensation, that it is "in the mind," that its *esse est percipi*.

WARMTH, HEAT, AND PAIN

In each case he attempts to show that the appropriate sensible quality cannot be supposed to have "a real existence" in the external thing to which we ascribe it. Thus the thing is slowly divested of its qualities until it approaches the status of an invisible intangible somewhat. The first argument tries to show this for the case of heat. Intense heat is painful, or, as he says, is "a pain." But pain is an experience, a sensation; it is "in the mind." So the same thing is true of intense heat; and so of heat in general. Heat does not have a "real being" in the things we call "hot."

To this we shall wish to object that intense heat and the pain that it causes are not the same thing. Intense heat is painful, in the sense that something that is very hot will cause pain in anyone who is sufficiently near it. This is not the same as to say that intense heat *is* the same thing as *pain*.

But this does not take us far. Hylas himself is made to object that pain is not so much heat as the consequence or effect of it. So what Berkeley sees as the force of the argument must lie in what Philonous is made to reply to this. This is, essentially, that when we put our hand near the fire, we feel one sensation and not two. Both the heat and the pain are immediately perceived. "Seeing therefore that they are both immediately perceived at the same time, and the fire affects you only with one simple, or uncompounded, idea, it follows that this same simple idea is both the intense heat immediately perceived, and the pain; and consequently, that the intense heat immediately perceived, is nothing distinct from a particular sort of pain."[17]

What is essential here is the premise that heat is something which is *immediately* perceived. We can see why Berkeley thinks this. Suppose you are asked whether something is hot. Incautiously, you put your hand near it, and reply "Yes, it is painfully hot." What makes you say this is a painful sensation in your hand. Berkeley supposes that "heat" is the name we give to this kind of sensation. If the sensation is intense we call it "pain" or "painful heat." But whether it is intense or not, it is heat; heat is a sensation: it is something of which we are directly or immediately aware.

Now we would all agree that in the sentence "I can feel a painful burning in my hand" the phrase "a painful burning" is used to refer to a sensation, and that so does "a warmth" in the sentence "I feel a warmth in my hand." But someone who says "I can feel the warmth of the fire" is doing something more than simply to record the fact that he is having a sensation of warmth. He is claiming to feel a warmth that emanates from the fire; he is saying there is such a thing to be felt, and that others could or would feel it too; so he is saying that the fire is, quite objectively, warm. We should conclude from this that if immediate perception is a matter of having sensations, perceiving the warmth of a fire, is not a case of *immediate* perception.

We should notice that in a curiously circular way Berkeley's belief that what we call heat is a sensation confirms him in the rightness of that belief. For if heat is a sensation, then to say that heat is in the fire can only be to say that the fire is having sensations of heat, and this is as absurd as to say that the burning coals are in pain.

THE RELATIVITY-ARGUMENTS

The arguments used by Locke to show that ideas of secondary qualities are not really in the things to which we ascribe them have been called "relativity arguments." For they consist in pointing out that how things look and feel and taste sometimes depends on the state and situation of the observer, and this is sometimes put by saying that ideas of such qualities are relative to the observer. Berkeley takes over these arguments, and extends the method of argument to ideas of primary qualities as well. We shall examine the best known of them.

First we must notice that Hylas allows Philonous to attribute to him a principle which is of some importance for the discussion of the argument. It is: "Those bodies . . . upon whose application to our own, we perceive a moderate degree of heat, must be concluded to have a moderate degree of heat in them, and those, upon whose application we feel a like degree of cold, must be thought to have cold in them."[18] Philonous speaks as if this principle were an inevitable consequence of supposing that heat and cold have "a real being" in bodies, and it is the principle rather than the supposition which he attacks directly. Suppose now that one of your hands is hot and the other cold, and that you plunge both into tepid water. Then the water will feel hot to one hand and cold to the other. So, according to the principle, we ought to conclude that the water is both hot and cold at the same time, which is absurd.

Now why does Philonous take the principle to be a consequence of the supposition that he wants to discredit? It is because we do sometimes claim to know what temperature things are, and to know this by "the evidence of our senses." So if we want to say that heat and cold have a real being in bodies, we must be prepared to say that we sometimes know that a body has some degree of heat or cold *really* in it. But this does not mean that we are committed to saying that every body, upon whose application to our own we feel a moderate degree of heat, really does have a moderate degree of heat in it. "It feels hot" is a prima facie reason for supposing the thing to *be* hot, but we do not and need not take it to be a conclusive one. If on the other hand someone says "I can feel that the water is hot," that is a conclusive reason for saying that it is hot, because it logically entails that the water is hot. So, roughly speaking, if in the statement of Hylas' principle we take "perceive" in its ordinary sense the principle is correct, but if we take it to mean "immediately-perceive" it is incorrect, and this is what the experiment with the bucket of water shows. It follows that we can make the same objection to this argument as we made to the earlier one; if to immediately-perceive something is just to have sensations of some kind, then to say that we perceive something to have such and such a temperature is not to speak about immediate perception. And, more importantly, to say "The water is hot" is not to say anything *about* sensations (even when, as will be sometimes but not always the case, we are prompted to say it by having sensations.)

It is not hard to see that the same objection can be brought, *mutatis mutandis*, against all of Berkeley's relativity arguments.

Consider, for example, the discussion of colors. Again, Hylas is made to say that "Each visible object hath that colour which we see in it."[19] And again we must distinguish between two ways of taking this. In the ordinary sense of "see," what we see must have the color we see it to have. "I can see that it is red" logically entails that it is red. But Philonous takes this admission in a much stronger sense. He takes it as equivalent to saying that a visible object has whatever color it looks to have (to anyone, under any circumstances). He has no difficulty in showing that this stronger statement is false. But he then concludes that "all colours are equally apparent, and that none of those which we perceive are really inherent in any outward object."[20] This simply does not follow. Because sometimes things — outward bodies — do not really have the colors they look to have, it does not follow that no color is inherent in any outward object at all.

What is interesting, however, is that Berkeley seems himself to have been fully aware of this. In the *Principles*[21] he says that if we consider those arguments which are allowed to show that colors and tastes exist only in the mind, we shall see that they show the same thing of extension, figure, and motion. But, "it must be confessed, this method of arguing doth not so much prove that there is no extension or colour in an outward object, as that we do not know by *sense* which is *true* extension or colour of the object." Now plainly the "method of arguing" in question does not show this either. What it shows is, at most, that we are sometimes mistaken about what the true extension or the real color is. But why, if Berkeley is aware that his arguments do not show that things have no colors or smells or shapes or sizes of their own, does he pretend in the *Three Dialogues* that they do?

The answer is, I think, that he uses them for a certain rhetorical purpose which becomes clear at the beginning of the *Third Dialogue*. We find Hylas here in a state of extreme skepticism. He says, "There is not one single thing in the world whereof we can know the real nature, or what it is in itself." Philonous is gently derisive. "Will you tell me I do not really know what fire or water is?" No, Hylas says. "You may indeed know that fire appears hot, and water fluid; but this is no more than knowing what sensations are produced in your own mind, upon the application of fire and water to your organs of sense. Their internal constitution, their true and real nature, you are utterly in the dark as to *that*." We can see how Hylas has come to this curiously boasted despair. He has been convinced that the sensible qualities we ascribe to things are sensations "produced in our own minds," and that nothing like them can belong to or inhere in external things. So he concludes that we cannot know what those external things are really like. We only know what kinds of sensations they produce in us. "They [i.e., the real things or corporeal substances which compose the world] have none of them anything in themselves, like those sensible qualities by us perceived. We should not therefore pretend to affirm or know anything of them as they are in their own nature."

Philonous now says that this skepticism is the result of Hylas' belief in external bodies and material substance. And the way out of the skeptical position which he recommends is that of going on and giving up that belief. For if what we ordinarily think of as external things are really nothing but collections of ideas, then they have no hidden nature for us to be ignorant of. This confirms our earlier statement about the origins of immaterialism. You start with Locke's position. According to this, to some of our ideas there correspond nothing similar in the external world. You extend this to all ideas: or, to put it differently, you say that all sensible qualities are secondary ones. The notion of a material thing as something to which we refer our ideas now becomes both embarrassing and unnecessary, and its place is taken by the collection of ideas previously said to be of it. Its place as a hypothetical cause of those ideas is taken over by God.

But this means that if we are in Hylas' skeptical

position we need not go on; we may equally prefer to go back. Instead of saying, with Berkeley, that all sensible qualities are secondary, we can disagree with Locke in a more fundamental way and say that none are. (And it should be clear too from what we have said that the quickest way for Hylas to retrace his steps is for him to go back on his acceptance of the suggestion that, to speak "in truth and strictness," we perceive only what we perceive immediately. For it is this principle, with the inevitably associated doctrine that we perceive only sensations, that has led him into skepticism; and it is this doctrine that is strikingly common to Berkeley and Locke.)

Let us then return briefly to the topic of immediate perception. It is clear that at least one thing that Berkeley is anxious to stress is that, in a very large and important class of cases, someone who says "It's hot in here," or "That is red," or "This is heavier than that," says so because he has or has had certain sensations. And it seems that he also wishes to stress that these cases are not only important; they are in some sense fundamental. There may be and doubtless are other ways of finding out whether a room is hot than the way indicated here, but this method is basic; as we said above, it provides the test by which other tests must be tested. It is then true, within certain limits, and putting aside certain difficulties about the concept of a sensation, that we ascribe qualities to things *on the basis of* our sensations. But it does not follow that what we say in ascribing a quality is about our sensations. If one speaker says "It's hot in here" and another replies "Surely not, you must have a fever," the latter denies what the former says but does not deny that the former feels hot. Now Berkeley may of course introduce "immediate perception" as a technical term and use it in any way he pleases. But if he uses it in such a way that we can be said to immediately perceive only sensations, nothing follows about seeing and touching. In particular, it is left open that we see and touch external objects; the *esse* of these is not shown to be *percipi*. What persuasive force Berkeley's arguments have is almost entirely due to his using his technical term to mean either "immediately perceive" or "perceive" (i.e., in the ordinary sense) according as it suits his purpose.

There remains another argument to consider. But since this is of a rather different character from those we have so far considered, let us stop here and ask, "If these were the only arguments for $E = P$, how would his claims for immaterialism look?" Before answering, we must say something about God.

God and Causation

I AM (Berkeley says) given ideas of which I know that I am not the cause. I can frame images, think of something, and then stop thinking of it, as I choose. That *these* ideas obey my will shows that my will is a

sufficient cause and explanation of them. But if I open my eyes and look in the garden, I see a tree whether I will or not. So some of my ideas must have a cause other than myself. This cause cannot be matter. Nor can it be any idea or set of ideas, for ideas are passive and not causal agents. The cause must then be a spirit. Now only a very powerful spirit could give me all the ideas of sense that I have, and only a wise and benevolent spirit would give me them in such lawful and regular sequences. So we must suppose that there is such a spirit. Since it has some of the attributes assigned to God in Christian theology, I call it by that name.

But what, if anything, Berkeley has proved is that there is *something* which is the cause of all our sensations. We will agree to *call* it "God." God, then, is not an idea or a combination of ideas (and, consistently enough, Berkeley denies that we can imagine or frame an idea of him). What bespeaks his existence is not something *in* the world but *that there is* a world at all. About this notion, we must notice two things.

First: God plays the same role in immaterialism that matter does in Locke's account. (It too, notice, is invisible, intangible, odorless, and silent, and it too is curiously pervasive). Berkeley of course denies that matter can be evoked equally well to explain the fact of our having sensations. His chief reason is the curious one that matter is dead, inert, insensible, and so has no ideas to give us. But he sometimes says instead that we have no idea of matter, so the proposed explanation would not mean anything. (You can say "Something causes my ideas of sense, and I am going to call it 'matter'," but you cannot *then* go on to explain your having ideas of sense by saying that matter causes them.) It is true that we have no idea of God either. But (he says) we have a *notion* of him; the idea ("in a larger sense") of a spirit causing ideas is familiar to us from our own experience in framing images.

Second: in Locke there are many different material things, in Berkeley only one God. So let us notice that Berkeley's argument for God's existence is formally fallacious in a way that is relevant to this apparent difference. Given that all my ideas of sense have a cause which is a very powerful spirit, it does not follow that there is a very powerful spirit which is the cause of all my ideas of sense. The argument is fallacious in the same way as is "All human beings have a father, therefore there is someone who is father of all human beings." Given, in other words, that there are spirits who cause ideas of sense in us, Berkeley has no right to suppose there is exactly *one* such. For all he has proved, there could be any number. And, it is quite clear, for all he *could* prove. For we are as completely cut off from the domain of such powerful spirits as we are from Locke's material substances. And now the gap between Berkeley and Locke can be made vanishingly small. For suppose — and this must be, for Berkeley, just as good a supposition as any — that for each sensible object there is a spirit and that he gives us just those ideas of sense which belong to the combination of ideas which constitute that sensible object. Now if we bear in mind that neither "spirit" nor "matter" (in the philosophical conception) mean much more than "putative unsensed cause of sensations," we see that the difference between Berkeley's world-picture and the picture which he wanted to replace is very small indeed.

The idea of a spirit for each sensible object is of course fanciful and absurd. But if we rid our minds of the cloudy associations of Christian theology (as Berkeley plainly did not) we shall perhaps agree that the idea of *one* spirit for *all* sensible objects has no more to recommend it.

"*Unperceived Objects*"

WE have now seen that the claim which Berkeley makes for immaterialism, that it is the only world-view, the only way of looking at the sensible world, which does not lead to gross paradoxes and foolish skepticism, is quite unfounded. It is clear also that we have been given no conclusive reasons, nor anything like such, for accepting it. But it seems we can say more than this. It seems that immaterialism has paradoxes of its own.

For, to make the obvious objection, if apples, stones, trees are collections of ideas, how is it possible for them to exist when no one is looking at them or otherwise perceiving them?

Berkeley's official reply to this is well known. He agrees that $E = P$ has the consequence that sensible objects cannot exist unperceived, but denies that this is in any way paradoxical, since, he says, they never do exist unperceived. God is always perceiving everything.

Now this defense is quite inadequate. First, if Berkeley is right, we never perceive anything but *our own* ideas. It follows that no one can ever perceive anything that anyone else does, and that God cannot in particular. But what we ordinarily suppose is that the very things we perceive will continue to exist when neither we nor anyone else is perceiving them, or rather that it makes sense to suppose that they will. Our objection is that Berkeley is committed to denying just this.

Also, God is introduced into the argument as a cause of ideas, and the proof of his existence does not enable us to see why he should perceive anything, let alone everything, or indeed what is meant by speaking of his perceptions. The two roles which God plays in immaterialism, that of a cause of sensations and that of ubiquitous observer, are quite unrelated and merely juxtaposed.

But there is yet a more powerful argument against allowing Berkeley to bring in God here. The objection we are considering, fully stated, is this. To say

there is a sensible object of such-and-such a kind at place so-and-so and that no one is looking at it or touching it or . . . (etc.) is to say something, which, whether or not it is true, is perfectly intelligible and self-consistent. But to admit this is precisely to admit that $E = P$, as Berkeley seems to understand it, is false. It is to admit that sensible objects can (logically) exist "without the mind." And even if everything is in fact perceived by God, this will not help. If, as we are suspecting, Berkeley is committed to denying the existence of unperceived things *a priori*, it is no defense for him to say that there are *in fact* no unperceived things. To use God to any advantage here, he would have to have shown that it was impossible for a sensible object not to be perceived *by God* (that the *esse* of a sensible thing is not just *percipi* but *percipi a Deo*). But the arguments for $E = P$ do not mention God at all.

The common suspicion that Berkeley appeals to God just to get himself out of a difficulty is then justified. Certainly in his defense it must be said that he has an independent argument for God's existence. But the independent argument does not help his case.

We must now notice that if we take him at his own words, he *cannot* meet this objection. He writes, "The table I write on, I say, exists, that is, I see and feel it; and if I were out of my study, I should say it existed, meaning thereby that if I was in my study I might perceive it, or that some other spirit actually does perceive it. There was an odour, that is to say, it was smelled; there was a sound, that is to say, it was heard; a colour or figure, and it was perceived by sight or touch. *This is all I can understand by these and the like expressions.*"[22] (My italics.) Now — ignoring the reference to "if I were out of my study" — we see that he is saying that by "There was a sound" he can understand nothing more than that a sound was heard. So he cannot understand or attach any meaning to "There was a sound which no one heard." Yet this is something which we might say, believe, or even know to be true.

It is natural now to make the following objection on his behalf: any reason we could have to suppose that there was a sound is *ipso facto* reason to suppose that a sound could have been heard (not "could have been heard by anyone who was suitably situated," since some people are deaf). Quite so; but this is to give up $E = P$ and to defend instead the weaker thesis that, where sensible things are concerned, *exists* means *to be perceivable*. And we shall see that there is some reason to think that this is what Berkeley *should* have said, and even to suppose that this is what he really *meant*. At least, this is the thesis toward which some of his most interesting arguments tend.

The Desert-Island Argument

IN the *Principles*[23] and again in the *Dialogues*[24] there is an argument designed to show that there is a formal contradiction involved in the idea of a sensible object existing unperceived. This argument, though (of course) fallacious, throws considerable light on Berkeley's motives for asserting $E = P$. Set out schematically, it comes to this:

(1) It cannot be supposed possible for sensible objects to exist without the mind unless it is possible for us to conceive them as so existing. (2) But to conceive a sensible object as existing without the mind we should have to conceive it as unconceived. (3) And to do this we should have to think about it without thinking about it, which is plainly impossible. (4) Therefore, we cannot suppose it possible for a sensible object to exist without the mind, or unconceived. (5) Therefore, we cannot suppose it possible for a sensible object to exist unperceived, either.

Let us first consider the argument up to (4). It is true that we cannot think of something without thinking of it. And it follows that if we think of something as "unthought-of" we are thinking of it as having a characteristic which it lacks. But it does not follow that we cannot suppose without absurdity that there are things which no one is thinking of. A thing *can* be "unthought-of" as long as it does not occur to someone to think that it is.

But the characteristic *being unthought-of* is an unfamiliar one. Let us then approach the fallacy in a different way.

Suppose someone says "I never make remarks about myself." This is a remark about himself, and so his making it makes it a false one. So no one, in making this remark, *could* be saying something true. But obviously it can be true of someone that he never makes remarks about himself. So then what the man in our example says of himself is something that could be true of him, even though, if he says it, it is false. (Notice that if someone else says of him "He never makes remarks about himself," this remark is not subject to the same peculiarity, and yet it is in one obvious sense the same remark as he made.) So we see that the peculiarity of his remark did not lie in *what he said* but in the relationship of *what he said* to *his saying it*. We can say that his statement is self-refuting. And obviously it is one thing for a statement to be self-refuting in this kind of way and another thing for it to be logically absurd.

Now suppose someone says "No one is now thinking of St. Paul's Cathedral. No one is 'conceiving' it; it is not in anyone's mind." It is arguable that this is self-refuting in the same way as is the statement we have just considered. But this does not mean that it is absurd or self-contradictory to suppose that there are things out of anyone's mind. Berkeley has confused self-refutingness with logical absurdity. But perhaps we can see from this what he is getting at. If someone claims that every sensible object is being perceived, we cannot refute him directly. We cannot hold up something and say "This is not perceived, look!"

But it seems that Berkeley thinks that we cannot refute him at all. We cannot refute him either by saying, for example, "There is a tea-pot in that cupboard which no one is now perceiving." For Berkeley would say that we were then *thinking* of the tea-pot. This brings us to step (5) in the argument. Surely, we may wish to say, it is one thing to think of something and another to perceive it. But there are indications that Berkeley would not have admitted this. It seems that he sometimes uses the word "perceive" in such a wide sense that to think of something — or at least of something that really exists — counts as perceiving it.

This conception of thinking must now be looked at. But to anticipate a little: suppose that for Berkeley to think of something, e.g., St. Paul's, is always to *imagine* it, and this in the sense of calling up a visual image of it ("in the mind's eye"). Then he will not allow any difference between your thinking of St. Paul's and your imagining yourself looking at it. And this would explain why he advances the desert-island argument and why he is willing to allow $E = P$ to stand or fall by it. "You may think," he argues, "that it is possible for a sensible object to exist unperceived. But just try to *imagine* a sensible object existing unperceived. What you will do — all you can do — is to imagine yourself perceiving it."

Ideas and Images

IN the *Principles*[25] Berkeley says that the objects of human knowledge are ideas, and that ideas are of three kinds. Ideas of the first kind are "imprinted on the senses." He calls these "ideas of sense." Ideas of the third kind are "formed by help of memory and imagination." Let us call these images. Between ideas of sense and images there are two important differences. There is a difference about their causation. "I find I can excite ideas [images] in my mind at pleasure. ... It is no more than willing, and straightway this or that idea arises in my fancy. ... "[26] But "the ideas actually perceived by sense have not a like dependence on my will. When in broad daylight I open my eyes, it is not in my power to choose whether I shall see or no. ... "[27] Since my ideas of sense are not creatures of my will, there must be "some other will or spirit that produces them." But with this difference there goes another. "The ideas of sense are more strong, lively, and distinct than those of the imagination; they have likewise a steadiness, order, and coherence, and are not excited at random, . . . but in a regular train or series, the admirable connection whereof sufficiently testifies the wisdom and benevolence of its author."[28]

Now these passages contain an important clue for the understanding of immaterialism. Berkeley is at pains in them to ward off the objection that he allows for no difference between what is real and can be touched and seen and what is merely imaginary. If seeing a horse and imagining a unicorn are equally a matter of having ideas, does not this obliterate the distinction between horses, which really do exist, and unicorns, which do not? Berkeley replies that he can allow for this distinction as well as anyone. If you are having ideas of a horse which are imprinted from without, you cannot make these go away by an act of will. But if you imagine a unicorn, your ideas will be, at least relatively, faint, weak, and unsteady, and you will be aware that they are excited in yourself at your own pleasure. But we must notice how much is tacitly conceded in this distinction. For apparently Berkeley regards what happens when we see something as *sufficiently like* what happens when we think of something for it to be possible to distinguish between them qualitatively. Seeing something and thinking of it are apparently regarded as species of the same genus. It is all a matter of having ideas; the difference lies only in the kind of ideas they are. To think of the sun is to have a mental image of it; and to have this is *like* seeing the sun; it is perhaps like seeing the sun *very dimly* or obscurely.

It should be clear that this conveys a totally mistaken picture of what it is like to see something and also of what it is like to think of something. We may well be in doubt sometimes whether we are seeing something or not. We may ask "Do I really see a mouse there, or is it just a piece of screwed-up paper?" But no possible doubt is represented by the question "Am I seeing a mouse or am I just thinking of one?" "I am seeing a mouse" and "I am thinking of a mouse" are not alternative hypotheses. There is no fact of which we could ask which of these is the right explanation of it. Hence there could not be criteria for determining whether a given "idea" is an idea of sense or an idea of the imagination.

Now what gives rise to this curious confusion is a certain doctrine of how thinking of something is possible. According to this conception, if we are to think of the sun by night, when the sun is not visible, we need a representative of the sun. For Berkeley this is an image. But how do we come by these images? Berkeley's answer can be found at the beginning of the *Principles*[29] and elsewhere. The central point is that some images are "copies" or "resemblances" of ideas of sense and the others are derived from such by processes of composition and division. And we have here an underlying theory which is of considerable importance for understanding Berkeley. We can think of (conceive) something only if we can frame images of it. An image is a *picture* of a possible idea of sense; it is a copy or resemblance. And it seems that sometimes he wishes to conclude from this that ideas of sense are the only things we can think about, apart, of course, from spirits. But in any case he supposes that to determine what a word means we must *generally* consider what images it excites in us. This is why

Berkeley so often entreats his reader to *look into his thoughts a little*. He is at such times not merely asking that his reader reflect, or consider, but asking him to find out whether he can attach images to certain expressions. Can he, for example, attach any image to — can he picture what is meant by — "material substrate"? Berkeley is sure that he cannot. But then either this phrase stands for a spirit (which it plainly does not) or it is meaningless, a piece of empty jargon which the learned delude themselves that they understand.

This conception of how "thinking is possible" and the associated conception of how words are able to stand for things I shall call the picture theory. We must not read more into the theory than is there. Berkeley does not say, nor does he think, that all words stand for or call up images. Some words stand for nothing, and some stand for what he calls "notions." Nor does he think that every time we hear a word uttered it calls up an image in our minds. The theory comes to no more than that a large and important class of words have meanings which can be adequately and exhaustively specified by saying what images or pictures go with them. But this is enough to give it an important bearing on $E = P$.

THE DOCTRINE OF ABSTRACT IDEAS

Berkeley often says that those who defend the philosophical conception of matter do so because they believe that some words stand for *abstract* ideas. And in the Introduction to the *Principles* he explicitly discusses this belief. It will help our enquiry to consider what he says about it.

The materials for his discussion occur in Locke's *Essay*. As Locke makes clear, the doctrine of abstract ideas arises because of the question "How do words become general?" It supplies the answer: by becoming the signs of general ideas; and it tries to show that we come by these general ideas by a process of abstraction. We start with particular ideas of various particular red things, for example. Because these ideas are all of something red, they must have something in common. And we are supposed to be able to somehow separate and discard all their features except this one; and so we can frame an *abstract* idea of red. The common adjective "red" is now held to be a sign of or a name for this abstract idea; it is the name we give to the abstract idea when we have framed it.

The chief thing to notice about this account is its extreme obscurity. *How* exactly are we supposed to be able to get one abstract idea from several particular ones, and *what* exactly is it that we are supposed to get? If we can abstract *red* from some of our ideas, does this mean that we already have the idea *red* without knowing it? We may suspect that this whole account is an unrealizable metaphor from chemistry; i.e., we are invited to think of ourselves distilling general ideas or extracting them from some particular ones by some kind of chemical process.

Let us, then, look more carefully at the problem: how do words become general? Well, words don't exactly *become* general; some words just *are* general, and we say that a word is general when it applies or could apply to more than one thing. But Locke's problem is this: if a word means something to us because it calls up an idea in our minds, and if the ideas that can be called up in our minds are derived from experience, and if everything that we experience is a particular so-and-so, then how is it that general words mean something to us? What idea is it that "red" calls up in our minds and in calling up which it means something to us? It is clear that given Locke's premises about how words come to have meanings, general words do provide a difficulty; and, of course, it is clear, too, how these premises suggest the answer. General words call up general ideas.

Now the short answer to the problem is that we do not need to suppose that to understand a general word we have to have some special idea called up in our minds. First, such words function in sentences. So we should be considering not, e.g., "man" but "That is a man" or "There is a man at the door." Secondly, and very crudely, we understand such sentences because we know what men are or what they are like or because we know within certain limits how to recognize them and pick them out from things that are not men.

Unfortunately this answer is less obvious than it should be because the problem of general words becomes mixed up with another one. It is easy to suppose that (a) all men have something in common, (b) it is in virtue of detecting this something in a man that we are able to say truly and with reason "That is a man," (c) this something is what "man" means. Let us coin the word "man-ness" for this alleged detectable characteristic. Then "man-ness" is, as "man" is not, a proper name; it is the name of a feature (an abstract entity). And throughout his discussion we find Locke systematically confusing general words with such abstract nouns. Thus, he asks: how come we by general terms; or, where find we those general natures they are supposed to stand for?

Muddling together these two problems makes Locke's question difficult to answer. For he wishes to say that the general word calls up an idea in the sense of some kind of image; but he also thinks of the idea that the word signifies as an abstract idea. These two requirements cannot be met simultaneously. Hence the frequent vagueness and the occasional absurdity of his account of how we "frame" abstract general ideas. He wishes to say that the general word stands for an image, but an image that has the same relation to the word "man" as an image of some particular man has to that man's name. There is no such idea.

Berkeley's criticism of Locke, as so often, consists in implicitly holding Locke to some one of the tangled and mutually inconsistent strands of his account.

We can, he says, imagine or represent to ourselves the ideas of various things we have perceived, and we can variously compound or divide them. We can imagine a man with two heads; or imagine a hand or a nose separated (i.e., abstracted, taken away) from the rest of the body. But what we so imagine is always and necessarily, he insists, something that we could conceivably perceive, and thus something that could conceivably exist. "But I deny that I can abstract one from another, or conceive separately, those qualities which it is impossible should exist so separated; or that I can frame a general notion by abstracting from particulars in the manner aforesaid."[30]

It is clear from this, as well as from his frequent use of such words and phrases as "prescinding," "precision," and "mental separation," that Berkeley is taking "idea" in the sense of "visual image" and that he is taking "conceiving *x*" as equivalent to "framing an image of *x*." And he is able in this way to make a devastating criticism of Locke's account. The process of abstraction is supposed to issue in a certain kind of idea. But there could not, Berkeley points out, be an idea of that kind. Consider, he says, for example, the idea that is supposed to be signified by "man"; since all men are colored it must be of something colored, but it cannot be of anything white or black or red or indeed of anything with any particular color at all. But how could there be such an idea?

It is sometimes objected on Locke's behalf that many images are much more schematic and much more "fuzzy" than Berkeley's account would suggest. But this is, I believe, to miss the point of his objection. It is true that if I say that I have a visual image of a man I do not need to be able to answer the question "What color is he?" I can, quite intelligibly, reply "No particular color, just a man." (A child's drawing of a car need not be of a car of any particular make. This is the same kind of logical point.) But Berkeley is not saying, or at least he does not need to say, that images must be completely specific in every possible way. He is saying, rather, that in so far as their features are specifiable it must be possible to specify them *consistently*. And he is perfectly right in thinking that abstract general ideas would not satisfy this requirement.

Berkeley is, however, not content with criticizing Locke's answer to his own question. He himself offers an answer to it, and an answer which has very considerable merits. In order to explain how we understand such a word as, e.g., "triangle," we do not, he says, need to appeal at all to the notion of an abstract general idea of *triangle*. If the word does call up an idea in our minds, it will be the idea (image) of some particular triangle, i.e., of a triangle of some particular size and shape. And this idea can be supposed to *represent* all figures of the same kind, i.e., all triangles. Insofar as our interest in the idea is that it is an idea of a triangle, it can be called a general idea. Thus Berkeley does not deny that there are general ideas, only that there are abstract general ones.

The great merit of this is that Berkeley sees very clearly where, so to speak, the generality *belongs*. A general word is one which applies *generally* — applies to each and every thing of a certain kind or class or sort. It is not a word which names a peculiar "general" thing. In the Draft to his Introduction he makes this point in a way that could hardly be improved on. "It is one thing for a proposition to be universally true, and another for it to be about universal natures or notions." A theorem in geometry about triangles is universally true, in the sense that it holds of all triangles whatsoever. But we do not need to suppose that it is about some abstract or universal thing called *Triangle*.

Further, Berkeley quite correctly points out that Locke's difficulties come largely from his having taken for granted that general words were like proper names. " . . . It was thought that every name has, or ought to have, *one only* precise and settled signification, which inclines men to think that there are certain *abstract determinate ideas*, which constitute the true and only immediate signification of each general name. And that it is only by the mediation of these abstract ideas, that a general name comes to signify any particular thing." Whereas, he says, there is no one thing which is *the* thing which a general name signifies; each of them signifies indifferently a great number of things.

THE POINT OF BERKELEY'S INTRODUCTION

What, however, is the discussion of abstract ideas in aid of? It seems that Berkeley wishes to draw two morals from his discussion.

First, he thinks that the belief in abstract ideas had led men not to ask themselves what they meant by certain words, by giving them an excuse not to do so. Some words, and indeed most or all of those which were important in science and philosophy, had been supposed to stand for abstract ideas; and abstract ideas had been supposed to be mysterious and recondite things. And as long as this was so, it was naturally felt to be useless to inquire what these words meant or how they were used. Consider, for example, the case of arithmetic. It has "been thought to have for its object *abstract* ideas of *number*. Of which to understand the properties and mutual habitudes is supposed no mean part of speculative knowledge."[31] But, Berkeley is clear, "there are no ideas of number *in abstract* denoted by the numeral names and figures." An account of how numerals are used must

relate them to the particular concrete things which we have occasion to count and measure.

The general moral is, then, what is explained by Berkeley when he says: "He that knows he has none other than particular ideas, will not puzzle himself in vain to find out and conceive the abstract idea, annexed to any name." But he has a special reason for urging the importance of this moral, a reason which is connected with immaterialism. Words must refer somehow, he thinks, to things that could be experienced; or, what he thinks comes to the same thing, to experiences, to ideas of sense or to images. To allow abstract ideas to mediate between words and ideas is to set this principle at nought, and in effect to proceed on the assumption that those words are meaningless.

From this he collects another moral. We are to beware of language; in philosophizing, we must endeavor to "lay aside the veil of words." Words are apt to impose on the understanding; therefore, "whatever ideas I consider, I shall endeavour to take them bare and naked into my view, keeping out of my thoughts, as far as I am able, those names which long and constant use hath so strictly united with them." And one advantage that is supposed to accrue from this is that "so long as I confine my thoughts to my own ideas divested of words, I do not see how I can be easily mistaken. The objects, I consider, I clearly and adequately know. I cannot be deceived in thinking I have an idea which I have not." Where his ideas are concerned, he thinks, questions can be answered, and answered with certainty, by nothing more than an "attentive perception" of what passes in his understanding.

This recommendation will seem an obscure one. But it becomes more intelligible if we bear in mind his conception of thinking and the theory of language that goes with it. The meaning of a word is something to be explained in terms of images and ideas. Berkeley is anxious to insist that the words we hear spoken and see written do not always call up or excite ideas in us. And he insists too that some words do not have ideas "annexed" to them at all. But there is no doubt that he takes it to be a general rule that very many words do stand for images. You understand what the word means only if you know what images and ideas belong to it. We can see how this conception both supports and is supported by $E = P$. Suppose, for example, the question arises what the word "apple" means. Well, simply imagine an apple; imagine yourself looking at one, or touching it, or eating it. Then, first, what you imagine will be a perceived apple (the desert-island argument). Secondly, what are actually present to the understanding are certain images, which are copies or representations of the sensations you would have if you were seeing or touching or eating an apple. So, Berkeley thinks, these sensations must be what "apple" refers to. To talk about an apple, or about anything imaginable, must be to talk about sensations. But is not an apple a material thing? This is either to say, in a misleading way, that among the sensations in question are certain touch-sensations of hardness and texture, or it is nonsense. And it is especially nonsense if it means that there is a piece of insensible stuff which has the sensible qualities that the apple is supposed to have. For such a thing is *unimaginable*. We do not and could not know what it would be like to come across such a piece of stuff. In the nature of the case, there can be no images which would "cash" such an alleged conception. So the phrase "material substance," used in the way in which philosophers want to use it, is strictly nonsense.

This connection between the rejection of abstract ideas and the rejection of matter comes out in a very clear way in the *Principles*.[32] Berkeley has just said that the vulgar opinion, "strangely prevailing among men," that houses, mountains, rivers, and such things have an existence distinct from their being perceived by the understanding, is one that involves a contradiction. (For these are things which we perceive by sense; and we perceive nothing by sense except our own ideas; and these clearly cannot have such an independent existence.) But how, he asks, does this strange opinion arise? It arises because of the doctrine of abstract ideas. "For can there be a nicer strain of abstraction than to distinguish the existence of sensible objects from their being perceived, so as to conceive them existing unperceived?" Anything (he says) that could exist — and anything, then, that is capable of being perceived — can be imagined or conceived. But these are the only things that can. And he seems to conclude that to imagine or think of a sensible object just *is* to imagine how it would look or feel or taste or sound or smell. "Hence as it is impossible for me to see or feel anything without an actual sensation of that thing, so is it impossible for me to conceive in my thoughts any sensible thing or object distinct from the sensation or perception of it."

We are now in a position to see why he is so certain that to see the truth of $E = P$ it is enough to "look into our thoughts" and consider what we mean when we say of some sensible thing that it exists; why he says, mistakenly, that "There was a sound" means the same as "A sound was heard." For we can see how he arrives at these accounts of what the expressions mean. To find out what is meant by saying (for example) "There is a table in my study" we must lay aside the veil of words and consider what imaginable situation would make us say this. We shall then imagine a situation in which we are having the relevant ideas of sight and touch. And this shows us what the sentence means. If we could not imagine how things would look and seem if there were a table there, we should not know what it meant to say there was a table there; the sentence would be a set of empty words.

IMMATERIALISM AND VERIFICATIONISM

I want now to suggest that we can distinguish between two quite different sets of considerations which tend Berkeley toward the central theses of his philosophy. He himself did not so distinguish them, doubtless, but that is no reason why we should not.

In reading him it is impossible not to be struck by the way in which he, as it seems carelessly, takes for granted the very thing which to us seems so absurd and shocking — the thesis that apples and stones are literally ideas or sensations or combinations of them. For what are sensible objects, he asks, "but the things we perceive by sense, and what do we perceive besides our own sensations or ideas?"[33] Here, at the very beginning of the *Principles*, he is assuming — for of course the question is a rhetorical one — the very thing we should expect him to try to prove. And this is by no means an isolated instance. Throughout his Introduction he speaks as if it were obvious that practically all words refer to ideas, while yet continuing to speak as if some of them referred to triangles, lines, and men. Again, he says[34] that the sun he sees by day is the real sun and the one he imagines by night is the idea of the former. But (it should occur to us) what he imagines by night is not an idea or image of anything, but the sun itself. The idea is what we frame *in* imagining the sun (if we have strong and clear visual images, as obviously Berkeley had). If it is correct to speak of imagining the idea of the sun, why not also speak of seeing the idea of it, i.e., of seeing that idea of sense which we have, as we should ordinarily say, *in* seeing the sun? But of course he thinks that this *is* equally correct.

The clue to this practice is provided by Philonous. "I do not pretend to be a setter-up of new notions. My endeavours tend only to unite and place in a clearer light that truth, which was before shared between the vulgar and the philosophers; the former being of opinion, that *those things they immediately perceive are the real things*; and the latter, that *the things immediately perceived, are ideas which exist only in the mind*. Which two notions being put together, do in effect constitute the substance of what I advance."[35] So immaterialism is not self-contained. Berkeley is writing in and taking entirely for granted a whole tradition of philosophizing; and the central thesis of that tradition is that what we really perceive, what we are directly aware of, are sensations and images — ideas — which are copies, or representations, of things outside us. In this tradition it is to these ideas that we primarily give names; it is to these that words primarily refer. And we must suppose that he was so much "inside" this tradition that he could not ever call its basic tenets into question.

Suppose now that someone is systematically taught to call seeing an apple "seeing the idea of an apple"; to call touching an apple "touching the idea of an apple"; and so on. And suppose he now hears it suggested that the real apple is something quite distinct from what he sees and eats and touches, but which (somehow) *underlies* what he sees and eats and touches. He might very well reply that this conception of a *real* apple is an empty and absurd one. The word "apple," he might say, is being mis-applied. We give that name to just those things which we *do* see and touch (and what do we see and touch besides ideas?) So what could be understood by the phrase "a real apple," if a real apple is sup-posed to be distinct from anything we see and touch or could see and touch? How are we to imagine or conceive these real apples? Is it not obvious (he might ask) that unless the phrase marks out certain ideas it marks out nothing? And again, how could anyone know that these real apples exist or know anything about their nature? The suggestion is not merely false; it is empty. Given that we see those ideas which we call ideas of an apple and touch and taste the ideas which go with them, what does it matter whether there is a real apple there or not? How would the world be different? And what, finally, is meant by saying that the real apple *under-lies* the apple we see and touch? Is it not clear that this is an unrealizable metaphor? For it does not underlie it in the way that the table (for example) does. So (he might sum up) it is not merely that the champions of this suggestion *do not* explain to us clearly what they mean; a little reflection will make clear to us that they *could not*.

Now if we make allowances for his acceptance of the thesis, commonplace among educated men of his time, that we perceive only ideas, we shall see that the case described above is almost exactly Berkeley's case. And we can say that his philosophy represents an attempt to square that thesis with the demands of a tough-minded and sensible common-sense frame of mind. Naturally, the attempt does not entirely succeed. The awful implications of the accepted thesis are not entirely exorcised. Or, to put it differently, although Berkeley sometimes speaks as if "We have ideas-of-sense of an apple" were just a way of saying "We see apples," he does sometimes seem to regard it as saying something different. Sometimes the former is a strict way of saying the latter, but sometimes he speaks as if the latter were, strictly speaking, false, or at least misleading. Thus he is compelled to say that, strictly speaking, we do not see and touch the same thing, and do not see and touch the same thing as other people. There is no place in immaterialism for the conception of a sensible world which we *share* with other human beings. But the interest of his philosophy lies in his having made the attempt. For the methods of argument he deployed are available against more genuine bogies. Berkeley himself deployed them, with varying degrees of success, in discussions of the nature of scientific theories and of scientific theoriz-ing; of theories of motion; of mathematical concepts and especially the concepts involved in the differ-ential calculus; and the psychology of human vision.

15

Hume

A. G. N. FLEW

DAVID HUME WAS BORN in Edinburgh in 1711. His family was well-connected on both sides, though its estate of Ninewells in Berwickshire was small. Hume's father died in 1713, leaving three children to their mother, "a woman of singular merit, who, though young and handsome, devoted herself entirely to the rearing and educating of her children." In 1723, a few weeks before his twelfth birthday, David was admitted to Edinburgh University along with his elder brother John. He left, without taking a degree, in 1725 or 1726. The next few years were spent studying at home: "My studious disposition, my sobriety, and my industry gave my family a notion that the law was a proper profession for me. But I found an insurmountable aversion to everything but the pursuits of philosophy and general learning, and while they fancied I was poring over Voet and Vinnius, Cicero and Vergil were the authors which I was secretly devouring."

In 1734, after a certain Anne Galbraith had accused him of fathering her third child conceived out of wedlock, Hume entered the office of a West Indies merchant in Bristol. This venture was brief and half-hearted. He withdrew to France: "During my retreat in France, first at Rheims, but chiefly at La Flèche, in Anjou, I composed my *Treatise of Human Nature*." At La Flèche he had contacts with the famous Jesuit college which had educated Descartes. In 1737 he returned to London, to arrange publication. But even before the first two volumes appeared early in 1739, he had returned to Ninewells.

In 1745 the electors preferred William Cleghorn to the already "notorious infidel" Hume for the Professorship of Ethics and Pneumatical Philosophy at Edinburgh. In the same year he had accepted the job of tutor to the young Marquess of Annandale, who turned out to be certifiably insane. In 1746 Hume served as secretary to General St. Clair in an abortive raid on the coast of France, and in 1747 accompanied him on a military embassy to the courts of Vienna and Turin. In 1749 Hume returned to Ninewells, but removed to Edinburgh in 1751. (In the same year Glasgow preferred James Clow to Hume for its Professor of Logic.) In 1752 Hume became librarian to the Faculty of Advocates in Edinburgh, and was thus able to start work on his *History of England*. By 1761 his literary reputation was sufficient for all his works to be admitted to the *Index librorum prohibitorum* in Rome.

In 1763 the Earl of Hertford asked him to be his secretary on his embassy in Paris. This was an inspired appointment, for Hume was immediately lionized by the whole of

Paris society, while he did the formal side of the job well enough to be left for a period as *chargé d'affaires*. He returned from France in 1766 with Rousseau in tow. He made great efforts to arrange for him an acceptable retreat in England. The impossible Rousseau repaid all this kindness with animosity and abuse. In 1767 Hume accepted the important Undersecretaryship of the Northern Department of the Secretary of State in London. This post he resigned in 1769 to retire finally to Edinburgh. In 1775 he was struck with a fatal wasting disease of the bowels. Unshaken in his assurance of annihilation, continuing to receive friends as affably as always, and to send corrections of his works to the printers, he followed faithfully the family motto "True to the end." He died in 1776.

IN ORDER TO SEE the philosophical works of Hume in the perspective of his life's work, and perhaps also even to appreciate more fully the point of some of his actual philosophical doctrines, it is as well to realize what part they played in his total literary effort. Similarly, in order to gain any understanding of Hume's philosophical development, we need to have a picture of the relations between the various philosophical writings themselves. It is therefore convenient to begin with an annotated check list of his chief publications.

First, in 1739 Hume published the first two Books of his *A Treatise of Human Nature*, following these with the third Book in 1740. This was described on the title page as "An attempt to introduce the experimental method of reasoning into moral subjects." In two hackneyed sentences of his autobiography he records: "Never literary attempt was more unfortunate than my *Treatise of Human Nature*. It fell deadborn from the press, without reaching such distinction as even to excite a murmur among the zealots." This was his largest and most wide-ranging philosophical work, and the one by which — to his own later exasperation — at least his general philosophy has usually been judged.

Second, in 1740 there appeared *An Abstract of a Treatise of Human Nature*. This, like the *Treatise* itself, was anonymous, and referred to the author in the third person. But J. M. Keynes and P. Sraffa in their edition[1] established finally that the author must have been Hume. The *Abstract* is only a pamphlet. But it is very significant as a review of what Hume himself in 1740 considered to be the most important new moves made in the *Treatise*.

Third, in 1742 the first fifteen *Essays, Moral and Political* appeared in Edinburgh, again anonymously. They were successful. Other editions and more essays followed.[2] These were the first of Hume's works to bear his name. These urbane, rather slight, pieces are relevant to us mainly as indications of Hume's lifelong consistent concern for human studies. "In these four sciences of Logic, Morals, Criticism, and Politics," he had written in the Introduction to the *Treatise*, "is comprehended almost everything which it can any way import us to be acquainted with, or which can tend either to the improvement or ornament of the human mind."

Fourth, in 1748 appeared the *Philosophical Essays concerning Human Understanding*, to which Hume in 1758 gave their present title, *An Enquiry concerning Human Understanding*. We shall refer to this either as the first *Enquiry* or as the *EHU*. In the autobiography Hume states: "I had always entertained a notion that my want of success in publishing the *Treatise of Human Nature* had proceeded more from the manner than the matter, and that I had been guilty of a very usual indiscretion in going to the press too early. I therefore cast the first part of that work anew in the *Enquiry concerning Human Understanding*. . . . " In a letter of 1751 he wrote: "I believe the *Philosophical Essays* contain everything of consequence relating to the understanding which you meet with in the *Treatise;* and I give you my advice against reading the latter."[3] And even as early as 1740 Hume had confessed his dissatisfaction with the *Treatise* to his friend Francis Hutcheson: "I am apt, in a cool hour, to suspect in general that most of my reasonings will be more useful by furnishing hints and exciting people's curiosity than as containing any principles that will augment the stock of knowledge that must pass to future ages."[4] Yet when his philosophical doctrines at last began to attract systematic attention it was upon the *Treatise* that the fire was concentrated. This is true of Thomas Reid's *Inquiry into the Human Mind* (1764).* The same was true of "that bigoted silly fellow" Beattie's *Essay on the Nature and Immutability of Truth* (1770). This is now remembered only because Kant used it as a source about the *Treatise* and because Sir Joshua Reynolds commemorated it and its author in an offensive painting. Exasperated by this concentration, Hume wrote the repudiation that first appeared posthumously in his definitive edition (1777) of *Essays and Treatises on Several Subjects*. (This includes all the works he wished to preserve, apart from the *History* and the *Dialogues*.)

Yet if we compare the first *Enquiry* with the *Treatise* we find that the former is by no means simply a revised and rewritten version of Book I "Of the Understanding": "Pieces where some negligences in

* Hume also spelt the word "inquiry." But it is common present practice which I have followed in referring throughout to Hume's *Enquiries* but to Reid's *Inquiry*.

his former reasoning, and more in the expression, are, he hopes, corrected." Certainly there is a very great improvement in style. But the content, too, is obviously different. Several subjects — such as substance, space, time, and personal identity — which are treated at length in *Treatise* Book I are either omitted altogether or dealt with very cursorily in *EHU*. The latter contains a section "Of Liberty and Necessity." This subject was dealt with in the *Treatise* in Book II "Of the Passions." There are also two whole sections, § X "Of Miracles" and § XI "Of a Particular Providence and of a Future State," which have no original in the *Treatise* as published. However, we know, from one of Hume's letters to his friend the future Lord Kames, that the manuscript once included some "reasonings concerning miracles" which Hume excised along with some other things: "which I am afraid will give too much offense, even as the world is disposed at present . . . I am at present castrating my work, that is, cutting off its nobler parts, that is, endeavouring it shall give as little offense as possible. . . ."[5]

In *EHU* § I, which corresponds to the *Treatise* "Introduction," Hume proclaims as one (perhaps his main) purpose something scarcely even hinted anywhere in the earlier book. He is concerned, like Locke, "to enquire seriously into the nature of human understanding." But Hume's intentions are also here explicitly polemical and secularizing. Whereas the *Treatise* is — as befits a treatise — detached, this *Enquiry* is aggressively engaged. It brings academic philosophy into the field to support a rational and, in Hume's view, therefore secular world outlook. This it does by raising what is "the justest and most plausible objection against a considerable part of metaphysics; that they are not properly a science, but arise either from the fruitless efforts of human vanity, which would penetrate into subjects utterly inaccessible to the understanding; or from the craft of popular superstitions, which, being unable to defend themselves on fair ground, raise these entangling brambles to cover and protect their weakness. Chased from the open country these robbers fly into the forest, and lie in wait to break in upon every unguarded avenue of the mind, and overwhelm it with religious fears and prejudices."

All this presents a problem to the interpreter. In the face of Hume's own protests to concentrate on the *Treatise* while neglecting the *EHU* would indeed be "a practice very contrary to all rules of candour and fair-dealing." Yet, in spite of these protests, to ignore the earlier in favor of the later work is out of the question. For this *Enquiry* omits or abbreviates many of the explorations of Book I of the *Treatise*, explorations which are indeed "useful by furnishing hints and exciting people's curiosity." Perhaps the appropriate approach is a compromise; to regard the *Treatise* as the fortunately preserved notebooks recording early philoso-phical investigations, and the *EHU* as the first public expression of Hume's mature philosophy. We shall then not be tempted to think of the latter merely as a rewriting of the former, but be on the alert to notice any further changes of substance over and above the obvious gross additions and omissions.

Fifth, late in 1751 or early in 1752 came *An Enquiry concerning the Principles of Morals*, "which is another part of my *Treatise* that I cast anew." This second *Enquiry* (*EPM*) covers afresh the ground of Book III "Of Morals." In this case Hume has revised, rearranged, and rewritten his material so thoroughly that it is scarcely possible to give suitably diagrammatic indications of the differences between the two books. But it is in this case not disputed that there has been genuine and substantial development.

Sixth, certainly in 1752, came the *Political Discourses*. This was "the only work of mine that was successful on the first publication." These are much more substantial and important than the *Essays, Moral and Political*. They seem to have had considerable influence on the Founding Fathers of the United States of America. (Incidentally, Hume himself early formed and consistently maintained a strong sympathy with the national aspirations of the American colonists.) These *Political Discourses* include several historically important contributions to political economy.[6]

The essay "Of the Populousness of Ancient Nations" is a milestone in both historical and demographic enquiry. But this and the others are relevant to us here primarily as further indications of Hume's constructive concern with and for social studies.

Seventh, in 1754, he published in Edinburgh a history of the Stuarts which ultimately became the last volume of his *History of England, from the Invasion of Julius Caesar to the Revolution in 1688*. In the following years till 1762 he wrote and published volumes on the earlier periods. (Hume wrote his *History* "as witches use to say their prayers — backwards.") During and after his period of official employments (1763–1769) he was offered opportunities and inducements to complete the work by carrying the account right up to his own time. The story goes that his final refusal was couched in devastatingly exhaustive terms: "I must decline not only this offer, but all others of a literary nature, for four reasons. Because I'm too old, too fat, too lazy, and too rich."[7]

Of course, this *History* has long since become obsolete, although it was a popular book for a century or more. It was a very characteristic product of the Enlightenment, and played its part both in that and in the general development of historiography. We need to notice here only the sustained attempt in it at a clinically naturalistic detachment. Voltaire remarked: "Mr. Hume, in his *History*, is neither parliamentarian, nor royalist, nor Anglican, nor Presbyterian — he is simply judicial . . . we find a

mind superior to his materials; he speaks of weaknesses, blunders, cruelties as a physician speaks of
epidemic diseases."[8]

Eighth, in 1757, came *Four Dissertations*. The
first of these, *The Natural History of Religion*, is
what its title partly suggests, an essay at the detached consideration of the origin and development
of religion as a natural phenomenon. The second,
"Of the Passions," covers the same ground as Book
II of the *Treatise*, often in the same words. But it
omits the main thing of interest left from this book
after the transfer of the discussion on liberty and
necessity to the first and that on reason and conduct
to the second *Enquiry*, namely, the attempt systematically to apply to psychological phenomena the
distinction between ideas and impressions and the
principle of the association of ideas. In the *Abstract*
Hume had boldly hoped: "if anything can entitle
the author to so glorious a name as that of an
'inventor' it is the use he makes of the principle
of the association of ideas." The other two dissertations are aesthetic, "Of Tragedy" and "Of the
Standard of Taste." Originally the fourth was to have
been "Some Considerations previous to Geometry
and Natural Philosophy." But Hume withdrew
this and substituted two others. He then replaced
these by the present fourth. Of those withdrawn
two survive, "Of Suicide" and "Of the Immortality
of the Soul."

Ninth, posthumously in 1779, appeared the
Dialogues concerning Natural Religion. These Hume
had begun at least as early as 1751. But his own caution and the pressure of his friends prevented him
from publishing them in his lifetime. The whole
story is pieced together in N. Kemp-Smith's definitive edition.[9] Kemp-Smith argues — I think decisively — that Philo is throughout the mouthpiece
of Hume. E. C. Mossner accepts this, and adds arguments for the identification of Demea with Dr.
Clarke and Cleanthes with Bishop Butler.[10] This
survey of Hume's total literary output will already
have suggested certain difficulties in presenting his
philosophical thinking. In addition to these peculiar
problems arising from the existence of both *Treatise*
and *Enquiries*, there is the more general one presented by richness and complexity. The range of
problems considered by Hume is much wider than
that treated by most of the other great philosophers
of the modern period. In dealing extensively not
only with general philosophy but also with morals,
politics, aesthetics, and the philosophy of religion
he resembles Kant rather than Descartes, Locke,
Leibniz, or Berkeley. The complexity does not come
mainly from any inadequacy of expression or intri-
cacy of mind but from the fact that he has several
objectives which it is not always easy, or even
possible, to reconcile.[11] So in this chapter we shall
not attempt to cover everything. Instead we select
a few themes, trying to pick out those of the greatest
historical interest, those most characteristic of Hume,

and those of most relevance today. When in doubt
we give weight to Hume's own explicit and implicit
judgments of relative importance. Inevitably this
method must involve that some themes will engage
disproportionate attention while others, often both
interesting and important, will be ignored entirely.
Yet this is much to be preferred to the distant
generalities which would result from an attempt to
cram in everything.

Psychological and Logical Empiricism

IN *Treatise*, *Abstract*, and first *Enquiry* Hume begins
the main business by proclaiming his empiricist
principle: "The first proposition is that all our
ideas, or weak perceptions, are derived from our
impressions, or strong perceptions; and that we can
never think of anything we have not seen without
us or felt in our own minds."[12] This, he suggests, is
an improved version of what Locke was after in
denying the existence of innate ideas. Impressions
comprise "all our sensations, passions, and emotions, as they make their first appearance in the soul."
Ideas are "the faint images of these in thinking and
reasoning."[13] "Impressions and ideas differ only in
their strength and vivacity."[14] Together these make
up the whole class of "perceptions." Ideas are
always copies of impressions. They are thought of,
traditionally, as mental images. All this provides the
grounds for a method of challenge: "When we entertain . . . any suspicion that a philosophical term is
employed without any meaning or idea . . . we need
but enquire, 'From what impression is that supposed
idea derived?' "[15]

The first thing to notice is that this is a psychological, not a logical, empiricism. Hume is making an
assertion about what men, as a matter of contingent
fact, cannot do. This is appropriate to the fundamental stated objective of the *Treatise*, which is to
develop a new science of man in hopes that success
here will revolutionize our understanding of other
subjects too. Hume proposes[16] "to march up
directly to the capital or centre of these sciences, to
human nature itself. . . . There is no question of importance whose decision is not comprised in the
science of man, and there is none which can be
decided with any certainty before we become acquainted with that science." We are "pretending . . .
to explain the principles of human nature. . . ."*

The second point to remark is that in the *Treatise*
Hume takes it for granted that mental images must
play an essential part in the significant use of lan-

---

* "What is this but a Scottish version of Kant's Copernican
Revolution?" asks H. H. Price.[17] There are far more similarities — beneath gross differences of style and temperament —
between Hume and Kant than are generally recognized, or
perhaps than Kant himself fully appreciated. It is here instructive to compare Continental reactions to Kant "the all-
destroyer" with the traditional English-speaking tendency to
fly to him as a refuge from the terrible Hume.

guage. Ideas *are* thoughts, and no word can be employed meaningfully unless it is associated with an idea. It is significant that in paying tribute to "one of the greatest and most valuable discoveries that has been made of late years, in the republic of letters" Hume understates Berkeley's achievement. For Berkeley in fact did more than assert "that all general ideas are nothing but particular ones, annexed to a certain term, which gives them a more extensive signification, and makes them recall upon occasion other individuals, which are similar to them."[18] He argued further that words could be meaningful without benefit of the actual or dispositional occurrence of any mental imagery at all.[19]

To support this psychological empiricism Hume appeals to two sorts of evidence: first, examination of his own experience; and, second, the experience of those born blind, deaf, or otherwise defective experientially. "Those who would assert that this position is not universally true nor without exception have only one and that an easy method of refuting it; by producing that idea which, in their opinion, is not derived from this source."[20]

The inadequacy of Hume's principle to support his method comes out clearly if we consider this last sentence quoted. It is all very well to support a psychological generalization by citing evidence, and then to challenge all comers to produce a counterexample. But you cannot properly proceed to use a mere generalization as your ground for rejecting as illegitimate any "supposed idea" for which no parent impression can be produced. Yet this is precisely what Hume proposes to do: " . . . if no impression can be produced, he concludes that the term is altogether insignificant."[21]

Something sounder can nevertheless be developed from this heads-I-win-tails-you-lose procedure. The psychological can be transmuted into a philosophical thesis — and this provides a paradigm of the sort of transposition which is often rewarding to the student of Hume. Consider Hume's own example of the man blind from birth. The psychological thesis is that because he has never enjoyed visual sensations he is unable to form visual mental images. This may well be true. But how was Hume in a position to know? Psychological facts cannot be known *a priori*: "As the science of man is the only solid foundation for the other sciences, so the only solid foundation we can give to this science itself must be laid on experience and observation."[22] Suppose such a blind man did sometimes have yellow mental images. How could he identify them as such and tell us about them if he had never seen any yellow things?

At one moment the *Treatise* gets very warm indeed: "To give a child an idea of scarlet or orange, of sweet or bitter, I present the objects, or, in other words, convey to him these impressions."[23] The point is that the man blind from birth could not understand any of our purely visual terms, simply because the meaning of these can only be given by reference to visible things. If now we generalize this we get a principle of logical empiricism: No term can be understood by anyone unless its meaning can be given in terms of his experience, and no term can have any public meaning in a public language except what can be given by reference to the public world. Such a principle is logical, not psychological. Its truth, if it is true, depends not on whether certain contingent facts obtain about people, but entirely on the meanings of the terms employed to state it.

A principle of logical empiricism could serve Hume's methodological purposes admirably. It could, where a psychological generalization could not, support his challenges to explain in terms of human experience the meanings of allegedly significant expressions. It could also spare him some of the embarrassments to which his psychological empiricism gave rise. Thus in the *Treatise* he distinguishes simple from complex perceptions. He insists that whereas complex ideas do not have to be copies of complex impressions the simple ideas of which they are composed can only be derived from simple impressions. The logical analogue would be a distinction between terms which can be defined verbally and terms which can be defined only ostensively. Now in both *Treatise* and *Enquiry* he asks whether we could have an idea of a particular shade if we had had impressions only of the shades bracketing it on a color card. He allows that we could, admits this as an authentic exception to his rule, but laughs it off brazenly as only a little one: "this instance is so singular that it is scarcely worth our observing and does not merit that for it alone we should alter our general maxim."[24] This is scarcely a difficulty at all for logical empiricism. The expression referring to the intermediate shade, unlike a mental image of that shade, would obviously be complex, not simple.

It is worth noticing certain differences between the treatment in the *Treatise* and in the *Enquiry*. The former makes much of ideas as essential to the significant employment of words, the latter largely drops this. The *Enquiry* still says that "all our ideas . . . are copies of our impressions."[25] But it is not as insistent on a literal psychologizing interpretation as the *Treatise*, which speaks of "exact representations" which "differ only in degree."[26] Again, while the *Treatise* takes it that impressions are always and only involved in actually feeling and seeing and ideas in merely imagining, remembering, or thinking, officially their only — and hence presumably defining — difference there lies in their different vivacity. (Therefore the maximum concession in the *Treatise* to disturbing facts, such as eidetic and hallucinatory imagery or auditory percepts so faint as to be mistaken for imagings, is: "that in particular instances" ideas and impressions "may very nearly approach to each other."[27]) In the *Enquiry*, though the "two classes . . . are distinguished by their different degrees of force," this distinction seems to be regarded not so much as defining as a mark of the fundamental division between thinking and experience. (Thus the later book can afford to concede that in "disease or madness" ideas and impressions can become "altogether undistinguishable."[28]) Again, the *Enquiry* contains hints of a quite fresh distinction, between language and the world: "All the colours of poetry ... can never ... make the description be taken for a real landscape."[29] Finally, the paragraphs which take the place of discussion of simple and complex ideas entertain the incongruously Cartesian thought: "What never was seen ... may yet be conceived, nor is anything beyond the power of thought, except what implies an absolute contradiction."[30]

Of course, all this is largely a matter of nuances. Yet it does suggest that the mature Hume was beginning to edge away from his first extreme and rather unstable form of psychological empiricism. He seems to be recognizing some of its inadequacies and, perhaps, realizing that the really fruitful point is that the range of human understanding must be limited ultimately by the range of human experience: "though our thought seems to possess ... unbounded liberty ... it is really confined within very narrow limits ... all this creative power of the mind amounts to no more than the faculty of compounding, transposing, augmenting, or diminishing the materials afforded us by ... experience."[31]

Hume's Fork

IN the *Treatise* Hume proceeds next to elaborate subdivisions within his two categories, to introduce the notion of the association of ideas — the mental analogue of gravitational attraction between corporeal atoms — and to apply his principle to the tricky notions of substance, abstraction, space and time, mathematics, and existence. Where Locke compromises, Hume insists radically: "We have therefore no idea of substance, distinct from that of particular qualities, nor have we any other meaning when we either talk or reason concerning it."[32] Unlike Berkeley, Hume has no intention to substitute for occult Lockean substrata a Divine Agent presenting and sustaining our perceptual impressions.[33] Similarly, "the idea of existence is not derived from any particular impression. The idea of existence is the very same with the idea of what we conceive to be existent."[34] It is only in Part III that he reaches the subject "Of Knowledge and Probability." In the *Abstract* he passes to this directly, with only a sidelong mention of "our idea of substance and essence." In the *Enquiry* he moves via a section, mostly omitted from the definitive edition, in which he displays his associationist notions by applying them to literary criticism.

The treatment of knowledge and probability in the *Enquiry* itself differs considerably from that in the *Treatise*. It opens:

> All the objects of human reason or enquiry may naturally be divided into two kinds, to wit, *relations of ideas* and *matters of fact*. Of the first kind are the sciences of geometry, algebra, and arithmetic, and, in short, every affirmation which is either intuitively or demonstratively certain. ... Propositions of this kind are discoverable by the mere operation of thought, without dependence on what is anywhere existent in the universe. ... Matters of fact ... are not ascertained in the same manner, nor is our evidence of their truth, however great, of a like nature. The contrary of every matter of fact is still possible, because it can never imply a contradiction ... [35]

In the *Treatise*, though such a distinction is adumbrated in Book I[36] and developed in Book II[37], it is only set visibly to work in Book III. It serves there as a framework for the analysis of moral judgments.[38] This is the instrument nicknamed for its more aggressive employments "Hume's Fork."

It is a dichotomy belonging in its developed form unequivocally not to psychology but to logic. It obtains between kinds of proposition, not sorts of perception. The differentiae are: that whereas one kind can be known *a priori* and cannot be denied without self-contradiction, the other kind can be denied without contradiction and can be known only *a posteriori*. Any suspicion that the phrase "either intuitively or demonstratively certain" might be intended to allow room for some criterion of the truth of propositions about the relations of ideas other than the test of non-contradiction is removed later. Hume then makes it clear that the distinction he has in mind is that between those necessary propositions whose truth can be known immediately from an understanding of the meanings of their terms, and those which "cannot be known. . . without a train of reasoning and enquiry."[39]

There is no suggestion now that ideas are mental images. If propositions about the relations of ideas were about the relations between mental images they would belong to the other category. Propositions do not become *a priori* merely because the matters of fact which they purport to state are psychological. (Not but what many philosophers seem to have mistaken it that they did.)

Hume's division is intended to be both exclusive and exhaustive. Yet he provides two differentiae. Each of these separately would certainly make such a classification possible. But it is not obvious — and it is certainly not shown — that the use of the two different differentiae must always give the same results. Presumably Hume would have met this objection by challenging his opponent to produce some proposition which can be both known *a priori* and denied without contradiction. He might also have added, what at least once he seems to suggest in defense of his principle of psychological empiricism,[40] that he had found so many cases where his assumption worked, and none where it did not, that it was good methodological sense to proceed at least provisionally as if it always would. But he would have been better advised to put the emphasis on the word "known," and to insist that it is only on the basis of experience that any matter of fact could properly be said to be known.

The first use here of Hume's new analytic tool is to present a revised account of the nature of mathematics. The examples of propositions about the relations of ideas are drawn from geometry and arithmetic: "*That the square of the hypotenuse is equal to the square of the two sides* is a proposition which expresses a relation between these two figures. *That three times five is equal to the half of thirty* expresses a relation between these numbers." Such propositions can be discovered *a priori* and are necessarily true, and "Though there never was a circle or a triangle in nature, the truths demonstrated by Euclid would forever retain their certainty and evidence."[41] Hume also sketches an account of applied mathematics: "Every part of mixed mathematics proceeds on the supposition that certain laws are established by nature in her operations, and abstract reasonings are employed either to assist experience in the discovery of these laws or to determine their influence in particular instances. Thus it is a law of motion, discovered by experience, that the moment or force of any body is in the compound ratio or proportion of its solid contents and its velocity. . . . Geometry assists us in the application of this law. . . ."[42] This is very thin. But it is a by-blow offered here rather by way of incidental illustration than as a full-dress exposition. Perhaps the suppressed and lost essay on geometry would have filled in the outline, although there is very good reason to believe that it too was unsatisfactory.*

Nevertheless this represents a considerable advance on the treatment in the *Treatise*. That asserts that "geometry falls short of that perfect precision and certainty, which are peculiar to arithmetic and algebra."† The trouble with geometry is that "its original and fundamental principles are derived merely from appearances."[45] Hume's contention arises logically directly from his own first principles. For if such geometrical concepts as "circle," "straight line," and "point" are to be construed as mental pictures, then they cannot, however idealized, be the ideal notions of mathematics. A mental picture of a point must have extension as well as position. This comes out excellently in his challenge to "our mathematician to form, as accurately as possible, the ideas

of a circle and a right line. . . . I then ask if upon the conception of their contact he can conceive them as touching in a mathematical point, or if he must necessarily imagine them to concur for some space."[46] Unable to see how ideal geometrical concepts could be derived from experience or how any concepts could occur without mental imagery, Hume had no option but to argue[47] that really there is no such creature as an ideal geometrical notion. So the mathematicians are mistaken in their definitions.*

This position is buttressed by considering difficulties about infinite divisibility. These all arise from the proposition "Everything capable of being infinitely divided contains an infinite number of parts; otherwise the division would be stopped short by the indivisible parts, which we should immediately arrive at."[49] This is one of those beguiling propositions which can seem obvious until some devastating Hobbist points out that it is quite mistaken:" For to be divided into infinite parts, is nothing else but to be divided into as many parts as any man will."[50] This false start largely vitiates Hume's treatment of space and time, though that did perhaps provide Kant with one or two stimulating suggestions.

The *Enquiry* has little to say about space and time. But it makes clear that Hume was still troubled by paradoxes of infinite divisibility, which are considered as providing grounds for some skepticism even within the demonstrative sciences: "Reason here seems to be thrown into a kind of amazement. . . . She sees a full light which illumines certain places, but that light borders on the most profound darkness. Yet still reason must remain restless and unquiet, even with regard to that skepticism to which she is driven by these seeming absurdities and contradictions."[51] So in a backsliding footnote he suggests that they might possibly be avoided "if it be admitted that there is no such thing as abstract or general ideas, properly speaking, but that all general ideas are in reality particular ones attached to a general term. . . . " In the same note, in a passage excised after the second edition of 1750, he adds: "the ideas . . . which are the chief objects of geometry are far from being so exact and so determinate as to be the foundation of such extraordinary inferences."[52]

The second use of the new analytic tool in the first *Enquiry* is for the examinations of the logic (and then the psychology) of arguments from experience. It is this part of Hume's thought which, in the eyes of posterity as well as, apparently, in those of the author of the *Abstract*, has done most to "shake off the yoke of authority, accustom men to think for themselves, give new hints which men of genius may carry further and, by the very opposition, illustrate points wherein no one before suspected any difficulty."

---

* By 1772 Hume himself could not remember much about it: "I happened to meet Lord Stanhope . . . and he convinced me, that either there was some defect in the argument or in its perspicacity; I forget which; and I wrote Mr. Millar that I would not print the Essay."[43]

† It is instructive to compare this account with that given by J. S. Mill.[44]

* It is instructive to compare the position of Plato, who also could not see how they could be derived from experience, but who insisted that they were genuine, and was thus led to argue that they must have been acquired in a previous life.[48]

In the end it is this distinction between propositions about relations of ideas and propositions about matters of fact which shapes the conclusions of the first *Enquiry* and becomes the framework of Hume's whole mature philosophy. In the last part of the final section he reviews all main subjects of "reasoning and enquiry" and concludes: "When we run over libraries, persuaded of these principles, what havoc must we make? If we take in our hand any volume — of divinity or school metaphysics, for instance — let us ask, *Does it contain any abstract reasoning concerning quantity or number?* No. *Does it contain any experimental reasoning concerning matter of fact and existence?* No. Commit it then to the flames, for it can contain nothing but sophistry and illusion."[53] This exhilarating purple passage epitomizes everything in Hume which made him the spiritual father of logical positivism.[54]

Arguments from Experience

HAVING allocated mathematics to one side of the great divide Hume turns his attention to the other.

> The contrary of every matter of fact is still possible, because it can never imply a contradiction.... *The sun will not rise tomorrow* is no less intelligible a proposition and implies no more contradiction than *It will rise*. We should in vain therefore attempt to . . . demonstrate its falsehood. . . . It may therefore be a subject worthy of curiosity to enquire what is the nature of that evidence which assures us of any real existence and matter of fact beyond the present testimony of our senses or the records of our memory. . . . All reasonings concerning matter of fact seem to be founded on the relation of cause and effect.[55]

But "the mind can always conceive any effect to follow from any cause, and indeed any event to follow upon another; whatever we conceive is possible, at least in a metaphysical sense. . . . "[56] So when again it is asked, "*What is the foundation of all our reasonings and conclusions concerning that relation?* it may be replied in one word, *Experience*. But if we still carry on our sifting humour and ask, *What is the foundation of all conclusions from experience?* this implies a new question which may be of more difficult solution and explication."[57]

The exposition in the *Enquiry* is far neater than that in the *Treatise*. It centers on the logical relations of two representative propositions. "When a man says, *I have found, in all past instances, such sensible qualities conjoined with such secret powers*, and when he says, *Similar sensible qualities will always be conjoined with similar secret powers*, he is not guilty of a tautology. . . . You say that the one proposition is an inference from the other; but you must confess that the inference is not intuitive, neither is it demonstrative."[58] The crux is that the nerve of all

arguments from experience seems to be a move from *All known x's are* φ to *All x's are* φ. "There is required," Hume remarks, "a medium which may enable the mind to draw such an inference," adding darkly, "if indeed it be drawn by reasoning and argument."

Yet where is this medium, that is, middle term, to be found? "That there are no demonstrative arguments in the case seems evident, since it implies no contradiction that the course of nature may change and that an object, seemingly like those we have experienced, may be attended with different or contrary effects." The alternative is one of the sort which "regard matter of fact and real existence. . . . But . . . we have said that all arguments concerning existence are founded on the relation of cause and effect, that our knowledge of that relation is derived entirely from experience, and that all our experimental conclusions proceed on the supposition that the future will be conformable to the past." So to try to prove that in this way "must be evidently going in a circle, and taking that for granted which is the very point in question."[59] (Whatever Hume's intentions in attempting "to introduce the experimental method of reasoning into moral subjects," experiments in his book are not what would rate as such with scientists. "Experimental" can be taken as equivalent to "experiential.") Modestly he concludes: "I want to learn the foundation of this inference. . . . Can I do better than propose the difficulty to the public . . . ?"[60]

This has come traditionally to be known as "the problem of induction." But words like "problem" and "difficulty" are not apt. For in spite of Hume's show of modesty, and regardless of what else can be said around and above, what is presented here is not a difficulty or a problem but a demonstration. Elsewhere Hume rightly insisted that: "nothing can be more absurd than this custom of calling a difficulty what pretends to be a demonstration, and endeavouring by that means to elude its force and evidence."[61] It is a demonstration of the impossibility of deducing universal laws from any evidence which can be provided by experience. Even the word "induction" can be misleading here, unless it is interpreted widely to cover all such evidence and not restricted to some one procedure such as induction by simple enumeration. It should also be noticed that the impossibility is not restricted to one time direction. Attention tends to be concentrated on arguments drawing from premises stating what has been found to hold so far, conclusions covering what will happen in the future. Really Hume's point is logical and timeless. It holds equally for all arguments of the same form, including both those moving from premises about what is happening here to conclusions covering what is happening simultaneously somewhere else, and those — of particular interest to the future historian — moving from premises about some present and some past events to conclusions about other past events. "A man finding a watch or any other machine in a desert island would conclude that there had once been men in that island."[62]

Attempts to escape the force of this demonstration are perennial. One favorite move is to suggest that some principle of the uniformity of nature might serve as the missing premise. This is sometimes offered as a synthetic *a priori* truth and sometimes presented as an article of scientific faith. Hume himself never really doubted that nature, beneath all appearances of irregularity, is at bottom completely orderly, in the sense that its every feature is explicable in terms of general laws. This conviction was not inconsistent with recognizing, as he did, the subsistence of a great deal of variety in things. Hume's objection to the suggested supplementary premise in its first interpretation would have to be that there is no room for propositions which both express matters of fact and can be known *a priori*. In the second interpretation his objection would have to be that he was not looking just for a middle term which would produce a valid deduction, but for one which would do this and which could itself be established.

But now suppose we continue on our own account to render down that formidable principle of the uniformity of nature into the sort of precisely stated premise required to complete the syllogism. We shall get something like: *For all values of x the class of all known x's always constitutes a representative sample of the class of all x's.* The really fundamental trouble with this is, neither that it belongs to some outlaw category, nor that it is "known" only by faith, and hence not known. It is that abundant experience has shown it to be simply untrue.

Another favorite move is to argue that though from nonuniversal premises universal law conclusions cannot be *demonstrated* they can nevertheless be shown to be *probable*. This is a much more subtle business. For while in the everyday sense of "probable" it is only too true, since they can constitute the best possible evidence for accepting such laws as reliable, to say this misses Hume's point. Whereas if "probable" is used in some purely mathematical sense, defined in terms of samples and populations, our premises cannot be made to entail even the modified conclusion, unless we can command the help of a further premise stating that examined cases are in fact representative of all cases.[63]

We must accept the core of Hume's argument as a demonstration. But we do not have therefore to concede that the nerve of all experiential arguments consists in an irredeemably failed deduction. It is possible, for instance, to proceed hypothetico-deductively, developing universal hypotheses consistent with — though not of course derived or derivable from — our necessarily limited experience. We may then with a greater or lesser degree of assurance proceed to entertain these until and unless experience shows them to have been false.[64] We may

also take a hint from the fact that Hume himself finds it natural to speak of the *presumption*[65] or the *supposition*[66] rather than the *assumption* "that the future will be conformable to the past." We might urge that it was reasonable: not to assume, much less to insist, that all well-tested and so far unfalsified generalizations must hold good in the future; but to presume, with whatever degree of skepticism may in each particular case seem appropriate, that they will in fact do so. In this case we can be well aware that our presumptions may in many instances turn out to have been mistaken.* To anyone who asks *why* it is reasonable to allow experience to shape our presumptions, what can we say except that to do this is a part, and a large part, of our paradigm of what it is to be a reasonable man? For "none but a fool or a madman will ever pretend to dispute the authority of experience or to reject that great guide of human life."[69]

Custom and Instinct

THE conclusion which Hume himself draws is "that in all reasonings from experience there is a step taken by the mind which is not supported by any argument or process of the understanding. . . . " But "If the mind be not engaged by argument to make this step, it must be induced by some other principle of equal weight and authority. . . . This principle is custom or habit. For wherever the repetition of any particular act or operation produces a propensity to renew the same act or operation without being impelled by any reasoning or process of the understanding, we always say that this propensity is the effect of *custom*." This is "a principle of human nature which is universally acknowledged."[70] It is a principle of animal nature too: "animals, as well as men, learn many things from experience . . . it is impossible that this inference of the animal can be founded on any process of argument or reasoning. It is custom alone which engages animals, from every object which strikes their senses, to infer its usual attendant. . . . "[71] "All inferences from experience, therefore, are effects of custom, not of reasoning."[72]

This involves a subtle and, as it is actually presented, questionable shift from one sort of subject to quite another. Starting from an enquiry into the logical nature and status of arguments from experience Hume slides across into discussing the psychology of learning. This move, which to him does not present itself in quite this light, is apparently mediated by the assumption that only a conclusion of

---

* "So that it is not Nature that is uniform, but scientific procedure; and it is uniform only in this, that it is methodical and self-correcting."[67] But in this unqualified form the epigram is too trim to be true. For it is a contingent fact about nature that things so far have had the regularities they have been discovered to have; and natural science could certainly have been more difficult than it is. It could, after all, have been as difficult as psychology appears to be.[68]

reasoning can be reasonable. Thus he makes much of the fact "that the most ignorant and stupid peasants, nay infants, nay even brute beasts" are able to learn from experience, although quite incapable of offering reasons adequate to justify the step of supposing "the past resembling the future."[73] Yet it is entirely possible for it to be reasonable to do something without the agent being aware of, or even capable of appreciating, the good reasons which could be deployed in support. It is also — and perhaps this is still more to the point here — both possible and necessary, since no chain of justification can be without an end, for something to be reasonable though there is no room for any further supporting reasons.*

Nevertheless, though we may insist that the principle of arguing from experience can be justified adequately and ultimately by reference to a paradigm of rational behavior, we can still find a place for Hume's appeal to custom and instinct. For by it we are enabled, as he was, to see man as a part of nature, and human learning as involving — as well as a whole lot else — the same fundamental psychological principles as animal learning. Attempts thus to connect human with animal psychology are typical. There are three whole sections in the *Treatise* and this one in the first *Enquiry* in which after considering some aspect of human nature Hume turns to see how far the same ideas can be applied to animals.[75] In seeing learning in particular as thus grounded in basic biological dispositions Hume sometimes seems to have been tempted to romanticize the "wisdom of nature" in securing "so necessary an act of the mind by some instinct or mechanical tendency." Yet never-sleeping skepticism is there to add: "which *may* be infallible in its operations."[76] (Our italics.)

The Necessity of Causes

WE have already heard Hume arguing that no conclusion of fact can be demonstrated, because the contradictory of any factual proposition is always logically possible; or as, significantly, he always says himself, "conceivable, or possible in a metaphysical sense." There are thus no *a priori* limitations on what sort of thing may be the cause of what, or what sort of cause is required by what. The significance of this contention comes out best, as is so often the case, from considering what it commits him to reject. In the *Treatise* he applies it to destroy the argument that "thought or perception" could not possibly result simply from the motions or collisions of atoms. Whether or not such a hypothesis does

or does not happen to be true, "to consider the matter *a priori* anything may produce anything."[77] Later, as we shall see, he is emboldened to invade the territories of natural theology and, "persuaded of these principles," to make havoc there in the traditional habitat and continuing refuge of the unwarranted *a priori*.

In the *Treatise* Hume also considers the possibility of proving the causal axiom itself, the "maxim . . . *Whatever begins to exist must have a cause of existence*." Applying his earlier rather gauche version of the same fundamental principles he concludes that it is not possible. He then proceeds to dispose briskly of a job lot of arguments from Hobbes, Clarke, and Locke which purport to demonstrate what cannot be demonstrated. For the contradictory of this maxim is conceivable, involves no contradiction: just as there can be bachelors although every husband must have a wife, so there might conceivably be bachelor events though every effect must have a cause.

Since the maxim cannot be known *a priori*, "that opinion must necessarily arise from observation and experience."[78] Hume never in the *Treatise* provides an explicit account of how this is supposed to happen, and the whole subject is omitted from the *Enquiry*. But he repeats that the principle arises from experience, and suggests[79] that it has the same grounds as our conclusions "that such particular causes must necessarily have such particular effects."* There are indications implicit throughout his published writings, and an outright affirmation in a letter, that he never for a moment intended to question the *truth* of the maxim. "I never asserted so absurd a proposition as that anything might arise without a cause."[82] Presumably he considered it to be a generalization, formed on the basis of experience of regularities in the world.[83]

But if it is not necessarily true either that certain sorts of things must have certain sorts of causes or that every event must have some sort of cause, the questions arise: "Why we conclude that such particular causes must necessarily have such particular effects?"[84] and "What is our idea of necessity, when we say that two objects are necessarily connected together?"[85] "But as it is more probable that these expressions do here lose their true meaning by being wrong applied, than that they never have any meaning,"[86] Hume becomes committed to search for the parent impression. It is not to be found by examining the universe around us. This reveals only contingent conjunctions, never necessary connections.

---

* Hume remarks of the justification of behavior: "It is impossible that there can be a progress in infinitum, and that one thing can always be a reason why another is desired. Something must be desirable on its own account, and because of its immediate accord or agreement with human sentiment or affection."[74] But the same can be generalized to apply to all chains of justificatory reasoning.

* I am therefore unable to agree with Kemp Smith[80] that Hume thought that belief in the truth of this maxim was on all fours with the (unevidenced) natural belief in the independent existence of material things. A further reason for rejecting this view is that Hume apparently allows that the vulgar believe in objectivity of chance, which is on his view the opposite of causal necessity[81] and this, if universal causality were a matter of "natural belief," they surely could not do.

It must, therefore, be derived from some internal impression, or impression of reflection. There is no internal impression which has any relation to the present business but that propensity, which custom produces, to pass from an object to the idea of its usual attendant. . . . Either we have no idea of necessity, or necessity is nothing but that determination of the thought to pass from causes to effects and from effects to causes, according to their experienced union.[87]

"This connection, therefore, which we feel in the mind . . . is the sentiment or impression from which we form the idea of . . . necessary connection."[88] It is thus a perfectly legitimate idea. But it is one we misapply by projecting it out of its proper psychological nest and onto the external world: "the operations of nature are independent of our thought and reasoning . . . objects may be observed in several instances to have like relations, and . . . all this is independent of and antecedent to the operations of the understanding. But if we go any farther and ascribe a . . . necessary connection to these objects, this is what we can never observe in them but must draw the idea of it from what we feel internally in contemplating them."[89]

All this, like the rest of the contents of the *Treatise*, is offered as a contribution to "the science of human nature"; and certainly when he wrote the *Abstract* Hume rated it as one of the triumphs of his use of that "principle of the association of ideas" which he had dared to hope might make him the Newton of the moral sciences. As the three basic principles of this association "are the only ties of our thoughts, they are really *to us* the cement of the universe, and all the operations of the mind must, in great measure, depend on them." But though Hume's psychological intentions must never be forgotten, our concern here is with "his logics."[90] (Italics his.)

Having shown that there cannot be *logically necessary* connections between events, he searches for the source of the misconception, and suggests that it is due to the projection of an idea of *psychological necessity*. This is a curious explanation. Once, but only once, he comes near to suggesting that really there only is psychological necessity: "the necessity which makes two times two equal four, or three angles of a triangle equal to two right ones, lies only in the act of the understanding by which we consider and compare these ideas."[91] Such a heroic move would be consistent with a radically psychological interpretation of the notion of relations of ideas. But it is not typical of the *Treatise*, and finds no place in the generally less psychological atmosphere of the first *Enquiry*. If no such move is to be made we should surely either receive some account of the transformation of a psychological into a logical idea or be prepared to look elsewhere for sources of the misconception. Consider then the argument: All *A*'s cause *B*'s, and an *A* is occurring; therefore, neces-

sarily, a *B* will occur. When in such an argument "we conclude that such particular causes must necessarily have such particular effects" we may be misled to mistake the "necessarily" to qualify not the inference but the conjunction of *A*'s and *B*'s in the non-linguistic world and hence may "say that two objects are necessarily connected together." Which Hume has demonstrated to be impossible.

In the *Treatise* we can find some materials for a logical analysis of the concept of cause.[92] They are treated rather perfunctorily. In the *Enquiry* Hume omits them to concentrate on discussion "Of the Idea of Necessary Connection," which clearly was always his prime concern here. Thus he notices that it is usually held "absolutely necessary a cause should precede its effect," and diffidently offers an argument against the view that it might sometimes be simultaneous. But he never asks whether an effect could precede its cause and why not — and hence is never led to make much of the diagnostic practicality of the notion.[93] Again, he is prepared to allow that spatio-temporal contiguity is also essential. But in this case he returns later to argue that certain potential causes and effects cannot be spatially contiguous because they cannot have any spatial characteristics at all: "A moral reflection cannot be placed on the right or on the left hand of a passion. . . ."[94] This argument — characteristic more of Professor Ryle[95] than of Hume — is interesting as showing how close Hume was to emancipating himself from the prejudice, on which even Newton had always insisted, that the idea of "action at a distance" was an absurdity.* The definitions finally offered are reconstructive rather than descriptive.

We are given a choice of two, "presenting a different view of the same object and making us consider it either as a philosophical or as a natural relation."[97] The labels are confusing: *philosophical relations* hold between things, loose and separate; *natural relations* obtain between ideas linked by the principles of association. "Philosophical" should be associated with natural philosophy, including science and perhaps mathematics, while "natural" refers here to human nature. The first version defines "a cause to be an object followed by another, and where all the objects similar to the first are followed by objects similar to the second." The second is "an object followed by another, and whose appearance always conveys the thought to that other."[98]

It has often been suggested that Hume's account of causality is circular.[99] This charge is supported usually from the *Treatise*, where the second clause of the second definition runs, "and so united with it that the idea of the one *determines* the mind to form the idea of the other."[100] (Our italics.) But for

* Newton said, " . . . that one body may act upon another at a distance through a vacuum, without the mediation of anything else by and through which their action and force may be conveyed from one to another, is to me so great an absurdity that I believe no man who has in philosophical matters a competent faculty of thinking can ever fall into it."[96]

critics to "direct all their batteries against that juvenile work" is precisely what Hume in the famous posthumous repudiation slated as "a practice very contrary to all rules of candour and fair dealing."[101] In any case, examination of usage in the *Treatise* suggests that — despite "some negligences . . . in the expression" — *determination* is to be construed not as a synonym for *causation* but rather as referring simply to a peculiar impression generated by a regular associative transition. It is more rewarding, and less peripheral to Hume's prime purpose, to notice that in the *Enquiry* Hume adds a codicil to his first definition: "Or, in other words, where if the first object had not been, the second never had existed."

This introduces something quite new. Ignoring for the moment the question of time direction, the original testament is a bald statement of constant, but possibly coincidental, conjunction, which could be expressed as a material implication: $\sim(A.\sim B)$. i.e. not as a matter of fact A and not B. But the codicil is a subjunctive conditional: if A were not, B would not be. Subjunctive conditionals, as has become notorious, cannot be deduced from material implications alone. Yet all causal propositions entail some subjunctive conditionals, as do all propositions expressing laws: (theoretical *law* is the sibling of practical *cause*). For if A's are the sole causes of (are all lawfully but not inversely connected with) B's then we can deduce that if no A were to have occurred no B would have occurred. The upshot is that an analysis of the concept of cause (or law) in terms only of material implication cannot be complete.

Of course Hume never thought that it was. The first definition was intended only to epitomize his account of causation as a philosophical relation. There he is surely right to insist that the only relevant relations which it makes sense to talk of discovering by observation in things can be expressed as material implications. The same applies to the results of experiments, though Hume himself has little to say of experiment, in the Baconian sense of "putting Nature to the Question." The codicil belongs if anywhere to the account of causation as a natural relation. Yet it cannot be deduced even from this second epitomizing definition. We can find a hint in the *Treatise*: "Perhaps it will appear in the end that the necessary connection depends on the inference instead of the inference depending on the necessary connection."[102] Suppose that some universal (i.e., All . . .) empirical, and all causal sentences are so used that they license the inference to appropriate subjunctive conditionals; as all universal necessary propositions (e.g., "All husbands are male") license the inference to the appropriate subjunctive conditionals (e.g., "if there were to have been a husband, he would have been male"). Such empirical universal law propositions will not be equivalent to, nor even deducible from, those universal empirical generalizations — statements of mere constant con-

junction — which can in most languages be expressed in the very same words. No more than these universal generalizations themselves are, as Hume has shown already, either equivalent to or deducible from the necessarily limited evidence. If this is on the right lines then universal law statements and causal propositions may be empirically supported, but not demonstrated. Presumably it is the factitious necessity of these, and the genuine necessity of the valid inferences drawn from them, which is then misguidedly projected onto the nonlinguistic world. As his psychological ambitions moderated, Hume came sometimes extraordinarily close to such a view: "When we say . . . that one object is connected with another, we mean only that they have acquired a connection in our thought, and gave rise to this inference by which they become proofs of each other's existence."[103]

Hume's discoveries are so revolutionary that search for anticipators is inevitable. Certainly many of the points he makes can be found earlier elsewhere separately — some seem to have been unearthed[104] as far back as the fourteenth century, in Nicholas of Autrecourt.* Hume's importance and claims to originality lie chiefly in bringing things together in an explosively forceful way, and in pursuing metaphysical and methodological consequences radically. Descartes, Malebranche, Berkeley, even Leibniz, had all insisted that *true* power and energy could not be observed in things: "it is in vain we search for it in all the known qualities of matter. In this opinion they are almost unanimous. . . . "[105] But they were inclined to infer that since matter is really inert *true* causes are to be found only elsewhere, in the shape of spiritual agents, and in particular, God. Hume drew the different conclusion: "Either we have no idea of necessity, or necessity is nothing but that determination of the thought."[106]

It may at first be puzzling that, after treating "power" and "necessity" as virtual synonyms, Hume is not embarrassed to notice both a sense in which all matter possesses power, and sensations from which some sort of idea of power obviously might be derived. There is in fact no call for him to be disturbed. For neither of these possible ideas represents the sort of power or necessity he is concerned to deny to things. "The *vis inertiae* [power of inertia] which is so much talked of in the new philosophy" [science], is to be analyzed exclusively in terms of the observed and observable phenomena summarily labeled by the expression; "as, when we talk of gravity, we mean certain effects. . . ."[107] As for the sensations accompanying effort, "which are merely animal, and from which we can a priori draw no inference," these are no more indigestible than the experience of "an act of volition."[108] This is one of the places in the *Enquiry* where Hume's continuing commitment to genetic psychology obscures logical

* There is no reason to believe that Hume had ever heard of this forerunner.

issues. His chief and constantly reiterated concern is to show that it is impossible to know *a priori* what will cause what. To this the legitimacy of these two further ideas of power presents no serious threat. Consideration of one of them provides welcome occasion to suggest the illegitimacy of projecting anthropomorphic notions onto either inanimate nature or God.

Liberty and Necessity

THE contention that to act predictably and to act of your own free will were not necessarily incompatible was old even in Hume's day,[109] so old that we should be shocked to see philosophers blandly assuming without argument the opposite. Hume's claim that he "puts the whole controversy in a new light" is differently grounded, on "giving a new definition of *necessity*."[110] His first move is to urge that "the constant and regular conjunction of similar events" is, in fact, to be found in the moral just as much as in the natural sphere. He supports this in two ways: by direct appeal to what he takes as indisputable facts of common knowledge; and by arguing that it is a necessary presupposition both of everyday life and of moral science. It is perhaps permissible to doubt whether there are universal, as opposed to statistical, laws to be found everywhere in the human field. Certainly the associated methodological issues are subject to continuing controversy. However, Hume's second and crucial move does not depend on the first.

It consists in showing that necessity, construed as he construes it, is not by itself incompatible with liberty, "a power of acting or not acting according to the determinations of the will."[111] Part of the trouble of this, "the most contentious question of metaphysics, the most contentious science," has, he suggests, been this. People find in "the operations of their own minds . . . nothing further than constant conjunction . . . and the consequent inference," but believe that there must be a great deal more to necessity than this. They conclude that men are not subject to the same necessities as other parts of nature.[112] In fact they are. For there are regularities in human thinking, volition, and behavior which permit inferences.*

The *Treatise* does not suggest this etiology. Except for a mention of a scholastic distinction[115] it equates liberty with chance, a notion which "is commonly thought to imply a contradiction, and is at least directly contrary to experience."[116] Nor is the object of the exercise presented in the *Treatise* as "a reconciling project."[117] The first *Enquiry* introduces

* "But when . . . we change *will* into *must*, we introduce an idea of necessity which assuredly does not lie in the observed facts, and has no warranty that I can discover elsewhere . . . what is this Necessity save an empty shadow of my own mind's throwing?" T. H. Huxley[113] wrote what was for its time an unusually appreciative book on Hume.[114]

contemptuous references to controversy which has "turned merely upon words." Similar phrases are found in both the would-be popular *Enquiries*, and might easily be misinterpreted as mere playing to the gallery. In fact they indicate genuine failure to appreciate that not all questions which are in some sense verbal are as trivial and merely verbal as a dispute about — say — whether to accept gifts as well as donations.[118] Hume had none of the interest in semeiotic shown by Hobbes, Locke, Berkeley — or Plato. This was peculiarly unfortunate. For perhaps the greatest weakness of his philosophy is the lack of anything even approaching an adequate account of the nature of *a priori* propositions. What he provides is an odd liaison between not very genuinely introspective psychology and incongruously Cartesian talk about conceivability. He needs something much better than this if he is to have any hope of showing and not merely suggesting that the two differentiae defining Hume's Fork must always yield identical results. Until that is done, an opening remains for speculation that it may after all be possible to know *a priori* some truths more substantial than those whose contradictories involve contradictions. And hence, perhaps, for the metaphysical deduction of some tenuous outline of a Being onto which officious Revelation might pin more intrusive attributes.

The first *Enquiry* also introduces, or restores, a discussion of the theological implications of Hume's determinism. God must be "the ultimate Author of all our volitions . . . we must, therefore, conclude either that they are not criminal or that the Deity, not man, is accountable for them."[119] It is an ancient dilemma, though none the less forceful for that. Hume's response is characteristic and significant. The first option is ruled out: moral distinctions are rooted "in the natural sentiments of the human mind." The "inextricable difficulties, and even contradictions" found in all attempts to escape the second give good reason to philosophy to "return, with suitable modesty, to her true and proper province, the examination of common life."[120]

Miracles and the Religious Hypothesis

HUME was raised in a strict school which stressed harshly, and at the same time and with the minimum of equivocating apologetic, both the logically inescapable consequences of omnipotence, and the essential meaning of that great moral scandal of both traditional Christianity and of Islam, the doctrine of Hell. This is not important only biographically. For while he emancipated himself early and entirely, he retained a lifelong interest in both the natural history and the philosophy of religion. His views here are integral to his whole philosophical position, just as that position itself provides methodological basis and philosophical framework for the work in history and the moral sciences generally. Neither this nor their intrinsic importance seems to be adequately appreciated even yet. In his own day and after he was notorious as "Mr. Hume, the atheist." The later fashion among hostile critics of glossing serious arguments as gimmicks in a lifelong publicity hunt found distinguished adherents[121] well into our century.* Some critics, taking for granted that total emancipation which Hume achieved only by labor and genius, even now virtually ignore his contribution.[122]

Little of this is to be found in the *Treatise*, thanks to the castration of the manuscript. Still there are daring hints. To illustrate views on the psychology of belief he cites a phenomenon which must present a problem to all unbelievers who have enjoyed the friendship of spokesmen for Hell and God's goodness. The problem is the frequent this-worldly humanity of such spokesmen toward "those very people whom without any scruple they condemn to eternal and infinite punishments."[123]

By the time the first *Enquiry* was written things were different: "I think I am too deep engaged to think of a retreat."[124] The notorious argument about miracles is essentially defensive, a check to all "impertinent solicitations" from "the most arrogant bigotry and superstition."[125] It is concerned primarily with evidence rather than with either fact or faith. Experience is "our only guide in reasoning concerning matters of fact," and "A wise man therefore proportions his belief to the evidence."[126] The section is divided into two parts, to mark two phases in the argument. The first proceeds *a priori* from the concept of the miraculous: "from the very nature of the fact."[127] A miracle would be more than a very unusual event. For in its this-worldly aspect it must involve "a violation of the laws of nature."[128] But this means that there must be a tension between opposing elements in the evidence needed to prove such an occurrence — for the evidence which tends to establish the law must weigh against the evidence for the occurrence of the exceptional event, and vice versa.

> The plain consequence is (and it is a general maxim worthy of our attention) that no testimony is sufficient to establish a miracle unless the testimony be of such a kind that its falsehood would be more miraculous than the fact which it endeavors to establish. And even in that case there is a mutual destruction of arguments, and the superior only gives us an assurance suitable to that degree of force which remains after deducting the inferior.[129]

In the second part the future historian deploys, within the strategic framework provided by this *a priori* argument, four sorts* of *a posteriori* consideration. He concludes: "we may establish it as a maxim that no human testimony can have such force as to prove a miracle . . . so as to be the foundation of a system of religion."[131]

This final clause is emphasized heavily. For Hume is ready to concede that "there may possibly be miracles, or violations of the usual course of nature, of such a kind as to admit of proof from human testimony"; and were such a thing to be shown to have happened, "philosophers . . . ought to search for the causes whence it might be derived."[132] This concession is remarkable. For it seems to involve a shift: from Hume's characteristic position, which allows miracles to be logically possible but points to difficulties, springing from the very nature of the concept, about evidence; to that of a modern scientific naturalist, who might insist that, while any describable event is of course logically possible, there is no room for such a concept, since a law to be a law at all must be without exception.

As Hume's argument is officially defensive, it is up to his opponents to justify their concept of miracle. Yet he could have urged that any concept of miracle which is to do the trick required must contain the tension upon which his argument is based. For to serve as a medium sufficiently extraordinary to convey an inference from this-wordly evidence to transcendental conclusions a miracle has to be much more even in its this-worldly aspects than a very unusual event. The scientific naturalist's appeal to his meaning of the word "law" may, unless further supported, appear merely arbitrary — as may any appeal to definitions, even to those implicit in the discourse of the best people. Hume's argument, like his arguments earlier about the idea of necessities in things, touches a deeper level before it returns — perhaps not altogether aware of what is involved — to using the word in that same scientific naturalist's way.

Throughout this section "Of Miracles" Hume is at pains to make provocatively clear how low he rates as evidence the support offered for the miracles of the Judaeo-Christian tradition in general, and in particular for the alleged physical resurrection of Jesus Christ. This was to attack what in his day was accepted universally to be the foundation of the Christian religion.† Nevertheless this was only to

---

* It is a grave handicap to the interpretation of Hume to be unable to appreciate that and why anyone of goodwill and integrity could possibly find the doctrines of the Christian religion not only quite implausible but also sheerly repellent. Just as it is a handicap too to have so little interest in matters of morals and moral philosophy that you have to screw yourself up to the point of briefly considering what was always one of Hume's own major interests.

* The fourth is actually presented as *a priori*, though Hume clearly had in mind a different and weightier *a posteriori* consideration.[130]

† Thus Butler in his *Analogy of Religion*, first published in 1736 at the very time when Hume was working on *THN*, could claim without any fear of contradiction: "It is an acknowledged historical fact, that Christianity offered itself to the world, and demanded to be received, upon the allegation, i.e., as unbelievers would speak, upon the pretence, of miracles, publicly wrought to attest the truth of it, in such an age; and that it was actually received by great numbers in that very age, and upon the professed belief in the reality of

do in a new and perhaps more open way what Deists had been doing for some time. But in the following section Hume outlines a plan of attack against something that previously was common ground to all parties: the argument from design.* Since Hume takes it "that the chief, or sole, argument for a divine existence . . . is derived from the order of nature."[137] the two sections are complementary. The first urges that there could not be evidence adequate to prove the occurrence of miracles, which in turn authenticate a religious revelation. The second suggests that we cannot legitimately elaborate any system of natural (as opposed to revealed) religion, which might make probable the occurrence of some sort of miraculous revelation. In the second Hume is as circumspect as in the first he is provocative. This goes some way to explain why the section with the more limited objective seems always to have drawn the heavier fire.

Yet in spite of the Aesopian expression it should be fairly easy to see what Hume is driving at.[138] The argument under examination starts from "the order of nature where there appear such marks of intelligence and design that you think it extravagant to assign for its cause either chance or the blind and unguided force of matter . . . . From the order of the work you infer that there must have been project and forethought in the workman."[139] The first move now is to insist that any argument of this sort could at most prove a strictly finite deity. "If the cause be known only by the effect, we never ought to ascribe to it any qualities beyond what are precisely requisite to produce the effect." The inferred entity can only be credited with "that precise degree of power, intelligence, and benevolence" manifest in the world. " . . . nothing farther can ever be proved, except as we call in the assistance of exaggeration and flattery to supply the defects of argument and reasoning."[140] Suppose this restriction is granted. Surely Hume the empiricist is the last person to object to arguments grounded on experience: from houses back to builders; from watches to watchmakers? "Why then do you refuse to admit the same

* Butler: "There is no need of abstruse reasonings and distinctions, to convince an unprejudiced understanding, that there is a God who made and governs the world, and will judge it in righteousness . . . to an unprejudiced mind ten thousand instances of design cannot but prove a designer."[136]

these miracles."[133] It was primarily on these same grounds of miracle and prophecy that Butler, whom Hume greatly respected, himself urged the claims of Christianity to the assent of rational men: " . . . these two are the direct and fundamental proofs: and those other things, however considerable they are, yet ought never to be urged apart from its direct proofs, but always to be joined with them."[134] It is interesting to compare the relevant part of a Canon of the Vatican Council of 1870: *Si quis dixerit . . . miracula certo cognosci numquam posse nec iis divinam religionis christianae originem rite probari: Anathema sit.* (If anyone shall say . . . that miracles can never be known for certain and that the divine origin of the Christian religion cannot be duly proved thereby: Let him be cast out!)[135]

method of reasoning with regard to the order of nature?"[141]

The crux lies in "the infinite difference of the subjects."[142] Whereas we are familiar with houses and watches, builders and watchmakers, and know from experience that the one in fact does not come into existence without the other, "The Deity is known to us only by his productions, and is a single being in the Universe, not comprehended under any species or genus, from whose experienced attributes or qualities we can by analogy infer any attribute or quality in him."[143] Furthermore: "It is only when two species of objects are found to be constantly conjoined that we can infer the one from the other; and were an effect presented which was entirely singular, and could not be comprehended under any known species, I do not see that we could form any conjecture or inference at all concerning its cause."[144]

Hume thus presents as crucial two parallel differences between the two cases. Both the supposed effect and the inferred cause must be unique. The God of the theists is unique, "a single being . . . not comprehended under any species or genus." He is transcendent and incomprehensible. His ways are not our ways. But these characteristics — and they are surely defining characteristics — rule out all possibility of employing any such notion in the work of explanation and prediction, as we may employ such notions as those of unobserved building workers or postulated particles. The universe is also unique, and that again by definition. Of course in one sense, the sense in which one may say that the extra-galactic nebula in Andromeda is another "universe," this is not so. But the universe which is supposed to point to a Great Designer embraces everything there is, including every other "universe," and excluding only the putative Designer himself.

The consequence of this essential uniqueness of both putative cause and alleged effect is, as Hume finally dares to insinuate, that in natural theology all arguments from experience must break down. Theism cannot constitute a hypothesis from which any effects different from or additional to those already predictable without its aid may be deduced. This is because God must be so unlike any familiar objects that we can have no experiential analogies to guide our expectations. Nor may we even argue that it is immensely *improbable* that a universe like this has come about without Design. For, as C. S. Peirce once remarked, universes are not as plentiful as blackberries. We cannot have any experience to guide us here. So in this unique case we cannot have any grounds for saying that anything is *either* probable *or* improbable.

It may be helpful to contrast with "the religious hypothesis" of the natural theologians the case of a straightforwardly finite and anthropomorphic god called in to account for some but not all phenomena. Suppose we postulate a sea-god Poseidon with the familiar attributes of human despots. We deduce that he would protect his flatterers and afflict those who defied or ignored him. We organize some marine experiments to test our hypothesis. The status of the Poseidon concept is now similar to that of the particles postulated in the kinetic theory of gases. Surely there was nothing unsound in principle about the hypothetico-deductive methods employed in that piece of theory construction? "Why then do you refuse to admit the same method of reasoning with regard to the order of nature?"

It is clear how the reply must run. The atomic hypothesis in the kinetic theory of gases is legitimate and potentially explanatory because, thanks to our experientially based prior knowledge of mechanics, it is possible to make definite deductions about the macrocosmic effects of microcosmic transactions between the particles postulated. With appropriate alterations much the same will apply to the Poseidon theory of shipwrecks. But the god Poseidon is no more God than the Andromeda nebula is the universe. It is precisely his anthropomorphic characteristics which exempt the Poseidon hypothesis from Hume's attack. They enable us to infer that crews neglecting the propitiatory procedures must expect trouble. It is precisely the essential uniqueness of the God of the theists which exposes "the religious hypothesis" to that onslaught.* It makes it impossible to draw parallel legitimate inferences about the observable effects of his suppositious behavior.

Neither the objection we have been considering nor the reply presented themselves to Hume himself in quite this fashionably modern scientific form, in terms of hypothetical entities in theory construction. Yet he certainly was considering theism as and only as a possible explanatory hypothesis: "a particular method of accounting for the visible phenomena of the Universe."[146] All this must be seen as one exceptionally important part of Hume's general project to introduce Newtonian principles into "moral subjects." Here in particular Hume wanted to carry Newton's ideas and methods much further than the master himself would have approved. When Hume dismisses "the supposition of further attributes" as "mere hypothesis" this description carries the peculiarly Newtonian overtones.[147] Newton was not always as clear and correct as he might have been about the proper place of hypothesized entities in science: "Whatever is not deduced from the phenomena is to be called an hypothesis; and hypotheses, whether metaphysical or physical, whether of occult qualities or mechanical, have no place in experimental philosophy. In this philosophy particular propositions are inferred from the phenomena, and afterwards made general by induction. Thus it was that the impenetrability,

the mobility, and impulsive force of bodies, and the laws of motion and gravitation were discovered."[148]

The *Dialogues* develop the objections to natural theology indicated in the first *Enquiry*. Even in the earlier book Hume makes it clear that and why he has no time for attempts at proof *a priori* here: "Whatever *is* may *not be*. No negation of fact can involve a contradiction. The nonexistence of any being, without exception, is as clear and distinct an idea as its existence. . . . The existence, therefore, of any being can only be proved by arguments from its cause or its effect, and these arguments are founded entirely on experience."[149] In the *Dialogues* Cleanthes reiterates this: "I propose this argument as entirely decisive, and am willing to rest the whole controversy upon it."[150] But since Hume is now seriously essaying the dialogue form, and not (as elsewhere)[151] merely using anonymous reported speech as cover for the expression of dangerous thoughts, he does here give slightly more attention to the sort of degenerate neo-Thomism represented by Demea.* Thus he objects that "the words . . . *necessary existence* have no meaning or, which is the same thing, none that is consistent." In any case no good reason can be given for "the great partiality" of insisting that "the material universe" cannot while God must possess this exotic pseudo-attribute. Again: "Did I show you the particular causes of each individual in a collection of twenty particles of matter, I should think it very unreasonable, should you afterwards ask me what was the cause of the whole twenty."[154]

However, the main concern of the *Dialogues* is with "the religious hypothesis," the sort of natural theology best represented in Hume's own day by Bishop Butler, the Cleanthes of the *Dialogues*. It was partly in hopes of securing Butler's private advance opinion that Hume castrated the manuscript of the *Treatise*. On this main concern the *Dialogues* add a great deal, by developing and meeting objections to the fundamentals sketched in the first *Enquiry*. Thus, where the *Enquiry* only mentions the so-called problem of evil in the course of an argument about the "true and proper province" of philosophy,[155] the *Dialogues* makes much more of it. Philo, who can with qualifications be regarded as the mouthpiece of Hume himself, demands: "Why is there any misery at all in the world? Not by chance surely. From some cause then. Is it from the intention of the Deity? But he is perfectly benevolent. Is it contrary to his intention? But he is almighty. Nothing can shake the solidity of this reasoning, so short, so clear, so decisive; except we assert that these subjects exceed all human capacity. . . . "[156] In this assertion Philo would be happy to concur so long as the moral of theological

---

* Thus Butler insists: "Upon supposition that God exercises a moral government over the world, the analogy of His natural government suggests and makes it credible that this moral government must be a scheme quite beyond our comprehension; and this affords a general answer to all objections against the justice and goodness of it."[145]

* Not that any other version could have detained him very long once given his analysis of the notion of *cause*. This point is well taken by Fr. F. C. Copleston.[152] But it is hard to follow him in his hopes that what has been removed by logical analysis may be replaced by "metaphysical analysis."[153] *Plus ça change, plus c'est la même chose.*

silence is accepted sincerely by all and not just exploited, as it usually is, as a weapon to silence the hostile critics of positive theology while the dogmatists press on unabashed. Philo insists that "this entrenchment" is absolutely impregnable. But he continues still more confidently to urge that even were "pain or misery in man *compatible* with infinite power and goodness in the Deity" their existence must be fatal to "the religious hypothesis," considered simply as an argument from experience. "You must *prove* these pure, unmixed, and uncontrollable attributes from the present mixed and confused phenomena, and from these alone. A hopeful undertaking." (Hume's italics.)*

Again, while appreciating the enormous impact of the appearances of final causation, particularly in living things, Philo first develops the basic points made already in the *Enquiry*: " . . . order, arrangement, or the adjustment of final causes is not, of itself, any proof of design; but only so far as it has been experienced to proceed from that principle."[158] In any case: "I would fain know how an animal could subsist, unless its parts were so adjusted."[159] The really curious thing about the argument from design is that it professes to find its most convincing evidence precisely in this field. Yet all experience suggests that living things grow and are not made. We know that this was puzzling Hume as early as 1751.[160] Recognition of the overwhelming impact of these appearances of final causation and emphasis on this curiously neglected fact of experience are two threads running right through the *Dialogues*.

Again, Philo is at pains to underline his willingness to attribute to the universe itself whatever principles of order experience may lead us to formulate, rather than gratuitously to hypothesize something outside the universe to which the imposition of those principles of order might be credited.[161] This is the nerve of the scandalous "Stratonician atheism." Hume presumably found it in the account of Strato in Bayle's *Continuation des Pensées Diverses* (1705). Yet this move provides another paradigm of Hume's program of applying generally and systematically the methodological parsimony of Newtonian physics.

Mitigated Skepticism

"THE reader will easily perceive that the philosophy contained in this book is very sceptical, and tends to give us a notion of the imperfections and narrow limits of human understanding." This sober comment in the *Abstract* offers a better clue to Hume's skepticism than any of the dramatizing purple passages so often quoted from the *Treatise*. But the best account is presented in the final section of the first *Enquiry*. Hume there marshals his grounds

and demarcates a position with the assurance of maturity and without the distraction of exciting digressions.*

He begins with a crisp cooling card for Descartes. Once doubt all our opinions and faculties and it is impossible to justify those faculties "by a chain of reasoning deduced from some original principle which cannot possibly be fallacious or deceitful." There is no such pre-eminent privileged principle anyway. Nor, "if there were, could we advance a step beyond it but by the use of those very faculties of which we are supposed to be already diffident. The Cartesian doubt, therefore, were it ever possible to be attained by any human creature (as it plainly is not), would be entirely incurable. . . . "[166] More moderately interpreted as a program of questioning caution, such "antecedent scepticism" is nevertheless very good sense.

The traditional grounds "of scepticism with regard to the senses" are passed by as "trite" and "only sufficient to prove that the senses alone are not implicitly to be depended on . . . we must correct their evidence by reason and by considerations derived from the nature of the medium, the distance of the object, and the disposition of the organ, in order to render them, within their sphere, the proper criteria of truth and falsehood."

But there are other and "more profound arguments against the senses, which admit not of so easy a solution." It is "evident that men are carried by a natural instinct or prepossession" (what Descartes called "a certain spontaneous inclination") to "suppose an external universe which depends not on our perception," and to take "the very images presented by the senses to be the external objects."[167] "But this universal and primary opinion of all men is soon destroyed by the slightest philosophy. . . . " For the "table which we see seems to diminish as we remove further from it" while "the real table, which exists, independent of us, suffers no alteration."[168] The trouble is: we cannot deny that there is an independent external world; while "the slightest philosophy" shows that the images or perceptions of the mind cannot be identified with things outside.

It cannot "be proved that the perceptions of the mind must be caused by external objects. . . . " Thanks mainly to his analysis of causality Hume could not accept the judo move by which this difficulty is converted into an argument for the

---

* This, as T. H. Huxley notices,[157] neatly turns the tables on Butler.

* Important though they are, the enquiry "What causes induce us to believe in the existence of body?"[162] and the investigations "Of Personal Identity"[163] are undoubtedly digressions in a Part entitled "Of the sceptical and other systems of philosophy." There is thus no call to abuse Hume for omitting them from the first *Enquiry*; especially as he had already admitted, in his second thoughts on the *Treatise*, that "upon a more strict review of the section concerning personal identity . . . I must confess I neither know how to correct my former opinions, nor how to render them consistent."[164] We have been unable to squeeze in any treatment of the themes of either of these digressions. But for the former we are fortunate to be able to refer to a fine study by H. H. Price.[165]

universally present agency of God, "some invisible and unknown spirit." Nor is he quite prepared to take the radically phenomenalist line, that the question whether there are objects independent of and additional to all actual or possible sense data is without meaning. "It is a question of fact whether the perceptions of the senses be produced by external objects resembling them."[169] Such issues are to be settled by appeal to experience though "here experience is and must be entirely silent," for "the mind has never anything present to it but the perceptions. . . . "[170]

Hume proceeds to borrow Berkeley's argument that if secondary qualities are subjective primary must be too. In his last edition as the last sentence of this part he added: "Bereave matter of all its intelligible qualities, both primary and secondary, you in a manner annihilate it and leave only a certain unknown, inexplicable something as the cause of our perceptions — a notion so imperfect that no sceptic will think it worthwhile to contend against it."[171] The skeptical upshot of Hume's philosophy of perception thus parallels the outcome of his critique of natural theology,[172] "The whole . . . resolves itself into one simple, though somewhat ambiguous, or at least undefined, proposition; that the cause or causes of order in the universe probably bear some remote analogy to human intelligence."*

Corrosive skepticism also threatens enquiries less easily abandoned. "All abstract reasonings" are endangered by the paradoxes of the infinite afflicting "the ideas of space and time." Nor are "reasonings concerning matter of fact" immune. The popular objections again are weak. They cannot stand against the demands of "action, and employment, and the occupations of common life." The profounder, philosophical, objection is that all inferences from experience are simply a matter of "custom, or a certain instinct of our nature, which it is indeed difficult to resist, but which, like other instincts, may be fallacious and deceitful."[173]

Momentary contemplation of "the whimsical condition of mankind" is all very well.[174] But this "Pyrrhonian or excessive scepticism" must not be allowed to get out of hand. It is altogether too easy for "the craft of popular superstitions . . . to . . . raise these entangling brambles to cover and protect their weakness."† In any case the object of the whole

exercise is to establish new foundations for the sciences — and particularly the human sciences — in a study of human nature. It is precisely from that study that Hume would derive his own mitigated skepticism: "Nor can there remain any suspicion that this science is uncertain and chimerical unless we should entertain such a scepticism as is entirely subversive of all speculation, and even action."[176] Pyrrhonism is therefore dismissed as idle, subversive, and contrary to the most fundamental instincts of our nature. However, Pyrrhonism "corrected by common sense and reflection" may help to produce that "degree of doubt and caution and modesty which, in all kinds of scrutiny and decision, ought forever to accompany a just reasoner." It may also help to persuade us to confine "our enquiries to such subjects as are best adapted to the narrow capacity of human understanding."[177]

Apart from greater compactness and directedness of the argument, and the omission of all the dramatics of doubt, the only indication here of development between *Treatise* and *Enquiry* consists in the considerably diminished emphasis on instincts and propensities. This emphasis is entirely consistent with the wholeheartedly psychologizing program of the *Treatise*. There it keeps forcing on Hume's attention the embarrassing problem of providing appropriate grounds for distinguishing the laudable instincts of those who proportion their belief to the evidence from the deplorable propensities of "the bigotted and superstitious." This must be absolutely insoluble so long as he sticks to strictly psychological terms. Yet even in the *Enquiry* Hume cannot quite bring himself to insist consistently and unequivocally that excellent empirical grounds really are excellent grounds. He still writes "All inferences from experience . . . are effects of custom, not of reasoning"[178]; "we cannot give a satisfactory reason why we believe . . . that a stone will fall or fire burn. . . . "[179] Traces of Cartesian rationalism rejected consciously still remain. We remember that the *Treatise* was composed in France. Indeed the background of Hume's general philosophy was as much French as British. Thus it was in France, not in Britain, that Pyrrhonian skepticism had been taken seriously. Again, the occasionalism Hume attacks is that of Malebranche, not the version which Berkeley labors to distinguish.

The Foundations of Morality

IT is different with Hume's moral studies. In the Introduction to the *Treatise* he lists "some late philosophers in England, who have begun to put the science of man on a new footing." He mentions Locke, Shaftesbury, Mandeville, Hutcheson, and

---

* Both passages are among the last sentences he added to his works. He is at pains to emphasize the emptiness of the second conclusion and particularly that it can "afford no inference that affects human life, or can be the source of any action or forbearance."

† It is precisely such paradoxes of the infinite as those which worried Hume which are deployed in Arnauld's *Logique de Port Royal* — with which Hume was certainly familiar — to support the uncongenial moral: "*Il est bon de le fatiguer à ces subtilités, afin de dompter sa presomption, et lui ôter la hardiesse d'opposer ses faibles lumières aux verités que l'Eglise lui propose, sous pretexte qu'il ne peut pas les comprendre.*" ("It is good to wear him out with these subtleties, in order to tame his presumption, and to take away from him the

audacity by which he opposes his feeble lights to the truths which the Church proposes to him, on the pretext that he is unable to understand them.")[175]

Butler, but, significantly, not Berkeley. Kemp Smith has argued convincingly from evidence both biographical and internal "that it was through the gateway of morals that Hume entered into his philosophy," and that it was chiefly the recently published works of Hutcheson which when he was "about eighteen years of age . . . opened up . . . a new scene of thought."[180] The key structural ideas of Hume's approach to morals are given at the end of the first *Enquiry*, as part of the triumphant concluding survey of all sound subjects: "Morals and criticism are not so properly objects of the understanding as of taste and sentiment. Beauty, whether moral or natural, is felt more properly that perceived. Or if we reason concerning it and endeavor to fix the standard, we regard a new fact, to wit, the general taste of mankind, or some such fact which may be the object of reasoning and enquiry."[181]

His starting point is "the reality of moral distinctions." Any attempt to deny this he regards as perverse, fantastical, and disingenuous. So the question arises "whether they be derived from reason or from sentiment."[182] As often, he inclines more to what he takes to have been the general position of the ancients. In the first of the four appendices to which most of the philosophy in the second *Enquiry* is relegated, he allows that: "One principal foundation of moral praise being . . . the usefulness of any quality or action, it is evident that reason must enter for a considerable share in all decisions of this kind. . . . " Yet this cannot be the whole story. "Utility is only a tendency to a certain end; and were the end totally indifferent to us we should feel the same indifference toward the means. It is requisite a sentiment should here display itself in order to give a preference to the useful over the pernicious tendencies." This is identified here as a general benevolence: "This sentiment can be no other than a feeling for the happiness of mankind, and a resentment of their misery. . . . "[183] The *Treatise* allowed only a restricted benevolence extended through the mechanisms of sympathy, asserting "that there is no such passion in human minds as the love of mankind merely as such, independent of personal qualities, of services, or of relation to ourself."[184] But any question of this sort is unimportant compared with Hume's primary contention, that "After every circumstance, every relation, is known, the understanding has no further room to operate nor any object on which it could employ itself."[185] When all the work of description is done there is still the preference to be felt, the decision to be taken, the action to be performed.

This primary thesis belongs not to the psychology but to the logic, or perhaps one should say the metaphysic, of morals. The nature, and the compelling force, of Hume's argument may be appreciated better if its harsher and more provocative expression in the *Treatise* is also called in evidence. There he urges that "reason alone can never produce any action or give rise to volition." Nor, by the same token, is it ever capable alone of inhibiting any sentiment or performance. For reason merely demonstrates abstract connections of ideas, or enables us to learn the brute relations of things. To know propositions is just to know propositions. It is not to prefer, to act, or even to refrain. The explicative part — though not of course the intrusively normative element — of Hume's conclusion dramatized is thus made a necessary truth: "Reason is, and ought only to be, the slave of the passions, and can never pretend to any other office than to serve and obey them."[186] Officially "passion" is being used so widely as to cover every inclination which could conceivably provide any motive for doing or not doing anything.* Thus, the most impassive contemplation of some proof in set theory must constitute one more exemplar of reason enslaved to passion — albeit only to the soft innocuous taste for mathematics.

When Hume turns to morals he applies the same distinction: "Morals excite passions, and produce or prevent actions. Reason of itself is utterly impotent in this particular."[187] He considers the program, projected by Locke and attempted by Spinoza, for a sort of moral geometry proceeding from self-evident and necessary premises. This he dismisses as chimerical, first, because there simply are no relations able to supply the premises required, and, second, because no such pure deductive system could be capable of bridging the gulf between abstract knowledge and practical obligation. "We cannot prove *a priori* that these relations, if they really existed and were perceived, would be universally forcible and obligatory."[188] A similar situation obtains in the complementary case of "matter of fact, which can be discovered by the understanding."[189] For virtuousness and viciousness are not, nor yet are they deducible from, characteristics of situations in themselves. "Vice and virtue, therefore, may be compared to sounds, colours, heat and cold, which", he takes it, "are not qualities in objects, but perceptions in the mind. And this discovery in morals, like that other in physics, is to be regarded as a considerable advancement of the speculative sciences; though, like that too, it has little or no influence on practice."[190]

It is from this context that we have to understand the remark which has recently and deservedly become famous.†

In every system of morality, which I have hitherto met with, . . . the author proceeds for some time in the ordinary way of reasoning . . . when of a sudden I am surprised to find that, instead of the

---

* Compare the made-to-measure senses of "want" and "disinterested" employed at the end of the section "Political Anatomy" in Chapter 9 of this volume.
† Just how recently we may appreciate if we notice that G. E. Moore made no use of this passage in *Principia Ethica* (1903).

usual copulations of propositions *is* and *is not*, I meet with no proposition that is not connected with an *ought* or an *ought not*. This change is imperceptible; but is, however, of the last consequence. For as this *ought* or *ought not* expresses some new relation or affirmation it is necessary that it should be observed and explained; and that at the same time a reason should be given, for what seems altogether inconceivable, how this new relation can be a deduction from others which are entirely different from it.[191]

What Hume is doing is to insist that it is essential to distinguish between, on the one hand, pure calculating or detached describing, and, on the other hand, engaged preferring or practical prescribing. His point can be, as it usually is, rated as one of logic, not merely inasmuch as it is not, as to the very careless reader it might appear, one of psychology, but rather because there is a logical gulf between the concepts concerned — prescriptions cannot be deduced from pure descriptions only. The principle of this impossibility is not — like some formulation of the law of non-contradiction — a fundamental condition of any communication. Nor, obviously, is it grounded on a difference which has been and is recognized universally, and which is in fact always marked in every part and every use of every language. It is only and precisely because this was not, and is not, the case that it needed Hume to see clearly that crucial importance of the dichotomy. Vigilance and energy will remain necessary if this most fertile and illuminating distinction is not to be neglected or obfuscated.[192] Once it has been sharply drawn the proposition *A* (*pure*) is *cannot entail an* ought, can be seen to be necessarily true. The impossibility is indeed a matter of "inexorable logic."[193] To attempt to deny it must be obtuse if not actually irrational. Denial is not just something to be respectfully accepted as the reasonable corollary of a difference in presuppositions and world outlook.

The second *Enquiry* contains no passage to correspond to this famous paragraph. But the idea of a great divide between fact and value remained a constant in Hume's thought. Thus, in one sense, that in which Moore spoke of the naturalistic fallacy,[194] he is the very fount and origin of anti-naturalism: "nothing can be more unphilosophical than those systems which assert that virtue is the same with what is natural, and vice with what is unnatural."[195] But in another more general sense — like that in which Warburton the friend of Pope and future Bishop of Gloucester railed at the *Natural History of Religion* as designed "to establish naturalism, a species of atheism, instead of religion"[196] — Hume was unreservedly naturalistic. He believed firmly in an order of nature: it is a mark of the vulgar, not of the philosopher, to believe in the objectivity of chance. He had no more patience with the old established division of history into sacred and pro-

fane than Hippocrates showed toward the sacredness of "the Sacred Disease."[197] For stories of miracles or claims to revelations Hume had no time; he had no room for any bifurcation into a natural and a supernatural order. The "will of the Supreme Being" rates merely perfunctory mention in the second *Enquiry*.* Theological ideas are introduced only to provide an example of how a principle which could not be tolerated in the solid affairs of common life may find sanctuary among these mental shades; and to detect their distorting influence intruding to warp "reasoning, and even language . . . from their natural course."[200] The "true religion" advocated in the first *Enquiry* and the *Dialogues* amounts to little more than a disguised rejecting of the whole dark business as a welter of troublesome superstitions.†

There is a third, rather artificial, sense in which Hume could be called naturalistic. This is derived from the fact that his thought provides so central a place for human nature. Hume's analysis would reduce experimental reasoning to a matter of fundamental custom, and the necessity of causes to the projection of felt human habits onto the world. Similarly, here his argument drives to the conclusion that while reason "discovers objects as they really stand in nature" human preference "has a productive faculty; and, gilding or staining all natural objects with the colours borrowed, raises, in a manner, a new creation."[201] Morality is thus both man-centered and man-made.

But Hume does not mistake it that this makes morality unimportant or arbitrary. Quite the contrary. It is precisely because it is rooted in universal human desires, human needs, and human inclinations that it becomes supremely important: "these principles . . . form, in a manner, the party of humankind against vice or disorder."[202] For the same reason, "Though the rules of justice be artificial, they are not arbitrary."[203] In another, our third, sense they are supremely natural. In the essay entitled simply "A Dialogue," usually and rightly printed together with the second *Enquiry*, he considers the problem presented by the apparent variation of moral sentiments as between one culture or subculture and another. He insists that there is a basic uniformity beneath the superficial diversity: "the principles upon which men reason in morals are always the same though the conclusions which they draw are often very different . . . there never was any quality recommended by anyone, as a virtue or a

---

* One is reminded of C. D. Broad's remark[198] about *The Foundations of Ethics*[199] by Sir David Ross, Provost of Oriel: "In the last two pages the Provost relieves the Gifford Trustees from all imputation of breach of trust by referring in civil terms to his Creator."
† It was one of the "once-born" Hume's most serious limitations that he had no sympathy for the "twice-born"; and also that he would never give its due to that simple piety and dedication of character which often has so little to do with fears of eschatological frightfulness.

moral excellence, but on account of its being useful or agreeable to a man himself or to others.[204]

Rooting morality thus directly in human nature solves for Hume the problem of how it is possible for "It is my duty" to be a good, albeit perhaps defeasible, reason for doing something. (It was not open to him, as it might have been to a less secular moralist, to call on sanctions in a further life in order to provide us with a theoretically overwhelming interest in even the most uncongenial of our duties.) Hume seems sometimes to have been ambitious to do even more, to prove that moral obligation is really and unreservedly an indefeasible reason for action. "What theory of morals can ever serve any useful purpose unless it can show . . . that all the duties which it recommends are also the true interest of each individual? The peculiar advantage of the foregoing system seems to be that it furnishes proper mediums [i.e. middle terms] for that purpose."[205]

The *Treatise* contains many scandalous expressions, calculated to give the greatest offense to any naturally Kantian spirit, referring to the necessary limitations of the role of reason. In the second *Enquiry* most of this "enfant terribilisme" is dropped, although the substance of the relevant argument is little changed. (The *Treatise* was, in this respect, Hume's *Language, Truth and Logic*.) Kant's own recognition of the validity of this argument later presented itself to him — typically — not as supporting a definite if tautological conclusion but as setting an insoluble problem: "But *how** pure reason can be practical in itself without further motives drawn from some other source . . . all human reason is totally incapable of explaining this, and all the effort and labour to seek such an explanation is wasted."[206]

This argument leads Hume to say such things as: "It is not contrary to reason to prefer the destruction of the whole world to the scratching of my finger."[207] and "Actions may be laudable or blamable, but they cannot be reasonable or unreasonable."[208] Against such paradoxes one wants to protest in the name of common usage if not of common sense. Hume himself corrected Locke's division of all arguments into demonstrative and probable on the grounds that it was a paradoxical offense "to common use" to "say that it is only probable that all men must die." He introduced the third term "*proofs*, meaning such arguments from experience as leave no room for doubt or opposition."[209] By the same token he might have allowed us to employ the words "reasonable" and "unreasonable" in such instances as he cites.

Comparison of the two cases can be instructive. For in both the concession could be verbal only, or it could be more. In the former case, to become more than merely verbal it would have to involve a commitment to the position that the strongest experiential evidence really does constitute excellent grounds to support an empirical conclusion. In the

* His italics.

latter, the merely verbal concession would allow the use of "reasonable" and "unreasonable" as synonyms for "laudable" and "blamable," adding the caveat "that reason, in a strict and philosophical sense, can have an influence on our conduct only after two ways."[210] A substantial admission would allow that a man's conduct may be described as reasonable, not merely in virtue of his discovery of relevant facts and consequences and his eschewing of plans of action which must be self-frustrating, but also because he displays a concern for impartiality, consistency, and general rules. To all those things Hume was always, at least in theory, very much devoted; and all are surely involved in the idea of reasonable conduct. A concession on these lines need in no way prejudice his main original point. These concerns must modify choosing and doing, and all action has to have its motives. Hume himself does actually go a large part of the way to providing such a sense of "reasonable." In considering the importance of "general rules" in the direction of our moral sentiments he refers to "what we formerly said concerning that reason, which is able to oppose our passion; and which we have found to be nothing but a general calm determination of the passions."[211]

However, it would be wrong to allow currently fashionable interests to distract attention from the stated program of Hume's moral investigations. These cover many issues which belong to moral philosophy, in the narrowest modern sense. Besides the contributions already considered, there is the account of promising as a form of performatory utterance. This is accompanied by suggestions on how conventions similar to those on which all language is grounded can give words power to generate obligations, without themselves constituting or presupposing any antecedent contract and promise.[212] This analysis is put to work forthwith in a critique, too little appreciated nowadays, of the political doctrine of the social contract.[213] Again, there is a broadside, owing some of its power to Butler, against the Hobbist doctrine of the total selfishness of man, whether presented as pure psychology or as the result of "a philosophical chemistry."[214]

Of course, there are the two importantly different and much canvassed definitions of "virtue" and "vice." "So that when you pronounce any action or character to be vicious you mean nothing but that from the constitution of your nature you have a feeling or sentiment of blame toward it,"[215] and virtue is "whatever mental action or quality gives to a spectator the pleasing sentiment of approbation, and vice the contrary."[216]

But these definitions are not displayed by Hume as the trophies of a purely logical analysis. This interpretation is at least excusable in the *Treatise*, although it should seem strange that in this piece of straight subjectivism Hume should apparently have forgotten everything he has been saying and is just about to say about the difference between judgments of fact and decisions of value. For he seems to be defining the word "vice" in terms simply of "a matter of fact" which "lies in yourself, not in the object." Nevertheless, one might say that Kant was not the first philosopher to think that some psychological facts are not as other facts are (being about the fundamental structure of the human mind, and hence — apparently — somehow *a priori*). But, coming to the *Enquiry*, there is no such excuse. Here Hume claims: "The hypothesis which we embrace is plain. It maintains that morality is determined by sentiment." He then gives the definition quoted, and continues: "We then proceed to examine a plain matter of fact, to wit what actions have this influence. . . . If you call this metaphysics . . . you need only conclude that your turn of mind is not suited to the moral sciences."

What Hume has been attempting is — in modern terms too — moral science, not moral philosophy. This is made perfectly clear from the beginning: "As this is a question of fact, . . . we can only expect success by following the experimental method and deducing general maxims from a comparison of particular instances."[217] It is (as he argued himself in a passage unfortunately excised from the editions of 1764 and after), entirely consistent with these principles that a definition should first appear quite late.[218] It should be read not as abstract logical analysis but as an epitome of all the concrete particulars considered previously. It is an indication of the profound mutual isolation of the humanities from the sciences in British education and culture that Hume's Newtonian ambitions here should in practice be so largely ignored. It is one effect, and also in some small part a cause, of this isolation, that the bridging opportunities offered by study of such undichotomized and unfragmented men are rarely exploited by teachers of philosophy.

Hume's wholeness is seen too in his manifest generous concern for moral practice as well as moral theory. He was attempting moral science, and no one could have emphasized more clearly the distinction between study of fact and decisions of value. But he never thought — what is not true — that the pursuit of understanding is inconsistent with practical engagements: "Man is a reasonable being, and, as such, receives from science his proper food and nourishment. . . . Man is a sociable no less than a reasonable being. . . . Man is also an active being."[219] To be a scientist and nothing else is impossible: our easily fashionable cult of noninvolvement ensures only that our own particular involvements are self-centered, complacent, and irresponsible. For involvements of some sort are the inescapable prerogative of our humanity. Hume was attempting, in the second *Enquiry*, descriptive analytical empirical moral science. He was not broaching a program of moral reform. This may account for some at least of the exceptions to a general utilitarianism which Jeremy Bentham — that archetypal Fabian — saw in Hume's *Treatise*, and thought unnecessary. Yet on occasion Hume was ready even in this *Enquiry* positively to advocate the best moral principles of his age, while his own life approached "as nearly to the idea of a perfectly wise and virtuous man as perhaps the nature of human frailty will permit."[220] He was also prepared, where he saw the need, radically to rethink accepted moral ideas. Thus, after giving many hints that his usual preference for certain classical against (supposedly) Christian ideas extended here too, he wrote the notorious essay "Of Suicide." In this he argues that it is absurd to try to derive an absolute embargo on suicide from any idea of what is or is not natural, or from some difficult notion that such (or any) action would involve the illegitimate frustration of Omnipotence. He suggests that suicide can, on the contrary, sometimes be a right or even a duty.* In all this Hume was obedient to his own most characteristic maxim: "Be a philosopher; but, amidst all your philosophy, be still a man."[222]

* An experience in France in 1746 caused Hume to sigh: "Alas! We live not in Greek or Roman times."[221]

16

French Eighteenth-Century Materialism

E. A. GELLNER

JEAN LE ROND D'ALEMBERT (1717–1783) was the illegitimate son of Mme de Tencin and the Chevalier Destouches. Shortly after his birth he was abandoned by his mother on the steps of the baptistry of Saint-Jean-Le-Rond in Paris. Luckily, he was claimed by his father, who found foster parents for the child and arranged for his education at the Jansenist College de Mazarin. Exposure to the intense Jansenist-Jesuit conflict evoked in d'Alembert a lifelong distaste for metaphysical argument.

After briefly studying law and then medicine, d'Alembert concentrated on the study of mathematics, and after publishing the *Traité de Dynamique* in 1741, he was accepted in the Académie des Sciences. The *Traité* reveals that d'Alembert was influenced by both Descartes and Bacon. He accepts unproved axioms as the basis of his system of mechanics, but he maintains that the process of deduction must be supplemented by experimental investigation and that the validity of conclusions must be experimentally verifiable. Metaphysical assertions, therefore, cannot express certain knowledge.

D'Alembert, with Diderot, worked on the projected French translation of Chambers' *Cyclopaedia*, and, with Diderot, he became co-editor of the more ambitious *Encyclopédie*. In 1751, he published his *Discours Preliminaire* to the *Encyclopédie*, a purely philosophical work. D'Alembert still expresses his allegiance to the Cartesian tradition (he believes that, given a sufficiently broad perspective, nature can be reduced to one principle, "one great truth"), but he is more concerned with his development of Locke's theory of sensation. He maintains that it is not through the construction of hypotheses but through a careful study of physical phenomena that one attains knowledge of the universe, and that it is sense impressions which ultimately are the basis of all human understanding. He traces complex concepts and creations of science and art to original sense impressions, and he also claims that while there may be absolute moral values, moral judgments are in practice determined by social necessity.

In 1757, d'Alembert quarrelled with Rousseau, and withdrew from the *Encyclopédie*. He apparently cared less for public strife than some of his more famous contemporaries, but his personal integrity was never compromised, and he continued to support the *philosophes*. His belief that sense experience (which is common to all men) is the source of knowledge was naturally linked with a strong faith in the value of education. He never abandoned his researches in art (especially music), philosophy and science. Of special interest to philosophers are the *Eléments de la philosophie* (1759) and *Mélanges de littérature et de philosophie* (1753–67).

D'Alembert professed himself a deist, believing, with some skeptical reservations, that intelligence cannot be explained without assuming the existence of an intelligent cause. There is strong evidence, however, that in the late 1760's he was converted to atheism by Diderot. He died unrepentant, and as an unbeliever was buried in a common unmarked grave.

Denis Diderot (1713–84) was born in Langres of conservative middle-class parents and, like La Mettrie, he was expected to enter the Church. In 1728 he was sent to study in Paris. After achieving a Master of Arts degree, he remained in Paris, to the dismay of his family, to study according to his own interests and to enjoy the company of his free-thinking friends (among them Jean Jacques Rousseau). He worked as a translator, and became familiar with the writings of Locke, Shaftesbury, and the English deists. In 1746 his *Pensées Philosophiques*, a defense of deism, was published; this won him for the first time the unwelcome attention of the police. But Diderot was not turned from his rebellious course. He agreed to become coeditor (with d'Alembert) of the *Encyclopédie*, and in 1749 his *Letter on the Blind for the Use of Those Who See* was published. This original and imaginative essay examined the influence of the senses upon ideas, and advocated a materialistic and atheistic interpretation of nature. Diderot went to prison for five months.

In 1751 the first volume of the *Encyclopédie* appeared; it was very quickly recognized as a revolutionary publication. Thanks to the unpopularity of the Jesuits (who were the most eager to see the work suppressed), the project, although not approved, was allowed to continue. It is enormously to the credit of Diderot that he continued to work on the *Encyclopédie* during this time and again during the crisis which followed the publication of Helvetius' *On the Mind* (1759). The work was often both dangerous and tedious, and it must be noted that Diderot's friends (and colleagues) caused him almost as much trouble as his enemies. Nevertheless, for twenty years the *Encyclopédie* was Diderot's chief concern. It was successfully finished, and is a remarkable document — the embodiment of the knowledge, thought, and ambitions of a remarkable generation.

Diderot also found the time to write on aesthetics and moral philosophy, and to compose plays and stories. Among the most interesting of his later writings, at least to philosophers, is *d'Alembert's Dream*, an exciting presentation of materialist thought. Perhaps the most striking aspect of Diderot's materialism is that it includes a concept of the evolutionary process (with no barrier between animate and inanimate matter).

Diderot's last years were mainly taken up with the pleasures of family life, but he was not an entirely subdued grandfather. It should be mentioned that before he died he travelled to Russia and spent five lively months at the court of Catherine the Great.

Paul Dietrich (or in its commoner Gallicized form, Paul Thiry), Baron d'Holbach, was born in Edesheim in the Palatinate in December 1723. Little is known of his parents. The main family influence in his life was his maternal uncle, Franciscus Adam d'Holbach, from whom he inherited both title and wealth.

This uncle, the son of an episcopal tax collector at Speyer, moved to France, where he acquired a fortune and with it also a title of nobility. He died in 1753. Thus Baron d'Holbach was, as Naville points out, a *nephew* of a parvenu, and not a *son*, as Rousseau mistakenly describes him.

After studying at Leyden, where he was a friend of John Wilkes, d'Holbach settled in Paris in 1749. He did not contribute to the first volume of the *Encyclopédie*, which appeared in 1751, but did contribute, anonymously, to the second volume, which appeared in 1752, and is described by Diderot as a person "to whom we are greatly indebted, and who is extremely versed in Mineralogy, Metallurgy and Physics. . . . "

D'Holbach's friendship with Diderot was probably the most important intellectual alliance of his life. He continued to assist the *Encyclopédie* both by articles and otherwise, and in turn it is claimed that his own *System of Nature* is to some degree a cooperative work — in particular, certain passages are attributed to Diderot.

D'Holbach's initial contribution to the thought and work of the enlightened circle of *encyclopédistes* was that of an expert on various branches of natural science and a translator of works in these fields from the German. But his most characteristic and celebrated role in the movement was that of being the *maître d'hôtel* of philosophy: the Thursday and Sunday dinner parties at his Paris house, and his country residence of Grandval, were the social center of Enlightened thought. His salon was described as the *café de l'Europe*.

During the first decade of his Paris activity, until 1760, his intellectual production centered mainly on the translation and popularization of scientific works: he prepared more than four hundred articles for the *Encyclopédie*. It was during the second decade, from 1760 till 1770, that the center of gravity of his work shifted to the massive production and editing of antireligious books. This work found its culmination in his masterpiece, the *System of Nature*, published in 1770. (The early editions were all attributed to a certain M. Mirabaud, then already deceased.) Subsequently, his work was preoccupied mainly with the ethical, social and political implications of his materialism: with the further elaboration of this aspect of the ideas already found in the *System*.

D'Holbach, by extending, systematizing, and bluntly stating the full force of current ideas, presented, in Diderot's words, "a philosophy that is clear, definite and frank. . . . His philosophy is all of one piece." He died in 1789, the year which saw the beginning of the events for which the ideas of his circle have since been praised or blamed.

Julien Offroy de la Mettrie (1709–51), the first and most extreme of the French materialists, was born in St. Malo on Christmas day. His well-to-do parents determined that the boy should become a member of the clergy, although this decision was more the result of financial than sentimental considerations). La Mettrie, therefore, received a good preparatory education, studied with a Jansenist tutor in Paris, and then, after all, became fascinated with medicine. He studied physics and anatomy in Rheims, and in 1733 traveled to Leyden to study with Dr. Boerhaave, the famous disciple of Spinoza. La Mettrie was clearly not unsympathetic to the materialist point of view in 1742. In that year he contracted a fever, and observing his own symptoms, he became convinced that thought is strictly a function of our physical mechanism. He began to work on *A Natural History of the Soul*, in which, under the guise of an interest in Aristotelian metaphysics, he argued that motion, sensibility, and intelligence are material phenomena which exist without dependence upon a prime mover, a first cause, or any nonmaterial agent. He further developed this thesis in *L'Homme Machine* (1748), a frankly anti-Cartesian and antireligious polemic whose title alone was sufficient to provoke the devout.

The ethical writings of La Mettrie did little to redeem his dubious reputation. In *Discours sur le Bonheur* ("Discourse on Happiness") he maintained that self-love and happiness are the essence of virtue, and that the "moral law" is the product of social necessity and natural feelings of sympathy; he concluded that both virtue and vice are subject to necessity. This serious book, which anticipated the work of Helvétius, did not receive the attention it deserved, perhaps because La Mettrie's enthusiastic endorsement of sexual pleasures had already alienated many of his potential readers; he was considered rather too eccentric, or too physical, to be a serious philosopher.

La Mettrie lived his last years at the court of Frederick the Great, and it was generally reported that he brought on his own death by overindulging his liking for *pâté aux truffes*. It is not probable that one pâté, no matter how rich, would kill a healthy man, but the story delighted his enemies.

By all accounts, La Mettrie was a man of agreeable character. His writings testify to his spirit and intelligence.

François Marie Arouet de Voltaire (1694–1778) was neither the most profound nor the most radical of the *philosophes*, but he was certainly the most formidable protagonist of Enlightenment thought. His passionate and satiric attacks upon obscurantism in general and Christianity in particular represent the spirit of an era that has often been called, somewhat inaccurately, "The Age of Voltaire." After learning of the brutal execution of the Chevalier de la Barre, Voltaire expressed frankly his dearest ambition: "I am tired of hearing that twelve men were able to establish Christianity; I should like to prove that one is capable of destroying it." Christianity was not destroyed, and the downfall of *L'ancien regime* was the work of many, but there seems no doubt that the wit of Voltaire was the most effective single weapon in the struggle.

Voltaire's philosophical views were inspired by his early study of skeptical writings, especially the works of Bayle and Fontenelle, and developed to maturity during his stay in England (1727–29). Here he was impressed by and absorbed the empiricism of Locke and the arguments of the English deists. He was equally impressed by the benefits to be gained from the government's policy of toleration and the maintenance of a sound economy based on private commercial interests. These influences formed his philosophy, which changed little thereafter, and which is elegantly expressed in *English Letters, Charles XII, Essay on the Manner and Spirit of Nations, Louis XIV, Zadig, Micromegas, Candide*, and the *Philosophical Dictionary*.

Voltaire was in many ways admirable but not in all. He was unwilling to consider theories more extreme than his own, and he was able to speak of La Mettrie as a "person of no importance"; he attacked (without refuting) the atheism of d'Holbach and Diderot. A personal slight could evoke the fury that was usually directed against general wrongs. His abuse of the Jewish religion was inextricably linked with abuse of the Jewish people, with this prejudice Voltaire fell miserably short of his own ideals.

Voltaire was, therefore, not a man free of serious faults, but his contemporaries estimated rightly that he was a man who ardently wished, and for the most part ardently worked, for the improvement of the human condition. When, after thirty years of exile, Voltaire returned to Paris, in the winter of 1778, his welcome was glorious. A few weeks later he met death with less enthusiasm, but more patience, than he had faced life.   (Editor)

WE SHALL BE EXAMINING in this chapter an important facet of the European philosophical tradition. It is represented most clearly and characteristically by a group of French philosophers of the eighteenth century. The group contains some of the most famous names in French literature and includes, among others, La Mettrie, Voltaire, Diderot, d'Alembert, and d'Holbach. These writers cannot be said to form a philosophical school, nor were they all philosophers in the modern sense of the word. Some, like Voltaire and Diderot, were literary men; some, like d'Alembert, scientists and mathematicians. But each in his own way gave expression to a certain characteristic point of view that may be called the syndrome of progressive thought. We shall first take a general survey of this syndrome and then consider in more detail one particular manifestation of it — the work of d'Holbach.

Major Themes of the Enlightenment

THE characteristics of the syndrome of progressive thought are anti-clericalism and hostility to religion; rejection of supernatural or "spiritual" explanations of phenomena; an insistence or preference for explanations of phenomena in terms of the structure and activity of matter; a positive expectation that everything in nature and man can be explained in natural intramundane terms; determinism; empiricism in epistemology; hedonism and/or egoism in psychology; belief in reason as the guide and arbiter of life; rejection of the authority of tradition; utilitarianism in ethics, and utilitarianism and/or democracy in politics; pragmatism with regard to the theory of truth; relativism; and belief in the power of education and of government and in the possibility of deliberate improvement of human life.

Manifestations of this syndrome tend to be more sharply articulated in Roman Catholic countries than elsewhere, and not surprisingly; for its elements were first assembled in opposition to Roman Catholicism. Perhaps the manner in which they were assembled owes something to the Church's *example*, as the selection of the constituents plainly owes almost everything to its *opposition*.

It would be wrong and, so to speak, parochial to erect a general typology of thought along the lines of adherence or opposition to the elements listed.* The alignment of views for and against the progressive syndrome, as I have called it, is rooted in a historical situation rather than in some universal and basic dualism.

The expression "materialist", as used in common speech, owes much of its meaning to the syndrome described. To say that someone is materialistic or is a materialist in his views, policies, or practices is not normally a way of saying that he proposes theories about matter being the only constituent of the universe. Rather, it is a way of implying that his thinking has some of the characteristics on our list. A man may come to be called a materialist because he allows only for hedonic or egoistic motivation in men, or because he allows no considerations other than the specification of tangible advantages to influence policy, or because he refuses to allow the possibility of inexplicable or unpredictable factors influencing events.

"Materialism" in a narrower and more technical sense can be defined as the doctrine that only matter exists, and hence that all other phenomena and features of the world are explicable as manifestations of the organization and movement of matter.

Materialism in the narrower sense is indeed *one*

---

* This is similar to the division into tough- and tender-minded suggested by William James, whose dichotomy in fact seems to owe something to the contrast described here.

of the constituents of the set of beliefs and attitudes which make up materialism in the broader and looser sense.

The reason for the use of the same term to describe both the wider and the narrower "materialism" — as often happens when we get an ambiguous term designating a doctrine or attitude — is that materialism in the narrower sense is held to be the crucial and most important among the materialist doctrines in the wider sense. Both adherents and opponents have supposed that materialism in the narrower sense is the premise from which the wider set of ideas can be deduced. In fact, it is not even clear whether all the doctrines of the wider set can easily be made consistent with materialism in the narrower sense (or, in some cases, with each other), let alone whether they are deducible from it.

The set of ideas that I have described as the progressive syndrome are the fruit of the French eighteenth-century Enlightenment. The individual ideas are not on the whole original; they generally have far older roots and a longer history. But their joint crystallization in a connected system of ideas constituting a characteristic and easily distinguishable outlook is the work of thinkers who, if not always French by nationality or residence, wrote in French and made their first and strongest impact on the climate of opinion in France. Their influence in preparing the ground for the French Revolution is a commonplace of history books.

It would, of course, be a very misleading simplification to suggest that there was a general consensus, or even a clearly discernible majority opinion, among the many active writers of the period. Nevertheless, certain themes stand out — either by being upheld more often or more effectively, or by standing out more conspicuously in opposition to preceding orthodoxies, or by being seen in retrospect to be the premonitions or sources of ideas that were later to become widely accepted or influential. Those themes are the ones found among the items on our initial list.

On that initial list, we *named* a large number of doctrines. It might also be useful to indicate the general contents of the "progressive thought syndrome" by a somewhat shorter list of actual formulated tenets.

There is, first and foremost, hostility to revealed religion: the world is knowable and known through human experience and thought, and its nature is *not* something contained only in an exclusive, privileged, and unimpugnable communication vouchsafed to some particular tradition or institution. Similarly, the bases of morality and politics are something to be sought in human experience and reason.

There is naturalism. By this I mean the denial of fundamental discontinuities in nature — for instance, the denial of the discontinuity between animal and human nature, or between the physical and mental aspects of man. This also involves the denial of supernatural intrusions into the realm of nature, and hence of the need or permissibility of invoking them in explaining the phenomena of nature.

There is materialism (in the narrower sense) — the insistence that there exist explanations of natural phenomena — including human and mental ones, in terms of the organization and activity of matter. It should be noted that this last idea can be seen as a corollary or justification or expression of the naturalistic and empirical vision of man, and it is in this capacity, rather than as an independent position, that it tends to be incorporated. For instance, La Mettrie's celebrated *L'Homme Machine* is concerned less with the thesis that gives it its name and notoriety than with the preaching of an empirical and medical, rather than an *a priori*, attitude to human phenomena, and with the establishment, on such a basis, of a continuity between man and the rest of nature; in other words it is concerned with the denial of the legitimacy of invoking some special principle or substance with regard to man's behavior. It should also be noted that if this interpretation is correct — if materialism in the narrow sense is, in the internal economy of the outlook, a corollary or support of empiricism and naturalism rather than an independent thesis — then the essence of the outlook contained in "materialist" eighteenth-century works is *not* deeply shaken by certain features of modern science which are sometimes invoked against it — as examples, the recognition of psychogenetic factors in medicine, or the existence of irreducibly statistical laws in physics, or the shadowy nature of the modern physicists' equivalents of the notion of matter, or the possibility of its substitution by energy. Such phenomena would only strike at the heart of the characteristic eighteenth-century outlook under discussion *if* they were also incompatible with the empiricist, antirevelational and antitraditional view of enquiry, and with the unitary view of nature. But it is doubtful whether there is indeed such a conflict.

What is the significance, in the history of philosophy, of this outlook? Its formulations do not quite reach the first rank among the great philosophical works of history.* The individual ideas are generally not new, and their implications are not always worked out with the kind of thoroughness or rigor that, even if he inherits his premises from someone else, can place a thinker in the front rank.

Why then is the "materialism" of the Enlightenment nevertheless of great importance? Its real significance lies in the fact that it crystallized, blended, articulated, and diffused an outlook which is still a part of the basis of the Western, educated man's vision of the world. Its achievement was the propagation of ideas and the sifting, fusing, and clear articulation of them. This is no mean achievement, even if not combined with the introduction of new

* For instance, they receive no discussion in Bertrand Russell's *History of Western Philosophy*.

ideas or with a truly rigorous exploration of the implications of old ones. And it should be added that if the outlook is with us still — if indeed it is the main constituent of our view of the world — then so are its difficulties and contradictions. We tend to be (not all of us, perhaps, but those professionally concerned with ideas) more clearly aware of the difficulties and inner incompatibilities of that outlook. There are two reasons for this: First, the mere passage of time, the accumulation of experience in trying to live with, or by, the ideas of the Enlightenment, have brought those incompatibilities or difficulties to light.* Second, the comparative decline in the intellectual and social significance of the opponent of the outlook in question — Christianity, and, in particular, Catholicism — has aided the emergence of oppositions *within* the Enlightened outlook. Ideas, like men, combine in opposition to external enemies, and their differences re-emerge when the external threat recedes. For instance, one of the striking and persistent inner strains within the outlook arises from the conflict between its radical empiricism, the insistence on the senses as the *sole* source of knowledge, and what may be called absolute materialism, the view that the structure and activity of independently and continuously existing matter is the only ultimate reality and explanation of other phenomena. The allegedly unique channel of information does not seem suited to convey information about the nature or even the existence of the allegedly unique existent. This difficulty remains inherent in the general modern outlook; empiricism in the sense that experience is the only arbiter of doctrines about reality (if not their source) is with us still, and so is the conviction that of the paradigm of explanation is one in terms of the structure and activity of, if not always matter, then at least of something independently existing and possessing a structure. The opposition between the model of *information* (through *experience*) and the model of *explanation* (by means of a *structure* and activity of something existing independently of experience) is not easy to overcome and remains with us.†

The claim that the significance of the Enlightenment's philosophy lies in its having forged and formulated the main element of the outlook of the Western European secularized intelligentsia until

this day and also to a large extent — even if it is not always officially recognized — of Western society at large, calls for some qualifications. But these qualifications do not contain any substantial emendation concerning that which was central to the men of the Enlightenment, their attack on religion. The view that historic, revealed religion is false and harmful when it obstructs nonreligious inquiries has been largely incorporated into the outlook of Western man. The fact that religious institutions, practices, and adherence survive in no way contradicts this, for the religion that has survived the onslaught of the Enlightenment has adjusted itself so completely that it tacitly recognizes the justice of the attack. The religion that was attacked by the men of the Enlightenment was, or contained theories concerning the nature of the world, of man, of society; these were either in conflict with empirical or naturalistic theories, or ruled out the possibility of such theories altogether. Contemporary religion no longer presumes to prejudge or interfere with the findings and inquiries of the sciences. Inquiries, not merely into inanimate and biological nature, but into man and society, or even into the sociology of religion itself, are no longer resented or resisted. They are tolerated or welcomed. It is unlikely that many contemporary investigators of, say, the applicability of the cybernetic model to psychology — and presumably there are Roman Catholics among them — felt that they were committing impious acts or undermining religion. (I doubt whether "dabbling in cybernetics" has been the content of even a single confession.) Yet in the eighteenth century, men were driven to put forward something like the cybernetic hypothesis, partly just *because* if it were true, it would undermine religion and facilitate empirical inquiry into man and nature. Ascertaining the truth of the man-machine idea was deemed a necessary step in the liberation of inquiry.

The religion that has survived the onslaught of the Enlightenment is careful to restrict its claims to the realms, whatever they are (and their nature and locale vary), that do not prejudge the results of free and empirical inquiry; or to make quite plain that the truth it offers, whatever its subject matter, is different in kind and source from ordinary truth; or to restrict itself to the realm of values, where, admittedly, the outlook of the Enlightenment also made claims, but far less successfully. And even in the last field, it is noteworthy that the weightiest arguments — if not the only ones — in discussions of policy or legislation that affect moral issues, are utilitarian arguments. And note that this reduction of religion to noninterference was all that the Enlightenment really required; even that height of eighteenth-century impiety, *Le Système de la Nature*, which we shall examine in more detail as the quintessence of enlightened thought, does not demand more.

It is a truism to say that European society has undergone a process of secularization in the past

---

* For instance, the political history of the twentieth century makes it less tempting to suppose that when freed from transcendental religious prejudices, men will thereafter cooperate rationally and harmoniously in the interests of general human happiness.

† It would of course be incorrect to say that it was only the passage of time that brought the conflict to light. In eighteenth-century *British* thought, the awareness of the conflict was crystal-clear and central: No one could accuse the tradition of Berkeley and Hume of being oblivious to it. The fact that British eighteenth-century thinkers could devote themselves to clarifying this issue and working out its implications is presumably connected with the fact that they did not have to be concerned with combating Roman Catholicism.

two hundred years or so. This is not the place to examine the social significance of this assertion; but, on the intellectual plane, it means, roughly, that people have replaced religious ideas by others *largely drawn from the set that can be found, assembled, and systematized in the "System of Nature."*

Later thinkers who have set out to give secular answers to problems such as those of morality, of the relation of mind to body, or of the freedom of the will have generally drawn on some of the many ideas from the set found, ordered, and often succinctly and forcefully stated in the *System of Nature*. (To say this is not to say that the text itself has persisted in being influential; it has not. On the contrary, it has been rather unjustly neglected. But the complex of ideas of its time, which it summed up more forcefully than any other work, continues to be a kind of matrix from which secular thinking draws many of its crucial premises.)

Many intellectual biographies in and since the eighteenth century have contained as their crucial episode the confrontation with the issue — to *believe* or not to believe? The precise nature of the tempting or beckoning *faith* does not here concern us. What do concern us are the beliefs of *dis*belief; the world picture which was generally assumed to be the alternative to faith was something rather like that of the *System*.

It has generally been assumed that the kind of residue or alternative that remains if faith is abstracted or abandoned must be something like the vision of the *System* — naturalism, determinism, empiricism, materialism, utilitarianism — fused as best one can.

It is easy and somewhat cheap — although also correct — to remark, as many have, that many of the ingredients of this outlook require as much *faith* as does religious belief. What is less obvious is whether the kind of "materialistic" outlook found in the *System* is indeed the only, or natural, alternative to a conventionally religious view of the world. Roughly speaking, modern man tends to assume as obvious that if religion is false, then the world must be something like the picture of the *System*. This seems to me at least questionable, although it is very difficult to visualize what a radically different, yet seriously tenable, secular view would be like. But it is questionable nevertheless: one need only reflect on how much this particular secular alternative owes to the religion it combated. In its particular views, it owes it a great deal by opposition; and in its general structure it may well owe it as much by more or less unconscious emulation.

Modern Themes Not Present in Enlightenment Thought

THE claim that the Enlightenment forged and first formulated the modern outlook as it manifests itself both in shared presuppositions and in formal philosophies does not, as indicated, call for qualification on the grounds that religion has survived its attack. If the characteristic eighteenth-century outlook fails to excite or stimulate today, it is partly because its exponents have done their work so well and successfully. What they preached has become common ground, shared even by the successors of their erstwhile opponents.

But the claim does call for some qualification on other grounds. There are certain prominent constituents of our modern climate of opinion which were either lacking or inadequately incorporated in the beliefs of the Enlightenment. It is their absence, as well as the success and hence the platitudinization of the outlook, which gives to the outlook of the Enlightenment that slightly stale and unexciting taste which, for many people, it has. It is worthwhile to specify the *lacking* constituents that were to be added later.

1. There is what may be called historicism and sociologism: a certain awareness of the continuity, unity, flow, and growth *in* the world. That awareness was later inspired by the consideration of either human or biological history, and is often lacking among the men of the Enlightenment, who were rather inclined to have what one might call a "two basic states" view of the universe — *before* and *after*, as it were, the Enlightenment. (Before, there was darkness and superstition; afterward, there was light. The "dual state" vision is perhaps itself something inherited from religion.)

With the replacement of the somewhat *simpliste* dual state view by theories of historical growth or evolution, there also came a more tolerant and, as it were, *functional* interpretation of those errors which the enlightenment had fought. This made it impossible to see them purely as errors fathered on us by fear or imagination and exploited by priests and tyrants for their own ends. This greater sophistication or understanding and/or tolerance is reinforced by what may be called the "sociological" outlook: If ideas are to be seen primarily as social, rather than individual, functions, then part at least of the weeding operation carried out by men of the Enlightenment was misguided. If societies or nations are supraindividual unities, they may well speak to the individuals who compose them through those seemingly absurd legends or dogmas or institutions that did not stand up to the enlightened critique. Thus the relativism that *was* present in the Enlightenment, but which was not thoroughly followed up, received an impetus and development that led to the partial undermining of the critical Enlightened outlook itself.

2. Another notable constituent in the modern outlook was lacking in the Enlightenment, and indeed lacking among the views with which it grappled: a pessimism based, not on a religious doctrine of original sin, but on a quite secular view of man.

This vision of man formulated metaphysically by Schopenhauer, aphoristically by Nietzsche, and clinically by Freud is something which is alien to Enlightened thought and which constitutes a grave problem for it. The Enlightenment was not necessarily given to attributing a fundamentally good moral substrate to man, as Rousseau did, but it saw man as at least morally neutral and capable of rational and indeed virtuous, behavior, once it could be freed from superstition; and even if motivated by self-interest, enlightened self-interest would lead to a rational harmony.

The idea that the enemy of rationality and happiness is *within* and deeply rooted, a kind of cosmic or biological or fundamental bloody-mindedness, is something which, if true, badly upsets the rationalistic and optimistic world-view of the Enlightenment. If true, it shows that enlightenment is not enough. The aims it offers humanity — rational, harmonized happiness — are in fact shown not to satisfy our real strivings; the means it offers — the removal of superstition and prejudice and tyranny — are shown to be inefficacious.

3. There is, finally, the Existentialist tradition, in a broad sense of the term. This arose in reaction, not to the Enlightenment itself, but to the "enlightened," rationalist elements in Romantic post-Enlightenment philosophy — that is, to the belief that reason was the clue to nature, history and life and that the previous ideas of the priests, etc., and such people were not false but constituted a kind of lisping reason.

The essence of Existentialism is the attempt to shift issues of general and fundamental conviction from the realm of inquiry and objective truth to the "subjective" realm of *decision* or *commitment*. It first did this either in the interests of religion — to save it from condemnation as false *theory* about the world, comparable to those of scientific inquiry — or as a reinterpretation of it, to save it from travesty in the hands of its rationalizing defenders.

This movement is of great significance from the viewpoint of understanding the subsequent history of the ideas of the Enlightenment, for it re-establishes the discontinuity which the Enlightenment attacked, and it does so in a new way that evades the arguments of the Enlightenment. The Enlightenment insisted on seeing man and things human as parts of nature and hence amenable to human reason and investigation: it concentrated its attack on dualistic doctrines which maintained that the human mind, destiny, or values were manifestations of something extranatural and unamenable to unaided thought and scientific study. Existentialism re-establishes religious conviction, not by any dualistic ontology or super-science, or by claims of the presence of extranatural, spiritual stuff or whatnot, but by claiming that the manner in which our ultimate commitments are made is and must be different from the manner of empirical or scientific inquiry. Though Existentialists may

sometimes express themselves quasi-ontologically, as though postulating a category of existence consisting of self-choosing or self-conscious beings, this does not really amount to the claim that there exists a special and further *stuff* in the world; the special existence is produced by the act of choice.

If this idea is valid — and it is hard to see how one could judge it — it turns the flank of the enlightened, naturalistic insistence on the unity of nature. It does so, not by saying anything about nature or by denying its unity as an *object* of observation, but by insisting that ultimate or most general convictions are not about *objects* but are a choice within a *subject*. Hence the dualism, the discontinuity denied by the Enlightenment and perhaps required by religion, reappears, but not as a rift *in* nature.

Existentialism has since assumed both religious and atheistic forms, but in either case it maintains this new rift and fundamental dualism between conscious subjects and objects of consciousness and this kind of dualism, unlike the old religious or Cartesian dualism, is something that evades the critique of the Enlightenment.

We are now in a better position to reassess the balance-sheet of the Enlightenment's conflict with religion — an aspect which, after all, was central to it. The religious doctrines that survive the onslaught of the Enlightenment among the educated tend to be, in the main, *reformulated* religious doctrines — reformulated with the aid of either the socially functional view of knowledge or the Existentialist reassessment of faith as something not cognitive or descriptive at all. (There are also more straightforward "fundamentalist" and anti-rationalistic theologies; dogmatism or the denial of reasoning is easy.) So religion survives through certain ways of thought with which the Enlightenment was not familiar and which, in part, arose in order to evade its arguments. The old, forthright theology which dogmatized about this and another world is not much in evidence. Religious assertions are now made, not merely with regard to some "other realm," but also in some "other sense." In other words, the unity and self-sufficiency of the natural world is not often seriously challenged. Sophisticated modern religion, when not simply dogmatic, tends to have either an Existentialist, a sociological, or a pragmatist coloring.

The essence of the "materialist" outlook to be considered is, I think, to be seen in the insistence on the unity, continuity, self-sufficiency, and necessity of the natural world, and in the accompanying idea that human salvation is to be sought in that world, and that doctrines contrary to that unity are harmful. If this is indeed the essence of the outlook, then the subsequent additional ingredients of the characteristic modern *Weltanschauung*, which we have indicated, can be seen, first, as the extension of that continuity to social phenomena and to dualistic, transcendental beliefs themselves, the implications being that apparently irrational social forms and convictions also share in the general necessity of nature and cannot be discounted as mere aberrations; and hence, on quite irreligious (socio-epistemological) grounds, religion must be respected rather than exorcised; secondly, there is the realization that the unity and continuity of nature require one to see man, his aims, and conduct, as of a piece with biological nature, and the implications of this tend to be a pessimism in morals which in fact conflicts with the optimistic anticipation of secular salvation characteristic of the Enlightened outlook. Finally, there is the establishment of a new kind of discontinuity, based not on some kind of dualistic ontological claim, as hitherto, but on a kind of dual *aspect* of man, as object and also as a choosing (and, possibly, cognizing) agent.

The Ideology and its Impact

WE have, so far, described the materialism of the Enlightenment as an outlook, a set of connected, but not necessarily consistent, ideas. We have also suggested that its importance lies in having first brought together, formulated, and disseminated the characteristic modern world-outlook, with the certain qualifications that have been indicated. A propagated general outlook which consciously incorporates certain values, and aims at an alteration of human life and society is sometimes referred to as an ideology. The work of the Enlightenment was certainly the promulgation and propagation of an ideology; indeed, the term originates from the period, and some of the later participants in the movement were known as the *Idéologues*.

But to say this is not to denigrate either the ideas or the work of the Enlightenment. The term "ideology" is far too easily used in a pejorative way. What it properly designates is something which is indispensable to any society, and which is not, as such, necessarily bad or good. The men of the Enlightenment have, moreover, acquired a certain bad name as being the prototypes of thinkers who wish to remold man and society in the image of their own abstract ideas without regard to reality — to propagate the need for continuity in social life and for piecemeal rather than total reform. The term *philosophe*, designating the fashionable and influential thinkers of the period, is sometimes used as meaning an intellectual reformer of such a kind. The excesses of the French Revolution, or indeed the Revolution itself, are blamed on them and their teaching by those who do not approve of it.

The high valuation of the work of the Enlightenment, and indeed the claim that it is the source of our modern view of things, will of course not appeal to those who believe that philosophy can and should be detached and neutral. For such people, the philosophy of the Enlightenment must seem a travesty of philosophy; indeed, it is difficult to see how they can account for its existence.

But if the philosophy of the Enlightenment was an ideology or a propagated outlook calculated to transform society, it was *also* a philosophy in the narrower, technical sense. It contained doctrines on many matters, such as the limits of meaningful discourse, the criteria of morality, the relation of mind and body, which philosophers, who believe in the existence of a narrow, neutral, and ideologically uncommitted subject called "philosophy", consider to be properly philosophical questions in their own preferred sense. The ideologies of the Enlightenment not only contained such doctrines, but contained them in an *essential* way. They were connected in many logical ways, as premises and as corollaries of the "ideological" elements. The two aspects were quite inseparable, and indeed remain so.

My own view is that the separability of allegedly technical philosophy from questions of our outlooks on man, society, and the world — a separation which is sometimes claimed as an achievement and credit of the academic philosophy of our own century — is an absurdity. But if one took such a view, then indeed the claims made for the philosophy of the Enlightenment — that it was the first expression and powerful stimulus of the general modern outlook — collapse. What *is* true, perhaps, is that as "pure" philosophy it is not quite in the first rank but as a *philosophy*, a way of looking at the world, it is in fact both of the utmost importance and of great merit.

Something further should perhaps briefly be said about the subsequent history of the outlook. Two fates can undermine the vitality of an idea: either success or failure. The "materialism" of the Enlightenment has had to suffer both.

More specifically, the materialism of the Enlightenment has had comparatively little impact on Britain, and its immediate impact on Germany has been in the main to produce a reaction rather than to stimulate imitation. The failure to impress itself on Britain is still perceptible: the "enlightened" complex of ideas does not operate as a unity within the Anglo-Saxon tradition. Its "progressives," generally to the surprise of Continental observers, work for rational reconstruction of society on "enlightened" lines — roughly, choosing ends by reference to human well-being and seeking guidance about the means from experience, without also being *ex officio* anticlerical. The explanation of why the complex of anticlericalism and materialism in the narrow sense did not fuse in Britain with utilitarianism, empiricism, and democracy is partly to be sought in the absence of a dominant Roman Catholic Church, and partly in the fact that the individual ideas of the Enlightenment were already present and were not imported from the *philosophes*. The land of Hobbes did not need to learn of materialism or egoism, the land of Hume did not need to learn of empiricism, nor the land of Bentham to be taught the consistent application of utilitarianism to social thinking.

But if, in the short run, the outlook of the Enlightenment either failed to impress itself on France's neighbors or produced a philosophic reaction, in the long run it provided the model or the main strand in the thinking of other societies when they in turn came to be shaken by the economic and political changes of the modern world. Fused with some later elements, with Marxist, romantic, and other ideas, the Enlightenment continued and still continues to provide the alternative world view in places where the local religious views lose their hold. This secular vision, evolved in the West when religion was being sapped from within the society, continues to be the paradigm of a secular alternative in those lands where religion is being undermined by the external impact of the West and by the emulation of it. The successors of the *philosophes* in the nineteenth century were men of the Western world* who turned away from their own local form of the religious *infame* and sought salvation in mundane aims and by mundane means; their successors in our century are to be found among the agents and justifiers of modernization throughout the world. The ideas of the Enlightenment are not the only constituent in their outlook; there are also historical ideas, mystiques of the community, and other elements. Still, the notions of the Enlightenment are an indispensable ingredient.

It is not unusual to sneer at the outlook typified by *The System of Nature*, which will be examined in more detail, by saying that it expresses a religious *attitude* toward a nonreligious vision of the world. Enthusiastic rationalism of this kind is claimed to be out of date. It is not entirely clear to me why this combination — secular views held with religious fervor — should be so inferior to the alternative, the combination of religious formulas with nonreligious indifference. It is often said that the retention of unenforced laws undermines the respect for law as such, and it is at least possible that the respectful retention of the incredible beliefs may undermine intellectual curiosity and respect for truth, the drive toward understanding the world, without much fundamental inquiry is unlikely to occur. The allegedly comic fervor implicit in the open adherence to a systematically secular view of the world may at least be credited with seriousness in its attempt to understand the world, and in its attempt at consistency. It may be better to inherit the all-embracingness and enthusiasm of faith without its content, rather than the reverse.

The System of Nature

THE eighteenth-century French thinkers were both numerous and prolific. A full account of the views

* Including its marginal lands.

even of those who can be characterized, in some sense or another, "materialists of the Enlightenment," would be impossible in a limited space. It is customary and appropriate to take some writer or work as epitomizing the thought of the period. If one wished to concentrate on anticlericalism alone, without a total rejection of religious ideas, one might choose Voltaire. If one were to choose a single *work* as both typical and influential, it would be appropriate, and customary, to take the cooperative *Encyclopédie*. But there would be obvious disadvantages in using a cooperative work of this kind, without the claim to consistency or restriction to general principles. For purposes of examining a coherent, systematically expounded *philosophy*, it is best, from consideration of both merit and a kind of unity, to take Baron d'Holbach's *Le Système de la Nature*, and in particular the first of its two volumes. Its views are more radical than most of the publicly expressed views of the time; it is, however, essentially a coherent, frank, and passionate systematization of the largely shared ideas or of their logical conclusions of the most influential group of intellectuals of the time.

There is a sense in which *The System of Nature* can be said to *tell a story*. It is not merely a vision of the universe and man, and an exhortation, but it is a kind of dramatic presentation of a conflict of two forces: it is almost a narrative. The battle it describes is, of course, unfinished. The intention of the book is to make us see its true character, to make us understand the nature of the two contestants, and to enlist our support for good against evil and to aid its victory. We are conducted along the various points of the front line, the doctrines of man, of knowledge, of morals, and so on.

The two forces engaged in this fundamental crucial conflict are two ways of thinking: the religious and the naturalistic (which includes materialism and empiricism). The former is both wrong and very harmful. The latter is both true and immensely beneficial to humanity.

The work consists of the delineation and demonstration of the true and beneficial view and style of thought, and of an analysis and refutation of the main features of the mistaken and harmful view. It also consists of a pathology of thought, a diagnosis of how the harmful type of thought comes to exist and have a hold on humanity; and, to a lesser extent, it also includes what may be called a rationalist theory of Grace — that is to say, an account of how the true, rationalistic, materialistic manner of thinking can be restored and establish itself amongst men. (This part of the doctrine is among its weaker aspects. So is the rationalistic doctrine of Original Sin — the attempt to account for how mistaken or meaningless and harmful doctrines have come to be so pervasive and powerful.)

The important features of the wrong and harmful type of thinking are: belief in God, in spiritual forces of any kind, in a nonmaterial element of man, in free will or any other exceptions to natural regularity, in innate ideas or any nonsensuous mode of knowledge, in the belief in divine creation or interference, and in the upholding of moral values other than those based on actual human needs and interests.

The particular object of attack is not merely the Christian, and in particular the Roman Catholic vision of the world, but also what the author considers its buttressing by "modern" philosophers (above all, Descartes and his followers): the main dualistic doctrines to the effect that there is an independent thinking substance in addition to extended matter and that there are modes of knowing other than through the senses. In general, one might say that what is under attack is any doctrine that impugns the unity and exhaustiveness of nature — any doctrine that adds an extramundane religious realm to the totality of nature or that introduces some fundamental rift or discontinuity inside it (such as the discontinuity between matter and thought or between determined and free events).

The System of Nature is, of course, itself dualistic in its fundamental *sociology*, for it envisages two fundamental polar possibilities for man and society (though, of course, mixed, intermediate positions are possible and occur, and indeed may be the commonest fate of mankind): a state of rationalist salvation, when man, free or freed from superstition and prejudice, is guided by the trinity of nature, reason, and experience to happiness, and on the other hand the degenerate or unregenerate state when religious and spiritualistic superstition leaves man in misery under the domination of priests and tyrants. The most important social variable, so to speak, is the manner of *thought* (though this itself appears to be dependent on education and government). Materialistic, rationalistic, naturalist thought liberates man and society and leads him to happiness; religious thought leads him to error and misery.

In as far as *The System of Nature* distinguishes between the religious view proper and its more recent metaphysical supports, even if it classes them together as variants of the same basic intellectual sin, it can be seen as the anticipation of Comte's positivism and the distinction between the religious and the metaphysical stage which humanity passes through before attaining *positive* thinking.

The Nature of the Universe

THE preface of *The System of Nature* opens with what is, in effect, the most central idea of all contained in the work: "Man is unhappy only because he is ignorant of Nature." The preface goes on to point out that man is so enslaved by prejudice that one might suppose him forever condemned to error. A dangerous germ has entered all his ideas and

makes them unstable, obscure, and false: the pursuit of the transcendental, the desire to indulge in metaphysics rather than physics. Man despises realities in order to contemplate chimeras. He neglects experience and fails to cultivate his reason, but feeds instead on conjectures and systems; he claims to know his own fate in the imaginary regions of another life, and does not attempt to make himself happy in the world he inhabits.

In brief, the source of evil is ignorance, and ignorance is not accidental but the product of one pervasive error — extranatural beliefs and interests, and the inhibition of inquiry into nature by natural means. Hence, the author calls for a fight against religion and metaphysics in the interests of natural *knowledge* and the happiness it will bring.

One should note that this preface, which in its way sums up the book as a whole, quite unwittingly introduces a crucial ambiguity into the notion of that *Nature* which is its subject. One might have begun with a positive description of it — a unity, governed by laws, without inner repetitions, etc. — and proceeded deductively from its general features, imitating the procedure of Spinoza's *Ethics*, with whose vision *The System* has obvious affinities. But such a procedure, though orderly and logical, would obscure the fact that "nature" here also has another meaning: namely, that which is found out by natural means, by the application of reason to experience, *whatever it turns out to be*. In other words, the main premise of the *System* can also be seen to be an epistemological one rather than an ontological one: perhaps, one should say, the recommendation of a cognitive strategy rather than the postulation of a cosmological picture. (And more than this, the recommended epistemic strategy could itself in turn be seen as the corollary of an ethical premise and a sociological one — of the exclusive valuation of happiness and of the conviction that it is furthered by naturalistic inquiry and hindered, above all, by religious and metaphysical conviction.)

The System, like most other systems of ideas, *can* be arranged as a deductive argument from premises, but it is in fact more correctly represented as an interlocking system of ideas which support each other. Some of these ideas are, of course, more crucial than others, and can be singled out as premises; but it is important to remember that they in turn can figure as conclusions inferred from other parts of the system, even if those other parts to some extent in turn depend for their proofs on them. The belief in the beneficial power of knowledge, and in the maleficent power, almost exclusively and predominantly, of ignorance, superstition, religion, and transcendentalism, is one such premise within *The System*, and perhaps the most important.

The first chapter does in fact give us a positive description of that *Nature* which is the object of inquiry and, one might add, of reverence.

The universe, that vast assembly of all that exists, nowhere presents us with anything but matter and movement: it displays nothing but an immense and uninterrupted chain of causes and effects: some of these causes we know because they strike our senses immediately; others we do not know, because they act on us only by effects far removed from their first causes. . . . the sum total [of diverse matter, its properties and manner of acting, and the systems constituted by them] we call *nature*. . . . Thus nature, in its widest sense, is the grand total resulting from the assembly of the different materials, their combinations, and the different movements we see in the universe.

D'Holbach also uses "nature" in a more special sense: "Nature, in its narrower sense, or as applied to each individual being, is that which follows from its essence, that is to say, the properties, combinations, movements, and manner of acting which distinguish it from other beings."

He thus distinguishes between *particular* natures and the general system (the *universal* nature) to which everything that exists is necessarily tied. A very significant *Nota Bene* ends the first chapter. It disclaims any interpretation that would seem to personify nature, which is an abstract being; the note explains how expressions frequently used in the book, such as "Nature required . . . " or "It is natural . . . " can be translated in a manner not suggesting a personified nature. It should be noted that these translations are not very convincing to a modern critical philosopher: they employ either the notion of essence or the legislative, "compelling" idea of law of nature. So, indirectly, the reinterpretations of "nature" offered by d'Holbach still seem tainted with the anthropomorphism that he strives to reject.

The second chapter concerns itself with movement. Movement is made central both to nature — being the agent of all the necessary changes which constitute it — and to cognition — being the only carrier of information. "To know an object is to have felt it: to have felt it is to have been moved by it." Two conflicts seem latent in d'Holbach's thought here, first, between his "contact" theory of knowledge and his materialism, and secondly, between his essentialist manner of speaking (behavior seems to emanate from the essences of things) and the exclusiveness of communicated motion as the agent of change. For the emanation of all properties (including those of change) from the essences of things suggests an entelechy rather than a mechanism.

A distinction of great importance for d'Holbach is between external and internal movements. External movements are perceptible, consisting of the transfer of the whole mass of some body from one place to another. Internal movement is hidden and depends on changes in the essence, the molecular structure of a body. For his argument this type of movement is essential in helping to explain biological and psychological change and activities without recourse to some principle other than natural, deterministic movement.

D'Holbach also distinguishes between simple (one-cause) and complex (many-cause) movements. All movement is a necessary consequence of the essences and properties of things or of the causes that act on them. (One might, as indicated, suspect conflict between his Leibniz-like essentialism and his prescriptive notion of law, but interaction can also be covered by necessary laws that can be said to "inhere," and perhaps this would be the solution adopted.) Everything in the universe is in movement; it is of the essence of nature to act. The notion of *nisus* (striving) is stressed, which is to bring harmony to the preceding thesis and the appearance of occasional rest in the world.

Movement is pervasive and inherent in nature; no impulsion external to the world is required. The supposition of creation from nothingness is but words without meanings attached to them. These notions become even more obscure if the creation is attributed to a spiritual being. Matter is sufficient. Matter and movement are facts and sufficient ones. He adds a doctrine of the diversity of substances, invoking Leibniz. Nature in its endless change is compared to a phoenix, ever reborn from its own ashes.

The third chapter expands his view of matter. What emerges again is both a sensualist view of matter — we distinguish substances by the various effects produced in us — and also a different theory only questionably compatible with the former, a specification of primary qualities called "general and primitive": extension, mobility, divisibility, solidity, inertia. Moreover, all properties are claimed to inhere in their substances necessarily "in the rigorous sense of the word," and yet *movement* is also said to be responsible for all change. (The problem of squaring the necessity of all truths with the existence of temporal change is not raised.) Mankind is castigated for having formed inadequate conceptions of matter in the past (that is conceptions calling for extranatural explanations of the properties of matter). An "eternal circle" theory is put forward: the sum of existence remains the same, but everything changes.

The fourth chapter opens with some interesting observations on the psychology and logic of explanation: Men are not surprised by effects of which they know the causes (the implication being that only ignorance invokes extranatural explanations). But d'Holbach also makes the observation that men do not seek causes of effects with which they are familiar. "It takes a Newton to feel that the fall of bodies is a phenomenon worthy of all attention." This seems to be a sign of another latent tension in his thought, "Is a sense of mystery, a need for further explanation, pathological or profound?"

He wishes to say the former with regard to religious explanation or awe, and the latter with regard to scientific ones; but the differentiae are not adequately worked out. Natural, scientific explanations are of course, for him, those that are materialistic, monistic, and based on experience. But, one might object, their materialism and monism are not in fact things given by experience; and they are, in fact, frequently transcendent, though perhaps not anthropomorphically so. The chapter reaffirms that there can only be natural explanations.

He sketches a physics and a sociology ("*morale*") in terms of dispositions of matter and bodies in relation to each other: "attraction and repulsion, sympathy, antipathy, affinities, and relations." To exist is said to be the undergoing of the changes proper to some determinate essence.

Necessity is the infallible and constant connection of causes with their effects. (And, of course, it is claimed to be all-pervasive.) Man necessarily desires what is or what seems useful to his well-being, for instance. There cannot be independent energies, isolated causes (in other words, no extranatural interventions, no miracles). The examples given are, interestingly, one from physics and one from sociology — a whirlpool of dust and political convulsion.

The fifth chapter is concerned mainly with the notion of order. The real problem d'Holbach seems to face here is how to combine his orderly, deterministic view of nature, one that finds *inside* nature the explanation of all phenomena, with an avoidance of any possibility of a theistic argument from design. The main device employed for this end is the distinction between (real) order of nature, which is inherent in things, universal, and inescapable, and that which men *call* order, which is a subjective or relative notion men project onto things which have a certain conformity with their aims. This latter notion has a contrast, an antithesis, *disorder*, which men also project onto things.

This pair of contrasted notions is "abstract and metaphysical," and corresponds to nothing outside us. (It is interesting to note that d'Holbach here considers the notion endowed with an antithesis to be metaphysical and meaningless, while the contrastless notion of order-of-nature, which covers *everything*, does, according to him, apply to reality.) Apparent disorder is (1) only apparent, (2) a transition to a new order (as in illness or death). Miracles and monsters are denied. *Chance* is but an illusion of ignorance.

Anthropocentrism and anthropomorphism are denied. It is ignorance that has led to explaining nature in terms of intelligence. But such an intelligence would require organs, etc. Intelligence is only a characteristic of organized beings. There is no need for nature (as a whole) to have it simply because it also produced it, as wine does not have the characteristics it produces in us. . . . It is but empty words and anthropomorphic inferences which lead to attribution of intelligence to the universe. (And how about the attribution of order and necessity? One might ask, is *that* not anthropomorphic? D'Holbach attributes both more and less to nature than the theists do. He *gives* it power so as to eliminate the need for extramundane interferences, and *denies* it constituents that destroy its unity and which could appear to be intrusions from some other realm. For him, explanations must be both intranatural and materialistic.)

The Nature of Man

THE sixth chapter deals specifically with man; it explicitly sets out to apply the general ideas, which are claimed to have been established earlier, to the "beings who interest us most." Notwithstanding some nonfundamental differences, we shall see *man* falling under the same rules as those to which everything is subject. D'Holbach's special kind of "essentialism," the view referred to earlier that everything has an "essence" which *is* its special manner of acting, and the determinism associated with this are both applied to man. There is reference to the hiddenness and complexity of the human manner of acting.

This (hidden operations) is the origin of mistaken — voluntaristic, spiritualistic — views of man which are rooted in the idea that he moves himself, that he can act independently of the laws of nature. Careful examination will remove this illusion. There are two kinds of movement, inner and outer; and in a complex machine, the inner ones may be well hidden. Spirituality, immateriality, immortality — those vague words — are then invented to account for hidden movements. Thus, according to religious, spiritualist theories, man becomes double — gross matter and simple pure spirit. This dualism d'Holbach denies. But has man existed for all time? he proceeds to ask. We don't know, but probably not. Man is tied to the particular conditions which have produced him.

There follows an attack on dualistic theories. These are but the invention of words to hide ignorance. The dualism that most philosophers accepted in d'Holbach's time is based only on unnecessary superstitions. Man is a material being organized to feel, think, and be modified in a manner suitable to himself, to his organization, the combination of substance assembled in him. And why suppose nature sterile and incapable of creating new beings? — In other words, why invoke external or "spiritual" agencies to account for them? Then follows an invocation to man: Accept your ephemeral nature! All is change in the universe. Nature contains no constant forms. The conclusion is that man has no reasons for supposing himself privileged (unique) in nature.

The seventh chapter continues the assault on the

"spiritualist system" (the religious and Cartesian doctrines of the soul). It stresses the uselessness of the gratuitous assumption of duality, of differentiation of inner and outer activity, of the notion of an imperceptible, indivisible, unextended inner stuff. This is an unintelligible and merely negative idea. Only material causes can act. One has invented an infinite intelligence in the image of a finite one, and explained the union of the latter with body by reference to the former, failing to see that neither can move matter. (Here he gets close to admitting that we do at least have an image of the finite intelligence at any rate. But, he asks, how and where is this extensionless body located and connected with matter? It is through failure to respect experience and reason that men have obscured ideas, have failed to see the soul as a part of the body, and have created a being in the image of wind. But politically the idea is useful to theologians, for it makes the separable part of man available to punishments and rewards. In fact, the "soul" is the body seen relative to certain functions.

The paradoxes of general dualism are elaborated by him: Can God not endow matter with thought? And if not, are there then two eternal beings? Primitives explain what they do not understand animistically. We have done this for man and nature.

Chapter 8 proceeds to carry out the program of a unitary vision of man by establishing the thesis that all our intellectual faculties are derived from sensing. (We thus see that sensationalism plays a double role in the system — a positivistic one, eliminating empirically uncashable ideas, and also an antidualistic one in philosophical anthropology.)

The faculty of *feeling* (in a broad sense) may seem inexplicable, but it is not different in this respect from gravity, magnetism, electricity, elasticity. He proceeds to define feeling in terms of physiological modification and to argue for the importance of the nervous system: the sensibility of the brain derives from its *arrangement*. Milk, bread, and wine become the substance of man. He repeatedly remarks on this point. (D'Holbach's materialism has its own doctrine of transubstantiation.)

Sensation is defined as the impact made on our senses; *perception* as its transmission to the brain; an *idea*, the image of the object causing the sensation. (Thus the theory is both causal and sensationalist.) This is then worked out with regard to the individual senses.

This is the only way in which we receive sensations, perceptions, ideas. These modifications produce further ones in our brain, which we call thoughts, reflections, memory, imagination, judgment, will, actions; these all have sensation as their basis. To have an accurate idea of thought, reflect on what happens in us in the presence of any object: we combine impressions. Thoughts have beginnings, ends, duration, a history like all other events; how, asks d'Holbach, can the soul be indivisible?

Memory, imagination, judgment, and will are defined in conformity with this. Understanding is the capacity of apperceiving outer and inner objects. The sum of faculties is intelligence. One manner of using them is reason.

Everything is in the brain, which is sufficient to explain mental phenomena. Invoking spiritual being of which we have no idea does not help. (Everything is thus reduced both to sensation and to brain — empiricism and materialism — thus doubly exiling spiritualism as unintelligible and as alien stuff.)

The soul is affected by events — hence it is material. (The connection of materialism with causality and intelligibility is that materialism is made to follow from possibility of explanation, as well as from possibility of experiential contact, of sensation.)

The ninth chapter begins with a reaffirmation of diversity, necessary diversity. There are no two strictly identical beings. Hence men differ: hence they are unequal, and this inequality is the basis of society. Mutual need is the consequence of inequality and diversity. Our diversity leads us to be classified according to our moral and intellectual characteristics. These are physically caused. Parentage and nurture determine us. Man's temperament is but the arrangement of his parts. Then follows another attack on dualistic spiritualism. (Not even man himself may be seen anthropomorphically. Existentialism later, and Kant at the same time, maintain dualistic, non-naturalist views of men at the price of at least partially opting out of science.)

Spiritualism makes *morals* (d'Holbach rightly uses this in a broader sense that includes the whole study of man and society) a conjectural science. Materialism, on the other hand, gives us knowledge and control. Man is alterable. The theologians will always find man a mystery, attributing his behavior to a principle of which they can have no idea. Our discoveries, in terms of the materials that enter into man's constitution, will lead us to improve him. There follows a phlogiston theory of the psyche along with an electrical theory of nervous communication. Fire and warmth are indicated as principles of life.

Science is based on truth, and truth depends on the fidelity of our senses. Truth is conformity between objects we know and the characteristics we attribute to them. It is attained by well-constituted senses with the aid of experience. How can one check on defective senses? By multiplied, diversified, repeated experiences. In brief, truth is the just and precise association of ideas. Error is faulty association of ideas. (Thus we have both a coherence and a correspondence theory of truth. The checking-by-accumulation-of-experiences is of course compatible with both.) Prediction also is based on experience and analogy. (D'Holbach does not ask how this is squared with his doctrine of necessary diversity.)

Our faculty of having and recalling experience, foreseeing effects so as to avoid harmful ones or to procure those useful to our survival and happiness (our sole aim), constitutes *reason*. (A very pragmatic and utilitarian definition — but one which is not open to a Humeian critique!) Sentiment, our nature, may mislead us, but experience and reflection lead us back to the right path. Reason is nature modified by experience, judgment, and reflection. It presupposes a moderate temperament, an *esprit juste*, a controlled imagination, knowledge of truth based on sure experience, prudence, and foresight. Thus few men are indeed rational beings! Our senses are the only means of telling the truth of opinion, the usefulness of conduct. Man's only aim is happiness and self-preservation. It is important to know the true means: his own faculties. Experience and reason show him he needs other human beings.

Moral distinctions, all manners of judging men and their actions, are based on utility and diversity, not on convention nor on the chimerical will of a supernatural being. Virtue is what is constantly useful to human beings in society. Our duties are the means that experience and reason show up to our ends. To say we are obliged is to say that without those means we shall not reach our ends.

Happiness is the state in which we wish to persist. Pleasure is transient happiness. It depends on a certain inner movement. Hence pleasure and pain are so close. Happiness cannot be the same in all men; hence moralists disagree. Ideas men form of happiness also depend on habit. Most of what men do depends on habit. A footnote illustrates this by expanding a learning theory of criminality: *c'est le premier pas qui coûte* ("it is the first step that counts").

We are so modified by habit that we confuse it with nature. This is the origin of the fallacious theory of innate ideas. But the physical and moral phenomena are explicable by a pure mechanism. Hobbes is quoted in support. Habit explains the almost invincible attachment of men to useless and harmful usages. (No facile refutation of the *philosophe*, as failing to see the importance and force of *habit*, is possible. He is fully aware of it — he just does not like what is contemporaneously habitual.) Education is inculcation of habit at an early age when organs are flexible. A theory of conditioning, of transmission of culture, is put forward.

Politics is in fact so vicious because it is not based on nature, experience, or general utility but on the passions, caprices, and particular utility of those who govern. To be useful, politics should operate according to nature, that is to say, it should conform to the essence and aim of society. (An empiricist essentialism?)

Men have, formally or tacitly, made a pact to help and not to harm each other. But given their pursuit of temporary and selfish caprices and passions, force is necessary, and it is called the law. As large societies cannot easily assemble, they are forced to choose citizens to whom they accord confidence. This is the origin of all government, which to be legitimate must be based on free consent of society, without which it is only violence, usurpation, brigandage. These citizens are called sovereigns, chiefs, legislators, and according to form, monarchs, magistrates, legislators. (Thus the attempt is made to derive a moral, critical theory of politics from a neutral naturalism.)

Society can revoke the power it has conferred when its interest so requires. It is the supreme authority, by the immutable law of nature which requires that the part is subordinated to the whole. Thus sovereigns are ministers, interpreters, trustees, and not absolute masters or proprietors. By a pact, be it tacit or expressed, they have bound themselves. (Thus d'Holbach has a double "contract theory" — among citizens themselves, and between them and government.)

To be just, laws must be for the general good of society and ensure liberty (pursuit of one's happiness without harming others), property (enjoyment of the fruits of one's work and industry), and security (an enjoyment of one's person and goods under the protection of the law as long as one keeps one's pact with society). Justice or equity is essential for society's happiness; it prevents exploitation.

Rights are what is allowed by equitable laws. A society that does no good has no rights over its citizens. "*Il n'est point de patrie sans bien-être: une société sans équité ne renferme que des ennemis, une société opprimée ne contient que des oppresseurs et des esclaves.*"* Through failure to know this we get absolute government, which is nothing but brigandage. A man who fears naught soon becomes evil. (*This* diagnosis of the current corruption of those in power is not in harmony with d'Holbach's optimistic prognosis, expressed elsewhere and implicit throughout, of the social behavior of enlightened man. The political implications of d'Holbach's views inevitably fluctuate between democracy and paternalism.) Hence one must limit the power of chiefs. Also, the weight of administration is too great to rest on the shoulders of one man. Power corrupts. Sovereigns must be subject to laws and not vice versa. (Thus, in effect, we get a double diagnosis of such ills: ignorance and concentration of power. D'Holbach assumes, too easily perhaps, that the removal of the one and of the other will go together.)

Government affects the physique and morals of nations. Government affects all other social variables. *Mores* are the habitudes of people. No habit, however abominable, is without the approval of *some* nation. Some religion is found to consecrate even the most repulsive usages.

The passions of the governors are reflected in the governed. One cannot destroy passion in the hearts of men, but let us direct them toward objects useful to them and society. Let education,

---

* "There is no nation without well-being: a society without equity includes only enemies, an oppressed society contains only oppressors and slaves."

government, and the laws habituate and fix them within limits set by experience and reason. Nature as such makes us neither good nor evil. Man is a terrain on which weeds or useful grain can grow. Education and other environmental influences mold him.

For man to be virtuous, he should have a motive for virtue; education must give him reasonable ideas; public opinion and example must show him virtue as estimable. In fact, the reverse is the case. Man must pursue his own well-being and hence the means to it. It is useless and perhaps unjust to ask a man to respect virtue if only harm comes of it. Some savages flatten the heads of their infants, thus distorting nature. So it is with institutions. Religion leads men to seek happiness in illusions. Public opinion gives us false ideas of glory and honor.

Authority generally believes itself interested in maintaining established opinions. Prejudices and errors which it holds necessary for its maintenance are supported by force, which never reasons. Princes, puffed up by false ideas of grandeur, are surrounded by flatterers. Courts are the real centers of people's corruption. This is the real origin of moral evil. Thus all conspires to make man vicious. Habit reinforces this. Thus most men are determined for evil.

The tenth chapter attacks the doctrine of innate ideas. Our inner organ, which we call our soul, is purely material, as was shown by the manner in which it acquires ideas through impressions made by material objects on our senses, which are themselves material. All faculties we call intellectual spring from sensing. Moral qualities are explicable by laws applicable to a simple mechanism.

The ideas of Descartes and Berkeley are attacked. To justify their monstrous opinions, they tell us that ideas are the only objects of thought. But ideas are *effects*. Though it is difficult to reach the causes, can we suppose that there are none? If we have only *ideas* of material objects, how can we suppose that the causes of our ideas are immaterial? To suppose that man, without aid of outer things and objects, can have ideas of the universe is like saying a blind man could have a true idea of a picture he had never heard spoken of.

It is easy to see the origin of these errors. Forced by prejudice or fear of theology, men start from the idea of a pure spirit — and then fail to see how this can interact with body. And seeing that the soul does have ideas, they conclude that it draws them from itself.

Yet there are certain phenomena supporting these views: *dreams*. D'Holbach then gives a casual account of dreams. Dreamers are compared to waking theologians. But dreams prove the opposite from the spiritualist dogma. The soul of a dreaming man is like a drunk or delirious man.

If there were a being in the world capable of moving itself by its own energy, it would have the power to arrest or suspend movement in the universe — to

be an exception to general determinism. (D'Holbach as usual fuses his determinism with an essentialism — his view that causal and other properties flow from the very nature of beings — or an essentialist mode of expression.)

The difficulty of understanding the capacities of a human soul causes attribution of incomprehensible qualities. For instance, our thought and imagination can survey the vast universe. In reality, it is only as an effect of our senses that we have ideas: it is only through modifications of our brains that we think, will, act. (Sensationalism and physical determinism are fused by him.) From this, a verification principle, in effect, of meaning, is extracted and declared to be but the inverse of Aristotle's dictum about what is found in the mind being first in the senses. If a word or an idea refers to nothing sensible, then it is meaningless.

The profound Locke has brought this principle to light, to the regret of the theologians. Others, too, have seen the absurdity of the system of innate ideas. How is it that he and they have failed to see that their principle undermines theology? But, alas, prejudice — especially of the sacred kind — is strong. Moralists should have seen the absurdity of innate moral sentiment or instinct.

D'Holbach offers an empiricist theory of geometrical and logical truth in order, again, to avoid the theory of innate ideas. He applies the denial of innate ideas to abstract ideas — goodness, beauty, order, intelligence, virtue, etc. — and offers an empiricist theory of their significance. All men's errors and disputes spring from abandoning the evidence of experience and the senses, and allowing themselves to be led by allegedly innate ideas. To think of objects that have not acted on our senses is to think of words (only), to use imagination (in a void) — for example, the word *God*. Theology, psychology (i.e. the contemporary study of a psychic stuff), and metaphysics are pure sciences of words. They infect the study of morals and politics. But men have need of truth. This consists of knowing the true relation they have to things that can influence their well-being. Those relations are known only with the aid of experience. Without experience there is no reason; without reason we are but blind men who act by chance. But how to acquire experience of ideal subjects never known or examined by our senses? How to know their effects on us? By making morals depend on these transcendental things, one makes morals arbitrary, abandoning it to the caprices of the imagination.

Men vary, but beings of the same species are roughly similar, though never identical. Here the book develops an individual relativism. No proposition, however simple, evident, and clear, can be the same in two men. (Thus, the isolation of the individual is arrived at from his "organized-matter" nature, rather than from sensationalism.)

To ask that a man thinks like us is to ask that he

be organized as we are. Men must vary. Their chimeras and religions also vary. Men kill and persecute each other for words devoid of sense. But man devoted to experience, reason and nature would only occupy himself with objects useful to his felicity. If man must have illusions, let him leave others to theirs. Thus tolerance is derived from determinism, relativism, and positivism. (But this relativism is not turned back upon d'Holbach's own position.)

The eleventh chapter discusses the doctrine of liberty. The notion of freedom (from laws of physics) it holds to be a corollary of the spiritualist view of soul. The self-origination view of ideas and of action are tied up. He goes on to remind us that the soul is but the body envisaged relatively to some functions more hidden than others, and stresses determinism. Our life follows a line decreed by nature.

Yet people believe in the notion of freedom, a notion which is a basis of religion and is allegedly required by society for responsibility. For man to be free would require that all things lose their essences (natures) for his sake (in other words, that they should not be governed by necessary laws. This shows, incidentally, that d'Holbach's terminological "essentialism" can really be seen as a manner of affirming a determinist, law-bound view of nature, and no more.) Man is determined by his pursuit of well-being and survival, and is informed by experience. The will is, as indicated, a modification in the brain which disposes to action. Thus will is ever determined. The will is, for instance, determined by thirst and water, and by the knowledge of the water being poisoned. This model, he claims, helps explain all phenomena of will.

When will is in suspension, we deliberate. To deliberate is to love and hate alternately. We are often in balance between two motives. Our manner of thinking is necessarily determined by our manner of being. The errors of the philosophers are due to seeing will as a first cause rather than going a step further back in the inquiry.

The partisans of liberty have confused constraint with necessity. Thus man can be free of constraint without being (metaphysically) free. Saying that man is not free is not to say that he is always like a thing moved from outside. He can be moved from inside. It is only the complexity of our inner movements that obscures the truth of determinism.

Education is necessity displayed to children. Legislation is necessity displayed to members of the body politic. Morals is the necessity of relations subsisting between men, shown to reasonable men. Religion is necessity of a necessary being, or necessity shown to the ignorant and pusillanimous. The theologian and tyrant necessarily persecute truth and reason. Education is generally so bad because it is based on prejudice. When it is good, it is then unfortunately contradicted or destroyed by the evil there is in society. The great art of the moralist would be to show men and those who regulate their

wills that their interests are the same, that their reciprocal happiness depends on the harmony of their passions. Religion would only be allowed if it fortified this, if indeed a lie could be of real aid to truth. It is religion and power which make men evil. This shows we must go to the roots if we wish to effect a cure. (Government and religion appear to be the roots of reform.)

Fatalism (i.e. d'Holbach's position) is the necessary, immutable eternal order of nature. The theory of liberty only springs from the fact that in some cases we see causes and in others we do not. In man, liberty is but the kind of necessity enclosed within him. He quotes in support of this, "*Volentem ducunt fata, nolentem trahunt*" ("The fates lead the willing, and drag the unwilling") — which gets very close to a theory of freedom as recognition of necessity.

The twelfth chapter examines the view that the system of fatalism is dangerous. For beings whose essence is to conserve themselves and make themselves happy, experience is indispensable; without it, there is no truth, which is, as indicated, the knowledge of the constant relations existing between man and the objects acting on him. Truth itself we desire because we hold it useful; we only fear it when we suppose it will harm us. But can truth really harm us? No, it is on its utility that its value and its rights are based. It can be disagreeable to some individuals and contrary to their interests, but it will always be useful to the human species, whose interests are never the same as those of the men who, being dupes of their passions, think it in their interest to plunge others into error. Utility is thus the touchstone of systems, of the opinions and the acts of men. It is the measure of the esteem and love we owe to truth itself: the most useful truths are also the most estimable. Those we call sterile and despise are those whose usefulness is limited to being the amusement of men who do not have ideas, manners of feeling, and needs similar to our own.

Utility is also the measure of *this* system itself. Those who know the harm done by superstition will recognize the value of opposing it by truer systems, founded on nature and experience. Only those interested in established lies will see it with horror. Those who do not perceive — or only feebly — the misery caused by theological prejudice, will see it (our system) as sterile.

Let us not be surprised by the diversity of judgments, for men's interests vary. But let us look at the system with the eyes of a disinterested man, free from prejudice and concerned for the happiness of the species. We shall then assess it more correctly. (The argument then proceeds from the premise that control requires knowledge of true causes.)

The argument from freedom to responsibility is mentioned. But, it is claimed, we *can* impute an act even to determined beings. We can still distinguish useful from harmful acts, and we cannot but approve and disapprove. Laws are made to maintain society and to prevent the associated men from harming each other. The tools of punishment are to society as drains are to a house. A utilitarian deterrent theory of punishment is expounded.

The system of fatalism would not leave crimes unpunished, but would mitigate the barbarism of punishment — which is inefficacious anyway, only wasting criminal lives (more useful employed on forced labor) and making criminals more cruel and so on. The facility with which one deprives men of life is an index of the incapacity of legislators. The paradox of determinism is avoided by stressing that we do not have the freedom to choose to be passive. Let it not be said that man is degraded by being compared to a vegetable or a machine. A tree is a useful and agreeable object. Nature herself is a machine.

Everything is necessary. Nature distributes (what we call) order and disorder, and pleasure and pain. She provides remedies for ills. Evils are due not to wickedness but to the necessity of things — a neutral nature from which all emanates. Let us submit to necessity! And a paean to determinism follows.

The thirteenth chapter deals with the doctrine of the immortality of the soul, with the dogma of a future life, and with the fear of death. The soul grows and declines with the body — in other words, it is identical with it. Origins of "soul," i.e., of reduplication-of-the-self theories, are discussed. The illusoriness of immortality is shown from the fact that soul is sensation, and from the notion of organism. An organized being is compared to a clock. Once broken, it cannot work. Similarly, we cannot exist without our bodies. As Bacon says, "Men fear death as children fear darkness." Even deep sleep gives us ideas of death. Death is sleep, the cessation of ideas. Fear of death is an aid of tyranny. But it does not frighten the wicked, only the good. The effect of religious fanaticism is that men show themselves at their worst. For the wicked also apparently go to heaven: Moses, Samuel, David, Mahomed; Saints Cyril, Athanasius, and Dominic, and other religious brigands. (A footnote points out maliciously that Berkeleyans and Malebranchists do not need Resurrection.)

The Foundations of Morality

THE fourteenth chapter maintains that education, morals, and laws suffice to restrain men. It is not in an ideal world, but in the real world, that one must seek solutions and cures. It follows from what has been said earlier that it is education, above all things, that provides the cure. Good government has no need of lies.

Men are bad because government is bad. Society is the war of the sovereign against all, and of all against all. In a footnote d'Holbach remarks that he is not saying, like Hobbes, that the state of nature is a state of war; men are by nature neither good nor bad, but can become either.

The fifteenth chapter continues these themes: Man cannot be happy without virtue. Utility, as already said, should be the unique measure of human judgments. To be useful is to contribute to the happiness of one's fellows. This being so, let us see whether our principles are advantageous.

Happiness is sustained pleasure. For an object to please us it must be in harmony with our "organization." Our machine has need of continuous movement — hence the taste for (theatrical) tragedies, excitement, coffee, alcohol, spirits, executions, etc. (In a footnote he remarks that religion is the *eau-de-vie* of the people.) To be happy without interruption would require infinite forces. For d'Holbach, this follows from his view that sensations are functions of inner activities.

Interest is what each of us deems necessary to his felicity. Interest is the unique motive. Hence no one is disinterested. Sometimes we do not know enough of a man's motives to see this, or do not ourselves attach value to the same object as he does. We admire interest which results in benefice for humanity. A good man is one whose true ideas have shown him his interest in a manner leading to action that others love and approve in their own interest. This is the true basis of morality. There is nothing more chimerical than interests placed outside nature or innate instincts. Psychological egoism is thus postulated. Morals would be a vain science unless it showed virtue to be in one's interest. Obligation can only be based on interest. Harmony is shown to obtain through the existence of mutual need. We need other people, require their affection, approbation, and so forth. Virtue is but the art of making oneself happy through the happiness of others. Virtue and happiness are thus connected. Virtue is essential to society, and so is interest. But in fact (that is, in our bad times) virtue is not recompensed. The explanation of this is that society corrupts, and the good man retires out of its way. (The virtue-is-recompensed view is thus altered and made to hold only in a rational society.) Yet even now there are some virtuous men.

The sixteenth chapter discusses the errors of men concerning (the nature of) their happiness and the true source of their ills, as well as the remedies that others have wished to impose on them. Happiness is only the fruit of the harmony of desire and circumstance. Power, supreme power, is useless without knowledge of how to use it for happiness. Princes and their subjects are so often unhappy only because they lack knowledge. Hence, ascetic declamations — against power, riches, and pleasure — are frivolous, ineffective, and beside the point. The power of man over man must be based on the happiness that the power provides. Without it, it is usurpation. Rank and power are justifiable (only) by utility.

If we consult experience we see that the source of

human ills is to be found in illusion and in sacred opinion. Ignorance of natural causes produces the belief in gods. And men have prejudices no less dangerous and harmful concerning government. They dare not demand happiness from kings. Nations adore the origin of their miseries.

We find the same blindness in the science of morals. Instead of being based on the real relations among men, it is based on imaginary ones, and on relations between man and imaginary beings. The notion of a "supreme good" is a chimera. Diverse ills require diverse cures. Those who combat human desire have mistaken the natural state of man for a disease. Yet there are some happy men — even among the poor. The world is not, even now, so very terrible. Do not men cling to life?

The seventeenth chapter maintains that "true ideas founded on nature" are the only remedy against human ills, and contains a recapitulation of Part One of the work and a conclusion. It is when we cease to take experience as our guide that we fall into error. Our errors become particularly dangerous and incurable when they have the sanctions of religion. We then refuse ever to retrace our steps, and suppose that our happiness depends on closing our eyes to truth. If moralists have failed, it is because their remedies have ignored nature, reason, experience. (This is d'Holbach's Holy Trinity. Note that the second is but a systematic regard for the third, and the third is the revelation of the first, and the second and third are somehow *specially* legitimate parts of the first.)

Only passions are the real counterweights of passion. Reason, fruit of experience, is but the art of choosing what passions to listen to for our own happiness. Education and legislation is their canalizing to useful ends. Religion is the dissemination of chimeras.

Reason and morality have no hold over man unless they show him his true interest. Man is only wicked because he feels it almost always in his interest to be so. Make men more enlightened and happy and you will make them better. An equitable and vigilant government will soon fill its state with honest citizens by giving them motives for doing good. A footnote quotes Sallust: "*nemo gratuito malus est*" ("no one is bad for no reason"), and adds: "*nemo gratuito bonus*" ("no one is good for no reason"). If we seek the origin of our ignorance of morals and motives we find it in false ideas of speculation, such as the dualistic theories of man which have supposed the soul free.

The conclusion is that all human error follows from having renounced experience, the testimony of the senses, and right reason, and from having allowed oneself to be guided by frequently deceitful imagination and ever suspect authority. Man will always misunderstand his true happiness so long as he fails to study nature, learn its immutable laws, and seek only in it the remedies of the evils that follow from his present errors.

The System of Nature, *Volume II*

IT is impossible, in a limited space, to give the same kind of summary for the second volume of *The System of Nature* as we have of the first; and it is also less necessary. The second volume does not add to the positive picture provided by the first. It concerns itself largely with further diagnosis and refutation of theological, spiritualistic, dualistic doctrines, and with the social conditions and consequence of both truth and error. The general themes are often restated.

> Nature is self-existent; she will always exist; she produces everything; contains within herself the cause of everything; her motion is a necessary consequence of her existence; without motion we could form no conception of nature; under this collective name we designate the assemblage of matter acting by virtue of its peculiar energies.[1]

Or again, elsewhere

> The simplest observation will prove [to man] incontestably that everything is necessary, that all the effects he perceives are material; that they can only originate in causes of the same nature. . . . Thus [the human] mind, properly directed, will everywhere show [man] nothing but matter, sometimes acting in a manner which his organs permit him to follow, and others in a mode imperceptible to [our] faculties. . . . [Man] will see that all beings follow constant, invariable laws, by which all combinations are united and destroyed . . . the great whole remaining ever the same. Thus [he will be] cured of idle notions with which he was imbued . . . [and of the] imaginary systems; he will cheerfully consent to be ignorant of whatever his organs do not enable him to compass. . . .

The passages which discuss the psychological and social possibility of atheism, and which concede that so philosophical an outlook is unsuited (at any rate, at present) for the generality of men, are interesting as expressions of the state of mind of an enlightened intelligentsia which is confident of the truth of its vision but does not feel that it can share it — for a long time, at any rate — with the common run of humanity. Truth *is* salvation; but not as yet, it appears, for everyone.

Towards the end of the second volume there are a number of declamatory passages that well convey the spirit of the work, even if they are stylistically atypical. Thus, the penultimate (thirteenth) chapter contains the following *confessio fidei*, to be made by the devotee of nature to the theologians:

> We only assure ourselves of that which we see; we yield to nothing but evidence; if we have a system, it is one founded upon facts; we perceive in ourselves, we behold everywhere else, nothing but matter; we therefore conclude from it that

matter can both feel and think; we see that the motion of the universe is operated by mechanical laws, that the whole results from the properties, is the effect of the combination, the immediate consequence of the modification, of matter; thus we are content, we seek no other explication of the phenomena which nature presents. We conceive only a unique world, in which everything is connected; where each effect is linked to a natural cause, either known or unknown, which it produces according to necessary laws; we affirm nothing that is not demonstrable. . . .

The final chapter repeats the doctrine of the utility of mundane truth before giving us the celebrated "Code of Nature," another declamatory passage (sometimes, on stylistic grounds, attributed to Diderot). What is false cannot be useful to men, and that which ever harms them cannot be founded on truth, and should ever be proscribed. (This authoritarian Utilitarianism was not brought into harmony with d'Holbach's earlier tolerant relativism.) So it is a service to the human spirit to lead it out of the labyrinth of imagination where it cannot find certitude. Only nature, known by experience, can lead him out and give him the means that are at our feet.

But men defend their own blindness, for light hurts them; and they defend themselves against their own liberation. But the friend of nature (i.e., the enlightened man) is not the enemy of men!

Listen to nature, who says (and here follows the *Code of Nature*, which I reproduce only in very abbreviated form):

Be happy, seek happiness, without fear. Do not resist my law. Vain are the hopes of religion. Free yourselves from the yoke of religion, my proud rival. In my empire there is freedom. Tyranny and slavery are ever banished from it. Follow my laws — human sensibility should interest you in the fate of others. Be just — equity is the pillar of humanity. Be a citizen — for a homeland is necessary for security, pleasure, well-being. In brief, be a man. Do not indulge in self pity or be tempted by the transitory pleasure of a crime. Vengeance is mine* [says *nature*! — once again reminding one of someone else]. Do not doubt my authority. See the miserable ones [the ambitious ones, or the indolent rich] . . . . "

How preferable this is to the dogma of supernatural religion, which harms man, which covers itself with a cloak of utility when attacked by reason, claiming to be linked to morality while in fact it is at war with it. It is this artifice that has seduced the learned.

---

* "Car, ne t'y trompe pas, c'est moi qui punis, plus sûrement que les Dieux, tous les crimes de la terre; le méchant peut échapper aux lois des hommes, jamais il n'échappe aux miennes."

The morality of nature is the only morality offered by the disciples of nature. The friend of man cannot be the friend of the gods, the scourges of man. (In other words, atheism is a condition of humanism. Does it follow that the majority, unfit as yet for atheism, cannot be true "friends of man"?)

Nature — the sovereign of all beings! And you, its adorable daughters — virtue, reason, truth! Be our sole divinities. Be man's teacher.

The final passages of the *Code of Nature*, as well as the prose that follows it just before the end of the book, have a kind of stoic rather than (or as well as) a "progressive" ring: they invite man to accept his condition bravely without seeking spurious consolation, rather than stressing the hope of mundane salvation and improvement.

Thus the final passage of the book invokes nature to "console thy children for [the] sorrows, to which their destiny submits them, by those pleasures which wisdom allows them to partake; teach them to be contented with their condition; to banish envy from their minds; to yield silently to necessity: conduct them without alarm to that period, which all beings must find, let them learn that time changes all things, that consequently they are made neither to avoid its scythe nor to fear its arrival. . . . . "

This type of stoicism is perhaps a more logical corollary of the worship of nature — seen as an all-embracing and exhaustive, self-sufficient, and necessary unity — than the "progressive," happiness-through-enlightenment-and-secularism outlook that is more generally characteristic of *The System*. (Indeed, in earlier periods, an ethic of acceptance had been characteristically associated with the kind of vision of nature preached by *The System*.)

In these final passages of the book, the emergence of such an alternative moral outlook alongside the main, progressivist, Enlightenment one, can perhaps be seen partly as a survival and/or as a perception of the consistent moral implications of the general vision, but mainly it can be seen, no doubt, as a defense against an expected counter-attack by the adherents of religion — a counter-move which would attempt to seduce man into illusory consolations by stressing his mundane ills and mortality.

Conclusion

IN essence, *The System of Nature* is a recipe for salvation: the progressive, secular salvation of man through understanding and acceptance of a unitary and physical nature of which he is a part, and a part like any other; a salvation by positive knowledge. Fused with this progressive panacea, as a kind of minor supporting theme, there is also an older recipe, salvation by acceptance, the avoidance of false hopes.

The two are fused in that they both militate against religious, dualistic, anthropocentric or anthropomorphic views of the world. *The System* is, of course, not merely the recommendation of a positive remedy, it is also the diagnosis of the disease: the source of all human ills is ignorance and false and meaningless beliefs, religion and nonmaterialist doctrines in general.

In elaborating this simple vision, *The System* formulates, as indicated at the beginning, many if not all of the themes that have become familiar and have been elaborated in modern thought. For instance, the verification theory of meaning, the behaviorist analysis of mind, the view that religious assertions are meaningless, that religion is an intoxicant of the people, and many others are found clearly stated. Moreover, the manner in which these ideas, which individually may not be original, are made interdependent has a characteristic modern ring.

The System does not really deal adequately with the problems that his modern outlook has to face. For instance, at its root there are two premises that are used alternatively and which are perhaps not consistent: *materialism* in a narrow sense — the all-exhaustiveness of matter, a theory about the world — and *empiricism*, the view that all knowledge and indeed all psychic life is based on sensation, a theory about cognition and about mind. Both ideas are used as sticks with which to beat religion and metaphysics, but their mutual compatibility is not explored sufficiently. As formal philosophy, this fails to reach the level of Hume or Kant. The compulsive insight of materialism — that what exists must exist in space and occupy a part of it, and that all else can only be an aspect of it — is made use of, but it is preached rather than critically explored.

This might be expressed by saying that no harmony is brought about between the paradigm of *explanation* — in terms of structure of matter — and of *information* — in terms of sensing (though sensing is defined in part in terms of impact, modification, etc., the activity of thought, and hence of explanation, is in turn derived from sensing).

There are other (to us) obvious conflicts within the system — between its determinism and call to arms and its hope of human liberation by human effort. One might say that both its theory of Grace and its doctrine of Original Sin are weak: it does not succeed in explaining how, in a determined universe, men will free themselves from the religion and tyranny that have poisoned their lives; nor does it convincingly explain how, in a world in which truth (materialistic truth), virtue, usefulness, and happiness are so closely connected in the very nature of things, the unspeakable and pervasive evils of spiritualistic doctrines could have gained the hold over man that they appear to have. It is, of course, easy to analyze the outlook of *The System*

as an all-embracing religion turned inside out; it is also, I think, correct. But this, as such, is not something of which the author or authors need be ashamed — nor would they have been. It is indeed, in a sense a "religion"; but that by itself does not prove it to be a false one.

The System has still other weaknesses: not only does it oversimplify the roots both of evils and of salvation, but it naïvely overestimates the prospects of human harmony and reasonableness once the chains of superstition have been removed. There are in it, mixed up with its anticipations, some views that now seem, or are, archaic, such as an empiricist theory of mathematical truth, the phylogistic theory of psychology, and the doctrine of the qualitative differentiation of all objects. (This is used only as a premise for relativism, and *not*, as some others have used it, as a premise for the impossibility of scientific understanding of the world.) There is, again, a curious gap between its positivistic and deterministic scientific program on the one hand, and, on the other, its essentially normative, prescriptive, evaluative sociology. (Its statements about man and society hover uncomfortably between analysis and prescription.) There is a tension between the democratic-liberal and the progressive-paternalistic implications of its politics.

There are other conflicts still: Between the empiricism on the one hand and the determinism and the essentialist manner of speaking on the other; between the doctrine of the irreducible diversity of things and the doctrine of the intelligibility of nature; between its relativism and the absoluteness with which its own central doctrines are maintained. There is a conflict between the optimistic view that truth is not only useful but also manifest, and the more pessimistic view that the truth is not something acceptable to humanity at large, in view of the tyrannical power of habit. This conflict between enlightened truth and the power of antiquated popular custom perhaps brings out most clearly how the men of the Enlightenment were the prototypes of later, similarly alienated intelligentsias throughout the world. Professor Réné Hubert, in his excellent *D'Holbach et ses Amis*, remarks at the end[2] that the diffusion of d'Holbach's views has endowed France with its dogmatic village atheists. Perhaps so. But a more important consequence of the diffusion of those views has been the endowment with them of a wider world, the "men of two worlds"; the men who bring a new Enlightenment, fashioned in large part from the ingredients present in *The System*, with which they attempt to reform and reeducate populations whose ingrained and habitual beliefs are of the kind which *The System* combated.

17

Kant

G. J. WARNOCK

IMMANUEL KANT WAS BORN at Königsberg in April of 1724 and died in the same town in February, 1804. The whole of his life was spent in his native province. From 1740 onward he was a member of the University of Königsberg, except for a short period during which he was a private tutor, and at the time of his death he had been professor of logic and metaphysics there for over thirty years. He never married, and his long life was quite uneventful except intellectually.

It is curious to observe the ways in which he did, and he did not, escape from the powerful influences of his early years. His parents were Pietists, and his schooling was strictly religious; his philosophical education was in the tradition of speculative metaphysics. He retained throughout his life a deep respect for religious faith and a remarkably stern, uncompromising sense of morality; he retained also an affection for, and much of the style of, traditional metaphysical argument. But in spite of this he rejected completely the particular claims both of religious teachers and of metaphysicians, and he has often been regarded as the most damaging critic of both.

He did not, in the manner of Berkeley or Hume, for instance, arrive at his philosophical conclusions easily or soon. The works on which his fame securely rests were published in the ten years after he was 57.

In person, Kant was very short and remarkably thin, with a disproportionately large head. However, he took great pains with his appearance and enjoyed some reputation for elegance of dress. He was always very careful of his health, with the deliberate intention of living as long as possible. For one so apparently frail, he succeeded very well.

KANT WAS A PROFESSOR, and he wrote like a professor. The writings of some of his predecessors, of Descartes, for example, or Berkeley or Hume and perhaps even of Leibniz, are such that they can be read with enjoyment by ordinary men and — no doubt within limits — understood with comparative ease. In their way, they are contributions to literature as well as to philosophy. Not so with Kant. He sometimes expressed, with agreeable humility, a hopeless wish for the literary skill and force of Rousseau, but he was partly unable, and also partly unwilling, to give to his own writings a pleasing and perspicuous form. The bent of his mind was naturally, as well as by long training, academic, and besides this he firmly believed, on principle, in the value of aiming at *thoroughness* rather than elegance. As a result, his chief writings are formidably and unbendingly professional, elaborately schematic, ponderous with technical terms, and exceedingly laborious to read and to understand. This is due in part, of course, to the genuine difficulty of the problems with which Kant grappled. He really was, as he set himself to be, both thorough and profound. But it remains, one may feel, a misfortune in the history of philosophy that so powerful a thinker should have commanded so little art in conveying his thoughts.

Kant's highly professorial style both of thinking and writing is liable to give the impression that his interests were also narrowly academic. He is sometimes represented simply as debating the merits of, and seeking to mediate between, two rival philosophical schools — empiricism, regarded as culminating in Hume, and rationalism, as represented particularly by Leibniz. But the fact is that this particular debate, in which certainly Kant was greatly interested, emerged out of a problem of much deeper and more general concern. In this problem the at least apparent antagonists whose conflict Kant wished to bring to some conclusion were, on the one side, not Hume, but Newton, and on the other side, not Leibniz, but the essentials of morality and religion. This was not a domestic quarrel within the field of philosophy, a quarrel in which the general public had nothing at stake; it was a conflict, Kant thought, between far more formidable powers. It was an issue involving the deepest interests of every man. And it was, above all, the task of philosophy to come to terms with it.

It is not difficult to grasp in outline how Kant saw this conflict. In his early days he had both written and lectured on the physical science of his time, and it never occurred to him to question for a moment the solidity of its main conclusions. He disagreed with Newton on certain philosophical points but he believed that in general Newton and his great predecessors had undoubtedly laid hold of the key to the understanding of the natural world. The world was to be regarded as a mechanical system of bodies operating in accordance with mathematically formulated laws: to explain scientifically a natural occurrence was to produce a law or laws such that, given the antecedent condition of the system, just that occurrence could be shown necessarily to have ensued. Perhaps no philosopher has accepted more wholeheartedly than Kant the essential rightness of the "scientific world-view" — taking physics, understandably enough, as the ideal of a science, and Newton, again with good reason, as its ideal expositor.

But not only that; Kant thought also what Newton at least would not explicitly have claimed: that the gospel of science committed its devotees to the view that not only were their presuppositions and methods correct in their own field, but also that their scope and application could not be restricted. It must, he thought, be dismissed as unscientific to suppose that any limit might be reached in nature beyond which scientific inquiry could be pushed no further, or that there might be natural occurrences not susceptible to scientific explanation. Neither of these beliefs, he held, could properly be accepted by a thoroughgoing believer in scientific method, who must believe that that method could be applied at any point to answer any question, and that what could not be learned in this way could not be knowledge at all.

But if so, Kant thought that he discerned an inevitable conflict with many fundamental human convictions. The belief that God has created the world and shapes it for his purposes implies the admission that at least one happening — the act of creation — falls outside the order of nature and cannot be brought within the scope of any natural law. It implies that the course of nature cannot fully be understood in scientific terms alone. The very existence of God is not a scientifically demonstrable fact. It is a matter of even more immediate and evident concern that if we are to suppose, as we must, that human beings are responsible creatures who are morally answerable for what they do or omit to do, we have to suppose that they *can* act, or fail to act, as they choose and as their obligations demand of them. Yet can we suppose this if we are also to believe that all that occurs, occurs necessarily — that in just those conditions in which any event takes place, no other event *could* have taken place? It appears that if we accede to the claims of science to operate and formulate laws without bounds or restrictions, we may have to regard religious faiths as superstition and moral convictions as illusory. Yet how, except in a spirit of arbitrary dogmatism, can we say at what point scientific inquiry must end?

Since the time of Hobbes and Descartes, at least, it had been a primary interest of most philosophers to provide some kind of resolution of these apparent conflicts. A quite recent attempt, and perhaps the most ambitious of all, had been made by Leibniz.*

* Leibniz's writings, before the edition of 1768, were only fragmentarily available to Kant. He had been brought up on the versions put forth by Wolff and Baumgarten. His first

Leibniz had persuaded himself that the view of the world presupposed in the system of Newtonian physics was, in its foundations, "contrary to reason" although it "satisfied the imagination"; therefore, he held, it could not be seriously put forward as the literal truth. Reason, he believed, could not accept "atoms and the void." To speak briefly, he then went on to devise a doctrine according to which the Newtonian view of the world might (with modifications) be accepted as a manner of speaking — that is, of recording what *appears* to be the case; while contrasted with this was to be the rationally acceptable, logically demonstrable account of what is *really* the case. There appears to be a world of material bodies in space and time, a world that can indeed be viewed as a mechanical system. What really exists is an infinite assemblage of immaterial, nonspatial, and even nontemporal *Monads*, created by, and in some sense subject to the direction of, God. In the apparent world there is rigorous causal determinism; in the real world of Monads there is no such thing. Yet God so orders the real and the apparent that no conflict arises at any point. The system of science holds true as an account of appearances; the truths of religion and morality apply in their different sphere, in God's creation as it really is. Finally, since God in creation must have chosen to create the best among the many worlds that He might have created, the world as it exists must be the best of all possible worlds.

Now it appears that Kant became gradually more and more dissatisfied with this and all similar attempts to solve his leading problem. Characteristically, such attempts consisted in trying to excogitate theories of what was really the case in such a way that the essential truths of morality and religion could be put forward as really (though sometimes in peculiar senses) true, while the rival corpus of scientific theory could be regarded as an account of mere *phenomena*, of the merely apparent. But in such undertakings Kant found great difficulties. For one thing, the alleged rational demonstrations of the true nature of reality were never conclusive and were sometimes demonstrably faulty. For another, whereas the allegedly merely "apparent" truths of science formed a generally accepted, well attested, and steadily developing system, metaphysical theory had the look of a chaotic battlefield. It was a scene of incessant conflict, incessant disagreement, illusory victories, and indecisive defeats in which nothing whatever could be taken as definitely established, and there appeared to be no prospect of any sure progress being made. Finally, was there not a manifest absurdity in seeking in this way for the foundations of morality and religion? No one's moral convictions could really be supposed to be dependent on the outcome of refined but chaotic meta-

physical argument, and religious beliefs were already far more secure than the fragile metaphysical structures called in to support them.

For this complete lack of solid progress in metaphysics, two possible explanations might be considered. It might simply be the case that metaphysical problems were so extremely complicated and difficult that no one hitherto had been clever and pertinacious enough to solve them; if so, there would be nothing for it but dogged persistence, in the hope that the proper solutions would eventually be found. Alternatively, there might be something radically wrong with the procedures that had been followed, even perhaps with the very questions that had been posed. Metaphysicians might have been attempting, not merely the difficult, but actually the impossible. If so, it would not be surprising that nothing had been achieved; and moreover, it would be essential to desist forthwith from further attempts to go on in the same old way and instead to re-examine the nature of the whole undertaking. It was at this point that the influence of Hume was evidently decisive: "David Hume, who can be said to have begun the assault on the claims of pure reason which made a thorough examination of them necessary."

Through the prompting of Hume's arguments, Kant came to believe by the early 1770's that both schools among his predecessors — Rationalists and Empiricists alike — had accepted certain principles from which it *followed* that metaphysical theories must be illusory and impossible. The great merit of Hume — and Kant rated his merits very high — was that he had seen this to be so and had deliberately drawn the necessary conclusion. So long as those principles stood, the subject called philosophy must abandon the speculative ambitions of deductive metaphysics, must turn instead to "the experimental method" and become what we might now regard as a satellite of empirical psychology and sociology. It was part of Hume's program to effect just this transformation.

It was in this way, then, that Kant was brought to the conviction that the fundamental question for a philosopher of his time must be the question of whether philosophy itself is a genuine subject: "My purpose is to convince those who find it worth their while to occupy themselves with metaphysics: that it is absolutely necessary to suspend their work for the present, to regard everything that has happened hitherto as not having happened, and before all else first to raise the question: 'whether such a thing as metaphysics is possible at all.' "[1] This is the essentially Kantian "critical" question. And this question brings him to the starting point of his three great *Critiques: The Critique of Pure Reason* (1781), *The Critique of Practical Reason* (1788), and *The Critique of Judgment* (1790).

thorough acquaintance with Leibniz's own work seems briefly to have revived his faith in metaphysical theory; but not, as we shall see, for long.

The Critique of Pure Reason

LET us ask, first, exactly why Kant supposed that the very possibility of metaphysics must be called into question. Here we may well follow closely his own explanation.

One of the most striking passages in Hume's inquiries had been his investigation of the concept of causation. It is, as Hume and Kant agreed, generally supposed that when it is asserted that *A* causes *B*, what is meant thereby is that if *A* occurs, *B necessarily* ensues. A causal connection, one might say, is distinguished from a chance correlation or coincidence precisely as being necessary. Now Hume asked by what right we suppose, in such a case, that given the one occurrence, the other is necessary. Do we learn this by observation? No, for what we learn by observation is at best that when *A* occurs, *B* in fact does ensue; strictly, we learn only that in fact this *has been* the case. We do not learn that it always will be, still less that it is necessarily so. Do we then discern by reason that *A* and *B* are connected necessarily? No, for we are required by reason to accept as necessary only those propositions the contradictories of which are, or imply, impossibilities — that is, contradictions. But the denial of a causal statement is never a contradiction; although fire boils water, there is no contradiction in supposing that it should not. But if so, we have *no* right — we simply are not in a position — ever to assert that any pair of events is connected necessarily. When we do assert this we are mistaking, according to Hume, our own habitual, confident expectations for features of the world.

This argument rests, as Kant saw, on a general doctrine, which Hume indeed was anxious to insist upon generally. This is the doctrine that any true proposition is *either* a truth of reason, necessary in that its negation would be contradictory, *or* a truth of fact, established as such by observation or experiment and, even if certainly true, not necessarily true. On this dichotomy, Hume based (as did the logical positivists after him) the charge that "divinity and school metaphysics" must be senseless and illusory. For these were not experimental sciences founded on empirical evidence; nor did they consist in the formal elaboration of theorems whose denials would be demonstrably contradictory. Yet there is, Hume held, no third possibility; hence, they must simply be dismissed as "sophistry and illusion."

Now Kant entirely agreed with Hume that if this dichotomy were valid and exhaustive, then there could be no such subject as metaphysics had been traditionally supposed to be. There would be only, on the one hand, empirical sciences, and, on the other, formal exercises in calculation. All necessary truths, all truths demonstrable *a priori*, would be on this view merely analytic; all synthetic truths, all assertions of matters of fact, would correspondingly be merely contingent. But the aim of the metaphysi-

cian was to formulate doctrines that would be both synthetic and demonstrable *a priori* — arrived at by reasoning but substantially true of the world; if so, he must either abandon his pursuits or show cause why Hume's dichotomy should not be accepted. He is called upon, before going on in the traditional style, to establish the credentials of his subject, which Hume challenged.

Kant himself, however dubious he may have been of the status and the claims of traditional metaphysics, was never seriously inclined to believe that Hume's dichotomy was in general tenable. He held that when he stated it, Hume had simply not realized the extent of the havoc that its acceptance would occasion. Certainly, in metaphysics there were supposed to occur propositions that were both synthetic and *a priori*; but in Kant's view such propositions certainly did occur also in some central parts of mathematics and of physical science. Thus, the weapon with which Hume sought to destroy "school metaphysics" would, if effective, destroy at the same time mathematics and science — disciplines which, whatever may be the case with metaphysics, no sane man could be prepared to regard as mere "sophistry and illusion." The question with which Kant sets out, therefore, in his scrutiny of the credentials of metaphysics, is not the question whether there can be synthetic *a priori* propositions; for he is quite certain that there can be and are many such propositions. Rather, he asks how it is that we are in a position to assert them — what sorts of truths these are, and how they can be established. The three fields in which they are found, or are alleged to be found, are mathematics, physical science, and metaphysics. By asking exactly what it is in the first two fields that makes possible the assertion of synthetic *a priori* truths, Kant hopes to discover whether such truths can be established also in the third, and if so how. This three-stage inquiry is clearly reflected in the three main divisions of the first *Critique* — the *Aesthetic*, the *Analytic*, and the *Dialectic*.

It is now possible to summarize the general strategy of Kant's subsequent argument. It will be observed that it is marvelously neat, enormously ambitious, and, in the outcome, astringently paradoxical.

First, what sorts of things are synthetic *a priori* propositions? Kant's view may be briefly indicated as follows. In the course of human experience we find, whether by simple observation or by deliberate experiment, that certain events occur and certain features are present which it is possible and often easy to suppose might have been otherwise. Such things we record, of course, in *contingent* assertions; and it is evident that we can know such assertions to be true only if we have found that our experience does in fact comprise the events or the features alleged. In contrast with this, by examining the concepts we employ, we are able to state certain other propositions that we can see or show to be *necessarily* true in that their denial would involve conceptual or logical inconsistency; and here we have, of course, no need of empirical confirmation. But there is, Kant holds, a third class of propositions, whose existence none of his predecessors had explicitly recognized — certain propositions that must be true if human experience is to occur at all, propositions that state, in Kant's phrase, "the conditions of the possibility of experience," or, as we might say, its fundamental defining characteristics. Now such propositions will not be analytic — for it is not analytic that any such thing as human experience does occur; the supposition that it does not implies no contradiction. But equally they will not be ordinarily contingent, for if the truth of a certain proposition is a condition of the very possibility of experience, there will clearly be no place for consulting the verdict of experience as to whether or not that proposition is true. On the assumption that any experience occurs at all, such a proposition could be asserted *a priori*. But if propositions of this class are not analytic and are not contingent, then they are precisely what Hume and the rest had rejected or ignored — namely, synthetic *a priori* propositions.

Kant's next point, a crucial one, can be expressed as follows. Such propositions, he says, say something about the world; but they are really based on something about ourselves. What the world is to us is the world as we experience it; our capacities for experience therefore impose a restriction on the *kind* of world that *our* world could be. If so, the question, "what are the conditions of the possibility of experience?" is most illuminatingly approached, not primarily by asking "what is necessarily true of the world that we experience?" but rather, "what are the general conditions of any possible employment of our human faculties?" It is true, Kant says, that in detail "our knowledge must conform to objects"; but it is also true that in general "objects must conform to our knowledge." That is: Any world of which we could have experience — and no other kind of world could be a subject of significant discourse — must be such that the faculties we have could be employed in experience of it.

An objection may naturally occur to one at this point, which serves to bring out a distinction that for Kant is fundamental. Surely, one may think at first sight, it is quite fantastic to assert that "objects must conform to our knowledge"; for how could it possibly be that the nature of our faculties should determine, or even influence in any way, what is the case in the world? Surely we are simply obliged to take the world as we find it; it would be a gross absurdity to suppose that it must somehow accommodate itself to our needs or our demands. Now, Kant feels the full force of this objection and to meet it he draws and insists upon a vital distinction between the world as it is *in itself* and as it *appears to us*. What exists, exists: its nature simply is what it is; with that, we ourselves can have nothing

to do. It is, however, equally certain that what exists *appears* to human beings in a particular way, and is by them classified, interpreted, categorized, and described in a particular manner. If our sense-organs had been radically different from what they are, certainly the world would have appeared to us as being radically different; if our languages and modes of thought had been utterly different, the descriptions of the world that we should have given would also have been different from those that we now give. Thus, though our faculties and capacities make no difference at all to the nature of what exists in itself, they do partly determine the character of the world as it appears; they determine the general *form* that it has; for whatever the world may be in itself, it appears to us in the way that it does because we are what we are. It is, then, with the world as appearance that Kant is concerned; it is objects as *phenomena* that must "conform to our knowledge." But this is not a cause for complaint or lamentation. For the desire to know, or even to talk, about the world as it is in itself is a desire without sense. It amounts to the desire to perceive without the employment of any particular mode of perception, to describe without the use of any particular descriptive vocabulary. In perception and thought we necessarily employ those faculties and propensities that we have; our subject-matter is, unavoidably, the world as it appears to one possessed of those faculties. In determining the general character — in Kant's phrase, the form — of this phenomenal world, it is thus with those faculties that we must be primarily concerned.

Next, Kant contends that our human faculties can be classified as follows: (1) *sensibility*, employed in sensation and perception; (2) *understanding*, employed in the making of statements, the acquisition of knowledge; and (3) *reason*, employed (we may say baldly for the moment) in reasoning. He next effects an ambitious combination between this triad, and the previously mentioned triad, mathematics, natural science, and metaphysics. This works out as follows:

The synthetic *a priori* truths of *mathematics* state the conditions necessary for the occurrence of *perception*.

The synthetic *a priori* truths of *natural science* state the conditions necessary for the occurrence of *discursive thought*.

The propositions of *metaphysics* express certain beliefs or ideals which are practically indispensable to the employment of *reason*.

It will be observed that the third step here is asymmetrical with the others. In mathematics and natural science, it seems, we have demonstrable truths; in metaphysics, however, we have only beliefs or ideals. This is indeed Kant's view; and thus, in a manner that we shall shortly investigate, he comes close in the end to that very conclusion of Hume's which he seemed at the outset disposed to challenge. But we must first look more closely at the stages in Kant's campaign.

THE TRANSCENDENTAL AESTHETIC

Unfortunately, the argument of the Aesthetic is very much confused. It seems clear that Kant is primarily interested in the concepts of space and time, arguing that the spatial and temporal character of the world is a consequence of the nature of our sensibility. However, he has also, as we have seen, a thesis about the synthetic *a priori* character of some parts of mathematics; and he does not distinguish clearly, or even at all, between truths in mathematics and truths about space and time. This is apt to make his case look much less interesting than it really is.

It is, I believe, not difficult to see that Kant's argument for the synthetic *a priori* character of mathematics is weak. (1) In geometry he seems to have taken it for granted — no doubt in common with all his contemporaries — that a system of geometry is essentially a set of assertions about space, is thus fact-stating, and is therefore synthetic. It can be argued that here he has failed, excusably no doubt, to distinguish between a calculus and its application. (2) He seems also to have been greatly impressed by the fact that, in the current textbooks of geometry, the formal demonstrations simply would not work out without an appeal to "intuition," to what we can see to be so. He regarded this, oddly perhaps as it seems to us, not as a defect in the exposition, but as proof that geometry cannot be analytically developed. And (3) in arithmetic he urges more than once that the expression on one side of a valid equation does not necessarily lead us to think (does not "contain the thought") of the expression on the other. But this excursion into mathematical psychology is not relevant to the logical character of the theorems of arithmetic. The weakness of these and some other points has led some critics to conclude that Kant's problem here does not arise — that there is, in this field at least, no need to ask how it is that we are able to make synthetic *a priori* assertions, since there is actually no good reason to suppose that we do.

This, however, is a mistake. This criticism would be effective only if the logical character of pure mathematics were Kant's genuine and exclusive concern. But this is not so. He was interested mainly — although without quite realizing that this is a different question — in the logical status of the concepts of space and time.* And here there undoubtedly are problems of considerable difficulty and importance.

The essence of Kant's problem may be expressed

as follows. We are no doubt naturally inclined to think of space and time as being simply given features of the world. It just is the case, we think, that we find ourselves in a space of three dimensions, and that events occur successively in a single and irreversible time order. But, Kant points out, there are certain further considerations which seem to be inconsistent with the idea that all this is a brute fact about the world. For one thing, we seem to find it *inconceivable* that space and time might have been, or might become, fundamentally different from what they are. It is a fact about the world that elephants are gray in color; we can easily suppose, however, that they might have been black, or pink or blue. If it were similarly just a fact about the world that space has three dimensions, it ought to be no less easy to suppose that it might have had two or four or seven, but can we really make head or tail of such alleged possibilities? Do we know what a world in seven dimensions would be like? For another thing, we are evidently prepared to make assertions about space and time for which, if these are merely assertions of fact, we surely have not the necessary evidence. We are prepared to assert, without any qualification, that there is only *one* space; what evidence have we for so vast a claim? We take it to be certain that in any part of the universe the nature of temporal sequence will be the same as it is in our vicinity; but by what right could we make assertions of fact about vast tracts of the universe which we have never inspected, which perhaps are inaccessible to our inspection? It appears, then, on reflection, that we do not really treat assertions about space and time as ordinary assertions of fact — as assertions to which alternatives are perfectly conceivable and for which we require the warrant of empirical observation. We do not humbly investigate the universe we live in, prepared to encounter and to accept any species of spatial or temporal characteristics whatever. On the contrary, it appears rather that we approach the universe with the postulate that whatever it may anywhere contain, its contents *shall* be in a three-dimensional space, and that whatever events may at any time be found to occur, they *shall* all have their places in a single time series; and it appears also that this postulate is for us the only one that is fully and genuinely intelligible.

How can this be? In answer, Kant appeals to his distinction between the world-in-itself and the world-as-appearance. Clearly, he says, we cannot make any demands upon the world-in-itself; that has whatever character it has quite indifferently to any postulates or assumptions that we may make. But the case is otherwise with the world-as-appearance. For of this we can say that it can *only* appear in a form that we are capable of perceiving. Does it not seem, then, that the spatial and temporal character which we demand that our world must have must be determined by the form in which we are capable of perceiving it? We are in no position to say that

---

* One might say that he was trying to explain the *applicability* of mathematics to objects and events, our notions of space and time being presupposed in such application.

space and time as we conceive of them are — still less, that they *must* be — universal features of the world in itself; but if our sensibility is such that we are able to perceive *only* what has such a spatial and temporal character, then we can (as we do) assert that *our* world, the world as it appears to us, *must* in all its parts be thus spatial and temporal. We may say, then, that "Time and Space, taken together, are the pure forms of all sensible intuition, and so are what make *a priori* synthetic propositions possible. But these *a priori* sources of knowledge, being merely conditions of our sensibility, just by this very fact determine their own limits, namely that they apply to objects only in so far as objects are viewed as appearances, and do not present things as they are in themselves."[2] In no other way, Kant holds, is it possible to explain how we could make *a priori*, in advance of observation, synthetic assertions about the general character of the world as a whole and at all times.

With this thesis Kant makes a serious and interesting attempt to grapple with a serious and genuine problem, a problem, moreover, which he was perhaps the first philosopher to discern. It can be argued, however, that his discussion is incomplete. He seems to imply that given the nature of our "sensibility," *anything* must appear to us under the forms of space and time: he seems also to imply — here at least — that there is no need to bring in anything *except* our sensibility. But both these implications may be challenged. For, first, though it is certain that we naturally do, for example, see and treat the objects that we encounter as three-dimensional, as being located in a three-dimensional space, the fact that we do this is not dependent solely upon us; it is at least imaginable that there should appear to us mere kaleidoscopic patterns of color such that, however strongly we might be disposed to construe appearances as three-dimensional, it would be impossible or at any rate quite pointless for us to do so. The fact that we bring to our perception of the world a predisposition to perceive it as three-dimensional — and not merely, say, as a succession of two-dimensional patterns — is scarcely a more important fact than the fact that what we perceive is such that we *can* successfully do this. Second, it is not only a matter of our sensibility, our modes of perception; it is not only, as one might say, that we cannot imagine how a world of four or seven dimensions would look. The fact is that we should also not know how to talk about it. This seems particularly evident in the case of time. The notion that any event can be located uniquely at some place on a single time-scale, and that movement on this scale is in one and only one direction, is inextricably built in, not only to the use of such words as "past" and "future," "before" and "after", but also to all talk about remembering, expecting, hoping, to most talk about action, and in general to the use of tenses in all our verbs. Thus, in Kant's terms, the character of space and time could be said to be determined as much by our "understanding" as by our "sensibility"; they are forms of description scarcely less than forms of intuition. Kant was probably led to neglect, or at least to minimize, this point as a result of his somewhat confused concern with mathematics. Partly he seems to have assumed here, no doubt inadvertently, that spatial and temporal concepts have their predominant, if not their only, use in the application of mathematics; and partly, less excusably, he may have wished to preserve the seductive symmetry of his argument by making his separation of sensibility from understanding not only correspondent with, but as sharp and complete as, the distinction between mathematics and natural science.

THE TRANSCENDENTAL ANALYTIC

So far, then, Kant has argued as follows. In the field of discourse about space and time and objects and events in space and time, it appears that we are able to make assertions having a peculiar logical character — assertions, namely, that, though genuinely about the world, are yet made *a priori*. Kant has tried to account for this by the proposition that space and time are "forms of intuition," modes, that is, in which the world necessarily presents itself *to us*, in virtue of the nature of our perceptual faculties. Spatial and temporal concepts are then *a priori*, or "pure," concepts, not learned from, but rather brought to, the course of our experience; they are "formal" concepts *already* applied in the perception by us of any "matter" whatever. Kant now moves on to consider what synthetic *a priori* assertions there are or could be, associated, not as before with our "sensibility," but with our "understanding"; and first of all, he wishes to identify the pure, *a priori*, or formal concepts in this field.

The argument by which, in the text as we now have it, Kant arrives at his list of the concepts in question is at once obscure, strained, artificial, and thin. It appears to be as follows: The concepts of which we are in search are those (other than spatial and temporal concepts) which express the general *form* of human experience. Now just as the spatial and temporal forms of our experience were traced to the character of our sensibility, these other forms are to be traced to the character of our understanding. We have seen how the world must appear to us, for us to perceive it; we have now to ask what general form it must have if it is to be for us the object of discursive thought and of knowledge, and what this form is will be determined by the character of our understanding. Now we already have in our possession, so Kant assumes, an ancient, well-established, formal classification of the operations of the understanding — namely, the logician's list of forms of judgment. Surely, then, the required new list of formal concepts, since this is also to be a classification of the functions of the understanding, will be capable of being systematically derived from the logician's list. "In this manner there arise precisely the same number of pure concepts of the understanding which apply *a priori* to objects of intuition in general, as, in the preceding table, there have been found to be logical functions in all possible judgments. For these functions specify the understanding completely, and yield an exhaustive inventory of its powers. These concepts we shall, with Aristotle, call categories."[3] Kant goes on rather rashly to congratulate himself upon the superiority of his tidy procedure over the haphazard, "rhapsodical" method he thought he discerned in Aristotle.

It would be tedious to go into the numerous questions and objections raised by this passage; it is not important enough to detain us long. Two comments may be made. First, Kant does nothing to counter the obvious objection that, though he and the logicians may have a common interest in "form," their subject-matter is evidently different, and that, more importantly, there is no reason to suppose that the grounds for their formal distinctions will be the same or even analogous. Formal distinctions are made by both grammarians and logicians, in part in the very same field, that of sentences, but since their reasons for making distinctions are different, their classifications are neither the same nor even symmetrical. But is there any more reason to look for symmetry between the formal distinctions of the philosopher and the logician than there is between those of the logician and the grammarian? Second, it can be established from Kant's correspondence that the alleged derivation of categories from forms of judgment occurred to him only *after* he already knew what his list of categories, pure concepts, was to contain. This whole section has the air, then, of a hopeful *coup de théâtre* rather than of a passage organic to the original plot.

Kant passes from this to a far more important examination of the question of how it is that we can assert *anything* of the world *a priori* — except that, as is now taken to be sufficiently explained, it must appear to us under the forms of space and time. His argument here, of which his first and second editions present substantially different versions, is difficult and obscure. I think, however, that it can without serious distortion be reduced to the following outline.

It is clearly an essential fact about human existence that each human being has, and is aware of himself as having, his own personal and more or less continuous experience of a world. Furthermore, each human being supposes that this world of which he has experience is the same as that which is the object of the experiences of others. There are as many diverse experiences as there are human beings; yet there is only one world, a world public to the experience of them all. Now Kant's main point here is essentially this: that if all this is to be so, then the world must necessarily be *orderly*. For suppose the contrary. If,

for example, when I had at some moment the experience describable as that of seeming to see a tiger, my experience in subsequent moments could be of any sort at all; if I should then seem to see nothing, or stars, or a human face, or an empty landscape, or a tea pot, or merely vague patterns of color, and if such unpredictable chaos were quite general, then clearly it would be impossible to make any *distinction* between merely and momentarily seeming to see a tiger and actually seeing a tiger that was really there. It would be in fact, in general, impossible to make any distinction between my private experiences on the one hand and real things or actual happenings on the other; what it is that is *really* perceived would be an unanswerable question. Such a question, indeed, could not even be asked. The very notion of a real physical world existing independently as the *object* of my experiences could not be formed; nor, surely, could the notion of "my own" experiences and of "myself," since these notions get their sense by contrast with what is objective and external.

Similarly, if the course and character of my experiences afforded me no clue to what the experiences of others were or might be or could be, it would be impossible to form the supposition that there was *one* world, *of* which we all had experience. The very supposition that something really occurs in the world implies that certain particular experiences are or might be had by any or all human beings; but if the experiences of any one person were consistent with any experiences whatever for others, then the notion of there being a common world could not arise.

In this way, then, whatever in particular the character of the world may be, we may say *a priori* that our experience of it — and therefore the world itself also — must at least be in some way orderly. For if not, the very idea that there existed a world and that there existed individual beings having their own experiences of it, could not possibly arise; there could be no talk of a world, of other persons, or of ourselves. Order of some kind is thus the most general and fundamental of the "conditions of the possibility of experience." And it is in this way that Kant offers an answer to the fundamental question of how it is that we can say that there are "categories" which necessarily apply to the world. What we have to consider is: What kind of world it must be which could be the *common* object of the personal experiences of *many* individuals, or an object of personal experience for *any* individual. For

the *a priori* conditions of a possible experience in general are at the same time conditions of the possibility of objects of experience. . . . . .[4] Concepts of objects in general thus underlie all empirical knowledge as its *a priori* conditions. The objective validity of the categories as *a priori* concepts rests . . . on the fact that, so far as the form of thought is concerned, through them alone does experience become possible. They relate of necessity and *a priori* to objects of experience, for the reason that only by means of them can any object whatsoever of experience be thought.[5]

But can we be more specific than this? Kant believes that we can. In particular, he believes that he is now in a position to demonstrate *a priori* three propositions — propositions, in fact, that he takes to be fundamental principles of physical science. It is worth observing clearly how large a claim Kant is here putting forward. He is claiming, in effect, for physical science (for him, the science of Newton) a position so fundamental that its first principles are necessary for the very existence of human experience — conditions, that is, not only of the possibility of scientific inquiry but at the same time of the possibility of any experience at all. The claims of the scientific outlook have never perhaps been pitched higher than this. No one has ever nailed his colors so firmly to Newton's mast.

Unfortunately, Kant's arguments do not prove as much as he claims. In his *Analogies of Experience* he argues, first, that our experience, experience of the human kind, must exhibit the type of order that enables us to refer our experiences to things conceived of as having permanence and duration — that is, to *substances*; but this sound conclusion he appears to interpret, quite arbitrarily, as equivalent to the principle of the "conservation of matter". Second, he argues that a world exhibiting the orderliness essential to objectivity must be such that causal laws can be framed and applied to it. However, his argument does not really suffice to prove what he appears to claim; that there must be completely *universal* causal determinism. It proves only that there could not be universal chaos. And third, he offers a highly unconvincing argument intended to establish the overambitious conclusion that perception of things as coexistent entails that they must also be supposed to be interacting members of a single dynamic system. Now the fact is, I think, that Kant is here overplaying his hand very much as he had done in the *Transcendental Aesthetic*. There he had attempted to deal, as it were at one blow, simultaneously with space and time and with mathematics, both topics being connected without distinction with the nature of our sensibility. Here he has also attempted to deal at one blow with the foundations of ordinary experience and the foundations of science, referring both without distinction to the nature of our understanding. This is unfortunate, for the weakness of his treatment both of mathematics and of science may appear, since he nowhere makes the required distinctions, to be a weakness in the whole of his case. In the present case, while he may be correct in his implication that scientific theories make use of certain fundamental principles which are neither analytically true nor

subject (in the context of a given theory) to experimental confirmation, he does not establish either that such principles *must* be those that the Newtonians had adopted or that those principles express conditions necessary to any experience whatever. It does not follow from this, however, that he is altogether mistaken in asserting that there *are* certain propositions which must be true if our experience of the world is to be what it is, for there could be such propositions, even if they do not figure in the foundations of Newtonian theory; and it is this, no doubt, that Kant would wish chiefly to insist upon.

We may conveniently sum up the purport of Kant's argument so far by asking to what extent he has provided, as he undertook to provide, an answer to Hume. It had been Hume's contention, as Kant understood it, that we can say what *must* be the case only when we are dealing with "relations of ideas" and when the denial of what we say would be "contrary to reason" in the precise sense of being or implying a contradiction. Outside this area, in the realm of matters of fact, we may say simply that everything can happen; nothing is impossible; and hence we can at best establish what contingently is the case or even, more strictly, what has been found to have been the case. Now if, Kant says, we are discussing what exists as it is in itself, then we are indeed in no position to say that things *must* be like this or that. But if we are referring to the world only as a possible object of human experience, the case is otherwise. For human beings are beings equipped with particular faculties, capacities, and modes of thought, and it is not true that in a world inhabited and known by such beings anything whatever is possible, for only a particular *kind* of world could present itself as an object of experience for them. In particular, according to Kant, what they can perceive must be spatial and in time; what they can experience and speak of as a single common and objective world must be orderly and predictable in such a degree as to render coherent, in a sense to bring within a single system, the diverse successions of their individual experiences. If the various conditions presupposed in this were not satisfied there would result, not experience of a very extraordinary and intractable world, but simply *no* world and *no* experience — none, at least, the nature of which is conceivable to us, and it is idle to trouble our heads over the inconceivable. Now we may think that Kant's sharp distinction between sensibility and understanding, between forms of intuition and categories, is vulnerable. We may find obscure and artificial the arguments by which he attempts to work out in detail what are the "conditions of the possibility of experience." But we may still find great value in the penetrating insight that only a certain *kind* of world could be for us an object of discourse and experience, and that in this sense we can say that, in certain general respects, *our* world *has* to be as it is. Again, we may rightly feel that Kant's detailed table of categories is exceedingly artificial and contrived, quite without the finality and neatness which he hopefully claims for it; nevertheless, the general contention that there *are* categories was an important advance on the current tradition of Empiricism. How this is so may be sketched as follows. A collection of plants or animals, for example, does not, as Aristotelianism perhaps implied, dictate to us the principles of its own classification; an aggregate of observational data does not, as Bacon appears to have hoped, directly present us with its own explanatory theory. Similarly, Kant urged, the "matter" of human experience does not dictate to us the form of its own interpretation. Very much as the scientist approaches observational data with certain theoretical concepts and principles already in mind, so human beings bring to the diverse successive items of their experiences a predisposition to construe them in particular ways — as being, in fact, experiences *of* material things and objective happenings, describable in principle by everyone in a common vocabulary, and locatable in one common space and time. If so, then there will indeed be fundamental concepts which would be better regarded as imposed upon, than as abstracted from, our experience; and there will be certain very general propositions about our experience, which would be better regarded as defining its essential character than as merely recording the actual details of its course. Kant's perception of this was both profound and truly original.

Now Kant was originally concerned to establish these things in order to show that his predecessors had accepted a false dichotomy: they had supposed that all propositions were either merely contingent or merely analytic; and Hume, at least, had argued, rightly on this supposition, that therefore there could not be significant doctrines of the kind alleged to constitute traditional metaphysics. Kant's argument evidently implies, however, that metaphysics cannot be thus dismissed, for the essential supposition is false. However, he now discerns reasons of his own for concluding that, even so, there can be no such thing as a science of metaphysics. On this he was as convinced as, and a good deal clearer than, Hume himself.

THE TRANSCENDENTAL DIALECTIC

The general ground for Kant's own rejection of metaphysical theories is not difficult to state. He has argued that there can indeed be demonstrable propositions having the peculiar logical character of being both *a priori* and not analytic; and it is this kind of proposition that, if possible, the metaphysician must establish, for he is neither a mere analyst nor yet an empirical researcher. However, Kant's asking the previously neglected question of *how* such propositions can be established has yielded the answer that they owe their peculiar logical status to the fact that they express "conditions of the possibility of experience"; they can be proved if it can be shown that this is what they do. But this answer can be seen to be fatal to the claims of the metaphysician. For first, Kant takes it to be perfectly clear in fact that there is *no* metaphysical doctrine whose truth is in any degree a condition of the possibility of experience; and second, such doctrines, he thinks, are always supposed in principle to be independent of experience altogether, to be established, that is, by pure reasoning alone. In either case, it appears that, whether in fact or in principle, the doctrines of metaphysicians cannot be made out to be synthetic *a priori* truths; and if so, they can make no use of the way of escape that Kant had opened between the horns of Hume's dilemma.

Nevertheless, it never seriously occurred to Kant to dismiss metaphysics without more ado. He rightly thought it necessary to explain how intelligent men should so persistently have pursued what are evidently illusory objectives; he though it proper to examine more precisely the errors into which they had been betrayed; and, more surprisingly, he wished to suggest that such labors as theirs were very far from useless, and were even unavoidable.

The essence of the situation, as Kant saw it, is this: It is, understandably and properly, a persistent desire of rational beings to construct some picture of the world and of their own place in it that will be rationally satisfactory, will satisfy the demands of reason. But, Kant holds, it is in principle impossible that the corpus of what is *known* should satisfy these demands; and conversely, it is unavoidable that any picture of the state of things which *does* seem to satisfy reason's demands should yet have the defect that it cannot be known to be true. The central difficulty he states as follows: What reason may be supposed to demand of an account of reality is that it should be complete and comprehensive; of an explanation of the state of things, that it should be final and unconditional. Anything less than this will exhibit, so to speak, loose ends that will inevitably occasion intellectual discontent. However, Kant points out that our actual knowledge must always and necessarily be incomplete and that our explanations can never be more than conditional. If so, there arises "a natural and unavoidable dialectic of pure reason" — a conflict, "inseparable from human reason," between what we demand and what we are in a position to achieve.[6] Metaphysics, in Kant's view, is the natural, persistently repeated, but necessarily vain attempt to supply what our reason demands but can never have.

Such attempts are characteristically made, Kant proceeds, in three main fields, which he calls the psychological, the theological, and the cosmological. We have, of course, some knowledge of the nature of human beings as they exist in the actual conditions of human life. But we have also, as thinking beings, a natural hankering to know more than this. What, we want to ask, is a person really and essentially, quite apart from the temporary and contingent conditions of the bodily existence of everyday life? It is in the attempt to answer this question that theories of the soul have been devised — theories purporting typically to prove that the soul in itself is a simple, indestructible substance, capable of existing and retaining its identity eternally when all the transitory circumstances of mere bodily existence have been removed. But Kant shows that the arguments in favor of any such view not only do not, but could not, suffice to prove it, for the conclusion purports to be a substantial conclusion of fact, which cannot be arrived at by mere analysis; yet clearly we, in this life, neither have nor could have the substantial evidence on which it would have to be founded, if only because the scope of the alleged conclusion necessarily transcends both the conditions and the temporal limits of human experience. Again, in theological reflection we may seek to attribute the contingent existence of the world to the creative act of a Supreme Being whose existence (if it is not itself to stand in need of explanation) must be supposed necessary. Yet, though we may perhaps form the bare concept of such a Being, it is evident both that nothing encountered in our actual experience could suffice to prove that such a Being exists and also that its actual existence could not be proved *without* experience, by merely verbal or conceptual maneuvering. Moreover, in both these cases it is not only that what is sought to be proved is too vast and ambitious for any available evidence to support it; it is also that, in so far as we attempt to speak of "the unconditioned" — what is not and could not be encountered in our experience — the words that we use can be given no positive sense: we do not even clearly understand what we are *trying* to prove.

Cosmological speculation, Kant holds, is in even worse case. Here, as he powerfully argues in the *Antinomies*, it is not only that we are impelled to put forward theses that we cannot establish; we are or can be naturally led to formulate equally plausible theses that stand in plain conflict with each other. For example the evident difficulty in the idea of an absolute beginning of existence, of the existence of things as suddenly supervening upon absolutely *nothing*, may plausibly incline us to hold that something must have existed always — it is impossible, we may think, to accept the idea of the universe beginning to exist *ex nihilo* at a particular time. But against this, is it not equally difficult to make sense of the implied conclusion namely, that, up to any given moment an *infinite* period of time must have *completely elapsed*? Is it not indeed a contradiction to speak of the history of the universe up to the present as both completed and not finite? Again, we may argue that the universe must be held to be infinite in extent, since we could never have any possible ground for the conclusion that beyond any

given object there are no more objects; yet does it not on the contrary seem equally evident that for any pair of objects that actually exist, the distance between them must, however large, be definite and finite? We can only escape from the resulting vacillations, Kant argues, if we renounce altogether the attempt to speak without restriction of the universe *as a whole*. For us, the bounds of the *known* world both in space and time may be thought of as *to be* indefinitely extended; we are, however, in no position to assert of the bounds of the universe itself either that they are or that they are not infinitely extensive.

In these and other ways Kant argues in detail that the natural inclination of rational beings to push their inquiries to the limit is doomed to perpetual disappointment. It expresses indeed the natural but incoherent desire of beings whose existence is limited and conditioned to free themselves from all limits and all conditions — though they cannot of course really conceive what such freedom would be. It is as if human reason attempts to throw off its humanity. Nevertheless, Kant holds that the labors of metaphysicians are in a certain way indispensable, and also, even more importantly, that their doctrines are not *completely* without foundation, though their proper foundation is not at all what has usually been supposed.

On the first point, Kant suggests that the metaphysicians' ideal — the rational ideal of *complete* knowledge, of *final* explanation — is essential at least as a guide and an incentive to all our intellectual undertakings. It might well be impossible to persist in the systematic accumulation of knowledge unless it were supposed that the task was in principle completable, that advance was being made toward some attainable goal. If no such ideal were ever formulated, it might be that even legitimate, limited researches would languish and be abandoned. There is thus *some* function for the "ideas of Reason"; they serve, so to speak, as targets for our aspirations. Even so, the critical thinker should remind himself sometimes of the distinction between facts and ideals, however great the temptation may be to try to disregard it; though he may often fall into, he must always also escape from, the snares of intellectual overambition.

But what foundation, then, does Kant for his own part propose for metaphysics? We may state it in this way. Consider, for instance, the idea that the universe as a whole is the creation of an omnipotent and benevolent Deity; that its history is destined in the end to realize that Deity's purposes; and that men in particular are free, rational, and immortal spirits to be held answerable, if not in this life, then in eternity, for all that they freely do or omit. Now we have here a typical set of metaphysical theses. There is, Kant insists, no question at all of this picture of things being proved or known to be correct, since it utterly transcends what our experience can furnish. However, by thus "denying knowledge," we "leave room for faith." This ideal picture of things can be *accepted*, and moreover accepted confidently; for the utter impossibility of proof carries with it the equal impossibility of disproof. But is there reason, then, why it should be accepted? Kant's answer is that the acceptance of some such picture is indeed imperatively demanded — not by arguments, however, but by our *moral convictions*. That the world should be directed by the just purposes of God is not a theoretical but a moral demand. That men are answerable for their vices and virtues, and that vice and virtue, here or hereafter, will find their deserts, we have no theoretical reason to assert; but our moral convictions oblige us to believe it. In general, Kant insists, if there is any reason at all to accept accounts of the world and of our place in it which transcend the very limited scope of our actual experience, if there is ever good reason for saying more than we know, that reason will be moral rather than intellectual; in his own terms, *practical* and not theoretical. We must, then, "seek, in the practical use of reason, sufficient grounds for the concepts of God, freedom and immortality. These concepts are founded upon the moral use of reason, while speculation could not find sufficient guarantee even of their possibility."[7] In this way, Kant effects a very striking reversal of the orthodox tradition among his predecessors. Whereas they had been apt to suppose that metaphysics must supply the intellectual foundations of religion and morality, he contends that metaphysics and religion themselves can rest only on the sense of moral conviction. And he would have argued that although he is obliged to admit that there is strictly no such thing as metaphysical knowledge, it is far less dangerous to religion and morality to make this admission than to attempt to base them on *illusory* theoretical foundations. It is better to confess that we have only faith than to purport to have knowledge where actually we have none. In his next work he passes to the examination of that "practical use of reason" to which, as he thinks, we must turn when we come to the end of our theories.

Kant's Philosophy of Morals

THE distinctive feature of Kant's moral philosophy could be said to be its unbending rationalism. It is reason in man, Kant holds, that makes him a moral being, and it is the faculty of "practical reason" to which the moral philosopher should attend. Now it is not difficult to see why Kant should assign to reason this central role. He held it to be evident that the demands of morality are peculiarly and characteristically *unconditional*, absolute, or "categorical"; that the principles of morality are *invariant*; and that morality imposes its demands on free and respon-

sible beings alone. If so, he argued — in direct opposition to Hume — that moral distinction *must* be "derived from reason" and not from a "moral sense" or any other feeling, sentiment, desire, or passion whatever. For if the demands of morality were to be determined by any human feelings or desires, they would plainly be conditional upon the circumstance of human beings actually having those feelings and desires; they would also have to be, held to be in principle variable, contingently upon changes in the sentiments of human beings. Furthermore, if moral conduct were to be explained as issuing from any desire or feeling, there would ensue, Kant held, the contradictory conclusion that a man might act morally (whether well or ill) without being free; for in so far as our behaviour is the outcome of our desires, it is a mere aspect of the order of nature, an item in the natural succession of causes and effects, and being naturally determined in this way cannot be called "free." If, however, the principles of morality are *rationally demonstrable*, they will be seen to be independent of empirical contingencies; their demands will be binding on us on the sole condition that we are rational beings; and our moral decisions, founded upon reason and not on desire, will be properly regarded as being unique in, or more strictly as falling quite outside, the natural order of events, and hence can be significantly held to be free.*

It is worth noticing that Kant makes much of the claim that his doctrines are simply a systematic formulation of views already explicit or implicit in the common moral consciousness; and in this claim there is certainly some truth. It cannot, indeed, be maintained that all societies at all times have adopted to moral matters an attitude of the Kantian kind. There are, and have been, primitive societies of which this would obviously be untrue, and even of the highly civilized societies of classical antiquity there is reason to say that questions of human character and conduct were there considered in a subtly, though still markedly, different light. But in what may be vaguely designated as Western societies of the Christian era, some Kantian attitudes do seem to be quite common. The moral "ought" seems often to be felt to be distinguished precisely as being absolute and unconditional. It seems often to be held that "moral worth" can be ascribed only to actions performed, not from any desire or inclination of the agent to perform them, but solely from a sense of duty, from the rational conviction that they ought to be done. It seems also very generally to be assumed that the principles of morality are themselves

---

* It is often forgotten that these opinions, so characteristic of Kant's maturity, had not always been his. In his *Inquiry into the Distinctness of the Principles of Natural Theology and Morals* (1764), Kant wrote that "the judgment 'This is good' is completely indemonstrable and a direct effect of the consciousness of the feeling of pleasure associated with the conception of the object"; and he then spoke favorably of Hutcheson's concept of a "moral feeling."[8]

unchanging and universal, however the details of their application may change and however various the attitudes of individuals or societies may be in different places or periods. In so far, then, as Kant was attempting to lay a firm foundation for such convictions as these, his claim to some support in what he calls the "common understanding" may well be granted.

It is not in fact surprising that this should be so. For, though Kant himself insists that the moral law is "autonomous," self-sufficient, and in particular independent of religious belief, the moral outlook which he actually expounds is clearly that of the somewhat rigorous Christian sect in which he grew up — an outlook which itself is sufficiently characteristic of at least Protestant Christianity, and which is therefore widespread, though not always explicit, in modern Europe. Now it is natural for the believer to suppose that the laws of God for men are unchanging, that they oblige absolutely, that nothing whatever could override their demands upon us. Kant takes exactly this view of the moral law, with the important difference that he seeks to derive it, not from God as legislator and judge, but solely from man himself as a rational being. It could indeed be said that his major difficulty — perhaps also the prime cause of his ultimate failure — is that he is attempting to expound a Christian view of morality while explicitly repudiating its religious foundations. He is attempting to set forth the idea of God's law without reference to God. If so, it is neither surprising that much of what he says should find support in the common moral consciousness of contemporary Europe, nor perhaps that his system should make on us, in the end, the impression of being oddly without content, as if hanging in the air.

The starting point of Kant's own exposition is found in the notion of a "good will." In assessing the moral worth of an action we should attend, Kant insists, not to the talents or abilities of the agent (which, in that they might be employed for evil purposes, are themselves morally neutral) nor to the actual results of the action (which may be determined by contingencies beyond the agent's control), but solely to the direction of the agent's will. Now, to exercise a good will is to set one's self to act simply and solely "for the sake of duty"; and this is to set one's self to act, not so as to achieve any particular result nor yet to fulfil any desire, but solely in order to conform with a moral "maxim." Thus, in Kant's view, the problem of moral decision is essentially that of distinguishing right maxims from wrong ones; for once we are assured that a maxim is right, we know that what morality demands of us is simply that we should direct our wills to conforming with it. What actually ensues is not of strictly moral concern.

How, then, are maxims to be tested and distinguished? Kant's answer is, he thinks, simple and conclusive. If, as he assumes, the principles of moral-ity are always and everywhere the same, it follows that what is a right maxim for one must also be a right maxim for any other; it must be such that it could be, and should be, accepted and acted upon by anyone at any time in the appropriate circumstances. "I do not, therefore, need any penetrating acuteness in order to discern what I have to do in order that my volition may be morally good. . . . I only ask myself: Can I will that my maxim become a universal law? If not, it must be rejected, not because of any disadvantage accruing to myself or even to others, but because it cannot enter as a principle into a possible universal legislation."[9] It is impossible, Kant is here saying, for a rational being rightly to propose to himself to act upon any principle if he cannot also will that others should act upon it. "There is, therefore, only one categorical imperative. It is: Act only according to that maxim by which you can at the same time will that it should become a universal law."[10] There are many particular maxims, Kant believes, that command unconditionally, but these are all strictly derivative from *the* categorical imperative. Another way, perhaps, of stating what that imperative requires is that it demands of a rational being *consistency of judgment*: the rules by which his own conduct is determined cannot by him be arbitrarily restricted from application to the conduct of others also.

Kant goes on to argue that his essential point can also be stated in the formula that "man and, in general, every rational being exists as an end in himself." To use another person "merely as a means" is, he implies, to ignore that person's position as himself an independent and rational judge of his own actions — whether by actually forcing him to act as one desires or by manipulating his judgment by means of deliberate deception. Thus, conversely, to treat him as an end is to allow to him (of course within such limits as may be set by his own obligations) the same right and opportunity of choice and decision that one claims for one's self. This amounts, Kant appears to say, once again to the requirement of consistency in one's attitude to one's own case and to that of others. In using another person merely as a means, I claim for myself a special and superior position which it is not possible that everyone should enjoy; my claim, therefore, "cannot enter as a principle into a possible universal legislation"; and therefore it must be in conflict with the demands of morality. Kant adds that any rational being inevitably does regard himself as an end in this sense; therefore all do; and therefore none can rationally refuse to recognize the force of the categorical imperative. This leads in turn to Kant's striking conception of a "kingdom of ends." The whole class of rational beings may be thought of as a community of independent and essentially equal judges of conduct — indeed of *legislators* for conduct, in so far as each will hold and offer as universal those maxims that he approves and adopts for himself. The moral law is then precisely that set of principles of conduct which, thus laid down by each for all, will render the relations of each with all consistent, coherent, and systematic. "Morality, therefore, consists in the relation of every action to that legislation through which alone a kingdom of ends is possible."

So far, Kant would claim to have established the essential nature of morality on the assumption that moral beings do really exist and that moral behavior does really occur. But this assumption, he thinks, cannot be made lightly. He regards it as a perfectly intelligible suggestion that our whole apparatus of moral concepts — all our moral convictions, responses, feelings, and attitudes — may be simply ill-founded, mere figments of the human mind imported into a situation where actually no such things can have any application. We may, for example, suppose ourselves and others to be under certain obligations, to have certain duties, to be susceptible to moral commendation or blame; yet our actual situation may be such that these suppositions are really quite out of place. Indeed, Kant holds, there is a strong *prima facie* reason to think that this is so. For we have to suppose, as he had argued in the first *Critique*, that necessity reigns throughout the whole of nature; we have to concede to the scientist that there are laws of nature and that nothing occurs that is not in conformity with these. But if so, and if human actions fall within the general class of natural occurrences, how is it possible to suppose that any human actions are *free*? But if no human actions are free, it cannot be proper to hold human beings responsible for what they do, and if so, they cannot properly be regarded as subject to the demands, the "imperatives," of the moral law. If all that occurs *has* to occur, there is no room left for talking about what *ought* to occur. If free will is an illusion, morality itself is an illusion also.

But Kant also maintained, more surprisingly perhaps, that if once the will is supposed to be free, it then cannot possibly be suggested that morality is an illusion: "If freedom of the will is presupposed, morality together with its principle follows from it by the mere analysis of the concept." Here his argument seems to have been that what is meant by "free" is not merely "lawless"; an action would not be rightly called free if it occurred merely at random, unpredictably, inexplicably; a free act, properly so called, is an act that must be *explained* in a particular manner, namely by reference to an agent's rational decision. But Kant has already argued that rational decision is identical with moral decision, that the demands of morality and rationality are one and the same thing. Hence, if to be a free agent is to be a rational agent, it is necessarily to be a moral agent also. A "free" will is not a will subject to no law, but a will directed by reason; and this is a will subject to the demands of morality. Thus, Kant claims, "We have finally reduced the definite concept of morality to the idea of freedom."[11] There remains, then, the question of whether freedom of the will can rightly be ascribed to human beings.

Now Kant held, as we have just observed, that there was some reason to conclude that it cannot. For he held that freedom must be definitely excluded from any field in which natural causation was universal; and he held also that natural causation must be supposed to hold universally throughout the whole of nature. Does it not follow, then, that the notion of freedom in human conduct must be held to be excluded? Kant thought not, and his reason was, essentially, that human beings were not wholly to be included within the natural order. That "nature" in which he believed that we must suppose all occurrences to be causally determined was, of course, the world of *appearances*; we cannot, he held, make this, or indeed any other, general supposition about the world-in-itself. But when we speak of nonhuman things, we are speaking of appearances only, and hence the nonhuman world must be held to be *wholly* subject to causal determination. Now I can also regard the movements of my own limbs, and for that matter the succession of my thoughts, perceptions, and feelings, as appearances, as merely items in the natural order. However, besides this, "man really finds in himself a faculty by which he distinguishes himself from all other things, even from himself so far as he is affected by objects. This faculty is reason." It is preeminently in the exercise of reason that we find in man *activity* ("spontaneity", in Kant's phrase) as distinct from mere happening; and this activity cannot be wholly — even if it can be in part — explained in terms of causes and their effects. Genuinely to reason in a certain manner is not merely to be caused to have certain thoughts; and to be conscious of reasoning is not merely to be aware of the mental effects of certain causes. Man as a reasoning being is thus unique in the order of nature, and indeed, Kant holds, in so far as he exercises reason he cannot be included, cannot include himself, in the world of appearances at all. But since, in Kant's view, the exercise of the will (as distinct from the operation of mere inclinations or desires) is an exercise of reason — "practical" reason — it follows that in exercising his will man is not merely part of the order of nature, and hence in this field there is no conflict with natural causation. For man has "two stand points from which he can consider himself . . . first, as belonging to the world of sense, under laws of nature, and, second, as belonging to the intelligible world under laws which, independent of nature, are not empirical but founded only on reason."

But at this point Kant encounters a curious, but for him inevitable, obstacle to further discussion. He is prepared to assert that by distinguishing man who is a member of the "intelligible world" from man who is merely part of the "world of appearance," we *can* ascribe the exercise of free will to man. He is even ready to assert that we *must* do so if we wish to make any use of rational reflection and decision in determining our conduct; we cannot, as it were, adopt entirely the attitude of mere passive spectators of the events of our own lives and the workings of our own minds. However, Kant also insists that we cannot claim to *know* that the will is free, for this would be a claim to have knowledge of things-in-themselves, namely, of men as members of the "intelligible world"; and it was, of course, a leading thesis of the first *Critique* that no such claim could possibly be well founded. That the will is free is not, in Kant's view, an empirical proposition about the world; but neither is it a synthetic *a priori* proposition expressing a condition of "the possibility of experience." Thus, though the belief in free will is indispensable to rational action, it remains only "an idea of reason, whose objective reality in itself is doubtful." Further than this inquiry cannot possibly go. Therefore, the conclusion is that "we do not indeed comprehend the practical unconditional necessity of the moral imperative; yet we do comprehend its incomprehensibility, which is all that can be fairly demanded of a philosophy which in its principles strives to reach the limit of human reason."[12]

Let us now ask, first, how far Kant can be held to have succeeded in laying bare the "principle," the essential nature, of morality. On this it may perhaps be said that he succeeded too well in meeting his own theoretical demands; the difficulties he encounters are the direct results of his very consistency. He insisted at the outset that any satisfactory account of moral principles must be such as to make clear that, and show how, these are invariant and unconditional—"categorical." This being so, he could not represent moral distinctions as dependent upon any mere fact about human beings, about what their desires or needs or preferences might be. Nor was he willing to make their force conditional upon anything else outside themselves, such as, for example, a religious faith. Thus he was led to the idea that the whole of morality must, in effect, be extracted from the definition of man, for only in this way would it be possible to establish that man as such, independently of all the contingencies of his varying circumstances, was subject unconditionally to the demands of morality. Now man as such is a creature who possesses reason. If so, Kant's problem was that of seeking to exhibit *moral* behavior and *rational* behaviour as being one and the same.

It might well be held that what a rational being is committed to as such is the avoidance of *inconsistency*. No statement, no theory, no argument, no practical policy can be rationally acceptable if it is inconsistent. So it is not surprising that Kant's various formulations of the supreme principle of morality all amount to a demand for consistency in practice and principles. Those principles of conduct which I propose for myself can be rationally accepted only if first, I can without inconsistency, also apply them in assessing the conduct of others and second, they are such that they could be adopted without inconsistency by any (and therefore by all) such beings as I am. And this is exactly what is involved in the notion of the "kingdom of ends." Those principles of conduct can be rationally — that is, consistently — adopted which are such that every member of the community of rational beings could apply them in his own practice and employ them also in judging the practice of all the rest; such principles alone can "enter into a possible universal legislation" and thus be accepted by all without conflict arising.

Kant concludes at this point, in words already quoted, that "morality therefore consists in the relation of every action to that legislation through which alone a kingdom of ends is possible." But it should now be clear that this conclusion embodies a very bold and quite unargued assumption. For it is apparent that he is here claiming not only, as he reasonably could, that his test of universal acceptability without conflict suffices to rule out certain principles as unacceptable, but also that it definitely identifies certain principles — *the* principles of morality — as demanding acceptance. But in order to make this latter claim, it is necessary to suppose that certain definite principles alone would make possible a "kingdom of ends," and that they alone could be accepted and applied by each and all. Kant clearly does suppose this, but he offers no argument in support of the supposition, and in fact the uniqueness in this respect of certain principles of morality seems to him to be simply assumed. Yet surely the assumption is exceedingly unplausible. For instance, in the important field of sexual behavior, it seems evident that there are numerous and widely various policies and attitudes, not all of which strike us as equally desirable, but which are all *possible* in the sense at least of not being, in Kant's rather formal sense, inconsistent and unworkable if generally adopted.

We may also make the point in another way. Basing his argument upon the sole consideration of man as a rational being, Kant is perhaps in a position to lay down what men should *not* do — namely, they should not adopt principles of judgment or conduct which lead to or involve inconsistency. However, it is by no means clear that this suffices to determine in any positive way what they *should* do.* It could be thought to determine this only if one were to make the additional and unplausible assumption that there is only one way of avoiding inconsistency. In the same fashion, we are of course in a position to say that a proposition that embodies or implies a contradiction cannot be true, but thereby we have no warrant for

* It has been maintained by certain commentators that Kant claims only to express the "form" of morality and would not have claimed that his theory in any way specified its content. But the fact is that he attempts to break down this very distinction — to demonstrate, that is, how it is possible to derive definite moral principles *a priori*, from "formal" considerations alone.

concluding that any particular proposition *is* true simply because there would be no inconsistency in asserting it.

To assess Kant's discussion of the notion of freedom is considerably more difficult, and is indeed a task that cannot well be done briefly. A number of separable, but interrelated, questions arises.

First, is Kant right in taking what is certainly the traditional view that there is a *prima facie* incompatibility between acceptance of universal causal determinism and the supposition that men are free and responsible agents? This is a question that has been voluminously argued, and philosophers are still sharply divided on its answer. I should like to state here, somewhat dogmatically, that in my opinion Kant is right. To suppose that for every item of human behavior there is a completely sufficient physical or pyschological causal explanation does not indeed directly contradict explanations of human behavior in other modes — such as those in terms of an agent's own reasons and decisions; it does, however, *undermine* them in a sense, as a psychopath's or hypnotized person's own explanation of his curious conduct is undermined, shown up as not the "real" explanation, by knowledge of the causes which in fact produce his pathological or peculiar behavior. And it is, I think, clear that in so far as we are genuinely able to explain human action as simply the effect of antecedent causes, we do in fact cease to regard the person concerned as genuinely answerable for his behavior. If, for example, his behavior has been undesirable, we think rather of modifying his future behavior by remedial treatment than of blaming or punishing him for what he has done. That there is accordingly a problem there, having the form of an "antinomy," seems to me to be a correct supposition.

Second, I think that Kant is also correct in connecting the notion of free will, as he does, with that of being a reasoning creature. It is clear that an act which is free in the required sense — an act for which the agent may properly be held responsible — cannot merely be "lawless" or causally inexplicable. For of course an inanimate object's behaviour might be regarded as thus inexplicable without our being for that reason in the least inclined to attribute any exercise of freewill to the object in question or to hold it "responsible" for the way it behaves. It is less clear that Kant is right in his further contention that *desire* cannot here be the central concept. It might well be urged that precisely those persons are free who are able to do what they desire — that freedom, as Hobbes said, "signifieth [properly] the absence of opposition" to our acting as we wish. And in a sense of course this is true. But it does not follow that those who can do — are free to do — what they desire exercise *freewill*, or are responsible for what they do. For example, they may be advanced psychotics; and if we were to allow freedom to such persons — to permit them, that is, to act as

they desire — we should obviously not render them responsible beings, nor would we restore to them the power of responsible decision. To have a free *will* in Kant's sense, then, is something more than simply to be free; it is to have not simply the power to act as one desires but the capacity to reflect and to decide how one is to act — possibly, though of course not necessarily, in opposition to one's own desires and inclinations. And it seems fair to say that this capacity to decide, this capacity *not* to act forthwith in accordance with one's dominant desire, does imply the capacity to think, to reason. If so, there is justice in Kant's identification of a rational being, a being possessed of freewill, and a morally responsible being.

Now, however, we come to two points at which Kant seems open to serious criticism. He holds, with justice, that to regard men as rational and responsible beings is not to regard them as ordinary items in the natural order, their behavior determined wholly by laws of nature; he holds that if we are to regard their behavior and our own as rational and responsible, we have actually to consider men as excluded in part from the "world of sense," as thereby "distinguished from all other things." Now Kant goes on to say that to regard men in this way is to regard them as belonging to the "intelligible world," the world of things-in-themselves. But this last step seems to be unwarranted. Kant has distinguished between appearances as conditioned by our perceptual and conceptual apparatus, and what exists (necessarily indescribably) as it is in itself; he now distinguishes between man as a mere physical and psychological phenomenon, and as a being capable of rational decision and action, but the second distinction seems to be quite different from the first. It should be quite evident, in fact, that this is so. For he distinguishes man from all other items in the "world of sense" on the positive ground that man has, as other beings have not, the capacity to reason; things-in-themselves, however, cannot be distinguished from appearances by possession of any positive characteristic, since (necessarily) they cannot be characterized in any way. Indeed, if it were the case that man *qua* rational being was to be identified with man as a thing-in-himself, it would have to be concluded that we could not only *know* nothing, but could even *say* nothing about man *qua* rational being. Kant, rightly of course, does not accept this. But if not, it must be conceded that he is mistaken in supposing that to consider man as a rational being is to consider him as a thing-in-himself; to suppose this is to run together two different distinctions.

It follows that, although it may be true as Kant says that freewill is only "an idea of reason whose objective reality in itself is doubtful," this is not so for the reason Kant has in mind. The positive assertion that man has free will could not, in his view, be known to be true, since he regarded it as an assertion about the "intelligible world," which he has to regard as inaccessible to knowledge. If, however, man as the possessor of free will is not to be identified with man as a thing-in-himself, the general inaccessibility to knowledge of things-in-themselves will not be a reason for concluding that we cannot know that man possesses free will. This is not to say, however, that there may not be other reasons for that conclusion.

Finally, we must ask whether Kant really succeeds in resolving the *prima facie* "antinomy," the apparent conflict, between free will and universal causal determination. I suggest that he does not. He argues, it will be remembered, that there are different "standpoints" from which a man may be regarded. His body may be regarded simply as a physical object; its movements and its states may be observed and described as one would observe and describe those of any material thing; and further, Kant holds that his mind may be similarly regarded as a mere set or succession of psychological states and occurrences. But we adopt a different "standpoint" from this when we regard a man as thinking, choosing, deciding, acting; we describe him and his behavior in different terms — terms that have no application to inanimate objects — and of course we can explain what he does in different terms also. We ask not what caused his limbs to move in a particular way but, perhaps, why he chose to act as he did. Kant believes that, from the first standpoint, we can and must concede that causation rules completely and universally; the successive states of a man's body and mind, regarded simply as physical and psychological phenomena, must be allowed to be without exception or remainder the effects of antecedent causes. However, he holds that we are under no such necessity when we adopt the second standpoint. For here, since we are no longer regarding man as a mere natural object, we are not committed to asserting of him all that is true in general of the natural world; in so far as we distinguish men from mere natural objects, we do not have to concede that their states and their doings are wholly determined by laws of nature. In this way, Kant thinks, it is open to us to admit that man as an item in the "world of sense" is subject to causal necessity while also proceeding on the supposition that regarded from the other point of view he has free will.

Now there is certainly merit in Kant's distinction between his two "standpoints." One might perhaps express his point by saying that we may regard a man either as a *thing* or as a *person*: if as a thing, we may proceed to apply to him those concepts by which things in general are described and their behavior explained — among others, of course, the concepts of cause and effect; but if as a person, we may proceed to apply the very different concepts of intention, decision, reason, action, and the rest — concepts that apply *peculiarly* to persons and which thus serve, as Kant says, to distinguish persons "from all other things." However, if Kant is to resolve his problem

in this way, what he needs to establish is not merely that his two standpoints are different but that they are actually *independent*. He appears, in fact, to have assumed that they are. For he seems to assume that in considering what we are to say of man from one point of view, it does not matter what we may have said of him from the other; he assumes that the possibility of conflict is removed simply by virtue of the difference in point of view. But it is certainly very far from clear that this assumption is justified. It is at least possible to maintain that if, regarding a man's behavior simply as a set of physical and psychological occurrences, we could explain it *completely* as the natural effect of certain physical and psychological causes, we should then think it impossible also to speak of his behavior in terms of reasons, decisions, and the rest. It is possible to maintain that our modes of describing and explaining the actions of persons proceed on the general supposition that it is *not* possible to explain human behavior exhaustively in causal terms, and that, if one seriously holds that this *is* possible, one ought to abandon the vocabulary peculiar to persons as being ill founded. But this, of course, is to maintain that Kant's two standpoints, though certainly different, are not independent — that what we are inclined and accustomed to say from one of them may be affected, and might even be totally undermined, by what we are inclined or obliged to say from the other. If so, then Kant's attempt to escape from his antinomy would not succeed. For although he is right in saying that we *do* regard persons as distinguished from all other things, and have indeed an extensive vocabulary marking this distinction, it might be urged that we should simply be mistaken in doing this if it were also possible, as he concedes that it is, to explain human behavior exhaustively in the same terms as that of other objects in the world. It is only if this is *not* possible, it might be said, that persons are rightly distinguished from all other things.

Now if this criticism is well founded — and there is not space enough here to attempt to decide this — it attacks Kant's position at a very deep level. For to resolve the apparent "antinomy" between the claims of science and morality was certainly among Kant's major purposes, and it was by means of one of his central doctrines that he undertook to do this — namely, by the distinction between "appearances" and things-in-themselves. By means of this distinction, he hoped to allow the claims of science to offer the whole truth about the natural order, and at the same time to preserve the essentials of morality by removing morality from that arena altogether; in the world of things-in-themselves there was to be room not only for faith but for moral convictions and moral responsibility, whereas knowledge and necessity were to reign in the phenomenal world. But if what has been suggested in the preceding paragraph is correct, such a removal of moral notions from the natural order may be fatal to them: so far from establishing that they may be employed without question or challenge, it may lead to the conclusion that they cannot rightly be employed at all. To repeat: It is certain that to regard men as rational, free, and responsible agents is *different* from regarding them as merely among the objects of scientific investigation; but it cannot be assumed that they can *rightly* be regarded in that way, *whatever* the scientific investigation of human behavior may reveal. If so, it may well be held that Kant was misguided in his employment, to solve one of his major problems, of one of his major philosophical doctrines. If that is so, it may be held in turn that his ethical theory, though a deeply serious and most impressive intellectual effort, is a failure in the end.

The Critique of Judgment

KANT's third *Critique*, his last major piece of philosophical writing, may be more briefly dealt with. It may well be thought a rather unsatisfactory performance. Though it contains a number of extremely interesting points, it lacks the firm structure of Kant's other works, and its general outline is not easy to discern. Paradoxically enough, this is due in large part to what appear to be Kant's efforts to impose on this part of his work the "architectonic" of the other *Critiques*, and his attempts also to articulate it very closely with them. The contrivance by which he seeks to achieve these ends makes the outcome, not clearer, but if anything more obscure. The internal "architectonic" of the third *Critique* seems chiefly to result in repetition, substantially the same points being made several times under seemingly arbitrarily different headings, whereas the general relation of the work to what has gone before is really more complex and less systematic than Kant represents it to be. We may begin by attempting to unravel this relationship.

The fact seems to be that Kant wished to extend and "complete" the work of his first two *Critiques* in two different ways, but was determined, if possible, to represent these two ways as being one and the same. In the first place, he had had the idea from an early stage that his philosophical territory as a whole consisted of three divisions — "the theory of taste, metaphysics, and moral theory." Now it could be said that the first *Critique* had dealt with metaphysics, the second with moral theory; if so, it would seem that a third work was now called for, to be devoted to the "theory of taste," or aesthetics. But besides this, Kant later came to have much in his mind another threefold division — namely, that between reason, understanding, and *judgment*. He now — in the Introduction to the third *Critique* — wishes to say that the *Critique of Pure Reason* (in spite of its title, and in spite of the fact that the speculative use of reason is the topic of the *Dialectic* in that work) was concerned in particular with the faculty of *understanding*; and that the *Critique of Practical Reason* was concerned with the faculty of *reason*. "The function of prescribing laws by means of concepts of nature is discharged by understanding and is theoretical. That of prescribing laws by means of the concept of freedom is discharged by reason and is merely practical." But now Kant wishes further to distinguish *judgment* as a separate faculty — a "middle term" — between understanding and reason, and he accordingly believes that a third *Critique* should be devoted to this faculty, as the earlier two had been to understanding and to reason.

He thus has two motives for planning a third *Critique*. First, he wishes to add the study of aesthetics to the studies of metaphysics and ethics; and second, he now wishes to add a critique of *judgment* to those which have dealt with understanding and reason.

Now it is by no means evident that the two motives are really one and the same, nor even that they would naturally lead in the same direction. Let us suppose that the scope of aesthetics is sufficiently clear; we have then to ask how it is related to the "critique of judgment"; and here we have first to try to make out what Kant now means by "judgment."

In the first *Critique*, Kant has said that to "judge," to make a judgment or assertion, was to apply a concept to a particular instance, or to apply a rule, principle, or law to a particular case. But there, as he now thinks, he had accepted a tacit restriction; he had tended to think only of the situation in which one applies to a particular case a concept or rule that one possesses *in advance* — in which, for instance, already possessing the concept "pink," one judges that "this is pink" on encountering an appropriate instance. This he now distinguishes under the name of *determinant* judgment. Different from this, he thinks, and raising problems of its own, is what he now calls *reflective* judgment — judgment in which "only the particular is given and the universal has to be found for it." Instead of applying a known principle *to* some assemblage of facts, one may, for example, discern a previously *un*known principle *in* an assemblage of facts; instead of finding some particular that falls under one's concept, one may have to find the concept under which a particular falls. In particular — or so Kant's examples seem to imply — the problem of the scientist is characteristically not that of applying to observational or experimental data principles or laws already known, but of discerning in those data what the principles or laws should be. Scientific advance, at any rate, though not its application, is, he seems to say, the work of the reflective judgment; and the faculty thus exercised surely deserves, and has not yet received, close examination.

At least part of what Kant has in mind here could be expressed as follows: He now shows himself to be clearly aware, in supplementation of what he had said in his first *Critique*, that although the general requirement of order which is a "condition of the possibility of experience" may be also a presupposition of scientific inquiry, it is something far too general to determine the procedure of any particular science; the actual laws of a science are not just deductions from or applications of the general proposition that there are laws. But neither are they simple summaries of observed facts. The formulation of such laws, in fact, demands the exercise of a peculiar kind of thinking which Kant now calls "reflective judgment," by which some aggregate of facts is comprehended within a system or theory, the system or theory being in a sense the *invention* of the thinker himself.

However, in the light of what has been said above, it is perhaps not very surprising that, after this introduction, Kant does not in fact proceed to that detailed examination of "reflective judgment," or of the character of scientific theorizing, which his opening pages might naturally have led one to expect. Instead, the discussion soon shifts rather abruptly to "the analytic of aesthetic judgment" — to that other inquiry, that is to say, with which Kant hoped to complete his philosophical work, and with which he had actually been concerned before the general idea of a "critique of judgment" had occurred to him. But although this transition is certainly abrupt, Kant does not leave his two discussions unlinked; he does not change the subject without apology. The link that he provides may well be felt to be highly artificial, but it is not wholly lacking.

First — although this is perhaps not a point of major importance in itself — Kant suggests that *pleasure* is connected in a peculiar way with the exercise of reflective judgment. In the attempt to discern unity and system in some agglomeration of empirical facts, he suggests that the fact of success yields a special kind of pleasure or satisfaction — no doubt particularly to the successful theorist, but also to those who are merely his spectators. "Just as if it were a lucky chance that favoured us, we are rejoiced (properly speaking relieved of a want) where we meet with such systematic unity under merely empirical laws." It is not perfectly clear whether Kant would wish to say that such theoretical successes yield actual aesthetic satisfaction, or whether he means merely to suggest an analogy or resemblance. In any case, he does evidently mean to say that the exercise of reflective judgment in science, and perhaps in general, is closely related to the enjoyment of aesthetic satisfaction; and indeed this is an eminently defensible proposition.

There is, however, another link which, for Kant at least, is much more important. It is provided by what he calls the concept of "purposiveness" or "finality." Kant has argued, reasonably enough, that reflective judgment has to proceed on the general supposition that it can be successfully exercised; for example, in attempting to frame a scientific theory that will comprehend some aggregate of phenomena, one cannot help starting with the

supposition that there is *some* system, some principle or law, to be discerned in one's data. Now this, Kant holds, is to regard the phenomena in question as "purposive"; it is to employ a "principle of finality"; it is, one might also say, to think of the phenomena as having been *arranged with the plan* of exhibiting some particular type of order. This is not to say, he insists, that we have to believe that the natural world actually is deliberately organized, or that it actually does serve any purpose; we have to think of it as organized but not by an actual organizer, as having a plan but not as having been actually and deliberately planned; we must presuppose in nature "purposiveness without a purpose." '

What Kant has in mind may perhaps become clearer — and it will also become clear in what direction he is moving — if for the rather strange expression "purposiveness without a purpose" we substitute the expression "design." In the exercise of reflective judgment, and in particular in scientific inquiry, we presuppose that natural phenomena exhibit design, and in our theories we attempt to bring such design to light. But this is not to accept the theist's "argument from design"; for we need not assume an actual designer, or any actual *purpose* in the course of nature. It is simply design that we are in search of; and, as has been already briefly remarked on, success in the search for design in nature yields a special pleasure or satisfaction.

It is now, of course, open to Kant simply to suggest that we have here also the key to aesthetic judgment: it is the perception of *design* in an object and the peculiar pleasure to which this perception gives rise that is expressed when we pass on it a favorable aesthetic appraisal. Kant thus proceeds to the "critique of taste" on the supposition that aesthetic judgment is at least a case, and perhaps the central one, of the exercise of that "reflective judgment" which had at first seemed to be an unconnected topic. In this way his two interests are brought together, and the critique of taste can be allowed to constitute by far the major part of his *Critique of Judgment*.

Kant takes it for granted — too easily indeed, as most philosophers have done — that aesthetic judgment as such is concerned with *beauty*. He begins by making some valuable distinctions between beauty and some other notions with which beauty is apt to be confused.

First, beauty must not be confused with goodness. A book, an action, a custom, or indeed a person may have aesthetic merit without moral worth, or conversely, moral worth without aesthetic merit.

Second, what is pleasant or agreeable may not be beautiful. Though the beautiful pleases, not all that pleases is beautiful. Kant holds that a color, for instance, may please the eye, a sound the ear, or a taste the palate, without any of these being any more to be considered *beautiful* than is the hot bath which is so pleasant on a cold morning.

Third, what is beautiful may be entirely useless, and in any case the question whether an object is beautiful or not is independent of the question of what its purpose is or what use it has. We may even, Kant emphasizes, be struck by the beauty of an object which we do not and perhaps cannot identify at all; in such a case we are, *a fortiori*, not at all concerned with the usefulness of an object of that kind. On this point Kant is refreshingly anti- "functional" in his aesthetic views. For the same reason, Kant emphatically distinguishes the notion of beauty from that of perfection. It has been held, as he says, that just those objects have aesthetic merit that are perfect of their kind. However, just as to assess the utility of something requires that the object and its end be identified, so to judge the perfection of something demands knowledge of what that thing is and what its state should be. But aesthetic judgment does not require this. An *objet trouvé* may well be judged to be beautiful though it is not an object of any particular *kind* and so is not, *a fortiori*, a perfect specimen of that kind of object. It might, of course, be added that, conversely, there would in fact be no inconsistency in judging some object to be a perfect specimen of its kind and yet denying that it was beautiful: we might well see no beauty, for example, in the perfect gorilla.

Next, Kant dwells at length on the peculiar logical character of aesthetic judgments. Such judgments oddly combine, as he points out, some features of both subjective and objective assertions. On the one hand, if an object gives me personally no aesthetic satisfaction, it is useless to point out that critical opinion is against me or to show that the object satisfies the aesthetic criteria laid down by distinguished theorists of art. I may thus be induced to keep my opinion to myself, or even to worry about the deficiencies of my taste, but I cannot, while remaining personally unpleased and unimpressed, sincerely assert that I now realize the object to be beautiful. There is no such thing as compelling agreement to such an assertion; that an object is beautiful is not to be *proved*. On the other hand, we do speak of our aesthetic judgments as if they were in some way objective. If I do hold some object to be beautiful, I regard as mistaken those who assert that it is not. I do not dismiss the question as merely a matter of taste; in fact, I may assert that those who disagree with me display *bad* taste or none, and this is to contend that their aesthetic judgments are commonly *wrong*. But what can be meant here by "right" and "wrong," since it is admitted that there is actually no method of proof?

Kant's solution runs thus. A beautiful object, he suggests, is such that the contemplation of it stimulates the harmonious interplay of both the understanding and the imagination. In aesthetic judgment we do not, as we do in the exercise of mere understanding, stop short at the mere identification of the thing or the comprehension of its properties and use; but neither does our imagination roam uncontrolled in a mere play of formless and undisciplined fantasy. The object leaves the imagination free, yet it does not leave it without any control. For though the object may have no particular purpose, and may indeed remain quite unidentified, it must exhibit "purposiveness without a purpose" — that is, design or (in the words of a later generation) "significant form." It is the finding of such significant form, which is yet not significant of anything in particular, which both gratifies the understanding and stimulates the imagination; and it is from the complex interplay of these two faculties that there arises that peculiar species of pleasure that prompts the judgment "That is beautiful." Such a judgment cannot be proved, for it is practically analytic to say that the free play of the imagination cannot be compelled or prescribed. However, it is prompted by nothing idiosyncratic in the speaker, since the faculties of understanding and imagination are common to all. Hence it can make, as the judgment "This is pleasant" cannot, a justified claim upon the assent of all others.* Kant adds that there can be no method or set of rules for producing objects that please in this way, and for that reason artistic creation preeminently requires, as does all creative thinking in some degree, *genius*, and not merely a skill or talent or marked ability to learn. Kant appears to recognize clearly enough that what he says of the artist, *mutatis mutandis*, will apply to the theorist of genius also: this, indeed, is implied in his general account of "reflective judgment."

From the beautiful Kant turns, in the fashion of his time, to the sublime. What he says here is mainly of interest as throwing light on, and in a certain respect also modifying, his philosophy of morals. There are some objects, he says, which, while they powerfully stimulate the imagination, yet lead the reason to entertain ideas that far outrun the imagination's capacity. The vast extent of the heavens, for example, or the colossal violence of a storm at sea, may call up in us the notions of infinite size and infinite power; and here, though we may be dissatisfied with the actual inadequacy of our imagination to picture such notions, we may yet be exalted by the consequent realization that "we esteem as small in comparison with ideas of reason everything which for us is great in nature as an object of sense." If so, though we may improperly give the name "sublime" to the *objects* that excite us in this peculiar way, it is the preeminence of the power of human reason to which sublimity really belongs. Reason outruns the capacity of imagination; "sublimity, therefore, does not reside in any of the things of nature, but only in our mind, in so far as we may become

---

* It will be observed that Kant, like most theorists of art in the last century, comes down strongly on the side of *form* as being the only proper criterion of beauty; color he regarded as merely sensorily agreeable. It was this prevailing attitude from which, conspicuously, Turner suffered, and of which some would say his work provides the refutation.

conscious of our superiority over nature within, and thus also over nature without us (as exerting influence upon us)."[13] But it is as moral agents that we chiefly rise above the "influence" of nature. The conception of the moral law is therefore the leading instance of the sublime: it is for this above all that we properly feel *respect*, and in this that we properly find (what Kant had earlier seemed to deny) a pleasure that is close to the pleasure of aesthetic enjoyment. Kant now goes so far as to say that while aesthetic and moral merit must still be distinguished, "the beautiful is the symbol of the morally good" and "teaches us to find, even in sensuous objects, a free delight apart from any charm of sense."[14]

Finally, in Part II of the *Critique of Judgment*, Kant turns to an examination of *teleology*. It is clear enough what leads him to do this. He has sought to explain aesthetic judgment as the perception of design — "purposiveness without a purpose" — in objects, whether artifacts or products of nature. But it had sometimes been maintained — and perhaps it still is — that it is possible to discern design, even in the sense of purposiveness *with* a purpose, in some natural objects or even in nature as a whole; and this is to claim, in Kant's terms, a field for the exercise of "reflective judgment" extending far beyond aesthetics and also beyond the field of that ordinary scientific theorizing to which Kant had alluded in his Introduction. It is therefore of importance for him to decide on the merits of this claim. Moreover, as will be observed, he now takes the opportunity to restate with the utmost emphasis his thesis (already mentioned) that metaphysics and religion must be founded, so far as any foundation can be supplied, on our recognition of the moral law and of its demands.

Kant argues first that there are certain kinds of natural phenomena which we are powerfully impelled to regard as purposive — namely, *organisms*. When we consider the phenomena of organic growth, reproduction, and adaptation, it is natural to us to think of the phases of such processes as being directed to the *end* of achieving, continuing, or maintaining the existence of the organism in its final form. We think of the embryo, for example, as growing the way it does because of what it *is to become*; the pruned tree puts out new shoots *in order to* survive. Now, in Kant's view, to think of organisms in this way is not only natural but actually necessary, for he thinks there is no other way in which their behavior can be understood. We do not think of valleys as having been formed for the *purpose* of accommodating rivers, for in such a case another quite clear explanation is available: we can attribute the formation of valleys, in part at least, to the mere mechanical action of the rivers themselves. But if we consider, Kant says, even so familiar a phenomenon as the growth of grass, it is wholly impossible to conceive how the mere "mechanism of nature" should precisely and specifically lead to this result. Far more,

then, is it impossible to conceive of any mechanism to account for the existence and reproduction of all the diversified species of animals. Kant mentions, in a famous passage, the idea that perhaps all species of animals might, by the operation of more or less chance agencies, have evolved in their diverse ways from some single primal form, but he held — rightly at that time — that there was no sound evidence for this supposition, which he regarded merely as "a daring adventure on the part of reason"; and besides, he would not entertain the idea that living organisms might have been originally produced from inorganic matter — this idea he very flatly declares to be "contrary to reason." Thus, since he is sure that there are many objects of nature that cannot be — and, he adds, never will be — satisfactorily accounted for as exhibiting merely the effects of antecedent causes, he holds that we cannot dispense with the idea that some natural processes are governed by what their product is to be; and this is to regard those processes as intrinsically *purposive*.

However, Kant insists that this idea can only be "regulative." Although we may make no headway with any attempt to explain the development of, say, the human embryo in ordinary causal terms, and are thus obliged to interpret the process in terms of its final result, we do not *know* that there is no mechanism sufficient to explain all that we observe. If we suppose that all that occurs in nature is in fact the effect of antecedent causes, and also that there are in fact some natural processes that can only be understood by reference to their final outcome, we are involved in a plain contradiction. Kant's view is that on the one hand we must always *look for* a causal mechanism in nature, but on the other hand, where we cannot find or even conceive of such a thing, we have to fall back on the idea of a purposive process; and in proceeding thus, there is no inconsistency. We cannot know that what we call organisms *are* not mechanisms; but so long as we cannot understand an object *as* a mechanism, we must explain it in the available alternative manner. It is at this point that a "teleology of nature" suggests itself to us and can properly be accepted as a guide to understanding, experiment, and research.

But we may, Kant next observes, be impelled to carry this idea further: "We are entitled, nay incited, by the example that nature affords us in its organic products to expect nothing from it and its laws but what is final when things are viewed as a whole."[15] It is quite natural to us, as Kant points out, to speak of "the wisdom, the economy, the forethought, the beneficence of nature." This may be nothing more than a figure of speech, a rhetorical personification of nature "herself," and as such it does neither good nor harm. There is, however, a related argument which seeks to attribute wisdom, economy, forethought, and beneficence, not just to nature, but to a supernatural author of nature. This argument calls for examination.

It is commonly intended, of course, to establish the existence of God. As such, Kant discerns in it fatal weaknesses. For one thing, since the supposed *end* of Creation must be, if the argument is to have any content, something that *we* can understand and should value as an end, the conception of the supposed Designer must inevitably be infected with arbitrariness and anthropomorphism. But more seriously, we do not actually find in nature evidences of design that are capable of supporting the required conclusion. It would be most natural, Kant suggests, to attribute the often confused phenomena that we actually observe in nature to the agency of a plurality of gods on the Greek or Roman model, each powerful but not omnipotent, and liable also to be sometimes at odds with the other deities. The belief in one God, omnipotent and omniscient, is not really required by what we find in the world. With respect to the world as we actually know it, the notion of a single Designer cannot be more than an "idea of reason," a notion that we set before ourselves to guide our search for system and unity in the laws of nature; we cannot suppose that we *know* anything of such a Being or that we have conclusive reason for asserting its existence. The argument from design in nature seems to supply such a reason only if the deficiencies of the actual evidence are surreptitiously glossed over with an eye to the desired conclusion.

Moreover, Kant goes on, although the bare idea of a supreme designer may serve to set the target for research into the system of nature, from a religious point of view the "argument from design" is not only inadequate, it is also unnecessary. For what, in that argument, must be supposed to be the end of Creation? We cannot, Kant argues, find or even imagine anything in nature that could seriously be assigned to that preeminent position except *man* — and man, furthermore, not in those respects in which he is himself merely a part of the natural order but in that respect in which he is unique, in his capacity as a *moral agent*. It is man's power of rational choice that distinguishes him from all other things and which alone entitles us to assign to his existence that "worth" which a supposed end of creation must have. But if so, Kant argues, we already have the best possible ground on which to argue for the existence of God, quite independently of whether the *rest* of nature exhibits many or few or even any marks of design.

It must be carefully observed that Kant is not here maintaining that man's moral convictions positively require the existence of God. On the contrary, he holds that just as it would be contemptible to observe the precepts of morality merely for the reason that God might punish delinquency, so it would be no less contemptible to offer disbelief in God's existence as an excuse for ignoring one's moral obligations: it is not true that if there is no God, then everything is permitted. It is rather that if there is no God there is no reason to regard as *practicable* the achievement of the goal that morality itself sets before us — namely, an ultimate coincidence of happiness with moral deserts. It is possible, and indeed obligatory, for us to strive to do our duty even if we do *not* believe that those most morally deserving of happiness will best achieve it; nevertheless, a conviction of the reality of moral obligation naturally suggests that the goal may ultimately be achieved, and this in turn leads on to the idea that there is a God who intends it to be achieved, and a life after death in which its achievement will be found. This does not afford us, Kant insists, a *proof* of the existence of God; still less can we, with our empirically conditioned concepts and human categories, claim any knowledge of God's nature. Nevertheless, our moral convictions do afford us, so he maintains, a ground for belief in, and a comparatively definite analogical conception of God, as no other supposed evidences do. Thus, of the three grand objects of metaphysics — God, freedom, and immortality — it is, contrary to the traditional view, freedom that is really fundamental. For the notion of freedom (as Kant had argued in the second *Critique*) involves the conception of the moral law, and it is from reflection upon this that we obtain the only assurance that can be obtained — still far short of demonstration — of the doctrines of religion. It is incidentally far better, Kant observes, to make religion in this way dependent upon morality than, by making morality seem to depend upon theology, to infect our moral convictions with all the uncertainties and deficiencies to which theology is inveterately liable. Thus, Kant's third *Critique* culminates, as do also in a sense the first and second, in the assertion of the primacy of the moral law.

Kant himself expressed the view that his third *Critique* formed the culmination of his whole critical enterprise. It seems, however, that posterity has not been misguided in attaching much greater importance to the first and second. Indeed, Kant's reflections on aesthetics and teleology reveal much insight as well as great ingenuity, but they can hardly be said to rival his earlier works in range and penetration. His philosophy of morals may have been, as I have suggested, ultimately a failure; nevertheless it cannot be denied that Kant saw very clearly just what were the demands that he was called upon to meet, and he attempted, in his analyses of the concepts of duty and freedom, to grapple seriously with problems that are too often glossed over, or not even envisaged. There *are* theoretical difficulties implicit in many common attitudes to moral problems; there *is* a sense in which the legitimacy of moral concepts in general can be questioned and stands in need of defense; the notion of the moral law is *not* a straightforward one. It was Kant's great merit that he keenly felt this to be so, and that he faced the resulting problems squarely and with pertinacity.

But doubtless it is in his first *Critique* that Kant's

philosophical power is most fully displayed. In that work it could be said that he dealt the conclusive blow at the species of "transcendent," speculative metaphysics which had bulked so large in the earlier history of philosophy. Although (as indeed Kant foresaw) this work of criticism may have to be repeated often enough in the face of renewed speculative flights, there is a sense in which all later criticism of such metaphysics retraces — at its best — the path which Kant's *Dialectic* had mapped out. His criticism was not unsympathetic; at times, indeed, one almost feels that he was deeply reluctant to reach the conclusions to which his own argument was leading him; that argument is, however, all the more effective for being motivated by no emotional antipathy. And on the positive side, there is permanent value, and still much work to be done, in Kant's vast enterprise of eliciting from human experience those permanent, pervasive, perhaps even "necessary," features and principles that fix and determine its fundamental character. It was in this analytical, unspeculative "metaphysic of nature" that Kant saw the true field of strictly philosophical activity — a field neither already preempted by the natural sciences nor beyond the scope of rational argument and demonstration. The tasks of philosophy have been, and can properly be, envisaged in many different ways and from many diverse points of view. At a time when the aspirations of philosophy are tending to become somewhat overcautious, too negatively conceived, it might well prove most salutary to reconsider, and if possible to reanimate, the constructive, exploratory tasks that Kant pursued and commended and on which, in his own cumbrous, overingenious, but most powerful style, he actually succeeded in casting so much light.

18

Hegel

J. N. FINDLAY

HEGEL WAS BORN at Stuttgart in the Duchy of Wurttemberg in 1770. He claimed descent from one of the refugee Protestant families who had fled from Austria during the Counter-Reformation. He was educated at Stuttgart Gymnasium, and afterwards at Tübingen University (1788–1793), where he became a deep friend of the poet Hölderlin and of the philosopher Schelling. The French Revolution occurred while Hegel was at the University, and excited and moved him and his friends; later on it was to become for him the type of political abstractness carried to self-destroying extremes, of which the concrete unity of the ancient city-state was the happy antithesis. From 1793 to 1800, Hegel held tutorial positions at Bern and Frankfurt, and began to work out his own ideas. In this development he was of course much influenced by Kant, and by the contemporary thought of Fichte and Schelling; it is, however, important to realize how much he was influenced by his deep studies of Greek philosophy, by his reading of Spinoza, and by his ponderings over the ethical and philosophical meaning of the New Testament. His *Early Theological Writings* reflect this last preoccupation.

From 1801 to 1803 Hegel taught philosophy at Jena and cooperated with Schelling in producing a *Critical Journal of Philosophy*. His friend's unprincipled methods of philosophizing led, however, to a break-away, and in 1807 Hegel published his first great original work, the *Phenomenology of Mind*. From 1808 to 1816 Hegel was rector of a gymnasium at Nuremberg, where he wrote his *Science of Logic*, published in 1812–13–16. From 1816 to 1818, Hegel held a philosophical chair at Heidelberg and published in 1817 (later editions 1827 and 1830) his *Encyclopaedia of the Philosophical Sciences*, a compendium of his system, consisting of a Logic, a Philosophy of Nature, and a Philosophy of Spirit. From 1818 to 1831, Hegel held a philosophical chair in Berlin, where he published his *Outlines of the Philosophy of Right* in 1820. He died of cholera in 1831. After his death his lectures on Aesthetics, History of Philosophy, Philosophy of History, and Philosophy of Religion were published by his students, who also added valuable supplements (*Zusätze*), based on lecture notes, to the *Encyclopaedia* and the *Philosophy of Right*.

HEGEL IS BY GENERAL ADMISSION one of the most important philosophers; by general admission he is also one of the hardest. To present him briefly in language largely akin to his own would be a major undertaking; to present the gist of his views in language understandable in our own age, and in a critical modern perspective, is almost superhumanly difficult. The reasons for this difficulty are many. Hegel presents his thought in a barbarous diction of his own devising where terms are not merely oddly but shiftingly used: a thought or form of being is said, for example, to be "mediated" when it involves any sort of internal or external relatedness; it is said to be "posited" *both* when it is explicitly recognized and *also* when it enjoys a contextual or relative status; it is said to have "moments" whenever it exhibits distinguishable aspects; and to show "totality" of each of these "moments" mirrors its total structure. The entities mentioned by Hegel are, moreover, usually described as in a state of active self-transformation: they repel themselves from themselves, they "swing round" into their counterparts, they collapse into immediacy, they fall to the ground, they come together with themselves, and so on. The pained puzzlement provoked by these queer locutions is often only equalled by the dreamlike, schizoid quality of the thoughts lying behind them, to which one can with difficulty penetrate. Thus, Hegel devotes much space to developing the strange fantasy of a topsy-turvy noumenal world, a world lying behind the phenomenal order but at every point *inverting* its relations, so that the noumenal north corresponds to the phenomenal south, the noumenal acid to the phenomenal base, noumenal goodness and happiness to phenomenal unhappiness and badness, etc.[1] Beside such a mad picture, Locke's account of an underlying substance which merely is *we know not what* seems positively innocent and straightforward.

But not only are the individual phases in Hegel's thought hard to interpret; the transitions between them, and the sequence they form, are in the last degree difficult and extraordinary. For Hegel's main philosophical originality lies in the fact that he does not offer us one *single* set of concepts and principles, a single notional schema in terms of which things are to be understood, but rather a long array of such schemes, adopted and discarded in turn, and arranged in what Hegel holds to be a fixed order of philosophical adequacy or "truth." Hegel does not merely offer us an atomistic pluralistic view of things, but *also* one that is continuous and monistic; he does not merely see things mechanically and materialistically, but *also* teleologically and vitalistically; he is not content to sketch various forms of metaphysical and theological dualism, but also to dissolve them in an extreme of atheism and humanism. And not only does he offer us many such conceptual schemes, but he also seeks to combine or reconcile them in what seems a barely intelligible fashion: thus, one has to stomach a necessity that none the less embraces contingency in itself, or an "infinity" which is an attribute of what is, from another point of view, finite. And the transitions from one such conceptual scheme to the next do not follow formulable patterns; they resemble, rather, a descent of "tongues" obeying ever new grammar. Hardly has a definite picture been formed than Hegel shakes the kaleidoscope and a wholly new pattern forms itself by slips, slides, and changes of perspective too numerous and too subtle to mention. Sometimes one does not know whether one is *in* a definite thought-phase or in process of moving to the next: things fixed in quality at the beginning of a paragraph may be freely variable at its end, the rigorously distinct atoms of one paragraph are the flowing segments of the next, and so forth. One's difficulty is increased since Hegel uses this kaleidoscopic shaking method, not merely in developing notions and points of view, but also in describing and accounting for the world. The forms of nature, the experiences of the individual mind, the interplay of nations in history — all these are dealt with in the same radical "transforming" fashion, the very reverse of what we should normally think of as coherent and "logical." Hegel has described the course followed in his own *Phenomenology of Mind* as a "highway of despair"; to some it would seem, rather, to be a sort of philosophical Buchenwald, with new forms of senseless intellectual torment crowded into each instant.

The difficulty of studying Hegel has been increased further by the fact that while he may have "inspired" many, he has been objectively studied by few. While many have found in him the taking-off ground for their own speculative flights, few have been troubled to read him with the dispassionate, scholarly care so readily accorded to Aristotle or Kant. Many have simplified him into an "objective idealist" of the type of Kant, with the redundant "thing-in-itself" mercifully omitted, quite forgetting the many passages where Hegel commits himself to an almost materialistic realism.[2] Some have made of him an orthodox Christian theist, forgetful of the passages where God and his acts and persons are dissolved into pure logic, and where there is an almost savage insistence on the necessary "death" of the divine and on the transformation of religious pictures into philosophical varieties. Others have made of him a transcendent, timeless absolutist after the manner of Bradley, forgetful of his insistence that the absolute is nothing if not historic, actual, and contemporary, that it is self-conscious only in Man, and that its supreme form is philosophy. Yet others have held him to be a mere empiricist, forgetful of the extremely high level of abstraction and generality to which all notions are raised in his treatment, things being brought together in a single perspective that no empiricist would think akin. Yet others have looked on him as a mad rationalist, or have sought, by patching and perfecting his arguments, to make him even more madly so, ignoring the extent to which Hegelian "necessity" covers many subtle relations of mere suggestion, notional approximation, or graduated affinity. The multitude of interpreters and interpretations has so settled upon the body of Hegelianism as completely to cover and obscure it: instead of views which, if difficult and at times absurd, are at least always interesting, one has had views as one-sidedly intelligible as they are naïve and jejune. To free the flesh and bones of Hegelianism from this bombinating cloud of interpretation might well seem an impossible task, especially when one recurs to the difficulty of Hegel's original writings and to the vastly greater difficulty of the current translations.

To relegate Hegel to the mere limbo of the historically influential would, however, be gravely regrettable; for this reason a study of his thinking has been included in the present volume. Hegel's diction, though immensely difficult, is with some pain masterable, and, when mastered, reveals his thought as abounding in originality and illumination, and as endowed with a strange power of seeing important affinities among things apparently most diverse and disparate, and of raising to the level of philosophical significance ideas even of the most specific and empirical cast. Hegel is able, perhaps fantastically, but interestingly, to see an analogy between mutually soliciting forces and mutually recognizing persons, between an electric shock and an angry retaliation, or between Kant's categorical imperative and the impartially decapitating guillotine. Hegel is also able to *differentiate* his notions as richly as he is able to unify them. For most philosophers, e.g., moral judgments are a fairly homogeneous class of phenomena, instances of one readily delineable concept, whereas for Hegel they form a large *family* of attitudes, developed at times in completely opposed ways, yet all tending to a common limiting pattern. If this is empiricism, it is empiricism of an acceptable type, one that uses experience in forming its *notions* rather than in settling the truth of its *assertions*. Hegel is further gifted with a remarkable diagnostic and prognostic faculty: he can see just what is the secret motive and advantage of a philosophical position, just where and how it will develop its characteristic rubs and difficulties, and just how it will consequently be transformed into, or replaced by, other forms of thought. Hegel uses this diagnostic power in his remarkable History of Philosophy, an unrivalled study of the uneasy transitions rather than the stable positions of philosophical thought. Sometimes he exercises this faculty in regard to the future. Thus, he entirely foresees, and with as much completeness sees *through*, what Mill was so elaborately to argue in regard to the syllogism's being a mere *petitio principii*, or in regard to inductive inferences' being really reasonings from particulars to particulars.[3]

And if Hegel extends this understanding of thought to the regions of nature and history, he has at least shown the continuity of these various spheres, that philosophizing does not differ abruptly from breathing, eating, and fighting. The ability to form both such very general and such very specific concepts, and to lend them philosophical significance, is certainly a power that countervails against much that is unacceptable or nonsensical.

There are other directions in which Hegel's thought has contemporary relevance. It is above all valuable for having put in its place the sort of rigid thought that obtains in an artificial calculus, where meanings are sharp, basic assumptions explicit, and rules of inference exhaustively directive. This kind of thought, called by Hegel the thought of the understanding, obviously agrees neither with the actual nor with the ideal form of human discourse. Our actual discourse practically never employs notions so sharp that there are not contexts where we are tempted both to apply them and deny them application, and even to find illumination in doing so — "That's true in a *way* (unspecified) but in another way not true" — and its interest is not so much in connections of strict entailment as in those involving a rather loose *parity* or *analogy*. To calculate is not, in ordinary discourse, to evince reason — it is not reasonable to add up figures rightly or to reach the right conclusion in *Barbara* — whereas one does evince reason in one's less charted flights of analogical or hypothetical thinking. And it is not even the *ideal* of thought that one should at all times be calculus- or syllogistically-minded, though it may be right in certain exhaustively argued, rigidly abstract fields. To be thus minded is to cut off the suggestiveness of one's concepts — the things that their application makes it reasonable to add on, or to pass over to, although not *obliging* one to do so. And it makes it impossible for one to experiment among modes of speech and thought, and to compare them as regards adequacy and effectiveness, since such experiment and comparison obviously cannot be considered in the modes of speech and thought in question. Obviously, in philosophy everything that is significant and creative must occur in the interstitial pauses, the marginal discussions which occur *outside* of formalized argument — thus the *philosophy* in *Principia Mathematica* is all written in English — while the formal, deductive element will be valuable largely in showing us what a mode of speech or thought involves, or to what it precisely leads, and so in providing the *raw material* for philosophical judgment or decision rather than that judgment or decision itself. All this is exactly what may be collected from the statements and practice of Hegel, for whom no notion is fixed and no argument grossly clinching. In philosophy, that essentially unsettled subject, to combine a sentence with its negative will very often have an illuminating, stimulating force, and there will be no arguments having substance and interest that will not also permit deductive evasion. If Hegel has perhaps exercised too far his philosopher's right to be unfixed in his notions and unclinching in his arguments, he has at least steered clear of that final regimentation of thought which certainly spells the death (if, for some, *Liebestod*) of philosophy.

Hegel is also of contemporary interest in that his furthest excurions into what seems the transcendent or the transcendental, really only serve to illuminate what is a matter of actually present, wholly commonplace, concretely experienced fact. In a circuitous, high-level manner, Hegel really practices what is now called analytic philosophy, rather than metaphysics or theology. For the seemingly Platonic entities which are said by him to antedate nature and mind, or which are the unchanging objects of religious devotion, prove in the end to be merely the dummy bridges or the painted obelisks terminating some Palladian vista. Hegel is in a sense the supreme positivist, since for him the absolute has no being outside of concrete human experiences, even if he does make it present *par excellence* in the experiences of artists, religious worshippers, and philosophers. What Hegel does, however, suggest is that in a satisfactory description of what is concretely "there," there will have to be a certain amount of queerness and a marginal meeting of extremes, which to the understanding (as to contemporary thought) might seem unacceptably mystical.

What has been said in commendation of Hegel does not, of course, dispose of the large element of sheer nonsense, sometimes conscious and wanton, in his writings, and of the difficulty and pain that such nonsense must occasion. One can plead only that most philosophies involve absurdities, due chiefly to the routine use of devices that are only at times illuminating, and that in Hegel very great illumination must be weighed against great nonsense. In what follows we shall almost entirely ignore the historical affiliations of Hegel's thinking, which was in any case an autochthonous growth, begotten more out of his own personal broodings over the mysteries of Christianity and on the strange arguments of the Platonic *Parmenides*, than from the philosophers who went before him in time. Practically everything in Hegel corresponds to something said by Kant, and was prepared for by Fichte and Schelling, and yet it is all audaciously and timelessly original. No philosopher before Hegel had, e.g., tried to make the way in which philosophical truth was reached an indispensable part, or even the whole, of such truth: no one before him had sought to incorporate transformed errors into his final view of things. These positions may be questionable, but are certainly of the highest philosophical interest.

We shall, in the rest of this essay, first say something about Hegel's characteristic "dialectical" method of philosophizing, then about the two central notions of his system: the "Idea," on the one

hand, and mind or spirit (*Geist*), on the other. We shall then try to give an articulate impression of his main philosophical productions: (a) the *Phenomenology of Mind*, worked out in a book of the same name, first published in 1807; (b) the Logic, worked out in two versions, the three volume *Science of Logic* of 1812–1816 and the briefer "Encyclopaedia" *Logic* of 1817; (c) the Philosophy of Nature, dealt with in the second part of the *Encyclopaedia of the Philosophical Sciences*; (d) the Philosophy of Mind or Spirit, dealt with in the third part of the *Encyclopaedia*, part of whose content is also covered by the *Philosophy of Right* (1820), Hegel's theory of morals and the state.

Hegel's Dialectical Method

HEGEL's characteristic method of thought is *dialectical*, a method by means of which various, one-sided, "abstract" notional approaches (and forms of being which embody these) show up their own inadequacy and internal discrepancy so as to be "overcome" in notions of a more adequately explanatory, many-sided, and "concrete" character. It may be noted that the terms of dialectic are *notions*, not propositions in which something is maintained or asserted. The historical origins of the method need not here be considered. Obviously the Socratic dialectic and the dialectic of the second part of the Platonic *Parmenides* are among its remote ancestry; less remotely, it was inspired by the Kantian antinomies with their reconciling solutions, and by Fichte's concatenated use of such antinomies, where reconciling solutions provoked ever fresh contradictions. From Kant and Fichte Hegel also derived the characteristic triadic pattern of his dialectic: the "immediate," tranquil, usually finitist Thesis; the "mediated," uneasy, often badly infinite Antithesis; and the Synthesis, which in a fair proportion of cases brings the two previous members together in harmony, thereby providing the thesis for a new triad. But Hegel's dialectic is not uniformly triadic, nor are all his triads of one type, nor are the words "Thesis," "Antithesis," and "Synthesis" of frequent occurrence in his writings.

Perhaps the best hint as to how the dialectic was meant to operate is to be found in a passage from the Introduction to the *Phenomenology*. There, Hegel says that each dialectical phase represents precisely the *experience* of the phase that went before it; it is the *retrospective comment* or *observation* upon what was contained in some notion. This comment, or the reason that provoked it, was not part of the content of the earlier phase; it was implicitly *in* it, but not consciously *put* or *posited* in it, nor explicitly *there* for it. Dialectic is therefore nothing but the reflective retreat of our thinking, its continuous self-comment upon its prior performances, the full sense and motive of which can be plain only when the retreat has been *completed* (as Hegel thinks it can be). Until this has been done, the sense and motivation of the dialectic in a sense goes on "behind its back"; it can be plain only to some super-dialectician who has already been through the whole argument. Dialectic therefore somewhat resembles the modern practice of passing from things said in an *object-language* to remarks made in a *metalanguage*, which comment on the previous saying; it is clear that much that is revolutionary may emerge in the process. Thus it is possible to prove in a metalanguage the unprovability of a statement affirming its own unprovability: its unprovability at *one* level of discourse becomes its provability at the *next*. That Hegel practices this method of metalinguistic, or rather metaconceptual, retreat, may be illustrated by many examples. Thus, the notion of being includes in its explicit content the sharpest possible contrast with not-being or nothing — it *means* or *claims* to be something quite different. But the external observer necessarily sees that it can do nothing to back up this claim, that the two notions melt together in their empty abstraction. For him, therefore, the one *passes* into the other. Retrospectively, however, this case of passage introduces him to the new notion of *becoming*. It is therefore always by seeing what is true *of* a notion, though not present *in* it, that the dialectic progresses. And it involves, further, that we put our newly acquired notion back onto the level of the previous one, that we incorporate into our text what has first been inscribed in the margin. It is as if the English commentary to one section of *Principia Mathematica* were formalized in the next section with a new commentary added, and that the whole book were written in this manner. The analogy is of course not exact, nor could metalanguage always be confounded with object-language in the manner indicated. It may, however, enable us to understand better what Hegel thought he was doing, and the pattern to which his dialectical steps largely conform.

Hegel thought, however, that the successive moves of his dialectic were all *necessitated by what* went before them. Though not following in the manner of a mathematical demonstration — where "abstract identity" mediates various equational steps — they are nonetheless the logical outcome of their predecessors. Furthermore they operate in this manner, in a peculiarly rigorous sense, in that each dialectical phase can have only *one* appropriate successor, so that the members of the dialectic form a continuous, unbranching chain, called by Hegel *Wissenschaft* or systematic science. The working out of the dialectic therefore resembles the successive formation of the natural numbers out of their predecessors. The claims to a unique, strict law of succession in the dialectic are not, however, borne out by Hegel's actual practice, nor is it conceivable that they should be. Obviously there are always very different comments that can be made upon some notion, each indicating an alternative dialectical route of advance. And Hegel has, in fact, developed the same parts of the dialectic very differently in different treatments — for example, matter and form are quite differently placed and treated in the *Science of Logic* and in the *Encyclopaedia*. And even at a given dialectical phase, the comment of Hegel goes further than recognizing what was implicit at some earlier phase; very often it recognizes *wants* or *deficiencies* at that stage and then suggests how such a want or deficiency can be *remedied*. Thus, the dialectic sees it as a defect of scientific knowledge that it cannot rationally determine the whole of its object; it then passes to the notion of volition, where such determination is precisely possible. Obviously there is more to such a thought-transition than the mere recognition of what was previously there. The procedure involves, rather, as Trendelenburg maintained in certain famous criticisms, that one starts with certain initial abstractions and then proceeds to undo them, regularly bringing in features from a richer experience. This means that the dialectic, to the extent that it can be successful, cannot be the mere logical consequence of its point of origin, but must involve elements of the unpredictable and the novel, often empirically derived, even if they are not without some logical connection with this point of origin. A dialectical step must be motivated, must have reasons of some sort, but they must be reasons that incline rather than necessitate, and the new notion reached must involve traits that could not have been excogitated from the old.

There is, further, at many points in the dialectic, great play with the notion of opposition or contradiction: the comment passed on some notion (or form of being) is one identifying it with its contradictory or contrary, or affirming the impossibility of distinguishing or separating it from the latter. It is Hegel's constant attempt to show that just in so far as something is merely *A*, it is also and for that very reason not-*A*. That fact has made his dialectic seem to so many critics nugatory and eristic. The way in which Hegel manages the transition from a term to its contradictory or contrary is, however, by no means absurd, for it is not absurd that we should be able to say *of* a predicate or notion the precise opposite of its actual content. Thus, the notion of what is perfectly definite and specific is also one of the most indefinite and unspecific of notions. Hegel constantly shows that while what is "put" or "posited" in a notion may be *A*, yet it may be right to affirm from this the very negation or contrary of *A*, or to recognize that while the notion may claim to differ from or exclude *A*, it does not, in fact, establish that claim; so it must yield place to a notion that actually is what it only claims to be. A few instances will suffice to show the working of this extraordinary mode of antithetical thinking. Pure being, we are told at the beginning of the dialectic, claims to be the absolute opposite of mere nothing, the absolute absence of any sort of being. It cannot, however, substantiate this claim, since both notions are so void of determinate content that they melt without trace into each other. Only when the notion of *Bestimmtheit* (determinateness) is added to that of mere being, can the claim to other than mere nothing be substantiated or be more than a mere claim. In the same way, at a later stage of the dialectic, the notion of the merely possible claims to be something quite different from that of the wholly impossible. The merely possible is, however, that for whose existence certainly necessary conditions are still lacking, and that for which such conditions are lacking is impossible rather than possible. The inadequate notion of the merely possible therefore challenges us to form a more adequate notion of the really possible, which will successfully exclude the impossible. In the same way, to take yet another example, the merely universal, conceived of as wholly exclusive of and antithetical to the individuals that share in it, becomes itself merely an exalted, paradigmatic individual, and therefore challenges us to form a better notion of the universal, which shall *not* be thus absurdly exclusive. The "swinging over" of a notion into its contrary, when made an object of dialectical comment, would not therefore seem to involve a breach of elementary logical laws. Hegel does not locate contradictions in the *explicit* content of ordinary notions — if he did, such notions would obviously be inapplicable to anything. The contradictions are rather the emergent products of a higher-order philosophical reflection, which sees such notions as attempting a task they do not perfectly perform, and which sees, further, how they can be made to be or to do what they only pretend to or strive thereafter. The contradictions are evoked by a special art which has also the power to lay them to rest; it is an art of necromancy tempered by exorcism.

Philosophical reflection, on Hegel's view, takes three closely connected forms: (1) the form of the abstract understanding; (2) the form of dialectic proper; (3) the form of reason or speculative thought. The understanding, for Hegel, is the thought that would have all its notions exact and definite, which lays down all that they do and do not contain, which wholly ignores what is not thus part of a notion's explicit content, and which makes that content so firm and fixed that it can then function in a formal calculus that mechanically brings out its relations to other notions similarly precise. Notions so docked and trimmed by the understanding are admitted by Hegel to be both necessary and admirable. It is only by sharp abstractions, which cut through the rank variety of things like a scythe sweeping through grass, that intellectual mastery can be had at all. But the understanding has a negative aspect in virtue of which it is death-dealing and pernicious. For by shedding a bright light in a narrow circle, and by keeping this light fixed throughout a particular inquiry, it makes us ignore the shading of our abstractions into other abstractions, and ignore their need to be supplemented by these latter if a satisfactory view is to be had. Thus, the useful abstractions of legality are useful only if supplemented by the parallel abstractions of morality, the quantitative abstractions of mathematics require treatments that recognize quality, and so on and so forth. When the understanding fixes the roving focus of the mind to a single direction or distance of abstraction, it at once robs its view of sense and solidity and so permits the contradiction-finding comment in which dialectic proper consists. To overcome such dialectic, the mind must recapture in philosophy that constant shuttling among and mixing together of abstractions which is so much a feature of ordinary thought. There must be a philosophical reason which, at a higher level, mirrors the unthinking reasonableness of ordinary life. For example, just as our unthinking reasonableness glides easily from a discrete to a continuous way of treating space and time, so must our philosophical reason learn to regard them as essentially continuous in discretion, only able to exhibit one of these antithetical characters in so far as they also exhibit the other. The notions of this philosophical reason will differ from those of unreflecting reasonableness only as they clearly distinguish and intelligibly combine features obscurely and shiftily mixed together in unreflective thinking.

Hegel in his practice therefore simply recognizes the tendency of our notions to become senseless and to generate contradictions and puzzles, when artificially held apart from their completing context and so shorn of their normal use and life. He is not, in fact, maintaining anything very different from Wittgenstein, who compares the philosopher to a man who *stares* at his linguistic tools, instead of making use of them, and who therefore finds them profoundly puzzling and bereft of their normal significance. To employ the verb "to be" in ordinary contexts is by no means puzzling; but to ask what being may be in the abstract is to be faced by a surd that is not obviously different from its contrary nothing. Hegel only differs from Wittgenstein in that he holds the whole passage from prephilosophical reasonableness to philosophical reason, by way of the abstractions of the understanding and their dialectical breakdown, to be philosophically essential and enriching. It is only by separating off various one-sided abstractions and then overcoming their one-sidedness in a reasonable result, that a specifically *philosophical* insight becomes possible at all. The function of contradiction in the dialectic must, however, not be exaggerated. There are very many instances where dialectical comment consists merely in recognizing an incompleteness or inadequacy in a notion and then passing on to another notion where this defect is remedied.

Further Peculiarities of the Dialectic: Its Culmination in the "Idea"

HEGEL'S dialectic is curious in three remaining respects, which will require special notice and attention: (1) it is for the most part systematically *triplex* or *triadic*; (2) it is *ontological* as well as notional — that is, it applies to things and forms of being, and not merely to concepts; (3) it terminates in a *crowning notion* which, treated in the abstract, Hegel calls the "Idea" or the "Absolute Idea," and, treated concretely, the "Absolute Mind" or "Spirit" (*Geist*). We must say a little on each of these points.

The triadicity of Hegel's dialectic is, as we have said, largely a legacy of the Kantian antinomies and of Fichte's method in the *Theory of Knowledge*. It professes to go from a first position (or Thesis) to an opposed second position (or Antithesis), and then on to a third mediating position (or Synthesis).* This triadic arrangement fairly represents the notional pattern of *much* of Hegel's dialectic. Thus, the Logic, the study of the Idea in and for itself, swings over into the Philosophy of Nature, the study of the dirempted, self-alienated Idea, and returns to the Philosophy of Spirit, the Idea that has absorbed its "other" into itself. In the same way, "being determinate" (or "finite") swings over into an abstractly endless qualitative progression and returns to "being-for-self," in which finitude and infinity are harmonized. As often as not, however, the triadic scheme does not rightly represent the actual form and motivation of Hegel's thought-content. Very often a notion *B* remedies some inadequacy in a notion *A*, and itself reveals an inadequacy that is remedied by a notion *C*, and so on, without there being anything naturally triadic in such a development. Thus, "mechanism" develops into "chemism," and "chemism" into "teleology," without forming a natural triad. To a large extent the triadicity of Hegel's dialectic represents an external mold into which his thought-material is artificially cast, an artificiality increased by Hegel's determination to have only one line of advance upon which every philosophically significant notion must find its unique place. Hegel's artificial triadic scheme is in fact the source of the considerable element of sheer imposture which has at all times been patent in his thinking: he must pretend always to be swayed by uniquely compelling reasons, even if he has in fact only one out of many possible inclining motives, or perhaps no genuine motive at all.

Hegel's dialectic is further peculiar in that it not only professes to apply to notions and categories of thinking, but also to concrete natural and spiritual *forms of being*. In the Logic, we deal dialectically with such categories as being and number, but in the Philosophy of Nature we deal dialectically with such things as inertia, electricity, and plant-physiology. And in the Philosophy of Mind we not only deal with such forms of individual and social mind as mesmerism, habit, and property but with such seemingly *historical* forms of being as Roman political life, Oriental art, or Jewish and Christian religion. Hegel's dialectic, it would seem, not merely operates in our thinking but in the world. And this would seem to entail that the contradictions and oppositions that beset our thought are also at large in the world, a position seemingly at variance with established logical laws. But in actual fact the terms entering into the Philosophies of Nature and Mind are as much *notions* as those entering into the Logic, only more specific ones: whether we explore plant reproduction or Roman jurisprudence or sacramental penance we are studying phenomena raised into the universality of thought, and pried loose from particular historic individuals or occasions. Hegel's doctrine does, however, mean that there are in some sense *real analogues* to the hard abstractions, the uneasy passages, and the reasonable integrations met with in dialectic. There are, Hegel thinks, certain "low and untrue existences" exemplifying one-sided and abstract categories; although they presuppose the presence of completing categories *somewhere*, they may not embody these themselves. Thus, there are in the world many things embodying the one-sided, abstract category of contingency, of which a philosophical explanation is in consequence impossible. In the same way, there are real states more or less analogous to the unstable thought-transitions between various more stable positions — for example, the experience of pain, revolutions in societies, planetary movements, etc. Hegel finds it helpful to speak of these as actual, manifest contradictions. Since they are actual and manifest, they cannot be self-contradictory in the manner meant in formal logic, although it may be illuminating to speak as if this were so. There are, likewise, real states that resolve the contradictions just mentioned. Thus, Christianity, the absolute religion, combines all the opposed religious principles that went before it. In so talking of real abstractions, real contradictions, and real resolutions of conflicts, Hegel is no doubt speaking analogically or metaphorically. He may, however, be resting himself on a real affinity between thought and existence, between the manner in which thought retreats self-critically to ever new vantage points, which both contain and override what went before, and the manner in which new forms of existence shape themselves out of, and stand relieved upon a background of previous forms, of which they are in a sense the criticism.

The whole point of the dialectic would, however, be lost if we disregarded its outcome, the notion which Hegel regards as comprehensively explanatory, in which all less explanatory notions are taken up, and in which the self-critical retreat of thought reaches its equilibrium. This notion is, for Hegel, only

* We have said before that Hegel hardly ever uses these terms.

reached at the *end* of the dialectic, but it may be argued that the whole self-criticism of the dialectic involves it from the start and would be unintelligible without it. In all dialectical comment, Hegel's final conception provides the implicit standard: it is by comparison with it alone that successive stages of thought are held to be inadequate. And it is because dialectical systems like the Marxist one acknowledge no such implicit standard that their attempts to improve upon Hegel reduce to such nonsense. It may help us, therefore, to try to formulate Hegel's standard conception in advance, even though such a procedure might be one that he himself would reprobate.

Hegel's all-explanatory notion is, in abstract form, the "Absolute Idea," in concrete form "Absolute Mind" or "Absolute Spirit." The content of this notion may be said to be that of *self-conscious rationality*, pursued wholly for its own sake and aware of itself as the *goal* or *end* of all forms of activity and existence. Such rationality is held by Hegel to be involved in all thought and all being; it is present wherever mere multiplicity is brought under a governing universal or rule. It is present in external nature in what Hegel calls a virtual or implicit form; it exists there *an sich*, in itself, not *für sich*, manifest to self, as it can be only for a conscious intelligence. Hegel's theory of nature is Aristotelian in inspiration; he sees its dispersed spatio-temporal multiplicity as everywhere dominated by "forms," universals of varying grades of abstractness or richness, from the dead monotony of gravitation and inertia to the rich, mobile specificity of organic forms. Nature, says Hegel, is the system of *unconscious* thought. He follows his predecessor Schelling in calling it *petrified* intelligence. In nature there may be what Hegel calls active universality, subordinating spatial and temporal "outsideness" to itself, but it is not as yet universality free and disengaged, as it can only be in mind. For Hegel, mind *is* liberated universality and the activity that liberates it: it simply *is* the self-disengagement of universals from their immediate sensuous shells, their self-enjoyment in consciousness, and their subsequent going-forth to a more exhaustive mastery of the sensuous natural world. This going-forth occurs both in the theoretical efforts of cognition, which subjects the world to an ever closer web of interlocking necessitation, and also in the efforts of the will, where the same world is subjected to an interlocking scheme of rational practice.

Hegel holds, further, that this power of the self-disengaging universal is essentially *interpersonal* or *social*. Once we move away from the immediacies of sense, we can frame no notion and entertain no thought that is not such that *everyone* could share it. He goes further, and holds that the very meaning of the first person pronoun "I" is implicitly universal: it expresses a rule-governed unity, which, although it may appear to be the function of a particular mind, is essentially shareable and public. I may *try*, Hegel maintains, to mean by the word "I" a particular, finite person, but I cannot ever *succeed* in meaning just this: for my words to be generally comprehensible, the subject who utters them must of necessity be *the* subject, an *I* who is also a *we*. Hegel therefore interprets the varied applicability of demonstrative expressions, such as "I," "now," "this," etc., as showing that they all have a real universal meaning.[4] Hegel maintains, further, that the thinking self or mind is endowed with what he calls "true infinity" and also "absolute negativity." Whatever I determinately am, I can divest myself of such determinates in thought; I can conceive of myself as being quite otherwise determined. I can make even what seems most intimately mine be *not* myself, and myself *not* what is thus negated, achieving by such a double negation the most *positive* consciousness of my own being.[5] Hegel holds that even insanity shows traces of this rational impersonality — in imagining himself to be Julius Caesar and not a bank-clerk, the madman at least realizes that he can be *anything*.[6] It will not, however, be in the ravings of the insane, but in the disciplined life of the sane, that rational impersonality will be most plainly manifest; it will be seen in the science that imposes canons and categories on the material of experience and disassociates itself from all bias and prejudice, and in the morality that does the same with regard to the material of private interest and impulse.[7] In all this Hegel is obviously borrowing from Kant's idea of the transcendental self, which expresses itself in the same way in the categories of the understanding and in the categorical imperatives of morality. What he says may not be much in line with contemporary views of the use of the pronoun "I", but it seems more in line with our *actual* use of the pronoun. It may be nonsense to say that I might have been at the battle of Cannae, or have been a Cro-Magnon man or even an animal, but it is a nonsense that we regularly commit and that is certainly involved in the understanding of events remote in space or time or of the states of mind of other persons.

The rationality in which the dialectic terminates is, however, a rationality that essentially involves the presence of what is, from a superficial point of view, *irrational*, of what Hegel calls the "Other" or "Other-being" (*Anderssein*). There is a vein of irrationalistic dualism in Hegel's idealism which distinguishes it from almost all other forms of idealism and rationalism. Hegel believes rationality to be essentially *active*: it is not an order tranquilly dominant over multiplicity, but rather the universal in action (*das thätige Allgemeine*), universality in *process* of achieving such dominance.[8] It is on Hegel's view necessary for our rational being that we should be at first plunged in the dispersed violent life of the senses, that we should have experiences satisfying no rational expectation and cohering in no rational pattern. Only by starting with what is thus rude and violent can we rise to that pursuit of the universal in which science consists. In the same way, it is only if we start with many interests and passions, having no initial harmony either among themselves or with the interests and passions of others, that a coordinating, practical rationality can emerge at all, or the still higher rationality of law and morality.[9] Rational life for Hegel demands opposition; it requires "the seriousness, the suffering, the patience, and the labor of the negative."[10] Hegel further implies that it is in one sense hopeless to look for a *complete* subordination to reason of the irrelevances, irrationalities, and resistance of brute fact and personal impulse, for with such subordination, rationality would no longer have a task to accomplish, and would therefore cease to be. This view of rationality as essentially involving an endless "ought" is one that Hegel took over from Fichte, who himself derived it from Kant's view that the demands of reason are "regulative" rather than "constitutive." However, Hegel was to give these doctrines a novel twist, thereby rising to his new notion of the "Absolute Idea."

In the notion of the Absolute Idea, *teleological* explanation plays a dominant part. The opposition between reason and its "other" is resolved, not by holding it to be illusory (though it is in a sense this), but by holding it to exist *for the sake* of reason itself. It is *in order* that there may be rational conscious life that there exists a world of inert matter, subject to many ill-coordinated forces, which only in the fullness of time produces unified organisms, to whose bodies the world presents problems, as it also presents questions to their minds. Likewise, it is *in order* that there may be rational, conscious life that there exist many distinct persons, not at first having any community of interest or insight, and only rising to such a "universal self-consciousness" after much fratricidal strife. It is likewise *in order* that there may be rational, conscious life that there have been long historical processes of development, which can only be understood as leading to ever more advanced rational embodiments. For Hegel, moreover, rationality plays throughout the world-process the role of an immanent Providence: reason is credited with a deep-going cunning (*List*) by means of which it can use the most untoward and fortuitous of circumstances to secure its own needed widenings of horizons. Hegel undoubtedly thinks of his rational end as in some sense endowed with an *active power* to make itself actual. It is, despite appearances, not at the beck of circumstance, nor a nebulous aspiration framed in the "soft element" of thought, but a power to which men and things cannot help lending themselves, even if half-consciously. It is this essential *submissiveness* of the world to reason that Hegel has expressed in the famous saying, "The Rational is the Actual, and the Actual the Rational."

Hegel's Absolute Idea consists then, in the clear vision of the world as subordinated throughout to the single goal of rational activity. In this clear vision, the antithesis between rational activity and its "other" is in a sense abolished since the other exists merely for the sake of reason and is in *this* sense wholly rational. (It is important to stress that this "overcoming" of the irrational is in a sense also its perpetual "preservation.") The Absolute Idea is therefore aptly described by Hegel as "the eternal vision of itself *in* the Other."[11] Hegel says, in this connection, such remarkable things as "The realization of the infinite End consists solely in the overcoming of the illusion by reason of which it seems as yet unaccomplished. . . . The Idea in its process makes itself this illusion, places an Other over against itself, and its activity consists in this: to overcome this illusion."[12] And as a concrete phenomenon, the Absolute Idea expresses itself in the three forms of absolute mind or spirit: art, religion, and philosophy.

Hegel's dialectic is therefore guided by the assumption that the retreat of thought to ever higher self-critical vantage points will at length end in the vision of itself, of pure rationality, as the *final cause* of everything. This assumption goes some way toward explaining the triadic form of the dialectic, upon which we previously commented. For the system involves throughout (1) rationality in the abstract; (2) the abstract "other" of rationality; (3) rationality in the concrete, or rationality that has "overcome" and absorbed its "other." We shall not here attempt a comprehensive criticism of the notion just set forth, but shall postpone this until the actual pattern of Hegel's system has been sketched. Suffice it to say that the explanation of things in terms of the "Idea" and "Spirit" is a far more many-sided and subtly original way of regarding the world than would be ordinarily covered by such a term as "idealism."

Hegel's Phenomenology of Mind

THE *Phenomenology of Mind*, Hegel's first major work, forms a necessary introduction to his whole system. It purports to set forth a line of development necessarily to be followed by the *individual* mind in rising from the immediacies of sense to the philosophical realization of its own rationality as the explaining "truth" of everything. Once it has achieved this realization, the mind can then go on to frame for itself a systematic round of pure notions, a logic, a theory of nature, and a theory of mind, all formed and molded in the medium of pure thought. But though Hegel may *say* that the course of the *Phenomenology* is necessary, a paradigm for all minds to follow, he in fact jumps hither and yon among the most varied attitudes and historical phases, among all of which he discerns the most far-fetched and fascinating connections. The *Phenomenology* is more to be admired for its poetic vividness and for its superb empirical richness than for its *a priori* consequence.

The *Phenomenology* begins with a *Vorrede* or Preface of great but difficult beauty, where Hegel sets forth the nature of the "scientific" dialectic that he hopes to develop, contrasts it with the thought of his contemporaries, and then sketches the portrait of the sole actor in the ensuing drama: rational mind or spirit. Of this, he beautifully says:

> The living Substance is further than Being, which is in truth *Subject*, or, what is the same, which is truly actual only in so far as it is the movement of positing itself, or the mediation of a becoming-other-than-self with self. It is, as Subject, the pure, *simple negativity*, and in this fashion the rending apart of what is simple or a doubling of opposed factors, which again is a denial of this indifferent diversity and of its contrariety. Only this *self-reinstating* identity, or this reflection-into-self in other-being — not an *initial* unity as such, nor anything *immediate* as such — is the True. It is the becoming of itself, the circle which presupposes its end as its goal and as its beginning, and which is only actual through being carried out and in its End. . . . We must say of the Absolute that it is essentially a *result*, that it only is at the *end* what it is in truth.[13]

This absolute result the *Phenomenology* reaches in three dialectical phases: (A) Consciousness, in which the mind confronts objects seemingly quite alien to itself; (B) Self-consciousness, in which the mind faces objects which are mirror-images of itself, other minds, members of a common society; and finally (C) Reason, where mind more and more daringly and successfully unmasks the foreignness of things and comes to see in them nothing but the conditions of its own rational subjectivity. Divisions (A) and (B) are fairly simply subdivided, but Division (C), with which the *Phenomenology* is mainly concerned, has *four* major subdivisions: (AA) The Certainty and Truth of Reason; (BB) Mind or Spirit (*Geist*); (CC) Religion, and (DD) Absolute Knowledge or Philosophy. We shall briefly indicate the content and main turning-points of the above divisions.

In (A), consciousness, Hegel begins with what he calls sense-certainty, which is more or less like what Russell called "knowledge by acquaintance." Sense-certainty is the consciousness we have when we apprehend the "immediately given," without as yet attributing to it any character, nor connecting it with what may lie beyond. Such sense-certainty *purports* to be unfathomably rich in its content and irrefragable in its certainty, but a very small withdrawal of the mind to a higher vantage point reveals it to be neither. For one cannot say *what* is confronting one in sense-awareness without going beyond the immediate occasion, nor can its mute certainty survive the passing instant. Consciousness accepting its conceptual role in the face of the given, then becomes "sense-perception," which transforms

the given into a number of distinct things, having many distinct properties or aspects. The dialectical problem is now to reconcile the assumed underlying unity of the thing with its variety of aspects: one or other must go by the board. By an ineluctable movement, thought is forced beyond sense to the explanatory concepts beloved of the "scientific understanding," the third phase of consciousness: it pierces beneath to the unseen *forces* and *laws* of which the sensible world is taken to be the "outward expression." Hegel now takes one of his most characteristic steps. When the world of sense has been whittled away into a web of interlocking scientific abstractions, the dialectical observer suddenly sees that what lay behind the things of sense always really was the mind itself — that is, the mind *masquerading* as gravitation, electricity, etc. What is *implicit* in scientific understanding therefore becomes *explicit* in "social self-consciousness"; the mind now has as its object its own self, it becomes an "I that is a We, a We that is an I." Science, on Hegel's view, is a mere anticipation of social life: to be aware of mind obscurely illustrated in things is to be ready to see it, more clearly illustrated, in the behavior and discourse of intelligent beings.

In (B), self-consciousness, Hegel begins by giving a remarkable sketch of various primitive forms of social life: of the life-and-death struggle where the humbling vision of a rival consciousness is inseparable from the impulse to wipe it out, which develops into the milder manifestations of class-consciousness, of lordship and serfdom, in which the "other person" is allowed to survive but becomes demoted to permanent inferiority. Hegel is perceptive in realizing how the deeper rational consciousness of ourselves as involving both a ruling (or rational) and a subjected (or nonrational) function presupposes the primitive division of persons into the ascendant and the dependent, and the crude Nazi concepts that attend on this division. It is the conflation of master and slave into the single individual's own self-consciousness to which the dialectic next turns: Hegel studies in masterly fashion the three historical attitudes of the Stoic, the Skeptic, and the other-worldly Christian. Stoicism represents that boundless inward freedom of rational subjectivity which is *indifferent* to variations of status: for Stoicism, Aurelius the Emperor and Epictetus the poor slave are as one. But the dialectical observer sees the *lack of all content* in this abstract Stoic reasonableness, a lack of content that becomes explicit in the sheer *negativism* of Skepticism, with its repudiation of all theoretical and practical commitments. But the dialectical observer again sees the secret *duplicity* of this skeptical negativism, since the Skeptic remains, in his nonphilosophical dealings, committed both to common sense and morality. This duplicity then becomes fully explicit in the unhappy *two-world* consciousness of medieval Christendom, with its contrast between the qresent transitory unreasonable world (in which a man's "self" is placed), and the unchangeable reasonable divine world *yonder* (*jenseits*), with which man's only links are the arbitrary and mysterious outpourings of *sacramental grace*. In this elaborate self-humiliation — *mea culpa, mea culpa, mea maxima culpa* — the dialectical observer, however, sees an element of *pretence*: the Unchangeable and Divine is not really so alien to the corrupt sinner as he gives it out to be. The God before whom the divided consciousness prostrates itself, and which it projects into an extreme metaphysical or historical remoteness, is really that divided consciousness's implicit rationality, since this God can in the last resort demand nothing that is not true or good. The rational post-Reformation consciousness therefore simply makes explicit the unity between the rational and the worldly that the divided Catholic consciousness sacramentally symbolizes. It is to the nondualistic post-Renaissance consciousness that the dialectic accordingly passes.

Reason, the third major phase studied in the *Phenomenology*, is said by Hegel to be characterized by "idealism," by which he does not, however, mean an idealism like that of Berkeley, which merely affirms all things to be "my idea" while leaving their content otherwise unaltered: it rather means a mood of unbounded *self-confidence* in the rational penetrability of the world. "The mind," says Hegel, "first merely divining itself in the reality, or only in a general way knowing it to be its *own*, proceeds in this sense to take general possession of the property assured to it, and plants the sign of its sovereignty on every height and depth." In the following section (AA), entitled "The Certainty and Truth of Reason," Hegel first deals with various forms of rational *observation*, each of which represents an *appropriation* by mind of the content of the environing world. This appropriation begins with the classification and description of the inorganic, rises to the classification of organisms, passes on to the introspective classifications of empirical psychology, and ends up with two kinds of psycho-physical observation, greatly vaunted in Hegel's time: the pseudo-science of physiognomy started by Lavater and the even more spurious science of phrenology originated by Gall. Hegel writes lengthily and devastatingly about phrenology, and then uses it to pass by a *tour de force* to certain rudimentary forms of *ethical* life. The phrenologist, he tells us, who reduces all mind to a configuration of the skull-bones, is in a confused manner seeing that even skull-bones — i.e., all matter — express rational spirituality. What this vision implicitly portends is explicitly stated in the rich reality of life in a social community, where the "other" is always another *person*, a sharer of common notions and ways of acting. This forms the content of a section entitled "The Realization of Rational Self-Consciousness Through Itself." Hegel does not here pass immediately to reason in the form of organized ethical life, but proceeds first to give a

remarkable series of studies of varying forms of *rational egoism*, true products of the romantic age in which he lived. There is "Pleasure and Necessity," a study of the paradoxes and dilemmas of pure hedonism; "The Law of the Heart and the Madness of Self-conceit," a study of a Bohemian mood associated with Rousseau and his *Nouvelle Héloïse*; and finally "Virtue and the Way of the World," a study of romantic moralism, of a sort not unknown in the Victorian Age but quite unknown in the present. This leads on to a third subsection enigmatically called "Individuality which is real to and for itself," in which the first subdivision bears the still more enigmatic title of "The Spiritual Kingdom of Beasts, or the Affair itself." This last is a remarkable study of the secret interestedness of seeming disinterestedness, as instanced, for example, in the embittered wars of "unprejudiced" scholars. Hegel is then led on to consider two forms of ethical high-mindedness, one that puts forward detailed moral prescriptions and one that merely criticizes such prescriptions in a Kantian manner. The sections sketched have the complex internal interplay of a novel, pressed into the abstract mold of a philosophy.

In (BB), a section entitled "Mind" or "Spirit" (*Geist*), Hegel spirals in a complicated way from the primitive reasonableness, consisting in conforming to the laws and customs of one's own community, through a long consideration of "self-estranged," individualistic, "cultured" life, where traditional standards are questioned and where religion wages an embittered war with critical "enlightenment," to the purely inward reasonableness of the morality of conscience. What is important about this pattern is that Hegel here makes the ethics of social conformity dialectically prior — that is, *less* developed — than the ethics of inward conscientiousness, an order to be reversed in the later *Philosophy of Right*. Here conscience, torn, split, and inwardly contradictory, is a higher phenomenon than social conformity; there the contrary will be maintained. Hegel's study of the ethics of custom dwells interestingly on the unavoidable conflicts natural to a customary ethics, with brilliant examples drawn from Greek tragedy. The interest of the study of the battle between rationalistic enlightenment and religious faith lies in Hegel's view of the *mock* character of the whole conflict, the religious person really believing in the same sort of ultimate subjugation of the world to reason that the rationalist also affirms. The whole interchange between these antagonists is an elaborate *ignoratio elenchi*, the rationalistic party elaborately demolishing the *factual* truth of various religious propositions which the religious party never understood in this sense. For Hegel, the higher critics of the Enlightenment are the purifiers rather than the subverters of religion; in the deepest mysticism there should always be a Voltairean tinge. Hegel's treatment of conscientious morality is mainly interesting for the view that it is essential that consciences should *differ*, that they represent an inward, personal exercise of judgment that cannot by its nature be brought under rule. Hence the supreme state of conscientious morality is, for Hegel, not conformity, but tolerance, the forgiveness (*Verzeihung*) mutually accorded by men with totally different ways of life. It is at this point that moralistic conscientiousness passes over into religion, which represents precisely the profound rationality that can override even the most opposed and diverse human attitudes and vocations.

The section (CC) gives Hegel's dialectical treatment of religion, a treatment he was greatly to elaborate in the later lectures on the Philosophy of Religion. Here for the first time Hegel expounds his view of religion as a translation into the medium of "feeling" and "picture-thinking" of the philosophical truth that rational subjectivity is the final cause of everything. The religions of Persia, India, and Egypt, with their sensuous, perceptual, and geometrical emphases, are seen as the necessary precursors of what Hegel calls the "Art-Religion" of the Greeks, where the ideal of rational subjectivity, and its mastery over its "Other," finds a perfect sensuous embodiment in the marble form of the god. But the Greek god expresses this ideal in too perfect, too immediate a manner: it bears no trace of the anguish and labor of the sculptor, nor of the contrast between the ideal of perfect beauty and the collapsing civic life which is first inspired to struggle toward it. (Hegel believes that Greek art rose to its highest only when the city-state began to decay.) Yet, for the dialectical observer, both this contrast and this anguish are parts of the whole spiritual achievement, since rational harmony can be nothing without deep irrationalities to be overcome. It is in Christianity, the absolute or revealed religion, that one has the perfect imaginative embodiment of *all* aspects of the notion of rational subjectivity.

Christianity is the "revealed religion" *par excellence*, since, for it, the "eternal essence" or pure idea of rationality can be nothing unless revealed. As a mere abstraction or withdrawn ideal, it is nothing: it must be an ideal for *someone*, who, in so far as he thinks of it, must be "put" as different to it but who, as thinking of it and also loving it, does away with this difference. The begetting of the Son by the Father "before all worlds," and their reunion or mutual recognition in the Spirit merely express in religious language the factors necessarily present in rational subjectivity.

> We accordingly distinguish three aspects, the *Essence*, the *Being-for-self*, which is the other-being of the Essence and for which the Essence exists, and the *Being-for-self* or knowing itself *in the Other*. The Essence beholds only itself in its Being-for-self, it is in this externalization only with itself; the Being-for-self that excludes itself from the Essence is the *knowledge of its own Es-*

sence. It is the word, which being spoken externalizes the speaker and leaves him emptied, but which is as immediately apprehended, and has its being only in its self-apprehension. So that the distinctions that are made are just as immediately resolved as made, and as immediately made as resolved, and the True and Actual lies just in this circular movement.[14]

The Creation expresses the same necessity as the Begetting of the Son, only more concretely. It expresses the necessity that rationality, if it is not to be an abstraction, should be confronted with a multitude of brutally existent, mutually opposed, inert, unreflecting entities, which will provide it with a real "other," over which it can then win a real victory. And the creation of man represents the necessity that rational subjectivity should at first not be fully explicit, but should lie latent in the finite subject, whose particularity makes it just as possible to be irrational as rational. The fall of man represents that necessary presence of the irrational without which rationality could not be exercised; this is even more poignantly put by attributing wrath — irrationality — to God Himself. And the Incarnation of the Divine Man means the descent of rational subjectivity into the particularity of sense and determinate personal existence, without which it would be an abstraction, whereas the Death and Resurrection of the same Divine Man signify the triumphant re-emergence of rational subjectivity, having overcome and reduced to communicable universals everything that was particular and sensuous. The Christian story, therefore, merely projects on to an imaginative screen the timeless schisms and reintegrations involved in rational self-consciousness. This timeless sense becomes evident even to the religious consciousness when its God-Man loses His sensuous immediacy, and survives only in the memory and worship of the religious community. The Word, on Hegel's view, is more truly incarnate in the worshipping Church than it ever was in Galilee. All this might seem, from an obdurate Kierkegaardian viewpoint, to represent no more than a gross "logicization" of Christianity; with equal justice it might be looked on as a profoundly illuminating Christianization of logic. Certainly we understand the source and significance of Hegel's philosophy much better when we have studied his comments on Christianity.

In (DD), the final sub-section of Reason, the *Phenomenology* passes on from religion to philosophy. The overreaching presence of rational subjectivity, even in what seemed most alien to it, and which religion grasped in an externalized, imaginative form, rational subjectivity now sees in its *own* form, in the form of notions, or in the form of "self." It becomes clear that the object, the "other," in whatsoever guise it may make its appearance, exists only to be taken up into rational subjectivity and is, in this sense, one with it. At the same time, rational subjectivity looks understandingly back on the whole development it has undergone; the phenomenological observer is at last one with the actual experient. This development is seen, not as a personal history, but as a timelessly necessary sequence of stages; in a sense philosophy must abolish time.* Rational subjectivity will now also look back upon, and sum up, various *philosophical* points of view that have led up to its accomplished self — that is, the various subjectively oriented philosophies from Descartes to Hegel. Having summed up all these, it must then press onward to the purely notional treatment of categories and forms of being in which the system proper will consist. The *Phenomenology* accordingly ends with a programmatic forecast of the ensuing system.

Hegel's Logic

HEGEL's Logic exists in two expositions: that of the earlier *Science of Logic*, the occupation of Hegel's years as a schoolmaster at Nuremberg, and the so-called "Lesser" *Logic*, which forms the first part of the Hegelian *Encyclopaedia*. This Encyclopedia *Logic*, even with the valuable Additions (*Zusätze*) from Hegel's lectures, is a work so condensed as to be unintelligible without the longer book. In many ways, however, it is the superior exposition, and has also been translated with some beauty. We shall follow it mainly in the ensuing sketch.

Hegel's Logic purports to be the study of the pure Idea, or the Idea dealt with in the abstract medium of thought. It presents a series of pure categories or "thought-determinations" in terms of which reality may be characterized; these range from "being," the most abstract and empty of all, to the "absolute idea," the notion of rational subjectivity as the explanatory "truth" of everything. This series of categories is dialectical — in other words, it moves in a steady sequence of triads forming larger triads, from concepts that manifest some explanatory flaw when surveyed from a higher vantage point, to concepts less and less inadequate, until a crowning phase is reached. After this the series continues to develop, but no longer as pure logic; the notions it deals with — for example, inertia, sensation, etc. — are much too "concrete" to count as categories. The whole development of the Logic is therefore entirely *abstract*; it is, as Hegel says, "the realm of shadows, the world of simple essences freed from all sensuous concretion."[15] If Hegel sometimes calls it a *concrete* development, this refers only to its increasing richness of aspects and to its necessary relation to possible application. It is a mere concession to

picture-thought when the realm of shadows is identified with the Creator-God of religion.

The Logic is triadically divided into (A) the Doctrine of Being, which deals with categories involving only what is superficially or immediately "there," and not with anything unmanifest; (B) the Doctrine of Essence, involving always an antithesis between what is outwardly manifest and what is "deeper down" and essential; and (C) the Doctrine of the Notion, where this contrast between surface and depth has been superseded and where indwelling universals explain everything. We shall now try to give some clearer indication of the content and pattern of these three divisions.

THE DOCTRINE OF BEING

The Logic begins with the notion of pure being, the notion of something as being merely "there," while nothing more is said of it or predicated of it. It corresponds on the plane of thought to the dumb confrontations of sense-acquaintance, in which *something* stands indubitably before us, but something which as yet is we know not what. Modern logic may find no place in its schedules for such a direct acknowledgment of being, but this is a fault of that logic, not of Hegel's treatment. Hegel holds that we must begin our study of categories with this simple notion, since, of all notions, it is the most abstract; everything whatever, when emptied of determinate content, or not as yet given it, becomes the abstraction of a mere *ens*, of which no more is predicable. As used in ordinary thought, this simple notion of entity is of course quite innocuous; it is a mere preliminary to further characterization. But the metaphysical understanding "fixes" the notion in an unwarrantable manner in order to provoke dialectical comment.

It is plain, in fact, that although this notion of mere entity purports to be something wholly different from the opposed notion of absolute nonentity or nothing, it affords no purchase for this distinction. The Eleatic *eon*, of which we cannot but think, differs in no assignable particular from its contrary *mē eon*, of which we cannot think at all. As metaphysical abstractions, the two notions are indistinguishable; we must therefore progress to some notion *not* so metaphysically abstract. Such a notion Hegel first finds in "becoming," a notion that arises dialectically when we reflect on the *transition* between our two previous notions: the mere being that could not be kept apart from, and therefore *passed over* into, nonentity, and the nonentity which similarly passed over into being. (This becoming or passage is, of course, the mere notional blue-print of becoming *in time*.) But the dialectical commentator finds logical instability as well as emptiness in this latter notion, and accordingly passes to the stabler notion of "being determinate" (or *Dasein*), a being thought of as one with a certain quality or deter-

* This purely philosophical abolition of time is, of course, quite different from the real abolition believed in by Mc-Taggart and certain other Hegelians.

mination, and which pertains to a *Something* set off by its quality from otherwise qualified somethings. In this whole section Hegel has abolished the Eleatic ontology, much as Plato did in the *Sophist*. That which is, if it is to be conceived at all, *must* manifest qualitative contrast, and this surely is an acceptable conclusion.

Being determinate is now said by Hegel to lead on to an "infinite qualitative progression." The transition is difficult, and its character can only be indicated. Each determinate entity seems to be of the quality it is *without* regard to the qualities that other determinate entities exhibit. The dialectical observer sees, however, that each qualified entity *depends* for its quality on the other qualified entities which hem it in and show it up, and that it has, in a sense, *these others within itself*, as conditions of its own determinateness. This implicit presence of *all* qualities in each determinate entity then becomes explicit in the category of "*Alteration.*" Things alter in quality because their nature secretly includes all other qualitative possibilities. And such alteration is in principle indefinite or infinite — a step that may present difficulty — no determinate form of being can be envisaged to which some contrasting other will not forthwith appear. This unending reference of each determinate form of being to ever other contrasting forms is said by Hegel to be a case of the "*bad infinite.*" It is bad because the dialectical observer can discern a conflict in it: (1) it always purports to go beyond any and every finite determination; (2) it never, in effect, goes beyond any and every finite determination, but merely exchanges one for another.

By a mere reversal of notional perspective, the dialectical observer can, however, see in the bad infinity something that deserves to be called "truly infinite": the infinitude of the *freely ranging variable*, that which must always have *some* finite value or other but which is not bound down to any *one* such value. *Plus ça change, plus c'est la même chose* is the maxim for this kind of infinite: it is the infinity of that which remains itself despite boundless variability. In a low form, it is seen in the indefinite applicability of a variable or formula like a/b or $a = 2y$; in a high form it is seen in the self-conscious subject that remains itself despite indefinite change in content. Such true infinity is then renamed by Hegel "being-for-self" and is said to be the synthesis of pure being and being determinate.

In the notion of being-for-self, qualitative distinctions have been set aside or ignored: each thing that is for self has the same free variability as any other and is therefore a mere *unit*, something numerically, but not qualitatively, distinct from other units. This, says Hegel, is the sort of abstraction that has inspired many sorts of physical and metaphysical *atomism*; to us the *Tractatus* of Wittgenstein, with its "colorless" simple objects capable of any combination, comes most readily to mind. But the di-

alectical observer sees in this conceptual situation the germs of the new categories of "*quantity.*" For the rigid distinctness of units, for which no ground of distinction is postulated, is in effect *no* difference. The units cannot be held apart; they melt into each other, and their bounding lines become arbitrary. We therefore move to the categories of pure quantity, where discreteness of units always presupposes underlying continuity, and continuity possible discreteness, and where, instead of rigidly distinct units, we have something that can be increased or decreased without limit, and without affecting basic character.

The dialectical development of quantity follows much the same lines as the previous development from being to being determinate, and from being determinate to being-for-self. If abstract being is nothing except as further determined to being this or that, so pure quantity is nothing except as determined to this or that definite "*quantum.*" And as being determinate necessarily alters into a bad infinitude of qualitative states, so does determinate quantity necessarily pass into a "*bad infinite quantitative progression.*" It is, says Hegel, the nature of quantity to "push on" beyond *any* definite limit, while nonetheless never transcending *all* such limits. This sort of endless passing beyond barriers, and piling of Pelion upon Ossa, may seem "awful" to the understanding; but reason sees in it nothing but an "awful wearisomeness" (Wallace's happy rendering.) And just as the bad infinity of qualitative alteration is resolved in the true infinity of being-for-self, so is the bad quantitative infinity resolved in the true infinity of the "*quantitative ratio,*" a relation among quantities which can preserve its identity despite boundless variation of those quantities. The ratio 1/2 is, for example, illustrated by 2 : 4, 3 : 6, 4 : 8, and so on, and concentrates a whole infinite progression in a nutshell.

The Doctrine of Being ends with an important, historically influential section on "measure." A measure is a qualitative quantum, a fixed set of ratios or proportions upon which some definite quality is thought of as being founded. To many small variations of ratio, no qualitative variations correspond, in the same way that a slight lengthening or thinning of a feature will not change a man's general expression, although plastic surgery will. Hegel now develops the interesting notion of a "*nodal line of measure relations,*" in which long ranges of variation of quantitative ratio which do *not* involve qualitative changes suddenly pass over dramatic "nodes" where there is a temporary breakdown of measure-relations and their supervenient qualities, followed by the emergence of *new* measure-relations and *novel* qualities. Of this famous "transition from quantity into quality," Hegel gives numerous examples: (1) the transition from the solid through the liquid to the gaseous state as temperature increases; (2) the sudden transitions from tone to tone as strings are lengthened or shortened; (3) the sudden change from being "thin on top" to being bald, or from being a number of grains to being a heap; (4) changes in ethical rating of behavior from "avarice" through "good economy" to "prodigality"; (5) changes in a state's constitution and manner of life with variations in population and size of territory. In all these cases, Hegel *confounds* instances where the relation of qualitative to quantitative variations is interestingly *logical*, as in the case of baldness and the grains, and cases where the relation is merely *empirical*, as in the relation of sensible qualities to physical ratios. Hegel's doctrine has been much made use of by the Marxists in their account of the way in which small social changes at length lead to major revolutions; such doctrines derive rather from what is confused in Hegel's doctrine than from what is logically important.

The nodal line of measures ends, however, in the same bad infinite progression as did the qualitative and quantitative infinite progressions. The dialectical commentator now seeks light in a wholly different direction. He abandons the purely descriptive, surface approach, characteristic alike of our qualitative and quantitative notions. He is to plunge beneath the surface of appearance, into the new dimension of "substrates" and "essences."

THE DOCTRINE OF ESSENCE

In the Doctrine of *Essence*, Hegel deals with categories involving a distinction between "surface" and "inner nature," between the qualities and quantities that are overtly shown and the unmanifest laws, dispositions, substrates, etc., that condition such a manifestation. Hegel rightly holds that thought cannot master the empirically given without postulating much that is not palpably there. These categories of essence are all spoken in terms of "positedness" (*Gesetztsein*) and "reflection." They occur in pairs, and are significant only in their mutual bearing; so they may be said to be "posited" by one another, or to reflect light into one another. If the surface phenomena reflect or "posit" a dispositional essence, this dispositional essence itself reflects upon or "posits" appropriate surface phenomena.

The initial concept in essence, corresponding to that of pure being in the field of being, is that of "*identity*." Identity is the *deeper* kind of being that can, by its nature, be *differently* shown in varying actual or imaginary circumstances. It is not the identity of formal logic so much as the identity of Locke and Hume. Such identity "reflects into" or "posits" the opposed category of "*difference*"; there cannot, in Hegel's use, be identities that are not manifest in different forms, nor different forms that do not manifest *some* underlying identity. Hegel speaks as do ordinary persons, who draw no clear distinction between numerical and specific identity, or between difference of individuals and difference of aspect.

The dialectic now develops by drawing out the hidden implications of the notion of difference. At first this takes the form of mere "diversity", where the different things are taken as being independent of, and quite indifferent to, each other. "I am a human being, and around me are air, water, animals, and all sorts of things. Everything is thus put outside of every other." But the dialectical observer sees that this mutual indifference can be only a sham, that each different form of the same thing only is what it is by virtue of its contrast with the other forms. When this comment is written into his first-order thought, he rises to the new category of "opposition" (*Gegensatz*), of which contradiction (*Widerspruch*) is the most extreme form. The things or states of the world are now thought of as representing opposed or contradictory forms of the same underlying essence. ("Contradiction" has for Hegel the ordinary, rather than the formal-logical meaning.)

By an extreme *tour de force*, Hegel now moves to the logical relation of the "ground" to the "grounded." The dialectical observer sees that each opposed form in which an essence reveals itself, involves "totality" — in other words, they involve, in a sense, *both* themselves and their opposites. Thus, positive electricity so involves its opposite (negative electricity) and negative electricity, its opposite (positive electricity) that both are in effect equipollent; each stages the *whole* conflict in itself. This, however, is precisely what we mean by the relation of a necessary and sufficient ground to the thing grounded by it, a case where, according to Hegel, "Grounded and Ground are one and the same content, their difference being the merely formal difference of simple relation to self and of mediation or positedness." From a view of the world as a mere *diversity* of forms, we have therefore progressed, by way of a view of it as a great *battleground* of opposed forms, to a view of it as a system of *mutually grounded* forms, each having the others (or some of them) as a necessary background. In this grounded, contextual view of the world, we apply the new category of "*existence*." Existent things "form a world of mutual dependence and an unending connection of Grounds and Grounded. The Grounds are themselves existents, and the existents are both Grounds and grounded in many directions." In essence's development from identity to ground, Hegel treats, on the side, the logical laws of identity, noncontradiction, excluded middle, sufficient ground, and the Leibnizian identity of indiscernibles. He contrasts the *formal* interpretation of these laws, acceptable only to the diremptive understanding, with more fluid, rational interpretations according to which they are only half-truths. Carefully read, Hegel's statements are valuable rather than monstrous.

The dialectical observer now picks on the notion

of a *"thing"* as a salient example of existence or grounded being. This thing emerges when we stress the "reflection-into-self" — that is, the self-relatedness — of the grounded existent. A thing is in this aspect something that has being in its own right and which *includes* its whole grounding context in its essence. But a thing must also be thought of as having a reflection-into-other-things about it, or a necessary relativity to them, by virtue of which it may be said to have *"properties"* that are not wholly one with its being. The relation of an existent thing to its properties differs from that of a mere *ens* to its characteristic quality: a thing can possess or lose properties, whereas an *ens* vanishes if its quality changes. Once, however, a thing's properties are recognized as being *jointly* dependent on that thing and other things, they become loosened from their allegiance to that thing, and to make explicit this looseness is to recur to the contemporary notion of "matters," or the concept of electricity, temperature, odor, and so on, as queer stuffs or fluids capable of migrating from thing to thing. Such "matters" readily take revenge on the things to which they first owed allegiance, since they are themselves thinglike, they demote the thing to a mere aggregate of "matters," a common locus of interpenetrating charges, odors, calorific and frigorific fluids, etc. The category of the thing is accordingly said to "break down," as not reconciling the self-dependent unity of the thing with the multitude of its properties or "matters." This breakdown being acknowledged, we advance to the notion of "phenomenal being" (*Erscheinung*) — that is, to the notion of "an indefinite multiplicity of existents, whose being is purely mediation, and which do not accordingly rest on themselves but have validity only as moments." In phenomenal being, everything takes in everything else's washing, and *is* no more than this traffic.

Concerning phenomenal being, Hegel's most interesting discussion is of the three forms of "essential relationship" (*Verhältnis*): (1) The Whole and its Parts; (2) Force and its Expression; and (3) Inward and Outward. In the first, we have a form of thought where it is not clear *which* is the unseen explanatory essence and *which* the manifest datum to be explained. We tend *both* to make the whole the datum in which the parts are merely postulated, and the parts the datum for which the whole is postulated. However we proceed, we become involved in contradictions. The diremption into parts dissolves the whole, whereas the bringing of the parts together ruins them as parts. The dialectical observer now sees how these defects may be removed in the relation of a force to its expression, since a force is *not* thought of as being dissolved or lost in its expressions, but as active and present in them. The dialectical observer notes, however, the imperfect identity between a force and its expression which is shown by the fact that the former is not thought of as *by itself*

capable of going over into the latter, but as needing *conditions* that will *solicit* it from without. He therefore passes on to the more satisfactory relation of the *inward* to the *outward*, where a thing's essence is thought of as *including* all the conditions that might stimulate it into functioning in various ways, so that it *is* able to function in those ways and cannot lay claim to unrealized capacities to which unkind circumstances have denied expression. Deeply considered, the matters of fact in this world simply are *because* they are: the grounding conditions that lead up to them only do so *because they are, in essence, the things themselves*. Hegel is here advancing something like a coherent view of the existent world, although he seems to concentrate the whole universe of conditions into its most insignificant part rather than to lose the latter, Spinozistically, in the former. The view of things now reached is that of the new category of actuality (*Wirklichkeit*).

Hegel relates the notion of actuality to the three modal notions of "possibility," "contingency," and "necessity." The actual is not the self-contradictory concept of the merely possible, that which only *seems* possible because it is superficially self-consistent, and has been cut adrift from its complement of conditions. The actual involves, not merely the *inward* possibility of self-consistency, but also the complete set of *external* conditions without which it would be *really* impossible, and which may therefore be called its *real* possibility. In the same way, the actual is not the merely contingent, that which is, but which could possibly *not* have been. It is to be noted that Hegel *does* allot a considerable role to such pure contingency on the "surface" of nature: he holds it to be wrong and unphilosophical to think that everything can be given a fully necessitating explanation. But such purely contingent things are, from the Hegelian viewpoint, *incompletely actual*, a point to be remembered in interpreting the famous sentence, "The Actual is the Rational, and the Rational the Actual." The actual is, however, declared to be the "absolutely necessary," in the sense that, though demanding countless seemingly external conditions, it nonetheless embraces all these in its "notion" and so is, in a sense, *causa sui* — self-produced.

Hegel now applies the notion of the absolutely necessary to the three Kantian categories of substance and accident, cause and effect, and reciprocal interaction. The absolutely necessary is thought of first as the one Spinozistic substance whose nature is the *power* mediating the connection of its modes. But since it is wholly present in each of these modes, the dialectical observer can also see it as an interaction of many independent, mutually influencing substances, each being active or passive in relation to the others. This pluralistic, causal vision, involving as it does the most complete mutual adjustment among the interacting substances, leads on, however, to the vision of them as forming a sort of pre-established harmony, a mutual conspiracy, in which each substance exists merely to evoke and be evoked by the other substance so that all form a system which is as much *one* as many. (Hegel's version of *Wechselwirkung* is not quite the same as Kant's.)

The dialectical observer now takes a momentous step: he sees the implied "truth" of mutual necessitation to be simply "freedom." Each substance in provoking and being provoked by all the others is in reality only giving rein to its own nature. "It then appears that the members linked to one another are not really foreign to each other, but only elements of one whole, each of them in its connection with the others being, as it were, at home with and combining with itself." When what is here implicit is made fully explicit, we pass from the categories of essence to those of the "notion," where, instead of the complex interrelations of mutually necessitating factors, we have the freely developing self-differentiation of a single reality.

THE DOCTRINE OF THE NOTION

Thought at the "notional" level is said to be distinct from thought at the levels of essence and being owing to its thoroughgoing *totality*: each of the "moments" distinguished in a notion involves all the others and so is in a sense the *whole* notion. The development of a notion is also not the straight passage from one thought-position to the next that we met in the sphere of being, nor the ordered swing from correlative to correlative that we encountered in the sphere of essence. It is, rather, as if the same sentence were repeated again and again with a varying emphasis so as to give rise to an ever richer understanding. The notion of anything is, if one likes, its essence, but it is no longer opposed to its surface immediacy, nor is it provoked into manifestation from without. And while it is, from one point of view, a phase of subjective life, it is also, from another point of view, the indwelling "form" of the object. What is, of course, here in question in not any *particular* notion or thought-pattern, but the descriptive peculiarity of *a* notion of thought-pattern as such.

Thought at the notional level is an inseparable unity of three distinct moments: "universality" (*Allgemeinheit*), "specificity" or "particularity" (*Besonderheit*), and "individuality" (*Einzelnheit*). To form a notion like "man" is essentially to distinguish something *universal* or *common*, but it is also to be willing to *specify* this universal in a variety of ways and to *apply* both universal and specifications to definite *individual cases*. Only in this absolute triunity can the three functions of the notion be anything. The diremptive understanding tries to make nonsense of the notion by cutting off its three moments from each other, but this nonsense shows itself in the fact that an aspect isolated so instantly becomes the whole notion. Thus, an isolated universal really is a sort of individual, and an isolated individual must have form-*copies* in itself. The notion of reason is said to be self-specifying and self-individualizing — in other words, it is part of its nature to have specific and individual differentiations — and there is no problem of "how it comes by them." Hegel's famous doctrine of the "concrete universal" amounts to little more than a thoroughly acceptable rejection of any Platonic chorismus between the genus, the species, and the individual instance. It does not imply that the detail of species and individuals can be "read off" from a study of the abstract universal.

The dialectical observer now sees in the distinct, but closely combined, notional aspects of the universal, the species, and the individual the possibility of a fascinating range of notional forms, of "*judgments*" in which the distinctness of the moments is mainly emphasized — and of "*syllogisms*" where the stress is rather upon their union. Hegel does not think of these judgments and syllogisms as merely subjective forms; like their component notions they are operative in the world. And Hegel arranges them in a remarkable dialectical series beginning with judgments and syllogisms, where the relations among universal, species, and individuals are external, plausible, and contingent, and rising to judgments and syllogisms where the relationship is one of complete coincidence and absolute necessity. Thus, in the realm of the judgment, we start off with merely factual assertions like "This wall is green," where subject and predicate have the most peripheral of overlaps and end with critical value-judgment. As an example, take the assertion "*Hamlet*, by such and such features of its structure, is a magnificent tragedy." Here, the subject is approved as conforming to a standard or notion intrinsic and peculiar to itself and is therefore merely declared, with an accompaniment of delight, to be what it is. (As a theory of value-judgments, this is certainly interesting.) In the same way, syllogisms start with the mere linkage of contingent, plausible premises, leading to conclusions lightly controverted — the inference, for example, that the moon must fall on the earth since it is an unsupported body — and end with syllogisms like the disjunctive, where a universal first deploys itself in its full range of species in order to gain a clinching hold on the individual case. In this part of the Logic, Hegel gives a remarkable review and reinterpretation of the patterns of formal logic, a review that inspired the two great logics of Bosanquet and Bradley.

The dialectical observer now takes a remarkable step: he sees in the complete union of the individual, the species, and the genus, to which judgment and syllogism have alike worked up, the new category of the "*object*". The factors of the notion have been shown to be the same totality differently stressed; and this totality simply is the object. The object here introduced seems to be the notion merely seen in an inverted perspective. If the notion can be regarded as universality that cannot *but* be specified and individualized, the object, inversely, is the individual essentially exemplifying what is specific and generic. Objectivity is "immediacy," but it is a sort of immediacy into which all sorts of conceptual meanings and their syllogistic relations have been concentrated. The object is further said by Hegel, for reasons not wholly clear, to reveal itself both as one *total* object or world and also to break itself up into many subordinate objects, each similarly divided. Objects and worlds now work themselves out in the three ascending phases of "mechanism, "chemism," and "teleology."

To think of objects most simply is to think of them mechanically — that is, as being mere *aggregates* of subordinate objects — and as themselves forming similar aggregates, the implication of the term "aggregate" being that objects are as such indifferently and externally assembled. This results in their character being merely the result of such inner aggregation, whereas their power to act involves no spontaneity but depends wholly on external or internal *pushes*. Such "pure mechanism" the dialectical observer sees to be self-contradictory, since it refers the explanation of movement even further back, and since the supposedly independent objects show themselves to be completely dependent on others both for their character and behavior. The observer is therefore moved to think of objects *chemically* — as having a *measure* of independence — but also as having a necessary *bias* or *affinity* toward each other. Objects chemically conceived will be thought of as necessarily passing from states in which *unity* is asserted at the expense of separateness (states of chemical neutrality), to states in which *separateness* is asserted at the cost of unity (states of chemical isolation). But since neither state is thought of as being more fundamental than the other, this passage can only be a perpetual oscillation, and it can only be external accident that can put the chemical objects in either state. The dialectical observer now sees that the negation of externality half-achieved in chemism is fully achieved in the notion of "end" or "final cause": here an object can make use of other objects to bring itself about, and can so rise to genuine independence.

Teleological thinking is, in the first instance, *finite* in character. It explains behavior in terms of an end which is *subjective*, in as much as it is the end of a particular mind or organism, having a definite contingent content, and related to an external objective situation. The situation is in a state F, it can be brought to the state G by the means M, and the "subjective end" is precisely that it should be brought from F to G by way of M. In such finite teleology, the end is such that it naturally lays hold of the appropriate means, but the operation of the means in realizing the end is *wholly mechanical*: the subject presses the button, as it were, and the nonpurposive machinery does the rest. Such finite teleology is, accordingly, not completely explanatory, and it has the further defect of leading to a bad infinity. For each finite end, once realized, becomes a mere situational object or means, which must be made use of in a new teleological process.

The dialectical observer now resolves this bad infinity by making the end "truly infinite," and by identifying it, not with any particular content, *but with purposive activity as such*, whereas all finite ends, and the means adopted to realize them, become merely the necessary conditions of such purposive activity. Such purposive activity becomes an "end-in-itself", a sort of game played for various finite mock goals, which is accordingly *always* fulfilled, whatever the variation of such finite goals and means. "The Good, and absolutely Good, is eternally accomplishing itself in the world: and the result is that it need not wait upon us, but is already by implication, as well as in full actuality, accomplished." With this step, the dialectic reaches the *Idea*, which is simply that organizing purposiveness for which the whole world exists to make possible. This Idea is "*truth*" or the "*true*," in the special Hegelian sense of a conformity of an object to its notion, for, seen in the perspective of infinite teleology, *all* things conform to their notion. The Idea, Hegel tells us, is what religion envisages when it imagines everything in the world to be dominated by the Divine Providence.

The Idea is now developed in three forms: one "immediate," the Idea as life, one duplex and "reflective," the Idea as knowledge and will, and one absolute, the Idea as the final unity of the subjective and the objective. In life we see organizing purposiveness specified in a number of distinct functions and individualized in one concrete organism: it manifests an "absolute negativity" by virtue of which it can vary its form and materials without loss of identity. But since it has this "absolute negativity" only in "immediate" form, there are limits to its free variability: the organism is mortal and dies. The dialectical observer now sees the idea more stably incarnated in the forms of knowledge and will. In knowledge, the subject seeks to dominate the objective world by swathing it in an ever closer web of definitions and theorems; it cannot, however, quite remove the crude "givenness" of empirical fact. In will, the subject seeks to remold the object practically, encountering only *one* difficulty: the object cannot ever *perfectly* conform to the demands of the subject if the latter's remolding activity is to continue. But when it is seen that the object's partial recalcitrance to the mind is demanded by mind's own rational activity, such recalcitrance becomes, by a change of perspective, the most perfect conformity between the mind and its object. This and this only is the point that Fichte failed to see. To realize it is to reach the Absolute Idea.

Hegel winds up by saying that there is nothing at all to contemplate in his Absolute Idea beyond (1) the whole system of categories of which it represents the final development, and (2) the characteristic dialectical method by means of which that system has been developed. To see the Absolute is merely to *understand* the nature of the philosophy that one has so far been engaged in.

From the Absolute Idea, the dialectical observer now advances to the realm of nature by the simple expedient of *abandoning the abstraction* within which the Logic has run its course. This transition is made in somewhat obfuscating language: the idea is said to "let itself freely go" or to "release its specificity" in the forms of nature. But we are told further that the reason *why* the universal thus determines itself, why the infinite becomes finite, or why God creates a world (the three questions are equated) is simply that "God as an abstraction is not the true God."[16] In other words, the abstract categories of the Logic have sense only as applied to the concrete detail of nature and mind, in which detail there must be much that is, rationally speaking, arbitrary, and whose postulation can accordingly be said to be, in a mythic sense, "free."

Hegel's Philosophies of Nature and Mind

ONLY the briefest sketch can now be given of the remaining parts of Hegel's system: (A) the Philosophy of Nature; (B) the Philosophy of Subjective Mind; (C) the Philosophy of Objective Mind; and (D) the Philosophy of Absolute Mind.

In (A), the Philosophy of Nature, the dialectical observer lets his eyes run over nature as the necessary "other" of mind, which, being thus other, is in every respect most completely unmindlike, since it is characterized throughout by the most extreme *externality* among its phases, of which space and time are the accomplished illustration. The dialectical observer then sees the forms of nature arrange themselves in an ascending series: from those in which mutual externality is most salient through forms in which there is something like a "field-unity" overriding this externality until we rise to the almost mindlike unity of the organism. The dialectic proceeds from *Mechanics*, covering such topics as space and time, matter, motion, gravity, and planetary dynamics, through *Physics*, covering such topics as the elements, cohesion, sound, heat, electricity, magnetism, and chemical interaction, to *Organics*, with its three divisions of the geological, the botanical, and the zoological.

Hegel's Philosophy of Nature is, in the best sense of the word, a "dialectical materialism" — that is, a dialectical passage from unorganized dispersed materiality to the complete organization and concentrated unity of the organic and the mental. And it is a genuine materialism, since Hegel does not think that nature is the product of a pre-existent mind but that it antedated all mind in time. There were, Hegel admits, long geological ages when there was neither life nor mind in the world.[17] Teleologically, mind may come first, but temporally it comes last. And in filling in the detail of the *Naturphilosophie*, Hegel meticulously cites the findings of contemporary science, which his philosophical interpretations neither supplement nor distort. For example, the notion that he tried to prove that there could be only seven planets is a pure libel: he knew of both Uranus and the asteroids. His philosophical interpretations of nature are, in fact, mere assessments of their significance in relation to his key notion of rational subjectivity. In saying that light represents the *ideality* of matter in the same way that gravity represents its *reality*, he is neither undermining nor "deducing" gravity or light. It is strange that Hegel's Philosophy of Nature should have been so much maligned, for it is at least as interesting as the cosmology of Whitehead.

In (B), the Philosophy of Subjective Mind, the dialectical observer sees mind coming into being as the "truth" of nature and matter — the "truth," Hegel remarks, being that matter has no "truth." Nature was always mind "petrified" and implicit: the development of mind merely brings out what was hitherto latent. The development of subjective life is then studied in the three divisions of Anthropology, Phenomenology, and Psychology. In Anthropology mind appears in the form of "soul," not as yet detached from its bodily frame and circumstances and profoundly influenced by diurnal, seasonal, climatic, and similar variations. At this level, the whole of a subject's ambient world is condensed into a massive life of *feeling*, in which there is not yet any clear discrimination of characters, nor any opposition between thought and the world. At this level, too, there is much of that interpenetration and long-distance communion of minds, telepathy, clairvoyance, mesmerism, etc., which the understanding regards as "abnormal," but in which speculative reason merely sees an additional demonstration of the mastering "truth" of mind. In phenomenology, mind is seen as *conscious*, opposing itself alike to environing objects and to other conscious subjects. The dialectic here resumes some of the early sections of the *Phenomenology of Mind*. In Psychology, finally, mind emerges as rational: we have a more concrete study of the knowledge and will whose abstract profile has been sketched in the Logic. Possibly the most interesting section of this Psychology is the remarkable treatment of language.[18]

In (C) the Philosophy of Objective Mind, we have Hegel's legal, ethical, and political philosophy. The doctrine is briefly sketched in the *Encyclopaedia*, and more elaborately so in the *Philosophy of Right*. The dialectical observer is made to see mind, which has emancipated itself from nature, going forth to found a "second Nature," a world of its own, consisting of varied legal, ethical, and political institutions. The foundation of all this world is seen to be the "absolute negativity," the pure freedom of the rational will, the will that really seeks only itself and its own rationality but which has at least *this* positive relation to its impulses: it presupposes them as the raw material for its controlling, organizing activities. To exercise this pure will is to be a person, and the directive it issues is accordingly *that one should be a person oneself and should respect the like personality of others.* This abstract pattern of "right" is then followed out through the complex forms of property, contract, civil, and criminal torts, as studied in the classical jurisprudence, ending with a discussion of punishment. Hegel here unfolds his well-known theory of punishment as a sort of counter-assertion of a man's inherent rationality, which in some way cancels out the denial of rationality of which he, in his crime, has been guilty. In having momentarily injured his own rationality, a man must wish that his own injurious will should itself be injured.

This connection between transgression and injury must, however, remain imperfect and contingent as long as judge and criminal remain mutually external: it can lead only to the bad infinity of a vendetta among persons, none of whom acknowledges his rationality in the other. Such a bad infinity can be resolved only when judge and transgressor come together in the same person, which enables the dialectic to shift from the open forum of law to the inner forum of conscience. This shift does not, however, resolve all conflicts, for the conscientious morality that purports to be a man's inner rationality can do nothing to *prove* that it is so. Since it applies no uniform procedures, it can do nothing to secure general acceptance. Beyond emptily professing its sincerity, it can, in fact, do nothing to differentiate such sincerity from the most deplorable hypocrisy that merely masks wickedness with casuistry. Rationality must accordingly shift to a free acceptance of *Sittlichkeit*, the particular specification of the universal rule of right that is enshrined in the customs and institutions of the society to which a man, in fact, belongs. Only in this way can the rule of right be at once inward and personal yet freed from the abstractness that must lead to conflicting applications or developments. Hegel is not here *denying* the abstractly universal rule of right; he is only saying that it must be specified and individualized in some actual set of social usages.

The morality of *Sittlichkeit* is now studied in three ascending phases: (1) the morality of the closely-knit family, (2) the morality of the loosely-knit, individualistic civil community, and (3) the morality of state life. It is well known that, in his treatment of the last, Hegel gives what is very much a sketch of the prevailing Prussian Constitution. This led to the charge that his Philosophy of Right was not grown in the "garden of science" but on the "dunghill of servility." Hegel's "state idea," toward which he thinks of all historical constitutions as tending, involves first, a hereditary constitutional monarch, then, a monarchically appointed system of state officials, and finally, a bi-cameral legislature representing the landed, aristocratic "estate," on the one hand, and the commercial "estate," on the other. It is important to stress that, whatever its limitations, Hegel's state idea gives no countenance to authoritarian rule. Its monarch is bound both by the constitution and laws and by the advice of his officials. He is, in fact, merely there to give those last decisions without which the state idea would be emptily abstract. And constitution and laws are alike based on the respect for persons that constitutes Hegel's rule of right; this rule they may specify and apply but it cannot override. One cannot, for example, deny rights to certain individuals merely on account of race, religion, or other peculiarities. The State idea does indeed exclude any universal supranational authority since the universal, for Hegel, necessarily involves opposed forms. And it involves the possibility of clashes among such forms, in which each side has some show of justification, and it assigns positive value to such clashes. Nowhere, however, does Hegel condone mere aggression among states, any more than he allows tyranny within them. His state idea was not realized in imperial Germany, much less in Hitler's realm of horror.

The treatment of objective mind ends up with a section on universal history, which was elaborated in the popular *Lectures on the Philosophy of History.* Here the dialectical observer sees the whole of history as embodying the "Cunning of Reason," as revealing the gradual approximation to the "developed State Idea," through many imperfect democracies, despotisms, etc., and by way of countless individual arbitrarinesses and contingencies. This Philosophy of History represents a philosophical reassessment of the facts of history, as the Philosophy of Nature represents a reassessment of the facts of natural science; but in neither case does Hegel seek to fill in gaps, or to forecast or distort the facts. To criticize his treatment is to criticize his teleological interpretation in general.

In (D), the last part of the Philosophy of Mind, Hegel deals with "absolute mind," or mind aware of its own rational subjectivity as completely accounting for everything. This consciousness appears in the three forms of art, religion, and philosophy. In art, rational subjectivity sees itself victorious over "sensuous immediacy," which it has managed completely to suffuse or penetrate with a set of imaginatively suggested notions or meanings. In religion, its victory over its "other" is set forth in pictures and stories, and is appreciated by means of "feelings" rather than by clear concepts. In philosophy, we have the clear conceptual understanding of the absoluteness of mind, which is itself mind's final absoluteness. These three forms each have their own history, in which the dialectical observer sees a continuous, rational thread. This is slowly unwound in Hegel's masterly *Lectures on Aesthetics*, his *Lectures on the Philosophy of Religion*, and his *Lectures on the History of Philosophy*.

Concluding Remarks

IN our remaining space we can voice only a few general criticisms of Hegel, although many of his weaknesses will have been obvious from the previous account. Of the interpretations of his work we need say nothing: many of them have not merely scant support in his writings — they have no support at all. His views are, in particular, very different from those of the so-called Anglo-Hegelians — a fact well known to such a thinker as Bradley, but which, in the deep fog of uninterest that at Oxford always masks and muffles all but its own most immediate preoccupations (and which is, in fact, the charm as much as the fault of the university) — tended to be lost sight of. We shall comment briefly on Hegel's dialectical method, say a little about his general teleological interpretation, and speak finally of his notion of rational subjectivity.

Of the dialectical method — as the retreat of thought to ever higher vantage points from which it can survey and appraise its own procedures and assumptions and consider them both as regards their internal and mutual consistency, their broad, overall effectiveness and their ability to yield us a rich understanding of the matters we have on hand — it is plainly the characteristic method of philosophy, which can only make its specific contribution in so far as it *steps aside* from its wonted ways, *suspends* its customary presuppositions, *stops* the mechanically revolving wheels of well-oiled calculi, and proceeds to ask, in stumbling confusion, whether all it has been doing is as it should be. That it may reach the happy conclusion that it has been thinking in the best of all possible ways and that its doubts and hesitations have been themselves confused is not to the point. Philosophy remains a recourse to "second intentions," and to such intentions endlessly reiterated. There is, however, nothing in all this which entails that dialectical comment should satisfy Hegel's typical requirements; that it should be unbrokenly unilineal; that it should proceed uniformly in triads; and that it should tend, lastly, to a limiting point of appeasement. Hegel's dialectical practice has, in fact, established none of these things. It will be plain to anyone who will examine the course of the dialectic as stated above that it has often vacillated hither and yon in the most unsystematic manner; that, while it has generally pursued lines of important and deep analogy, these lines have also varied in their importance; that there has been caprice and arbitrariness in its changes of theme; that it has sometimes separated topics that belonged together; and that it has even gone back upon its tracks. Thus, the treatment of ground and existence constantly brings in causal notions that are officially brought in only at a later point. In the same way, the treatment of teleology would have followed more naturally on the treatment of causality and necessity in the Doctrine of Essence, the whole treatment of notion, judgment, and syllogism having only been sandwiched between them to satisfy the absurd demands of unilinearity. Obviously, the dialectic could have followed a different line or could have pursued several such lines concurrently. It is plain, too, that the triadic arrangement of the thought-material is often quite artificial — an art-form rather than a pattern of argument. And it is plain, lastly, that Hegel's determination to find a point of appeasement in his notions of the "idea" and "spirit" requires more than a dialectical justification. Hegel really only finds certain modes of thought or being inadequate because the "idea" and "spirit" covertly represent his standard of adequacy.

We turn, therefore, to consider the main motive of the dialectic: the notion of mind or rational subjectivity as the *final cause* of everything. The appraisal of this notion is difficult, since final causality remains such an obscure notion. It can, of course, be *metaphysically* interpreted, as some of Hegel's language tempts us to do. We can think of the Idea as some sort of immaterial agent that embraces all the categories in its timeless perfection but nonetheless carries out a gratuitous self-embodiment in time — in the ascending patterns of nature and mind — moved by what seems an unintelligible motive. If this is Hegel's notion of the Idea's final causality, it belongs entirely to the realm of picture-thinking and is one to which no clear meaning can be attached. But that this *is* Hegel's view may be doubted. For it makes nonsense of his view of the realm of notions as a realm of shadows whose sheer *abstractness* motivates the transition to the realms of nature and mind. If the Idea were what this picture presents it as being, it would not need to become concretely embodied at all. The picture also conflicts with Hegel's reiterated statements that the Idea is nothing far off and transcendent, but actual and present, and that the self-consciousness of God or the Absolute Idea exists only *in man*.

What meaning can we then give to the assertion that the Idea, the notion of rational subjectivity, is the final cause of everything? It can be interpreted as meaning (a) that everything in the world in some manner contributes to the fuller realization of rational subjectivity, or that there is at least a preponderating tendency in the world which works in this direction. Alternatively, (b) it may be taken as meaning that it is rational to *view* the things and events in the world *as if* tending in the direction in question. The first interpretation gives Hegel's idealism an empirical, factual meaning, one to which the detail of experience *could* be relevant. The second interpretation gives it a purely philosophical meaning: it recommends the adoption of a particular notional framework or emphasis, in terms of which things may be regarded. It seems plain that *both* interpretations fit Hegel's statements. That his teleological idealism *has* empirical consequences is shown by his glad acceptance of the reported facts of telepathy and by his theodicistic view of history. And that he also regards it as a *philosophical* way of viewing the world is shown by his doctrine that it is in *philosophy* particularly that the idea becomes explicit. There is, however, no inconsistency between interpretations (a) and (b). A philosophical way of viewing the world may involve emphasizing certain facts in that world, whereas a doctrine attributing a preponderant tendency to the world is so essentially vague, so little capable of precise refutation or establishment, that it involves little beyond a selective emphasis on what may be the same body of facts. To be a Hegelian in fact means to be a consistent rationalistic *optimist*, to lay stress on all the indications of deepening rationality in the world, and to understress, or explain away, whatever seems of a contrary tendency. That such rationalistic optimism is itself rational is, however, quite arguable: in a sense it is, and in a sense it is not. To use Kantian language, it may be justified as a *regulative* presumption, not, however, as a *constitutive* axiom. In other words, it may be rational to proceed *as if* the world is such, or as if it could be made such, as to accord maximally with the demands of reason and yet leave room for the possibility that it may only do so to a quite feeble extent. For the "demands of reason" cover such things as simplicity in science and harmony among individual wills, which not only can, but must, have endlessly varying degrees, for all of which it is, in a sense, reasonable to prepare.

The degree to which the facts fit in with our rational presumptions is also exceedingly indeterminate: the German concentration camps, for example, provided extraordinary examples of cooperation, fortitude, and piety, but they also provided the supreme instance of senseless wickedness.

It is, however, in his key notion of *Geist* or mind, meaning what is rational rather than what is merely subjective, that Hegel has perhaps made his most valuable contribution to philosophy. For this notion binds together things that really belong together, and which modern philosophy has too often kept apart. For it binds together the logical and the ethical, which are plainly members of the same family, and it connects both with the most elementary conscious and social experiences in which they undoubtedly have their roots. To examine an object from all sides and recognize it as being this or that, to test phenomena exhaustively so as to show their conformity to a common formula, to give impartial attention to all the evidence collected, to examine a practical project in the most varied lights and pronounce on its overall desirability, to consider a policy from the point of view of the most varied interests, to judge a work of art as subordinating clamant detail or irrelevant titillation to the clear presentation of some subject — all the activities described may be said to be doing the same thing in different ways, to be digging out the elusive universal from the phenomena of first regard, to be exercising reason or rationality. That our varying standards of taste, truth, and practice hang together and have no other source but features that are fundamental to the "mind" and present even in the most elementary experiences is something certainly deserving emphasis. And if rational subjectivity is not the end or "truth" of the world, it is at least the source of all that can have value or interest in it.

19

John Stuart Mill

J. P. DAY

JOHN STUART MILL was born in London on May 20, 1806. He was the eldest son of James Mill, the philosopher, economist, and historian. From his third to sixteenth year he was subjected by his father to an extremely intensive education that was intended to equip him to be the leading apostle of the second generation of Benthamites. Mill found particular value in the instruction he received in logic and political economy, and did not miss the complete absence of any in religion. Even his father's severity as a teacher was not an unmitigated evil, for Mill attributes most of his success in life to this formidable preparation against it. He relates that his reading of Bentham and Hartley were crucial points in his intellectual development; he also made a study of the British empiricist philosophers. James Mill's circle included Bentham, Ricardo, George Grote, and John and Charles Austin, whose acquaintance John Mill was consequently able to enjoy. His education was rounded off by a year in France as the guest of Jeremy Bentham's brother, Sir Samuel Bentham.

In 1823, Mill entered the Examiner's Office of the East India Company, where he was employed for the next thirty-five years. He considers that the administrative experience which he thereby acquired was of substantial value to him in his writings on social theory. Much of his spare time during the next eighteen years was spent on propagandist activity for the "philosophic radicals," a group around his father who believed in an amalgam of Benthamism, associationist psychology, and Ricardian economics. In 1822 he established the Utilitarian Society, and between 1824 and 1828 he contributed extensively to the *Westminster Review*, the house-organ of philosophic radicalism. Between 1825 and 1829, he was also active in the London Debating Society, where he encountered the Coleridgeans, Maurice and Sterling, the latter of whom became his most intimate friend. So began a period of revolt against Benthamism and the eighteenth century, which was accentuated by his reading such authors as Goethe and Carlyle.

In 1826, Mill underwent a mental crisis that was probably brought on by overwork and emotional starvation. He owed his recovery in part to reading Wordsworth, and learned the lesson that the feelings have a claim to cultivation no less than does the intellect. In 1829–1830, he made the acquaintance of the St. Simonians and their ideas, which stirred him to fresh thoughts on economics. Above all, the latter year saw the beginning of his friendship with Mrs. Harriet Taylor, the dominant intellectual influence of his life and the joint author with him of such major works as the *Political Economy* and the *Liberty*. The years 1834–1840 were mainly occupied with editing the *London Review* (later the *London and Westminster Review*), and the extent of his reaction against the tenets in which he had been educated is indicated by his description of his editorial policy as being "to free philosophic radicalism from the reproach of sectarian Benthamism." His father, "the last of the eighteenth century," died in 1836, and in the following year Mill came under yet another powerful new influence, the positivism of Comte.

The final period of Mill's life, which extends from 1840 to his death, was marked by a return from what had been excessive in his reaction against Benthamism. Partly under the influence of de Tocqueville's account of representative government in the U.S.A., he and Harriet became less of democrats than they had been, though at the same time they became more socialistic, as Mill understood that ambiguous term. In 1851, he and Harriet married, her first husband having died two years previously. In 1856, Mill was promoted to Chief of the Examiner's Office, but he retired two years later. Shortly after his retirement, Harriet died unexpectedly at Avignon, where Mill spent most of the rest of his life in the company of his step-daughter, Helen Taylor. From 1865 to 1868, he served as M.P. for Westminster, and did his most effective work on behalf of Irish land reform and, notably, women's suffrage. He had also become elected Rector of St. Andrew's University. He died at Avignon on May 8, 1873.

Mill wrote much, and not only on philosophical questions. His principal philosophical works divide into the constructive and the critical. Each class comprises one treatise and half a dozen essays, namely the following, listed in order of publication: (i) Constructive: *On the Definition of Political Economy, etc.* (1836 repr. 1844 in *Essays on some Unsettled Questions of Political Economy*); *A System of Logic, etc.* (1843, 8th definitive ed. 1872); *On Liberty* (1859); *Utilitarianism* (1861, repr. 1863); *Theism* (in *Three Essays on Religion*, 1874). (ii) Critical: *Bentham* (1838, repr. 1859 in *Dissertations and Discussions*, Vol. I); *Bailey on Berkeley's Theory of Vision* (1842, repr. 1859 in *Dissertations and Discussions*, Vol. II); *Dr Whewell on Moral Philosophy* (1852, repr. 1859 in *Dissertations and Discussions*, Vol. II); *Auguste Comte and Positivism* (1865); *Examination of Sir William Hamilton's Philosophy* (1865, 3rd definitive ed. 1867); *Berkeley's Life and Writings* (1871, repr. 1875 in *Dissertations and Discussions*, Vol. IV).

Naturally, the constructive writings are the more valuable. Mill himself rightly considered the *Logic* and the *Liberty* to be his best works. It is in fact the former which is his most important contribution to philosophy. Its importance is certainly in part historical. In the first place, as Leslie Stephen says, "Mill's *System of Logic* may be regarded as the most important manifesto of Utilitarian philosophy." But its historical significance is even more far-reaching than this, and proceeds from the fact that the treatise came to occupy the same sort of commanding position on the philosophical map as had been held by Locke's *Essay Concerning Human Understanding* a century and a half earlier. There are, indeed, many interesting parallels between the two books. For example, Mill's empiricist war on intuitionism corresponds to Locke's empiricist polemic against innate ideas, and both philosophers share a deep concern for the social sciences. Above all, both works are thorough and comprehensive and say something worthwhile on practically all of the many topics that they touch on. This is not to say that Mill's contributions to these topics are all equally valuable. Thus, at one extreme, his philosophy of mathematics is sharply at variance with modern views, whereas, at the other extreme, Bk. VI of the *Logic* provides what is even now one of the best introductions to the philosophy of the social sciences. Indeed, the importance of the *Logic*, like that of the rest of Mill's works, is by no means only historical, and much of the book can be, and is, still read with profit today.

The *Theism* is not discussed here. This is partly because Mill did not revise it, but more because its value is in any case dubious. In this essay, Mill aims " . . . to consider what place there is for religious beliefs on the platform of science; what evidences they can appeal to, such as science can recognize, and what foundation there is for the doctrines of religion, considered as scientific theorems." But has this program any point? Whatever the logical status of religious and theological utterances may be, they certainly are not scientific theorems, so that small profit is likely to accrue from treating them as if they were and, in particular, from trying to test their truth by the rules of "inductive logic."

Most of Mill's nonphilosophical works are on economic and political science. The chief of them are the *Principles of Political Economy* (1848, 7th definitive ed. 1871), which is his greatest book after his

Logic, and the *Considerations on Representative Government* (1861), which is his main contribution to politics. They contain valuable discussions of two topics which lie outside the scope of this chapter, but which are yet of philosophical interest; namely, the cases for and against private property and democracy respectively. The latter discussion is to be found in the *Thoughts on Parliamentary Reform* (1859, repr. 1867 in *Dissertations and Discussions*, Vol. III) and in the *Representative Government*, I–VIII. The former discussion is to be found in the *Political Economy*, II, i, ii, and in the *Chapters on Socialism* (1879), which are materials for a book about socialism that Mill was working on when he died. A third topic of some philosophical interest is women's rights, which is treated in the *Enfranchisement of Women* (1851, repr. 1859 in *Dissertations and Discussions*, Vol. II) and in the *Subjection of Women* (1869). But Mill's views on this question are really just applications of the doctrine of justice expounded in the *Utilitarianism*, V.

The plan of the chapter is as follows: The first nine sections are devoted to Mill's logic, philosophy of science, and metaphysics. They are based mainly on the *Logic*, except for the ninth section, which is based mainly on the *Examination of Hamilton*. The last three sections are devoted to Mill's moral and political philosophy, and are based mainly on the *Liberty* and the *Utilitarianism*. The other philosophical works mentioned above are considered in the course of the exposition and criticism of these four.

The Meaning of Words and Propositions

MILL declares that an analysis of the meaning of words is a prerequisite of an analysis of the meaning of propositions, and his treatment of these topics shows that he believes further that to analyze the meaning of a proposition *is* to analyze the meanings of its constituent words. Consequently, what is valuable in his theory of meaning is his account of the meaning of words (in which he is considerably indebted to the Scholastics and to Hobbes), whereas what he has to say about that of propositions is weak.

Mill makes his best points about words in what he says about "names," particularly in distinguishing "connotative" from "nonconnotative" names. He does not think that all words are names, and adduces as instances of words that are not names "subsidiary words" or "parts of names," like adverbs. But he certainly interprets "names" widely, including among them adjectives and "many-worded names," such as "the present prime minister of Great Britain."

He holds the distinction between connotative and nonconnotative names to be the most important division of names, and explains it as follows. Nonconnotative names merely "denote" — that is,

refer to — a subject or attribute: for example, "Harold Macmillan" and "whiteness." On the former, he remarks that all such proper names are nonconnotative, so distinguishing them from other "individual names" such as "the present prime minister of Great Britain." Connotative names, on the other hand, both denote a subject and connote an attribute: for example, "man" and "white" respectively. On the former, he remarks that all such general names are connotative. He explains that he means by the "connotation" of a name the attribute(s) possession of (all of) which is necessary and sufficient to giving a thing that name: thus, "man" connotes, implies, or involves animal life, rationality, and a certain form. He adds that the connotation of many common names is indefinite, since such nouns are often vague. The "meaning" of a name, he continues, is its connotation and not its denotation. The opposite theory is confuted by the consideration that although "morning star" and "evening star" denote the same thing, they are not rightly said to mean the same thing.

Mill next points out that to "define" a word means to state its connotation, so nonconnotative names, such as proper names, are indefinable. He holds that what are defined are always words, not things, as some have thought. Yet there is a genuine distinction corresponding to this spurious one, namely, that whereas some definitions simply give the connotation of a word, others do this and also tacitly assert the actual or possible existence of things possessing these attributes. Mathematical definitions, he says, are in the latter class, and we shall notice the significance of this thesis below in the section on "The Nature of Mathematical Truth."

Mill accepts that "proposition" is to be defined as "discourse, in which something is affirmed or denied of something," and hence that all propositions are in subject-predicate form. The most important division of propositions he holds to be that into "verbal" (or essential, or analytic) ones, and "real" (or accidental, or synthetic) ones. The former merely attribute to the subject some property connoted by the subject-term, and so are uninformative (except about the meaning of that term). But the latter attribute to the subject some property not so connoted and so are factually informative. Thus, Mill's distinction between verbal and real propositions rests on his doctrine of connotation. Finally, he tells us that all real propositions assert the existence of, or relations of coexistence, sequence, causation, or resemblance between things.

According to modern ideas of meaning deriving from Wittgenstein, the main defect of Mill's theory is that he puts the relation between, and hence the relative importance of, the meaning of words and the meaning of propositions the wrong way round. For today it is held that it is the latter notion which is primary, since it is in terms of it that the former notion must be explained. The meaning of a proposition is not the sum of the meanings of its constituent words; rather, the meaning of a word is the parts that word can play in the propositions of which it can be a constituent. Further, Mill plainly interprets "names" much too widely. Adjectives like "white" and descriptive phrases like "the present prime minister of Great Britain" are not correctly called names; nor are "subsidiary words," such as adverbs like "truly," properly called parts of names. But others of his points are both true and important. It is true that proper names are not connotative whereas common nouns are. Mill is also right that the "meaning" of a word means its connotation and not its denotation, and in the reason he gives for rejecting the opposite opinion. And he is right again in saying that many, and perhaps most, common nouns are vague.

On the other hand, it is of course untrue that all propositions are or can be expressed in subject-predicate form, and that propositions are restricted to asserting either existence or the few relations that Mill lists. Moreover, the validity of the distinction between "real" or synthetic and "verbal" or analytic propositions has been disputed recently. However, the upshot of these discussions seems to me to be, not that the distinction is unsound, but that it is sometimes harder than Mill recognizes to say to which class a given proposition should be assigned.

The Utility of Formal Logic

MILL views the difference between deduction and (ampliative) induction in the light of his distinction between "real" and "apparent" inference. All immediate deductive inferences, such as "All men are mortal, therefore no men are immortal," are apparent because the conclusion asserts no more than the premise and simply paraphrases it. But all inductive inferences, such as "All examined men are mortal, therefore all men are mortal," are real, because the conclusion does assert more than the premise.

Mill holds all mediate deductive inferences to be expressible in subject-predicate form: all Euclid, he says, could be so expressed. He takes the mood *Barbara* as paradigm in his discussion of syllogism, and in this it will be convenient to follow him. The axiom of syllogism is traditionally held to be the *dictum de omni et nullo*, which asserts (in the case of *Barbara*) that "whatever can be affirmed of a class, may be affirmed of every object contained in the class." But Mill objects that this is no axiom but a mere identical proposition, namely, "Whatever is true of certain objects, is true of each of these objects." The real fundamental axiom of (affirmative) syllogisms has two forms, corresponding to the "speculative" and "practical" aspects of real propositions. Viewed under the former aspect, "All men are mortal" means "The attributes connoted by 'man' are always accompanied by the attribute mortality." But viewed under the latter aspect, it means "Ditto are a mark (or evidence) of ditto." The two corresponding forms of the fundamental axiom are "Things which coexist with the same thing coexist with one another" and "Whatever has any mark, has that which it is a mark of."

Mill dissents both from those who value syllogism on the ground that we prove by it most of our truths and from those who regard it as worthless because it is circular. Nevertheless, the latter are certainly right in holding syllogism to be circular. Thus, consider the argument "All men are mortal; Churchill is a man; therefore Churchill is mortal." Its conclusion only asserts part of what is asserted in the premises, so that it is circular, and mediate no less than immediate deductive inference is apparent, not real.

We may discern in this argument two stages, only the second of which is explicitly stated above, and the unexpressed first stage of which is "All examined men are mortal, therefore All men are mortal." Of these two stages, only the first is (real) inference: the second is rather an "interpretation" of the generalization, or an application of it to a particular case. However, it is equally permissible to infer in a single stage from particulars to particulars without passing through a generalization. Thus: "All observed men are mortal; Churchill is a man; therefore Churchill is mortal." Children, animals, and uneducated persons always, and educated people often, reason thus. The situation here respecting the generalization "All men are mortal" is like what Dugald Stewart points out it often is respecting mathematical axioms. For Mill thinks that the capacity to reason in the two-stage way turns on the ability to use language. Beasts, etc., cannot reason thus because, having no language, they cannot formulate or remember generalizations. But they can make inarticulate inferences from particulars to particulars, since in these the reasoning proceeds *according to*, not *from*, the generalization, and therefore does not need to be formulated verbally.

Mill's notion of the utility of deductive or syllogistic logic follows from his conception of syllogistic reasoning. He holds that its value, considered as a "mode of verifying any given argument," is threefold. First, the major premise being a "memorandum we make of the inferences which may justly be drawn in future cases" (or, considered in its practical as opposed to its speculative aspect, a direction for drawing them) we need rules for applying it correctly to new cases as they arise. Our situation is like that of a judge whose office it is to interpret or apply laws. The utility of the rules of syllogistic logic is that they insure that we do this correctly: their purpose is to maintain consistency between what we remember and our conclusions.

Second, we have just seen that every inference from particulars to a particular may be regarded as an induction followed by a deduction. And another advantage of reasoning this long way round is that we are less likely to go wrong in another way. For if we reason thus, we cannot overlook the fact that evidence that all observed S are P is only good enough to establish that X, which is S, is P, if it is also good enough to establish that all S are P. Whereas if we reason from particulars to a particular, we are quite likely to overlook this truth.

A third advantage of the two-stage mode of reasoning is that the middle term in syllogism makes explicit the points of analogy involved in all applications of generalizations to fresh cases. Thus, compare with the two-stage inference to Churchill's mortality, above, this argument: "Socrates, Plato, Wellington, and Palmerston are mortal; therefore Churchill, who resembles them, is mortal." The former argument specifies, as the latter does not, the respects in which Churchill is like the others, namely, in respect to the attributes connoted by "man." And formal logic keeps us on the right track by reminding us that if this resemblance does not hold our conclusion will not follow, since we shall have committed the fallacy of four terms.

Mill represents the latter argument as typical of analogical inference as opposed to inductive inference proper, which is typified by the former argument. The essential difference, besides the one just mentioned, is that in inductive, but not in analogical, inference, there is shown to be a constant conjunction between the point(s) of analogy (for example, the attributes connoted by "man") and the moot attribute (mortality). For to establish a generalization such as "All men are mortal" is to do just this.

As a result of these considerations, Mill reaches the following conclusions respecting the meaning of "logic." He equates logic as a whole with the "logic of truth," and represents formal logic or the "logic of consistency" as that part of the whole which is about the way in which we reach true conclusions in new cases by applying true generalizations to them. This develops the preliminary account of the study with which Mill introduces his treatise. He there states that his object is " . . . to attempt a correct analysis of the intellectual process called Reasoning or Inference, and of such other mental operations as are intended to facilitate this: as well as, on the foundation of this analysis, and *pari passu* with it, to bring together or frame a set of rules or canons for testing the sufficiency of any given evidence to prove any given proposition." He explains that he includes induction as well as deduction in reasoning and that he understands by "other mental operations" naming, definition, and classification. But his formula naturally excludes the establishment of propositions directly by observation, as opposed to indirectly by reasoning. He also equates logic as he defines it with philosophy of science, since science in his view consists essentially in inferences from observations. On whether his formula provides a correct definition of "logic," Mill observes that the question of what the correct definition may be is much disputed among logicians and that at any rate, his formula summarizes correctly the contents of his own *Logic*. Finally, on the value of the study as he defines it, his opinion is that although "mankind judged of evidence, and often correctly, before logic was a science, or they never could have made it one," nevertheless the bulk of them "require either to understand the theory of what they are doing, or to have rules laid down for them by those who have understood the theory."

To comment: For a start, it is plainly wrong to say that deductive reasoning is not (really) reasoning. It is correct and usual to call it so, and Mill is mistaken in saying that the practice is an "abuse of language." Indeed, as we have just seen, he himself sometimes admits as much. When he denies it, he is of course tacitly equating "reasoning" with "ampliative reasoning," which, however, is just as erroneous as the much more common habit of identifying "reasoning" with "explicative (or deductive) reasoning." And his worry about the fallaciousness of deductive reasoning on the score of its circularity is the obverse of the much more common worry about the fallaciousness of inductive reasoning because of its noncircularity. The answer to both worries is that it is pointless to complain of a thing for being what it is and not another thing.

Next, it is untrue that all mediate deductive inferences can be expressed in syllogisms, if only because it is also untrue that all propositions can be expressed in subject-predicate form.

It is true that syllogism is circular when "circular" is used to mean that an argument's conclusion is included among the premises. For suppose that A, E, I, and O propositions are read in denotation, in the modern fashion. Then, "All men are mortal" will mean "Socrates is mortal and Wellington is mortal and Palmerston is mortal . . . etc." And the argument "All men are mortal; Churchill is a man; therefore Churchill is mortal" will be circular because "Churchill is mortal" will be one of the conjuncts included among "etc." However, this is so only if the major is interpreted in this way. But Mill's view is that it is to be read in connotation to mean "The attributes connoted by 'man' are always accompanied by the attribute mortality." And on this interpretation the argument is not circular. The circularity of syllogism, consequently, is not a matter with which Mill ought, in consistency, to concern himself at all.

It will hardly escape notice that Mill discusses syllogism entirely in terms of the application of a generalization to a new case. But this, of course, is only one sort of syllogism. The major need not be a generalization; it may be a description like "All (the) men in the room are tall," or a necessary proposition like "All men are animals."

A large issue latent in Mill's discussion of syllogism is that of the meaning or use of generalizations. He seems to waver between three views. (1) The intensional (or connotative) interpretation, which is the only one he explicitly states; (2) the extensional (or denotative) interpretation, which is implicit in his charge of circularity in syllogism; and (3) the rule of inference interpretation. This view is implicit in his doctrine that we (sometimes) reason according to, not from, the generalization — for what one reasons according to can only be a rule, not a statement.

As for Mill's opinion that beasts reason, the objection which he brings against the view that they generalize and then deduce (namely, that they have no language) surely bears equally strongly against his own view that they reason inarticulately from particulars to particulars. For "reasoning" means advancing some proposition as reason for another, and where there is no language there are no propositions and, consequently, no reasoning. The temptation to ascribe reason to animals and infants is easily explicable by the resemblances between (some of) their overt behavior and that of genuinely rational beings.

On the other hand, it seems to me that Mill is right in saying that all inductive inferences about particular cases may be regarded as proceeding *via* a generalization, and that his account of the advantages of the two-stage procedure over inference from particulars to particulars is both true and important.

I have two remarks to add about his notion of the scope and value of logic. Although there are those who equate "logic" with "formal logic," most logicians appear to share Mill's view of the scope of the study. For most logic textbooks follow the tripartite pattern which Mill initiated: a part on language, a part on deduction, and a part on induction and methodology. As for the utility of logic, or at any rate of his *Logic*, it is necessary to add to what has been said above that in his *Autobiography* Mill strikes a more practical note. There he tells us that his treatise was intended to be a blow on behalf of the progressive school of experience and association against the conservative, *a priori*, and intuitionist school, of which he regarded Whewell and Hamilton to be the leading members in Great Britain.

The Nature of Mathematical Truth

THE last remarks apply with particular force to Mill's philosophy of mathematics. For he offers them in deliberate opposition to the *a priori* and intuitionist philosophy of Whewell, believing that the prestige of intuitionism rests mainly on the erroneous opinion that it provides the true theory of mathematics and physics and hence, that "to expel it from these, is to drive it from its stronghold." What Whewell means by saying that the axioms of geometry, as an example, are known *a priori* by intuition, or are self-evident, is that to understand their meaning is to see their truth, so that it is un-

necessary, as it is also indeed impossible, to establish their truth *a posteriori*. I shall outline in turn Mill's views on geometry and on arithmetic.

The propositions of geometry, says Mill, consist of (1) principles or premises that are either (a) axioms or (b) definitions; and (2) theorems, which are deductive conclusions from (1) and consequently apparent, not real, inferences. There are three axioms; (i) "Things which are equal to the same thing are equal to one another"; (ii) "The sums of equals are equal"; and (iii) "Lines, surfaces or solid spaces, which can be so applied to one another as to coincide, are equal." They are all generalizations from experience or enumerative inductions — in other words, they are established by direct induction from observed cases. They are also exactly true, the reason for their truth being their universal scope: thus (i), being about all things, is universal in the sense of being about things in all times and places or throughout all nature. Mill gives a similar account of the status and truth of the principles of deductive logic (for example, the law of contradiction, "An affirmative proposition and the corresponding negative proposition cannot both be true"), and of inductive logic (namely, the law of causation, "Every event has a cause").

The case is significantly different with the (incorrectly so called) definitions like "A circle is a figure bounded by a line (the circumference) which has all its points equally distant from a point (the center) within it." For although these too are generalizations from experience, they are unlike the axioms in being not exactly, but only approximately, true. The reason why it is incorrect to call them definitions is that from definitions properly so called, only verbal propositions follow. But in geometrical definitions there is a tacit assumption that objects conforming to them exist. This, however, is strictly false, since the world contains no circles, etc., exactly like those defined by Euclid.

The position respecting the truth of the theorems is therefore this: They are "hypothetically" or "conditionally true" (i.e. what is now called valid), in the sense that they must be true if the premises are true, and in this sense alone can they be called "necessary." But they are not actually (exactly) true because some of the premises, namely the definitions, are not (exactly) true.

Finally, since both axioms and definitions are about nature, "geometry is a strictly physical science" like mechanics, and its three axioms are laws of nature — specifically, laws of resemblance.

Mill's account of arithmetic is very similar. The chief differences are the following: The axioms of arithmetic are two, namely, the first two of the three given above for geometry. Its (incorrectly so called) definitions are the definitions of the numbers, for example, "$2+1=3$," which assert that there exist collections of objects (for example, a lot of two pebbles and a lot of one pebble) which can be put together in one collection of objects (namely, a lot of three pebbles). They are only approximately true because they all assume that $1 = 1$, or that all the numbers are numbers of the same or equal units. This, however, is sometimes false: 1 lb. troy and 1 lb. avoirdupois do not make 2 lb. troy, or avoirdupois, or any other weight. Whereas the axioms are natural laws of resemblance, the definitions are natural laws of coexistence, and theorems — for example, "$79,105 + 3,824 = 82,929$" — are assertions about the ways in which a certain collection might have been formed by putting together other collections (or by withdrawing collections from collections). Mill's thoroughly empirical approach to arithmetic is further revealed by his account of the meaning of the "names of numbers" or numerals. For example, he holds that "2" denotes all pairs of things, and connotes the way in which single objects must be put together to make that particular sort of collection.

Mill's philosophy of mathematics is generally considered to be the least acceptable part of his logic, and indeed he enjoys on this account a certain *succès de scandale*. It is of some interest that it bears a marked resemblance to Hume's mathematical philosophy as given in his *Treatise*, which, however, has escaped the criticism that Mill's has incurred. At the least, Mill's theory has the merit of having provoked his secular godson, Lord Russell, into trying to devise a better one.

It is clear that Mill identifies geometry with Euclidean geometry, and his account of the three classes into which its propositions fall is broadly correct. Today, the theorems of Euclidean geometry are held to be derivable from the axioms and definitions of, notably, Hilbert rather than from those of Euclid himself; and the theorems of arithmetic from the axioms and definitions of Peano.

But comparison of Mill's axioms with Hilbert's and Peano's readily shows that Mill's are quite inadequate. Further, they are not, as Mill alleges, empirical generalizations. For it is a mark of empirical generalizations that they can be disproved by observed exceptions; yet Mill's axioms lack this mark. Thus, consider his geometrical axiom "Things which are equal to the same thing are equal to one another." And suppose someone were to claim that it is disproved by the following facts: When one rod is placed beside a second, their ends coincide; and when the second is placed beside a third, their ends coincide; but when the first is placed beside the third, their ends do not coincide. Would his claim be allowed? Plainly not. The facts would be explained in some other way, as that the first rod changed in length when it was placed beside the third. And so generally: No observed fact would be allowed to count as a disproof of the axiom. Actually, it is a necessary and *a priori* truth, its necessity deriving from the fact that equality is a transitive relation.

Mill's account of geometrical and arithmetical definitions is open to similar objections. They are not

approximately true generalizations about things and events. Euclid's definition of "circle" is not about tree-trunks, car-wheels, etc., although this is not to deny that in applied or physical geometry such terms may be given physical interpretations, as when "straight line" is interpreted as the path of a light-ray. That Mill's specimen arithmetical definition "$2 + 1 = 3$" is not an empirical generalization about assemblings of lots of pebbles, etc., is apparent from the same sort of consideration as that given above about axioms: namely, that no apparent exceptions derived from experience of counting collections of objects would ever be admitted as a disproof of this proposition. Similarly, Mill is in error in thinking that "$1 = 1$" is sometimes false because numbers are not always numbers of the same units. On the contrary, it is always true, and the point that Mill seems to be after is the quite different one that calculations in applied arithmetic are not reliable unless the things are rightly counted to begin with. One condition that must be fulfilled for this to be so is that the things all be of the kind that it is required to count; and if one counts a pound troy when one is supposed to be counting pounds avoirdupois, or conversely, this condition is evidently not satisfied.

In what he says about theorems, Mill's distinction between necessary truths and necessary consequences is correct and illuminating. Both necessary and contingent truths may have necessary consequences, and the necessary consequences of necessary, but not of contingent, truths must themselves be necessary truths. And since Mill holds mathematical axioms to be empirical generalizations and therefore contingent, he is consistent in saying that mathematical theorems are necessary only in the sense of being necessary consequences. But his further contention that mathematical theorems are strictly false (or only approximately true) because some mathematical principles, namely the definitions, are strictly false (or only approximately true) is open to objection on two counts. First, we have seen that mathematical definitions are not in fact strict falsehoods or only approximate truths. And second, if they were, it is fallacious to think that valid conclusions from (strictly) false premises cannot be true.

Finally, it is quite untrue that geometry is a physical science like mechanics, and that its axioms are a sort of laws of nature. Indeed, there runs throughout Mill's discussion a fatal failure to distinguish between pure arithmetic and the applied arithmetic of counting and calculating, and between pure geometry and the applied geometry of, for example, geometrical optics.

The Proof of Causal Laws

SINCE deductive reasoning is only "apparent" and an "interpretation" of inductions, the central problem of logic is to elucidate the nature of inductive or "real" inference and to formulate the conditions of its soundness. The formulation of these conditions of legitimacy is the task of "inductive logic," the function of which is to lay down "practical rules, which may be for induction itself what the rules of the syllogism are for the interpretation of induction." But we must first consider what induction is.

Mill defines "induction" as "generalization from experience," although he admits that deductions from generalizations, such as the conclusion of the two-stage argument to Churchill's mortality are also called inductions. He observes further that generalization is a method of discovery as well as of proof, although it is the latter aspect which is the more important one. He also distinguishes induction from two operations with which it has been confused, notably by Whewell. The first of these is description. One of Whewell's definitions of "induction" is as "colligation of facts": thus, Kepler made an induction when he accepted the proposition "All observed positions of Mars lie (more or less) on an ellipse." But Mill objects that this was description, not induction, and that induction only came into the case when Kepler inferred from this proposition to "All positions of Mars do ditto." The other operation is the employment of the "hypothetical method." Another of Whewell's accounts of induction is that is consists in framing a hypothesis or guessing the solution and then seeing whether the consequences of the hypothesis fit the facts; as when Kepler, after numerous attempts, lighted on the idea that the orbit of Mars is an ellipse, and found that the observed positions did indeed lie more or less on this curve. But Mill rejects this conception of induction as inverse deduction also, principally on the ground that Whewell's doctrine takes no account of the question of proof.

Mill distinguishes two main types of inductions: causal laws and empirical laws. The former he identifies with "uniformities of succession," not with the much smaller class of generalizations that explicitly assert causation; we will consider these in the present section. Within the latter he selects three sub-types for discussion, as will more fully appear in the next section.

According to Mill, causal laws are properly proved by the law of universal causation conjoined with the experimental methods. The law of causation is the proposition "Every event has a cause." By "cause," Mill understands "immediate, unconditional, and invariable antecedent event"; his notion is thus a development of Hume's and Brown's. It will be convenient to represent antecedent events by A, B, C, etc., and subsequent events by X, Y, Z, etc. To say that A is an "unconditional" antecedent of X means that when A occurs, then X occurs, whatever else happens, that is, A is a sufficient condition of X. Thus, night is not called the cause of day because day would not succeed night if, for example, the sun were extinguished.

Mill enumerates five experimental methods. In the method of agreement, we prove that A is the cause of X by establishing that X (say, prosperity) is always preceded by A (say, free trade). In the method of difference, we prove that A is the cause of X by establishing that (1) when X (say, a man's death) did not occur, A (say, his being shot through the heart) did not precede; (2) when X did occur, A did precede; and (3) there was no other difference between situation (1) and situation (2) besides the absence of X and A in (1) and the presence of X and A in (2). In the method of concomitant variations, we prove that A is the cause of X by establishing that an increase (or diminution) in X (say, prosperity) is always preceded by an increase (or diminution) in A (say, free trade). This method therefore resembles that of agreement, except that whereas the latter deals with the presence or absence of A and X, the former deals with variation in degrees of A and X. It is by the former that we establish numerical laws, such as Boyle's and Ohm's. The joint method of agreement and difference is explained by its name and by what precedes, and the method of residues may be ignored.

The proof of causal laws by the law of causation conjoined with the experimental methods possesses two important features. First, the type of proof is demonstrative, not empirical, proof. Thus Mill writes, "A general proposition inductively obtained is only then proved to be true when the instances on which it rests are such that, if they have been correctly observed, the falsity of the generalization would be *inconsistent* with the constancy of causation." The word that I have italicized plainly indicates that Mill is thinking of deductive proof. Second, the type of induction involved is eliminative, not enumerative, induction. We prove that A is the cause of X not by accumulating observed constant conjunctions of A with X, but by eliminating all other possible candidates for that title, as B, C, etc. However, Mill recognizes that only the method of difference possesses these two features, and he prizes it above the other methods accordingly. What impairs the probative force of the method of agreement is "plurality of causes" — that is, alternative causes. For example, death is caused by being shot through the heart, or by cancer, or . . . etc. Hence, if X occurs without A's preceding, we cannot eliminate A, since it may yet be true that A causes X when it does precede it. Hence further, causal laws evidenced by the method of agreement must be proved in a different way. (See the next section.)

The law of causation, the principle of induction itself, stands on the same footing as the principles of mathematics and formal logic: it is an enumerative induction that is true because, although its scope is of the maximum width (being about all events), yet no exception to it has been found. Mill concedes, incidentally, that enumerative inductions of less than universal scope are in various degrees probable, but not true or certain. The result is that causal induction is "scientific" and indirect, not prescientific and direct. We establish the proposition "A is the cause of X," not by direct induction, by accumulating evidence of a constant conjunction between A and X, but by indirect induction, by deducing it from a wider and better established induction, namely, the law of causation. This is revealing both of Mill's indebtedness to Whewell's account of the "consilience of inductions" and of his own conception of "inductive logic"; for he writes: "To test a generalization, by showing that it either follows from, or conflicts with, some stronger induction, some generalization resting on a broader foundation of experience, is the beginning and end of the logic of Induction."

Most of what Mill says about the meaning of "induction" is correct, and he is in the right in his instructive controversies with Whewell. But he includes far too much under "causal laws." It is wrong to equate those, for instance, with laws of succession; here, Mill is presumably following Kant. Again, it is false that the laws of functional dependence established by the method of concomitant variations are laws of succession or of causation: they are nontemporal. Had he seen these points, Mill would not have exaggerated the importance of causation in induction as he does, claiming that "the notion of Cause . . . is the root of the whole theory of Induction."

Mill's doctrine of the experimental methods owes much to Bacon, Hume, and Herschel. It is open to the following main criticism. We will take it that we are interested in establishing the causes of effects rather than the effects of causes. Now, for this purpose, the method of agreement is not an eliminative method at all. For what it eliminates are candidates for the style of necessary condition, whereas, as we have seen, Mill means by a "cause" a sufficient condition. (A is a sufficient condition of X if, whenever A occurs, then X occurs; and A is a necessary condition of X if, whenever A does not occur, then X does not occur.) The method does, however, provide enumerative evidence about sufficient conditions. The method of difference, on the other hand, does indeed eliminate candidates for the style of sufficient condition. It follows that Mill is right in rating the method of difference higher than the method of agreement, but wrong in the reason he gives for doing so. The reason is, not so much that the latter method is frustrated by the existence of alternative causes (although this is true), as that it is not an eliminative method of proving causation at all. Similar remarks apply to the method of concomitant variations as to the method of agreement.

There is also a decisive objection to Mill's doctrine of the principle(s) or ground(s) of induction — namely, that it (they) will not afford a demonstrative proof when conjoined with the data yielded by the methods. It is to be observed, first, that the law of causation, though necessary, is not sufficient to make causal proofs formally valid. There is need of another premise, which Professor von Wright calls the postulate of completely known instances, and he formulates it thus: "[first] certain categories of simple properties can be left out of consideration as being *irrelevant* to the eliminative method of induction, and . . . [second] in each single case we are able to judge whether the information about the instances, which has been taken into account, represents complete knowledge as to all the remaining relevant properties or not." There are indications that Mill half saw the need for this second principle, as when he remarks that in establishing the causes of chemical phenomena, we take no account of the positions of the planets because these are judged to be irrelevant.

But even if Mill had explicitly adopted this second principle it would have availed him nothing, because neither principle can be shown to be true or probable. In the case of "Every event has a cause", the reason is simply that this form of words is not of the type that can be true or probable — that is, it is not a statement. That it is not a generalization, as Mill maintains, can be shown by the same sort of objection as was made to his account of mathematical axioms and definitions. For suppose I adduce what I claim to be an exception, an uncaused event, say cancer. Will my claim be allowed? Patently not. I shall be told that cancer is not an uncaused event but an event the cause or causes of which are not yet known. And so generally with any alleged exception. But not only is this form of words not a generalization; it is not any kind of statement. It is rather, in my view, a rule for investigators which happens to be couched in a rather misleading grammatical form. And a rule cannot, of course, be true or false, probable or improbable.

As for the postulate of completely known instances it seems clear enough that we know neither of its clauses to be true or probable. Some, indeed, argue for the first clause; Keynes, for example, maintains that we know *a priori* that place and date are always inductively irrelevant, this truth being the principle of the uniformity of nature. But for my part, I am unable to see that this proposition is either true or known *a priori*. The second clause is even more plainly false. We frequently judge circumstances to be relevant when they are not and (what is much more serious) exclude them from consideration as irrelevant when they are not. To say this is not to deny the important truth that previous judgments of (ir)relevance are essential to making inductions of all sorts, not merely causal ones. But it is to deny that these judgments are infallible.

Finally, Mill's "proof" of causal laws is circular in the following sense. On the one hand, he says that the law of causation, "Every event has a cause," is proved true by enumerative induction from the fact of the existence of numerous true causal laws, such as "Malaria is caused by *anopheles*." On the other hand, he says that such a causal law is properly proved true by the method of difference — that is, by a deductive argument in which it is shown to follow necessarily from true premises, one of which is the law of causation.

The Proof of Empirical Laws

MILL recognizes that causal laws, or uniformities of succession, are not the only type of generalizations. There are also empirical laws, and he considers how three sorts of these are proved.

The first sort is uniformities of coexistence not dependent on causation. By an "empirical law" Mill means a generalization that has not been deduced from and so explained by a law of wider scope. Accordingly, he distinguishes empirical laws both from "derivative laws," which have been so explained, and from "ultimate laws," which are not so explainable. All uniformities of succession are derivative laws because they are deducible from the law of causation. But only some uniformities of coexistence are derivative laws; first, because there is no law of coexistence corresponding to the law of causation (as it might be, "Every property has an unconditional invariable concomitant property"); and second, because only some of these uniformities fall under the law of causation, namely, simultaneous effects of the same cause — for example, high water at any point on the earth's surface and high water at the point diametrically opposite to it. Hence, some uniformities of coexistence are ultimate.

Since there is no law of coexistence, these ultimate uniformities cannot be established by eliminative induction and must be established by enumerative induction. The question is, how probable are they? Mill takes as an example the generalization "All crows are black," and observes that the degree of its probability is the degree of the improbability that an exception to it should not have been observed. There are two possibilities. First, blackness may be a "property of kind" among crows. In this case, the probability of the generalization is the improbability of the existence of a kind — nonblack crows. By a "(natural) kind," Mill means a class possessing indefinitely many common properties in addition to those connoted by its name; thus, the classes of diamonds and of men are kinds, whereas the classes of white things and of Christians are not. The second possibility is that blackness in crows is not a property of kind but is accidental. In this case, the probability of the generalization is the improbability of the existence of a single nonblack crow. In fact, the existence of neither the nonblack kind nor the nonblack individual is particularly improbable. Now, since empirical laws are (by definition) explained by no wider law, they are not acceptable at all unless their scope is restricted to the limits of time, place, and circumstance within which the evidence for them has been observed. If all the observed

black crows have been in Europe, we cannot generalize that all crows, only that all European crows, are black. Subject to this provision, the degree of probability of ultimate uniformities of coexistence varies directly as their scope. Thus, whereas a generalization of the widest scope $(2+1 = 3)$ is true or certain, one of narrower scope (All crows are black) is only probable in some degree.

A concept cognate with "natural kind" is "natural class." Mill observes that in the latter, "natural" means simply "good"; specifically, good for the purpose of scientific classification. This purpose is so to group individuals that the greatest possible number of true generalizations can be asserted about each class. Thus, whereas "land-dwelling animal" is a bad or artificial class, "mammalian animal" is a good or natural class because one can assert about its members, not only that they are all mammals, but also that they are all vertebrates, warm-blooded, etc. There is therefore a significant connection between induction and classification.

The second sort of empirical laws that Mill considers is causal generalizations evidenced by the method of agreement. We have seen that Mill believes the existence of alternative causes to rule out the possibility of demonstrative and eliminative proof of causal generalizations by this method. It is indeed precisely because causal generalizations so established are not deducible from the law of causation that they are mere empirical laws.

Nevertheless, Mill holds that causal generalizations may be shown by the method to be probable, provided that the examined instances are varied and numerous. The joint effect of variety and number is this: If we have a large number of occurrences of X agreeing in no antecedent except A, the possibility of alternative causes is excluded by the consideration either that A is the cause of X or X has as many alternative causes as we have observed occurrences, which latter alternative, however, is very improbable. The effect of number alone is to rule out the possibility that when X is constantly preceded by A, this is a case not of causation, but of coincidence. The reasoning here resembles that which we employ to discover and prove that dice are not true. If I throw a die 600 times and it falls with ace uppermost 400 of these times, I conclude that this is almost certainly because it is untrue. All such reasoning, according to Mill, presupposes Laplace's principle of inverse probability.

The third type of empirical laws that Mill discusses is what he calls "approximate" (proportional or statistical) generalizations — for example, the nonnumerical sub-type "Most dark-eyed persons are dark haired" and the numerical sub-type "51 per cent of births are male births."

He argues that these, like causal generalizations established by the method of agreement, are proved by taking a sample large enough to eliminate chance. Suppose I know that a bag contains very many balls, some black and some nonblack, and that I wish to know what proportion are black. I take a large random sample, find that 80 per cent in it are black, and infer that (about) 80 per cent in the bag are black too. Chance is eliminated in this sense. Although it is *possible* that the observed result is due to the composition of the population being, say, 80 per cent nonblack and to my selection of this highly unrepresentative sample being fortuitous, it is nevertheless very *improbable*; indeed, the supposition that the composition of the population is any proportion other than (about) 80 per cent black is more improbable than the supposition that it is that proportion. Here again, the argument is inverse reasoning in the calculus of probabilities, and requires some principle of inverse probability as well as some large-number theorem of the calculus.

Mill thinks that although proportional generalizations are useful for the purposes of practical life, in science they must be regarded as "merely provisional" and replaced when possible by universal ones. For example, the unqualified proportional generalization, "Most persons who possess uncontrolled power employ it ill" should be replaced by the corresponding qualified universal one, "All persons who possess, etc., employ, etc., unless they are persons of unusual strength of judgment and rectitude of purpose."

My first criticism of these doctrines is that it is untrue that the degree of probability of ultimate uniformities of coexistence varies directly with their scope. Indeed, other philosophers hold the scope of generalizations to be a determinant of their probability, but they maintain in flat opposition to Mill that their probability varies *inversely* with their scope. It seems to me that scope does not affect inductive probability at all, and that the only connection between the two concepts is that it is more difficult to establish a generalization with a given degree of probability the wider its scope. It is harder to establish that most men very probably like beer than that most Englishmen very probably do.

Passing to what Mill says about causal generalizations established by the method of agreement, it is to be noted, first, that he is right in saying that the argument by elimination of chance which he describes is used to discover and prove causation. An interesting example is the reasoning employed in experimental parapsychology.[1] But in going on to say that the argument is inverse reasoning in the calculus of probabilities, he lays himself open to the objection that in that case it cannot be *inductive* argument, as he claims, since all reasoning within this calculus, whether direct or inverse, is deductive.

The same objection holds against his account of the proof of proportional generalizations: as Professor Kneale truly says, "All ampliative induction may be described as the making of inferences from samples, but not all inference from samples is inductive." Mill implicitly recognizes a distinction between two senses of "probable," namely, the inductive and the casual. We have just seen that he wrongly holds the criterion of the former to be the scope of the generalization; the criterion of the latter he rightly holds to be the degree in which the quantifier in the major premise of a proportional syllogism approaches to universality. Contrast, for instance, the inference-patterns, "Most *S* are *P*, *X* is an *S*, therefore *X* is probably *P*" and "Nearly all *S* are *P*, *X* is an *S*, therefore *X* is very probably *P*." Contemporary philosophers of science[2] dissent from Mill's contention that statistical laws and theories are only provisional, and regard them as no less (or more) permanent that universal ones, Mill here reflects the prejudice of his age. His ideal of science is the celestial mechanics of Newton as perfected by Laplace, and Newton's is the type of a universal or "deterministic" theory.

My final criticism of Mill's inductive philosophy as a whole is that it is too complicated and draws distinctions where there are no differences. For we have seen that he argues that causal laws are rightly established by the method of difference, which proves them true by eliminative demonstrative induction; that ultimate uniformities of coexistence are proved probable by enumerative problematic induction, their probability depending on their scope; and that both causal generalizations evidenced by the method of agreement and proportional generalizations are proved probable by inverse deductive reasoning in the calculus of probabilities, their probability depending on the number of the observed instances. But I suggest that the truth is simpler — that generalizations like "Lead-poisoning is a cause of death," "All crows are black," and "Most dark-eyed persons are dark-haired" are all normally established by enumerative induction, the degree of their probability depending on the variety and number of the observed instances.

Deductive vs. *Experimental Science, and the Proper Method of Political Economy*

MILL's philosophy of the social sciences, notably of political economy and political science, is the culmination of his *Logic*. But to understand it, we must first consider what he says about the distinction between deductive and experimental science, the sciences of human nature in general, and erroneous methods in the social sciences.

Mill teaches that the advantage of deductive over experimental science is that of indirect over direct induction, namely, that generalizations can be more securely established by being connected deductively with wider and better evidenced generalizations. A science normally becomes deductive when it becomes mathematical, when its laws are numerical laws stating relations of functional dependence between measured variable magnitudes; for mathematics represents deductive reasoning in its highest development.

Whether a science is deductive or experimental is also intimately connected with the existence of conjunct part-causes and resultant mixed effects. This occurs when X is caused by A and B, a case which must, of course, be distinguished from that of alternative causes, in which X is caused by A or B. Part-causes are conjoined in two modes, the mechanical and the chemical. Take, for example, the respective cases in which two equal and opposite forces act upon a body and keep it in equilibrium and the case in which hydrogen and oxygen combine to form water. Conjunction in the former mode is the general rule, and is best called composition, as in mechanics. Generally speaking, the experimental methods are powerless to establish the causes of mixed effects. In the example of chemical conjunction, the only reason why it is possible to establish experimentally that the combination of hydrogen and oxygen is the cause of the presence of water is that it so happens that in certain conditions these elements are reproduced from the compound. And in mechanical cases, the situation is quite hopeless. How could one discover by the method of difference, the only method that really proves causation — that the cause of a body's remaining at rest is its being acted upon by two equal and opposite forces? It is because of composition that we may say, not that heavy bodies, for instance, fall or that an increase in demand causes a rise in price, but that heavy bodies *tend* to fall or that *ceteris paribus* an increase in demand causes a rise in price. For the latter locutions recognize, as the former do not, that the operation of one cause may be modified or defeated by that of another. Moreover, if we express ourselves in the former manner, we involve ourselves in the absurdity of admitting that there are exceptions to laws of nature — in the behavior of balloons, for instance. Social phenomena are the most intractable of all to the experimental methods. This is not only because conjunction of causes obtains here on a grand scale, but also because it is not a practical possibility to vary and hold constant the conditions at will as the method of difference requires. Hence, we can only employ the deductive method.

In this method there are three stages. First, the induction by the experimental methods of the laws of the separate causes. Second, the deductive working out from these laws and "collocations" of facts of theorems or consequences. It is at this stage that compound part-causes are added together. Third, the verification of these consequences by seeing whether they fit the observed facts. If they do, the laws are said to "explain" these facts. A classic example is Newton's explanation of Kepler's laws of planetary motion by his laws of motion and gravitation. Verification is essential because the laws of

some of the separate causes may have been omitted, and because errors may have occurred in the deduction.

By the sciences of human nature, Mill means the sciences of man considered as a creature with a mind, not human physiology and the like. He considers that these studies can only be rescued from their backward, "empirical" state by applying to them the methods of the advanced (physical) sciences. Hence too, his philosophy of the human sciences is a special case of his philosophy of science in general. Mill first considers the objection that there can be no sciences of human nature because men's wills are free, so that there can be no laws of human nature. He disposes of it satisfactorily in the Humean way: "We may be free, and yet another may be perfectly certain what use we shall make of our freedom."

Mill says that the science of human nature is not an exact science because, although the laws of the main phenomena are known, those of the "perturbations" are not; it is therefore like tidology rather than astronomy. Its laws are proportional generalizations which, if the science is to be properly established, need to be deduced from and explained by "the universal laws of human nature." These are the laws of mind — the laws of association, for example; for Mill's conception of psychology is entirely his father's and Hartley's. They are ultimate and universal, the first principles of human nature. However, the empirical laws of human nature are deducible, not directly from these first principles, but from certain "middle axioms," which are the laws of "ethology" (or the science of formation of character), and which are derivative from the ultimate laws. Finally, Mill is satisfied that the laws of the behavior of men in society are the consequences of the laws of the behavior of men individually.

Mill criticizes two erroneous methods in the social sciences. The first is the experimental method, exemplified in political science by Macaulay's criticism of James Mill's *Essay on Government*. We have just noticed the objections to this method, namely, that the existence in social phenomena of the composition of causes, and the impracticability of experimental control over conditions, render the method of difference inapplicable. We may, indeed, employ observation as opposed to experiment, but history is not so obliging as to present us with the sort of facts we need, such as, if we are investigating the causes of prosperity, two nations differing in no respect save that the one has free trade and prosperity whereas the other has neither. There remain the methods of agreement and concomitant variations, but these are frustrated by the prevalence in social phenomena of alternative as well as conjunct causes.

The other faulty method is the "geometrical" one, which errs in misassimilating the social sciences to geometry, in which there is no composition of causes. The most notable example is Benthamite political science as delivered in James Mill's *Essay*. The Benthamites attempt to explain political phenomena by deducing them from the *single* principle that "the majority of any body of persons will be governed in the bulk of their conduct by their personal interests." But this ignores the existence of equally important counteracting causes: the conduct of rulers, for example, is determined as much by habit and tradition as by interest.

The Benthamites are nevertheless right in holding the proper method of the social sciences to be deductive and not experimental. Only, it must be the "physical" deductive method, which employs as premises a *number* of laws of different causes. There are two ways of using this method, the direct and the inverse, which differ over verification. In the former, as we have seen, we verify our deductions (which are usually general statements rather than singular ones) by seeing whether they fit the facts. But in the latter we verify empirical laws previously obtained by generalization, by seeing whether they are deducible from the principles of human nature. Mill owns that he derives his notion of the inverse method from Comte. In social phenomena, the existence of conjunct causes and mixed effects may be called, in a physiological metaphor, the "consensus" of social facts.

The direct method is impracticable when the conjunct causes are very numerous, so that it can only be applied to those social phenomena which are mainly and immediately the effects of a few causes. This is the case with economic phenomena, for example. Here, the main, immediate causes (laws) are very few — namely, the "psychological law" that "a greater gain is preferred to a smaller" and the "perpetually antagonizing principles to the desire of wealth, namely, aversion to labour and desire of the present enjoyment of costly indulgences." In *pure* political economy, we reason from these principles, well aware that they, and hence the theorems, are strictly false. The principles of economics are thus like the definitions of geometry. The economist's "definition of 'man' as a being who invariably does that by which he may obtain the greatest amount of necessaries, conveniences and luxuries with the smallest quantity of labour and physical self-denial with which they can be obtained in the existing state of knowledge" is only approximately true of real men, just as Euclid's definition of a circle is only approximately true of tree-trunks. When we *apply* the pure science, however, we correct our conclusions by making due allowance for additional causes or laws — for instance, we recognize that labor may not move from one place to another, although wages are slightly higher in the second place, on account of sentimental attachment to the first place. Mill's own *Political Economy*, it should be noted, is a work of both pure and applied science. The sort of causes most often overlooked when the social sciences are applied are those relating to national and period characteristics. For example, economists assume too readily when applying their science that all men compete as keenly as do Britons and Americans. These characteristics form the subject of a separate study, "political ethology" (a branch of ethology). Only those social facts can properly be studied apart from the rest in which the laws of political ethology are of secondary importance. This is not the case with political facts, for which reason, among others, "there can be no separate Science of Government," and political problems must be treated as problems of "general sociology."

Notice first that Mill distinguishes the deductive from the hypothetical method. The difference is that whereas in the former the premises are obtained by induction, in the latter they are simply assumed. But he holds, mistakenly, that hypothetic inference is only justified when the assumed premises are proved, and that this only occurs when they imply *and are implied by* true conclusions. Thus, Mill's ideal of hypothetic inference, like his ideal of (causal) inductive inference, is deductive inference.

Mill is right on the whole in saying that the method of difference is inapplicable to social phenomena on account of the composition of causes and the impracticability of controlling the conditions, and that the method of the social sciences must therefore be deductive. Some, however, think otherwise. Economics, for example, has its protagonists of the experimental method, notably the German historical school in the last century and the "institutionalists" in this one. But Mill would have said, correctly, that the attempts by the latter to discover the laws of, say, trade-cycles by analyzing statistics and discerning tendencies, fail through confusing mere empirical laws or trends with genuine laws, and thereby falling into the same fallacy as many "philosophers of history." (See the next section.) On the other hand, he somewhat underestimates the methods of agreement and concomitant variations. His own treatment in his *Political Economy* of production, although not of distribution and exchange, relies on these methods.

Mill has been criticized for his "methodological individualism" and his "methodological psychologism." Professor Britton renders the former "All that goes on in society is to be explained by the laws of the nature of individual men"; considers whether it is a truism or a falsism; and opts for the latter. Professor Popper, however, considers it a truism, and I agree with him. On the other hand, Professor Popper rejects Mill's "methodological psychologism," and on this there are two things to be said. First, Mill's associationist psychology is obviously inadequate. However, this matters less when it is realized that his contention really is that the principles of the social sciences are not so much "psychological" laws as certain universally accepted laws of human nature. But second, these principles certainly include laws of nonhuman nature too. For example, the laws of diminishing utility and of diminishing returns are often included among the principles of economics, but although the former is about human nature, the latter is about land and other natural resources.

Again, Mill is right in holding, against Comte, that economic facts can and should be studied apart from social facts as a whole. The analogy with the natural sciences is helpful here: the physical sciences do not study "natural phenomena as a whole." A physicist studying what happens to a man ejected from an airplane considers only those properties of the man traditionally called "primary." Similarly, the economist studying labor-migration considers men only as producers, distributors, and exchangers of wealth.

Finally, Mill is again right in saying that the principles of economics are, or rather, include, approximately true inductive laws of human nature. This is the general view of the classical economists; it is implicit in the economic works of Ricardo and explicit in the methodological works of Senior, Cairnes, and Bagehot. The principles are approximately true in the sense that Mill's principle — that "a greater gain is preferred to a smaller" — is strictly true, not indeed of all men always as it states, but of most men on most occasions. Nor is it open to question that economic principles are empirical generalizations rather than theoretical assumptions. Indeed, it has been pointed out that a leading difference between the natural sciences and, not only economics, but the social sciences generally is that whereas the principles of the former tend to be theoretical assumptions that cannot be established directly by observation of instances, those of the latter are always inductive laws that can be so established.[3]

The Proper Method of General Sociology and of Political Science

MILL distinguishes two types of sociological inquiry. In the first, we attempt to discover the causes, or effects, of events within a "state of society." But in the second, we investigate the causes of the sequence of states of society. The latter is the problem of "general sociology" or "the general science of society," a study not to be confused with particular social sciences such as political economy. Mill follows Comte in calling the first study "social statics" and the second "social dynamics." A typical discovery of the former is the existence within any "state of society" of an association between the form of government and the other main social facts, a finding that has an important bearing on the perennial question "What is the best form of government?" By a "state of society" is to be understood the simultaneous state of all the "greater social facts" —

that is, the political, legal, intellectual, moral, and other such conditions. Again, whereas in social statics we establish laws of coexistence, in social dynamics we establish laws of succession. The former are derivative laws, but the latter are laws of causation to which the former are subordinate. "The fundamental problem, therefore, of [general sociology], is to find the laws according to which any state of society produces the state that succeeds it. . . . " Society — that is, man — develops or progresses. This is because there is reciprocal causation between men and the circumstances in which they are placed. In consequence, the boundaries of states of society are generations.

The Continental "philosophers of history" have tried, with some success, to discover such laws of succession — for example, the tendency of masses to prevail over individuals. Their discoveries are the fruits of the deeper study of history initiated in the nineteenth century and of the compilation and analysis of statistics. But, says Mill, these philosophers have fallen into the error of mistaking such tendencies for laws of nature, whereas they are in fact only empirical laws. And empirical laws cannot be used for long-range prediction until they have been verified by being deduced from the ultimate laws of psychology and ethology. We have seen that this is the procedure of the inverse deductive or historical method. The justification of this method is that it is plainly impossible to deduce laws of historical development directly from laws of human nature and from circumstances. Moreover, there is the greater need for verification by deduction because sociologists have but few instances (that is, few societies) to generalize from, so that the direct inductive evidence for their empirical laws is weak. Even so, it is practically never possible to show that an empirical law is a necessary consequence of the ultimate laws and the conditions, only that it is a probable or possible consequence of them.

Explaining and verifying the empirical laws would be much easier if it were possible to establish some "middle principle" between them and the ultimate laws. And fortunately this is possible. For there is one sphere of social facts of predominant importance, in the sense that development in all the other spheres depends on development in it — namely, thought. This is not because man is predominantly a truth-pursuing animal in the way that he is, as we have seen in the preceding section, predominantly a wealth-pursuing one, but because the effectiveness with which he can pursue his other aims depends on the extent of his knowledge. The last consideration gives the real reason why "every considerable change historically known to us in the condition of any portion of mankind, when not brought about by external force, has been produced by a change, of proportional extent, in the state of their knowledge, or in their prevalent beliefs." Consequently, the required middle principle, on which the laws of the other spheres of social facts depend, is the "law of the successive transformations of human opinions." Mill considers that a serious candidate for this title is Comte's "law of the three stages," which asserts that human thought on all subjects passes through the following phases. In the first or theological stage, men explain facts in terms of the will of some god. In the second or metaphysical stage, they explain them in terms of the operations of some abstraction such as "Nature." But in the third or positive stage, men explain facts simply in terms of their mutual relations, as expressed in inductive laws of succession and resemblance. For Mill thinks that Comte's vast generalization is supported, not only *a posteriori* by the evidence of history, but also *a priori*, in the sense of being what the laws of psychology would lead us to expect.

Mill's criticism of the "philosophers of history" for mistaking trends for genuine laws, and for making long-range predictions from them, is perfectly sound, and the moral has recently been forcibly reinculcated by Professor Popper. It is an application of the truth which Mill repeatedly stresses, that it is justifiable to extrapolate from an empirical law only a very short way with respect to time, place, or circumstances.*

On the other hand, I question whether long-range predictions from empirical laws that have been "reduced" to laws of human nature in the way that Mill advocates are in much better case, since such "indirect verification" by reduction does not amount to much. To prove, say, de Tocqueville's famous trend to social equality by showing it to be possible, in the sense of *not incompatible with* the laws of human nature, is to set one's standards of proof very low.

Mill's view of political science impresses me as quite mistaken. It is, as we have seen, that there can be no science of government separate from "general sociology," because here considerations of national character and of the age are not secondary, as they are in political economy.

First, I submit that this sort of cause is no less secondary in politics than in economics. Consequently, there is no more need for, say, "nineteenth-century political science" and "twentieth-century political science" than there is for "German political economy" and "French political economy." There can be, and indeed is, a universal science of politics as of economics.

Second, I disagree with Mill about the inapplica-

* Professor Popper charges Mill with "historicism", or a belief in the existence of *unconditional* trends, and attributes this error to Mill's failure to notice that trends are deducible from and explainable by, not laws alone, but laws *and* "initial conditions", which latter may and constantly do alter. I do not think that this charge can be sustained. Mill is fully aware that empirical laws must be reduced to true laws *and* what he calls "collocations" of variable facts or circumstances; so his position on this important point is substantially the same as Professor Popper's.[4]

bility of the direct deductive method to political facts. Observe, for a start, that his criticism on the "geometrical" method is met by adopting the "physical" method. If his father had enriched the premises of his *Essay* with the laws of the chief modifying causes, Mill's criticisms would not have touched it. There is nothing in his criticism to show that *both* forms of the direct deductive method are unsound, so that we must employ the inverse method. And in fact, the "physical" method is the right one for political facts for the same sort of reasons as it is the right one for economic facts. (See the preceding section.)

On the question of the separability of political science from general sociology, it is necessary to add two remarks. First, the former considers men as members of *political* societies, or societies possessing governments, whereas the latter is supposed to consider them simultaneously as members of societies of all sorts. Second, although the former study is both possible and actual, the failure of the attempts to found the latter indicate that it is not possible to do so. It is not in fact practicable to study social phenomena "as a whole"; and this is why there can be, and are, social sciences, but there is not, and cannot be, a "general science of society."

Finally, Mill's own practice in his most considerable political work, the *Representative Government*, is largely inconsistent with his methodological doctrine. For the method he uses there is a compromise between the "mechanistic" theory of politics, which uses the direct deductive method, and the "naturalistic" theory of politics, which uses the historical method. Moreover, the former predominates in his treatment. Thus, on the one hand he argues deductively that democracy is ideally the best form of government from such principles of human nature as "each person is the only safe guardian of his own rights and interests." On the other, he argues that democracy or any other form of government will not work unless certain basic conditions are satisfied, as that the citizens "should be willing and able to fulfill the duties and discharge the functions which it imposes on them." This, indeed, is a law of "social statics." But since Mill considers such laws of coexistence to be subordinate to the laws of succession of "social dynamics," he is to be found arguing along "historical" lines that "the one indispensable merit of a government . . . is that its operation on the people is favourable, or not unfavourable, to the next step which it is necessary for them to take, in order to raise themselves to a higher level."

The Nature of Things

MILL holds a metaphysical theory about the nature of things which is of the sensationalist or phenomenalist variety, and which he admittedly derives from the idealism of Berkeley. This metaphysical theory is introduced into a discussion in which he is attempting something different, namely, to offer a rival psychological account to Hamilton's intuitionist one of how it is that men possess that familiar but complex conception, nature or the external world. It will be convenient to consider his psychological theory first.

Mill describes the belief, the origin of which is to be explained, as follows: The terms "the external world," "body," and "matter" are collective expressions for the sum of things, a typical item of which is the orange on my side-board. In our conception of this orange, and of things like it, Mill discerns three main features. First, we regard its existence as permanent, "real" or "external." In this, it differs radically from the sensations that we have when we perceive it, for the existence of these is fugacious, "ideal," or "in the mind." That is, the orange does not cease to exist when no one perceives it, unlike sensations which do not exist unless they are experienced. Second, we conceive the orange to be the cause of our having the sensations that we have when we perceive it. Third, whereas the sensations that A has when he perceives the orange are private to A in the sense that only A can logically have A's sensations, the orange is a common or public object in the sense that it can be perceived by anyone.

According to Hamilton, our belief in the existence of an external world of things possessing the properties just specified is intuitive. Mill, on the other hand, maintains that it is acquired. His view derives in part from his general opposition to intuitionism; in this respect, his criticism of Hamilton's theory of the external world parallels his criticism of Whewell's philosophy of mathematics. Mill aims to show that the belief may have resulted from the operation of known laws upon known facts, and that if it had so resulted it would naturally appear intuitive.

The known laws and facts in terms of which Mill couches his explanation are partly psychological and partly physical. The psychological ones are these. First, the fact that men can conceive of possible sensations — when they have experienced a sensation of a certain sort under conditions of a certain kind, they can anticipate or expect that they would have a sensation of that sort if conditions of that kind were to recur. Second, the laws of association of ideas. Third, the existence of minds possessing the powers of having sensations, of remembering having sensations of certain sorts under conditions of certain kinds, and of expecting that they would have sensations of those sorts if conditions of those kinds were to recur.

Each of these three factors requires comment. As to the first, Mill observes that his possible sensations are "contingent sensations" or "conditional certainties" and not "mere vague possibilities." To say that a (factual) sensation of a certain sort (namely, the kind one has when one touches an

orange) is now feelable by A, is to say that if some necessary condition were satisfied (say, A's having first a [kinesthetic] sensation of the kind one has when one extends one's hand), then A would certainly have a (tactile) sensation of the sort in question. Thus, Mill equates "possible sensation" with "sensation which anyone would have if some necessary condition were satisfied." (See below, however.) Viewed in the light of recent discussions of the meanings of "can" and "if," this point will be seen to be not trivial.[5]

As for the second factor, inferences by association are not conscious inferences *from* a general rule and some other premise, but unconscious inferences from particulars to particulars *in accordance with* a rule. Hence, when I infer from the existence of a group of simultaneous possibilities of sensation the existence of a permanent, public, etc., object (say, a mountain), I am doing the same kind of thing as I do when I infer from its faintness that the mountain is several miles distant, and say (what is strictly speaking false) that I see that it is so. For another point in which Mill agrees with Berkeley is the doctrine of the "acquired perceptions of sight."*

With regard to the third factor, Mill, again like Berkeley but unlike Hume, holds that a phenomenalist account of minds or persons will not do. For he considers that that which can remember actual sensations and anticipate possible ones cannot itself be no more than a set of possible sensations. He propounds no alternative theory about the nature of mind.

The physical factors on which Mill bases his explanation are two: first, the fact that sensations occur; second, the fact that they occur in order. For sensations succeed one another and sometimes coexist. But more, certain sorts of sensations regularly coexist in stable groups, and certain sorts of stable groups regularly succeed certain other sorts of stable groups in stable sequences.

The stable groups are composed predominantly, and sometimes exclusively, of possible sensations, not actual ones. The reason for this has been indicated above. That which a certain sort of actual sensation (say, the sort of visual sensation one has on seeing an orange) regularly coexists with is not another sort of actual sensation (say, the sort of tactual sensation one has on touching an orange). For a sensation of the latter sort does not occur until a third sort of actual sensation has occurred first (namely, the sort of kinesthetic sensation one has on

* Stereoscopic vision is a controversial subject, but the view of most psychologists today seems to be that although what Berkeley and Mill say is true, it is not the whole truth. Thus, most psychologists do not dispute that our perception of distance and depth depends largely on automatic and unconscious inferences from such "cues" as the degree of faintness of the object seen. But they point out that this is not the whole story, since in ordinary binocular vision we should still perceive distance and depth to some extent if all such cues were absent, notably because of the operation of retinal disparity.

extending one's hand). Hence, that which the first sort of actual (visual) sensation regularly coexists with is, not the second sort of actual (tactual) sensation, but a sort of possible (tactual) sensation. "This is what is meant by saying that a Body is a group of simultaneous possibilities of sensation, not of simultaneous sensations."

Similarly, the stable sequences are composed predominantly, and usually exclusively, of groups of possible sensations, not of groups of actual ones. Only a small minority of causal laws, namely, some physiological ones, state that one sort of actual sensation is the unconditional invariable antecedent of some other sort of actual sensation. The great majority of them such as "Fire melts ice," state that one sort of group of possible sensations is the unconditional invariable antecedent of some other sort of group of possible sensations.

According to Mill, there are two stages in the genesis of the belief in the external world. The first is the formation of the conception of a group of simultaneous possibilities of sensation. This arises from experience. It is by experience that *A* learns that if he were to have a visual sensation of a certain sort, then if he first had a kinesthetic sensation of a certain sort, he would have a certain kind of tactile sensation. The second is the formation of the conception of a thing or body. This arises from the operation of the laws of association upon the conception of a group of simultaneous possibilities of sensation, and Mill accounts for the properties we impute to bodies as follows.

The reason we attribute permanent or real existence to things is that permanence is a property of possible sensations, although not of actual ones. But the conception of a group of possible sensations is that which we transform into the conception of a real thing. And by association we simply transfer the permanence that characterizes the former to the latter. We think of things as common or public for a similar reason. Possible sensations, unlike actual ones, are public, for a possible sensation is a sensation that anyone would experience under certain conditions. Here again, by association, we transfer to our conception of bodies the publicity that attaches to the groups of possible sensations in the conception of which the conception of bodies originates. The notion of things being the causes of sensation originates as follows. We have seen that groups of possible sensations succeed one another regularly, so that each sort of group has some other sort of group for its unconditional invariable antecedent. Hence, by association, we come to think of sensation itself as having an unconditional invariable antecedent in the same way as do groups of possible sensations, and of matter as that which exercises this causal function.

From these psychological considerations, Mill turns abruptly to metaphysics, and propounds his own theory on the nature of things in the following words: "Matter, then, may be defined, a Permanent Possibility of Sensation. If I am asked, whether I believe in matter, I ask whether the questioner accepts this definition of it. If he does, I believe in matter: and so do all Berkeleians. In any other sense than this, I do not. But I affirm with confidence, that this conception of matter includes the whole meaning attached to it by the common world, apart from philosophical, and sometimes from theological, theories."

The most conspicuous defect in Mill's psychological theory is perhaps his omission of a feature of the order of our sensations which, as Hume points out, is of great influence in inducing us to form the conception of things or bodies that exist externally or really, namely, what he calls the "constancy" and "coherence" of some of them. Mill's neglect of this valuable clue, provided by his great predecessor in the empiricist tradition, is surprising.

Mill's metaphysical theory comprises two assertions. The first is that his definition of "matter" as "a permanent possibility of sensation" agrees with the common conception of the nature of things, if not with the philosophical one. Mill's claim to be with the vulgar in this matter of matter and against the philosophers is the same as Berkeley's, and it is equally unacceptable in the case of both philosophers. For there are in fact radical differences between things as ordinarily conceived and things as defined by Mill.

Thus, the former exist actually whereas the latter exist potentially. This difference tends to be obscured in Mill's discussion for two reasons. First, it may be thought that we have actual existence in both cases, that which exists actually being in the former case a thing and in the latter case, a possibility or set of possibilities. But the last contention is fallacious. For to say that there is a possibility of snow is simply to say in other words that snow exists potentially: it is not to say that a possibility, or anything whatever, exists actually. Second, Mill's practice of prefixing "permanent" and "simultaneous" to "possibilities of sensation" strongly suggests that these possibilities exist actually, for these adjectives are usually applied to actual, not to potential, existents, as when we speak of "simultaneous shots" or "the permanent way."

There is a possible reply to this objection which turns on an ambiguity in Mill's definition of "matter." He usually writes as if a thing, say the orange, were the (set of) *sensations* which anyone would have if he first had certain other sensations. However, he also says explicitly that contingent sensations are conceptions that men form because they are capable of expectation. So, his real account of the nature of the orange is not the one just given, but is anyone's *conception* of the sensations which he would have if he first had certain other sensations. On this account, the objection just made does not hold, since conceptions exist actually. However, it is open to other, equally decisive, objections. Thus, conceptions exist only in the minds of their conceivers, whereas things (are said to) exist "without the mind." Again, whereas things are permanent, the conceptions in question are short-lived, for no one dwells in imagination for long on such thoughts as that of the tactile sensation he would have if he were first to have the sort of kinesthetic sensation that goes with extending one's hand.

Another objection holds against both of Mill's definitions of "matter." This is that whereas things are common, both possible sensations and conceptions of possible sensations are private. As to the latter, it is clear that A cannot have B's conception or anticipation, or conversely. But the privacy of possible sensations is perhaps less evident, and we have seen that Mill himself insists on the publicity of possible sensations as contrasted with the privacy of actual ones. He is nonetheless mistaken in this, for it is no less logically true that any particular sensation which is feelable by A is feelable only by A than it is that any particular sensation which is felt by A is felt only by A.

I suggest that Mill was led astray here by ambiguities in "sensation" and "feel." As to the first, "sensation" is ambiguous as between "particular sensation" and "sort of sensation." Now, the latter is indeed common in the sense that the same sort of sensation is feelable by both A and B. But it seems pretty clear (though not perhaps so clear as to settle the question conclusively) that Mill holds that the orange on my sideboard consists of (anyone's conception of) the *particular* sensations which he would have if certain conditions were satisfied, not (anyone's conception of) the *sort* of sensations he would have if certain conditions were satisfied. And possible particular sensations, to repeat it, are no less private than are actual particular sensations. It is to be noticed that this is the right form in which to express Mill's doctrine. For he is in the main, like Berkeley, a factual and not a linguistic idealist or phenomenalist. Formulated linguistically, Mill's doctrine would be: Any statement about the orange means the same as a conjunction of statements about (anyone's conception of) the sensations he would have if certain conditions were fulfilled.

As to the second ambiguity, "feel" is in one use a verb of perception taking a common object, but in another use a verb of sensation taking a private object. Thus, compare (1) "the orange which anyone would feel if he first extended his hand" with (2) "the sensation which anyone would feel if he first had another sensation." In (1), "the orange" means "the particular orange," and "feel" is a verb of perception. In this sense of "feel," numerically the same object (one and the same orange) is feelable by both A and B. But in (2) "the sensation" means "the sort of sensation," "another sensation" means "another sort of sensation," and "feel" is a verb of sensation. In this sense of "feel," only qualitatively

and not numerically the same object (the same sort of sensation) is feelable by both A and B. It seems likely that Mill was misled into believing in the publicity of contingent sensations by his unconsciously misassimilating (2) to (1).

But in any case, the fact is that Mill himself, in his psychological theory, insists on the difference between the conception of a set of contingent sensations and the conception of a physical object. For the aim and upshot of that theory is to show how the laws of association so operate upon the former conception as to transform it into a different conception, namely, that of a thing. And if this is so, Mill cannot be right in asserting, in his metaphysical theory, that the two conceptions are the same. In fact, it is the metaphysical thesis which is the false one, as Mill sometimes shows himself to be dimly but uneasily aware.

As to the cause of his mistake, I surmise that it is simply the genetic fallacy. For, as I have just said, his psychological theory represents the conception of a possible sensation as that in which the conception of a thing originates. But saying that the latter therefore *is* (really only) the former is like saying that a man is (really only) so much carbon, hydrogen, oxygen, and nitrogen.

The second assertion comprised in Mill's metaphysical theory is that "matter exists" is true if "matter" is taken to mean "[conceptions of] sets of contingent sensations" but false if it is taken to mean anything else, such as and more particularly "external existents."

If "matter" is taken to mean "external existents," the question "Does matter exist?" may be interpreted in different ways. First, as a factual question: On this interpretation, it is like "Do moas (still) exist?" Second, as a theoretical question: Here, the existence of the external world is regarded as a hypothesis designed to explain the occurrence and order of sensations. On this interpretation, the question is like "Does the ether exist?" Third, as a philosophical question: Here, the real existence of things is regarded as a commonsense belief which is implicit in our common ways of speech. On this interpretation, the question is like "Does mind exist?"

In his metaphysical theory, Mill takes the question in the factual way. It is clear from the context that he does not interpret it in the theoretical way. It is also clear that he cannot be interpreting it in the philosophical way, since his own psychological theory shows that taken in *this* sense he holds the answer to the question to be affirmative: this, he agrees, is what men think and say, and the object of his psychological theory is to account for the existence of the belief.

Now, if the question "Does matter exist?" is taken to be factual, the first part of Mill's second assertion (namely, that the answer to the question is affirmative if "matter" is taken to mean "[conceptions of] contingent sensations") is warranted and true. For we are all directly aware of the existence of our own expectations of sensations. But, on the same interpretation of the question, the second part of Mill's second assertion (namely, that the answer to the question is negative if "matter" is taken to mean "external existents") is not warranted. For though it may *be* false that matter, in this sense of "matter," exists, it is logically impossible to *establish* that it is false or true. For the only way to establish that a thing of a certain sort does or does not exist is to observe it or fail to observe it; but it is self-contradictory to speak of observing or failing to observe a thing to which is imputed the property of existing when no one observes it. Hence, the second part of Mill's second assertion is pointless. It is not competent in him to "attack the belief in Matter as an entity *per se*."

The source of Mill's error lies in his taking the question "Does matter exist?" in an illegitimate — that is, the factual — way. It is strange that he should slip into doing this in his metaphysical theory because, as I have said above, in his psychological theory he interprets it in a legitimate way, namely the philosophical one.

The Right to Liberty of Thought

THE problem that Mill sets himself in *Liberty* is to define the proper bounds of society's power over the individual. "Society," of course, is a wider term than "the State," and the power that Mill is concerned with includes not only the physical coercion and threats employed, notably, by governments, but also the "moral coercion of public opinion." His reason for addressing himself to the problem is his concern about a general tendency, which he thinks he sees, to an increase in society's power over the individual, and also at the danger of a "tyranny of the majority" latent in democracy. For his reading of de Tocqueville's *Democracy in America* had convinced him that it is quite gratuitous to assume that only minorities have "sinister" or class interests or are likely to legislate in these interests.

Mill's solution to his problem consists in asserting "one very simple principle. . . . That the only purpose for which power can be rightfully exercised over any member of a civilized community, against his will, is to prevent harm to others." He excludes, besides members of uncivilized communities, minors. This is Mill's "principle of individual liberty." He grounds it, not on "abstract [or natural] right," but on "utility in the largest sense, grounded on the permanent interests of a man as a progressive being." That is, men have an absolute right to be free from constraint with respect to all of their acts that do not harm others, because the general "well-being" is thereby maximized.

The sphere of individual liberty comprises accord-

ingly those of a man's acts which "affect only himself . . . directly and in the first instance." Mill divides this sphere into two parts, for each of which there is a corresponding right to liberty. First, the inward life, with respect to which there is an absolute right to "freedom of opinion and sentiment on all subjects" and to the expression thereof, since this is "practically inseparable" from the former. Second, the outward life, with respect to which there is an absolute right to the liberty of "doing as we like, subject to such consequences as may follow." By the last qualification, Mill means "the inconveniences which are strictly inseparable from the unfavourable judgement of others" — for example, the fact that men shun the company of the offensively drunk. Corollaries of this second right are the absolute rights to the liberties of contract and association. Mill then attempts to prove his liberty-principle as a whole by proving in turn the rights to liberty of thought and of action.

He proves the existence of the first right from the consideration that free thought and discussion is a necessary condition of men's obtaining the maximum of knowledge. For there are only three possible cases. First, that in which the suppressed opinion is true and the protected, opposed opinion false; here it is obvious that the suppression deprives men of knowledge. The common argument that those who silence discussion assume their own infallibility is correct, since one cannot be sure that an opinion *is* true unless it is open to anyone to refute it if he can. Second, the case in which the suppressed opinion is part of the truth and the protected, opposed opinion is the complementary part of the truth. For instance, the doctrines of parties of order or stability and of parties of progress or reform divide the truth between them in this way. Here, the case against suppression is substantially the same as in the first case.

Third, the case in which the suppressed opinion is false and the protected, opposed opinion is true. Even here, the suppression deprived men of knowledge, although in a less obvious way. For knowing an opinion to be true presupposes knowing the reasons, not only for, but also against it; but the latter evidently prerequires the liberty to propound views opposed to the protected opinion. Knowing an opinion to be true also presupposes understanding its meaning, but unless it is freely discussed, it ceases to have meaning and becomes "a dead dogma, not a living truth." The doctrines of Christianity, Mill thinks, are now in this situation.

Finally, Mill tells us that free thought is needed not only, or mainly, to form great thinkers but "to enable average human beings to attain the mental stature which they are capable of." His proof of the existence of an unconditional right to free thought and expression that does not harm others is that the latter is a necessary condition of men's obtaining the maximum knowledge, which in turn is a necessary condition of their mental development or "self-realization," which in turn is a constituent of the general well-being.

Mill's theory belongs to the family of liberal, not democratic, theories of limited government. In particular, it resembles Lock's attempt in his *Letter Concerning Toleration* to prove the right to religious liberty by defining the respective spheres of interest of Church and State.*

We must now consider Mill's account of the meaning of "liberty." In one place he writes "Liberty consists in doing what one desires." But this is much too wide to serve as a definition, since it carries the paradoxical consequence that all actions are free — for doing what one wishes is the same thing as acting. Mill means rather "doing what one desires without restraint by others"; and this is much nearer the truth, although still too wide, since an acceptable definition needs to be qualified with respect to the *sorts* of restraint imposed by others. That this is what Mill really intends is clear from the opening sentence of his essay, in which he explicitly connects "social liberty" with the power exercised by society over the individual.

My main criticism is that his argument is not adapted to prove his thesis. This is (or *ought* to be) that men have an *absolute* or unconditional duty not to restrain each other from expressing thoughts that do not harm others, as distinct from themselves. To establish this on utilitarian grounds, Mill must show that the general well-being is *always on balance* maximized by this policy. Consider this illustration. A man proposes to publish a true criticism of a false protected doctrine, and the penalty for doing so is crucifixion. Mill must show that the effect on the general well being is better if the man is not restrained by a friend, say, than it is if he is. This involves comparing (1) the increase in well being caused by men's increasing their knowledge, less the decrease in well being caused by the man's crucifixion with (2) the nondiminution in well being caused by the man's escaping crucifixion, less the decrease in well being caused by the loss to society of new knowledge — and similarly for all actual and possible cases. But Mill shows only that *one* of the consequences (namely, self-realization) of the policy that he advocates increases well being.

Although he does not prove it, Mill's thesis may nevertheless be true. The relevant question is, are there any exceptions to it? Mill himself adduces one, namely, when the circumstances are such that expression of the opinion constitutes an instigation to a mischievous act. But since such instigations obviously harm others, they fall outside the scope of his principle and so cannot be exceptions to it.

Since I cannot think of any exception, I am inclined to think that the principle is true. In the illustration just given, for instance, I should not consider myself morally justified in restraining the man from publishing his criticism.

In conclusion, it is interesting that in *Liberty*, Mill does not argue that case for free thought which his *Logic* leads one to expect him to argue. We have seen that he accepts Comte's intellectual interpretation of history, according to which progress in the intellectual sphere of life is the predominant cause of progress in all the other spheres. One might therefore have expected Mill to advocate free thought on the ground that it is a necessary condition of progress in the intellectual sphere. This is, in fact, the case for it that Bury puts up in his *History of Freedom of Thought*.

The Right to Liberty of Action

MILL'S proof of the existence of the individual's absolute right to liberty with respect to acts that do not harm others, which is largely derived from von Humboldt, is as follows, Development of personality, or self-realization, is a *constituent* of the general well being; and liberty of action is one of the two necessary conditions of self-realization, the other being "variety of situations." In addition, self-realization is a *cause* of increased welfare, since those who develop themselves induce the undeveloped to do likewise by setting "the example of more enlightened conduct, and better taste and sense in human life."

Mill contends that the right is unconditional because the general well being is always on balance maximized if the right is respected. Consider, for example, prohibition of selling, and hence of using, alcoholic beverages. Mill's contention is that from the standpoint of the general well being, the first of the following situations is better than the second: (1) the self-realization for which free sale is indispensable, less the harm caused by excessive drinking; and (2) the absence of harm caused by excessive drinking, less the loss of self-realization caused by prohibition. And so similarly for all actual and possible cases.

Mill thinks that his contention is greatly strengthened by the consideration that restraints on this liberty tend not to promote the individual's interests *at all*. The reason is that although it is an important truth that men are in general the best judges of their own interests, it is by no means true that they are the best judges of the interests of others. Prohibition, as we have just seen, has at any rate *one* beneficial consequence, the restraints on self-regarding acts tend to be like the Puritan legislation against plays and concerts, which had no good result whatever. Further, Mill observes that such restraints are impracticable as well as wrong, since men will not stand for them.

---

* A recent example is Lord Russell's suggestion that there is a *prima facie* case against society's interference with the production and distribution of goods in which private property is not possible. Such goods are, roughly speaking, "mental" goods.[6]

Naturally, Mill intends his principle to cover prevention. If a policeman sees one man load a gun and aim at another, it is of course his right and duty to restrain the former *before* he harms the latter. Thus, the principle asserts that society is justified in restraining the individual only from doing those of his acts that harm, or certainly or probably will harm, others.

Mill considers and rejects the objection that there are, in fact, no acts that affect only the agent directly and in the first instance. He thinks that the supposed difficulties are satisfactorily met by drawing the appropriate distinctions. Thus, although no one ought to be punished for being a drunk, a policeman is properly punished for being drunk on duty, since the effect of his incapacity will be certain, or probable, harm to others.

Mill thinks that the great enemies of self-realization are "the despotism of custom" and "the tyranny of opinion." These forces are now so strong that self-development of any kind is desirable, even in undesirable directions, in order that society may be familiarized with the existence of a variety of characters and so induced to tolerate such a situation.

Although the current tendency is to curtail liberty unjustifiably, there are cases where liberty is excessive. Mill believes that the liberty of parents to do wholly what they will with their children rests on the erroneous view that the latter are as much "theirs" as are their own limbs, so that those of their acts that affect their children are really self-regarding acts.

In conclusion, Mill touches on two important questions respecting the proper limits of governmental intervention which do not strictly involve his liberty-principle. First, there is "authoritative" or coercive governmental interference with industry and trade. The case for such interference is usually based on the principle that where there is harm to others (ruin through competition, for example) there should be restraint, but Mill's liberty-principle asserts, not this, but that where there is no harm to others there should be no restraint. In fact, Mill maintains on utilitarian grounds that *laissez-faire* should be the general rule, but with large exceptions. Second, there are "unauthoritative" or noncoercive interventions by government — for instance, governmental supply, but not monopoly, of education. The liberty-principle evidently does not apply here, since there is no infringement of liberty. Nevertheless, Mill thinks that there are three other cogent objections to this sort of intervention: that, generally speaking, the citizens are the persons best fitted to run the businesses in which they are interested; that even when they are not the most fit persons, it is still best that they should do it "as a means to their own mental education"; and, above all, that to permit these interventions is to increase governmental power beyond what is either necessary or desirable.

It will be perceived that Mill's proof of an absolute right to liberty of action is indeed adapted to prove an unconditional or absolute right, and so escapes the main objection that I brought against his proof of an absolute right to liberty of thought and expression. The question whether his principle respecting freedom of action is in fact true may be settled more simply in the same way as is the corresponding question about free thought, namely, by seeking exceptions. Here too, since I can find none, I am inclined to think that the principle is true. To take stock instances: it is not clear to me that, provided no others are harmed and the agents involved are adults, it is morally justifiable to restrain physically the would-be suicide, to prohibit the sale and so the use of opium, or to imprison those who voluntarily engage in homosexual practices.

Fitzjames Stephen points out that Mill's liberty-principle, conjoined with his doctrine mentioned above about the "inconveniences strictly inseparable from the unfavourable judgment of others" on a man's self-regarding conduct, involves serious consequences. As, for example, that society is morally justified in refusing to employ a habitual drunkard, but not morally justified in infringing his liberty by threatening him with a fine if he is drunk. The man himself might argue, not unreasonably, that if it is wrong for society to inflict on him the small harm of a trifling threat for being habitually drunk, then *a fortiori* it is wrong for it to inflict on him for this misconduct the very great harm of chronic unemployment.

A few words in conclusion about Mill's teaching on the value of liberty. He evidently thinks social liberty a good thing, in which he is clearly right, for we all say so, including the apologists of tyranny; else why should they defend it on the ground that the citizen is *really* free when he is being coerced by government? The only question then is why is it, or what makes it, a good thing? Mill's answer, as we have seen, is: Because the liberties of thought and action, which jointly make up liberty as a whole, are necessary conditions of self-realization, which is a constituent of the general well being. But while this seems true so far as it goes, I do not think it is by any means a complete account. As we saw earlier, it is arguable that liberty of thought is good for the reason that it is a necessary condition for the advancement of knowledge. And there are two further reasons worth mentioning. First, that liberty and constraint usually cause a feeling of spontaneity and frustration, respectively, which men respectively consider a great good and a great evil. Second, that liberty favors morality and character to some extent at least, since constraint sometimes, though doubtless not always, destroys morality by removing choice and weakens character by eliminating responsibility. There may well be still more reasons why liberty is a good thing.

The Meaning and Truth of the Principle of Utility

"IT is the business of ethics," says Mill, "to tell us what are our duties, or by what test we may know them." He adds that such a test is "the *means* . . . of ascertaining what is right and wrong, and not a *consequence* of having already ascertained it" (my italics).

His primary objective in *Utilitarianism* is to explain the meaning and prove the truth of "the first principle of morals," namely, the utility (or greatest happiness) principle that, if true, is the test of the rightness and wrongness of actions. He is also concerned with defending the "inductive school of ethics" against the "intuitive" one. The chief protagonists are Bentham and himself, and Kant and Whewell, respectively. The latter maintain moral principles to be *a priori* self-evident truths, whereas the former maintain both the first principle and "secondary principles" to be, or to be logical consequences of, *a posteriori* true generalizations.

The utility-principle is the judgment that happiness is the only thing desirable as an end (or the only intrinsic good), and/or that actions are right as they tend to produce happiness, wrong as they tend to produce unhappiness. In the latter formula, "actions" means "*classes* of actions" (homicide, for example), not particular actions. The test of the rightness (or wrongness) of a *particular* action is *usually* its membership in a class of actions, most of which produce happiness (or unhappiness). Hence, a particular action belonging to such a class is *usually* wrong, even though it produces happiness. But it is *sometimes* right if it produces happiness, even though it belongs to a class of actions most of which produce unhappiness. (As an example, homicide is sometimes justified.) Hence, the test of the rightness of classes of actions may be applied to particular actions too; but the normal test of the rightness of particular actions cannot be logically applied to classes of actions too.* By "happiness" is meant "pleasure and the absence of pain," and "the general happiness" as opposed to the agent's own. All desirable things other than happiness are desired as *means* to the production of pleasure or the prevention of pain.

The test of the *rightness* of actions being as described, the motive of the agent cannot be the (or a) test of that. But it is the test of the *goodness* of the agent. On the utilitarian view, a man is good or virtuous if his motive is to promote the general happiness. This does not mean, however, that the good man is always trying to make everyone, or a

large number of other people, happy. Few are in a position to be public benefactors: the objects of the beneficence of most are restricted to a few other people.

Pleasures differ in kind (or quality) as well as in intensity (or quantity), and one pleasure may be more desirable than another, either because it is more intense or because it is of a higher kind. One kind of pleasure is higher than another when the former is preferred to the latter by all or most competent judges, who are those who have had experience of both kinds. In fact, such judges normally prefer those pleasures which accompany the exercise of the higher faculties.

The proper policy for the legislator is to make such laws and social arrangements as insure that the individual will promote the general happiness in promoting his own, and to use the forces of education and opinion to cause the individual to associate the general happiness with his own. In this way, the legislator will provide men with an "artificial" sanction or inducement to produce general happiness: but they also possess a "natural" sanction to do so in their social feelings — in other words, their "feeling of unity with all the rest."

Mill replies to the objection against utilitarianism, that there is no time to estimate the certain or probable effects of a particular action on the general happiness, as follows. We normally do not need to make such estimates since, as we have seen, all we usually ought to do in judging of the rightness of a particular action, is to note that it belongs to a class of actions that tend to promote happiness or unhappiness. The proportional generalizations that give this information about classes of actions are the "secondary principles" of morality; and one sense in which utilitarianism is an empirical, inductive, and "scientific" philosophy of morals is in its insistence that these secondary principles are empirical generalizations. Most moral questions about particular acts are thus soluble simply by applying secondary principles. But not all. For when the case falls under two conflicting secondary principles, the first principle must be applied directly to the particular act. For example, a military conscript considering the rightness of disobeying an order to join up might regard his case as falling under two conflicting secondary principles: "Homicide is generally wrong" and "Obedience to the laws is generally right." He must then estimate the direct effects on the general happiness of his obeying and disobeying the order respectively, and decide accordingly.

Mill considers that a logical consequence of the utility-principle is the equality-principle, that we ought to count "one person's happiness, supposed equal in degree (with the proper allowance made for kind) . . . for exactly as much as another's." A logical consequence of this "equal claim of everybody to happiness" is in turn "the equal claim to all the

---

* Since Mill's meaning on this issue is disputed, I should add that I take my account from that part of his essay on Whewell's moral philosophy which is devoted to replying to Whewell's objections against the utility-principle, and which contains the clearest statement of his view of the matter.

means of happiness." These equal claims are not, of course, unconditional rights to an equal share of happiness and of the means to it. For they are frequently overridden by considerations of general utility; and rightly so. For example, the claim to equality of income may be rejected on the score that the general happiness is promoted more by the first state of affairs than by the second: (1) greater national wealth and inequality of income as a necessary inducement to producing it; and (2) equality of income and consequently less national wealth. The meaning of Mill's equality-principle is rather that "all persons . . . have a [moral] *right* to equality of treatment, except when some recognized social expediency requires the reverse."

Thus far on the meaning and implications of the utility-principle; now for the proof of its truth. Mill prefaces it with the remark that it is not a proof in the ordinary meaning of the term because questions of ultimate ends are not amenable to such proof. The proof is this: (1) One's own happiness (or pleasure) is the only thing desired for itself by each person. Therefore, (2) the general happiness (or the happiness of all) is the only thing desired for itself by all. (3) Being desired entails being desirable (or good). Therefore, (4) the general happiness is the only intrinsically good thing; and/or (5) the test of the rightness of actions is their tendency to promote the general happiness.

Mill provides the following elucidations of propositions (1) and (3): (1) is a "metaphysical" necessity, by which he means an inductive law of psychology.* He anticipates the possible objection to (1), that other things besides happiness — for instance, virtue — are desired for themselves, by asserting that such things are indeed desired for themselves, but as being *parts* of happiness. For happiness is a "concrete whole," made up of parts or elements; we have seen earlier that another such constituent which is desired for itself is self-realization. We have also seen earlier that yet other things are desired as *means* to happiness. And according to Mill, the way in which virtue, as one example, comes to be desired for itself or as a part of happiness is "by association with what it is a means to." Similarly, the miser comes to love money for its own sake by constantly associating the idea of money with the idea of the goods that money is a means of procuring. Proposition (3) Mill explains by analogy: as "seen" entails "visible," so "desired" entails "desirable."

To comment: There is an obvious parallelism

* Some interpret this as meaning that (1) is a *logical* necessity or analytic truth. But though Mill sometimes uses "metaphysical" as equivalent to "logical", he also uses it as equivalent to "psychological"; and that, I submit, is its sense here. If (1), the main premise of his proof, is analytic, Mill's position is an intuitionist one, since the utility-principle is then a logical consequence of a "self-evident" truth. In fact, however, the claim that the first principle of morals is a logical consequence of an empirical generalization indicates the other and main sense in which utilitarianism purports to be an inductive and "scientific" ethical theory.

between Mill's championship of the progressive school of experience against the conservative intuitionists in the philosophy of morals and in the philosophy of mathematics. Nor will it escape notice that Whewell is a leading antagonist in both battles.

The fact that Mill gives no information about how to compare higher and lower kinds of pleasures of different intensities radically vitiates his utility-principle. For suppose I have to decide between two actions: reading poetry to a friend and thereby giving him high-grade pleasure of moderate intensity, and playing pushpin with him and thereby giving him low-grade pleasure of great intensity. Mill gives no guidance about which action will maximize happiness or, consequently, about which I ought to do. The introduction of differences of quality as well as of quantity in pleasures is one of Mill's chief departures from Benthamism.

Mill is mistaken in thinking that his equality-principle is a logical consequence of his utility-principle. For suppose I have to decide between two actions, the former of which will give to one man twice the amount of pleasure that the latter action will give to each of two men. According to Mill's utility-principle, it is indifferent which I do — but according to his equality-principle, I ought to do the latter action. The two principles are coordinate, so that the utility-principle is not *the* first principle of Mill's moral philosophy, as he claims.

Notwithstanding his protestations to the contrary, Mill's putative proof of his utility-principle is in fact a proof in the ordinary meaning — that is, a deductive proof. To be precise, and to use Sidgwick's terminology, what it purports to do is to deduce a value judgment, the principle of *universalistic ethical* hedonism, from a descriptive statement, the principle of *egoistic psychological* hedonism.

The main premise (1) in Mill's proof is false, and arises from the following confusion. If I desire virtue, for example, I foresee that if I acquire it, I shall have the pleasure of fulfilled desire. But it does not follow that when I *seem* to desire virtue, what I *really* desire is the pleasure of fulfilled desire. For I have no reason to anticipate the pleasure of fulfilled desire on acquiring virtue unless I desire, not that pleasure, but virtue. Hence, it is false that the only thing men desire is their own pleasure.

The inference from (1) to (2) is invalid and commits the fallacy of composition. "The general happiness" means "The happiness of each and all," and "Each desires his own happiness" does not entail "Each and all desire the happinesses of each and all." Again, (3) is false and commits the naturalistic fallacy — the fallacy of believing that a descriptive statement can entail a value judgment. For whereas "desired" is a descriptive word, "desirable" is an evaluative one, and means "good." Mill is led into this fallacy by the erroneous analogy he draws between the relation of "desired" to "desirable" and "seen" to "visible."

His discussion of how things other than happiness come to be desired as ends betrays an ambiguity in his use of the key word "happiness." In the strict and narrow sense, it means, as we have seen, "pleasure and the absence of pain." But in the wider sense, it means that, and also virtue and self-realization and fame, etc.

Although Mill signally fails to prove the truth of the utility-principle, it may yet be true. But rather than investigate this question by seeking exceptions, I shall conclude by showing why his critics are dispensed from this trouble, and by simultaneously indicating a radical defect in *Utilitarianism*. Briefly, there is a far-reaching inconsistency between Mill's notion of the nature of ethical philosophy and his primary objective in the essay. According to Mill, the aim of the former, to repeat it, is "to *tell* us what are our duties, or by what test we may know them" (my italics). Mill, like Bentham, writes as a reformer and uses his standard of morality to criticize existing institutions and practices. The questions whether, or how far, his principle and its consequences square with "the morality of common sense" does not concern him. But in that case, the question of the *truth* of his principle cannot arise — though that of its goodness certainly does. Hence, Mill's main aim in *Utilitarianism*, which is to prove the truth of the utility-principle, is misconceived, and any attempt by a critic to establish its truth or falsity would be misconceived also.

20

Schopenhauer

RICHARD TAYLOR

ARTHUR SCHOPENHAUER WAS BORN on February 22, 1788, in Danzig, and was destined by his father for a life of commerce for which, however, he had no temperament. He was partly educated in England, and forever exhibited some of the intellectual habits characteristic of British thought, particularly clarity of style. Only a man whose thoughts are trivial and insipid, he observed, feels the need to wrap them in obscure and imposing terminology, just as one lacking physical beauty feels the need of gaudy apparel to cover his embarrassing nakedness. He followed the odious life of commerce for a time, but was released from it by his father's death, to devote himself wholly to learning. His mother, Johanna Schopenhauer, was a novelist of considerable reputation in her day, and between her and the son there arose a spirit of competition that grew into pronounced enmity. Schopenhauer predicted, rightly, that she would be remembered to posterity only as his mother. He nevertheless dedicated to her his book on *The Basis of Morality*. Among philosophers he venerated Immanual Kant, acknowledged a great debt to Plato, but heaped scorn on most of the rest, particularly the professors of his own time and culture. These he dismissed with such mordacious epithets as "windbags." He described Hegel as a "stupid and clumsy charlatan" and Fichte as an opportunist whose deliberate scheme was to caricature Kant and thereby "wrap the German people in philosophic fog." The great influence of these two, in particular, and his own relative obscurity during most of his life combined to confirm him in his opinion of the utter worthlessness of most of mankind. One of his most original and inspiring writings, *The Basis of Morality*, remains to this day relatively unknown. It was submitted to the Danish Royal Society of Sciences for a prize, but despite the fact that it had not a single competitor, it was rejected, partly because of the author's declared contempt for some of his contemporaries who were then widely considered illustrious. Although Schopenhauer's thought attracted little attention at first, he finally began to receive some of the admiration he so richly deserved, and there was even created a demand for his popular essays, which were, and have been ever since, widely read. Schopenhauer himself never doubted that the turgid philosophical systems then so much in vogue would some day be eclipsed by the profundity and clear truth of his own. He died, having finally tasted some of the recognition he craved, at the age of seventy-two.

S CHOPENHAUER, LIKE PLATO and Aristotle, distinguished between those who live *for* philosophy and those who live *by* it. The former are the lovers of wisdom for its own sake and the latter the sophists, or what Schopenhauer contemptuously referred to as professors of philosophy. The philosopher sets understanding and wisdom as his ultimate goal, whereas the sophist or professor uses philosophical thought — usually that of other men — as a means to some personal and worldly end. The true philosopher, accordingly, derives his problems from the world and life, creating the thought from which the sophists and professors subsequently derive their livelihood. These latter, having no genuine perplexity and hence no original philosophy, make their way in the world, for themselves and their families, as critics, disciples, and epigones.

Schopenhauer, by these standards, was clearly a genuine philosopher. He dedicated himself wholly to the elaboration of his own highly original and profound philosophy and, despite his vast erudition, took his problems from the world rather than books. He was never established as a professor, failed in his one brief attempt at lecturing, and was never beholden to authorities. Decades of obscurity did not divert him from his true love, which was the truth as it appeared to his eyes and understanding. His chief work, *The World as Will and Idea*, was written before he was thirty, and he regarded all his subsequent thought as further elaboration and confirmation of it. The second edition of this work, appearing late in his life, contained some fifty additional essays written over the course of years, each of them a further development of the ideas contained in the original. His life work thus presents a consistency and order that is rare, and precious, in any philosopher. His disdain for the thought of his contemporaries helped to free his mind from prejudices and presuppositions, giving his philosophy an uncommon freshness, penetration, and originality. No significant aspect of experience escaped his interpretation, and things ordinarily deemed beneath the notice of philosophy — such as noise, sex, and the anatomy of animals — fall into place in his system.

It is almost a rule in the history of philosophy that highly original and inspired thought is pressed by its inventor to extremes, and carries absurdities in its wake which become very apparent to subsequent generations. Schopenhauer's philosophy is no exception. His earlier writings, infused with the enthusiasm of a youthful thinker who was able to see the importance of his basic insight without appreciating its limitations, abound in extremes and fanciful hypotheses that can now only appear to us as absurd. At times the boundaries between science, philosophy, and poetry seem quite obliterated in his thinking. Gravitational force, for example, was regarded by Schopenhauer as an expression of will in inanimate bodies, and the growth, development, and behavior of plants he interpreted in the same fashion, even to the point of appearing to ascribe motives and purpose to them. Yet one can hardly help thinking that had Schopenhauer not been so obsessed with the concept of the will that he sometimes applied it in fantastic ways, he might have missed some of the invaluable insights that this idea suggested, and which were in many cases original with him.

The Kantian Background

SCHOPENHAUER's philosophy begins with the distinction between what is and what is rationally knowable, a distinction that is as old as philosophy but one which Schopenhauer thought had not been properly made before Kant. The knowing subject's world is comprised of his perceptions, which are the product of understanding applied to the data of sense, together with his rational interpretations of these, which are the product of reason. This implies that the knower's apprehension of reality is conditioned throughout, that is to say, is relative to his sense, understanding, and reason, these being what the knower himself contributes to thought and experience. Reality cannot, accordingly, be known by sense, understanding, and reason, as it is in itself, but only as it is grasped, and thereby limited and conditioned, by these faculties. Thus arises the distinction between the *phenomenal* world, or the world as it is experienced and rationally understood, and the *noumenal* world, or the world as it is, independently of the knower's rational apprehension of it.

According to Schopenhauer, the world then, is rationally knowable only in so far as it is capable of being sensed and rationally interpreted. The senses, for example, are obviously not windows through which a mind perceives a world, but are bodily organs that entirely transform the stimuli acting upon them, producing purely bodily effects called sensations. Nor is the mere existence of these sensations within the body equivalent to the perception of things, which is the work of understanding. Not until the light of understanding is shed upon sensation does any perception of things arise. Sensations, however, can be understood only within the framework of the understanding, which is no more a mere light than the sense organs are mere windows. The understanding imposes upon the phenomena of sense certain fixed relations of time and space, together with universal causal connections, as Kant had maintained. Thus, and thus only, can a knower understand a world revealed to him by sense; namely, as phenomena, or appearances, connected by certain necessary relations of time, space, and causality, these being thought of always as necessary simply because they are not derived from experience, but imparted to it. And human reason itself, finally, can render no judgment of reality without presupposing a ground or sufficient reason for any truth, and it must itself derive its materials for judgment from the phenomenal world, conditioned by understanding, which is in turn conditioned by sense.

Schopenhauer drew three important results from these distinctions. The first is that what unthinking men call "reality" is a phenomenal world, which is at bottom an illusion, partly created by one's own sense and understanding, and therefore an illusion that cannot be banished by these. Schopenhauer graphically expressed this result by calling the phenomenal world an "idea," or something that exists only in the understanding. The second result is that the spatial and temporal relations between phenomena, together with their universal causal connections are the knower's contributions to experience, and cannot therefore be asserted of reality itself. Thus arises the necessity of all such relations; namely, that they are conditions of experience, and not ideas derived from experience. Schopenhauer expressed this result by calling these relations a "veil of Maya" spread between ourselves and reality, our phenomenal world being the resultant of this ever-present veil, and the noumenal world lying always beyond it. And the third result is that the noumenal world, or reality, as it is in itself, unconditioned by the contributions of a knowing subject, can be known, if at all, only immediately, that is, only by one's own identity with it.

Will as the Thing in Itself

KANT had declared that the noumenal world, being rationally unknowable, is not knowable at all, though he conceded that we could guess what it ought to be on the basis of clues afforded by our moral notions. He noted, however, that a man is himself both a phenomenon and a noumenon, in so far as he is both a perceivable body in space and time, causally related to other bodies, and a subject that perceives, thinks, wills, and acts. Indeed, a man can be, Kant thought, and even should be, regarded as an ultimate cause or source of his own moral conduct, even though such a conception would be senseless as applied to anything merely as an object or phenomenon.

Seizing upon this, Schopenhauer claimed that we can in fact know reality, as it is in itself, because each of us is, in his own true nature, that reality. We do not know our true nature by sense, reason, and understanding, certainly, for these testify what we are only as phenomena. We are nevertheless perfectly aware of our underlying nature, simply by our identity with it. With respect to ourselves the veil of Maya is pierced, and we apprehend ourselves, not through the distorting portals of space, time, and causality, but intuitively, in our true and innermost nature. And what we are, we find, is not just a physical, animal body, nor even this together with thought and

reason, but *will*. Indeed, Schopenhauer maintained that our thoughts, no less than our bodies, are themselves nothing but the expressions of this will, that our bodies and all bodily behavior, voluntary as well as involuntary, is simply the mirror of this will. This was Schopenhauer's basic metaphysical principle, the "single idea" that *The World as Will and Idea* was declared, in its preface, to express. We know what ultimate reality is, as will, because we are ourselves not merely an expression of a will but identical with the will that underlies all phenomena. The greatness of Schopenhauer's thought consists in the ease with which he appeared to find confirmation of this sweeping metaphysical claim. He thought it rendered intelligible what other philosophies did not. Without the light of this hypothesis, the world seemed to him but a conglomeration of more or less unconnected things, but understood as the expression of will, the whole of nature appeared intelligible. Schopenhauer's speculations thus constitute a unified philosophy, into which diverse things fit like the pieces of a puzzle. He himself compared his approach to that of a cryptographer or translator of a hitherto unknown alphabet, who rightly concludes that he has the key when what was before meaningless becomes suddenly intelligible.

That will of which the world and most clearly the organic world is the expression is essentially a primordial, ungrounded force, and a blind one. That it is ungrounded means only that there is no further cause or ground for its existence, as of course there cannot be, since it is itself an ultimate reality. To say that it is blind means that it has no ultimate goal or end other than existence itself. It is in this sense that Schopenhauer thought it could be described, though somewhat misleadingly, as self-caused, a description that theologians have always reserved for God, conceived as an ultimate reality outside the world. The will exists neither in space nor time, for these Schopenhauer considered phenomenal distinctions, nor does it stand in ordinary causal relations to any objects, for the same reason. There is, accordingly, but *one* will; not in the sense that this is one thing among others but rather that distinctions of multiplicity, which presuppose phenomenal space and time, do not apply to it. He likewise thought of the will as infinite and eternal; not, again, in the sense of being greater and more durable than other things, but in the sense of being beyond temporal and spatial distinctions altogether.

That the inner nature of existence cannot be grasped by reason and sense follows obviously, Schopenhauer thought, from the demonstrations of Kant's transcendental aesthetic. But that it can be grasped intuitively, within the knowing subject himself, by that subject's identity with it, is something he thought Kant himself had only barely failed to see. Standing upon the intellectual tradition of Greek philosophy and Renaissance science, and in the moral tradition of Christianity, we are apt to think of ourselves as essentially rational, guided by our thought toward those ends that we have examined and found to be good. In short, we think of our will as guided by our thought and reason. Plato and Aristotle thought that this subordination of the appetites to reason is what makes us distinctively human, while other philosophers — Hegel, for instance — have never doubted that, whatever might be the ultimate nature of reality, at least it is rational. But according to Schopenhauer, the exact opposite is true. Thought and reason follow upon the will, and emerge much later, in the life of the individual, the species, and the evolution of life.

Whatever reservations one might have concerning Schopenhauer's metaphysical characterization of the will, it is nonetheless greatly to his credit that he stressed this aspect of nature and to that extent counteracted the excessive rationalism of his predecessors. His voluntarism had the further effect of emphasizing what is by now becoming increasingly taken for granted, namely, man's kinship with all living things, a kinship which previous philosophers had almost unanimously minimized or denied altogether, and which is now only reluctantly admitted by those who want to find in human nature a difference, not of degree, but of kind. There can be little doubt, too, that seemingly diverse phenomena do become intelligible in the light of this voluntarism, while theories of rationalism leave them in darkness. Thus, the infant cries for food long before it has any concept of nutrition, and asserts its will to live long before it has any notion at all of what life has to offer. Spiders make their elaborate, gossamer webs in accordance with the finest principles of structural engineering, and ant lions dig their traps without any knowledge of the insects that will fall into them. They are guided entirely by instinct, which Schopenhauer interpreted as comparable to motive and will but without reason. Birds construct nests, sometimes spanning continents to do so, without ever having seen eggs. Men's goals likewise emerge, Schopenhauer declared, with a strict uniformity throughout history, prior to any clear idea of what they are or any intellectual appreciation of their worth or worthlessness. Indeed, it is not until the emergence of man, the most recent and refined product of the evolutionary process, that any intellectual apprehension of ends arises at all. We do not, with the growth of intelligence, finally survey various possible ends and then select some of these to become real. On the contrary, according to Schopenhauer, we first will our ends and declare them to be good simply because they are willed. We then cast about for whatever means will achieve them. Every man, for example, like everything else that lives, naturally wills life, and the perpetuation of life, both through himself and his offspring, without giving any thought to whether or not it is a good. Schopenhauer was struck by the fact that a man still wills life in the face of any proof that it is not good, and with his last breath,

he gasps for another — just as fishes, thrown up on land, gasp at the air that is suffocating them, and even keep doing so after their heads have been severed. A man, alone among all other creatures, can sometimes take his own life in a moment of dementia or despair, but the will that is in every cell of his body protests no less, pressing to life so long as any glimmer of it can be held. Thus does a decapitated criminal, his end most irrevocably effected, still tremble when the earth is finally thrown over him.[1] Thus do decapitated fowl flap about revoltingly, the will to live only gradually subsiding, even in the face of this fate. The head of the Australian ant, Schopenhauer notes, will sometimes attack its own severed thorax and abdomen as its nearest adversary, the latter meanwhile defending itself bravely with its sting, such is the determination of everything to live on whatever terms. The beggar, oppressed by want, his body riddled with sickness, some of his senses destroyed, still clings to life with the eagerness of a youth, as though expecting some imminent emancipation which he nevertheless knows is not coming. Schopenhauer noted how men view with instinctive shock and terror the deliberate preparation for the execution of any man, and rejoice at his deliverance by reprieve, prior to any consideration of the worth of the life that is at stake and, sometimes, in the clear knowledge of its worthlessness. We are gripped with fascination and dread at the sight of an impending suicide, even in the knowledge that hundreds are perishing daily all around us. Sometimes a whole nation is held suspenseful while men struggle against time and overwhelming odds to rescue some child who was hitherto unknown, and who will never be heard of again. In these other lives we see without reflection the expression of our own natures, and in their extinction we see the frustration, not of the desire for the world's great satisfactions, which do not even occur to us, but just of the will to live that is the same in all.

The Will in Nature

THE will which is the true nature of man is also, Schopenhauer believed, the secret of existence itself, the noumenon that becomes objectified in that totality of phenomena we call the world. It thus seemed to him to provide an ultimate, or metaphysical, explanation of existence. Empirical science, he noted, neither supplies nor seeks ultimate explanations, being concerned only with the relations between observable things in nature. It explains particular phenomena in terms of their relations to other phenomena, but does not explain the phenomena themselves. Hence science has no place for the concept of a noumenon or ultimate cause, which is, accordingly, a metaphysical concept. Science and philosophy do not, then, offer competing explanations, but rather explanations at different levels, for there is nothing in Schopenhauer's philosophy that casts doubt upon the discoverable connections between phenomena.

Thus, purely physical explanations are, in Schopenhauer's terminology, either *morphological* — that is, descriptive of things — or *etiological* — that is, descriptive of (particularly the causal) relations between things — the uniformity of such relations then becoming expressed as laws of nature. Combustion, for example, can be morphologically explained as a process of rapid oxidation. Given instances of combustion, on the other hand — such as the igniting of a given match at a given place and time — can be etiologically explained in terms of certain preceding changes sufficient to produce them. Similarly, an oak tree can be morphologically explained by a plant physiologist, and the existence of a particular oak can be etiologically explained in terms of the acorn from which it arose, and the conditions under which it sprouted and grew. In such cases no ultimate explanation is achieved or sought, for we can still wonder why, for instance, an oak or anything else arises under such conditions, why there is any phenomenal world at all, why the world assumes the forms that it does, and what underlies the forces and changes it exhibits.

Such questions of ultimate explanation have always been answered theologically. Thus, God is postulated as a being, separate from the world, and possessed of intelligence, power, and, of course, benevolence. He is supposed to produce the world from nothing, to impart motion to it, and, guided by eternal principles of goodness, to design the whole and all its parts in consonance with an unvarying purpose. Now Schopenhauer's metaphysical explanation is not wholly different from this, except that, in his philosophy, the ultimate cause is deprived of such qualities as would render it divine, and is accordingly called a will rather than a god. Thus, the will is deemed uncaused, or, what means the same thing, the ground of its own existence. It is declared to lie outside the phenomenal distinctions of space, time, and causality. It is claimed to be powerful — even, indeed, omnipotent — and to be the ultimate source of all motion and change. It endows all things, and most manifestly living things, with their forms and capacities. The properties that Schopenhauer denied of the will, but which would be essential to God as theologians conceive of him, are benevolence, intelligent purpose, and separate existence. The will and phenomenal nature were thought of by Schopenhauer as coeval, such that neither could exist separately and independently of the other. While all apparent design and purpose in nature can be understood as the expression of will, the will itself is deemed blind, that is, to have no ultimate purpose, good or bad, beyond life and existence themselves. Nature was even regarded by Schopenhauer as the creation of the will, except that it is not a creation in time, life and existence being

eternally assured to the will. Such creative activity he deemed free, in the original sense of that word; for the will, being an ultimate cause, can be subject to no determination from without.

Thus, Schopenhauer's philosophy embodies what purports to be metaphysically explanatory in traditional theology, and eliminates only what he found to be in no way suggested by experience — particularly the ideas of intelligence and benevolent purpose. He believed his metaphysics to be confirmed by all our experience, and by science, the more it reveals to us, but particularly by the forms of living things, which he thought were in all cases the very mirrors of the will manifested in them.

No living form, Schopenhauer noted, is too bizarre for nature to attempt as the expression of will. All creatures have assumed precisely the forms that express their wills and characters, and appeared to him as those very wills become visible. These visible forms of animals seemed to him to be related to those aspects of their environment that are the objects of their wills exactly as any act of will is related to its motive or purpose. Thus, the heads of most beasts are directed to the earth, where the objects of their wills lie, while exceptions to this seek their food from trees or from the air. Waterfowl that wade and seek their food from the muddy bottoms have elongated legs and, correspondingly, fantastically extended necks, while predatory birds have talons, together with piercing mouthparts and digestive systems to match. Some creatures endeavor to perpetuate their existence by attack, some by flight, some by protective apparatus, some by mimicry, and so on. In each we find exactly the form and structure corresponding to this will and character. Timidity is perfectly embodied in the hare, whose outer ear is grotesquely elongated to catch any threatening sound and whose legs are perfectly made for evasion and fast retreat. Rapaciousness is expressed in the whole form of hawks and other predatory creatures, which by their very natures act in perfect consonance with their structures. Hardly anything is ever given to living things superfluously, every organ subserving the ends with which their wills endow them and displaying this will visibly before us. The tropical ant eater possesses heavy, shovel-like claws, a weirdly elongated snout, a glutinous narrow tongue, and no teeth, being directed throughout to the nests of ants which are its nourishment. Should the remains of such a creature be discovered ages hence. Schopenhauer speculated, by a race of men to whom ants and termites were unknown, it would appear to them as a mystery, an incomprehensible miscarriage of nature. To us, on the other hand, its perfect adaptation to its purpose is so manifest as to make it appear as the expression of a will in relation to its motive, just what we expect it to be as soon as we know its mode of life. This animal wills the destruction of ant nests, without plan, reason, or forethought, and this will finds its expression in the precise form, capacities, and instincts that the creature exhibits.

This is, of course, one of the more controversial of Schopenhauer's claims. Men of science have, since the seventeenth century, looked with suspicion on all attempts to describe biological phenomena teleologically, a suspicion that has been carried so far that many contemporary psychologists endeavor to explain even human behavior after the nonpurposeful models of physics and chemistry. Nonpurposeful explanations of living things are achieved, it is widely believed, when these are described etiologically and mechanically, that is to say, in terms of cause and effect, without recourse to such expressions as "in order that" and all others suggestive of purpose, intent, or motive. Thus, instead of saying after the manner of Schopenhauer that the ant eater has a glutinous tongue *in order* to prey on ants and termites, one can say, it is claimed, that *because* it has such a tongue, it does in fact prey upon ants and termites. Similarly, it is said that certain water fowl feed from the bottoms of streams only *because* they happen to have acquired pendulous legs that enable them to, and not that they are possessed of such legs *in order* to feed thus. It is, in fact, the main significance of Darwin's work that he seemed, and still seems to many, to have provided just such nonpurposeful but nevertheless adequate explanations.

While such descriptions are doubtless adequate for the understanding of inanimate things, they seemed to Schopenhauer, as they have to many others, wholly inadequate for the understanding of living things. We can indeed say that the snow melts because the sun heats it, without supposing that the sun shines in order to achieve such results, but concepts of purposes or ends seemed to Schopenhauer necessary for the manifest teleology of living things. It does in fact seem far-fetched to suppose, for instance, that the infant cries for food and nurses at the breast simply because it finds itself possessed of mouth and vocal cords. We can hardly avoid supposing that, in some sense, it is because it needs nourishment that it has a voice to make this known and a mouth and digestive system wherewith to receive it. Its mother likewise nourishes it, and possesses the means whereby to do so, in order that it may live. Whatever speculative theory of nature one might endorse, hardly anyone can fail to view the matter in that way. And so it is, Schopenhauer thought, in the case of all living things. We do not find mere chance adaptations of this or that part to some aspect of the environment. We find the adaptation of the entire organism to some end or purpose, suggesting that the structure of an animal, which is complex, results from the single mode of life that is in some sense willed, rather than vice versa. It was this seeming direction of the *entire* animal organism to a single end that struck Schopenhauer as most significant. A nonpurposeful theory might explain a particular adaptation on the part of a given species in terms of such notions as

accidental variation, the survival of the fittest, and so on, but it seemed to Schopenhauer incredible beyond serious consideration to suppose that the entire complex structure of any animal could, even as a result of millions of accidents over ages of time, finally assume just those interrelationships that would bestow on its possessor, quite by accident, that single mode of life which it is found to pursue. A hawk, for example, has not only talons with which to prey on smaller things, but a correspondingly effective beak, appropriate digestive system, keen eyes, and all its parts mutually adapted to swift flight and pursuit. That one of these structures might have resulted from the chance operations of nature, and the animal then have gradually come to use it merely in virtue of finding itself in possession of it, is perhaps believable; but it did not seem believable to Schopenhauer that such a combination of structures, all subserving one single obvious end, could have such an accidental origin. It seemed even less credible to him if one supposed such accidents to be endlessly multiplied. He found the same doubt confirmed by the structure of every animal. A striking case in point is the stag beetle. This insect, in transforming itself from grub to adult beetle within the prepared cavity of a log, leaves an empty space within the wood which is its place of lodgement, and this suitably shaped space subsequently accommodates the huge horn that then develops upon the insect's head. It can hardly be supposed, Schopenhauer noted, that the horn appears simply because the insect happened to leave a space there. Rather, we must suppose that the space was prepared just in order that the horn could develop. Schopenhauer could not resist finding in these and similar phenomena something at least analogous to a motive or end, and an act of will to which it is related. Generalizing upon such examples, he said that what is invariably found in all living things is a structure more or less elaborately adapted to a mode of life, and hardly ever a mode of life that is then adapted to whatever structure this or that animal happens to possess or acquire.

Of course, the criticism can be made that Schopenhauer's explanation of animal forms as the objectifications of will is scientifically barren; that is, that it is neither a law of nature, nor a theory from which any laws can be derived, or any predictions made. This is true but beside the point, for Schopenhauer's theory purports to be a metaphysical explanation of certain phenomena and not an etiological law connecting phenomena with each other. If, as he claims, living things are the objectification of a will that is blind, unconditioned by phenomena, and hence unpredictable, it is hardly surprising that the assertion of this should be useless for the purposes of prediction. It is perhaps significant to note, too, that even Darwin, who is widely supposed to have banished teleology from nature altogether, was unable to dispense with it. At the foundation of his theory is the concept of the "struggle for survival." If this is significantly different from what Schopenhauer called "the will to live," it is hard to see what that difference is.

The Meaninglessness of Life

IN calling the will "blind" Schopenhauer meant only that it has no further end than the perpetuation and proliferation of life itself; and life, as contrasted with living *for* something, he considered the essence of meaninglessness, or what he sometimes called "vanity." This meaninglessness eludes us so long as we have great goals to claim our attention or projects upon which to exercise our wills and egoism, for we assume that these goals move us by their own worth. We do not consider the possibility that they are deemed worthy only because they are, blindly and without ultimate justification, sought after. There is thus created an illusion, Schopenhauer thought, laid upon us by our very nature, which philosophy can exhibit but from which it cannot liberate us. So long as a man wills, as it is his nature to do, he desperately pursues the fulfillment of those desires with which his nature endows him, notwithstanding any purely intellectual understanding of their worthlessness and the vanity of pursuing them.

This idea can be nicely illustrated with the ancient myth of Sisyphus. Sisyphus, according to this story, was condemned by the gods to a fate which was to consist of rolling a heavy stone to the top of a hill, the stone then always rolling back to the bottom, to be pushed again to the top by Sisyphus, eternally. Perhaps nothing serves better than this image to exhibit the idea of vain, meaningless toil. Nor does its meaninglessness result from the fact that it is onerous, for Sisyphus' labors would be made no more worthwhile if he were endowed by the gods with an overwhelming desire to perform them. His work would then be exactly the same, but his attitude would be different. He would no longer feel condemned but would instead have a profound desire to pursue, with all this strength, this meaningless and unending task, and would deem himself free to just the extent that nothing hindered him from it. Hence, from an illusion produced by his will, he would consider his project to be a good, notwithstanding its endlessness and vanity, and to be supremely worthy of all his effort.

There is no need of mythology to illustrate this thought, however, for Schopenhauer believed that it is proclaimed by everything around us, and that human existence is often best viewed against the vast panorama of nonhuman life that surrounds us. Thus, in certain parts, the woods are filled every year with mayflies, more appropriately called the ephemeral flies, which appear all at once from the lakes and streams. In a few days they litter the ground with their corpses, meanwhile having accomplished the only thing they were brought forth for, to scatter countless eggs, just in order that this scene might be briefly repeated another year. Certain insects burrow in the darkness of the earth for years; a few to emerge finally for a short flight in the sun and to deposit their eggs, only that more may burrow again for years, to repeat this pointless episode through eternity. Herrings and salmon appear from the ocean every spring, turning the foreign fresh-water streams into a violent turbulence, struggling against the torrents and every obstacle, tumbling over each other in wild desperation, oblivious to a hundred predators lining the shore to scoop them at pleasure, goaded to the spawning for nothing else than to insure that the cycle of this meaningless spectacle might never cease. Schopenhauer found this basic feature of life epitomized in the ground mole. This animal digs in the darkness through its whole existence, in peril the moment it shows itself forth, struggling only for the privilege of one more breath, feeding on the worms that can only nourish it on through another moment of toil. The same drama, the same law, the same primordial will to live and to perpetuate life simply for its own sake, seemed to Schopenhauer to be repeated in every species. Every living thing responds to an urge that was inflicted upon it without choice, as though inspired by some god, always to grasp for more life and to fill the whole of nature with its own kind, but without any ultimate justification at all.

Schopenhauer thought that the purposelessness or vanity of this striving does not become wholly evident, however, until we note that nature's productions are effortless, and hence that no individual living thing, considered by itself, has any significance whatever apart from its own will to live. Deriving the thought from Plato, he expressed this idea by saying that nature cares only for the forms and species of things and is wholly indifferent to their members. Life is always assured to the will, even though it is snatched from its living embodiments as casually as it was originally bestowed. Life, both human and subhuman, arises in such profusion as to stagger our thought, and yet it is swept into nothingness as if by whim. The creatures of which we just spoke sometimes perish in masses as if at a signal, but without notice, and it is shortly as if nothing had happened. Nature still presents the same general appearance, and the species persist unaltered. Schopenhauer compared the life of a man to the journey of someone riding a raft upon swift, turbulent rapids, struggling to avoid every shoal and rock throughout the whole course of the journey, only to reach the escarpment at the end, from which he is hurled down into an eternal nothingness. The life of a man and of every other creature he found to be mainly a struggle against death; and yet time by itself rushes every living thing along to its death as its only possible ultimate goal. If one were to step afresh into our world, having the faculties to appreciate what he found, he could contemplate one of nature's living works, whether it were a man or a contemptible fly, only with awesome admiration. It would appear to him so exquisitely designed, so painstakingly harmonized in all its parts, so delicately adjusted to its purposes, a work of artifice so elaborate, as to make it seem some sort of final end. Yet that individual thing is by Schopenhauer's philosophy nothing but an effortless expression of an infinite will, and counts in nature for nothing, being obliterated by the merest vagary. Innumerable creatures perish in the woodlands from a chance spark, and small animals play guilelessly amidst the ubiquitous threats that can extinguish them at a stroke. We are so accustomed to viewing animal life in this light that we no longer see anything incongruous in it; yet Schopenhauer claimed that it is no different with human life. If we declare human nature to have some special transcendent worth — to be, in Kant's terms, an "end in itself" — it is from our own wishful thinking. It is not from the lessons of nature and history, for these contradict us daily. A man is often felled at the height of his powers by a bacterium; a civilization is robbed of one of its geniuses by the most trivial trick of fate; cities are abolished by earthquakes; millions are slaughtered at the caprice of a tyrant and their bodies piled into pits and burned like grasshoppers. And yet it is shortly as though nothing of importance had happened, the will to live persisting in what remains, quite unabated. Men claim that human life is a unique good, even the image of something divine, in spite of the testimony that is constantly before them. They do not realize, Schopenhauer thought, that this very declaration issues from nothing more than their will to live, which they share with all living things, that this will has no goal beyond life itself, and that, life always being assured to this will, no individual life has the slightest intrinsic importance or worth.

Religion

THE vanity of life seemed to Schopenhauer to be the testimony of experience, and yet nearly all of man's religions and popular metaphysics have denied it. They have, Schopenhauer thought, arisen from the very need to deny it. Theologians say that man, alone among all other creatures, has a unique or transcendent value that is not to be compared with anything else. They say that every single man has a soul created from nothing by a god; that this soul not only blesses him with a spark of the divine nature, thus setting him apart as an image of God, but also guarantees him, alone among creatures, a chance for an endless life. Philosophers, following these same fancies, invent arguments to demonstrate that what we actually find in the world is no real indication of what is going on there. They say that man's mind or rational soul gives him a kind of freedom, a *liberum arbitrium indifferentiae*, that is possessed by nothing else in the world; that he may use this freedom for the pursuit of good or evil; and that, unlike anything else, he possesses a unique moral sense or conscience by means of which he draws the distinction between moral good and evil. They then attempt to reconcile what we find in the world with what religion declares we ought to find by declaring the former to be somehow illusory. Leibniz even described the world as the best of all possible ones, or precisely what we should expect a wise and benevolent god to create. What Schopenhauer found, in short, in religion and popular metaphysics, is the denial of the most pervasive and ineradicable facts of experience, a denial which renders *faith*, or the belief in things unseen, the highest religious virtue.

When the founders of world religions, such as Gautama Buddha or Jesus Christ, penetrate beyond such wishful thinking and declare the world to be infected with suffering and evil, and man's will to be the source of some of that evil, their teachings are soon wrapped up in a rosy optimism by successive generations of disciples and epigones until it becomes, at their hands, essentially the opposite of what it originally was. Schopenhauer regarded the original teachings of Christianity, as well as those of the Eastern religions, as utterly pessimistic, noting that the very symbol of Christianity is an instrument of torture.

This religious distortion of things, and the ease with which men embrace the faith to receive it, can be explained, Schopenhauer thought, through an understanding of human nature as the expression of will. For the will is a will to live, and can accordingly be satisfied only with the promise of endless life. The thought that one should be living, and so profoundly willing life against every threat and obstacle, only to face inevitable annihilation at last, is one from which every man recoils in terror. The utter certainty of it makes it hardly less terrible to him. It is from just this calamity that religion holds out hope of salvation, and upon this hope rests its entire strength and appeal. That its claims should be contrary to both reason and experience makes hardly any difference at all, in the face of an almost irresistible appeal to the will. It is thus a naïve distortion, he thought, to think of religion as representing man's attempt to supplement his knowledge and to explain what his experience of the world leaves mysterious, as though our primary purpose were to know rather than to will. Thoughts about the gods do not originally arise in men's minds as answers to speculative questions about the world and the heavens. They arise as the ideas of possible deliverers from what men instinctively dread, which is the ultimate and total frustration of the will in death. Nature teaches most forcibly that the annihilation of any individual thing is of no account, that a man is no exception to this, and that one's tenure of existence is most temporary. But the will of each man declares with the same force that, in his case at least, this shall not be so. We find no promise from nature that it is not so and find, in fact, the clearest assurance that it is. Men thus invent their gods, as just those beings who can overturn this verdict of nature and seize from the grave its victory. Theologians then endow these gods with whatever powers will make this possible, this being, indeed, the substance of the theological task. If, Schopenhauer observed, men should ever become convinced of their mortality by the clear evidence of science and their own experience, their lively interest in religion would evaporate with that conviction. It is in fact not possible that they should become thus convinced, however, for they have not been, despite the fact that human mortality has long since been as clearly established as any conclusion of science could possibly be. And similarly, Schopenhauer noted, if there should somehow be discovered a means whereby every man could automatically be guaranteed an endless life, religion would forthwith lose its interest, being rendered superfluous to the need that originally evoked it.

Death

THE death of any individual, from which religion promises to redeem one, cannot be regarded in Schopenhauer's philosophy as an evil, however. It appears so only to the uninformed will. As Lucretius and others have pointed out, death, if it is what it so plainly appears to be, is simply the beginning of eternal nonexistence, and obviously nothing can suffer evil through its sheer nonbeing. For anything to suffer, the first condition is that it should exist. That an eternity should drift by during which this or that individual should no longer live cannot by itself be any more a source of dread, if one views the matter rationally, than that an eternity should have elapsed before that individual arose, the two states being perfectly identical and perfectly empty. Each of us becomes dust, to be sure, but it is no different from the dust whence we arose. We know that there was an endless time before we came into existence, and we view this eternal nonexistence with complete equanimity. The will that then found its expression in us finds no way of changing this nor, indeed, have we any desire to change it. But once alive, and filled with the will to live, the eternal emptiness that awaits us in death fills us with unthinking fear, as though this impotent specter contained something of surpassing frightfulness. Nor is it the pain of death that a man fears, for all suffering belongs to life and lies clearly on this side of death; besides, men will often cling to life through the most hideous torment and, with their final agonized breath, try to draw another. Clergymen and poets declaim upon the sorrow, even the injustice, in the thought of the mind or soul of a man sinking with him into the darkness of the grave, and they are thus moved to declare that this must not be so, that God cannot justly permit it to be so. They fail to see, Schopenhauer pointed out, that the same injustice and sorrow, if there were any, would also attend the thought that the same soul or mind should have lacked existence through that endless time before it arose. Yet they never say that this must not be so, or that God would not permit it to be so, nor do they see the least sorrow or injustice in the evident fact that it is so.

Death, Schopenhauer observed, is nothing but the dissolution of the individual organism, and that individual is only a phenomenal thing, and not an ultimate reality. The inner nature of the individual, the will that underlies and finds its expression in him, is no individual thing at all, for it lies beyond the distinctions of time and space altogether. It is thus untouched by his death, and is evidently indestructible in its very nature, life forever being assured to it. We men are like the dreams that arise and sink away in the night, the dreamer meanwhile remaining quite unchanged by this procession across his consciousness. In the birth of a man we see the expression of a will in an animal body. In his death we see the final dissolution of that finite expression; but there is no death of the will itself that was thus briefly manifested. When we suppose, then, that in death one's self or ego or true inner nature perishes while the world remains, we are reversing the real order of things. Schopenhauer claimed that it is one's world, as a phenomenon, that perishes with one's body and brain, while his true nature, which is no phenomenal ,individual thing, remains untouched.

Schopenhauer's assurance that death is an illusion does not, of course, furnish any reassurance at all to those who dread the prospect of their own inevitable decay. The reason for this, it seems clear, is that each man craves the perpetuation of his own individual identity, and Schopenhauer claimed, in effect, that such identity is an illusion, that the distinction a man draws between himself and other things is no real distinction, and hence that the indestructibility of the will itself is the highest guarantee of the indestructibility of any man's true nature. Now, however dubious this might seem as a metaphysical principle, and however irrelevant it might seem to the solicitude each man has for his own being, and his relative indifference to the perpetuation of lives other than his own, it should be pointed out that the concept of death has never been made very clear by other philosophers, and that the concept of the identity of a thing, whether of a man or anything else, is similarly vague and even paradoxical. Some philosophers, like Locke, have maintained that one's personal identity is but the consequence of his having memory, while others have insisted that one's having memories, which he recognizes as his, is only the consequence of a personal identity that is already presupposed. There is, in any case, apparently no agreement among philosophers as to what this absolute individual identity consists in, and this is at least a negative reason for suspecting that Schopenhauer might have been right in declaring that it does not even exist, that it is only an idea wrought by man's own thinking. One might suppose that the idea of the individual identity of a thing would be clear as it is applied to things simpler than persons, but this too is doubtful. Many simple plants and organisms, and indeed the cell constituents of all living things, multiply simply by splitting in half, and here it is quite obvious that nothing new is created. Instead, as Schopenhauer would express it, something already existing has received a new phenomenal variation. When one of those halves, now more or less arbitrarily taken to be an individual in its own right, perishes, and the other divides once more — a process that is going on perpetually throughout our bodies and throughout all nature, and that expresses the essence of all growth and reproduction — we do not suppose that anything has really been annihilated or anything else created, but only that what already existed has expressed itself in a new arrangement. Looked at in this way, the death of anything appears not as a single, final event, but as a process that begins with birth. Perpetual renewal, gain and loss, growth and decay, are inherent in every living thing. One's birth, likewise, does not now appear as a sudden beginning of what had no reality before, but simply as a dramatic event in a history that had no beginning but reaches back to the beginning of time. As one's lifeless nourishment becomes part of his living substance, as it is incorporated into his body, his dead excrement ceases to be such. In these commonplace processes may be revealed the whole nature of birth and death, as changes within a beginningless and endless process of change or, according to Schopenhauer's philosophy, as variations upon a life or will that is changeless. Nothing begins absolutely, nothing ceases absolutely, and that which is expressed in all change, that which is reality itself, changes, according to Schopenhauer, not in the least. This idea, of the one in the many, is as old as philosophy, and however difficult it is to understand it, that difficulty should not blind us to the difficulties of denying it.

The Metaphysics of Sexual Love

THE ceaseless proliferation of life, its endless multiplication, and the urgency with which this is pursued by everything that lives struck Schopenhauer as a mystery upon which previous philosophers had shed little light. How quickly, Schopenhauer thought, the mystery dissolves and the explanation leaps up when we penetrate beyond phenomena to the will that underlies them. We find that every living thing is, like ourselves, moved by an irrational impulse,

whether conscious or not, to perpetuate itself. But vastly exceeding that is the determination each thing has to perpetuate its kind. This impulse Schopenhauer considered to be essentially the same in all living things, including those without either consciousness of feeling, and to be the very focus of the will. Some creatures perish in the act of procreation or shortly afterward, while everything appears to direct most of its life's energy, in one way or another, to that end. Thus did Plato rightly regard *erōs* as an aspiration to immortal life; but he erred, according to Schopenhauer, in supposing that *erōs* is the inspiration to reach some goal that the intellect and reason could contemplate. We are not drawn from in front toward any goal that exists, but impelled from behind toward a goal that is merely the product of that impulse.

Schopenhauer found displayed in all living things, in their response to the sexual impulse, a bondage to something quite unknown to them, and it seemed obvious to him that human beings were no exception at all. We view with amused fascination the behavior of adolescents as these desires begin to be uncomprehendingly but nonetheless compellingly felt. Sexual desire, in all its numberless expressions, has been the primary ingredient of poetry, song, and humor since these began. Any allusion to it, however vague and dimly hinted, is always instantly recognized and always raises a smile, just because of the consciousness all men have both of its ineluctable appeal to the will and its absurdity to the intellect. Animals battle rain, cold, and every obstacle to gain the goal of procreation, having no real conception of what it is and usually no knowledge whatever of what constrains them so — something, which, moreover, could only appear to them, from the standpoint of their own interest, as trivial in comparison to its cost. It appeared to Schopenhauer no different on the level of man, except that men have a clear intellectual comprehension of what they take to be the goal, namely, the act of procreation itself — which is, however, not the goal at all, but only a means. They represent it to themselves as something quite sublime and deserving of all the effort it claims. Men even suppose that, unlike lower creatures, they first perceive sexual union as an inestimable good and then direct their wills to the attainment of it, as though the opposite were not perfectly obvious. No man ever chooses this goal, or selects the impulse to be driven toward it. Sexual desire expresses itself, even in men, before there is any clear knowledge at all of the means to its gratification. The perniciousness of this was considered by Schopenhauer to be appalling beyond reckoning. The highest claims of duty, as in famines and wars, subside in its presence. Things that men have learned should have an absolute claim on their conduct — such as honor, veracity, and justice — are almost casually jettisoned in favor of this prior claim laid upon them by nature, the moment a chance for its fulfillment is seen or even hinted at. Thrones have been abandoned to it, fortunes squandered, and few of the most ordinary men can think without shame upon how their own petty affairs are ceaselessly muddled by it. Cupid finds ways, Schopenhauer noted, of slipping locks of hair even into the manuscripts of philosophers and into the portfolios of cabinet ministers.

If one tries to understand this turmoil from the standpoint of the individual and his own interests, it seems senseless; but if one regards the individual himself as the expression of a will that cares nothing for him but is directed only to the perpetuation of life, then, Schopenhauer claimed, what was mysterious becomes clear, and the explanation of sexual passion unfolds. Thus, a man, free and beholden to nothing beyond his own weal and well being, in a single stroke of matrimony multiplies without end his burdens and cares. He does this lightly and with a gay heart, for the sake, he imagines, of pleasing and thereby possessing that woman so lovely as to deserve all sacrifice; but hardly has he gained her than every other woman charms him more. It is not so with the woman, however, whose inclination is to cleave to her husband — not, however, as she imagines, for her own sake or his, but in the interests of her children, born and unborn. Thus, a man who for one reason or another — such as age, want of strength, or excess of intellect — cannot be easily envisaged as a father, cannot really appeal to any woman, whatever may be his other merits. Another, who can easily fill the role of fatherhood, will hardly be without a mate, whatever he may lack of taste, culture, or wisdom. A man, Schopenhauer observed, is by nature inclined to inconstancy, and a woman to constancy — precisely because he can sire a hundred children in a year, and she bear only one, to which one she is, moreover, quite irrevocably committed for years. Thus does every woman react, instinctively, to every other woman with enmity and the spirit of competition, even in areas having no connection with family life, and even though that other may pose no threat to her at all. Nothing appears to her more blameworthy, more indicative of faulty character, than an outside woman who unsettles the stability of a family union — particularly where the passions are enlisted, for no man's will is secure against these. A man, on the other hand, is hardly ever cast in that role, and seldom condemned if he is. In contrast to the woman, a man's initial reaction to any woman of suitable age is one of gallantry and ingratiation, even though she may be entirely unknown to him and plainly destined to remain so; while to any other man his natural reaction is one of indifference. The delights that passionate love holds out, however, and which are the thinly disguised theme of all romantic story and song, are claimed by Schopenhauer to be the most nebulous and evanescent of any, being utterly extinguished in the instant of their final brief attainment. They are pursued with nonetheless unabated ardor, even in the full knowledge of this, showing well enough that they arise from the will even in opposition to the intelligence. What at one moment overwhelms the seeker as a sublime goal, to be gained at all effort and cost, is found illusory in its reality — just because the means was mistaken for the end, and was misconceived as an end for the individual himself. The real end, the perpetuation of the species, which is of no passionate concern to any man and which, in fact, he usually endeavors to frustrate if he can, is nevertheless achieved with dreadful effectiveness, and with no concern whatever for its cost to those who are the instruments of it. It is for this reason, Schopenhauer claimed, that marriages of convenience, as well as those arranged by parents, are generally, but unreasonably, condemned. In such unions, we assume passionate love to be at most only a subordinate motive, and we instinctively deem the sheer perpetuation of the race, and all that is necessary to this, paramount. Yet it is just such marriages of convenience, intellectually arrived at, that are usually happiest and most durable, and that do in time result in genuine and abiding affection, just because they are contrived with a view to the interests of the parties involved. Passionate love, on the other hand, serves no real interest of those who are so mysteriously swept up in it, and in fact often renders those interests quite hopeless in its determination to achieve its own impersonal end. It thus forms the basis of the least stable unions, eventually converting wedlock into a howling discord and establishing each of its partners with a detested companion for life. We nevertheless, sensing the greater urgency of the ultimate end, which is the perpetuation of the race, and the relative insignificance of those who are its means, approve this very passion as the only acceptable motive. We cheer the elopers as they flout wisdom and prudence, congratulate them when all cool deliberation and intelligence are swept aside, as though sensing that the very meaning of life, which is nothing more than life itself, were fulfilled by their folly. It is thus, as Schopenhauer expressed it, the immortal part of man, or his true nature, that gazes into the eyes of his lover, while what is mortal in him, his own individuality, desires everything else but counts for nothing.

Pessimism

THE philosophy of pessimism, with which Schopenhauer's name is always associated, is not merely an attitude that one just accepts or rejects according to his temperament. It is a solemn rational conclusion that Schopenhauer drew from what seemed to him the facts of experience. One is apt to think of an optimist as simply a man who likes living, and a pessimist as one who complains against life, but that is altogether superficial. The love of life does not require that life should be good. It requires only that it should be willed. And since men and all living things do by their very natures will life, the question can still be asked whether it is in fact something good that is thus willed.

Schopenhauer thought not. Indeed, the evil of the world seemed to him its most salient, positive, and ineradicable feature. But the intellectual apprehension of this fact, however certain, does not by itself turn one away from the world and life, and it did not do so in Schopenhauer's own case. He lived it to the fullest, pursuing much the same ends that all other men rush after — honor, recognition, comfort, and longevity — in the full conviction of his own folly and the vanity of life, never taking even the first step on that path to salvation that he had so carefully described. This indicates no hypocrisy, however, for the explanation is implied in his own philosophy; namely, the strength of his own will, his bondage to it, and its complete independence from his thought and reason.

A philosophy of optimism, which men everywhere are strangely exhorted to approve quite without any inquiry into its truth, requires that life, or at least human life, have some ultimate meaning or purpose beyond the mere perpetuation of life. It requires that we be able to apprehend this purpose intellectually, that we be free to pursue it, and that it is worthy of our effort. But Schopenhauer found support for none of these claims in anything we see or know. Theologians make claims of this sort, relating human life and meaning to some divine purpose or plan that is guaranteed to be good; but no theologian dares to suggest that these are the lessons of life. He speaks, instead, of faith, of things hoped for but unseen, and he finds a ready response to this appeal in the hearts and wills of believers.

Moreover, if a philosopher of optimism is to be true, there must be genuine, positive goods in the world, and they must prevail, or give some promise of prevailing, over their opposites. But again, nothing seemed to Schopenhauer less likely to be true. The concept of a *summum bonum*, or complete and final good, is in Schopenhauer's philosophy simply an absurdity, for it could consist only in the complete satisfaction of the will, which he considered to be as insatiable as time is endless. If one tries to form an image of a satisfied will, the idea that he gets is that of effortless inactivity wherein all desire has subsided. But far from being the image of a good, this is the picture of boredom, which is one of the acutest forms of suffering. It is therefore not without reason, Schopenhauer thought, that it is sometimes imposed upon prisoners, in the form of solitary confinement, as one of the severest penalties. But even apart from a supreme good, there seemed to Schopenhauer no reason for thinking that the world presents even a balance of goodness over evil. Goodness is everywhere the evasive quality, the fleeting element, the one that is continually pressed into oblivion. Theologians and many philosophers

have invented ingenious arguments, always predicated on the goodness of God and intended to confirm that goodness, to the effect that goodness does prevail, that it is even identical with existence itself, and that evil is something only negative, accidental, and illusory; but Schopenhauer thought that such arguments are merely born of wishes. It is never our senses that teach us that the world is good, but simply our wills that will our existence and its fulfillments, which then seem good for that reason alone. Almost without exception we find that things are lovely, throughout nature, in proportion to their rarity. Ugliness is the norm, toward which all things tend, almost as though it were a law of nature. Flowers appear briefly and wither quickly, the more quickly as they are more lovely; but the dirt and manure from which they spring endure almost indestructibly. Precious gems are often of exquisite beauty, but they must be sought out from the obscure corners of the earth, whereas the bleak and colorless rocks and sands are everywhere at our feet. Hideous caterpillars transform themselves at last into nocturnal moths whose loveliness fills us with awe, but so ephemeral is their tenure of life that nature does not even give them mouths and they starve in hardly a few hours. Here and there one occasionally sees a rare act of pure sweetness and kindness, without ulterior motive, on the part of some man; but it is never what was expected, and one can count on his fingers the clear instances of it seen in his lifetime. Cruelty and malice, on the other hand, are always at hand, and ulterior or self-regarding motives are taken for granted. Genius appears here and there, accidentally, among men, but it is forever engulfed in the ocean of stupidity that gives no hint of being accidental or illusory. Indeed, a man of genius can be rendered an idiot by the slightest physiological disturbance — a slight unbalance of salts in his blood or the malfunction of a small gland; but a dolt cannot be made a genius by all the powers of heaven and earth, so durable is that state. Men otherwise destined for art, science, or philosophy are made hopelessly moronic by a momentary shortage of oxygen to their brains at birth or by the infections of insignificant viruses in infancy. One never hears of an opposite fate from similar causes. Thus do virtually all men arise and live through their lives with the uniformity of clockwork, their routine existence accompanied by a few trivial thoughts and insipid emotions, while only here and there, on a continent of millions, appears a fleeting sample of original power and genius.

The same rule, the same tendency to what is worse, Schopenhauer found in the lives of individuals. Thus, health and the joy of life are best exhibited in small children and morons, who know so little and who are in every sense protected from the world that philosophers of optimism assure us is an unadulterated goodness. If a man in the fullness of years and experience were to exhibit the joyousness of a child he would appear to everyone as an utter fool, as one who by that time should have learned better. Pain, anxiety, and suffering are what are positive, what are actually felt, while pleasure and happiness are the negative, illusory states. Indeed, the mere absence of the former is everywhere recognized as sufficient for the latter. We can easily form the clearest mental image of a man suffering, in a numberless variety of ways. No novelist needs to strain to fill an entire volume with the elaboration of such states, carrying us chapter by chapter through one trial and ordeal after another. Thus it is the Biblical story of Job that has the flavor of reality, and not the story of the paradise in which our race was begun, short-lived as that was. No clear image of positive and enduring pleasure and happiness can even be concocted except only in so far as it expresses mere absence of pain and suffering, nor can any extensive description of it possibly be given without soon becoming insipid. We are satisfied to call a man happy simply upon learning that he is emancipated from suffering and pain. One test of this is to conjure in the mind an image of a man enduring violent pain, which is a simple task, and then to try placing beside it the image of a man receiving pleasure of similar magnitude and duration, which is something that cannot be done. Our experience furnishes abundant materials for the former but almost none for the latter. Thus did Dante describe hell most vividly, Schopenhauer noted, in a manner immediately comprehensible by anyone, but turning to the task of describing heaven he found almost nothing to say and was obliged to rest content with a description of utter boredom and nothingness. This is, in fact, the popular conception of heaven in the minds of those who trust in God to supply the details of that abode, their imaginations failing. Buddhist literature is filled with the most graphic descriptions of suffering, but can find only one word with which to describe the salvation from it, namely, "nirvana," which means, literally, nothingness. Every engrossing drama carries its hero through trials, heartbreak, and defeat. These are no sooner conquered, however, than the curtain is hurriedly lowered, there being simply nothing to portray of the happiness that is then supposed to ensue. Youth, health, and vigor are good, but no one feels them, or attaches any positive qualities to them, nor are they in any way sensed until they are lost in sickness and age — and these are felt most acutely. Similarly, in the realm of desire, it is our wants and cravings that we feel. The satisfaction of them is felt only indirectly, as the quiescence of those wants, which were positive and real.

Such considerations as these, which anyone can easily multiply, Schopenhauer considered as confirming his thesis that it is our nature simply as living beings to will, blindly and without ultimate purpose, and thus to be made miserable by trifling frustrations, but to be made entirely happy by nothing at all, not even the gratifications provided by a lifetime. And for just the same reason the intellectual understanding of evil leaves us quite unmoved, and quite incapable of drawing from pessimism any practical conclusions for action. The mere knowledge that the philosophy of pessimism is true has no tendency to prevent us from acting as though the exact opposite were true, and Schopenhauer's own life reflected little of his pessimism. Men are moved only by an appeal to the will, and it is the nature of all living things, just as living, to will life.

Freedom

PHILOSOPHERS who conceive of individual men as ultimate realities rather than as phenomenal expressions of a deeper reality have usually supposed either that an individual man is the ultimate source of his own voluntary behavior or that all his behavior is determined by the relations of cause and effect between phenomena, whether subjective or objective. It is to the former view that most theories of absolute free will belong and to the latter most theories of determinism; but Schopenhauer's view does not exactly coincide with either.

To assert that a man has an absolute free will with respect to some of his acts amounts to saying that he alone is the cause of them but that nothing makes him do them. This, however, entails that he has a free and spontaneous will, a *liberum arbitrium indifferentiae*, which means that some things occur without any reason or explanation at all. Thus, on this view, if a man freely commits a murder, then there is a reason or explanation for the murder, for we can point to the murderer and say that he did it or that he made it occur — but there is no possibility of saying why he did it or what made him do it. We can only say something to the effect that his will, which was free, inclined him to it, but that nothing inclined or determined his will. Now this theory, in all of its innumerable forms, Schopenhauer rejected as inconsistent both with the facts of experience and with the principle of sufficient reason, which seemed to him obviously valid for all phenomena. According to the principle of sufficient reason there are, in the case of any event, certain others that etiologically explain its happening, and Schopenhauer found it difficult to see why human behavior should, in the whole order of nature, be considered an exception to this principle. When a man does something we are rarely tempted to suppose that there is no explanation for his doing it, though the complete explanation may not, of course, be known, even to him. We have, moreover, a general idea of what the explanation is, for we find that men everywhere act in accordance with their characters, together with the motives that present themselves to them. Thus Schopenhauer thought that men form no exception to the scholastic principle *operari sequitur esse*, which means that everything acts in accordance with what it is. Iron acts in certain ways under certain conditions and cannot act otherwise, simply because it has the nature of iron rather than of copper or zinc. So likewise, a hawk or a mouse cannot act otherwise than it does under the circumstances into which it is thrown, simply because the one has the character of a hawk and the other that of a mouse. And so it is with men, too; each acts as a man and, more importantly, as the kind of man he is. The greedy man acts greedily when presented with an opportunity for greed, while the unselfish, sweet, or compassionate man acts unselfishly, sweetly, or compassionately, having the character of just such a man.

To suppose, on the other hand, in accordance with a simple determinism, that human behavior consists only in bodily motions that are the causal effects of events occurring within or without the agent — that they are, for instance, the mechanical effects of stimuli or of choices, volitions, nerve impulses, and so on — is altogether too superficial and does no justice to the realization each man has that his conduct arises from himself. Schopenhauer did not think of men, any more than of other creatures, as phenomenal robots or puppets drawn hither and thither by such events as happen to occur in and about them. He thought of them as living things whose whole lives derive their impetus from a will that is the essence of their being. This profound inner source of human conduct is well recognized by the various theories of free will and self-determination whose error consists only in their supposition that individual men, as the authors of their own behavior, are the ultimate sources of it, and that they are thus neither caused nor wholly conditioned, but act, willy nilly, this way and that, as their private free wills happen to incline them.

According to Schopenhauer's philosophy, each man is the objectification of a will that expresses itself in his basic character, this character, in turn, being reflected in his basic purposes, his conduct, and even his physiognomy. This will is, to be sure, unconditioned, uncaused, dependent upon nothing for its reality and its nature, being instead the ultimate ground of all life and existence. It is, accordingly, by definition free. But this gives no individual man a free will, in the sense of his having ultimate dominion over that very force that animates him and determines what he is. Man's freedom, according to Schopenhauer, belongs to his *esse*, that is, to his nature or character, and not to his acts. His character being the immediate expression of will, there is no reason why it should be what it is — it might as well have been something else. But given the character or nature that one has, his acts are but the consequences of that character and are in nowise free in themselves. One's phenomenal character, moreover, is quite obviously determined throughout, just as in the case of any inanimate thing. Whether, for example,

one is male or female, and whether, accordingly, he has the temperament, passions, and role appropriate to the one or the other, is a matter in which no man has a voice. Similarly, with respect to one's time and place of birth, his ancestry (and hence his heredity), his body and nervous system with such powers and defects as these possess, and the formative influences of his youth — in none of these things does a man ever suppose himself to have any hand at all. Man's freedom, then, is reserved entirely to his noumenal character, or his true inner nature, which is the arbitrary and unconditioned expression of will. A man is therefore appropriately described, not as a being that *has* a free will, but rather as one who *is* the free expression of will.

Schopenhauer thus concluded that by one's acts one learns the kind of man he is — heroic if his deeds turn out to be those of strength and heroism, or timid, weak, and vacillating if they turn out to be actions befitting that character; or compassionate and deep-feeling if such a man he be, or the reverse if such is the character so manifested. One's remorse, or occasionally his pride and exultation, in the contemplation of what he has done, do not then arise from the belief that he might, given the person he is, have done otherwise, but rather from the sharp *reminder* these deeds provide, the reminder of just what he is. One is never tempted to think, when viewing the things he has done, that they might be undone; hence the acute poignancy of the remorse, if they are deeds he cannot view without shame. And the remorse is deeper in proportion as there is no future possible compensation for the evil in them. The most profound remorse of all, accordingly, results from the realization that these acts could not have been otherwise, and that they betray, utterly, what one is, what he can in no way help being, and what he is destined to remain.

Nor need we, Schopenhauer thought, take seriously any theory of special acts of will, or volitions, as an attempt to make the individual agent an ultimate author of his conduct. Such acts of will, whatever they may be, must nevertheless be events, and hence part of a phenomenal chain of cause and effect. Whatever, then, might be their consequences in action, they are themselves the consequences of other events, and their antecedents must therefore reach back into an infinity of time, rendering them of small significance indeed so far as an agent's dominion over his voluntary behavior is concerned. But in fact, Schopenhauer claimed, an act of will is not something at all separable from the act itself into which it is supposed to issue. To *will* an act, as distinguished from merely contemplating it or deliberating concerning it, is simply to *do* the act in question. One does not will to walk and then find himself walking as a result, or will to speak and then hear himself speaking in consequence of this. Rather, he wills to speak in speaking and wills to walk in walking. The will of a man is thus not some reserve force within him, disposed in this way or that in accordance with his varying inclinations and motives. It is the very essence of his life, his being, his action, and, manifestly, the source of those very inclinations and motives themselves. To imagine the will to be subservient to one's inclinations, motives, and desires would be like imagining the very motions of the planet that carries us about in space to be at the mercy of us who are its mere passengers.

The fundamental character of a man, which according to Schopenhauer's view expresses itself in all his behavior, is, moreover, not subject to change. His phenomenal character may change, and indeed cannot help changing — for one inevitably grows older, gains new motivations as older ones subside, embarks upon this role and that, and in these superficial ways ceases to be what he has been. But what he is, in a deeper sense, or the kind of person he is has its source in his will, which is invariable through life. One rarely doubts this when contemplating the characters of others, nor is he much inclined to doubt it when viewing his own past works. Only when one considers his present self and is repelled by what he finds is he tempted to suppose that he is now going to make of himself something quite different from what he has heretofore been, without troubling to ask himself what it is, in this case, that is going to act upon what. And yet, Schopenhauer insisted, he soon discovers anew what he is and learns that it is fundamentally not one whit different than before, as no one else would have been tempted to doubt in the first place.

There is, of course, within this framework still room for a perfectly clear conception of freedom. Anything is deemed free, Schopenhauer noted, just to the extent that it is not frustrated, constrained, or impeded; and a will, whether fixed and determined or not, is nonetheless subject to frustration, constraint, and impediment. Thus, a river flows freely if it is not dammed or otherwise obstructed. Similarly, a nation is considered free to the extent that it is not subject to external domination. It matters not at all to the freedom of that nation — though it may matter greatly to its citizens — whether its government is tyrannical or not. Or a hawk, similarly, whose will is to prey upon small animals, is made unfree by whatever circumstances render it incapable of realizing that end. No question arises, in such cases, of whether any will is free, independently of tendencies, goals, or purposes, or the impediments to their realization. It is just so, Schopenhauer claimed, in the case of an individual man. To the extent that his will is not impeded, to that extent is he free, and no question arises, or can even be made meaningful, whether that will is itself free, in this sense. Nor, of course, is it relevant to the question of his freedom what direction his will happens to take, however crucial that may be to determining what kind of man he is.

These rather unusual theories of Schopenhauer's anticipated, in important respects, certain conceptions of the will that have been gaining increasing acceptance in recent years, though Schopenhauer is rarely recognized as the father of them. The force of irrational influences in the formation of character, and the small role played by reason in this respect, is now generally recognized. It is also no longer widely supposed that acts of will are things that are separable from acts themselves, or that they are subjective, mental events transpiring within the agent and issuing in bodily movements that are called acts. To act voluntarily or from one's own will is, many thinkers now insist, not to will to act and then to act, but rather, simply to act. It can hardly be doubted that this insight was fairly original with Schopenhauer, and that it is of lasting significance.

At the same time, it is in the application of his voluntarism to the problem of freedom that a great contradiction in Schopenhauer's philosophy seems to lie. A man's character, according to this philosophy, is absolutely fixed. Yet Schopenhauer also taught that one can gain release from suffering only by freeing himself from the bondage to his will, whereupon all craving and willing cease, and one then views existence contemplatively and aesthetically. Such a conquest of the will would seem to be not only a change of character, the possibility of which Schopenhauer denied, but a complete transformation of it. And even if this did not seem quite impossible, according to Schopenhauer's principles, it is still unclear, in the light of those same principles, what could possibly act upon the will to produce this diminution of its force, since Schopenhauer claims throughout his philosophy that the will is the only thing that ever does act and that it is never acted upon. Schopenhauer tried to overcome this difficulty by suggesting that the salvation from willing results from the will turning upon itself and overcoming itself. It is difficult to attach any clear meaning to this, however, except as a metaphor. It was essential for him to deny completely the possibility that a man could emancipate himself from his will by the use of his reason, an idea that has been prevalent in philosophy ever since Plato set it forth as expressing the essence of a just or virtuous man. And yet it is difficult to see how Schopenhauer's conception differs significantly from this one. Had he simply denied the possibility of any release from willing, and accepted the fatalism that this implies, his philosophy would have remained entirely consistent, and pessimistic throughout.

Ethics

THE ethical theory Schopenhauer derives from his philosophy is unique in the history of thought, being at once a denial of moral philosophy as traditionally conceived and an explanation of the basis of moral judgments.

Traditionally, moral philosophy has been considered something non-empirical and *sui generis*, a science concerned more with ideals than with facts. Experience, it has been assumed, can only teach us what is, not what should be; it can inform us what men do but not what they ought to do. Kant carried this assumption so far as to declare that it would make no difference at all to a true theory of morals whether any man in fact behaved morally or not. It is the task of moral philosophy, then, according to this approach, to discover what men's duties and obligations are, basing itself entirely upon reason or conscience rather than upon empirically discoverable facts of human nature.

Schopenhauer regarded this task as misconceived from the outset. Such notions as moral obligation and duty, he thought, considered independently of any empirical considerations such as contracts and laws, have no application whatever in human affairs except on the assumption that men's wills are free to choose among alternatives and that men can decide among various competing motives which shall claim their effort. This assumption, of course, he rejected. One's behavior is the product of his will, and this is something that is given to him, not something he selects. More precisely, one's conduct is the resultant of his character, which has its source in his will, together with his motives. Given these, the course of action one "chooses" is already clearly determined. The most pervasive and stable motives, moreover — such as greed, vanity, altruism, the love of honor or possession, and so on — are in their various combinations fairly fixed in every man from the start, a fact that seemed to Schopenhauer quite evident to anyone so long as he is considering the behavior of other men, and equally evident to them when they are considering his. Our motives are not *chosen* by our reason or intelligence, nor can they even be thought of in that way without the absurdity of the idea leaping up. One's motive or end being given, reason and intelligence are employed only in the discovery of means or devices for its fulfillment. It is this that distinguishes men from other creatures; namely, that while the lower animals, guided by motives that are the product of their wills, aim at their ends through instinctive response, men aim at them through intelligent contrivance. The instinct of an animal does not select the motive itself, however, and no more does the intelligence or reason of a man do so. One's motives are the product of his will, and are in fact one of its clearest expressions. As the spider constructs its web instinctively, and with no knowledge of engineering, guided by the motive of entrapping its prey, so also the vain and greedy man was vain and greedy long before he ever gave thought to greed and vanity. He employs his intellect solely to the satisfaction, never to the selection, of those motives. The sweetness of a sensitive and compassionate soul, similarly, arises not from reflection, nor from the quiet study of

moral treatises, but from something far deeper, from the will or nature of that person himself. It is for this reason that learning and the gifts of intellect have no correlation whatever with virtue and rectitude. Every man of sense, accordingly, before he places his trust in another, knows enough to inquire into that man's heart, that is, his motives and will, rather than his reason, and regards with proper indifference his achievements in learning, which have no influence upon this.

Schopenhauer nevertheless found a task for the philosopher in the realm of morals, and that is to describe the source, in human nature, of that profound condemnation and commendation expressed in moral judgments. This he found in the three basic springs or motives of human behavior, namely, *egoism*, or self-love, which is the impulse to one's own weal and good; *malice*, or the impulse to others' woe or hurt; and *compassion*, or the impulse to another's weal or well being. Now, each of these Schopenhauer considered a distinct and basic motive and not one which — like the love of honor, for example — is derivative from something more basic. Egoism, whose role in determining behavior is so pervasive that the total absence of it in any man would make him seem an anomaly in our eyes, is selfishness, that is, the impulse to one's own good, as an end in itself, rather than as a means to some further end. Malice, similarly, is disinterested nastiness, that is, the impulse to hurt others, without any expectation of actual benefit to oneself. And pure compassion, which like all lovely things is exceedingly rare, is sweetness, sympathy, or what Schopenhauer called loving-kindness, without ulterior motive; that is the inclination to the weal or joy of other creatures, whether human or other, without hope of reward or gain for oneself.

Now, each of these motives appeared to Schopenhauer to be a fundamental ingredient of human nature, such that the total absence of any one of them would be an aberration. Yet egoism is plainly the most reliable one, and the clearest expression of the will to live. It is unhesitatingly allowed as the presupposition of all laws and prescriptions of penalties, and indeed of everything pertaining to human relationships, even those, such as within the family circle, wherein it would be expected to have least force. Marriage, which is sentimentally spoken of as a union of love, is nonetheless realistically assumed in laws to be a union of two self-regarding wills each with its own jealously guarded rights and prerogatives; and such in fact it almost invariably is. Nor does the most egregious egoism or self-concern ever strike us as really abnormal. Wealthy men walk past beggars, whose plight they could relieve effortlessly, and then bend down to pick a trivial coin from the walk, for themselves. This occasions no real astonishment in anyone, despite the plain incongruity of the situation. When some poor soul is felled on the street of a great city, whether from illness or drink, it can by no means be assumed that any of the indurate multitude who must step over him to get on with their petty rounds will stop to assist him, although he is eventually removed as an obstruction to traffic. Nor are there many, Schopenhauer maintained, who do not derive some satisfaction from the positive ruin of another, provided some benefit rebounds to themselves in the form of, say, a small legacy or a barely significant improvement in their worldly position.

Schopenhauer nevertheless found nothing inherently immoral in egoism, which is entirely self-regarding, nor anything necessarily pernicious in its fruits. The impulse to one's own weal and well being ordinarily results, at worst, in unfeeling indifference to others, while it often, quite accidentally, brings benefits to them. One must often serve others, in order to use them effectively in the advancement of his own interest, an idea that is expressed in the phrase "enlightened self-interest." As an incentive to action, then, egoism is neither uniquely moral nor immoral but simply amoral.

Expressions of egoism are, however, aesthetically quite repellent, and rightly regarded as the mark of boorishness and lack of civilized graces. This is the basis for the natural aversion people have toward adolescents; particularly boys, whose total unconcern for others is usually quite evident. Schopenhauer also regarded it as the foundation of all gentle manners. Just as all civilized persons require clothing to cover their repulsive nakedness, so also are manners and all the usages of civilized social intercourse needed to cover over the egoism which always repels. Yet while something is thus hidden from the eyes, nothing is hidden at all from the intellect by this device. Just as everyone knows that the finery of the gentleman conceals a nakedness that he could not exhibit without shame and humiliation, so aesthetically repellent is it, so also everyone knows that just beneath the usages and courtesies of the parlor and all social gathering lies an unvarying egoism which, never abolished, is covered over just for decency's sake, to avoid offense. Thus do all people sense a certain hypocrisy in gentle manners which, like the fashions of clothing, tend to become formalized. Yet they are a device of concealment without which Schopenhauer thought the most elementary forms of civilized life would be quite impossible.

Malice, on the other hand, Schopenhauer conceived to be the very *basis* of immorality, and to exist only in human nature, being quite foreign to all other creatures — an observation that led Gobineau to describe man as *l'animal méchant par excellence*. We do indeed find pain and suffering throughout nature, but only in men do we sometimes find these the very purposes of action, such that malice becomes deliberate and disinterested. The cruelty of one animal toward another is the product of uncomprehending indifference, not deliberate choice, whereas in man Schopenhauer found it to be sometimes a chosen aim. Thus have public executions always drawn crowds — not, of course, for the moral lesson they are officially meant to impart, but for the satisfaction of seeing deliberately imposed suffering. Tales of violence are always guaranteed a wide audience, the more so if they are true, for the fascination that is found in the suffering of others is quite limitless. A man who prepares his own destruction atop a high building always attracts onlookers, and from the unabashed malice of some of these there always arise chants and exhortations to him to jump. Nor, Schopenhauer thought, can this impulse to cruelty possibly be regarded as entirely an artificial product of social life and civilization. It is, in the strictest sense, an *original* sin, which advanced culture endeavors to combat, but seldom implants. Children feel malice long before they have any capacity for compassion, delighting in the misery, stupidity, or deformity of others, and teasing and tormenting whatever is within their reach, without any hope of benefit thereby and often at considerable trouble to themselves. Thus does every feral animal rightly and instinctively flee from men, and men only, being cajoled to approach even the friendliest human gesture only after long and patient training, and even then with a distrust that never quite vanishes. Men's instinct to hunt is an original one which, though often conjoined with the love of the out-of-doors, has nevertheless an independent motivation; for many who care nothing for the beauties of nature still go to great cost and preparation for the pleasures of hooks, guns, and traps. Nor can the impulse to gossip, Schopenhauer believed, and to share with others the satisfaction of contemplating the defects of others, spring from anything but an original malice. One must be taught to praise, and only with effort can he find real satisfaction in the achievements of others, while epithets of scorn and execration rise spontaneously to the lips. Rage sometimes bursts forth, explosively, having every semblance, in Schopenhauer's comparison, to a latent charge that required only a spark to release it. Sweetness and loving kindness are never explosive, never suggest the idea of a latent, pent-up charge. They must, on the contrary, always struggle to find any expression at all.

Schopenhauer declared malice to be the one and only common element in every act that is the source of immediate moral revulsion, and hence the very basis of immorality. A man might, and in fact commonly does, injure others in response to his own insatiable selfishness, and this we disparage but our sense of morality is not outraged by it. The pain he causes is the result of his unfeeling indifference, and he seems to us more like an insensitive animal than a satan. But that a man should, knowing what pain is, make the pain in another creature the very object of his will, always stirs in us the deepest moral revulsion.

Now when we consider human nature, so generously endowed with egoism and malice, it might seem that any incentive directly opposed to these would be impossible, and many philosophers have, like Hobbes, declared it to be so. Yet Schopenhauer believed that it does actually exist, here and there, and rarely. Sympathy or compassion, as the words themselves suggest, is the imaginative identification of oneself with the sufferings of others, the feeling, with them, of their pain and anxiety. By the inhibition of one's own will which thereby results, one's egoism and malice, with which sympathy is wholly incompatible, are overcome and cancelled. Tender souls are sometimes appalled at the suffering of some poor and perhaps worthless creature, and in highly civilized nations there are even established societies devoted to alleviating the sufferings of all animals, entirely without hope of reward or gratitude. There sometimes even appears a holy man — a Buddha or a Christ — who by a dramatic act or otherwise identifies himself with the very sufferings of the world, and thus is planted the seed of a religion. We look at a child, whose feelings have been senselessly crushed by something perhaps trivial, or at the lover, suffering the torment of rejection, at the insane, whose torment is incomprehensible to themselves, at dumb animals whose expressions sometimes bespeak their unutterable pain, at the sick, and the dying; and here, sometimes, the web of Maya that separates the *me* from the *thou* is sundered. We see, fleetingly, the identity of our will with that of the suffering creature before us. Our own ego is momentarily extinguished, and loving kindness wells up in spite of ourselves. Or we see a man, bent upon revenge, even justified in his thirst for it, having the power of it in his hands, immune to all fear of reprisal — but one who nevertheless hesitates at the last moment, restrained by the same dim feeling of compassion. The only plausible and realistic explanation for this, according to Schopenhauer, is that he envisaged the suffering he was about to inflict, that he saw a bit beyond the illusory separation between himself and his victim, that he imaginatively identified his own will with that of another — in short, that he felt a compassion that crippled his own egoism. Here we are in the presence of something with which the traditional precepts of moralists and clerics have nothing to do; and yet our hearts are filled with profound approbation. Here, according to Schopenhauer, and here alone, we find the basis of genuinely moral conduct. Without it, we have at best civilized behavior, motivated by hope of gain, fear of penalty, or more commonly mere habit. But in the presence of genuine compassion, however faint, we find ourselves constrained to approval which has no regard for our own interests. Our selfishness bows helplessly; not from great expectations of its consequences, which may be trivial, nor from the perception that here some moral rule is exhibited — for compassion is a feeling and thus subject to no

rule — but from the transcendent beauty of the motive itself, and the truth suggested by it, that the inner nature or will of all living things is the same. "Ought" and "ought not," categorical imperatives, commandments of gods, considerations of utility, thoughts of rewards or punishments, or of the dogmas of religion or the casuistry of priests, have here no relevance at all. There is only the command of the heart, which knows no philosophy, but before which all dogmas and systems of morals give way and collapse.

Salvation

THE role that Schopenhauer assigns to compassion in ethics gives also the clue to his scheme of salvation. Compassion is a prompting of the heart — that is, of the will — and not of the intellect or reason which only perceive and do not feel. The effect of compassion is the partial and momentary extinguishing of the individual will itself, resulting from its identification with the suffering will of another. This is clearly the first step of deliverance — to see beyond the phenomena of individuality separating the "me" from "thou," to penetrate the veil of Maya and grasp the reality beneath it, the common will that unites all things. This thought is not foreign to religion, of course, and Schopenhauer found it perfectly expressed in the Sanskrit formula of Hindu literature, called the *Mahavakya* or "great word," *Tat twam asi*, meaning "this thou art." Compassion, however, accomplishes this realization only imperfectly, for it is rare, fleeting, and quite at the mercy of external circumstances. Nevertheless, in this experience Schopenhauer thought he found the partial extinction of the individual will. He concluded, therefore, that it is possible, and that at least here one can be in a small degree released from his bondage to a groundless source of existence and, thereby, from suffering. He found this same quiescence of the will, though imperfectly, in the contemplation of beauty, for aesthetic contemplation and restless craving are impossible to combine, and yet the former is sometimes possible to a sensitive soul. In the quiet perception of painting, of natural beauty, and above all, of music, which Schopenhauer deemed the very language of the will, the ground of existence is lost, suffering is put behind one, and the mind approaches an awareness of something eternal and immutable, something that ordinarily eludes us just because it has no reference to the will and hence no bearing upon individual cravings. Final deliverance, however, could only consist of a total and permanent release from this bondage, an ideal that Schopenhauer did not deem possible in life, for life is itself the expression of will. He did, nevertheless, find it achieved to a high degree in the lives of the saints, particularly those of Eastern religions. It is the teaching of Buddhism, for example, as it is

Schopenhauer's, that life is essentially suffering, that this suffering arises from grasping or craving, particularly the craving for existence, and that the release from this suffering can accordingly only come from the release from blind craving itself. The Buddhist ideal is the state of Nirvana, wherein all desire, willing, and craving are put to rest and, with them, individuality. This is an ideal that the Buddhist represents as realizable, though perhaps not entirely in this life. Now to us this overcoming of the will looks like the abnegation of life itself, which it is, and thus, we are apt to think, of all of life's goods. But this is only because we imagine that these goods are such, independently of our craving for them. For Schopenhauer, as for the Buddhist, salvation is the victory over, and the annihilation of, the world, which is nothing, of life, which is suffering, and of the individual ego, which is an illusion.

21

Nietzsche

ARTHUR DANTO

NIETZSCHE'S LIFE WAS NOT a happy one by ordinary standards of felicity; indeed, it was rather tragic: he endured great suffering, physical and emotional. Toward the end, his work began to be known — Georg Brandes lectured on his philosophy in Denmark in 1888 — but he was insulated by insanity from the recognition his work achieved after that, and during his productive years his thought was generally unknown and, save by a handful of readers, unappreciated and largely misunderstood. Nor was he fortunate in the posthumous notoriety and influence his writings came to enjoy.

Friedrich Wilhelm Nietzsche was born in Röcken, Germany, on October 15, 1844. He was named after the then King of Prussia, but he later dropped the "Wilhelm" and in general repudiated his German origins: he liked to pass himself off as of Polish (and noble!) descent, although he counted himself a "Good European." His books are filled with anti-German critical shafts, and he was in fact something of a Francophile. His father, a Lutheran pastor, died when Nietzsche was four. Nietzsche was trained in classical philology at Bonn and later at Leipzig, and made an immense impression upon one of his professors, the distinguished Friedrich Ritschl. It was in great measure due to Ritschl's enthusiastic recommendation that Nietzsche secured the post of professor extraordinarius at the University of Basle in 1869. Since he was only twenty-five, it is clear that he was regarded as a man of singular promise. At Basle, he lectured on classical philology and ancient philosophy, and formed important friendships with, among others, the student of primitive Christianity Franz Overbeck, the historian Jacob Burckhardt, and most particularly with Richard Wagner, who was at the time living in Tribschen, near Lucerne. Nietzsche regarded Wagner as the agent through which German culture would achieve the heights of tragic greatness once before realized in Greece, and this was part of the polemical message of *The Birth of Tragedy out of the Spirit of Music*, published in 1872. Meanwhile, Nietzsche became a Swiss citizen, was promoted to full professor at Basle, and served, briefly and disastrously, as a medical orderly with the Prussian forces in the Franco-Prussian War of 1870. From 1873 to 1876 he published a series of *Unzeitgemässe Betrachtungen* ("*Thoughts out of Season*"), including *David Strauss: Confessor and Scribbler* (1873), *On the Utility and Disutility of History for Life* (1873), *Schopenhauer as Educator* (1874) and finally *Richard Wagner at Bayreuth* (1876). By this time he was quite thoroughly disillusioned with Wagner as a person and as an influence on German life, and a growing breach was made definitive with the publication, in 1878, of Nietzsche's first aphoristic work, *Human, All-too-Human*.

Nietzsche resigned from Basle in 1878 on grounds of poor health, and thereafter he lived an increasingly solitary and crushingly lonely life, nursing his ravaged body and painfully producing his major works in the ten-year period from 1878 to 1888. These included two appendices to *Human, All-too-Human* (*Mixed Opinions and Sayings* [1879] and *The Wanderer and his Shadow* [1880]); *Die Morgenröte* (1881); *The Gay Science* (1882); *Thus Spake Zarathustra* (published in four separate instalments from 1883 to 1885); *Beyond Good and Evil* (1886); *Genealogy of Morals* (1887); *The Wagner Case* (1888). In 1888, he also did *Twilight of the Idols* (published in 1889), *The Antichrist* and *Nietzsche contra Wagner* (published in 1895), and *Ecce Homo* (not published until 1908). During this period he also wrote a massive body of material, some of which was gathered together by his sister Elizabeth and published, first in 1901, under the title *The Will to Power* — a name Nietzsche once considered for his major but unachieved systematic treatise. In addition, new prefaces and appendices to earlier books were added as these went into fresh editions.

In 1882, he spent some time with a woman whose spirit and intelligence he vastly admired. This was Lou Andreas Salomé, a sort of intellectual adventuress. As with all Nietzsche's relationships, his involvement with Lou Salomé was complex and unsatisfactory, and his romantic ambitions came to nothing. Despite hints in *Ecce Homo* that he was something of a ladies' man, Nietzsche must have been essentially unattractive to the opposite sex, and his protracted celibacy was not altogether a matter of choice. In fact, he proposed marriage on a variety of occasions to different surprised women who did not find it difficult to reject him. There is almost definitive evidence, however, that he did not die a virgin; the disease causally responsible for his madness and his death was a venereal infection, apparently contracted during his student days in what must have been for him almost a unique sexual adventure.

Nietzsche's insanity began dramatically in January, 1889. In the remaining years of his life he was pretty much the helpless ward of his sister, whose mission in life it now became to establish her brother's reputation as a sage and prophet, and to edit and publish his writings. She set herself up as the chief authority on Nietzsche's meaning and as something of a high priestess to the Nietzsche cult, and managed, in the course of her editorial labors, to introduce a variety of distortions it would be difficult not to regard as unscrupulous: she modified and suppressed and rearranged Nietzsche's manuscripts and letters, and certainly did no service to scholarship, whatever may have been the consequences of her efforts for Nietzsche's growing reputation. Nietzsche died at Weimar on August 25, 1900.

Despite the hortatory fierceness of his writing style, despite the militancy of his moralistic messages and the easily misunderstood and overemphasized passages in which ruthlessness, cruelty, and suffering are commended and kindness and charity are condemned, Nietzsche was himself anything but a brute. There is overwhelming evidence that he was a gentle person, of sweet disposition and capable of great considerateness and courtesy — a soft-spoken man with a disarming sense of humor. He was a bit of a crank on dietary matters, but otherwise quite reasonable and sane. True, one has the sense of impending madness when one reads some of the particularly shrill and egomaniacal passages in *Ecce Homo*, written in the months before his collapse. But at the same time he was also writing the *Götzendämmerung*, which is perhaps his most sustained piece of philosophical prose. Here, as elsewhere when Nietzsche's life and work are concerned, one can hardly make an unqualified assertion.

It is a current fashion in the history of philosophy to treat Nietzsche as a moralist and as an uncompromising critic of religion and of the social institutions of his time. While it is true that he was these things, moralizing covers but a fraction of his published utterances, and by any common criterion of what constitutes being a philosopher, Nietzsche certainly qualifies as such. For he thought deeply, and often originally, about most of the main topics and problems that have always concerned philosophers, and he had something to say about them all: not merely about good and evil and how men ought to live, but about truth and beauty, mind, body, and matter; what there is and our knowledge of what there is; science, art, and religion; and philosophy itself.

He undertook to give a radical reinterpretation of philosophical activity, it being his view that philosophers before his time had misconstrued their own achievement and had supposed themselves to be giving an objective reading of things when in fact they were imposing upon the world a willed structure that was a projection of their own tacit moral prejudices. And in contrast with this, he felt that he himself was making a fresh start in philosophy, and that it was only part of his work to be destructive. But for that reason, he did not believe his own philosophy easy to understand, and time and again he insists upon the novelty of his ideas and cautions his readers to move carefully and not try to assimilate his theses to the very conceptual structures it was his task to put in question. But because he was also a master of German prose, an artist with words, a fertile inventor of ringing phrases and memorable aphorisms — and because, again, he was given often to the use of an inflammatory and overdramatized vocabulary — he was frequently taken up by a philosophically naïve audience that found him all too easy to "understand." And he has been — for reasons in part his own fault — singularly unfortunate in his disciples and influence. Murder has been committed in his name, and whatever he might have thought of it had he lived to see it, he was regarded both by some Nazis and some enemies of Nazism as the philosophical inspiration of that disastrous movement. He has been appealed to as a supreme justifier of intellectual bohemianism and of irrationalisms of all varieties; he has inspired rebellious and arty youth of the past several generations; and he has been the solace of all sorts of obscurantists. And except for a handful of sympathetic critics, philosophers have tended to acquiesce, by default, in this interpretation of his work.

Yet there is a less noisy, more analytical Nietzsche, whose work might easily have been taken as a contribution to technical philosophical movements, the members of which have by and large ignored him as one of their own. He shares the distinction of having discovered, independently, what we know as the pragmatic theory of truth, the view that our criterion for a proposition being true is its success as an instrument for the organization and anticipation of experience: it is true if "it works." But unlike his American counterparts, he lacked the patience, and probably the logical acuity, to work out the implications of his invention, and indeed he hardly understood what he had done. For like many innovators, he tended frequently to be dominated by conceptions which his own invention was meant to supersede; and although he clearly had the pragmatic theory of truth, he *believed* in the correspondence theory of truth and dramatically announced that "Everything is false" when he ought to have realized that he had merely found a new conception of truth. And from this misconception a good deal of his philosophy was generated.

One cannot, accordingly, present his philosophy and be wholly faithful to his intentions at the same time. It is due to recent developments in analytical philosophy that we are able to appreciate, today, much in his philosophy which must have been obscure, if not unintelligible, to his contemporaries and even to himself. In what follows, I shall therefore try to reconstruct his main philosophical ideas. From the historical point of view, of course, it would be wrong to represent Nietzsche as a dispassionate, careful analyst. His writings are too untidy for that; he wrote too much and on too many topical issues, and with too much heat and color to satisfy such a portrait. Like his own life, the structure of his thought is sober in contrast with the surface of his brilliant expositions and his pyrotechnical expression. But I shall endeavor to support my interpretations of his thoughts, wherever possible, with his own words; and by this device of ample quotation I hope to remedy, in some measure, whatever *historical* distortions a systematic treatment of his thought might entail.

Perspectivism

PHILOSOPHERS and plain men alike are often inclined to believe that there is an objective structure to the world, antecedent to any theories we may have about this structure, and that a theory is true or false in accordance with whether it correctly describes this structure or not. But this conception of an objective and independent world structure which human beings may hope to succeed in describing, as well as that theory of truth which asserts a relation of correspondence between the world and sentences purporting to assert facts about it, are violently contested by Nietzsche. Indeed, he attached, as we shall see, an importance to the refutation of these views far in excess of what most philosophers, who might agree that the correspondence theory of truth is inadequate or wrong, would have supposed the issue merited. When he speaks of truth, he means truth in the sense just specified, and when he says, as he often does, that "everything is false," he means that the alleged relation of correspondence between sentences and reality does not hold, and that, in just this sense of true, nothing is true. He was a thoroughgoing conventionalist in matters of human knowledge, and his celebrated attack against philosophical theories that maintained the existence of an objective *moral* order in the world was but a special case of a more general attack against any theory whatsoever that maintains the existence of *any* order in the world. What we *believe* to be true is likely to be whatever happens to have made it possible for us to live in a coherent way: he writes that "Truth is that sort of error without which a particular class of living creatures could not otherwise live"[1]; but his view was that this "error" had gotten to be inimical to life and, as one who, in his words, was an "Aye-sayer" to life, he felt it to be his main philosophical task to expunge this error, to put in question this concept of truth, and to release mankind for better things. His purposes were always therapeutic and prophetic, and it would badly misrepresent him not to appreciate his analyses in their motivating spirit; but I shall come to that later, and begin by clarifying the claims I have just ascribed to him.

As with Hume, to whose analyses his own bear many resemblances, Nietzsche held an anomalous attitude toward the so-called "common-sense view" of things. On the one hand, he regarded it as strictly speaking a fiction, for it is but one of an indefinite number of possible "interpretations" of the world, and Nietzsche argued that no sense can be given to the notion of a *correct* interpretation, for no interpretation is or can be *true*. But for this very reason, it cannot be invidiously contrasted with any allegedly correct view of reality. Yet philosophers have often drawn such a contrast, have found the views of common sense wanting, and have opted for quite contrary views of what reality must be like. In particular, there is a long tradition whose claim it was that the world in reality is far different from what common sense supposes it to be, for common sense is based upon the senses; and not only are the senses deceptive in principle, but reality itself is not accessible to them. But in this regard, Nietzsche wishes to sponsor the common-sense view, for it has been elaborated over a long period of time, and men are able to live, in a practical way, in accordance with it: it is a *useful* fiction which philosophical interpretations — no less fictional than it — are not. "The apparent world is the only one: the 'real world' is merely a lie."[2]

By "real" he has specifically in mind what philosophers have said reality to be: fixed, unified, and eternal, underlying but separable from what changes, from diversity and temporality. The senses do not lie, he insisted. He does not mean that illusions do not occur, but that their occurring is irrelevant to this issue: insofar as the senses reveal "becoming, passing away, change" they do not lie.[3] The characteristic philosophical distrust of the senses he sometimes attributes to a general contempt for the body and for animal existence: a turning away from life. Common sense, to repeat, is an interpretation. But "there are no facts (*Tatsachen*) only interpretations"[4] and no world *an sich* apart from an interpretation: "As though a world would be left over once we subtracted interpretations."[5] He writes: "The world which we have not reduced in terms of our own being, logic, and our psychological prejudices and presuppositions, does not exist as a world *an sich*."[6] So it is no criticism of common sense to point out that there are alternative views: the question is whether they are viable. The viability of common sense cannot readily be questioned: we *live* by it. Nietzsche's problem was whether it could nonetheless be attacked in the *name* of life, rather than, as with most philosophers, in a life-abnegating spirit. He felt it could be, but that an immense (and obvious) risk was involved. So he felt his philosophy to be dangerous. His difficult philosophical stance involved both a criticism of common sense (the view of the "herd") as well as a defense of it against all "life-denying" philosophical and religious criticism.

Nietzsche is often taken to be an arch irrationalist, a reputation based in large measure upon his celebration of dionysiac frenzy in his influential early work, *The Birth of Tragedy*. I cannot here untangle that brilliant, confused essay on Greek art and culture, but in it Nietzsche unmistakably distinguished between unlicensed dionysianism, which he, and according to him, the Greeks, found horrendous, and *hellenized* dionysianism. It was the latter he espoused, and he paints a ghastly picture of what happens when "art, in some form, particularly as religion or science, did not appear as a prophylactic against barbarity."[7] Reason as such is not contrary to life. But often life is depreciated in its name, and when Nietzsche impugns *Vernunft*, he does so when it is regarded, as by the Eleatics or Platonists, as in essential conflict with the senses and the passions, or when our ordinary view of things is unfavorably dismissed in favor of a view of things purportedly more in conformity to "reason." Indeed, "we possess science today strictly insofar as we have decided to *accept* the testimony of the senses — to the extent that we sharpen, arm, and learn to think through them."[8] And, he continues, "The rest is miscarriage and not-yet-science: I mean metaphysics, theology, psychology, and theory of knowledge. *Or else:* formal science, sign-theories: like logic and that applied logic, mathematics."[9]

In view of some customary appraisals of him, this is a remarkable passage. For while Nietzsche is often appealed to by existentialists and others who find positivism repugnant, the fact is that his views on many of the chief questions of philosophy are very much in the later spirit of logical empiricism. That school, it is well known, subscribed to a theory in accordance with which those propositions alone are meaningful which are of either of two classes: propositions which are verifiable by means of experiences, and propositions which are true in virtue of formal rules. Whatever sentence is of neither of these kinds is meaningless, and metaphysical utterances in particular fall, according to them, into this latter class. This was almost exactly Nietzsche's view. His affinities to contemporary analytical philosophy run even deeper. He felt that the entire tendency on the part of "reason" to posit entities, to ascribe to the "real" world "unity, identity, permanence, substance, cause, thinghood, being"[10] is due to certain inherent features of our language: "Language, at its origin, belongs to an age of the most rudimentary form of psychology. We enter into a realm of gross fetishism when we become conscious of the fundamental presuppositions of the metaphysics of language, or, in plain words, of 'reason.' . . . I am afraid we shall not get rid of God because we still believe in grammar."[11] The so-called categories of the understanding, which Kant, for example, felt could not be derived from anything empirical, are in fact built into the structure of our speech. As regards the idea that there is a world of permanent objects, "every word and sentence we utter speaks in its favor."[12] So to the degree that the common-sense view is embedded in ordinary language, and to the degree that Nietzsche's contention is correct that metaphysicians have mistaken certain general features of their language for generic traits of existence, they have based their rejection of common sense on exactly the presuppositions of common sense. But once the "true world" is seen to be no more than a skeletel reduplication of the general features of the "apparent world," it is immediately revealed as "an idea become useless and superfluous" and "Therefore a refuted idea. Let's get rid of it."[13] Meanwhile, once rid of the conception of the "true world," we have nothing against which to contrast the "apparent world," and the latter concept, deriving its only significance from a spurious contrast, is thus itself a spurious concept: "with the true world we have also gotten rid of the apparent world."[14]

One might think that if a useless idea is for that reason refuted, a useful one would accordingly be confirmed. But Nietzsche wishes to insist that, for all its patent utility, common sense is nonetheless false, and the notion that there are real and isolable entities in the world is plainly a common-sense belief. "There are no things," he writes, "that is our fiction."[15] But it is not a fiction we could easily get on without in common life or, for that matter, in science. "We operate with things which do not exist: with lines, surfaces, bodies, divisible times and spaces."[16] These concepts have a *use*, but they do not denote concrete entities nor, in Nietzsche's employment of the expression, do they "explain."

The concept of the atom is a case in point: "In order to understand the world, we have to be able to calculate; in order to be able to calculate, we require constant causes. Because we find no constant causes in reality, we invent some for ourselves, e.g., the atom. This is the origin of atomism."[17] It is tempting to suppose that Nietzsche speaks here of what philosophers today term "theoretical entities" — entities, typically unobservable, which are postulated as part of a general theory by means of terms which cannot be explicitly defined in the language of observation, nor reduced in any simple fashion to sets of observation sentences. But he has in mind a more sweeping thesis, one in accordance with which *all* references to concrete entities have the role of theoretical terms: "We have arranged for ourselves a world in which we can live — with the acceptance of bodies, lines, surfaces, causes and effects, motion and rest, form and content. Without these articles of faith, no one now would be able to live! But this by no means constitutes a proof. Life is no argument. Amongst the conditions of life, error might be one."[18] These "articles of faith" are, then, inherent in the language we speak, are "inherited and have finally almost become the condition of the human species."[19] So once again, in the required sense of "true," common sense is not true for all its unquestioned utility. "Innumerably many beings," he speculates, "who reasoned differently than we, perished: yet theirs might have been closer to the truth!"[20] What Nietzsche means is something like this. Consider a generalization "All *A*'s are *B*'s." Unless an individual were able to disregard differences, and able to regard similar things as the same, he would never have arrived at such generalizations. But he might nonetheless have seen things more as they are, no two things in the world being quite alike. Yet his sensitivity, inhibiting his power to generalize, might have made it less easy for him to survive than those of his fellows with coarser sensibilities, the inductive achievements of whom are the consequence of cruder apprehensions. There would, again, be little chance for one who actually *saw* the world as sheer flux: "every hesitancy in drawing inferences, every propensity to skepticism, is already a great danger to life."[21] So our general conceptual scheme is a tissue of "lies and frauds,"[22] but because of its practical indispensability we term it "true." "What, really, are mankind's truths? They are the *irrefutable* errors of man."[23] Irrefutable, certainly, by experience, for experience, or the experience of the survivors, at least, naturally conforms to them. They are not, in quite the Kantian sense, *a priori* forms of intuition, but are, rather, the perceptual and linguistic presuppositions that have survived with the species whose survival they have helped make possible. "Through immense stretches of time," he wrote, "the intellect produced only errors. Some of these proved useful preservatives of the species. Whoever hit upon or inherited these fought the fight for himself and his descendants with greater success."[24]

Consider, again, the concept of cause and effect. Nietzsche offers an analysis of it very like Hume's. But unlike Hume, who hesitated to speak of what are the "hidden springs" of occurrences, Nietzsche violates, as indeed he has violated all along, his self-avowed dictum that we cannot correctly say what the real world is like. Our notion of cause and effect is built up out of recognitions of constant conjunctions of events: "A certain thing is each time followed by a certain other thing — we, when we perceive and wish to name this, name it Cause and Effect. We fools! We have but seen the *image* of Cause and Effect. And this picture makes it impossible for us to see a more fundamental connectedness (*Verbindung*) than constant sequences."[25] But we are, to the extent even that we speak of a certain "thing" following a certain other one, already hopelessly committed to our perspective on the world, for "in truth," he contends, "a continuum stands before us from which we isolate a pair of fragments, just as we perceive a movement as isolated points and therefore do not properly see but infer it . . . there is an infinite set of processes in that abrupt second which evades us."[26] We impose, thus, an alien order upon a world which, in dionysian terms, he speaks of as "to all eternity chaos, not in the sense that necessity is absent, but that order, structure, form, beauty, wisdom are absent . . ."[27] So "let us guard against saying that there are laws in nature. There are only necessities."[28]

But what can he have meant by "necessities"? How are we to speak of these save with reference to some sort of structure, and what then happens to the vision of unstructured chaos? Often, when Nietzsche says there are no laws, he means no *moral* laws, as when he says there is no design, he means no *divine* design or purpose. Then, I suppose, his reasoning is this. Since "chance" contrasts with "design," nothing can happen by chance if nothing happens by design. But then, since chance is a contrary of necessity, Nietzsche illicitly concludes that if things don't happen by chance, they happen of necessity. Perhaps all he meant by "necessity" then was "not by chance," for to admit chance would be to admit design. But what more positive sense could be given to this notion is hard to say, unless with reference to causal laws which, we have been told by him, are fictions. As we shall see, he rejected the notion of determinism altogether. So his is a dark saying indeed.

It is not difficult to see that antimetaphysical strictures notwithstanding, Nietzsche subscribes to a definite enough thesis as to how the world in reality is, and opposes this to the common-sense view. But how to describe the world as it really is cannot but be taxing. For the language we have to do it with commits us to a metaphysics he deems false and at odds with the way things are. But we have no other language. Other philosophers have since felt similar problems: one thinks, for instance, of Russell's pursuit of a logically perfect language by means of which we might finally liberate ourselves from the "metaphysics of the New Stone Age," inherent, Russell implied, in the tyrannical grammar of everyday speech. Nietzsche never sought a new language as such, but his sometimes frenzied use of poetic diction, of "dithyrambs," might be taken as attempts to crack the grip of linguistic habits. The incapacity of ordinary language to house his own visions might serve, again, to explain why he felt his philosophy hard to understand. Strictly speaking, it ought to be impossible to understand, or nearly so. How are we to understand a theory when the structure of our understanding itself is called in question by that theory? And when we have succeeded in understanding it, in our own terms, it would automatically follow that we had misunderstood it, for our own terms are the wrong ones.

Finally, we can appreciate why Nietzsche felt his philosophy was dangerous. Just to get men in a position to understand his philosophy is to put them in a disadvantageous position so far as survival is concerned. Nietzsche says, over and over again and in a variety of ways, that all we think we know is false, that "nothing is true," but all the while he holds that something would be true if only we could say what it was — true, at least, in the sense of corresponding with reality, but a reality we have not the means to describe. He still believed in truth in that sense, though he had worked out a different notion of truth altogether, a pragmatic notion of truth wherein sentences are better or worse instruments for the organization and anticipation of experience. Yet he could not bring himself to accept this theory, and remained victimized by a conception of truth and reality he had set himself up to criticize, castigating common sense, science, and philosophy as interpretations, saying that *everything* we claim to know is interpretation, without quite realizing that he, too, was offering an interpretation and not the bare truth. When he did realize this, as I think he did, it was a liberating thing.

Philosophical Psychology

NIETZSCHE considered himself a pioneer psychologist, a first explorer of "the great forest and primeval wilderness" of the human mind.[29] His writings are celebrated for the empirical psychological insights they contain, which are of unquestioned originality and penetration. I have space only to outline his contributions to what today we would call *philosophical* psychology, the logical analyses he offered of mental concepts. His primary target here was the concept of the ego, his claim being that it is ontologically superfluous, and metaphysically pernicious, to suppose there is such an entity as the self. It is a supposition, however, which is naturally generated out of certain distorting structural features of language and a general predisposition in our part to regard whatever happens as the *action* of an *agent*. Our first mistake is to misconstrue mental activity as the action of a special agent (the self), and our second mistake is to export this idea into the world at large, our conception of the world then being an illicit projection of a model which is not even adequate for representing mental behavior. "Reason," he says, "believes generally that wills are causes. It believes in the ego as a being, a substance, and *projects* this belief in ego-substance onto all things. It first *creates* thereby the concept of thing ... Being, construed as cause, is thought into things, *shoved under*: the concept of 'being' follows from, and is derived out of the concept of 'ego.' In the beginning stands the great fatality of an error, that the will *is* something that *effects*, that the will is a *power* ... Today we know it is only a word."[30] His diagnosis is roughly as follows. Tacitly accepting the assumption that when something happens, it is done by some agent, we conclude, from the fact that thinking takes place, that it is an action, and that there must accordingly be an agent. This is the self. The ego then is an inferred entity, not a primitive datum, and supposing it to act by means of the exercise of a will has colored our whole conception of causality. But these notions will not bear up under scrutiny. "A thought comes when 'it' will, not when 'I' will,"[31] so it is hardly the case that I cause my own thoughts. And the concept of the will itself, though philosophers apparently regard it "as though it were the best known thing in the world,"[32] is utterly ·obscure. The phenomenology of volition is exceedingly complex; it is not remotely clear what we are describing when we speak of acts of will, and yet "We believed ourselves to be causal in the act of will: we thought that here, at least, we had caught causality in the act."[33] But we have done no such thing, and have but lapsed into the error of false causality.

He draws our attention to the fact that we are only likely to credit the will as having caused an action, a bit of bodily behavior, when it was an *expected* one, in contrast, e.g., to an unanticipated twitch. But what is involved is only this. We have learnt to expect certain more or less predictable modes of behavior from our bodies. These are more or less invariantly accompanied by certain recurrent thoughts and feelings. The latter are then taken to be the *causes* of the acts they accompany. But both the thinking *and* the action are indifferently indicated by the same term, "I." So we get the notion that there is a self which underlies both, an agent which exercises the will and, by so doing, causes its body to move, at once commanding and obeying. We aquiesce in a false sense of power henceforth regarded as freedom. It is this conception of action which is projected onto the world, the concept of *thing* being "shoved under" the surface, surface changes then

being regarded as the *actions* of things. As we have seen, Nietzsche was suspicious of the concept of *things*. One of his tasks as psychologist was to account for our having hit upon such a concept. He often seems to have felt that if you could find such an account, you pretty well refuted the concept. The concept of free will he regards as having been due to a "logical rape."

Nietzsche was not a philosophical determinist. He insists that the idea of cause and effect, useful enough in practice, "should not be objectified the way the natural scientist does ... in conformity to the reigning mechanistic doltishness."[34] Cause and effect would then be another fiction unrecognized as such and taken for true. Properly, it has a use "for the purposes of communication and understanding," *not* explanation: "In reality an *sich*, there are no causal ties, no necessities, no psychological unfreedom. There is no following of effect upon cause, there reigns no "law." We alone have invented the causes, the continuities, the connections, the relativity, the coercion, the numbers, the laws, the freedom, the grounds, the purposes. So if we impose this conventional world (*Zeichenwelt*) onto, and mix it up with the *an sich*, we tend, as we have always tended, to mythologize."[35] We must, he says in an unpublished note, "Put away ... two popular concepts, Necessity and Law. The first imposes a false coercion (*Zwang*), the second a false freedom on the world. 'Things' do not behave themselves in conformity to law or with regularity."[36] The popular scientific image of an orderly world of things, the behavior of which is in every instance determined by causally sufficient conditions, is due to the same habit of thought and language, Nietzsche concludes, which is also responsible for the concept of inner freedom. Both are myths mistaken for facts. But then the problems arising in connection with either concept are almost what a latter generation termed "pseudo-problems." The point is not to try to solve them but to show how the concepts which give rise to them ever came about. We *may* continue to employ these concepts, but can do so with philosophical immunity only so long as we recognize that they may have served, may continue to serve, a certain purpose in communication and coping, but have neither metaphysical warrant nor "truth."

But Nietzsche is not exclusively preoccupied with the natural history of mental *concepts*: his psychology is often concerned with the natural history of mental *facts*, and with the role these may play in the economy of human life. Philosophers, such as Descartes, for example, frequently begin their inquiries with introspective accounts, but Nietzsche finds the phenomenon of introspection, and our capacity not merely for having thoughts but for being *aware* that we have them, altogether puzzling matters. It is true that we have this awareness, at least sometimes, but what *purpose* does it serve? "It first becomes a problem for us when we begin to appreciate the degree to which it is dispensable."[37] For our mental life, introspectively revealed, might have gone on just as it does go on, only we might not have been *conscious* of its going on: "we could think, feel, will, remember; we could likewise 'act' in every sense of the term, and yet none of this need ever have 'come into consciousness' (to put it metaphorically)."[38] It is true that a great deal of our acting and thinking goes on without our reflecting on the fact that it is going on. The question then is what *extra* function is served by such reflectings when they do in fact occur. For "The whole of life might be possible without its seeing itself in a mirror, so to speak. And actually even now the largest part of life is played off without this mirroring — even, indeed, our thinking, feeling, and volitional life, however painful this may sound to the older philosopher."[39] Nietzsche puts the matter almost *this* way: in response to what need did self awareness arise? The assumption being that whatever kinds of things we in fact do must have been evolved in response to some vital need.

In answer he offers "an extravagant hypothesis": "The strength and subtlety [of self-awareness] stand in proportion to the capacity for communication of a man (or an animal). The capacity for communication is in turn proportional to the *necessity to communicate*."[40] He is not saying that we reflect only when we need to communicate, but that the phenomenon of self-awareness developed as a partial means to satisfy the need for communication in the species. Once having developed, men may "squander it," as he puts it, just as, whatever may have been the needs in response to which language developed, men may, once they have the use of language, speak idly. His interesting claim here is that reflecting — ostensibly a private operation — is *social* in origin, a response to a social need. The recluse, the "wild-beast sort of man," would neither require nor develop it. His point is that men are the most vulnerable of animals, and the most in need of constant care by their fellows. But then they must be able to express their needs in order to have others minister to them, and this requires that we "know ourselves." Thinking does not require that we be aware of our doing so: "Man, like every living creature, thinks continually but does not know it; the thinking which becomes conscious of itself is the smallest part." *Conscious* thought requires an ability to identify and express its content. To the old question whether there can be thought without words, Nietzsche has a plain answer. No thought that we are ever *aware* of can be nonverbal, for we need language to identify it. But then we cannot detect nonverbal thoughts by introspection. The incapacity to express our needs intelligibly would expose us to nonsurvival, and all successful expressions must be publicly understandable, must be, accordingly, put into the language which all members of the group can grasp. So the "development of consciousness goes hand in hand with the development of language" and "it is only as a social animal that man becomes conscious of himself."[41]

There is, thus, nothing in consciousness which is not publicly understandable, inasmuch as the words we use to express our introspections to ourselves are just the words we have learnt to use to express our needs to others, and must be understood by others as a condition for the successful application of them by ourselves to our own inner states. "My notion is that consciousness does not belong to the individual existence of men but rather to what is the community-and-herd-nature ... Consequently, each of us, with the best will in the world of *understanding* himself as individually as possible, of 'knowing himself,' will always bring into consciousness what is 'non-individual,' our averageness ... Our thought, through the character of consciousness ... is always translated back into the perspective of the herd."[42] So even if, in fact, "our actions are, at bottom, to an incomparable degree personal, unique, and absolutely individual," still, "as soon as we translate them into consciousness they no longer appear so."[43]

This analysis has a contemporary ring: one remarks analogies to the theses against the existence or possibility of "private languages" in Wittgenstein's *Philosophical Investigations*, or to the purported resolution of the problem of "other minds" in the work, say of P. F. Strawson, who writes, "There would be no question of ascribing one's states of consciousness or experiences, to anything, unless one also ascribed, or were ready and able to ascribe, states of consciousness, or experiences, to other entities of the same logical type as that thing to which one ascribes one's own states of consciousness. The condition of reckoning oneself as a subject of such predicates is that one should also reckon others as subjects of such predicates ... If *only* mine, then *not* mine at all."[44] Nietzsche would have accepted these analyses, but he would hardly have concurred in the total acceptance of ordinary language often implicit in these writers and their contemporaries. He was concerned to revise and overcome ordinary language and common sense, and nothing he writes is quite free from visionary moral intentions. "Everything that becomes conscious," he writes, "becomes thereby shallow, small, relatively stupid, and is but general signs — *herd* signs."[45] One cannot, and, if this analysis is sound, *logically* cannot express one's uniqueness; whatever comes into words is flattened out and can only be understood in the most general way. Literally, one cannot *talk*. Scant wonder, then, that Nietzsche did not expect his essentially (to his way of thinking) fresh and *unzeitgemassige* (untimely) ideas to be grasped, and felt that at best he was addressing an unborn generation, of superior beings, to whom his message might come through. One might very nearly characterize him as that philosopher most frustrated by the limitations of language in the entire history of the subject. He felt his message to be unfamiliar and frightening, that its frightfulness was a result of its unfamiliarity, but that we are likely to develop in a salutary direction only so far as we can expose ourselves to the frightening and the new. What we term "knowledge," he contended, is a kind of reaction to fear: faced with the unfamiliar, men seek to assimilate it to pre-existing modes of thought. That which even philosophers regard as "the known" (*Das Bekannte*) is "that which we are accustomed to, so that we no longer wonder at it. It is the commonplace, is any kind of rule that is fixed, whatever we are at home with."[46] This is not what he wanted for himself. In this sense of "knowledge," he did not want to be "known." And he tried to make two points, the first being that the obvious and ordinary way of looking at things is but *one* way, and that what is obvious and what is the case may very well be distinct, so that everything we claim to know may be false. The second is this: if we can just succeed in putting our perspective "in perspective," and get people to see the possibility of another way of reading the world, they might be liberated for a novel and, perhaps, a better perspective.

A first move in this direction is to rid ourselves of the philosophical prejudice that we have a direct and certain knowledge of our own inner states, that our judgments here are incorrigible and privileged. "Error of errors!" he writes: "The known is the familiar, and the familiar is what is most difficult to 'know,' that is, to see as a problem, as alien, as 'outside us.'"[47] But this is illustrated over and over again with our mental life, upon the knowledge of which we are inclined to vaunt ourselves. Consider the case of dreaming, to begin with. During sleep "our nervous system is, through manifold inner causes, in a state of excitation . . . and thus there are hundreds of occasions for the mind to be surprised, and to seek the causes of this excitation. The dream is *the search for and representation of* the apparent causes of each stimulated excitation."[48] Suppose, to use his example, a man's feet are bound in sleep. Because of the stimulation, he dreams there are snakes coiled about his feet. The dreamer infers that "these snakes must be the cause of the sensations which I, the sleeper, have."[49] We often incorporate such things as sharp, sudden noises into a dream, so that the dreamer "explains it from *afterwards*, so that he thinks he first experiences the conditions responsible for the noise, and then the noise itself."[50] Briefly, the dream image, which is an effect of certain stimuli, is taken by us for the *cause* of these. "I maintain," he speculates, "that as man reasons while asleep, so also he reasoned when awake, for many millenia. The first *causa* which entered the mind . . . satisfied him and passed for truth."

This *type* of mistake is one we are always lapsing into, he asserts. It is termed "The Error of Imaginary Causes" — one of the "Four Great Errors."* We commit this error when "The representation (*Vorstellung*) which a given state *produces*, is misconstrued as the cause of that state."[53] This does not happen merely in dreams, nor is it a residue of primitive but superseded ways of reasoning. We do the same thing when awake, and whenever we sustain feelings which "stimulate our causal instinct" and move us to seek for *reasons* accounting for these feelings. We seek for motives. But motives are just imaginary causes. It is the feeling itself which causes the interpretation we give of it, and the interpretation is perversely taken as the cause of the feeling: a motive is just an interpretation of a feeling. There thus arises "a habit in favor of a certain kind of causal interpretation which in fact inhibits, and even excludes, an inquiry into causes."[54] (Note the inconsistency in Nietzsche's use of "cause," a notion, like so many others, which he repudiates only to employ himself, and in a sense seldom different from the one he impugns.) The final explanation of this falsifying proclivity is the general predisposition we have to "reduce something unfamiliar to something familiar," which, "besides giving a sense of power, relieves, comforts, and satisfies."[55] For we are such that "any explanation at all is better than nothing"[56]; and the "causal instinct is conditioned and stimulated by the feeling of fear."

So our accounts of our mental lives, as our accounts of phenomena generally, are aimed more at comfort than at deep understanding: they are genial falsifications, blandly accommodating, shielding us from the truth about ourselves and about the world. Once again, this puts us at no mean advantage in contrast with those who, like Nietzsche in his own image of himself, saw more honestly and deeply. "The common man, similar to his fellows, was and will always be at an advantage. The more exquisite, finer, singular person, the one it is difficult to understand, simply remains alone, succumbs in virtue of

---

* The other three are the errors of "Confusing Cause and Effect", "False Causes", and "Free Will". These are discussed in the *Götzen-dämmerung*, a late work translated as *The Twilight of the Idols*. Professor Walter Kaufmann, in the introductory remarks to this selection in *The Portable Nietzsche*,[51] makes the important point that the word "idols" (*Götzen*) is used as Bacon used it: "idols" are habitual patterns of belief which prevent men from seeing the truth. Nietzsche's four idols do not otherwise correspond, save in number and purpose, to Bacon's list. It is worth noting that the subtitle of the book, "How one Philosophizes with a Hammer", sounds a good deal less forbidding when we realize the hammer is to strike graven images. And even less forbidding still when Nietzsche writes, in a slightly heavy, Teutonic sort of funnyness, that "the eternal idols which are here touched, as with a tuning fork — there are in general no idols which are older, more convinced, more inflated — and none more hollow" so that we "hear, as an answer, that famous hollow sound which testifies to bloated entrails".[52] All of "knowledge", on his analysis, is a matter of habit. The "idols" are but pernicious habits. Habits as such are neither good nor bad, but there are good habits and bad ones.

uniqueness to mischance, and rarely reproduces. One must summon an immense counter-power in order to cross this natural, all-too-natural *progressus in simile*, this duplicating of mankind, in alikeness, commonness, averageness, herd-likeness — in common!"[57] And this meant forcing the familiar into an unfamiliar light, seeing it as a problem. His most sustained effort in this direction was concerned with the concept of morality.

Morality and Religion

THAT our most fundamental beliefs should all, on Nietzsche's view, be false, is not by itself an objection against them. "It is here," he remarks, "that our new language perhaps sounds strangest."[58] The real issue, he adds, "is how far a belief supports and furthers life, maintains and indeed disciplines a species. We are basically inclined to maintain that the falsest beliefs (to which belong the synthetic *a priori* judgments) are the least dispensable." Philosophers, who at times conceive their task to be the identification of the most generic traits of existence, have at best succeeded, instead, in rendering explicit one or another concept which is "at bottom a pre-conceived dogma, a fancy, an 'inspiration,' or at most a heart's desire made abstract and refined, and defended with reasons sought after the fact."[59] So "every great philosophy so far has been . . . the self-confession of its originator, a kind of unintentional *memoires* unrecognized as such."[60] But this, he says, is nowhere more plain than in moral philosophy.

Nietzsche repeatedly insists that there is no objective moral order in the world: "There are no moral phenomena, only moralistic interpretations of phenomena."[61] He credited himself with being the first to recognize that "there are altogether no moral facts,"[62] and he urged each philosopher to take, along with himself, "a stand beyond good and evil — to put beneath himself the illusion of moral judgments."[63] Our moral codes and categories serve not to describe the world, but rather as instruments to get on in it, and with one another. And the proper task for the moral philosopher is to understand, rather than to pass, moral judgments, to be a self-aware critic instead of an unwitting victim of the prevailing moral currents. In view of his own undisguised and unremittant moralizing, it is somewhat amazing that Nietzsche should have supposed himself to have succeeded where other philosophers had failed, to see morality "as a problem" and to view it objectively and from beyond good and evil. His philosophy has moreover been considered a prime specimen of the self-confessional sort of thinking he officially eschewed. It is very *à la mode* to say of him that his philosophy may not be separated from his life and remain intelligible or meaningful. But he would himself have regarded this as blameworthy,

a defect in him and not a virtue. And as regards his moralizing, he might have said, in self-defense, that he *had* gotten beyond good and evil in the sense in which these values were assigned in his own era and tradition, even if he had not quite gotten outside morality as such. And he might have said further that his moralizing, his enjoining against and criticism of the prevailing moral system, was based upon, and closely connected with, his general objective analysis of the role and function of moral judgments. I shall endeavor here to sketch the main features of that analysis, indicating where his familiar moralistic theses connect with it, and shall not deal intrinsically with the latter, for they are almost so well known as to require little more than bare mention.

Morality is a coercive mechanism, not only in the sense that it prohibits certain modes of action and sanctions others, but in the sense that it operates to re-enforce the prevailing schema for understanding or interpreting the world. It does this indirectly, chiefly, on Nietzsche's analysis, by acting to repress the only sorts of forces — the "life-conditioning passions" (*lebenbedingende Affekte*) — out of which might be generated new perspectives. "All the old moral monsters are unanimous on this, that *il faut tuer les passions*."[64] But these passions "must be further developed if life is to be further developed."[65] This does not commit Nietzsche to the advocacy of unqualified *laissez-aller* in the emotional domain. "Every morality," he writes, "is a bit of tyranny against nature, even against 'reason'." But he adds, "This is no objection against them."[66] First, because the passions are sometimes "merely fatal, where they drag their victim down with the weight of their stupidity,"[67] and secondly because moral restraint is causally responsible for the emergence of a great deal that makes life worth living: "Whatever is of freedom, subtlety, daring, dance, and masterly firmness, that is or ever was in the world, be it in thinking or ruling, or in speaking and persuading, in art as in ethical conduct, is made possible primarily by this 'tyranny of such arbitrary laws.' Indeed, and in all seriousness, the probability is not slight that this is 'nature' and 'natural' — and *not* any *laissez aller*."[68] So the point is to "spiritualize" rather than to extirpate the passions, though this involves certain risks. Still, "To *annihilate* the passions and desires, merely in order to forestall their stupidity and the unpleasant consequences of their stupidity, strikes us today as merely an acute form of — stupidity."[69]

There are two main types of moral perspective, master-morality and slave-morality. The latter is generated by fear and by inadequacy. In any given group, certain individuals will tend to dominate over the rest in virtue of having traits of character which their fellows lack; and these leaders are resented and feared by those obliged to defer to them.

Each of these two groups assigns a different meaning to the word "good." For the masters it designates just those qualities which *they* possess, in virtue of which they enjoy pre-eminence in the group. It contrasts with "bad" (*Schlecht*). It is analytic that masters are "good," in this sense; and whoever is not "good" is "bad." For the slave, "good" means exactly what "bad" means in the moral vocabulary of the masters. It contrasts with "evil" (*Böse*), a term which is extensionally equivalent to the word "good" in the masters' language. Masters may be good (in their sense) and evil (in the slaves' sense) but they cannot be good and *bad*. Slaves may be good (in their sense) and bad (in the masters' sense), but they cannot be good and *evil*. For if they were evil, they would be masters and not slaves. Masters tend to call good such traits as "love of enterprise, foolhardiness, vengefulness, guile, rapacity, power-seeking"[70] and in general, whatever they admire in themselves; they are "value-determining,"[71] and impose their own values on the world. Slaves, who fear those who possess such traits, call both them and their possessers "evil," restricting "good" to such things as "pity, the warm heart, the kind and helping hand, patience, caring, humility, friendliness. . . ."[72] Slaves are impotent and cannot impose their terms on the world. So their morality, as already indicated, is based on weakness rather than strength.

Nietzsche embroidered upon these distinctions in *The Genealogy of Morals*, the title of which, incidentally, illuminates some of his intentions. These were, in part, to show that moral systems develop over time and out of given social circumstances, and are not presented from on high; that they are of human rather than divine provenance; and that they are to be justified, if at all, by their use and consequences in human life, rather than with appeal to external authority — ideas perhaps more shocking to the nineteenth century than to our own.

The master type, of unquestioned utility to the group when it is threatened from without, is feared, in time of peace, by those who were protected by its bellicosity in adverse times. For the qualities which make good warriors persist in peace-time, and are felt as threatening when the external avenues for using them are closed off. But fear is complicated by *resentment* on the slave's part, whose attitude toward his erstwhile protector is apt to be hostility. It is a hostility which cannot be discharged, however, in the healthy way in which the master releases his aggressive drives. It can only, in the slave's case, be discharged through devious channels. Historically, Nietzsche argues, this has taken place through getting the master-type to accept, for *himself*, the same system of values which originated in slavish powerlessness. The strong have thence come to disapprove of, and regard as reprehensible, the precise set of traits deemed "good" in the masters' normal code. They have been led to take toward

themselves the identical attitude taken toward them by slaves: they have been forced into the slaves' perspective. This "transvaluation of values" then causes an intense self-hatred on the part of nature's aristocrats. How could this ever have happened? Nietzsche answers that it is the work of *religion*, the achievement of priests, those "most impotent of men."[73] Through the instrument of religion, the *ressentiment* felt by the disenfranchised has won a spectacular revenge. Our moral code, and particularly the moral code of Christianity, for all its emphasis on charity and love, is the combined product of fear and hatred of the object of fear. The Christian concept of love has arisen "out of the cauldron of unslaked hatred."[74]

There can be little doubt that Nietzsche admired the master-type. He allows that there is a component of barbarity in their nature: "there is a beast of prey in all these distinguished races, an unmistakable blond beast."[75] This deserves a brief comment, in view of the notoriety the expression "blond beast" acquired during the Nazi's pre-emption of Nietzsche as their official precursor. First *"blonde Bestie"* very likely means "lion," the king of beasts: if lions were, *per accidens*, black, Nietzsche might have had deep meaning for current racist agitation on the fringes of Islam, and been anathema to Nordics. At all events, it was not just Aryans to whom it applied: "distinguished men," for Nietzsche, included "Roman, Arabic, Germanic, Greek nobles, Homeric heros, Vikings."[76] Nor by "race" did he mean *any* member of these listed groups: there were slaves *and* masters amongst Romans, Greeks, Arabs, etc. As we shall see, the distinction did have a *kind* of biological basis for him. Meanwhile, Nietzsche didn't approve of these types *in virtue* of their bestiality. He was only prepared to accept it as an undesirable concomitant of something intrinsically desirable, somewhat in the way he felt that the passions may be stupid without this being a sufficient reason for extirpating them nor, for that matter, a sufficient reason for preserving them.

Not even the weak are averse to the infliction of suffering upon others: this is something which is "human-all-too-human," and mankind has never found the spectacle of cruelty distasteful. Nietzsche is seldom more tongue-in-cheek than when he elaborates this theme: "To witness suffering is pleasant. To inflict it even more so. This is a hard saying, but it expresses a powerful old human-all-too-human axiom. . . . There is no festivity without cruelty: so teaches the longest, oldest history of mankind. Even in punishment there is something so very *festive*."[77] A great many of our institutions exist for the rationalization of cruelty: he cites in evidence the fact that exacting a certain quantum of pain from someone who has wronged one is obviously regarded a sufficient compensation. To be sure, he points out in one of his famous passages, there is no disciplining of men without cruelty. Man is the animal that makes (and keeps) promises, and this involves the acquisition of a "memory of the will."[78] But this "is never done without blood, torture, and sacrifice. . . . How much blood and shuddering is at the base of all 'good things.' "[79] So the difference between weak and strong, in the end, has little to do with any basic differences or degrees of purity of spirit. It lies chiefly in the ability of the strong and the disability of the weak to discharge their aggressiveness on others. But this is a crucial difference. For the minds of the weak are "poisoned" as a consequence, and they must find devious ways of voiding hostility. And *one* way in which they have succeeded in this we have already indicated: getting the healthy to accept as their own the ethics of the maimed, via the agency of religion.

This has produced a remarkable psychological phenomenon. To begin with, the strong are no *less* strong for having accepted this morality. It is only that their drives are differently channelled. In particular, they no longer blithely discharge their energies in violence. But since "all instincts which are not discharged outwardly *turn themselves inward*,"[80] there occurs something which Nietzsche terms "internalization" (*Verinnerlichung*), and with this there "first emerges what one later calls the 'soul' ":
"The whole inner world, originally small, as though confined between a pair of membranes, receives depth, width, and height as the external behavior of man is inhibited."[81] And moreover, "Man, lacking external enemies and resistances, and forced into a restricted narrowness and ethical regularity, impatiently tore at himself, persecuted, gnawed at, molested himself. Wanting to rend someone, he dashes against the bars of his cage . . . Man makes of himself a torture chamber, an uncharted and dangerous wilderness."[82] This self-punishment is the phenomenon of *bad conscience* (*Schlechtes Gewissen*) which Nietzsche portentously stigmatizes as "the greatest and most disastrous disease, of which mankind to this day has not been cured: the sickness of man suffering from himself, within himself."[83]
One might infer that Nietzsche will take the sort of stand currently taken by supporters of a certain view of psychological therapy, advocating wholesale release of aggression in the interests of mental health. But again he draws up short of what his subsequent reputation encourages one to believe about him. "There can be no doubt that bad conscience is a disease," he says, but adds immediately: "Yet it is a disease in the sense in which pregnancy is one."[84] One wants to reply that pregnancy is not a disease in *any* sense, and Nietzsche concedes that with the advent of *Schlechtes Gewissen* humankind "awakened an interest, a tension, a hope, nearly a conviction to the effect that with man something was being announced and prepared, as though man were not an end but a way, an incident, a bridge, a great

promise. . . . "[85] And this is indeed the message about man announced by his Zarathustra (to which I shall turn later). Since we know that Nietzsche espoused the ideal of a superman, and since the emergence of bad conscience has been a historically necessary condition for this possibility, he cannot be understood as wholly condemning it, nor, for that matter, wholly condemning slave-morality nor advocating master-morality and the savage excesses of the blond beast. He nonetheless does object to the attitude of those in the grip of bad conscience. For they tend to exaggerate beyond measure their own alleged worthlessness, chiefly because, in accepting religion, they have accepted an entire theological package. But this includes a perfect God to whom they owe their existence. Now in view of this debt, and in view of the impossible disproportion between divine goodness and *their* unworthiness, the former can be to some degree discharged and the latter to some degree reduced by taking on a special burden of self-inflicted pain. (We saw above how pain pays off debts in the legal logic of mankind.) Even so, the matter is hopeless.
"This is a sort of madness of the will, a spiritual insanity. . . . Man's will to find himself guilty and worthless and inexpiably so; . . . man's will to erect an 'ideal' — that of the 'Holy God' in the light of which he could be assured of his own absolute unworthiness. What a mad, sorrowful animal man is!"[86] Zarathustra's message that "God is dead" is meant to shatter this impossible guilt, to restore man to a sense of dignity but not complacency by replacing this guilt-producing contrast by another and benign one between what man is and what he might become.

It is important to stress that the strong alone suffer from bad conscience. It is a symptom of strength, but a strength turned inward and against its possessor. The weak have no talent for asceticism. Nietzsche finds ascetics attractive. His theory is that energy in the human psyche is conserved through all its transformations, so the strong cannot but express their strength whatever may be the available channels. "To demand that strength not express itself as strength . . . is as absurd as the demand that weakness express itself as strength."[87] To think any such demand is capable of being satisfied is due, once more, to archaic modes of thought and to structural features of language of a misleading sort, in accordance with which we tend to think of strength as the activity of an agent the way, for example, we think of flashing as the activity of lightning. We think the latter, Nietzsche insists, in virtue of the fact that we say that lightning flashes. But flashing is not separable from lightning: lightning just *is* the flashing, and comparably, the strong just are what they do: they cannot both be strong and not act in strongish ways. To demand that they desist is thus to ask the impossible. For just these reasons, the weak do not abstain from violent behavior by *choice*, as they might represent the matter to themselves. But *thinking* that this in fact is what they do, they assume the right "to call the bird of prey to account for being a bird of prey."[88] The notion of free choice is thus built into the grammar of our language. Using a subject and a verb together — for example, *a x*'s — we are led to suppose that "*a* doesn't *x*," though false, is possible since *a* is one thing and *x*-ing is something else, and *a* may *x* or not. But Nietzsche's point is that *a* just *is* the *x*-ing, so if *a* doesn't *x*, it *cannot x*, and if it does *x*, it cannot do other. But there are ways and ways of *x*-ing, and yesterday's barbarian is today's unhappy anchorite, his power turned against himself. Our ethico-religious system has thus re-routed cruelty, but has not abolished it. Nor can it be abolished without life itself being abolished, for life itself is cruelty. "Life itself is *essentially* appropriation, injuring, overpowering the alien and the weak. It is oppression, hardness, imposing one's form. . . . Life just is will-to-power. . . . Appropriation does not simply belong to a perverse or imperfect or primitive society: it belongs *in essence* to living things, as a basic organic function. It is a consequence of the will-to-power which is but the will to life."[89] "Will to power" is a central, organizing concept in Nietzsche, but one he tended more to use than to analyze; so it is not very clear what he meant by it. But this much can be said: it is the defining trait of living matter and, he sometimes suggests, of *all* matter:* a drive to master and transform the environment on the part of each thing. It is not to be identified with *conatus*, i.e., a tendency on the part of each thing, to retain its integrity: "self-preservation is merely an indirect and frequent *consequence* of this."[91] It was for this reason, incidentally, that he polemicized against Darwin, his thesis being that we don't struggle, so to speak, to maintain a marginal existence, save in exceptional circumstances: life is not a struggle to survive but to prevail, and "the general aspect of life is neither need nor starvation, but far rather richness and profusion. . . . Where there is struggle, it is struggle for power."[92] But then neither is life to be characterized in terms of maximizing utility in accordance with a spontaneous preference for pleasure over pain: "The will-to-power is the primitive affect-form, and all other affects are merely its derivatives . . . men do not strive for pleasure, but pleasure comes in when they achieve what they strive for: pleasure accompanies, it doesn't move

anything."[93] It follows, in a somewhat extended use of the term, that cruelty is a necessary concomitant of life. To be alive is to be overpowering something, and if *A* overpowers *B*, *B* is overpowered by *A*: and this is cruel for *B*.

Were it not for moral mechanisms and social restraints, re-enforced by religion, the weak would in the nature of the case perish before the will-to-power of the strong. But Nietzsche contends that the strong are, at best, rare and untypical: "Mankind, like every other type of animal, produces a surplus of the abortive, diseased, degenerate, feeble, and the necessarily suffering: the successful instances are the exceptions amongst men."[94] The unhappy fact is, moreover, that often the most excellent representatives of the species fail to survive, or survive, often, as social misfits. "The species does not grow in perfection," he laments, "the weak are always prevailing over the strong."[95] Yet Nietzsche is not nostalgic for some state of nature where the healthy brute overpowers those in whom the will-to-power courses less fully. Already in the *Birth of Tragedy* he rejected unlicensed brutality as too horrific to bear contemplation. There is no point in all that suffering. But the ascetic ideal, in which hunter and prey are one, *gives* a point to suffering, and this is something of positive value. "Man, the animal, had heretofore no meaning. His life on earth had no purpose. 'What is man for?' was a question without an answer. Man did not know how to justify, to explain, to affirm himself."[96] True enough, the Christian ideal is hostile to life, is "in opposition to the fundamental presuppositions of life."[97] As much might be said of religions generally. Yet even if it is a will *against* life, it is a will, and "man would rather will nothingness than not will."[98] It is not suffering but meaningless suffering which men object to, and in giving a meaning to suffering, religion has not been a total disaster.

The ascetic ideal is but one of a *family* of ideals to which men subscribe, in accordance with which the human being, and human life generally, is esteemed as of little worth in comparison with some transcendent and purportedly valuable entity. So it is possible for one to be highly critical of religious beliefs and at the same time share religion's depreciatory estimation of human life. To take a stand against religion in the name of reason or truth is to be victim to the identical attitude embodied in the religious outlook on life, so the ascetic ideal has a wider application that might at first sight appear. "This ideal is *their* ideal," he says of such critics, "they are not free spirits by a long shot, *for they still believe in truth*."[99] It is just at this point that his own views on knowledge and truth connect with his moral ideas. He contends, in a crucial passage in *Die Fröhliche Wissenschaft* (added in 1886) that we are still pious (*fromm*) insofar as we still believe in truth. But this is to believe in a "real"

---

* At one point he offers, strictly as a metaphysical hypothesis, the thesis that "all active force may be defined as will-to-power". For "will can naturally only affect will" and perhaps the world, "seen from within", is just "will to power and nothing else".[90] This ambitious thesis was worked at piecemeal for a long time, and Nietzsche left behind a scattered set of exceedingly opaque jottings on the subject, many of which may be found in the posthumously assembled work, somewhat shadily edited by his sister, *Der Wille zur Macht*.

world independent of human contrivance and "Insofar as one affirms this 'other world' — well? must one not thereby deny its opposite, namely *this* world? *Our* world? . . . Even we knowing ones of today, we godless and antimetaphysical ones, even we take our fire from a torch which a belief of a thousand years kindled, the belief of Christ's which was also Plato's belief, that God is truth, that truth is divine." Zarathustra calls out that God is dead, and if God is truth, then truth is dead as well. He adds, to the passage just quoted: "But what if this were increasingly unworthy of belief, what if nothing any longer proves itself divine . . . what if God turns out to be our most enduring lie?" In the *Genealogy of Morals* he concludes: "From the moment that we deny the God of the ascetic ideal, *another problem presents itself*: that of the value of truth. The will-to-truth demands a critique [and] is experimentally put in question."[100] This, we have seen, was his own critical task in philosophy. His own view was that there is no "true," no "real" world, that the "apparent" world is the only one. Echoing a famous sentence of Dostoevski, he writes: "Nothing is true, everything is permitted." (*Nichts ist wahr, alles ist erlaubt.*) And this *is* "freedom of spirit" — "For the belief in truth has given notice."[101] If everything is permitted, fresh ideals can be found for human life, restored to a fitting dignity. If the world is of our making, so to speak, and if there is no other world than this, we can make another one and remake ourselves along with it. Nietzsche felt himself, and mankind through him, to be suddenly open to immense possibilities: "Every hazard is permitted the inquirer. The sea, *our* sea lies open there. Perhaps there has never been so open a sea!"[102]

Superman and Eternal Recurrence

I HAVE so far been chiefly concerned with the negative, destructive part of Nietzsche's philosophy. There is, to be sure, implicit throughout, a set of positive theories about the world, truth, knowledge, and the human psyche, but Nietzsche seems to have been unwilling or unable to write down a sustained constructive account of what he believed ought to replace the theories he attempted to discredit, so one is obliged to reconstruct this by the hints and contextual suggestions which complement the few opaque fragments of a positive nature. But even as a moral prophet he is persistently unsatisfying to those who might wish to know the content of that bright future he foresaw for us once we are relieved of the truncating pressures of the prevailing epistemo-ethical perspectives. And this indefiniteness and vagueness remains despite the fact that one of his books, and indeed that work of his which he regarded as his masterpiece — *Thus Spake Zarathustra* — was ostensibly devoted to the articulation of his specific vision of what might lie before us. It is not

difficult to see how that book, and his writings generally, should have become a hospitable quarry for elitists and crackpots, anti-intellectualists, know-nothings, and advocates of brutality and instinctuality, none of whom were prepared to heed the cautions and qualifications Nietzsche posted at each turn. *Also Sprach Zarathustra* has almost tragically lived up to its subtitle — "a book for all and for none." And lacking, as we do, any specific and single recipe for reading his message, we can do little more here than emphasize the lack of such a recipe, and to point up the essential vagueness of his teaching.

The *historical* Zarathustra (Zoroaster) believed the world to be the scene of conflict between good and evil, the latter taken as objective forces. Nietzsche's Zarathustra, of course, did not believe this. But since he was the first to make this fundamental error, he should, Nietzsche says, be the first to rectify it.[103] This is his reason, allegedly, for picking Zarathustra as the spokesman for his philosophy.

Zarathustra announced the relativity of all values:

> Many lands saw Zarathustra, and many peoples. Thus he discovered the goods and evils of many peoples. No greater power did Zarathustra find on earth than good and evil. . . .
>
> Much that one people held good, another held to be scorn and disgrace: thus I found. Much I found named evil here which there was bedecked with royal honor. . . .
>
> Truly, man gave themselves all their good and evil. Truly, they took it not, they found it not, nor did it come to them as a voice from heaven. . . .
>
> Till now there were a thousand goals, for there were a thousand people. Only a yoke for the thousand necks is lacking, the *one* goal is lacking. Humankind has yet no goal.[104]

Zarathustra sees it as his task to provide this "one goal" for mankind, and the doctrine of the superman* is to serve this purpose. "Look: I teach you the superman!," Zarathustra intones: "The superman is the meaning of the earth."[105] But no specific characterization is really given of the superman except by contrast with other kinds of men, in particular the "last man" (*der letzte Mensch*), the man who is like everyone else and happy to be happy: "We have invented happiness! — says the last man, and blinks."[106] But Zarathustra, like Nietzsche, is not at all contented with the way man is:

> Man is something that shall be overcome. What have you done to overcome him?

---

* I use the familiar word "superman" for Nietzsche's *Übermensch*, in part because it is in use, in part because any alternative is not very much better and would at best have the negative value of avoiding wholly extrinsic connotations of the expression. "Overman" is graceless and puzzling. "Higher man" would perhaps be most accurate and least offensive. But I shall be conservative and stay with "superman."

All beings have created something higher than themselves. And you would rather be the ebb of this great flood, and rather return to the animals than overcome man?

Man is a rope, tied between beast and superman — a rope across an abyss.

What is great in man is that he is a bridge and not a goal: what can be loved in man is that he is an *Übergang* and an *Untergang*.[107]

The words "*Übergang*" and "*Untergang*" are difficult to translate and at the same time preserve the rhythm of Nietzsche's writing. But the idea is simple enough: we can only go on to something higher by perishing as *merely* human beings. The notion is essentially the *Stirb und werde* of Goethe's *Faust*, or of the biblical grain of corn. In a way, then, Nietzsche hardly differs in what he urges from what the ascetic ideal does, namely a certain contempt for ourselves, a sense that our worth consists not in what we are but in what we might, with effort, become. The difference between his ideal and the ascetic ideal is that *his* dissatisfaction with man, if internalized by his hearers, is not ultimate, and does not lead to an increasing self-depreciation. For the contrast is not between what we are and some impossible idealized standard we cannot compare with, but between us and some ideal capable of achievement if we work to actualize our potentialities. But to go higher we must rid ourselves of what is "human, all-too-human" in us.

But having said so much, it is difficult to see what exactly these potentialities are. Zarathustra lists the sorts of persons he admires, but these[108] are transitional figures, men who "prepare the way," and not supermen. Nietzsche at various times expressed admiration for such men as Cesare Borgia, Napoleon, and Goethe; and we have noticed his ill-concealed admiration for the instinctual, physical, "masterful" type in whom the will-to-power runs strong. But it would be a mistake to identify any of these as supermen, though very possibly they all exhibited traits of a sort he admired. But Zarathustra says,

Sultry heart and cold head: where these join together, there the roaring wind springs up, the "Savior."

Truly, there were those who were greater and more highborn than those whom the people named saviors, those violating roaring winds!

Yet you, my brothers, must be saved from those greater than all the saviors, if you would find the way to freedom!

There was never yet a superman. Naked I saw them both, the greatest and the least of men:

They were all-too-similar to one another. Truly even the greatest I found — all-too-human![109]

We may, if we wish, regard this as a recipe for superman: a sultry heart plus a cold head, minus the human-all-too-human. And this recipe in a way echoes the achievement of Greek tragedy at its highest point, a fusion of the dionysian and the apollonian. And the plea of Zarathustra, and presumably Nietzsche himself, is that we should sacrifice ourselves (*Untergang*) in order to bring about (*Übergang*) a higher human type. And the mechanism of this going-under and going-over is the will-to-power. But precisely what steps we must take to do this he leaves unstated. He only says, negatively, that contemporary institutions seemed inimical to it, tending simultaneously to cool the heart and fuddle the head, leaving a massive residue of the human-all-too-human.

The teaching of the superman strongly suggests that Nietzsche subscribed to the view that higher and higher levels of human excellence might be reached, the superman being a limit toward which mankind approaches as the human-all-too-human approaches zero. And from this one might infer a commitment to some theory of creative evolution, providing the basic human material available at any given time were not too thoroughly debased. Certainly Nietzsche did not discount the possibility, and indeed the imminent danger, of human deterioration to the point where nothing further might happen in the way of achievement — a leveling off, a total mediocritization. This indeed is the danger of the "last man." And this lends, he felt, a certain urgency to his teaching:

It is time that man sets himself a goal. It is time man planted the seed of his highest hope.

The ground is still rich enough for this. But one day the ground will be poor, and tame, and no high tree can grow from it any more.

Woe! The time comes when man no longer hurls the shaft of his longing beyond mankind, and his bowstring forgets how to twang!

Woe! The time comes when man cannot beget a star. Woe! The time of the most despicable man comes, who cannot any longer despise himself.

Look! I show you *the last man*.[110]

To speak metaphorically, there is an increase in entropy, but it is not inevitable. So we have a picture of human history with low points and high points, it being up to us to decide which. But it is just here that we find it difficult to square this view with another one, the doctrine of eternal recurrence, the theory that Nietzsche perhaps cherished more than any of his other ideas.

The eternal recurrence idea, roughly, is that whatever in fact happens, has happened infinitely many times and will re-happen an infinity of times, *exactly* in the same way in which it happens now. So, strictly speaking, there is really no "last" man but rather an infinity of last men. And strictly speaking there is no single person Nietzsche, but instead an infinite number of *exactly* similar Nietzsches, mirroring one another throughout time. And, like the superman, the doctrine of eternal recurrence is taught by Zarathustra:

> You would say "Now I die and vanish." And "Now I am a nothing." Souls are mortal as bodies.
>
> But the knot of causes, in which I am tangled, returns again — and creates me again. I belong myself to the causes of eternal recurrence.
>
> I come again, with this sun, this earth, this eagle, this snake — not to a new life or a better life or a similar life:
>
> I come eternally again to this same life, in what is greatest and what is smallest, and teach again the eternal recurrence of all things.[111]

It is hard to know what to make of this notion, not merely with regard to any intrinsic difficulties in it — and there are many — but with respect to the radical sort of conventionalism Nietzsche appeared to espouse and continued to espouse after the publication of *Also Sprach Zurathustra*. Things are allegedly fictions, solidities arbitrarily projected onto a markless flux; in nature, even assuming there are things, no two of them are alike; laws are simply conventions, of sheerly human contrivance; there are in the world no causes and no effects — these are propositions which Nietzsche seems over and over again, with minor variations, to have insisted upon. He regarded the doctrine as the most scientific of hypotheses and, indeed, sought in science for confirmation of it. But then, consonantly with his views on science, this "law," as part of science, would be a conventionalist fiction. Yet the idea excited him deeply, and we must try to determine what reasons he felt he had in support of the doctrine, and then what was his attitude toward it, assuming his reasons were sound. That is, to put the matter pragmatically, we must see what difference its being true or false would make to him — although he seldom discussed the possibility of its being false. One of the first occasions on which he mentions it conveys pretty well how he felt:

> What if a demon were to creep after you one day or night, in your loneliest loneness, and say: "This life which you live and have lived, must be lived by you once again and innumerable times more; and there will be nothing new in it, but every pain and every joy and every thought and every sigh, and everything unspeakably small and great in your life, must come again to you, and all in the same series and sequence . . . the eternal

hourglass will again and again be turned — and you with it, dust of the dust!" — Would you not throw yourself down and gnash your teeth and curse the demon who spoke to you thus? Or have you once experienced a tremendous moment, in which you would answer him: "Thou art a god and never have I heard anything more divine!"[112]

The doctrine is by and large presented in just such fanciful terms in Nietzsche's published writings, or hinted at, or stated obliquely with no particular effort at argument or proof. And perhaps Nietzsche came in time to believe he *had* proved it: it often happens that a certain theory is presented by a philosopher in a programmatic manner, and afterward is simply presupposed in his writings without his ever having worked it out in detail. But Nietzsche did leave behind some purported arguments, presumably elaborated around 1881, the time at which he was composing *Die Fröhliche Wissenschaft*. The following extract is perhaps the most detailed statement of it in his *Nachgelassene Werke*:

> The total amount of energy (*All-kraft*) is limited, not "infinite": let us beware of such excesses in concepts! Consequently, the number of states (*Lagen*), combinations, changes, and transformations (*Entwicklungen*) of this energy is tremendously great and practically immeasurable, but in any case finite and not infinite. But the time through which this total energy works is infinite. That means the energy is forever the same and forever active. An infinity has already passed away before this present moment. That means that all possible transformations must already have taken place. Consequently, the present transformation is a repetition, and thus also that which gave rise to it, and that which arises from it, and so backward and forward again! Insofar as the totality of states of energy (*die Gesammtlage aller Kräfte*) always recurs, everything has happened innumerable times. . . .[113]

This is an exceedingly opaque piece of writing, and one is rather put off by the two occurrences of "consequently" (*Folglich*) which appear in it: are they to be taken as literary or logical? I assume the latter, since this passage is offered as an argument. But then it turns out to be rather a poor argument. Let us try to reconstruct it. To begin with, we list three propositions which Nietzsche felt to be true and interconnected:

1. The sum-total of energy in the universe is finite.
2. The number of states (*Lagen*) of energy is finite.
3. Energy is conserved.

These propositions are clearly independent. The truth of (3) is compatible with the truth *and* falsity of (1), and conversely. And (2) might be false even if both (1) and (3) were true. Nietzsche seems to regard (2) as *entailed* by (1), but it is not. To be sure, he has not specified how the term "state" is to be used, and pending such restrictions it is very difficult indeed to know whether (2) is true or false. But one could give a wholly natural interpretation of *Lagen* in which (1) and (3) are true and (2) would be false. Imagine some conservative energy system the total energy of which has some finite number, say 6, where some of the energy is kinetic. Suppose again that the kinetic energy increases, so the potential energy decreases, but at a rate such that the first approaches 6 while the latter approaches 0. These limits could be approached indefinitely without being reached, and there could in principle be an infinite number of "states" of kinetic energy, having a different magnitude at every instant, without the recurrence of any single magnitude. On such a model, (1) and (3) would be true and (2) false. So we must regard (2) as independent of (1) and (3).*

But how do (1) through (3) entail that any single *Lage* occurs an infinite number of times? The answer is that they do not. We need also

4. Time is infinite.
5. Energy has infinite duration.

Now, suppose there were exactly *three* energy-*lagen*, *A, B, C*. And suppose that each of these occurred for a *first* time a finite time ago, say at *t*-3, *t*-2, and *t*-1. Say that *A* had the earliest first occurrence of the three, at *t*-3. Then, before *t*-3, no *lage* of the three possible *lagen* our model supposes could have existed. But from (4) it follows that there must have been time before *t*-3. And from (5) it follows that there must have been energy before *t*-3. But from (3) it follows that the amount of energy before and after *t*-3 is the same. But on our hypothesis, at least *one* of the three possible *lagen* must exist if energy exists, these being the *only* energy *lagen*. Hence at least *one* of these *lagen* must have existed before *t*-3, or, what comes to the same thing, there can be no first occurrence for *each* of the *lagen*. Hence at least *one* of them must have occurred an infinite number of times. But quite apart from the fact that we do not know which of the three it is, it is nonetheless the case that so far we at best can prove that one of them occurred an infinite number of times, and this is compatible with the possibility that *two* of them happened a finite number of times.

Suppose *A* has occurred an infinity of times before *B* occurs. *B* would mark a cut-off point temporally behind which stretches an infinitude of occurrences of *A*. But what sense would it make to say that *A* occurs an infinite number of times though nothing

else happens? Would it not be more appropriate to speak of one event of infinite duration? Nietzsche would rule this out as constituting an equilibrium, and his point is that if an equilibrium is ever reached, it would persist eternally. If there were only *A* through an infinity, nothing could bring about a change, for there is nothing but *A*, and to bring in something from outside would violate (3). So let us add

6. Change is eternal.

But the simplest sort of change would be an alternation of a pair of events, *A* and *B*. With our model and (1) through (6) we can prove that at least *two lagen* have occurred an infinite number of times. And this is still compatible with the possibility that *one* of the three possible *lagen* occurs a finite number of times. But now imagine we have an infinity of alternations . . . *A-B-A-B-A-B-A-B* . . . , and at a new cut-off point *C* occurs, so that *C* had a first occurrence a finite time ago. Nothing is so far incompatible with this possibility. But if we add something like

7. Principle of sufficient reason,

we can perhaps rule out a first occurrence for *C*. That is, there must now be a sufficient condition for *C*. But then it must be either *A* or *B*, these being all our model allows. Then since each of these things has happened an infinity of times, if either of them is a sufficient condition for *C*, *C* must have occurred an infinite number of times.

By repeated applications, we can increase our model by any finite number and prove that nothing can have occurred for a first time. But then nothing can in the future occur for a first time either. Of course we can hardly regard this as a proof of the impossibility of creation *ex nihilo* since we have pretty much had to assume this with (3), (4), and (5).

We can, then, reconstruct Nietzsche's argument with a melange of *a priori* and empirical propositions, each independent of the others and each of which could be separately denied. But further discussion is out of place here and we turn to the question of why Nietzsche thought the doctrine so important.

To begin with, it would be incompatible with the idea that the entire course of history approaches some goal, has some "meaning." For let *G* be such a goal. Then either *G* cannot ever occur, or *G* has occurred an infinity of times. Hence to accept the doctrine entails a rejection of *certain* religious interpretations of history. On the other hand, it is not the sole alternative to these, and the doctrine is compatible with the possibility that each iterated transformation (*Entwicklung*) has a goal.

Secondly, the doctrine can support a certain kind of optimism. For there can be no *permanent lage*, no infinitude characterized by *A-A-A-A* . . . Hence, the "last man" doesn't really constitute a danger

---

* The ancient theory of cosmic return sometimes maintained that there were a finite number of atoms, hence a finite number of combinations of atoms. This would surely be unexceptionable, but Nietzsche has rejected atomism as a fiction. He uses instead *All-kraft* and *Lage*. It clearly doesn't follow from the fact that the sum is finite that there is a finitude of parts. The sum of the series $1 + \frac{1}{2} + \frac{1}{4} + \frac{1}{8} \ldots$ is a finite number, 2. But it hardly follows that there is a finite number of members in the series.

of the sort envisaged by Zarathustra. But then, by the same criterion, the doctrine can support a certain kind of pessimism. The detested institutions will appear again and again. Yet, as in certain forms of Mahayana Buddhism, a Buddha appears at a critical moment in each cosmic cycle, so a Nietzsche must appear, again and again, when humankind is at its lowest point, enjoining upon his fellows a fresh effort. Does it matter that we shall all pass away, return again, pass away again. The answer is it does not. What counts is the effort, the will-to-power, the joy in overcoming, not for what it leads to, but in itself. And man should "accordingly" cherish this for its own sake, the importance of all goals being radically diminished when, like Sisyphus, we see we must do the same things over and over again: "My formula for greatness in men is *Amor Fati*: that one should not wish things to be otherwise, not before and not after, in the whole of eternity."[114]

"My doctrine states," he writes in the *Fröhliche Wissenschaft* period, "So live that you must desire to live again. This is your duty. At any rate you will live again. He for whom striving gives the greatest feeling, let him strive. He for whom rest gives the greatest feeling, let him rest. He to whom order, following, obeying gives the greatest feeling, let him obey. He must only be clear as to what gives him the highest feeling, and be shy of no means! Eternity is worth it!"[115] So act (or so be) that you would be willing to act in just that manner (or be just this way) an infinity of times. In this way, perhaps, men might feel free of *ressentiment*. In each accepting ourselves, we should each accept one another. In existentialist terms, it is a plea for authenticity. Though why this plea could not be made independently of the doctrine of eternal recurrence is difficult indeed to say. But that doctrine does, Nietzsche seems to feel, rule out the possibility of *another* and *different* life, say in heaven or hell. In place of that view, think how liberating, he argues, the doctrine of eternal return would be. "Let us," he adds, "stamp the form of eternity upon our lives."[116] Think, he tells us, "what effect the doctrine of eternal damnation has had!"[117] "*This* life is your eternal life."[118]

22

The Philosophy of Science, 1850-1910

PETER ALEXANDER

ERNST MACH WAS AN AUSTRIAN PHYSICIST, born in 1838 at Turas in Moravia. He made contributions to mechanics, electricity, acoustics, optics, hydrodynamics, and thermodynamics, and undertook psychological investigations of space and time, hearing, vision, and aesthetics. He published papers on such diverse subjects as the photographing of projectiles in flight, the chemistry of the ripening of grapes, and the place of classics in secondary education. He studied at Vienna and was appointed to a chair of mathematics at Graz in 1864, a chair of physics at Prague in 1867, and a chair of physics at Vienna in 1895 which he held until 1901. In that year he was made a member of the Austrian house of peers. He died in 1916.

Heinrich Rudolf Hertz was born in 1857 in Hamburg. His first interest was in engineering. He studied in Berlin under Helmholtz and Kirchhoff, who both thought very highly of him. He made important contributions to the study of electricity and magnetism, and became professor of physics at the technological institute at Karlsruhe in 1885. In 1889 he became professor of physics at Bonn, but he was dogged by ill-health and died in 1894. He was awarded many scientific prizes for his work in physics.

Jules Henri Poincaré was born into a distinguished family in 1854 at Nancy. He was first trained as a mining engineer, but his most important work was in mathematics. He taught first at Caen and then, from 1881, at the University of Paris, where he lectured on physical mechanics and, later, on mathematical physics and astronomical mechanics. He was elected to the Académie Française in 1908 and died in 1912.

Pierre Maurice Marie Duhem was born in 1861 in Paris. He studied in Paris, showing an early interest in thermodynamics, to which he was later to make original contributions. From the earliest times, he wrote an enormous amount on the history of science, and published work on almost all branches of mathematical physics. He became a lecturer in the Faculty of Sciences of Lille University in 1887 and at Rennes in 1893. From 1895 until his death in 1916 he held a chair at Bordeaux University. In 1900 he was elected a *correspondant* of the Académie des Sciences.

THE WORK DONE in the philosophy of science during the period from 1850 to 1910 is important because it began an extensive revision of prevailing views about science, which had developed largely from those of Francis Bacon. This revision was in the direction of greater faithfulness to the way in which scientists actually work and a closer examination of existing theories. It was partly the result of the growing interest among working scientists in the philosophy of their subject and a growing reluctance to entrust it to scientifically naïve philosophers.

There were, of course, differences among those who took what we may regard as the accepted view, but there were common features that appeared with striking regularity among the variations. Scientific investigation was held to begin in free and unprejudiced observation, to proceed by induction to laws that were empirical generalizations, and to reach, by further inductions from groups of laws, statements of wider generality sometimes referred to as "theories." Laws and theories were held to be further supported by comparing consequences deduced from them with statements of the results of observations. There were different accounts of what could be achieved by this method. Among scientists, it usually went unquestioned that its purpose was to discover the nature of observable objects regarded as constituents of the external world and the relations actually holding between them. Where these relations were described with the help of unobservable entities like forces or atoms, these were similarly regarded as constituents of the world whose properties could be discovered and would explain phenomena by providing hidden connections between them. On the other hand, philosophers, largely under the influence of Berkeley, Hume, and Kant, tended to regard all this as suspect and to see the business of science as the mere relating of our experiences in such a way as to allow prediction.

Superficially, the work of the philosopher-scientists of this period appears to constitute a closer application of the views of empiricist philosophers to the work of scientists and an attempt to win scientists to them. But, in fact, most of the views about the methods and aims of science prevailing among both philosophers and scientists were questioned by these men or by those who later came under their influence. Among the most important figures were Ernst Mach, Heinrich Hertz, Henri Poincaré, and Pierre Duhem; there can be little doubt that they contributed greatly to the approach of the subject now usually adopted in England and America and that they laid the foundations of diverse views within this approach. We can see this influence in the work of Karl Pearson;[1] in the interest of the Vienna Circle in records of bare sensation and the formalization of scientific theories, as well as in their rejection of metaphysics;[2] in the anti-inductivism of Karl Popper[3] and his disciples; in the operationism

of P. W. Bridgman,[4] the "conceptualist pragmatism" of C. I. Lewis,[5] and even the linguistic approach of Ludwig Wittgenstein.[6] Its effect on scientific theorizing itself is perhaps most strikingly exhibited in the Copenhagen interpretation of quantum theory.[7]

Mach, Hertz, Poincaré, and Duhem all made original contributions to various branches of science, and their interest in philosophical problems arose largely through perplexities and dissatisfactions about certain trends within science. They were concerned less with any implications that scientific conclusions may have for a general philosophical view of the world than with the logical structure of scientific theorizing and theories and with the delineation of the methods permissible in science. It was their work in this field which constituted a reaction against current philosophical accounts of science and which had an effect upon the development of scientific and philosophical thinking.

I propose to give a brief account of the leading views of these four scientists followed by a critical discussion in an attempt to bring out their permanent contributions to the philosophy of science. Since it is impossible here to do full justice to their views and arguments, I have selected those topics that appear to be of most interest in themselves.

Ernst Mach

ALTHOUGH Mach wrote on psychology, physiology, aesthetics, and chemistry, as well as on several branches of physics, his work is not as diverse as this list suggests, for there runs through most of it a concern for the philosophical and logical questions raised by scientific investigation. His historical studies of mechanics and optics are directed toward the confirmation of his philosophical conclusions by reference to the actual work of scientists. Moreover, these conclusions were such as to encourage free movement from one field to another; he held that there are no fundamental, "natural" divisions between the various branches of science but that such divisions are merely arbitrary and convenient. This view depends upon a special conception of "subject matter" that is perhaps unfamiliar to many scientists even now, and for which he makes a case that merits consideration. However, he regards himself as directly combating mechanism and reductionism; in accepting this latter view, some of his philosophical descendants have gone beyond him. The culmination of this view about the subject-matter of science is to be seen in the publication, by the remnants of the Vienna Circle, of the *Encyclopaedia of Unified Science*.

Influenced in his early days by Kant and Fechner, Mach soon reacted against their noumenalism and turned toward Hume and Avenarius in company with Helmholtz, Petzoldt, Kirchhoff, Boltzmann, and W. K. Clifford, contemporary scientists who shared his interests. The attitude he adopted under these influences during the late 1860s remained his for the rest of his life, to be modified and developed but never rejected. The influence of Kant, however, never wholly disappeared. His philosophy of science is sensationalistic, conventionalistic, and anti-metaphysical. The ideal of science is to stay as close to experience as possible, since "all knowledge of nature is derived in the last instance from experience,"[8] and science's aim is the complete and exact description of phenomena.

In one of his earliest works,[9] Mach asserts that the fundamental propositions of mechanics are neither wholly a priori nor wholly discoverable in experience. This statement becomes clearer when we see that the a priori element is the law of causality or sufficient reason which is merely "the presupposition of the mutual dependence of phenomena."[10] Scientists need some such presupposition as an article of faith to justify their search for the forms of this dependence, but logically, such a law can never be finally established by observation owing to the limited possibilities of observation. However, if this law is regarded as a statement about the world, it can neither be wholly a priori, for Mach accepts the empiricist premise that the truth of statements about the world can only be known finally by observation. The a priori core of the law of causality is formal and empty, but the skilled observer can give it content by describing actual dependences in nature.[11] The principle of conservation of energy, which is a fundamental proposition of mechanics, is a form of the principle of excluded perpetual motion, which in its turn is a form of the law of causality. This law is older than the whole of mechanics in the form "Nothing can come out of nothing" or "Every event has a cause," and so the principle of conservation of energy is not uniquely connected with mechanism or a product of the mechanical view.[12]

In *The Science of Mechanics*, Mach argues, with the help of historical examples, that many propositions of mechanics which have been thought to be a priori are in fact examples of "instinctive knowledge," obtained largely through haphazard and unconscious experience. Much of his account of scientific method may be regarded as an attempt to remove this sort of confusion. He says[13] that the failure to distinguish "what is a priori, what empirical and what hypothesis" may result in a peculiarly inaccurate and unscientific treatment of mechanics. If we regard perfectly respectable mechanical propositions as a priori when they are in fact derived from experience, we may think that mechanics is more broadly a prioristic than it is and admit, superfluously and illegitimately, propositions having no possible basis in experience. Hence his principal and often expressed aim is "the elimination of all superfluous assumptions which cannot be controlled by experience and, above all, of all assumptions that are metaphysical in Kant's sense. . . ."[14] and to guard against "the encroachments of metaphysical methods."[15]

His method involves two procedures. He seeks to show, by his historical studies, that the conclusions accepted by scientists, though they involve one or two formal principles, are otherwise based entirely on observation, even when this is not obviously so. Then he attempts, by giving logical reconstructions of scientific theories, to show that this is clearly the *correct* procedure. He is not issuing a prescription, dogmatically asserting what science *ought* to be, but recommending his view because it appears to be consistent with the ideals implicitly accepted by working scientists. They are concerned only with aspects of the world accessible to exact investigation, and such aspects are just those that are accessible to observation.[16] An extension of scientific principles and concepts beyond the boundaries of possible sense experience is scientifically *meaningless*. Space and motion are meaningful because they represent observable relations between bodies: a body can be said to have a given position or to move in space only in relation to another reference body. Thus Newton "acted contrary to his expressed intention only to investigate *actual facts*," and so descended into the physically meaningless when he talked about absolute space and motion, which are "pure things of thought, pure mental constructs, that cannot be produced in experience."[17] Mach accepts Newton's expressed intention and regards the principle that metaphysical statements must not appear in science as an aspect of the principle of economy.[18]

SENSATIONALISM

The "actual facts" which science seeks to investigate are discoverable by observation, and the key to Mach's account lies in his analysis of facts and observation.

The world I observe apparently consists of animate and inanimate bodies together with my own feelings, memories, moods, and so on. The most primitive attempt to describe this world reveals that its relatively permanent "bodies" can and must be analyzed into relatively impermant, simple elements such as colors, sounds, tastes, etc. These Mach calls their "ultimate component parts" because I am unable to analyze them further. I must not ask, like Locke, what accounts for the coherence of certain elements into groups which I call "bodies." The answer could only be in terms of a substratum beyond my experience and so unknowable.[19] The question is illegitimate and the answer meaningless because evidence about the world can be obtained only through sense-experience and so there is no possible means of bringing evidence for this, or any other, answer to the question.

The mistake involved in asking such questions is that of forgetting that when we talk of *bodies* we are talking on a different level from that on which we talk of the elements into which we analyze them. The ideas of relative permanence and independence are appropriate to the level of bodies and not to that of elements. A billiard ball is appropriately regarded as a sphere when we are playing billiards but not when we are examining it under a microscope; for, as Mach puts it, "summary comprehension and precise analysis, although both are provisionally justifiable and for many purposes profitable, cannot be carried on simultaneously. . . . Colours, sounds and the odours of bodies are evanescent." When we embark on analysis we leave relative permanence behind.[20]

Now, a color, or any other "element," is, as far as I can know, just one of my sensations. All my knowledge of the world comes to me through my sensations, so the world is, for me, composed of my sensations. I can have no warrant for regarding them as signs of something other than themselves because I can have no means of knowing even of the existence of this something other, let alone of its characteristics. A thing is merely "a thought-symbol for a compound sensation of relative fixedness." Sensations are logically prior to things because I can analyze things into, or "construct" them out of, sensations, but I cannot perform the reverse operations. "Properly speaking the world is not composed of 'things' as its elements, but of colours, tones, pressures, spaces, times, in short what we ordinarily call individual sensations."[21] The senses do not represent things correctly or incorrectly because they do not represent at all.[22]

Mach analyzes my "ego," composed of my body and my volitions, feelings, thoughts, memories, and so on, in a similar way. There are, in my experience, three sorts of complex, namely, external bodies, my body, and my mind. None of these is completely independent of the others but only relatively so. External bodies depend upon the position of my body and the condition of its sense organs and may even depend upon my mind, by way of my body, as when "powerful ideas burst forth into acts."

Each element of the three complexes is a sensation, whether it be a pain or desire, the color of my finger, or the color of an external object. Distinctions between the three complexes are merely arbitrary and practical and "the ego can be so extended as ultimately to embrace the whole world." It follows that there is no real distinction between the subject matters of different branches of science, since all are searching for the relations between sensations. The physicist studies the relations within and between external body complexes, the physiologist those within living body complexes, and the psychologist those between both these complexes and mind complexes.

As Mach points out, the word "sensation" may mislead. The fundamental term is "element," which is neutral as between the different complexes. A color may be an element in complexes studied by both physicists and psychologists. Considered in its dependence upon temperature or a luminous source or other colors, it is a physical object; considered in its relations to the retina or a piece of thinking, it is a sensation; but the color remains in itself unaltered, whichever set of relations we attend to. "Not the subject matter, but the direction of our investigation, is different in the two domains."[23] There is no opposition between the physical and the psychical, but a simple identity of certain elements; in the sensory sphere everything is at once physical and psychical,[24] but colors are in themselves neither physical nor psychical.

Mach asserts the complete parallelism of the physical and the psychical, but rejects Fechner's view, which was an early influence, that they are two aspects of one reality. This is metaphysical, since it refers to an unknowable *tertium quid*. The elements given in experience are always of the same kind: if we stress certain relations, we see them as physical; if we stress other relations, we see them as psychical.[25]

This, Mach holds, does not commit him to solipsism. We can justify our normal belief in the sensations of other people and in the possibility of agreement, which is essential to science, by an argument from analogy. This is a perfectly respectable form of argument in physics and here allows me to infer, on the grounds of the similarity of other people's behavior to mine, that they have sensations similar to mine. This makes the behavior of others *intelligible* to me and is the most economical way of doing so.[26] Agreement between observers can be achieved by relying on many different observers when "accidental" divergences, due to the color blindness of one or the astigmatism of another, become obvious; the divergences can be discounted by taking only what is common to the reports of all observers. The sense organs "are treated as physical instruments, each with its peculiarities, its special constants, and so forth, from which the results, as finally indicated, have to be set free."[27]

Mach also rejects idealism, the idea that the world is *created* by the senses, and Berkeleyanism, as far as it asserts the dependence of the "elements" upon an unknown cause (God) external to them. Both these ideas are metaphysical, for they make assertions which could never be tested by experience.

Physiological considerations lead Mach to conclude that space and time are just as much sensations as sounds and colors. He attempts to show that they are reducible to movements of the eyes and other bodily movements. All sensations are accompanied by time sensations, but only some sensations are accompanied by space sensations. The space and time of physics, although originally derived from these sensations, do not coincide exactly with them but stand for functional dependences upon one another of the elements characterized by the sensations and involve standards of measurement external to the sensations.[28] Space and time are not more real or objective than colors, sounds, and temperatures, but are merely well-ordered sets of sensations; they are "forms of the dependence of phenomena on one another."[29]

This affects his views on cause and effect. Echoing Hume, he enunciates a *principle of continuity* which underlies most scientific work. "When once the inquiring intellect has formed, through adaptation, the habit of connecting two things A and B, in thought, it tries to retain the habit as far as possible, even where the circumstances are slightly altered. Whenever A appears, B is added in thought."[30] The popular notion of cause, which is also that of Mill, is too primitive and assumes too great a simplicity in nature by suggesting that we can isolate single events as cause and effect. Mach proposes to replace it by the mathematical conception of function, the dependence of the characteristics of phenomena on one another. The law of causality is "sufficiently characterized by saying that it is the presupposition of the mutual dependence of phenomena." This has the advantage of drawing our attention to all the elements in the complexes we study and helping us to see the interconnection of the whole world. There is neither cause nor effect in nature. They are "things of thought, having an economical office,"[31] arrived at by abstracting those elements of phenomena that help us to describe what we take to be important.

Mach's principle makes no reference to space and time because spatial and temporal relations are merely two sorts of dependence of phenomena upon one another.[32] Instead of representing every phenomenon as a function of other phenomena *and* of spatial and temporal positions, we can represent it as a more complex function of other phenomena.

Teleological explanations are not to be despised. Euler maintained that phenomena may be explained by reference to purposes or ends as well as physical causes, as when he presumed, *a priori*, that all phenomena exhibit a maximum or a minimum character. Light, for example, travels in straight lines. He also held, however, that we can discover the nature of this maximum and minimum only by observation. Mach urges that such explanations may be useful aids to investigation, especially in biology, by reference not to the purposes of, but to the end achieved by, a given function of an organism. We must never confuse causal and teleological accounts nor regard teleological accounts as final and sufficient, but where there are gaps in our causal accounts it would be foolish to neglect *any* clues to understanding that may be afforded by a consideration of ends. Kepler, through his knowledge of the purpose of the eye, arrived at the idea of accommodation over a century before its mechanism was understood.[33]

There is no clear division between biology and physics, nor between teleological and causal methods of investigation. In chemistry, certain theoretically possible combinations are not formed because they are less resistant to attack than certain other combinations and, on the other hand, all biological phenomena are in principle describable in causal terms. Teleological accounts are merely provisional but help us to describe phenomena while we search for more precise causal descriptions.[34]

THE COURSE OF SCIENTIFIC INVESTIGATION

Fundamental to Mach's account is his belief that scientific investigation is carried out for practical ends.[35] This does not mean that all such investigations must have an immediate practical application but rather that no conclusion is of interest unless it is logically possible that it be applied. This is bound up with his objections to metaphysics. If we are faced with two alternative explanations such that the acceptance of one rather than the other could make no difference to our ways of dealing with the world, then there is nothing to choose between them. The explanations are metaphysical and, in a scientific context, no better than no explanation. One consequence of this, as we shall see, is Mach's demand that a scientific theory should have predictive power; while there is nothing strange or new about this demand, the weight Mach gave to it was unusual.

Conscious scientific investigation begins in practical needs but is preceded by "instinctive" knowledge of natural processes. The scientist asks his first questions against a background of such knowledge.[36] Mechanical experience precedes mechanical science. We develop machines, tools, mechanical skills in a haphazard and accidental way long before we come to understand, or even question, the principles underlying them. This is both a historical account of the beginning of all science and a description of a process which occurs whenever a new question is investigated.

In order that knowledge shall not die with a generation it must be communicated. This necessitates the description of facts, processes, and techniques, and, since description involves generalization, depends on recurrence. This is the beginning of the enunciation of laws. At first we shall be able to formulate laws covering only small numbers of facts and the rest will appear "uncommon, perplexing, astonishing or even contradictory to the ordinary run of things." This leads us to search for resemblances and recurrences of elements among our unsystematized experience. The ideal of science is that we should see everything as part of the ordinary run of things, that we should achieve "a unitary conception of nature."[37] We achieve this when we see everything as composed of a limited number of elements, when everything is familiar to us, there are no surprises, no problems, and everything is explained.

This is all a matter of description, and the ideal

of science is the most complete, precise, and economical description of facts. The facts are observable and the relations we seek are resemblances and differences between their observable elements. We describe as economically as possible when we refer only to those observable elements and do not go beyond sense-experience. Such descriptions remove the necessity of waiting for new experiences and of making further experiments and, since they are general, allow us to infer what will happen in given circumstances, to *predict* future occurrences.

Instinctive knowledge is extremely primitive but not innate. It is formed in, and constantly tested by, experience; when the tests have not failed, certain statements are accepted without question and become the axioms of science. "The greatest advances in science have always consisted in some successful formulation, in clear, abstract and communicable terms, of what was instinctively known long before, and of thus making it the permanent property of humanity."[38] Mach seeks to support this by considering the axioms of Archimedes' statics. For example, the statement that magnitudes of equal weight acting at equal distances from their point of support are in equilibrium appears to be self-evident and *a priori*.[39] But a great deal of experience underlies this assumption. It shows, among other things, that the color of the lever arms, the position of the spectator, and so on, have no influence, and, on the other hand, that the lengths of the arms, as well as the weights, are relevant. How else could we have learnt these things? Although we usually overlook the fact, all our judgments of relevance are dependent upon experience, but, because of the wealth of experience from which such judgments or "axioms" are conclusions, we are entitled to accept them as self-evident though not as infallible. It is important that we realize the nature of these so-called axioms.

Natural laws are built up with the help of instinctive knowledge and are like that knowledge in being abridged descriptions, comprehensive and condensed reports about facts.[40] Their value is that they "save experience," for they allow us to predict in advance of experience. In this respect, Mach refers to them as "rules" for the making of predictions.[41] Galileo's laws of falling bodies are "simple and compendious directions for reproducing in thought all possible motions of falling bodies."[42] The index of refraction for two media allows us to construct every conceivable case of refraction: it is a rule "for the reconstruction of great numbers of facts . . . embodied in a single expression."

However, laws are never complete reproductions of facts but involve abstraction. The law of refraction allows us to reconstruct the fact of refraction only on its geometrical side. Laws are thus to some extent *conventional*, for we choose those formulations which help us to deal with those aspects of the phenomena with which we happen to be concerned.[43]

Before a law is accepted it may be entertained as a hypothesis. This is unobjectionable if it is then subjected to test. Mach sometimes gives the impression that hypotheses do not have an important function in science, but that is not his real view. In an approving passage, he shows how Galileo made hypotheses about the manner in which bodies fall but, unlike Aristotle, went on to make observations to test them. Indeed, he says, concerning the same passage: "Without some preconceived opinion the experiment is impossible because its form is determined by the opinion." Newton, on the other hand, he praises for not making hypotheses about the *causes* of phenomena and for aiming merely to describe the actual facts.[44] Elsewhere he roundly condemns the construction of hypotheses "behind the facts where nothing tangible and verifiable is found" and says they are mental artifices or expedients having nothing to do with the phenomena. All hypotheses of fluids or media are superfluous to the theories of heat and electricity.[45]

Mach is objecting to two things, first, to untested, though testable, hypotheses figuring in scientific conclusions and, second, to explanatory hypotheses involving unobservables — for example, atoms, being regarded as asserting the existence of unobservable entities. In general, hypotheses are dangerous when more reliance is placed upon them than upon the facts themselves.[46]

Mach's account of theories is perhaps his most influential contribution to the philosophy of science. The business of the scientist is primarily to describe phenomena rather than to construct theories, although theories may be useful aids for this purpose. Through experience we form abstract concepts, such as "red," "square," and "smooth," which we can use independently of one another and of particular objects. A report of a fact using only such abstract implements is a *direct description*; contrasted with this is a theory, or *indirect description*, in which we appeal to a description already formulated and say that a new fact is "not in one but in many or all its features like an old and well-known fact." Light behaves like a wave motion or an electric vibration, a magnet as if it were laden with gravitating fluids. That is, we treat light as if its behavior depended on waves, even though we can never verify this, as the behavior of a stretched string observably does. Theories must be accepted neither in their own right nor as having equal dignity with direct descriptions and our aim must always be to replace a theory by a direct description which "contains nothing that is inessential and restricts itself absolutely to the abstract apprehension of facts."[47] Theories are auxiliary and transitional. The real achievements of mechanical physics are the exact quantitative treatment of physical connections and the elucidations of physical processes with the help of more familiar mechanical analogies, such as the *flow* of an electric current. The finished description must be free from theory, just as a finished building must be free from unsightly scaffolding.[48]

Theories are constructed with the help of memory and comparison alone. A new fact is transformed into an "old acquaintance" when we find a system of resemblance between it and a familiar fact. The theory points to features we failed to see immediately in the new fact and so provides a practical and quantitative advantage by speeding up the investigation, but it can tell us nothing which we could not eventually learn from observation alone. A fruitful theory may even retard investigation if we take it to represent the new fact more completely than it does. The particle theory led physicists to regard the path of light as an undifferentiated straight line, thus delaying the discovery of its periodicity.[49]

The quantity (*mn*) of heat supplied to a substance is the product of its mass (*m*) and its increase of temperature (*n*). Black's substantial theory of heat regarded *mn* as the quantity of a *substance* transferred, and at this time this was a helpful picture. But the picture was inessential. What was essential was the quantitative relation between various products, *mn*, in complex situations involving transfer of heat between several bodies, for instance, the fact that if a quantity of heat disappears from one point an equal quantity appears at another.

This last statement, a direct description of phenomena, was retained when the substantial theory was superseded, after the work of Mayer and Joule, by the theory that heat was a motion, and it is the description which is important and not the various attempts to *explain* the relation by unobservable substances or motions. The "motional conception of heat is now as inessential as was formerly its conception as a substance," since neither theory describes what occurs beneath the surface revealed to us in observation. A new theory about heat is not a discovery of the truth about heat but a proposal for a new way of talking about heat which better enables us to visualize its quantitative relations. The theory we adopt is dictated by convenience and historical accident. "It is perfectly indifferent, and possesses not the slightest scientific value, whether we think of heat as a substance or not. The fact is, heat behaves in some connections like a substance, in others not."[50] We are dealing in analogies.

Mach strongly criticizes atomism, the ideal of which is "the reduction of all physical processes to the motions of atoms," on similar grounds. Atoms are not realities behind phenomena but provisional economical tools invented for the purpose of representing phenomena and assisting prediction. They are not formed by the principle of continuity and are, moreover, "invested with properties that absolutely contradict the attributes hitherto observed in bodies." The atomic theory has nothing to do with the phenomena *themselves* but is "a mathematical *model* for facilitating the mental reproduction of facts." If we take the atom for a real entity, causally

connected with the phenomena, we take the tools of science for the objects of investigation, a mistake which becomes easy when an excessive formal development occurs.[51] We must not expect to get out of atoms any more than we put into them, that is, any more than we can get from sense experience.

A further argument against atomism depends on Mach's view of space. The intuition of space is essentially bound up with the organization of the senses, so that "we are not justified in ascribing spatial properties to things which are not perceived by the senses." We are not justified, therefore, in regarding the atoms as situated and organized in space.[52]

In general, we cannot by means of a theory discover rules for phenomena which cannot be perceived in the phenomena themselves. "In a complete theory, to all details of the phenomenon details of the hypothesis must correspond, and all rules for these hypothetical things must also be directly transferable to the phenomenon." A theory may contain more than we have observed in the phenomena but that *more* concerns the phenomena only if it is observable in the phenomena. We can only discover which features of a theory represent features of the phenomena by observing. The theory may tell us where to look or what to look for but it never removes the necessity for looking.[53]

Mach defines a "perfect theory" when he says "A systematic representation [theory] of a class of phenomena is perfect when a complete survey of all the phenomena possible to that class can be developed from the fundamental propositions, when no phenomenon arises to which there does not correspond a construction from the fundamental propositions and vice versa."[54] This does not, of course, mean that every statement in the theory must itself correspond to some observation or be verifiable, even in principle, but only that any derived statement which is testable must be tested and that any observable statement must be derivable from the theory. We must not suppose that the untestable statements of the theory have any physical meaning or existential import.

EXPLANATION

It is a consequence of Mach's account that he identifies scientific explanation with description. Explanation's task can be no more than the description of the relations between phenomena, or, ultimately, between the elements of phenomena. The need to support "weaker thoughts by stronger thoughts" is the need of causality and the "moving spring of all scientific explanations," but causal explanation is neither more or less than "the statement or description of an actual fact or of a connection between facts" in terms of elements.[55] Only the unfamiliar requires explanation, and if we put our description of the unfamiliar in familiar terms the need for explanation vanishes. But another important feature in explanation is relative simplicity: explanation involves the analysis of complex phenomena into simple ones — that is, the discovery in a phenomenon of known simpler phenomena.[56] A fact is clear to us "when we can reproduce it by very simple and very familiar intellectual operations such as the construction of accelerations, or the geometrical summation of accelerations."[57]

The basic explanatory units are Mach's "elements" and that is why the attempt to explain feelings, for example, in terms of the motions of atoms — that is, by mechanical principles — is misconceived and circular. It is an attempt to explain the more simple and immediate by the more complex and remote.[58] Mechanical principles are merely ways of describing relations between elements. A feeling is just one of the elements in terms of which we explain, so to explain feelings by mechanical principles is to attempt to explain what does not need explaining. The postulated sensations, feelings, and willings of others are tools for the prediction of their behavior and not descriptions of occurrences, observed or unobserved.[59] Atoms are invented symbols for just those complexes of sensational elements which we treat in physics and chemistry.

In explaining we are not, however, reducing the unintelligible to the intelligible. The simplest facts, our basic elements, are themselves unintelligible because they cannot be further analyzed. "Understanding consists in analysis alone." Explanation has to stop somewhere and no ultimate explanation is possible; where we stop is a matter of taste, convention, and economy. The most we can hope for is to reduce uncommon unintelligibles to common unintelligibles. We tend to believe that mechanical facts are more intelligible than others, and, therefore, more fundamental, but this is the result of the historical accident that, because mechanics is older than the rest of physics, we are more familiar with mechanics. Mach quotes with approval from the physicist J. R. Mayer, "if a fact is known on all its sides, it is, by that knowledge, explained, and the problem of science is ended."[60]

We can now see more clearly the point of what Mach says about theories. They are never themselves explanations, since they contain concepts whose correspondence with existents can never be verified. They can help us to find explanations, that is, more complete descriptions, by pointing the way to new facts. An explanation is always a description of facts, but we can never know whether theoretical statements describe anything or not.

SCIENTIFIC METHOD

Mach's historical studies, and his account of science, led him to the conclusion that there is no one scientific method. No method is excluded from science as long as it is a method of arriving at facts or a more complete description of facts. He rejects the view that scientists always proceed by inductive reasoning but, on the other hand, he believes that most suggestions for investigation come, by whatever roundabout route, from experience.

He is, however, aware that accident, metaphysical theories of the structure of the universe, or beliefs about God's purposes may play important roles in scientific investigation. "The happiest ideas do not fall from heaven but spring from notions already existing," and accident should not be disregarded but purposefully used.[61]

Many of the principles of mechanics were the product of theological speculation but are nevertheless sound. This is because the stimulus for both scientific investigation and theological speculation is the desire for a more comprehensive view of the world. Although the form of these principles of mechanics was theologically determined, only experience can give them content and only when they are so given content are they of scientific interest.[62] Other coherent world systems are similarly able to contribute to science.

The formation of hypotheses is seldom the result of "artificial" scientific methods, but is an unconscious process occurring in the very infancy of science. The only fundamental method in science is "the method of change or variation" by which new ideas develop out of old ones. Even prejudice is not to be condemned outright. It sometimes has an economical value, for "no one could exist intellectually if he had to form judgments on every passing fact of experience, instead of allowing himself to be controlled by the judgments he has already formed."[63]

Philosophical theories have been especially fruitful in contributing to science, and Mach mentions particularly the theory of irrationals, conceptions of conservation, and the doctrine of evolution. This procedure is unexceptionable in science if the philosophical theories are so adapted as to be amenable to testing by the accepted scientific methods of observation.

Heinrich Hertz

HERTZ was a brilliant physicist who, just before he died at the early age of thirty-seven, wrote a book on mechanics which is a classic of the philosophy of science. Whereas Mach before him discussed mainly the observational basis of science and Poincaré after him was more interested in the logical status of laws, Hertz stressed the *systematic* character of scientific theories and perhaps had a clearer view of the whole than either. In the 4th edition of *The Science of Mechanics*, Mach discusses Hertz's book and expresses considerable agreement with it. Hertz is more liberal toward metaphysics than Mach and holds that metaphysical conceptions can be of great assistance to science. However, he considers it important that we should be clear about the logical character of the statements we use and do not mistake metaphysical for empirical statements.

His starting point is largely Kantian, for he divides mechanics into that part which depends on the formal necessities of our thought and that part which depends on experience, and adds that certain features of mechanics depend upon our arbitrary choice.[64] His study of scientific theories is largely concerned with the disentangling of these three features. A scientific theory is an artificial deductive system which corresponds to observable nature if it is correct and fails to correspond if it is not. It can be set out as an axiom system, in which may be deduced conclusions which can be tested for correspondence by observation. Of course, Hertz is asserting not that this is how theories are historically constructed but that they can be reformulated to exhibit this logical character. *The Principles of Mechanics* is such a rational reconstruction of one theory.

Hertz gives an important place to prediction but goes beyond Mach's view that theories are merely aids to prediction. When we test the consequences of a theory we test that theory as a whole and not just the equations derived from it. If these consequences are confirmed, we are entitled to say that any unobservable, theoretical entities involved in it are at least possible existents and that the theory is a possible description of nature. Thus he allows meaning to theoretical concepts beyond the purely formal meaning they obtain from their position in a deductive system.

Hertz's philosophy of science, as he explains in his Preface, was developed to meet certain problems which arose in science itself. Physicists are agreed, he says, that "the problem of physics consists in tracing the phenomena of nature back to the simple laws of mechanics," but here agreement ceases since it is by no means clear what these simple laws are. It is generally thought that they are Newton's laws of motion, but a clear understanding of these depends upon a clear understanding of the concept of *force* and there is disagreement among physicists about this. There are two possible ways of dealing with such a situation. We might undertake an analysis of the concepts which are not clear with a view to clarifying them or we might reconstruct our theories taking as fundamental only concepts about which we *are* clear. In this way Hertz is led from dissatisfaction about a concept to the analysis of a whole theory.

The most important problem for science is the anticipation of future events. We do this on the basis of experience of past and present events for forming "subjective images of external objects" such that "the necessary consequents of the images in thought are always the images of the necessary consequents in nature of the things pictured." A theory is thus a collection of such images with their relations, which forms a picture, or model, of things and their relations in nature. Observation shows us whether it is an accurate picture. But for an acceptable theory the conformity between nature and our thought need only be in the respect indicated in the above quotation. We have no means of knowing finally whether our images are in conformity with nature in any other respect. The image of the constituents of gases as minute, perfectly elastic spheres is satisfactory if its consequences correspond to the observed behavior of gases, whether actual gases are composed of such particles or not. However, the more evidence of this sort we have, the greater is the probability that they are so composed.

There may, of course, be alternative theories which give the same consequences and there is nothing to choose between them if they fulfil the following three requirements. (1) They must be *logically permissible*, i.e., consistent with "the laws of our thought." (2) They must be *correct*, i.e., their relations must not conflict with the observable relations between external things. (3) They must be appropriate — that is, simple — in the sense of containing the fewest possible superfluous or empty relations. This last is a strictly comparative requirement; of two theories we should accept the more appropriate. The permissibility of images depends upon the nature of our minds, their correctness upon our experiences, and their appropriateness upon our "notations, definitions and abbreviations," the conventional part of our images.

The word "principle" has been variously used in mechanics and Hertz fixes its meaning for his purposes. For him, principles are any selection from among mechanical propositions such that the whole of mechanics can be developed from them by deduction without further appeal to experience.[65] This leaves us a certain freedom, for by choosing as fundamental different propositions from among those accepted in mechanics we can give various representations of mechanical theories — that is, various images of things. That is, we may set out the verified and accepted propositions of mechanics in different ways according to our view about the probable structure of the world. These images must be tested for permissibility, correctness, and appropriateness.

Hertz now outlines three possible representations or images, two of them drawn from the history of mechanics and the third his own. This, he argues, is superior in certain respects to the others.

The first image is the customary representation of mechanics adopted by most textbooks at the time. It followed closely the historical development of the subject and its fundamental concepts were space, time, force, and mass. Force was regarded as the cause of motion and independent of it. This image is unsatisfactory in respect of permissibility owing largely to the lack of clarity of the term "force" but this in turn depends partly on "the unessential characteristics which we have ourselves arbitrarily worked into the essential content given by nature"[66] — on our definitions and notations, rather than on the necessities of our thought or the contribution of experience. The image passes the test of correctness, but fails to satisfy the condition of appropriateness because of the indefiniteness of the idea of force: it embraces all the natural motions but "includes very many motions which are not natural." It is not simple because many of the forces used cannot be objects of direct perception. In astronomy, gravitational forces enter only as transitory aids to calculation and appear neither in observation statements nor in conclusions.[67] Physics has been compelled, especially in the more recent conceptions of atomism and magnetism, "to fill the world to overflowing with forces of the most various kinds." In Mach's language, this image lacks economy.

The second image is of more recent growth and was in Hertz's day coming into favor among the more enlightened physicists, Helmholtz among them. Instead of basing natural phenomena on innumerable actions-at-a-distance between atoms it bases them on transformations of energy. It avoids the difficulties attached to the conception of force by taking space, time, energy, and mass as fundamental. Force is introduced by definition as an aid to calculation. Energy, it is claimed, depends only on positions or velocities,[68] so all the basic concepts depend only upon direct experience.[69] Thus this image is superior to the first in appropriateness. Hertz has some doubts about its correctness, but stills them temporarily by arguing that motions with which it cannot deal probably do not occur in nature. The real difficulties occur when we examine its logical permissibility. The problem is to define energy in terms of "simple, direct experiences." Physicists favoring this image have regarded energy as a substance but this raises difficulties in connection with potential energy, which it is difficult to treat as a substance. For example, it is sometimes necessary to ascribe negative potential energy to a system, or to regard the potential energy of a finite quantity of matter as infinite.[70] Thus, although the second image looks, at first sight, more promising than the first, the difficulties attached to it warrant a search for a better one.

The third image that Hertz develops in *The Principles of Mechanics* starts with only three independent fundamental conceptions, time, space, and mass. That is, he attempts to derive the whole of mechanics from kinematics, the abstract study of motion, without using force and energy except as convenient devices for calculation. Kirchhoff had already asserted that three independent concepts are necessary and sufficient for mechanics.[71]

Hertz at once points out that it is impossible to understand all the motions of bodies by bringing them under simple laws in terms only of what can be directly observed. The "totality of things visible and tangible do not form a Universe conformable to law, in which the same results always follow from the same conditions." We have to presuppose "behind the things which we see, other invisible things — to imagine confederates concealed beyond the limits of the senses." The first two images met this necessity by creating the concepts of force and energy, respectively. But these are entities quite unlike any we meet in experience. Hertz's "confederates," beyond observed motions and masses, are simply more motions and masses of the same kind differing from observed motions and masses only in being unobservable. These fill the gaps, provide the connections between the phenomena. Force and energy may then be regarded as merely actions of mass and motion not necessarily "recognizable by our coarse senses." This image, according to Hertz, fits the work of recent scientists. Forces connected with heat have been traced back to the concealed motions of tangible masses; Maxwell has made convincing the account of electro-magnetic forces in terms of concealed masses; Kelvin's theory of vortex atoms is a dynamical explanation of forces; Helmholtz has used concealed motion in his treatment of cyclical systems. Hertz merely generalizes this procedure.

Time, space, and mass are objects of experience, and the experiences by which they are to be determined can be specified. Between these concepts, taken in various combinations, there are certain permanent relations which we also discover in experience. We find that the connection of all three together can be summarized in Hertz's "Fundamental Law," analogous to the ordinary law of inertia. It is: "Every natural motion of an independent material system consists herein, that the system follows with uniform velocity one of its straightest paths." This law is derived from experience and represents the only fundamental appeal to experience needed for mechanics. From it, together with the three concepts and the hypothesis of concealed masses, the whole of mechanics may be derived by purely deductive reasoning.[72] This constitutes an explanation of mechanical phenomena. Further appeals to experience are necessary to establish the correctness of the system but these concern the deduced conclusions and not the premises.

Other concepts are introduced into the system by definition, i.e., as conventions of the system. Force, for example, is not a hidden entity but merely "a mathematical aid whose properties are entirely in our power," and so it ceases to be mysterious as it was in the first image. When two bodies belong to the same system the motion of one is determined by that of the other, but it is convenient to divide the determination into two steps. We may say that the motion of the first determines a force and that this force determines the motion of the second. Force is a "middle term" between two motions, entering both as a cause and as an effect and so not fundamental. The general properties of force follow as a necessary consequence of thought from the fundamental law, since it depends entirely upon motions whose properties are described by that law.

Mechanics has a mathematical form and a physical content just as "2 apples + 2 apples = 4 apples" has; just as the mathematical statement "2 + 2 = 4" is independent of the existence of apples or their properties, so the mathematical form of mechanics is independent of its physical content.

The Principles of Mechanics is divided, to exhibit this independence, into two parts. Book I, entitled "Geometry and Kinematics of Material Systems," contains the mathematical form, draws out the implications of the fundamental ideas, space, time, and mass, and is "completely independent of experience." "All the assertions are *a priori* judgments in Kant's sense. They are based upon the laws of the internal intuition of, and upon the logical forms followed by, the person who makes the assertions; with his external experience they have no other connection than these intuitions and forms may have."[73] Book II, entitled "Mechanics of Material Systems," consists of the application of the mathematical form to experience through the fundamental law.

Space, time, and mass (in the form of mass particles) are, in the first book, *a priori* concepts which have, as it were, a life of their own, that is, they have logical consequences, depending on logical rules we all accept, which we can draw out without reference to experience. In terms of these concepts, Hertz constructs purely mathematical definitions of "path," "direction," "magnitude," "straight," "the straightest paths of the system," "velocity," "acceleration," "energy," and so on.

In Book II, the "ideal" concepts of space, time, and mass are regarded as "symbols for objects of external experience."[74] The statements of this book must "be in accordance with possible, and, in particular, future experiences," the connection with experience being made by the fundamental law. The correctness of the whole depends, therefore, upon the correctness of this law in application to experience made possible by three rules about the measurement of space, time, and mass given at the beginning of Book II. These are not new definitions but "the laws of transformation by means of which we translate external experience — that is, concrete sensations and perceptions — into the symbolic language of the images of them which we form, and by which conversely the necessary consequents of this image are again referred to the domain of possible sensible perceptions."[75] The fundamental law and these rules, added to the system of Book I, allow us to deduce statements with external reference or, as Hertz says, statements which "represent possible experiences"[76] and are testable by direct experiment. This is sufficient for continuous motions and action by contact; for apparently discontinuous motions and actions at a distance a further essential feature is the hypothesis of concealed masses.

One of the main advantages Hertz claims for his system is that it shows Hamilton's treatment of

mechanical problems with the aid of characteristi functions to be an integral part of the geometrica element in mechanics and not a branch independen of the usual mechanics. Another advantage is that th fundamental law avoids the mystery involved in th suggestion, in Gauss' principle of least constrain of deliberate intention in inanimate nature. Hertz i thus on the side of Mach and Poincaré in wishing t eliminate metaphysics as far as possible from scienc even if he does not think it can be entirely eliminatec

In discussing the permissibility, correctness, an appropriateness of his image, Hertz places mos emphasis on its superior permissibility, since h undertook its construction mainly because certai elements of the other two images were obscure an unintelligible. He does not claim that it is the only or even the best possible, image of mechanics bu merely that it is more intelligible than the others.' There is justice in his claim of logical rigor. He als claims that it is correct — that it includes all natur: motions without exception, although it has th character of a hypothesis, constantly open to refut: tion or further confirmation. He anticipates tw possible criticisms, first, that it limits the possib connections to continuous ones and, second, that th account of force in terms of concealed motions ma fail to cover some of the forces in nature. H replies to the first criticism that "All connections of system which are not embraced within the limi of our mechanics, indicate in one sense or anothe a discontinuous succession of its possible motions but it is a fact of experience that "nature exhibi continuity in infinitesimals everywhere and in ever sense."[78] This he accepts as a tentative hypothesi He replies in a similar way to the second criticisn His view that all forces in nature can be treated : the effects of concealed motions is a hypothes awaiting refutation. He takes heart from the fact tha distinguished physicists, including Lord Kelvi tend more and more to accept the hypothesis.

Hertz also claims greater simplicity for his imag than for the other two. From past changes we ca deduce future ones by applying the fundamental la without knowing the positions of all the separa masses of the system or introducing arbitrary an probably false hypotheses. Moreover, its concel tions are so closely "adapted to nature" that th essential relations in nature are represented by simp relations between ideas. It lacks simplicity only whe concealed masses are introduced, but he argues th: even this lack of simplicity is not to be attributed nature but to the incompleteness of our knowledg The complications are a necessary result of the speci assumptions. Hertz stresses that the appropriatene under consideration has no reference to practic applications or the needs of man but concerns tl objective knowledge of nature. The "usual represen ation" of mechanics has been devised expressly facilitate practical applications and so is likely to l more appropriate in *this* sense. "Our representatic of mechanics bears towards the customary one somewhat the same relation that the systematic grammar of a language bears to a grammar devised for the purpose of enabling learners to become acquainted as quickly as possible with what they will require in daily life."

Having dismissed the second image as a satisfactory alternative to the first, Hertz concludes his Introduction with a summary comparison of the third image with the first. There is, after all, nothing to choose between them in respect of permissibility and appropriateness since the first image might be recast in a better logical form and might be rendered more complete by suitable additions. Their correctness is therefore the sole basis of choice between them and this depends upon the facts. Both images cannot at the same time be correct; one or both must be false, because the first assumes "as the final constant elements in nature the relative accelerations of the masses with reference to each other" and the third assumes "as the strictly invariable elements of nature fixed relations between the positions." Moreover, there either are or are not concealed motions. If our perceptions were more detailed and precise we should know which are the constant elements in nature; as it is we can reach a decision only on the grounds of probability. Simplicity is on the side of the third image and there is evidence, from electric and magnetic forces, that the first image yields only approximately true statements. Hertz expects more positive evidence in favor of the third image from further knowledge of an all-pervading medium (the ether) "whose smallest parts are subjected to rigid connections," to motions in which the supposed actions at a distance will be traced. On these grounds he concludes for the third image.[79]

This conclusion perhaps requires some further elucidation, since Hertz appears to waver between different reasons for rejecting the first image. He originally criticizes it on the connected grounds of appropriateness and permissibility but not on grounds of correctness, and finally argues that the basis of choice between the first and third images is their correctness. That this is not a real inconsistency can be understood only by referring again to a very fundamental notion in Hertz's account of science. The permissibility and appropriateness of a theory depend upon us, its correctness does not. This means that, as long as we retain those relations which correspond to experience, we are free to reconstruct a theory in any way we please in order to improve its logic or to make it more simple. Hertz's third image is not just such a reconstruction of the first because it uses different basic concepts but is superior to the first, *as it stands*, in respect of these two characteristics. However, this is not a final and fundamental reason for rejecting the first and accepting the third, since the first image might be revised to produce an image of equal permissibility and appropriateness to the third but retaining space, time, force, and mass as basic concepts. This would leave correctness as the final ground of choice between them. As far as the available evidence goes, both images are correct, so there is nothing to choose between them, except that Hertz has actually performed his reconstruction whereas the supporters of the first image have still to do theirs, but future evidence will, Hertz supposes, support one image rather than the other and make possible a choice between them on grounds of correctness. Thus, although he was led to produce his reconstruction by a lack of appropriateness in the first image, he never loses sight of the fact that there are many ways of overcoming this lack.

Henri Poincaré

POINCARÉ approached scientific method as a mathematician and his conclusions about it are partly determined by this. Philosophically he was influenced by Kant and Mach, although he seldom acknowledges a debt to Mach. Superficially his account appears to vary greatly from that of Mach but it is a development in the same tradition.

Science is basically inductive, depending on generalizing from observed particulars, and scientific induction is based upon a belief in a general order, independent of us, in the universe, and in this it differs from mathematical induction, which is based upon our direct intuition of the mind's power to repeat indefinitely an act once performed.[80] Just because scientific induction is based upon the belief in a general order its conclusions always lack certainty, because whether the order is absolutely general remains open to doubt however much order we have found.

The scientific method consists in observation and experiment but because the scientist cannot observe everything he must select. Although he must do so on some principle, Poincaré scorns the idea of selection on grounds of morality or practical utility.[81] The best scientists are moved by disinterested curiosity but their selection need not therefore be arbitrary or capricious. There is a hierarchy of facts, the most interesting and valuable of which are those which "can be used several times, those which have a chance of recurring," for "the more general a law is, the greater is its value."[82] It is fortunate that there are such recurring facts. In a universe in which there were eighty million chemical elements, uniformly distributed, there would be no chemistry, perhaps no science.

The facts that have the greatest chance of recurring are simple facts. There is a greater chance that the few constituents of a simple fact will be united again than that the many constituents of a complex fact will be. On the other hand, what appears simple to us largely depends upon familiarity; "facts which occur frequently appear to us simple, just because we are accustomed to them."[83] Scientists have sought simple facts in different directions but especially in the very small and the very great. The physicist finds it in atoms, the biologist in cells, and the astronomer in the immense distances between the stars, which can be regarded as points by comparison with these distances.

As soon as we have found regularities we lose interest in them and look for differences instead of similarities; it is the exceptions which are puzzling, which demand investigation, and are most instructive. If we have only two distant points on a curve and wish to establish the shape of the curve we should be more likely to find evidence that the curve is a straight line if we plotted more points near the first two. These points would differ very little whether the curve was a straight line or a parabola and errors might obscure even this difference. It would be more instructive to take points near the center since here the difference between different curves is likely to be greatest. If our hypothesis is that the curve is a straight line we test it by choosing those points which are most likely to falsify it. This is an economical procedure because if the curve is not a straight line, one point in the center is more likely to show us this than several points at the extremities. In general, "when a rule has been established, we have first to look for the cases in which the rule stands the best chance of being found at fault." When we find irregularities we try to bring them, in turn, under some rule. Science seeks not merely to enumerate similarities and differences but to show that similarities underlie differences. The economical tendency of science is both a practical advantage and a source of the intellectually appreciated beauty we find in order.[84]

The aim of science, then, is generality, the discovery of laws covering many diverse facts, and its method is to proceed from simple facts by generalizing. The scientist is thus not interested in facts as such but in the relations between them. The importance of a fact is determined by the return it yields. This means two things. A recorded conclusion may save time and effort by making it unnecessary to repeat the work which led to it and it may allow us to foresee other facts, that is, to predict. The more a conclusion helps us in these two ways the more valuable it is.

Poincaré argues that although the methods of demonstration in mathematics differ from those in physics, their methods of discovery are very similar.[85] He seeks to show this by long discussions of mathematics. His discussions of geometry are perhaps most helpful for understanding his conclusions about the physical sciences. Like Mach, he holds that the space of geometry is not the same as the space of sense experience and that, in general, mathematical ideas do not come directly from experience. We can arrange conditions in which things which look equal

to a third thing do not look equal to one another. We invent the mathematical continuum to remove this disagreement with the law of contradiction so that things equal to the same thing are equal to one another *whatever* our senses tell us.[86] This is an axiom in analysis rather than geometry, of a kind which Poincaré calls "analytical *a priori* intuitions."[87]

There are, however, certain specifically geometrical axioms, such as those of Euclidean geometry; for example, that through one point only one parallel can be drawn to a given straight line.[88] These were once regarded as stating fundamental properties of the observable space in which we live but the development of non-Euclidean geometries during the nineteenth century casts doubt on this by showing that coherent systems of geometry could be based on the denial of certain of these axioms. Our understanding of space and geometry was greatly increased when it was shown that the theorems of non-Euclidean geometry, superficially very different from those of Euclidean geometry, are nevertheless logically related to them and can be interpreted in such a way as to be translatable into them. Moreover, the construction of non-Euclidean geometries has turned out to be more than an intellectual exercise. Although they were developed in a purely abstract way they have been found to have physical applications just as Euclidean geometry has.[89]

In view of this it does not make sense to regard Euclidean geometry as the true description of the space in which we live. The difference between the applicability of Euclidean and Lobatchewskean geometries is a function of the scale on which we are working. Terrestrial triangles are too small to show the properties of Lobatchewskean triangles, and Euclidean geometry may be regarded as applicable to limiting cases in which departures from Lobatchewskean theorems are small enough to be negligible.

Geometrical axioms, Poincaré concludes, are neither synthetic *a priori* truths, for if they were we could not conceive of their contradiction and non-Euclidean geometry would be impossible, nor experimental truths, for that would rob geometry of its exactness. They are in fact *conventions* or disguised definitions. Our choice of convention is guided by observation and experiment and limited by the necessity of avoiding contradictions. Some conventions are more useful that others but questions about their truth are meaningless, like the question whether the French language is true and the English language false. "One geometry cannot be more true than another: it can only be more convenient."

Euclidean geometry remains the most convenient for ordinary purposes. It is simplest in itself, it accords with our mental habits, and it sufficiently agrees with the properties of natural solids which we can compare and measure by means of the senses. It has a special fitness because of our education.[90] We build up our concept of space from experience "by studying the laws by which . . . sensations succeed one another."[91] It is derived not from isolated sensations but from the relations between sensations, including muscular sensations as well as those of sight and touch. In our world, sensations succeed one another according to laws *most conveniently* expressed in Euclidean geometry, but we can imagine worlds in which they succeeded one another in ways most conveniently expressed in non-Euclidean geometry, which beings educated in those worlds would no doubt have discovered. If we were translated to one of those worlds we could still use Euclidean geometry although it were not the most convenient, and non-Euclidean geometries can be used to express the laws by which our sensations do in fact succeed one another. It is familiar and obvious that the points, lines, and triangles of Euclidean geometry are idealizations of the rough points, lines, and triangles of our experience. Poincaré concludes that "we do not *represent* to ourselves external bodies in geometrical space, but we *reason* about these bodies as if they were situated in geometrical space."

We must not suppose Poincaré to be saying that the axioms of geometry are, because they are conventional, arbitrary. There are good reasons, connected partly with our education but also with the kind of world in which we live, for choosing one set rather than another. But there is no possibility of experimental support for Euclidean geometry, for experiments teach us only about the relations between bodies and not about the relations of bodies to space or of different parts of space to one another.[92]

Poincaré now turns to mechanics and finds a conventional element in the physical sciences generally. On the whole he accepts the English view of mechanics as an experimental science against the French view of it as a deductive, *a priori* science but regards this dichotomy as a little misleading owing to the failure of scientists to distinguish between the experimental, mathematical, conventional, and hypothetical elements in mechanics.[93]

The principle of inertia, that a body under the action of no force can only move uniformly in a straight line, is accepted in mechanics and is a particular case of the more general principle that the acceleration of a body depends only on its position and that of neighboring bodies, and on their velocities.[94] In neither form can it be either an *a priori* or an experimental truth. It cannot be *a priori* since the Greek view of motion conflicted with it. It cannot be an experimental conclusion since we cannot experiment with bodies acted upon by no force and there are situations in which its more general form could never possibly be falsified. For example, if the acceleration of a molecule which we cannot see appears to falsify the principle, we can always suppose that this acceleration depends upon the positions and velocities of other invisible molecules whose existence we have previously not suspected, and so

safeguard the principle. Thus it may be verified experimentally in certain cases but "may be extended fearlessly to the most general cases; for we know that in these general cases it can neither be confirmed nor contradicted by experiment."[95] Such principles first appear as experimental truths but become transformed into definitions. Although experiment serves as a basis for them, it will never invalidate them because they have become definitions.[96]

Poincaré uses an extended illustration to show how scientific conclusions are conventional. If the earth were always enveloped in thick clouds so that we had no knowledge whatever of the sun, the planets, or the stars, we could explain the flattening of the earth at the poles, Foucault's pendulum experiment, and related phenomena either by the hypothesis that the earth rotates or by a more complex hypothesis involving real centrifugal forces and a medium, such as the ether, exercising a repulsive action. More complicated explanatory devices could always be added if either hypothesis failed to fit the facts. There would be no grounds for arguing that one hypothesis was truer than the other, for all the phenomena could be explained on either. But just as Copernicus urged that the Ptolemaic system was not wrong but merely unnecessarily complicated, we could prefer the view that the earth rotates as the more economical view. There would be no means of discovering whether it really did or did not rotate.[97]

Experiment contributes to mechanics by showing which principles will be convenient. Mechanical statements are of two kinds, at least. Some are summaries of experimental results and are approximately verified for relatively isolated systems; others are postulates of greater generality, applicable indeed to the whole universe, rigorously true and beyond the reach of experimental test, their certainty being conferred upon them by us. The resemblance between geometry and mechanics, however, ends here. Experiments which lead us to regard one set of geometrical axioms as more convenient are not performed on the objects with which geometry deals, whereas the experiments which lead us to choose a convention in mechanics are performed on objects which are the same as, or analogous to, the objects with which mechanics deals.[98]

Poincaré calls the experimental conclusions "laws" and the conventional postulates "principles," and when he extends his account to cover every branch of science he makes it clear that he does not mean to say that the whole of science is conventional, since principles are not the whole of science. A primitive law, which is an experimental conclusion, always approximate, about the relation between two facts, is decomposed into an absolute principle and a revisable law connected by an invented concept. The empirical proposition (1) *The stars obey Newton's law* is broken up into (2) *gravitation obeys Newton's law* and (3) *gravitation is the only force acting on the stars.* Gravitation is an invented, ideal, concept and

(2) is a definition beyond the reach of experimental tests but (3) is open to test because it predicts verifiable facts. Propositions such as (3) always remain and are the non-conventional parts of scientific theories.[99]

"Experiment is the sole source of truth" and only through experiment can we obtain new knowledge. The role of mathematical physics is to direct our generalizations. In order that observations may be used it is necessary to generalize because only then can we predict. But when we generalize we also correct; if we have a number of points on a graph we generalize by drawing a smooth curve but we do not always draw the curve exactly through every point. We correct an experimental result rather than sacrifice the smoothness of the curve. This involves the presupposition that the law we seek is best represented by a smooth curve. In fact, no experiment is possible without preconceived ideas, although most of them are unconscious. In order that we should not be misled by them we should try to bring out the assumptions we make and so control them.

Every generalization presupposes a belief in the unity and the simplicity of nature. Poincaré justifies the first belief by saying that if "the different parts of the universe were not as the organs of the same body, they would not react one upon the other." The second is more difficult since we have a choice of generalizing any fact in an infinite number of ways. When we have no evidence in favor of one way of generalizing rather than another we choose the simplest without implying that the others are absurd. Usually, we take every law to be simple until the contrary is proved.[100]

Every generalization is a hypothesis and should be submitted to verification as soon as possible. If observation falsifies a well-considered hypothesis, this is important but not merely because we have removed the necessity of entertaining one more hypothesis. It may mean that we have ignored or failed to find some relevant circumstances so that we may be on the verge of a discovery. The result of falsification is thus not purely negative. If the experiment were made without the hypothesis it would probably happen that nothing extraordinary would be noticed and no stimulus be provided for a search for an unrevealed relevant factor.

Hypotheses, however, may be dangerous if they are accepted unconsciously or if they are unnecessarily multiplied. If they are tacit and unconscious we may not notice that, in a given situation, it would be advisable to regard them as falsified. Mathematical physics is valuable here because precision demands that we formulate *all* our hypotheses. It is a sound methodological principle to use as few hypotheses as possible because an experimental falsification of a statement derived from a number of hypotheses does not tell us which of these to reject, whereas a single hypothesis can be falsified conclu-

sively. Conversely, if the experiment is successful, we may mistakenly think we have confirmed all the hypotheses.

Poincaré distinguishes three kinds of hypotheses. When we make judgments of relevance we accept certain very general hypotheses, to the effect, for instance, that the influence of very distant bodies is negligible. These form the common basis of theories of mathematical physics and are the last that should be abandoned. They are *natural and necessary*. Calculation from two alternative hypotheses may lead to the same testable conclusions so that experiments cannot distinguish between the hypotheses. This is true of the alternative hypotheses that matter is continuous and that it has an atomic structure; experimental verifications cannot prove the real existence of atoms. Such hypotheses are *indifferent* and are not dangerous if they are seen for what they are, namely, useful artifices for calculation or pictorial aids to understanding. Direct generalizations from observations, open to test by further experiments, will always be fruitful, whether they are accepted or rejected. These are *real generalizations*.[101]

In experiment we try to "decompose" complex phenomena into elementary ones, with respect to time and space, to connect each moment in the development of the phenomenon with immediately contiguous moments and each point in space with immediately contiguous points. We accept as true *by and large* the hypothesis that there is no action at great distances. We also decompose complex phenomena in another way — complex bodies into elementary bodies and complex events into elementary events. Because observable phenomena may be decomposed in this way and regarded as due to large numbers of elementary phenomena similar to each other, they are conveniently described by differential equations and this accounts for the ease with which scientific generalization takes a mathematical form. Mathematical physics depends on the approximate homogeneity of the matter studied and allows us to "divine the result of a combination without having to reconstruct that combination element by element."[102]

Physical theories are ephemeral but this does not make them valueless. Fresnel's theory of light involved the movement of an ether; Maxwell's theory, which superseded it, did not. But Fresnel's theory was valuable because it enabled him to predict optical phenomena and this was his real object. He was not concerned to verify the existence of the ether or to discover its real nature, and his theory can still be used as a device for facilitating prediction because its differential equations remain true even though the theory as a whole is no longer accepted.

These equations express relations, which it is the aim of theories to discover, but the objects between which the relations hold are forever inaccessible to us. On one theory the differential equations refer to the motions of the ether, on another to electric currents, but to reject the first and accept the second is not to say that we have discovered that motions of the ether do not exist whereas electric currents do, but rather to say that the new theory is more helpful than the old. "Motion" and "electric current" are "merely names of the images we substitute for the real objects which nature will hide forever from our eyes."[103]

Theories show us the real relations between real objects and to this extent tell us truths about nature, but it is the structure of the theories rather than their content which corresponds to the world and constitutes these truths. When a theory is superseded, the content is replaced; but any true relations it has taught us remain. Thus the many different theories about the dispersion of light all give the same equations. Because of this, and because their premises have common features which are true, the different theories are simultaneously true in the only way in which theories can be true. The test of this truth lies in the verifiable applicability to the world of the relations it contains. The perfectly elastic spheres of the kinetic theory cannot be verified experimentally but the relations it gives between gaseous and osmotic pressures can be. "It will be said that science is only a classification and that a classification cannot be true but only convenient. But it is true that it is convenient, it is true that it is not only for me but for all men; it is true that it will remain convenient for our descendants; it is true finally that this cannot be by chance."[104]

Questions about the actual existence of theoretical entities, such as atoms and the ether, "are not only insoluble, they are illusory and devoid of meaning,"[105] because they are questions about what could never be observed and so are metaphysical. Such questions have at most a metaphorical sense and the scientist must recognize this. Mathematical theories in physics cannot reveal to us the real nature of things but can co-ordinate the physical laws we discover through experiments. If everything happens as if the ether exists then the theory of the ether is satisfactory for science. It is a possible explanation of those phenomena that can be deduced from it but a possible explanation is not necessarily *the* explanation, i.e., the correct explanation. To show that it was *the* explanation we should have to show that it was true in its entirety, but this is never possible. Moreover, there is no objection to using, as Maxwell does, irreconcilable and even contradictory theories about different phenomena in the same field. Even contradictory theories may be useful instruments of research and our suspicion of them is based on the mistaken idea that theories set out to explain.[106]

In the history of science we can discern two opposing trends. There is a movement toward unity and simplicity when we discover new relations between apparently unconnected objects, and a movement toward diversity and complexity when, with the help of better techniques, we discover new phenomena as we extend our knowledge in breadth and depth. If the first tendency wins, science is possible because "the true and only aim is unity," but if the second wins it is not. But there is no *a priori* method of showing which will win. Poincaré argues, with the help of the growing unification of the studies of light, electricity, and magnetism, that there are signs of a continued victory for the tendency toward unity. Certainly the victory is won only with a loss of simplicity, but unity is essential and simplicity only desirable.[107]

Pierre Duhem

DUHEM made original contributions to physics and was also a considerable historian and philosopher of science. His interest in the history of science was based largely on the belief that it is impossible fully to understand a scientific concept without a knowledge of its history and the problems it was designed to meet.

In the philosophy of science he regarded himself as a positivist and sought to show that science and metaphysics were logically independent but historically dependent. Like Mach he took a conventionalist view of scientific theories but was nearer to Hertz and Poincaré in his interest in the broad logical and systematic characteristics of theories rather than in the problems of perception and observation connected with their verification. His work is notable for the wealth of historical detail which he brings to support his conclusions about scientific theories. It must be said, however, that his enthusiasm for systematic theorizing led him to undervalue much of the work, especially on the atomic theory, which was going on during his lifetime.

He begins his work *The Aim and Structure of Physical Theory* with a discussion of the fundamental question whether it is the aim of physical theory to *explain* experimental laws or merely to summarize and classify them. His answer that its aim is *not* to explain depends upon his definition of "explain," which he states on the first page and which he appears to think needs no justification or discussion. "To explain . . . is to strip reality of the appearances covering it like a veil, in order to see the bare reality itself."[108] The observations on which physical science depends are unable to take us below sensible appearances to the hidden reality, and the subject-matter of laws is these appearances and not "material reality." The only study which can take us below the surface of sensible appearances is metaphysics; if the aim of physical theory were to explain, it would not be an autonomous science but would be subordinate to metaphysics, and agreement upon scientific questions would be impossible between adherents of different metaphysical views. But we justifiably desire universal consent for scientific theories. Duhem shows, by a historical examination of Aristotelian, Newtonian, atomistic and Cartesian metaphysics, that physical theories purporting to rest on metaphysical beliefs always involve laws which are dictated by the facts and which cannot be derived from metaphysical considerations. Behind the alleged explanations of science there always lies something unexplained.[109]

An aim which is not open to these objections Duhem finds in the view that physical theory is "a system of mathematical propositions, deduced from a small number of principles, which aim to represent as simply, as completely, and as exactly as possible a set of experimental laws." He supports this view by distinguishing the four fundamental operations by which a physical theory is constructed.

1. We select from among the physical properties we wish to represent those which can be regarded as simple and as combining to form the rest. With the help of measurement we represent these by mathematical symbols which have no intrinsic connection with the properties they represent but serve merely as signs.
2. We connect these symbols in a small number of propositions which serve as principles in our deductions. These do not claim to state real relations between the real properties of bodies but are arbitrary and convenient, and are controlled only by the requirement of logical consistency. These Duhem calls "hypotheses."
3. We combine hypotheses according to the rules of mathematical analysis. Again, the only requirements are those of logic and mathematics, and no real relations between properties are implied by these combinations.
4. The consequences we draw from the hypotheses are translated into statements about the physical properties of bodies, the methods of defining and measuring these properties serving as a kind of "dictionary" by means of which we perform the translation. We compare the resulting statements with the results of experiment; if they agree the theory is a good one, if not it is a bad one.[110]

"Thus," concludes Duhem, "a true theory is not a theory which gives an explanation of physical appearances in conformity with reality; it is a theory which represents in a satisfactory manner a group of experimental laws," and "agreement with experiment is the sole criterion of truth for a physical theory." The theory is tied to the phenomena at each end but in between there is no correspondence between the theory and the facts. It is like an airplane journey from point A to point B when we are indifferent to the time taken and the conditions of the journey. Our course does not matter so long as we start at A and arrive at B. The theory, like the airplane,

does not touch ground at any point between A and B but merely makes one of many possible connections between them.

The utility of theories is fourfold. They contribute to intellectual economy by enabling us to deduce large numbers of experimental laws from a few hypotheses or principles instead of having to learn and remember all the experimental laws. They allow us to classify laws in a methodical way into "family groups," and this helps us to apply them, to choose the right tool for a given job. Moreover, we feel that the more complete and consistent a theory becomes the more "natural" is this classification, that is, the more closely do the relations it establishes between the data of observation correspond to real relations between things. Finally, theories enable us to predict, to anticipate experiment. Success in this is the best indication of the naturalness of the classification.

Theories which set out to explain, and not merely represent, consist of two parts, one explanatory, the other representative, which are strictly independent of one another. It is the representative part which is important and fruitful and which may be common to rival theories. The explanatory part contributes nothing and the progress of physics is largely constituted by the dropping of the explanatory parts of theories and the consequent removal of points of unnecessary dispute. But, because the explanatory element in a theory is often replaced by a different explanatory element, historians of science have sometimes mistakenly thought that the progress of science is toward better explanations. Indeed, this progress would be more rapid if scientists themselves would admit that explanation is no part of their business.

Duhem, following Pascal, distinguishes two types of minds and two corresponding views of science. French scientists have, on the whole, abstracting minds; English scientists (e.g. Kelvin) tend to have visualizing minds. Duhem's view of physical theory commends itself naturally to abstracting minds but the visualizing mind will look more favorably upon the English method of using a pictorial representation or mechanical model, instead of a mathematical theory, as the device for connecting observations. One advantage, among many disadvantages, of the English method is that it emphasizes the fact that the scientist is not seeking explanations.[111]

But models appeal to the imagination rather than the reason and are not "dominated by logic"; they serve neither as explanations nor as rational classifications of physical laws. In consequence this view suffers from the severe disability that consistency and unity are not demanded by it; two conflicting models may be used for two groups of laws, even if the two groups are related. "Thus, in English theories we find those disparities, those incoherencies, those contradictions which we are driven to judge severely because we seek a rational system where the author has sought to give us only a work of imagination."[112] For various different purposes the material molecule is represented by spherical masses connected by spiral springs; by rigid, concentric, spherical shells held in that position by springs in a jelly-like ether; or by rigid shells each containing a gyrostat rotating around an axis on the shell. Each situation is treated in isolation from the others and an appropriate model constructed, no attempt being made to link them in a logical system. Duhem criticizes Poincaré for praising the English method, because, apart from its lack of rigor, fewer advances have been made with its help than is usually supposed. It is more useful as a method of exposition than as a method of discovery.[113]

On the other hand, if physical theory is simply a classification of experimental laws there is no logical ground for condemning one system of classification, but two different systems must not be confused. Duhem quotes Poincaré on this with approval. "Two contradictory theories can, in fact, both be useful instruments of research, provided that we do not mix them together and provided that we do not seek the bottom of things in them."[114] Nevertheless, we all, even the English physicists, prefer unified systems and tend to regard non-unified theories as provisional.

Duhem devotes the second section of his book to the structure of physical theories. The demand for logical rigor leads him to assert that theoretical physics is mathematical physics, which begins by representing observable appearances by numbers and algebraical symbols.[115] This does not mean that physics can study only the quantitative aspects of things, for the varying intensities of qualitative characters can be symbolized in this way. In the interests of economy, certain qualities of things are regarded as primary, as the irreducible primitive elements into which complex phenomena are analyzable. These elements should be as few as possible, and since physical theory does not seek to explain, it is not necessary to assert that the elements are ultimate in nature, *incapable* of further analysis, but only that we have not succeeded in analyzing them further. Their primacy is purely relative.

In the next stage the physicist works only with his symbols, seeking relations between them which will serve as principles for deductive development. This deductive development, the third stage, consists in adding further symbols representing initial conditions and deducing consequences, again in symbolic form, which can be "translated" back into the language of observation. The methods of measurement constitute a "dictionary" which makes the translation possible. A description of a phenomenon in observational language states a *practical* fact; that description translated into the symbols of the theory states a theoretical fact. Because the translation is an approximation involving abstraction and idealization, one practical fact may be represented by an infinity of theoretical facts. The deduced theoretical facts, on translation, give us practical facts, verifiable by observation and used to test the theory, but it is essential that the predicted practical fact should be definite enough for the experiment to check it unambiguously. The usefulness of predictions therefore depends upon the sensitivity of our instruments and powers of observation.[116]

A physical experiment consists of two parts, observation and interpretation. When an experimenter is observing a spot of light on a scale this may not be all he is doing; he may also be interpreting what he observes as the concluding step in measuring the electrical resistance of a coil. Observing requires only attentiveness and good eyesight but interpreting requires, in this example, knowledge of electrical theory. Duhem distinguishes between "the facts really observed" and the interpretations of them usually reported in scientific papers, which use accepted theories. Interpretation "substitutes for the concrete data really gathered by observation abstract and symbolic representations which correspond to them by virtue of the theories admitted by the observer."[117]

Laws of physics state relations between symbols which derive their meanings from the theories of which they form a part. The pressure and volume of a gas connected by Boyle's Law do not name the pressure felt and the size seen in ordinary experience but are symbols invented in the course of constructing an elaborate theory of gases. Common-sense laws, such as "The sun rises in the east," are either true or false, but scientific laws, stated in symbolic terms, are neither. They are, rather, approximate, representing more or less well the relations they are intended to represent. Many different theoretical laws will represent the same facts. "In order for each of these laws to be accepted, there should correspond to each fact not *the* symbol of this fact, but some one of the symbols, infinite in number, which can represent the fact; that is what is meant when the laws of physics are said to be only approximate." Since no physical law can *ever* do more than approximate to a group of facts, there can be no such thing as the one true law covering those facts. Because the symbols used in physical laws are always too simple to represent reality completely, the laws must always be provisional.[118]

Perhaps Duhem's most important contribution to the understanding of physical theory is his account of the testing and, especially, the falsification of hypotheses. In this, his view is a development of Poincaré's view. If empirical generalizations, such as "all swans are white," are taken as the pattern of a scientific hypothesis, it is clear that, although it can never be conclusively confirmed, one negative instance will conclusively refute it. But this is too simple a model, since a scientific hypothesis can never be tested independently of other hypotheses. A hypothesis is always part of a theory and it is along with other statements of the theory, and perhaps other statements of the theory, and perhaps other theories, that the hypothesis is used to make predictions. An unfulfilled prediction indicates something wrong with the hypothesis *or* some other hypothesis of the theory *or* another theory that has been assumed. The negative instance falsifies *something* conclusively but can give us no more certainty than that, for it does not uniquely identify the statement or statements which should be rejected. "In sum, the physicist can never subject an isolated hypothesis to experimental test, but only a whole group of hypotheses; when the experiment is in disagreement with his predictions, what he learns is that at least one of the hypotheses constituting this group is unacceptable and ought to be modified; but the experiment does not designate which one should be changed."[119]

In consequence, Duhem holds, there can be no crucial experiments in physics. As we are never able to compare two independent and conflicting hypotheses, we can never design an experiment which will conclusively decide between them. When we wish to do this, we always have to confront the whole theory in which one hypothesis is embedded with the whole theory in which the other is embedded, and when a complex theory rather than a single statement conflicts with an experimental result there is always the possibility of modifying the theory somehow so that it no longer conflicts. There is one exception to this which, however, seldom occurs. If two theories differ only in one statement it is logically possible to design an experiment to refute one of the theories conclusively. Duhem mentions this mainly for the purpose of stressing that this crucial experiment cannot conclusively *establish* the other theory since alternative theories, which the experiment does nothing to refute, are always possible.

Duhem rejects the view that scientific laws are arrived at by induction. Outstanding exponents of this view are Newton and Ampère, but their scientific work shows that their conclusions were not reached by this procedure. Their work, rather, supports Duhem's "symbolic representation" view of theorizing. No experiment in physics involves merely generalizing from observations; it also involves interpretation based upon the acceptance of a great deal of theory.

Only the conclusions of a theory can be directly tested by experiment. Its intermediate steps are not meant to be translated into practical facts and need have no physical meaning, for no operation can be devised for testing them. Even some concepts which appear to have a physical meaning do not. In a theory about gases we can consider the absolute temperature as varying between zero and infinity but no operational meaning can be given to this because, by definition, there could be no thermometer capable of measuring 0 degrees on the absolute scale.

Poincaré and E. Le Roy argued that certain fundamental hypotheses of physical theory cannot be contradicted by experiment because they are really *definitions*. For example, the statement that the acceleration of a freely falling body is constant defines "freely falling," and a body which appears to conflict with the statement leads us to say that it was not falling freely; it does not lead us to reject the law. But against this Duhem argues that certain hypotheses are regarded as uncontradicted by negative instances, not as a logical necessity, but only because they cannot be tested in isolation and we are free to choose which of the hypotheses under test to reject. This does not mean, of course, that the unrejected hypotheses need never be rejected in the face of new experiments, since the revision of the theory in which they figure may involve their revision either as a consequence of the revision of other statements or because a modification of just these statements will give the desired coincidence with experiment. We tend to leave definitions alone but we may modify them, since they are attempts to represent symbolically concepts formed in every-day experience, and new experiments may show that accepted definitions do not adequately do this. Indeed, the most sweeping and fruitful advances in physics are often the consequences of such modification, as in the work of Einstein.[120]

Hypotheses are not the conclusions of inductions nor are they the products of sudden creation. They are slowly and painfully evolved by a process of modification and testing and may be assisted, as Duhem shows by tracing the development of the Newtonian theory of universal gravitation from ancient Greek science, by metaphysics or astrology. Hypotheses are seldom *chosen* by the physicist; he just finds himself working with a hypothesis, whose origins may not be clear to him. The only conditions imposed by logical considerations are that no hypothesis shall be self-contradictory, that there shall be no inconsistency between hypotheses, and that they shall allow the mathematical deduction of testable consequences.[121]

Comment

IT is striking that the scientists of this period who were interested in the philosophy of science were mainly physicists. This was perhaps partly due to the fact that physics was more highly developed than the other sciences, which meant that it provided more relatively complete and independent theories for philosophical examination; much modern philosophy of science consists of the analysis of theories. Because of the extent of its development, physics had begun to impinge on other branches of science, and philosophical problems are always likely to arise on the borderlines of different studies. Moreover, the philosophical problems raised by physics tend to be sharper, more dramatic, and, because of the relative homogeneity and lack of complexity of its subject-matter, more easily handled. But, whatever the reasons, in spite of the very great advances resulting from the work of this period, the fact has, in one way, had an unfortunate effect on the philosophy of science. This is the prevailing tendency to regard the philosophy of science as identical with the philosophy of physics and to treat physical theories as the ideal patterns of all theories, even those of biology and psychology. Philosophers have been inclined to neglect any special study of the biological and social sciences and even, sometimes, to recommend the reductionist view that statements in these sciences can be reduced to purely physical statements.[122]

This is doubtless partly due to Mach's explicit rejection of the view that there are real differences between the various branches of science, based on his assertion that sensations constitute their common subject-matter. Even if we accept Mach's sensationalism, we are not therefore committed to regarding the philosophy of physics as constituting the whole of the philosophy of science. It is possible, and even likely, that different methods may be necessary for relating the different *sorts* of sensations dealt with by, say, physics and psychology, and that radically different kinds of theories may arise out of them. The statement that, because what is observed is basic to all sciences and can always be analyzed into elementary sensations, therefore no ultimate distinction can be made between branches of science, smacks of the *a priori*. What is needed to remove this suggestion is surely an examination of fruitful theories in these different branches to discover to what extent they are comparable to theories in physics.

However, there is no need to accept sensationalism. There are well-known general objections to this view, but we are interested here in those which are especially relevant to the philosophy of science. The first concerns the meaning to be attached to "subject-matter." Science begins with problems and it is reasonable to argue that part of its subject-matter is whatever raises these problems. But scientific problems are raised by bodies and processes and not by sensations, except perhaps in psychology, where we may enquire into the mechanisms by which sensations occur. Sensations just follow one another and there is no reason why one rather than another should follow any given sensation. The bent appearance of a straight stick half immersed in water raises a problem because calling it "a straight stick" implies that except under special conditions it will remain, and continue to look, straight in the future. When it does not look straight, we want an explanation. Admittedly, we can, if we like, analyze both the straight look and the bent look into complexes of sensations, but then we lose this implication; what right have we to be surprised if the second complex follows the first? It is only when we interpret the first in such a way as to give it priority and talk of "a straight stick" instead of sensations that we can ask how it comes about that what *is* straight *looks* bent. The problem is raised not merely by what we see but by the implications of our descriptions of what we see. Different kinds of bodies and processes raise different kinds of problems suitably studied by different branches of science.

The second objection concerns the relation between observations and laws, and depends upon the fact that there are different kinds of scientific laws. The view that laws relate sensations is more convincing as an account of laws which refer to "constitutive" properties, such as those of shape, than as an account of laws which refer to "dispositional" properties, such as solubility. The shape of a crystal is permanently available for observation but its solubility is not, since it always has shape but is not always dissolving. It is even less convincing when applied to laws which are clearly idealizations rather than generalizations from observed instances. Boyle's Law states that the volume of a gas at constant temperature is inversely proportional to its pressure, but no actual gas obeys this law exactly. It is said to apply to perfect gases, and can be made to apply to actual gases only with the use of a specific correction for each gas. Many of the most interesting and fruitful scientific laws are of this sort and cannot be regarded as abridged descriptions of observed facts. Even less can they be regarded as statements of the relations between our sensations. They are more like inventions than discoveries, more like statements about atoms than Mach allows. Indeed, his real view appears to involve a conflict consequent on his half realizing this. We misrepresent him in two ways if we merely say that he regarded laws as abridged descriptions of observed facts. In the first place, they are for him predictive and so refer to past but unobserved facts and to facts that may be observable in the future; a mere summary of actual observations could not be predictive. In the second place, he holds that they depend upon abstraction; in his notes added to the fourth edition of *The Science of Mechanics* (1901) he talks of Galileo's laws of motion as having been arrived at by "abstracting or idealizing" and says that "our mental representations of the facts of sensual experience must be submitted to *conceptual* formulation" (Mach's italics.)[123] He also says, in several places, that we "complete in thought facts that are only partly given."[124] If all this is difficult to reconcile with his official sensationalism, it at least indicates a greater awareness of the nature of scientific laws than is sometimes attributed to him.[125] Hertz, Poincaré, and Duhem, in their reference to the use of abstract symbols, were clearer about this.

In view of the fundamental position given by all our authors to observation it may be questioned whether they can be regarded as objecting to inductivism, and certainly they are not as thoroughgoing anti-inductivists as some modern philosophers of science.[126] Nevertheless, they laid the foundations of anti-inductivism, chiefly by their insistence that theories are not reached by induction but are conventional, invented conceptual systems linked with experience only through the methods of testing them. They agreed that theories may be *suggested* by observations but also that they may be, and have been, suggested by metaphysical or theological systems or in some more fortuitous way.

Further, they all, even Mach, had doubts about the possibility of "pure" observation, unprejudiced by implicitly accepted hypotheses. Empiricists have at times hoped to find certainty by isolating some core of experience about which we could not be mistaken, and Mach's sensationalism springs partly from this. It was hoped, especially by members of the Vienna Circle, that "basic propositions" or "protocol statements" could be found which, because they were merely records of immediate sensations, would be incorrigible. I can be mistaken in thinking I am seeing a red book but not in thinking I am having a specific color-sensation but, as soon became evident, immediately I try to make even the simplest statement recording my sensation I rely on past experiences, which I may misremember, and on hypotheses, which may be false. The correctness of the statement "This is red" or "I am having a sensation of red" depends on the correct relating of my present sensation with past ones in connection with which I used the word "red." No statement can be utterly singular, making no reference to past or future experiences: no description can refer only to what is before me now.

The more complex a description is, the more does it depend on past experiences, formulated or unformulated hypotheses, beliefs, and even theories. The simplest formulation of the problem of the straight stick which looks bent involves hypotheses about the past and future behavior of the stick, the implications of straightness, rigidity, and so on. Mach makes various scattered remarks suggesting that he saw this without realizing its full significance, as when he says that "description presupposes the interdependence of the descriptive elements"[127] and when he asserts the value of prejudice.

Duhem correctly distinguishes between the observational and interpretive parts of an experiment, but this need not conflict with the view that there is no such thing as pure observation, free from interpretation. A statement may be an observation statement relative to a given theory without being free from *other* hypotheses or theories. What we must demand, to avoid begging any questions, is that the observation statement should be free from, i.e., should not presuppose, the theory for which it is used as evidence.[128] Of course, it must be *possible* to interpret the observation statement in terms of the theory, otherwise it could not be used to test the theory, but this is only another way of saying that statements which are neutral as between the theory

under test and alternative theories must be deducible from these theories and open to observational testing. Indeed, it is perhaps true that a difference between scientific and metaphysical theories lies in the deducibility from scientific theories, but not from metaphysical theories, of testable statements which can be accepted as true even if the theory is not, but not as false if the theory is accepted as true.

This has connections with Popper's views that falsifiability is the criterion for this distinction and that the one ground for accepting a hypothesis is the failure of strenuous efforts to falsify it. Empiricists, including Bacon and Mill, have often stressed the value of the falsification of scientific hypotheses, but mainly as a means of eliminating false hypotheses. Our authors, especially Poincaré and Duhem, went farther and gave it a more positive value as leading to the discovery of hitherto unnoticed factors.[129] Moreover, Poincaré says that we must "look for those cases in which the rule stands the best chance of being found in fault" and illustrates the procedure by the example of the construction of a graph, quoted above.[130] This is important because it is often easier to find confirming than refuting instances unless we design our method in such a way that refuting instances will not be missed or ignored. Moreover, in spite of their expressed devotion to observation as the basis of all scientific investigation, they had the germ of the idea that an important method in science is the hypothetico-deductive method according to which scientific investigation begins not with bare observations but with hypotheses, consciously or unconsciously entertained, which the observations are meant to test. Mach says, "Without some preconceived opinion the experiment is impossible because its form is determined by the opinion. . . . The experiment confirms, modifies or overthrows our suspicion,"[131] and Poincaré that even if we wish to make an experiment without preconceived ideas this is impossible because we can never free ourselves from preconceived ideas.[132]

The value of falsification is, of course, that it can be conclusive, since one negative instance conclusively falsifies a general statement, whereas no collection of positive instances can conclusively establish it. However, as Poincaré and, in greater detail, Duhem showed, this conclusiveness cannot give us a very valuable kind of certainty since hypotheses are usually parts of theories and what we test is the whole collection of statements composing the theory. The falsification of the whole collection leaves us still to make the choice of the hypothesis to be rejected, and it may even be open to us to modify a previously accepted definition used in the theory instead of one of the hypotheses we regarded as under test. We can conclude with certainty only that some part of the theory must be modified but not that any given statement in it must be.

Although it is clear that induction as a procedure

is much less important than has been formerly supposed, it seems that the relation underlying this procedure is involved in the testing of theories and that positive confirmation, as well as falsification, is taken note of by scientists. Because the fulfilment of a prediction is less conclusive than its non-fulfilment it does not follow that it is of no importance. We must distinguish between the fact that a prediction has been fulfilled and the fact that it was fulfilled while we were doing our best to ensure that it would not be. The second fact gives us more right to rely on the first fact and the first gives us some right to rely on the general statements from which the prediction was made. The observation statement lends some support to the general statement deduced from the theory and since observation statements are particular we depend here on the inductive relation of particular statement to general statement. The more confirming observation statements we have, in circumstances favorable to falsification, the more strongly is our general statement, and so our theory, confirmed.

Concerning the hypothetico-deductive method, it is by no means certain that hypotheses must always precede observation, as distinct from the description of our observations. It is sometimes argued that even in noticing a similarity between two things, we depend upon our already having the concept of similarity and *interpreting* these things as similar. The disadvantage of this view is that it makes the process of concept formation mysterious, and difficult to understand and explain. This disadvantage is not shared by the alternative view that concepts are formed *from* experience, that similarity, for example, is perceived. In less primitive scientific contexts, however, it is surely true that unsystematic and haphazard observation may suggest hypothesis and that observations made with one hypothesis in mind may lead to the formation of other hypotheses concerning matters to which the first hypotheses is irrelevant. We may notice things even when we are not looking for them or thinking about them, or when we are looking for something else.

Although the work we are considering involves difficulties in so far as its basis is sensationalistic, it contributed greatly to our understanding of theories by stressing, through the idea of their conventionality, the notion that they can be regarded as systems analogous to pure deductive systems. The development of the method of "rational reconstruction" as a means of exhibiting the logical structure of theories, by treating them as abstract calculi interpreted with the help of empirical concepts and allowing the deduction of observationally testable consequences, was considerably assisted also by the work of Frege, Russell, and other mathematical logicians, who gave us the technique for making the method precise.[133] It is valuable because it makes clear the logical relations holding between observation statements and theoretical conclusions and forces us to make explicit

our unstated assumptions. It may even have the practical advantage of leading to the discovery of unrealized implications, that is, new predictions. The method has sometimes been mistakenly criticized on the grounds that it does not make clear the procedure by which theories are constructed, but this is to ask it to do what it was never intended to do; both aims are valuable, but the failure to distinguish them can lead to nothing but misunderstanding.

One consequence of the conventionalist account of scientific theories is that it has sometimes led people to the conclusion that different theories are alternative and equally valid ways of talking about phenomena and that there is, therefore, no sense in saying that they are true or false or even probable. This was encouraged by explicit statements of Poincaré, but even he argued that there is some justification for regarding acceptable theories as true in the limited sense that they mirror real relations between phenomena. Various linguistic accounts of scientific theories have arisen, partly, no doubt, under the influence of comparisons made by our authors between different theories and different languages and Mach's reference to rules for predicting phenomena. Among these are accounts of theories as "language systems," as systems of rules for inferring, and as maps with the help of which we find our way about among the phenomena.[134] It is impossible to discuss these in detail here but it may be said that they do less than justice to the explanatory function of science and that many scientists who are familiar with them are not convinced that they correctly represent the extent and nature of scientific achievement.

Mach errs in the direction of extreme formalism, as when he says that hypotheses of fluids or media are superfluous to theories of heat and electricity. It has been argued that physical theories are purely mathematical and that the terms of the mathematical structure get their meanings purely from the positions they occupy in this structure. But theories can be *applied*; indeed, that is their whole point, and in order that they may be applicable at least some of the abstract mathematical terms must be given physical meaning as well, that is, must be interpreted. This is a logical requirement and not just a convenient device for explaining a theory to the layman: the subtlest and most complex system of pure mathematics will not give testable consequences without such interpretation. Hypotheses about fluids and media are interpretations of the mathematical systems which form the backbone of theories of heat and electricity and even if these particular interpretations are inessential to those theories, *some* interpretation is essential. This increases the plausibility of the view that as we improve our theories and find better and better interpretations for our equations we are arriving at closer and closer analogies for structures and processes in nature.

The predictive function of theories is important,

indeed essential, for whatever else it does a theory must make some reference either to events in the future or to unobserved but observable events in the past. But when Mach asserted that theories were no more than convenient devices or rules for the prediction of future experiences he perhaps overestimated the importance of this function. Hertz, Poincaré, and Duhem were right to insist that this is not their only important function, that good theories at least represent true relations and that this is the reason why they have predictive power. The fact that alternative theories have relations in common which are retained when a theory is rejected suggests that these relations have some special claim to be regarded as corresponding to actual relations in the phenomena, even if the entities between which they hold remain mysterious. The fact that we may never be able to eliminate alternative theories implies that there is a conventional element in theories but not that they are arbitrary or that there is no non-conventional element.

Can we go further and say that scientific theories also explain? Duhem answers this with a firm "No!" because, he holds, only metaphysics can point to the hidden realities underlying the phenomena which science studies, and this is the only kind of explanation he admits. Mach's reply is less firm. There is no possibility of giving explanations which are ultimate and which make things intelligible. The only way to make things intelligible is by analysis and we cannot continue our analysis beyond sensations. Theoretical entities, such as atoms, are not explanatory because their existence cannot be confirmed; and even if it could we could still ask for explanations of *their* behavior. Scientific explanation, therefore, can only be the complete description of phenomena and this always leaves the basic elements unexplained and so unintelligible.

Against Mach and Duhem it can be urged that they take too narrow a view of what constitutes an explanation. In the ordinary way we accept explanations of different sorts, depending on the kind of thing to be explained and the extent of our knowledge. We regard a piece of behavior as explained when we are told the motives which led to it; an explosion when we discover that someone lit a match in the garage. Whether we accept an explanation as satisfactory or not depends on our knowledge; satisfactoriness is relative. If we know a great deal about behavior and psychology we may not be satisfied until we discover how a person came to have the motives attributed to him. If we already know that explosions are often caused by the lighting of matches in garages we may not be satisfied until we discover the relevant properties of inflammable vapors. Some explanations involve showing a connection between the event to be explained and other events, and this is none the less an explanation because we can continue to ask for explanations of those other events. The fact that there can be no

ultimate explanation does not imply that *no* explanation is possible.

If the events given in explanation are observable the explanation looks very like mere description, although even here the *connection* is postulated rather than observed; if unobservable events are given in explanation then *they* are postulated and the explanation consists in showing that these postulated events are such that they would give rise to just those observed events which require explaining. There is some justification for regarding this as the way in which science explains, as Hertz did. Explanations involving unobservables are analogous to those involving observables but differ in that we may never be sure that the postulated events occur. That is, science may be regarded as putting forward possible explanations, as Poincaré admits, and even, when many apparently unrelated consequences of a complex theory have endured the strain of severe testing, probable explanations. Of course, a possible explanation may not be *the* explanation, but it does not follow that it is not explanatory but only that it may not be *true*. Science can be said to have an explanatory character even if it can never claim to have found *the* explanations it is seeking.

Thus, although our authors, with the exception of Hertz, denied that the aim of science is to explain rather than describe, they put into our hands the method of exhibiting its explanatory character by means of rational reconstructions which show us how our invented concepts are linked with the phenomena, that is, how they could explain what we observe. Even if we cannot finally discover the truth, light either is or is not a wave motion, and if it is, this explains certain phenomena involving light because the phenomena can be deduced from the wave motion. If other phenomena involving light cannot be deduced from the theory this shows that light is not a wave motion, at least of the kind postulated. Metaphysical explanations are different. In a sense they are too powerful since they do not, like scientific explanations, explain why this rather than that event occurs; they explain indifferently anything that may occur and their truth forbids nothing. A good metaphysical theory can be accepted whatever observable events occur: a good scientific theory can be accepted only if certain observable events occur and certain others do not.

This lies behind the desire to eliminate metaphysics from science; it depends upon the view that the essential character of science is that it is controlled by, and testable in, experience. Hertz appears to have thought that science depends somewhere on untestable assumptions. Mach, Poincaré, and Duhem were more definite in their attempts to eliminate such assumptions. But none of them went to the lengths of some of their later admirers, especially the members and adherents of the Vienna Circle,[135] who regarded metaphysical statements as meaningless, not only scientifically but in a wider sense, to the extent of regarding them as unworthy of consideration by philosophers. Duhem clearly thinks there is an important place for metaphysics;[136] Hertz says "A doubt which makes an impression on our mind cannot be removed by calling it metaphysical; every thoughtful mind as such has needs which scientific men are accustomed to denote as metaphysical" and considers it worthwhile to defend science against metaphysical criticisms.[137] Mach thinks it a defensible pursuit of philosophy to search for broad general pictures of the world such as cannot be reached by science and refers to theology as a branch of knowledge.[138]

The difficulty attached to the elimination of metaphysical statements as meaningless, not only from science but from philosophy as well, is that any proposed criterion of meaningfulness is likely to exclude statements which many people regard as meaningful, and what right have we to do this? When reasonable people claim to find meaning in theological or metaphysical statements and spend time and effort in discussing them, it is difficult to avoid the suspicion that those who do not find them in the least meaningful may be failing to understand what is understandable. This is a problem which goes beyond our present field, but however unsatisfactory we may find the positivist solution, it has made us more cautious about relying, in science, upon statements which are not testable by observation, and about distinguishing, among those statements which we do accept, between those which are testable and those which are not. Whether we accept or reject metaphysical statements it can only conduce to better understanding if we see those statements we do accept for what they are.

Metaphysical statements have been, and still are, important for science in another way because they may develop into or suggest scientific theories, as Mach and Duhem went to considerable trouble to show.[139] We cannot, of course, argue from this that, since it would be shocking to suppose that scientists were influenced by meaningless collections of words, some metaphysical theories must therefore be meaningful. They may be meaningful but this argument does not show it, for suggestions for scientific theories may be found in dreams, fairy stories, meaningless noises, or, indeed anywhere. In favor of inductivism it can be said that even if theories are not arrived at by the strict inductive method of arguing from observed instances to generalizations, they may nevertheless sometimes be suggested by observations, either systematic or unsystematic, logically relevant or logically irrelevant. The fact that scientific theories are often at variance with common sense does not militate against this view, since what is suggested may look very different from what suggests. The purely mechanical models of Kelvin and the other English physicists do not deserve the scorn poured upon them by Duhem because these devices may be fruitful in suggesting new interpretations and new directions of investigation. Moreover, even metaphysical theories often contain concepts which are such that they could be suggested by observations or derived from them by paying attention only to certain features of what is observed and extrapolating or idealizing.

Finally, it may be said that the importance of the work of this period is that it has drawn our attention forcibly to the logical problems involved in scientific investigation and theorizing and has suggested techniques for approaching these problems. It has made us more cautious about the kinds of statement to which we attach weight and about the kinds of problem which we regard as scientific. It has led us to consider the distinction between metaphysical and scientific statements and, within science, the distinction between theoretical and observation statements. Of course, it has left many problems, such as the question of what we mean by "observation" in science, but because of the great clarification it produced those problems appear, at least, to be manageable.

23

F. H. Bradley

W. H. WALSH

FRANCIS HERBERT BRADLEY was born in London in 1846 and educated at the University of Oxford; his father was an Evangelical clergyman. Bradley failed to get first-class honours at Oxford, but his talents were recognized by Merton College, which appointed him to a fellowship in 1870. His fellowship carried with it no teaching duties and was tenable for life provided the holder did not marry; Bradley held it until his death. Soon after getting it he fell ill with a kidney disease and was never again in very good health, a fact which goes some way to explain his recluse-like life. He spent most of time either in Oxford, where he was seldom seen outside Merton, or in France; he corresponded, and entered into public controversies with, distinguished contemporaries like William James and younger men such as Bertrand Russell, but had few personal contacts with philosophers. Bradley admired French literature, detested George Eliot and thought Gladstone the incarnation of evil because he failed to rescue General Gordon. His pastimes are said to have included shooting cats with a revolver from the windows of his rooms in college. Bradley was appointed to the Order of Merit in 1924 and died in the same year.

EW PHILOSOPHERS HAVE EXPERIENCED such variations of reputation as F. H. Bradley. Universally acknowledged to be the presiding genius of British philosophy in the opening years of the century, and widely if less warmly admired for the rest of his lifetime, his fame fell rapidly after his death in 1924. In the 1930's he was commonly singled out for attack as a typical metaphysician which meant, for those who made the accusation, that his main philosophical contentions were not so much false as meaningless. Bradley, according to the view most prevalent in avant-garde philosophical circles at that time, was the last of a long series of speculative thinkers who had attempted the task of determining by purely *a priori* methods what must be the nature of that reality which underlies all appearances and which is, by definition, empirically inaccessible. Bradley called this supposed reality by the mysterious name of "the Absolute" and professed to prove various surprising things about it, but in fact the proofs were all fallacious, and the "positive news about absolute reality," to use a phrase of his own,[1] which Bradley claimed to give, was news from nowhere. It was added that he might not have been betrayed into these appalling confusions had he not been wedded to a logic which was viciously out of date. Bradley's reputation at this time certainly touched its lowest point;* more recently it has improved, partly perhaps because British philosophers have again begun to read his works instead of being content to abuse them from a distance, partly because of a more general change in the whole philosophical climate, and it is now common to acknowledge his analytical powers and the independence of his mind. It remains true, nonetheless, that there is little or no appreciation of his work as a metaphysician; the results of the "sceptical study of first principles" which he thought must lie at the center of any sound philosophy are still widely thought of as an unfortunate mistake.

I propose in this essay to enquire to what extent this side of Bradley's reputation is deserved, which means in effect asking if the account of his metaphysics given by his critics is correct. To that end I shall devote the first part of what follows to an outline of his leading metaphysical doctrines, as stated in *Appearance and Reality*, introduced by a brief summary of his earlier work in ethics and logic. I shall then go on to consider in the light of this the justice of some of the things that have been said about him.

Bradley came on the English philosophical scene at a time when it was full of life and movement. Only a few years earlier the views of John Stuart Mill, favoring utilitarianism in ethics, associationism in logic, and a form of naturalism in metaphysics, had been virtual orthodoxy; now they were everywhere

* A fellow-undergraduate, now a distinguished teacher of another subject, once said in my hearing that he would be ashamed to belong to the same college as Bradley.

subject to criticism. The critics were led by men like T. H. Green in Oxford and Edward Caird in Glasgow who were students of the classical German philosophers and believed that many of the contentions of Mill's "school of experience" depend on arguments whose inadequacies had long ago been exposed by Kant and Hegel; only the persistent ignorance and insularity of the English enabled them to continue to pass as respectable. Bradley joined with scarcely concealed pleasure in the task of dissipating the "mass of inherited prejudice" which obstructed philosophical advance, showing formidable powers as a controversialist from the first. It would be wrong, however, to suggest that he was at any time a merely negative thinker. He wanted not merely to destroy the doctrines to which he was opposed, but to state alternatives to them, and for this task he was in many ways better equipped than any other opponent of empiricism. Not only was he master of an incomparable philosophical style, at once lucid and eloquent; his capacity for self-criticism and awareness of the need for the strictest intellectual rigor in any piece of philosophical reasoning were altogether superior to those of Green or Caird. The latter were content to suggest rather than to prove that, despite first appearances, the universe is permeated by spirit; for all their freedom from strict religious orthodoxy, a certain piety entered into their philosophical outlook. Bradley's thought was hampered by no such consideration: he was ready to follow an argument wherever it took him. As some of his early admirers were to find to their discomfort, it sometimes took him to strange and unwelcome conclusions.

Bradley's earliest published work, his essay on *The Presuppositions of Critical History*, attracted surprisingly little notice; it was only with the publication of *Ethical Studies* two years later in 1876 that he began to gain attention. We need not summarize his ethical views at length here, but can confine ourselves to two points about them. First, though one of Bradley's main motives in writing the book was obviously to show up what he took to be the shoddy character of the moral philosophy of the self-styled "advanced thinkers" of the time, utilitarianism was by no means his only target. Certainly he argued that notions like that of the greatest sum of pleasures, along with the accompanying political idea of the individual supposed to be real apart from all social relations, cried out for critical analysis, which would show that they could be held to only by a combination of vicious abstraction with an obstinate refusal to think. But Mill was not the only philosopher to be a prey to such abstraction. The Kantian theory of "duty for duty's sake" was riddled with contradictions as surely as the hedonist's idea of "pleasure for pleasure's sake": nothing was gained if we eschewed a one-sided sensationalism only to embrace an equally one-sided rationalism. This suspicion of abstraction in any form was to remain one of the leading elements in Bradley's thought. To avoid it in ethics we must look at the realities of the moral world and see the moral agent as operating inside a living community, by whose traditions and practices his mind was shaped, though he might well help to modify them in his turn. Only thus could the moral law be exhibited as what it is commonly taken to be in practice, not an alien abstraction but a "concrete universal." In this positive theory of ethics we have the prefiguring of one of Bradley's main metaphysical ideas: he saw the universe as well as the moral world as a unity in diversity, the components of which were real only so far as they belonged to something wider than themselves, while that something could not be what it was without them.

The sentiments as well as the language of *Ethical Studies* were to an important degree Hegelian; yet it is doubtful whether Bradley was even at this stage the simple Hegelian he was often alleged to be. He had certainly moved a long way from Hegel when he published his next book, *The Principles of Logic*, in 1883. Not only did he argue, in explicit opposition to Hegel, that logic could be treated as a "special science" in relative isolation from metaphysics: he chose in his detailed treatment of logical questions to discuss them "from a level not much above that of common sense," to use his own description. So far from detracting from its merits, this procedure gave his work a freshness and a down-to-earth quality which are conspicuously lacking in the corresponding volume by his smoother and more orthodox colleague Bernard Bosanquet. The astonishing thing about Bradley's *Logic*, indeed, is the extent to which it remains readable and pertinent even today.

The plan of the book is similar to that of *Ethical Studies* in so far as it is Bradley's aim in it to expose two opposite errors: that committed by the British empiricists when they sought to reduce judgment and inference to psychological operations with ideas, and that embodied in the traditional logic, which compressed mental operations into a few pre-ordained forms. Against the first Bradley argues, with complete cogency, that the idea with which logicians are concerned is not a part of anyone's mental history; judgment is not a psychological union of two ideas, but the reference of an ideal content to reality. Against the second he makes a variety of points which have become commonplaces in logic, despite the underlying differences in Bradley's attitude to formalism and that of most subsequent logicians. He points out, among other things, that the grammatical subject of a statement is not necessarily identical with its logical subject; that not every proposition can be taken as attributing a predicate to a subject; that universal statements are best analyzed as hypotheticals; that the view that all deductive inference is syllogistic is patently false. Russell was clearly not a student of Bradley's *Logic* for nothing.

It must be confessed that Bradley himself set relatively little store by these technical innovations. They were important to him not for their own sake, but only so far as they contributed to the solution of what he regarded as the main problem for the philosophical logician, the discovery of whether any form of statement is adequate to express the full and precise nature of fact. Bradley put this problem in his own way by asking whether we can anywhere find a judgment which is wholly categorical. His answer in the *Logic* was an unqualified "no." Whether we take the simplest judgment of sense or the most complicated judgment of science, we find in every case that their truth is conditioned by something which lies beyond them. The reality they seek to express is a fragment torn from a wider context, a part of a whole whose existence cannot be ignored when it comes to assessing truth. There is, moreover, a further difficulty to be considered. Not only is it practically impossible for a man to get at the fact he wants to express in entire independence of the wider reality it implies: the means of expression he possesses to bring out the nature of that fact are one and all fatally deficient. Human thought and language are irremediably general and abstract, and hence unsuited to do justice to the individuality of the real. Accordingly no statement a man makes can quite mean what it says or say what he means. This is the background to the famous declaration at the end of the *Logic* that "unless thought stands for something that falls beyond mere intelligence . . . a lingering scruple still forbids us to believe that reality can ever be purely rational. . . . Our principles may be true, but they are not reality. They no more *make* that Whole which commands our devotion, than some shredded dissection of human tatters *is* that warm and breathing beauty of flesh which our hearts found delightful."[2]

It is clear enough that these conclusions depend not merely on a clear-cut and decided view of the nature of thought, but also on a firmly-held view of the nature of things; clear again that there can be no adequate justification of such a view so long as we remain within the bounds of logic as Bradley conceived them. To round off his logic (and his ethics, too for that matter) he needed to set out his metaphysics, and this he did in *Appearance and Reality* in 1893. We must now give a brief account of the main arguments of that work.

Appearance and Reality

'APPEARANCE AND REALITY' is divided into two parts, of which the first is much the shorter. It comprises, in effect, an examination of a number of well-known metaphysical ideas, the result of which is in every case a clear failure. It may be useful to try to give some idea both of the candidates summoned and of the kind of test to which they are forced to submit.

The candidates are really familiar enough figures, though they appear in a slightly misleading guise: they represent views of the world which are associated with common sense, popular science, or popular religion. Bradley found these views in general currency in his own time, as they have continued to be in our own, and believed that the first object of a metaphysician must be to expose their general inadequacy. His procedure was to take the leading ideas of which the view under examination consisted, and to ask whether it could form part of a tenable theory of first principles, capable of giving a coherent interpretation of experience. Bradley's verdict in each case was that this requirement could not be satisfied: the view under examination, when we came to think it out, was seen to dissolve in contradictions. Whatever the practical utility of the ideas it involved (and Bradley laid special stress, as we shall see, on their value as qualifying "appearances"), they could not be said to aid us in giving a description of things as they really are.

We must now try to elaborate and illustrate this very abstract account. Among the notions which Bradley examines in this part of his work are these. First, the view, common enough among philosophically-minded students of natural science, that we can get at the truth of things by distinguishing two sorts of qualities in them, primary and secondary, the first of which indubitably characterize them while the second are derivative and subjective. Secondly, the common-sense idea that the familiar categories of thing, quality, and relation, together with the everyday notions of space and time, suffice for a full and adequate description of the world. Third, the slightly more sophisticated idea that whatever difficulties may be involved in ascribing reality to the external world, the self or soul is palpable and intelligible fact. Perhaps the most attractive feature of Bradley's procedure is the impartiality with which he conducts his examination: so far from being biased in favor of the self, as some of his readers no doubt hoped that he would be, he subjects this particular idea to the most devastating of criticisms, showing that those who fall back on it have little or no conception of what it really involves. As an example of his detailed treatment we may select what he has to say about the common-sense notion of things. Everybody would agree that a thing is a unitary something to which a diversity of properties is attributed; the difficulty is, however, to see how the unity and diversity are related. A thing, as we see on reflection, is not merely the sum of its properties, but equally it is nothing when taken apart from its properties. The properties, again, make up a plurality, but not a mere plurality: there is order and relation among them, the order of temporal succession, for instance, or of spatial juxtaposition. Yet what sort of a thing is this relatedness of properties which is thus thought to give unity to the thing? On the one hand it is nothing apart from the

properties: that qualities appear in certain relations is not just an external fact about them, but depends on what they are, or rather on the nature of the thing to which they belong. This seems to make relatedness of the properties itself a higher-order property, and thus to leave the problem of the unity of the thing where it was. On the other hand we cannot follow Leibniz in denying the reality of relations altogether: the notions of property and relation are born together. Yet how the two notions can be harmonized is not apparent. Quality implies relation, and relation quality, but the two ideas are for all that obstinately diverse. To use either without the other is ruled out; to use both, as of course we commonly do, is "a makeshift, a device, a mere practical compromise, most necessary, but in the end most indefensible."[3]

It will be useful at this point to pause and ask what is the principle underlying this argument, both because of its initially puzzling character and because the answer will take us to the very center of Bradley's metaphysics. Most of us would be ready to agree that the notion of a thing is somewhat vague, both in what precisely it includes and in what it applies to. Most of us, again, might on reflection be got to agree that there is, after all, a relation, not easy to specify, between the properties a thing has and the relations in which it stands. But to most people the relatively unthought-of character of these ideas, even their possible incoherence, is no obstacle to their successful use: after all, are there not many true propositions in which they function, e.g., "there is a black telephone on my desk"? What then was Bradley's objection to them? One answer, though not an adequate one, is that he was considering not so much the everyday as the metaphysical use of the ideas in question. It would never have occurred to him to deny that the statement about the telephone was or might be what he called a "finite truth," true enough for practical or everyday purposes: the passage quoted above, which comes from a discussion of "the machinery of terms and relations," makes that clear enough. The problem of metaphysics, however, is not practical but theoretical; provisionally it may be said to be that of giving a description of the world in terms which are fully coherent. In tackling that problem we cannot be content to make do with unexamined notions: metaphysics must be pursued in a spirit of full self-criticism or not be pursued at all. The trouble about the metaphysics of common sense is that it does not satisfy this requirement.

We may well imagine a follower of Professor Moore replying to this that even if common sense does not examine its ideas, it very well might, with results which could perfectly well be satisfactory. The trouble is, however, that Bradley and Moore have different notions of what it is for an idea to be satisfactory in metaphysics. At the beginning of part II of *Appearance and Reality*, where he makes explicit the criterion used in the rejection of popular theories in his first part, Bradley lays down the principle that "ultimate reality is such that it does not contradict itself."[4] To many more recent philosophers these words would suggest no more than the truism that no one true statement of fact can be inconsistent with any other. But that Bradley means more by them than that is shown by such alternative formulations as that "the character of the real is to possess everything phenomenal in a harmonious form,"[5] or again that "reality . . . has a positive nature exclusive of discord."[6] These phrases imply that, for Bradley, the world is not merely, as Wittgenstein put it, "everything that is the case"; it is everything that is the case seen as constituting a single self-differentiating system. And his point against Moore is that a world of things, or of qualities and relations existing side by side, could not be construed on these lines. Such a world, like that imagined by Hume in which all events are loose and separate and every perception a substance,[7] would be at best a loose aggregate, not an intelligible unity in diversity. Ideas which conduce to no better result than this can scarcely be pronounced metaphysically satisfactory.

A skeptic might still enquire why Bradley was so sure that reality is "harmonious" in the peculiar sense just explained. Why will it not do to see things in the Moorean or, if we prefer it, the Russellean and Humean way? Bradley's answer to this question is that we know that reality is individual, which means in effect individuated but undivided, and know it on the strength of two pieces of evidence. The first is the occurrence of the state of "feeling," a term which Bradley uses to designate the primitive form of experience which is presupposed by, and develops into, thought proper. Feeling is not strictly a form of awareness or apprehension, since the distinction of self and not-self is not made at this level; it might, however, be described without too much inaccuracy as a quasi-awareness, a state in which a certain content is presented or appears. Now the peculiarity of feeling, and the point Bradley finds significant about it, is that this content is at once manifold and unitary. We can be said in feeling to experience a totality, but a totality whose parts are not discriminated, and indeed cannot be without moving outside feeling proper. The world as it comes to us in feeling, our immediate point of contact with reality, is thus a whole whose parts are at once indubitably there and yet do not exist in separation; that this was, so to speak, our original intuition of the real seemed to Bradley highly significant. But he did not rely on the argument from feeling alone. Feeling is a transitory and unstable state: it scarcely comes before we are at work transforming it into something else. As soon as we take cognizance of the felt totality, a process which itself involves sharply discriminating subject from object, its elements fall apart and the original whole is dissolved. But the memory of it is not entirely lost, if Bradley is to be believed. For though

the world which relational thought constructs on the basis of feeling neither is nor can be, for reasons which have already been indicated, either fully individuated or fully integrated, it remains thought's aspiration to reconstitute the whole which it necessarily breaks up, to restore the innocence, as Bradley picturesquely puts it, which existed before the Fall. Nothing short of system, and system carried down to the level of individual detail at that, will satisfy the intellect as an ideal of knowledge, nor is its operation affected by the evident fact that it could not be attained unless the intellect as we know it were to commit suicide in transforming itself into a "higher intuition."[8] Given that it is in the nature of the human mind to seek truth, that it has this ambition to comprehend reality as an individual whole would certainly afford a presumption that this is how it really is.

The Absolute

I SHALL not stop now to try to assess the value of these arguments, but shall proceed at once to exhibit the bearing of the whole topic on Bradley's concept of the Absolute. Few ideas in philosophy have occasioned more misunderstanding, yet it is at bottom quite unmysterious. The Absolute, to put the matter most shortly, is simply Bradley's name for what I called above "everything that is the case seen as constituting a single self-differentiating system." To speak of the Absolute is not to draw our attention to a new entity, occupying a region somewhere beyond the range of sense-experience; it is rather to urge on us a certain way of looking at familiar facts. The particular things and events of everyday life, though not illusory, are nonetheless misconceived if taken as fully real; to comprehend them properly we need to see each of them in a different light. We need to take every allegedly separate element in the world as a fragment torn from a wider context, every apparent reality as part of a wider reality within which it evidently falls. The one reality to which all that is belongs, is for Bradley a single self-differentiating and self-individuating system. It is, in short, the Absolute.

To round out this brief summary of Bradley's metaphysics it will be useful to notice and comment on three assertions which Bradley makes about the Absolute in his chapters on "The General Nature of Reality" at the beginning of part II of *Appearance and Reality*. The first is that the Absolute must contain all its appearances: "we may say that everything, which appears, is somehow real in such a way as to be self-consistent."[9] The second is expressed in the statement that "the Absolute is one system, and its contents are nothing but sentient experience."[10] The third is that it is harmonious not merely in the theoretical way in which Spinoza's *Deus sive Natura* might be said to be harmonious, but also as excluding what Bradley calls "practical defect and misery."

As will be noticed, each of these assertions is no more than general: detailed knowledge of the Absolute, as Bradley is never tired of insisting, is precluded by the fact that the "higher intuition" spoken of above is an idea, not a reality. Each of them, as will appear, readily gives rise to misunderstanding.

The point of saying that everything which appears must belong to the Absolute is, I think, twofold. First, it is to emphasize that appearance is not illusion. "Our appearances no doubt may be a beggarly show," Bradley writes in a not too happily phrased passage, "and their nature to an unknown extent may be something which, as it is, is not true of reality. That is one thing, and it is quite another thing to speak as if these facts had no actual existence, or as if there could be anything but reality to which they might belong."[11] We have seen earlier that if we try to operate with a concept like "thing" or "time" in a metaphysical way we are led to contradict ourselves. But though our thought is thus ultimately incoherent, it does not follow that it is sheer error. We may not succeed in qualifying the real, but at least we succeed in qualifying appearances. We are not, that is to say, simply misconceiving things, or talking about something which has no existence except in our own imaginations, when we use these concepts. Nor is it the case that every such concept is equally far from ultimate truth: as Bradley was to argue in a later chapter, there are degrees of truth and reality, measured by the twin tests of coherence and comprehensiveness. There are problems here to which we shall need to return; meantime, we may note a second aspect of the dictum that the Absolute contains all its appearances, namely that it serves to express Bradley's rejection of any sheerly transcendent reality. The Absolute, however remote it sounds, is not a Kantian thing-in-itself or a Spencerian unknowable: it is something continuous with, and immediately relevant to, what goes on here and now. This is not to say that it is simply the sum of what goes on here and now, supposing that idea to be capable of clarification: such a "shallow Pantheism," as Bradley calls it,[12] would have no more worth than a doctrine of "empty transcendence." The Absolute is certainly more than those of its appearances which we know, but it both includes these appearances and would not be what it is without them.

The view that reality is "sentient experience" is peculiarly liable to misinterpretation, as Bradley himself points out. The meaning we naturally attach to it is that nothing exists except experiencing subjects, souls, or selves, which would make Bradley subscribe to a version of the idealism of Berkeley. Such a view could hardly be more mistaken, for the distinction between the experiencing subject and the "external" world he experiences, as we have already had occasion to notice, arises inside experience rather than antedates it. Self and not-self are distinguished within an original felt totality; to think of the totality as itself the "adjective" of a subject is to confuse levels disastrously. Bradley is as much of a realist as he is a subjective idealist; he echoes Kant and anticipates Wittgenstein in arguing that the notion of the self makes no sense except by contrast with what is not the self. Of what then does his idealism consist? I suggest, in affirming that reality comes to us in the form of immediate feeling, in which what is potentially subjective can no more be dispensed with than can what is potentially objective. To isolate either and set it up as reality is to make a wholly unjustified abstraction. Bradley's idealism recognizes this point; realist epistemologies do not.*

The third of Bradley's assertions about the Absolute is altogether more difficult. The concept of the Absolute, as we have hitherto expounded it, is so used by Bradley that the Absolute is the name of that wider reality within which everything that exists must be thought to fall if we are to think of it coherently. The Absolute here is what must be supposed to be whether we like it or not. Spinoza reached a similar position when he argued that the existence of any finite thing carried with it the existence of an infinite substance. But though Spinoza was prepared to allow that there was a sense in which his infinite substance could be spoken of as "perfect" (roughly, that of being complete and self-contained), he notoriously refused to ascribe to it any moral or aesthetic predicates. For him, God or nature was neither good nor bad, neither beautiful nor ugly, neither admirable nor the reverse. Bradley, by contrast, believed that "our main wants — for truth and life, and for beauty and goodness — must all find satisfaction"[13] in the Absolute; in short, that what is supremely real is also supremely valuable. We may well ask what arguments he had for so bold and far-reaching a conclusion.

We may notice at once that he never pretended to have any *direct* argument. He did not, that is to say, suggest anything so crude as that the Absolute must have value because we should be dissatisfied with it otherwise. The "wants" of our nature reveal nothing about how things are, and it is the purpose of metaphysics to say how things are, to satisfy the intellect and not, for example, the will or the sensibility. Nothing but confusion could come from mixing up what ought to be with what is. But though a direct argument for ascribing value to the Absolute could not be found, Bradley believed that the conclusion could be established by indirect means, by showing the impossibility of the opposite view. Suppose, he said, that it were the case that there were unsatisfied desire or practical unrest in the Absolute, or a balance of pain over pleasure there: such a state of affairs would not be compatible with theoretical harmony. It would not be compatible because unsatisfied desire, for instance, involves

* Compare in this connection the concept of a wholly objective sense-datum, developed by Moore and Russell as part of a realist answer to Bradley.

"an ideal element not concordant with presentation but struggling against it,"[14] or again, "the struggle of diverse elements, sensations or ideas, barely to qualify the self-same point."[15] Remove this discord and this struggle (and to speak of the universe as theoretically harmonious supposes that they must be somehow removed), and unsatisfied desire disappears. Bradley expresses some reservations about the applicability of this line of reasoning to pain, regarding it as a bare possibility that pain might be compatible with harmony and system, but clearly thinks it otherwise compulsive.

We may well wonder whether Bradley's indirect argument does not reintroduce the principle he condemned in rejecting a direct approach, for the "idea" which reality fails to accommodate in unsatisfied desire is not an idea of what reality is, but of what it ought to be. To pursue this matter here would, however, clearly be inappropriate: we must be content to refer to Bradley's detailed chapters on such topics as error, evil, and goodness for an elaboration of his point of view. Nor can we carry this outline account of his metaphysical doctrines further. There are, of course, many discussions of importance to which no reference has been made in the present summary, notably those of the crucial chapter on "Thought and Reality" which reiterate the skeptical conclusions of the *Logic* about the rationality of the real. It was this part of Bradley's work which caused those who stood nearest to him most embarrassment,* for it was here that he diverged most from orthodox Hegelianism. It remains true, nevertheless, that the divergence struck most of Bradley's critics as a domestic issue inside the idealist school: his work was, in their view, open to attack whatever the rights and wrongs of this matter. We have perhaps given a sufficient account of Bradley's metaphysics for the purpose of understanding these independent critics, to whose arguments we must now turn.

Bradley's Critics

THE criticisms of Bradley I want to consider were nearly all originated by Bertrand Russell and G. E. Moore. These two philosophers, each of whom had been briefly under Bradley's spell as an undergraduate, combined in the early part of their career in the negative work of overthrowing what they took to be false doctrine; later their paths diverged, and it became apparent that the standpoints from which they had directed their criticisms were by no means identical. It turned out that Russell had attacked Bradley in the interests of science, whilst Moore did so in the name of common sense.

In one important respect Moore and Russell

* Caird went so far as to say that the conclusion of *Appearance and Reality* amounted to "a manifest self-contradiction".

were at one. They both believed that a primary reason for Bradley's reaching untenable, and indeed absurd, conclusions, was his reliance on an inadequate logic. Bradley, they held, was at bottom an adherent of the subject-predicate logic of tradition, whatever he might have had to say against traditional logic. It was this, for instance, which blinded him to the need for an independent logic of relations, an appreciation of which would have saved him from much nonsense on the subject of relation and quality. Again, Bradley inherited from Hegel a deplorable tendency to confuse the "is" of predication with the "is" of identity, and both with the "is" of existence. His attitude to logic was faulty in yet another way, in so far as he set too much store by logical considerations, allowing himself to be led by them into condemning whole aspects of the world of whose existence and validity he might have been convinced by simple observation.

The repetition of these and other charges about Bradley's deficiencies in logic was certainly a powerful factor in diminishing his reputation. As time went on it was increasingly believed that those who accepted the "new" logic, as it was called, must be philosophically at an enormous advantage over their more old-fashioned colleagues; the very great prestige which Russell deservedly acquired as a result of his work in mathematical logic worked in his favor in metaphysics too. The idea got about that Russell and Moore were wielders of powerful new tools, the possibilities of which were totally unknown to Bradley. Yet if we look at the facts it is hard to substantiate this impression. Only the very slightest acquaintance with his writings is needed to show that Bradley was far from being simple-minded in logic: the innovations he introduced into logical doctrine are sufficient testimony to that. It is true that he held that every judgment, whatever its ostensible form, should be rephrased to read "Reality is such that . . . "; but it was metaphysical argument (to the effect that a plurality of reals is impossible), not logical naïveté, which led him to that conclusion. It is true again that there are passages in his writings where he seems momentarily to play on different senses of the verb "to be," but it is hard to think that the apparent equivocation plays any real part in his argument. So far as it occurs, it belongs to a preliminary stage of dialectical sparring rather than to the serious deployment of a case. As for the charge that Bradley placed too much reliance on logic and too little on observation, this is really part of a more general complaint that Bradley's philosophy flies in the face of common sense, and will be best considered as such when we deal with the criticisms of Moore.

Russell's objections to Bradley turned partly on method, partly on detailed execution. As regards method, Bradley was, he thought, altogether too sanguine in hoping to construct an overall theory of reality. Experience had shown in the past that such theories could never be definitely established —

there were always some competent philosophers to be found who objected to them — and something different was needed if philosophy was to become scientific. Russell thought his own "logico-analytic" method supplied that something different; its introduction, he argued, would give us "piecemeal, detailed and verifiable results" in place of "large untested generalities recommended only by a certain appeal to the imagination."[16] Roughly, Russell proposed to investigate what a later philosopher has called "limited and precisely defined philosophical questions about the elucidation of known facts," instead of indulging in "very general and abstract metaphysical speculations about possible facts or about the world as a whole."[17] He thought that the right way of going about these questions was to introduce a carefully defined technical vocabulary in which to discuss them. And he suggested that though this would make philosophy less generally attractive, because more professional, it would give the subject an intellectual respectability which it lacked altogether when practiced by a Bradley.

This is not the place to attempt any estimate of Russell's own philosophical achievement; we can remark only in connection with what has just been said that later "analytic" philosophers have been less ready to believe that philosophical problems can be tackled "piecemeal" and less disposed to think that the way to advance the subject is to introduce new technical terms into it. The notion that philosophy can be turned into a science if it limits its attention to critical problems and is content to accept second-order status is perhaps still philosophical orthodoxy in Great Britain; to that extent Russell's views have prevailed. But it is increasingly hard to justify, and if justification by results were demanded, it is hard to see where they can be found. One conclusion we might draw from reflection on the experience of the last forty years is that philosophical analysis cannot have the metaphysical neutrality which some of its early practitioners thought its greatest attraction. Whether he likes it or not the analyst accepts a certain point of view, has his own conception of the world as a whole, and his work convinces only those of his readers who share it.[18] Why, then, Bradley should be condemned for consciously attempting to formulate a "constructive" philosophy is not evident.

One suspects that Russell's real objections to Bradley lay not so much in what he attempted as in the conclusions he came to. For after all Russell had a metaphysical doctrine of his own, embodying a distinctive way of looking at the world. His view was in many ways the precise antithesis of Bradley's. Bradley argued that no fact was intelligible in isolation: to understand anything you had to pass beyond it, eventually seeing it in relation to the universe as a whole. Russell maintained that to understand any fact, you had, unless it were already simple, to reduce it to its basic elements: every fact must ultimately be built up out of atomic facts. Bradley's universe was close-knit, every part of it having a bearing on every other; Russell's consisted of a plurality of separate reals whose relations were purely external. Now Russell of course had detailed arguments against accepting Bradley's point of view: he rejected Bradley's account of relations and held that Bradley's case for the coherence theory of truth was anything but watertight. Unfortunately, his arguments rest on assumptions which Bradley was not prepared to grant, such as that we can make a sharp and absolute distinction between questions of logic and questions of fact, or again, that if there is to be truth anywhere, some statements must be absolutely and finally true. I am not wishing to say here that Russell was wrong to make these assumptions: my point is rather that his making them was bound up with his having a particular conception of reality. The reason why Russell and Bradley made so little impression on each other in their various controversies was not that either was stupid but that neither had any use for the other's way of looking at the world. To Russell, Bradley's talk of unity in diversity was simply confused, and the appeal to feeling to give sense to this idea quite without effect. To Bradley, Russell was obtuse in failing to see the obvious fact that all relations fall within a wider whole which must eventually determine them. We shall have to ask at the end of this chapter what lesson is to be drawn from this failure of two very able men to attain mutual comprehension.

Before turning to Moore it will be useful to consider another group of Bradley's critics, who were influenced by Russell though they were singularly blind to certain aspects of his thought. To the logical positivists, whose ideas briefly dominated British philosophy in the late 1930's, Russell was the supreme example of a virtuous analytic philosopher, Bradley the supreme example of a misguided metaphysician. Bradley as they saw him was a man who professed to tell us what things were really like, and to do so on the strength of purely rational considerations; the propositions he put forward thus claimed to be at once factual and *a priori*. But since all ordinary facts were open to empirical investigation, the facts which Bradley claimed to reveal must be of a very special nature. They must be facts about "reality" as opposed to "appearance," where reality is understood to be beyond the reach of the senses. Bradley showed his own cloven hoof in this matter by saying that the subject of his metaphysical propositions was the Absolute. But we had only to enter into the simplest reflection, his critics said, to see that this was no more than an empty phrase. Ask yourself only how you would set about deciding the truth or falsity of any pretended statement about the Absolute, and you would see at once that it must be a "pseudo-proposition," grammatically correct no doubt but lacking all "literal significance." As for the question how a presumably intelligent man could persuade himself that the truth might be otherwise, the answer must once more be through bad logic, though anti-scientific bias and a hankering after the comforts of religion might perhaps be contributory factors.

The short answer to this is that the logical positivists had entirely failed to understand what Bradley meant by "the Absolute"; not surprisingly perhaps, since they clearly regarded his work with aversion and kept as far away from it as possible, but inexcusably just the same. They took the term to designate a singular entity, and, since they could find nothing in their own experience for it to apply to, decided that it must be intended to name something supersensible. The Absolute was, perhaps, a secularized version of God. We do not need to read much of *Appearance and Reality*, however, to see that the idea of the Absolute involves something quite different from that of the God of popular religion, assuming that the latter is taken to be a person or spirit belonging to another world. For "the Absolute" is not the name of a particular of any sort but of a complex organization; its grammar, to use a fashionable term, is akin to that of "the social system" rather than to that of "the Pope." We can no more be acquainted with the Absolute than with the Spirit of the Age. But this is not enough to show that the first phase is meaningless, any more than the second is.

It is, of course, open to defenders of the logical positivists to reply that even if "the Absolute" has a meaning, there may still be nothing for it to apply to. The argument here is that the single system of intelligible reality within which Bradley thought everything must fall simply does not obtain. It is just not true that there is one great fact which embraces all other facts, one self-differentiating whole which includes everything else as its parts. This is certainly a respectable view but it is not self-evidently correct: the case for it has to be argued against a Bradley or a Hegel. And this means that any hope of finding a short way of dismissing these philosophers as mere metaphysicians, intellectual charlatans, must be abandoned. To deny on these grounds that "the Absolute" has any application is in fact to assert the correctness of an alternative way of looking at the world, i.e., of a rival metaphysical view.

The low reputation of Bradley's metaphysical work in the immediate pre-war period depended in part at least on misconception. But it does not follow that recognizing the misconception will automatically lead to his being taken seriously again as a metaphysician. It is true that some of the prejudice which used to be felt against Bradley's type of view has been dissipated, and that analytic philosophers themselves have questioned the value of some of the weapons (e.g., the analytic/synthetic dichotomy) which were used to attack him. Nevertheless,

much prejudice about Bradley does remain, and it is often quietly assumed that even if the sticks used to beat him are not all they were originally cracked up to be, they are at any rate good enough for this particular purpose. There is, moreover, a further reason why few students of philosophy in Great Britain today set much store by the positive doctrines of *Appearance and Reality*, namely that they were condemned not merely by Russell who was, many would now allow, a metaphysician *malgré lui*, but also by Moore, who is still widely thought to be the epitome of every philosophical virtue. We must now go on to consider the basis of Moore's criticism.

To Moore, Bradley was a conspicuous illustration of an all too common tendency among philosophers, the tendency to build elaborate systems on the supposition that what everyone knows to be true is false. We have seen how Bradley, in the first part of his book, examined certain concepts which are in common use and argued that they could not be true of reality: thing, quality, relation, space, time, motion, change, causality were among the concepts subjected to this treatment. None of these ideas, said Bradley, could be taken as it stood as being applicable to the real. Moore took this statement to mean that no propositions embodying any of these concepts could in any circumstances be true. If Bradley were right, no such assertion as that this came before that, or that this is beside that, could ever be truly made. Moore's case against Bradley was that we had only to realize this clearly to condemn his whole philosophy, for whatever doubts there might be about individual instances, it was absolutely certain that there were some true propositions of the types cited or referred to.

Moore's argument here rested on a robust belief in common sense, of which he posed quite openly as the champion. His defense of common sense should not, however, be misunderstood. He was certainly not committed to the view that every common-sense opinion is correct; it was only certain basic beliefs he was prepared to endorse, such as that there is a material world, that other people exist, and that some things happened in the past. Moore maintained that, however ingenious a philosopher's skeptical arguments against these beliefs might be, they could not prevail over them: it would always be more rational to suspect the arguments than to give up the beliefs. And that skeptical philosophers themselves failed to abandon them was shown by their continuing to write as if other people and things existed in the very course of speculating whether they might not be disembodied spirits and the only existents in the world.

A different, and in some ways more cogent, version of Moore's argument has been put forward by more recent philosophers. According to this, we must distinguish sharply between doubting particular propositions and doubting whole classes of propositions. Take statements about the past as an example.

We can legitimately ask whether *any particular* statement of this kind is true, because we assume we know what it would be like for it to be true: we measure the case under examination against others we have already decided to be in order. But now suppose we get into the position of wondering whether it might not be the case that *each and every* statement about the past is false. The saving condition is now removed, and we no longer have a standard by which to decide the issue. A general doubt of this kind is accordingly senseless, since it could arise only if we first assume it to be without justification.

Now Moore and his followers[19] regularly suppose that Bradley, in the first part of *Appearance and Reality*, was engaging in just this sort of doubt; as I have already said, they take him to assert the falsity of many statements whose truth everyone else in the world takes for granted. The question is, however, whether they have any warrant for this interpretation. Did Bradley actually mean to assert, as Moore says he must if we are to attach any meaning to his statement that time is not real, that there are no temporal facts? He certainly admits, and indeed emphasizes, that a concept like time "qualifies appearances," and he insists repeatedly that appearance is not illusion. Appearances, he maintains, "exist" or "are" or "are facts" ("occur" might have been a better word), though they are not real "in their character as presented." Moore finds this position self-contradictory, since "by far the commonest and most important" of the conceptions for which the term "real" stands is that according to which to say of something that it is real is to deny that it is imaginary or non-existent.[20] Moore goes on to suggest that Bradley might have falsely believed that time exists on the ground that it is thought of. A more charitable interpretation might be built on the following points.

First, that despite his language Bradley is not so much concerned with things as with ways of taking them:* when he says that time is not real he does not mean that there are no such things as temporal situations, but rather that you cannot give an account of the world which will be finally coherent if you characterize it in temporal terms. To deny reality to something, on this account of the matter, is to say that a certain theory is not intelligible (compare Plato and Parmenides for this association of reality with intelligibility). When Bradley said in *Ethical Studies* that "the individual apart from the community is not anything real"[22] he was not making a statement about the existence of particular people, but maintaining forcibly that a way of thinking about man and his social relations was indefensible. Second, that truth and reality for Bradley are qualities which can be present in different degrees, as intelligibility can. Moore uses "real" and "true" as what might be called all-or-nothing words: a thing

is either real or unreal, a theory either true or false. This assimilates "true" and "real" to "existent," yet there are obvious usages of the words for which the assimilation cannot be made, e.g., "a true comrade," "a real friend." Bradley's concept of truth, like Plato's concept of *alētheia*, is clearly connected with these uses. Third, that when Bradley says that time, though not real, is nonetheless appearance he is meaning that we are not simply deluded when we frame temporal statements; we really are talking about something, and we are not getting it wholly wrong. Nor for that matter is he committed to denying that concepts may be applied with greater or less propriety at the level of appearances. The truth is the whole, perhaps; but not every way of talking which falls short of the whole is equally near to it, nor, given a particular way of talking, does the fact of its falling short license us to use it as we please. In other words, there are everyday truths and falsehoods for Bradley as for the rest of us. The only point on which he wants to insist is that none of them is finally true or finally false. But this is a metaphysical point which common sense can afford to ignore so long as it sticks to practice and does not engage in theory.

What this comes to is that there is no conflict between Bradley and common sense, only between Bradley and common sense *philosophy*, which is by no means the same thing and whose credentials are by no means so obviously impeccable. To reiterate loudly that we all know that there was a war not so long ago, and thus that there is at least one true statement which can be made about the past, is certainly not to answer Bradley, since he is ready to accept the point. In one sense Bradley's philosophy, like Wittgenstein's, "leaves everything as it is." But in another sense it changes things profoundly. A man who is convinced of Bradley's point of view will see the world with fresh eyes, since he will see it in an entirely different perspective. The ordinary facts of everyday life will remain, but the construction put on them will shift significantly; instead of taking them as complete and final truth, Bradley would have us fit them into an overall picture of reality as a whole. And if he were asked why we need to attempt any such overall picture, he would reply that we do not: we can stick to practical affairs and eschew metaphysics if we choose. But if we are to engage in metaphysics, nothing short of a coherent description of the world as a whole will satisfy us. Metaphysics is an intellectual pursuit; it is theory, and we do not need to theorize in these matters if theory is not to our taste. To object to a particular metaphysical theory in the name of unsupported common sense is not, however, to urge a rational objection to it, but to indulge in a species of misologism.

This is not to say that we have a straight choice between rejecting Moore and accepting Bradley. Bradley himself appears to have thought that his own metaphysical position, despite its admittedly unsystematic presentation, was compulsive. He believed

* *Cf.* in this connection: "In our First Book we examined various ways of taking facts."[21]

both that he could show the self-contradictory character of all alternative views, and the inevitability of his own. "In all cases," he writes in one passage, "that alone is valid for the intellect, which in a calm moment the mere intellect is incapable of doubting. It is only that which for thought is compulsory and irresistible — only that which thought must assert in attempting to deny it — which is a valid foundation for metaphysical truth."[23] There can be no doubt that Bradley believed that his own metaphysical arguments would satisfy this test. But it is surely significant that other philosophers have used the same procedure and arrived at very different conclusions: Aristotle used it in establishing the validity of the laws of contradiction and excluded middle, Descartes in the *cogito* argument. It is significant, again, that Russell, who is by no means insensitive to logical considerations, could make nothing of Bradley's arguments about relations. The lesson to be learnt from these facts must, I think, be that Bradley has overstated his case. To appreciate his metaphysics we need not merely to follow his arguments, but also to share his fundamental point of view and see the world as he saw it. To become a Bradleian you have, at least, to see sense in Bradley's intuition of reality as a single, self-differentiating, self-individuating system. Admittedly, metaphysics is not a matter of intuition and nothing more; if it were it would be indistinguishable from poetry. Metaphysics is an attempt to give conceptual expression to a certain way of looking at the world, and no metaphysics will convince unless it can claim intellectual coherence. But mere intellectual coherence is not enough here, nor in judging whether it is present can we entirely abstract from the point of view with which it is bound up. What seems coherent to a Russell will not seem coherent to a Bradley. That this must be so was half-recognized by Bradley when, in the preface to *Appearance and Reality*, he "transcribed" from his "notebook" the famous words "Metaphysics is the finding of bad reasons for what we believe upon instinct, but to find these reasons is no less an instinct." What bearing the acceptance of the idea would have on the question of the possibility of metaphysical *truth* is a serious matter, but one which we cannot take up here.

24

Pragmatism

H. S. THAYER

C. S. PEIRCE WAS BORN in Cambridge, Mass., in 1839. He was the son of Benjamin Peirce, a distinguished mathematician and professor at Harvard. As a child Peirce showed great intellectual precocity. He was taught privately by his father and also attended Cambridge High School. He entered Harvard in 1855 and was graduated in 1859; but he failed to distinguish himself academically at the university. Peirce later obtained a Bachelor of Science degree, graduating *summa cum laude* in chemistry. He entered the United States Coast survey in 1861 and spent thirty years of his life in this service with some intermissions in 1864–1865 and 1869–1870 when he lectured at Harvard. On receipt of a modest inheritance, he retired in 1887 at the age of 48, and devoted the rest of his life to logic and philosophy. He never obtained a regular university post, in spite of his obvious talents and the efforts of influential friends. He seems to have been of a cross-grained and bohemian temper, which alienated the respectable people who controlled academic appointments. He spent the last part of his life in poverty and had to devote a good deal of effort to dodging his creditors. He died in 1914.

William James was born in New York City in 1842. As a boy, he was educated in England and elsewhere in Europe. In 1864, he entered Harvard Medical School, and was graduated with a medical degree in 1869. During his undergraduate career he went with Agassiz as a field naturalist to the Amazon basin, but neither the career of a naturalist nor that of a physician proved to be to his taste. In 1872, he was appointed to teach physiology at Harvard. This led to his interest in psychology and philosophy, and his achievements in those fields established his permanent fame. He died in 1909.

John Dewey was born in Burlington, Vt., in 1859 and was educated at the University of Vermont and Johns Hopkins University. From 1888 to 1904, he taught at the Universities of Minnesota, Michigan, and Chicago. At Chicago, he became internationally famous as the director of the school of education. In 1904, he moved to Columbia University where he worked for the rest of his career, retiring from his teaching post in 1930. He died in 1952.

THE ORIGINS OF PRAGMATISM are clear in broad outline and obscure in fine detail; for the more conspicuous features lend themselves to easy, and by now familiar, reportage. Thus, in a word, pragmatism is a method of philosophizing, often identified as a theory of meaning that was first stated by Charles Peirce in the 1870's;* was revived primarily as a theory of truth in 1898 by William James; and was further developed, expanded, and disseminated by John Dewey and F. C. S. Schiller.

The broad outline is helpful. As a guide, it directs us to where to start looking if we want to find out about pragmatism. For most purposes, this is enough. That there should be considerable uncertainty about some of the more specific formative conditions in the historical evolution of pragmatism is another matter; and for most purposes, it is of historical interest only. Much of the obscurity over these historical details derives from one or both of two influential factors.

First, it is odd that the founders of pragmatism were neither very clear nor very consistent in the accounts they gave concerning the historical origins of their doctrine. As a partial explanation of this fact, the founders of pragmatism did not entirely agree about what pragmatism stood for as a philosophic position or as a nucleus of ideas. Peirce and James took a catholic view of the historical ancestor of pragmatism. Socrates, Aristotle, and even Spinoza, Locke, Berkeley, Hume, Kant, Mill, and an assorted variety of scientists, were all credited with a philosophic conduct above the call of special doctrines, particularly becoming to pragmatism. Dewey saw Francis Bacon as "the prophet of a pragmatic conception of knowledge."[2] With a genial hospitality for the past, James referred to pragmatism as "a new name for some old ways of thinking,"[3] thus sounding a note of gracious deference and generosity. But surely pragmatism was more than the invention of a name — an ugly one to boot, as James acknowledged.[4]

The second factor beclouding the historical development of pragmatism is a firmly established, inaccurate generalization, namely: Pragmatism is a doctrine holding that the meaning and truth of thought is determined (somehow) by criteria of practical *usefulness*. Some of the colloquial and uncritical language with which the leading pragmatists stated their views would seem to support this generalization. But even conceding this much, and granting also that the founders of pragmatism grossly overestimated the extent to which the language they used was free from ambiguity and divers interpretations, this way of characterizing pragmatism is a mistake. What is especially at fault here lies not so much in a misrepresentation of the

essential as in an essential irrelevance. The conception of human thought and knowledge as subject to a norm of practical results, where a standard of usefulness is also a test of significance in matters rational, goes way back as a sagacious deliverance of long standing in Western philosophy. It is by far a more ancient and venerated doctrine than anything yet to be found in pragmatism.

The ancient doctrine is as old as the human race. It has its origins in primitive magic and religion; it received ample and various dramatic and philosophic expressions in classical Greek literature; in the disillusioned and despairing Hellenistic world, it became a dominant thesis in the several competing philosophies (or "schools") of salvation; through Augustinian Christianity, it continued to be reiterated by any number of Franciscan schoolmen throughout the Middle Ages; it found its way into the pronouncements of the early champions of modern science and the "new knowledge." The contexts are different, but the upshot of the deliverance was much the same: knowledge is power; the value of thought lies in its practical uses. The dictum holds for any interpretation of practical uses, sacred or profane, whether it be taken as recommending the subservience of all things to a moral aim or to material gain. For the theologically minded, what is more practical than the salvation of one's soul? How else is intelligence to be justified but as an auxiliary and derivative instrument to this end?

To identify pragmatism as a philosophic rationalization of the spirit of modern industry and big business because of an alleged emphasis upon the practical and useful in thinking, or as a philosophy of power, is to forget history. Ironically, the theologians who have most severely indited pragmatism as a crass version of modern utilitarianism show a surprisingly short memory in this respect. For, on its own premises, there is no more recalcitrant form of utilitarianism to be found than Western theology.

While pragmatists do make considerable *use* of the notions of useful and practical results in judging certain kinds of human activities, these are not exclusive preoccupations. To be committed to a preference for useful over useless pursuits in the business of living is not a pertinent sign or criterion of pragmatism or its manifestation. It is less than informative to single out pragmatism as a philosophy of the useful; for on the whole, the characterization is useless.

It is not the purpose of the following pages to present a historical survey of pragmatism or to throw new light upon its emergence from the background of the prevailing vicissitudes of nineteenth-century thought. Rather, the concern here is with an analysis of some of the most significant contributions and critical developments of pragmatism.

---

* In a later reflection upon pragmatism, Peirce wrote to James (1904) ". . . pragmatism solves no real problem. It only shows that supposed problems are not real problems."[1]

The Main Lines of Development

PRAGMATISM, it was remarked at the outset, was conceived as a method of philosophizing, subject to certain qualifications to be dealt with shortly. The method that pragmatism is regarded to have introduced into philosophy is a procedure for deciding and ruling upon the meaning of beliefs, ideas, and uses of language. Roughly, the method to be followed is to ascertain and formulate the distinct empirical consequences that result from using, experimenting with, or acting upon a given idea in given circumstances. The resulting consequences, if any, are then to be interpreted as indicative of the meaning, if any, of the idea under consideration. The *formulation* of those consequences is understood as a schema or translation, in part or in whole, of the meaning of the idea, its "pragmatic significance."

Peirce described the method as characteristic of the experimentalist's procedure in the laboratory: "Whatever assertion you may make to him, he will either understand as meaning that if a given prescription for an experiment ever can be and ever is carried out in act, an experience of a given description will result, else he will see no sense at all in what you say."

And generally: "If one can define accurately all the conceivable experimental phenomena which the affirmation or denial of a concept could imply, one will have therein a complete definition of the concept."[5]

Peirce thought of the method as applying primarily to the use of language and as a way of clarification and analysis of assertions and concepts.* But when James took up the method, pragmatism was not confined to these limits, nor was the method itself quite the same. Peirce's recommendation to study the logical consequences of concepts under certain prescribed conditions became converted into an evaluation of the moral, psychological, and social effects of ideas. The analysis of meaning shaded off into an appraisal of the value and truth of ideas. Peirce's "maxim," as he called his method of analysis, became James' "universal mission."[7] In looking away from first principles, *a priori* or metaphysical antecedents in which to ground meaning and truth, the pragmatic method of analyzing experimental implications was to issue in a philosophy of experience, of thought, and of action.

Peirce's laboratory, then, was rebuilt into a hotel by James; pragmatism was the corridor; and "innumerable chambers open out of it."[8] But it was not very clear whether the corridor really led to the chambers or whether most of the odd inhabitants of

---

* There is much in common in the motives that led Peirce to enunciate his maxim of pragmatism and Wittgenstein to the well-known injunction to ask, not for the *meaning* of a sign — as if the meaning was an object coexistent with the sign — but for the *use* of the sign; in many cases "the meaning of a word is its use in the language."[6]

the chambers ever used the corridor at all. Schiller, one of the proprietors of the establishment, noting that hotels are manmade and that man is the measure of all things, instigated a continuous rebuilding program according to which each and all of the residents, beginning from their own chambers, would proceed to remake the hotel, each according to his own measurements and in his own way. Presumably all kinds of possible rooms were to be added, requiring all kinds of possible corridors. The future of the hotel was to be novel, expanding, and wide open. But Dewey, with more sober forethought, reasoned that wide-open hotels are not hotels at all; and seeing the danger of either a general collapse of the whole structure or its degeneration into a slum for recluses, he began to tear down the flimsy beehive compartments and to expand the corridor. Since one socializes best in corridors, private chambers were abolished; rooms were to have windows but no doors. But the corridor was the essential thing; it was restored with some of its Peircian furnishings of the laboratory and called "inquiry." If Dewey could have had his way, the hotel and the corridor would have become a single unit.

Leaving this picturesque mythologizing, let us return to take a less fanciful and more incisive look at the formation of pragmatism. Here, Peirce has left a valuable record of the events that led to the first conscious expression of pragmatism. His account suggests that pragmatism was not regarded as a surprisingly novel doctrine at its inception and that it came from, and was fashioned out of, cooperative deliberation. Thus, the mention of Bain and the presence of Chauncey Wright are clues to important influences upon the early history of pragmatism.[9]

"It was in the earliest seventies that a knot of us young men in Old Cambridge, calling ourselves, half-ironically, half-defiantly, 'The Metaphysical Club,'—for agnosticism was then riding its high horse, and was frowning superbly upon all metaphysics—used to meet, sometimes in my study, sometimes in that of William James." The membership in the "Club" included Oliver Wendell Holmes, Jr. (the future Chief Justice) and Nicholas St. John Green, a lawyer and disciple of Jeremy Bentham, who, in particular,

... often urged the importance of applying Bain's definition of belief, as "that upon which a man is prepared to act." From this definition, pragmatism is scarce more than a corollary; so that I am disposed to think of him as the grandfather of pragmatism. Chauncey Wright, something of a philosophical celebrity in those days, was never absent from our meetings. ... Wright, James, and I were men of science, rather scrutinizing the doctrines of the metaphysicians on their scientific side than regarding them as very momentous spiritually. The type of our thought was decidedly British. I, alone of our number, had come through the doorway of Kant, and even my ideas were acquiring the English accent.

Our metaphysical proceedings had all been in winged words . . . until at length, lest the club should be dissolved, without leaving any material *souvenir* behind, I drew up a little paper expressing some of the opinions that I had been urging all along under the name of pragmatism. This paper was received with such unlooked-for kindness, that I was encouraged, some half-dozen years later . . . to insert it, somewhat expanded, in the *Popular Science Monthly* for November, 1877, and January, 1879.[10]

It is of some interest to compare this description with the one in which Locke recounts the occasion that prompted his writing the great *Essay* and tells of the group of friends who met in the early 1670's, just two-hundred years before the "Metaphysical Club" was born.[11] Locke's "Club" was discussing the principles of morality and religion, but its members soon found that their conversations were hedged about with difficulties. What was needed, as Locke goes on to explain, and as the *Essay* attempts to accomplish, was a clarification, linguistic and conceptual, of the Understanding — of how and with what sort of "objects" it works and is "fitted to deal with." The popular reception of the *Essay* made it one of the most influential sources of the kind of problems that have since dominated modern philosophy: it was critical in spirit (aimed at removing "the rubbish which lies in the way to knowledge"), conscious of the uses and intellectual abuses of language, and concerned with the nature of knowledge.

Peirce had come to philosophy through Kant but it should be noted that in point of this critical philosophizing about the limits and certainty of knowledge, Locke and Kant are kin. Peirce's modest start, his now famous paper, "How to Make Our Ideas Clear," is the spiritual heir of this same critical quest.

Peirce's Theory of Inquiry

PEIRCE'S account of the function of thought — roughly, what we do and why we do it when we can be said to think — is remarkable on several counts. The novelty of the construction alone is of great interest, though not of exclusive importance.

Much of the outward form of the theory has affinities with an older idealism: that thinking is a means to establishing an equilibrium and restoring our momentarily severed connections with "reality"; that every thought (or belief) is but a partial half-truth falling short of the totality of Truth; that the goal of thought is the cessation of thought in one's becoming one with the Whole. But beneath the guise of these familiar and once engagingly respectable influences, Peirce effects a radical recasting of our interpretation of the function of thought. Most noteworthy in this respect is the attempt to construe thought within a more inclusive theory of organic behavior.

The resulting hypothesis, and the core of the theory, is that thought is one intervening phase of a single behavioral process mediating between a phase of sensory stimulation and a phase of purposeful resolution. As a process the occurrence, span, and termination of which will differ under differing stimulus conditions plus our humanly inherited equipment for response, the sequence of phases will exhibit variations in manifestation and in their grading off from one to another. Nonetheless, specific and describable operations occur within the phase of thought and afford classification and analysis of the "fixation of belief" and of logic in a broad sense.*

In brief and in general, for Peirce *doubt* is an irritating condition usually originating externally from surprise.[13] Doubt is a state of uneasiness and hesitancy; habits of action — and thereby in some cases action itself — have come up against an interfering obstacle. The resolution of doubt, or the removal of an obstacle, is attained by *belief*. Thus doubt occasions a struggle to attain a state of belief. This struggle Peirce calls "inquiry." Inquiry, or thought, "is excited by the irritation of doubt, and ceases when belief is attained: so that the production of belief is the sole function of thought."[14] Belief not only brings doubt to an end but also contains a reference to action. This is not to say that belief is action nor that belief always produces action. Belief, says Peirce, is the establishment of a habit — that is, a rule of action. Belief has these three features: It is an item of awareness (that is, we are conscious of our beliefs); it destroys the irritation of doubt; and it produces a habit.

It should be clear that, according to this view, doubt is not a condition we can will into existence. Doubt and belief are like physical pain in this respect: they occur or not regardless of what we will. Thus, when philosophers ask us to entertain doubts about the existence of the world, they are asking what is in fact impossible, if "doubt" is taken in Peirce's sense. He calls this the "Cartesian error". Descartes' skeptical doubts were not genuine (Peircian) cases of doubt at all. At best, most so-called philosophical doubts possess a heuristic value indicating what might be learned if we were to examine in a detached spirit some of our most ingrained and sluggish convictions. But Peircian doubt has little in common with such sophisticated reflectiveness, and were a man to have such doubts about the existence of the world, or of his mind, the

---

* That is, as a general theory of signs, semiotic, the "philosophy of representation."[12]

pathological results would be beyond philosophic repair by Cartesian "proofs."

What has come to be regarded as a characteristically *pragmatic* consideration is introduced by Peirce into his theory of inquiry as follows. Since belief produces a habit, beliefs are to be distinguished by the habits resulting from them. Belief is, or contains, a resolve to act in a specified way under certain conditions. Habits, or rules of action, thus provide the criterion for two sorts of determinations concerning belief: (1) Beliefs will differ or not depending on whether the rules of action they provide will differ or not; (2) the significance of a belief is determined by the rule of action it prescribes. An analogue of (1) is Peirce's doctrine that differences among signs will consist in the differences among the logical interpretants of signs; and an analogue of (2) is his doctrine that the "ultimate" logical interpretant of a sign, concept, or proposition ("the real meaning") is a habit.[15]

The rationale behind both (1) and (2) need not be confined merely to beliefs and habits. Indeed, (1) and (2) are special applications of two historical precursors: (1) is an instance of the venerable principle called by Leibniz the "identity of indiscernibles," here used by Peirce to maintain that beliefs differ only if some of their properties or practical or experimental consequences differ; and (2) is an instance of the injunction, "By their fruits shall ye know them," which, Peirce notes, is part of the ancestral history of pragmatism.

As habits provide the criterion by which we can distinguish different beliefs or avoid making false (or merely verbal) distinctions, a similar procedure applies to habits. Habits are to be distinguished, and their significance understood, by action.

> ... the whole function of thought is to produce habits of action ... to develop its meaning, we have, therefore, simply to determine what habit it produces, for what a thing means is simply what habits it involves ... What the habit is depends on *when* and *how* it causes us to act. As for the *when*, every stimulus to action is derived from perception; as for the *how*, every purpose of action is to produce some sensible result. Thus we come down to what is tangible and conceivably practical, as the root of every real distinction of thought, no matter how subtle it may be; and there is no distinction of meaning so fine as to consist in anything but a possible difference of practice.[16]

Peirce illustrates these remarks, or "the principle" they are aimed at eliciting, with an aperçu of medieval disputation on the doctrine of transubstantiation. Can we rightly suppose that the objects in this case are "really" flesh and blood while possessing the sensible qualities of bread and wine? We mean by "wine" that which has certain sensible effects, and to talk of something having just the sensible properties of wine while really being blood "is senseless jargon." This is not to argue, as did an eleventh-century dialectician, Berengarius of Tours, that the accidents of bread or wine cannot continue to remain while the substances are entirely changed. For Peirce is not speaking about substances underlying accidents but rather about situations in which language is used correctly or senselessly. We fall into jargon when, given a certain set of stimuli that (without any noticeable or specifiable deviation from past situations) have correctly occasioned the use of "wine", we exchange that use for another — namely, "blood" — without any evident reason or justification for departing from the uniformity of word usage.

While there is room for demurring over details of the illustration and of Peirce's rather free assignment of meanings and meaningfulness alike to objects (wine), words ("wine"), concepts, and ideas, still the general intention is clear. Clarity of thought and our use of language is a function of certain kinds of habits of behavior in certain kinds of situations leading to certain kinds of sensible results. A cryptic and often quoted comment of Peirce's is "our idea of anything is our idea of its sensible effects."[17] And from this Berkeleian-sounding phrase, it is but a short step to Peirce's maxim of pragmatism.

Peirce's Pragmatism

> Consider what effects, that might conceivably have practical bearings, we conceive the object of our conception to have. Then our conception of these effects is the whole of our conception of the object.[18]

IRONICALLY, this most famous and often repeated of Peirce's statements of pragmatism is probably the least clear recommendation of how to make our ideas clear in the history of philosophy. Peirce himself takes note of his use "five times over of derivatives of *concipere*,"[19] explaining that recrudescence as an emphatic attempt to indicate that he was concerned here with "intellectual purport." Concepts are to be explained by concepts, not by images or actions. While this may not excuse the inelegance of his formulation, it is a noteworthy addendum. Access to the meanings of concepts is gained only through traffic with concepts.

"Clarity of apprehension," to use Peirce's expression, or *meaning*, is had by a replacing (or translation) of concepts with concepts. A replacing, one might add, of unclear concepts with clear ones. But the addition is trivial counsel pending agreement upon some criterion of clarity (or meaning). One approach to a criterion is hinted at in the above maxim: replace our initial conception of an object with a conception of the conceivable practical bearings or effects of that object. But this advice, to be effective, must await elucidation of "concept," "conceivable practical effects," and "conception of conceivable practical effects." Alas, however, the wanted elucidations are not to be found in Peirce's writings. There are scattered comments bearing upon these matters, but they are often recondite and apparently at variance with one another. A putting of the pieces together would be a major undertaking, laudable for what it might contribute to our understanding of Peirce, but not to be embarked upon here. Still, some observations concerning the maxim of pragmatism are worth registering.

1. Peirce's pragmatism, often said to be a "theory of meaning," was regarded by Peirce himself as a maxim, rule, and method for ascertaining the meaning of signs. But pragmatism is not concerned with the meanings of all signs; it is concerned "merely [with laying] down a method of determining the meanings of intellectual concepts, that is, of those upon which reasonings may turn."[20] Exactly what the limits are upon this class of concepts is not clear. Peirce bars "names of feelings," like "red" and "blue" apparently because feelings are subjective, indeterminate, and the practical effects of feelings effect nothing more than other feelings. Other terms, such as those designating individual objects, are also to be excluded from pragmatic analysis,[21] along with nondescriptive logical components of sentences, such as "and," "or," "if-then," and the like.

Despite much uncertainty as to if and how pragmatic analysis of meaning applies to a considerable portion of discourse, two points are evident. Pragmatic meaning is not ubiquitous, nor is the application of the pragmatic rule to hold for all kinds of communication. Peirce inclines to a view of kinds of meaning among which the pragmatic is but one. Second, pragmatic determination of meaning does not apply to words or word usage in general but more directly to *concepts*, or what Peirce calls "the intellectual purport" of words. For Peirce, the broadest category of instruments of communication is that of *signs*. Words, concepts, and certain standardized forms of overt behavior are each kinds of signs. As a broad description, then, pragmatism is a theory, or set of procedural rules, for clarifying (or determining) the meaning of certain classes of signs.

While the pragmatic maxim is aimed at an overall clarification of "ideas," its most immediate application and assessible results may be found in the province of language and linguistic usage.

2. In saying that our conception of an object turns upon conceiving its "practical bearings" or "effects," Peirce did not intend to expound a doctrine of crass utilitarianism. Some of the more uncautious statements of James lend themselves to that interpretation so that one might say that the "meaning" of a concept, or of an object, is its practical use for some individual. Nor was it Peirce's intention to suggest that all thought (or conceiving) issues in action or that the "purport" (or "interpretation") of concepts lies in acts. Thought, says Peirce, may ultimately apply to action, but it will be "to *conceived* action."[22] Peirce repeatedly emphasized that pragmatism was not a philosophy of action nor one in which meaning is somehow wedded to action. His attempts to disassociate his view from such misunderstandings and from some of the developments James and others were giving to what they called "pragmatism" eventually led him to rebaptize his own position as "pragmaticism," a word ugly enough, he commented, to be safe from kidnappers.

3. Pragmatism is a method for achieving clarity of our ideas, for "determining the meanings of intellectual concepts." But what are meanings? We get no very clear-cut answer from Peirce. But then, for all his erratic brilliance, this is not to be wondered at; for we get no completely satisfactory answer from philosophy at all, the clearest of traditional answers proving clearly inadequate. But we can, if a little lamely, give Peirce credit for having anticipated much of what seems to be sound in recent critical advances upon the fringes of a theory of meaning.

So firmly rooted in the philosophic past are several dominant ways of thinking and talking about *meaning* that we tend to acquiesce to them, almost as second nature, while we are still cutting our philosophic teeth and know no better. Prominent among these and ancestor of them all is the Aristotelian treatment of meanings as stated essences, which, despite many vicissitudes of theorizing over the long interval, reappears (for example) in Locke's view of meanings as ideas. In each case, as an essence stated or as an idea named, a meaning is easily construed as an entity or object of some sort. It is then but an easy step to regard the meaning of a term as the object named by the term (be the object an essence or an idea). But this step invites confusion, as Plato first pointed out with the term "nonbeing" — for "nonbeing" names nothing, yet is meaningful — and as Frege and Russell along somewhat different lines have also shown. If much of contemporary discussion of meaning has taken a negative turn, pointing out where not to look and how not to talk when considering questions of the meaning of "meaning," the effect has been salutary in disenthralling us with some of the more stubborn misconceptions of the past.

For Peirce, meanings are not objects, essential or otherwise; nor are they ideas, mental images, or otherwise. In spite of an ample number of very different descriptions Peirce gave from time to time of what he initially intended by the "pragmatic rule," one professed motive stands out: the pragmatic rule is a proposed procedure for the analysis and definition of some of the signs* (or terms) necessary for the communication of knowledge and the attainment of true belief.

* Here the word "sign" is intended to cover the fluctuation already noted between Peirce's speaking of the meaning of "concepts," "ideas," and "words." Henceforth, to save multiplying words, we will often let "sign" stand for "concept," "idea," "belief," "word," in discussing Peirce. This follows Peirce's own view that the inclusive category of vehicles of communication is that of "signs."

Peirce applies this rule to our ideas of "hardness," "weight," "force," and "reality." Thus, we mean by the sign "hard thing," a thing that will not be scratched by many substances. "The whole conception of this quality, as of every other, lies in its conceived effects."[23] We mean by "force" "what is completely involved in its effects" or "if we know what the effects of force are, we are acquainted with every fact which is implied in saying that a force exists, and there is nothing more to know."[24] The principle behind these uses, however, invites closer scrutiny.

The sign "hard," says Peirce, means "will not be scratched by many substances." Peirce does not mistake meaning and naming; the meaning of the word "hard" is not its extension nor the class of things that will not be scratched by many substances. The "will not be scratched" refers to a certain *operation* — namely, a scratch test — and to certain results of the test always to be observed or expected.* To speak of some object O as hard, is to say "if a certain operation under certain circumstances is performed on O, then such and such results will occur," where, of course, the operation, circumstances, and results are specified. This is to provide a conditional explication of "hard," and of explications of "intellectual concepts," Peirce writes that he found them taking this form: "Proceed according to such and such a general rule. Then if such and such a concept is applicable to such and such an object, the operation will have such and such a general result; and conversely."[28]

Note that the operation (scratch-testing, for instance) is a general procedure or "rule" and the result will be general and capable of "a definite general description." Obviously, any single operation if carried out will be subject to any number of individual and local conditions ("this metal at this time, place, and temperature, scratched with this substance . . . " etc.). These peculiar, contingent, individual conditions making specific operations possible, however, are just what do not count in the explication of *hard* or other concepts. What is wanted is the "definite general description." That description, too, is what Peirce elsewhere seems to mean by our "conception of the effects" or "practical bearings," or our idea of the "sensible effects" of any object. These sensible effects are not to be taken as private[29] and varying from observer to observer; they are the publicly shared effects. In the same way, the common denominators of operations, of results, and of results described (or forecast) figure in the pragmatic determination of concepts.

In sum, Peirce's rule turns out to be an injunction,

hence, a maxim, to translate and explicate a sign by providing a conditional statement of an experimental situation in which a definite operation will produce a definite result. Thus, let T be such a term, $ExpS$ the experimental situation, O some operation, and R the result. The method of learning, or "gaining a perceptual acquaintance with the object of the word" or illustrating the meaning of T, is actually to instigate $ExpS$ and O, producing R. The analysis and explication of T consists in showing that $T_1 = T_2$ and "T_2" refers to the conditional statement, "If $ExpS$ and O, then R." Call this last statement S. Then for Peirce, the "whole meaning" of T is expressed by T_2, and T_2 is equivalent in meaning to S. Thus in the case of the predicate "hard," the pragmatic method of determining meaning can be formulated roughly as:

T_1 ("hard") $= T_2$ and $T_2 = S$ where S is the conditional statement of the form, "If such and such $ExpS$ and if O (i.e., scratch test), then R (i.e., will not be scratched).

The same procedure is in principle extendible from predicates to statements containing one or more predicates.

Peirce refers to this pragmatic method of conditional explication of signs as a "prescription" or "precept." The conditionals are recipes informing us of what we are to do if we wish to find out the kind of conditions to which the sign applies. That the method is the very substance of what has come to be known as "operationalism" has by now become a familiar observation. But it is ironical that this aspect of Peirce's work should have to be singled out as meriting attention by way of its appealing resemblance to operationalism; for operationalism, at its inception, as a theory of defining the meanings of concepts in physics, was far less rigorous in its formulation and considerably muddier in its obscuring of essential details than its Peircian forebear. A more suggestive connection of ideas, and one deserving study, is the striking resemblance of Peirce's method of determining the meaning of concepts to the "method of determination of terms by reduction statements" devised more recently (1936) by Carnap.

There are, it must be observed, two uncertain points in Peirce's maxim for clarifying concepts, and each is vital to our understanding of the meaning of that maxim itself. The first is that the notions of the *conceivable* or *possible* consequences or "practical bearings" of concepts are left unexplained. Peirce's statement of the maxim informs us that our *conception* of the *conceivable* practical bearings (or sensible effects) of an object is "the whole" of our conception of the object. But surely this sense of "conceivable" is not intended to cover every *logically possible* practical bearing of an object. The meanings of concepts could hardly get settled this way. As in the case of words ending with "able," modalities of physical or logical possibility and necessity will

---

* It also refers to a certain universal "general" trait existing in things. Peirce's "scholastic realism," which often crops up in his writings and to which references continue to be made,[25] holds that ". . . *some* general objects are real"[26] and that there is experimental evidence for this position. A familiar pronouncement is "General principles are really operative in nature. That is the doctrine of scholastic realism."[27]

govern their use. While Peirce advanced a doctrine of "real possibility," its relation to his analysis of the meaning of "intellectual predicates" is not easy to follow.[30] The second difficult point in Peirce's method of clarifying meanings is his use of conditional statements of the sort discussed above. The problem here is simply one of how disposition terms (like "hard") and contrary-to-fact conditional statements, in which the "whole meaning of an intellectual predicate"[31] is expressed, are to be interpreted. So far, the problems facing an adequate theoretical analysis of contrary-to-fact conditional statements have stoutly resisted most attempts at effective penetration.[32]

4. Whatever the sense of "conceivable" or "possible" in Peirce's talk of conceivable and possible effects that concepts and statements must have if pragmatically meaningful, the primary motivation is clear: since statements have consequences, it is a class of stated, confirmable, experimental consequences that statements *mean*. The translation of any term or statement into the conditional form discussed earlier is a translation resulting in an assertion that, on experiment, a certain operation, if performed, will lead to certain confirmable results. From such considerations, it follows that to have meaning, a statement must be confirmable — that is, be in principle, or "conceivably," capable of experimental verification. A further, but less certain, conclusion suggests itself and seems occasionally to come from Peirce: the (pragmatic) meaning of any statement is the procedure of its verification, the so-called "verification theory of meaning."

Finally, it is a characteristic of Peirce, and of his meaning theory, to maintain that the meaning of a sign has reference to an indefinite number of confirmable consequences. To say "X is hard" means, according to Peirce, "to predict that no matter how often you try the experiment" of scratching X, "it will fail every time." The limited number of experiments upon X that we may care to try in a day or a lifetime are each singly or as a finite whole degrees of confirmation of the statement "X is hard." A limited number of such tests may make the meaning of the statement *clear* to those of us who cannot reckon in any other way. But what the meaning is and how it is prompted or taught differ in this respect: the records of actual confirming instances are ordinarily merely a subclass of the meaning of the sign or term. For the statement asserts, or means, that it is *always* the case, *whenever* you try, that X *will* not be scratched. Thus, understanding the meaning of a sign, we will know how to supply a confirming instance of the sign. But knowing how to confirm and knowing the meaning of a sign are not the same. Knowing the meaning involves understanding an assertion about an "innumerable series" of confirming instances.

Inquiry and Truth

WHILE thought or inquiry has as its sole purpose the production of belief, there are several characteristic methods by which belief can be attained. Only one of these methods, that of science, takes into consideration a right and wrong way of fixing beliefs; it is used by those who wish not only to believe (since all of us do) but to have their beliefs "coincide with fact." Now Peirce regarded it as a psychological fact that to hold some belief B and to think B *is true* are the same mental acts.[33] Thus, for us all, the sum of our beliefs and an enumeration of what we think to be true come to one and the same order of thoughts. But which of any of our beliefs are in fact true or false is a matter to be determined on grounds other than the act of believing or the satisfaction thus incurred. For while a belief may in fact be false, as soon "as a firm belief is reached we are entirely satisfied."

Truth, then, is not identified with belief, nor is the subjective satisfaction accompanying believing a test of truth at all. The key to the pragmatic definition of truth is the concept of reality. Pragmatic meaning and truth overlap and coalesce with the idea of the Real — not reality as the sum and substance of all that *is*, be it noted, but the *concept* of the Real. We *conceive* the real to be the cause of thought and belief. Truth, argues Peirce, is accordingly *conceived* as a characteristic of the belief we would possess if it were affected by nothing but the real and with the real as the only object represented in these beliefs.[34] Such a belief will be "final"; unlike ordinary opinion it will be free of the accidental, human, subjective elements of error. For Peirce, then, a true belief, a belief that represents a real object, and what is thought to exist in the final opinion are pragmatically equivalent. To distinguish a true conception of a thing and the thing as *real* is simply to "regard one and the same thing from two different points of view, for the immediate object of thought in a true judgment *is* the reality."[35]

The "final opinion" is simply part of what Peirce took as an ideal of the endless application of scientific method to belief. Hence, his well-known definition of "truth":

The opinion which is fated to be ultimately agreed upon by all who investigate is what we mean by truth, and the object represented by this opinion is real.[36]

Truth is that concordance of an abstract statement with the ideal limit towards which endless investigation would tend to bring scientific belief, which concordance the abstract statement may possess by virtue of the confession of its inaccuracy and one-sidedness, and this confession is an essential ingredient of truth.[37]

On Some Criticisms of Peirce's Definition of Truth

IN more recent discussions of pragmatism, the above definitions of truth have achieved a prominence considerably out of proportion to the importance Peirce himself attached to them. For he scarcely discusses them, and, apparently, never took an interest in developing a comprehensive explanation or theory of truth. But Peirce's two definitions have an important place in the history of pragmatism for, James' view of truth aside, they are revived by Dewey and incorporated into his conception of truth as "warranted assertibility" (see below).

The two definitions of truth have been variously criticized: the notion of a final opinion "fated" to be agreed upon seems a little mysterious. Is there such an opinion? How do we know that endless investigation will be led to one opinion rather than a few or many? And how do we know that a finally agreed upon opinion will be true? It is not necessary to try to consider each of these questions here. It is enough to point out how each is derived from, and continues to perpetuate, a fundamental misconception concerning Peirce's definitions.

Peirce did happen to believe in an ultimate purpose of thought and of the universe. The evolution of thought, especially the history of science, exhibits purpose. What that purpose is, however, we do not know.[38] But these beliefs, while important for Peirce's metaphysics, are not *asserted* in his definitions of truth. It is a mistake to read the definitions as assertions or predictions about some future state of affairs in which a final opinion *will* be agreed upon. Peirce was describing what is *meant*, pragmatically, by calling an opinion *true*; he was not speculating about the existence of opinions fated to be agreed upon.

It was a mistake of this kind that led Russell to conclude that Peirce's definition of truth is of no philosophic importance.[39] Russell argues that the idea of an opinion "ultimately agreed upon by all who investigate, if taken in a chronological sense of 'ultimately,' would make 'truth' depend upon the opinions of the last man left alone as the earth becomes too cold to support life."[40] But this dismal prospect of man's sorry state, which atom bomb warfare may prevent us from anticipating, fails to be relevant to Peirce's definition. For the definition does not assert that the meaning of "truth" entails the existence of a final opinion of living men. Peirce's definition does not commit him to believing that there will, in fact, ever be a final opinion at all. Nor does it follow from the definition, as it does from Russell's reading of it, that no one will ever know what "truth" means except the final investigator in the final moment of his enjoying his final opinion.

It does follow from Peirce's definition that no single belief can be known with certainty to be true. But this is hardly a novel thesis. Where novelty is

evident is in Peirce's suggestion that this same thesis — or some specific expression of it within and relevant to the contexts of statements — adds to the truth of statements. This is an application of Peirce's *fallibilism*. He goes further than maintaining that all human opinion (and presumably, any statement of fact) is subject to an element of inaccuracy and error. He thinks that a "confession of inaccuracy and one-sidedness" incorporated into a belief or statement is "an essential ingredient of truth." A further beneficial effect of fallibilism, according to Peirce, is that the confessed fallibility of our beliefs works as a permanent stimulus to further inquiry. Peirce once commented that the only infallible statement is that all statements are fallible.[41]

Peirce, and Dewey following him, took this idea of confessed inaccuracy very seriously. They saw it as, in principle, not only a condition of the truth of assertions, but an essential characteristic of scientific method. Fallibilism is a reflection upon the so-called self-corrective tendency of scientific method.*

The question, then, of the meaning of "truth" was thought, by Peirce, to be capable of a meaningful answer by describing those conditions that will and do serve as a kind of model for interpreting the term. Ideally, the conditions described are just those that are implied by and exhibited in our use of the term, its "practical bearings," and the scope of its relation to "conceived action."

In stating his view of what truth is, Peirce not only made use of a not-too-sound analogy of beliefs, like a series of numbers, tending to a limit, but also employed the idea, familiar in the analysis of scientific concepts, of *ideal conditions*. Thus, to take a famous example, in Euclid's *Elements*, a *point* is defined as "that which has no part." If we wanted to use Euclidean geometry in making measurements upon a field, we would look in vain for those objects that could rightly serve as points according to the definition. We might find scatterings of birdshot and several boulders on the field, but no points. In a metaphysical mood we might conclude that points do not exist. But in our concern to measure the field, this stratagem occurs to us: we could construe Euclid's points as objects of a certain minimum volume, say birdshot. In a semantical mood, we could even define "part" as at least twice the volume of one piece of birdshot. Thus, semantics defies metaphysics, and points are restored to existence.

But this last triumph of strategy aside, we could proceed with our measurements, having points of a sort to work with, while denying in candid strictness that points "really" exist. The feature of most interest concerning the birdshot in the illustration is the approximation to points; they, more than

---

* Thus Peirce says, "certain methods of mathematical computation tend to correct themselves . . ." It is "one of the most wonderful features of reasoning and one of the most important philosophemes in the doctrine of science . . . that reasoning tends to correct itself."[42]

boulders, come closer to being points by some standard of minimum volume applied equally to birdshot and boulders. To deny that points exist as ideal Euclidean objects is not to protest that statements (or concepts) of these, or of any other ideal objects, are without use or significance. This would be a ruthless empiricism under which empirical science would never have got started. As in the above illustration, statements of ideal conditions can be supplemented with other statements more directly geared to existing objects through which the informative value and regulative function of ideally stated conditions is kept intact. The benefits of this procedure for actual investigations of existing facts can be invaluable — ideal conditions come through pragmatically as standards of relevance in assessing what aspects of what subject matters are of most concern to the inquiry in hand and in conferring upon the inquiry at hand divers utilities in simplifying certain calculations and suggesting certain theoretical goals and pursuits.

The concept of truth, for Peirce, is to be understood in a similar spirit as referring to those ideal conditions wherein opinion (or statement) stands in a certain relation to real objects as a result of inquiry. And existing opinions (or statements) are, by the same view, regarded as more or less approximating these ideal conditions.

The meaning of truth in general, as Peirce defines it, or that meaning narrowed down to particular working cases of the sort outlined above, has a twofold purpose. In general, the idea of truth represents an ideal of scientific progress; truth is our conception of what our beliefs would be if they represented (or were affected by) nothing but reality. This is the ideal of finished scientific knowledge. In its application to any of our beliefs at any one time, however, the idea of truth is to serve as a working standard of criticism, a norm for appraising the reliability of beliefs, and a constant reminder that no claim to the discovery of truth can be honored without its submission to impartial experimental investigation, and that no belief is in principle exempt from the community of inquiry and the pressure of continual testing.

We have looked as long as we have at Peirce's definition of truth because it and the topic of truth occur repeatedly in later discussions of pragmatism. But this is to have strayed beyond the limits Peirce set for pragmatism as a method of settling disputable meanings or avoiding meaningless disputes.

As the foregoing pages have attempted to review, such, in substance and in retrospect, was Peirce's contribution to the founding of pragmatism: a biologically orientated theory of inquiry issuing in an analytically empirical and experimental criterion of meaning. And such in substance were the ideas that lay unnoticed for twenty years until James gave them a new reception with results unforeseen, and mostly unintended, by Peirce.

William James

IT was in a lecture of 1898 that James first invoked pragmatism, crediting the idea to Peirce. For James as for Peirce, pragmatism was but one of many philosophic themes encountered and pursued over a lifetime.

In the background of James' pragmatism was his scientific training in medicine, his teaching of physiology and later of psychology, and his great *Principles of Psychology* (1890). Further back was his early ambition to become a painter, an articulate observer of color and shape and expressive details — a versatility James never lost as a writer. Anticipations of his pragmatism can be found in the *Psychology*, in several early articles, and in *The Will to Believe* (1897); and no sharp line divides the pragmatism from later ventures into "radical empiricism" (although James notes that pragmatism and radical empiricism can be taken as logically independent doctrines).[43]

Pragmatism and its forerunner, the will to believe, had their philosophic initiations in a moment of trial and personal crisis when James was in his late twenties. From his medical studies and readings in science, the idea began to force itself upon James that man is a mechanism doomed from the start to action in a mechanically closed universe. From this idea, like the universe it represented, there seemed to be no escape; the prospects of suicide or madness apparently hung equally in the balance for him. Other fears accompanied this insufferable conviction or followed from it; one such experience of horror and dread is described in *The Varieties of Religious Experience* (1902).[44]

An entry James made in his diary in 1870 is most revealing of the crisis and the healing that came by way of a decisive philosophic commitment; it is an illuminating instance of James' personally tried and personally "proven" view of the function of philosophic thought and belief.

I think that yesterday was a crisis in my life. I finished the first part of Renouvier's second "essais" and see no reason why his definition of Free Will — "the sustaining of a thought *because I choose to* when I might have other thoughts" — need be the definition of an illusion. At any rate, I will assume for the present — until next year — that it is no illusion. My first act of free will shall be to believe in free will. For the remainder of the year, I will abstain from the mere speculation and contemplative *Grüblei* in which my nature takes most delight, and voluntarily cultivate the feeling of moral freedom, by reading books favorable to it, as well as by acting. For the present then remember: care little for speculation; much for the *form* of my action; recollect that only when habits of order are formed can we advance to really interesting fields of action — and consequently accumulate grain on grain of willful choice like a very miser. . . . *Principiis obsta* — Today has furnished the exceptionally passionate initiative which Bain posits as needful for the acquisition of habits. I will see to the sequel. Not in maxims, not in *Anschauungen*, but in accumulated *acts* of thought lies salvation. . . . I will go a step further with my will, not only act with it, but believe as well; believe in my individual reality and creative power. My belief, to be sure, *can't* be optimistic — but I will posit life (the real, the good) in the self-governing *resistance* of the ego to the world. Life shall be built in doing and suffering and creating.[45]

The affirmation of free will, of action, of creative life, buttressed by reading in Renouvier and Darwin and by his own incipient pragmatism, saved James.

This early and private record of James' thought is impressive as a disclosure of central motives and circumstances in the making of his pragmatism. But it would be a mistake to treat the passage just quoted as in any way relevant to assaying the truth or adequacy of his later published views on pragmatism — a mistake illustrative of the so-called genetic fallacy and not uncommon among sociologically and psychoanalytically-minded historians of ideas. The passage helps explain James' pragmatism, not explain it away. It throws much light on how pragmatism, as James conceived the doctrine, could function as an invaluable guide to the acquisition of "creative" and "satisfactory" acts of thought and belief. It also helps to explain the shift in content and direction that James brought upon Peirce's original formulation of pragmatism: fundamentally, a shift from the analysis of meanings of ideas to an analysis of their value or moral uses, a matter to be commented upon below.

For James, accordingly, pragmatism was more than a critical maxim for achieving clarity of meaning; it provided a method for resolving moral, religious, and metaphysical problems; hence, freeing us "from abstraction and insufficiency, from fixed principles, closed systems, and pretended absolutes and origins," and directing us to "concreteness and adequacy, towards facts, towards action and towards power."[46]

We shall be helped to a better critical understanding of these ideas by an interim reflection upon some points of historical interest in their evolution.

Empiricism and Pragmatism

A NOTABLY favorite thesis of empiricism is that all ideas are derived from experience. Different accounts of how this derivation occurs, from the most simple to the most complicated, are but variations wrung from essentially the same empirical theory. In Locke and Hume, the thesis receives more than usual emphasis by way of being, in addition to a statement of principle, a practice of critical philosophical analysis.

Historically, the notion of *derivation* was flexible enough to suggest the complementing of one piece of theory with another: from thinking of ideas as causally derived from experience to thinking of the meaning of ideas as reducible (or translatable) to events (or terms) of immediate experience. Contemporary versions of reductionism are linguistically based, envisioning a reduction by means of logical constructions of the descriptive terms of science to terms referring to immediate sense data. This term-for-term reduction has its parallel in the psychology of eighteenth-century empiricists with its reduction of ideas to simple sensations.

But reductionism,* of old or of late, has proved capable of turning its otherwise innocent pursuit of explanation into a scouting party of criticism — from explaining how ideas are derived from sensations (of old) or how theoretical terms are constructed from sense data reports (of late) to critical raids upon such of these ideas or terms that fail to stand up under reductive explanation. To fail in reductive explanation, be it an idea (of old) or a unit of language (of late), is to fail to show any traceable lineal descent from sense experience; the penalty is an implication of bastardy, in this case "meaninglessness." Thus are the plowshares of reductive explanation converted into swords of criticism. Santayana, seeing that much behind the psychologizing tendencies of British empiricists, labeled it a "malicious psychology."

For Hume, the reductive approach is clear. Beginning with an account of the origins of ideas as "derived" from impressions, the explanation is subtly worked over into a critical test of the meaningfulness of those ideas or beliefs that purport to be about matters of fact. Examining the idea or belief in the *self*, or *causality*, Hume asks from what impressions these are derived. Finding none, the idea is meaningless or the belief false (note the encroachment of truth under the criterion of meaning). On the other hand, a "justified" belief in the self or in causality — namely, Hume's, as against unjustified rationalism — fits the reductive bill. So Hume has

---

* To avoid a possible misunderstanding, it should be added that the above comments on *reductionism* have nothing to do with the idea, dating from Aristotle, of certain portions of a science being reducible to others — where fundamental definitions and laws of one science (for example biology) are shown to be logically derivable from another science (for example physics). Rather, the thesis here alluded to (and one that James supported and advocated in rough outline) is that of providing terms or descriptive reports of immediately experienced data as translations of the abstract, general, and theoretical concepts of a science or system of knowledge. So translated, the latter often complex notions are *reducible* to the former, and can in principle be dispensed with in favor of a language of simple empirical observations. As a program, reductionism in this sense has achieved only fragmentary success; the model of effort and ingenuity in sketching the program for physics and psychology is Carnap's *Der logische Aufbau der Welt* (1928).

been read, perhaps not correctly,[47] as maintaining that a reductive uncovering of the experiential causes of ideas and beliefs about the world is a test of meaning and validity.

Both Peirce and James took an alternative course in giving priority to the *consequences* of ideas and beliefs when questions of truth or meaning were under consideration. This was not an alternative to empiricism, but rather a fundamental shift and a resulting revision within the theory and among the practices of empiricism. One could continue to affirm sense experience as "the original" of ideas and immediate experience as the cause of thought and stimulus to inquiry. But ideas and beliefs were no longer to be regarded as somehow reflections or products of presumably simple and inspectable impressions; nor were ideas to be construed as images, usually said to be the less "vivid" semblances of antecedent sensations. Imagining, believing, thinking, having ideas, each and all, do have causes and are, perhaps, "derived from experience." For the pragmatist, however, the experiential causes of ideas and beliefs may be necessary conditions of their *occurrence* but not a sufficient condition in the analysis of what they *are* — *viz*: what (in any case) they mean, or whether they are true or false.

For Peirce, James, and Dewey, the weakest and most troublesome points in traditional empirical theory were three: its interpretation of sensation (or sense data); its interpretation of ideas (thinking and mind); its persistent attempt at a reductive analysis of mental phenomena. In short, empiricism, to the pragmatist, was suffering from a faulty philosophical physiology, psychology, and method of analysis.

There are important differences between Peirce, James, and Dewey about how the positive steps of revision were to proceed. Peirce, we have seen, appealed to a criterion of the conceivable consequences — that is, the class of confirming instances, under standard test conditions, as one right way of determining the meaning of signs (ideas, beliefs, predicates, statements). And the "justification" or truth of signs, as "confirming instances" suggest, is undertaken in an analogous though not identical way. The appeal is never to a particular test case, a single operation, a single result, or a single sense experience, as giving the meaning of a term. Meaning (as well as verification) is not had that way; particular tests, or particular sense experiences, are at best but intimations, or signs, of meaning. Meaning is found in the "generals" only; it is found in a kind or form of operation and result (expressed by conditional statements); meanings are (present) in formulas, not in specific actions or events but in rules of action. Peirce's pragmatic empiricism, his "critical common sensism," comes from Kant rather than from British empiricism.* While he rejects the *Ding an sich* and,

* Though the influence of Berkeley is important and also that of the Scottish "Philosophy of Common Sense."[48]

evidentally, the synthetic *a priori* — which normally would stand as a rejection of Kant altogether — he writes that he was led to the maxim of pragmatism from reflection upon Kant's *Critique of Pure Reason*.[49] The view of meanings as general, as expressed in formulas prescribing *kinds* of operations and results, as found in forms and rules of action, is directly linked to Kant. The word "pragmatism" as a name for this outlook, Peirce says, was a translation of Kant's *pragmatisch*. It does not mean "practical" but empirical or experimental. For Kant, practical laws are "given through reason completely *a priori*"; pragmatic laws are "empirically conditioned," based on and applying to experience.[50]

A neat point of comparative differences between Peirce and James is found in a comment by James on the meaning of "pragmatic." James neglects the strict allegiance to Kantian use that Peirce intended for "pragmatism." Altogether contrary to Peirce's efforts to rid pragmatism of associations with the practical or with actions, James remarks that the history of the idea shows what pragmatism means: "The term is derived from the same Greek word *pragma* meaning action, from which our words 'practice' and 'practical' come."[51]

James, remaining closer to British empiricism than either Peirce or Dewey, gave the principle of consequences a thoroughly nominalistic application. This, too, is a divergence from Peirce. Indeed, reading Peirce, one is struck, by the frequency of his incursions upon nominalism, usually brief, acrid, and none too clear. While Peirce dissented from James' *Will to Believe* and his account of truth, the underlying discord is realism vs. nominalism; it divides James' pragmatism from Peirce's pragmaticism. What counted as the "consequences" of thought or belief for James was just that level of experience which excluded generality, and thus meanings, for Peirce, viz: practical effects, sensations, conduct, actions. To James, it is this level of live differences of choice, chance, and resolutions that is most "meaningful"; it is there that the value of philosophic concepts is found and tested. In a phrase that permanently shocked some of his British critics, James spoke of the "cash value" of ideas, referring to both meaning and truth.

Now since the level of live differences finds men differently situated, with differences of needs, wants, and satisfactions, the "value" — the meaning and truth — of ideas is subject to the same range of local and relative differences. That this must be the case follows, for James, from the psychological observation that the primary function of thought and of ideas is to bring and keep us in satisfactory relations with the world of persons and things in which we live and move and have our being. The observation stems from James' functional psychology. His "functional method" consists in the analysis of mental phenomena as processes or activities (rather than as objects or entities) to be distinguished and so described by the difference their presence makes in relation to other processes or exhibits in experience. The approach is seen in James' general description of the *mental*, or the presence of mind in phenomena, at the beginning of the *Psychology*:

"The pursuance of future ends and the choice of means for their attainment are thus the mark and criterion of the presence of mentality in phenomenon." And the thoroughly purposive nature of thought, for James, is evident here as well.[52]

At bottom, and in the most dramatic exemplifications of its function, thought is an instrument of survival. But in any case, the circumstances in which survival of a man or men or a society is a major concern are amply variegated. Furthermore, as sages have been wont to remind us, survival is but one among many human interests and does not invariably take first place. So it is that thought is called upon to assist in the satisfaction of many kinds of interests. And so, too, according to James, the value of thought — or the specific products of thought, ideas, beliefs — is to be judged on each of numerous occasions by a standard of effectiveness and efficiency as means. But means to what? Means, says James, "that will carry us prosperously from any one part of our experience to any other part, linking things satisfactorily, working securely, simplifying, saving labor." [53,54]

The Moral Basis of Truth

THE chief characteristic and innovation of James' pragmatism has already been alluded to several times. This is the moral and psychological focus in which he attempted to assimilate meaning and truth — to see them each clearly but through a single glass. Peirce favored keeping questions of *meaning* and *truth* distinct, and regarded pragmatism as a method of explicating meanings, not as a theory of truth. But James took pragmatism to be both a *method* for analyzing problems, for discerning meanings, as well as a *theory of truth*. It is this view, or the several converging views of truth developed by James, that is regarded as typifying his "pragmatism."

It was James who made the philosophical world aware of pragmatism and who gave pragmatism its mother tongue. Ideas and beliefs he portrayed as "plans of action," theories were "instruments" or "modes of adoption to reality." His appeal to the "pragmatic method" of solving problems contained the now familiar watchwords: "practical consequences," "practical differences," and the "useful" and "workable."

A reason for these idioms, impelling and reflected in them, is not far to seek. James was first and foremost a moralist concerned with working out an effective and reasonable philosophy of human thought and behavior — not a "philosophy of life," but a live philosophy. Moral interests dominate his popular writings and are observable as motivating even his most technical philosophic papers. Moral objectives guide James' account of philosophy: "The whole function of philosophy ought to be to find out what definite difference it will make to you and me, at definite instants of our life, if this world-formula or that world-formula be the true one."[55]

It is in this medium of moral interests facilitated by the terminology of value that James' view of truth was formulated and promulgated. The following characteristic pronouncements attest to this:

> Truth is one species of good, and not ... a category distinct from good, and co-ordinate with it. *The true is whatever proves itself to be good in the way of belief.* (James' italics).[56]
> "The true" ... is only the expedient in the way of our thinking, just as "the right" is only the expedient in the way of our behaving .... Expedient ... in the long run and on the whole."[57]

He continues to reiterate the idea in each and all of the locutions commented upon above; the "true" is that which is valuable, useful, expedient, workable, successful, profitable, etc. While each of these terms is applicable to a wide range of referential conditions, the extremities in outline are evident: at the one end, reference is directed to conditions of adaptation and survival; at the other, to any improvement in "life's practical struggles" or any yield of "vital benefits." The notion of truth is thus allied with and a part of James' view of the practical function of thought. That thought (which includes believing and willing and even talking) is a means to the satisfactory organization of experience, we noticed earlier. "Truth," then, refers to such of those means that work *efficiently* and *satisfactorily* and "falsehood," to those that do not. Moreover, "true" (and "false"), like "good" and "value" (or "not good" and "valueless"), will admit of no absolute and universal application, since their reference to means is relative to those circumstances in which our differences of needs determine differences of satisfactions, and differences accordingly in what means we regard as useful or useless: "to a certain degree ... everything here is plastic."[58]

The venerable thesis of ethical relativity, while shunned by many, has rarely (since Herodotus) been looked on as an anomaly. But James' casting of truth in a like mold seemed to strike most contemporary philosophers as queer. James was alert to this, saying, "I am well aware how odd it must seem to some of you to hear me say an idea is 'true' so long as to believe it is profitable to our lives. That it is *good*, for as much as it profits, you will gladly admit."[59] But this was not the only novelty occasioning misunderstanding nor the one most basic. In point of fact, James does not seem to have been fully aware of how far he had departed from customary nomenclature and traditional doctrine in issuing his new version of truth.

Trouble over Truth

A SPANIEL at the heels of the new doctrine, and always a nuisance, was James' disinclination to give his ideas a rigorous and explicit formulation, to free what he meant from the ambiguities and unguarded language of his more popular accounts of truth, even overcoming his own indecision about what was to count as an admissible object of reference for the word "truth" and what was not. The conciliatory spirit of the man worked against the precise settling of his thought. The meaning of truth was kept malleable while James tried to adapt his view to what he felt was sound in Bradley, Royce, and Peirce on one side, and Dewey, the Chicago school, and Schiller on the other. To fail at this was to fail at the impossible; James eventually gave up trying and turned to other philosophical pursuits, leaving pragmatic truth for Dewey to work out as best he could.

As matters stood, the meaning of truth as good, with some reshuffling of James' exposition, came to this: the truth of an "idea (opinion, belief, statement, or what not)"[60] is (1) its agreement with reality; (2) its workableness, or that concrete difference that its being true makes in anyone's actual life;[61] and (3) the process of verification.

James set forth a functional description of the conditions in which truth as agreement with reality occurs:

> To "agree" in the widest sense with a reality *can only mean to be guided either straight up to it or into its surroundings, or to be put into such working touch with it as to handle either it or something connected with it better than if we disagreed.* Better either intellectually or practically! And often agreement will only mean the negative fact that nothing contradictory from the quarter of that reality comes to interfere with the way in which our ideas guide us elsewhere. To copy a reality is, indeed, one very important way of agreeing with it, but it is far from being essential. The essential thing is the process of being guided. Any idea that helps us *deal*, whether practically or intellectually, with either the reality or its belongings, that doesn't entangle our progress in frustrations, that *fits*, in fact, and adapts our life to the reality's whole setting, will agree sufficiently to meet the requirement. It will hold true of that reality.[62]

The description helps to give an apt picture of intellectual practice, uncovering the circumstances and motives that might usually prompt our assent to an idea, to our calling it "valuable" for a given purpose, even to calling it "true." But the description is something less than revealing of what the word "true," once so elicited, might mean, beyond being a vague adjective of approval for the serviceability of an idea.

Had James been more painstaking in developing the pragmatic meaning of *agreement*, he might have avoided some of the harsher rejections of his doctrine and some of the confusion it engendered. He remarks, for example, that of an idea or belief proved useful to us in our dealings with the world, we can say, " 'It is useful because it is true' or that 'it is true because it is useful.' Both phrases mean exactly the same thing."[63] Perhaps with a certain interpretation and restriction upon "useful," a case can be made for the equation. But "useful" in its ordinary ill-defined plenitude of uses makes the equation startling; it was rejected by many readers for the simple reason that while most true beliefs may be useful, it is by no means evident that because a belief is useful, it is true. Similar statements from James that truth is what "works" or "pays" among our ideas and beliefs were also vehemently condemned.

The many critical rejections of James' version of truth turned for the most part on one underlying objection, one forcibly put by Russell.[64] James seemed to have yielded to subjectivity and irrationality, and seemed to justify sheer irresponsible expediency in so conceiving — or misconceiving — the criterion of truth. Like the alarmed Plato combating Thrasymachus in the *Republic*, Russell proceeded to "examine" pragmatism by analysis and caricature.

Indeed, Russell's caricatures of the pragmatic doctrine of truth eventually reached a wider audience than the literature being parodied. One, or something like it, went: Imagine a group of philosophers to be pondering the truth or falsehood of such recondite and vexing beliefs as that Caesar crossed the Rubicon, that the earth is round, that the moon is made of green cheese. Each of the philosophers prudently attempts to adduce and survey the evidence upon which his beliefs concerning these troublesome matters are founded. Each, that is, except for the pragmatist who happens also to be present. Instead, he asks himself what, in each case, will be profitable or useful to believe. Beliefs that will "pay" he calls "true" and those that will not "pay" he calls false. If, for example, he should happen to own a share in a firm doing business in cheeses — thus deriving an income allowing him to philosophize at leisure — he may find it profitable to believe that nature's sublime satellite of the earth is made of cheese. The proverbial child who cries for the moon, our pragmatist might cleverly point out, is really crying for cheese. While other philosophers look to the world, or to those portions of it that are relevant for the confirmation of belief, the pragmatist looks at himself and confirms beliefs according to his needs and purposes. Hence the subjectivity of pragmatic truth. Hence, too, the irrationality of it all. For if truth is merely what we want, or think we want, to believe, the once eternal separation of truth and falsehood becomes as fluid, confused, and ephemeral as the conditions that generate belief; just as fanciful as wishing; just as chancelike and changeable as the sundry stings and delights that prick on the tender quick of life.

Furthermore, as Russell has pointed out, while it may be good, or profitable, for students taking an examination to believe that the earth is round, it may be profitable for the teacher who must grade the examination papers for most of the students to believe that the earth is flat. The result is a chaotic conflict of profit interests and conceptions of truth.

The caricature (as well as the moralizing it prompts) is unjust, however, and essentially so since its critical motivation is mistaken. James was cognizant of the need for objective and socially shared controls over what to count as truth and what to count as falsehood among those ideas that can take such a count at all. Controls are thought of as present in each and all of the senses of *agreement with reality*, which, we lately noticed, is a condition of truth according to James. The chief shortcoming in James' account of truth — aside from its confinement to a level of introductory generalizing — is not in its denial of objective conditions under which ideas are determined true or false but in the assumption that the conspicuous nature of the controls in question required little or no supplementary buttressing with explanations.

But that ideas do or do not agree with reality and that agreement — and thus truth — is not a matter of private desires or sheer willing it so is evident from James' warning: "Our experience . . . is all shot through with regularities . . . one bit of it can warn us to get ready for another bit, can 'intend' or be 'significant of' that remoter object . . . truth is manifestly incompatible with waywardness on our part. Woe to him whose beliefs play fast and loose with the order which realities follow in his experience; they will lead him nowhere or else make false connections."[65]

James, then, was not espousing a subjective doctrine of truth nor on the whole unconsciously lapsing into one. Truth as a species of good, as "whatever proves itself to be good in the way of belief," is in fact subject to objective conditions of occurrence, and in principle, subject to objective procedures of verification, as the word "proves" was no doubt supposed to suggest.

James' Wager: The Right to Believe and Right Beliefs

JAMES appeared to be one of those philosophers willing to engage in a specious justification of religious beliefs. So at least his *Will to Believe* was judged by its critics. For James was thought to have argued that where the evidence is equally indecisive for each of two contradictory opinions (for example, God exists or God does not exist), we have a right to adopt the religious attitude. Furthermore, the "vital good" that is supposedly gained from believing is lost to the disbeliever and lost as well to the skeptic who, by suspending belief, is also in fact taking a decisive position.

It is curious that, in spite of James' repeated and emphatic statements, several important points are usually ignored when the argument has been paraphrased and examined for its flaws. James insists that the argument holds only in those cases and for those persons where the beliefs in question are "live" — that is, involve a willingness to act upon them — and where the option or decision between two incompatible and live beliefs is also live, forced, and momentous. To some, the beliefs that there is a god and that there is no god are alike in that they are neither alive, urgent, nor important. In general, James' argument was limited to those situations in which someone feels compelled to decide between two important beliefs, where the evidence for either admits of no arguable settlement one way or the other. Situations of this kind occur infrequently, James maintains; usually, on most questions, we do not feel forced to choose between complete belief or disbelief in an idea, from which all shades of doubt are excluded. It is a mistake, therefore, to suppose, as some have, that James' argument fails by not accounting for cases where we accept or reject a belief tentatively. For such cases are excluded at the outset from the province of his argument.

The argument of *The Will to Believe*, with some modification and amplification, reappears in James' *Pragmatism*. James continued to maintain that certain ideas might be justified, or "true," on grounds other than direct confrontation with facts or by the accustomed procedures of empirical reasoning. Seen in connection with the view of truth as *workableness*, James reasoned that since the "work," or function, of ideas and beliefs is to help us establish satisfactory relations with our environment, those who needed to believe in the Absolute, God, Freedom or Design had a right to do so, provided only that the need was real and the working of belief beneficial. The belief was then to count as pragmatically true. Both Peirce and Dewey were, among others, critical of James' strong, but not wholly clear, affirmation of this "right" to belief. James could say, "On pragmatistic principles, if the hypothesis of God works satisfactorily in the widest sense of the word, it is true."[66]

James later regretted the license that this loosely stated condition of *workableness* seemed to permit. For almost any belief could be passed off as true; one had only to *believe* that the results of believing were beneficial. Standards of veracity thus go slack on the very occasions in which, ordinarily, they need the tightest rein, where passion and personal interests are most in play. An obvious weak link in the argument was how "real needs" and "beneficial workings" were to be determined and how they were to be distinguished from those mistaken or feigned. But this is precisely the question of truth standards — or the threat of their slackening — just remarked on.

In partial defense of his contending our right, under the appropriate conditions, to believe that "the Absolute exists," James said: "Of two competing views of the universe which in all other respects are equal, but of which the first denies some vital human need while the second satisfies it, the second will be favored by sane men for the simple reason that it makes the world seem more rational."[67]

There are several interesting points in this thought that, while open to criticism, will help us to get a clearer view of an otherwise hidden and important feature of James' theorizing about truth.

1. In the first place, there is the standing difficulty, as lately observed, of confusing the cause of a belief with its truth. This is a difficulty that Peirce, James, and Dewey usually take pains to avoid by making the *consequences* of a belief, rather than its origins, the test of its truth. James, however, was less consistent, so it would appear, than Peirce or Dewey in this respect. The appeal to a "vital human need" as somehow justifying belief in the Absolute, or God, looks suspiciously like an appeal to the origins of the belief — *how* it arose — as conferring truth upon it. Vital needs, we should reply, may explain *why* we believe what we do, but they in no way determine the truth or falsehood of *what* we believe. And even if truth is taken as the *workableness* of a belief, a vital need is of itself no guarantee of the workableness of a belief. Following James, one might hold very roughly that a belief "works" when it satisfies some need. A need, once felt, may prompt a belief; but the fact that a need is felt provides no basis whatever for determining how it is best, or most workably, satisfied. This is a problem for inquiry, as Dewey has emphasized, and one of the tasks for inquiry is an accurate interpretation of the nature of the need, as it occurs, as well as how the need, once understood, is to be satisfied. Truth or falsehood thus characterizes the inquiry into needs and their satisfaction (the inquiry produces a satisfactory result — that is, one that is "true" — or it does not — that is, one that is "false"), but truth is neither a property of a need nor of the satisfaction that results from a belief.

2. Suppose, as James asks us to imagine, there were two theoretical views of the universe, θ_1 and θ_2, in all other respects equal, except that θ_1 denies the vital human need to believe "the Absolute exists," whereas θ_2 affirms this belief. James says that we shall favor θ_2 because it makes the world seem more rational. But furthermore, as a hypothesis that works (is needed and is beneficial), the belief in the Absolute is "true."

There is something amiss in this matter of a choice between θ_1 and θ_2, namely: the artificiality of the conditions laid out for our choosing. Let B stand for the belief "the Absolute exists." The question then is, what distinguishes θ_1 from θ_2 except that B is denied by the former and affirmed by the latter? If, but for this one exception, θ_1 and θ_2 are, as James says, "in all other respects equal," then nothing distinguishes them and they collapse to one theory θ. The choice then comes down to this: Shall I choose θ and not B, or shall I choose both θ and B? Since in either of the imagined cases I *am* choosing θ, we can eliminate this much from the question of choice. But the choice to be decided then reduces further to: Shall I affirm or shall I deny B?

But perhaps James intended something else by stating the condition that the two theories were "in all other respects equal" except for the one affirming and the other denying B. Perhaps he did not mean that the theories were equal in the sense of being identical, aside from B. James might have meant something else by the word "equal" — for example, that the two theories were of equal explanatory power, yet not identical as constructions nor one reducible to the other. But if he meant something like this, then the point of his example is vitiated. For if θ_1 and θ_2 differ in any other way in addition to differing over accommodating or failing to accommodate B, then our choice of one over the other will be guided by other considerations as well. The choice between θ_1 and θ_2 will no longer turn simply upon B; and the vital human need that B is said to satisfy will figure at best as one remote predilection to be reckoned in among any number of more immediate rational motives influencing our choice of one theory over the other.

Whatever James really meant by the example of two competing theories being in all respects "equal" but for B, the point just considered comes closest to representing what is actually involved in a choice between theories. Outside of philosophy, it is to be seriously doubted that a choice between theories ever rests upon the acceptance or rejection of a single isolated statement. James' example pictures θ_1 in which B is denied and θ_2 in which B is affirmed. But to deny or affirm B is to deny or affirm any one or all of numerous interrelated and logically connected statements linked to the statements "B is false" and "B is true," respectively. The decision to be made in choosing θ_1 or θ_2 will then involve more than a decision to accept or reject B, since the affirmation or denial of other related statements coming under other theoretical deliberations are all equally at stake.

The reason for thinking a belief like "the Absolute exists" is justified or workable (or for thinking it unjustified) is therefore far less simple than James' argument would suggest.

3. Ordinarily, beliefs of the metaphysical and religious kind that James was considering — "the Absolute exists," "God exists," etc. — are understood to be assertions of the existence of certain

kinds of objects. The beliefs entail statements of existence,

$$S_1: \text{``}(\exists x)\,(x = \text{the Absolute})\text{,'' or } S_2: \text{``}(\exists x)\,(x = \text{God})\text{''}$$

saying there is something and it *is* the Absolute or it is God. Either of the statements S_1 or S_2 is true, if in fact the object said to exist does exist, and false otherwise. Mankind has long been divided between those who think these statements (especially S_2) true and those who think them false. The division is due to two related questions: What kind of object is it that is alleged to exist?; does it exist? (or: what is it that the words "Absolute" and "God" purport to name and do they name?) Obviously no intelligible answer to the second question could be given until the first has been settled. We must agree on what S_1 and S_2 say there is (or what kind of object each asserts to exist) before we can attempt to arrive at a verdict concerning their truth or falsehood. And, depending on how the first question is answered, we may or may not arrive at an answer to the second.

James' approach to these questions differs in a novel way from the above. His interest throughout is not upon the question of the existence of objects, or kinds of objects, but upon the *belief* in the objects and how beliefs function. On the subject of religious belief, James' empirical outlook, his pragmatic method, and his acumen and learning in psychology work together in the development of his analysis. Regarding the question of the existence of the Absolute, or of God, as speculative and confined largely to the discussions of philosophers and theologians, James turned instead to facts. The facts, in this case, are instances of human belief: James' functional analysis is directed to exploring and discerning what difference the presence of belief makes in the life experience of men. This is to ask, pragmatically, "what conceivable effects of a practical kind the object [the *belief*] may involve." James did not cease to argue that certain metaphysical and religious beliefs could be "justified" by their effects in organizing, stimulating, and adding a sense of value to human life and experience. But that argument, whatever we may think of it, and the concern with justification do not detract from the fruitfulness of James' method of analysis, nor should doubts about the former blind us to the value of the latter. James' method continues to recommend itself as a way of clarifying the nature of religious belief and the function of religious language.

The pragmatic analysis of the meaning of metaphysical and religious beliefs and assertions effects a major recasting of their stated content. The older expressive forms, preserved in S_1 and S_2, come out under the new translation thus:

"The Absolute exists" = "some justification of a feeling of security in the presence of the universe exists." The concepts "God," "Freedom," and "Design" all mean "the presence of promise in the world."[68] S_2, "God exists," comes out to be something close to "there is something, and it promises better things in the future."* Not only does the traditionally religious language undergo a change in meaning, but the other components of traditional statements like S_1 and S_2 are also affected, particularly the word "exists." For in the context of religious beliefs, to say "God exists," "Design exists," etc., is to say "there is a justification for such and such a feeling (or belief)." In this context, "x exists" is translated "belief in x is justified" (where "x" is "promise in the world"). And it was because he construed the *justification* of a belief as consisting in the effects of believing upon the life experience of the believer that James' doctrine seems at first so startling. For it follows that belief in God may be true (or justified) for some persons and not for others. And, further, as we have seen, in judging the truth of the statement "God exists," the question of whether there is in fact an existing God is not of paramount importance. But these conclusions are startling and perplexing just to the extent that we fail to take note of James' departure from other more traditional modes of discussing religious beliefs and religious language, and James' analysis of belief becomes additionally confusing if we overlook his replacement of the notion of truth as the correspondence of a belief to fact by his own view of truth as the workableness of beliefs.

James' Legacy: An Uncompleted Theory

JAMES' pragmatic theory of truth was left in a rough and unfinished state of development. While he turned his attention to other matters, the theory was taken up by Dewey and underwent a patient and thorough reformulation. James was quite willing to leave the defense of pragmatism to others; he had grown tired of the seemingly endless critical controversy that had raged ever since the inception of the theory in 1907.

One piece of stated but unfinished business in James' account of truth was to prove of importance in the subsequent development of Dewey's pragmatism, and is of some intrinsic interest on its own. This calls for a final word, though controversial details are best deferred to the later discussion of Dewey's theory.

The "dictionary" definition of truth, as James calls it, is that ideas are true by virtue of their agreement with reality; failing to agree with reality, ideas are false. We have been seeing how James gave a pragmatic interpretation of this notion of *agreement*. The relative character of truth and falsity in James' theory comes by way of identifying truth with the

* "This vague confidence in the future is the sole pragmatic meaning at present discernible in the terms design and designer."[69]

usefulness of ideas (or the "value" of ideas in "leading" us to other looked-for ideas and experiences). Relativity is encountered here, just as with *usefulness* and because of it; for things are useful or not relative to certain purposes, in certain situations, for certain persons, etc. Ideas, like instruments or plans, are of help to us or not, subject to a similar range of provisions in any particular case. Let us follow Dewey in calling this complex of conditions, in which ideas (or beliefs) are put to work and their usefulness is tested, a *situation*. Situations, of course, will always include human agents and one or more of various human interests and purposes, along with any number of other sorts of conditions. We can then say that for James and Dewey, the truth of ideas and beliefs is relative to the situations in which ideas and beliefs occur. In any one situation, the truth or falsehood of an idea does not exist as some property peculiar to the idea itself, nor in a relation between the idea and some fact — *truth*, for the pragmatist, is rather a characteristic of the performance of an idea in a situation. But even this way of putting the matter can be misleading; for if we are to gain a clear view of what is most distinct and original in the pragmatic theory, what needs to be especially stressed is the part about *performance*. Truth or falsehood is not a trait that ideas, beliefs, even statements display in isolation from any or all situations. Traits of a situation do not necessarily inhere in its parts, nor do the characteristics of a situation survive among some of its isolated fragments — and ideas, beliefs, or statements, each taken on its own like single facts and purposes, are fragments of situations. Truth and falsehood are located, then, not in ideas, beliefs, or statements, but in and among situations; it is how ideas perform, how beliefs function, how statements are used in situations that occasions their truth or falsehood.

This emphasis upon the performance or workableness of ideas as constituting their truth is an application of James' *functional* method of analysis. The principle to be followed is that of discovering what practical and accountable differences the presence of a given idea makes within a given situation. Such, for James, is the way to get at the *meaning* of ideas. In the case of *truth*, we are directed accordingly to consider how ideas affect the situation in which they occur with respect to the purposes and interests involved. But this is to observe and talk about performances, or operations *of* ideas in relation to all the other constituent conditions of a situation. Fundamentally, truth or falsehood (just as usefulness or uselessness) pertains to *operations* rather than to the things operating. Specifically, where our choices and purposes are clear, ideas, beliefs, or statements that operate effectively relative to those purposes are "true"; if ineffective or obstructive in operating to the same end, they are "false."

From this, it follows that judgments of truth and falsehood are relative; in this case, relative to situations and to what proves effective, and to what ineffective in the operative conceptualization taking place therein. We may differ of course in what we adjudge to be cases of truth or falsehood, because of differences, for example, among our respective interpretations of a situation. Sizing up situations differently, we shall be led to differences over what to commend as the pragmatically effective rational conditions and operations thus exhibited, and what not. Even where no such disparity of interpretations exists, we may still find that the effectiveness of the ideas, beliefs, and statements under judgment remains a debatable matter. But the prevailing relativity thus acknowledged in our judgments of truth and falsehood is not to be thought of as a yielding to subjectivity and a giving up of definite judgments altogether. How we size up situations is subject to those critical canons of evidence and inference that generally govern our talk about the world.

Describing a *situation* is an empirical affair of recording and interpreting observed data, even making predictions. The resulting description allows, we have seen, judgments of the truth or falsity of certain conceptual features of the situation thus described. The value and accuracy of such judgments depends in part upon the description. But descriptive appraisals of situations are themselves subject to similar critical considerations of effectiveness and relative usefulness according to a further order of purposes and interests. To render a description of a situation is itself the occurrence of a situation.

The orientation of judgment remains in all outward respects the same; the focus always is upon how ideas operate or perform in given contexts, relative to some working purpose and point of view. The contexts, indeed, may differ as we have seen, being different under different interpretations, or different depending upon whether it is a situation, a judgment of a situation, a judgment of a previously judged situation, etc., that is under consideration and being judged. But, once having granted this relativity of contexts and of rulings upon useful and useless conceptualizations, and granting too the various working purposes to which pragmatic judgments of truth and falsehood are perforce confined, the resulting judgments of truth are just as absolute and objective as any that could be desired.

Strictly speaking, if one hazards a strict interpretation of James on this matter, it is not ideas, beliefs, or statements that are true or false but the occurrence or assertion of these in relation to other circumstances within situations. Truth or falsehood each characterizes a certain manner of operating peculiar to ideas, beliefs, or statements — namely: their use or uselessness in a context — but this is to characterize a complex of occurring and related events rather than any one single piece of the complex. The words "truth" and "falsehood" are used to describe or comment upon certain selected features of situations

— it is the occurrences and uses of ideas, beliefs, and statements that are selected; and their effects and usefulness in the situation as a whole are the objects of comment. James says that "The truth of an idea is not a stagnant property inherent in it. Truth happens to an idea. It *becomes* true, is *made* true by events. Its verity *is* in fact an event, a process, the process namely of its verifying itself, its veri-*fication*. Its validity is the process of its valid-*ation*."[70]

The relevance of this statement to our present reflections is clear. To call an idea "true" is, relative to a given purpose, to approve of the manner in which an idea performs and the consequences of its use in a given context.

Dewey

WE have hitherto considered the development of pragmatism as a philosophy occupied with certain fundamental questions of meaning and truth and the formulating of a theoretical method for analyzing and resolving those questions.

In turning to Dewey, we witness the coalescence of the critical and scientific motives of Peirce's pragmatism and the moral implications and ideals that James had found pragmatism capable of suggesting and inspiring. But those outlooks are not only combined in Dewey; they are intensified and sustained in the course of a long lifetime devoted to an exploration and analysis of their respective consequences in a variety of philosophic contexts, and to their continuous expansion and supplementation under inquiry responsive to new currents of thought.

This is not to convey the impression that Dewey started out in philosophy as a disciple of Peirce and James and spent the rest of his days weaving a synthesis of their teachings on pragmatism. Dewey's philosophic career began under the influence of Hegelian idealism and neo-Kantism. His early interests appear to have been primarily in epistemology, at the time a mixture of doctrines and questions of psychology and logic concerning the nature of thinking and judgment.

Dewey's long lifetime of ninety-three years spanned three major revolutions. Born in the year that saw the publication of Darwin's *Origin of the Species* (1859), a witness to the effects of the theory of relativity in physics, Dewey died in 1952, when men throughout the world were desperately struggling to realize the fact that a new atomic age had suddenly and ominously arrived. These three revolutions furnish a cardinal insight into Dewey's thought — for they had their origins within science, but their most violent impact and disturbing effects continue in the sphere of social and moral experience. Despite several major intellectual changes and vicissitudes of interest, one singularly acute and fixed concern can be observed threading the seventy years of Dewey's productive philosophical activity. The persevering theme is the relation of science and human values. As a young man in his thirties, Dewey was already pointing out that this was "one of the most pressing of contemporary problems."[72] In his sixties, the same problem was forcibly advanced as the central theme of *Reconstruction in Philosophy*[71] — carefully formulated by a man who, over the interval of years, had gained a penetrating understanding of the nature of human problems and had evolved a theory for inquiring into them. Again, when he was 86 and looking back on this earlier work, Dewey restated his conviction that the reconstructive task of philosophy lies in bridging the separation and in establishing continuity between morals and science.[73]

Dewey's own recommended reconstruction of this problem, as we shall see, was worked out within what he called "instrumentalism"; indeed, it forms the very core of instrumentalism itself. For Dewey, the separation of science and ethics into distinct kinds of experience and intellectual attitudes is the greatest misfortune and most serious intellectual error of the present century. In place of this cleavage, he continued to advocate a marriage via the theory of inquiry and inquiry as evaluation.

In a study of the historical development of pragmatism, Dewey notes this point of difference between Peirce and James: "Peirce wrote as a logician and James as a humanist."[74] While this difference is not to be too finely drawn, and while in the evolution of pragmatism there is a mixing of these ancestral strains, let us recognize and make use of this distinction in fixing our attention on Dewey. The distinction is traceable enough in the history of pragmatism to be descriptively accurate, and it directs us to two basic and simultaneously evolving aspects of Dewey's pragmatism, namely: a *theory of logic* and a *guiding principle for ethical analysis*. The distinction neither repudiates nor overlooks the metaphysical, political, and aesthetic commitments that go with each or both of these theoretical developments of pragmatism; nor does it ignore the divers subject matters in which these developments of theory occurred (notably in Dewey's work in psychology and educational theory).

Here, in viewing pragmatism as a theory of logic and a principle of ethical analysis, we are also made aware of two sides of Dewey's interest in philosophy. On the one side was his concern with a number of detailed and technical philosophic problems calling for equally technical solutions; on the other side was Dewey's concern with larger social problems confronting the modern democratic society undergoing an industrial and technological revolution.

Accordingly, Dewey's writings — or those most expressive of his pragmatism — can roughly be divided in this way: those of a technical and logical nature fall under the heading of instrumentalism, "a theory of the general forms of conception and reasoning"[75] (a theory that does not exclude moral judgments or set them off as a radically different kind from judgments of fact); and those in which Dewey is concerned with questions of value in human conduct and experience and in which the general pragmatic principle of *consequences* is developed as a method of social criticism and evaluation. Here it is the nature of the various consequences, in and for human life, of institutions, customs, social arrangements, and ideas that occupy Dewey's attention and from which his critical suggestions are offered. This is one of the primary and always necessary critical functions of philosophy as Dewey viewed it — the task of critically evaluating experience as a part of the "continuous reconstruction of experience," a task he also regarded as the "articulation and revelation of the meanings of the current course of events."[76] Indeed, in this expanded form as a principle of ethical analysis, Dewey's pragmatism gave him a way of evaluating philosophy itself:

"There is . . . a first rate test of the value of any philosophy which is offered us: Does it end in conclusions which, when they are referred back to ordinary life-experience and their predicaments, render them more significant, more luminous to us, and make our dealings with them more fruitful?"[77] The history of pragmatism begins with Peirce, who wrote as a logician, and James, who wrote as a humanist and educator; its Hegelian synthesis was achieved in the disenchanted Hegelian Dewey, who was both logician and humanist.

Instrumentalism

"INSTRUMENTALISM" is the name Dewey gave to what are in fact several interrelated and carefully elaborated theses concerning the function of thought in situations. That is, if the earlier comment on situations is recalled, "instrumentalism" is Dewey's theory of those conditions in which reasoning occurs and of the forms, or controling operations, that are characteristic of thought in attaining and establishing future consequences.

James had regarded ideas, concepts, and theories as instruments, whose function and value lay in their capacity to lead us to future facts and experiences. Dewey's instrumentalism was initiated as an attempt to provide a complete description and systematic analysis of this instrumental interpretation of reasoning:

Instrumentalism is an attempt to constitute a precise logical theory of concepts, of judgments and inferences in their various forms, by considering primarily how thought functions in the experimental determinations of future consequences . . . it attempts to establish universally recognized distinctions and rules of logic by deriving them from the reconstructive or mediative function ascribed to reason. It aims to constitute a theory of the general forms of conception and

reasoning, and not of this or that particular judgment or concept related to its own content, or to its particular implications.[78]

The theory was developed over many years and in many writings: into it went the products of Dewey's reflections on logic and the nature of thought, his own contributions to psychology, the influence of the biological and functional aspects of James' *Psychology*, and the influence of Peirce. The definitive statement came in 1938 when *Logic: The Theory of Inquiry* was published.

The theoretical core of Dewey's instrumentalism is found in his theory of *inquiry*. This theory comprises two objectives but, because Dewey treats them as interrelated, they are sometimes subject to an imperceptible grading off of the boundary between them. When this happens, the more ardent followers of Dewey have seen a desirable fusion; but the critical reader runs into confusion. The first objective is that of presenting a "natural history of thinking" as faithfully as the empirical facts will permit. This, in short, is a description of how thought occurs and how intelligence "works" in situations. So conceived, social, biological, and psychological information would be relevant to the articulation of a general theory of logic.

The other objective of the instrumental theory of logic is both a generalization from and reflection upon the first, with an aim to uncovering and accounting for the assumptions and implications that appear to be involved in and suggested from achieving the first objective. This latter objective differs from the former in being of a more "theoretical" and explanatory character. The "mediative function" of thought in situations, its instrumental role in establishing consequences, when recognized calls for a further explanation of the kind of conditions that initiate the function of thought and those characteristic of the termination of that function. The second objective, then, has to do with the distinctive traits of situations within which the function of thought begins and eventually ends.

The two key concepts of Dewey's logical theory are *situation* and *inquiry*. The concept of the *situation* is, evidently, the most fundamental logically, for by means of it "inquiry" is defined. On the other hand, in practice, inquiry comes first, for it is only through inquiry that situations can be known or discussed at all.

Concerning *situation*, Dewey writes: "What is designated by the word 'situation' is *not* a single object or set of objects and events. For we never experience nor form judgments about objects and events in isolation but only in connection with a contextual whole. . . . In actual experience there is never any such isolated singular object or event; *an* object or event is always a special part, a phase, or aspect, of an environing experienced world — a situation."[79]

That objects are to be construed as parts of a *context*, or aspects of an "environing *experienced* world," implies that among the objects to be included in situations are living organisms, creatures experiencing situations. Logical theory will be concerned with human situations, or more accurately, with contexts in which human intelligence, purposes, and action affect what is experienced. But not every human situation is of concern or relevant to logical theory. Any one of these "contextual wholes," because contextual and whole, exhibits some pervasive trait or quality according to Dewey. And it is only certain kinds of situations that can be said to *qualify* as logical, namely: those that are "indeterminate" or "doubtful" and in which *inquiry* is a natural development.

Dewey's conception of inquiry is heavily indebted to Peirce's theory; for Dewey, as for Peirce, inquiry is a process by which doubtful or unsettled situations become settled. The goal of inquiry is the attainment of belief; the product or outcome of competent inquiries is knowledge.[80] More than Peirce, Dewey describes the process of inquiry and the situations in which the process occurs in a language thick with borrowing from the biological, social, and evolutionary movements of thought on the immediate historical scene.

Inquiry is defined as: *The controlled or directed transformation of an indeterminate situation into one that is so determinate in its constituent distinctions and relations as to convert the elements of the original situation into a unified whole.*[81]

The Pattern of Inquiry

A BRIEF look at what Dewey calls "the pattern of inquiry" will help fix our attention on something more concrete and bring out what is important and so far only suggested in the theory we are considering. Thinking, or the activity of inquiry, is a process having certain phases occurring within certain limits: it starts with a "perplexed, troubled, or confused situation at the beginning and a cleared-up, unified, resolved situation at the close."[82] The troubled situation in which inquiry begins has "biological antecedent conditions" in a "state of imbalance in organic-environmental interactions,"[83] a state of disturbed equilibration.[84] This situation of disequilibrium, or imbalance, is indeterminate "with respect to its *issue*"; it is *confused*, meaning "its outcome cannot be anticipated"; it is *obscure* because its final consequences cannot be clearly foreseen; it is *conflicting* "when it tends to evoke discordant responses."[85]

Situations, it will be remembered, are "contextual wholes" possessing various qualitative traits. For Dewey, it is the "immediately pervasive quality" that makes any situation a "whole" and unique or individual.[86] While the list of experienceable qualities is endless, so that situations may be tragic, amusing, red, noisy, etc., the kind of situation with which we are concerned at present is one whose pervasive quality is *indeterminate* or *doubtful*. It is the whole *situation* that is indeterminate, doubtful, disturbed, or confused. Dewey takes great pains to guard us from identifying the doubtfulness of situations with some allegedly subjective sense of doubt as a "state of mind" or an event in a human brain. He writes:[87] "It is the situation that has these traits. *We* are doubtful because the situation is inherently doubtful. Personal states of doubt that are not evoked by and are not relevant to some existential situation are pathological."*

Inquiry proper commences when an indeterminate situation begins to yield "suggestions"; organic interaction, says Dewey, becomes inquiry when consequences begin to be anticipated. The first stage of inquiry consists in the recognition that the situation is a problem. "To see that a situation requires inquiry is the initial step in inquiry."[89] The indeterminate situation becomes a problematic situation. Formulation of the problem is the beginning of the transformation of the situation by inquiry. How and how adequately the problem is formulated has two major consequences: (1) It identifies the situation, correctly or not, as to the specific sort of problem it presents, and it interprets the situation as posing a question for which an answer is to be sought; (2) formulation of the problem suggests the scope and character of the ensuing inquiry necessary for the attainment of a solution. How the problem is conceived determines what data and suggestions are relevant, what irrelevant to the inquiry; "it is the criterion for relevancy and irrelevancy of hypotheses and conceptual structures."[90]

The second stage of inquiry consists of the formulation of hypotheses or possible relevant solutions to the problem. Hypotheses, or "ideas," are anticipations of consequences; they take a conditional form, being forecasts of what would (or will) happen if certain operations are performed with respect to certain conditions. Facts and observations will function as "suggestions" — that is, to suggest ideas; and ideas will function as suggestions of possible operations and consequences. Ideas may even suggest other ideas, facts, and observations. The "function" of ideas here consists in their use, or suggested use, as means to the resolution of the problem. "Reasoning" is an examination of ideas in an attempt to discern the relevancy and pertinence of their function within inquiry and its movement toward a solution. Reasoning is thus called by Dewey an examination of *meanings*.[91] Reasoning operates with symbols, with propositions; and propositions develop the "meaning-contents of ideas in their relations to one another."[92] Reasoning is the fourth stage in the process of inquiry; it concludes in the

---

* Some difficulties in this assignment of inherent doubt to situations are discussed by Thayer.[88]

fifth and last stage with an "experiment" or testing of the idea (or meaning) to which reasoning has led. The experiment may be immediately evident or may require more or less elaborate operations for its carrying out. The kind of experiment required and the success of its outcome will depend upon the initial character of the problematic situation and the inquiry that has taken place. Reason terminates with what is or is not an "answer" to the problematic situation. The "test" of that answer is whether it in fact is a solution of the problem. Inquiry then concludes or must retrace its steps or start over again. But a "successful" conclusion, when reached, marks a transformation of a problematic situation into one that is clear, untroubled, and settled.

Truth

WHEREAS Dewey had once tended to define truth as the "working" or "satisfactory" product of thought, "the verified" idea or hypothesis,[93] he later preferred to speak of *warranted assertibility*. The assertion warranted by inquiry is to be thought of as related to the indeterminate situation in much the same way that a solution is related to a problem. The conditions imposed by a problem must be met by an answer; the problem determines the conditions of an answer, but the answer resolves the problem. This occurrence of conditions *met* and *resolved* is the cardinal feature of truth for Dewey. To have *met* the conditions of a problem precludes chance and sheer guesswork and immediate knowledge as well; inquiry or interpretation and analysis of the problem will have intervened to produce an answer, a warranted assertion.

In general (and the idea of truth is a very general one for Dewey) truth is found in the relation between the first stage of inquiry (the problematic situation) and the final stage (that of judgment, resolution, and transformation). *Truth* characterizes the relation that these two phases of particular inquiries bear to one another: the relation of problem (or question) and solution (or answer). The relation, we may add, obtains *in* a situation *between* that initial state of conditions whose pervasive quality is designated as *problematic*, and that later state of conditions whose quality is designated as *determinate, complete, closed, solved*. If we call the first state of conditions C_1, and the latter state C_2, then truth may be defined as the relation between any occurrence of the kind C_1 and C_2 such that C_2 resolves or answers C_1. Here, C_2 is, or is formulated by, a warranted assertion. The warranted assertion represents, as an answer, a case of knowledge or true belief. His "analysis of 'warranted assertibility,' " Dewey said, "is offered as a *definition* of the nature of knowledge in the honorific sense according to which only *true* beliefs are knowledge."[94]

While Dewey tried to avoid using the words "true"

and "false" and to keep clear of the correspondence theory, his attempts were not altogether successful. We may try to get along with other words, in analyzing human knowledge, but the notions of truth and falsehood have a peculiarly fundamental position and continue to make themselves felt throughout any such analysis. Inventing linguistic substitutes for this particular pair of old terms is a temporary expedient at best and of questionable value, since whenever the new locutions are themselves up for consideration they get explained and understood by reverting to uses of the old terminology. There is as well an obvious (if not obviously analyzable) sense in which ascriptions of *truth* contain, at the least, a reference to some correspondence between that which is *said* to be true and the conditions that are supposed as the prerequisites and criteria for anything to be true.

Thus, in the course of a series of critical exchanges with Russell,[95] Dewey was led to a restatement of his theory of truth according to which, and as a result of pressure, a notion of *correspondence* was restored to grace. The statement remains one of the few and most direct of Dewey's pronouncements on truth.

My own view takes correspondence in the operational sense it bears in all cases except the unique epistemological case of an alleged relation between a "subject" and an "object": the meaning, namely, of *answering*, as a key answers to conditions imposed by a lock, or as two correspondents "answer" each other; or, in general, as a reply is an adequate answer to a question or a criticism — as, in short, a *solution* answers the requirements of a *problem*. On this view, both partners in "correspondence" are open and above board, instead of one of them being forever out of experience and the other in it by way of a "percept" or whatever.

Dewey concludes:

In the sense of correspondence as operational and behavioral (the meaning which has definite parallels in ordinary experience), I hold that my *type* of theory is the only one entitled to be called a correspondence theory of truth.[96]

This statement of his theory of truth also casts some light on a cardinal doctrine of Dewey's theory of knowledge: that inquiry effects an existential transformation of subject matters inquired into; that knowledge brings about a change in the thing known.

Concerning this part of his theory, Dewey has sometimes been compared[97] with Marx, who wrote: "The truth, i.e., the reality and power of thought, must be demonstrated in practice. Philosophers have only *interpreted* the world in various ways, but the real task is to *alter* it."[98] But it is not at all clear what insight this comparison is supposed to supply. For Dewey, philosophic interpretations *have* altered the world, but as obstacles to intellectual progress. And for Dewey, as for any sane thinker, the real problem is how to alter the world for the better. But the method Dewey proposes for this purpose is to be found in the writings of Dewey, not in Marx. Dewey, like Peirce, once invoked a Biblical phrase in expressing his instrumentalist view of truth — "By their fruits shall ye *know* them."[99] However, in the present climate of Western opinion, critics of Dewey have found it convenient to classify him as a disciple of Marx rather than of Christ.

In any event, in speaking of knowledge (or the result of inquiry) as effecting a change in the things known, Dewey is not to be taken as arguing that knowing is an occult force mysteriously transforming the object of knowledge so that we are barred from "really" knowing what it is "in itself." Rather, our understanding of and relation to conditions that are *problematic* is not the "same" as our relation to those conditions when viewed according to a known or hypothesized *solution*. The conditions that make for a puzzle are not the "same" after we know the answer. For, before we know the answer, the conditions are puzzling; and after we know the answer, the conditions are not puzzling, and we may sometimes wonder why we thought them puzzling at all.

"Truth," then, for Dewey seems to refer in general to those conditions that make the difference between what is a problem and what a solution; "truth" refers to just that set of conditions and operations that render a problematic situation unproblematic.

Inquiry as Evaluation

JAMES regarded truth as an aspect of *good*. Dewey agreed, with qualifications that cannot be adequately covered here, that establishing warranted conclusions of inquiry is an act of evaluation. The pattern of inquiry reviewed earlier can be interpreted as the stages of a reflective evaluation of a situation with a view to discovering what consequences, if instituted, will answer to what is "needed" or "lacking." In this respect inquiry is a continuous activity of transforming existent situations, in which deficiencies and wants and specific moral perplexities are felt, by bringing about conditions that contribute to sufficiency, stability, and satisfaction. Relative to the former conditions, these latter are specific *goods*; relative to the situation in which deficiencies and ills are problems, inquiry is directed to finding "the right course of action, the right good."

Discovery of the right course of action, in such cases, requires an evaluation of inquiry itself. Judgment, for Dewey, with which inquiry closes, involves an appraisal of the adequacy and "value" of the intermediate course of inquiry and of the propositions that are being prepared for a final settlement.[100] Judgment involves an evaluation of the means being for-

mulated in inquiry (that is, propositions) with respect to their relevance to the problem and to its solution. The warranted assertion of inquiry is the result of judgment; it is the evaluated solution that terminates inquiry. In this sense inquiry concludes with what *ought* to be or is the *right* solution to the problem. In that sense, too, all inquiry is evaluative and aims at the establishment of a good. The good aimed for is "the meaning experienced . . . in a unified orderly release in action."* Not all situations are of an obvious "moral" character; but all inquiries are evaluations of situations and of the bearing of future consequences in the attainment of goods.

For Dewey, inquiry is not only essential to the moral reconstruction of experience, it is a paradigm of moral activity itself.

A moral situation is one in which judgment and choice are required antecedently to overt action. The practical meaning of the situation — that is to say, the action needed to satisfy it — is not self-evident. It has to be searched for. There are conflicting desires and alternative apparent goods. What is needed is to find the right course of action, the right good. Hence inquiry is exacted. . . . This inquiry is intelligence. . . . *Moral* goods and ends exist only when something has to be done. The fact that something has to be done proves that there are deficiencies, evils in the existent situation. . . . Consequently the good of the situation has to be discovered, projected and attained on the basis of the exact defect and trouble to be rectified. . . . The process of growth, of improvement and progress, rather than the static outcome and result, becomes the significant thing. Not health as an end fixed once for all, but the needed improvement in health — a continual process — is the end and good. The end is no longer a terminus or limit to be reached. It is the active process of transforming the existent situation. Not perfection as a final goal, but the ever-enduring process of perfecting, maturing, refining is the aim of living. Honesty, industry, temperance, justice, like health, wealth and learning, are not goods to be possessed as they would be if they expressed fixed ends to be attained. They are directions of change in the quality of experience. Growth itself is the only moral "end."[102]

Inquiry is a sign and condition of human growth. It was not surprising that Dewey should find in inquiry the possibilities for a genuine religious outlook — one wanting only an imaginative projection of the essentially communal function of inquiry and its premium on socially shared experience. Nor was Dewey ineffective in giving expression to this intellectual deliverance; it was not a resuscitation of the

---

* The full passage is important: "Good consists in the meaning that is experienced to belong to an activity when conflict and entanglement of various incompatible impulses and habits terminate in a unified orderly release in action."[101]

eighteenth-century religion of Reason but a reasonable faith in intelligence. In place of the divisive forces in modern society effecting and preserving intellectual and social class differences in the dry husks of orthodoxy, inquiry as thus interpreted by Dewey is a radical agent of unification and social cohesion. In inquiry, men achieve communion.

Dewey would not be too happy with the comparison, but in his ability to find moral, metaphysical, and religious significance in the fact of "science," in inquiry and intelligence — in his reinterpretation of the classic vision of human excellence realized in the act of knowing — he is in the company of Aristotle, St. Thomas, and Spinoza.

In the very definition of inquiry, its role is cast as bringing order and coherence into otherwise conflicting and discordant experience. Coherent experience is communicative and communal. For Dewey, religion has its vital source and spreading roots in the life and shared experience of the community. Inquiry, since it is the compelling resource of human growth and renewal of values, is thus a fit object of religious reverence, just as its continuous workings are objects of liberal enjoyments.

Pragmatism and a Problem about Truth

WE have not ventured to survey the many controversial issues that have been raised and discussed concerning Dewey's instrumentalism. An adequate conspectus of the critical objections to Dewey's ideas would take us too far off the present course and would require a separate study in itself. It is hoped that the above account of the theory of inquiry and truth is clear enough to dispel some of the more longstanding doubts as to what Dewey was saying and what he attempted to achieve.

One problem, however, ought to be mentioned here, for it has been a matter of controversy about as longrunning as the history of pragmatism. This is the question of the pragmatists' view of truth. For many readers of Dewey (and of James), the pragmatists appear to interpret judgments of truth as resting upon and as expressioning mere personal satisfaction. For convenience, we can sum up most of the objections to this alleged pragmatic doctrine of truth in one argument that, historically, represents the paradigm case against pragmatism: If ideas or beliefs are true or not, depending on whether or not they "work" or their consequences are "successful" or "satisfactory," then (1) we can never know whether an idea is true or false, since we can never know *all* of the consequences or far-reaching effects; (2) the same idea can be both true and false, since it may prove satisfactory at one time, unsatisfactory at others, or may satisfy some persons while dissatisfying others; and (3) we can never know whether the pragmatic definition of truth is justifiable or useful, since to try to judge that definition will require making true statements about it and its consequences. But true statements in this case will be ones that work or have satisfactory consequences, and this, for reasons (1) and (2), leads to an infinite regress and insuperable difficulties.

The paradigm case, if taken seriously, might lead one to suspicions about the sanity of the spokesmen for pragmatism.

Thus, consider the following example: Suppose you are asked, "Did you have a poached egg for breakfast?" Most persons, when asked, will try to remember. But the pragmatist will have to take time out for an experiment. He will first try to believe that he *has* eaten a poached egg and observe the consequences of his belief; he will next believe the negative of his first belief and consider its consequences. He will then compare the consequences of the two beliefs, and his answer to the question will depend on which of the consequences he finds most "satisfactory." This way of getting at truth is surely absurd. It is not only absurd but impossible for the logical reasons (1), (2), and (3) just given. What is worse (for the pragmatist), this kind of example[103] is not only logically convincing as dissuading would-be pragmatists, it is very persuasive as rhetoric. For what young philosopher, in earnest professorial moments, could bear to witness this difficult and austere abstraction called "truth" going limp or to pieces over the breakfast table and poached eggs?

On the larger social and ethical consequences of pragmatism, the paradigm case alarms us to these dangers: truth and falsehood will be determined by the desires and interests of men with power; the state, police, or politicians will decide what consequences of what ideas are "successful" or "satisfactory." Pragmatically, then, pragmatism is a socially disastrous philosophy.

What is most wrong with the paradigm is an undeclared and uncritical use of the concepts of "successful" or "satisfactory" consequences of ideas or beliefs as somehow referring to private, wilful, and subjective episodes in the mind. But for Dewey, satisfaction and desiring are not "subjective" events and are not to be viewed according to an early and outmoded mentalistic psychology. The concept of "satisfactory consequences" need not be construed as replaceable by concepts descriptive of mental conduct, "desires," "wishes," and the like; nor need it be construed as synonymous with certain expressions designating purely subjective and private mental events, as if the Cartesian concept of mind were the only available basis for a manageable and intelligible use of such language.

In Dewey's theory of inquiry, it is a mistake to interpret "satisfactory consequences of ideas" as somehow entailing "subjective" or "private" items of behavior in contradistinction from something else called "objective." For ideas, or hypotheses, must *satisfy* the conditions of a situation that is problematic. The consequences of ideas are satisfactory or not relative to the conditions of some specific problem situation. This sense of *satisfactory* does not call for trading on a theory of subjective mental events, nor does it call for a subjectively directed mental conduct language at all — no more so than when one is said to "satisfy" the requirements of an examination. When a man satisfies the requirements for military service, it would scarcely be credible to say that this means he has produced "desired effects" or an instance of *liking* in either his own mind or in that of his examining officer. Or, in order to borrow money from the bank, one must satisfy the banker of one's ability to pay back the loan with interest. But it is seriously to be doubted that one "satisfies" bankers by appealing to their tender feelings and humane desires. The "satisfaction" is just as impersonal and unsubjective as is the "interest" on the loan. In much the same sense, satisfactory hypotheses and theories in science are not so called because they happen to be pleasing to some scientist.

The trouble with the paradigm case against pragmatism lies in its defective strategy in relying upon defective assumptions. Yet to venture to remove the threat by exposing it in this fashion is not to abolish all lingering doubts about pragmatism. For there is even the unresolved question of why pragmatists should have such difficulty in exorcising the paradigm once and for all. It is ironic, considering that pragmatism began as a program for achieving conceptual clarity, that pragmatists would run into such difficulties in making themselves understood.

Some Pragmatic Consequences of Pragmatism

FROM its inception, pragmatism was never intended as a philosophy or an amalgamation of doctrines into a school and a new orthodoxy. By those who contributed most to its development, pragmatism was conceived as a way of philosophizing — a method for dealing with problems; it was not proposed as a system of philosophy nor as a calling for devotees and disciples. Indeed, much of its influence is to be found in disciplines outside professional philosophy.

The following remarks are devoted to indicating several ways in which pragmatism has evolved and continues to be operative, as one among other philosophic approaches upon the current intellectual scene.

Peirce's principle of fallibilism is one of the links connecting pragmatism with several current forms of critical empiricism. Peirce held that no statement about facts is self-certifying, indubitable, or ever finally verified. He once said that all reasoning about fact "is of the nature of judging the proportion of something in a whole collection by the proportion found in a sample."[104]

Roughly stated, the pragmatic analysis of experience, perception, and thought has always emphasized the inferential character of these activities; the study of these forms of behavior is the study of the specific functions of organic and socially conditioned habits, leading principles, and anticipated consequences as these occur in certain kinds of contexts and are prompted by certain kinds of purposes. From Peirce on, pragmatists have taken an increasing interest in various forms of inferential behavior exhibited in the use of signs, language, and action. Early in the present century, a number of remarkably suggestive philosophic advances were made by James, Dewey, and G. H. Mead concerning the nature of mind, the use of mental conduct language, and the analysis of the self and intelligent conduct. Finding a similar development emerging quite independently in recent British philosophy (notably in Ryle's *The Concept of Mind*),[105] Americans have of late begun to take a new interest in this period of their own philosophic past — a past suddenly made respectable by a coincidence in Oxford.

A related field of contemporary interest has been the study of the inferential nature of empirical statements and their justification. Following Peirce's work, F. P. Ramsey in several important papers and C. I. Lewis in a major work have each attempted to set forth distinctively pragmatic theories of the probable character of empirical knowledge.[106]

Recently, a more radical extension of fallibilism to *all* statements has been proposed in the spirit of a more thoroughgoing pragmatism. On this view, the cleavage in meaning and truth between *analytic* and *synthetic* statements is repudiated or viewed as a matter of degree (and as relative among statements within a given conceptual system).[107] While this critical rejection of the traditional analytic-synthetic distinction was motivated by technical problems of *meaning* and *reference*, its relation, even if unintended, to fallibilism is clear. For one effect of waiving the distinction is to give up the notion of "logically true" statements as immune to any possible revisions coming by way of experience. The effect is to dispossess logical laws of the "necessarily true" status they were once thought to enjoy. And this is to restore a connection between logic and ontology. However, since the proposal is controversial at present, it is best left unpursued here.

One other respect in which pragmatism is alive deserves notice. This is the proposal, elaborated carefully by Dewey and more recently by C. I. Lewis, that the "logic" of moral judgments and procedures of evaluation is of the same objective character and follows the same standards as those that govern the testing and verification of empirical hypotheses in the sciences.

Allied more than not with the critical spirit of modern British "analysis" concerned with the topology of the philosophic uses and misuses of language; allied, too, with logical empiricism in its pursuit of a responsible philosophic grasp of the structure and procedures of scientifically warranted knowledge; and proposing to extend the objective procedures for evaluating knowledge — claims to evaluating social and moral experience and ideals — pragmatism contains latent possibilities for important syntheses of current trends in philosophy. Whether synthesis is to be looked for in philosophy as a renewal of vitality or avoided as encouraging ersatz products is an open question.

Venturing to predict the future of pragmatism, or even the future of philosophy, would be futile.

Pragmatism is a creature of the times, and recently the times have been hard. Philosophy is currently subject to a dilemma of forces besetting civilization generally; routine patterns work against variety; we grow more informed in mind while weaker in imaginative nerve. However, a situation in which hope is no less rational than despair can nourish new intellectual currents; and if the present dilemma in philosophy is no occasion for laughter, neither is it one for tears.

25

G. E. Moore

A. R. WHITE

MOORE WAS BORN in London in 1873. From 1898 to 1904, and from 1911 to 1939, he lived at Cambridge as a Fellow of Trinity College and subsequently as Professor of Philosophy in the University of Cambridge. During 1940–1941, he lectured at various American universities. He was a Fellow of the British Academy and received the Order of Merit. He died in 1958.

THE NAMES OF G. E. MOORE and Bertrand Russell are traditionally linked. They were fellow undergraduates at Cambridge in the 1890's and remained as colleagues there much of their working lives. Together with Wittgenstein, they constitute a famous Cambridge triad whose influence on contemporary thought has been immense. Moore and Russell have always had a lot in common, and each has admitted the other's influence. Together they revolted from the Hegelianism and idealism common in the Cambridge of their youth; together they accepted what common sense and the sciences assert; both gave their attention to what they called an "analysis" of what is said in such assertions. But whereas the prolific and elegant writings of the publicist Russell soon became popular throughout the world, Moore's small output, with its crabbed style, won favor more slowly and, then, mainly in English-speaking countries. This is in some measure due to the fact that while Moore was interested in problems connected with our ordinary use of language and our common-sense beliefs, Russell shared the interest of many continental philosophers in the language and theories of mathematics and the natural sciences. It is, I think, possible and of some interest in this connection to characterize Wittgenstein's early *Tractatus Logico-Philosophicus* as Russellian and his later *Philosophical Investigations* as Mooreian.

Because philosophical thinking in Europe at the beginning of this century was dominated by an idealism borrowed from Hegel, Moore's fame for a long time rested partly on an article, "The Refutation of Idealism," which he published in *Mind* in 1903. This is largely a historical accident, for his objections to idealism were basically the same as those which he also felt against some of the quite different theses of Hume (compare "Hume's Philosophy," 1909, reprinted in *Philosophical Studies*, 1922), namely: that by an "abuse of language" they arrived at conclusions that "fly in the face of common sense." These objections spring from a view of the method of tackling philosophical problems which contemporary English-speaking philosophers, who might deny every one of the particular solutions to which the method led Moore, are united in practising. It is by his advocacy and practice of this method that Moore merits a place in the history of philosophy.[1]

Philosophical Method

MOORE's main philosophical work consists not in investigating either the *truth* or the *meaning* of what is said in ordinary life — or in science — which as such he believes to have a well-known meaning and to be in many cases certainly true, but in giving what he calls an *analysis* of this meaning. He investigated the views of other philosophers to see what these views could mean and whether they are true, because they are often attempted analyses whose results deny the commonly accepted truth and meaning of what they analyze.

In the opening pages of an article on "Necessity" in 1900, he said,

> My primary object in this paper is to determine the *meaning* of necessity. I do not wish to discover what things are necessary; but what that predicate is which attaches to them when they are so. Nor, on the other hand, do I wish to arrive at a correct verbal definition of necessity. That the word is commonly used to signify a great number of different predicates, which do actually attach to things, appears to me quite plain. But this being so, we shall be using the word correctly, whenever we apply it to any one of these; and a correct definition of necessity will be attained if we enumerate all those different predicates which the word is commonly used to signify; for the only test that a word is correctly defined is common usage. The problem which I wish to solve is different from either of these. . . . The question which we must answer . . . is quite different from either of the two questions: Is he using the word correctly? or: Has the thing in question that predicate? For there may be no doubt at all that we should answer yes or no to either of these questions. . . . My main object is not to discover whether any or all of the propositions of the form "A is necessary" are true or false, nor yet whether they are correctly expressed; but what their *meaning* is.[2]

This contrast between the truth and the meaning (in the sense of the correct use) of what we say and its meaning in another sense, which he later usually calls analysis, was repeated in a programmatic essay of 1925, "A Defence of Common Sense." He singled out as the chief difference between himself and other philosophers that he was "not at all sceptical as to the *truth* of such propositions" as we assert in our common-sense beliefs, and that he considered the way we express them to be "the very type of an unambiguous expression, the meaning of which we all understand"; but what puzzled him was their analysis. He supposed further, that a reason for this difference was that other philosophers were "confusing the question whether we understand its meaning (which we all certainly do) with the entirely different question whether we *know what it means*, in the sense that we are able to *give a correct analysis* of its meaning."

In his autobiographical remarks of 1942, when he was describing what had been his "main stimulus to philosophize," he tells us: "I do not think that the world or the sciences would ever have suggested to me any philosophical problems. What has suggested philosophical problems to me is things which other philosophers have said about the world or the sciences. . . . First, the problem of trying to get really clear as to what on earth a given philosopher *meant* by something which he said, and, secondly, the problem of discovering what really satisfactory reasons there are for supposing that what he said was true, or, alternatively, was false."[3]

Because Moore had no doubt of the meaning or truth of what he wished to analyze, namely, what is said by common sense, he was able to appeal to these deliverances in support of his own analyses and in refutation of the analyses of other philosophers. Before considering his view of analysis, therefore, it is important to get quite clear about the details of his attitude to the meaning and truth of what is analyzed — that is, about the details of what is often called the appeals to ordinary language and to common sense, respectively, especially as these two have been frequently confused or assimilated even by his admirers.

THE APPEAL TO COMMON SENSE

Part of the awe or contempt with which ordinary people regard philosophy is due to the paradoxical nature of many of its conclusions. Ever since Zeno's denial of the possibility of motion, philosophers have commonly asserted that many of the things which we all believe are quite mistaken. They have told us that the furniture of the world ceases to exist when it is not perceived, that we cannot be sure that life is not a dream, that we have no good reason for believing that the sun will rise tomorrow, that nothing we say is wholly true, and that thought and reality are one. With the reign of nineteenth-century idealism, this venerable tradition of contradicting the "beliefs of common sense" reached its peak. One of the startling things about Moore was his apparent philosophical naïveté in assaulting this position. Such naïveté had not been known since the rather despised Scottish 'common sense philosophy' of the eighteenth century with which Moore has many, perhaps unconscious, affinities.

Moore very frequently took some of the statements of common sense as undoubtedly true: "It seems to me that we do in ordinary life constantly talk of *seeing* such things [*sc.* that that is a door, a finger, etc.] and that when we do so, we are neither using language incorrectly nor making any mistake about the facts — supposing something to occur which never does in fact occur."[4] He used them moreover as a touchstone of truth; a reason for accepting a philosophical view is that it is in accordance with common sense, and a reason for rejecting it is that it "flies in the face of common sense." Speaking about a philosophical theory with which he sympathized, he once said, "I actually know that this is a thumb, and if the proposition that 'This is a thumb' could be shown to be inconsistent with the Sensum Theory, I should say the Sensum Theory was *certainly* false."[5]

But his acceptance of common-sense statements was not uncritical; he agreed that some such statements are certainly mistaken and that any such might be. In deciding whether there was good reason to accept as true any given statement of common sense he seems to have used five principles or criteria, of which the first — and possibly the second — is also a criterion for calling a statement a statement of common sense at all. *First,* he uses a criterion of universal acceptance — that is, that there are many things, such as our belief in the existence of material objects like tables and chairs, which "we certainly all do, in ordinary life, constantly believe."[6] *Secondly,* we may distinguish a criterion of compulsive acceptance, for Moore draws attention to the fact that there are many beliefs, such as those just mentioned, which we cannot help holding, even if at the same time we hold beliefs inconsistent with them. *Thirdly,* various kinds of inconsistency flow from the denial of various of the beliefs of common sense. A philosopher may, for instance, use an argument that presupposes the truth of the belief he is attempting to disprove — as do those who, while denying the reality of time and yet talk of "what we constantly believe," presuppose that things do happen in time. Another philosopher may presuppose the truth of the *type* of belief to be disproved as when Hume "declares that we cannot, in ordinary life, avoid believing things which are inconsistent with them [*sc.* the skeptical views that we never know any external facts]; and, in so declaring, he, of course, incidentally implies that they are false, since he implies that he himself has a great deal of knowledge as to what we can and cannot believe in ordinary life."[7] Or a philosopher may use arguments that rest on grounds far less certain than those common-sense beliefs he is attacking. Furthermore, we are often able to show a philosopher who denies a statement of common sense that it "is consistent with something else which he holds to be true, whereas his original view is contradictory to it."[8] *Fourthly,* Moore held that a special type of inconsistency arises in attempts to deny certain beliefs of common sense, for these beliefs "have this peculiar property — namely, that *if we know that they are features in the 'common sense view of the world', it follows that they are true*; it is self-contradictory to maintain that *we* know them to be features in the common sense view and that yet they are not true." Indeed, some of these statements must be accepted because "to say that there is a 'Common Sense view of the world' is to say that they are true."[9] *Fifthly,* Moore often asks us to accept a common-sense belief on the ground that one can see "by inspection" that it is "self-evident."

But although these are five good reasons for accepting a common-sense statement as true, he insisted that they do *not prove* it true and that indeed it *may* be wrong. They do not prove it true for the simple reason that such a statement is ultimate and self-evident, that is, "it is not an inference from some proposition other than itself."[10] For Moore held that since and because there are many statements which are accepted as true on the evidence of others, there must be some which are accepted without evidence; and typical examples of these latter are the laws of logic and some of the statements of common sense. Thus, the five criteria are not intended, *per impossibile*, to *prove* any statement of common sense to be true, but to serve as the best reasons there could be for accepting them. They are, as he said quoting Mill, "considerations capable of determining the intellect either to give or withhold its assent."[11] If we consider together a statement of common sense and its philosophical denial, Moore is confident that the application of the five criteria will show that while neither statement is provable there are far better reasons for accepting as true and for claiming to know the common-sense statement rather than its rival.

Having established that it is thus reasonable to take many such statements of common sense as true, he could justifiably appeal to these in his own favor and against many philosophical views.

THE APPEAL TO ORDINARY LANGUAGE

As well as accepting the truth of those common-sense beliefs which he wished to analyze, Moore felt justified in assuming that there was no doubt about the meaning of the expressions used to convey them. Hence he frequently appeals to the ordinary use — or uses, for there are often several ordinary uses of the one word — of the expressions, such as "know," "see," "good," "real," "time," whose meaning he is examining on the grounds that the ordinary use of an expression that occurs in everyday language like English is well known to those who understand that language and that it is a use we all constantly employ. Nor was Moore's interest in the ordinary use of our everyday expressions at variance with his occasional display of unconcern about "verbal questions"; for what interested him was not the philological fact that one word and not another is used in a certain way, but the philosophical fact that it is in this way, and not another, that the given word is used.

Though he felt neither difficulty in understanding nor doubt about the correctness of the ordinary use of everyday expressions, he was very puzzled by the expressions often used by philosophers, which, although partly unexplained neologisms, are mainly unexplained alterations of the meanings of everyday words. Such tampering with ordinary language seemed to him a main cause of the contradictions of common sense in which philosophy frequently issued as well as of the self-contradictions within philosophy itself.

Moore, then, appeals in various ways to the expressions of our ordinary language whose meanings he is examining; *either* (1) by taking them as an indication that we all believe so and so because "the language we use constantly implies" it; *or* (2) by using them to interpret the strange language of philosophers; *or* (3) by using them to refute the doctrines of philosophers on the grounds that (a) such doctrines often involve "an abuse of language," as when a philosopher says "that our wills can properly be said to be free even if we *never* can, in any sense at all, do anything else except what, in the end, we actually do do";[12] (b) when interpreted in ordinary language, philosophical doctrines are often seen to be either inconsistent with common sense or internally inconsistent. Perhaps the best summary statement of the way he appeals to ordinary language against philosophers is expressed in a sentence in *Principia Ethica*: "I shall try to produce an agreement that the fundamental principle of Hedonism is very like an absurdity, by showing what it must mean if it is clearly thought out, and how that clear meaning is in conflict with other beliefs, which will, I hope, not be so easily given up."[13]

MEANING

We saw that Moore accepted and appealed to both the truth and the meaning of many things that are said in common sense; what he found baffling and worth investigating about them is what he has called an *analysis* of their meaning. But before examining exactly what he meant by such an analysis, some of his uses of "meaning" and his theories about it need to be considered. For ambiguity and outright fallacy here are the sources of many of the things which have puzzled both him and his commentators.

1. First of all, to the question "What do we mean when we talk of the 'meaning' of an expression?" Moore throughout his life assumed an answer that has been very common from the earliest times of philosophy and which is predominant also in the work of Russell and the early Wittgenstein. I call this the *concept theory* of meaning, for it is the view that the meaning of an expression is a peculiar sort of nonphysical and nonpsychological entity, namely, a concept — or a proposition, as it is called when the expression is a complete sentence — for which the expression stands, or names, signifies, or expresses, and which is "called up before the mind" of anyone who understands the expression. As early as 1910, Moore realized some of the difficulties in such a theory; for instance, what and where are the concepts for which expressions referring to imaginary things like centaurs stand, or for which the expressions of false beliefs, such as "The battle of Waterloo was fought in 1812," stand? But despite this, he never abandoned the theory because to him as it has to others, it seemed to give an easy and obvious solution of certain problems about meaning, such as how to distinguish between the words or images that express something and the something that is expressed, how to account for the fact that, as we say, two expressions

may express the same thing, how to explain what we mean when we speak of "unexpressed thoughts," what it is that synonymous expressions have in common, what it is that we are examining when we examine the meaning of an expression, and, finally, what the word "meaning" refers to.

Because of this concept theory of meaning, Moore speaks of what he wishes to analyze (the *analysandum*) as either the meaning of an expression or the concept (or proposition) for which the expression stands, or, sometimes, the object or fact that the expression names.

2. Secondly, Moore often, as he confessed in 1942, "in giving analyses, used the word 'means' and thus [gave] a false impression,"[14] for we have seen that he wished neither to look for the meaning of an expression — which he assumed was well known — nor to show a philological interest in the expression as such. The use of the word "meaning" as a synonym of "analysis" has had the result that when he wished to contrast an inquiry or a doubt about the meaning of an expression with an inquiry or a doubt about the analysis of the meaning of an expression, he often put it as a contrast between one sense of knowing the meaning of an expression and another sense of knowing the meaning of an expression. And this has led some readers to think that he sometimes felt doubtful about the meaning, in the ordinary sense, of some everyday word.

ANALYSIS

Now if by "meaning," in the sense in which he did feel there was a legitimate doubt about the meaning of what we ordinarily say, he intended to speak of an analysis of the meaning of the expressions we ordinarily use, what is such an analysis? The answer to this, I believe, is that Moore held, often at the same time, three views about what analysis — or knowing the meaning, in the technical sense — was.

He seems to have thought of it as *either* being able to say what it is that *we see before our minds* when we see the meaning of an expression, that is, the concept conveyed by it — with perhaps the hint that what we see is the property common to all those things in regard to which the expression is correctly used; *or* being able to say what the constituent concepts are into which the concept can be *divided* and which compose it; *or* being able to say how the given concept is related to and *distinguished* from other concepts which are conveyed either by the same or by different expressions.

When he took the first, or *inspection*, view, he said, for example, in regard to the notion of *good*, "whoever will attentively consider with himself what is actually before his mind when he asks the question 'Is pleasure (or whatever it may be) after all good?' can easily satisfy himself that he is not merely wondering whether pleasure is pleasant."[15] When Moore is trying to get us to understand the meaning of

"correspondence" in order to see whether or not it is like the meaning of "truth," he says that "the essential point is to concentrate attention upon the relation *itself*: to hold it before your mind, in the sense in which when I name the colour 'vermilion,' you can hold before your mind the colour I mean."[16] Similarly, the burden of his charge against the idealists was that they failed to see the difference between, for example, "blue" and the "consciousness of blue," and this because "they have not been able to hold *it* and *blue* before their minds and to compare them."[17]

In Moore's earliest works we are told that "a thing becomes intelligible first when it is analysed into its constituent concepts,"[18] for example, the analysis of a sensation into the object of the sensation, the awareness of the object, and a relation of these two elements; the analysis of belief into the act of belief and the object of belief. Though this *division* view of analysis remains in some of his latest work — where we are told that "the expression used for the *analysans* must *explicitly mention* concepts which are not explicitly mentioned by the expression used for the *analysandum*" and must also mention the "method of combination" of these concepts[19] — it is best known in *Principia Ethica* of 1903. Here he is led to the conclusion that because "a definition [i.e., analysis] states what are the parts which invariably compose a certain whole" the notion of *good* has "no definition because it is simple and has no parts."[20]

The occurrence of what I have called the *distinction* view of analysis alongside the division view is of some historical interest since the division view, which has a very long philosophical history, predominated among Moore's early analytic contemporaries — Russell, the Vienna Circle, and the early Wittgenstein — whereas the present tendency, due considerably to the later writings of Wittgenstein and the work of Ryle, is toward the method of distinction.

Now Moore seems to have used "distinction" and "distinguish" both in the sense of merely separating out and enumerating the various meanings of a given expression such as "good" or "see" and in the sense of relating any one of these meanings to, and distinguishing it from, the other meanings of the same expression and the meanings of other expressions pertinent to the given expression. The importance of the first, or preliminary, kind of distinction, which he often practised, is stressed in the Preface to *Principia Ethica*, where he criticizes philosophers who "are constantly endeavouring to prove that 'Yes' or 'No' will answer questions, to which neither answer is correct, owing to the fact that what they have before their minds is not one question but several to some of which the true answer is 'No,' to others 'Yes'." The second kind of distinction, which alone is analysis, is exemplified by his comment that the commission of the famous naturalistic fallacy in ethics involves "that those who commit it should not recognise clearly the meaning of the proposition 'This is good' — that they should not be able to distinguish this from other propositions which seem to resemble it; and, where this is so, it is, of course, impossible that its logical relations should be clearly perceived."[21]

The general picture that Moore had of a philosopher analyzing the meaning of an expression is that of someone staring (inspection) at an object in front of his eyes (before the mind) and, therefore, in some sense, knowing what it is. But in another sense he does not know what it is, either because he cannot see the various parts of which it is constituted and the way they are put together (division), or because he cannot see how the object is related to and distinguished from other things (distinction).

Contemporary philosophers who have taken over Moore's contrast between knowing the meaning of an expression and being able to analyze that meaning have put it in linguistic terms as the contrast between knowing how to use an expression and being able to describe or give the rules of that use. We have seen that Moore's concept theory of meaning led him, on the other hand, to describe the contrast as that between having a concept before the mind and being able to see or say something about it, such as how it is constituted from, or related to and distinguished from, other concepts. The advantage of his formulation seemed to Moore to be that we can analyze concepts without necessarily paying attention to the linguistic terms in which they are expressed and, ideally at least, even without there being any linguistic expression of them. But, as we would expect, when we realize the mistakenness of the concept theory, his actual treatment has had to be in terms of the linguistic expressions of the concepts. A striking example of this is his examination of the question whether "existence is a predicate."[22] His purpose was to show that, despite their grammatical similarity, "Tame tigers exist" is logically different from "Tame tigers growl," "Tame tigers jump," "Tame tigers are friendly." His method is to point out that other statements and questions that are appropriate to "growl," "jump," "friendly," and are not appropriate to "exists." We can say, for example, "All (or most) tame tigers growl, jump, are friendly," but we cannot sensibly say "All (or most) tame tigers exist"; we can say "Here's a tame tiger and he growls (or does not growl)" but it is absurd, because either pleonastic or self-contradictory, to say "Here's a tame tiger and he exists (or he does not exist)."

Furthermore, Moore was quite clear that even if we could analyze a concept without reference to any verbal expression, yet "in order to *give* an analysis you must use verbal expressions." Here, however, he usually assumed that what we have to do is to find a collection of constituent concepts which together make up, are identical with, the concept to be

analyzed; and, therefore, in practice to find a verbal expression which is synonymous with or a translation of, that is, expresses the same concept as, the verbal expression of the concept to be analyzed. This led him into the most frightful difficulties about synonymity and the identity of concepts,[23] which issued in the famous "paradox of analysis," namely, that if the concept which provides the analysis is identical with the concept to be analyzed we have said nothing, whereas if it is different we have given a false analysis.

This "translation" approach to analysis, which characterized the work of analysts up to the 1930's, is partly due to the concept theory of meaning and partly to two of Moore's theoretical views of analysis, namely as an inspection of some concept before the mind and as a mental division of that concept into its parts. In much of his actual practice, however, where analysis is regarded as the attempt to distinguish, by way of similarity and difference, one concept from another — one meaning of an expression from other meanings of that expression and the meanings of other expressions — he rightly did not insist on looking for concepts equivalent to the given concept or for expressions synonymous with the given expression. And it is this distinction view of analysis which has won favor with philosophers since just before the 1939-1945 war.

Applications of the Method of Analysis

THE two fields of philosophical problems that mainly interested Moore were ethics and the theory of perception. In both fields he kept coming back again and again to the same difficulties and offering almost the same variations on his earliest solutions. Although these solutions are nowadays generally thought unacceptable, the particular fields provide the best region in which to see his method and approach at work.

ETHICS

Taking "What is good?" as the central question of ethics, Moore distinguished the sense in which the question demands an inquiry into the analysis of the notion of "good" from the senses in which it seeks to know either what things are good or what kinds of things are good. Though he did in his first ethical work, *Principia Ethica*, attempt a brief answer to the question "What kinds of things are good?" most of his work here and elsewhere is devoted to the problem of analysis. He further distinguished various senses of the word "good" as a preliminary to analyzing one central sense, which he variously termed as "intrinsically good," "good in itself," "good for its own sake," and "good if quite alone."

Now the actual results he arrived at in his analysis of the meaning of "good" provide a good example of the workings of his method, since these results are rather different according to which of his three views of analysis he took.

First, under the influence of the inspection method and the translation approach, he demanded an analysis in terms of the identity of some other concept with the concept of *good* and then objected that this could not be given because any attempt to do so either committed what he called the "naturalistic fallacy" or at most gave a logical equivalence and not an identity of two concepts. Now we shall see that although Moore's naturalistic fallacy argument successfully rejects all the notions suggested as identical with *good*, and thus led him to say that *good* is unanalyzable, in fact it analyzes *good* by the method of distinguishing it from other concepts. The lack of identity of *good* with any other concept seemed to him to follow also from the fact that if the analyst of *good* will "attentively consider what is actually before his mind" and "if he will try this experiment with each suggested definition in succession, he may become expert enough to recognise that in every case he has before his mind a unique object."[24]

Secondly, under the influence of the division method, he said in *Principia Ethica*[25] that "a definition states what are the parts which invariably compose a certain whole; and in this sense, the notion 'good' has no definition because it is simple and has no parts."

Although for these reasons he usually said that *good* is unanalyzable, in practice he used the method of distinction to try to show its analysis. In *Principia Ethica*,[26] we are told that in order to advance in analysis we must become aware that the notion of *good* is "different from other notions" and that to "fail to recognise clearly the meaning of the proposition 'This is good' [is to fail] to distinguish this from other propositions which seem to resemble it." The use of the "naturalistic fallacy" argument is, I believe, to show that all the theories of ethics overlook or deny important distinctions between *good* and other notions. The *name* that Moore gave to the fallacy is misleading as regards his method, for he did not wish merely to say that *good* is not identical with any "natural" characteristic but that it is not identical with anything else. He said, for example that "even if it [i.e., *good*] were a natural object that would not alter the nature of the fallacy . . . only the name would not be so appropriate."[27] Thus he is able to take the misidentification of *good* with any metaphysical concept as another instance of this fallacy. Indeed, he says of two nonethical notions: "If I were to imagine that when I said 'I am pleased' I meant that 'I' was exactly the same thing as 'pleasure,' I should not indeed call that a naturalistic fallacy, although it would be the same fallacy as I have called naturalistic with reference to Ethics."[28]

We can avoid talking of concepts and still adhere to the naturalistic fallacy argument by saying that whatever *A* may be, it is always significant and not idle to say that *A* is good or to ask whether *B*, which has the characteristic *A*, is good. Moore himself sometimes put the argument this way, and those who used it before him often did so. Because of his concept theory of meaning, the conclusion that Moore drew from this argument was that "good" is the name of a unique, simple, nonnatural concept or characteristic; whereas the correct conclusion, I think, is that "good" is used evaluatively, not descriptively, so that however completely one has described something it always remains to be evaluated. The proposed descriptive analyses in terms of pleasure, self-realization, God's commands, etc., which he rightly combated, really only give the criteria by virtue of which we may call things good; hence it is not self-contradictory, although in some instances decidedly odd, to admit that something has any or all of these characteristics and yet refuse to call it good or to set any value on it.

One particular distinction which Moore always felt was most dangerously overlooked is that between "good" and various attitudinal notions such as "approve," "like," "be pleased with." He therefore devoted much energy to attacking "subjective" views, that is, views which regarded "This is good" and "I (or someone or most people) approve of this" as synonymous. His fundamental objection to these views was that they seemed to deny the dictum "Once good, always good" in so far as according to them two men, or the one man at different times, who had different feelings toward the same thing might, without contradicting each other, say the one that it was good, the other that it was bad. Moore sometimes mistakenly held that this conclusion of the subjectivist argument is contrary to common sense. But, of course, if "good" and "bad" are interpreted in the subjectivist way, then the conclusion is not contrary to common sense, since it only says that one person may approve what another does not. What the conclusion does go against is our ordinary use of "good" and "bad," which precludes the correct application of "good" and "bad" to the same thing at the same time in the same respect.

The apparent strength of his arguments against these subjectivist views, which, I suspect Moore considered the most plausible and worrying attempt to define *good*, seems to have confirmed him in his belief that it is indefinable. The fact that owing to his concept theory of meaning he thought that "the sense in which the word 'good' is used" could be paraphrased as "the characteristic of which the word 'good' is the name," prevented him, apart from some *obiter dicta*, from fully realizing until 1942 that "good" might not be used to describe or name anything, and thus not to describe an attitude, but in some quite different way. In 1942[29] he faced a view raised by Stevenson from which "it would follow that 'good' in this usage" — and, Moore adds later, in any usage — "is not the name of any characteristic at all," but is only emotive or expressive of the speaker's attitude. Though he felt grave doubts about this view, particularly because he did not see how it allowed a person who said "This is good" to contradict or say something "logically incompatible" with a person who said "This is not good," he there shows himself rather inclined to think it might be the correct view.

PERCEPTION

Assuming that the things we express by such words as "I hear a clock," "I see an inkstand," "This, which I see, is a book," "This, which I feel, is a shirt," are often undoubtedly true and their meaning quite clear, Moore bent his energies to giving an analysis of their meaning. Since he concentrated on examples of *visual* perception, I confine myself to this.

Generally, the problem of the analysis of such statements is to say what we mean when we see a particular material object — for example, a book. Put in the *inspection* terminology, we have to state what exactly it is that we know or judge or have before the mind when we know or judge or have before the mind such things as "This is a hand" or "I see a dog." The psychological flavor which he sometimes gave to the inspection view is clearly exemplified in his 1910–1911 lectures, where the attempt to describe what sense perception is is given as the attempt to describe "what is it that happens in our minds" when we see a material object. He wished to "analyse . . . the *mental* occurrence — the act of consciousness — which we call *seeing*" because "all of us who are not blind can directly observe this mental occurrence, which we mean by seeing."[30] This is the sort of approach that Wittgenstein later criticized by saying "It shows a fundamental misunderstanding, if I am inclined to study the headache I have now in order to get clear about the philosophical problem of sensation," for "We are interested in the concept and its place among the concepts of experience."[31]

Moore's *distinction*, and even his *division*, methods of analysis escape this tendency to psychologism; but they are bound up, in the case of perception, with an initial step that he held to be inevitable, namely: the assumption of something called a *sense-datum*. In the division method the concept of the object seen is to be divided into the concept of a sense-datum and of some *thing* to which the sense-datum is related in a baffling way. The distinction method proceeds from the assumption that when we see an opaque material object, e.g. a book, we *ipso facto* see, in a second sense, a particular part of it, say, the surface turned toward us, and also see, in a third sense, a sense-datum, e.g. a particular colored patch. Our task then is to distinguish and relate the three concepts covered by the one word "see" and the three concepts covered by their respective grammatical objects, namely, the "material object," the "part of the surface of the material object," and the "sense-datum."

Since Moore's whole treatment of the problems of perception is affected by his introduction of sense-data, and since the legitimacy of this introduction is widely queried among contemporary philosophers, it is important to see his reasons for introducing them. I believe that at least six such reasons can be discovered in his writings. I shall label these in my own way.

1. *The method of restriction* is the favorite among philosophers and psychologists generally. Just as the first two senses of "see" are distinguished by the extent of the objects that are respectively seen — for example, the whole of the desk or just a facing surface — so the third sense is restricted to what we "actually" or "directly" see. We are told that "the mere fact that an object is *directly apprehended* is a sufficient condition for saying that it is a sense-datum."[32] On the question of what in fact is directly seen Moore was much less sure. Sometimes he included colors, their size and shape and spatial relations, at another time he restricted himself to patches of various color, size, and shape and the space they occupy, at another time he allowed even "a transparent glass cube."

He also used the traditional arguments from perspective and environmental conditions to conclude that *what* a person directly sees who looks at something under certain conditions, e.g. a penny flat in front of the naked eye, is often different from what a person directly sees who looks at it under other conditions, e.g. the penny endwise seen through colored spectacles; and in at least one of these cases different from the penny which is seen. What is "directly seen" is the sense-datum.

2. *The method of selection* is exemplified by a famous passage in "A Defence of Common Sense."[33] where Moore says:

And in order to point out to the reader what sort of things I mean by sense-data, I need only ask him to look at his own right hand. If he does this, he will be able to pick out something (and, unless he is seeing double, *only* one thing) with regard to which he will see that it is, at first sight, a natural view to take that that thing is identical, not, indeed, with his whole right hand, but with that part of its surface which he is actually seeing, but will also (on a little reflection), be able to see that it is doubtful whether it can be identical with the part of the surface of his hand in question. Things *of the sort* (in a certain respect) of which this thing is . . . I mean by sense-data.

The difficulties this passage has rightly caused many people are due, I think, to Moore's supposition that a sense-datum is a peculiar sort of *entity*, which we at first wrongly identify *with* another thing, the surface of the hand, for example — but later come to think can be distinguished from it. I shall later suggest that, on the contrary, "sense-datum" is a word we may use to talk about how something looks to us, and that our problem is what to identify what we see *as*, and not what to identify what we see *with*.

3. *The method of the ultimate subject.* When we say, for example, "This, which I see, is an inkbottle," Moore admitted that we are saying something about an inkbottle and that it is therefore *a* subject of our assertion. But he held that we are also saying something about a sense-datum, which is, therefore, also *a* subject of the assertion. Furthermore, he held that it was the "ultimate" or "real" or "principal" subject both because it is, as the previous method appeared to show, what we pick out in a perceptual judgment and because "if there be a thing which is the inkstand at all, it is certainly *only* known to me as *the* thing which stands in a certain relation to this sense-datum. It is not given to me in the sense in which this sense-datum is given."[34]

4. *The linguistic method.* In 1957[35] Moore argued that "I cannot see, in the common sense, any physical object without its 'looking' somehow to me"; but to say that something looks so and so to me "means" or is "merely another way of saying" that "I directly see" a so and so entity, which we may call a sense-datum; therefore, seeing a material object implies seeing a sense-datum. This translation from "looks" to sense-data, which Moore thought so obviously correct, has been one of the chief objectives of the modern attack on the legitimacy of sense-data.

5. *The method of intentionality.* Quite early, Moore allowed that there are more kinds of sense-data than those apprehended by the five physical senses. In 1914[36] he gave a list of five experiences or "mental events" whose members he felt had some intrinsic resemblance which permits us to call them all "sensory experiences." These experiences were either the having of sensations proper or the having of hallucinations and illusory sense experiences or the having of three different kinds of image, namely, waking images, dream images, and after-images. Each of these experiences was analyzed into two components, not counting the person who has the experience, namely, the experience and the object *of* which there is the experience. The object of the experience is in each case called a sense-datum. Similarly, at other times, "having a pain" is regarded as having an experience *of* something, and pains are then regarded as another kind of sense-data.

The distinction which is basic to this method — namely; the distinction of an experience and that thing of which it is an experience, was used by Moore in his famous attack on idealism in 1903, for the burden of that attack was that the idealists had failed to distinguish in a sensation — for example, the sensation of blue — between the consciousness of the object and the object — or, blue itself.

6. *The method of after-images.* In all Moore's late works, after-images take pride of place as an exemplification of sense-data, perhaps because they seem to point indubitably to the existence of something which *ex hypothesi* cannot be a material object or any part of one and which, furthermore, seems capable of ostensive definition. We are told to "stare at a lighted electric lamp for a little while, and then close your eyes" and "the after-image which you will then see is a specimen of the sort of thing I mean by a sense-datum."[37]

Having for all these reasons come to the conclusion that there exist both material objects and sense-data, both the inkbottle we see and the different and special objects which you and I see, either when we both really see an inkbottle or when we are having a hallucination of one or an after-image of one, etc., Moore then devoted an enormous amount of his time to attempting to answer two questions, namely, (1) How are these sense-data related to our perception of them? or, as he often put it in Berkeleian form, is the *esse* of sense-data *percipi*? and (2) How is the sense-datum related to the material object in those cases where there is both a sense-datum and a material object? But to neither question did he ever give an answer which really satisfied him.

The second question, which interested him more, he put in three different ways, each of which has its special pitfalls. The way just mentioned — "How is the sense-datum related to the material object?" — as well as a second way — "What am I saying about the sense-datum when I say 'This is a penny'?" — have the disadvantage both of introducing technical language (and thus, perhaps, manufacturing a problem) and of enticing us into regarding the sense-datum in too existential and material a way. These two dangers are avoided by a third formulation which puts the problem as "What do we mean by saying 'This is a chair' and 'I see a chair'?" or, more specifically, "What do we mean by the 'is' in 'This is a chair . . . '?" It is not the fault of this formulation that Moore jumped to the conclusion that the "is" is that of identity and had to go to desperate lengths to extricate himself from the ensuing difficulties.

For instance, he first asked whether in saying "This, which I see, is such and such a material object" — for example, "This is a penny" — I could be *identifying* a sense-datum *with* either a material object or a part of the surface of a material object; and then gave various reasons for answering the first alternative with an emphatic "No" and the second with a hesitant "No." He then concluded that it is mistaken to say that the sense-datum *is* a part of the surface of a material object and "silly" to say it *is* a material object. He also felt forced to deny that the word "this" in "This is a penny" can refer solely to the sense-datum, for otherwise we would again be saying that the sense-datum *is* a material object. He therefore often suggests[38] that the word "this" must here be "short for a definite description," such as "the object of which *this* [in another sense] is part of the surface," and the last "this" may in turn be short for another definite description such as the object to part of whose surface this, in a third sense referring to the sense-datum, has some specific relation. It was not until 1957 that he saw that the statement "*This* sense-datum *is* a part of the surface of a physical object" is often undoubtedly true even if the sense-datum cannot be *identical with* any such surface; and he never saw how — as I shall shortly point out — that "This sense-datum *is* a material object "can also be true despite the nonidentity of the sense-datum with the material object.

Having convinced himself that the sense-datum is not identical with either a material object or a surface of a material object — and further, mistakenly, that it *is* not a material object or a surface of one — he sometimes looked around, in a despairing and not very wholehearted manner, for some other relation between the sense-datum and a part of the surface of a material object. But no convincing solution here suggested itself, though several were glanced at.

Since I have suggested that underlying Moore's analysis of the notion of visual perception are two mistaken assumptions, namely that "sense-datum" is the name of a peculiar sort of entity and that the "is" in "This sense-datum *is* a material object or a part of the surface of a material object" must be that of identity, I shall briefly mention how I think the perceptual statements "This, which I see, is a penny" and "I see a penny" are to be analyzed. We may, I believe, answer the question "What do you see?" in two different but equally correct ways. We may *either describe* what we see by using the typical sense-datum terminology of colors, shapes, etc. — for example, a thin brown line — as well as the language of "looks," "appears," etc., *or* we may *identify* what we see by talking of material objects, such as pennies, or of parts of such objects or of hallucinations and after-images of them. It is possible for two people to agree on their identification answer to the question and yet have quite different description answers; for though what they both see is correctly identified as a penny, it looks different to each. Furthermore, when we talk of "seeing a part of the surface of a penny" rather than of "seeing a penny," we are not, as Moore thought, using a different sense of "see," but are more *precisely* identifying what we see. Compare "This is a Master's gown" and "This is the gown of a Master in Arts of the University of Oxford." Thus "This, which I see, is a penny" and "This, which I see, is part of the surface of a penny" may both be true at once.

Finally, when we say "This, which I see, is a so and so," the word "this" refers to what we have described, and the word "is" is used to *identify* it *as* a so and so and not to *identify* it *with* anything. Nor is *what* we describe — the "sense-datum" we "directly see" — an object or entity over and above the material object or after-image with which we correctly identify it.

Conclusion

VERY few philosophers today would accept the solutions in ethics or in the theory of perception to which Moore's method of philosophizing led him, but the whole tenor of contemporary English-speaking philosophy echoes his approach to these and other problems. It is hardly possible for anyone writing in this tradition now to deal as cavalierly with what "common sense" believes as did the great metaphysicians of the past. Everyone now is an analyst of some sort, whatever views he may hold about the nature of philosophy. And it is worth emphasizing that Moore insisted that he had never regarded analysis as the *only* proper business of philosophy; he approved of attempts to "give a general description of the whole Universe," including the chief kinds of good things. However much Moore's view of what the meaning of a word is may be rejected by contemporary analysts, they accept as a commonplace his distinction between knowing the meaning of a word in the sense of being able to understand it and knowing its meaning in the sense of being able to give an analysis of that meaning and being able to say what that meaning is.

The seemingly unbridgeable gap that yawns between English-speaking and Continental European philosophers of today is the gap between those who have been influenced by Moore and the later Wittgenstein, and those who continue to philosophize in the traditional metaphysical manner. In whatever way and to whatever extent this gap may close in the future, Moore's contribution was that of setting many philosophers off on a new path. Without a knowledge of Moore's views, it is not possible to understand properly what is happening in English-speaking philosophy today.

26

Bertrand Russell

D. J. O'CONNOR

BERTRAND RUSSELL WAS BORN in 1872 of a titled family. His grandfather, Lord John Russell, was active in politics in Victorian times and became Prime Minister. Russell was privately educated as a boy and later went to Cambridge, where he studied mathematics and philosophy. His pacifist activities during World War I resulted in a prison sentence which he used to write *An Introduction to Mathematical Philosophy*. In 1931 he succeeded to the peerage vacated by the death of his brother. He lectured on philosophy, politics, and social affairs all over the world and wrote voluminously on philosophy, mathematics, science, politics, morals, religion, and education. He was a Fellow of the Royal Society and received the Order of Merit. In 1950 he was awarded the Nobel Prize for literature. In his last years he was active in the campaign for nuclear disarmament and was imprisoned by the British government for his activities in promulgating his views. Russell died in 1970.

USSELL'S FIRST WRITINGS on philosophy were published over sixty years ago; his most recent appeared in 1959.[1] It is natural to expect that his views would have changed considerably during so eventful a period in the history of philosophy. They have indeed changed, and in such important ways that it is extraordinarily difficult to give a clear and accurate account of Russell's philosophy in the compass of one chapter. I have therefore chosen for discussion first, those features of his thought which have remained central and unaltered during his philosophical career and second, the most recent versions of those important doctrines which have changed. When a philosopher has written twenty books and over fifty papers on philosophical subjects, any brief summary of his views will distort some points, even important ones, and pass over many more in silence. But I hope that by explaining the principles on which I have selected topics for discussion, I may help the reader to put this account into a proper perspective.

Professor C. D. Broad once remarked, "As we all know, Mr. Russell produces a different system of philosophy every few years."[2] Russell's fertility of invention and his constant willingness to re-examine problems on which he has already published his views do seem at first to the student of his writings to give some substance to Broad's remark. But a closer acquaintance with his work soon reveals that Russell's basic outlook has changed very little and that where there have been changes, these are often due rather to changes of interest than to revisions of his former opinions. Russell himself has explained how his interests have changed and how these changes of interest were related to developments in his thinking.[3] At the age of 15, he became interested in the philosophical problems connected with religion — the classic trio of divine existence, immortality, and free will. At first, he retained his belief in the existence of God while rejecting free will and immortality. "After a time, however, I came to disbelieve in God and advanced to a position much more like that of the eighteenth-century French *Philosophes*. I agreed with them in being a passionate believer in rationalism; I liked Laplace's calculator; I hated what I considered superstition; and I believed profoundly in the perfectibility of man by a combination of reason and machinery."[4] Some of these early attitudes have survived. He is still a firm believer in reason and a hater of superstition; but what he has learned from the twentieth century has dimmed the buoyant optimism that he inherited from the eighteenth.

In 1890, he went up to Cambridge to read mathematics. But his interest in philosophical problems remained. And when he had finished the mathematical tripos, he spent a further year reading for the moral sciences tripos. Here he was heavily influenced by the then fashionable doctrines of Kantian and Hegelian idealism. Some of his early philosophical

work was written under these influences. Russell has written of one of these that "It seems to me now nothing but unmitigated rubbish";[5] and of others, including his book *An Essay on the Foundations of Geometry*, that they were "somewhat foolish" or "misguided."

Fortunately, his wanderings in the jungles of idealism did not last long. Russell gives part of the credit for his conversion to the influence of G. E. Moore. But his own critical and skeptical temper and his sound scientific training would hardly have allowed him to remain long in confusion. The absolute idealist position embodied a doctrine on the nature of relations which, if true, would have rendered natural science and mathematics impossible. Russell was led to revise his views on this and other idealist doctrines partly through his work on the philosophy of Leibniz (published in 1900) and partly by a growing interest in the philosophy of mathematics and in mathematical logic. He refers to the year 1900 as "the most important year in my intellectual life." It was in this year that he met Peano at the International Congress of Philosophy in Paris and learned of the new concepts and methods which were to revolutionize the foundations of mathematics. Inspired by Peano's work, he spent the next twelve years working on mathematical logic and its associated philosophical problems. This work culminated in the publication, jointly with A. N. Whitehead, of the three volumes of *Principia Mathematica* (1910–1913). This classical revolutionary work belongs more to the history of logic and mathematics than to the story of philosophy proper and we need not consider it here. But it affected Russell's philosophy in two ways. First, it convinced him of the importance of mathematical logic as an analytical tool for philosophy. Second, it provided some specific examples of logical doctrines with philosophical bearings. These included the theory of types and the theory of descriptions (which we shall discuss below) and the doctrine that all pure mathematics is a development of logic and uses only concepts that can be defined in logical terms. This controversial thesis provides, if true, a solution of the problem of the *a priori* and a refutation of Kant. The question is a technical one of great complexity, and philosophers of mathematics are still divided on its truth. It is probably fair to say that the theory is likely to prove nearer to the truth than any of its rivals.

After his main work in logic was completed, Russell's interests centered on more traditional problems of philosophy, particularly those of the theory of knowledge, of mind and matter, and, later, of language and meaning. *The Problems of Philosophy* (published in 1912 and still one of the best introductions to philosophy) represents his starting point. It was a conservative position. He accepted the existence of universals in the Platonic sense and took up an attitude of critical common sense to questions about minds and physical objects. A skeptical Cartesian approach shows through the writing, however, and points the way to his later doctrines. His later work, starting with *Our Knowledge of the External World* (1914), moves rapidly away from this position of philosophical conservatism. This move was governed by two principles of method which have been features of Russell's work ever since. (1) He took great care to consult the latest findings of all the sciences before making up his mind on any philosophical issue. (2) He consciously adopted Ockham's razor as a maxim. This dictum, usually attributed to William of Ockham, in the form "Entities are not to be multiplied without necessity" (*Entia non sunt multiplicanda praeter necessitatem*)* is taken by Russell to be a basic principle of any scientific philosophy. He states it also in the form "Whenever possible, substitute constructions out of known entities for inferences to unknown entities."[6] We shall see below how he applies it.

These two principles have guided his work over the last fifty years. They provide a basic unity for his thinking and at the same time explain its changes. Because science develops so rapidly, the first principle has tended to make the details of his thought somewhat vulnerable. But his willingness to take science seriously and his competence in scientific matters have given his philosophy a more genuinely empirical flavor than that of most of his contemporaries. He shows a proper disdain for those philosophers who treat problems on which science has something to say without familiarizing themselves with the scientists' findings. "A great many philosophical questions are, in fact, scientific questions with which science is not yet ready to deal. Both sensation and perception were in this class of problems, but are now, I should contend, amenable to scientific treatment and not capable of being fruitfully handled by anyone who chooses to ignore what science has to say about them."[7] Two of Russell's major philosophical works, *The Analysis of Mind* (1921) and *The Analysis of Matter* (1927), show very markedly the influence of contemporary scientific theories.

In the most influential of his later books, *An Inquiry into Meaning and Truth* (published in 1940), he turns his attention to questions of language, truth, and verification, and to the connections between them, which he had treated rather sketchily in earlier books. Finally, in 1948, his latest important book on philosophy, *Human Knowledge*, takes up in its two final sections the problems of induction and probability. He had not previously dealt with these except for a brief chapter on induction in *The Problems of Philosophy* nearly forty years earlier. His work in *Human Knowledge* on what he calls "nondemonstrative inference," is interesting and important, but, rather surprisingly, it has not yet received

* It is not found in Ockham's works in this form, but the sentiment is expressed by him in other ways.

the detailed criticism that would enable us to come to a fair summary estimate of its value.

We may summarize Russell's philosophical career by saying that his *method* has remained unchanged since his rejection of idealism. The *content* of his philosophy has changed, though less than some of his critics have suggested. Each of his philosophical works published since 1912 has exemplified some major change of interest, but important changes of doctrine have been few. There are two important ones: (1) his abandonment of a Platonic theory of universals; (2) a resolute attempt to make the principles of "neutral monism" solve the problems of perception and the body-mind relationship. Since the publication of *The Analysis of Matter* in 1927, he has altered the direction of his interest without seriously amending the content of his doctrines. We shall be concerned below first with Russell's method and then with the outlines of his mature philosophical theories.

Method

RUSSELL has been a consistent advocate of the use of scientific methods in philosophy. This is, of course, a slogan that other philosophers have adopted, and until we know what is meant by "scientific method," it tells us little. Philosophy for Russell is an activity that shares some of the characteristics of both religion and science. Like religion, it takes for its subject matter the nature of the universe and man's place in it; but like science, it tries to solve the problems presented by its subject matter by strictly rational methods. However, it is clear that not all rational methods are equally appropriate. Plato, Spinoza, Hume, and Bradley, to name only a few, have all used what they conceived to be the method of reason on human experience, and arrived at very different conclusions. Russell explains[8] that "there are two different ways in which a philosophy may seek to base itself upon science. It may emphasize the most general *results* of science and seek to give even greater generality and unity to these results. Or it may study the *methods* of science, and seek to apply these methods with the necessary adaptations to its own particular province. Much philosophy inspired by science has gone astray through preoccupation with the *results* momentarily supposed to have been achieved. It is not results but *methods* that can be transferred with profit from the sphere of the special sciences to the sphere of philosophy."

But what is meant by "the methods of science"? Experiment, measurement, and the formulation of hypotheses may all be spoken of as scientific methods. Scientists use them and could not get along without them. But the use of *these* methods leads to particular concrete findings about the world, to just those *results*, in fact, that Russell rightly holds to be largely irrelevant to philosophy. Philosophical theories must take account of such findings only in that they set limits to the probable solutions of philosophical problems. It is not these methods that Russell has here in mind.

What does he have in mind, then? To answer this question we must remember that though "science" may refer to empirical sciences like chemistry or biology, it may also refer to the *formal* sciences of logic and mathematics. It is these formal sciences that Russell has chiefly in mind. Consider the special character of philosophical statements. They are (a) general and (b) *a priori*.[9] In saying that they are general, Russell means that they do not deal with any particular region of the universe, spatial or temporal, and that they have no specific subject matter. Nor are they concerned with the universe as a whole. There is, in fact, no such thing as "the universe" which can be meaningfully spoken of. "Philosophical propositions," he says, "instead of being concerned with the whole of things collectively, are concerned with all things distributively; and not only must they be concerned with all things, but they must be concerned with such properties of all things as do not depend on the accidental nature of the things that there happen to be, but are true of any possible world, independently of such facts as can only be discovered by our sense."[10] And in saying that philosophical statements are *a priori*, he means that they "must be such as can neither be proved or disproved by empirical evidence."[11] Now it is clear that propositions that are true, general, and *a priori* are propositions of logic, and that philosophy, so conceived, "becomes indistinguishable from logic." "Logic" is used here in the sense of symbolic or mathematical logic, the science which Russell himself did so much to establish. The task of the scientific philosopher then becomes the application of the principles and methods of logic to the problems of philosophy. Russell's actual philosophical practice is somewhat less austere than this program suggests; he sometimes interprets the word "logic" in a more liberal sense.

We shall see below what this amounts to in practice. In the meantime, however, it will be helpful to notice some other features of Russell's method that contribute to its scientific character. In the first place, Russell has always used a skeptical approach to his problems. An early book, *The Problems of Philosophy*, starts with the question: "Is there any knowledge in the world which is so certain that no reasonable man could doubt it?" And one of his objects in the book is to find a way of arranging the items of our knowledge in an order of credibility so that the logical connections (or the lack of them) between the first items in the list and the later ones can be clearly seen. The same attitude can be traced in all his later work.[12] He regards it as an important advantage of the method of logical analysis that by examining the basis of our beliefs, we can be brought to see "the mutual independence of propositions that had been thought to be logically connected. . . . As logic improves, less and less can be proved."[13] However, he insists on the importance of avoiding an insincere skepticism. It is one thing to show by adopting skepticism as a philosophical policy that "from A it is impossible to deduce B, although, hitherto, it has been thought possible and although it has been held that this was the only good reason for believing B. But if, in fact, a man is going to go on believing B just as firmly as before, his skepticism is insincere. . . . But if we are unwilling to profess disbeliefs that we are in fact incapable of entertaining, the result of logical analysis is to increase the number of independent premises that we accept in our analysis of knowledge."[14]

A second characteristically scientific feature of his work is the tentative and provisional nature of his conclusions. He is careful, particularly in his later books, to make more modest claims for his findings than most philosophers are willing to do. As an instance of this, consider the conclusion of his paper *Logical Atomism*, where he has been sketching his theory of the nature of mind and matter. "The above summary hypothesis would, of course, need to be amplified and refined in many ways in order to fit in completely with scientific facts. It is not put forward as a finished theory but merely as a suggestion of the kind of thing that may be true." Many other examples could be given. This passage, moreover, hints at another way in which Russell's philosophy may properly be called scientific. Although no scientific findings should be part of the premises of a philosophical theory, (1) they can properly serve as negative evidence to refute it, should the theory trespass injudiciously on the territory of science, and (2) we may reasonably ask that a philosophical statement be sufficiently detailed and explicit to be consistent with the present state of science. Doubtful as the corpus of science may be at any time, it is at least more worthy of belief than any part of philosophy.

The last feature of Russell's work that justifies his claim that philosophy can be "scientific" is his deliberate rejection of any attempt at building a unified philosophical "system" in the manner of classical metaphysics. He recommends instead that philosophical problems should be treated *one by one* by the methods of philosophical analysis. Russell claims that his method represents "the same kind of advance as was introduced into physics by Galileo the substitution of piecemeal detailed and verifiable results for large untested generalities recommended only by a certain appeal to imagination."[15] This method may in time result in a system, when its various findings coalesce into a coherent and mutually supporting body of knowledge. This happens also in science. But neither the scientist nor the philosopher can profitably make system-building his aim. A system of knowledge is an orderly edifice of true propositions that have themselves to be established laboriously and one by one.

Russell is primarily a mathematical logician turned philosopher. Although, as we have seen, he was interested in philosophy from his boyhood, it was not until he had found a way of using his logical discoveries in the solution of philosophical problems that he developed the characteristic methods and doctrines for which he is now known. He wrote of *Principia Mathematica*: "The technical methods of mathematical logic, as developed in this book, seem to me very powerful and capable of providing a new instrument for the discussion of many problems that have hitherto remained subject to philosophical vagueness."[16] We may conveniently divide Russell's teaching on "logic as the essence of philosophy"[17] into (1) general principles and (2) specific techniques for effecting logical analyses. The general principles are four: A doctrine about language; a theory of logical form; a theory of logical analysis as a method for displaying logical form; and a theory of "logical atomism" which directs the process of analysis. Let us look briefly at each of these in turn.

1. Russell's attitude to the natural languages, in which most thinking, writing, and communication is carried on, is ambivalent. On the one hand, he believes that there is a sense in which natural languages are a guide to the nature of the world that they are used to talk about. "There is, I think, a discoverable relation between the structure of sentences and the structure of the occurrences to which the sentences refer. I do not think the structure of nonverbal facts wholly unknowable, and I believe that, with sufficient caution, the properties of language may help us to understand the structure of the world."[18] This must be so because alternative attitudes to language are either obviously false or self-refuting. On the other hand, he is acutely aware of the many ways in which language can mislead thinking. "The influence of language on philosophy has, I believe, been profound and almost unrecognised. If we are not to be misled by this influence, it is necessary to become conscious of it and to ask ourselves deliberately how far it is legitimate."[19] Moreover, he explains that a natural language is ill-adapted to expressing many philosophical matters, and, in consequence, "philosophers who have been dependent on it have frequently been misled by it."[20]

There are two main aspects of any language: its vocabulary and its syntax. Vocabulary is treacherous to the philosopher because words in natural languages are usually vague and often ambiguous as well. We have therefore to attend constantly to the exact senses in which words are used in philosophical discourse. This sort of attention and the type of analysis of meanings that follows from it has been a standard philosophical procedure since Aristotle. Russell believes in addition that philosophical confusions over problems like those of substance and universals may be laid to the discredit of the peculiarities of natural vocabularies. It is, however, to the *syntactical* features of natural languages that

Russell attributes many of its philosophical failings.

2. He came to this view early in his career as a result of his criticism of the Hegelian idealists and of his studies in the philosophy of Leibniz and in mathematical logic. He showed in particular how the subject-predicate structure of sentences masks the real logical structure of the propositions that they embody and leads to false and fantastic metaphysical theories like Leibniz's monadism and absolute idealism. This concept of *logical form* is most obviously required in the application of symbolic logic to natural languages. Any piece of valid deductive reasoning about any subject matter is valid in virtue of its logical form. We may exemplify this by simple instances taken from a primitive stage of logic. It is obvious to intuition that statements (A) and (B) are valid implications:

A. If all buttercups are dicotyledons and some yellow flowers are not dicotyledons, then some yellow flowers are not buttercups.

B. If all intellectuals are admirers of Proust and some philosophers are not admirers of Proust, then some philosophers are not intellectuals.

But the validity of (A) and (B) is in no way bound up with their subject matter. For replacing the terms "buttercups," "dicotyledons" and so on by variables X, Y, and Z, we have:

C. If all X's are Y's and some Z's are not Y's, then some Z's are not X's.

This is as obviously valid as (A) and (B), and it represents their common logical form. We understand (C) as saying "Whatever X, Y, and Z may be, if all X's are Y's, etc." We may thus replace the variables by any terms we please, and we shall obtain, provided we replace them consistently, further implications which will also be valid and whose validity will depend on their being substitution instances of the valid form (C).

One of the tasks of symbolic logic is to find ways of testing the validity of such argument forms which may, of course, be of very much greater complexity and subtlety than (C). But to do this, we must first find ways of representing any piece of discourse which is expressed in a natural language so as to bring out its underlying structure or logical form. It is important to notice that logical form, expressed in logical language, is *neutral* between natural languages in the same way that (C) is neutral between (A) and (B) above. An Englishman, a Russian, and a Chinese could each translate equivalent pieces of discourse into the same logical language. For example, the mutually translatable sentences

> All men are mortal.
> *Omnes homines mortales sunt.*
> *Alle Menschen sind sterblich.*

are all representable in logical language as

$$(x)\,(fx \supset gx)$$

The language of *Principia Mathematica* was an immense step forward toward the provision of an "ideal" language by means of which we can dissect out and display the logical skeleton common to all natural languages. The realization that the grammatical form of a proposition may misrepresent its logical form is entirely the work of Russell, and it has proved an invaluable notion in developing the technique of logical analysis.

3. Logical analysis for Russell is a process of clarifying concepts and propositions, whether of science, philosophy, or common sense, which are the source of obscurity and confusion. Translation into an ideal language is only one way of doing analysis. But to carry out this program completely, we have first to perfect our logical language. There are great technical difficulties in the way of such a project, and few logicians, Russell least of all, would claim that the ideal language had been completed.

One of these difficulties that arose in the foundations of mathematics contributed indirectly to an important development in Russell's theory of language. The point may be illustrated simply by the following paradox, which, though it is not the one that occasioned his original difficulty, is sufficiently similar to it to bring out the point at issue.[21] Consider the following sentence:

> The sentence printed inside a rectangle on this page is false.

This sentence (let us call it "*S*") refers to itself, and says of itself that it is false. But if *S* is false, what it says is not true. That is to say, *S* is not false. And assuming, as is usually done, that every sentence is either true or false, this means that *S* is true. But if *S* is true and says of itself that it is false, it must be false. Thus supposing *S* to be false, we are forced to conclude that it is true and vice versa.

If the way in which we use language leads to paradoxes of this kind, we may reasonably suppose that in some way or other we are using it wrongly. In this case, it is not difficult to see why the paradox arises. It is because *S* refers *to itself*. Russell resolves the paradox by distinguishing between "orders of proposition," or, what comes to the same thing, between levels of language.[22]

We may distinguish level 1 sentences about the world, level 2 sentences about level 1 sentences, and so on. S_1 might be, for example, "It is raining." Then S_2 in level 2 may say something true or false about S_1 — for example, "S_1 is in English," "S_1 is ungrammatical," "S_1 is false," "S_1 is true," and so on. Every sentence in a properly ordered language will refer either to a sentence on the language level *immediately below it* or, if it is of level 1, it will say something about the nonlinguistic world. Only by observing some such distinction as this can we avoid contradictions. This is one of the basic notions

underlying Russell's famous "theory of types." Though the theory was originally designed to avoid inconsistency in the foundations of mathematics, its extension to natural languages proved to be both fruitful and controversial. Not only propositions but words also (or rather their meanings) may be of different logical types.

All words are of the same logical type; a word is a class of series, of noises or shapes according as it is heard or read. But the meanings of words are of various different types; an attribute (expressed by an adjective) is of a different type from the objects to which it can be (whether truly or falsely) attributed; a relation (perhaps expressed by a preposition, perhaps by a transitive verb, perhaps in some other way) is of a different type from the terms between which it holds or does not hold. The definition of a logical type is as follows: *A* and *B* are of the same logical type if and only if, given any fact of which *A* is constituent, there is a corresponding fact which has *B* as a constituent which either results by substituting *B* for *A*, or is the negation of what so results. To take an illustration, Socrates and Aristotle are of the same type, because "Socrates was a philosopher" and "Aristotle was a philosopher" are both facts; Socrates and Caligula are of the same type, because "Socrates was a philosopher" and "Caligula was not a philosopher" are both facts. To love and to kill are of the same type because "Plato loved Socrates" and "Plato did not kill Socrates" are both facts. It follows formally from the definition that, when two words have meanings of different types, the relations of the words to what they mean are of different types; that is to say, there is not one relation of meaning between words and what they stand for, but as many relations of meaning, each of a different logical type, as there are logical types among the objects for which there are words. This fact is a very potent source of error and confusion in philosophy.[23]

A very important consequence of this view is that we have, if we accept it, a criterion for distinguishing meaningless from meaningful sentences. Why is the sentence

Prime numbers are nutritious.

neither true nor false but simply without meaning? Because, Russell would say, prime numbers are of different logical type from, say, herrings or oranges. A result of this point of view is that when we consider statements, we have to do more than ask: Is it true or false? We have first to ask: Is it meaningful or not? This original and promising thesis proves, however, to be difficult to apply in detail, and it has attracted criticism.[24] True to his scientific program of tentative and undogmatic philosophizing, Russell admits that his theory may be defective. "I have never been satisfied that the theory of types, as I have presented it, is final. . . . But I hope that, in time, some theory will be developed which will be simple and adequate and at the same time be satisfactory from the point of view of what might be called logical common sense."[25]

4. Russell's logic rests on and gives support to a certain view of the world which may not unfairly be called metaphysical. We can indeed accept the logic without the metaphysics. Many logicians do so; but Russell himself accepts both. This view of the world was named by Russell himself "logical atomism." He has adhered to the view consistently since his first formulation of it. He wrote of it in 1943: "I think that almost everybody in the philosophic world disagrees with me on this subject but I am quite impenitent, because I never find arguments brought against my logical atomism. I find only a fashion and a dogma."[26] The principle underlying this doctrine is one that has guided all of Russell's philosophical writing since his early rejection of idealism. In his latest philosophical book, he explains the principle in this way: "Taking it for granted that, broadly speaking, science and common sense are capable of being interpreted so as to be true in the main, the question arises: what are the minimum hypotheses from which this broad measure of truth will result?"[27] In addition to this principle of method, a version of Ockham's razor referred to above, two beliefs formed the basis for his logical atomism: (1) his belief that the new logic elaborated in *Principia Mathematica* was a language that would "show at a glance the logical structure of the facts asserted or denied";[28] (2) his belief, dating from his reaction against Hegelianism, that the world is fundamentally *plural*. This belief was based partly on empirical grounds and partly on his realization of the importance of *relations* for mathematics and science. If the monism of Hegel (or any other variety) is correct, relations must be as illusory as the idealists had claimed they were. But since relations are required to guarantee the truth of mathematics and science, monism must be false. The world must therefore consist of a number of different entities.

But what is the nature of these entities? Russell's answer is that they are *atomic facts*. An atomic fact consists of a particular qualified by a property — for example, This is white — or two or more particulars related by a relation — for example, *A* is larger than *B*; *A* is between *B* and *C*. — (Relations may, of course, connect two, three, four, or any number of particulars.) But what does he mean by a particular? He certainly does not mean the individual things of our everyday experience — tables, trees, stones, animals, people, and so on. These are complex and not such as to be the result of analysis. (They are indeed only "*prima facie* complex entities." For on analysis, they dissolve, as we shall see later, into "logical fictions" — series, classes, and the like.) The complex entities at which analysis arrives are atomic facts consisting of particulars qualified by

properties or standing in relations. As to "particulars" themselves, Russell gives different accounts in different places. He first says that they are "such things as little patches of colour or sounds, momentary things — and some of them will be predicates or relations and so on."[29] Later, he defines "particulars" as "terms of relations in atomic facts," and "proper names" as "words for particulars."[30] These later definitions exclude properties and relations, which then become, so to speak, the glue that sticks the particulars together in the various logical patterns in which atomic facts can exist. It is, in fact, difficult to work out a clear *positive* concept of what "atomic fact" means for Russell, because it is difficult to be clear about the meaning of "particular." (Perhaps space-time points have the best claim to this status.) It is easier to get a negative account of the concept. Atomic facts are those that *appear* to offer no further ground for analysis (although Russell admits that "it is perfectly possible to suppose that complex things are capable of analysis *ad infinitum* and that you never reach the simple."[31])

Atomic facts are thus complex to the extent that they are built out of particulars and properties or relations. But they have at least a relative simplicity in representing the limit of analysis. Moreover, their simplicity is mirrored in their form of representation in the ideal language of mathematical logic. If we let $a, b, c \ldots$ stand for particulars and $f, g, h \ldots$ stand for properties and relations (that is, for one-place predicates and two-, three-, four-, or n-place predicates) we may represent

1. This is white.
2. *A* is larger than *B*.
3. *B* is between *C* and *D*.

respectively as

1'. $f(a)$
2'. $g(ab)$
3'. $h(bcd)$

and so on. Such formulas represent atomic propositions of our logic, that is to say, propositions that do not contain other *propositions* as components. We may then contrast with these the *molecular* propositions built up out of them by logical connective words like "not," "and," "if . . . then," and "or," and quantifiers like "for all x" or "there is an x such that. . . ." Given the two atomic propositions*

4. This is red.
5. This is extended.

we might build up molecular propositions:

6. This is red and this is extended.
7. If this is not extended, this is not red.
8. For every x, if x is red, then x is extended.

and so on. Russell's logic is such that the truth or

---

* Supposing, of course, that these are genuine atomic propositions.

falsity of these molecular propositions is known once we know the truth or falsity of the atomic propositions out of which they are constructed.*

This is a bold and striking doctrine, but it is clear that it is little more than a program for a theory about language and the world. To show in detail how our uses of language at all levels, from the simplest to the most complex, are constructible on this pattern is an enormous task that has not yet been seriously attempted. Russell would of course agree that a doctrine of atomic propositions and their combinations, even supplemented with the theory of logical types and language levels, is still a very long way from a complete theory of language. His critics have tended to treat what is no more than a foundation as if it were the completed structure.[32]

These then are the main principles on which Russell's philosophical method rests. How does he apply them? We may best understand this by examining answers to specific philosophical problems. And as an introduction to this, we may look briefly at two very characteristic analytic devices which are used by Russell in tackling these problems. The first is the method of logical constructions; the second is the theory of descriptions. We have already seen that he states his principle of intellectual economy, Ockham's razor, in the form "Whenever possible, substitute constructions out of known entities for inferences to unknown entities." In other words, let us try to explain the world in terms of those features of it with which we are directly acquainted; and let us avoid supposing the existence of any things with which we are not (or cannot be) directly acquainted, unless facts or logic force us to do so. Russell came to appreciate the use of this maxim in the course of his investigations into the foundation of mathematics. For example, plane geometry deals with entities like points and straight lines. But it is clear that these are not objects of experience. The dots and strokes on paper by which we represent them do not have the properties by which these geometrical concepts are defined. A point, for example, is defined by Euclid as that which has position without magnitude at all. It is possible, however, using a method first worked out by A. N. Whitehead,[33] to analyze the concept *point* in terms of entities that *do* occur in our experience. Consider, for example, a series of concentric spheres diminishing in volume and arranged one inside the next like a series of Chinese boxes. It is found that such a *series* (that is, the *set* of spheres together with the relation which orders them) constitutes an entity which satisfies all the logical requirements of the geometrical concept, *point*.[34] We have thus substituted an empirical concept for a nonempirical one without any loss of essential meaning. Russell

admits that such a replacement may seem at first clumsier and less transparent to intuition than the familiar concept of which it is the analysis. "Very often the resulting statement is more complicated and difficult than the one which, like common sense and most philosophy, assumes hypothetical entities whose existence there is no good reason to believe in. . . . But it is a mistake to suppose that what is easy and natural in thought is more free from unwarrantable assumptions."[35] We shall see below how Russell uses logical constructions in tackling some philosophical problems.

The theory of descriptions gives a method for analyzing certain philosophically puzzling kinds of statement. The analysis removes the puzzle by exhibiting a complex logical form which is disguised in ordinary language by a simpler but misleading grammatical form. The puzzle arises from the difference between proper names and uniquely descriptive phrases which, in English, usually take the form "the so-and-so."* If, to use one of Russell's examples, we say

Scott is the author of Waverley.

the "is" here is the "is" expressing identity; that is to say, both "Scott" and "the author of *Waverley*" denote the same object. Logicians assumed at one time that if two phrases denote the same object, one can be substituted for the other in any statement without affecting the truth or falsity of that statement. But this is clearly not always so. *Waverley* was published anonymously, and many people, including King George IV, wanted to know if the statement "Scott is the author of *Waverley*" was true. But obviously, they did not want to know if the substitution statement "Scott is Scott" is true.

The sentence, on Russell's theory of descriptions, is analyzed as a conjunction of *three* propositions:

1. There is an x such that x wrote Waverley.
2. For all y, if y wrote *Waverley*, y is identical with x.
3. There is not an x such that x wrote *Waverley* and x is not identical with Scott.

(or, in less formal language: One and only one person wrote *Waverley* and that person was Scott.) This analysis removes the dangers of assuming that phrases embodying definite descriptions like "the author of *Waverley*" or "the tallest mountain in Africa" are *proper names*. Such an assumption can lead to false and extravagant metaphysical beliefs in the following way. A proper name, if it is used meaningfully, must refer to an object. Suppose we consider sentences like

---

* In the case of (8), we assume that this can be read as a conjunction as follows: If a_1 is red, then a_1 is extended *and* if a_2 is red, then a_2 is extended *and* . . . *and* if a_n is red, then a_n is extended.

* Such phrases can be used in other senses. For example, in "The whale is a mammal," the phrase "the whale" is not a definite description. Russell's theory is intended to cover only definite descriptions.

The golden mountain is in Africa.
The present King of France is bald.
The oldest dragon in Ireland is carnivorous.

If the subject terms in these statements are construed as proper names, the statements will not even be meaningful unless there are entities to which the names refer. But the statements are clearly meaningful. Thus it seems to follow that there must be entities *of some kind or other* (though doubtless not things in the real world) for which the definite descriptions stand. The Austrian philosopher Meinong (1853–1921) was led into a belief of this kind, a belief that evinces, as Russell remarks, "a failure of that feeling for reality which ought to be preserved in even the most abstract studies."[36]

The theory of descriptions removes the need for such fantastic hypotheses by showing that definite descriptions are not proper names. It does this by offering an analysis of the sentences in which they occur. The theory has, of course, met with criticism, but Russell in his most recent philosophical writings has defended his theory very forcefully and convincingly.[37] Nor is it the only device which has been suggested for meeting these problems in the philosophy of language; the German logician, Gottlob Frege (1848–1925), proposed another. But it remains a classical example of a technique for logical analysis and, in F. P. Ramsey's phrase, a paradigm of philosophy.*

We have so far been considering Russell's philosophical method without looking at his views on the traditional problems of philosophy — body and mind, the external world, truth, universals, and the rest. It may indeed prove in the long run that it is his method rather than the specific content of his theories that will have the greater influence. But the theories themselves are among the most original and controversial in twentieth-century philosophy. We shall not have space to consider them all, but I have chosen three groups of topics for discussion: (1) body, mind, and the problem of the external world; (2) truth; (3) nondemonstrative inference.

Mind, Matter, and the External World

IN the years following his early idealist period, Russell's philosophical views were, in general, those that would be endorsed by educated common sense. But he showed considerable logical sophistication where these views seemed to lead, as they so often do, to difficulties and contradictions. *The Problems of Philosophy*, published in 1912, marks his closest *rapprochement* with common sense. Most of his

characteristic doctrines appear in the books published after that date, starting in 1914 with *Our Knowledge of the External World*. In these later books he accepts the findings of common sense as long as they withstand criticism. Too often, however, they fail in his eyes to do so.

Perhaps the most celebrated and the most criticized of Russell's philosophical theories is his "neutral monism." Versions of this theory were suggested in the nineteenth century by Ernst Mach and later by William James. Russell was at first critical of these suggestions, but came later to work out his own version of them. The basic principle of the theory is that there is no fundamental difference in nature between mental events and physical events. And since "mind" and "matter" are, for Russell, logical constructions out of mental and physical events respectively, there is at bottom no difference between mind and matter. The theory, if acceptable, rids philosophy of the dualism between mind and body introduced by Plato and reaffirmed in the seventeenth century by Descartes. Moreover, it is a theory with a distinctively "empirical" flavor, which preserves the economy of assumptions demanded by Ockham's razor. It can claim to keep closer than most theories to the facts of experience, since we do not infer any entities (such as minds or physical substances) that do not occur in the catalogue of things of which we are, or can be, directly aware.

Let us suppose for the purposes of illustration a simplified universe[39] consisting of two spheres, S_1 and S_2, and a single observer, O. We may suppose S_1 to be red and S_2 to be green and each to be 1 foot in radius and to be situated 10 feet from the other. O is equipped with normal sense organs and central nervous system and can move about freely in the universe. We omit for simplicity any considerations of O's observations of his own body. Further, we suppose that the edge of the universe is where both objects vanish according to the ordinary laws of perspective. (The universe will therefore be roughly spherical.) We may then consider S_1 and S_2 as centers from which radii diverge in all directions. Each of these radii can be viewed as a series of *aspects* of its central object. Each aspect, that is to say, is the appearance that the object would present from that point were an observer to be present there. And each point in space will consist of an intersection of a radius of S_1 with a radius of S_2. Thus every point in the universe will consist of a pair of aspects, one of S_1 and one of S_2 (or, in the cases in which the radii are in the same straight line, a single aspect of either S_1 or S_2). Russell calls a view of the world from a given place a "perspective." The physical universe will then consist of the set of all perspectives.

If in addition O is present at a given point, the aspects of S_1 and S_2 at that point become members of another series, the experiences of O. The total experience or mental history of O will then be the

* The uses of the theory of descriptions do not lie only in the application to the problems mentioned above. For example, the theory has an important bearing on the ancient philosophical question "Is existence a predicate?"[38]

temporally ordered series of the aspects of S_1 and S_2 from the points at which O is successively situated. Thus aspects are collected into two different kinds of "bundles." On the one hand, those consisting of the aspects of S_1 make up the physical object S_1, while those consisting of all the aspects of S_2 make up the physical object S_2. On the other hand, those aspects occurring in O's experience as he moves from one space-time point in the universe to another make up his mental history. There is no difference in the materials collected; it is simply the collections of which they form a part that determine whether we count them as mental or physical. In the simplified universe sketched here, all the aspects of the objects would be physical and only those also occurring in O's experience would be mental.

This artificially simplified universe can be complicated to introduce all the objects and all the observers of our real highly complex world without any change of principle. Russell himself illustrates his theory in several ways. In *The Analysis of Mind* he says,

When I look at a star, my sensation is:
1. A member of the group of particulars which is the star, and which is associated with the place where the star is;
2. A member of the group of particulars which is my biography, and which is associated with the place where I am.

The result is that every particular of the kind relevant to physics is associated with *two* places: e.g., my sensation of the star is associated with the place where I am and with the place where the star is. This dualism has nothing to do with any "mind" that I may be supposed to possess; it exists in exactly the same sense if I am replaced by a photographic plate.[40]

[He also gives a more picturesque and metaphorical explanation to make the same point by] the analogy of the Post Office directory, which classifies people in two ways, alphabetical and geographical. In the first arrangement, a man's neighbors are those who come near him in the alphabet; in the other, they are those who live next door. In this manner, a sensation may be grouped with a number of other occurrences by a memory-chain, in which case it becomes part of a mind; or it may be grouped with its causal antecedents, in which case it appears as part of the physical world. This view affords an immense simplification.[41]

The simplicity of the view of the world that follows from the theory is, of course, on Russell's view of philosophic method, its major advantage. Simplicity is, indeed, a virtue in a theory but only if the theory accounts for the facts that it is designed to explain. Does neutral monism do this?

It seems that it does not. In the first place, the contents of our sense experiences (or what Russell calls "percepts") do not constitute the whole of any normal mind. There are also images, both of memory and imagination, emotions, felt dispositions, and so on. And common sense will want to add "consciousness" as a common feature of all the elements of mental life. Sense perception, memory, reasoning, volition, desire, and so on are all very different in their respective natures, but all of them, according to common sense and many philosophers, share the property of being "conscious states." It is notoriously difficult to make such a catalog of mental contents that will satisfy even a minority of philosophers. But it is clear at least that the materials out of which our mental lives are built do not consist of percepts alone. Russell spends a good deal of time and ingenuity (particularly in *An Analysis of Mind* and *An Outline of Philosophy*) in trying to show that introspections, imagination, memory, desire, emotions, and other *prima facie* "mental" happenings can all be reduced to images and percepts plus the operation of certain causal laws. He argues with some plausibility that the notion of consciousness as a sort of mental stuff or a pervasive mental quality is indefensible.[42] "Mind is a matter of degree, chiefly exemplified in number and complexity of habits." But the critical reader gets the impression that Russell's demand for economy in explanation has here prevented him from doing justice to the facts. His account has been severely criticized, and Russell himself has acknowledged the force of some of these objections, though without renouncing neutral monism. Professor Stace points out[43] that the neutral entities in Russell's system are just aspects that can be constituents of both mind and matter. Images, on the other hand, are purely mental, while aspects that remain unperceived are purely physical. And if this is so, Russell has not avoided either dualism or a fundamental distinction between the mental and material worlds. This is perhaps one point in Russell's philosophy where Ockham's razor has shaved too closely and removed essential tissues along with the metaphysical fuzz it was designed to eliminate.

In his later work,[44] Russell expresses himself differently on mind and matter. Mental events, of which "mind" is a collection, are what can be known without inference; matter is knowable only as the result of inference. And "consciousness" is to be analyzed in terms of the more basic concept of "attention" or "noticing."[45] This can be regarded as a more cautious version of neutral monism which, though less detailed than his earlier version, is still compatible with its basic ideas. But if the theory is a failure, the failure lies rather in the oversimple account of mind than in the ingenious analysis of matter. To look more closely at his theory of material objects, we must examine Russell's account of sense perception.

Russell had originally accepted a view of sense perception (derived from Brentano and Meinong)

according to which there are three distinguishable elements in every occurrence of sensing a physical object: the mental act of sensing, the sensory content, and the object sensed. If I look at a tomato, I am *aware* of a *round red patch* which I believe to be caused by (or in some other way related to) the *tomato* I am perceiving. The three italicized phrases stand respectively for act, content, and object. Russell criticizes these distinctions in the first chapter of *The Analysis of Mind*. He first abandons the notion of a mental act. "The first criticism I have to make is that the *act* seems unnecessary and fictitious. The occurrence of the content of the thought constitutes the occurrence of the thought. Empirically, I cannot discover anything corresponding to the supposed act; and theoretically I cannot see that it is indispensable." Moreover, Russell thinks that we are apt to be misled here by grammar. The fact that we say "I see" or "he hears" and so on, predisposes us to take for granted that there is a *subject* that does the sensing or thinking or whatever it might be; and therefore that these are *activities* of the subject. "It would be better to say 'it thinks in me' like 'it rains here'; or better still, 'there is a thought in me.' This is simply on the ground that what Meinong calls the act in thinking is not empirically discoverable or logically deducible from what we can observe." The further question of the distinction between sensory content and the object sensed is best discussed in the context of his general theory of sense perception.

Russell's views on perception have shown some changes between the publication of *The Problems of Philosophy* in 1912 and his later work. But of the three main types of philosophical answer to the problem of our perception of the external world, naïve realism, the causal theory, and phenomenalism, he has always espoused some version of the second, though with sidelong glances from time to time at the more austere charms of the third. The phenomenalist account of the external world explains it as an ordered set of percepts, actual and possible, and nothing more. This is congenial to Russell's desire for intellectual economy. At times, as in his account of material objects as logical constructions from their aspects, he appears to be taking a phenomenalist point of view. But his scientific training and outlook triumph over his passion for austerity. In Chapter XX of *The Analysis of Matter*, he states the case for phenomenalism very fully and carefully. He rejects it only because it is at variance with the scientific concept of cause in that it postulates action at a distance in space and time. A phenomenalist's world is discontinuous in a way that seems to be incompatible with the truth of physics. Russell therefore abandons the theory.

No philosopher has paid more attention than Russell has to the evidence of physics and physiology in their bearing on the problems of perception. This is in accordance with his general approach to philosophy and his belief that well-established scientific theories, though never indubitable, are always to be taken seriously when they seem to be relevant to philosophy. Not only does he reject phenomenalism because of its inconsistency with physics; he rejects naïve realism for the same reason.

> We all start from "naive realism," i.e. the doctrine that things are what they seem. We think that grass is green, that stones are hard and that snow is cold. But physics assures us that the greenness of grass, the hardness of stones and the coldness of snow are not the greenness, hardness and coldness that we know in our own experience but something very different. The observer, when he seems to be observing a stone, is really, if physics is to be believed, observing the effects of the stone upon himself. . . . Naive realism leads to physics, and physics, if true, shows that naive realism is false. Therefore, naive realism, if true, is false; therefore it is false.[46]

Thus he is left, by elimination, with the causal theory of perception.

His version of the causal theory may be summarized in the following three propositions:

1. Physics and physiology give us very good reason to believe that material objects, as they exist in the world unperceived, must be very unlike our percepts. For example, "a table does not look like a vast number of electrons and protons, nor yet like trains of waves meeting and clashing. Yet that is the sort of thing a table is said to be by modern physicists."[47]
2. Any person has good reason to believe that other people perceive a world of material objects very like (though not quite like) the world that he perceives.
3. What anyone perceives *directly* (a "percept" in Russell's language) is the end product of a complex causal chain of physical and physiological events. This is an event *in the brain* of the person who is perceiving. Thus, what we are most directly aware of are events in our own brains.

This last statement has always been a stumbling block to Russell's critics. But it looks less paradoxical if we attend to his explanation. We must distinguish between two kinds of space: the public and neutral space of physics and the private and personal space of our perceptions. The objects I see are arranged in my visual field, which is part of my perceptual space. Perhaps it is more accurate to say that my percepts make up or constitute my private sensory space by the way they are ordered. This space is private to me and no one can share it. And it would be absurd to say that my percepts are *in my brain*, if by that I mean that they are in my brain *in perceptual space*. My brain does not form part of my perceptual space, since I cannot, except in very unusual circumstances, ever see my brain. But my brain does have a location in public physical space, like any other physical object. And the events which are the immediate occasion of (and indeed the necessary and sufficient conditions of) my perceiving *do* occur in my brain. Moreover, we have excellent evidence from physiology for believing that the nature, location, and structure of these brain events occurring in physical space completely determine the nature, location, and structure of the percepts occurring in our private perceptual space. And since the only public and communicable sense of the phrase "located in" refers to location in physical space, we are justified in saying that percepts are located in our brains.

There are two points on which objection will naturally be taken to this. The first is that we do not ordinarily use the word "see" in this way. The second is that the word "percept" is being used, misleadingly, in a double sense. Russell admits the first point but justifies his unusual use of "see." "The usual sense implies naive realism, and whoever is not a naive realist must either eschew the word 'see' or use it in a new sense. Common sense says: 'I see a brown table.' It will agree to both the statements: 'I see a table' and 'I see something brown.' Since, according to physics, tables have no color, we must either (a) deny physics, or (b) deny that I see a table, or (c) deny that I see something brown. It is a painful choice; I have chosen (b), but (a) or (c) would lead to at least equal paradoxes."[48]

The second objection is perhaps more serious. Russell seems to use the word "percept" in two senses. In the first sense, a percept is what other philosophers (and Russell himself at one time) call a sense-datum or a group of sense-data. That is to say, for example, if I am looking at a tomato, the round red bulgy patch that I am directly aware of is a percept. A percept in this sense is private to the percipient and can have no location except in the private sensory space of that percipient. On the other hand, when he says that "percepts are in my head" and that "my head consists of percepts and other similar events"[49] he seems to be using the term in the sense of "events that are occurring in my brain and therefore physically located there in public space." And so, for Russell, "I see X" means "I am directly aware of percepts whose necessary and sufficient conditions are certain brain events; and these brain events are the final stage of a causal series in whose ancestry some of the events constituting X are a necessary part." It is a complex analysis of a simple phrase. But on any version of the causal theory of perception, the analysis of "I see X" will be complex. Russell's account would be clearer if he did not use the word "percept" in this ambiguous way. Let us distinguish these two senses of "percept" as *M*-percepts and *P*-percepts, respectively. He now has on his hands two correspondingly related analyses of the concept "material object." Objects are not substances but logical constructions from percepts. On one interpretation, a piece of matter is an ordered set of

its appearances, its *M*-percepts. On the other, "a piece of matter is a system of events"[50] and if the piece of matter is perceived, some of those events will be *P*-percepts, brain events of the type described. And so, to revert to the question that started this discussion of perception, the distinction between content and object becomes the distinction between *M*-percepts and *P*-percepts. Russell seems to think that the distinction is unimportant enough to be disregarded (presumably because every *M*-percept has its corresponding *P*-percept and vice versa). But many philosophers would dispute this.

Truth

AS in the case of perception, so in the case of truth Russell's loyalties to one of three main theories have always been clear. He has been a persistent critic of the pragmatic theory of truth and, since his rejection of Hegelian idealism, of the coherence theory as well. Most forms of idealism define truth in terms of the fitting of a judgment in the coherent system of all true judgments. Some of Russell's early papers written in the first decade of the century,[51] criticized the theory very effectively and did much to account for the disrepute into which it has since fallen. The pragmatic theory of truth analyzes "*P* is true" in terms of the consequences of our belief in *P*. If our belief proves expedient, "on the whole and in the long run" in William James' phrase, then *P* is true. The first of Russell's criticisms of the theory was published in 1909 in a review of James' *Pragmatism*, and thirty years later he was still attacking more sophisticated versions of the theory.[52] His most important objection is put succinctly as follows: "The essential point on which I differ from pragmatists is this: pragmatism holds that a belief is to be judged true if it has certain kinds of *effects*, whereas I hold that an empirical belief is to be judged true if it has certain kinds of *causes*."[53] The causes in question are, of course, the complex relations which the contents of our true beliefs have to the facts they purport to reflect. Russell, in other words, accepts the "correspondence theory of truth." This theory can take many different forms, and, like most expressions of a common-sense point of view in philosophy, it is extraordinarily difficult to state in a form that will be immune to obvious objections. In particular, we have to be clear on three points: (1) about the exact meaning of "belief" or "proposition" or "judgment" or whatever it is we hold to be capable of correspondence with fact; (2) about the meaning of "fact"; and (3) about the exact nature of the relationship that constitutes correspondence between belief (or proposition or judgment or whatever it may be) and fact.

His views on the problem have appeared in three main stages. An early version of the correspondence theory is given in *Philosophical Essays* (1910) and

The Problems of Philosophy (1912). This is a fairly complex analysis that we need not examine here, as Russell later abandoned it under the influence of his principle of intellectual economy. The second stage is represented by *The Analysis of Mind* (1921) and *An Outline of Philosophy* (1927). The views advanced in these books show some of the main features of his final version, which appeared in *An Inquiry into Meaning and Truth* (1940) and *Human Knowledge* (1948). It is this last account that we shall examine.

In an early discussion of the problem,[54] Russell states three conditions that an adequate account of truth must satisfy: first, it must allow for the possibility of error; second, it must make truth a property of beliefs and statements (with the consequence that, in a mindless world, there could be no truth or error); and third, it must make the truth of a belief dependent upon something external to and independent of the belief itself. These criteria are, of course, essential to a correspondence theory of truth, though they are compatible with some other theories too. Russell's final version of the correspondence theory conforms to these conditions. It tries first to account for the simplest instances of true and false beliefs, before attempting to explain more complex cases. This procedure is in accordance with his usual philosophical method. It is clearly sensible to proceed in this way with so complicated a problem, though Russell finds

> that most of the writers who concern themselves with a definition of "truth" proceed in a quite different manner. They start with what is complex or questionable, such as the law of gravitation or the existence of God or quantum theory. They do not trouble their heads with plain matters of fact, such as "I feel hot." This criticism applies not only to pragmatists, but equally to logical positivists. Philosophers of almost every school fail to investigate our knowledge of particular facts, and prefer to start their investigation with our knowledge of general laws. I think this is a fundamental error which vitiates most of their thinking.[55]

This scrupulous determination to start from the simplest cases and to explain the complex only in terms of the simple already accounted for requires a long preliminary investigation. The first two-thirds of *An Inquiry into Meaning and Truth* is taken up with a discussion of the meaning of words and of sentences, the nature of belief, and the foundations of our knowledge. The outcome of this inquiry, so far as it concerns the problem of truth, is as follows.

Truth is a property of beliefs and only in a derivative sense a property of sentences. If we then take as a rough preliminary definition of "true" and "false" that true beliefs are those that correspond (and false beliefs those that fail to correspond) with facts, we have three concepts to analyze: fact, belief, and correspondence. Russell leaves the term "fact" undefined. "Fact, as I intend the term, can only be defined ostensively. Everything that there is in the world, I call a fact. . . . Facts are what make statements true or false."[56] They are, he explains in the same context, independent of our knowledge or experience. And though Russell also considers an alternative version of the correspondence theory which makes truth consist in correspondence between belief and *experience* rather than between belief and *fact*, he dismisses it. For since there are facts which are not experienced, if truth consisted in correspondence between experience and belief, some beliefs, namely those referring to unexperienced facts, would be neither true nor false. And so the law of excluded middle would be broken. Rather than contemplate so drastic an amendment to the laws of logic, Russell rejects the theory.[57]

But though he leaves "fact" unanalyzed, he has a good deal to say about "belief." He observes that the concept "has an inherent and inevitable vagueness which is due to the continuity of mental development from the amoeba to *homo sapiens*."[58] Animal beliefs, evinced in behavior, are no less worthy of the title than the convictions expressed in language that we rather optimistically take to be the standard cases of belief. "The simpler kind of belief, especially when it calls for action, may be entirely unverbalized. When you are traveling with a companion, you may say: 'We must run; the train is just going to start.' But if you are alone you may have the same belief, and run just as fast, without any words passing through your head. I propose, therefore, to treat belief as something that can be pre-intellectual, and can be displayed in the behavior of animals."[59] Most of our beliefs are, in fact, unverbalized, and consist in no more than those bodily states of tension, muscular adjustment, and expectation by which we, like other organisms, adapt ourselves to our environment. "A belief, as I understand the term, is a certain kind of state of body or mind or both. To avoid verbiage, I shall call it a state of an organism, and ignore the distinction of bodily and mental factors."[60] It is, however, a characteristic of all beliefs, verbalized or preverbal, that they have what Russell calls "external reference." They are each *directed* to some fact, real or supposed. If the fact exists, the belief is true; if not, it is false. The fact (or set of facts) corresponding to a given belief (which Russell calls its *verifier*) is the state of affairs that satisfies the expectation embodied by the belief.

But this is vague and metaphorical. What is the precise relation, the *correspondence*, of belief to fact such that the belief having this relation to a verifier is true? To explain this, Russell appeals to the relation between sign and *significatum*, or thing signified. This is a relation established by association of the sign with the significatum. It is in this way that clouds come to "mean" rain, smoke comes to "mean" fire, red lights to "mean" danger, and so forth. And in this way, too, we learn the meanings of words, and of all the other signs in which our beliefs are clothed

— images, bodily feelings of expectation, and so on. Russell uses the word "significance" for the meaning of sentences and other complex expressions of belief which are built up according to rule from simple signs having *meaning*. Thus, our beliefs acquire significance by their embodiment in meaningful signs. But, of course, a belief can be significant without being true. The significance of a belief is the symbolic expression of a *potential* fact which, if it existed, would make the belief true. It is what forms the content of our beliefs and enables us to judge if a given fact, occurring in our experience, is the verifier of a particular belief. It is easy enough to see, in the case of a simple facts of experience ("This is cold," "I have a toothache," and so on) what correspondence between belief and fact amounts to, on this account. It consists basically in a relationship of the sort established between a sign and what it signifies. The occurrence of the sign involves an expectation that is satisfied by the occurrence of the significatum. (I see a flash of lightning and this sets up a bodily state of expecting thunder. This belief-expectancy is satisfied by hearing the anticipated peal of thunder. I think to myself "The traffic light will turn green in a moment"; the event satisfies my expectation.)

This is what Russell means by "correspondence" in the case of simple beliefs. But the matter is more complicated in the case of statements or beliefs of a less primitive kind. And it is these, of course, that provide the interesting cases. Consider, for example, the kind of general statements that are important in science, or artificially simplified cases of these like "All men are mortal," "All green leaves contain chlorophyll," and so on. Here many verifiers are needed: "This leaf is green and contains chlorophyll," "That leaf is green and contains chlorophyll," and so on, for an indefinite number of instances. These cases go beyond the problem of truth, and raise problems of nondeductive inference that are discussed below.

Russell gives his general account of truth in the following words:[61] "Every belief which is not merely an impulse to action is in the nature of a picture, combined with a yes-feeling or a no-feeling; in the case of a yes-feeling it is 'true' if there is a fact having to the picture the kind of similarity that a prototype has to an image; in the case of a no-feeling, it is 'true' if there is no such fact. A belief which is not true is called 'false.'" To make this account sufficiently broad, we have to interpret "picture" to include not only images (which are often unimportant or non-existent in the thinking of some people) but also sentences and other symbolic clothing for our beliefs. And even then, it fits the more elementary types of belief far better than it fits the complex beliefs involved in science and which require languages, natural or artificial, for their expression. Russell goes further than most philosophers have done in making the correspondence theory intel-

ligible in detail. If his account is inadequate, it seems to be because he has not given the same time and care to the superstructure of his theory as he gave to its foundations.

Nondemonstrative Inference

RUSSELL's early work on logic was on formal or deductive logic. Roughly speaking, this branch of logic deals with forms of inference having the following property: if the form is valid, it is impossible for the premises to be true and the conclusion to be false. However, there are many inferences which are not of this type. In our reasonings about matters of fact and experience it is possible for the premises of our beliefs to be true and the beliefs themselves false; and however careful and "correct" our reasoning may be on such matters, the conclusion can never be more than probably true. We all feel certain that arsenic will poison us, that bread will nourish us, and that the sun will rise tomorrow. But on the evidence we have for them, these beliefs can never be more than very probable. Such inferences are, moreover, of great practical importance, both in our everyday living and in the development of natural science. Philosophers and logicians have therefore to take account of them. Unfortunately, the problems that they present have proved very intractable. Russell discusses this problem first in *The Problems of Philosophy*. He points out that men, like other animals, have a natural tendency to assume that their future experience will be like their past experience in many respects. But this is simply in virtue of an animal tendency to be guided in our expectations of the future by our memories of the past. "We all know that these rather crude expectations of uniformity are liable to be misleading. The man who has fed the chicken every day throughout its life at last wrings its neck instead, showing that more refined views as to the uniformity of nature would have been useful to the chicken."[62] The question for the philosopher therefore is not what *causes* our expectations but what *justifies* them. If our beliefs about the future based on our experience of the past were always completely reliable, this question would not arise. But since it does arise, we must try to find some principle or principles — or perhaps some technique — that will enable us to test the reliability of our inductive expectations at least to the extent of being able to estimate *how probable* it is that a given expectation will prove correct.

In his early discussion of the problem in *The Problems of Philosophy* Russell does offer an inductive principle which purports to do this job. We need not examine it here, as he later abandoned it. Two things about it are noteworthy. First, it is a very complicated principle. It is stated in two forms, one applicable to single events and another to scientific laws, and each of the forms is in two parts. (Russell's formulation takes twenty lines of print.) Second, if we ask what reason we have to believe it, Russell answers "we must either accept the inductive principle on the ground of its intrinsic evidence or forgo all justification of our expectations about the future."[63] Such a view is obviously open to criticism,[64] and Russell seems soon to have abandoned it. In his philosophical writings over the next thirty-five years he does not deal seriously with the question.[65] In 1943, replying to his critics in *The Philosophy of Bertrand Russell*, he confesses that the problem of inductive inference is still unsolved. "It is clear that induction is needed to establish almost all our empirical beliefs and that it is not deducible from any or all of the principles of deductive logic."[66] He concludes that the inductive principle must be one of the independent premises of our knowledge. "What exactly this principle should be is a difficult question which I hope to deal with at some not distant date if circumstances permit."[67]

This promise is redeemed in *Human Knowledge*, published in 1948. Parts V and VI of the book contain a careful discussion of probability and the postulates of scientific inference. It is not possible to give an intelligible précis of the complex argument in a short space. What follows is a summary of his conclusions. Why do I believe that lemons taste sour? For two reasons: (1) I have tasted a fair sample of lemons and they have all tasted sour; (2) everybody else who has done the same and has reported their experience agrees with me. I therefore believe (a) that the next lemon I taste will be sour, and (b), more rashly, that all lemons taste sour. Now if this is to rank as a piece of reasoning which *justifies* my belief about lemons and is not just a *causal* explanation of why I hold the belief, I am assuming the truth of a general principle of induction which may be roughly stated: If I have found properties A and B always associated together in the past, it is probable that I will find them so in the future; and the oftener this has happened in the past, the more probable it is that it will happen so in the future. Now this principle can hardly be claimed to be self-evidently true, nor can it be deduced from the laws of logic. Because of this, reasoning in accordance with this principle has occupied, according to Russell, "a very peculiar position in most accounts of scientific inference; it has been considered to be, like the hangman, necessary but unpleasant, and not to be talked of if the subject could possibly be avoided."[68] Russell tries to remove this scandal to philosophy. Basing his work on some results of J. M. Keynes,[69] Russell concludes* that provided that certain conditions are satisfied, a form of this inductive principle can be derived from the mathematical theory of probability; the principle will then no longer have to be accepted as an indemonstrable but unobvious presupposition of inductive reasoning.

* It should be added that not all logicians have so favorable a view of Keynes' work as Russell has.

Russell sets out these conditions in a number of "postulates." He arrived at these after examining a wide variety of the inductive arguments which are ordinarily accepted as reliable by science and common sense. He asks: If we are to accept (as we all do) this type of argument as satisfactory, what extralogical principles are we tacitly assuming? He concludes that the following five postulates are sufficient:[70]

1. *The postulate of quasi-permanence.* Given any event A, it happens very frequently that, at any neighboring time, there is at some neighboring place an event very similar to A.
2. *The postulate of separable causal lines.* It is frequently possible to form a series such that, from one or two members of the series, something can be inferred about all the other members.
3. *The postulate of spatio-temporal continuity.* When there is a causal connection between two events that are not contiguous, there must be intermediate links in the causal chain such that each is contiguous to the next.
4. *The structural postulate.* When a number of structurally complex events are arranged about a center in regions not widely separated, it is usually the case that all belong to causal lines having their origin in an event of the same structure at the centre.
5. *The postulate of analogy.* Given two classes of events A and B, and given that, whenever both A and B can be observed, there is reason to believe that A causes B, then if, in a given case, A is observed, but there is no way of observing whether B occurs or not, it is probable that B occurs; and similarly, if B is observed but the presence or absence of A cannot be observed.

It will be seen that these are not principles of logic but general assumptions about the way nature works. Accordingly, as Russell remarks, "they state only probabilities, not certainties."[71] He lays no stress on the particular formulation that he gives to these postulates. But he does claim that the success of our common-sense and scientific generalizations from experience presupposes that nature has some such permanent patterns of behavior as these postulates describe.

The problem of "justifying induction" has attracted a good deal of attention in recent philosophical writing. Some philosophers have argued very plausibly that it is senseless to ask for a proof that inductive reasoning *in general* is a rational activity. We may ask of a particular piece of such reasoning whether it conforms to established inductive procedures, just as we may ask if a given piece of deductive reasoning is valid (that is, whether it conforms to the rules of formal logic). But to ask the general question: Is induction rational? would be just as silly as to ask: Is deduction rational? Our *standards* of rationality are provided by correct reasoning, deductive and inductive. To ask: But are these procedures really rational? is like asking of a standard foot rule: Is it really a foot long? Russell, in his later treatment of induction, is perfectly aware of this. His question is not: How are we to justify induction? (though in an early book, *The Problems of Philosophy*, he did discuss this question). His question is simply: What must the universe be like if inductive reasoning is to be successful? And to this question, his answer is a good deal more detailed and informative than those of earlier philosophers.

Ethics

IT is probably fair to say that most philosophers who have written about ethics have not experienced any passionate convictions about right and wrong. Aristotle, Hobbes, and Hume wrote influentially on these subjects, but there is little evidence in their writings or in their behavior of that hunger for righteousness of which the Gospel speaks so favorably. But this is not surprising, nor necessarily discreditable to the philosophers. Few people are responsible for their enthusiasms. In any case, there is an important logical distinction between first-order and second-order activities. We properly distinguish between doing science and reflecting critically on the scientists' findings and procedures, and between feeling and expressing moral approvals and disapprovals and critically examining the logic of the sentences in which these emotions are expressed.

But Russell is unusual among philosophers in taking morals, both in its personal and its social aspects, very seriously indeed. He cares little about moral philosophy, for reasons that will become obvious when we consider his views. But human good and evil do greatly concern him. His first book was on political questions, and one of his latest concerns morals and politics.[72] In over fifty years of writing, he has published as much on society, morals, and happiness as he has on the philosophical and logical matters for which he is more famous. Indeed, there could be no better evidence for his concern for human happiness and the good life than his most recent activities. In his ninetieth year, he suffered imprisonment in an effort to save his country from the disastrous fate which he and many of his countrymen see as the outcome of the foreign and nuclear policies of their present rulers.

Russell's ethical teaching has two sides, personal and social. He defines the good life as "one inspired by love and guided by knowledge."[73] And in offering this definition, he is thinking mainly of the intelligent coordination of human wishes. Love demands that the wishes of others shall as far as possible be satisfied; knowledge ensures that we adopt the most efficient means to their satisfaction and select for satisfaction only those wishes which are not incompatible. The knowledge Russell refers to here is factual and scientific knowledge. He does not believe that there can be any such thing as "ethical knowledge."[74] Only that knowledge is relevant to ethics which can tell us what things are desired and how these desires can most efficiently be satisfied. A natural objection of the common-sense moralist is that some desires are "right" and some are "wrong" and that an important task of knowledge in ethics is to tell us which is which.

This Russell denies. "Primarily, we call something 'good' when we desire it and 'bad' when we have an aversion from it."[75] By this he means that our behavior springs from desire and that though our "official" views on good and evil tend to be affected by childhood training and by public opinion, human nature is sufficiently common and stable to determine a wide class of common human goods — food, shelter, health, bodily comforts, sex, social and family ties, intellectual and aesthetic activities, and so on. But he means as well, something which is of more consequence for academic ethics. Statements of value to the effect that something is good or bad in itself (and not just as a means to some further end) are not genuine statements at all. They are neither true nor false and state nothing. They merely evince or express our attitudes, wishes, and approvals as a dog expresses his when he snarls or wags his tail. "When we assert that this or that has 'value,' we are giving expression to our own emotions, not to a fact which would still be true if our personal feelings were different."[76]

At other places in his writings on ethics, he holds a view superficially similar to this but which should be carefully distinguished from it. A moral judgment like "slavery is an evil institution" *states* my attitude toward slavery. " 'I ought to do so' primarily means 'This is the act toward which I feel the emotion of approval.' "[77] This view, which equates moral judgments with statements about the speaker's attitudes, is clearly different from that which says that my moral judgments are not genuine statements at all but are merely *expressions* of my attitudes. The first is usually classed as a type of *subjective* theory about ethics; the second is usually called an *emotive* theory. Russell seems to combine both of these approaches to ethics without distinguishing them clearly; but, especially in his later writings, he puts more emphasis on the second. We shall therefore concentrate on this view, which is the more defensible of the two.

His chief reasons for holding these views are (1) the great variability of moral judgments between different times, places, and persons; (2) the impossibility of finding a way of deciding between conflicting judgments of value. "Since no way can even be imagined for deciding a difference as to values, the conclusion is forced upon us that the difference is one of tastes, not one as to any objective truth."[78] We may postpone for the moment considering whether these reasons are good ones. In the meantime, it will help us to understand Russell's point of view if we examine some obvious common-sense objections to it.

Surely, it may be said, there are at least two good reasons why it must be wrong to say that statements of value describe no state of affairs but merely express the speaker's attitude. No doubt, if I say sincerely "Bullfighting is wrong," I am indeed expressing my disapproval of bullfighting. But I am doing more: First, I am making a statement intended to have a *universal* reference and not merely a *personal* one. After all, nobody forces me to watch bullfights or to take part in them. In making the statement, I intend to imply that this kind of conduct should be avoided *by everyone*. Second, I am moreover making a statement which, though I believe it to be true, I also believe to be capable of denial and to be open to argument. No one can sensibly question an expression of attitude except either to query its sincerity or to inquire how the attitude came to be formed. But if an *aficionado* of the bull ring were to say to me, "No, I don't agree that bullfighting is wrong," he is not doing either of these things. Nor is he merely expressing his own favorable attitude to the ritual torture of bulls.

Russell has an answer to the first objection. He agrees that a moral judgment "must have an element of universality."[79] And he goes on to explain: "I should interpret 'A is good' as 'Would that all men desired A.'" The element of universality in moral judgments lies in the fact that those who make such judgments necessarily wish that the preferences they express be shared by their fellows. But such judgments have no property analogous to the claims to objectivity and to truth which are implicit in judgments of fact. Persuasion in matters of ethics must therefore be of a different kind from persuasion in matters of science. In factual questions, we appeal to objective and publicly verifiable evidence, admitted as such by all competent judges. In questions of value, we persuade by preaching or propaganda. "According to me, the person who judges that *A* is good is wishing others to feel certain desires. He will therefore, if not hindered by other activities, try to rouse these desires in other people if he thinks he knows how to do so. This is the purpose of preaching and it was my purpose in the various books in which I have expressed ethical opinions. The art of presenting one's desires persuasively is totally different from that of logical demonstration, but it is equally legitimate."[80]

What, then, would Russell say to the second of the two objections mentioned above? Here he confesses very candidly to a feeling of uneasiness with his position. If he is right, he cannot, he thinks, be prepared to argue for his views; all he can consistently do is to recommend them by any means that the arts of persuasion have found to be effective. He considers a charge of inconsistency brought against him by some of his critics.[81] It is suggested that he is inconsistent in that "although I hold ultimate ethical valuations to be subjective, I nevertheless allow myself emphatic opinions on ethical questions." But, of course, he is not being inconsistent in any ordinary logical sense. He has nowhere affirmed a statement whose implications can be shown to amount to a formal contradiction. The most his critics can properly claim is that it is pointless for a subjectivist in morals to propagate his views. If "cruelty is evil" is a proposition of the same logical standing as "I dislike the taste of oysters" or if it is merely like evincing my dislike of oysters as a food, is not uttering this sentence doing no more than making public a trivial and inconsequential piece of autobiography? No. Russell could properly claim that it is much more than this. Making my moral opinions public is a necessary step in persuading others to adopt them. Indeed, it might well be argued that an enthusiasm for propagating one's opinions on questions of morals is a necessary part of what we mean in saying that we hold the opinions at all. We should not know what to make of someone who claimed, on interrogation, to believe that cruelty to animals was bad but failed ever to show any disapproval or distaste at instances of such cruelty or to comment adversely on conduct of this kind or to dissuade others from it.

But the second objection has still to be faced. Russell expresses the difficulty thus: "All of this may be true, I shall be told, *provided your desires are good*; if they are evil, rhetoric in their defence is an art of the devil. But what are 'good' desires? Are they anything more than desires that you share?"[82] On his own theory, of course, they are no more than this. But does this mean that moral judgments are therefore beyond argument? Russell is inclined to agree, though reluctantly, that this is so. "Suppose for example, that someone were to advocate the introduction of bull fighting into this country. In opposing the proposal, I should *feel*, not only that I was expressing my desires but that my desires in the matter are *right*, whatever that may mean. As a matter of argument, I can, I think, show that I am not guilty of any logical inconsistency in holding to the above interpretation of ethics and at the same time expressing strong ethical preferences. But in feeling I am not satisfied. I can only say that, while my own opinions as to ethics do not satisfy me, other people's satisfy me still less."[83]

Mere moral feelings fail to satisfy Russell because, quite properly, he sees in them, *taken by themselves*, no basis for rational argument. But is it true that there is no ground for argument at all over such questions? We cannot indeed prove that our moral feelings are justified in the same way in which we justify a judgment of fact. But there are facts that enable us to do something analogous to this. In spite of wide variations in human tastes and temperaments, men and women do recognize that there are sources of happiness and misery common to us all; and most of us do feel, to some degree at least, sympathy with the joys and sorrows of other sentient creatures. We therefore tend to recognize that some moral attitudes and emotions are "justified" in terms of such common human preferences. There is thus a sense in which moral judgments, even as Russell interprets them, can be supported by reasons. Professor Edwards makes this point very clearly in discussing Russell's doubts about the justification of his own moral attitude to bullfighting:

> Russell first maintains in general terms that moral judgments are nothing but the expression of a desire on the speaker's part. He then says that he somehow feels that when he says "the introduction of bull-fighting in the United States would be a bad thing" he is doing something more than expressing his desire or that his desire is somehow objectively superior to that of a person who desires the introduction of bull-fighting. My theory or Russell's own theory, supplemented by a consideration of the *reasons* for moral judgments, easily clears up the source of this dissatisfaction without any surrender to intuitionism. "The introduction of bull-fighting into the United States would be a bad thing" in addition to expressing something concerning the speaker, makes some such objective claim as, "The introduction of bull-fighting would lead to avoidable pain for innocent animals and to an increase in cruelty and indirectly to the strengthening of illiberal forces and tendencies; moreover, though it would produce a certain amount of pleasure among the spectators, this very pleasure would reduce their capacity for other and deeper pleasures." Russell's desire *is* objectively superior in the sense that its satisfaction would prevent the suffering of innocent animals, certain increases in cruelty, and the strengthening of illiberal forces, etc. The satisfaction of his opponents' desire would have altogether different consequences. This is, I think, what Russell means by "superior" in the sense of referent. If the facts concerning bull-fighting are as I described them a moment ago it is clear that Russell is right.[84]

Finally, let us return to the question whose consideration we deferred. Do the facts that (1) there are wide variations in moral judgments among equally sincere and intelligent men and that (2) there are no agreed methods of settling such differences of opinion prove that an emotive theory of ethics is correct? If *S* is a certain statement about whose truth there is wide disagreement and which has no known method of decision, it is still clearly possible for *S* to be true (or false) in the straightforward factual senses of these words. The early history of science can give us abundant examples of this: the shape of the earth, the distances of the stars, the constitution of the sun, the causes of fevers — the list could be a very long one.

As soon as an appropriate method of solving the problem is discovered, disagreement is resolved on its solubility, though not necessarily on the details of its solution. Our present question therefore becomes: Is there any good reason to suppose that an effective method of deciding moral disputes is in principle impossible to find because of the nature of these disputes? Or are we faced with a problem like any other unsolved scientific problem — like the problem of the causes and cure of cancer, for example? Here there is good reason to believe that the problem is soluble in principle although the scientists are still searching for the answer.

It can fairly be said that nearly all moral philosophers would now agree that the problem is not analogous to an unsolved problem of science. And most of them would agree that there are good reasons to suppose that an effective method of decision is in principle impossible to find. But even if we concede that Russell's account of moral judgments is consistent with these facts, it is certainly not necessitated by them. Moreover, if we concede, as many moral philosophers at the present time would do, that moral judgments are *basically* expressions of moral emotions, we are not therefore forced to conclude that moral questions are therefore *entirely* beyond the reach of reason and that in their public aspects they are no more than an appropriate field for preaching and propaganda. Let us recall two points that have already been emphasized: (1) human beings do share many needs, desires, and ideals, and many of these can be simultaneously satisfied; (2) a knowledge of the relevant facts in each case of moral decision will help us to decide how far our desires can be consistently satisfied without thwarting or being thwarted by the satisfaction of the desires of others. This will not solve all our problems, but it gives us a wide and important field for the use of reason in ethics.

Conclusion

IT has been necessary in so short a survey as this to omit any consideration of a great many of Russell's doctrines, including some of those for which he is especially remembered. His achievements in logic and in the philosophy of mathematics would have given him an assured place in the history of philosophy had he written nothing else. And we have not discussed his theories of space, time, and causality, nor his very original solution to the problem of universals. His very influential writings on education, sociology, and politics have also had to be ignored. No philosopher of the twentieth century has had anything like Russell's breadth of interests, scientific background, and philosophical insight. And certainly none of them can show anything like the beauty, clarity, and wit of his handling of language. The literary virtues of his writings alone won him the Nobel Prize for literature in 1950.

He differs, too, from many philosophers in having a very distinctive moral flavor to his writings. Even if we disagree with the detail of his arguments, we can absorb, to our advantage, a certain quasi-religious reverence for truth and objectivity which is the mark of the true philosophic mind. No one is more contemptuous than Russell of the superstitious extravagances of conventional religion, and in his lighter writings he has had a good deal of fun at their expense. And yet, in his attitude to the world there is something of a religious attitude of a detached and impersonal kind, reminiscent perhaps of Spinoza more than of any other great philosopher. An eloquent if overrhetorical example of this is the famous essay "A Free Man's Worship."[85] A more mature and revealing passage occurs at the end of "My Mental Development," written in 1943.[86]

My intellectual journeys have been, in some respects, disappointing. When I was young, I hoped to find religious satisfaction in philosophy; even after I had abandoned Hegel, the eternal Platonic world gave me something non-human to admire. I thought of mathematics with reverence and suffered when Wittgenstein led me to regard it as nothing but tautologies. I have always ardently desired to find some justification for the emotions inspired by certain things that seemed to stand outside human life and to deserve feelings of awe. I am thinking in part of very obvious things, such as the starry heavens and a stormy sea on a rocky coast; in part of the vastness of the scientific universe, both in space and time, as compared to the life of mankind; in part of the edifice of impersonal truth, especially truth which, like that of mathematics, does not merely describe the world that happens to exist. Those who attempt to make a religion of humanism, which recognises nothing greater than man, do not satisfy my emotions. And yet, I am unable to believe that, in the world as known, there is anything that I can value outside human beings and, to a much lesser extent, animals. Not the starry heavens, but their effects on human percipients, have excellence; to admire the universe for its size is slavish and absurd; impersonal non-human truth appears to be a delusion. And so my intellect goes with the humanists, though my emotions violently rebel. In this respect, the "consolations of philosophy" are not for me.

Nevertheless, the fact that, for Russell, truth is mind-dependent does not mean, as we have seen, that it is, in any sense, man-made. Reverence for logic and fact is perhaps the most vivid moral lesson that remains with the student of his philosophy. He believes that we ought to be rational; that is, he passionately recommends rationality as a guide to living. And echoing a sentiment of David Hume, he defines this ideal as follows: "Perfect rationality consists, not in believing what is true, but in attaching to every proposition a degree of belief corresponding to its degree of credibility. In regard to empirical propositions, the degree of credibility changes when fresh evidence accrues."[87] Truth is thus an ideal to be striven after rather than attained. "All human knowledge is uncertain, inexact and partial. To this doctrine, we have not found any limitation whatever."[88] But inexact and partial as our best knowledge may be, it is none the less something to be pursued:

"I think that we can, however imperfectly, mirror the world, like Leibniz's monads; and I think it is the duty of the philosopher to make himself as undistorting a mirror as he can. But it is also his duty to recognise such distortions as are inevitable from our very nature. Of these, the most fundamental is that we view the world from the point of view of the *here* and *now*, not with that large impartiality which theists attribute to the Deity. To achieve such impartiality is impossible for us, but we can travel a certain distance towards it. To show the road to this end is the supreme duty of the philosopher."[89]

27

Logical Positivism

R. W. ASHBY

A. J. AYER WAS BORN in 1910. He was educated at Eton and was a classical scholar at Christ Church, Oxford. He spent some time after graduation in Vienna studying with the Vienna Circle and on his return to England became a lecturer in philosophy at Christ Church in 1933 and a Research Student there in 1935. In 1936 he published *Language, Truth and Logic* which introduced a radical version of the doctrines of the Vienna Circle to the English-speaking world. He served during the Second World War in the Welsh Guards and in military intelligence. After the war, he returned to Oxford as Fellow and Dean of Wadham and in 1946 became Grote Professor of the Philosophy of Mind and Logic at University College, London. In 1960 he went to Oxford as Wykeham Professor of Logic. Professor Ayer has lectured at many American universities and in several foreign countries, including China, Peru, and the Soviet Union. He is the editor of the Pelican Philosophy Series to which one of the best known contributions is his own book *The Problem of Knowledge* (1956).

Rudolf Carnap was born in Germany in 1891. In 1926 he became a lecturer in philosophy in Vienna, where his work and influence contributed greatly to the development of the Vienna Circle. He left Vienna to become professor of philosophy at the University of Prague. In 1936 he accepted an invitation to go to America and became Professor of Philosophy at the University of Chicago, a post he held until 1954, when he went to the University of California at Los Angeles. His many publications have ranged over a wide field in scientific philosophy. The earliest concerned philosophical problems of physics and geometry (*Der Raum*, 1922, and *Physikalische Begriffsbildung*, 1926). The very influential *Der Logische Aufbau der Welt* was published in 1928 and *The Logical Syntax of Language* in 1934. Carnap's later work dealt with semantics and with the logical problems of induction and probability. He died in 1970.

Hans Reichenbach was born in Hamburg in 1891 and educated at Erlangen and Stuttgart, where he studied physics and philosophy. In 1926 he was appointed to a post at the University of Berlin. When the Nazis took power in Germany in 1933 Reichenbach left the country and taught for five years in Turkey at the University of Istanbul. In 1938 he was invited to a post at the University of California at Los Angeles, where he taught for the rest of his life. He died in 1953. Reichenbach's considerable output includes books on symbolic logic, probability, and the philosophy of science. *Experience and Prediction* (1938) and *The Rise of Scientific Philosophy* (1951) are readable non-technical accounts of his philosophical position.

Moritz Schlick was born in 1882 and studied physics at the University of Berlin. His doctoral thesis, written under the supervision of Max Planck, concerned a topic in optics. He soon became interested in the philosophical problems of science and in 1917 published a monograph on *Space and Time in Contemporary Physics*; it was one of the earliest essays on relativity theory and one of the first attempts to introduce the theory to non-physicists. He was appointed to a professorship at Kiel in 1921 and in the following year was invited to Mach's old chair at the University of Vienna — the professorship for the philosophy of the inductive sciences. Here he became the central figure of the Vienna Circle, a group of like-minded scientists and philosophers which made Vienna a world center for philosophy in the 1930's. Schlick visited America in 1929 to teach at Stanford and in 1931 to teach at Berkeley. In 1936 he was murdered on the steps of the university by a former student who appears to have been insane. The authorities of the day, subservient to clerical opinion to which Schlick's doctrines were anathema, made little attempt to punish the murder.

AT THE UNIVERSITY of Vienna the tradition of empiricism — which had flourished with the teaching of Ernst Mach — was continued by Mach's successor, the well-known physicist L. Boltzmann. In 1922 Moritz Schlick was appointed to the same professorship in the philosophy of the inductive sciences, and around Schlick gathered a group which during the following years met regularly to discuss philosophical questions. All the early participants had received a training in a discipline other than philosophy. Schlick had studied physics, and had written a thesis (concerning a problem in theoretical optics) under the supervision of Max Planck at Berlin. He maintained close contact with Planck, Einstein, and Hilbert, and in 1917 published a book entitled *Raum und Zeit in der gegenwärtigen Physik* — (Space and Time in Contemporary Physics). In the following year he published another book, *Allgemeine Erkenntnislehre* (General Theory of Knowledge), which was concerned with the theory of knowledge, and anticipated many of the distinctive features of the philosophy that was later held in Vienna. Freidrich Waismann and Rudolf Carnap, among the most active members of the group, both had an appreciable knowledge of mathematics, and Hans Hahn, Karl Menger, and Kurt Gödel were primarily mathematicians. Otto Neurath was a sociologist, Victor Kraft a historian, and Felix Kaufmann a lawyer. Philipp Frank, who was a regular and active visitor, was a professor of physics at Prague. The vitality and coherence of the group stemmed from the fact that the members had a common interest and a common method of approach; they wished to unify the special sciences and to make philosophy scientifically tenable, by the practice of logical analysis. The group came to be known as the Vienna Circle, and its philosophy was called consistent empiricism, logical empiricism, or logical positivism.

The most direct influences upon the philosophy of the Vienna Circle were the empiricism of Hume, Mill, and Mach (not the French positivism of Comte*), the views of scientific method expressed by Poincaré, Duhem, and Einstein, the axiomatics of Peano and Hilbert, and the mathematical logic of Frege, Schröder, Russell, and Whitehead. The greatest single influence upon the Circle during its earlier years was Wittgenstein's *Tractatus Logico-Philosophicus* (1921, translated into English 1922). This work presents a philosophy of logical atomism which differs from Russell's in important respects,[1] and at the same time advances a number of original and far-reaching theses on a variety of philosophical topics. It proclaims: "The object of philosophy is the logical clarification of thoughts. Philosophy is not a theory but an activity. A philosophical work consists essentially of elucidations. The result of philosophy is not a number of 'philosophical propositions', but to make propositions clear. Philosophy should make clear and delimit sharply the thoughts which otherwise are, as it were, opaque and blurred."[2] The *Tractatus* evoked an immense amount of discussion in the Vienna Circle. Many of its doctrines were taken up and developed; others were rejected. Schlick regarded its conception of philosophy as marking a decisive turning point in the history of the subject. We shall have occasion to

* Auguste Comte (1798–1857), who invented the name "positivism" for the view that all knowledge consists in a description of the coexistence and succession of phenomena, held that there are six basic sciences — mathematics, astronomy, physics, chemistry, biology, and sociology — and that each of these, although it presupposes, is not reducible to the preceding one. The Vienna Circle held, as one of its main contentions, the doctrine of the unity of science, i.e., the view that the concepts and laws of all the special sciences are logically reducible to the concepts and laws of one system of science. Neurath and Carnap's "thesis of physicalism" was a particular version of this view.

discuss some of the doctrines of the *Tractatus*, and some of the other main influences upon the Vienna Circle, when we examine the distinctive features of the philosophy of logical positivism.

In 1929 the Vienna Circle issued a publication *Wissenschaftliche Weltauffassung: Der Wiener Kreis* (The Vienna Circle: Its Scientific World-Conception) which announced the aims and methods of the group. Its principal aim was to bring about a unification of the special sciences and of all knowledge accessible to man. The method to be employed was logical analysis, and this was to be used (a) negatively, to eliminate metaphysical statements from the natural sciences, mathematics, and human knowledge generally, (b) positively, to clarify the concepts and methods of the sciences, and to show that all human knowledge is constructed from the data of experience. A first attempt to carry out this last-mentioned aim had already been made by Carnap in his *Der logische Aufbau der Welt* (Logical Construction of the World), 1928.

From this time on, the logical positivist movement expanded rapidly. A similar group — including Hans Reichenbach, Richard von Mises, Kurt Grelling, and at a later time Carl Hempel — was formed in Berlin. An existing journal was renamed *Erkenntnis*, and used by the logical positivists for the publication and discussion of their views. A series of monographs under the collective title *Einheitswissenschaft* (Unified Science) and a series of books under the title *Schriften zur Wissenschaftlichen Weltauffassung* (Writings Concerning the Scientific World-Conception) was also published during the 1930's. Carnap's *Logische Syntax der Sprache* (Logical Syntax of Language), 1934 and Karl Popper's *Logik der Forschung* (Logic of Scientific Discovery), 1935 originally appeared in this series of books — although Popper was not a member of the Vienna Circle, and was in some important respects opposed to its philosophy. Congresses were held at Prague, Königsberg, Copenhagen, Paris, Cambridge, and in 1939 at Harvard University, and contact was maintained with sympathetic groups in Poland, Holland, and Scandinavia. In England the movement was first represented by A. J. Ayer, whose *Language, Truth and Logic* was published in 1936. In the United States the philosophers most sympathetic to the movement were Ernest Nagel and Charles Morris. But while the logical positivist movement was gaining more widespread support, the original Vienna Circle was breaking up. At the beginning of the 1930's Carnap and Frank became professors at the University of Prague, and Feigl went to the United States. Hahn died in 1934. In 1936, Schlick was murdered by an insane student, and after his death the regular meetings of the Circle came to an end. By 1938, mainly on account of the political situation in Vienna (the Nazi authorities later prohibited the sale of logical positivist literature), Neurath had left for Holland, Waismann for England, Carnap, Menger, and Gödel for the United States. After that time logical positivism was the work of isolated individuals or smaller or less coherent groups than the Vienna Circle. The most distinctive features of the philosophy of logical positivism will be examined in the following sections of this chapter.

The Rejection of Metaphysics

IN *Wissenschaftliche Weltauffassung: Der Weiner Kreis* the authors say*

> If anyone asserts "There is a God," "The first cause of the world is the Unconscious," "There is an entelechy which is the leading principle in living beings," we do not say "What you say is false"; rather, we ask him "What do you mean by your statements?" It then appears that there is a sharp division between two types of statements. One of the types includes statements as they are made in empirical science; their meaning can be determined by logical analysis, or, more precisely, by reduction to simple sentences about the empirically given. The other statements, including those mentioned above, show themselves to be completely meaningless, if we take them as the metaphysician intends them. Of course, we can frequently reinterpret them as empirical statements. They then, however, lose the emotional content which is the very thing which is essential to the metaphysician. The metaphysicians and theologians, misinterpreting their own sentences, believe that their sentences assert something, represent some state of affairs. Nevertheless, analysis shows that these sentences do not say anything, being instead only expressions of some emotional attitude.

This passage is characteristic of logical positivist writing on metaphysics. The logical positivists set out to show that all metaphysical statements are cognitively meaningless, that all metaphysical speculation is pseudo-speculation. In this way they sought to bring about a more radical elimination of metaphysics than had been envisaged by any earlier school of anti-metaphysicians. They took encouragement from some of Wittgenstein's remarks in the *Tractatus*,[3] but their opposition to metaphysics stemmed from an interest different from his — namely, from their interest in purifying natural science and mathematics. Wittgenstein maintained that the structure of the world was something which could be *shown* in the structure of language, but could not be *stated*. He said, "There is indeed the inexpressible"[4] and he concluded the *Tractatus* with the remark "Whereof one cannot speak, thereof one must be silent." Neurath typified the different position of the Vienna Circle when he said that with

* Carnap, Neurath, and Hahn.

regard to metaphysics one should indeed be silent, but not *about* something.[5]

The logical positivists[6] argued that a language consists of a number of words which make up its vocabulary, and rules of syntax, including rules which determine how the words may be put together to form sentences. Consequently there are at least two ways in which a sequence of words may fail to express a genuine statement. Either one or more of the words may have no sense, or the sequence may be counter-syntactical. The sequence

> Twas brillig and the slithy toves
> Did gyre and gimble in the wabe

fails in the first way, whereas the sequence

> Was by stabbed Brutus Caesar

fails, in ordinary English, in the second way. The logical positivists claimed that the sentences of transcendental metaphysics must fail in the first way, and that most, if not all, of them fail in the second way as well. Such sentences contain words which are supposed to represent transcendental entities or properties, e.g., "being," "non-being," "noumena," "substance," "inherence," "emanation," and for this reason they are not analyzable into sentences about anything we could possibly experience. This alone, according to the logical positivists, is sufficient to show that such words and sentences are without sense. The special terms of metaphysics, they said, are as meaningless as the words "tove" and "wabe," and for the same reason, namely that they have not been given an empirical application. Moreover, many of the sentences of traditional metaphysics fail in the second way as well, i.e., by being counter-syntactical. For example, "I am," as it occurs in Descartes' "I think, therefore I am," commits the error of supposing that the existential use of the verb "to be" represents some kind of property, and of employing this use of the verb together with a name or referring expression. In Heidegger's remark "We know the Nothing" the word "nothing" occurs as a name, although the only intelligible use of it is that which corresponds, roughly speaking, to the negative existential quantifier in logic; e.g., we can say intelligibly, although falsely, "We know nothing," i.e., "it is not the case that there is an x such that we know x." The expression "the being of being," as it occurs in the writings of many metaphysicians, commits the double syntactical error of treating "being" as a predicate and then applying this predicate to itself — to speak of "the being of being" is as senseless as, or more senseless than, speaking of "the length of length." The fact that the traditional grammatical syntax of natural languages allows, and even encourages, such errors was regarded by the logical positivists, as by Russell and Wittgenstein before them, as a main source of metaphysics. What determines the rules and forms of logically correct syntax? This question,

as we shall see, was answered differently by different members of the Vienna Circle. Here it is sufficient to say that the logical positivists held that the logical syntax of an informative sentence or statement* is shown by the method of its verification. Their two main reasons for rejecting metaphysics — that metaphysical terms are senseless and that metaphysical sentences are counter-syntactical — both rested upon the view that to be cognitively meaningful a statement must be, in principle, empirically verifiable.

The Principle of Verifiability

THE Vienna Circle supposed that it had derived its principle of verifiability from Wittgenstein, partly from the *Tractatus* and partly from remarks made by Wittgenstein in private conversations with Schlick and Waismann. In the *Tractatus* Wittgenstein said, "to understand a proposition means to know what is the case, if it is true."[8] This says, in effect, that to understand a proposition is to know what content it has, and to know what content it has is to know what would be the case if the proposition were true — and both of these contentions are plainly tautological. It was also Wittgenstein's view that every proposition is a truth-function of atomic propositions — this was the principal contention of logical atomism, and is sometimes called the thesis of extensionality. Further, an atomic propostiion, according to the *Tractatus*, is an arrangement of names or primitive signs and "The references of primitive signs can be made clear by elucidations. Elucidations are propositions containing the primitive signs. Thus they can only be understood, if one is acquainted with the references of these signs."[9] The Vienna Circle took this to mean that primitive signs must refer to objects of acquaintance, and these objects are, by definition, the objects that we directly experience. This seemed to lead inevitably to the supposition that Wittgenstein's "elementary sentences" expressing atomic propositions are observation sentences.[10] And since the Vienna Circle also accepted the thesis of extensionality, they concluded that the meaning of every genuine statement is completely expressible by means of observation sentences alone. Moreover, Wittgenstein was reported as saying, in his conversa-

---

* The logical positivists tended to speak indifferently of sentences, statements, propositions. It is sometimes important to distinguish these: e.g., a sentence belongs to a particular language, it is meaningful or not, but it is not properly said to be true or false, it is not verifiable, and does not stand in logical relations to other sentences; a statement or proposition may be expressed by different sentences in the same or in different languages, but does not itself belong to a particular language, it is properly said to be true or false, it is verifiable or not, it does stand in logical relations to other statements or propositions. A statement is sometimes said to be whatever is expressed by an indicative sentence, whether the sentence is cognitively meaningful or not, while a proposition is said to be whatever is expressed by a cognitively meaningful sentence.[7]

tions with Schlick and Waismann, that in order to get clear how a sentence is used, what its meaning is, one of the questions to be asked is "How would one verify such an assertion?" Said against the background of the prevailing empiricism at Vienna, it seemed scarcely plausible that Wittgenstein meant by this anything other than verification by experience; and in any case, as Schlick later remarked, "no other kind of verification has been defined."[11] The claim that for a statement to be meaningful, in the cognitive sense, it must be *empirically* verifiable was made explicitly by Waismann, Schlick, Carnap, Neurath, and other logical positivists, in articles in *Erkenntnis* and elsewhere, from 1930 onwards.[12]

The plausibility of this claim may be seen in the following way. Consider as an example the statement "There is a palmetto lampshade in the next room." It certainly seems correct to say that a person understands this statement only if he knows what kind of observations would verify it. For suppose a person born blind was told that the word "palmetto" is used as a color word, and that he was told what kind of color this use of the word signifies. And suppose that he then discovered that he had the ability to use the word correctly in conversation and argument, and, strangely enough, that whenever a particular object was referred to he could always say correctly whether or not it was palmetto in color. Nevertheless, although he could use the word correctly in all other contexts, he would not, since he was born blind, know what it is like to have a visual experience of seeing palmetto or any other color. In this case, it seems certain that we would say, because of the last-mentioned fact, that he did not understand the meaning of the word "palmetto" — not in the sense of "understand" in which we understand the word. And the same seems to be true of all basic predicates, i.e., the predicates in terms of which all others are understood. Hence it seems to be at least a necessary condition for understanding a descriptive statement that one should be able to recognize the sensory experiences that would verify it.

Before we consider in detail what the logical positivists meant by "empirical verifiability," it will be convenient to consider here the logical character of their principle of meaning. Suppose that a metaphysician says "Reality enters into but transcends all change." It is not *prima facie* evident that this statement cannot have a method of verification — that there cannot be special non-sensory experiences which would, in a sense, verify it. Indeed, metaphysicians and mystics have recommended forms of intellectual or physical discipline whereby, they claimed, anyone who wished to could come to have just such experiences as are here in question. The different replies that might be made to this suggestion bring out some possible views of the logical status of the verifiability principle: (a) It might

be said that it is impossible for human beings to have experiences radically different in kind from those which they now have. But if this were more than a tautology, following from an implied definition of the term "human being," it would be an assertion of contingent psychological fact. The logical positivists did not wish to base their criterion of meaning on such an insecure foundation; they claimed that the essential difference between their empiricism and the earlier empiricism of Hume and Mill and Mach was that it was based not upon psychological assumptions but upon considerations of logic. (b) It might be allowed, as Ayer once did,[13] that it is significant to say that mystics may have non-sensuous experiences, but maintain that we have no grounds for supposing that those experiences are cognitive if we have no reason to think that the "object" of such experiences could be described in ordinary empirical terms. The statement "Mystics have experiences which we do not have, which they describe by the sentence 'Reality enters into but transcends all change'" is verifiable by ordinary empirical methods, whereas the statement "Reality enters into but transcends all change" is not verifiable in ordinary empirical terms. Consequently this metaphysical statement is one which we cannot understand, and therefore we cannot regard it as reporting a cognitive experience. But to this the mystic may answer that he can describe in empirical terms the kind of discipline he recommends, so we can understand his method, and if we are not prepared to carry out the appropriate procedure of verification then of course we shall not understand his metaphysical statements. In our reluctance to follow him there is still the implicit and dogmatic belief that no procedure would result in our having experiences radically different in kind from those which we now have. (c) Schlick,[14] Ayer at one time,[15] and some other logical positivists claimed that the verificational theory of meaning was in effect a statement of the sense of (cognitive) "meaning and understanding" that is actually accepted in everyday life. For example, Schlick says that the verificational view is "nothing but a simple statement of the way in which meaning is *actually* assigned to propositions, both in everyday life and in science. There never has been any other way, and it would be a grave error to suppose that we believe we have discovered a new conception of meaning which is contrary to common opinion and which we want to introduce into philosophy."[16] But this assertion — that the verificational criterion is the one actually employed in everyday practice — is an assertion of fact that might well be false, and one which, in any case, needs to be confirmed by sociological investigation. Again, this is not the way that the logical positivists, for the most part, wished to set up their criterion of meaning. (d) Finally, the logical positivist may regard the verifiability principle as a decision or recommendation or prescription for the use of the expressions "cognitive meaning" and "understanding." He may claim that this decision prevents radical confusion and helps to promote clarity in the discussion of many philosophical questions. As we shall see, Carnap[17] took this view of the status of the verifiability requirement, and Ayer takes the same view in his most recent remarks on the subject.[18] Whether, in fact, the verifiability principle, when regarded as a prescription, does have the advantages claimed for it, may perhaps be decided by considering first some different versions of the principle, and then by reviewing the recent history of philosophy. We shall undertake the first task, but the second must be left to the discernment of the reader.

From the various formulations of the verifiability principle given by the logical positivists, together with some of their incidental remarks, it appears that at different times they held, or considered, at least four different views concerning cognitive meaning.

1. Schlick's much quoted sentence "The meaning of a proposition is the method of its verification"[19] together with his remark that P. W. Bridgman's book *The Logic of Modern Physics* (1927) "is an admirable attempt to carry out this programme for all concepts of physics"[20] may suggest that Schlick at one time identified the meaning of a proposition with the operations involved in verifying it. In his book, Bridgman held that the meaning of a term or concept is literally the set of operations which must be performed in order to apply the term in any particular case. For example, according to this view we know what we mean by "length" when we have decided upon a standard procedure for obtaining a certain kind of quantitative result. Bridgman says, "In general, we mean by any concept nothing more than a set of operations; the concept is synonymous with the corresponding set of operations"[21] and "The proper definition of a concept is not in terms of its properties but in terms of actual operations."[22] In a later article[23] he allows that we may understand by the meaning of a concept more than a set of operations, but he insists that the specification of a method of application is a necessary condition for a concept to have any meaning at all.

Bridgman admits that the statement "meanings are operational" says nothing until restrictions are imposed upon the kind of activities that are to be regarded as operations. He begins by allowing "physical operations" (e.g., the use of instruments) and "mental operations" (e.g., counting). Later he also allows "pencil and paper operations" (e.g., the manipulation of mathematical and logical signs) and even "verbal operations" (e.g., verbal definition and substitution). But why just these activities and not others are regarded as operations is not made clear. The only ground recognized by Bridgman for defining a concept in terms of one kind of operation rather than another is the pragmatic one of producing the desired result. Consequently it seems that,

in many cases at least (e.g., where the desired result is to record the apparent color of an object), direct observation should be allowed as a legitimate operation. But in that case the present account would no longer be a distinctively operational theory of meaning; it would have become, at least in part, the same as the second view we shall consider, and open to the same objections.

In accordance with his general view, Bridgman maintains that the meaning of a concept is determined by an unambiguous set of operations and that where the operations are different the concept is different. For example, "the operations by which length is measured should be uniquely specified. If we have more than one set of operations, we have more than one concept, and strictly there should be a separate name to correspond to each different set of operations."[24] Thus length determined by the use of a measuring rod is a different concept from length determined by optical methods. And presumably there are different concepts of optical length, according to the instruments, calculations, and theory employed. This has the unfortunate effect of multiplying the number of concepts used in science. Moreover, it follows that a result obtained by one set of operations cannot be checked by carrying out a different set of operations; but in scientific work this is a common and useful practice. It is pertinent to ask how, according to Bridgman's view, "the same set of operations" is to be defined. A unique set of operations can be specified, e.g., by an actual demonstration with a particular measuring rod. But how are we to know what is to count as the same set of operations on another occasion? Are the operations the same if a different but similar measuring rod is used? And, if so, how similar must the two measuring rods be? And how similar must the movements of the two rods be, if the same operations are to be repeated? In particular cases "the same set of operations" can be defined in operational terms. For example, suppose that $O_1 O_2$ and $O_3 O_4$ are two sets of measuring operations with the same ruler. Then there is a further operation, viz: the use of a protractor at the point in each set of operations at which the ruler is moved along, in terms of which it can be decided whether $O_1 O_2$ and $O_3 O_4$ are the same set of operations. But now we want to be able to repeat the operation of using the protractor, and we need to know what is to count as using the protractor in the same way on different occasions. And if this is defined in terms of some further operation, still another definition will be required to determine when this further operation is being repeated. This shows that "the same set of operations" cannot be defined in operational terms without involving either an infinite regress or circularity.

But whatever may be the force of these objections to Bridgman's view, it seems at least certain that Schlick did not himself hold an operational theory of meaning. He stresses that by "the method of verification" he means the logical possibility of verification, not any actual procedure of verification. As he remarks on a later page, "You cannot even start verifying before you know the meaning, i.e., before you have established the possibility of verification."[25]

2. In an early article Schlick says, "In order to understand a proposition we must be able exactly to indicate those particular circumstances that would make it true and those other particular circumstances that would make it false. "Circumstances" means facts of experience; and so experience decides about the truth and falsity of propositions, experience verifies propositions. . . . "[26] According to this view, for the statement "It will rain tomorrow" to be meaningful it is not sufficient that its truth or falsity should be decidable in *some way or other*, e.g., by obtaining reports from a meteorological office. For the statement to be understood by any particular person it is necessary that he should be able, in principle, to establish its truth or falsity by having the relevant experiences. And, it seems, what the statement means to any particular person is that under certain conditions he would have experiences of a certain kind.

This immediately raises the objection that if the present view were correct, all cognitive meaning would be essentially private. The same sentence could not have, or could not be known to have, the same meaning for two different speakers, since there is no way of deciding whether different persons have qualitatively similar experiences. The present version of the verifiability principle apparently leads to a radical form of solipsism, according to which every descriptive statement — including every statement ostensibly about the external world, about the experiences of other persons, about the past and the future — refers only to the private experiences of the speakers. Schlick attempted to avoid this conclusion by distinguishing between the content and the form of human experience.[27] The content, he said, is essentially private and incommunicable — it can only be lived through. But we are able to decide whether different persons use the same descriptive words on the same occasions and in the same logical order. And so, Schlick claimed, the form or structure or order of our experiences is expressible and communicable, and that is all that is required for the purpose of scientific knowledge. Carnap, at one time, held a similar view.[28]

It seems, however, that this distinction between content and form will not save Schlick's early view from a collapse into solipsism. For if the meaning of every descriptive word or phrase is to be found, in the last analysis, in private experience, then this is so not only for qualitative words but also for the relational words by means of which we describe the form or structure of our experiences. And, apart from the solipsistic objection, it is evident that other absurdities result from identifying the meaning of a word or sentence with some sensory experience or set of experiences. For example, if the meaning of the sentence "This is red" were identified with an actual occurrence of the sensation of red, then the sentence would be meaningful only when it was true; in other words, it would not be possible to use this sentence to express a significant but false statement. There is, however, no point in pursuing these objections any further, since Schlick and other logical positivists subsequently held different and more tenable versions of the verifiability principle.

3. By the middle of the 1930's most of the logical positivists explained the notion of verifiability by saying that a statement is verifiable — that it has a method of verification — if it stands in a specified logical relation to some set of observation statements. To show that this relation holds is to show the logical possibility of verifying the original statement, and at the same time to reveal its cognitive content or meaning. It seemed that the objection of solipsism could now be avoided, since, as we shall see, it appeared that observation statements could be formulated in such a way that they were not the private property of any one observer.

In this case, the verifiability principle was effectively "neutralized." It was still held that to be significant, a statement must refer to experience; but it was supposed that it was not necessary for it to refer to the experience of the person who makes the statement on any given occasion. Observation statements express logically possible evidence and hence any statement suitably related to a set of observation statements is verifiable and significant even if no one is ever in a position to verify the observation statements in question. But in their early accounts, Schlick, Waismann, Carnap, and others held that the meaning of any statement is completely determined by the circumstances that would verify it. Thus Waismann said "Anyone uttering a sentence must know in which conditions he calls the statement true or false; if he is unable to state this then he does not know what he has said. A statement which cannot be verified conclusively is not verifiable at all; it is just devoid of any meaning."[29] The requirement of conclusive verifiability was, in effect, the requirement that the logical relation between any genuine statement and the relevant set of observation statements must be that of logical equivalence. For the original statement to be conclusively verifiable by appeal to observation statements it must entail and be entailed by those observation statements. Consequently the verifiability principle was now faced with the objection that a statement which covers an unlimited number of cases, e.g., the statement "Every gas at constant pressure expands when heated," is not logically equivalent to any finite number of observation statements and therefore is not conclusively verifiable, even in principle. The present version of the principle would exclude as meaningless all universal statements, including all statements expressing scientific laws. It would also have the paradoxical consequence that while an existential statement, e.g., "Humans exist" may be significant, its denial could not be significant. For to deny that humans exist is to assert "For all x, it is not the case that x is human," and this is a universal statement. Some of the logical positivists attempted to meet this difficulty by regarding a universal statement as the logical product of (that is, a conjunction of) some finite number of singular statements.[30] And Schlick adopted the view[31] that scientific laws are not statements, but rules for scientific procedure and prediction; e.g., according to this view, the previously mentioned law about gases is really a rule of the form "If anything is a gas at constant pressure and heated (expect, infer that) it expands." But there are serious objections to these alternatives. In the first place, it is not plausible to suggest that the meaning of "all" or "every" can be expressed by some finite conjunction of singular statements unless it is added "and these are all the instances there are," i.e., roughly, "Every other event is not an instance of the kind of question." But this is another universal statement, and although the same kind of analysis may be given again, an unanalyzed universal statement will always remain. Secondly, if scientific laws are regarded as rules, they are neither true nor false, and cannot be confirmed or disconfirmed by empirical evidence. On this view, scientific knowledge must be radically reconstrued, so that it is no longer thought of as being, for the most part, a corpus of true or highly confirmed universal statements.

Carnap[32] and others also objected that a singular statement about a material object, like a statement of scientific law, is not conclusively verifiable; e.g., the statement "This is a sheet of paper" is not conclusively verifiable, since the number of predictions that can be based upon this statement is not finite. And if statements of scientific law and statements about material objects are not conclusively verifiable, it seems that most statements about past and future events and about other people are also not conclusively verifiable. Finally, even if these objections were met, it cannot be held that statements of these various kinds are conclusively verifiable, unless it is also held that observation statements are conclusively verifiable. And, as we shall see, many logical positivists argued that observation statements are not conclusively verifiable.

Popper[33] had proposed falsifiability rather than verifiability as the criterion of a *scientific* statement, and it was sometimes suggested by the logical positivists that this might be adopted as a criterion of *significance* for all genuine statements. But again there are difficulties. For example, according to the present criterion, a universal statement, of the form $(x)fx$, is significant because it is falsifiable, and to falsify it we must be able to assert an existential statement of the form $(\exists x)\sim fx$. But, according to the criterion, this existential statement is significant (and, *a fortiori*, can be asserted) only if it is falsifiable, and to falsify it we must be able to assert significantly the original universal statement. To break out of this circle, it is necessary to have an independent criterion of significance for either universal or existential statements.

4. To meet the preceding objections, the later formulations of the verifiability principle require that any genuine statement should be related to some set of observation statements in such a way that the observation statements provide not conclusive verifiability but confirmability for the original statement. In other words, the original statement should entail certain observation statements, so that the truth of the latter is a necessary condition for the truth of the former, but it is not required that there should be a finite set of observation statements that entails the original statement.

At the beginning of two important articles entitled "Testability and Meaning" (1936–1937), Carnap says,

> If by verification is meant a definitive and final establishment of truth, then no (synthetic) sentence is ever verifiable. . . . We can only confirm a sentence more and more. Therefore we shall speak of the problem of *confirmation* rather than of the problem of verification. We distinguish the *testing* of a sentence from its confirmation, thereby understanding a procedure — e.g., the carrying out of certain experiments — which leads to a confirmation in some degree either of the sentence itself or of its negation. We shall call a sentence *testable* if we know such a method of testing for it; and we shall call it *confirmable* if we know under what conditions the sentence would be confirmed. As we shall see, a sentence may be confirmable without being testable; e.g., if we know that our observation of such and such a course of events would confirm the sentence, and such and such a different course would confirm its negation without knowing how to set up either this or that observation.

According to Carnap, the adoption of a criterion of significance is a matter of choice and convenience in the construction of a language suitable for philosophical purposes. He considers four different criteria — complete testability, complete confirmability (degree of) testability, and (degree of) confirmability. All of these, according to Carnap, exclude metaphysical sentences. The last-mentioned criterion, degree of confirmability, is the most liberal, and allows as significant empirical statements of the various kinds that were excluded by the requirement of conclusive verifiability. Each of Carnap's criteria determines a more or less restrictive form of empiricist language; and this, according to his view, is the same thing as a more or less radical form of empiricism.

Carnap is largely concerned in these articles, as in many of his later writings, to give a technical analysis of the formal features of such languages. He considers, among other things, formal methods of defining or otherwise "introducing" descriptive predicates. In particular, he shows[34] that *dispositional* predicates — e.g., "soluble," "fragile," "visible" — cannot be explicitly defined in terms of non-dispositional predicates. To overcome this difficulty he devises what he calls "reduction sentences." One kind of reduction sentence says that if an object is placed in certain experimental conditions, then it has a certain dispositional property if and only if it reacts in a certain way. For example, if we write "Wx" for "x is placed in water," "Sx" for "x is soluble," and "Dx" for "x dissolves," then the form of one kind of reduction sentence is:

$$Wx \supset (Sx \equiv Dx)$$

(that is: If x is placed in water, then x is soluble if and only if x dissolves.)

Although, according to Carnap, a dispositional statement is not logically equivalent to any set of non-dispositional statements, we can by means of a reduction sentence provide a rule for testing whether any object has the dispositional property in question. Although the dispositional predicate cannot be explicitly defined in terms of non-dispositional predicates, the reduction sentence provides a rule for introducing it into the language.

Ayer, in the first edition of *Language, Truth and Logic*, adopted what he called the "weak" sense of verifiability. He says that a statement is verifiable in this sense "if it is possible for experience to render it probable," if some observations would be "relevant to the determination of its truth or falsehood."[35] This amounts to saying that a statement is verifiable and meaningful if some observation statement(s) can be deduced from it, perhaps in conjunction with certain additional premises, without being deducible from these additional premises alone. But this formulation, as Ayer recognizes in the second edition of his book,[36] permits any meaningless and any metaphysical statement to be verifiable. For suppose that N is any nonsensical statement, and O some observation statement: from N and the additional premise *if N then O* the observation statement O can be deduced, although O cannot be deduced from the additional premise alone. To meet objections of this kind Ayer introduces a number of conditions; he says (1) "a statement is directly verifiable if it is either itself an observation statement, or is such that in conjunction with one or more observation statements it entails at least one observation statement which is not deducible from these other premises alone," and (2) "a statement is indirectly verifiable if it satisfies the following conditions: first, that in conjunction with certain other premises it entails one or more directly verifiable statements which are not deducible from these other premises alone; and secondly, that these other premises do not include any statement that is not either analytic, or directly verifiable, or capable of being independently

established as indirectly verifiable."[37] These conditions are designed to prevent obviously meaningless statements from being verifiable, and at the same time to allow the verifiability of theoretical statements in science. It has been shown[38] that Ayer's conditions are not entirely successful in these respects, and even more elaborate qualifications have been proposed;[39] but it is not clear whether even the most complex formulations of the confirmability criterion of significance are free from objections of the same kind.

Observation Statements

THE formulations of the verifiability principle considered in the last two sections essentially involve the notion of a basic observation statement. This was a topic about which the members of the Vienna Circle, as well as other logical positivists, held widely differing views. We shall consider briefly the questions that were asked about observation statements, and the principal answers that were given.

It seems obvious that if there are to be any empirical statements at all, there must be some which are direct descriptions of experience. Thus, while a statement about the British Constitution refers to experience only indirectly, a statement about an individual citizen, or perhaps about the appearances of an individual, refers to experience directly. Some writers[40] have argued that it does not make sense to speak of a person "verifying" a statement which describes his present experience. But if any statement is to be indirectly verifiable, there must be *a* sense in which some statements are directly verifiable. The main questions that were asked about observation statements were: (1) Do they refer to private sensory experience or to material objects? (2) Can the speaker be mistaken about their truth or falsity, i.e., are they corrigible or incorrigible? (3) Are they, in fact, true or false statements about experience, or are the sentences which seem to express them simply verbal responses to acts of observation? It will be seen that these are not independent questions, and that a particular answer to one of them may determine the answer given to another.

The early view, held by Schlick[41] and others, and based upon Wittgenstein's account of "elementary sentences," was that observation sentences are those which can be compared directly with the private sensory experience or sense-data of the speaker. But this view, taken in conjunction with any of the versions of the verifiability principle we have considered, seemed to lead directly to solipsism. At one time Carnap[42] supposed that it was a factual question whether observation sentences — or "protocol sentences," as they were often called by members of the Vienna Circle — refer to the simplest sensations and feelings, or to gestalts of single sensory fields, or to material objects. Later,[43] however, he came to hold the view that this is not a factual, but a linguistic question, the answer to which depends entirely upon our choice of a form of language for reporting our observations. This change in Carnap's view was due mainly to criticisms advanced by Neurath.[44]

Neurath was the first of the Vienna Circle to reject the correspondence theory of meaning and truth that is presented in the *Tractatus*. Wittgenstein has said "Reality is compared with the proposition"[45]; "To the configuration of the simple signs in the propositional sign corresponds the configuration of the objects in the state-of-affairs."[46] According to Neurath a fact is not something independent of language; to say that something is a fact is simply to assert an indicative sentence. Criticizing the theory of the *Tractatus*, and the early logical positivist view of observation sentences that was based upon it, Neurath says "Sentences are to be compared with sentences, not with 'experience', nor with a 'world', nor with anything else. All these senseless duplications belong to a more or less refined metaphysics and are therefore to be rejected."[47] At this time Hempel[48] held the same view. Sentences are not to be thought of as *describing* experience, either directly or indirectly. Nevertheless some sentences are reports of acts of observation, in the behavioristic sense of being verbal responses to those acts. Such protocol sentences, according to Neurath, may have whatever form we find most convenient for the purpose of science. He suggests that a protocol sentence should contain a name or description of an observer and some words recording an act of observation; he gives as an example "Otto's protocol at 3.17 {Otto's word thought at 3.16: (In the room at 3.15 was a table perceived by Otto)}."[49] In this example, it is supposed that the entire quoted sentence is written down by Otto at 3.17, simply as an overt verbal response; it is supposed that the sentence in the outer brackets was Otto's private verbal response ("word thought") at 3.16, and that the sentence in the inner brackets records Otto's perception of a table in the room at 3.15. In the example, the word "Otto" is repeated, instead of using "my" and "me," in order that the components of the protocol may be independently tested, e.g. by being found in the protocols of other observers. The protocols of different observers may conflict, and when this happens at least one of them is to be rejected. According to Neurath, it is a matter of convenience and decision which of the conflicting protocols should be rejected, and therefore no protocol is incorrigible. The aim of science is to build up a coherent system of sentences, including the protocol sentences we find it most advantageous to accept, but in this process no sentence at any level is sacrosanct. Every sentence in science is in the end accepted or rejected by a decision made in the interests of coherence and utility. This so called "conventional" view of science, and the coherence theory of truth and meaning which it implied,[50] was strenuously opposed by other logical positivists[51] on the ground that it was a complete abandonment of empiricism.

Neurath and Carnap held that if protocol sentences were regarded as describing a content of experience, they could be understood only solipsistically. But every protocol sentence, they contended, is equivalent to certain sentences of physics, including sentences reporting the physical states of the observer. This intertranslatability of the protocol language of every observer with the language of physics permits protocol sentences to be understood inter-subjectively; and it is only when protocol sentences are understood in this way that they are of epistemological interest. This was part of a more general thesis, namely that every significant sentence in any language or science can be translated into sentences of the physical language, i.e., the physical language is a universal language. Neurath and Carnap called this "the thesis of Physicalism"[52] and it was on this basis that they hoped for the unification of science.

Ayer, in the first edition of *Language, Truth and Logic*, held that observation sentences express statements about "sense contents" or sense-data. But he also held that no empirical statement could be incorrigible. An observation statement would be immune from the possibility of error only if the sentence that expresses it did no more than point to or indicate an experience; but, Ayer argued,[53] a purely ostensive sentence has no informative content and does not express a statement. In the second edition of *Language, Truth and Logic*, and elsewhere,[54] he advanced the view that a sentence which is a direct description of experience may be verbally incorrect, but it cannot express a statement about which the speaker may be factually mistaken. In his article entitled "Basic Propositions" he attempts to explain this view in the following way. Many descriptive sentences, e.g., "This is a table," may be used correctly, i.e., in accordance with the rules of the language and on the occasion that would be generally recognized as appropriate for their use, and yet the statements they express may turn out to be false. But in the case of a sentence which directly describes a present experience, e.g., "This is an oblong patch of brown," if the sentence is used correctly the statement it expresses cannot turn out to be false. Thus, a basic observation statement is one whose truth is guaranteed simply by adherence to the meaning rules of the language. In this sense, observation statements are incorrigible. Nevertheless, the fact remains that one may always be mistaken in believing that one has adhered to the meaning rules of the language. And in his most recent remarks on this subject[55] where he appears to be more inclined to regard material object statements as observation statements, Ayer seems to revert to the view that even if one uses an observation sentence correctly one may always be factually mistaken.

Logic and Mathematics

THE nature of the propositions of logic and mathematics, and the method of their validation, might
seem to provide the most serious difficulty for the
thoroughgoing empiricist and anti-metaphysical
philosophy of the logical positivists. The proposition
that no physical object can have two different
volumes at the same time, and the proposition that
the circumference of any circle is $2\pi r$, are plainly significant propositions — although, since their truth may
be demonstrated without appeal to experience, their
significance does not depend upon their being
empirically confirmable. Moreover, it seems that
such propositions are known to be *necessarily* true,
although their necessity could not be established
by any empirical method. Thus, the propositions of
logic and mathematics seem to provide us with
knowledge of necessary features of the world, and
yet they are validated not by appeal to experience but
by *a priori* reasoning. A logical or mathematical
proposition is validated by starting with some set of
initial propositions, the necessary truth of which is
transparent (obvious, self-evident, or set up by
convention), and then deducing from these initial
propositions other propositions, step by step, until
the required proposition is reached. An important
feature of the relation of deducibility is that it is
truth-transferring, i.e., if an initial proposition
is true then any proposition that is deducible from
it must also be true. Consequently, although the
truth of a highly complex proposition of logic or
mathematics may not be at all transparent, when the
proposition is considered by itself, the method by
which it is validated guarantees that it is necessarily
true.

In the nineteenth century, J. S. Mill had taken the
heroic course of saying that the peculiar necessity
attributed to the propositions of logic and mathematics is an illusion. According to Mill,[56] they
would have this kind of necessity only if they expressed the properties of such objects as are represented, for example, in the definitions of arithmetic
and geometry; but, Mill says, such objects exist
neither in the physical world nor in our minds.
Mill concludes that these propositions are in fact
very general empirical propositions. They, or at least
those that serve as the initial propositions in any
deductive proof in logic or mathematics, are established by simple enumeration and have been
supported by all human experience so far. This
unfailing empirical confirmation has misled us into
thinking that the propositions of logic and mathematics are necessarily true. The fact is, according to
Mill, that, like all empirical propositions, these
propositions are only contingently true, and their
truth cannot be known with a special kind of
certainty.

The logical positivists found this view unsatisfactory for the following reasons: In the first place,

no logician or mathematician supposes that in
order to be completely scrupulous he should attempt
to validate the initial propositions of his subject by
inquiring whether they have been confirmed by all
human experience. And no one supposes that the
axioms of logic and mathematics are propositions
of the kind that could be *more* highly confirmed,
although this would be an appropriate requirement
if Mill's view were correct. Moreover, the difference
between a proposition of mathematics or logic and
an empirical proposition is not essentially one of
generality, nor is it a difference of confirmability.
For example, "Every pair of straight lines that have
once met do not meet again, but continue to diverge" and "Every pair of straight lines is such that
each has breadth" are equally general; and if the
first were the kind of proposition that could be
empirically confirmed, it would have to be allowed
that these two propositions have been equally confirmed by all the evidence so far. Finally, the negation of an empirical proposition is itself an empirical
proposition, whereas the negation of a proposition
of logic or mathematics is a contradiction. The
meanings of the terms that occur in the latter type
of proposition are sufficient to preclude the possibility of finding a counter-instance and to guarantee
that the proposition is true. The logical positivists
claimed that this was the essential feature of propositions that can be validated *a priori*, and the correct
explanation of logical and mathematical necessity.

They gained powerful support for this view from
the extensional logic of Russell and Whitehead[57] and
Wittgenstein.[58] A theory of logic is said to be
"extensional," as opposed to being "intensional,"
when it consistently avoids any metaphysical or psychological interpretation of meanings, propositions,
properties, and relations of necessitation and contradiction between properties or propositions. For
example, in the logic of Russell and Whitehead
implication between one proposition and another is
understood not as a relation of necessitation but
simply as the negation of a certain conjunctive statement of fact (or as a disjunctive statement of fact).
Thus, the statement "This wire is copper" implies
"This wire conducts electricity" is understood to
mean simply "It is not in fact the case that both this
wire is copper and this wire does not conduct
electricity" (or "It is in fact the case that either this
wire is not copper or this wire conducts electricity").
This extensional interpretation of implication is called
"material implication"; in the symbolism used by
Russell and Whitehead the form of a statement of
material implication is expressed by the formula
$p \supset q$ and this is defined to mean simply $\sim(p.\sim q)$ or
$\sim p \vee q$. Wittgenstein (and, independently, Post)[59]
had realized that the extensional definitions of
implications, negation, conjunction, and other logical
relations may be represented by means of "truth
tables." Thus, in columns 1 and 2 below are listed
all the possible combinations of truth and falsehood

of any propositions that might be put in the place of p and q. The truth possibilities, or "truth-values," for q in column 2 determine the corresponding values for $\sim q$ in column 3. The truth-values listed for p in column 1, together with those listed for $\sim q$ in column 3, determine the corresponding values for $p.\sim q$ in column 4. The truth-values for $p.\sim q$ determine the corresponding values for $\sim(p.\sim q)$ in column 5. And since $\sim(p.\sim q)$ is the extensional definition of $p \supset q$, the truth-values in column 5 are repeated in column 6. Columns 1, 2, and 6 by themselves represent the extensional definition of implication:

1	2	3	4	5	6
p	q	$\sim q$	$p.\sim q$	$\sim(p.\sim q)$	$p \supset q$
T	T	F	F	T	T
T	F	T	T	F	F
F	T	F	F	T	T
F	F	T	F	T	T

Wittgenstein also used truth-tables as a means of exhibiting the logical characteristics of molecular propositions, and of showing that these characteristics were a consequence of the extensional definitions of the logical connectives that occur in the propositions. Thus, the truth-table below shows that $p \supset q$ is true for some combinations of the truth-values for p and q, but false for one combination. The table also shows that $p.(p \supset q) \supset q$ is true for every combination of truth-values for p and q, and that $q.\sim q$ is false for every combination of truth-values for q and $\sim q$:

1	2	3	6	7	8	9
p	q	$\sim q$	$p \supset q$	$p.(p \supset q)$	$p.(p \supset q) \supset q$	$q.\sim q$
T	T	F	T	T	T	F
T	F	T	F	F	T	F
F	T	F	T	F	T	F
F	F	T	T	F	T	F

A molecular proposition, such as $p \supset q$, which is true for some combinations of truth-values of its components but false for others, i.e., which is true in some circumstances but false in others, Wittgenstein called a "significant" (*sinnvoll*) proposition. A molecular proposition, such as $q.\sim q$, which is false for every combination of truth-values for its components, Wittgenstein called a "contradiction." A contradiction is false in every possible circumstance, and is therefore necessarily false. A molecular proposition, such as $p.(p \supset q) \supset q$, which is true for every combination of truth-values for its components, Wittgenstein called a "tautology." A tautology is true in every possible circumstance, and is therefore necessarily true. The truth-table method can be used to exhibit the tautological character of any proposition of the most fundamental part of formal logic. A truth-table shows, as in the above example, that the tautological character and necessary truth of such

a proposition is a consequence of the extensional definitions of the logical connectives, together with the order in which the component propositions occur in the molecular proposition. Wittgenstein also drew attention to the fact that since to assert a tautology is to assert something that would be true whatever the circumstances, and to assert a contradiction is to assert something that would be false whatever the circumstances, tautologies and contradictions cannot be used to make one factual assertion as opposed to another. They are, in this sense, uninformative.

Many of the logical positivists supposed that every proposition of logic is a "tautology" in Wittgenstein's sense,[60] although this was a program for research rather than an established thesis. But they were prepared to hold their view of the analytic nature of logical propositions independently of this particular thesis.[61] If there are some logical propositions (e.g., "Everything that is red is colored," "If A is larger than B, and B is larger than C, then A is larger than C") that are not analyzable as truth-functional tautologies, then these propositions are necessarily true not in virtue of the extensional meanings given to the logical connectives but in virtue of the meanings given to the descriptive predicates (such as "red," "colored," "larger than") that occur in them. The logical positivists adopted a similar position with regard to the propositions of mathematics.[62] Most of them held the Frege-Russell thesis that pure mathematics is reducible to logic, i.e., that all the concepts of mathematics can be defined in terms of the concepts of logic, and that all the theorems of mathematics can be deduced from these definitions by means of the principles of logic. But they also held that if this program could not be carried out, the propositions of mathematics could still be shown to be analytic. As Ayer remarks, if the Frege-Russell thesis is untenable, then the propositions of pure mathematics will "form a special class of analytic propositions, containing special terms, but they will be none the less analytic for that. For the criterion of an analytic proposition is that its validity should follow simply from the definition of the terms contained in it, and this condition is fulfilled by the propositions of pure mathematics."[63] The logical positivists claimed that the analytic nature of the propositions of logic and mathematics explained the fact that these propositions are not validated by appeal to experience. They are validated *a priori* by logical analysis of their meaning. Their truth is logically independent of any empirical evidence. But for the same reason, it was stressed, these propositions have no empirical content. They cannot be used to make any factual assertion.

If this view is correct, it has to be explained how logic and mathematics can be useful and give surprising results, and how it is that the propositions of applied mathomatics can apparently express knowledge of the world. These formal disciplines are useful, the logical positivists said, because they provide indispensable rules and techniques for deduction in empirical science and every-day life. As Wittgenstein had remarked in the *Tractatus*, "In life it is never a mathematical proposition which we need, but we use mathematical propositions *only* in order to infer from propositions which do not belong to mathematics to others which equally do not belong to mathematics."[64] These formal disciplines can give surprising results, it was argued, because without the techniques of deduction which they provide we do not have the intellectual capacity to discern all the implications of our definitions or initial propositions. Hahn said, "An omniscient being has no need for logic and mathematics. We ourselves, however, first have to make . . . successive tautological transformations, and hence it may prove quite surprising to us that in asserting a few propositions we have implicitly also asserted a proposition which seemingly is entirely different from them."[65] Finally, the logical positivists allowed that the propositions of applied mathematics may express knowledge of the world. But, they said, these propositions result from giving a physical interpretation to the formulas of a purely formal system.[66] When such an interpretation has been given, the resulting propositions are in effect empirical statements or hypotheses, and for this reason they do not have that immunity from empirical disconfirmation that is characteristic of the propositions of logic and pure mathematics. The logical positivists emphasized that the invention in the nineteenth century, by Lobachevsky, Bolyai, and Riemann, of systems of "hyperbolic" and "elliptical" geometry as alternatives to Euclidean geometry, had shown very clearly that it is an empirical question which of these systems of geometry is true of the physical world. Thus they endorsed Einstein's remark "As far as the laws of mathematics refer to reality, they are not certain; and as far as they are certain, they do not refer to reality."[67]

A closer examination of what the logical positivists said about the propositions of logic and mathematics shows that at least three different views were held at different times:

1. There is, first, the view that a necessary proposition (or, perhaps, the modal proposition which says that this proposition is necessary) is in fact an informative proposition about our usage of words or symbols. Ayer, in the first edition of *Language, Truth and Logic*, sometimes[68] seems to imply a view of this kind. Carnap, in his book *The Logical Syntax of Language*, contends to say that something *A* (a proposition, circumstance, fact, process, condition) is logically necessary or impossible or possible, is a misleading way of saying that the sentence "*A*" (in a specified language) is analytic or contradictory or not contradictory.[69] But this view is open to the objection that a necessary proposition of logic or mathematics is not about, i.e., does not

mention, the words or symbols by which it is expressed. The proposition "Everything that is red is colored" is not a proposition about the English words "red" and "colored." Moreover, if a "necessary proposition" were in fact informative about the usage of words it would be a contingent empirical proposition, i.e., the present view has the paradoxical consequence that there are no necessary propositions. We need not criticize this view in more detail, since it was soon rejected by the logical positivists.

2. A second view is that the sentences that apparently express necessary propositions really express rules of inference,[70] or prescribe how words or symbols are to be used.[71] Wittgenstein had suggested this view in the *Tractatus*, and at a later time he said that the sentence "The colours green and blue cannot be in the same place simultaneously" expresses a rule of (logical) grammar.[72] Hahn said that the sentences of logic (and mathematics) "say nothing at all about objects of any kind . . . they prescribe a method of speaking about things."[73] Ayer held the same view in an article entitled "Truth by Convention." The plausibility of this view can be seen from the following consideration. We can certainly argue:

> Everything red is colored
> This liquid is red
> Therefore this liquid is colored

Here the sentence "Everything red is colored" apparently expresses a major premise, and the argument makes use of a certain rule of inference. But we may argue more directly:

> This liquid is red
> Therefore this liquid is colored

And here the suppressed sentence "Everything red is colored" expresses not a suppressed major premise, but the rule of inference that is employed in the argument. Nothing more is involved, it is said, in accepting the sentence than a readiness to make the inferences that it prescribes. The principal objection to this view is that if it is correct the sentences and formulas of logic and mathematics do not express, and cannot be so interpreted that they express, *true propositions*. It is usually supposed that while in some contexts the formulas of logic and mathematics may be used as rules of inference, in other contexts they express necessarily true propositions. Moreover, some justification has to be given for the adoption of some rules of inference rather than others. And it is generally held that it is only because the formulas of logic and mathematics in some contexts express necessary propositions that their use on other occasions as rules of inference is justified.

3. The logical positivists often said that the propositions of logic and mathematics are derived from, or are consequences of, the definitions or other statements of the meaning of the terms that occur

in these propositions. This view was expressed by Hahn,[74] Hempel,[75] and Ayer, among others. Ayer, for example, in the Introduction to the second edition of *Language, Truth and Logic* insists that there are *a priori* propositions, and that it is a mistake to suppose that the sentences that seem to express them really express contingent propositions about linguistic usage or rules of usage. An important function of these sentences, Ayer says, is to illustrate or elucidate the usage of words. Nevertheless, the necessity of an *a priori* proposition depends upon the facts of linguistic usage, or presupposes the rules of usage. A similar view has been expressed by philosophers who were not at any time logical positivists. Strawson, for example, says that linguistic statements lie behind logical statements.[76] The principal obscurity of this view lies in the vagueness of such expressions as "depends upon," "presupposes," "lies behind." These words do not make clear exactly what relation is supposed to hold between contingent empirical propositions about usage, or rules of usage, and the necessary propositions of logic and mathematics. The relation cannot be that of entailment. Neither a contingent proposition about usage nor a rule of usage can entail a necessary proposition. If a contingent proposition C could entail a necessary proposition N, then, since entailment admits of transposition, $\sim N$ would entail $\sim C$; but in this case the contingent empirical proposition $\sim C$ is deducible from the contradiction $\sim N$, and this is absurd. Nor can it be supposed that a rule can entail a necessary proposition; it may be allowed that one rule may be deduced from another rule, but it cannot be the case that a necessary proposition is deducible from a rule, i.e., from something that is not a proposition. A satisfactory account of the relation in question has not yet been given.

Ethics

THE logical positivists were not very much concerned with the questions of moral philosophy. The various views relating to these questions that were held by them have also been held by philosophers who were not logical positivists (for example, by Russell). These views are therefore not especially characteristic of the philosophy of logical positivism.

In 1930 Schlick published a book (translated into English under the title *Problems of Ethics*) in which he contends that ethics is primarily a factual, not a normative, study. It is primarily concerned with the psychology of moral behavior. Schlick gives a new formulation of psychological hedonism, according to which it is not the thought of a future pleasure, but the present pleasure of an end-in-view, that determines our action. He says, "of the ideas which function as motives, that one gains the upper hand which finally possesses the highest degree of pleasant emotional tone, or the least unpleasant tone, and thus the act in question is unambiguously determined."[77] A moral evaluation of an action, Schlick says, is nothing but an emotional reaction to the expected consequences of the action.[78] His main conclusion is that "in human society that is *called* good which is *believed* to bring the greatest happiness."[79] It is a matter of fact, according to Schlick, that for the most part the greatest happiness of the individual coincides with the greatest happiness of society. Consequently the principal moral maxim for the individual is to seek happiness, or, as Schlick prefers to express it: "At all times be fit for happiness."[80] Thus in all important respects Schlick's view is very similar to classical utilitarianism.

Carnap, following Wittgenstein, rejected all the traditional theories of ethics. In the *Tractatus* Wittgenstein had said, "The sense of the world must lie outside the world. In the world everything is as it is and happens as it does happen. *In* it there is no value — and if there were, it would be of no value. . . . Hence also there can be no ethical propositions."[81] Carnap developed these remarks in his own way. Traditional moral philosophy, he said, "is not an investigation of facts, but a pretended investigation of what is good and what is evil, what it is right to do and what it is wrong to do."[82] Carnap argues that if moral sentences are regarded as expressing propositions, they do not express anything that is empirically verifiable; consequently if moral sentences are regarded in this way, they are metaphysical and meaningless. An intelligible interpretation of these sentences is that they express wishes or commands. Thus, Carnap says,

> The rule, "Do not kill," has grammatically the imperative form and will therefore not be regarded as an assertion. But the value statement, "Killing is evil," although, like the rule, it is merely an expression of a certain wish, has grammatically the form of an assertive proposition. Most philosophers have been deceived by this form into thinking that a value statement is really an assertive proposition, and must be either true or false. Therefore they give reasons for their own value statements and try to disprove those of their opponents. But actually a value statement is nothing else than a command in a misleading grammatical form. It may have effects upon the actions of men, and these effects may either be in accordance with our wishes or not; but it is neither true nor false. It does not assert anything and can be neither proved nor disproved.[83]

Ayer, in *Language, Truth and Logic* and elsewhere,[84] held a similar view, and one which is often thought to be most characteristic of logical positivism. Ayer rejects the subjectivist account that "morally right" means the same as "is generally approved" or "is approved by the speaker," on the ground that it is not *self-contradictory* to say that a particular action is generally approved or approved by the speaker and yet morally wrong. For the same reason, he rejects any other account (e.g., utilitarianism) that interprets moral words as representing empirical properties. Nor can these words represent non-empirical properties, for then moral sentences would be supposed to express nonverifiable propositions, and hence they would be meaningless. Ayer concluded that the function of moral words is simply to express the emotions of the speaker and to evoke similar emotions in others. He says, "if I say to someone, 'You acted wrongly in stealing that money,' I am not stating anything more than if I had simply said, 'You stole that money.' In adding that this action is wrong I am not making any further statement about it. I am simply evincing my moral disapproval of it. It is as if I had said 'You stole that money,' in a peculiar tone of horror, or written it with the addition of some special exclamation marks."[85]

A consequence of Ayer's "emotive" theory, as of Carnap's "imperative" account, is that when we make opposed moral pronouncements we do not formally contradict each other. If we are not expressing propositions at all, then we are not expressing propositions that contradict each other. In this sense, Ayer says, we never dispute about questions of value. Much of what passes for dispute about questions of value is really dispute about matters of fact, e.g., about the actual nature of an action and its circumstances and consequences. But although opposed moral pronouncements do not express a formal contradiction, they may nevertheless register a genuine and important difference of moral standpoint. It is also a consequence of these views that there can be no such thing as moral knowledge, in the sense in which knowledge is the justified acceptance of a true proposition. But it is a misunderstanding of the function of philosophical analysis to suppose that this consequence implies that nothing is good or evil, right or wrong, or that moral pronouncements are arbitrary or unimportant.[86]

The emotive or persuasive theory of ethics was developed by C. L. Stevenson in a number of articles[87] and in his book *Ethics and Language*. The imperative or prescriptive theory has been worked out in some detail by R. M. Hare in *The Language of Morals* and elsewhere.[88] But neither of these philosophers are committed to the more distinctive doctrines of logical positivism, and for this reason their views will not be considered here.

The Nature of Philosophy

AS we remarked at the beginning of this chapter, Schlick regarded Wittgenstein's view that "the object of philosophy is the logical clarification of thoughts" as marking a turning point in the history

of the subject.[89] Schlick's own view was that all knowledge is only of form, that it is through its form alone that knowledge represents the fact known.[90] Consequently, according to Schlick, the traditional problems of epistemology, so far as these are not reduced to problems of psychology, are to be replaced by questions concerning "the nature of expression, of representation, i.e., concerning every possible 'language' in the most general sense of the term."[91] In principle, all knowledge can be expressed in the statements of science. There is not, in addition, a special kind of knowledge to be expressed in distinctively "philosophical" statements. Schlick says, "The great contemporary turning point is characterised by the fact that we see in philosophy not a system of cognitions, but a system of *acts*; philosophy is that activity through which the meaning of statements is revealed or determined. By means of philosophy statements are explained, by means of science they are verified. The latter is concerned with the truth of statements, the former with what they actually mean."[92] Schlick argued that this function of philosophy could not be performed simply by asserting further statements; for the meaning of these additional statements would also have to be revealed or determined. Hence he held that philosophical analysis must terminate "in actual pointings, in exhibiting what is meant, thus in real acts; only these acts are no longer capable of, or in need of, further explanation."[93]

Carnap's and Neurath's view of the nature of philosophy departed from Wittgenstein's early doctrines in two important respects. In the *Tractatus* Wittgenstein had said, "Propositions can represent the whole reality, but they cannot represent what they must have in common with reality in order to be able to represent it — the logical form."[94] As we have seen, Carnap and Neurath rejected Wittgenstein's correspondence theory of meaning, and as a consequence of this they rejected his view that it is not possible to express propositions about the logical structure of language. Carnap had apparently done this in his early book *Der logische Aufbau der Welt*. And in his *Logical Syntax of Language* Carnap constructed two language systems; he formulated in detail the syntax of these systems, and showed that the syntax of the first could be formulated in that system itself. He claims, "our construction of syntax has shown that it can be correctly formulated and that syntactical sentences do exist."[95] Wittgenstein had also held that underlying the differences of the natural languages there is a common logical form, and that all the languages in which propositions about the world can be expressed must have the same logical structure.[96] Since Carnap and Neurath rejected Wittgenstein's theory of meaning, they also rejected this doctrine of the one language structure. They claimed that the form of protocol sentences is to be decided by us, with regard only to what is most convenient for the purpose of science. And in *Logical Syntax of Language* Carnap enunciated a "Principle of Tolerance" (with regard to the structure of language), according to which "it is not our business to set up prohibitions, but to arrive at conventions."[97] He said, "Everyone is at liberty to build up his own logic, i.e., his own form of language, as he wishes."[98] And he claimed that the principle of tolerance is of special importance in avoiding pseudo-problems in philosophy.[99] Moreover, since Carnap and Neurath also rejected Schlick's view that protocol sentences are to be compared directly with experience, they rejected his view that the clarification of meanings must terminate in "actual pointings" to experience. Consequently, according to them, philosophical clarification is nothing but the formulation of logical syntax. Carnap said at this time, "Philosophy is to be replaced by the logic of science — that is to say, by the logical analysis of the concepts and sentences of the sciences, for the logic of science is nothing other than the logical syntax of the language of science."[100]

In *The Logical Syntax of Language* Carnap made an important distinction between "object sentences" (e.g., "5 is a prime number," "Babylon was a big town"), "pseudo-object sentences" (e.g., "Five is not a thing, but a number," "Babylon was treated of in yesterday's lecture"), and "syntactical sentences" (e.g., " 'Five' is not a thing-word, but a number-word," "The word 'Babylon' occurred in yesterday's lecture").[101] The class of object sentences includes* the empirical sentences of everyday life and science, which we use to make assertions about the world. Pseudo-object sentences are formulated as though they refer to objects of some kind, but are logically equivalent to corresponding syntactical sentences. In other words, these sentences are disguised as object sentences, but are, in respect of their content, syntactical sentences. Syntactical sentences are explicitly about the form or order of words in a language. The manner of speaking in which we use pseudo-object sentences, Carnap called the "material mode of speech," and the manner of speaking in which we use syntactical sentences he called "the formal mode of speech." The material mode, he said, is not erroneous in itself and it often serves as a convenient abbreviation. But its use in philosophy is especially misleading, for three main reasons: (1) it suggests that something is being said about an object of some kind, when something different is being said about certain words or sentences, (2) it obscures the fact that philosophical

sentences are about, or are relative to, a particular language system or a number of language systems, (3) it misleads us into thinking that a factual assertion is being made, when very often a linguistic proposal or convention is being suggested. In the case of every philosophical sentence, Carnap said, translation from the material mode to the formal mode of speech safeguards against such confusions and reveals the syntactical content of what is being asserted. Some of Carnap's examples are: "The world is the totality of facts not of things"[102] is translatable into "Science is a system of sentences, not of names"; "A property is not a thing" is translatable into "An adjective (property-word) is not a thing-word"; "Identity is not a relation between objects"[103] becomes "The symbol of identity is not a descriptive symbol"; "Time is one-dimensional, space is three-dimensional" becomes "A time-designation consists of one co-ordinate, a space designation consists of three co-ordinates"; "The word 'day-star' designates the sun" becomes "The word 'day-star' is synonymous with the word 'sun' "; "The sentence '*S*' means that the moon is spherical" becomes "The sentence '*S*' is logically equivalent to, i.e., means the same as, the sentence 'the moon is spherical.' " Since Carnap at this time held that all sentences about designation and meaning are pseudo-object sentences and are translatable into purely syntactical sentences, he could hold consistently in terms of his own theory that all clarification of meanings is the formulation of logical syntax.

This purely syntactical theory of designation and meaning is untenable, and this can be seen in three different ways. In the first place, to say that the word "day-star" (or the expression "*die Sonne*") designates the sun, is plainly not to make an assertion about the word "sun." The word "sun" might not have existed in the English language, and it still would be true that the word "day-star" designates the sun. The expression "*die Sonne*," in German, would still designate the sun even if the English language did not exist at all. Thus the syntactical theory cannot specify any particular synonym for "day-star." And if it is said indefinitely that the word "day-star" is synonymous with some word in some language, for the alleged translation to be complete it must also be said that this unspecified synonym designates the sun. Thus, a purely syntactical translation cannot be given, and the "semantic relation" of designation cannot be eliminated. Similar considerations show that the meaning of a sentence cannot be explicated in purely syntactical terms. Secondly, even when a particular synonym is specified, to say that the word "day-star" and the word "sun" have the same meaning is not to say what either word means. The same is true of sentences. This shows again that semantic relations cannot be avoided. Thirdly, Carnap's allegedly syntactical expressions "property-word," "thing-word," "descriptive-symbol," "time-designation,"

---

* On p. 286 "5 is a prime number" is given as an example of an object sentence, and on p. 285 "Five is not an even but an odd number" is said to be a proper object sentence. But on p. 313 Carnap says, "Translatability into the formal mode of speech constitutes the touchstone for . . . all sentences which do not belong to the language of any one of the empirical sciences." Consequently it is not clear whether the class of object sentences is supposed to include analytic sentences as well as empirical sentences, or whether it is co-extensive with the class of empirical sentences.

and so on, are semantical expressions in disguise; for example, what makes the word "red" a property-word is not that it is listed under a certain syntactical heading, but that it is used to describe certain objects and not others. Carnap, influenced mainly by Tarski,[104] later recognized the legitimacy of semantics, and in his more recent work he has devoted a great deal of attention to the construction of semantic systems.[105]

Ayer combined the epistemological interest of British philosophy with a view of philosophical analysis that was derived mainly from Russell and Carnap. In *Language, Truth and Logic* he gives Russell's theory of descriptions and the theory of logical constructions, especially in its application to phenomenalism, as examples of the proper method of philosophy. But Ayer also says here, in agreement with Carnap, that "the purpose of a philosophical definition is to dispel those confusions which arise from our imperfect understanding of certain types of sentence in our language" and that philosophical theories such as those which he gives as examples of analysis may be regarded "as a revelation of part of the structure of a given language."[106] In *The Foundations of Empirical Knowledge* Ayer argues that the different theories of perception are not different empirical hypotheses but different forms of language for describing what we experience. The "sense-datum theory" evinces a preference for the sense-datum language.[107] Phenomenalism is the linguistic thesis that anything that can be said in the material-object language can also be said in the sense-datum language.[108] Here, and in a later article entitled "Phenomenalism," Ayer allows that a material-object statement does not entail any specific set of sense-datum statements; and that, perhaps, no finite set of sense-datum statements would be regarded as entailing a material-object statement. But, he argues, this lack of logical equivalence does not show that material-object statements and sense-datum statements are about different kinds of entities. It only shows that material-object statements are less specific, and, perhaps, not conclusively verifiable by appeal to sense-datum statements. The view that although philosophical analysis may fail to show logical equivalence, that it may fall short of formal demonstration, but nevertheless be an essential part of the work of clarifying our thought, is present in much of Ayer's later writing.[109] He also considers the functions or uses of certain types of linguistic expression, so far as this is relevant to the adoption of a general philosophical thesis. Thus, for example, he suggests that the use of temporal demonstratives, and the tenses of verbs, does not contribute to the factual content of a statement, but serves only to indicate the temporal position of the speaker in relation to the events he is describing.[110] If this is so, then there is not a distinct class of statements about the past, any more than there is a distinct class of statements about the present or the future. And consequently there is no special problem about the verifiability of a statement about the past, or about what is involved in understanding such a statement. Ayer's practice of analysis is less formal than Carnap's and that of many American philosophers, such as Goodman and Quine. But it is more concerned with questions of logic, and is aimed at more general results, than the practice of those philosophers who follow the later work of Wittgenstein and Austin.[111]

Epilogue

THE distinctive doctrines of logical positivism involved a wide range of philosophical problems that are still unsolved. To mention only some of the more general questions: What is meant by saying that a statement is empirically confirmable, or that one statement may be evidence for another? Is it simply a matter of convention which empirical statements we regard as basic? Is there an identifiable class of sense-datum statements? What is the nature of the difference between private experience and the public world? How is it that we can understand statements about the private experience of another person? Can the distinction between analytic and synthetic statements be made in purely extensional terms? What is the relation between statements about linguistic usage, or linguistic rules, and the necessary propositions of logic and mathematics? Does philosophical semantics provide an adequate account of the notion of truth? In what way, if at all, does one's choice of a form of language commit one to saying that certain kinds of thing exist? Since the 1940's the doctrines of logical positivism have been in part assimilated, and in part rejected, by more recent developments in philosophy — and logical positivism as a philosophical movement no longer exists. But the logical positivists contributed a great deal toward the understanding of the nature of philosophical questions, and in their approach to philosophy they set an example from which many have still to learn. They brought to philosophy an interest in cooperation, rather than the advancement of individual opinions. They adopted high standards of rigor and an attitude of detachment toward the issues they discussed. And they tried to formulate methods of inquiry that would lead to commonly accepted results. It is for these reasons that the spirit of the Vienna Circle was essentially one of optimism for the future of philosophy.

28

Existentialism

ALASDAIR MacINTYRE

SÖREN AABYE KIERKEGAARD WAS BORN in Copenhagen in 1813. He was brought up by his father in conditions of some severity; his father believed that he had sinned deeply before God and the young Kierkegaard was introduced to the notions of guilt and repentance both earlier and more intensely than most children. He became acquainted at the University of Copenhagen with the Hegelianism to which he was so averse, and later on he studied in Germany. Kierkegaard abandoned the course of studies which would have led him to the ministry of the established Lutheran church, and after a series of episodes which culminated in his breaking off his engagement to Regine Olsen he absorbed himself in what he believed to be his divinely appointed vocation: to show what it is to be a Christian. His use of pseudonyms and his attacks on other works he himself had written under other names were designed to make his activity as impersonal as possible. Nevertheless, he became notorious in Copenhagen for his eccentricity, and was caricatured in the comic paper *The Corsair*, as well as satirized by Hans Christian Andersen. Extremely dubious evidence has been used to assert that he was a hunchback, and equally dubious psychological explanations of Kierkegaard's withdrawn and controversial nature abound. At the end of his life he embarked upon a public polemic against the established church of Denmark and refused to receive the sacrament from a Lutheran pastor. He was a political conservative who welcomed the repression of popular movements in 1848. He died in 1855.

Martin Heidegger was born in Messkirch (Baden) in 1889. He was educated at Freiburg University, where he was a pupil of Husserl. His Catholic upbringing can be seen in his first work, a study of Duns Scotus in the light of Husserl, to whom in 1927 he dedicated *Sein und Zeit*, his own attempt to transcend Husserl's doctrines. In 1933 Hitler came to power. Heidegger joined the Nazi party, became Rector of Freiburg University, and in an inaugural address welcomed the new regime. He disowned Husserl (Husserl was a Jew) and he not only praised but participated in the destruction of academic freedom. This short but disagreeable episode was terminated by his voluntary resignation and retirement. For the rest of the Nazi regime and for some time after 1945 Heidegger lived in the mountains as a hermit. Since he has resumed teaching, he has restricted his pupils to a closed circle. The esoteric language of his published works reflects a mode of philosophical life at the other extreme from that of free and open critical debate.

Jean-Paul Sartre was born in Paris in 1905. He studied philosophy in Paris and Berlin, taught for a short time in a lycée in Le Havre, and joined the French Army in 1939. It was in the period which culminated in his experiences as a prisoner of war that he resolved to become a writer committed to the causes of democracy. His pre-war philosophical writings and his first novel, *La Nausée,* show the influence both of Heidegger and of Alexandre Kojève's lectures upon Hegel. His war-time and post-war plays express an imaginative concern with problems of guilt, responsibility, and freedom. In the post-war period Sartre's main enterprise has been the journal *Les Temps Modernes.* He was one of the founders of a small independent socialist party, in alliance with the Communist Party, in 1948. But this collapsed under the pressures of the Cold War. He was never a member of the Communist Party, which he criticized both for confused theory and for political and moral failure, but he often saw it as the only radical force in French politics. Sartre's expressed preference was for a rootless mode of life, the life of the café rather than of the bourgeois hearth. His works were sometimes unfinished: promised second volumes rarely appeared, and the announced final book in his sequence of novels *Les Chemins de la Liberté* appears never to have been written. An excellent account of the younger Sartre is contained in Simone de Beauvoir's memoirs. Sartre died in 1980.

"I AM NOT AN EXISTENTIALIST" — so Jaspers and so also Heidegger. When the very name is disowned by philosophers as central as these, but is conferred by their admirers at the same time upon figures as diverse as St. Augustine and Norman Mailer, Blaise Pascal and Juliet Greco, one almost despairs of arriving at a useful definition of "existentialism." We could probably find no single common characteristic shared by all those who have been called existentialist. We could certainly find little use even for a brief statement of doctrine shared by some of the central figures. For any formula wide enough to include the thought of Kierkegaard and Sartre, of Heidegger and Marcel, and pithy enough for our purposes, would be meaningless apart apart from the interpretations given to it by individual thinkers. "Existence precedes essence," for example, is like most philosophical slogans out of context susceptible of too many interpretations, and the use of such formulas to define existentialism is what has enabled both Dostoievski and Aquinas to be described as existentialists for purposes of controversy. But how then are we to define the field initially?

Some writers — William Barrett, for example — have wanted to characterize existentialism as part of an antirationalist revolt, against the Enlightenment, against deductive metaphysics, against Marxism, against positivism. But this is a dangerous half-truth at best. It stresses differences at the cost of ignoring resemblances. Sartre's social philosophy is one of the heirs of the Enlightenment, his ethics is first cousin to that of Anglo-Saxon analytical philosophy, his later writing is avowedly Marxist. Kierkegaard's hero was Socrates. Jaspers sees much to be praised in positivism. But it is not only that this kind of historical characterization irons out and ignores complexity. It is also that each of the leading existentialist philosophers is partly characterized as an existentialist because of his own stress upon what is specific to *his* thought, and not shared with others. "As a man is, so is his philosophy," said Fichte. One criterion of existentialist philosophizing is that the man is brought into the picture; his philosophy is commended partly because it is his. Hence the unfortunate tendency to oracular pronouncements and self-dramatization.

To discuss existentialism it is therefore necessary to be somewhat arbitrary, to select a list of names by most of which to define a particular intellectual continuity. Some of the names choose themselves: Kierkegaard, Jaspers, Heidegger, Sartre. Others fall into place by reason of their relation to the larger names: Bultmann and Camus, for example. Nor at least is there any problem about where and when to begin. The time and place are 1813 and Copenhagen, and the event is the birth of Sören Kierkegaard.

Kierkegaard's Interpretation of Christianity and of Ethics

KIERKEGAARD'S sense of a unique vocation thrust upon him connects his life with his writings. In his writings he is discharging this vocation by expressing what he has learned in his relationship with his authoritarian and guilt-ridden father, in his broken engagement, and in his dilemmas about Christianity and the church. The form of these dilemmas led him to conclude that truth, so far as it involves human existence, cannot be grasped by objective scrutiny or argument. These are certainly in place in mathematics and natural science. But they have no place in questions about how to live. Here all that rational argument can do is to present alternatives, to pose choices. Kierkegaard's writings take the form in part of such a presentation, the use of pseudonyms concealing the fact that it is one and the same man who is presenting the rival claims of contrasting and conflicting alternatives. To acquire the truth we have to choose between doctrines for which no logically coercive arguments can be advanced. For any argument derives its conclusion from premises which have to be vindicated, and if these premises are themselves derived as a conclusion from prior premises then these prior premises will in turn stand in need of vindication. Ineluctably we come to a point where not argument but decision is necessary.

On Kierkegaard's own view the most important application of this doctrine is to the characterization of authentic Christianity. Kierkegaard denies "that objections against Christianity come from doubt." They come from "insubordination, unwillingness to obey, rebellion against all authority." It follows that Christian apologetics is a mistake. But it is more than a mistake. It is a falsification of Christianity itself, which necessarily must appear to the ordinary reasonable man or to the philosopher as absurd and paradoxical. It would be a mistake, however, to take this as mere irrationalism. On the contrary, that Christianity must appear as absurd and paradoxical he asserts to follow from one of the two possible views of truth and reason between which we have to choose. These two views are outlined in the *Philosophical Fragments*, which begins from the paradox posed by Socrates in Plato's *Meno*. How is it possible to come to know anything? For either one knows already what one is to come to know or one does not. But if one already knows one cannot come to know; and if one does not already know, how can one possibly recognize what one comes across as being what one desired to know? The Socratic solution to this paradox is that we never in fact do come to know that of which before we were ignorant. Rather, it is that we recall that which we once knew but had forgotten. Truth lies dormant within us. We have only to elicit it. In this Socratic doctrine Kierkegaard sees the assumption of philosophy from Plato to Hegel: that a capacity for grasping the truth belongs to human reason, that what brings the truth to light for us on a given occasion is accidental (that it was this teacher, rather than that), that teaching is bringing out what was already present. Suppose, however, Kierkegaard argues, that this is not the only possibility. Suppose that we might instead be strangers to the truth, unable to grasp it with the resources of human reason. Then the truth would have to be brought to us from outside by a teacher capable of transforming us so that we can receive the truth from him, and such a teacher *ex hypothesi* must be more than human. But in what form will he have to come if he is to teach us? He will have to come in the form of a man, and of a man who impresses us not by his appearance or his power — for that would be not to teach but to dazzle us — but simply by himself and his teaching. He will have to come in the form of a servant. Thus Kierkegaard deduces from this assumption the necessity of a revelation in the form of God appearing as a man. His ironically veiled allusions to Christian doctrine gain from his emphasis that he is doing nothing but pursuing the consequences of one out of two possible alternative assumptions about the relationship of human reason to the truth. As to whether this assumption is true or not he cannot presume to say; he can only leave us to choose between philosophy in Platonic or Hegelian style on the one hand or the Christian revelation on the other.

It is characteristic of Kierkegaard that the brilliance of his prose style in the *Philosophical Fragments* may induce us to overlook the prosaic point that the truth which furnishes Plato with his central example in the *Meno* is geometrical truth and that this is precisely what Kierkegaard is not concerned with. And merely to notice this is for all the compellingness of Kierkegaard's delineation of the two alternatives to fall away. But this is not all. For when we have chosen Christianity, what on Kierkegaard's view have we chosen? What is Christianity? Christianity is inwardness, and "inwardness is the relationship of the individual to himself before God," and from this derives the kind of suffering which is involved in Christianity. Christianity is a matter of suffering for the believer, for it is to grasp oneself before a God where demands of faith and action invade one's ordinary standards by their absurdity, if judged by those standards. The inward acceptance of the absurd does not show outwardly; the knight of faith looks like a tax-collector. In *Fear and Trembling* Kierkegaard considers the type of action which outrages the public standards of ordinary morality but accords with the inwardness of faith because it is in obedience to a divine commandment. Clearly he has in mind his own breaking of his engagement to Regine Olsen, which he justified by referring to what he took to be his divinely appointed vocation; in fact he discusses the story of Abraham and Isaac. Abraham is commanded by God to sacrifice his son. This command runs counter not only to inclination, but also to duty. God commands the sacrifice of Isaac whom Abraham loves; indeed part of what makes it a sacrifice is that Abraham loves him. But Abraham has to break also with duty; his faith in God can make murder a holy act and not a crime. There is thus a rift between the highest human consciousness and the divine intrusion of the apparently absurd. But if at this point what Kierkegaard stresses is the dividing line between the ethical and the religious, there are other places, especially the book *Either/Or*, where he assimilates the religious and the ethical in order to contrast both or the latter with a category which he calls "the aesthetic." The aesthetic life is the life of the man who has no criterion but that of his own happiness. His enemies are pain and more especially boredom. The ethical life is the life of duty, of moral standards which admit of no exceptions in one's own favor. Romantic love, which lasts only as long as the appropriate feelings persist and is always flying off to new satisfactions, is characteristic of the aesthetic; marriage, with its commitments and obligations of an inescapable kind, is characteristic of the ethical. The case for the aesthetic in *Either/Or* is presented in the papers of an anonymous "A"; that for the ethical in the letters of an older man, Judge Wilhelm. The two cases cannot meet, for the first judges between the aesthetic and the ethical on aesthetic grounds and the second judges between them on ethical grounds. Yet there can be no criteria of judgment of a higher order beyond both the aesthetic and the ethical; all there can be is the reader's own choice. But here a reading of *Either/Or* raises an unavoidable doubt.

For Kierkegaard on the one hand insists that the choice between the ethical and the aesthetic is ultimate. It cannot be governed by criteria, for it is a choice of criteria. But on the other hand his descriptions of the two types of life are not neutral. He portrays the aesthetic life as essentially one in which the pleasures of hopefully traveling are destroyed by actually arriving. Hence the aesthetic life is concerned with possibilities which lose their point when they are actualized. But because they can never be actualized without this happening Kierkegaard could write of the aesthetic state of mind at its highest as "an imaginative inwardness which evokes the possibilities with intensified passion, with sufficient dialectical power to transform all into nothing in despair." The point of the ethical, by contrast, is found not in the future but in the present, not in the possible but in the actual, so that in the same passage Kierkegaard describes the ethical as "a quiet, incorruptible, yet infinite passion of resolve" which "embraces the modest ethical task."[1] Indeed, when Kierkegaard insists that he has made "A" cleverer than "Judge Wilhelm" he inadvertently reveals his conviction that one case can be more cogently presented than the other. But it is not just that the descriptions of the two alternatives are not framed in neutral terms. It is also the case that Kierkegaard explicitly affirms at times that one choice can be more correct than another. Sometimes he writes that all that one can do is to choose; at other times he writes that if only one chooses with sufficient seriousness and sufficient passion this will assure that one chooses the correct alternative. Thus, Kierkegaard wishes to argue both that there is no criterion for choosing between the aesthetic and the ethical and also that there is some sense in saying that one alternative is to be preferred to the other. We might rescue him from inconsistency by supposing him to be speaking from an ethical point of view when he says that the ethical is to be preferred and from a point of view at once meta-ethical and meta-aesthetic when he says that the choice is criterionless. But it is not clear that this is so — and when Kierkegaard speaks of his

own "point of view" he speaks of his motives and not about this — and Kierkegaard's possible inconsistency on this point would in any case be only one instance of a dilemma which must inform the views of all those who hold that truth is subjectivity. This dilemma is as follows.

If I hold that truth is subjectivity, what status am I to give to the denial of the proposition that truth is subjectivity? If I produce arguments to refute this denial I appear committed to the view that there are criteria by appeal to which the truth about truth can be vindicated. If I refuse to produce arguments, on the grounds that there can be neither argument nor criteria in such a case, then I appear committed to the view that any view embraced with sufficient subjective passion is as warranted as any other in respect of truth, including the view that truth is not subjectivity. This inescapable dilemma is never faced by Kierkegaard and consequently he remains trapped by it. One source of this dilemma lies in the confusions consequent upon Kierkegaard's equation of the distinction between the subjective and the objective with the distinction between the standpoint of the agent and that of the critic or spectator.

Kierkegaard is anxious to emphasize that the individual cannot without falsification conceive of his place in the world as that of an impartial spectator, an ideal and impersonal observer. He is always and necessarily a participant. As such his life is a series of decisions. The aesthetic, ethical, and religious stages are not so related that the individual who pursues one finds himself pushed by the very logic of what he does into a transition to another stage. Yet this is precisely how Hegel pictures the successive phases of human life in the *Phenomenology of Mind* and in the *Logic*. And Hegel is able to do this, is forced to do this, so Kierkegaard believes, because he pictures the individual as absorbed by the rational system which constitutes the universe and because he pictures the philosopher as the impartial observer of this rational system, seeing it as a timeless whole. It is clear at once both how Kierkegaard interprets Hegel's thought and why he has to react against it.

Kierkegaard's Relationship to Hegel

FOR Kierkegaard Hegel is the Hegel of the mature writings and especially of the Berlin period. Hegelianism is a philosophy which conceives of the universe as the articulation of a set of logical categories. These categories represent different phases in the rational self-development of the absolute idea. Every period in human history is the embodiment of some such phase, and the history of thought, especially the history of philosophy, is the idea coming to self-consciousness of its own rational nature. Nothing that occurs is contingent or arbitrary, once it is understood in the context of the systematic development of the idea, and the Hegelian philosophy is the total rational exposition of that context. Rational argument is the arbiter on every issue, for the coincidence of the rational and the real is complete. Even those individuals who apparently defy reason are by the cunning of reason made to serve its purposes. This explains the sense in which, according to Hegel, the philosopher is committed to envisage reality objectively and as a whole. For Kierkegaard this concept of philosophy is impossible because the philosopher is situated within the reality of which he speaks. He necessarily speaks from one particular, limited, contingent standpoint; his truths cannot be impersonal, objective or necessary. He cannot both be in the universe of which he speaks as an agent and grasp it as a spectator. But why not? The standpoint of the agent is often one from which it is wise to view the universe as impartially and impersonally as possible. It is simply untrue as a matter of empirical fact that we can never transcend our own immediate viewpoint. Agents who cannot do this are often less successful than those who can. If, then, what Kierkegaard was saying is so obviously false, assuming that he intended his words to be taken in their ordinary senses, how did he come to say it? The answer is surely that his vocabulary is badly infected by the Hegelianism which he is trying to reject and that Kierkegaard's use of such terms as "objective" and "subjective" is not intelligible outside a Hegelian context. But by borrowing a Hegelian vocabulary in order to attack a Hegelian position, Kierkegaard becomes himself involved in a kind of inverted Hegelianism. And this is a matter of substance as well as of vocabulary. For Kierkegaard's concept of human nature is already to be found in that portrait gallery of the varieties of human experience, the *Phenomenology of Mind.* When Kierkegaard depicts man as alien from the truth, forced to seek a truth which is at once an objective reality outside him and which he can only apprehend through experiencing his own subjective inwardness, he reproduces with extraordinary fidelity, although certainly unconsciously, Hegel's picture of what Hegel called "the unhappy consciousness."[2] His attempted refutation of Hegel turns out to rest on a doctrine which Hegel himself had recognized as one stage in the development of philosophy toward Hegelianism. Since Kierkegaard believes that his thought expresses the standpoint of genuine Christianity, and since Hegel in this section was describing attitudes which he took to have been historically identified with Christianity, perhaps this coincidence is not surprising. But it is worth dwelling upon it, since the Hegelian view reappears later in existentialist writers and may help to make intelligible some of the instability of existentialist thought.

Hegel's starting point is that human growth in rationality and knowledge is not a simple additive process. It is a process of contradiction and the transcendence of contradiction in which the human subject moves through alienation (*Entfremdung*) to reunification (*Aneignung*). The concept of alienation covers all those cases in which men do not recognize the products of human social life and thought as such, but falsely invest those products with independent power and reality. Whereas they are in fact akin to us, they appear as alien. An example is the attitude men take to the moral law. In reality the moral law expresses human ideals and norms. It is something made by men. But men see it as an objective authority, external to them, against which they are judged. However, as we progress rationally, we recognize the human character of such artifacts, and as we approach the complete appropriation of truth we can see our earlier false consciousness as a necessary moment of estrangement in our progress. These Hegelian concepts have been immensely influential; they are, however, inherently unstable. For they try to combine the possibility of seeing the world as a totally rational system with the possibility of seeing the world as the realm of the contingent and arbitrary where the individual has no guide. Yet to try to envisage both possibilities at once is to destroy the possibility of either. If we try to conceive the universe as a total rational system of which we ourselves are but a finite part, and of which our view is necessarily a finite and partial one, then for that very reason we must abandon any claim to completeness and finality for our own philosophy. But in that case we have not grasped the system as a final whole, and so we have no ground for asserting that there is such a system or that the universe has such a character. If, on the other hand, we try to conceive of ourselves as alienated and estranged in the Hegelian sense, we can only make sense of these predicates if we can assign some sense to the notion of not being or no longer being alienated and estranged. Alienation and estrangement are defined in Hegelian terms as not being or having or knowing what one *could* be or have or know. It follows that estrangement and alienation *can* be overcome; they cannot be the necessarily final word. They can only be moments in a possible progress toward a rational and systematic overcoming of estrangement. Hence, if one embraces those Hegelian concepts which imply a denial of the possibility of systematic, rational knowledge of the universe, one is driven toward the affirmation of such a possibility, just as much as if one affirmed the Hegelian system one would be driven also to affirm that one could not as a finite being be in possession of it.

These Hegelian concepts are therefore unstable in that if one uses them to deny the possibility of rational systematic knowledge one is driven toward something like the Hegelian system by the use of the concepts; whereas if one uses the concepts of system seriously one is forced in the end either to abandon them or to escape, as Hegel does in the *Logic*, by denying the finite limitations of the systematizer as himself only part of the system. A claim to an absolute extra-historical point of view is forced upon the serious Hegelian. When Hegel in the *Logic* explains that the thoughts which he is expressing are the thoughts of God, he develops his own positions in a way that makes him appear as all that Kierkegaard would condemn; but when Kierkegaard makes men totally alien to the truth and to the divine (except by grasping them through nonrational choice) what he is developing is precisely the other side of the Hegelian dilemma. There is thus built into the thought of Kierkegaard and of those who inherit his concept a basic instability about the enterprise of system-building in the Hegelian manner.

In Kierkegaard himself this oscillation is already evident. He professedly abjures system but is in fact one of the most rigidly systematic of thinkers. In spite of his complaint against Hegel that for Hegel Christianity is allowed to say only what the Hegelian world will permit it to say, much the same is true of Kierkegaard himself. Kierkegaard presents Christianity in terms of his own philosophical views and thus becomes all that he wants to abjure. For he wishes to stress the irremovable quality not only of the moral but also of the intellectual offensiveness of Christianity; and he does this by showing that Christianity cannot be rationally justified. To be a Christian is not to have reached a conclusion but to have made a choice. But since all religions and moral belief equally lack ultimate rational justification (including the beliefs both of rival religions and of atheism), the groundlessness of Christianity is not distinctive. It merely belongs to it as a member of the class of religious and moral beliefs. If this claim is made good, it provides a rational answer to the skeptic who has assaulted Christian faith by demonstrating that it is groundless. Of course it is. What else could it be? Thus Kierkegaard's argument renders Christianity easier to believe in that it would otherwise be in an age of skepticism. His hostility to apologetics cannot prevent the objective effect of his writings being quite other than he willed. And this has in general been Kierkegaard's fate. He despised professors and academics; but his writings fell into their hands and were used for purposes quite other than he orginally intended.

It is striking, however, that Kierkegaard did not merely fall prey to academic apologists, but also to academic secularizers. This too, however, is easily intelligible. On the one hand, Kierkegaard's own life may have consisted of the kind of religious self-dramatization which Ibsen portrayed in *Brand*; but on the other hand, Kierkegaard's type of religion reduces the content of religion to a minimum, Christianity consists in inwardness; the knight of faith outwardly appears like a tax-collector. What difference does it make to be a Christian, to be before God inwardly? The bareness of Kierkegaard's response to this question allows for an easy secularization of his central thesis.

Kierkegaard's Analysis of Dread

ONE major difficulty in understanding what the content of Christianity is for Kierkegaard is that his psychological analysis is of inner states which are, so far as they are comprehensible, secular. In *The Concept of Dread*, for example, Kierkegaard's stated theme is original sin; but he allows that original sin as a fact is beyond explanation. What he offers is an interconnected analysis of concepts such as freedom, genius, fate, individuality, and above all dread. Dread enters the argument from the outset. ("Dread" translates "*Angst*." Unamuno translated this in French by "*agonie*," Sartre by "*angoisse*." The psychoanalytic use of "anxiety" comes close to the meaning.) Before Adam fell, he was innocent. But — "Innocence is ignorance." Man in a state of innocence is not yet "determined as spirit." (That is, he has not a characteristically human awareness and intelligence.) He is undisturbed and peaceful, except that — there is something else which man might be. What is that something else? It does not yet exist. It is nothing. But this nothing haunts man and produces dread. Dread is not fear. Fear, so Kierkegaard asserts, always has a definite object. Dread, by contrast, has no such object; its object is nothing, "a nothing which is able only to alarm," a nothing which is "freedom's appearance before itself as a possibility." Kierkegaard describes the object of dread yet again as "something which is nothing."

So far we have a dramatically convincing description of a recognizable state of mind. But how does Kierkegaard use this to throw light upon his professed theme of original sin? Kierkegaard asserts that when he speaks of original sin, he is not speaking merely of Adam but of the entire human race. He asserts, indeed, that "man is an individual and as such is at once himself and the whole race. . . . " But then it at once occurs to us to ask, must each individual fall? Is sin the only alternative to innocence? Can we not discard our ignorance and remain good? Kierkegaard, who treats very patiently all kinds of abstruse problems about original sin, is completely impatient with these plain questions. Of one such, the question "what would have happened in case Adam had not sinned?" he remarks, "To the innocent man it never can occur to ask such a question, but the guilty man sins when he asks it; for with his aesthetic curiosity he would like to obscure the fact that he himself has brought guilt into the world, has himself lost innocence by guilt." Kierkegaard was presumably ignorant of the fact that he would have to count John Calvin among the aesthetically curious, since Calvin is prepared to speak seriously of what would have happened "*si Adam integer stetisset*" (if Adam had remained whole). The contrast with Calvin serves only to bring out how far Kierkegaard is prepared to go in avoiding awkward questions by treating them as signs not of doubt but of rebellion, not of problems but of sins. This procedure means that so far as the specifically religious content of the notions of sin and dread is concerned we come up against a blank wall of unintelligibility. What remains is an analysis of dread as an inseparable part of the human condition. What are we to make of this analysis?

The difficulty lies in the way in which Kierkegaard moves from treating dread as a highly specific emotion to treating it as something very general indeed. Sometimes dread is sharply contrasted with all other emotions; sometimes all other emotions are in danger of turning out to be forms of dread. When it is the burdensomeness of dread that is to be emphasized, the former is the case; when the omnipresence of dread is to be emphasized, the latter. So we are most implausibly informed by Kierkegaard that in children dread is found in the form of "a seeking after adventure, a thirst for the prodigious, the mysterious." The reasons why dread has to be omnipresent are perhaps twofold. First of all, Kierkegaard wishes to establish a necessary connection between certain very central features of human life and dread. Freedom and possibility necessarily involve dread, and freedom and possibility are necessary features of human existence. We thus find Kierkegaard establishing an *a priori* framework within which all the actual experiences of human beings have to be accommodated. There is nothing disreputable about this enterprise as such; it is simply that the Kierkegaardian framework is an uncomfortably and misleadingly constricting one.

We can bring out part of what Kierkegaard is doing by contrasting his view with that of Hume: "when a man is in a cheerful disposition, he is fit for business, or company, or entertainment of any kind; and he naturally applies himself to these and thinks not of religion. When melancholy and dejected, he has nothing to do but brood upon the terrors of the invisible world, and to plunge himself still deeper in affliction." Hume, like Kierkegaard, connects religion with apprehension. But whereas Hume wants therefore to connect religion with one particular frame of mind, Kierkegaard wants to show the pervasiveness of this frame of mind. That cheerful concern with the affairs of this world which for Hume constitutes the happy norm is for Kierkegaard a desperate attempt by men to conceal their dread from themselves. It is a mask, a disguise, an escape.

How could we settle the issue between Kierkegaard and Hume? It is certainly not a straightforward empirical matter. What we would need is a firm criterion for distinguishing between psychological realities on the one hand and mere rationalization, pretenses, and disguises on the other. And this requires a conceptual investigation which has never yet been carried through satisfactorily. It is the lack of such an investigation rather than any clearly established criteria which leaves us in doubt over Kierkegaard's conceptual psychology. Kierkegaard

hovers uneasily between an *a priori* elucidation of the concepts necessary to characterize our inner experiences and a transcript of his own private experience. The weakness of his account is that we do not get enough of either. His personal life limited absurdly his sense of the possibilities that were open; Kierkegaard is deeply ignorant of most of human life. His wish to speak of humanity as such forces an air of abstraction on to what could have been a moving personal recital; it is no accident that his *Journals* are often more illuminating than his published works. But if Kierkegaard is almost lost between the Scylla of autobiography and the Charybdis of *a priori* generalization, here also he gathers some of his force. For he does present a narrative which is both dramatic and yet concerns "Everyman." He does at least suggest both an intensity of purpose and a gift of psychological insight, especially when he deals with particular examples. Kierkegaard, as I have argued, is ambiguous in his attitude toward systematic thought. His attention to the individual case rescues him from a possible vulgarity into which some of his followers at once fall. It is therefore worthwhile to examine in turn the vulgarization and the genuine use of Kierkegaardian themes. A prime example of the latter is Heidegger; to view the former we have only to turn to Karl Jaspers.

Jaspers' Use of Kierkegaard

IF the concepts which Kierkegaard used to attack metaphysical system-building in the end betrayed him into the vices which he sought to exterminate, at least he was the unwitting victim of his own, or rather of Hegel's, concepts. But with Karl Jaspers (1883–   ) Kierkegaard's concepts are quite consciously put to the service of enterprises alien to Kierkegaard. For Jaspers' interest in Kierkegaard arose out of trying to solve problems of a kind with which Kierkegaard was never concerned. Jaspers was a practitioner of psychological medicine who in classifying psychiatric disorders began to connect them with fundamental attitudes to life and who became simultaneously dissatisfied with what he took to be contemporary philosophy's view of such attitudes — and also with what he took to be the scientific psychologist's attitude to mental disorder, and to normal personality. He saw philosophy as concerned to give an objective account of the universe, preoccupied with the vindication of the rationality of this or that *Weltanschauung* as against all others, and therefore committed to the view that all questions can be settled at the bar of pure reason. He saw psychology as concerned to give a wholly determinist, causal account of the origin of different types of personality, whether normal or disordered. Both these accounts share one and the same omission and both require the same Kierkegaardian corrective. What both omit is fundamental choice. We have to choose between different world-views and reason will not make the choice for us. Moreover, the study of a man's personality as it actually is, which is all that scientific psychiatry can view, omits what else that man could have become and omits also the fundamental choices which actualized one possibility for that man as against others. Jaspers therefore envisages behind the empirical self a true self whose situation is essentially Kierkegaardian. This authentic self is revealed to us in what Jaspers calls boundary-situations, moments of dread, of guilt, of awareness of death. For these moments force upon us consciousness of the necessity of choice. So far the development is not too unlike Kierkegaard's own. But from this point it is not just that Kierkegaard's thought is put to new uses. It is rather that while verbal tributes are still paid to Kierkegaard, everything that Kierkegaard hated returns.

For Jaspers' attitude to both science and rationalist metaphysics is really quite different from that of Kierkegaard. Kierkegaard's genuine mistrust of system leads him to see all thought as necessarily fragmentary and incomplete. Jaspers believes that philosophy can be an attempt to grasp being as such, "the comprehensive." While he nominally adjures "system," he does not mind being called systematic. Positivism is mistaken because it thinks that natural science is all-inclusive. Idealism makes equally totalitarian claims for the sphere of *Geist*. But if each will only concede that its own view is merely part of the truth then there is room for all in a wider synthesis. No philosophical view is false unless it claims to be final and exclusive. At this point, where Kierkegaard placed arbitrary, criterionless choice, Jaspers reintroduces the concept of an objective transcendent reality with which the whole history of philosophy is concerned. What does Jaspers have to say of this reality? The dominant criterion for what to say appears to be the consensus among other philosophers — but certainly not all other philosophers. His is a highly selective view of the history of philosophy. By now Kierkegaard is quite left behind. The "authentic self" is not defined by its acts of choice; its task is to interpret the signs of a reality beyond the merely empirical. Two of the key terms here are "communication" and "transcendence"; the former indicates an awareness of there being other people, the latter appears to be a pseudonym for God. Jaspers himself is a Protestant, but his characterization of the transcendent is general enough to be ambiguous between Platonism, Judaism, and Christianity. Yet at this point it must be confessed that any account of Jaspers which is lucid is for that very reason necessarily unfaithful. A great deal of Jaspers' thought cannot be reduced to the kind of religiose platitude to which I have reduced it because it is written in a high-flown German that resists decoding altogether. Moreover, Jaspers explicitly believes that philosophy must finally express itself in antinomies, in the opposing contrasts of rival views. He admires Nietzsche precisely for the contradictory qualities of Nietzsche's thought. Like other existentialist philosophers, he is extremely neglectful of the formal aspects of thought (Kierkegaard himself was to a limited extent an exception here; he was a keen student of Trendelenburg's version of Aristotelian logic) and so does not recognize that to admit contradiction into a system is to license any kind of utterance at all. It is perhaps partly for these reasons that Jaspers' cultural solutions are so empty of content. He sees a mediocre, scientist frame of mind overwhelming the West; the solution is a spiritual aristocracy that has assimilated inwardly the truths which the external social world has rejected. But what is the content of *this* inwardness? Kierkegaard's hidden faith loses all its particularity. Even with Kierkegaard it is difficult to grasp what the sense of being before God consists in. But to try to secularize and to generalize this sense is to see it evaporate. In Kierkegaard we may suspect a final lack of content in the solution, particularly if we are not ourselves Christians; in Jaspers the lack of content is there for all to see.

Heidegger's Debt to Phenomenology

IF Jaspers vulgarizes Kierkegaard, Heidegger makes a genuine use of him. But since Kierkegaard is only one of Heidegger's sources, we cannot begin here. We can begin only with Heidegger's critique of Husserl's phenomenology. The roots of phenomenology are in the work of Franz Brentano (1838–1916). Brentano was a critic of the associationist psychology which derived from the British empiricists and more particularly of the view that mental life consists of mechanically associated individual entities (Lockean ideas, Humean impressions and ideas). For Locke or Hume an assertion is a conjunction of ideas, an emotion is an inner occurrence ("Passions are original existences," wrote Hume), willing is an internal impression. For Brentano this omits the crucial constituent of mental life, its intentionality. Judging is judging that such-and-such. It is taking up an attitude toward an idea. Ideas are always themselves ideas of something. Feelings are feelings toward something. That something Brentano calls "the intentional object," borrowing the scholastic word "*intentio*." Brentano's way of putting the matter suggests that he is accepting the empiricists' characterization of the mental world, but both adding to their catalogue of items (ideas are not the only ultimate constituents of mental life, there are also judgments) and extending their view of the properties of ideas. But in fact the ascription of intentionality to mental states marks a far more radical breach with the traditional empiricist position.

Beliefs, emotions, desires are not just inner happenings which occur or do not occur. They have objects and they are part of an intelligible sequence in which the connections are not those of constant conjunction, but those of rules and concepts, reasons, and purposes. ("What led you to believe that?" "Why are you angry with him?" and "What do you want that for?" do not require causal answers.) Although beliefs, emotions, and desires need very different kinds of conceptual elucidations, it is common to all of them that they are directed upon objects which may but need not exist, that they are partially defined by an internal use of names and descriptions. The belief may be about something which I wrongly suppose to exist, the emotion concern an event about which I have been misinformed, the desire rest on a mistaken belief about the character of the object. But in each case, in order for the belief to count as a belief, the emotion as an emotion, the desire as a desire, something must be envisaged as an object, and this is what Brentano meant by an "intentional object." (There is no connection with the ordinary English use of "intentional.")

Brentano's central concern was to investigate the character of judging, believing, and the like. He was thus in fact engaged upon conceptual investigations, and later phenomenological writing often comes close to the methods of conceptual analysis used by such philosophers as Wittgenstein and Ryle. But Brentano's second theme separates phenomenology from all conceptual analysis. For Wittgenstein and Ryle are both essentially anti-Cartesian philosophers, while Brentano wishes to give a peculiarly Cartesian primacy to the contents of inner consciousness: here we have clarity and certainty, *Evidenz*. Thus, we may be in doubt as to our judgment about the external world, but we can be in no doubt when judging of our own inner selves.

Edmond Husserl (1858–1938) developed both of Brentano's main themes. In his early writings he argued against psychologism in mathematics; in his later he developed a fully fledged account of the "science of essences." Husserl's logical investigations go beyond Brentano both in rigor and in generality. But he retains both of Brentano's central positions, and the appeal to *Evidenz* has its heir in the "transcendental phenomenology" of Husserl's last years. For the earlier Husserl phenomenology does not commit itself to existential assertion. It elucidates essences, not existences; concepts, not objects. It says what anything would have to be like if it were to be of such-and-such a kind, but as to whether there are any beings of this kind it remains uncommitted. For the later Husserl there is an attempt to say what consciousness must be if its intentional acts and objects are what they are. There is an attempt at a new start on the path upon which Descartes set out with the *Cogito*. Husserl's earlier phenomenology had already led him to the doctrine that it is of the essence of objects to be objects "for" consciousness, to be correlative to states of mind. He came to view all that was not immediate experience as constituted by the meanings which are the intentional objects of consciousness. And so, while Brentano's doctrine of intentionality was extremely antisolipsistic, the Husserlian version is increasingly a solipsistic, or at least a Kantian one, in which consciousness somehow makes the perceived world.

This highly inadequate and distorted account of Brentano and Husserl is a necessary prelude to any discussion of Heidegger, both because of what Heidegger accepted from and what he criticized in Husserl. Heidegger begins by trying to go behind the questions posed by Husserl and Descartes. They had asked: "How can consciousness come to know a world outside consciousness?" Husserl had behaved as if it was clear that the investigation of conscious states of mind was one thing, the investigation of consciousness-in-the-world another. But whence this dualism? What makes us dualists? What is the "I" which poses the question "What can I know?" and what must be true of it for it to be able to pose this question? On Heidegger's view, although Descartes claims to be making a new start and Husserl claims that phenomenology is presuppositionless, both men take for granted their dualism of mind and matter, consciousness and the world, from the outset, rather than discover it. Heidegger's own attempt to start genuinely at the beginning with what is authentically primitive leads him to coin a new philosophical vocabulary, and to claim that this vocabulary is uninfected by earlier theorizing. Thus when Heidegger names the "I" which asks the Cartesian question he names it in its most primitive mode of being-in-the-world, "*Dasein*," literally "being there." What is the mode of being-in-the-world? It is a general movement toward things, reaching out after objects. Intentionality characterizes all awareness. But the mode of grasping the world which is knowledge is less basic than a more generalized grasping after things, in which we gradually build up concepts. After *Dasein*, human existence, comes the concept of things which are grasped as having a use, as tools, as instruments, the things which lie to hand. Then we come across things which resist use, which cannot serve our purposes. Thus we build up our categories.

Two philosophical traditions thus have to be disowned and not just one; not only is it wrong to start with consciousness and reach out to the world, but it is also wrong to try and capture the primitive reality of *Dasein* through the derivative concepts which we apply to the world of things, such as the concepts of cause and substance. We grasp *Dasein* as being-in-the-world or not at all. But is this victory over Cartesian dualism more than verbal? The great difficulty with Heidegger's *Sein und Zeit* (which is a far better book than those who have not read it generally allow) is that the perhaps warranted apprehension of traditional philosophical terminology is too often used to permit the invention of a new word (often a compound of hyphenated monosyllables, which thus gives an impression at once of the sophistication of the metaphysician and of the childlike simplicities of the nursery) to be a substitute for a solution to an old problem. But what then, to take up Heidegger's key word, is *Dasein*? Here Heidegger brings in his reading of Kierkegaard, and also of other Christian writers, especially of Augustine.

The Analysis of Dasein *in* Sein und Zeit

"DASEIN IST SORGE." *Dasein* is care, concern. (*Sorge* is a translation of the Latin *Cura*.) It is being-concerned-with. But what characterizes our concern is our finitude and the way in which our being is consumed in the moment-to-moment passage of time. We do not exist only for the present moment, however. Human existence is open toward the future. We confront possibility and we are filled with *Angst*. Here Heidegger follows closely Kierkegaard's analysis of dread. I can only avoid *Angst* by retreating to the less than human anonymity of "the One" (Heidegger's coinage from the ordinary use of "one does . . . " in place of "I do . . . " to express impersonality), by attending not to my own existence in its future reality but by envisaging myself as a unit along with other units. I can only overcome *Angst* by facing my existence in its totality, and for human existence that is to face the fact of my own death as the limit of possibility. Both conscience and guilt play their part here, for conscience informs me of what I might be and guilt of what I might have been. I cannot escape an inauthentic, harassed, and consumed existence except by continually living as one who knows that he is going to die. I am therefore confronted with a decision between the inauthentic existence of "the one" and authentic existence. Heidegger's account of *Dasein* is thus a blend of *The Concept of Dread* and *Either/Or*. We are no longer faced with choice as the key to truth; we are faced with a systematic and argued ontology — or at least with the prologue to such an ontology — in which choice has its place. The ontology is that of *The Concept of Dread* — without God. It is not that Heidegger explicitly denies that God exists. It is just that God is absent. Heidegger himself has indignantly repudiated the suggestion that he is an atheist. Nonetheless, all the concepts taken from Augustine and Kierkegaard are secularized, and with that secularization Heidegger frees himself from the problems created by Kierkegaard's theology. What he cannot free himself from, however, are the problems which he inherits from both Husserl and Kierkegaard.

The first of these is the solitariness of Heidegger's human being. The existence of other people in my world is certainly admitted; but it is not allowed to touch the concept of *Dasein*. Yet crucially human existence is social. We learn about ourselves from the mirror-image afforded by other people. We enter upon the use of a language which we did not invent but have to learn. Heidegger's own theory of language is not inconsistent with this; he stresses the context of mutual understanding in which a silence can be as meaningful as a spoken word. But nothing about the relationship to other individuals enters into the difference between authentic and inauthentic existence. And this makes it very difficult to understand what the content of authentic existence is. The concept is empty in the way in which Kierkegaard's concept of inwardness is empty. And the combination of the passionate enjoinder to choose authentic existence with the emptiness of that notion ought to make us ready for any sort of conduct from the Heideggerian which is at least chosen and involves brooding upon death. We should not be surprised that Heidegger was for a short period a Nazi, not because anything in *Sein und Zeit* entails National Socialism but because nothing in *Sein und Zeit* could give one a standpoint from which to criticize it or any other irrationalism.

Secondly, the concept of the logically and anthropologically primitive notion is as laden with philosophical assumptions as Husserl's dualism is. The primacy which Brentano awarded to inner perception is the ancestor of the primacy which Heidegger awards to *Dasein*. Heidegger never makes it clear why some concepts should be primary and others secondary and derivative. If he is claiming that the primary concepts are those that we do (as children, or as members of primitive societies) in fact acquire first, he appears to be simply wrong on points of fact. If he is claiming that his primary concepts *must* be acquired first, not only is his claim odd in the light of the facts (for how can what does not happen be necessary?) but he provides no arguments for his claim. Indeed, *Sein und Zeit* contains relatively few arguments.

What is worse is of course that Heidegger's account of human life, where it is not vacuous, is transparently false. Kierkegaard already had generalized the notion of dread into something difficult to pin down; Heideggerian *Angst* escapes altogether. And had Heidegger not been put by Sartre to quite new uses Heidegger's importance would not be what it is. To Sartre, therefore, we must now turn. But in order to understand Sartre we must place him in the total history which we are recounting.

Sartrian Ontology

JEAN-PAUL SARTRE was educated in the dull backwaters of Brunschvigian idealism and Bergsonian preoccupations which marked French academic philosophy so badly between the wars. His own successive readings of Heidegger and Hegel, together with the influence of such phenomenological writers as Merleau-Ponty, provided him with the materials for a series of episodes in each of which Sartre reissues an earlier existentialist theme, but in such a new context as to transform it. From Heidegger he takes his basic ontology. The world is divided into two species of being, "*être-en-soi*" (literally, "being-in-itself") and "*être-pour-soi*" (literally, "being-for-itself"). The former is the being of things, the latter that of people. Things simply are; they are complete in themselves. Human beings are incomplete; they are open toward the future, an as yet unmade future. The emptiness of this future has to be filled by the choices of the agent. Confronting the emptiness of his future the agent feels not only Heideggerian anxieties but elementary nausea. But the difference from Heidegger is profounder than this.

In Sartre's first novel, *La Nausée*, the protagonist, Antoine Roquentin, confronts the total meaninglessness of existence. This meaninglessness consists in the fact that things just are; they have no sufficient reason for being as they are. They are contingent. They are absurd. If we try to make sense out of existence we necessarily falsify. We tell stories about the past which impose a coherence that never could have existed. Is there, then, no way to lend life meaning and coherence (and with it perhaps dignity)? We can try to escape the meaninglessness of our lives like the bourgeois notables whose portraits Roquentin sees in the local galleries. They falsify human existence by pretending that it is solid and determinate, a matter of filling pre-existing roles, a matter of existence merely filling out an already determined essence. But the essence of man does not preexist his existence. Existence precedes essence. Is there, then, any way of escaping despair and nausea on the one hand or falsification upon the other? In *La Nausée* only one hint is given. Perhaps a work of art, a song or a book, may exist as geometrical forms exist, free from contingency. No clear sense is assigned to this possibility, and for an amplification of what Sartre might mean we have to turn to *L'Etre et Le Néant*. Here it becomes clear that the lack of meaning in life is connected with Sartre's atheism.

The notion of God is self-contradictory, the notion of a being who is an impossible blend of being-in-itself and being-for-itself. As one who makes choices and decisions, God must exist "for-himself"; as one who is complete and self-sufficient, God must exist "in-himself." He must have the freedom of a person and the fullness of a thing. This is a criticism of the concept of God which is very much to the point. It can easily be extracted from Sartre's terminology and posed as the old problem about predestination: how can the traditional concept of God avoid the charge that for God it is necessary that some things shall not yet have been decided and yet that for God it is necessary that everything is already decided? But Sartre is not interested solely in establishing the truth of atheism. He wishes, rather, to show that the concept of God embodies an impossible ideal

of self-sufficiency and meaningfulness against which we measure human life and find it contingent and meaningless. Human life has to be without a sufficient reason, because God is impossible. God is what man uselessly and hopelessly aspires to be.

The essential content of human nature for Sartre, then, is that it is an as yet undetermined project. It is open toward the future. It is the form of intentionality which has to be filled out with content. Sartre has in fact made the advance which Husserl attempted by cumbrous and Kantian arguments, but he has done it by simple assertion. Husserl wished to pass from analyzing the intentional form of consciousness to saying how consciousness was, or must be, in actuality. Sartre asserts that the intentional form is precisely what consciousness is. He uses this starting point to criticize both physiological and Freudian theories of emotion. Since emotions are intentional we must explain them by bringing into the picture their intentional objects. We must explain them as directed toward something which is an object of consciousness. What we cannot do is to bring into our explanation either antecedent physiological conditions or unconscious memories and motives, for they do not belong to the realm of consciousness as emotions do.

Man, as Sartre pictures him, is then absolutely undetermined by his physiological constitution. Actions cannot have causes but are the outcome of undetermined choices. There are regularities in human behavior, because a great deal of human behavior consists in living out routines and roles which, like the bourgeois worthies in *La Nausée*, we treat as if they were predetermined grooves along which we had to run. We behave as if we were determined; we present our choices as if they were unavoidable. In so doing we seek to deceive both ourselves and others. We are guilty of bad faith. The omnipresence of bad faith haunts Sartre's world. The waiter in the café, going about his job, is acting a part — the part of a waiter. The girl who refuses to admit to herself her would-be seducer's intentions and treats what she does as a series of happenings, not a series of actions, in which each episode follows the next without any responsibility on her part — she too is offered as a paradigm case of bad faith. So widespread is bad faith that it is difficult to understand the content of the concept of the "*acte gratuit*," the action not in bad faith. Indeed, in Sartre's series of novels *L'Age de Raison* the first protagonist, Mathieu, pursues with desperate ambiguity the possibility of an act that can truly be his own; when he dies in a hopeless last stand against the Germans in 1940, it is left unclear whether he achieved it. And this ambiguity in the novel seems to be a necessary consequence of the ambiguity of the concept. For on the one hand Sartre appears to treat bad faith as a purely contingent feature of human life which could be abolished; indeed, he urges us to turn from it. But his association of the concept with that of living out any socially recognized or recognizable role almost turns it into a necessary feature of human life. And this is entirely coherent with the doctrines of *La Nausée*; if the reality of human existence is to be meaningless, discontinuous, and incoherent, then any coherent way of life or action is necessarily a falsification. If, confronting the reality, we are necessarily to be overcome with anxiety and nausea, the retreat into falsification will become a central and characteristic feature of human life. Sartre's problem is that he is unwilling just to accept this. He wants to save us from it. The pattern of salvation appears very slowly in his writings and when it does appear it is a fascinating combination of Hegel and Kierkegaard.

Sartre's Picture of Human Relationships

HEGEL first appears on the scene as providing a model for human relationship. Sartre takes with great seriousness Hegel's remark in the *Phenomenology of Mind* that "Self-consciousness exists in itself and for itself, in so far as and by virtue of the fact that it exists for another self-consciousness; that is, it *is* only by being acknowledged or recognized." He thus breaks with the solitariness of Heideggerian man. Moreover, he takes from Hegel the dialectic of master and serf in the same portion of the *Phenomenology* and uses it to construct a psychology in which love between people is always deformed into mastering or being mastered. He is able to do this because he sees an ultimate distinction between my being a subject (what I necessarily am for myself) and my being an object (what I necessarily am for others). Sartre has a fascinating phenomenological analysis of what it is to be turned into an object by being looked at. If, therefore, I make someone else an object of my regard, I necessarily treat him as something that is now an object for me; in so doing I impose myself on him. I manifest not love but sadism. If, to correct this, I try to make myself an object of the other's regard I equally destroy the possibility of love, for now I substitute masochism. Imprisoned within the cycle of sadism and masochism, what way out can there be? Sartre offers a hint of a possibility of a way out, but in *L'Etre et Le Néant* he never specifies what it would be like. It remains as contentless as Kierkegaardian salvation. Or at least it only acquires content when Sartre turns to ethics and sociology.

In *L'Etre et Le Néant* what is said of human freedom is ambiguous. Freedom is a burden. "We are condemned to be free." During his time in a German prison camp after 1940 and later in the French Resistance, Sartre decided with immense seriousness to become a writer on behalf of democracy. A major preoccupation from then on is his attempt to link the freedom inherent in human nature with political freedom. In a short essay after the war (*L'Existential-

isme est un Humanisme*) Sartre argued that all moral principles rested upon the individual's choice; there are no objective grounds for morality. If I treat some consideration as morally cogent, it is because I have chosen to consider it cogent. There are no criteria governing such choices, and there can be none; for our fundamental choices are choices of criteria. Believers in objectivist theories of morals are yet another example of men in bad faith; they wish to shift the responsibility for decisions that are in fact their own on to someone or something else. Nonetheless, if I choose I choose as one who seeks to legislate not for himself as this particular individual but for himself as any man. I bring myself under some universal principle which I have chosen. In so doing I have to regard myself as legislator for all, and I have to limit the exercise of my own choice to those forms of action in which I do not infringe upon the freedom of others to choose similarly. The universal form of the moral choice determines a content for morality: respect the freedom of everybody. This conjuring of moral content out of moral form is of course more than merely reminiscent of Kant; and it invites all the criticisms to which the Kantian thesis has been subjected. Even if it be the case that any moral judgments, perhaps in order to qualify as moral, must always be of the impersonal form "Anyone in these circumstances ought . . . , " why does it follow that my judgments must have such a content that they enjoin respect for the freedom of all? "One ought always to respect the freedom of the propertied classes, even at the cost of the freedom of other classes" is a perfectly consistent and intelligible judgment which has in fact been advanced by many political theorists. The democratic ideal cannot be made to follow from the existentialist premises.

Sartre continues to remain obscure on this point in his later writings. But he provides a much more explicit account both of what we are to be saved from and of how we are to save ourselves. This account is rooted in Sartre's newly self-proclaimed Marxism, a Marxism surprising to those who remembered the immediate post-war philosophical debates between Sartre and orthodox Marxists. The Sartre of 1946 presents men as exempt from all causal determination, as unconditionally and limitlessly free in their choices. Pierre Naville as a Marxist accused Sartre of trying to separate men from nature altogether and of "a contempt for things." Lukacs argued that Sartre's concept of freedom portrayed not a necessary and essential characteristic of human nature but rather the contemporary indecision of the rootless bourgeois intellectual. Sartre's political agreement with the French Communist Party on many issues never exempted him from philosophical polemic. When, therefore, Sartre calls himself a Marxist, how far is he guilty of a *volte-face*? Only at the most superficial level. The Sartrian individual who is compelled to choose is a secularized version of Kierkegaard's individual, who is in turn perhaps Hegel's unhappy consciousness lifted outside the dialectic of history. Moreover, when the Sartrian individual enters into relationship with others, the patterns of his relationship are drawn, as I already noticed, from Hegel's account of the alienation of the unhappy consciousness. But the concept of alienation is difficult and probably impossible to use without implying something like its Hegelian context. The predicament of Sartrian man is often presented as the necessary predicament of all human nature; but Sartre's descriptions slide all too easily into those of contingent features of one form of human life, features which can be removed. So Sartre in the *Critique de la Raison Dialectique* presents a set of formulations in which bad faith and bad human relationships in general belong to the life of class-divided, and especially of capitalist, society.

The key expression, however, in describing our condition is no longer "bad faith"; it is "serialization." We are serialized by the routines and rigidities of our society: the perfect example of serialization is the member of a queue, who envisaged as such is only a unit in a series. Serialization will be overcome by a group which through its disciplined unity (bound together by a commitment to a rule the infringement of which carries the penalty of death) will break into a new form of society. Sartre's political science-fiction in the *Critique* scarcely deserves notice; what is of real interest is the attempt to construct a sociology which takes seriously the notions of freedom and activity as theoretical concepts. What attracts Sartre in Marx is precisely the notion that "Man makes his own history, but. . . . " What distresses him in later Marxism is the mechanical use of economic determinism. But his sociology suffers immensely from a lack of patience with facts, and there are only two aspects of it to which we need to attend closely.

The first is Sartre's general claim that existentialism and Marxism are complementary, not opposed. In the form in which Sartre makes it this claim is dubious, for all he wants to do is to make existentialism a reminder of the particularity, the contingency, and the power of choice annexed to individual human existence to the Marxist who will otherwise be too *a priori*, too inflexible, too determinist. But since Sartre never grapples properly with either the conceptual or the factual points at issue in controversies over determinism, it is difficult to assess the value of what he says. He jeers at attempts to reduce Flaubert to a social product of the Second Empire, but he does not say at anything like sufficient length what a renovated Sartrian Marxist would say about Flaubert. Moreover, he never separates out clearly what most needs distinguishing in his work, the conceptual and the empirical. The early Sartre ascribed to human existence as such, a freedom and a contingency whose almost unavoidable consequence was bad faith. But although bad

faith appears not to be inevitable, Sartre never appears to base his claims as to how widespread bad faith is upon empirical generalization. The later Sartre ascribes our fate of serialization to contingent features of human existence which belong to bourgeois society, not to man as such. But once again he appears not to derive his assertions from empirical generalizations but rather from conceptual considerations. In both earlier and later writings Sartre's plethora of lengthy examples suffers because he does not analyze with sufficient clarity the concepts which he is allegedly illustrating. The clue to the difficulty here perhaps lies in his novels and plays. His examples often tend toward small-scale works of imagination, and it may be that the philosophical arguments are better treated as elucidations of points in the novel and plays rather than *vice versa*. The examples would then appear as the core of the philosophical writings; and this would exemplify a constant existentialist theme, that of concreteness as opposed to abstraction. In France, at least, existentialism has above all informed a literary imagination and enjoyed a literary vogue. Not only Sartre is in point here but also Camus and Marcel.

The Vulgarizers: Camus and Marcel

WHY should I not commit suicide? Camus' philosophical essay, *The Myth of Sisyphus*, begins with this question and with the claim that this is the most central of all philosophical questions. But any claims that traditional philosophy might have either to assess this claim or to answer this question are disposed of very speedily. A few sentences from Aristotle are misread, the claims of traditional rationalism are disallowed, and characters as various as Don Juan, Kafka, and Dostoievski hold the stage. The essence of Camus' argument is simple; human life confronts an alien universe. The values of human life have no foothold. And therein lies its meaning. In giving way neither to falsely grounded hopes, nor to despair because such hopes are overthrown, we find the significance of human effort. We confront a world of the absurd, where contingency reigns, where there is no sufficient reason. And in the modern world the man who does this, who has been deprived of the false solaces of traditional rationalism, whether religious or antireligious, is the absurd man. He is among Dostoievski's characters, he is Kafka's hero, he is studied in Camus' novels. In fact, Camus' novels are far more interesting than his philosophical writings; but they exhibit just as clearly how the existentialist clothing of Camus' ideas is no more than clothing. The ideas themselves are old and familiar. For Camus is in fact an heir of the Enlightenment, an old-fashioned atheist, but an old-fashioned atheist who writes in a situation where theism can no longer be the main enemy because it was defeated too long ago. So he is preoccupied with old problems in a new setting: the nature of atheistic sanctity and virtue (*La Peste* and *La Chute*) and the dangers which arise from absolutizing and deifying the values of the rebellion against religion and tyranny since the Enlightenment (*L'Homme Revolté*).

If Camus is a conventional atheist behind his existentialist vocabulary, Gabriel Marcel is a conventional theist behind his. Marcel, in fact, would scarcely be counted an existentialist had he not been forced into controversy with Sartre's atheism. He was originally a disciple of Royce's personal idealism, and his phenomenological analyses of such states as hope and despair owe little to Husserl. Marcel's preoccupations have been similar to those of Karl Jaspers, although he has never constructed a system, for his philosophy is seriously antisystematic. Marcel distinguishes between what he calls problems and what he calls mysteries. Problems are characteristic of the natural sciences; they concern matters about which we can be objective, which are outside our personal existence. We can assemble all the data and we can offer a definitive solution. Mysteries are perplexities where we ourselves constitute part of the problem, where we cannot stand apart and be objective. There can be no definitive solutions here, and thus philosophy and religion, where a concern with mysteries is characteristic, are not problem-solving activities.

It is worth mentioning this aspect of Marcel at least because it focusses attention upon an assumption of much existentialist philosophy. It is often asserted by existentialists that problems which involve the character of human life or, more especially, which involve self-knowledge are problems where there can be no objective argument or discussion. This is perhaps partly due to a confusion between the problem of trying to be objective in arriving at self-knowledge (a real but not a philosophical problem) and that of trying to be objective in analyzing the concept of self-knowledge or speaking about self-knowledge (which is surely no special problem at all). But it is also perhaps due to the highly unsatisfactory way in which more orthodox philosophers discuss the problem. There is a real gap at this point in the philosophy of mind which the criticism of Cartesianism has done nothing to fill. And on the whole existentialists rush in where analytical philosophers fail to tread.

Theological Existentialism

THE relation of some theologians to existentialism is much closer than that of Camus or Marcel. If one begins with Kierkegaard himself, one is bound to pass at once to Karl Barth whose commentary on the *Epistle to the Romans* (1918) uses Kierkegaard's concept of fundamental choice and some of Kierkegaard's psychological analyses in order to elucidate St. Paul. Barth here marks a break not merely with the liberal neo-Kantian Protestant theology which he was explicitly attacking but even with the neo-Calvinism which he was avowedly defending. For Calvin, although he would have seen many decisions for the believer to make, would never have thought of decision as our way of coming to know the truth that God exists. When Barth makes all hang upon decision, however, he is at least faithful to traditional Protestant (and Catholic) orthodoxy in his description of the content of the Christian belief to which we have access by our decision. So far as he is a philosopher, Barth is an existentialist philosopher, but to characterize him as a philosopher at all is perhaps a mistake, since Barth derives the necessity of choice from the nature of Pauline Christianity, and although he uses philosophical arguments in the commentary upon *Romans*, he was later to express doubts about his own procedure in so doing. It is quite other with Rudolf Bultmann, who is a Heideggerian existentialist through and through.

Bultmann is a New Testament scholar who believes that the New Testament message stands in need of demythologizing. It is mythological because it presents an existential message, a message to do with *Dasein*, as though it were a cosmology. The pre-scientific cosmology of the New Testament is Gnostic in content: it pictures a three-story universe and man on the earth poised between God on the one hand and the powers of darkness on the other. This cosmology conceals what is essentially being said, which is that in the person of Jesus men are called upon to choose between authentic human existence in which the limits of our life are faced up to and, more particularly, our death is faced up to, and an inauthentic existence in which we are the prey of our own refusal to face up to *Angst* and *Sorge*. It is difficult to resist the suggestion that for Bultmann Jesus is an early and imperfect anticipator of Heidegger. Bultmann himself would deny this. He would argue that what makes his view distinctively Christian is the contention that we cannot make the transition from inauthentic to authentic existence by our own power. But about this it is clear that Bultmann believes that we can acquire the necessary power simply by a decisive choice. Therefore it is difficult to see what it is that Heidegger asserts we can do which Bultmann denies. At the very least it is clear that Bultmann is vulnerable to every criticism to which Heidegger is vulnerable, or at least to which the Heidegger of *Sein und Zeit* is vulnerable.

Bultmann is perhaps unique in the detail of his existentialist commitment. Many other theologies have plundered the existentialist vocabulary or have used distinctions or concepts which are characteristic of certain trends in existentialism. Particularly unfortunate is the kinship here between certain types of theology, especially perhaps that of Paul Tillich, and Heidegger's revival of ontology in his post-war writings. In those writings Heidegger passes from *Dasein* to *Sein*; he produces an aphoristic and enigmatic yet extended account of being, which while it is unique to him, uses concepts which are present in Sartre, in Kierkegaard, and elsewhere. It is thus perhaps better at this point to examine the themes of being and existence as they appear generally in existentialist writing in order to understand the roots of the confusion with which we are faced, and avoid being distracted overmuch by the details of particular existentialist expositions.

Existentialist Themes

BEING AND EXISTENCE

A. J. Ayer has castigated Sartre for the simple misuse of the verb "to be." It is quite true that Sartre, Heidegger, and others all use "being" and "nothing" as if they were the names of subjects which could have predicates ascribed to them. (The mistake is that of the Red King is Alice's world who thought that if nobody had passed the messenger on the road, nobody should have arrived first.) It is true also that they write as if being was a genus of which existence and non-existence were species. But it is untrue that these errors rest on simple confusion. They arise out of deep confusion. The basic existentialist confusion about existence arises perhaps from trying to say too many things at once. When the existentialist asserts that existence cannot be grasped in concepts, that it evades conceptualization, too often he puts the point rhetorically as Kierkegaard did: "What the philosophers say about Reality is often as disappointing as a sign you see in a shop window which reads: Pressing done Here. If you brought your clothes to be pressed, you would be fooled; for only the sign is for sale."[3] The point that philosophers deal in concepts, not in reality, is necessarily ambiguous. For "real" functions well as an adjective, but "reality" functions badly as a noun. When "real" is used significantly it is always in contrast to something else, and the force of "real" varies with what it is being contrasted with. In Madame Tussaud's one may look for a real policeman — rather than a waxwork model. In an argument one may ask whether an alleged exception to a rule is real — or only apparent. In looking at Van Meegeren's work one may ask how one can tell a real Vermeer from a forgery. But detach "real" from any such context and turn it into a noun and one is left without any clear sense. Among the meanings which existentialists appear to have intended to give to the contention that reality or existence cannot be fully conceptualized we can pick out at least two.

The first is the thesis that human existence evades conceptualization in a way that the existence of things does not. What is meant by this is perhaps that our characterizations of things are accurate or inaccurate, true or false, adequate or inadequate; we match up the description of the thing with the thing itself and there is an end to it. But in the case of people, how we characterize them, and the adequacy or otherwise of our characterizations, depends in part on how they characterize themselves. Moreover, the way in which we describe a thing will not of itself change the thing, but the way in which we describe people, if they become aware of it, may well change their behavior. The well-known phenomena of self-confirming and self-falsifying predictions are instances of this. That this is what some existentialists are speaking of when they speak of the impossibility of conceptualizing existence is suggested by their stress on the role of consciousness in human existence. But this is clearly not what Heidegger wishes us to attend to, for example, and the difficulty lies in explaining what he wishes to attend to without using his own language and so involving ourselves in his confusions. But a rational reconstruction might run something like this.

Let us begin with a lucid, even if mistaken, analysis of the concept of existence. Quine has argued that "to be is to be the value of a variable." The suggestion is that we are committed to asserting the existence of whatever we are committed to assigning as a value to a variable. The notion of existence is introduced after we are already familiar with the notion of a language containing variable expressions for individuals and for predicates. Such a language, if we take the notion of a variable seriously, must be a *formal* language. It therefore appears to follow from Quine's view that we can understand all that there is to understand about the notion of existence in terms which presuppose that anything that can be said can be formalized. This latter claim, even if true, has, however, to meet the difficulty that formalization is something that we do to and with statements and that we use alternative ways of formalizing statements in order to bring out different logical features of the structure of a given statement. What variables we are committed to, what values we are committed to assigning to them, will depend not just upon what we said in the initial statement (in some natural language) but also upon how we choose to formalize. And we have choices about formalization. There is no one single hidden logical form in a given statement which the logician only has to reveal. Michelangelo envisaged sculpture as chipping away the stone to reveal the form of the statue within; such a view of logical form seems to make the logician a Michelangelo. It follows from this that no one formalization of a given piece of discourse necessarily reveals the extent of our ontological commitments. And because we can never be sure that we have exhausted alternative possible ways of understanding we can never close the door on all further commitments. In other words, the question "What is there?" could never have a final answer.

It follows that no one way of talking (and one can include here with alternative modes of formalization, alternative ways of putting something in a natural language), nor even a number of different ways of talking, about a given subject-matter necessarily exhausts all that we want to say *is*. But it does not follow from this that *being* is a fish which the net of our concepts can never catch, that there *is* something which goes beyond everything our discourse and our concepts can identify, refer to, and characterize, namely existence itself. Because our language may always leave us with more to say it does not follow that there is something we can never say, something that lies beyond expression in conceptual form, something else which the word "existence" or the word "being" names. Yet just to this or to something akin to it most existentialist writers appear to wish to conclude. Sometimes, of course, they are merely making in dramatic form the familiar and correct point that "exists" is not a predicate in the sense that "is red" is a predicate. But whatever the starting point, or the logical force, of the consideration involved, the conclusion is the same, that over and above the existence of particular beings, there is something else, *being itself*.

Kierkegaard, Jaspers, Husserl, Heidegger, and Sartre all speak of being. In the case of Kierkegaard and of Sartre there is a reference back to Hegel's discussions. In the case of Husserl and Heidegger there is a reference back to the medieval scholastics as well. But in both these cases the use of "being" was controlled by a context which the existentialist writers remove. In Hegel's *Logic* the attempt is to set out those categories which are embedded in nature and spirit; the movement from one class of predicates to another is transformed into the self-movement of the absolute, and in the course of this transformation much nonsense gets talked along with some sense. But the original enterprise was not nonsensical or unintelligible. The medievals used and expounded Aristotle's treatment of being *qua* being in the *Metaphysics*, and Aristotle's treatment is at the opposite pole from any claim that being evades conceptualization. The Aristotelian account is an attempt to show the unity and the diversity of uses of the verb "to be." Just because being *qua* being is the most general of concepts it cannot be the name of a single elusive entity. The medieval use of Aristotle is complicated by the attempt to write into an Aristotelian schematism the Christian God. Every finite being exists in a particular mode, under particular limitations. God is not so particularized. Hence he is being without such modal limitations, and the scholastics referred both to this and to the Mosaic meaning of God as "I am that I am" when they spoke of God as *Esse Ipsum Subsistens* (subsistent being itself).

This scholastic willingness to speak of "esse" is entirely harmless so long as it is not detached from the Aristotelian (or earlier, the Platonic) framework in which it has a place. For we can assess the claims made about being in the light of the claims which we want to allow or disallow about the framework. But in the modern neo-Thomist revival Aquinas

was turned upside down as radically as Marx inverted Hegel, but unintentionally. For being was now presented as an independent subject-matter, but not as it is in Aristotle's *Metaphysics* as the object of conceptual enquiry. Rather, "being" is treated as the name of a *particular* subject-matter, albeit a very queer one, about which we can ask specific questions. This is not yet true, of course, in the nineteenth century.

The sobriety of the Aristotelian scheme is not lost in Brentano or indeed in Husserl. Kierkegaard's central positions do not depend on any of his Hegelian uses of "being." But with Heidegger and to a lesser extent with Sartre, being comes into its own. In Heidegger's later writings the starting point is from the question posed by Leibniz: why are there the things that there are rather than nothing? In Leibniz the answer to this question was the cosmological argument for the existence of God. In Heidegger the answer is that in the posing of the question we have not taken seriously the relation between being and what it is contrasted with, nothing. Heidegger proceeds to speak of being and nothing as contrasted powers, as well as contrasted realms. He allows that we can only speak of nothing as a thing, as something, at the cost of being unscientific. He concludes that the philosopher and the poet are here in a superior position to the scientific man. Of being and nothing he says that they are not objects; that logic cannot comprehend but presupposes them; that they are things which we scarcely grasp. Nietzsche with almost prophetic anticipation of Heidegger spoke of these concepts as "the last cloudy streak of evaporating reality"; Heidegger quotes him and argues that this bears testimony to the extremely elusive properties of being and nothing. Every accusation as to the indeterminateness of the concept of being is treated as if it were evidence of the indeterminateness of being.

Heidegger distinguishes between *Sein* (being) and *die Seienden* (existents). He in fact treats both terms as if they are names of objects, in spite of all his denials. But this is not his basic mistake, which is to suppose that because an expression is used in some one context with a particular grammatical form it can be transferred without change or loss of sense to any context in the same grammatical form. To take the most simple kind of change, Heidegger takes to be equivalent the assertions "He is afraid of nothing in particular" and "What he is afraid of is nothing." It is not only Heidegger who speaks like this. Tillich does so also, and in Tillich's writings existentialist and scholastic terminology meet in a new way.

For Tillich God is not *a* being, but Being-Itself. The medieval scholastics who spoke like this did so because they had produced proofs of the divine existence of a kind which led them to contrast the divine being with contingent beings in specific ways. Their careful Aristotelianism also restricted them in their use of negatives with the verb "to be." Not so Tillich, who can speak of the power of being to resist non-being, in a manner very similar to that of Heidegger.

Tillich's relationship to Heidegger is in no sense accidental, not so much because of a direct indebtedness but because Tillich like Heidegger begins from and tries to go beyond a Husserlian concept of philosophy. He believes that in analyzing the structure of the categories of thought, as Husserl did, the philosopher is driven to recognize that these are the categories of a finite being, and to recognize further an unconditional ground behind that thought and its objects. Something not unlike the cosmological argument appears in Tillich, but just because Tillich does not present an argument he is all the more difficult to grapple with. The resemblance to Heidegger comes out when Tillich uses his ontological assertions in psychological contexts. The power of being to resist non-being and the fear of the encroachments of non-being upon being are used vividly by Tillich in describing neurotic anxiety. Kierkegaard's Nothing which is the object of our dread is only to be appeased and driven away by a secure hold on our existence. We can all imagine a rendering of this into psychiatric terms at once less dramatic and more susceptible of questions about truth, falsity, and testing. Heidegger, similarly, is at his most convincing in his psychology and at his most wayward in his ontology.

The culmination of this waywardness lies in the kind of dialogue which has been carried on between Heideggerian existentialists and the upholders of degenerate modern versions of scholasticism. The attempt to call Aquinas an existentialist is bad enough in itself; but debates about the character of being and not-being, the treatment of existence as a genus of which these two are species by existentialist writers, the disputes over the relative priority of essence and existence, mark a depth rarely reached in the history of philosophy, which has its counterpart in a systematic misreading of the history of philosophy. So, for example, a contemporary book of readings in metaphysics is able to suggest that there is a single question, "What is being?", to which Parmenides, Plato, Aristotle, and Descartes all give rival answers, Parmenides saying that it is One, Plato that "It is, through the Ideas, One and Many," Aristotle that "It is Substance, or that which *particularly* persists; and thus, both one and many," and Descartes that "It is Substance, but according to the modes of thought and extension."[4] The scholastic author is very easily able to then give Heidegger credit for giving yet another answer to the same question. But what matters is that there is no such question, posed just like that. Parmenides, Plato, Aristotle, and Descartes posed different questions and elaborated quite different types of conceptual schemes in each of which "being" or some cognate term or terms has a place. But there is no simple,

identifiable use of "being" independent of linguistic or conceptual context which we can use to pose the question "What is being?" with a view to comparing rival answers.

Heidegger is not merely indebted to this version of the history of philosophy; he is himself an important and original contributor to it. To the criticisms of his perversions of language Heidegger's reply would be that he is certainly using language in ways that we are not used to, but this is not because he is an innovator but because he is trying to return to that primal simplicity of language in which alone the truth about being is laid bare. The only philosophical vocabulary pure enough for this task is that of the Greek pre-Socratics, and Heidegger sees this vocabulary as rooted in Homeric Greek. His method is to look for etymologies of the words which became "truth," "being," and the like and then to use his alleged etymological roots are prime evidence of what the word really means. Unfortunately he first mistranslates his authors and makes philological mistakes in his etymologies. But worse still, he never explains how etymologies could be clues to concepts. What Heidegger fails to grasp here is of the first importance.

The pre-Socratic Greek philosophers were not doing just one thing; they were grappling with attempts at physical theories, with religious cosmologies, and with conceptual puzzles. When Parmenides proves that change and multiplicity must be illusory, beginning from such premises as "What is is," he is making the first moves toward producing a logical grammar of the verb "to be." The groping with tenses, participles, and infinitives reflects an assiduous attempt to discover what you must commit yourself to if you are to say anything. Plato follows this up in dialogues such as the *Sophist*, where the problem of negative judgment is already treated in such a way as to enable us to dispose of all Heidegger's problems as to how we can speak of what is not. Heidegger insists upon treating pre-Platonic Greek writers not as making the earliest attempts at elucidations which Plato, Aristotle, and their successors could then use to improve upon, but as expressing final insights by means of definitive concepts. To do this he has to mistranslate at least one of Parmenides' uses of the verb "to be" and produce spurious etymologies for such expressions as "truth" and "to say."

What is unfortunate about these later writings of Heidegger is that they have helped to turn some contemporary Continental philosophy into a shared cult of ritual phrases rather than a serious conceptual enquiry. Heidegger's nonsense is harmful nonsense. But it is in fact not, strictly speaking, existentialist nonsense. Had *Sein und Zeit* remained Heidegger's testament, had we otherwise only Sartre's developments of Heidegger's thought and not Heidegger's own development of it, we would have had for criticism a much tougher and more interesting task. For the crucial *existentialist* thesis is not that existence is a realm beyond particular existents, but that existence, and especially human existence, is simply absurd. To this theme therefore we must now turn.

THE ABSURD

"The Absurd" has been the preoccupation of French, rather than German, existentialism. When Sartre calls existence absurd he appears to combine two main contentions. The first is that things have no sufficient reason for being as they are and not otherwise. The second is that things are contingent and not necessary. We can begin by considering the latter. An Anglo-Saxon analytical philosopher might be inclined to argue as follows. That the existence of material objects, including people, is contingent, that "Such-and-such an object exists" is always a contingent truth and not a necessary one, is itself a necessary truth. To wish that it were otherwise is therefore to wish that the denial of a necessary truth could be asserted as true. But the denial of a necessary truth expresses a logical impossibility, and just as we cannot make sense of that which is logically impossible, we cannot make sense of wishing that what is logically impossible should be so. For we cannot say what it is we would be wishing for. This argument, however, contains two important mistakes. The first is that it contains a very crude notion of what it is for an expression to have meaning or to make sense. Because an expression apparently denotes what it is logically impossible should be the case or exist, it does not follow that the expression does not have meaning. Indeed, it is a condition of our characterizing the expression as we do, it is a condition of our detecting the logical impossibility involved, that we should understand its meaning. This is true both in simple cases, like "round square," and in complex cases like those where a mathematician understands a formula as a preliminary to proving that it cannot be a theorem of a system because it is internally inconsistent. Such a proof may be long and laborious, and at a stage when the mathematician does not yet know whether the formula is or is not inconsistent he may well hope that it is consistent and can be proved to be a theorem, because, if it can be, certain other mathematical and even physical possibilities will be opened up. When he discovers the inconsistency he may then lament that it is so, and we should all understand him. So that there is nothing nonsensical about lamenting that necessary truths are what they are and not otherwise. Hence when Sartre laments the contingency of things, so far he does not violate sense. But to have shown this is not enough to vindicate Sartre.

When the mathematician lamented his inconsistency proof, the point of his lament was that were there not inconsistencies, other possibilities would open up. But for these, we might understand the words which the mathematician used to lament, but we would not understand his lament. We would not know what he had to regret. We should understand what he said, but not what he did. How are we to understand what Sartre does when he laments contingency? What possibilities are closed to him which would otherwise be open? What was the point of writing *La Nausée* or the relevant parts of *L'Etre et Le Néant*?

A reading of *La Nausée* suggests strongly that the contingency of things is lamentable precisely because they lack *therefore* a sufficient reason for being as they are. That this is so affects things and people differently. Things just *are* in all their nauseating fullness. They do not point beyond or outside themselves as do the contingent beings of Aquinas' "Third Way." Their being contingent is not a lack for them. Here there is nothing to lament. But with human existence the lack of a sufficient reason for oneself *and* for things being as they are means an imperfection, a Sartrian rendering of what Heidegger calls "fallenness." We are in a senseless world, of which we ceaselessly and inevitably try to make sense. This is the absurdity both of things and of ourselves. Can we make sense of lamenting the lack of a sufficient reason? Only if we suppose that if the universe were what Leibniz, or Hegel in his more rationalist metaphysical moods, said it was should we have possibilities opened to us which are now denied to us. But on Sartre's own showing, if Leibniz or Hegel were right we should cease to be free. Sartre of course speaks of us as condemned to freedom, so perhaps it is right to lament a state of affairs which entails our freedom. Yet at the same time Sartre clearly shows that all the possibilities of characteristically human life are bound up with the possession of freedom. So that about the Sartrian lament there is something false. What it is comes out very clearly if we compare the Sartrian picture of human naure in *La Nausée* with what Simone de Beauvoir says in her memoir about Sartre's life and attitudes at the time at which he was writing it. Sartre is there pictured as leading an eager, meaningful life, with many friends and projects. His fictional creature, Antoine Roquentin, has a meaningless, empty existence by contrast, and the power of Sartre's portrayal is in the claim that Roquentin is discovering the reality beneath the surface, the false solidity of social life hiding the metaphysical void. Yet Sartre does not behave as though this were true. His confidence in his own novel reaches far beyond Roquentin's desperate hope that writing a book might rescue him from contingency. What then induced Sartre's bad faith? (For Sartre's own behavior and its lack of coherence with his professed doctrines is a striking example of bad faith.) At least two reasons can be suggested.

The first is that Sartre is a disappointed rationalist. I do not by saying this point only to Sartre's well-known Cartesian tendencies. I mean, rather, that he continuously writes as if he expects something like the Cartesian or the Leibnizian or the Hegelian view of the world to be true, and is disappointed that it is not. Everything ought to be necessarily as it is, the parts all finite manifestations of a single rational whole, each with a sufficient reason for being what and as it is, which if we only knew it would provide a rational justification and explanation of a totally satisfying kind. The importance in Sartre's scheme of the human aspiration to the condition of God is only intelligible on this view. This also explains why when Sartre makes conceptual points long familiar from the writings of the British empiricists he does so with a sense of drama or even melodrama which is notably absent in Locke, Berkeley, and Hume. Or is this always true? When at the end of Book I of *A Treatise of Human Nature* Hume describes his experience of epistemological vertigo we are very close to the world of *La Nausée*: "I am confounded with all these questions, and begin to fancy myself in the most deplorable condition imaginable, environed with the deepest darkness, and utterly deprived of the use of every member and faculty."[5] What questions? Questions that make Hume "look upon no opinion even as more probable or likely than another." Why? Because all questions of likelihood rest upon inductive generalizations, and Hume has argued that we cannot justify inductive arguments. The arguments which Hume uses here amount, as has often been noticed, to pointing out that inductive arguments cannot be justified deductively, that we can find no clear and certain self-authenticating first principle from which to deduce what we need for inductive argument. In other words, the empiricist failure to justify induction rests upon an acceptance of rationalist standards of justification. Hume's empiricism is that of a disappointed rationalist. But at this point Hume turns to the solaces of friendship and backgammon; he invokes nature and the force of custom and habit. We argue inductively from custom and habit and there's an end on't. No amount of skeptical doubt can prevail against nature. This is the move that is not open to Sartre. For him custom and habit are falsifications, disguises. His discovery that the expectations of metaphysical rationalism are necessarily disappointed leaves him characterizing the world as lacking something. Where he ought to go a stage further back in the argument, and question the whole rationalist use of such terms as "sufficient reason," he retains this language and characterizes the world by saying that the world is such that the rationalist descriptions do not and cannot be applied to it. This is like supposing that when one has shown that animist forms of description do not apply to trees and rocks, one has adequately characterized trees and rocks. The refutation of primitive religion is no substitute for botany or geology; the refutation of metaphysical rationalism is no substitute for an adequate logic and conceptual psychology. But this

is not the whole story. There is another and a complicating factor. This is that the shock of the discovery that there are no sufficient reasons, no ultimate justifications (in the sense intended by rationalist metaphysics and also by a certain kind of theology which closely resembles it) is not private to Sartre. The question of ultimate justification for beliefs and standards remains relatively unimportant for most people when social forms are stable and social conflict is minimal. When, however, the support of custom and habit, which constitute civilized social life and are neither the work of nature as Hume thought or of self-deception as Sartre thinks, is withdrawn, as it has been in periods of rapid industrial change, of war, of prison camps and torture, of Nazism and the totalitarian state, people are forced to ask questions about justification which normally just do not arise. Moreover all their normal responses are put in question by extreme situations. What were socially approved and praised public acts, having familiar utilitarian justifications, become private gestures in a social void. The question "But what would happen if everybody acted like you?" has no more force when everybody has been acting much worse than you for a very long time. And something like this was the case in a large part of Europe from 1933 until 1945, to go no further afield.

In this situation the psychology of the absurd man, of the man who gestures in the void, becomes crucial. But Sartre's study of this man is defective in an important way. Consider two other studies of the psychology of the absurd or the extreme situation. The psychoanalyst Bruno Bettelheim, when put in Dachau and Buchenwald by Hitler, found that the way the prisoners reacted to the extremity of their situation was not what he would have expected on the basis of his past experience of and theorizing about ordinary life. So that when he began to theorize about the psychology of extreme situations it was in a context where concentration camp behavior was contrasted with "normal" behavior. Or take instead as even closer to Sartre's preoccupations the central character of Camus' novel *L'Étranger*. He has no normal human emotions or responses. Things happen to him and he performs actions, but all in an emotional vacuum. He neither hopes nor despairs. He is neither interested nor uninterested. He just is. The death of a mother, the wishes of a girl-friend, the chance killing of an unknown person — these are all the kind of events which have normal and standard, though not uniform, responses of various types. What are we to make of someone not characterized by these responses, and so radically lacking them that it is not enough to say that he is not sad or repentant? For him these are attributes that he scarcely understands. The words lack meaning for him. Why are we deeply moved by Camus' novel? In part, at least, by the contrast with ordinary human life. The meaning and point of the normal responses are thrown into sharp relief by this picture of a man who lacks them. But it is essential both to the structure of the novel and to our understanding of its central character that he should be abnormal and exceptional. Without this contrast with the normal we should be at a loss and the novel would be deprived of its point, just as Bettelheim's explanations of concentration camp behavior would lose their point if the backcloth of ordinary life were taken away. Yet this is the backcloth which is lacking in Sartre's philosophical writings, though it is certainly not lacking, at least by implication and sometimes by statement, in his novels after *La Nausée* and above all in his plays. And thus the absurdity which infects Sartrian man's existence is deprived of its point. But at the same time the vogue of Sartre is easily explained. He provides a picture of human existence which can easily be accepted by many uprooted and displaced people; he offers an explanation of why others do not see themselves like this, when he cites bad faith. Curiously, Sartre in his social philosophy identifies the deceptions of custom and habit with the social life of the bourgeoisie — curiously because probably the majority of those who recognize the application of Sartre's picture to themselves are rootless members of the bourgeois class. I do not think many French workers are Sartrians.

In Hegel "the unhappy consciousness" belongs to one historical phase, to one psychological type. It is the clue to one sort of man, not to men. It cannot be the clue to human nature, just because the problems of the unhappy consciousness can be resolved. Equally, when modern psychoanalysts recognize the experience of the absurd or Kierkegaardian dread or Sartrian nausea in their patients, they see these as symptoms of a condition that can be or needs to be cured. But in Sartre we are faced with a description of the human condition which suggests no alternative but the drastic, conceptually confused, political alternatives of the *Critique*.

CHOICE

To all this the reply might be that what is being underestimated is the extent to which Sartre in fact proves his points. For independent testimony can be adduced to support Sartre in such contentions as that no one else can choose moral principles for me, that in the end I can only stand firm on my choice of principles, and the like. Neither David Hume nor R. M. Hare are usually taken for existentialists, but Sartre leans heavily not only on Hume's thesis that we cannot deduce an "ought" from an "is," but even more upon a view of justification fundamentally similar to that of Hare. For Hare, when we have specified the consequences of acting upon the sort of principle we have chosen, when we have specified the way of life of which this principle is a part, the justification for principles is at an end.[6] Here we can no longer argue, we can only

decide. But this is apparently Sartre's ethical position also, and even Kierkegaard's. The view is the opposite of Aristotle's that deliberation and choice belong together — for Hare and Sartre alike, where there is no further room for deliberation, choice is in place. This choice is necessarily criterionless.

One reason why a point apparently of cold logic in Hume or in Hare becomes a dramatic point of controversy in Sartre is that Hume and even Hare are able to assume a social context of widespread moral agreement and Sartre is not. When we know what to choose morally, to be told that our choices have no further justification will not disturb us as it will when we do not know what to choose, and are looking for reasons to turn one way rather than another. But are Hare and Sartre in fact right? Are there criterionless choices and do they underlie moral principles? One could approach this in a number of ways. One would be to ask for examples of choices and to study the relationship of choice to criteria. Here it would perhaps turn out that actual examples of apparently criterionless choices seem always to be special and misleading cases, such as the choice of a numbered ticket from a hat in a raffle, where there must be no criterion for deciding between one ticket and another, because the whole point is that the selection shall be random. And this is to say that the choice is governed by a criterion, namely that each ticket shall have an equal chance of selection. In any case, choice of moral principles does not appear to be like *that*. Moreover, it follows from the Sartre-Hare view that a moral principle can (logically) have any content whatsoever. What moral principles one has depends on one's choices, and these, being not restricted by criteria of choice, can be of anything at all. But we are strongly inclined to say that if a man avowedly made it a moral principle that one ought always to walk about with one's hand on one's head we should find what he said unintelligible. If we discovered that he had a belief that doing this prevented some disease, or gave pleasure to himself or others, or was connected with some other recognizable human good, we should begin to understand. And this suggests strongly that the content of moral principles is not open for us to choose, just like that; that we are limited by the character of the concept of a good. But to admit this would involve Sartre in admitting his *bête-noire*, an objective moral order of some sort.

We can understand in any case an oddity in Sartre's position when we consider the fact that desires appear to play no role in providing criteria of choice. The reason for this is simple. Sartre thinks that desires and emotions themselves are chosen. If I am sad, he argues, it is because I choose to be. He pictures a man in a state of melancholy, who rouses himself to a state of interest and cheerfulness when someone else enters the room. But it does not follow from this, as Sartre supposes, that the man can be sad or not as he chooses. It would be much more natural to say that he can rouse himself from his sadness, if he wants something else badly enough, such as not to show his sadness to someone else. This absence of an account of desires and emotions as unchosen is linked, of course, to Sartre's unwillingness to give causal explanations of human behavior. The merit of Kierkegaard, Heidegger, and Sartre is that they do not omit the intentional element from their account of affective life; but insofar as they suggest that this is incompatible with giving a causal account, what they say is difficult to understand.

Existentialism: A Possible Explanation

IT is, however, not so difficult to understand how the existentialist position was arrived at historically. Consider the period in philosophy which began with Descartes and ended with Kant. In this period certain epistemological problems were posed but not solved. They could not be solved because of the assumptions which dominated the conceptual framework within which they were posed. There is the isolated, single knowing subject out of whose epistemological resources the whole of knowledge has to be reconstructed. There is the use of a deductive model in setting out the organization of our knowledge with the consequent search for logically guaranteed axioms, or for the hard data of sense-experience. There is the assumption that skeptical difficulties can be overcome, and a willingness to invoke God to overcome them when argument breaks down. Descarte's God bridges the gap between my ideas and the physical world. Kant's God bridges the gulf between duty and inclination. Hume's nature is very much a *deus ex machina*.

Hegel abandoned the epistemological assumptions of the Descartes to Kant era. But he appeared to make the price of a solution to the philosophical problems the acceptance of his system. And those who rejected the system were apt to retreat to the assumptions of an earlier age. With Kierkegaard this is at best implicit. Certainly we can see the choice between the ethical and the aesthetic as a replica of Kant's choice between duty and inclination, but with the rational basis removed. And more generally, the Kierkegaardian individual resembles the Cartesian "I" without the *Cogito*. This resemblance is reinforced by the explicit Cartesianism of Husserl which Sartre inherits. Sartrian man is Cartesian man in his theory of knowledge, and Kantian man in his ethics, with rational first principles having been replaced by criterionless choices. There is no God

or nature to guarantee the rationality of the universe; and there is the same absence of a background of socially established and recognized criteria, which is necessary to make the knowledge we possess and the way we come to possess it intelligible. Sartrian man is the heir of Descartes' lonely epistemological hero.

Is, then, existentialism a series of mistakes and nothing more? Even if this were all it would not be valueless. The saying that to be ignorant of the history of philosophy is to be doomed to repeat it is relevant here. In one sense, and quite another than that intended by the existentialists, a great deal of existentialism constitutes a *reductio ad absurdum* of certain philosophical theories. By forcing them to an unacceptable conclusion we obtain a much clearer view of what is wrong with them and also therefore of what we ought to say instead. But embedded in Sartre and Heidegger and Kierkegaard there are certain paramount insights, especially in the philosophy of mind. Disentangling them from the confines in which they are embedded belongs to the future history of philosophy rather than to the past history of existentialism. Sartre, for example, in his early essay on the emotions does not merely say of them that they are intentional: he expounds a whole theory of them as purposive attempts to change the world by quasi-magical means. My horror is an attempt to get rid of what horrifies me. Kierkegaard's analysis, in the course of his discussion of the aesthetic, of tragic pain and why we feel it, is a brilliant analysis of the difference between seeing what happens to a man as due to a flaw in him and seeing what happens to him as due to a flaw in the universe. Heidegger's secularization of Augustine on temporality and the experience of temporality is not inextricably bound up with his ontology. In every case there is a serious, if not a final, contribution to those studies which lie on the margin of philosophy and psychology.

The paradox of existentialism is that one of the great existentialist slogans has been to deny the possibility of constructing a philosophical system; that not one of the major existentialists has escaped doing this; and that with all of them the systematic form has done just what they said it would do, tortured and distorted their individual conceptual insights into less acceptable forms than they would otherwise have had. The lesson to be learnt is that in philosophy system is almost unavoidable; that to recognize this is to be able to use systematic forms without too much danger, but that to fail to recognize it is almost inevitably to fall victim to that which one professes to despise so much.

29

Contemporary British Philosophy

A. M. QUINTON

BRITISH PHILOSOPHY in the twentieth century has gone through three main stages. First of all, there is the realistic doctrine worked out by Russell and Moore in the first decade of the century in comprehensive opposition to the reigning idealism of the school of Green and Bradley. The main lines of this body of ideas are drawn clearly enough in Russell's *Problems of Philosophy* and Moore's *Some Main Problems of Philosophy* (both written before 1914, although Moore's book was not published until 1953). Between the wars, this realism was more or less the official academic doctrine despite the fact that its two founders moved away from it in different directions to inspire the other two main developments of the period.

The second stage may be called by Russell's name for it, the philosophy of logical analysis, since it is from Russell, together with the early Wittgenstein of the *Tractatus Logico-Philosophicus* (1922), that it principally derives. In the 1920's this philosophy took the form of logical atomism, as defined by Russell's lectures of 1918–1919 and most elaborately expounded in the *Tractatus*. Its ideas were the central ingredient of the thinking of the Vienna Circle and were reintroduced in the 1930's as logical positivism, most memorably in Ayer's *Language, Truth and Logic* (1936). What was perhaps the most substantial exposition of the ideas of this general movement in English came from the United States in C. I. Lewis's *Mind and the World-Order* (1929).

Linguistic philosophy is the most familiar name for the third stage, for the point of view of Wittgenstein, Ryle, and the ordinary language philosophers of Oxford that has dominated British philosophy since the second world war. Moore was in no sense the leader of this school, but the example of his practice in philosophizing, particularly in the later essays collected in *Philosophical Papers* (1959), was a very important influence on it, as was his insistence on the imperviousness of common-sense knowledge to the erosions of philosophical doubt. Wittgenstein's *Philosophical Investigations* (1953) and Ryle's *Concept of Mind* (1949), for all their differences, had in common a conception of philosophy as the elimination of metaphysical and skeptical paradox by attention to the actual meaning of language, a theory of meaning which found it in the use of words rather than in a realm of abstract entities and a theory of mind as present rather in the overt bodily activities of men than in their more or less inscrutable inner feelings.

In the last few years the hold of, at any rate, one crucial aspect of linguistic philosophy has conspicuously weakened. Since Austin's death in 1960 the hostile attitude to general and systematic theory implied by his more than Moorean dedication to detailed and piecemeal inquiry has largely disappeared. With Popper, Strawson, and Hampshire, the idea of systematic philosophy seems once more to be coming into its own.

Realism

THE realism that Russell and Moore elaborated together in the years before 1914 began negatively, as a comprehensive refutation of the main theses of the prevailing idealism. The fundamental principle of idealism was logical, the theory of internal relations which held that the nature of a thing was essentially constituted by its relations to other things. It followed from this that the truth about the world could not be obtained by the analytic understanding, which considered things in an artificial and so distorted isolation from one another, but only by the more synthetic reason, which apprehended things in their interconnectedness. The realist answer was a distinction between the essential and accidental nature of things. The essential properties and relations of a thing were those it had by definition, those which it must have if it were to be correctly identified as a thing of the kind it was. All its other properties and relations were contingent. They could be changed without the thing forfeiting its identity. The idealists applied their concept of internality to a wide field of topics. It was held to prove that, since everything in the world was somehow related to everything else, the world as a whole was a single substance, the sole complete and self-subsistent entity, whose parts could not be adequately conceived in abstraction from it. Applied to perception, it yielded epistemological idealism, the theory that subject and object in perception were not distinct and independent existences but two phases or aspects of a single experience. Applied to thought, it was used to discredit the distinction of particular and universal, both of which were seen as ultimately illegitimate abstractions from the only real object of thought, the concrete and systematic individual. Applied to belief, it was taken to show that truth did not consist in any external relation between heterogeneous propositions and facts but in the coherence, the systematic mutual implication, of judgments. Finally, it was held that the type of unity exhibited by the single concrete substance that was the world, Green's "eternal consciousness" or Bradley's "Absolute," was mental. Minds and societies of minds, although themselves still infected by abstraction and incompleteness, were the closest approximations amongst familiar things to reality, and certainly much closer than material objects.

Rejecting the internality of all relations, the realists vigorously resuscitated the victims of this principle. Moore, in the first classic text of realism, refuted epistemological idealism by distinguishing between the mental act of perception and its possibly and frequently physical objects. Russell revived the correspondence theory of truth by demonstrating the viciously regressive nature of the coherence theory and its inability to give reasons for choosing between mutually incompatible but internally consistent systems of beliefs. Mind-body dualism, entailed by the realist account of perception, was defended against the view that reality was exclusively mental in character. The more or less Platonic view of universals and propositions as self-subsistent abstract entities, neither mental nor physical, was supported by Russell as necessary to any adequate account of mathematical knowledge. The most thorough and sympathetic presentation of the realist critique, diffused in its first appearance through numerous writings of Russell and Moore, is to be found in A. C. Ewing's *Idealism: A Critical Survey* (1934), in which the whole argument is systematically set out.

The realists divided reality into the realms of the abstract and the concrete. The abstract realm of timeless universals and propositions was accessible to *a priori* insight and afforded knowledge of necessary truth. The concrete realm was an infinite plurality of externally related existences, some physical and some mental, of which we had contingent knowledge by perception and introspection respectively. Things and their properties were mutually irreducible. A concrete object derived its individuality from the substance that it contained over and above its characteristics, and a universal, on the other side, was something more than the collection of its instances. Truth consisted in the correspondence between a proposition, generally thought of as abstract but by Russell sometimes as mental, and a fact, usually treated as physical but presumably mental or abstract if introspective or necessary. Against the idealists who had held that all our beliefs, with the possible exception of the beliefs of idealist metaphysics, were corrigible and less than certainly true, the realists contended that certainty could be obtained in the field of necessary truth, by introspection and even by perception to the extent that its immediate deliverances were concerned. Generally speaking, realists favored the causal theory of perception of Russell's *Problems of Philosophy* which took the existence of an independent material world to be the simplest hypothesis capable of explaining the order of our sense-experience. Moore, though he always seems to have preferred this view, did at times hesitate between it and the phenomenalist theory that the material world could be simply identified with the regular pattern of actual and possible experience suggested by the actual course of our impressions. The problem, at any rate, attracted more of the attention of realists than any other. Self-knowledge was regarded as introspective and incorrigible; knowledge of the minds of others was accounted for by analogical inference. The mind itself was generally conceived as a substance, the subject of mental acts and the bestower of identity on the sequence of our mental states. But the substance theory of the mind evoked the same sort of hesitation as the causal theory of perception.

Realists were divided about the nature of causality.

On the one hand, the Humean theory of constant conjunction, favored by Russell, seemed to leave out the essential connectedness of cause and effect, but, on the other, the rationalist view that causation involved some sort of entailment of the effect by the cause seemed too close to the theory of internal relations. It was dissatisfaction with Hume that led Whitehead back to the acceptance of internal relations and it was on the basis of a rationalist theory of causation as entailment that Blanshard in his *Nature of Thought* (1939) was able to present the most plausible defense that the internal relations theory has received. More agreement was secured about the nature of induction, whose justification was based by realists on the synthetic and necessary truth of the principle of the uniformity of nature. Their theory of probability was provided by Keynes, who defined it, in his *Treatise on Probability* (1921), as an intuitable logical relation between evidence and hypothesis.

Idealist ethical theory had taken as the criterion of moral excellence the perfection or self-realization of the individual. In accordance with the idealists' preference for the more to the less inclusive and systematic, the realization of the individual was generally conceived as best achieved by his subordination of himself to the common good, to the demands of society or the state. Following Hegel, they rated the historically authorized wisdom of the community higher than the individual conscience. Realists took moral value to be ideal and self-subsistent, accessible to a special form of intuition and transcending social and historical actuality. Right action, furthermore, had intrinsic value, it did not derive its value from that of the ends, whatever they might be, to which it was directed. Moore, indeed, derived the rightness of actions from the goodness of their consequences, though he shared the more general opinion of the ideal nature of the good as something open to specifically moral intuition. Most realists were unconvinced by idealist reconciliation of moral responsibility with determinism. For the most part, they asserted that the human will had a contra-causal freedom and was a genuine initiator of events. On the whole, realists were more technical philosophers than the idealists had been. Their interests were largely confined to the hard central core of the subject and they had little to say about art, politics, and religion, that domain of the higher forms of human mental activity which the idealists, following the example of Hegel, had so extensively cultivated. Moore held that aesthetic, like moral, value (of which, indeed, it was a species) was an object of immediate intuition. The realist philosophy of politics asserted a comparable analogy between natural rights and moral obligations, seeing both as necessary truths, self-evident to rational insight. In the field of religion, realists were generally skeptical. But the criticisms they developed of traditional deductive arguments for the dogmas of religion at least assumed that it was on arguments of this kind that religious belief must rest if it was to have any rational justification at all. The realists had no general or *a priori* hostility to theology and metaphysics. In particular, they did not, like their positivist successors, question the intelligibility of metaphysical and theological propositions. Broadly speaking, they were sympathetic to the metaphysical enterprise of attempting to arrive by rational means at a general picture of the world, even if they did not much practice metaphysics, and they did not rule out the possibility that philosophical reflection might come to conclusions incompatible with common sense convictions even when they followed Moore in attaching a good deal of weight to those convictions. They were largely content to say that the results of traditional philosophical speculation had an insufficient rational foundation rather than they were false, let alone meaningless.

This somewhat negative open-mindedness about metaphysics derived from their general conception of philosophical method. They rejected the demonstrative ideal common to the classic rationalism of the seventeenth century and to idealists like Bradley and McTaggart. Unconvinced by purported proofs of the inconsistency of the fundamental organizing concepts of ordinary thought — substance, cause, matter, space, and time — they took the task of philosophy to be the search for the presuppositions or first principles of knowledge. The common stock of human convictions was not an unquestioned datum of philosophy. Rational inquiry could reveal both that there was more to the world than this common stock included — universals, propositions, and values — and less — no physical secondary qualities and no God, for example. But it could not totally demolish the foundation on which it was erected. It could only revise it critically in both directions and present it in a systematic way.

The most copious and representative of realists was C. D. Broad. The nearest he came to a comprehensive statement of his views was in his massive and imposing *Examination of McTaggart's Philosophy* (1933–1938), which is as much a substantive independent discussion of the main problems of philosophy as a critique of the most brilliantly articulated version of idealism. In other works, Broad defended the representative theory of perception, an anti-conventionalist theory of scientific knowledge, mind-body dualism, and a form of intuitionist ethics which combined ideas from Moore with those of the more deontological Oxford moralists. Approximately the same views were expressed in the numerous works of John Laird and A. C. Ewing, and in the writings of the distinguished historian of logic, W. C. Kneale. In the years when Russell and Moore were preparing their refutations of idealism in Cambridge, an analogous movement of thought was getting more slowly and cautiously under way in Oxford under the leadership of Cook Wilson.

Prichard, Cook Wilson's ablest follower, set out the position of this group in his *Kant's Theory of Knowledge* (1906), and it was developed at greater length in Cook Wilson's posthumous *Statement and Inference* (1926). The principal weakness of Oxford realism was its almost exclusively negative character, the outcome of an essential timidity under the pugnacious surface of Cook Wilson's personality and of the narrowly destructive temperament of Prichard. They were content to make minute and painstaking assaults on particular parts of the great loose structure of idealism and to assert such positive doctrines as they had to offer on the basis of their self-evidence. They were as hostile to Russell's logic as they were to Bradley's. Oxford realism was the philosophy of grammarians, dedicated to the pursuit of detail and correctness, and it has more than its respect for the established usage of words in common with the ordinary language philosophy of Oxford in recent times. Austin's known admiration for Prichard was strictly consonant with the fundamental lines of his attitude to philosophy. The ethical doctrines of the Oxford realists were more articulate and influential than their philosophical logic and theory of knowledge. Prichard was the first of the "Oxford moralists," and in the essays collected in *Moral Obligation* (1949) expounded the theory that any interpretation of the principles of duty which saw them not as self-evident but as derivable from propositions about the consequences to which their adoption would lead inevitably transformed them from rules of morals into counsels of expediency. W. D. Ross qualified the extremity of this position; first, by admitting the intrinsically consequential principle of producing as much good as possible into the set of *a priori* duties and, secondly, by introducing a *ceteris paribus* clause into the formulation of the self-evident principles in order to cope with the problem of the conflict of duties. E. F. Carritt applied the Prichardian doctrine to aesthetics and politics as well as to morals, and J. P. Plamenatz, in his *Consent, Freedom and Political Obligation* (1938), produced the most penetrating and fully worked out realist philosophy of politics.

Something should be said here about two philosophers who, though sharing many of the beliefs about particular issues of the analytic successors of the realists, remained in the realist camp as far as philosophical method was concerned: H. H. Price and W. T. Stace. Price began his career as a follower of Prichard but came to deviate from orthodoxy under the influence of Russell. In his great book *Perception* (1932), the most thorough and important treatise on this subject in a period when it was the recognized centre of philosophy, he presented a theory which was, in all but one vestigial respect, phenomenalist. For Price, a material object was a family of sense-data, actual and possible, but, in order to deal with the objection that phenomenalism turns unobserved actualities into systems of merely possible entities, he says that there must also be a categorically existing "physical occupant," a Lockean substratum pensioned off as a kind of metaphysical nightwatchman to keep things in being when no one is perceiving them. Price's sympathies in the philosophy of mind appear to be with a Humean theory, in which the mind is seen as a related sequence of experiences. In his *Thinking and Experience* (1953) Hume is drawn on again; in particular, his theory of general ideas, from which Price develops an account of the use of concepts in terms of readiness to form images, utter words, or behave appropriately which neither identifies it with any one of them nor with the apprehension of the abstract, intelligible objects of the classical theory of thinking.

Stace is perhaps even closer to Hume. In his *Theory of Knowledge and Existence* (1932) he elaborates a very comprehensive phenomenalism in which matter, space, time, and the theoretical entities of mathematics and science are constructed from the private, momentary sense-impressions that are our only true data. What is especially Humean about this enterprise is not so much its phenomenalism as the explicitly fictional status that Stace ascribes to the products of the construction. A noteworthy feature of his theory is that our conception of other minds is taken as prior to that of an independent, external world on the ground that the sense-data of others are essential to its construction. Stace perceived the ontological consequences of his distinction between the factual existence of data and the merely constructive existence of other things. In *The Nature of the World* (1940), his "essay in phenomenalistic metaphysics," he argued that the ultimate, concrete constituents of the world were "cells," conscious awareness of particular data. Everything real can be analyzed into complexes of cells. What cannot be so analyzed is ruled out as a metaphysical impossibility.

Orthodox realism had also had its metaphysician. Samuel Alexander's *Space, Time and Deity* (1920) was derived from an uncompromisingly realist theory of knowledge even if, for all its bulk and perseverance, it never came near being accepted as the official metaphysics of realism. Knowledge, for Alexander, was a particular kind of compresence between objects, one in which one of the related terms was a consciousness. The objects of consciousness were real independent things, not mental copies of them. On the other hand, we were not aware in knowledge of the full nature of the objects known but only of a selection of their total content made from a particular point of view. There were no mental objects to be present to introspection. Mental acts were enjoyed, not contemplated. The real stuff of the world, in Alexander's metaphysics, is space-time or pure motion from which space and time, conceived on their own, are more or less illegitimate abstractions. The characteristics that pervade space-time, and so everything real, are the categories. Alexander held

that the familiar empirical variety of the world arises from this indeterminate Aristotelian prime matter by a process of emergent evolution. A model for the process of emergence is provided by the relation of mind, as enjoyed mental activity, to its physiological foundation, the physical activity of the nervous system. From pure space-time, when its constituent point-instants are grouped appropriately, emerges the mechanical order of material things with primary qualities. At the next stage, the perceived order of secondary qualities arises, and from this, again, first life and then mind emerge. This is as far as things have got at present. "Higher" entities are conceivable, reaching up to the limiting case of deity, which, however, is an ideal terminus to the course of emergent evolution that can never be reached. As the appropriate ideal object of religious emotion, deity stands to the actual world in the fundamental relation of mind to body. This hierarchical picture of the world, seen as evolving into novel forms from a radically material or naturalistic foundation, has obvious affinities with the philosophies of Aristotle and Marx. It inverts the relation of mind to nature that is fundamental to the thought of Plato and Descartes and, through them, to that of most philosophers of the modern age, even those who would strenuously deny any such dependence.

The most imposing metaphysical product of modern British philosophy, the vast, rhapsodic, and inclusive system of A. N. Whitehead, is also realistic, both in its origins, for in his early philosophy of nature Whitehead was working in harmony with the standard realist rejection of subjectivism, and in its fundamental tendency, for in his furthest flights Whitehead never goes back on the presumption that mind is the product, not the constructor, of nature. Beginning as a mathematician, Whitehead was led to collaborate with Russell in the production of *Principia Mathematica* by his desire for a formal system that should embrace all forms of relatedness which are to be encountered in the world. The first application of this scheme of general ideas was in the philosophy of nature elaborated in a series of works from *Mathematical Concepts of the Material World* (1906) to his treatises of the early 1920's. Whitehead's natural philosophy is a sustained criticism of the apparatus of scientific ideas that we owe to the founders of modern science, in particular to Descartes and Newton. He does not deny the scientific usefulness of the conception of a purely mechanical nature composed of merely extended and enduring objects with exact spatial and temporal properties. What he questions is its philosophical ultimacy. A metaphysical system in which only the abstractions of mechanism are taken to be real commits the fallacy of misplaced concreteness. In these early books, Whitehead devised a method by means of which the neat abstractions of science could be defined in terms of the implicitly but not determinately material, spatial, and temporal events which are the actual objects of perception. It was from this method of extensive abstraction that Russell derived what he called "the supreme maxim of scientific philosophizing: wherever possible substitute logical constructions for inferred entities." Whitehead showed how the simply located points, instants, and particles of Descartes and Newton could be constructed out of perceived events overlapping each other in various ways.

The fallacies of simple location and misplaced concreteness underlie Whitehead's fundamental target: the bifurcation of nature into two unreal abstractions, the mechanical order of classical physics and the sensory order of perceived secondary qualities. Against the second of these, Hume's world of distinct, definite, unrelated sense-impressions, Whitehead argued that the basic mode of perception was not the "presentational immediacy" of idealized visual experience but rather the awareness of causal efficacy characteristic of tactual and organic sensation. The world as perceived is not an aggregate of distinct atomic elements but an organically interrelated system. The particles of the physicist shared with the discrete sensations of the empiricist philosopher a common, abstract, and mistaken atomism which left the relations of things unintelligibly arbitrary and led, by way of the problem of induction, to skepticism or irrational dogmatism.

In place of simply located material substance and discrete sensations Whitehead contended that the actual entities of which the world is composed were of the nature of rather short-lived but qualitatively complex and indeterminate feelings. These events or occasions were related to one another in the common order of extension or nature and also to the realm of eternal objects, of pure potentialities. An event took the form of a coming together of eternal objects, a "concrescence" or becoming concrete of possibilities, in which the event realized itself, achieved value by the fulfillment of its subjective aim, by deriving its character from its historical environment of other events. Whitehead laid a great deal of weight on the concept of "prehension." This was the appropriate activity of events which, as a relation to eternal objects, constituted their intrinsic character and, as a relation to other events, was at once perception and the converse of causation. The world, for Whitehead, is a continuing process of active, prehensive events driven on into novelty by a blind, undifferentiated creativeness. In its onward course, selected possibilities from the domain of eternal objects are actualized since the acquisition of characteristics is what the coming to be of events consists in. God is introduced to complete the system, being understood as a principle of limitation or concretion determining just which of the infinite possibilities allowed for by the realm of eternal objects are to be actualized.

Whitehead's description of his metaphysics as the philosophy of organism showed how far he had travelled from his realistic beginnings. His theory of the world as a prehensive unity of events is clearly, to the extent that anything is clear about it, a resuscitation of the cardinal presupposition of idealism, the doctrine of internal relations. In the huge melting-pot of his system all the great philosophies of the European tradition are boiled up together and all its laborious distinctions, the separations without which its persistent problems cannot even be posed, dissolve into a formless, if edifying, liquidity in the heat of Whitehead's enthusiasm. Easier to admire than to use, it has had little influence on the subsequent course of philosophy and remains the special and private concern of a circle of devotees.

Logical Analysis

DURING the inter-war years in Britain, while realism was the official form of academic philosophy, logical analysis, first in its atomist and then in its positivist stage, developed as an increasingly powerful opposition. By the early 1920's idealism, was in full retreat, at any rate outside Scotland, its most fertile field of recruitment. It was sustained as an effective philosophical force only by the isolated, if splendid, rearguard actions of McTaggart and Collingwood. With the publication of the great works of Russell's middle period, between *Our Knowledge of the External World* (1914) and *The Analysis of Mind* (1921), and of Wittgenstein's *Tractatus Logico-Philosophicus* (1922), logical atomism emerged with striking rapidity to occupy the vacant place and to cast a Jacobin shadow over the realist's triumph. The comprehensive scope of its challenge to realism was due to the special intensity of Wittgenstein's philosophical genius. He did not put forward a few piecemeal criticisms of the realist creed but set out a complete and integrated system of dissenting answers to all the major questions that it claimed to have settled. His blunt remark in his preface to the *Tractatus* — "the book deals with the problems of philosophy" — made a justified claim about the fullness of its reach.

In all its forms the philosophy of logical analysis consisted essentially in the application of the new formal logic of Frege and Russell to the radical empiricism of Hume. Hume's ideas had been continued or revived by Mill, Mach, and William James, and their inheritance by way of these intermediaries does something to explain the characteristic differences between the British, European, and American versions of the doctrine. This analytic and empiricist movement was logical in two principal respects. In the first place it took *Principia Mathematica* as its model for the proper form of a theory of knowledge and aimed to represent the whole of human knowledge in a logically articulated system in which everything was derived by explicit definitions and rules of inference from a minimum initial stock of undefined basic concepts and undeniable basic propositions. Secondly, it made use of three technical features of Russell's logic in order to carry out its analyses. (i) It adopted the principle of extensionality suggested by Russell's account of compound propositions as truth-functions of elementary ones, asserting that all compounds were no more than assemblages of these elements, and so went on to accept the Russellian classification of the possible forms of propositions. (ii) It made a generalized use of the technique devised by Russell for the analysis of definite descriptions, in which problematic expressions were eliminated in principle from discourse by the adoption of rules for translating sentences in which they occurred into sentences from which they were absent. By means of these definitions in use, references to material objects, minds, classes, and numbers were shown to be "incomplete symbols" and the entities to which they seemed to refer were reductively analyzed into the unquestionably empirical data of sensation. (iii) It took over, again in a generalized way, Russell's theory of types which added logical to grammatical limitations on the possible ways of combining expressions to form meaningful assertions. The logical paradoxes had led Russell to see that grammatically well-formed sentences could nevertheless be meaningless, and the logical analysts concluded that an essential preliminary to a theory of knowledge laying down conditions for the distinction between the true and the false was a theory of meaning to distinguish between the significant and the senseless.

The bible of the logical analyst movement was Wittgenstein's *Tractatus*. Like other sacred texts, it combined prophetic fervor with sibylline obscurity in a way that invited and received many conflicting interpretations. Expressed in pregnant aphorisms, it used familiar terms in new but unexplained senses. It seemed that Wittgenstein, assuming the posture of the founder of a religion rather than that of the exponent of a philosophy, was more unwilling than unable to make the task of understanding him an easy one. The book, whose English translations have a certain faded eloquence, was not diminished in its influence by the large variety of mutually inconsistent interpretations to which it gave rise.

Broadly speaking, the *Tractatus* sets out a general theory of language in relation to the world. It gives an answer to the Kantian-looking question: how is language, and so thinking, possible? Wittgenstein was not, as Russell supposed in his introduction to the book, projecting an ideal language in conformity with the most stringent standards of logical perfection. He was attempting, rather, to reveal the essential structure that must be possessed by any language capable of being significantly used and which must, therefore, be hidden behind the familiar surface of our actual language.

Its general outlines are best described in the order in which Wittgenstein himself set them out, although this is not the order of their logical dependence on one another.

1. To start with, there is an ontology, a theory of the ultimate contents of the world. For Wittgenstein, the world is composed not simply of objects but of objects arranged or configured in facts. These facts are distinct from and independent of one another. Objects are incomplete in the sense that they only exist in the relation to other objects that constitutes facts. There is a limit to an object's possibilities of combination. A possible combination of objects is a state of affairs and a fact is the actual obtaining of a state of affairs. He did not specify the concrete nature of facts; indeed he even implied that they may be unknown to us, but he did suggest that they are all of the same kind or level. Russell took them to be the occurrences of a particular kind of event, private and momentary sense-experiences. But although Wittgenstein seems to have come round to this view later, it is not contained in the *Tractatus*. Another gap in the theory that was filled by Russell concerns the classification of the objects of which facts are made. Wittgenstein did not distinguish them into kinds, but Russell divided them into particular objects, the simple, if non-persistent, entities referred to by unanalyzable names, and general objects like attributes and relations. In Russell's view, the names of simple objects were intelligible on their own but general terms could only be understood as "propositional functions," fragments of propositions of the form "x has the attribute F" or "y stands in the relation R to z."

2. The next, and crucial stage, was the theory of elementary propositions. These are the propositions which owe their meaning and truth not to their relation to other propositions but to their relation to the world. That there must be such simple, unanalyzable propositions if any propositions are to have a definite sense and not merely stand in internal logical relations to one another, is the cardinal axiom of Wittgenstein's philosophy. It may be seen as a highly generalized analogue of the traditional empiricist principle that if any concepts or propositions are to make sense some must be derived from experience of the world. What makes it possible for a sentence to express an elementary proposition is its being a picture of a possible state of affairs, a possible arrangement of objects which, if it obtains, constitutes a fact. The proposition, as an arrangement of names, pictures the state of affairs, as an arrangement of objects. If the objects it names are so arranged, then the proposition is true. Propositions and the states of affairs that they depict must have a common form, but this cannot itself be described in propositions, it can only be shown. Names, like objects, are incomplete and can only be combined in

a limited number of ways. Our ability to arrange names in ways in which objects are not arranged explains false belief, and our ability to rearrange them explains our understanding of sentences whose meaning has not been explained to us. If we are to think or speak at all, then, there must be fundamental propositions owing their meaning and truth to their pictorial correspondence to states of affairs and facts respectively. From this first principle Wittgenstein derived both his ontology of facts and objects, in one direction, and his theory of the non-elementary parts of language in the other.

3. Sentences that do not express elementary, pictorial propositions are either collections, overt or concealed, of elementary propositions or they express no propositions at all and are devoid of meaning. Those that do express compound propositions are all truth-functions of elementary propositions, generated from the latter by the operations of denial and conjunction and owing their meaning and truth-value wholly to that of their elementary components. To assert a compound proposition is to do no more than conjointly to assert or deny a collection of elementary propositions. There is nothing more to a compound assertion than what is contained by its elements. It follows that the logical concepts "not," "and," "if," and "all" are not descriptive of anything in the world, they are simply structural devices for the convenient assertion of elementary propositions, the ultimate bearers of meaning and truth. Wittgenstein's account of compound propositions is the pure, formal theory of reductive analysis and established the program of the whole movement. Philosophy conceived as the analysis of propositions becomes a search for the translations of various kinds of sentence into explicit truth-functions of elementary propositions.

4. Within the domain of compound propositions, there are two noteworthy limiting cases in which the truth-value of the compound remains the same whatever the truth-value of the elementary components. These are tautologies, such as "p or not-p," which are always true, and contradictions, such as "p and not-p," which are always false. The truth or falsity of these limiting cases is determined simply by their truth-functional structure; we do not need to know how things are in the world to tell whether they are true or false and, in consequence, they tell us nothing about the world. Their truth or falsity is thus of a degenerate kind which leads Wittgenstein to call them senseless, though this is not to say that they are nonsensical. In a fully explicit notation, where the elementary constitution of compound propositions would be made clear by the sentences expressing them, tautologies, true in every state of affairs, and contradictions, true in no state of affairs, would be superfluous. A particularly important class of tautologies is the laws of logic. These tautologous conditionals, like other tautologies, say nothing about the world. Their truth is determined by the

meaning and arrangement of the non-descriptive logical terms that occur in them. In these conditionals, the consequent is simply a repetition of some or all of the antecedent and, as laws of logic, they license the deduction of the consequent from the antecedent. Deductive inference, therefore, is no more than a reiteration, partial or total, in the conclusion, of what was asserted in the premises. Deduction gives no new information and in a fully explicit notation it would be dispensable, since we could tell what the logical consequences of a proposition were by simple inspection. Wittgenstein held mathematics to consist of equations which were dispensable in principle in the same way. The identity of meaning between expressions asserted by mathematical propositions would be conveyed by the identity of the expressions themselves. In general, logically necessary connections exist because we have different, alternative ways of saying the same thing. Obscurity of logical connection is the price we have to pay for the conveniences of abbreviation. Wittgenstein interpreted probability as a particular kind of logical relation between hypothesis and evidence. Take all the distinctly conceivable states of affairs relevant to the truth or falsity of hypothesis and evidence. The proportion of those states of affairs in which both are true to those in which the evidence, taken by itself, is true is the probability of the hypothesis on that evidence. Wittgenstein did not raise the question of the justification of induction, but he defined induction as the propensity to look for the simplest theories consistent with what we know already.

5. The abyss into which he cast all sentences that are not either elementary themselves or equivalent in meaning to some set of elementary sentences is not an entirely amorphous one. There are within it the makings of a threefold distinction between varyingly deplorable kinds of nonsense. (i) Least excusable is the nonsense of which traditional metaphysics is made up. "Most of the propositions and questions to be found in philosophical works are not false but nonsensical . . . [they] arise from our failure to understand the logic of our language." (ii) A more tolerable kind of nonsense is exhibited by the semantic sentences about the pictorial relations between language and the world which make up the *Tractatus* itself. With the fervor of Epimenides, he declares: "my propositions serve as elucidations in the following way: anyone who understands me eventually recognises them as nonsensical, when he has used them — as steps — to climb up beyond them." In other words, Wittgenstein's philosophy is indispensable nonsense and not just idle nonsense like traditional metaphysics. In an attempt to elude the self-destructiveness of this doctrine Wittgenstein maintains that philosophy is not a theory, does not issue in a body of assertible truths, but an activity, that of making the meaning of propositions clear. The ground for these puzzling conclusions is the

unargued and, in its literal sense, false contention that the relation between a picture and what it depicts cannot be depicted. (iii) Finally, there is what might be called deep nonsense, the transcendental or mystical profundities of morality and religion. "Ethics cannot be put into words." "God does not reveal himself *in* the world." "It is not *how* things are in the world that is mystical, but *that* it exists." In his detestation of traditional academic philosophy, Wittgenstein exaggerated its distinctness both from his own theory and from what he dignifies as the mystical. By far the greater part of it can be classified either as neutral and technical analysis of the kind he practiced himself or as spiritual edification.

Russell, as has been suggested already, did not accept this radical, systematic and closely integrated body of ideas without certain qualifications and additions. His main qualifications were his less dramatic theory of the relation of propositions and facts, which he saw as one of structural similarity, not picturing, and his much less neatly uniform and monistic account of the nature of facts. For Wittgenstein, all facts were atomic or elementary, simple objects in immediate combination. Russell felt constrained to admit negative and general facts as well, though he regarded the reduction of conjunctive and disjunctive ones as possible, and he had a good deal of difficulty with psychological facts of the kind represented by "*A* believes that *p*." Since these were not truth-functions of the believed propositions that they mentioned, it seemed that propositions would have to be accepted as simple objects, irreducible constituents of the world, unless some other technique of elimination could be found. Russell was inclined toward, but not wholly convinced by, the behavioristic theory of belief-propositions offered by the radical empiricism of William James.

Of most influence and importance was his traditionally empiricist interpretation of elementary propositions. These he understood to report the occurrence of sensations and images, Humean perceptions, and he consistently derived a sensationalist ontology from this interpretation, one which saw private, momentary sensory events as the real stuff of the world. Following James again, he described this theory of ultimate propositions and facts as neutral monism and directed his energies to the task of outlining the reduction of the material objects and minds of common and scientific knowledge to the elementary events of which they were composed. *Our Knowledge of the External World* (1914) expounds his theory of material objects as structurally regular systems of events, perceived (sensa) and unperceived (sensibilia). The system of events perceived or perceivable from a given place at a given moment he called a perspective, and he defined a mind, in so far as it was a percipient, as a series of perspectives which coincided in position with the successive locations of a brain and which were related by the peculiarly mental brand of "mnemic"

causation in which events can be influenced by temporally remote causes. In his *Analysis of Mind* (1921) this theory of matter and percipients was extended to cover mind as a whole, including its nonpercipient aspects. Consciousness, thought, belief, knowledge, emotion, desire, and will were, like perception, reduced in the end to complex arrangements of sensations and images. In some cases the reductive path to the empirical terminus led through reduction to bodily behavior, particularly where the unconscious mental states of Freudian psychoanalysis were concerned.

The philosophy of Russell's middle period took the characteristic form of a dissenting minority report to a rather rigidly systematic presentation of what were essentially his own ideas. His hesitant complications of the dogmatic symmetry of the *Tractatus* were paralleled in the 1940's by the friendly but fundamental critique of logical positivism contained in his *Inquiry into Meaning and Truth* (1940) and *Human Knowledge* (1948). The sadly brief career of F. P. Ramsey, who died in 1930 at the age of twenty-six, contained enough powerfully original work to show that a rather different reconciliation of the ideas of Russell and Wittgenstein than that provided by the logical positivists might have been achieved. In the short time available to him, Ramsey introduced important modifications of Russell's mathematical logic with his simplification of the theory of types and his elimination of extra-logical contingent assumptions from the system. Of particular promise were his suggestive studies in the philosophy of science, which included a theory of laws of nature as rules rather than propositions, his purpose here being to undercut the controversy about general facts, and some interesting ideas about induction and probability, in particular a suggestion that induction should be regarded, along with perception and memory, as one of the original sources of knowledge.[1]

The logical positivists of the Vienna Circle went further than Russell in the amendments they made to the doctrine of the *Tractatus*, though they took over its central portions more resolutely than he did. They adopted and considerably developed the view that all significant propositions about matters of fact could be reduced to elementary or basic propositions, the theory that logic and mathematics were analytic, and the dismissal as meaningless of metaphysical, religious, and ethical utterances. But they did not accept the ontological inferences that Wittgenstein and Russell had drawn from their theory of meaning. Furthermore, they insisted that there was no natural relation of similarity between propositions and facts, whether pictorial or structural; in their view the relation between the two was a purely conventional one. Agreeing with Russell that elementary propositions were reports of immediate experience, they formulated the requirement that all significant assertions should be, or be reducible to, direct reports of experience in the celebrated principle of verifiability. This stated that a sentence expressed a meaningful proposition only if its truth or falsity could be established by recourse to experience. At the other end of Wittgenstein's doctrine, so to speak, they took a very different view about the nature of philosophy. As ontology they rejected it along with the rest of metaphysics but as analysis, as a theory of the logical connections between propositions, they accepted it as a species of logic and so as safely included within the domain of the meaningful. Against the ontology of Russell and Wittgenstein they maintained that no metaphysical significance could be attached to the distinction between the simple, given, and unanalyzable on the one hand and the complex, inferred, and reducible on the other. Material objects and minds existed in just the same sense as the sensory elements out of which they were constructed. The only meaningful controversy that could arise about the existence of material things and minds was the empirical issue of whether there existed sensory elements related in the appropriate way.

A crucial difficulty remained, however. The interpretation of a particular type of proposition as given and not further reducible was ambiguous in status. It could be taken either as a proposition of analysis about the internal relations of discourse, to the effect that there was no class of propositions logically prior to the class interpreted as elementary, or as a proposition of semantics about the relations of language to the world. As analysis, a theory of elements seemed to be a convention or proposal to which there could be legitimate alternatives. As semantics it seemed unverifiably metaphysical. Acceptance of the former view led to Carnap's principle of tolerance and its application in devising languages with inter-subjectively verifiable statements about physical things as their basis. Fear of the latter, until it was dispelled by Tarski's theory of truth, encouraged the adoption of a kind of coherence theory which held the truth of a proposition to consist in its relation to other, conventionally adopted, propositions and not in the relation to the extra-linguistic world required by the doctrine of correspondence.

In Britain these ideas were lucidly and influentially set out by A. J. Ayer in his *Language, Truth and Logic* (1936). He expounded there a rather radical version of the common core of philosophical beliefs held by the analytic philosophers of the 1930's: a group that included, besides Ayer, R. B. Braithwaite and Max Black, adherents of Moore like C. Lewy, and two philosophers who were later to move off in notably new directions, Ryle and Wisdom. Most of them and the other contributors to their periodical *Analysis* at some time held most of the following views, which define an idealized normal analytic viewpoint comparable to the normal realism already outlined. There are no substances, since individuals,

analyzed in accordance with the theory of descriptions, are bundles of qualities. Universals, on the other hand, can be defined in terms of groups of particulars related by similarity. Meaning is verifiability in principle, and a proposition is true if it corresponds to the experiences that are conventionally laid down as verifying it. All necessary truth, in logic, mathematics, or philosophy, is analytic, determined by the meanings conventionally assigned to the elements of language. Only necessary truths and the basic propositions that describe immediate experience can be certain; complex empirical propositions can never be more than probable. Material objects are logical constructions out of sense-impressions. Minds are either constructions out of introspective experiences or second-order constructions out of the behavior of human bodies or both. In any case, the criteria of personal identity are physical. Causality is regular connection, and the theoretical entities of science are a further set of second-order constructions, analyzable in terms of the behavior of ordinary material objects and so, at the second remove, in terms of sense-impressions. The task of science, as of ordinary perceptual belief, is the prediction of sense-experience. That induction will yield true predictions is incapable of proof, but that it is rational is analytically determined by the meaning of the word *rational*. The probability of an event in given circumstances follows from the frequency with which events of that sort occur in circumstances of the given kind. There is good empirical ground for thinking all human action to be caused, but this does not prove it all to be unfree, a thing that could only be shown by universal constraint. Judgments of value are not statements of fact but are either expressions of emotion or imperatives. In neither case are they true or false. Religious and metaphysical utterances are unverifiable and so meaningless. Philosophy of the non-metaphysical sort consists of analytic propositions about the logical relations of different kinds of linguistic elements. More specifically, its job is to classify propositions into their different forms, to eliminate the metaphysical, and to trace the logical relations holding amongst the remainder.

The ideas of Russell's middle period and Wittgenstein's *Tractatus*, mediated through Continental logical positivism, were the main sources of this body of orthodox analytic doctrine. But the later teaching of G. E. Moore was an important influence and explains the differences of opinion and, even more, of emphasis between it and logical positivism proper. Moore's chief preoccupation in this period was with the problem of perception. He always regarded it as that of giving an account of beliefs about material objects in terms of the sense-impressions which were the evidence for them. Moore did not take the purpose of this inquiry to be the justification of beliefs about material objects, many of which, he held, we knew for certain to be true.

The task of a theory of perception was, rather, to give an analysis of propositions which, since we often knew them to be certainly true, we must in some sense understand already. The definition of this special variety of philosophical understanding, distinct from the ordinary understanding that is sufficient for knowledge and to be acquired from philosophical analysis, was a problem that greatly exercised Moore but which he was never to come very near to solving. The younger philosophers who advanced as a theory the identification of philosophy and analysis that Moore adopted in practice shared his concern both with the methodological issue and with the specific problem about perception from which it most pressingly arose. Throughout the 1930's, controversy continued within the school about the viability in principle and the articulation in detail of the phenomenalist reduction of propositions about material objects to propositions about sense-data and about the nature and justification of philosophical analysis in general. Ayer's *Foundations of Empirical Knowledge* (1940) expounded a phenomenalism that owed, as its author acknowledged, a great deal to Price's *Perception*. The view that statements about material objects could be translated without remainder into statements about sense-data was defended there against realists, on the one hand who maintained that the translation proposed was impossible, and formalists, such as Carnap in his physicalist and conventionalist phase, on the other, who maintained that it was unnecessary. The debates about analysis were less conclusive in their outcome. Generally speaking, its defenders moved away during the decade from an ontological interpretation which judged the success of an analysis by its power to reveal the form of the facts to one which defined an analysis as complete when it expressed the proposition being analyzed as an explicit truth-function of basic or elementary propositions. Moore's view that the aim of analysis was not to justify but to explain also became fairly widely accepted. This conviction of the clarificatory nature of philosophy has survived the rigorous and formal ideal of analysis with which it was originally associated. The detailed, informal analyses of the linguistic philosophers of the post-war period have been directed toward the understanding and not to the criticism of our common beliefs. In the years when the philosophy of logical analysis was undergoing its most lively development and exercising its largest influence, the agent of its destruction was being created. During the 1930's Wittgenstein was working out, and conveying by word of mouth to small groups in Cambridge, the radically new departure of his later philosophy. By the end of the war, the ideas later published in his *Philosophical Investigations* were widely enough known to become, on the resumption of philosophical activity, the dominating current of thought.

The Later Philosophy of Wittgenstein

AFTER the publication of the *Tractatus* Wittgenstein seems to have more or less given up philosophy until his return to Cambridge in 1929. From then until his retirement in 1947 he gradually worked out the profound, obscure, and inconclusive set of ideas published after his death in the *Philosophical Investigations* (1953). These new opinions were communicated orally to small groups of followers and manuscripts of his lectures circulated surreptitiously. Wittgenstein's dedication to esotericism both in the communication and in the expression of his thoughts ensured that they would be hard to understand and frequently misunderstood.

At first glance, obscurity seems to be all that the *Tractatus* and the *Investigations* have in common. Certainly they are obscure in different ways. While the earlier book is presented in a style of marmorean deductive rigor, with its constituent aphorisms expressed in the unvarying tone of a prophetic revelation, the later book is loose, colloquial, and varied in mood, with arguments cropping up here and there within a mass of questions, persuasive insinuations, and occasional vatic pronouncement in the earlier style. Furthermore, the content of the two books seems directly opposed. Where the *Tractatus* saw language as a logically rigid essence concealed behind the contingent surface of everyday discourse, a skeleton to be excavated by penetrating analysis, in the *Investigations* language is accepted as it actually and observably is, as a living, unsystematic, and polymorphous array of working conventions for a large and not simply classifiable range of human purposes.

Yet both are, in their very different ways, examinations of the same topic: the relation of language to the world. Although Wittgenstein came to reject most of the particular doctrines of the *Tractatus*, the fact that he spent so much of his time in the *Investigations* in refuting them, shows that even if the answers of the earlier book were wrong the questions that they were given to were not. And Wittgenstein did not abandon everything in the *Tractatus*. In particular, he reaffirmed, if in a new way, the earlier book's thesis of the impossibility of philosophy. What had been perhaps the least digestible feature of the *Tractatus*, its self-refuting contention that the sentences of which it was composed were meaningless attempts to say what could only be shown and at best a ladder to be climbed up on and then kicked away, took the form in the *Investigations* of the philosophical theory that it was no part of philosophy to propound theories but only to describe facts about language that were perfectly familiar already, arranging these familiar descriptions in a fashion designed to break the hold on our minds of philosophical confusions and paradoxes.

British philosophy in the last forty years would have been a very different, and poorer, thing

Wittgenstein had taken his own prohibitions literally. In fact, perfectly good sense can be made of most of the sentences in the *Tractatus*, and the *Investigations* is mercifully a great deal more than the tissue of detailed reminders about the actual use of words which the author believed that it ought to have been. It is full of large, original, and highly discussable philosophical theories and of arguments in support of them. In practice, even the most loyal of his disciples (and he exacted very high standards of loyalty) treat his passionate revulsion from the idea of himself as a philosophical theorist as the aberration which those who admire the rest of his work openly proclaim it to be. Historically considered, the two generations of British philosophers who have come under his influence have in effect simply ignored these self-denying ordinances. Making the exclusions from the body of his utterances that are needed to make the remainder intelligible, they have derived from each of his books a coherent and comprehensive philosophical system: from the *Tractatus* the logical analysis of the 1930's, from the *Investigations* the linguistic philosophy of the period from 1945 to 1960.

The system of the *Investigations* has three main parts which are broadly distinguishable despite their numerous and complicated interrelations. First, there is a theory of meaning in direct opposition to the logical atomism of the *Tractatus*, a theory which looks for the meaning of a word in its use, in public acts of communication between the users of language, and not in any objects for which it may be used to stand, whether these are understood to be in the world outside us or to be within our minds. Secondly, there is a theory about the nature of philosophy which is not, as we have seen, a matter of propounding theories but has rather the negative purpose of dispelling metaphysics, philosophy in its traditional sense, the confused and perplexed affirmation of paradoxical statements that are in conflict with ordinary common-sense beliefs that we know perfectly well to be true. Finally, there is a theory of mind, the part of the *Investigations* in which Wittgenstein breaks wholly new ground, which interprets our descriptions of mental acts and states not as referring to something private within our streams of interior consciousness but as governed by criteria that mention the circumstances, behavior, and propensities to behave of the persons described. If anything in Wittgenstein's earlier work anticipates his later theory of mind it is his cryptic disposal of the problem about the analysis of belief-sentences that caused Russell in his introduction to the *Tractatus* so much heart-searching.

The fundamental point of Wittgenstein's new theory of meaning is that the meaning of a word is not any sort of object for which the word stands. Certainly it is a feature of the meaning of some words to stand for things, but these, the proper names, constitute only a small, specialized, and unrepresentative part of language as a whole. And even in their case, the object they stand for is not their meaning, which is, rather, their conventionally established capacity to stand for objects. We are over-impressed, Wittgenstein believes, by the model of ostensive definition, the direct correlation of words with elements of the world and, underlying this, with the idea of pointing to an object as being a somehow self-explanatory way of giving the meaning of a word uttered at the moment of the act of pointing. But ostensive definition is just one conventional use of the act of pointing to things, which can also be used to give orders rather than introduce new words. That is to say, before pointing can give meaning to a word it must itself be understood as having meaning.

"What is the meaning of a word?" is a typically philosophical question; it calls for an inquiry we do not know how to conduct. To find out what meaning is, we should consider questions that arise about meaning outside philosophical discussions: how is the meaning of a word learned or explained, how do we tell whether someone understands the meaning of a word? If we approach the question in this way, by considering the common and familiar occurrences of the word "meaning," we shall see that to talk about the meaning of a word is to talk about the way in which it is used. To say of a man that he has learned or understands the meaning of a word is simply to say that he has learned or understands how to use it, that he has become party to a certain established social convention. The identification of meaning with the way a word is used is vague, but this is inevitable, for words are used in many different ways and have many different sorts of meaning.

The form of the original question suggests that there is one pre-eminent way in which words mean, and this assumption leads to such views as that the basic task of words is to describe, or, as in the *Tractatus*, to picture. But if we can only divert our attention from the misleading form of the original question and look at our use of words as it actually is in all its multifariousness, we shall see that language has many other uses than that of describing things. We use them to give orders, to express our feelings, to warn, to excite, to ask questions. It should not be assumed that there is some common element to all these different uses of language, some residual essence of meaning that is present in them all. The uses of language, in Wittgenstein's famous simile, are like games. Because we use one word to apply to all the vast variety of games, we are inclined to imagine that they all have some common property if only we could put our fingers on it. But this is not so. Games have only a family resemblance; there is a large collection of similarities only a few of which will obtain between any two of the practices we call games. To bring out this multiplicity of uses, Wittgenstein ran the two terms of his simile together in the notion of a language-game, this being a simplified model of some particular aspect of our language, studied in isolation by being conceived as the total language of some group of people. These are artificial abstractions from language as it is, since the uses of language overlap even more than most games do. The pieces, i.e., the words, we use in any one language-game may each be used in many different language-games as well.

Wittgenstein's insistence on the multiplicity of different uses of words has an egalitarian flavor. It is opposed to the idea that certain forms of language are specially privileged, meaningful in some unique, fundamental sense. He rejects, therefore, his earlier doctrine of elementary sentences made up of unanalyzable logically proper names and the atomic facts and simple objects supposed to correspond to them. No type of discourse is intrinsically simple or basic. Simplicity is always a relative notion, relative in particular to what we have a clear apprehension of already. There is not, therefore, any unique analysis of propositions into their intrinsically unanalyzable elements. What sort of analysis will be useful and provide a real clarification depends on the circumstances, on just what is problematic about the propositions under examination. Indeed, he would not accept "analysis" as a proper description of his later inquiries into meaning. The assumption that translation is the ideal technique for the clarification of meaning rests on another oversimplified image of the workings of language, one which treats language as a logical calculus, which is as confusing and irrelevant as that which sees the essence of significance to lie in picturing. The language we use is not, except in certain special technical areas, logically regimented in the manner of a calculus. It would be wholly unable to fulfil the purposes it now does if it were. The elasticity of language from a formal point of view is what makes it possible for us to convert it to new uses, to superimpose new tasks on to those it already has. He sums up his theory of meaning by saying that the language-games, within which alone words have meaning, are forms of life, modes of activity governed by systems of rules. A form of life involves attitudes, interests, and behavior; it is something far more comprehensive than the manipulation of a clearly specified calculus.

Wittgenstein's theory of meaning makes it clear that philosophy, understood as the clarification of meaning, will be something very different from the construction of a rigidly formal hierarchy of forms of discourse carried out in the *Tractatus*. It would have to be more complicated and more various in its technique than the philosophy of logical analysis with its ambition of arriving at exact rules of translation. But nothing said so far entails the extreme asceticism of the view of philosophy which he actually arrived at. Philosophy is not just any inquiry into meaning. It consists of inquiries

into meaning directed toward a particular purpose, the resolution of a special kind of perplexity or puzzlement. It is this condition of relevance to metaphysical confusions that distinguishes Wittgenstein's idea of the proper method of philosophy from Austin's. For Austin seemed to be interested in the rules of language for their own sake and displayed a corresponding Baconian empiricism about language in his actual philosophical practice. Many of the delicate discriminations in his writings are no more than associated with the philosophical problems he is concerned with and play no part in advancing the main line of argument. Wittgenstein's view is that men are naturally led into metaphysics, into the making of assertions which worry us by the collision between their apparent deductive inevitability on the one hand and their incompatibility with familiar and deep-seated common-sense beliefs on the other. He agrees with Moore that, in this collision, it is the metaphysical paradoxes that must give way. They are, he holds, the outcome of our misunderstandings of the logic of our language and arise from the misleading influence of insidious verbal analogies. We are led by the surface grammar of words, as he calls it, the overt likenesses between forms of discourse with very different uses, to assimilate and so misrepresent their depth grammar. The task of philosophy is to undermine these intoxicating analogies by the revelation of depth grammar, by recalling our attention to the actual working of the perplexing words in all its variety. He goes on to repudiate the metaphor involved in the phrase "depth grammar" by insisting that the facts about language from which misleading analogies divert our attention are not hidden in the ordinary sense of being concealed. The situation is rather that we ignore the pattern present in a whole range of uses by fixing our gaze on one particular, favored corner of it, as one might ignore the pattern in a carpet by looking at it in the wrong way. We do not need to look at the carpet with special instruments or to turn it over and examine its underside, which was roughly the proposal of the *Tractatus*, but to change our attitude toward it and to free ourselves from the constriction of a routine, mechanical response to it. Metaphysics is often produced by our considering words in strange connections which only occur in the writings of philosophers. In such cases, language is idling, there are no established rules for the use of words in these connections, and so we are compelled to resort to more or less untrustworthy analogies to provide a use for them. To overcome this kind of confusion we need to examine language at work, about its familiar everyday business.

Wittgenstein concludes that it is no part of the business of philosophy to reform language. It must leave everything as it is. He is not saying that language cannot be changed but rather that such changes must arise from the concrete needs of language users and not from abstract reflection about the nature of language. A further conclusion is that the philosopher must not simply replace old, bad, misleading analogies by new ones, for he seems to assume that these will be no improvement in the end on the theories they replace. What he must do is simply describe language about its everyday work, assemble reminders so that the actual pattern of uses is made clear to us. Everything in the pattern is perfectly familiar to us already; what the philosopher has to do is to make us aware of it as a pattern. Both of these conclusions have been criticized. In so far as philosophers in the past have been led into false or meaningless assertions by misunderstandings of the actual use of words, then to that extent proper, corrective philosophy will be concerned to clear up these misunderstandings by bringing that actual use into the open. But the original thesis about the causes of metaphysics is not very convincingly established. Furthermore, no very effective test of what is metaphysical in the bad sense is provided. Certainly there are philosophers who have revelled in the surprising and counter-intuitive appearance of their conclusions, Bradley and McTaggart, for example. But others, Aristotle and Kant are perhaps the most notable instances, have always aimed to reconcile their conclusions with the body of commonly accepted knowledge. Wittgenstein offers some tests for metaphysics, but they are of an imprecise and subjective character: the feeling of a particular sort of puzzlement, of not knowing one's way about. His rejection of the whole notion of philosophy as a criticism of ordinary ways of thinking is brought out in his attitude toward the problem of justifying kinds of belief. To discover what justifies a certain kind of belief, he says, all we have to do is to see what is generally accepted as justifying it. The role of philosophy, then, is purely negative. It is the removal of obstacles to understanding, not a business of making discoveries. In another of his influential similes, he likened philosophy to psychoanalytic therapy, which does not simply find out what is wrong with neurotics and tell them but gradually induces them to recognize the real significance of their words and actions. But, to turn to Wittgenstein's other conclusion, that philosophy must simply describe and remind, not theorize, the psychoanalyst has a theory himself about the nature of his patient's disorder which the patient can come to understand. Wittgenstein does not make out the case for a parallel in the situation of his metaphysical patients to repression or resistance to analysis. His view that philosophical analysis must use more various and complex techniques than the strict translation of the 1930's is better founded than his doctrines that it can only describe the established use of words, not explain, criticize, or attempt to improve on it, and that this description can only be safely carried out by the accumulation of exemplary reminders and not in any sort of general or theoretical terms. Certainly his account of previous philosophy as

pathological does not seem to have been confirmed by much therapeutic success. The problems he aimed to dissolve have obstinately refused to stay dead. History refutes his view that it is no part of philosophy to interfere with our existing use of words or with our existing standards of justifying argument. The language of modern science and the criteria of evidence that it opposed to reliance on authority, scripture, and the syllogism were the creation of the philosophers of the seventeenth century. Finally, his own practice makes clear that, despite the most strenuous efforts, no sort of philosophy can confine itself to the presentation of exemplary reminders. The purpose of assembling reminders is to correct a mistaken analogy, and to do this is inevitably to put forward a correct one. If the *Philosophical Investigations* had been merely the album of accepted uses of words it ought to have been according to its author's theory, it would not have had the large and generally illuminating influence it has had.

The particular philosophical problem that takes up most of Wittgenstein's attention in the *Investigations* is that of the nature of mind or, in his terminology, of the language in which we report and describe the mental states of ourselves and others. The metaphysical doctrine against which he is arguing here is that persistent dualism of mind and body, made explicit by Plato and Descartes, but, it would seem, rather deeply lodged in our ordinary way of thinking, which holds that mental states exist in private worlds of their own of which only one person is directly aware. The paradoxes arising from this theory are, first and foremost, the idea that we can never know what is going on in the mind of another person and also perhaps the older difficulty about understanding how things can act upon each other when they are as different from one another as mental and bodily states are according to this theory. The mistaken analogy that lies behind the skeptical absurdities of dualism is that between "I see a tree" or "I touch this stone" on the one hand and "I feel a pain" and "I understand this calculation" on the other. Just as the first two sentences report perception of and action on physical things so, it is supposed, the other two report mental perception and action. The world is then conceived as containing, alongside material objects and acts of manipulating them, mental objects like pains and mental acts or processes like understanding, meaning and thinking.

Wittgenstein maintains that our mental vocabulary does not refer to inner acts and states. It is not so much that he denies the existence of private experiences as that he denies that they could serve as criteria for the employment of mental words. In his view, to say that someone is in a given mental state is to say that he is in any of a large collection of publicly observable situations, that he is doing or disposed to do any of a large collection of publicly observable things. There is no one recurrent kind of thing of which a mental word is the name, nor is it the name of any kind of private thing. He supports this theory with two kinds of argument. In the first place, he examines in detail the working of a representative selection of mental concepts, and, secondly, he has a general argument to prove that a private language, referring to the experiences of which only one person is aware, is an impossibility.

The most important and suggestive particular concept he investigates is that of understanding. The dualist supposes that when someone under instruction says "now I understand," he is reporting a private experience of understanding. But whatever experience he may have, Wittgenstein replies, cannot be the sense, and thus the criterion of truth, of the man's remark. What decides whether or not he really does understand, let us say, long division, is whether or not he can go on to repeat the operation for himself, preferably on new material so as to rule out his having learnt by heart the arrangement of numbers making up the long division sum. To understand something is to be able to apply it. It might be thought that this objection could be countered by a further specification of the purported experience of understanding. Could the experience not take the form of the private awareness of some image or formula which gives the gist of the operation claimed to be understood? Against this suggestion Wittgenstein argues that an image or formula does not dictate its own application. It must itself be understood, and that it has been understood is something that only its correct application can establish. An image or formula as it stands can be interpreted or understood in different ways. Only its publicly observable application can show if the interpretation made of it is the correct one. Essentially the same argument is applied to the concept of meaning something by a word. What a man means by a word is not a private experience, in particular it is not an image which is itself a symbol that can be meant, i.e., used, in very different ways. The meaning a man attaches to a word is only to be discovered by considering the things to which he applies, and from which he withholds, the word and the verbal contexts, the statements and arguments, in which he employs it. It follows from this that thinking is not an interior process that accompanies speech and is the criterion of its being intelligent speech and not babbling. For to think what one is saying is no more than to mean what one is saying. The same general treatment is extended to cover concepts of emotion such as hope and fear. All these concepts derive their significance from the surroundings of the people to whom they are ascribed and not to some private events going on within them. The concepts considered so far all relate to higher forms of mentality and, primarily at any rate, can only be ascribed to creatures that are at least human beings to the extent of being users of language. An important feature of the "surroundings" in these cases is what

the people to whom they are ascribed will say. What sense is there, Wittgenstein asks, to the supposition that a dog is afraid of something that may happen next week?

Having argued that the publicly observable surroundings are in fact the criteria for our applications of mental words in these examples, Wittgenstein goes on to prove that this must be so, since there could not be a language whose use was wholly determined by private experiences. It might seem that I could resolve to utter a certain word whenever a sensation like this particular one I am having now took place. This decision would provide a criterion which I should apply whenever the same sensation recurred. But what could be meant, he asks, by the question whether a given sensation was the same as the one chosen as the criterion? We could only compare the present sensation with our memory of its predecessor, and how could we eliminate the possibility that our memory was playing us false? He concludes that language is an essentially social phenomenon. The making of noises does not become linguistic utterance unless it is governed by rules, unless there is an applicable distinction between the correct and mistaken use of words. With a private language, this condition cannot be satisfied, and the uttering of words introduced as names of private sensations would be just an "empty ceremony." It is for this reason that our mental words must be, as they are, connected with features of our situation which anyone can in principle observe. Every inner process must have its outward criteria.

The concept to which this treatment seems least applicable is that of pain, and Wittgenstein considers it at length. Here, as elsewhere, it is important to consider the way in which the use of the words under examination is learnt. Now, we learn how to use the words "it hurts" from other people who tell that we are in pain from our circumstances and behavior. But we do not tell that we are in pain ourselves in this way. In fact, Wittgenstein maintains, we do not discover or find out that we are in pain at all. It is not a thing we can be in doubt about and so not a thing of which it is appropriate to claim knowledge. We use no criteria for our utterances of "it hurts" and it is an incorrigible statement in the sense that we cannot be honestly mistaken about it. If I do hesitate about saying that I am in pain that shows that it is not exactly pain that I am suffering from but something like it, discomfort perhaps. Statements about pain in the first person, Wittgenstein says, are in fact extensions of natural pain-behavior, conventionalized alternatives to crying out which we are trained to adopt. They are not so much descriptions of pain but manifestations of it.

The will, in Wittgenstein's opinion, is no more private and internal than thought and feeling. The difference between my raising my arm and my arm's simply going up in the air does not consist in the presence in the former case of an interior act of will.

What commonly characterizes voluntary movement is the absence of surprise. Intentions, again, are not private states. I ordinarily know for certain what my intentions are, but this does not rest on any sort of interior observation. There is a parallel here, he asserts, with our knowledge of the movements and positions of our bodies. We do not have to look to see where our arms are but we do not tell by some recognizable feeling either.

The bearing of this theory of mental language on the metaphysical problem about our knowledge of other minds which inspired it is that there is no such general problem. For there could be no mental language with which I could talk about my own mind unless there were a public mental language and I had mastered it. He does not say that any statement about the mind of another person strictly and deductively follows from any set of statements about his behavior. Nevertheless, what others do and say provides all the ground that is required for the justification of our beliefs about them. To believe that other people have feelings in the way we do ourselves does not consist in the acceptance of a definite set of propositions. It is shown, rather, in the way in which we treat other people, in our attitudes of pity and concern for them, for example.

For many years the only access to Wittgenstein's ideas available to philosophers who were not in his immediate circle was provided by the writings of John Wisdom, a series of lively and entertaining articles brought together in his two collections *Other Minds* (1952) and *Philosophy and Psychoanalysis* (1953). When Wittgenstein's own writings were posthumously published it became clear that Wisdom was not simply a reporter of Wittgenstein's thinking but an original and indeed idiosyncratic developer of it. In the first place, Wisdom was more at home temperamentally with the view that there could be no solutions in the ordinary sense to philosophical problems than its first propounder ever was. It was a point of doctrine with Wisdom that no philosophical theory could be more than a half-truth. Consistently enough, this led him to be much more indulgent toward traditional metaphysical speculation than Wittgenstein had been. He seemed to see philosophy as a holding together in the mind of some sort of suspension of directly opposed theories: on one side the contentions of traditional metaphysics, on the other the equally general theses which Wittgenstein, in denying the metaphysical assertions, found himself inevitably committed to. For Wisdom, metaphysical propositions were not the worthless if symptomatic products of mistaken analogy. They were exaggerated representations of real logical affinities between different kinds of statement. The exaggeration involved was twofold: it was made up in part of a lack of qualification, a tendency to treat resemblances as identities, and in part in the expression in an ontological idiom of facts of a logical or conceptual nature. Confronted by two incompatible metaphysical doctrines, we will usually find that both are partly correct, since both bring real logical affinities to our notice. But every kind of statement is unique and has its own kind of logic, so none of these metaphysical comparisons can be fully endorsed. They should be understood, perhaps, as recommendations or decisions as to how words should be used rather than as descriptions of the actual nature of language as it is.

Wittgenstein's other leading follower and expositor, Waismann, stood in a more ambiguous relation to him. It was perhaps just because he owed so much to Wittgenstein that he was so emphatic about the differences between them. Thus, when he was criticizing Wittgenstein, he would do so on the basis of Wittgenstein's own theories and even use Wittgenstein's examples in doing so. His chief work, *Logic, Language and Philosophy*, which has not yet been published, was first drafted in the 1930's. It is an admirably lucid account of the later philosophy of Wittgenstein, much clearer and less devious than anything written by Wittgenstein himself. Waismann emphasized two particular aspects of Wittgenstein's philosophy: the conventionalist interpretation of logic and mathematics and the doctrine of the essential inexactness of language. He rejected as irrelevantly utopian the application to language of the formal ideal of a logical calculus. As he saw it, language was composed of a number of strata, of subjective reporting, perceptual description, and scientific theory, for example, within which strict relations of logical entailment and identity of meaning were to be found but between which looser relations prevailed. The characteristic problems of philosophy arose about these relations between strata at the "fracture-lines" between them.

Wittgenstein's direct successors have remained loyal to his idea of philosophy as an activity without statable results. The Oxford philosophers of ordinary language, on the other hand, have taken from him his positive doctrines about the nature of meaning and of mental concepts but have developed them in a more systematic way than he did. They have largely accepted his view about the nature of metaphysics and its causation by misunderstandings of the actual use of words. It has led them to an even closer attention than his to its actual working. If they have not followed him in ruling out the possibility of philosophical theorizing, many, under the influence of Austin, have been profoundly suspicious of anything very general in the way of theory. But they have been more impressed by its difficulty than convinced of its impossibility.

The Philosophy of Ordinary Language

OXFORD has undoubtedly been the center of British philosophical activity since the war. It has regained the position it had in the late nineteenth century in the epoch of Green and Bradley, which it lost to Cambridge soon after the turn of the century with the start of the philosophical careers of Russell and Moore and which Cambridge kept until the retirement of Wittgenstein in 1947. There is nothing surprising about this. If anything is odd it is that Oxford should have lost its commanding place. The Oxford system of studies ensures that philosophy is a substantial part, from a quarter to a half, of the work of about one student in five. As a result, the teachers of philosophy in Oxford are at least four times as numerous as those of any other university institution in Britain.

When the university returned to normal working at the end of the war, Ryle moved into the senior philosophical chair, which had been vacant since Collingwood's death in 1943, and Austin started the weekly discussions which soon came to be the place where new ideas were worked out and from which they were propagated amongst the younger philosophers. The philosophers of the ordinary language movement agreed with Wittgenstein on a number of general points. Both saw the task of philosophy as critical. They believed the proper objects of its criticism to be those general propositions about knowledge and the world, defiant of common sense, which constituted traditional metaphysical philosophy. They believed the proper method of criticism to be a demonstration, by careful attention to the ordinary uses of words, that these metaphysical propositions both embodied and rested upon misuses of language. But there were significant differences both of doctrine and method. The ordinary language philosophers did not share Wittgenstein's view that philosophy was a nontheoretical activity. They thought that the description of the use or meaning of words was as good and significant an employment of language as any other and so they had no objection to philosophical theorizing or even, in principle, to highly general philosophical theorizing. In practice, however, although Ryle was prepared to express a definite philosophy of mind in a single, uncompromising formula, Austin, convinced that oversimplification was the occupational disease of philosophers, concentrated, more influentially and so more representatively, on highly detailed negative criticism.

If they differed in this respect, Ryle and Austin agreed in rejecting Wittgenstein's idea of philosophy as a therapeutic undertaking aimed at the relief of a characteristic kind of intellectual perplexity. They regarded these puzzles more as incitements to the systematic task of establishing the informal logic of the ordinary use of expressions or, as Ryle also described it, of mapping the logical geography of concepts. In general terms, then, the method of the Oxford philosophers lay somewhere in between the professed method of Wittgenstein and the methods of the logical positivists of the 1930's. With the positivists and against Wittgenstein they believed that the job of philosophy was to set out the logical properties and relations of the various forms of discourse in a systematic way. But with Wittgenstein and against the positivists they rejected the ideal of linguistic perfection suggested by formal logic, concerning themselves with the description of language as it actually is rather than with the extrication of some ideal essence from it or with the proposal of a logically superior conceptual system as an alternative to it. In particular, as the phrase "informal logic" implies, they rejected the claims of standard formal logic to be an adequate instrument for philosophical analysis. They admitted the intrinsic value and interest of the construction of formal systems, their adequacy to the analysis of the detached and intellectualized languages of mathematics and theoretical physics, and their exemplary usefulness as language-games. But they thought that the formal logician's passion for economy led to an obliteration of distinctions which must be recognized if language was to be understood in the whole varied range of its uses.

Most of Ryle's main doctrines were foreshadowed in his first important essay, "Systematically Misleading Expressions" (1931).[2] Its chief purpose is to work out in detail some aspects of the Wittgensteinian theme that words do not have meaning in virtue of naming objects. Specifically, Ryle argues that even the grammatical subjects of statements, which at least purport to refer to something, do not always do so. At the end of the essay, he makes a brief statement of his ideas about the proper method of philosophy. Its task is to elucidate the hidden logical form of the assertions in which our beliefs are expressed. "Philosophy," he says, "is an exercise in systematic restatement." In the course of the argument he mentions amongst the class of misleadingly referential-looking expressions phrases that appear to refer to such mental entities as feelings, ideas, and concepts. The true logical subject of a statement seemingly about a man's feelings is the man himself, who is said by it to be in a certain state or condition, and not some metaphysically internal object.

Ryle's preoccupation with philosophical method has continued. Although he accepted the idea that philosophy was concerned with the revelation of logical form, he was suspicious from the beginning of the early Wittgensteinian theory that the logical form of a statement was determined by some natural correspondence of arrangement between the elements of the statement and the elements of the fact it stated. As he sees it, the inquiry is internal to language, a matter of distinguishing between grammatically similar assertions like "x is red" and "x is soluble" where the second statement implies a logically complicated array of statements of the same kind as the first. His preferred way of marking these differences was developed in his essay on "Categories" (1937).[3] Grammatically similar expressions are of different categories if they cannot be generally substituted for one another without absurdity, and if the statements in which they occur have differing implications or logical powers. Philosophy, in the fully worked-out view expounded in *Philosophical Arguments* (1945) and most notably applied in *The Concept of Mind* (1949), is a business of making explicit the rules which we follow unreflectively in our ordinary use of words, of "replacing category-habits by category-disciplines." A special form of this undertaking is considered in his *Dilemmas* (1956). Here philosophy is called in to adjudicate in conflicts between other forms of inquiry. Problems such as that about the freedom of the will are traced to a misapplication of concepts from the realm of scientific explanation in that of moral appraisal. The philosopher must settle these boundary-disputes by showing the limits of the proper application of the problem-generating notions.

Ryle has also continued to study the nature of meaning, the main subject of his early essay. His views are most fully elaborated in his contribution "The Theory of Meaning" to *British Philosophy in the Mid-Century* (1956). His chief purpose in this field has been to correct the errors of what may be called denotationism, a view which Ryle finds in its most unqualified form in Carnap's *Meaning and Necessity*. Where Carnap allocates two kinds of meaning, an intension and an extension, to each kind of expression, Ryle insists, first, that only the intension of a term can properly be regarded as its meaning and, secondly, that meanings are not any sort of objects and should not be spoken of as if they were. "The meaning of '*x*' " was one of the pseudo-referential terms examined in the early essay. In Ryle's view, to speak of the meaning of a term is not to talk about some abstract or Platonic object correlated with it but rather to talk of the job or function which has been conventionally assigned to it. In effect, his aim is to replace the doctrine of meanings as intellectually inspectable essences, common to Russell and the phenomenologists, by a behaviorist account of the matter. A term has meaning if there are people who understand it and their understanding of it consists in their readiness to produce it in selected circumstances, to associate it with a selection of other words, and to infer statements containing it from a selection of other statements. No Platonic third realm is mentioned in this theory, only the observable speech-habits of human beings.

In *The Concept of Mind*, Ryle's major work, his ideas about method are applied to a large but connected assemblage of philosophical problems. If his philosophical logic is directed against Platonism, his philosophy of mind is devoted to the demolition of Cartesianism. This is the theory that the world of our experience contains two radically different sorts of entity: physical things disposed in space, and mental or conscious things each proprietary to a particular mind. To Ryle, Cartesianism is a category-mistake which mistakenly infers from the grammatical form of our discourse about the powers and operations of the mind that alongside the common world of physical things there is a vast number of private mental worlds to each of which some particular mind has privileged access but which are sealed off from one another. Cartesian philosophers have mistakenly reified the apparent references of our mental vocabulary. What they take to be statements about actual occurrences in a host of private worlds are really about the dispositions of certain intelligent and sentient things in the common physical world. To talk about a man's beliefs or emotions is not to say what he is internally doing but is rather to speak in a compendious way about a large range of straightforwardly observable things that he is disposed to do. To say "*X* is angry" is to ascribe a disposition to him to shout, break things, and hit people; it is not to report a private event in his stream of consciousness. An important consequence is the rejection of any asymmetry between self-knowledge and knowledge of others. I find out about my own mental states, according to Ryle, in much the same way as I find out about the mental states of others. It follows that there is no privileged access to mental facts, that the difference between my knowledge of myself and of others is only one of degree.

Some critics have found the many illuminating inquiries into particular topics in Ryle's book more fruitful and persuasive than its general thesis. Among these may be mentioned his subordination of knowing that, the apprehension of propositions that philosophers have so much concentrated upon, to knowing how, the ability to perform specified tasks successfully. A connected point is his account of the intellect. He sees its employment not as an internal process prior and parallel to speech or other bodily activity but as the manner in which bodily activities are carried on, the readiness of the agent involved to correct errors and deal with accidents, something essentially adverbial, not substantive. An important chapter on perception denies that its immediate objects are sensations and, therefore, that sensation is the primary form of empirical knowledge from which beliefs about material things must be inferred. Although sensation is integral to observation, it is, Ryle believes, a logical mistake to regard it as itself a mode of acquiring knowledge. Also important in his attack on what he calls "the myth of volitions." Voluntary action is not distinguished from reflex or accidental bodily movement by following on an internal act of will. In a characteristic way he rejects this theory as giving rise to a vicious regress, since it can only answer the question it invites as to the voluntariness or otherwise of these supposed acts of will by postulating yet further acts of will in an unending series.

Ryle, although the largest figure in recent Oxford philosophy, is not the most characteristic. For the decade and a half after the war the tone of philosophical work there was unquestionably set by J. L. Austin, who died in 1960. For all his lively concern with the detailed peculiarities of ordinary speech, Ryle has always remained a systematic philosopher in the style of Russell, the early Wittgenstein, and the logical positivists, and despite its novelties of approach *The Concept of Mind* resembles the *Tractatus* and Carnap's *Logische Aufbau der Welt* in being an exercise in reductive analysis. With Austin, the philosophy of ordinary language comes definitely into its own. He described the discipline he invented, practised, and clearly believed to be the most needed, if not only possible, method of doing philosophy as "rational grammar" or "linguistic phenomenology." An immensely sophisticated refinement of the technique of G. E. Moore, whom Austin greatly admired, it also owed something to the technique of the Oxford realists deriving from Cook Wilson, in particular to that of Prichard. Behind it lay a belief that most previous philosophy had disastrously oversimplified the rules of discourse by extracting them from a small range of favorite examples. Austin's aim was to establish the rules of language by a really careful and detailed investigation of the actual use of words, guided by the widest and most varied stock of examples. With scrupulous exactness he did for its own sake what Wittgenstein had done with the more limited purpose of weakening the hold of seductive analogies and what Ryle was doing in a more cursory way as part of a systematic construction.

Much of Austin's early work was in the field of philosophical logic. In a very early paper, "The Meaning of a Word" (1940),[4] he argued, with Ryle, that a word's meaning was not any sort of object and therefore that there could be no general distinction between analytic and synthetic statements since, a meaning not being the sort of thing that has parts, there is not always an answer to the question "is the predicate of this statement part of the meaning of the subject?" Furthermore, there was no general answer to the question "what is the meaning of a word?", only specific answers of a various and complex kind to questions about the meaning of specific words. In a vein that anticipated Strawson's theory of reference, he held that entailment was not the only kind of implication and formal contradiction not the only kind of absurdity. With Ryle again, Austin attributed theories of universals to the unfounded assumption that if a word had meaning there must be an object which is the meaning of that word. Curiously enough, he took a directly opposite stand with regard to the problem of truth, defending the highly general theory that the truth of a statement consists in its correspondence to a fact against Strawson's view that to call a statement true is simply to endorse it and not to say anything about its relation to the extra-linguistic world.

Perhaps Austin's most original contribution to

philosophy was his theory of performative utterances, which he used to discredit the tendency of philosophers to suppose that the fundamental and usual employment of language was to state or describe. His attack on what he called "the descriptive fallacy" arose from an examination of the concept of knowledge undertaken in his celebrated essay "Other Minds" (1946).[5] Against such theories as Cook Wilson's, that knowledge was something unique and unanalyzable, he argued that its distinction from belief lay not in what it was in itself but rather in what one who claimed knowledge was doing as compared with someone stating a belief. To claim to know is to guarantee what one is saying and to give one's authority to others to believe it. It is not to describe a special attitude or state of mind. In Austin's view, it was correct to give this guarantee whenever there was no specific reason assignable for doubting one's beliefs. The general fact that men are liable to err was not a sufficient reason for withholding it. Austin compared "I know that x" with "I promise to do y" as being both performances rather than mere descriptions, emphasizing, with Wittgenstein, the multiplicity of uses to which language could be put. In time he came to reject as over-simple the original distinction between the performative and the constative. In his posthumous *How to do Things with Words* (1962) the contrast between merely saying things, truly or falsely, and doing things, "happily" or "unhappily," with sentences is developed into a more general theory, which distinguishes in any speech-act the locutionary element, what one actually says, the illocutionary element, the kind of act, promising or advising or requesting and so forth, which by convention the sentence in question is used to do, and the perlocutionary element, the actual effect of the speech-act, for the sake of which, perhaps, one originally made it.

Of comparable importance is the attack mounted by Austin in his lectures on perception, *Sense and Sensibilia* (1962), on the principal arguments used by philosophers like Price and Ayer to show that the immediate objects of perception were not material objects but sense-impressions. Their attempts to attach a definite meaning to the term "sense-datum" were undermined by an examination, of unprecedented delicacy, of the crucial words "look," "appear," and "seem." He subjected the inferences embodied in the argument from illusion to as searching and destructive a scrutiny as the premises from which it started. In particular, he questioned the belief that veridical and illusory perceptions were, from the perceiver's point of view, indiscriminable. An ingenious demonstration of the systematic ambiguity of the word "real" showed the unclarity of the contention that what we perceive is not reality but appearance. Austin went on to criticize the almost universal assumption of theorists of knowledge that knowledge has foundations. In his view there is no class of statements which always and by their nature constitute the ultimate evidence for our beliefs about the external world. No statements are basic in the sense of not being open to support by further, statable evidence.

Austin's chief remaining interest was in the assumptions underlying the traditional problem of free will. In his essay "A Plea for Excuses" (1956)[6] he said that philosophers should consider in detail the wide variety of ways in which responsibility is disclaimed or qualified. It is a mistake to suppose that there is a single, simple division of actions into the free and the unfree. Accident, mistake, inadvertence, and lack of intention are significantly different from each other. In "Ifs and Cans" (1956)[7] he criticized the attempts of some philosophers to interpret the statement "*X* could have done otherwise" in a way compatible with determinism by holding it to be either an ellipsis for "*X* could have done otherwise if such-and-such conditions had obtained" or equivalent to "*X would* have done otherwise if such-and-such conditions had obtained."

Of the other Oxford philosophers of the post-war period, undoubtedly the most important is P. F. Strawson. In his first writings he was mainly concerned with the application of formal logic to the problems of philosophy by Russell and his followers, the most notable of these in recent times being W. V. Quine of Harvard. Strawson maintained that formal logic was not a true anatomy of the concealed structure of our conceptual equipment but a simplified caricature produced by a desire for economy in computation. There are two main sides to his criticism. On the one hand, he showed how the logician distorts the ordinary sense of the formal words such as "if" and "or" in devising his calculi; on the other, he criticized the doctrine about reference embodied in Russell's theory of descriptions, and in the interpretation of general statements in Frege's quantification theory. Where Russell had taken a singular assertion with a non-referring subject or a general assertion with an empty subject-class to be false, Strawson held them to be neither true nor false. Though meaningful as sentences, they failed, in the circumstances, to make a statement, and the question of their truth-value did not, therefore, arise. Rather in the manner of Austin, Strawson said that the logicians were working with too small a set of distinctions. Confining themselves to the notion of entailment they decided that "the *A* is *B*" did and "all *A* are *B*" did not entail "there is something which is *A*." In his view neither entail it but both presuppose it, in the sense that neither can be used to make a statement unless it is true. The full development of the consequences of this theory of reference in his *Individuals* (1959) will be considered later. His theory of truth also had an Austinian flavor, despite its rejection by Austin, for it held that the function of the predicate "is true" was not to describe the statements to which it was applied

but to endorse or confirm them. There is no difference of descriptive content between "*p*" and "*p* is true," yet they differ in force or function. Both say *p*, but where the former does it simply the latter does in circumstances where it has already been said or implied. At the close of his *Introduction to Logical Theory* (1952) Strawson advanced an influential theory about induction. To the request for a justification of induction he replied that it could not be shown without circularity that induction would succeed. But the not wholly dissimilar proposition that induction is rational is analytic, since it gives a partial definition of rationality, and the necessary rationality of induction is all the justification it can have or requires.

The leading ideas of ordinary language philosophy have been applied by others in a wide variety of fields. Toulmin gave a performative analysis of probability[8] in which the function of the adverb in "probably *p*" was held to be that of making a guarded or qualified claim, considerations about observed frequencies being understood as evidence for the claim and not as a specification of its meaning. Warnock criticized the positivist identification of meaning with verifiability, making use of Strawson's idea that the significance of a sentence was prior to and distinct from its being used to make statements true or false. In his book on *Berkeley* (1953) he contended that statements about sense-data were neither, as in phenomenalism, part of the meaning of, nor, as in representationalism, contingent evidence for statements about material objects. The two were related rather as factual evidence to judgment in a judicial process. A somewhat analogous theory of the logical distinctness of categorical statements about material objects and the hypothetical statements about sense-data with which phenomenalists held them to be identical in meaning was urged in Berlin's vigorous critique of phenomenalism (in *Mind*, 1950). D. F. Pears applied the technique of Austin's philosophical logic in his demonstration of the vacuous and truistic nature of all general theories of universals,[9] all attempts to give a comprehensive explanation of why it is that a single predicate is applied to a number of different individual things. Such theories, he said, simply repeated themselves. In the end they asserted no more than that we call certain things "*F*" because they are all *F*.

Ryle's philosophy of mind was used by P. L. Gardiner[10] against idealist theories of historical explanation like Collingwood's which said that the historian's task was to relive the thoughts of past agents, and by A. G. N. Flew[11] to the contentions about the disembodied existence of the human soul made by philosophical theologians and students of psychical research. T. D. Weldon asserted[12] the emptiness of the very general principles with which political philosophers had tried to justify political obligation. H. L. A. Hart drew on Austin's theory of action in his important works[13] on the philosophy of law, examining responsibility, punishment, causal imputation, and the definition of law itself.

The most influential and widely discussed book in the field of ethics was R. M. Hare's *Language of Morals* (1952). It contained a much improved version of the non-descriptive theory put forward in the 1930's by Ayer and C. L. Stevenson. Agreeing with them, and with Hume, that there could be no valid inference from "is" to "ought", that judgments of value could not be deduced from wholly descriptive or factual premises, Hare interpreted judgments of value not as mere expressions of feeling but as implicit affirmations of universal imperatives. Factual reasons can be given for value-judgments, he held, but only in the light of antecedently adopted principles of value, and a man's ultimate principles must just be chosen. They are not true or false but sincere or insincere: sincere if the assertor directs his own conduct in accordance with them. Toulmin in his *Reason in Ethics* (1950) agreed with him about the logical distinctness of the descriptive and the evaluative but argued that the relevance of fact to value was determined not by freely chosen principles but by rules of evaluative inference whose acceptance as criteria of validity was as vital a part of the definition of rationality as the rules of deduction and induction. Comparable limitations on the rationally admissible scope of valuations were set out in the *Ethics* (1954) of P. H. Nowell-Smith. More recently, the descriptive-evaluative distinction itself, the accepted point of departure for most recent ethics, has come in for criticism, particularly in the writings of Mrs. P. R. Foot.[14]

Though its members sometimes protest that there never has been such a thing as a school of ordinary language philosophy, something came to an end with the death of Austin in 1960. Austin's three posthumous works will ensure it a lasting place in the history of philosophy, but the ablest of the generation which he influenced were already moving away from both his piecemeal approach and his rapt fascination with the established surface of language to a way of doing philosophy that was at once more systematic and more speculative. In Strawson's *Individuals* and Hampshire's *Thought and Action* the inquiry is pursued into the general nature and justification of the conceptual status quo with whose precise anatomy Austin was concerned. But before this latest phase in the development of British philosophy is considered, something should be said about the philosophers in a more direct line of descent from the logical atomists and positivists, inspired by Russell rather than Moore and more impressed by logic and scientific innovation than by the authority of common sense and ordinary language.

The Tradition of Logical Analysis: Popper and Ayer

ALTHOUGH Cambridge had little new to offer after the retirement of Wittgenstein, Oxford was not the only source of original ideas. It was in the post-war period that London for the first time came to occupy a position on the philosophical scene commensurate with its being the largest university in the country. This was largely due to the presence there of Popper and Ayer, who for all their differences were close enough in sympathy for "London philosophy" to be more than a geographical expression. Popper had never been a member of the Vienna Circle and was, indeed, strongly opposed to many of its central doctrines. He rejected the verificationist criterion of meaning, the view that individual sense-experiences were the foundations of knowledge and the belief that science and common knowledge were derived from the senses by induction. All the same he concentrated on the favorite problems of the positivists, using something like their criterion of meaning to mark off empirical science from metaphysics and offering alternative theories of the foundations and growth of knowledge, and he approached these problems in very much the same way, confident in formal logic and unhampered by the intellectual pieties of Oxford toward common sense and the ordinary use of words. Ayer, of course, had been the closest adherent and most effective expositor of the ideas of the Vienna Circle in Britain in the 1930's, and although he had always applied their methods to ordinary beliefs rather than to mathematics and natural science and came to modify his initial radicalism a good deal, he remained clearly in the positivist tradition.

Popper's ideas first appeared in his *Logic of Scientific Discovery* (1935, translated into English 1959), and although impressively developed and applied in the succeeding years, his fundamental convictions have remained unchanged. His two main problems are those of demarcating empirical science from metaphysics and of establishing the conditions of acceptability of scientific theories. The solutions he offers are connected by their joint dependence on the concept of falsification. The starting point is the fact that while theories, in virtue of their unrestricted generality, cannot be verified, the source of Hume's problem of induction, they can be falsified by a single negative instance. In Popper's view, a theory or assertion is empirical to the extent that it is open to empirical falsification. Unfalsifiable or metaphysical theories are not meaningless, as the positivists held, but simply unscientific. Theories are not formed by any mechanical inductive routine of generalization nor can they be justified by heaping up any amount of positive confirmation. They start as imaginative conjectures, and the aim of observation is to try to falsify them by discovering the falsity of the observable consequences that can be deduced from them. The scientific attitude is one of determined effort to falsify conjectures. If a theory passes unscathed the most stringent tests we can devise, then it is corroborated and so far worthy of acceptance, but its subsequent elimination and replacement always remains possible. The observable, potentially falsifying, consequences, whose deducibility from a theory proves its scientific status, are not incorrigible propositions about immediate experience but are statements about publicly observable things at particular places and times and are themselves further testable in the light of antecedently accepted theory. There is, therefore, no logical terminus to the process of testing, for two reasons: first, the unlimited number of basic statements entailed by a theory, and, secondly, the provisional and conventional nature of the acceptance of these basic statements.

Knowledge, then, is not a structure built up by inductive inference from the passively-received and indubitable deliverances of sensation. It is throughout conjectural, theoretical, and so active, a matter of putting imaginative questions to the world and energetically seeking a negative answer. Sense-experience may be causally related to our beliefs but it does not provide them ready made. Our conjectures about the world are free creations, and our natural propensity to form theories only becomes science when it is accompanied by a resolutely critical attitude to its productions, which concerns itself only with falsifiable beliefs and strives to discover which of them are in fact false. The growth of knowledge goes through three stages: first, the intuitive formation of a hypothesis, then, the logical derivation of its observable consequences, and finally, the exposure of these consequences to empirical test. If the hypothesis is falsified it must be revised or totally replaced; if it escapes falsification it is corroborated to the extent that the attempt to falsify it has been energetic. The more falsifiable a hypothesis is the more it is corroborated by successful exposure to tests. Popper shows that the falsifiability, simplicity, and empirical content of hypotheses vary together and are indeed the same thing looked at in different ways. A metaphysical statement is one where they are wholly absent.

The strength of this system of fundamental ideas is shown by the host of important consequences that Popper has drawn from it. The first of these is his rejection of the traditional empiricist theory of concept-formation. Hume believed that we acquire the concepts with which we classify things from their observed similarities. Similarity, Popper replies, is always similarity in a certain respect and from a point of view which must be adopted by an antecedent choice or decision. Concepts, then, are made, not found. Secondly, he defends a realistic interpretation of the theoretical entities of natural science against both the essentialism which holds that there

can be a complete and final explanation of events in terms of a set of ultimate, clear, and distinct essences, and the instrumentalism which regards theories as symbolic conveniences, formulas for the prediction of experience which are to be judged in terms of convenience rather than truth. Against essentialism he argues that the process of scientific discovery is continuous and incompletable; against instrumentalism that scientific theory gives genuinely new information about the structure of the world and is not merely a way of arranging tidily what we know about the order of our sensations. In conformity with this he interprets probability as an objective propensity of natural objects and not subjectively as a measure of relative ignorance. Thirdly, he is a mind-body dualist and an indeterminist. The conjectures of the scientific intelligence are genuine creative novelties, inherently unpredictable and not determined by the character of the scientist's physical environment. The thinking mind is not a causal mechanism. Similarly, judgments of value are held to record decisions or proposals; they are not determined by our given, natural preferences as in naturalistic ethical theories, though for his own part Popper opts for a characteristically falsificationist version of utilitarianism which chooses the elimination of human suffering as the goal of moral action.

What began as a theory of scientific method, using the concept of falsification to distinguish science from metaphysics and to give a noninductive account of the growth of knowledge, has thus developed into a general theory of knowledge which rejects both the empiricist account of concepts and of the incorrigible and sensory character of the ultimate evidence for our beliefs. Its insistence on the activity of the mind asserts the autonomy of the mind in the acquisition of knowledge and in moral action. Most notable of all, perhaps, is the social philosophy which Popper has presented in his *Open Society* (1945) and *The Poverty of Historicism* (1957), two sides of a sustained attack on historicism, the idea that the course of human history is subject to strict general laws of development. In the earlier book he examines in fascinating detail the views of Plato, Hegel, and Marx about history and society. A more systematic critique of historicism is contained in the later one. He argues that it rests either on a mistaken analogy between the procedure of social and historical inquiry it recommends and the methods of the physical sciences or else on the belief that scientific method is not applicable to human affairs at all. Agreeing with the view that science can be applied to human affairs, he argues that science does not yield laws of general development (evolution, for example, being not a law but a trend) and that a genuinely scientific theory of society, following the usual methods, will yield specific information about the unintended consequences of human actions. But there can be no overall theory of the historical process because this process is strongly influenced by the development of human knowledge, and the mind cannot predict its own future discoveries.

Popper does not believe that there is any unique philosophical method. Neither the minute examination of actual language practiced by Wittgenstein and the ordinary language philosophers nor the construction of logically ideal languages practiced by Carnap is adequate on its own, though both may have a subsidiary usefulness. Philosophy, as he sees it, is continuous with science. It has the same goal — the interpretation, not of language, but of the world — and must proceed by the same method — the critical examination of hypotheses. In particular, there is no hard and fast line in practice between science and metaphysics, although falsifiability distinguishes them in principle. A hypothesis, unfalsifiable at the time it was first put forward, may acquire scientific status by becoming accessible to testing through improvements of experimental technique or appropriate modifications of its content. Science, indeed, begins in more or less poetical myth. The crucial difference lies in the articulately critical attitude of the scientist. The kind of philosophy he is most concerned with, the theory of knowledge, is at its best when inspired by problems arising in the detailed work of the sciences, for left to its own devices it becomes academically scholastic. It proceeds by a combination of methods characteristic of all scientific thinking: observation, the historical scholarship which reveals the background to the present state of the problem, and logical analysis. His own theory is accompanied by an indeterminist metaphysics and issues in recommendations about both the conduct of thinking and the principles of personal and social action. Popper traces his dependence for the initial stimulus of his thought to Hume's account of the problem of induction, but his closest affinity is to Kant. His ideas about the relation of science and metaphysics, the intrinsically active nature of the mind, and the autonomy of human beings as rational agents constitute a powerful restatement in contemporary terms of Kantian themes.

Ayer's first two books systematized and made memorably accessible the principal doctrines of orthodox left-wing analysis as they had been progressively worked out by Russell, the *Tractatus*, and the Vienna Circle. The task of philosophy, as the logical analysis of discourse, was to classify utterances, to distinguish genuine propositions from others, and to explain the meaning and justification of propositions by their reductive analysis into basic statements about immediate experience. The principle of verification was used to show that religious, evaluative, and metaphysical utterances were not propositions. Genuine propositions were either necessary or contingent. If they were necessary they were analytic, true in virtue of the conventionally assigned meanings of their terms. This domain contained logic, mathematics, and the acceptable,

analytic residue of philosophy. Contingent propositions were either reports of immediate experience or truth-functional assemblages of such reports, analyzable into and inferable from them.

The introduction to the second edition of *Language, Truth and Logic* (1946) revealed some hesitancy and heart-searching about these positions but no large change of opinion. It specified in a summary way the main lines of Ayer's philosophical work since the war. Difficulties in the formulation of the chief instrument of analytic surgery, the verification principle, have led him to take a more tolerant view of metaphysical theories. Now treated on their individual merits, such things as theories of substance and universals have been reinterpreted by him as concealed logical analyses, often mistaken perhaps but at least not empty words. He also relaxed the stringent conditions he had originally laid down for a satisfactory philosophical analysis. The reductive ideal of definitions in use, of precise translations of statements about material things, past events, and other minds into propositions about immediate, present, subjective experience, was abandoned as too paradoxical in its consequences. In particular, the identification of past events with present and future experiences and of other minds with certain regularities in my experiences was given up. They could be defined in terms of past experiences and the experiences of others since these are not intrinsically unverifiable; it is only a contingent fact that I live at the time that I do and have the experiences I have. Ayer has not departed so far from his initial phenomenalism about material things, though he has given up the name. He has continued to hold that statements about the material world are somehow reducible to logically prior statements about sense-experience even if they are not strictly equivalent in meaning to any specifiable set of experiential assertions. Finally, he has substantially qualified the abruptness of his first version of the emotive theory of value, admitting that value-judgments are significant and can be logically articulated in arguments, but he has continued to insist that they are antonomous and not deducible from statements of fact and that since ultimate principles of value are not objective but must be chosen, they are neither true nor false.

In *The Problem of Knowledge* (1956) these new developments are brought together. Knowledge, he begins, is true belief accompanied by the right to be sure. It is not a special, infallible state of mind. The problems of epistemology are created by skeptical challenges to our conventional ideas about what constitutes this right to be sure. This leads on to a general theory of the nature of epistemological problems, foreshadowed in Wisdom's philosophical practice and in Waismann's idea of language strata,[15] but presented by Ayer with characteristic lucidity and explicitness. We can sort out our beliefs, he says, in such a way as to reveal a recurrent pattern in the logical relations between pairs of the resulting classes. All the evidence we have for causal connections, material things, past events, the experiences of others, and the theoretical entities of science is provided by particular conjunctions, sense-impressions, present events, the speech and behavior of others, and observables respectively. In each of these cases (and Ayer could have added others — values and preferences and the divine and the terrestrial), however, there is a logical gap between evidence and conclusion, facts of the first kind cannot be deductively inferred from evidence of the second kind. In this recurring situation, the skeptic denies that we have any right to be sure about facts of the kind inferred and even that we can attach any meaning to assertions about them. But there are other possible strategies. One is to deny the dependence, to hold, with intuitionism, that there is some sort of direct access to the questionable facts. Another is to deny the gap, the procedure of reductivism, which maintains that the statements embodying the conclusions can be translated without remainder into statements about the evidence available for them. Thirdly, there is the transcendentalist maneuver of invoking a principle of inference, which must be at once necessary and synthetic, to bridge the gap. Ayer's own preference is for what appears to be a somewhat diffident version of the last alternative. Described as "the method of descriptive analysis," it consists in admitting both the dependence and the gap and, by showing that skepticism is the only other possibility, taking the gap, as he puts it, "in one's stride."

The book's discussions of perception, knowledge of the past, and the philosophy of mind are not confined to this central problem about evidence. Ayer defends the primacy of the sense-datum language against recent objections and maintains that its statements are incorrigible and certain in being open to no more than verbal mistakes. His old hostility to the metaphysical concept of substance is expressed in his treatment of personal identity, which he no longer makes dependent on the identity of the body, and also in an essay on individuals where he argues for the thesis that a thing is simply the totality of its properties by supporting the possibility of a language in which all reference is performed by predicates. He has defended Hume's reconciliation of determinism with responsibility by the argument that the opposite of freedom is not causation but constraint and has recently advanced criticisms of both the prevailing interpretations of probability. In his London inaugural lecture, *Thinking and Meaning* (1947), he put forward a theory of the intellectual processes much like Ryle's; in his Oxford inaugural, *Philosophy and Language* (1960), he argued that the subject-matter of philosophy was not language but language in relation to fact. The follower of Russell in many things, Ayer has learnt from Russell the profitable lesson that the influence of philosophical ideas can be greatly extended by the style of their presentation. The Cartesian grace and clarity of his writing are unrivalled.

The Latest Phase: A Revival of System

THE Oxford philosophers, to the extent that they formed a school, were held together more by a unity of method than by allegiance to a body of doctrine. Some points of controversy within the group have been mentioned already — about truth and the status of ultimate moral principles, for example — and there are many others. Thus, few followed Ryle all the way in his identification of mind with dispositions to behavior or in his view that the notion of a sense-datum is logically incoherent. Until very recently no Oxford philosopher, with the exception of Ryle, has articulated his ideas into anything like a comprehensive system. Ryle has never been concerned to present his views in a systematic fashion, but throughout his work there is the common theme of hostility to non-concrete entities: sense-data, private mental states, the abstract universals and propositions of philosophical logic. Each of these suspect kinds of entity is interpreted by him in concrete terms. Perception is of public material things, mental life is dispositions to behavior, the thinking mind expresses itself in skilled linguistic and bodily activity.

But generally Austin's deep distrust of general formulas was taken as authoritative. His insistence on the minute investigation of particular issues on their merits and without the encumbrance of any theoretical prejudices led to a division of labor which left the broader consequences of philosophical inquiries to take care of themselves. Austin felt and communicated a sense that the whole work of philosophy needed to be done again from the beginning and that only the smallest corners of a large territory had been touched by the exact and patient methods he had devised. In his view it was far too early to draw any large doctrinal conclusions from what had been achieved so far.

In the last few years there has been some resistance to the restraints of the theoretical chastity he imposed. It has shown itself most impressively in two books published in 1959 in which philosophy is once more practiced in something like the grand manner. Strawson's *Individuals* is the more finished and careful of the two; Hampshire's *Thought and Action* the more comprehensive and ambitious. Both felt the time to be ripe for a move beyond piecemeal philosophical investigations to a more inclusive kind of philosophical theorizing. Strawson describes what he is doing as descriptive metaphysics, the attempt to elicit and explain the most general features of our conceptual system, those that underlie the massive, historically unchanging core of our way of thinking and speaking about the world. He regards it as continuous with the work of Aristotle and Kant and contrasts it with the more common revisionary metaphysics which seeks to replace our existing, inherited system of concepts with an ideal or at least improved one. Specifically, his book takes the form of a scrutiny of the whole range of our techniques of reference. Within the general field of individuals, of logical subjects or objects of reference, he picks out particulars as prior to and presupposed by the rest and again within the range of particulars he argues that material bodies and persons, who for him are a species of material bodies, are basic. Hampshire sees philosophy as a theory of man, whose business is to articulate man's distinctive powers and activities with reference to the interests and social background from which they arise. Since this background is constantly changing, philosophy can never be completed. Although he starts, like Strawson, from an account of the inevitable character of any system of concepts that can be used to express and communicate beliefs, he is particularly emphatic about its dependence on the fact that we are active and not just contemplative beings and he goes on to consider the whole active life of man in its interplay with the instruments at his disposal for understanding himself and the world. Unfortunately, both these remarkable books are hard to read. *Individuals* suffers from an excess of subtlety and a fondness for oblique modes of expression, *Thought and Action* from a lack of internal organization and an undue preponderance of assertion over argument. Comparable in scope and ambition to the most important recent contribution to philosophy from the United States, Quine's *Word and Object*, they are, however, worthy of the great interest and attention they have evoked.

Individuals is, in effect, a full development of the theory put forward in Strawson's important article of 1950 on referring. He argued there that singular terms or uniquely referring expressions could not be eliminated from language in the way proposed by Quine in his generalization of Russell's theory of descriptions. The requirement of uniqueness can only be satisfied by demonstrative terms such as "this" which refer only to what is currently observed, or by terms referring to entities located in a single spatio-temporal scheme. Furthermore, to secure a unitary scheme of this kind the basic objects of reference must be capable of reidentification. They must persist through time so that the momentary spaces of single observations can be linked together as one enduring space. He concludes that the basic particulars, by reference to which all other kinds of particular must be introduced, are material bodies, three-dimensional, enduring, and accessible to observation. Private states of mind, theoretical constructs, and such things as events and processes can only be identified by reference to bodies and persons. Extremely ingenious investigations of a purely auditory world and of a version of Leibniz's monadism in which spatio-temporal characteristics are seen as properties of objects confirm the primacy of bodies by showing that in these worlds the essential conditions of reference could not be satisfied. In a controversial chapter on persons, Strawson rejects both the Cartesian theory of mental substance and the view that a person is an unowned set of experiences. Why, he asks, do we ascribe our experiences to anything at all and why, in particular, do we ascribe them to the same thing that has our physical characteristics? He contends that I can only call some experiences mine if I am able to ascribe experiences to others and I am primarily distinguished from others as a body from other bodies. Predicates are ascribed to people in two ways, roughly speaking introspectively and behaviorally. To be able to apply them at all we must understand both aspects of their use. He thinks it conceivable that experience should continue after bodily death but only for a person who has been embodied.

In the second part of the book he moves on to the more general question of establishing that particulars are the primary logical subjects by showing the connection between the distinction of particular and universal and that of subject and predicate. Subject and predicate are grammatically distinguished as substantival phrase and verb and are distinguished by category in that the former is an instance of or is characterized by the latter. What connects these ways of distinguishing subject and predicate is that both ascribe a completeness to subjects that is not ascribed to predicates. He explains this completeness by tracing it to the presupposition, by the introduction of a particular into an utterance, of the contingent fact that the thing in question exists. The introduction of a universal presupposes only the significance of the predicative term, in other words, the tautology that something is an instance of the universal or that nothing is. Here a difficulty appears. Reference to particulars presupposes their existence, but statements of existence only have their familiar sense if the idea of reference to particulars is already understood. In a complex discussion Strawson argues that this general idea could be obtained from existentially non-committal assertions which had place-times as their subjects or, more realistically, from what he calls feature-placing statements like "it is raining" or "there is snow here." These would yield the general idea of a particular and thus give sense to the existential assumptions that lie behind the great mass of our references to particular things. Finally, Strawson rejects the nominalist view that non-basic particulars and non-particulars do not really exist and must be reduced to their ontological predecessors. He sees this inclination as a philosophical exaggeration of the facts about the order of dependence which he has set out.

The theory of language and of knowledge which forms the first part of Hampshire's *Thought and*

Action also asserts the primacy of material objects and persons. There can be no thinking without language, and it is essential to language that the world which it treats should be divided up into continuing things that are identifiable at different times and that there should be concepts of the resemblances between these things. These fixed requirements are, however, of a structural kind and they can be satisfied by many different specific systems of concepts. Hampshire's position about the specification of the fixed formal framework is radically conventionalistic. There is no natural and immutable set of empirical concepts; we have a choice here which is determined by our interests, and these are always changing. The empirically innocent eye is a myth, and the facts into which we divide the world cannot be analyzed into a natural, universal language of sense-impressions. This is shown by the fact that our primary empirical classifications turn on the possible uses and the causal origin of things rather than on their appearance. Our perceptual contact with the world is more a matter of agency than of contemplation. We perceive things by manipulating them in pursuit of practical ends, take the sense of touch as authoritative as to the reality of things, and are always conscious of ourselves as embodied agents in a world of other, more or less obstructive, bodies. It is from the flow of our intentions that we gain a sense of our own identity and, more generally, a sense of the passage of time. We cannot detach ourselves, as autonomous Cartesian subjects with a private inner life, from our situation as embodied intentional agents in the world. The central element in personality is not the merely contemplative intellect but the will. To be self-conscious is to be aware of one's situation in the world and of one's intentions.

He turns next to examine the concept of intention. We always know what we intend to do and it must always be possible to formulate our intentions in words even if we do not do so. Language and intention are mutually dependent. We have two sorts of knowledge about our future actions: intentional and predictive. In the one case we decide what we are going to do, in the other we discover it. The two kinds of knowledge are mutually exclusive: if I know predictively what I am going to do there is no room left for a decision and, on the other hand, I cannot predict my future decisions and intentions. The conventional nature of language entails that there is no natural division of the stream of reflection and conduct into particular intentions and actions. The interpretation of our active life is dependent on the system of concepts currently at our disposal. Hampshire contends that not all action is motivated by desire or directed toward wanted ends.

He considers next the bearing of his theory of action on human freedom. When we form an intention by making a decision, we cannot be sure that we will do what we intend to do, for it may be impos-sible; but we can be sure that we shall attempt to do it since we can always try. Lack of freedom consists primarily in the ineffectiveness of our intentions. The more we know about what limits their effectiveness the more chance we have of circumventing it. In particular, Freudian psychology is a liberating factor, since it is less a demonstration of our bondage to causality than an enlargement of our self-consciousness and a disclosure of hidden forces which, once revealed, we can resist. A second limitation on our freedom is set by the range of intentions that occurs to us. To identify these limits by reflection is to make them accessible to alteration. In particular, the range of our intentions is restricted by the character of our current conceptual scheme. We are made more free when this is modified, since a larger range of intentions is opened to us. What is crucial here is the way in which the agent's situation conventionally presents itself to him.

Evaluation is the subject of the final section of the book. The idea of goodness is one of the most general we have. It has no fixed content, but it is indispensable if there are to be reasons for action, and it is involved in the criteria for the application of many of our concepts. The concepts of morality, politics, art, and, above all, man himself are essentially disputable, permanently subject to question and revision. Philosophy, as a theory of the distinctive powers of man, is therefore incapable of completion. It transforms its own subject-matter. It does not describe an eternal, abstract human nature but gives reasoned prescriptions about the classification of the distinctively human powers, interests, and virtues. Morality is what is really important to us. Philosophical reflection prevents it from solidifying into custom or social convention. Its central element is the idea of the good man, and this must be derived from a philosophy of mind. The role of art is to surprise and disturb us, to break the hold on us of the familiar. To detach it from life is to trivialize it into mere entertainment. It is not clear just how Hampshire thinks the concept of the good man should be specified. Its concrete character is neither self-evident nor a matter of entirely free choice. What he seems to suggest is that the good man is the one in whom the distinctive human powers, in particular freedom and self-consciousness, are most developed. Neglecting the essentially social character of the moral end in his concentration on the good man to the exclusion of the common good, he appears, perhaps unwittingly, to be committed to taking the Faustian virtuoso as the ideal type of human being.

Hampshire's four main topics — language, intention, freedom, and excellence — move in a circle. Each influences the others, and he sees it as the task of philosophy both to study and to contribute to the history of their interaction. Its central subject is human nature expressing itself in the active pursuits of interests in a natural and social situation. Our purposes and our idea of our situation are determined by our system of concepts, but they also serve to determine it. *Thought and Action* is the most ambitious outcome so far of a preoccupation with the active side of human nature which has been a feature of most original philosophical work in Britain in recent years. It is marginally present in Ryle's rejection of intellectualism, his view that knowledge is an ability to do something rather than a passive state of contemplation, and in Austin's indictment of the "descriptive fallacy" and his consequent inquiry into the use of language to perform actions rather than neutrally register information. It is central to Popper's theory of thinking as a matter of creative conjecture, rational to the extent that it is accompanied by a determination to expose hypotheses to empirical testing and the social process of criticism, and it lies behind his opposition to determinism and his dualistic view of man and nature. Much of this recent interest in human agency stems from the short but very suggestive discussion of the subject toward the end of Wittgenstein's *Philosophical Investigations*, a discussion continued in Elizabeth Anscombe's *Intention* and effectively systematized in A. I. Melden's *Free Action*. It almost seems as if these very different philosophers are all contributing to a revival of something like Kant's way of drawing that most persistent of philosophical distinctions, that between nature and mind. Where Plato distinguished between the order of changing sensible existences and the eternal realm of logical essences and Descartes between the public world of extended matter and the private worlds of consciousness and feeling, these philosophers take agency to be the distinctive feature of human beings, prior to and more fundamental than their rationality and consciousness. The older dualisms have been powerfully defended in recent philosophy: that of essence and existence by Frege, Russell, and Quine, that of mind and body by Moore, Price, and Ayer. Wittgenstein and Ryle have devoted the greater part of their energies to the criticism of these older dualistic theories. In so doing they have prepared the way for the new distinction between man and nature, man as an embodied but active being in a passive nature. It is significant that the three most important of activist philosophers, Popper, Strawson, and Hampshire, all openly acknowledge the influence of Kant.

Notes

1. Early Greek Philosophy (*pages 1 - 13*)

1. Aristotle *Metaphysics* 983 *b* 6.
2. Aristotle *De Anima* 405 *a* 19.
3. See, for example, Diogenes Laertius, ii, 1–2. (The account is repeated in works of other ancient writers.)
4. Simplicius *Physics* 24. 13.
5. Quoted by Aetius, i. 3.4 (translated by Kathleen Freeman, — *Ancilla to the Pre-Socratic Philosophers*, Oxford, 1948).
6. Fragments 30 and 76 (Freeman, *op. cit.*). Fragment numbers in all cases refer to the arrangement of H. Diels in *Die Fragmente der Vorsokratiker*; the numbers here

used, those of the early edition of Diels, are given as alternatives in the sixth edition (edited by W. Kranz, Berlin, 1951).
7. Sextus Empiricus *Adversus Mathematicos* vii. 129.
8. Aristotle *Metaphysics* 985 *b* 23 (translated in *The Works of Aristotle*, edited by J. A. Smith and W. D. Ross, 12 vols., Oxford 1908–1952).
9. *Ibid.*, 986 *b* 21.
10. Fragment 11 (Freeman, *op. cit.*).
11. Fragments 4, 5, 6, 8 (translated — by J. Burnet, *Early Greek Philosophy*, 4th ed., London, 1930).

12. Fragment 8 (translated by G. S. Kirk and J. E. Raven, *The Pre-Socratic Philosophers*, Cambridge, 1957).
13. *Ibid.*
14. H. D. P. Lee's *Zeno of Elea* (Cambridge, 1936) gives the extant fragments with a translation and a very useful critical exposition of Zeno's doctrines.
15. Fragment 17 (Kirk and Raven, *op. cit.*).
16. Fragment 1 (Kirk and Raven, *op. cit.*).
17. Kirk and Raven, *op. cit.*, p. 367.

2. Socrates and Plato (*pages 14 - 35*)

1. *Theaetetus* 146 *c–d.*
2. 495 *e*–499 *b.*
3. 75 *b.*
4. 192 *d.*
5. 97 *b*–99 *c.*
6. Wilfrid Sellars: "Vlastos and the 'Third Man' Argument," *The Philosophical Review*, LXIV (195), 423.

7. 82 *b*–86 *d.*
8. 97 *a*–98 *c.*
9. 476 *d*–480 *a.*
10. 99 *c.*
11. 85 *e*–86 *d.*
12. *Phaedrus* 245 *c*–246 *a*; *Laws* 893 *b*–896 *d.*
13. 93 *d.*
14. 15 *b.*

15. 211 *a.*
16. 226 *b.*
17. 430.
18. 342 *a*–344 *b.*
19. *Protagoras* 324.
20. 580–587.

3. Aristotle (*pages 36 - 61*)

1. *The Works of Aristotle*, translated by various hands under the editorship of J. A. Smith and W. D. Ross, 12 vols. (Oxford, 1908–1952). All translations of passages from Aristotle in this chapter are taken from this work.
2. See, for example, I. M. Bocheński, *Ancient Formal Logic* (Amsterdam, 1951).
3. See Bocheński, *op. cit.*, pp. 63–71, and J. Łukasiewicz, *Aristotle's Syllogistic*, 2nd ed. (Oxford, 1957), ch. III.

4. 24 *b* 18–20.
5. Łukasiewicz, *op. cit.*, ch. I.
6. *Prior Analytics* 25 *b* 32–37.
7. *Ibid.*, p. 28.
8. *Ibid.*, 26 *a* 21.
9. *Posterior Analytics* 98 *b* 5–10.
10. *Ibid.*, p. 8.
11. *Prior Analytics*, 24 *a* 16.
12. Łukasiewicz, *op. cit.*, pp. 38 ff.
13. 72 *b* 18.
14. 24 *b* 22.
15. *Prior Analytics* 27 *a* 10–24.
16. For details, see Lukasiewicz, *op. cit.*, ch. III, pp. 54–66.

17. *Prior Analytics* 41 *b* 1.
18. *Prior Analytics* 25 *a* 1.
19. See T. L. Heath, *Mathematics in Aristotle* (Oxford, 1949), pp. 115–116; 144–146.
20. For example, *de Caelo* 271 *a* 35; 290 *a* 31.
21. 199 *b* 30.
22. *de Generatione et Corruptione* 329 *b* 1.
23. *de Caelo* 311 *b* 28.
24. *Ibid.*, 311 *a* 32.
25. *de Generatione et Corruptione* 334 *b* 31 ff.

26. *Ibid.*, 336 *a* 15.
27. For details, see J. L. E. Dreyer, *History of Astronomy from Thales to Kepler* (New York, 1953); T. L. Heath, *Aristarchus of Samos* (Oxford, 1913), ch. 13.
28. See *Metaphysics* 1073 *a* 17–1074 *a* 12.
29. For example, *de Caelo*, 269 *a* 20.
30. *Physics* 192 *b* 20.
31. *Physics* 216 *a* 19; *de Caelo* 313 *a* 15.
32. *Physics* 215 *a* 24, 216 *a* 15; *de Caelo* 277 *b* 4, 308 *b* 18; *Physics* 215 *a* 26.
33. *Physics* 215 *b* 23.
34. *Mechanica* 858 *a*.
35. *Physics* 215 *a* 19–22.
36. *Metaphysics*, 1026 *a* 21, 1064 *b* 1.
37. See T. L. Heath, *Mathematics in Aristotle* (Oxford, 1949).
38. The most convenient collection is in Book I of the *Metaphysics*, 990 *b*–992 *b*.
39. *Ibid.*, 1079 *b* 25.
40. Cf. *Phaedo* 96 *b*.
41. See, for example, W. B. Gallie, *Peirce and Pragmatism* (Harmondsworth, 1952), ch. 3.
42. A. E. Taylor, *Aristotle* (London, 1943), ch. II, p. 54.
43. *Categories* 2 *a* 11.
44. *de Generatione et Corruptione* Book II.

45. *Ibid.*, 329 *a* 26.
46. *Metaphysics* 1034 *a* 5–8.
47. Aristotle's main discussion is in Book IX of the *Metaphysics*. But it is conducted in very abstract terms and is more than usually difficult to follow.
48. *Physics* 194 *b* 16 ff. The same account recurs in Book V of the *Metaphysics*.
49. *Ibid.*, 195 *a* 16.
50. *Ibid.*, 198 *a* 25.
51. *de Anima* 413 *a* 21.
52. *Ibid.*, 412 *b* 18.
53. *Ibid.*, 414 *a* 19.
54. *Ibid.*, 412 *b* 6.
55. *Ibid.*, 411 *b* 5.
56. *Ibid.*, 413 *a* 4–7.
57. *Ibid.*, 414 *a* 18.
58. *Ibid.*, 425 *b* 24.
59. *Ibid.*, 425 *a* 27.
60. *Ibid.*, 417 *b* 22.
61. *Ibid.*, 428 *a* 20 ff.
62. *Ibid.*, 430 *a* 14–25.
63. A. E. Taylor, *op. cit.*, ch. IV, p. 120.
64. *de Caelo* 279 *a* 18.
65. *Metaphysics* 1072 *b* 4.
66. For example, *de Caelo* 285 *a* 29, 292 *a* 20, 292 *b* 1.
67. *Nicomachean Ethics* (hereinafter abbreviated *N.E.*), 1123 *a* 34–1125 *a* 35.
68. *Politics* 1278 *a* 20.

69. *N.E.* 1094 *b* 14–15.
70. *Ibid.*, 1103 *b* 27.
71. *Ibid.*, 1094 *b* 11 ff.
72. *Ibid.*, 1094 *a* 1.
73. *Ibid.*, 1097 *a* 35–*b* 15.
74. *Ibid.*, 1097 *b* 24–1098 *a* 18.
75. *Ibid.*, 1098 *a* 18.
76. *Ibid.*, 1095 *b* 32.
77. *Ibid.*, 1106 *a* 19.
78. For a good elementary discussion, see H. D. F. Kitto *The Greeks* (London and Baltimore, 1951), pp. 171–175.
79. *N.E.* 1102 *a* 5.
80. *Ibid.*, 1103 *a* 31–1103 *b* 2.
81. *Ibid.*, 1105 *a* 17.
82. *Ibid.*, 1138 *a* 31.
83. *Ibid.*, 1106 *b* 36.
84. *Ibid.*, 1110 *a* 7.
85. *Ibid.*, 1111 *a* 23.
86. *Ibid.*, 1145 *a* 15–1152 *a* 36.
87. Aristotle discusses this in Book VI of the *Ethics* before he considers the question of *akrasia*. But it is convenient for the purposes of exposition to reverse the order in which he takes these topics.
88. The whole argument of Book VI of the *Nicomachean Ethics* is concerned with these questions.
89. *N.E.* 1106 *a* 24.
90. Book X, ch. 6–9.
91. *N.E.* 1178 *a* 9.
92. See *N.E.*, ch. 3–5 of Book X.

4. Greek Philosophy after Aristotle (*pages 62 - 78*)

1. A. J. Festugière, *Epicurus and His Gods*, tr. C. W. Chilton (Cambridge, Mass., 1956).
2. See Diogenes Laertius ii. 134.
3. *De Divinatione* ii. 11. *Academica* ii. 96.
4. *De Fato* 17.
5. *Contra Stoicos* 5.17.
6. See Sextus Empiricus, *Adversus Mathematicos* viii. 9 and contrast N. W. de Witt, *Epicurus and his Philosophy* (Minneapolis, 1954), pp. 134 ff.
7. *De Natura Deorum* i. 43.

8. N. W. de Witt, *op. cit.*, pp. 142 ff.
9. Diogenes Laertius x. 58–59.
10. See Diogenes Laertius x. 70–73 and Sextus Empiricus *Adversus Mathematicos* x. 219, 224, 240.
11. *Placita* iv. 3. 11.
12. See Maxim 25 at Diogenes Laertius x. 148.
13. See Diogenes Laertius vii. 180 ff. for these details.
14. See Sextus Empiricus *Adversus Mathematicos* vii. 241 ff.
15. Cicero *Academica* ii. 145.
16. Diogenes Laertius vii. 73.

17. See S. Sambursky, *The Physical World of the Greeks* (translated by Merton Degut), (London, 1958).
18. See Cicero *De Officiis, passim*.
19. The list is taken from Diogenes Laertius ix 80 ff.; Sextus Empiricus, *Outlines of Pyrrhonism* i. 30 ff. gives the same list in a slightly different order.
20. *Adversus Mathematicos* vii. 159.
21. *De Optima Doctrina* ii. 45 K.

5. Augustine (*pages 79 - 97*)

1. *Contra Julianum* iv.14.72.
2. *Confessions* (hereinafter abbreviated *Conf.*) iii.4.7; vii.7.17.
3. *De civitate Dei* (hereinafter abbreviated *de civ. Dei*) xix.1.3.
4. *Ibid.*, xix.1.1–2.
5. *Conf.* vii.8.12–9.15.
6. *De Trinitate* (hereinafter abbreviated *de Trin.*), iv.16.21.
7. *Ibid.*
8. *Sermo* 150.3.4.

9. *Conf.* vii.20.26.
10. *De Trin.* xii.2.2.
11. *De quantitate animae* (hereinafter abbreviated *de quant. an.*) 33.72.
12. *De Trin.* xiii.5.8; *de Genesi contra Manichaeos* (hereinafter abbreviated *de Gen. c. Man.*) i.20.31.
13. *De libero arbitrio* (hereinafter abbreviated *de lib. arb.*) ii.13.

35–36; *de quant. an.* 33.76. *de moribus ecclesiae* (hereinafter abbreviated *de mor. eccl.*) i.25.47.
14. *De praedestinatione sanctorum* 2.5.
15. I Corinthians 13.12.
16. *In Iohannis Evangelium tractatus* xxix.6.
17. *Epistola* 120.3; *de Ordine* (hereinafter abbreviated *de ord.*) ii.9.26.

18. *De beata vita* 2.7.
19. *Soliloquia* (hereinafter abbreviated *Solil.*) ii.1.1.
20. *De lib. arb.* ii.3.7. The agreements and variations between these last three passages are interesting.
21. *Contra academicos* (hereinafter abbreviated *c. Acad.*) iii.11.24–25.
22. On all this, cf. *de Trin.* xv.12.21 and x.10.13–14.
23. *De Trin.* xv.12.21.
24. *Ibid.*, ix.3.3; x.3.5–10.14; xiv. 5.7–6.8; 10.13.
25. *Ibid.*
26. *Ibid.*, xiv.6.8.
27. *Ibid.*, x.4.6.
28. *De quant. an.* 13.22.
29. *De mor. eccl.* i.4.6.
30. *Ibid.*, i.27.52.
31. *De Genesi ad litteram* (hereinafter abbreviated *de Gen. ad litt.*) iii.5.7; xii.24.51; *de Trin.* xi.2.2.
32. *De quant. an.* 23.41–32–69.
33. *Ibid.*, 23.41.
34. *Ibid.*, 25.48.
35. *Ibid.*, 23.42.
36. *Ibid.*, 23.44.
37. *Ibid.*, 23.43.
38. *Ibid.*
39. Augustine deals with hearing at length in Book VI of his *De Musica*.
40. *De Gen. ad litt.* xii.16.32–33.
41. *De quant. an.* 33.71–72.
42. *Retractationes* (hereinafter abbreviated *Retr.*) i.1.2; cf. note *31* above.
43. *De Gen. ad litt.* xii.16.33; *de Trin.* x.5.7.
44. *Ibid.*, xii.24.50.
45. *Ibid.*, xii.21.44.
46. *Ibid.*, xii.2.3–4; 19.41.
47. *Ibid.*, xii.12.25.

48. *De Trin.* xi.4.7.
49. *Ibid.*, xi.9.16.
50. *De Gen. ad litt.* xii.11.22; 24.51.
51. *Ibid.*, xii.25.52; *c. Acad.* iii.11.26.
52. *C. Acad.* iii.17.37.
53. *Ibid.*, iii.11.25; 13.29.
54. *De lib. arb.* ii.8.21.
55. *Ibid.*, ii.8.22–24.
56. *Ibid.*, ii.12.33.
57. *De ord.* ii.3.10.
58. *De immortalitate animae* 6.10.
59. *De vera religione* 39.73.
60. *De lib. arb.* ii.9.25–10.29.
61. *Solil.* i.6.12; 8.15; 13.23; *de lib. arb.* ii.13.36.
62. *De Trin.* xii.15.24.
63. *Ibid.*, viii.3.4.
64. *Ibid.*, ix.6.9.
65. See my paper, "St. Augustine on Signs," *Phronesis*, II (1957), pp. 60–83.
66. *De Trin.* ix.7.12.
67. *Conf.* x.8.15.
68. *Ibid.*, x.12.19.
69. *De Trin.* xv.21.40.
70. *Ibid.*, xiv.11.14.
71. *Conf.* x.12.15.
72. *De Trin.* xv.21.40.
73. *Ibid.*, xiv.15.21.
74. *Conf.* i.1.1.
75. *Ibid.*, xiii.9.10; cf. *de Gen. ad litt.* ii.1.2; iv.3.7–4.8; *Ep.* 55.10.18; 157.9.
76. *De civ. Dei* xi.28.
77. *De lib. arb.* iii.19.54; 22.64, where Augustine is, however, discussing a special case only.
78. *Ibid.*, i.11.21.
79. *Ibid.*, iii.1.1–3.
80. *De Trin.* xi.5.9; cf. *Retr.* ii.15.2; *de Trin.* x.5.7–8.11.
81. I owe this illustration — which may derive from Mr. J. D. Mabbott — to Mr. P. T. Geach.
82. *De Trin.* viii.8.12; ix.2.2.

83. *De civ. Dei.* xiv.7.2.
84. *Ibid.*, xv.22.
85. *Ibid.*
86. *De doctrina christiana* i.27.28.
87. *De lib. arb.* i.5.11–8.18.
88. *De ord.* ii.8.25.
89. *De lib. arb.* i.9.19.
90. *Ibid.*, i.8.18.
91. *De Trin.* xiv.15.21; cf. note *75* above.
92. *De lib. arb.* i.6.15.
93. *Enarrationes in Psalmos* lviii.1.
94. *Ibid.*, cxlv.5.
95. *De lib. arb.* iii.5.17.
96. *De Trin.* xi.6.10.
97. *De Gen. c. Man.* i.16.26.
98. *De Trin.* xv.4.6
99. x.6.9–10.
100. *De lib. arb.* ii.3.7–15.39.
101. *De diversis quaestionibus* LXXXIII, 46.2.
102. *Conf.* vii.15.21.
103. *Ibid.*, xiii.38.53.
104. *De Gen. ad litt.* iv.12.22–23.
105. *Conf.* xi.10.12–14.17; *de Gen. c. Man.* i.2.3–4; *de Gen. ad litt.* v.5.12.
106. *Conf.* xi.14.17–16.21.
107. *Ibid.*, xi.16.21; 21.27.
108. *Ibid.*, xi.20.26.
109. *Ibid.*, xi.23.29–24.31.
110. *Ibid.*, xi.26.33.
111. e.g. *de Gen. ad litt.* v.4.9; vi.5.8–6.11; 11.18; *de Trin.* iii.8.13.
112. *De Gen. ad litt.* v.7.20.
113. *Ibid.*, ix.17.32.
114. *De Trin.* iii.9.16.
115. *De Gen. ad litt.* ix.17.32.
116. *Ibid.*
117. *Ibid.*, ix.17.32–18.35.
118. *Ibid.*, vi.13.24.
119. *De civ. Dei* vii.30.
120. i.2.7.

6. Thomas Aquinas (*pages 98 - 123*)

1. Quoted from E. Gilson, *Reason and Revelation in the Middle Ages* (New York and London, 1952), p. 10.
2. *De Veritate* 22.2.
3. *Summa Theologica* (hereinafter abbreviated *S.T.*) Part I, question 2, Art. 2 and *passim*.
4. *S.T.* II–II.1.4.
5. *S.T.* I.2.2.
6. On the impossibility of proving the Trinity by natural reason, see *S.T.* I.32.1.
7. See especially *S.T.* I.1.8.
8. *Summa Contra Gentiles* (hereinafter abbreviated *C.G.*) II.iii.
9. *S.T.* I.12.12.

10. For a detailed account of the rediscovery of Aristotle, see F. C. Copleston, *History of Philosophy*, II (London, 1959) and F. van Steenberghen, *Aristotle in the West* (Louvain, 1955).
11. *S.T.* I.84.6.
12. *S.T.* I.79.2.
13. See e.g. *S.T.* I.87.1.
14. See e.g. *S.T.* I.84, especially Art. 7.
15. *S.T.* I.78.4.
16. *C.G.* II.liv.
17. For a discussion of the complexities involved in the notions of matter and form, see Donald Williams, "Form and Matter, I

and II," *The Philosophical Review*, Vol. XLVII, 1958, pp. 291–312 and 499–521.
18. *S.T.* I.84.7.
19. *S.T.* I.16.1.
20. *Tractatus Logico-Philosophicus* 6.44.
21. *S.T.* I.85.2.
22. *S.T.* I.2.3. In *C.G.* I.xiii there is a more thorough and detailed discussion of the first proof.
23. *S.T.* I.2.3.
24. Copleston, II, p. 342.
25. *S.T.* I.2.3. Also *C.G.* I.xiii.
26. *In Boetii de Trinitate* Lect. II, question 2, Art. 3.
27. *S.T.* I.13.10.

28. Questions 4–20 of the first part of *Summa Theologica*.
29. *S.T.* I.7.1.
30. *S.T.* I.10.2.
31. *S.T.* I.9.1.
32. *S.T.* I.3.
33. *S.T.* I.14.1.
34. *S.T.* I.14.8.
35. *S.T.* I.14.8.
36. *S.T.* I.19.1.
37. *S.T.* I.20.1.
38. *S.T.* I.20. *C.G.* I.xxxvi
39. *C.G.* I.xiv.
40. *De Potentia* Ques. 7, Art. 5, Translated by T. Gilby in *Philosophical Texts of Thomas Aquinas* (Oxford, 1951).
41. *C.G.* I.xviii. Translated by A. C. Pegis in *On the Truth of the Catholic Church*, Vol. I (New York, 1961).
42. *S.T.* I.13.5.
43. *C.G.* I.xcii ff.
44. *S.T.* I.13.10.
45. *C.G.* I.xxx.
46. Copleston, II, p. 357 ff, and 349 ff.
47. Copleston, II, p. 395.
48. The notion of man as created in God's image is discussed in *S.T.* I.93.

49. *S.T.* I.19.1.
50. *S.T.* I.20.1.
51. *S.T.* I.79.8.
52. *S.T.* I–II.22.2 and 3.
53. *Ibid.*, 24.1 and 2.
54. *S.T.* I.98.2.
55. *Ibid.*
56. *Ibid.*
57. *S.T.* I–II.24.3.
58. *C.G.* II.lvii. Translated by J. F. Anderson in *On the Truth of the Catholic Church*, Vol. II (New York, 1961).
59. *Ibid.*
60. *S.T.* I.1.8. Also *S.T.* I.62.7.
61. *S.T.* I–II.6.1.
62. *S.T.* I.82.3.
63. *S.T.* I–II.17.1. We have given only the barest outline of Thomas' theory of freedom. It is discussed at length in *S.T.* I.82 and 83 and *S.T.* I–II.10 and 17.
64. *S.T.* I–II.10.2.
65. *S.T.* I–II.18.1.
66. *S.T.* I–II.18.5.
67. The arguments are found primarily in *S.T.* I–II, questions 18 to 20 inclusive.
68. *S.T.* I–II.18.4.
69. *S.T.* I–II.18.5.

70. *S.T.* I–II.90.4.
71. *S.T.* I–II.91.2.
72. *S.T.* I–II.96.5.
73. *C.G.* III.cxiv.
74. *S.T.* I–II.93.5.
75. *S.T.* I–II.94.2.
76. *Ibid.*
77. *S.T.* I–II.96.2, questions 90 ff.
78. *S.T.* I–II.96.2.
79. *S.T.* I–II.96.2.
80. e.g. *S.T.* I–II, questions 55 ff.
81. *S.T.* II–II.108.2.
82. For an illuminating discussion of the development of empiricism in the Middle Ages, see Ernest A. Moody, "Empiricism and Metaphysics in Medieval Philosophy," *The Philosophical Review*, Vol. LXVII, No. 2, April 1958, pp. 145–163.
83. The uses of demonstration in theology and elsewhere by Aquinas, Scotus, and Ockham are discussed in detail by Damascene Webering in *Theory of Demonstration according to William of Ockham* (New York, 1953.)

7. Ockham (*pages 124 - 140*)

1. *Quodlibeta*, translated by Philotheus Boehner, in *Ockham, Philosophical Writings* (London, New York, 1957), 6, 6.
2. *Summa totius logicae* (hereinafter abbreviated *S.T.L.*), Pars I, *Cap.* 12.
3. *Ibid. Cap.* 3.
4. *Ibid.*
5. *Expositio super Perihermenias*.
6. *S.T.L.*, Pars I, *Cap.* 1.
7. *Ibid.*
8. E. Moody, *The Logic of William of Ockham* (London, 1935).
9. I *Sentences*, 2, 4.
10. *S.T.L.*, Pars II, *Cap.* 30.
11. *Ibid.*
12. *Ibid.*
13. *Prologue to the Sentences*, translated by F. C. Copleston in *History of Philosophy*, Vol. III (London, 1953), 1, 2.
14. I *Sentences* (Copleston), 27, 3.
15. *Quodlibeta* (Copleston), 1, 14.
16. I *Sentences* (Copleston), 1, 3.
17. *Ibid.*, 41.
18. II *Sentences* (Copleston), 2.

19. *Ibid.*, 15.
20. *Quodlibeta* (Boehner), 6, 6.
21. *Quodlibeta* (Copleston), 5, 5.
22. *Quodlibeta* (Boehner), 6, 6.
23. II *Sentences* (Copleston), 2.
24. *Expositio super Libros Physicorum* (Boehner), *Prologue*.
25. *S.T.L.*, Pars I, *Cap.* 10.
26. *Ibid.*
27. *Op. cit.*, pp. 56–57.
28. Herman Shapiro, *Motion, Time and Place according to William Ockham* (London, New York, 1957), p. 22, note.
29. *Tractatus de Successivis*, ed. by Philotheus Boehner (New York, 1944), p. 47.
30. *Ibid.*, p. 37.
31. *Philosophia Naturalis*, trans. by Herman Shapiro in *op. cit.*, IV, 8.
32. I *Sentences* (Copleston), 3, 1.
33. *Ibid.*, 2, 9.
34. III *Sentences* (Copleston), 9.
35. I *Sentences* (Copleston), 2, 10.
36. *Ibid.*
37. *Summulae in Libros Physicorum*, 2, 6.

38. I *Sentences* (Copleston), 2, 9.
39. *Ibid.*
40. *Ibid.*, 38, 1.
41. *Ibid.*
42. *Tractatus de Praedestinatione et de Praescientia*, ed. by Philotheus Boehner (New York, 1945), p. 15.
43. *Ibid.*
44. *Quodlibeta*, 1, 10.
45. II *Sentences* (Copleston), 22.
46. *Ibid.*, 26.
47. *Quodlibeta* (Copleston), 1, 16.
48. *Ibid.*
49. I *Sentences* (Copleston), 1, 4.
50. II *Sentences* (Copleston), 5.
51. *Quodlibeta* (Copleston), 19.
52. II *Sentences* (Copleston), 22.
53. *Ibid.*, 26.
54. *Quodlibeta* (Copleston), 1, 16.
55. *Ibid.*
56. I *Sentences* (Copleston), 1, 4.
57. II *Sentences* (Copleston), 5, H.
58. *Ibid.*, 19, P.
59. *Quodlibeta*, trans. by Boehner in *Ockham, Philosophical Writings*, 13, 3.
60. *Ibid.*

8. Francis Bacon (*pages 141 - 152*)

All page references are to *The Works of Francis Bacon*, ed. by R. L. Ellis and J. Spedding (London, 1858–59), 6 vols. Where the original is in Latin, references to the English translations in this edition are given in parentheses. I have made some modifications in quotations from these translations.

1. I 131, 136, 189, 201, 204, 622 (IV 19, 25, 81, 92, 96, 321, 413), VI 637 (710).
2. I 134, 144, 210, 394 (IV 22, 32, 102, 252).
3. I 539 (IV 336).
4. I 145, 160, 218, 544 (IV 33, 51, 110, 341).
5. I 128, 144, 157, 180, 203, 633 (IV 17, 32, 47, 71, 95, 421).
6. III 84 (V 466).
7. I 231, 550, 567 (IV 122, 346, 362), *cf.* the distinction between astronomy and philosophy: III 748, 778 (V 524, 557).
8. I 176, 184, 227, 564 (IV 66, 75, 119, 360), III 238.
9. I 167, 568, 571 (IV 57, 363, 365).
10. I 235, 551 (IV 126, 347).
11. I 604 (IV 396). Bacon here follows the *De Rerum Natura* (1586) of Telesius.
12. I 220 (IV 112).
13. I 131, 139 (IV 20, 26).
14. I 365 (IV 247).
15. I 151, 163 (IV 40, 54).
16. I 168 (IV 58).
17. I 139 (IV 27), *cf.* I 211 (IV 103).
18. I 235 (IV 127).
19. I 230 (IV 121).
20. I 166, 644 (IV 56, 432).
21. I 248 (IV 137).
22. I 257 (IV 146).
23. I 266 (IV 154).
24. II 18, 75, 212, 302 (V 136, 196, 320, 398).
25. I 635 (IV 423).
26. *cf.* III 391.
27. I 268 (IV 155).
28. I 294 (IV 180).
29. I 396, 639 (IV 254, 427), II 17, 18, 88 (V 135, 136, 210).
30. I 217 (IV 109).
31. I 230, 234, 566 (IV 122, 126, 361), II 86 (V 209), II 450, III 22 (V 426), III 243, 735 (V 512).
32. I 141, 403 (IV 29, 263).
33. I 230, 248, 262, 266 (IV 121, 137, 150, 154), III 236.
34. I 205, 277 (IV 98, 164).
35. I 228, 230 (IV 120, 121).
36. I 270, 566 (IV 157, 361), III 236.
37. III 237.
38. I 206 (IV 98).
39. I 258 (IV 146).
40. I 233, 319 (IV 124, 204), II 380, III 15, 111 (V 419, 492).
41. I 277, 306, 317 (IV 164, 192, 202).
42. III 734 (V 511), *cf.* III 778 (V 556).
43. I 612 (IV 403).
44. I 201, 234, 320, 576 (IV 93, 126, 206, 369).
45. III 240.
46. I 256, 262, 268 (IV 144, 150, 155).
47. I 228 (IV 120), *cf.* I 168, 257 (IV 58, 146).
48. I 570 (IV 364), II 460, III 110, 735 (V 491, 512), VI 652 (726). *Cf.* Locke: *Essay Concerning Human Understanding*, Bk. IV, Ch. III, 25.
49. I 567 (IV 362), III 81 (V 463), VI 655 (730).
50. II 87 (V 210).
51. I 176, 566 (IV 67, 361), II 17 (V 135).
52. II 429.
53. I 260, 268 (IV 149, 155).
54. I 142, 175, 560 (IV 29, 66, 356), II 259 (V 354), III 21, 733, 777 (V 425, 510, 555).
55. I 168, 307 (IV 58, 193), III 15, 80 (V 419, 461), III 228.
56. III 79 (V 461), VI 654 (729).
57. III 86 (V 468).
58. III 93 (V 476).
59. III 114 (V 495).
60. III 82 (V 464).
61. III 83, 111 (V 465, 492).
62. III 18 (V 422).
63. I 234 (IV 126).
64. I 311, (IV 197), II 212, 243, 302 (V 320, 339, 398), III 22 (V 426), VI 651 (726).
65. On the void and density, I 347 (IV 231), II 243, 302 (V 339, 398), III 115, 243 (V 497, 518).
Compare Bacon's account of Hero's theory in *Cogitationes de Natura Rerum* III 15 (V 419) with his repudiation of it in *Novum Organum* I 347 (IV 231). The date of the *Cogitationes* is uncertain, but is almost certainly later than the 1604 assigned to it by Ellis and Spedding. Its discussion of atomism is in some respects more subtle than that of *De Principiis*.
On gases, II 213, 254 (V 321, 349) II 380.
66. I 329 (IV 214), VI 655 (729, 730).
67. II 493, and in the references under note *71*.
68. I 177, 329, 560 (IV 67, 214, 356), III 634, 733 (V 510).
69. I 346 (IV 230).
70. I 278, 610 (IV 165, 402), II 528, 602, III 25 (V 432).
71. I 310, 359, 606 (IV 195, 242, 398), II 380, 616. *Cf.* Ellis's Preface I 55, on the apparent inconsistency and its resolution.
72. I 277, 306 (IV 164, 191), II 429, 436, 644, III 19, 25, 114 (V 424, 429, 495).
73. II 82, 243 (V 205, 539).
74. *Cf.* Ellis's Preface to *De Principiis*, III 71–73, and Leibniz: "The Confession of Nature against Atheists" (1669), *Philosophical Papers and Letters*, ed. by Leroy E. Loemker (Chicago, 1956), I, 168–173.

9. Hobbes (*pages 153 - 169*)

1. *English Works of Thomas Hobbes* (hereinafter abbreviated *EW*), ed. by Sir William Molesworth (London, 1839–1840), 11 vols. Vols. VIII and IX. In quoting from Molesworth's edition I have often modernized spelling and punctuation.
2. *EW*, VIII, viii.
3. *EW*, VIII, xvi and xvii.
4. Rex Warner, *Thucydides: History of the Peloponnesian War* (London, 1954), p. 9.
5. Appendix I to *The Elements of Law*, ed. by F. Tonnies (London, 1889).
6. *Ibid.*, Appendix II.
7. The authority here is F. Brandt, *Thomas Hobbes' Mechanical Conception of Nature* (London, 1928).
8. *EW*, IV, 414.
9. *EW*, IV.
10. *EW*, IV, 414.
11. These, the third set of objections, are most conveniently found in *The Philosophical Works of Descartes*, translated by E. S. Haldane and G. R. T. Ross (Cambridge, 1931), 2 vols.
12. *Latin Works of Thomas Hobbes* (hereinafter abbreviated *LW*), ed. by Sir William Molesworth (London, 1845), 5 vols., V.
13. *LW*, II.
14. *LW*, II.
15. *EW*, II, xix–xx.
16. There is a good modern edition in English by S. P. Lamprecht (New York, 1949).

17. *EW*, IV, 237–238. Davys seems also to have omitted a very characteristic postscript, which Molesworth prints without annotation in another volume (*EW*, V, 435–436).
18. *EW*, V.
19. *EW*, IV, 279–384.
20. *EW*, III. There have been innumerable translations and editions. We therefore give all references to chapters, which are edition-neutral, rather than to pages, which are not.
21. *LW*, I.
22. *EW*, VII.
23. An account of this grotesque controversy can be found in G. C. Robertson's *Hobbes* (Edinburgh and London, 1886).
24. *EW*, VII.
25. *LW*, IV.
26. *LW*, II.
27. The best text is found only in the edition of F. Tonnies (London, 1889).
28. H. R. Trevor-Roper, *Historical Essays* (London, 1957), p. 238.
29. *EW*, X.
30. Ch. 46.
31. Ch. 1.
32. Ch. 34.
33. *LW*, I, lxxxix.
34. Ch. 6.
35. Ch. 11.
36. *EW*, I, 132.
37. On this and other questions of the relations between the metaphysical ideas of Galileo and Hobbes, see A. E. Burtt, *Metaphysical Foundations of Modern Physical Science* (London, 1932).
38. Ch. 1.
39. Ch. 3.
40. Ch. 4, 5, and 46 in *Leviathan*, Ch. 2–5 in *De Corpore*.
41. All quotations so far in this section are from Ch. 4.
42. Ch. 46.
43. Ch. 8.
44. *EW*, V, 258–259 and 266–268. For a recent discussion, see G. Ryle, "Ordinary Language," *Philosophical Review*, 1953.
45. *EW*, I, 15.
46. *EW*, I, 16.
47. *LW*, I, 25.
48. *EW*, I, 61.
49. *EW*, I, 36.
50. *EW*, I, 37.
51. *EW*, I, 37–38.
52. *EW*, II, 203: *cf.* 296 and *LW* II, 89–90.
53. *Mysticism and Logic* (Harmondsworth, 1953), p. 213.

54. *Leviathan*, Ch. 4.
55. Passages in III.1.2, III.2.2, III.2.4, and III.2.8.
56. For a contemporary discussion, see A. J. Ayer and R. Rhees, "Can There Be a Private Language?" in *Proceedings of the Aristotelian Society*, Supplementary Vol. XXVIII (1954).
57. *EW*, I, 15.
58. *EW*, I, 17.
59. *Leviathan*, Ch. 2.
60. Ch. 4.
61. *EW*, I, 60.
62. *Republic*, 596 *a*.
63. *EW*, VII, 346; *cf. Leviathan*, Ch. 46.
64. *Leviathan*, Ch. 6.
65. *Ibid.*, Ch. 34.
66. *LW*, II, 88–89.
67. *Cf.*, e.g., H. Feigl and M. Scriven (eds.), *The Foundations of Science and the Concepts of Psychology and Psychoanalysis* (Minneapolis, 1956), pp. 165–166.
68. *EW*, I, 34.
69. *EW*, I, 59.
70. *EW*, I, 63. For modern discussion of these, see G. Ryle, *Dilemmas* (Cambridge, 1954), and M. Black, *Problems of Analysis* (London, 1954).
71. H. Denzinger, *Enchiridion Symbolorum* (Freiburg im Breisgau, 1953), 884.
72. *Leviathan*, Ch. 44.
73. *Ibid.*, Ch. 5.
74. *Ibid.*, Ch. 21.
75. *EW*, V, 298–299.
76. *Essay Concerning Human Understanding*, II.21.21.
77. *EW*, IV, 277; *cf.* I, 130–131.
78. There is a convenient collection of references in Richard Taylor's "The Problem of Future Contingencies," *Philosophical Review*, 1957. I have published a fuller consideration of "Hobbes and the Sea Fight" in *Graduate Review of Philosophy* (Minneapolis, 1959).
79. R. C. Bradley's "Must the Future be what it is going to be" in *Mind*, 1959, should help to bring this elaborately protracted controversy to an end.
80. *EW*, I, 60.
81. *EW*, V, 435.
82. *EW*, IV, 256 and 255.
83. *EW*, V, 202.
84. Romans IX, 18–21.
85. *EW*, IV, 250; *cf. Leviathan*, Ch. 46.
86. *EW*, IV, 249–250.
87. See J. H. Randall, "Scientific

Method in the School of Padua," *Journal of the History of Ideas*, 1940.
88. *EW*, I, viii–ix.
89. *EW*, II, xiv.
90. *EW*, II, 3.
91. *EW*, II, 8.
92. Ch. 14.
93. *EW*, II, 11.
94. Compare *Second Treatise on Civil Government*, Ch. VIII, especially sections 100 ff.
95. Ch. 13.
96. *Ibid.*
97. Ch. 14.
98. *EW*, II, 172.
99. 496.
100. At the end of Ch. 31.
101. *EW*, I, 8.
102. *Leviathan*, Ch. 14.
103. *Ibid.*
104. *Ibid.*, Ch. 17.
105. *Ibid.*, Ch. 18.
106. *Ibid.*
107. *Ibid.*, Ch. 21. I owe this point to J. H. Warrender, *The Political Philosophy of Hobbes* (Oxford, 1957).
108. *Leviathan*, Ch. 20.
109. See Aage Bentzen, *Introduction to the Old Testament* (Copenhagen, 1948).
110. See, for instance, H. R. Trevor-Roper, *op. cit.* Ch. XIII–XVII.
111. *Leviathan*, Ch. 18.
112. *Ibid.*, Ch. 20.
113. *Op. cit.*, Ch. XI, § 137.
114. *Leviathan*, Ch. 9.
115. *Ibid.*, Ch. 29.
116. *Ibid.*, Ch. 21.
117. *A Brief View and Survey of the Dangerous and Pernicious Errors to Church and State in Mr. Hobbes' Book Entitled Leviathan* (London, 1674). On this and other contemporary criticisms see John Bowle, *Hobbes and His Critics* (London, 1951).
118. *EW*, II, 37: *cf. Leviathan*, Ch. 15.
119. *EW*, II, 55–56.
120. *EW*, IV, 249; *cf. EW*, II, 206–208 and *Leviathan*, Ch. 31.
121. *Leviathan*, Ch. 44.
122. *Ibid.*, *cf. EW*, IV, 357–358.
123. *Leviathan*, Ch. 15.
124. *Leviathan*, Ch. 13: *cf. EW*, II, 6–7.
125. *Discourse on Method*, Part I.
126. *Leviathan*, Ch. 13.
127. *Ibid.*, Ch. 6.
128. *EW*, II, 77; *cf. Leviathan*, Ch. 18.
129. *Leviathan*, Ch. 24.
130. *Ibid.*, Ch. 18.
131. *EW*, II, 72; *cf. Leviathan*, Ch. 16.

132. See the *Fifteen Sermons*, especially 1 and 5.
133. H. R. Trevor-Roper, *op. cit.*, p. 235.
134. E.g., *EW*, II, 198 *n*.
135. A. Farrer's edition (London, 1951), pp. 127 and 273.

136. *Leviathan*, Ch. 31.
137. *Ibid.*, Ch. 46.
138. *EW*, II, 213–215.
139. The most recent is J. H. Warrender, *op. cit.* Compare the critical notice of this in

Australasian Journal of Philosophy, 1958.
140. *Leviathan*, Ch. 15.
141. *Ibid.*, Ch. 32.
142. *Ibid.*, Ch. 38.

10. Descartes (*pages 170 - 186*)

1. Translated by Elizabeth Anscombe and Peter Geach in *Descartes: Philosophical Writings* (London, 1954).
2. *Meditations on First Philosophy* (Anscombe and Geach), *Fifth Meditation*.
3. *Ibid.*, *Second Meditation*.

4. London, 1956. Pp. 45–53.
5. "Dreaming and Scepticism," *Philosophical Review* (January, 1956), pp. 14–37.
6. *Meditations on First Philosophy* (Anscombe and Geach), *Second Meditation*.
7. *Ibid.*, *Third Meditation*.

8. *Principles of Philosophy* (Anscombe and Geach), Part I, LI.
9. *Ibid.*, L.
10. *Ibid.*, LX.
11. *Meditations on First Philosophy* (Anscombe and Geach), *Sixth Meditation*.

11. Spinoza (*pages 187 - 203*)

1. *A Treatise on the Correction of the Intellect*.
2. *Ibid.*
3. *Ibid.*
4. *Ethics*, translated by W. Hale White and A. H. Stirling (2nd edition, London, 1894), Part I, Prop. XVI, Cor. 3.
5. *Ibid.*, Part I, Prop. XVII, Scholium.
6. See *Ethics* (White and Stirling), Part V, Props. XXV–XXXIII.
7. Letter XXXII to Henry Oldenburg, in *The Correspondence of Spinoza*, edited by A. Wolf (London, 1928).
8. In the Oxford translation, edited by J. A. Smith and W. D. Ross.

9. *Ethics* (White and Stirling), Part IV, Appendix.
10. *Ibid.*, Part I, Prop. XVIII.
11. *Ibid.*, Part I, Prop. XV.
12. *Ibid.*, Part I, Prop. XVII, Scholium.
13. *Ibid.*
14. *Ethics* (White and Stirling), Part I, Prop. XV, Scholium.
15. *Ibid.*, Part II, Prop. XLIX, Scholium.
16. Letter XXXVI to John Hudde, in Wolf, *op. cit.*
17. *Ethics* (White and Stirling), Part I, Prop. XV, Scholium.
18. *Ibid.*, Part I, Def. 4.
19. *Ibid.*, Part II, Lemma VII, Scholium.

20. This is developed chiefly in the second part of the *Ethics*, from which the following quotations are taken. (White and Stirling translation.)
21. *Ethics* (White and Stirling), Part II, Prop. XIII, Scholium.
22. *Ibid.*, Part II, Prop. VII.
23. *Ibid.*, Part III, Prop. IX and Scholium.
24. *Ibid.*, Part IV, Appendix.
25. *Ibid.*, Part I, Appendix.
26. *Ibid.*, Part IV, Prop. XLV, Scholium.
27. The following passages are taken from Part V of the *Ethics* (White and Stirling).
28. *Ethics* (White and Stirling), Part V, Prop. XLII, Scholium.

12. Locke (*pages 204 - 219*)

1. *Essay Concerning Human Understanding*, Introduction, Section 2.
2. See Maurice Cranston, *John Locke: A Biography* (London, 1957), pp. 140–141.
3. *Essay*, Introduction 4.
4. *Ibid.*, Introduction 7.
5. *Ibid.*, Epistle to the Reader.
6. *Ibid.*, Book II. Chapter 1. Section 24.
7. *Ibid.*, IV.16.2.
8. *Ibid.*, IV.21.4.
9. *Ibid.*
10. *Ibid.*, Introduction 8.
11. *Works*, edited by Adam and Tannery, Vol. III, pp. 392–393, Letter 245.
12. It has been shown by Professor Yolton in his book *John Locke and the Way of Ideas* (Oxford, 1957) that his doctrine was widely accepted by Locke's British contemporaries.

13. *Essay*, I.3.2.
14. *Ibid.*, I.1.5.
15. *Ibid.*, II.1.2.
16. *Ibid.*
17. *Ibid.*, II.1.5.
18. *Ibid.*, II.1.5. *Cf.* also II.2.2.
19. *Ibid.*, Introduction 2.
20. *Examination of Malebranche*, 10.
21. *Essay*, II.1.4.
22. *Ibid.*, II.2.1.
23. *Ibid.*, II.1.25. (He repeats this criterion of simplicity at II.12.1.)
24. *Ibid.*, II.7.1.
25. Both accounts are given in II.15 of the *Essay*.
26. *Ibid.*, II.12.1.
27. *Ibid.*, II.8.7.
28. For a discussion of some of these difficulties see H. H. Price, *Perception* (London, 1933), Ch. II.
29. *Essay*, II.8.8.
30. *Ibid.*, II.8.9.

31. *Ibid.*, II.8.10.
32. *Ibid.*, II.8.13.
33. *Ibid.*, II.8.23.
34. *Ibid.*, II.8.9.
35. *Ibid.*, II.25.1.
36. *Ibid.*
37. *Ibid.*
38. *Ibid.*, II.23.2.
39. *Ibid.*
40. *Ibid.*
41. *Ibid.*, I.3.19.
42. *First Letter to Stillingfleet*.
43. *Essay*, II.23.5.
44. *First Letter to Stillingfleet*.
45. *Essay*, IV.6.11.
46. *Ibid.*, II.1.4.
47. *Ibid.*
48. Gilbert Ryle, *The Concept of Mind* (London, 1949), p. 16.
49. *Essay*, IV.3.6.
50. *Ibid.*, II.27.25.
51. *Ibid.*, II.27.9.
52. *Ibid.*, II.27.10.

53. *Ibid.*
54. See A. G. N. Flew, "Locke's Theory of Personal Identity," (*Philosophy*, 1951) for an excellent critical survey.
55. For an account of this controversy, see G. Humphrey, *Thinking: An Introduction to its Experimental Psychology* (London, 1951), Chapter II.

56. *Essay*, III.3.6.
57. *Ibid.*, III.4.6.
58. *Ibid.*, Introduction 2.
59. *Ibid.*, IV.1.2.
60. *Ibid.*, IV.3.8.
61. *Ibid.*, II.7.1.
62. He makes some severe comments on the formal logic of his day at IV.17.4–8 in the *Essay*.
63. *Ibid.*, IV.2.14.

64. *Ibid.*, IV.11.1.
65. *Ibid.*, IV.11.4.
66. *Ibid.*, IV.14.1.
67. *Ibid.*, IV.14.3.
68. *Ibid.*, II.29.5.
69. *Ibid.*, IV.15.3.
70. *Ibid.*, IV.9.1.
71. *Ibid.*, Chapters 18 and 19.
72. *Ibid.*, Epistle to the Reader.

13. Leibniz (*pages 220 - 235*)

1. *Monadology*, § 7.
2. *Third Letter to Clarke.*
3. *Fifth Letter to Clarke.*
4. *Third Letter to Clarke.*
5. *Monadology*, § 9. See also *Fourth Letter to Clarke.*
6. *Fifth Letter to Clarke.*

7. *New Essays*, Appendix.
8. *Ibid.*
9. *Die philosophischen Schriften von G. W. Leibniz*, edited by C. I. Gerhardt (Berlin, 1875–1890), VI, 123.
10. *Monadology*, § 45.

11. *Monadology*, § 32.
12. *Letter to Arnauld.*
13. *On the Ultimate Origination of Things.*

14. Berkeley (*pages 236 - 252*)

1. *Philosophical Commentaries* (hereinafter abbreviated *PC*), entry 491.
2. *Ibid.*, entry 540.
3. *Ibid.*, entry 553.
4. *Principles of Human Knowledge*, § 156.
5. *PC*, entry 751.
6. *Three Dialogues between Hylas and Philonous*, ed. by A. A. Luce and T. E. Jessop in *The Works of George Berkeley*, 9 vols. (London, 1948–1957), Vol. II, p. 172.
7. *Ibid.*, p. 173.
8. *Ibid.*, p. 224.

9. *Principles*, §§ 35–37.
10. *Ibid.*, § 37.
11. *Ibid.*, § 49.
12. *Dialogues*, p. 174.
13. *Ibid.*, p. 204.
14. *Ibid.*
15. *Ibid.*, p. 195.
16. *Principles*, § 4.
17. *Dialogues*, p. 176.
18. *Ibid.*, p. 178.
19. *Ibid.*, p. 183.
20. *Ibid.*, p. 185.
21. *Principles*, § 15.
22. *Ibid.*, § 3.
23. *Ibid.*, §§ 22–24.

24. *Dialogues*, p. 200.
25. *Principles*, § 1.
26. *Ibid.*, § 28.
27. *Ibid.*, § 29.
28. *Ibid.*, § 30. The second set of differences is reiterated in § 33.
29. *Ibid.*, § 1.
30. *Ibid.*, Introduction, § 10.
31. *Ibid.*, § 119.
32. *Ibid.*, § 5.
33. *Ibid.*, § 3.
34. *Ibid.*, § 36.
35. *Dialogues*, p. 262.

15. Hume (*pages 253 - 274*)

1. Cambridge, 1938.
2. The intricate story of the alterations, suppression, and additions in successive editions and collections may with some difficulty be unravelled from T. E. Jessop's *A Bibliography of David Hume and of Scottish Philosophy from Francis Hutcheson to Lord Balfour* (London and Hull, 1938). The least inaccessible place in which all Hume's essays may be found together seems to be the World's Classics edition (London, 1903), now out of print but often available second-hand.
3. *The Letters of David Hume* (hereinafter referred to as *Letters*), ed. by J. Y. T. Greig (Oxford, 1932), Vol. 1, No. 73. The spelling and punctuation of quotations from Hume in this chapter are slightly modernized.
4. *Ibid.*, No. 16.

5. *Ibid.*, No. 6.
6. Along with relevant extracts from his correspondence with Montesquieu, Turgot, and Adam Smith, they have been collected by E. Rotwein as *David Hume: Writings on Economics* (London, 1955).
7. E. C. Mossner, *The Life of David Hume* (London, 1954), pp. 555–556.
8. *Oeuvres Complètes* (Paris, 1883–1887), XXV, pp. 169–173.
9. Oxford, 1935.
10. "The Enigma of Hume" (*Mind*, 1936).
11. See Especially J. A. Passmore, *Hume's Intentions* (Cambridge, 1952).
12. *An Abstract of a Treatise of Human Nature* (hereinafter referred to as *Abstract*).
13. *A Treatise of Human Nature* (hereinafter abbreviated *THN*), ed. by L. A. Selby-Bigge (Oxford, 1906), I, i, 1, p. 1.

14. *Ibid.*, I, i, 7, p. 11.
15. *Enquiry concerning Human Understanding* (hereinafter abbreviated *EHU*), ed. by C. W. Hendel (New York, 1955), II, p. 30.
16. *THN*, Introduction.
17. In *Hume's Theory of the External World* (Oxford, 1940).
18. *THN*, I, i, 7, p. 17.
19. See especially *Alciphron* VII, § 14: this was first published in 1732.
20. *EHU*, II, p. 28.
21. *Abstract.*
22. *THN*, Introduction.
23. I, i, 1, p. 5.
24. *EHU*, II, p. 30.
25. II, p. 28.
26. I, i, 1, p. 3.
27. I, i, 1, p. 2.
28. *EHU*, II, p. 26.
29. *Ibid.*, II, p. 26.
30. *Ibid.*, II, p. 27.
31. *Ibid.*, II, p. 27.
32. *THN*, I, i, 6, p. 16.

33. See, e.g., Berkeley, *The Principles of Human Knowledge*, §§ 26 and 146 *ff*.
34. *THN*, I, ii, 6, p. 66.
35. *EHU*, IV, 1, p. 40.
36. I, iii, 1; iii, 7, p. 95; iii, 11, p. 124.
37. II, iii, 10, pp. 448–449; *cf*. 3, p. 414.
38. III, i, 1, p. 463 *ff*.
39. *EHU*, XII, iii, p. 171.
40. *THN*, I, iii, 2, p. 77.
41. *EHU*, IV, i, p. 40.
42. *EHU*, IV, i, pp. 45–46.
43. *Letters*, Vol. II, No. 465.
44. See Ch. 19, section on "The Nature of Mathematical Truth" in this volume.
45. *THN*, I, iii, 1, p. 71.
46. *THN*, I, iii, 4, p. 53.
47. *THN*, I, ii, 4, pp. 49–50; *cf*. iii, 2, pp. 72–73.
48. See *Phaedo*, 74 *ff*.
49. *THN*, I, ii, 2, p. 29.
50. *English Works of Thomas Hobbes* (Molesworth), I, 63. See Ch. 9, section on "Language, and its Abuses," in this volume.
51. *EHU*, XII, ii, pp. 165, 166.
52. XII, ii, p. 166.
53. *EHU*, XII, iii, p. 173.
54. See A. J. Ayer, *Language, Truth and Logic* (London, 1936; second edition, 1949): this passage itself is quoted in Ch. 2.
55. *EHU*, IV, i, pp. 40–41.
56. *Abstract*.
57. *EHU*, IV, ii, p. 46.
58. IX, ii, p. 51.
59. *EHU*, IV, ii, pp. 49–50.
60. *EHU*, IV, ii, p. 52.
61. *THN*, I, i, 2, p. 31.
62. *EHU*, IV, i, p. 41.
63. For a very elegant handling of these issues see P. F. Strawson, *An Introduction to Logical Theory* (London and New York, 1952), Ch. IX. Hume's distinction between the probability of chances and the probability of causes is relevant here (*EHU*, VI; *THN*, I, ii, 11 and 12). Disentangled from psychologizing about belief it will be seen to resemble closely that indicated in our text.
64. See K. R. Popper, "Philosophy of Science: A Personal Report" in C. A. Mace (Editor) *British Philosophy in the Mid-Century* (London, 1957).
65. *THN*, I, iii, 6, pp. 90 and 91.
66. *Abstract* and *EHU*, IV, ii, pp. 49–50.
67. S. E. Toulmin in *The Philosophy of Science* (London, 1953), p. 148.
68. See, e.g., M. Scriven, "A Possible Distinction between Disciplines" in *The Foundations of Science and the Concepts of Psychology and Psychoanalysis*, ed. by H. Feigl and M. Scriven (Minneapolis, 1956).
69. *EHU*, IV, ii, p. 50.
70. *EHU*, V. i, pp. 55–57.
71. *EHU*, IX, pp. 112–114.
72. *EHU*, V, i, p. 57.
73. *EHU*, IV, ii, pp. 52–53.
74. *An Enquiry concerning the Principles of Morals* (hereinafter abbreviated *EPM*), ed. by C. W. Hendel (New York, 1957), A, 1, p. 111.
75. *THN*, I, iii, 16; II, i, 12; II, ii, 12; *EHU*, IX.
76. *EHU*, V, ii, p. 68.
77. I, iv, 5, pp. 246–247.
78. *THN*, I, iii, 3.
79. *Ibid*.
80. See his *The Philosophy of David Hume* (London, 1941), pp. 409–410.
81. *THN*, I, iii, 12, p. 130 and 14, p. 171.
82. *Letters*, I, No. 91. For a recent discussion see G. J. Warnock, "Every Event Has a Cause" in A. G. N. Flew (Editor) *Logic and Language*, Vol. II (Oxford, 1953).
83. *THN*, I, iii, 13, p. 146 *ff*.
84. *THN*, I, iii, 2, p. 78.
85. *THN*, I, iii, 14, p. 155.
86. *Ibid*., p. 162.
87. *THN*, I, iii, 14, pp. 165–166.
88. *EHU*, VII, ii, p. 86.
89. *THN*, I, iii, 14, pp. 168–169.
90. *Abstract*.
91. *THN*, I, iii, 14, p. 166.
92. I, iii, 2 and 15.
93. See "Can an Effect Precede Its Cause?" in *Proceedings of the Aristotelian Society* Supp. Vol. XXVIII (1954) and the continuation controversy in *Analysis*, Vols. XVI and XVII.
94. *THN*, I, iv, 5.
95. See G. Ryle, *The Concept of Mind* (London, 1949).
96. *Third Letter to Bentley*.
97. *THN*, I, iii, 14, p. 170.
98. *EHU*, VII, ii, p. 87.
99. E.g., by J. A. Passmore *op. cit.*, p. 76 and A. N. Whitehead, *Process and Reality* (Cambridge, 1929), p. 128.
100. I, iii, 14, p. 170.
101. *Hume's Enquiries*, ed. by L. A. Selby-Bigge (Oxford, 1894, rev. 1902), p. 2. It is to be hoped that Professor Hendel will take the first opportunity of inserting this "Advertisement" into his edition.
102. *THN*, I, iii, 6, p. 88.
103. *EHU*, VII, ii, p. 86.
104. See F. C. Copleston, *A History of Philosophy* (London, 1953), III, pp. 135 *ff*.
105. *THN*, I, iii, 14, p. 159.
106. *Ibid*., p. 166.
107. *EHU*, VII, i, p. 84*n*.
108. *EHU*, VII, ii, p. 88*n*, and VII, i, p. 76.
109. *Cf*., e.g., Ch. 9, section on "Liberty and Necessity," in this volume.
110. *Abstract*.
111. *EHU*, VIII, i, p. 104.
112. *Ibid*., pp. 104 and 101.
113. In "On the Physical Basis of Life," *Lay Sermons* (London, 1871), p. 144.
114. *Hume* (London, 1894).
115. II, iii, 2, p. 407.
116. *Ibid*., 1, p. 407.
117. *EHU*, VIII, i, p. 104.
118. See "Philosophy and Language" in (Ed. A. G. N. Flew) *Essays in Conceptual Analysis* (London, 1956).
119. *EHU*, VIII, ii, pp. 108–109.
120. *Ibid*., p. 111.
121. See Selby-Bigge, *Hume's Enquiries* (1894), Introduction; and A. E. Taylor's "David Hume and the Miraculous" in *Philosophical Studies* (London, 1934).
122. Thus A. H. Basson in *David Hume* (Harmondsworth, 1958), after recognizing what has rarely been appreciated sufficiently, "that Hume's attitude to religion was one of the chief factors in his philosophical thinking" (p. 18), is still prepared to say "that Hume produced no serious philosophical writings after the *Enquiries*" (p. 150). He cites the *Dialogues* only twice, in a chapter on "Reason and Morals," and he ignores, except for one importantly incorrect reference to the argument "Of Miracles" (p. 18), even *EHU*, X–XI.
123. *THN*, I, iii, 9, p. 115.
124. *Letters* I, No. 58.
125. *EHU*, X, i, pp. 117–118.
126. *Ibid*., p. 118.
127. *Ibid*., p. 122.
128. *Ibid*.
129. *Ibid*., p. 123.
130. The fourth is actually presented as *a priori*, though Hume clearly had in mind a different

and weightier *a posteriori* consideration. For defense of this and other points of my interpretation of this much misunderstood section I must refer to my "Hume's Check" (*Philosophical Quarterly*, 1959).

131. *EHU*, X, ii, p. 137.
132. *Ibid.*, pp. 137–138.
133. *Butler's Works*, edited by W. E. Gladstone (Oxford, 1896), I, p. 309.
134. *Ibid.*, pp. 302–303.
135. H. Denzinger and C. Rahner, *Enchiridion Symbolorum* (Freiberg in Breisgau, 29th edition, 1953), § 1813.
136. *Butler's Works*, Vol. I, p. 371.
137. *EHU*, XI, p. 145.
138. If any defense or expansion of my interpretation is needed, I may refer to my "Hume and the Religious Hypothesis" in *Rationalist Annual*, 1959.
139. *EHU*, XI, p. 145.
140. *Ibid.*, p. 146.
141. *Ibid.*, p. 152.
142. *Ibid.*
143. *Ibid.*, p. 153.
144. *Ibid.*, p. 156.
145. *Op. cit.*, Vol. I, p. 162.
146. *EHU*, XI, p. 148.
147. *Ibid.*, p. 146.
148. *Newton's Principia*, Edited by Florian Cajori (Berkeley, 1946), p. 547.
149. *EHU*, XII, iii, pp. 171–172.
150. *Dialogues Concerning Natural Religion* (hereinafter abbreviated *DNR*), ed. by N. Kemp-Smith, 2nd ed. (Edinburgh and London, 1947), IX, p. 189.
151. E.g., *EHU*, XI.
152. *Op. cit.*, Vol. V, p. 311.
153. *Ibid.*, p. 287.
154. *DNR*, IX, pp. 190–191.
155. *EHU*, VIII, ii, p. 111.
156. *DNR*, X, p. 201.
157. *Op. cit.*, pp. 180–183.
158. *DNR*, II, p. 146.
159. *Ibid.*, VIII, p. 185.
160. *Letters*, I, No. 72.
161. *DNR*, VI, p. 174: *cf.* IV, pp. 160–162.

162. *THN*, I, iv, 2, p. 87.
163. *THN*, I, iv, 6
164. *THN*, App., p. 633.
165. *Op. cit.*
166. *EHU*, XII, i, pp. 158–159.
167. *Ibid.*, p. 160.
168. *Ibid.*, p. 161.
169. *Ibid.*
170. *Ibid.*, p. 162.
171. *Ibid.*, p. 164.
172. *DNR*, XII, p. 227.
173. *EHU*, XII, ii, pp. 164 and 166–168.
174. *Ibid.*, p. 168.
175. Part IV, Ch. 1.
176. *EHU*, I, p. 22.
177. *EHU*, XII, iii, pp. 169–170.
178. *EHU*, V, i, p. 57.
179. *EHU*, XII, iii, p. 170.
180. *Letters* I, No. 3. N. Kemp Smith *op. cit.* Part I and *passim*: quotation from p. vi.
181. XII, iii, p. 173.
182. *EPM*, I, pp. 3 and 4.
183. *EPM*, A I, pp, 104 and 105.
184. *THN*, III, ii, 1, p. 481.
185. *EPM*, A I, p. 108.
186. *THN*, II, iii, 3, pp. 414 and 415.
187. *THN*, III, i, 1, p. 457.
188. *Ibid.*, p. 466.
189. *Ibid.*, p. 468.
190. *Ibid.*, p. 469.
191. *Ibid.*
192. For a discussion of the status of this dichotomy see R. F. Atkinson and A. Montefiore, "*Ought* and *Is*" (*Philosophy*, 1958). It is perhaps ominous that Miss G. E. M. Anscombe's "Modern Moral Philosophy" should have appeared in the same issue.
193. Quoted by Atkinson and Montefiore *op. cit.* from A. G. N. Flew and R. W. Hepburn, "Problems of Perspective" (*The Plain View*, 1955).
194. *Principia Ethica* (Cambridge, 1903).
195. *THN*, III, i, 2, p. 475. *Cf.* J. S. Mill "Nature" in *Three Essays on Religion* (London, 1874).
196. Letter to A. Millar (quoted *Letters* I, No. 132*n*).

197. *Hippocrates*, ed. by W. H. S. Jones (London, 1932). Vol. II.
198. *Mind*, 1940, p. 238.
199. Oxford, 1939.
200. *EPM*, A I, p. 112; III, ii, p. 31*n*; A IV, p. 138.
201. *EPM*, A I, p. 112.
202. *EPM*, IX, i, p. 96.
203. *THN*, III, ii, 1, p. 484.
204. *EPM*, III, i, pp. 151–152.
205. *EPM*, IX, ii, p. 100; but *cf.* pp. 102–103.
206. *Groundwork of the Metaphysic of Morals* Ch. III *ad. fin.*; the passage quoted comes from H. J. Paton's *The Moral Law* (London, 1949), p. 129.
207. *THN*, II, iii, 3, p. 416.
208. *THN*, III, ii, 1, p. 458.
209. *EHU*, VI, p. 69*n*: *cf. THN* I, iii, 11, p. 124.
210. *THN*, III, i, 1, p. 459.
211. *THN*, III, iii, 1, p. 583: *cf.* II, iii, 3, p. 417; II, iii, 8, p. 437; and III, ii, 7.
212. *EPM*, III, ii, p. 30*n* and A III, pp. 122–123; *cf. THN*, III, ii, 2, pp. 489–491, and III, ii, p. 5. The expression "performatory utterances" derives from J. L. Austin, "Other Minds" (*Logic and Language* II), pp. 142 *ff*.
213. *Ibid.*, also in the *Political Discourses*.
214. *EPM*, A II, p. 114.
215. *THN*, III, i, 1, p. 469.
216. *EPM*, A I, p. 107.
217. *EPM*, I, p. 8; *cf.* III, ii, p. 34 and V, ii, p. 467.
218. *EPM*, I, p. 7: VIII, i, p. 83*n*.
219. *EHU*, I, p. 18.
220. Letter from Adam Smith to William Strahan, November 9th, 1776.
221. E. C. Mossner, *Life*, p. 203. The vicissitudes of this essay are recounted in Ch. 24 of the same book. I have attempted the acrobatic of standing on Hume's shoulders in "The Principle of Euthanasia" (*The Plain View*, 1957).
222. *EHU*, I, p. 18.

16. French Eighteenth-Century Materialism (*pages 275 - 295*)

I am greatly indebted to Professors John Lough and H. B. Acton and to Mr. T. Bottomore for background or bibliographical information, though of course the responsibility for the views expressed is mine alone.

1. Chapter VI.

2. (Paris, 1928), p. 99.

17. Kant (*pages 296 - 318*)

1. *Prolegomena to any Future Meta-physics*, translated by P. G. Lucas (Manchester, 1953), Preface.
2. *Critique of Pure Reason*, translated by N. Kemp Smith (London, 1933), A 39–B 56.
3. *Ibid.*, A 79–B 105.
4. *Ibid.*, A 111.

5. *Ibid.*, A 93–B 126.
6. *Ibid.*, A 298–B 354.
7. *Critique of Practical Reason and Other Writings in Moral Philosophy*, edited and translated by L. W. Beck (Chicago, 1949), Preface.
8. *Ibid.*, pp. 361–385.
9. *Ibid.*, p. 64.

10. *Ibid.*, p. 80.
11. *Ibid.*, p. 103.
12. *Ibid.*, p. 117.
13. *Critique of Judgement*, translated by J. C. Meredith, First Part, Second Book, Section 28 (Oxford, 1952).
14. *Ibid.*, Section 59.
15. *Ibid.*, Section 67.

18. Hegel (*pages 319 - 340*)

1. *Phenomenology of Mind*, p. 131, in the Jubilee Edition of Hegel's works, edited by H. Glockner (Stuttgart, 1951–1960), 26 vols. English translation: *The Phenomenology of Mind*, trans. by J. B. Baillie, 2nd ed. (London and New York, 1931), pp. 204–205.
2. See, e.g., *Philosophy of Spirit* (Glockner), p. 323.
3. See *Science of Logic* (Glockner), II, p. 155. English translation: *The Science of Logic*, trans. by W. H. Johnston and L. G. Struthers (London and New York, 1929), II, p. 330.
4. *Encyclopaedia*, § 20.
5. See, e.g., *Encyclopaedia*, § 382.
6. *Ibid.*, § 408, Addition.
7. *Ibid.*, § 23, §§ 485–486.
8. *Ibid.*, §§ 20, 215, 383.
9. *Ibid.*, § 475.
10. *Phenomenology* (Glockner), p. 24. Baillie translation, p. 81.
11. *Encyclopaedia*, § 214.
12. *Ibid.*, § 212, Addition.
13. *Phenomenology* (Glockner), pp. 22–24. Baillie translation, pp. 80–82.
14. *Phenomenology* (Glockner), pp. 584–585. Baillie translation, pp. 766–767.
15. *Science of Logic* (Glockner), I, p. 57. Johnston and Struthers' translation, I, p. 69.
16. *Philosophy of Nature* (Glockner), pp. 47–48.
17. *Ibid.*, p. 463.
18. *Encyclopaedia*, §§ 458–459, plus Additions.

19. John Stuart Mill (*pages 341 - 364*)

1. See A. G. N. Flew, *A New Approach to Psychical Research* (London, 1953), VIII.
2. See. *e.g.*, R. B. Braithwaite, *Scientific Explanation* (Cambridge, 1953).
3. See I. M. D. Little, *Welfare Economics* (Oxford, 1950), pp. 118 *ff.*
4. See *Logic*, especially III, xvi, 1–4.
5. See J. L. Austin, "Ifs and Cans," *Proceedings of the British Academy* (London, 1956).
6. Bertrand Russell, "J. S. Mill," *Proceedings of the British Academy*, Vol. XLI (London, 1955), pp. 57 *ff.*

20. Schopenhauer (*pages 365 - 383*)

1. See Albert Camus, "Reflections on the Guillotine," in *Resistance, Rebellion and Death* (New York, 1961), pp. 183–184.

21. Nietzsche (*pages 384 - 401*)

Except where otherwise indicated, the edition of Nietzsche's writings I have employed is *Friedrich Nietzsche: Werke in Drei Bänden* (Munich, 1956), edited by Karl Schlechta. The translations are in every case my own, but I have benefited from the excellent translations of Marianne Cowan, Francis Golffing, and Walter Kaufmann. Abbreviations used:

GT	*Die Geburt der Tragödie*	*The Birth of Tragedy*
MAM	*Menschlich, Allzumenschlich*	*Human, All-too-Human*
MR	*Morgenröte*	*Dawn*
FW	*Die Fröhliche Wissenschaft*	*The Gay Science*
Z	*Also Sprach Zarathustra*	*Thus Spake Zarathustra*
JGB	*Jenseits von Gut und Böse*	*Beyond Good and Evil*
GM	*Zur Genealogie der Moral*	*Genealogy of Morals*
GD	*Götzen-Dämmerung*	*Twilight of the Idols*
EH	*Ecce Homo*	*Ecce Homo*
AC	*Der Antichrist*	*The Antichrist*

Numbers in every case refer to aphorisms rather than to pages; Roman numerals indicate the chapter, where this information is relevant, e.g., where Nietzsche starts numbering his aphorisms afresh each time he has a new section or chapter in a book. Thus *GM*, II, 20 is *Genealogie der Moral*, part two, aphorism 20. In some cases, e.g., in *Götzen-Dämmerung*, he gives no numbers to the separate parts, though he numbers the aphorisms in each part. Here *GD*, III, 2 means to count the chapters until III and there find aphorism 2. Finally, in *Zarathustra*, Nietzsche numbers the chapters, but not the aphorisms. Here I indicate the aphorism by its German title, e.g., *Z, II*, "*Von den Priestern.*" I hope by these devices to enable the reader to locate a passage no matter what his edition.

1. *Nachlass*, 814.
2. *GD*, III, 2.
3. *Ibid.*
4. *Nachlass*, 903.
5. *Ibid.*, 705.
6. *Ibid.*, 769.
7. *GT*, 15.
8. *GD*, III, 3.
9. *Ibid.*
10. *GD*, III, 5.
11. *GD*, III, 5. Cf. *BGE*, 20.
12. *GD*, loc. cit.
13. *GD*, "*Wie die 'wahre Welt' endlich zur Fabel wurde.*"
14. *Ibid.*
15. *Nachlass*, 776.
16. *FW*, III, 112.
17. *Nachlass*, 896.
18. *FW*, 121.
19. *Ibid.*, 110.
20. *Ibid.*, 111.
21. *Ibid.*
22. *MR*, 117.
23. *FW*, 265.
24. *FW*, 110.
25. *MR*, 121.
26. *FW*, 112.
27. *FW*, 108.
28. *Ibid.*
29. *JGB*, 45.
30. *GD*, III, 5.
31. *JGB*, 17.
32. *JGB*, 19.
33. *Ibid.*
34. *JGB*, 21.
35. *Ibid.*
36. *Nachlass*, 776.
37. *FW*, 354.
38. *Ibid.*
39. *Ibid.*
40. *Ibid.*
41. *Ibid.*
42. *Ibid.*
43. *Ibid.*
44. P. F. Strawson, *Individuals* (London, 1959), pp. 105, 109.
45. *FW*, 354.
46. *FW*, 355.
47. *FW*, 355.
48. *MAM*, 13.
49. *Ibid.*
50. *Ibid.*
51. Kaufmann, Walter, *The Portable Nietzsche* (New York, 1954), pp. 463–464.
52. *GD*, *Verwort*.
53. *GD*, V, 4.
54. *Ibid.*
55. *Ibid.*
56. *GD*, V, 5.
57. *JGB*, 260.
58. *JGB*, 4.
59. *JGB*, 5.
60. *JGB*, 6.
61. *JGB*, 108.
62. *GD*, VI, 1.
63. *Ibid.*
64. *GD*, III, 1.
65. *Ibid.*
66. *JGB*, 188.
67. *GD*, III, 1.
68. *JGB*, 188.
69. *GD*, III, 1.
70. *JGB*, 201.
71. *JGB*, 260.
72. *JGB*, 260.
73. *GM*, I, 7.
74. *GM*, I, 11.
75. *GM*, I, 11.
76. *Ibid.*
77. *GM*, II, 6.
78. *GM*, II, 1.
79. *GM*, II, 3.
80. *GM*, II, 16.
81. *Ibid.*
82. *Ibid.*
83. *Ibid.*
84. *GM*, II, 19.
85. *GM*, II, 16.
86. *GM*, II, 22.
87. *GM*, I, 13.
88. *Ibid.*
89. *JGB*, 36.
90. *JGB*, 36.
91. *JGB*, 13.
92. *GD*, IX, 14.
93. *Nachlass*, p. 750.
94. *JGB*, 62.
95. *GB*, IX, 14.
96. *GM*, III, 28.
97. *GM*, III, 28.
98. *Ibid.*
99. *GM*, III, 24.
100. *GM*, III, 24.
101. *GM*, III, 25.
102. *FW*, 343.
103. *EH*, "*Warum Ich ein Schicksal bin,*" 3.
104. *Z*, I, "*Von Tausend und einem Ziele.*"
105. *Z*, "*Vorrede,*" 3.
106. *Z*, "*Vorrede,*" 5.
107. *Z*, "*Vorrede,*" 3–4.
108. *Z*, "*Vorrede,*" 4.
109. *Z*, I, "*Von den Priestern.*"
110. *Z*, "*Vorrede,*" 5.
111. *Z*, III, "*Der Genesende.*"
112. *FW*, 341.
113. *Nietzsche's Werke* (Leipzig, 1901), XII, 51.
114. *EH*, "*Warum Ich so Klug bin,*" 10.
115. *Werke* (Leipzig, 1901), XII, 116.
116. *Ibid.*, 124.
117. *Ibid.*, 119.
118. *Ibid.*, 126.

22. The Philosophy of Science (*pages 402 - 425*)

1. Karl Pearson, *The Grammar of Science* (London, 1892).

2. See, *e.g.*, *International Encyclopaedia of Unified Science* (Chicago, 1938–1952), and H. Feigl and W. Sellars, eds., *Readings in Philosophical Analysis* (New York, 1949).

3. Karl Popper, *Logik der Forschung* (Vienna, 1935), translated into English by Popper as *Logic of Scientific Discovery* (London, 1958): "Philosophy of Science" in *British Philosophy in the Mid-Century*, ed. C. A. Mace (London, 1957).

4. P. W. Bridgman, *The Logic of Modern Physics* (New York, 1927).

5. C. I. Lewis, *Mind and the World Order* (New York, 1929).

6. L. Wittgenstein, *Tractatus Logico-Philosophicus* (London, 1922; *Philosophical Investigations* (Oxford, New York, 1953).

7. See, *e.g.*, Niels Bohr, *Atomic Theory and the Description of Nature* (Cambridge, 1934).

8. *Popular Scientific Lectures* (hereinafter abbreviated *PSL*), translated, with additions, by T. J. McCormack (Chicago, 1943), p. 179.

9. *On the Definition of Mass* (1868).

10. *History and Root of the Principle of the Conservation of Energy* (hereinafter abbreviated *CE*), translated by P. E. B. Jourdain (Chicago, 1911), p. 61.

11. *Ibid.*, pp. 69–71.

12. *Ibid.*, p. 19 *ff*.

13. *Ibid.*, p. 81.

14. *The Analysis of Sensations* (hereinafter abbreviated *AS*), translated by C. M. Williams (Chicago, 1906), p. xii.

15. *The Science of Mechanics* (hereinafter abbreviated *SM*), translated by T. J. McCormack (La Salle, Ill., 1919), p. xi.

16. *Ibid.*, p. 465.

17. *Ibid.*, p. 229.

18. *Ibid.*, p. 481 *ff*.; *PSL*, p. 197.

19. *AS*, pp. 2–6.

20. *Ibid.*, pp. 7–8.

21. *SM*, p. 483.

22. *AS*, p. 10 fn.

23. *Ibid.*, pp. 9–13, 17–18.
24. *Ibid.*, p. 44.
25. *Ibid.*, pp. 61–62; *PSL*, p. 209.
26. *AS*, p. 33 *ff.*
27. *Ibid.*, pp. 344–345.
28. *Ibid.*, pp. 129, 136, 147, 245, 250, 348–349.
29. *SM*, p. 506; *CE*, p. 95.
30. *AS*, p. 57.
31. *Ibid.*, pp. 89–92; *CE*, pp. 60–63; *SM*, pp. 483–485.
32. *SM*, pp. 502–503.
33. *Ibid.*, pp. 455, 368.
34. *AS*, pp. 80–88.
35. *The Principles of Physical Optics* (hereinafter abbreviated *PPO*), translated by J. S. Anderson and A. F. A. Young (New York, 1953), pp. 57–58.
36. *SM*, p. 1.
37. *Ibid.*, p. 5.
38. *PSL*, p. 191.
39. *SM*, pp. 8–9.
40. *PSL*, p. 193.
41. *Ibid.*, p. 256.
42. *Ibid.*, p. 193.
43. *SM*, pp. 482–485.
44. *Ibid.*, p. 130, App., p. 522, p. 193.
45. *Ibid.*, pp. 493–496; *CE*.
46. *PSL*, p. 229.
47. *Ibid.*, p. 248.
48. Ibid., pp. 236, 257.
49. *Ibid.*, p. 241 *ff.*
50. *Ibid.*, pp. 166–171.
51. *Ibid.*, pp. 159, 207; *SM*, pp. 492–494, 505.
52. *CE*, pp. 86–87. But see *Space and Geometry*, translated by T. J. McCormack (Chicago, 1906), p. 138 and fn.
53. *CE*, p. 57; *AS*, pp. 311–312.
54. *PPO*, p. 7.
55. *AS*, pp. 334–355.
56. *SM*, pp. 483–484, 13.
57. *PSL*, p. 254.
58. *SM*, p. 507.
59. *AS*, pp. 311–312.
60. *CE*, pp. 55–58.
61. *PSL*, pp. 226, 260.
62. *SM*, pp. 460–461.
63. *PSL*, p. 228 *ff.*
64. *The Principles of Mechanics* (hereinafter abbreviated *PM*), translated by D. E. Jones and J. T. Walley (New York, 1956), p. 8.
65. *Ibid.*, pp. 1–4.
66. *Ibid.*, p. 8.
67. *Ibid.*, pp. 11–12.

68. *Ibid.*, pp. 15–16.
69. *Ibid.*, p. 18.
70. *Ibid.*, pp. 21–22.
71. In his Text Book of Mechanics. See *PM*, p. 25.
72. *PM*, pp. 25–28.
73. *Ibid.*, p. 45.
74. *Ibid.*, p. 139.
75. *Ibid.*, p. 141.
76. *Ibid.*, p. 30.
77. *Ibid.*, pp. 32–33.
78. *Ibid.*, p. 37.
79. *Ibid.*, pp. 39–41.
80. *Science and Hypothesis* (hereinafter abbreviated *SH*), translated by W. J. Greenstreet (New York, 1952, p. 13.
81. *Science and Method* (hereinafter abbreviated *SAM*), translated by Francis Maitland (New York, 1958), pp. 9, 15–16.
82. *Ibid.*, p. 17.
83. *Ibid.*, pp. 18–19.
84. *Ibid.*, pp. 21–23.
85. *Ibid.*, p. 285.
86. *SH*, p. 22.
87. *Ibid.*, p. 35.
88. *Ibid.*
89. *Ibid.*, p. 43.
90. *Ibid.*, p. 50.
91. *Ibid.*, pp. 57–58.
92. *Ibid.*, p. 79.
93. *Ibid.*, p. 89.
94. *Ibid.*, pp. 91–92.
95. *Ibid.*, p. 97.
96. *Ibid.*, p. 104.
97. *Ibid.*, pp. 115–117.
98. *Ibid.*, pp. 110, 135–139; *The Value of Science* (hereinafter abbreviated *VS*), translated by G. B. Halstead (New York, 1958), pp. 122–128.
99. *SH*, pp. 140–146. I am grateful to Professor S. Körner for help on this and other points.
100. *Ibid.*
101. *Ibid.*, pp. 152–153.
102. *Ibid.*, p. 159.
103. Ibid., p. 161.
104. *VS*, p. 135 *ff*; *SH*, p. 161 *ff.*
105. *SH*, p. 163.
106. *Ibid.*, pp. 215–216.
107. Ibid., p. 173 *ff.*
108. *The Aim and Structure of Physical Theory* (hereinafter abbreviated *ASPT*), translated by P. P. Wiener (Princeton, 1954), p. 7.
109. *Ibid.*, p. 18.
110. *Ibid.*, pp. 19–20.

111. *Ibid.*, p. 57.
112. *Ibid.*, p. 81.
113. *Ibid.*, pp. 91–99.
114. *Ibid.*, p. 101.
115. *Ibid.*, p. 115.
116. *Ibid.*, pp. 133–135.
117. *Ibid.*, pp. 146–147.
118. *Ibid.*, pp. 166–169.
119. *Ibid.*, pp. 185–187.
120. *Ibid.*, pp. 209–216.
121. *Ibid.*, p. 252 *ff.*
122. See. *e.g.*, articles by Carnap and Hempel in *Readings in Philosophical Analysis*.
123. *SM*, pp. 522–523.
124. *PSL*, p. 181, *AS*, p. 363.
125. See, *e.g.*, S. E. Toulmin, *The Philosophy of Science* (London, 1953).
126. *E.g.*, Karl Popper in works quoted.
127. *AS*, p. 253; *PSL*, p. 232. See also *VS*, p. 116 *ff.*
128. See, *e.g.*, P. K. Feyerabend, "Towards a Realistic Interpretation of Physics," *Proc. Arist. Soc.* 1957–1958; M. B. Hesse, "Theories, Dictionaries and Observation," and P. Alexander, "Theory Construction and Theory Testing," both in *British Journal for the Philosophy of Science*, 1958.
129. *SH*, pp. 150–151; *ASPT*, pp. 185–187.
130. *SAM*, p. 21.
131. *SM*, p. 523.
132. *SH*, p. 143.
133. See, *e.g.*, F. P. Ramsey, "Theories," in *Foundations of Mathematics* (Routledge, 1931); R. B. Braithwaite, *Scientific Explanation* (Cambridge, 1953).
134. See, *e.g.*, M. Schlick, *Gesammelte Aufsätze 1926–36* (Vienna, 1938); E. Hutten, *The Language of Modern Physics* (London, 1956); S. E. Toulmin, *The Philosophy of Science.*
135. See, *e.g.*, V. Kraft, *The Vienna Circle* (New York, 1954); A. J. Ayer, *Language, Truth and Logic* (London, 1936).
136. *ASPT*, Chapter I.
137. *PM*, p. 23.
138. *SM*, pp. 273, 457; *PSL*, p. 259.
139. *SM*, Chapter IV, Section 2; *ASPT*, Chapter VII.

23. F. H. Bradley (*pages 426 - 436*)

1. *Appearance and Reality*, 2nd edition (Oxford, 1897), p. 124.
2. *The Principles of Logic*, 2nd edition (Oxford, 1922), p. 591.

3. *Appearance and Reality*, p. 28.
4. *Ibid.*, p. 120.
5. *Ibid.*, p. 123.
6. *Ibid.*

7. Hume, *A Treatise of Human Nature*, edited by L. A. Selby-Bigge (Oxford, 1896), p. 233.
8. *Appearance and Reality*, p. 152.

9. *Ibid.*, p. 123.
10. *Ibid.*, p. 129.
11. *Ibid.*, p. 114.
12. *Ibid.*, p. 488.
13. *Ibid.*, p. 140.
14. *Ibid.*, p. 137.
15. *Ibid.*
16. *Our Knowledge of the External World* (London, 1914), p. 14.
17. M. Macdonald in *Philosophy and Analysis* (Oxford, 1954), p. 1, summarizing the first editorial of the periodical *Analysis* in 1933 by A. E. Duncan-Jones.
18. Compare F. Waismann, "How I see Philosophy" in *Contemporary British Philosophy*, 3rd series (London, 1956).
19. *E.g.*, M. Lazerowitz in *The Structure of Metaphysics* (London, 1955).
20. "The Conception of Reality" in *Philosophical Studies* (London, 1922), p. 211.
21. *Appearance and Reality*, p. 218.
22. *Ethical Studies* (Oxford, 1927), p. 173.
23. *Appearance and Reality*, p. 133.

24. Pragmatism (*pages 437 - 462*)

1. *The Collected Papers of Charles Sanders Peirce* (hereinafter abbreviated *CP*.), ed. by C. Hartshorn, P. Weiss, and A. W. Burks, 8 vols. (Cambridge, Mass., 1931–1958), Vol. 8, paragraph 259.
2. Dewey, John, *Reconstruction in Philosophy*, reprinted with new Introduction (Boston, 1948), p. 38.
3. The subtitle of *Pragmatism*.
4. *Pragmatism* (New York, 1907), p. vii.
5. *CP*. 5. 411–412.
6. Wittgenstein, Ludwig, *Philosophical Investigations*, translated by G. E. M. Anscombe (Oxford, New York, 1953), p. 43; *The Blue and Brown Books* (New York, 1958), p. 4.
7. *Pragmatism*, p. 2.
8. *Ibid.*, p. 54.
9. On Bain, see the study by Max H. Fisch, "Alexander Bain and the Genealogy of Pragmatism," in *Journal of the History of Ideas*, 15 (1954), pp. 413–414. On Wright's place in the history of pragmatism see Philip P. Wiener, *Evolution and the Founders of Pragmatism* (Cambridge, Mass., 1949), ch. 3; Gail Kennedy, "The Pragmatic Naturalism of Chauncey Wright," in *Studies in the History of Ideas*, Vol. III (New York, 1935), pp. 477–503; Morris Cohen, *Chance, Love, and Logic* (New York, 1923), Preface; selected writings and bibliographical references in *Chauncey Wright, Philosophical Writings, Representative Selections*, ed. by Edward H. Madden (New York, 1959).
10. *CP*. 5. 12–13.
11. The third paragraph of "Epistle to the Reader" in *An Essay concerning Human Understanding*.
12. *CP*. 1. 539.
13. *CP*. 5. 443.
14. *CP*. 5. 394.
15. *CP*. 5. 491.
16. *CP*. 5. 400.
17. *CP*. 5. 401.
18. *CP*. 5. 402.
19. *CP*. 5. 403.
20. *CP*. 5. 8.
21. *CP*. 5. 429.
22. *CP*. 5. 403n.
23. *CP*. 5. 403.
24. *CP*. 5. 404.
25. See Daniel J. Bronstein, "Inquiry and Meaning," in *Studies in the Philosophy of Charles Sanders Peirce*, ed. by Philip P. Wiener and Frederic H. Young (Cambridge, Mass., 1952), p. 47 *ff.*; Charles K. McKeon, "Peirce's Scottish Realism," in Wiener and Young *op. cit.*, pp. 238–250.
26. *CP*. 5. 430.
27. *CP*. 5. 101.
28. *CP*. 5. 483.
29. A point well emphasized by Justus Buchler, *Charles Peirce's Empiricism* (New York, 1939), p. 115.
30. See *CP*. 5. 453; 5. 457; 6. 364.
31. *CP*. 5. 468. See also *CP*. 5. 453.
32. For recent discussions, see R. M. Chisholm, "The Contrary-to-Fact Conditional," in Feigl, H. and Sellars, W., eds. *Readings in Philosophical Analysis* (New York, 1949); Nelson Goodman, "The Problems of Counterfactual Conditionals," in *Journal of Philosophy*, Vol. xliv, No. 19 (1947), pp. 113–128.
33. *CP*. 5. 375.
34. *CP*. 5. 384.
35. *CP*. 8. 16. Cf. also 5. 432.
36. *CP*. 5. 407.
37. *CP*. 5. 565.
38. *CP*. 5. 403.
39. See "Dewey's New Logic" in Paul Arthur Schilpp, *The Philosophy of John Dewey* (Evanston and Chicago, 1939), p. 144.
40. *Ibid.*, p. 145.
41. *CP*. 2. 75.
42. *CP*. 5. 574–575.
43. The Preface to *Pragmatism*, ix.
44. In the chapter on the "Sick Soul," disguised as the report of a "French correspondent."
45. *The Letters of William James*, ed. by Henry James (Boston, 1920), Vol. I. p. 147.
46. *Pragmatism*, p. 51.
47. For a different interpretation see John Herman Randall, Jr., "David Hume: Radical Empiricist and Pragmatist," in *Freedom and Experience—Essays Presented to Horace M. Kallen*, ed. by Sidney Hook and Milton R. Konvitz (Ithaca, 1947), pp. 289–312.
48. Cf. *CP*. 5. 439.
49. Cf. *CP*. 5. 3.
50. Cf. *Critique of Pure Reason*, A800, B828. The same fundamental distinction is made in *The Metaphysics of Morals*.
51. *Pragmatism*, p. 46.
52. *The Principles of Psychology*, 2 vols. (New York, 1890; reprinted 1950), Vol. I, p. 8.
53. *Pragmatism*, p. 58.
54. "Humanism and Truth," in *Mind* xiii (October, 1904). Reprinted in *The Meaning of Truth* (New York, 1909) and *Pragmatism*, enlarged ed. (New York, 1943).
55. *Pragmatism*, p. 50.
56. *Ibid.*, p. 76.
57. *Ibid.*, p. 222.
58. *Ibid.*, p. 61.
59. *Ibid.*, p. 75.
60. *The Meaning of Truth*, Preface, p. 1.
61. *Ibid.*, p. 1.
62. *Pragmatism*, pp. 212–213.
63. *Ibid.*, p. 204.
64. *Philosophical Essays* (London, 1910), ch. 5.
65. *Pragmatism*, p. 205.
66. *Ibid.*, p. 299.
67. From the Preface to *The Meaning of Truth*.

68. Preface to *The Meaning of Truth*. Also see *Pragmatism*, pp. 109, 115.
69. *Pragmatism*, p. 115.
70. *Ibid.*, p. 201.
71. *Andover Review* XIII (March, 1890). Also Morton White, *The Origins of Dewey's Instrumentalism* (New York, 1943), p. 6.
72. See pp. 173–174.
73. See the Introduction to the 1948 edition of *Reconstruction in Philosophy*, "Reconstruction As Seen Twenty-Five Years Later."
74. "The Development of American Pragmatism," in *Studies in the History of Ideas*, Vol. II (New York, 1925), p. 361.
75. *Ibid.*, p. 367.
76. *Reconstruction in Philosophy*, p. 213.
77. *Experience and Nature*, rev. ed. (New York, 1929), p. 7.
78. "The Development of American Pragmatism," p. 367.
79. *Logic: The Theory of Inquiry* (New York, 1938), pp. 66–67.
80. *Ibid.*, p. 8.
81. *Ibid.*, pp. 104–105.
82. *How We Think*, rev. ed. (New York, 1933), p. 106.

83. *Logic: The Theory of Inquiry*, p. 107.
84. *Ibid.*, pp. 26–27.
85. *Ibid.*, p. 106.
86. *Ibid.*, p. 68.
87. *Ibid.*, pp. 105–106.
88. Thayer, H. S., *The Logic of Pragmatism* (New York, 1952), p. 75 *ff.*
89. *Logic: The Theory of Inquiry*, p. 107.
90. *Ibid.*, p. 108.
91. *Ibid.*, p. 111.
92. *Ibid.*, pp. 111–112.
93. E.g., *Reconstruction in Philosophy*, pp. 156–157.
94. *Problems of Men* (New York, 1946), p. 332.
95. For a study of the exchange, and references to the literature, see Thayer, H. S., "Two Theories of Truth," in *Journal of Philosophy*, Vol. xliv, No. 19 (1947), pp. 516–527.
96. "Propositions, Warranted Assertibility and Truth," *Problems of Men*, pp. 343–344.
97. E.g., by Russell in Schilpp, *op. cit.*, p. 143, and *Freedom versus Organization* (New York, 1934), p. 192.
98. *Eleven Theses on Feuerbach*.

99. In *Reconstruction in Philosophy*, p. 156.
100. *Logic: The Theory of Inquiry*, p. 122.
101. *Human Nature and Conduct* (New York, 1922), p. 210.
102. *Reconstruction in Philosophy*, pp. 163–164, 169, 177.
103. Adapted from Russell, *A History of Western Philosophy* (New York, 1945), p. 825.
104. *CP.* 1. 141.
105. London, 1949.
106. See Ramsey's *The Foundations of Mathematics* (New York, 1950), esp. p. 156 *ff.*; see Lewis' *An Analysis of Knowledge and Valuation* (La Salle, Ill., 1946).
107. See W. V. Quine, *From a Logical Point of View* (Cambridge, Mass., 1953). Also, argued from a position claiming to be in the spirit of Dewey, Morton White, "The Analytic and Synthetic," in *John Dewey: Philosopher of Science and Freedom*, ed. by Sidney Hook (New York, 1950), pp. 316–330.

25. G. E. Moore (*pages 463 - 472*)

1. For a full explanation and documentation of what I say about Moore, the reader is referred to my *G. E. Moore: A Critical Exposition* (Oxford, 1958).
2. *Mind* IX, pp. 289–304.
3. In *The Philosophy of G. E. Moore*, ed. by Paul Arthur Schilpp (Evanston, 1942).
4. "Some Judgments of Perception," *Proc. Arist. Soc.* xix (1918), p. 7.
5. "The Nature of Sensible Appearances," *Proc. Arist. Soc. Suppl.* vi, p. 186.
6. *Some Main Problems of Philosophy* (London, 1953), p. 182.
7. "Hume's Philosophy," in *Some Main Problems of Philosophy*, p. 164.
8. *Principia Ethica* (Cambridge, 1903), p. 75.
9. "A Defence of Common Sense," in *Contemporary British Philosophy*, II, ed. by J. H. Muirhead (London, 1925), p. 207.

10. *Principia Ethica*, p. 143.
11. *Ibid.*, p. 74.
12. *Ethics* (London, 1912), p. 203.
13. P. 76.
14. In Schilpp, *op. cit.*, p. 664.
15. *Principia Ethica*, p. 16.
16. *Some Main Problems of Philosophy*, p. 279.
17. "The Refutation of Idealism," *Mind* xii, p. 450.
18. "The Nature of Judgment," *Mind* viii (1899), p. 182.
19. Schilpp, *op. cit.*, p. 666.
20. Pp. 7–8.
21. *Principia Ethica*, p. 61.
22. *Proc. Arist. Soc. Suppl.* xv (1936).
23. E.g., in Schilpp, *op. cit.*, pp. 660–667; "Russell's 'Theory of Descriptions'" in *The Philosophy of Bertrand Russell*, ed. by Paul Arthur Schilpp (Evanston, 1944).
24. *Principia Ethica*, p. 16.
25. P. 9.
26. Pp. 17, 61.
27. *Principia Ethica*, pp. 13–14.

28. *Ibid.*, p. 13.
29. *The Philosophy of G. E. Moore*, pp. 535–554.
30. *Some Main Problems of Philosophy*, pp. 29, 52.
31. *Philosophical Investigations*, translated by G. E. M. Anscombe (Oxford, New York, 1953), § 314 and p. 193.
32. *The Philosophy of G. E. Moore*, p. 639.
33. P. 218.
34. "Some Judgments of Perception," p. 13.
35. In "Visual Sense Data," in *British Philosophy in the Mid-Century*, ed. by C. A. Mace (London, 1957).
36. In "The Status of Sense-data," *Proc. Arist. Soc. Suppl.* xiv.
37. *The Philosophy of G. E. Moore*, pp. 629, 644.
38. E.g., "Some Judgments of Perception," p. 13; "A Defence of Common Sense," pp. 219–221.

26. Bertrand Russell (*pages 473 - 491*)

1. *My Philosophical Development* (London and New York, 1959).
2. *Contemporary British Philosophy*, 1st ser. (London, 1924), p. 79.
3. "My Mental Development" in *The Philosophy of Bertrand Russell*, ed. by P. A. Schilpp (Evanston, 1944), and *My Philosophical Development*.
4. *My Philosophical Development*, p. 35.
5. *Ibid.*, p. 41.
6. "The Relation of Sense Data to Physics," in *Mysticism and Logic* (New York, 1918), p. 150, and "Logical Atomism" in *Logical Positivism*, ed. by A. J. Ayer (Glencoe, Ill., 1959), p. 34. See also *Our Knowledge of the External World* (London, 1914), Lecture IV.
7. "On Scientific Method in Philosophy," in *Mysticism and Logic*, p. 94.
8. *Ibid.*, pp. 105–106.
9. *Ibid.*
10. *Ibid.*
11. *Ibid.*
12. See, *e.g.*, *Our Knowledge of the External World*, pp. 75–77, 258; *An Outline of Philosophy* (London, 1927), pp. 1, 163–167, 239: *An Inquiry into Meaning and Truth* (London, 1940), p. 16.
13. "Reply to Criticisms," in *The Philosophy of Bertrand Russell*, p. 684.
14. *Ibid.*
15. *Our Knowledge of the External World*, p. 12.
16. "Logical Atomism" in Ayer, *op. cit.*, p. 33.
17. The title of Lecture II of *Our Knowledge of the External World*.
18. *An Inquiry into Meaning and Truth*, p. 429.
19. "Logical Atomism" in Ayer, *op. cit.*, p. 38.
20. *Our Knowledge of the External World*, p. 108.
21. Russell and Whitehead discuss the logical paradoxes in section VIII of Ch. II of the Introduction to *Principia Mathematica*. A great deal of work has been done on this topic since the publication of *Principia Mathematica*.
22. *Principia Mathematica*, vol. I, p. 62.
23. "Logical Atomism" in Ayer, *op. cit.*, pp. 39–40.
24. See especially Professor Max Black's article "Russell's Philosophy of Language" in *The Philosophy of Bertrand Russell*, pp. 227–256.

25. "Reply to Criticisms," p. 692.
26. *Ibid.*, p. 717.
27. *My Philosophical Development*, p. 219.
28. "The Philosophy of Logical Atomism" Lecture II in *Logic and Knowledge*, ed. by R. C. Marsh (London, 1956).
29. *Ibid.*, Lecture I.
30. *Ibid.*, Lecture II.
31. *Ibid.*
32. E.g., Mr. J. O. Urmson in *Philosophical Analysis* (Oxford, 1956). Russell has rejected his criticisms on the ground that they rest on misunderstandings.
33. See his *The Concept of Nature* (Cambridge, 1920), ch. IV and C. D. Broad, *Scientific Thought* (London, 1923), ch. I.
34. See *Our Knowledge of the External World*, ch. IV.
35. *Ibid.*
36. *Introduction to Mathematical Philosophy* (London, 1919), p. 169.
37. The most thorough criticism is that of Mr. P. F. Strawson in his well-known paper "On Referring" in *Mind*, 1951. Russell discusses this and refutes Strawson's criticisms in *My Philosophical Development*, pp. 238–245.
38. See *Mysticism and Logic*, pp. 168–170. For Russell's account of the theory, see "On Denoting," *Mind*, 1905; *Principia Mathematica*, vol. I, Introduction, ch. III and pp. 173–187; *Introduction to Mathematical Philosophy*, ch. XVI; *Mysticism and Logic*, ch. X; and *My Philosophical Development*, pp. 83–85, 238–245.
39. I adapt this idea from W. T. Stace's illuminating discussion in *The Philosophy of Bertrand Russell*, pp. 259–260.
40. *The Analysis of Mind* (London, 1921), pp. 129–130.
41. *My Philosophical Development*, p. 139.
42. *The Analysis of Mind*, especially Lecture XXV.
43. In *The Philosophy of Bertrand Russell*, p. 363.
44. Especially in *Human Knowledge* (London, 1948).
45. *E.g.*, *An Inquiry into Meaning and Truth*, p. 61 and *Human Knowledge*, p. 217.
46. *An Inquiry into Meaning and Truth*, pp. 14–15.
47. *An Outline of Philosophy*, p. 134.

48. *The Philosophy of Bertrand Russell*, p. 705.
49. *The Analysis of Matter* (New York, 1927), p. 382.
50. *The Philosophy of Bertrand Russell*, p. 705.
51. Reprinted in *Philosophical Essays* (London, 1910). A later version of the coherence theory, advocated by some logical positivists, is criticized in ch. X of *An Inquiry into Meaning and Truth*.
52. In "Dewey's New Logic" in *The Philosophy of John Dewey*, ed. by P. A. Schilpp (Evanston, Ill., 1939), pp. 135–156, and *An Inquiry into Meaning and Truth*, ch. XXIII.
53. *My Philosophical Development*, p. 176.
54. *The Problems of Philosophy* (London, 1912), p. 121.
55. *My Philosophical Development*, p. 184.
56. *Human Knowledge*, p. 159. See also *An Inquiry into Meaning and Truth*, p. 367.
57. *An Inquiry into Meaning and Truth*, ch. XXI.
58. *Human Knowledge*, p. 160.
59. *Ibid.*, p. 161.
60. *Ibid.*
61. *Human Knowledge*, p. 170.
62. *The Problems of Philosophy*, p. 63.
63. *Ibid.*, p. 68.
64. See, *e.g.*, Paul Edwards, "Bertrand Russell's Doubts about Induction," *Mind*, 1949.
65. There are some rather sketchy references in *The Analysis of Matter* and a short chapter in *An Outline of Philosophy*.
66. *The Philosophy of Bertrand Russell*, p. 683.
67. *Ibid.*, p. 684.
68. *Human Knowledge*, p. 451.
69. In *A Treatise on Probability* (London, 1921), particularly Pt. III.
70. *Human Knowledge*, Pt. VI, ch. IX.
71. *My Philosophical Development*, p. 202.
72. *German Social Democracy* (London, 1896) and *Human Society in Ethics and Politics* (London 1954).
73. *What I Believe* (New York, 1925), p. 20.
74. *Ibid.*, p. 29.
75. *An Outline of Philosophy*, p. 239.
76. *Religion and Science* (New York, 1935), p. 242.
77. *An Outline of Philosophy*, p. 234.

78. *Religion and Science*, p. 250. See also *Human Society in Ethics and Politics*, p. 25.
79. "Reply to Criticisms," p. 722.
80. *Ibid.*, p. 724. See also *Human Society in Ethics and Politics*, p. 89.
81. E.g. by Professor Buchler in *The Philosophy of Bertrand Rus-*

sell, p. 514. Russell's quoted reply is given at p. 720.
82. *Ibid.*, p. 724.
83. *Ibid.*
84. *The Logic of Moral Discourse* (Glencoe, Ill., 1955), p. 214.
85. Reprinted in *Mysticism and Logic*, pp. 44–54.

86. In *The Philosophy of Bertrand Russell*, pp. 19–20.
87. *Human Knowledge*, p. 415.
88. *Ibid.*, p. 527.
89. *My Philosophical Development*, p. 213.

27. Logical Positivism (*pages 492 - 508*)

1. For a short account of these differences, see Russell, *My Philosophical Development* (London, 1959), Ch. 10. For detailed expositions of the *Tractatus*, see E. Stenius, *Wittgenstein's "Tractatus"* (Oxford, 1960) and G. E. M. Anscombe, *An Introduction to Wittgenstein's Tractatus* (London, 1959).
2. *Tractatus Logico-Philosophicus* (Leipzig, 1921), translated by C. K. Ogden (London, 1922), 4.112.
3. E.g., 4.003 and 6.53.
4. 6.522.
5. See *Soziologie im Physikalismus*, translated in *Logical Positivism*, ed. by A. J. Ayer (New York, 1959).
6. E.g., Carnap, *Überwindung der Metaphysik durch Logische Analyse der Sprache*, translated in *Logical Positivism*. See also Ayer, "The Genesis of Metaphysics," *Proceedings of the Aristotelian Society* (1933–1934).
7. For some reasons for this distinction, see Ayer, *Language, Truth and Logic*, Introduction to 2nd edition (London, 1946), pp. 5–9.
8. 4.024.
9. 3.261.
10. The Vienna Circle's interpretation of the *Tractatus* is disputed by G. E. M. Anscombe — see *An Introduction to Wittgenstein's Tractatus*, especially Ch. 1 and 12.
11. "Meaning and Verification," reprinted in *Readings in Philosophical Analysis*, ed. by H. Feigl and W. Sellars (New York, 1949), p. 148.
12. E.g., Waismann, "*Logische Analyse des Wahrscheinlichkeitsbegriffs*," *Erkenntnis* (1930); Schlick, "*Positivismus und Realismus*," *Erkenntnis* (1932), translated in *Logical Positivism*, and "Meaning and Verification," *The Philosophical Review* (1936);

Carnap, "*Überwindung der Metaphysik durch Logische Analyse der Sprache*," *Erkenntnis* (1932), (translated in *Logical Positivism* and "Testability and Meaning," *Philosophy of Science* (1936–1937).
13. In "The Principle of Verifiability," *Mind* (1936).
14. In "Meaning and Verification."
15. In *Language, Truth and Logic*, Introduction to 2nd edition, p. 16.
16. "Meaning and Verification" in *Readings in Philosophical Analysis*, p. 148.
17. In "Testability and Meaning."
18. In *Logical Positivism*, Editor's Introduction, p. 15.
19. *Ibid.*
20. *Ibid.*
21. *The Logic of Modern Physics* (New York, 1927), p. 5.
22. *Ibid.*, p. 6.
23. "Operational Analysis," *Philosophy of Science* (1938).
24. *The Logic of Modern Physics*, p. 10.
25. "Meaning and Verification," in *Readings in Philosophical Analysis*, p. 154.
26. "A New Philosophy of Experience," *College of the Pacific Publications*, Vol. 1 (Berkeley, 1932). Also included in *Gesammelte Aufsätze 1926–36* (Vienna, 1938).
27. See *Gesammelte Aufsätze 1926–36*.
28. E.g., in "*Die physikalische Sprache als Universalsprache der Wissenschaft*," in *Erkenntnis*, 1932, translated by M. Black as *The Unity of Science* (London, 1934).
29. "*Logische Analyse des Wahrscheinlichkeitsbegriffs*."
30. See J. R. Weinberg, *An Examination of Logical Positivism* (London, 1936), Ch. V.
31. "*Die Kausalität in der gegenwärtigen Physik*," in *Die Naturwissenschaften*, 1931; see Weinberg, *Examination of Logical Positivism*, p. 146.

32. See, e.g., *The Unity of Science* and "Testability and Meaning."
33. See *Logic of Scientific Discovery* (London, 1958), Ch. 1; also "Philosophy of Science — a personal report," in *British Philosophy in the Mid-Century*, ed. by C. A. Mace (London, 1957).
34. "Testability and Meaning," *Philosophy of Science* (1936), p. 439 *ff*.
35. *Language, Truth and Logic*, p. 37 and p. 38.
36. *Ibid.*, pp. 11–12.
37. *Ibid.*, p. 13.
38. See A. Church, review of *Language, Truth and Logic* (2nd edition), *Journal of Symbolic Logic* (1949); also D. J. O'Connor, "Some Consequences of Professor A. J. Ayer's Verification Principle," *Analysis* (1949–1950).
39. See R. Brown and J. Watling, "Amending the Verification Principle," *Analysis* (1950–1951).
40. E.g., M. Lazerowitz, "Strong and Weak Verification," *Mind* (1939 and 1950).
41. See Schlick, "Facts and Propositions," *Analysis* (1935), and "A New Philosophy of Experience."
42. See *The Unity of Science*.
43. See "*Über Protokollsätze*," *Erkenntnis* (1932).
44. See "*Protokollsätze*," *Erkenntnis* (1932), translated in *Logical Positivism*.
45. 4.05.
46. 3.21.
47. "Sociology and Physicalism," in *Logical Positivism*, p. 291.
48. "On the Logical Positivists' Theory of Truth," *Analysis* (1935), and "Some remarks on 'Facts' and Propositions," *Analysis* (1935).
49. See "Protocol Sentences," in *Logical Positivism*, p. 202.
50. See Hempel, "On the Logical Positivists' Theory of Truth," *Analysis* (1935).

51. See, e.g., B. von Juhos, "Empiricism and Physicalism," *Analysis* (1935), and Ayer, *Verification and Experience*, Aristotelian Society, 1936–1937.

52. See, e.g. Neurath, "Protocol Sentences" and "Sociology and Physicalism"; Carnap, *The Unity of Science* and "Logical Foundations of the Unity of Science," in *Encyclopedia of Unified Science* (1939).

53. See *Language, Truth and Logic*, Chap. V.

54. "Verification and Experience," *Proceedings of the Aristotelian Society* (1936–1937), and *The Foundations of Empirical Knowledge* (London, 1940), pp. 80–84.

55. *The Problem of Knowledge* (London, 1956), Ch. 2, sec. vi.

56. *System of Logic* (London, 1843), Ch. 5.

57. *Principia Mathematica* (Cambridge, 3 vols, 1910–1913; 2nd edition, 1925–1927). See D. J. O'Connor and A. H. Basson, *Introduction to Symbolic Logic* (Glencoe, Ill., 1960), I. Copi, *Symbolic Logic* (New York, 1954), and most modern introductory textbooks on symbolic logic for an extensional system similar to Russell and Whitehead's.

58. *Tractatus*, especially 4.25 *et seq.*

59. "Introduction to a General Theory of Elementary Propositions," *American Journal of Mathematics* (1921).

60. See, e.g., Carnap, "The Old and the New Logic," and Hahn, "Logic, Mathematics and Knowledge of Nature" (both in *Logical Positivism*; also Carnap, "Foundations of Logic and Mathematics," *Encyclopedia of Unified Science*.

61. See, e.g., Hahn, *op. cit.*, and Ayer, *Language, Truth and Logic*, Ch. IV.

62. See, e.g., Hahn, *op. cit.*; Carnap, *op. cit.*; Hempel, "On the Nature of Mathematical Truth" and "Geometry and Empirical Science," both in *American Mathematical Monthly* (1945), both reprinted in *Readings in Philosophical Analysis*.

63. *Language, Truth and Logic*, p. 82.

64. 6.211.

65. Hahn, *op. cit.*, in *Logical Positivism*, p. 159.

66. See Hempel, "Geometry and Empirical Science."

67. Quoted by Hempel at the end of "Geometry and Empirical Science."

68. E.g., at the bottom of p. 79.

69. *Logische Syntax der Sprache* (Vienna, 1934), translated by A. Smeaton, *Logical Syntax of Language* (New York, 1937), p. 303.

70. For a later exposition of this view, see K. W. Britton, "Are Necessary Truths True by Convention?," *Proceedings of the Aristotelian Society*, Supp. Vol. (1947).

71. See, e.g., Hahn, *op. cit.* For recent presentations and discussion of this view see also Max Black, "Necessary Statements and Rules," *Philosophical Review* (1958) also included in *Models and Metaphors* (Ithaca, N.Y., 1962), and Paul Edwards, "Do Necessary Propositions 'Mean Nothing'?" *Journal of Philosophy* (1949).

72. Wittgenstein is reported as saying this in his classes; see N. Malcolm, "Are Necessary Propositions Really Verbal?" *Mind* (1940), and G. E. Moore, "Wittgenstein's Lectures in 1930–33," *Mind* (1954, 1955), Section II, also included in *Philosophical Papers* (London, 1959). For Wittgenstein's later treatment of this topic, see his *Remarks on the Foundations of Mathematics* (Oxford, 1956).

73. Hahn, *op. cit.*, in *Logical Positivism*, p. 153.

74. Hahn, *op. cit.*

75. *On the Nature of Mathematical Truth*.

76. See *Introduction to Logical Theory* (London, 1952), Ch. 1.

77. *Problems of Ethics* (New York, 1939), pp. 38–39.

78. *Ibid.*, p. 78.

79. *Ibid.*, p. 87.

80. *Ibid.*, p. 197.

81. 6.41 and 6.42.

82. *Philosophy and Logical Syntax* (London, 1935), p. 23.

83. *Ibid.*, pp. 24–25.

84. "On the Analysis of Moral Judgements," *Horizon* (1949), reprinted in *Philosophical Essays* (London, 1954).

85. *Language, Truth and Logic*, p. 107.

86. See Ayer, "On the Analysis of Moral Judgements."

87. "The Emotive Meaning of Ethical Terms," *Mind* (1937); "Ethical Judgments and Avoidability," *Mind* (1938); "Persuasive Definitions," *Mind* (1938); "The Nature of Ethical Disagreement," in *Readings in Philosophical Analysis*; "The Emotive Concept of Ethics and its Cognitive Implications," *Philosophical Review* (1950).

88. "Imperative Sentences," *Mind* (1949); "Universalisability," *Proceedings of the Aristotelian Society* (1954–1955).

89. See "The Turning Point in Philosophy," in *Logical Positivism*, p. 54.

90. *Ibid.*, p. 55; see also *Gesammelte Aufsätze 1926–36*.

91. "The Turning Point in Philosophy, p. 55.

92. *Ibid.*, p. 56.

93. *Ibid.*, p. 57.

94. 4.12.

95. *Logical Syntax of Language*, p. 282.

96. See *Tractatus*, e.g., 2.1 to 4.002.

97. *Logical Syntax of Language*, p. 51.

98. *Ibid.*, p. 52.

99. *Ibid.*, sec. 78.

100. *Ibid.*, Foreword, p. XIII.

101. *Ibid.*, p. 286.

102. *Tractatus*, 1.1.

103. *Ibid.*, 5.5301.

104. See, e.g., "The Semantic Conception of Truth and the Foundations of Semantics," included in *Readings in Philosophical Analysis*.

105. See, e.g., *Introduction to Semantics* (Cambridge, Mass., 1942); *Meaning and Necessity* (Chicago, 1947); "Empiricism, Semantics and Ontology," *Revue Internationale de Philosophie* (1950).

106. *Language, Truth and Logic*, p. 62.

107. For reasons for this preference, see *The Foundations of Empirical Knowledge*, Ch. I.

108. *Ibid.*, Ch. V.

109. See, e.g., *Philosophical Essays* and *The Problem of Knowledge*.

110. See "Statements about the Past," *Proceedings of the Aristotelian Society* (1950–1951) (included in *Philosophical Essays*), and *The Problem of Knowledge*, Ch. 4, sec. v.

111. See Ayer, *Philosophy and Language*, Inaugural lecture, Oxford, 1960.

28. Existentialism (*pages 509 - 529*)

1. *Concluding Unscientific Post-script*, translated by W. Lowrie (Princeton, 1941), p. 228.
2. *The Phenomenology of Mind*, Section IV, B.
3. *Either/Or*, Diapsalmata.
4. *A Modern Introduction to Meta-physics*, ed. by D. A. Drennen (New York, 1962), p. 333.
5. *A Treatise of Human Nature*, I, iv, 7.
6. *The Language of Morals* (Oxford, 1952), pp. 68–69.

29. Contemporary British Philosophy (*pages 530 - 556*)

1. F. P. Ramsey, *The Foundations of Mathematics and Other Logical Essays* (London, 1931).
2. *Aristotelian Society Proceedings*, 1931–1932. Reprinted in *Logic and Language*, edited by A. Flew (1st series, Oxford, 1951).
3. *Aristotelian Society Proceedings*, 1937–1938. Reprinted in *Logic and Language*, edited by A. Flew (2nd series, Oxford, 1953).
4. Previously unpublished paper included in Austin's *Philosophical Papers*, edited by J. O. Urmson and G. J. Warnock (Oxford, 1961).
5. *Aristotelian Society Supplementary Volume*, 1946. Reprinted in *Logic and Language* (2nd series) and in *Philosophical Papers*.
6. *Aristotelian Society Proceedings*, 1956–1957. Reprinted in *Philosophical Papers*.
7. *Proceedings of the British Academy*, 1956. Reprinted in *Philosophical Papers*.
8. "Probability," *Aristotelian Society Supplementary Volume*, 1950. Reprinted in *Essays in Conceptual Analysis*, edited by A. Flew (London, 1956).
9. "Universals," in *Philosophical Quarterly*, 1950–1951. Reprinted in *Logic and Language* (2nd series).
10. *The Nature of Historical Explanation* (Oxford, 1952) and "Metaphysics and History" in *The Nature of Metaphysics*, edited by D. F. Pears (London, 1957).
11. "Can A Man Witness His Own Funeral?", *Hibbert Journal*, 1955–1956.
12. "Political Principles," in *Philosophy, Politics and Society*, edited by P. Laslett (Oxford, 1956).
13. *Definition and Theory in Jurisprudence* (Oxford, 1953); *Causation in the Law*, with A. Honoré (Oxford, 1959).
14. "Moral Arguments," *Mind*, 1958; "When Is a Principle a Moral Principle?," *Aristotelian Society Supplementary Volume*, 1954.
15. "Language Strata," in *Logic and Language* (2nd series).

Bibliography

1. Early Greek Philosophy (*pages 1–13*)

TEXTS

Diels, H., editor, *Die Fragmente der Vorsokratiker* (tenth edition, Berlin, 1961). The standard collection of the Greek texts.

Freeman, K., editor, *Ancilla to the Pre-Socratic Philosophers* (Cambridge, Mass., 1948).

Kirk, G. S.; Raven, J. E.; and Schofield, M., *The Presocratic Philosophers* (second edition, Cambridge, 1983).

GENERAL SURVEYS

Barnes, Jonathan, *The Pre-Socratics* (two volumes, London, 1979).

Burnet, J., *Early Greek Philosophy* (fourth edition, London, 1930; paperback, New York, 1957).

Furley, D. J., and Allen, R. E., *Studies in Pre-Socratic Philosophy* (two volumes, London, 1970).

√ Guthrie, W. C. K., *History of Greek Philosophy* (volume I, Cambridge, 1962; volume II, Cambridge, 1965).

Sarton, George, *History of Science* (volume I, Cambridge, Mass., 1960).

WORKS ON INDIVIDUAL PRE-SOCRATIC PHILOSOPHERS

Kahn, C. A., *Anaximander and the Origins of Greek Cosmology* (New York, 1960).

Kirk, G. S., *Heraclitus: The Cosmic Fragments* (Cambridge, 1954).

Lee, H. D. P., *Zeno of Elea* (Cambridge, 1936).

Kerferd, G. B., *The Sophistic Movement* (Cambridge, 1981).

Raven, J. E., *Pythagoreans and Eleatics* (Cambridge, 1948).

Thomson, J. F., "Tasks and Super-Tasks" in *Analysis* 15 (1954), pp. 1–13.

2. Socrates and Plato (*pages 14–35*)

TEXTS

Burnet, J., *Platonis Opera* (Oxford, 1899–1906). The complete Greek text of Plato's works.

The Loeb Classical Library publishes the Greek text of Plato's dialogues with English translations facing. The translations are by various hands.

The Collected Dialogues of Plato (edited by Edith Hamilton and Huntington Cairns in a complete translation by various hands, Princeton, 1961).

GENERAL SURVEYS

Crombie, A. C., *An Examination of Plato's Doctrines* (two volumes, London, 1962–63).

Gosling, J. C. B., *Plato* (London, 1973).

√ Guthrie, W. C. K., *History of Greek Philosophy* (volume III, part 2, volumes IV and V, Cambridge, 1972–78).

Gulley, N., *Plato's Theory of Knowledge* (London, 1962).

Santas, G., *Socrates* (London, 1979).

Shorey, P., *What Plato Said* (Chicago, 1933).

Vlastos, G., *Plato's Universe* (Oxford, 1975).

WORKS ON INDIVIDUAL TOPICS

Adkins, A. W., *Merit and Responsibility: A Study in Greek Values* (Oxford, 1960). Chapters 13 and 14 are on Plato.

Annas, J., *An Introduction to Plato's Republic* (Oxford, 1981).

Robinson, R., *Plato's Earlier Dialectic* (Oxford, 1953).

Ross, W. D., *Plato's Theory of Ideas* (Oxford, 1951).

Irwin, T., *Plato's Moral Theory* (Oxford, 1977).

Wedberg, A., *Plato's Philosophy of Mathematics* (Stockholm, 1955).

3. Aristotle (*pages 36–61*)

TEXTS

Smith, J. A., and Ross, W. D., Aristotle's *Works*, the Oxford translation (Oxford, 1908–52).
The Loeb Classical Library publishes the Greek texts with English translations facing. The translations are by various hands, as are the translations of the Oxford edition of the *Works*.
McKeon, R., editor, *The Basic Works of Aristotle* (New York, 1941, and later printings). Contains the Oxford translations of the major texts complete, and selections from the minor works.

GENERAL SURVEYS AND BACKGROUND

Ackrill, J. L., *Aristotle the Philosopher* (Oxford, 1981, paperback).
Allan, D. J., *Aristotle* (Oxford, 1952).
Barnes, J., *Aristotle* (Oxford, 1983, paperback).

Ross, W. D., *Aristotle* (second edition, London, 1930).

WORKS ON INDIVIDUAL TOPICS

Adkins, A. W., *Merit and Responsibility: A Study in Greek Values* (Oxford, 1960). Chapters 15 and 16 are on Aristotle.
Barnes, J.; Schofield, M.; and Sorabji, R., *Articles on Aristotle* (volumes I and II, London, 1975, 1977).
Cherniss, H., *Aristotle's Criticism of Plato and the Academy* (Baltimore, 1944).
Heath, T. L., *Mathematics in Aristotle* (Oxford, 1949).
Hesse, M. B., *Forces and Fields* (Edinburgh, 1961). Chapter 3 deals with Aristotle's physical theory.
Lukasiewicz, J., *Aristotle's Syllogistic: From the Standpoint of Modern Formal Logic* (second edition, Oxford, 1957).
Owens, J., *The Doctrine of Being in the Aristotelian Metaphysics* (Toronto, 1951).
Solmsen, F., *Aristotle's System of the Physical World* (Ithaca, N.Y., 1960).

4. Greek Philosophy After Aristotle (*pages 62–78*)

TEXTS

Epicureans, Stoics
Bailey, C., *Epicurus, the Extant Remains* (Oxford, 1926). The Greek texts with English translations.
Oates, W. J., *The Stoic and Epicurean Philosophers* (New York, 1957). Contains the complete Bailey translation of Epicurus' works as well as English versions of Epictetus, Lucretius, and Marcus Aurelius by various translators.

Plotinus
Armstrong, A. H., *Plotinus* (London, 1953; New York, 1962, paperback). Selections in English with a long introduction.
McKenna, S., *The Enneads of Plotinus* (London, 1956). An English translation.

Diogenes Laertius, Sextus Empiricus
Bury, R. G., *Sextus Empiricus* (Loeb Classical Library, four volumes, London and New York, 1939–57). Greek text with facing translation.
Hicks, R. D., *Diogenes Laertius* (Loeb Classical Library, two volumes, London and New York, 1925). Greek text with facing translation.

GENERAL SURVEYS

Epicureans, Stoics, Skeptics
Bailey, C., *The Greek Atomists and Epicurus* (Oxford, 1928).

Bochenski, I. M., *Ancient Formal Logic* (Amsterdam, 1951).
Schofield, M.; Burnyeat, M.; and Barnes, J., *Doubt and Dogmatism* (Oxford, 1980).
Sorabji, R., *Time, Creation and the Continuum* (London, 1983).
Mates, B., *Stoic Logic* (Berkeley, 1953, 1961, paperback).
Zeller, E., *Stoics, Epicureans and Sceptics* (London, 1893; New York, 1962).

Neo-Platonists
Wallis, R. T., *Neoplatonism* (London, 1972).
Whittaker, T., *The Neoplatonists* (Cambridge, 1928).

WORKS ON INDIVIDUAL PHILOSOPHERS

Epicureans, Stoics, Skeptics
De Witt, N. W., *Epicurus and His Philosophy* (Minneapolis, 1954).
Dillon, J., *The Middle Platonists* (London, 1977).
Rist, J. M., *Epicurus: An Introduction* (Cambridge, 1972).
———, *Stoic Philosophy* (Cambridge, 1969).
———, editor, *The Stoics* (Berkeley and Los Angeles, 1978).
Stough, C. L., *Greek Scepticism* (Berkeley, 1969).

Plotinus
Brehier, E., *La Philosophie de Plotin* (Paris, 1928).
Inge, W. R., *The Philosophy of Plotinus* (two volumes, London, 1948).

5. Augustine (*pages 79–97*)

TEXTS

The most convenient edition of the works is that of the Benedictines of Saint-Maur, for which no adequate substitute has yet been completed. It is reproduced, with a number of errors and alterations, in Migne's *Patrologia Latina*, Volumes 32–46. It is also contained, together with French translations, in the edition of the *Bibliothèque Augustinienne*, still in the course of completion.

A modern critical edition, of uneven standard, is now about half-completed in the series *Corpus Scriptorum Ecclesiasticorum Latinorum* (the "Vienna Corpus").
Details of the available translations may be found in the chronological tables of Peter Brown, *Augustine of Hippo* (see below).
Useful English versions of *Confessions* and the *City of God* are available in paperback in Penguin Classics.

GENERAL SURVEYS

Brown, Peter, *Augustine of Hippo: A Biography* (London, 1967).
Gilson, E., *The Christian Philosophy of Saint Augustine* (New York, 1960).
Markus, R. A., editor, *Augustine: A Collection of Critical Essays* (New York, 1972).

WORKS ON INDIVIDUAL TOPICS

Markus, R. A., "St. Augustine on Signs," *Phronesis* 2, 1957, pp. 60–83.
O'Connell, R. J., *St. Augustine's Early Theory of Man* (Cambridge, Mass., 1968).
———, *Art and the Christian Intelligence in St. Augustine* (Cambridge, 1978).

6. Aquinas (*pages 98–123*)

TEXTS

The complete Latin text of Aquinas' works is the Parma edition in 25 volumes (1852–73). There is also an American edition of this text (New York, 1948).
A critical edition of the Latin text, the "Leonine" edition, is still incomplete (Rome, 1882–   ).
A text of the *Summa Theologica* with facing English translation and extensive notes (by various hands) is available in 61 volumes (London 1964–80). This is the work, in the main, of members of the Dominican order.
A complete translation, in paperback, of the *Summa Contra Gentiles* is in five volumes (New York, 1956–57). The translators are Pegis, Anderson, Bourke, and O'Neil.
Pegis, A., *Basic Writings of St. Thomas Aquinas* (two volumes, New York, 1945). Selections, in English translation.

TRANSLATIONS OF SHORTER WORKS

d'Entreves, A. P., editor, *Aquinas: Selected Political Writings* (Oxford, 1948).
Foster, K., and Humphreys, S., editors, *Aristotle's de Anima with the Commentary of St. Thomas Aquinas* (London, 1951).
Blackwell, R. J., Spath, R. J., and Thirlkel, W. E., *Aquinas: Commentary on Aristotle's Physics.*.
Both these two last items are complete translations.

Maurer, A., editor, *On Being and Essence* (Toronto, 1949, paperback).

GENERAL SURVEYS

Copleston, F. C., *Aquinas* (Harmondsworth, 1955, paperback).
Gilson, E., *The Christian Philosophy of St. Thomas Aquinas* (New York, 1956).
Kenny, A., *Aquinas* (London, 1980, paperback).
———, editor, *Aquinas: A Collection of Critical Essays* (New York, 1969).

WORKS ON INDIVIDUAL TOPICS

Bobik, J., and Sayre, K. M., "Pattern Recognition Mechanisms and St. Thomas' Theory of Abstraction" in *Revue Philosophique de Louvain*, 1963.
Bochenski, I. M., "On Analogy," *The Thomist* 11, 1948.
Geach, P., *Mental Acts* (London, 1957).
Kenny, A., *The Five Ways* (London, 1969).
Lonergan, B., *Verbum: Word and Idea in Aquinas* (Notre Dame, 1967).
O'Connor, D. J., *Aquinas and Natural Law* (London, 1967, paperback).
Owens, J., "Aquinas on Infinite Regress," *Mind*, 1962.

BIOGRAPHY

Weisheipl, J., *Friar Thomas d'Aquino* (Oxford, 1974).

7. Ockham (*pages 124–40*)

TEXTS

The *Opera omnia philosophica et theologica* is in preparation, in 25 volumes, under the general editorship of E. M. Buytaert (St. Bonaventure, N.Y., and Paderborn). The first volume will be the *Expositionis in libros artis logicae prooemium et Expositio in librum Porphyrii de praedicabilibus*, edited by E. Moody.
The complete Latin text of Ockham's political works, under the title *Guillelmi de Ockham Opera politica*, is incomplete in two volumes. Volume I is edited by J. G. Sikes (Manchester, 1940), volume III by H. S. Offler (Manchester, 1956).
A selection of Latin texts with English translations facing is given in *Ockham: Philosophical Writings, A selection edited and translated by Ph. Boehner* (Edinburgh, 1957).

The following Latin texts exist in modern editions:
Summa totius logicae, edited by Ph. Boehner (St. Bonaventure, N.Y., 1951–54).
Quaestio prima principalis Prologi in Primum Librum Senteniarum, edited by Ph. Boehner (Zurich, 1941).
Tractatus de successivis, edited by Ph. Boehner (St. Bonaventure, N.Y., 1944). Attributed to Ockham, probably spurious.

Tractatus de praedestinatione et de praescientia Dei et de futuris contingentibus, edited by Ph. Boehner (St. Bonaventure, N.Y., 1945).
Breviloquium de potestate papae, edited by L. Baudry (Paris, 1937).

The following works of Ockham exist in print at present only in fifteenth-century editions:
Super quattuor sententiarum subtilissimae quaestiones (Lyons, 1495).
Summulae in libros Physicorum (Bologna, 1495).
Quodlibeta septem (Paris, 1487; Strasbourg, 1491).
Expositio aurea et admodum utilis super artem veterem (Bologna, 1496).

GENERAL SURVEYS

Boehner, Ph., *Ockham: Philosophical Writings* (Edinburgh, 1957). Boehner's Introduction, pp. ix–li, contains a useful summary of Ockham's philosophy.
Copleston, F. C., *Ockham to Suarez*, Volume 3 in *A History of Philosophy* (London, 1953).
Leff, G., *William of Ockham* (Manchester, 1975).

WORKS ON INDIVIDUAL TOPICS

Boehner, Ph., *Ockham's Theory of Truth* (St. Bonaventure, N.Y., 1945).
——, *Ockham's Theory of Signification* (St. Bonaventure, N.Y., 1946).
——, *Medieval Logic: An Outline of Its Development from 1250–c. 1400* (Manchester and Chicago, 1952). Discussions of Ockham throughout.
——, *Collected Articles on Ockham* (St. Bonaventure, N.Y., 1958).
Fuchs, O., *The Psychology of Habit According to William of Ockham* (St. Bonaventure, N.Y., 1952).
Guelluy, R., *Philosophie et theologie chez Guillaume d'Ockham* (Louvain, 1947).
Hamann, A., *La doctrine de l'église et de l'état chez Occam* (Paris, 1942).

Hochstetter, E., *Studien zur Metaphysik und Erkenntnislehre des Wilhelms von Ockham* (Berlin, 1937).
Jacob, E. F., *Essays in the Conciliar Epoch* (Manchester, 1953). Chapter 5 is on Ockham's political thought.
Menges, M. C., *The Concept of Univocity Regarding the Predication of God and Creature According to William Ockham* (St. Bonaventure, N.Y., 1952).
Moody, E., *The Logic of William of Ockham* (London, 1935).
Saw, R. L., "William of Ockham on Terms, Propositions and Meaning," in *Proceedings of the Aristotelian Society* 42, 1941–42.
Shapiro, H., *Motion, Time and Place According to William Ockham* (St. Bonaventure, N.Y., 1957, paperback).
Webering, D., *Theory of Demonstration According to William Ockham* (St. Bonaventure, N.Y., 1953).
Weinberg, J., "Ockham's Conceptualism," in *Philosophical Review*, volume 50, 1941.

8. Francis Bacon (*pages 141–52*)

TEXTS

Collected editions:
The Works of Francis Bacon, ed. by J. Spedding, R. L. Ellis, and D. D. Heath (7 vols., London, 1857–59). Containing a valuable preface and notes.
The Letters and Life of Francis Bacon, Including All His Occasional Works, ed. by J. Spedding (7 vols., London, 1861–74). A cheap edition has been published by "The World Classics" series (Oxford, 1901, 1937).

Selections and individual editions:
The Philosophical Works of Francis Bacon, ed. with an introduction by John M. Robertson (London and New York, 1905). This is a useful selection which has been reprinted from the texts and translations, and including the notes and prefaces, of the Spedding, Ellis, and Heath edition.
Francis Bacon, Selected Writings, ed. with an introduction and notes by Hugh G. Dick (Modern Library, New York, 1955).
Francis Bacon, Selections, ed. by M. T. McClure (paperback, New York, 1928).
The Advancement of Learning and New Atlantis, ed. with a preface by T. Case ("The World Classics" series, Oxford and London, 1906, 1951).
New Atlantis, ed. by A. B. Gough (Oxford, 1915).
Bacon's Essays and Colours of Good and Evil, ed. with notes and glossarial index (London and Cambridge, 1868). The *Essays* are available in paperback editions as well.

The Essays or Counsels Civil and Moral of Francis Bacon (Everyman's Library, New York, 1909).
A Harmony of the Essays by Francis Bacon, arranged by E. Arber (London, 1871).
Novum Organum, ed. by T. Fowler, with notes, an introduction on Bacon's philosophy, and a good bibliography (Oxford, 1878–89).
The New Organon and Related Writings, ed. by F. H. Anderson (New York, 1960). Available also in paperback.

GENERAL SURVEYS

Anderson, F. H., *The Philosophy of Francis Bacon* (Chicago, 1948).
——, *Francis Bacon: His Career and His Thought* (Los Angeles, 1962).
Broad, C. D., *The Philosophy of Francis Bacon* (Cambridge, 1926).
Farrington, B., *The Philosophy of Francis Bacon* (Liverpool, 1964).
Quinton, A., *Francis Bacon* (Oxford, 1980, paperback).
Taylor, A. E., "Francis Bacon" in *Proceedings of the British Academy* XII, 1927, p. 273.
Vickers, B., editor, *Essential Articles for the Study of Francis Bacon* (Hamden, Conn., 1968).

BIOGRAPHY

Sturt, M., *Francis Bacon: A Biography* (London, 1932).

9. Hobbes (*pages 153–69*)

TEXTS

Collected editions:
The English Works of Thomas Hobbes, ed. by Sir Wm. Molesworth (11 volumes, London, 1839; reprinted Oxford, 1961).
The Latin Works of Thomas Hobbes (Opera Latina), ed. by Sir Wm. Molesworth (5 vols., London, 1845; reprinted Oxford, 1961).
Other editions:
Leviathan, ed. by C. B. Macpherson (Harmondsworth, 1968). Of Hobbes, by far the best thing to recommend is *Leviathan*, and it is a delight to read.

Body, Man, and Citizen, ed. with an introduction by R. Peters (paperback, New York, 1962). Writings reflecting the interconnectedness of physics, physiology, and politics. Contains selections from *De Corpore*; the free-will dispute with Bishop Bramhall, *Of Liberty and Necessity; The Little Treatise; Human Nature;* and *Dialogue Between a Philosopher and a Student of the Common Laws of England*.
De Cive or The Citizen, ed. by S. P. Lamprecht (New York, 1949).

GENERAL SURVEYS

Peters, R., *Hobbes* (paperback, Harmondsworth, 1956).

Stephen, L., *Hobbes* (London, 1904).
Watkins, J. W. N., *Hobbes' System of Ideas* (second edition, London, 1973).

WORKS ON INDIVIDUAL TOPICS

Brown, K. C., editor, *Hobbes Studies* (Oxford, 1965).
Burtt, E. A., *Metaphysical Foundations of Modern Physical Science* (London, 1932).

McNeilly, F. S., *The Anatomy of Leviathan* (London and New York, 1968).
Spragens, T. A., *The Politics of Motion* (Lexington, Ky., 1973).
Trevor-Roper, H. R., *Historical Essays* (London, 1957). This contains a commentary on Hobbes' *Behemoth*.
Warrender, J. H., *The Political Philosophy of Hobbes* (Oxford, 1957).

10. Descartes (*pages 170–86*)

TEXTS

Collected edition:
Oeuvres de Descartes, ed. by C. Adam and P. Tannery (2 vols. and supplement, Paris, 1897–1910). This edition supersedes all other collected editions.
Individual editions and translations:
The Philosophical Works of Descartes, transl. by E. S. Haldane and G. T. R. Ross (2 vols., Cambridge, 1911, 1931). Also in paperback (2 vols., New York, 1955). This is the most complete translation available.
Another good translation is:
Descartes: Philosophical Writings, transl. by E. Anscombe and P. T. Geach (Edinburgh, 1954).
Descartes' Philosophical Writings, transl. by N. Kemp Smith (New York, 1953). This selection deals more fully with the *Rules for the Direction of the Mind*.

Réné Descartes Selections, ed. by Ralph M. Eaton (New York, 1927, paperback).

GENERAL SURVEYS

Kenny, A., *Descartes: A Study of His Philosophy* (New York, 1968).
Smith, N. Kemp, *Studies in the Cartesian Philosophy* (revised edition, London and New York, 1962).
———, *New Studies in the Philosophy of Descartes* (London, 1952).
Williams, B. A. O., *Descartes: The Project of Pure Inquiry* (Harmondsworth, 1978, paperback).
Wilson, Margaret D., *Descartes* (London, 1978).

BIOGRAPHY

Haldane, E. S., *Descartes: His Life and Times* (London, 1905).

11. Spinoza (*pages 187–203*)

TEXTS

Collected editions:
Spinoza Opera, ed. by C. Gebhardt (4 vols., Heidelberg, 1924). This is the standard edition in the original Latin.
Oeuvres Complètes de Spinoza (in French), ed. by R. Caillois, Madeleine Frances, and P. Misrahi (Paris, 1954). This volume also contains 150 pages of useful annotations, complete indices, and translations of two early biographies, by Colerus and Lucas, which provide essential source material for the life of Spinoza.
Correspondence of Spinoza, ed. by A. Wolf (London, 1928). Includes the biographies by Colerus and Lucas.
The Chief Works of Spinoza, transl. by R. H. M. Elwes (2 vols., New York, 1955), (paperback, New York, 1956).
Spinoza Selections, ed. by J. Wild (New York, 1930, paperback).

GENERAL SURVEYS

Bennett, J., *A Study of Spinoza's Ethics* (Cambridge, 1984).
Hampshire, S., *Spinoza* (Harmondsworth, 1951, paperback).
Joachim, H. H., *A Study of Spinoza's Ethics* (Oxford, 1901).
Wolfson, H. A., *The Philosophy of Spinoza* (two volumes, Cambridge, Mass, 1934; New York, 1958, paperback).

WORKS ON INDIVIDUAL TOPICS

Joachim, H. H., Commentary on *Spinoza's Tractatus de Intellectus Emendatione* (Oxford, 1940).
Parkinson, G. H. R., *Spinoza's Theory of Knowledge* (Oxford, 1954).
Saw, R. L., *The Vindication of Metaphysics: A Study in the Philosophy of Spinoza* (New York, 1951).

12. Locke (*pages 204–19*)

TEXTS

Collected Works (London, 1853, 1961)
Essay Concerning Human Understanding, edited by P. H. Nidditch (Oxford, 1975). This is now the standard edition.

GENERAL SURVEYS

Aaron, R. I., *John Locke* (second edition, Oxford, 1955).

Bennett, J., *Locke, Berkeley, Hume: Central Themes* (Oxford, 1971).
O'Connor, D. J., *John Locke* (paperback, Harmondsworth, 1952; New York, 1968).
Woolhouse, R. S., *Locke* (Brighton, 1983).
Yolton, J. W., *John Locke and the Way of Ideas* (Oxford, 1956).

WORKS ON INDIVIDUAL TOPICS

Alexander, P., *Ideas, Qualities, and Corpuscles* (Cambridge, 1985).

Gibson, J., *Locke's Theory of Knowledge and Its Historical Relations* (Cambridge, 1917; New York, 1960).

Gough, J. W., *Locke's Political Philosophy: Eight Studies* (Oxford, 1950, 1956).

Mackie, J., *Problems from Locke* (Oxford, 1976).

Martin, C. B., and Armstrong, D. M., editors, *Locke and Berkeley: A Collection of Critical Essays* (London, 1968).

BIOGRAPHY

Cranston, M., *John Locke* (London, 1957). The standard biography.

13. Leibniz *(pages 220–35)*

TEXTS

Collected editions:

Die Philosophische Schriften von G. W. Leibniz, ed. C. I. Gerhardt (7 vols., Berlin, 1875–90, 1960–61).

Leibniz: Philosophical Papers and Letters, ed. by L. E. Loemker (2 vols., Chicago, 1956).

Philosophical Writings, trans. and ed. by Mary Morris (London, 1934).

Translations of individual works:

The Leibniz-Clarke Correspondence, ed. by H. G. Alexander (Manchester, 1956).

The Monadology and Other Philosophical Writings, ed. by R. Latta (Oxford, 1898). There is a lengthy (and useful) introductory essay on Leibniz's philosophy.

Discourse on Metaphysics, trans. by P. Lucas and L. Grint (Manchester, 1961).

New Essays Concerning Human Understanding, trans. and ed. by P. Remnant and J. Bennett (Cambridge, 1981).

GENERAL SURVEYS

Broad, C. D., *Leibniz: An Introduction*, ed. by C. Lewy (Cambridge, 1975).

Rescher, N., *Leibniz* (Oxford, 1979).

Russell, B., *A Critical Examination of the Philosophy of Leibniz* (second edition, London, 1937, 1949).

Saw, R. L., *Leibniz* (Harmondsworth, 1954, paperback).

WORKS ON INDIVIDUAL TOPICS

Ishiguro, H., *Leibniz' Philosophy of Logic and Language* (London, 1972).

14. Berkeley *(pages 236–252)*

TEXTS

Collected editions:

The Works of George Berkeley, Bishop of Cloyne, ed. by A. A. Luce and T. E. Jessop (9 vols., London, 1948–57). With a good introduction and notes.

Other editions:

Berkeley: Essay, Principles, Dialogues, with Selections from Other Writings, ed. by M. W. Calkins (New York, 1929; 1959, paperback).

Berkeley: Philosophical Writings, ed. by T. E. Jessop (Austin, Tex., 1953).

The Theory of Vision and Other Writings, with an introduction by A. D. Lindsay (Everyman's Library, New York, 1910, 1957). Includes the *Essay Towards a New Theory of Vision, Principles of Human Knowledge,* and *Three Dialogues of Hylas and Philonous.*

British Empirical Philosophers, ed. by A. J. Ayer and Raymond Winch (London, 1952). Includes Berkeley's *Principles*, the first *Dialogue*, and parts of the second and third.

GENERAL SURVEYS

Bennett, J., *Locke, Berkeley, Hume: Central Themes* (Oxford, 1971).

Pitcher, G., *Berkeley* (London, 1977).

Tipton, I. C., *Berkeley* (London, 1974).

Warnock, G., *Berkeley* (second edition, Oxford, 1982).

WORKS ON INDIVIDUAL TOPICS

Armstrong, D. M., *Berkeley's Theory of Vision* (Melbourne, 1960).

Broad, C. D., *Berkeley's Argument About Material Substance, Proceedings of the British Academy*, XXVIII (London), 1942.

Luce, A. A., *Berkeley and Malebranche* (London, 1934).

——, *Berkeley's Immaterialism* (London, 1945).

Moore, G. E., "Refutation of Idealism," in *Philosophical Studies* (London, 1922).

BIOGRAPHY

Luce, A. A., *Life of George Berkeley, Bishop of Cloyne* (London, 1949).

15. Hume *(pages 253–74)*

TEXTS

Collected editions:

Philosophical Works, ed. by T. H. Green and T. H. Grose (4 volumes, London, 1874–75; out of print).

Individual editions:

The best available editions of the *Treatise on Human Nature* and *Enquiries Concerning the Human Understanding and Concerning the Principles of Morals* are edited by L. A. Selby-Bigge and recently revised by P. H. Nidditch (Oxford,

1902, 1975, 1978). Selby-Bigge's introduction makes some imputations against Hume's character. They betray a failure to understand his stated purposes and are not supported by the available biographical evidence (see E. C. Mossner, "Philosophy and Biography: The Case of David Hume," *Philosophical Review*, 1950).

Hume's Ethical Writings, ed. with an introduction by A. C. MacIntyre (New York, 1963, paperback).

Hume on Religion, ed. by R. Wollheim (London, 1963).

Political Essays, ed. with an introduction by C. W. Hendel (New York, 1953).

The Natural History of Religion, ed. by H. E. Root (London, 1956).

Dialogues Concerning Natural Religion, ed. by N. Kemp Smith (second edition, London, 1947).

GENERAL SURVEYS

Ayer, A. J., *Hume* (London, 1980, paperback).

MacNabb, D. G. C., *David Hume* (London, 1951). This is the best short introduction to Hume.

Penelhum, T., *Hume* (London, 1975).

Smith, N. Kemp, *The Philosophy of David Hume: A Critical Study of Its Origins and Central Doctrines* (London, 1941). An enormous and continuing expansion of Hume scholarship began with the publication of this massive comprehensive treatment.

WORKS ON INDIVIDUAL TOPICS

Beauchamp, T. C., and Rosenberg, A., *Hume and the Pro-blem of Causation* (Oxford, 1981).

Flew, A. G. N., *Hume's Philosophy of Belief: A Study of His First "Inquiry"* (London, 1961).

Gaskin, J. C. A., *Hume's Philosophy of Religion* (London, 1978).

Passmore, J., *Hume's Intentions* (Cambridge, 1953).

Price, H. H., *Hume's Theory of the External World* (Oxford, 1941).

Zabeeh, F., *Hume: Precursor of Modern Empiricism* (The Hague, 1960).

FURTHER REFERENCE

Hall, R., *Fifty Years of Hume Scholarship* (Edinburgh, 1978).

BIOGRAPHY

The Letters of David Hume, ed. by J. Y. T. Greig (2 vols., Oxford, 1932).

New Letters of David Hume, ed. by R. Klibansky and E. C. Mossner (Oxford, 1954).

The Life of David Hume Written by Himself, ed. by A. Smith (London, 1977).

Mossner, E. C., *The Life of David Hume* (second edition, Oxford, 1980). All previous biographies are superseded by this one. It is a splendid record of the life of a very admirable human being.

16. French Eighteenth-Century Materialism *(pages 275–95)*

GENERAL BACKGROUND

Becker, C. L., *The Heavenly City of the Eighteenth Century Philosophers* (New Haven, 1932).

Frankel, C., *The Faith of Reason* (New York, 1948).

Hazard, P., *European Thought in the Eighteenth Century* (London, 1954).

Hubert, R., *Les Sciences Sociales dans l'Encyclopédie* (Paris, 1923).

Mornet, D., *Les Origines Intellectuelles de la Révolution Française* (Paris, 1933).

Palmer, R. R., *Catholics and Unbelievers in Eighteenth Century France* (Princeton, 1939).

Picavet, Fr., *Les Idéologues* (Paris, 1891).

Spink, J. S., *French Freethought from Gassendi to Voltaire* (London, 1960).

The following contain selections from Holbach and other important figures of the Enlightenment:

Age of Reason Reader, ed. with an introduction by Crane Brinton (New York, 1956, 1961, paperback).

Les Philosophes (in English), ed. with an introduction by Norman L. Torrey (New York, 1960, paperback).

GENERAL STUDIES CONTAINING SPECIAL CHAPTERS DEVOTED TO D'HOLBACH

Lange, F. A., *History of Materialism* (Book I, Fourth Section, Chapter III) (London, 1880).

Morley, John, *Diderot and the Encyclopaedists* (Chapter XIV) (London, 1923).

Plekhanov, G., *Essays in the History of Materialism* (First essay) (London, 1934).

Willey, B., *The Eighteenth Century Background* (Chapter IX) (London, 1940).

WORKS OF D'HOLBACH

Le bon-sens ou Idées naturelles opposées aux idées surnaturelles (Amsterdam, 1772). Also published under the title, *Le bon-sens du curé Meslier*.

La religion naturelle, précédée de la correspondence de Voltaire et d'Alembert sur l'oeuvre du curé Meslier (Paris, 1881).

A Letter from Thrasybulus to Leucippe (London, 1826).

Common sense; or Natural ideas opposed to supernatural (New York, 1795 and London, 1826).

Le Christianisme Dévoilé (London, 1756). First published under the pseudonym Nicolas Antoine Boulanger.

Histoire Critique de Jésus Christ (1770).

La Contagion sacrée (London, 1768).

Système de la nature, ou des lois du monde physique et du monde moral (London, 1770; 2 vols. Paris, 1821).

The System of Nature; or the Laws of the Moral and Physical World (London, 1797).

———, with notes by Diderot, transl. by H. D. Robinson (Boston, 1868).

Système social; ou Principes naturels de la morale et de la politique, avec un examen de l'influence du gouvernement sur les moeurs (London, 1773).

La Politique Naturelle (2 vols., London, 1773).

Ethocratie ou le Gouvernement fondé sur les morals (Paris, 1776).

STUDIES OF D'HOLBACH

Hubert, R., *D'Holbach et ses Amis* (Paris, 1928).

Neville, P., *Paul Thiry D'Holbach* (Paris, 1943).
Topazio, V. W., *D'Holbach's Moral Philosophy* (Geneva, 1956).
Wickwar, W. H., *Baron D'Holbach, a Prelude to the French Revolution* (London, 1935).

"Kritisches Verzeichnis der philosophischen Schriften Holbachs," in *Archiv für Geschichte der Philosophie*, pp. 270-90 (1917).

17. Kant (*pages 296-318*)

TEXTS

Collected editions:

Sämtliche Werke, ed. by Preussiche Akademie der Wissenschaften (22 vols., Berlin, 1902-55). This is the standard edition of Kant's work. It also contains his correspondence.

——, ed. by E. Cassirer *et al.* (10 vols., Berlin, 1912-22).

——, ed. by K. Vorländer *et al.* (10 vols., Leipzig, 1920-29).

Translations:

Critique of Pure Reason, trans. by N. Kemp Smith (London, 1929, corrected 1933). This is the best available translation of the *Critique.*

Critique of Pure Reason, trans. by J. M. D. Meiklejohn, introduced by A. D. Lindsay (Everyman's Library, New York, 1934).

Prolegomena to Any Future Metaphysics That Will Be Able to Present Itself as a Science, trans. with an introduction by P. G. Lucas (Manchester, 1953). (The *Prolegomena* is Kant's own introduction to the doctrines found in the *Critique of Pure Reason.*)

Critique of Practical Reason and Other Writings in Moral Philosophy, trans. and ed. with an introduction by L. W. Beck (Chicago, 1949).

Moral Law, or Kant's Groundwork of the Metaphysic of Morals, trans. with analysis and notes by H. J. Paton (London, 1948, 1956).

Critique of Judgment, trans. by J. C. Meredith (Oxford, 1952). Contains analytical indexes.

Religion Within the Limits of Reason Alone, trans. with an introduction by T. M. Greene and H. H. Hudson (New York, 1960, paperback).

Perpetual Peace, trans. with an introduction by Lewis White Beck (New York, 1957, paperback).

"Idea of a Universal History from a Cosmopolitan Point of View," trans. by W. Hastie in *Theories of History, Readings from Classical and Contemporary Sources*, ed. by Patrick Gardiner, pp. 21-34 (New York, 1958).

Kant Selections, ed. by T. M. Greene (New York, 1929, paperback).

GENERAL SURVEYS

Broad, C. D., *Kant: An Introduction*, ed. by C. Lewy (Cambridge, 1978).

Körner, S., *Kant* (Harmondsworth, 1955, paperback).

Strawson, P. F., *The Bounds of Sense* (London, 1966).

Walker, R., *Kant* (London, 1979).

WORKS ON INDIVIDUAL TOPICS

Beck, L. W., *Commentary on Kant's Critique of Practical Reason* (London, 1938).

Bennett, J., *Kant's Analytic* (Cambridge, 1966).

——, *Kant's Dialectic* (Cambridge, 1974).

Ewing, A. C., *A Short Commentary on Kant's Critique of Pure Reason* (Chicago, 1950).

Paton, H. J., *Kant's Metaphysic of Experience* (2 vols., London and New York, 1936).

——, *The Categorical Imperative: A Study in Kant's Moral Philosophy* (London and New York, 1947).

Smith, N. Kemp, *A Commentary to Kant's Critique of Pure Reason* (London, 1923).

Weldon, T. D., *Introduction to Kant's Critique of Pure Reason* (Oxford, 1958).

18. Hegel (*pages 319-40*)

TEXTS

Collected edition:

Sämtliche Werke, ed. by H. Glockner (Jubilee edition, 26 vols., Stuttgart, 1951-60). Contains an analytical index and biography.

Translations of individual works:

The Phenomenology of Mind, trans. by J. B. Baillie (2d ed., New York, 1931).

The Science of Logic, trans. by W. H. Johnston and L. G. Struthers (2 vols., New York, 1929).

Hegel's Doctrine of Formal Logic (a good translation of part of the former), trans. by H. S. Macran (Oxford, 1911).

The Logic of Hegel, Part 1 of the *Encyclopedia of the Philosophical Sciences*, trans. by W. Wallace (Oxford, 1892).

Hegel's Philosophy of Mind, part III of the *Encyclopedia of Philosophical Sciences*, trans. by W. Wallace (Oxford, 1894).

Early Theological Writings, trans. by T. M. Knox (New York, 1948).

The Philosophy of Right, trans. by T. M. Knox (Oxford, 1942).

The Philosophy of History, trans. by J. Sibree (New York, 1956, paperback). Introduction by C. Friedrich.

The Philosophy of Fine Art, trans. by F. B. P. Osmaston (London, 1916-20).

History of Philosophy, trans. by E. S. Haldane (3 vols., repr. London, 1957).

The Philosophy of Hegel, ed. by C. J. Friedrich (Modern Library, New York, 1953).

GENERAL SURVEYS

Findlay, J. N., *Hegel: A Re-examination* (London and New York, 1958; New York, 1962, paperback).

Inwood, M. J., *Hegel* (London, 1983).

Singer, P., *Hegel* (London, 1982).

Stace, W. T., *The Philosophy of Hegel* (London, 1924; New York, 1957, paperback).

Taylor, C., *Hegel* (Cambridge, 1975).

WORKS ON INDIVIDUAL TOPICS

Ewing, A. C., *Idealism* (London, 1934).
Foster, M. B., *The Political Philosophies of Plato and Hegel* (Oxford, 1935).

McTaggart, J. M., *Studies in Hegelian Dialectic* (Cambridge, 1896).
——, *Studies in Hegelian Cosmology* (Cambridge, 1901).
——, *A Commentary on Hegel's Logic* (Cambridge, 1910).
Mure, G. R. G., *A Study of Hegel's Logic* (Oxford, 1950).

19. John Stuart Mill (*pages 341-64*)

TEXTS

20 (of 21) volumes of a new critical edition of all Mill's works have been issued by the University of Toronto (editors J. M. Robson and others) (Toronto and London, 1963-84)

GENERAL SURVEYS

Anschutz, R. P., *The Philosophy of John Stuart Mill* (Oxford, 1953).
Britton, K., *John Stuart Mill* (Harmondsworth, 1953, paperback).
Ryan, A., *The Philosophy of John Stuart Mill* (London, 1970).
Schneewind, J. B., *Mill: A Collection of Critical Essays* (London, 1968).

WORKS ON INDIVIDUAL TOPICS

Atkinson, R. F., "J. S. Mill's 'Proof' of the Principle of Utility," in *Philosophy* XXXII, 1957.
Cohen, M., and Nagel, E., *Introduction to Logic and Scientific Method* (New York, 1934). Chapter 13 is on Mill's methods of induction.
Jackson, R., *An Examination of the Deductive Logic of J. S. Mill* (Oxford, 1941).
Mabbott, J. D., "Interpretations of Mill's 'Utilitarianism'," *The Philosophical Quarterly* VI, 1956.
Nagel, E., *John Stuart Mill's Philosophy of Scientific Method* (New York, 1950, paperback). Nagel's introduction to this volume of selections from Mill's *System of Logic* is valuable.
Price, H. H., "Mill's View of the External World," *Aristotelian Society Proceedings* XXVII, 1926-27, pp. 109-40.
Urmson, J. O., "The Interpretation of the Philosophy of J. S. Mill," *The Philosophical Quarterly* III, 1953.

20. Schopenhauer (*pages 365-83*)

TEXTS

Collected edition:
Sämtliche Werke, ed. by A. Hübscher (7 vols., 2d ed., Wiesbaden, 1946-50).
Translations:
The Works of Schopenhauer, ed. by I. Edman (New York, 1928).
The Will to Live: Selected Writings of Arthur Schopenhauer, ed. by R. Taylor (New York, 1962, paperback).
Schopenhauer Selections, ed. by D. Parker (New York, 1928).
Selected Essays of Schopenhauer, ed. by T. B. Saunders (London, 1951).
The World as Will and Idea, trans. by R. B. Haldane and J. Kemp (3 vols., 8th ed., London, 1886). Both this and the following reference are translations of *Die Welt als Wille und Vorstellung*.
The World as Will and Representation, trans. by E. F. J. Payne (Colorado, 1958).
On the Fourfold Root of the Principle of Sufficient Reason and *On the Will in Nature*, trans. by K. Hillebrand (London, 1888).
The Basis of Morality, trans. by A. B. Bullock (London, 1903).

Essay on the Freedom of the Will, trans. by K. Kolenda (New York, 1960).

GENERAL SURVEYS

Copleston, F. C., *Schopenhauer, Philosopher of Pessimism* (London, 1946). Criticism is from a Roman Catholic point of view.
Gardiner, P., *Schopenhauer* (Harmondsworth, 1963, paperback).
Hamlyn, D. W., *Schopenhauer* (London, 1980).
Magee, B., *The Philosophy of Schopenhauer* (Oxford, 1983).
Zimmern, H. *Arthur Schopenhauer* (revised ed., London, 1932).

WORKS ON INDIVIDUAL TOPICS

Anscombe, G. E. M., *An Introduction to Wittgenstein's Tractatus*, Chapter 13 (London, 1959). Schopenhauer's influence upon Wittgenstein is discussed.
Stenius, E. *Wittgenstein's "Tractatus,"* Chapter XI (Oxford, 1960). Schopenhauer's influence on Wittgenstein is discussed.

21. Nietzsche (*pages 384-401*)

TEXTS

Collected works:
Gesammelte Werke, Musarionausgabe (23 vols., Munich, 1920-28).
Werke in drei Bänden (Munich, 1954-56), ed. by K. Schlechta.

Translations:
The Complete Works, ed. by Oscar Levy (18 vols., Edinburgh and London, 1909-13). Translation is not always reliable.
The Portable Nietzsche, trans. and ed. by Walter Kaufmann (New York, 1954; 1956, paperback). Contains the complete *Thus Spoke Zarathustra, Twilight of the Idols, The An-*

tichrist, and *Nietzsche Contra Wagner*, plus selections from other works, the notes and letters, and several pages of editorial comments.

GENERAL SURVEYS

Brinton, C., *Nietzsche* (Cambridge, 1941).
Copleston, F., *Friedrich Nietzsche* (London, 1942).
Danto, A. C., *Nietzsche as Philosopher* (New York, 1971).
Kaufmann, W., *Nietzsche* (revised ed., New York, 1956, paperback).

Mencken, H. L., *The Philosophy of Friedrich Nietzsche* (Boston, 1913).
Schacht, R., *Nietzsche* (London, 1983).
Stern, J. P., *A Study of Nietzsche* (Cambridge, 1979).
——, *Nietzsche* (London, 1978, paperback).

BIOGRAPHICAL STUDY

Lavrin, J., *Nietzsche: A Biographical Introduction* (London, 1971).

22. The Philosophy of Science, 1850–1910 *(pages 402–25)*

TEXTS

Mach, Ernst, *On the Definition of Mass* (1868). English translation by P. E. B. Jourdain included in *History and Root of the Principle of the Conservation of Energy*, 1911, q.v., p. 80.
——, *History and Root of the Principle of the Conservation of Energy* (Prague, 1872; English translation by P. E. B. Jourdain, Chicago, 1911; paperback, 1962).
——, *The Science of Mechanics* (Leipzig, 1883; 4th edition, 1901; first English edition, 1893; 4th English edition, Chicago, 1919; trans. by J. T. McCormack from the 4th German edition, 1962, paperback)..
——, *Die Prinzipien der Wärmelehre* (Leipzig, 1886). No English edition.
——, *The Analysis of Sensations* (Jena, 1886. First English edition, 1897; English edition, 1914, translated from the first German edition and revised and supplemented from the 5th German edition, 1906, by C. M. Williams; New York, 1959, paperback).
——, *Popular Scientific Lectures* (Leipzig, 1894. Fifth English edition, Chicago, 1943, translated with additions by T. J. McCormack, paperback). Contains lectures delivered between 1865 and 1897.
——, *Erkenntnis und Irrtum* (Leipzig, 1905). Lectures and essays, of which no English translation exists.
——, *Space and Geometry*. Three essays originally published in *The Monist*, 1901–3. Translated and collected under this title by T. J. McCormack (Chicago, 1906, paperback).
——, *The Principles of Physical Optics* (Leipzig, 1921. First English edition, 1926. English translation by J. S. Anderson and A. F. A. Young, New York, 1953, paperback).
Hertz, Heinrich, *Miscellaneous Papers* (First German edition, 1895. English translation by D. E. Jones, 1896).
——, *Electric Waves* (First German edition, 1892. English translation by D. E. Jones, 1893; New York, 1962, paperback).
——, *The Principles of Mechanics* (First German edition, 1894. English translation by D. E. Jones and J. T. Walley, New York, 1956, paperback).
Poincaré, Henri, *Science and Hypothesis* (Paris, 1902. First English edition, 1905. English translation by W. J. Greenstreet, New York, 1952, paperback).
——, *The Value of Science* (Paris, 1905. First English edition, 1907. English translation by G. B. Halstead, New York, 1958, paperback).
——, *Science and Method* (Paris, 1908. First English edition, 1914. English translation by Francis Maitland, New York, 1958, paperback).
——, *Dernières Pensées* (Paris, 1912). No English edition.

Duhem, Pierre, *The Aim and Structure of Physical Theory* (Paris, 1906. First English translation by P. P. Wiener from the second French edition of 1914, Princeton, 1954; New York, 1962, paperback).
——, *Les Origines de la Statique* (Paris, 1905–6).
——, *La Système du Monde* (Vols. I–VIII, Paris, 1913–58).

ANTHOLOGIES, SURVEYS, AND WORKS OF SPECIAL INTEREST

Braithwaite, R. B., *Scientific Explanation* (Cambridge, 1953; New York, 1960, paperback).
Bridgman, P. W., *The Nature of Physical Theory* (Princeton, 1936).
Broad, C. D., *Scientific Thought* (London, 1923; Paterson, N.J., 1959, paperback).
Campbell, N. R., *What Is Science?* (New York, 1952, paperback).
Carnap, R., *The Continuum of Inductive Methods* (Chicago, 1952).
Feigl, H., and Brodbeck, M., editors, *Readings in the Philosophy of Science* (New York, 1953).
Glymour, C., *Theory and Evidence* (Princeton, 1980).
Hanson, N. R., *Patterns of Discovery* (Cambridge, 1958).
Hempel, C. G., *Aspects of Scientific Explanation* (New York, 1965).
Hesse, M., *Structure of Scientific Inference* (London, 1974).
Kneale, W., *Probability and Induction* (Oxford, 1949).
Körner, S., *Conceptual Thinking* (Cambridge, 1955; New York, 1955, paperback).
Lakatos, I., and Musgrave, A., editors, *Criticism and the Growth of Knowledge* (Cambridge, 1970).
Mises, R. von, *Positivism* (Cambridge, 1951).
Nagel, E., *Structure of Science: Problems in the Logic of Scientific Explanation* (New York, 1961).
Newton-Smith, W., *The Rationality of Science* (London, 1981).
Pap, A., *An Introduction to the Philosophy of Science* (Glencoe, Ill., 1962).
Popper, K. R., *The Logic of Scientific Discovery* (London, 1958).
——, *Conjectures and Refutations* (London, 1963).
——, *Objective Knowledge* (Oxford, 1972).
Reichenbach, H., *Experience and Prediction* (Chicago, 1947; paperback, 1959).
——, *Philosophical Foundations of Quantum Mechanics* (Los Angeles, 1946).
Scheffler, I., *Anatomy of Inquiry* (London, 1964).
Schlick, M., *Philosophy of Nature* (New York, 1949).
Woodger, J. H., *Biology and Language* (Cambridge, 1952).

23. F. H. Bradley (*pages 426-36*)

TEXTS

Ethical Studies (Oxford, 1876; second edition, 1927; New York, 1954, paperback).
Principles of Logic (Oxford, 1883; second edition, 1922).
Appearance and Reality (Oxford, 1893; second edition, 1897).
Essays on Truth and Reality (Oxford, 1914).
Collected Essays (Oxford, 1935).

GENERAL SURVEYS

Church, R. W., *Bradley's Dialectic* (London, 1942).
Lofthouse, W. F., *F. H. Bradley* (London, 1949).
Passmore, J., *A Hundred Years of Philosophy* (London, 1957).
Wollheim, R., *F. H. Bradley* (Harmondsworth, 1959, paperback).

CRITICAL AND BIOGRAPHICAL STUDIES

Broad, C. D., "Mr Bradley on Truth and Reality," *Mind*, 1915.
Eliot, T. S., *Knowledge and Experience in the Philosophy of F. H. Bradley* (London, 1964).
———, "F. H. Bradley," in *Essays Ancient and Modern* (London, 1964).
Ewing, A. C., *Idealism: A Critical Survey* (London, 1936).
Manser, A. R., *Bradley's Logic* (Oxford, 1983).
Russell, B., *An Outline of Philosophy* (London, 1927).
Sidgwick, H., "Mr. Bradley and the Sceptics," *Mind*, 1894.
Stout, G. F., "Bradley's Theory of Relations," in *Studies in Philosophy and Psychology* (London, 1930).
Taylor, A. E., "Francis Herbert Bradley," *Proceedings of the British Academy*, 1924-25

24. Pragmatism (*pages 437-62*)

TEXTS

James, William, *The Will to Believe* (New York, 1897; paperback, 1950).
———, *Pragmatism* (New York, 1907; enlarged edition, including the "Preface" and three essays from *The Meaning of Truth*, 1943; paperback, 1955).
———, *The Meaning of Truth: A Sequel to "Pragmatism"* (New York, 1909).
———, *Radical Empiricism and a Pluralistic Universe* (New York, 1909, 1912, 1943).
———, *The Works of William James*, ed. by Frederic H. Burkhardt (Cambridge, Mass., 1975–   ). 13 volumes to date. To be the complete and definitive edition of James's writings.
Dewey, John, *The Influence of Darwin on Philosophy* (New York, 1910).
———, *Essays in Experimental Logic* (Chicago, 1916; paperback, New York, 1950).
———, *Reconstruction in Philosophy* (New York, 1920; enlarged edition, Boston, 1948; paperback, New York, 1950).
———, *Logic: The Theory of Inquiry* (New York, 1939).
———, *Problems of Men* (New York, 1946).
———, *John Dewey: Works*, ed. by Jo Ann Boydston (Carbondale and Edwardsville, Ill., 1969–   ). 25 volumes to date. To be the complete and definitive edition of Dewey's writings.
Peirce, Charles Sanders, *Collected Papers*, volumes 1-6 ed. by C. Hartshorne and P. Weiss, volumes 7-8 ed. by A. Burks (Cambridge, Mass., 1931-35, 1958). Volume 5 is of special interest.
Lewis, C. I., "The Pragmatic Element in Knowledge," *University of California Publications in Philosophy*, Volume 6, Number 3 (Berkeley), 1926.
———, *Mind and the World Order* (New York, 1929; paperback, New York, 1956).
———, *An Analysis of Knowledge and Valuation* (La Salle, Ill., 1946).
———, *Collected Papers of Clarence I. Lewis*, ed. by John D. Goheen and John L. Mothershead (Stanford, 1970).

GENERAL SURVEYS

Ayer, A. J., *The Origins of Pragmatism* (London, 1968).
Morris, Charles, *The Pragmatic Movement in America* (New York, 1970).

Rorty, Richard, *The Consequences of Pragmatism* (Minneapolis, 1982).
Rucker, Darnell, *The Chicago Pragmatists* (Minneapolis, 1969).
Scheffler, Israel, *Four Pragmatists* (London and New York, 1974).
Smith, John, *Purpose and Thought: The Meaning of Pragmatism* (New Haven, 1978).
Thayer, H. S., *Meaning and Action: A Critical History of Pragmatism* (New York, 1968; 2d edition, enlarged, Minneapolis, 1982).
———, "Pragmatism," *Encyclopaedia Britannica*, 15th edition, Volume 14, 1974, pp. 723-44.
White, Morton, *Pragmatism and the American Mind* (New York, 1973).

WORKS ON INDIVIDUAL TOPICS

Bernstein, Richard, *John Dewey* (New York, 1967).
Dykhuizen, George, *The Life and Mind of John Dewey* (Carbondale and Edwardsville, Ill., 1973).
Gallie, W. B., *Peirce and Pragmatism* (Harmondsworth, 1952, paperback).
Geiger, George R., *John Dewey in Perspective* (New York and London, 1958).
Hook, S., *John Dewey* (New York, 1950).
Moore, G. E., "William James' 'Pragmatism'," in *Philosophical Studies* (London, 1922; Paterson, N.J., 1959, paperback).
Nagel, E., "Dewey's Reconstruction of Logical Theory," in *The Philosophy of the Common Man*, ed. by Sidney Ratner (New York, 1940).
Perry, R. E., *The Thought and Character of William James* (Boston, 1936).
Quine, W. V., "Two Dogmas of Empiricism," in *From a Logical Point of View* (Cambridge, Mass., 1953).
Russell, B., *Philosophical Essays* (London, 1910). Chapters 4 and 5 are "Pragmatism" and "William James' Conception of Truth."
Schilpp, P. E., editor, *The Philosophy of John Dewey*, The Library of Living Philosophers, Volume I (Evanston and Chicago, 1939).
Wiener, P., *Evolution and the Founders of Pragmatism* (Cambridge, Mass., 1949).

25. G. E. Moore (*pages 463–72*)

BOOKS

Principia Ethica (Cambridge, 1903; 1959, paperback).
Some Main Problems of Philosophy (London, 1953; New York, 1962, paperback). The lectures contained in this book were written in 1910.
Ethics (London, 1912).
Philosophical Studies (London, 1922; Paterson, N.J., 1959, paperback). Contains eight of the most important papers published between 1903 and 1919 as well as two previously unpublished papers on ethics.
Philosophical Papers (London, 1959; New York, 1962, paperback). Eight papers written between 1923 and 1944, including "A Defence of Common Sense," "Is Existence a Predicate?" "Proof of an External World," "A Reply to My Critics," and "Russell's Theory of Descriptions." Also included are Moore's notes on Wittgenstein's 1930–33 lectures.
The Commonplace Book, 1919–1953 (London, 1963). Moore's notebook, edited by C. Lewy.

ARTICLES

"Necessity," *Mind*, volume nine, 1901, pp. 289–304.
"A Defence of Common Sense," *Contemporary British Philosophy*, II (London, 1925; reprinted in *Philosophical Papers*).
"The Justification of Analysis," *Analysis*, I, 1933, pp. 28–30.

"Is Existence a Predicate?" *Proceedings of the Aristotelian Society*, Supplementary volume XV, 1936. Reprinted in *Philosophical Papers*.
"A Proof of an External World," *Proceedings of the British Academy*, XXV, pp. 273–300. Reprinted in *Philosophical Papers*.
"A Reply to My Critics," in *The Philosophy of G. E. Moore*, edited by P. Schilpp (Evanston, Ill., 1942). Reprinted in *Philosophical Papers*.
"Russell's Theory of Descriptions," in *The Philosophy of Bertrand Russell*, edited by P. Schilpp (Evanston, Ill., 1944). Reprinted in *Philosophical Papers*.
"Visual Sense Data," in *British Philosophy in Mid-Century*, edited by C. A. Mace (London, 1957).

WORKS ON THE PHILOSOPHY OF
G. E. MOORE

The Philosophy of G. E. Moore, edited by P. Schilpp (Evanston, Ill., 1942). Articles on Moore's philosophy, with a reply by Moore.
Passmore, J., *A Hundred Years of Philosophy* (London, 1957). Chapter nine is on Moore and Russell.
Urmson, J. O., *Philosophical Analysis* (Oxford, 1956).
Warnock, G. J., *English Philosophy Since 1900* (Oxford, 1958).
White, A. R., *G. E. Moore: A Critical Exposition* (Oxford, 1958).

26. Bertrand Russell (*pages 473–91*)

TEXTS

A Critical Exposition of the Philosophy of Leibniz (Cambridge, 1900).
The Principles of Mathematics (London, 1903).
"On Denoting," *Mind*, XIV, 1905, pp. 479–93.
Philosophical Essays (London, 1910).
Principia Mathematica, Volume I (Cambridge, 1910). With A. N. Whitehead.
The Problems of Philosophy (London, 1912).
Our Knowledge of the External World (London, 1914; New York, 1960, paperback).
Mysticism and Logic (London, 1918; Harmondsworth, 1953, paperback).
"The Philosophy of Logical Atomism," in *The Monist*, 1918–19, nos. 28–29.
Introduction to Mathematical Philosophy (London, 1919).
The Analysis of Mind (London, 1921).
"Logical Atomism," in *Contemporary British Philosophy*, I (London, 1924).
Analysis of Matter (London, 1927; New York, 1954, paperback).
Outline of Philosophy (London and New York, 1927).
An Inquiry into Meaning and Truth (London, 1940).
"A Reply to My Critics," in *The Philosophy of Bertrand*

Russell, edited by P. Schilpp (Evanston, Ill., 1944; New York, 1963, paperback).
Human Knowledge (London, 1948).
Human Society in Ethics and Politics (London, 1954).
Logic and Knowledge, edited by R. C. Marsh (London, 1956). A Collection including "On Denoting," and "The Philosophy of Logical Atomism."
Why I Am Not a Christian and Other Essays (London and New York, 1957; New York, 1961, paperback).
My Philosophical Development (London, 1959).

WORKS ON THE PHILOSOPHY OF BERTRAND RUSSELL

Ayer, A. J., *Russell* (London, 1972, paperback).
Passmore, J., *A Hundred Years of Philosophy* (London, 1957), Ch. 9.
Sainsbury, R. M., *Russell* (London, 1979).
Schilpp, P., *The Philosophy of Bertrand Russell* (Evanston, Ill., 1944). A symposium with many excellent articles on Russell's philosophy, with a reply by Russell.
Watling, J., *Bertrand Russell* (Edinburgh, 1970).

BIOGRAPHY

Russell, B., *Autobiography* (three volumes, London, 1967–69).

27. Logical Positivism (*pages 492–508*)

TEXTS

Ayer, A. J., *Language, Truth and Logic* (London, 1936; second edition, 1946; New York, 1951, paperback).

——, *Foundations of Empirical Knowledge* (London, 1940; 1961, paperback).

Bridgman, P. W., *The Logic of Modern Physics* (New York, 1927).

Carnap, R., *Der Logische Aufbau der Welt* (Berlin, 1928).

——, *Scheinprobleme in der Philosophie* (Berlin, 1928).

——, *The Unity of Science* (London, 1934). A translation by M. Black of "Die physikalische Sprache als Universalprache der Wissenschaft," in *Erkenntnis*, 1932.

——, "Testability and Meaning, I-IV," in *Philosophy of Science, 1936–1937*. Reprinted in Feigl, H., and Brodbeck, M., *Readings in the Philosophy of Science* (New York, 1953).

——, *Logical Syntax of Language* (London and New York, 1937). Translation by A. Smeaton of *Logische Syntax der Sprache* (Vienna, 1934).

——, *Philosophy and Logical Syntax* (London, 1935).

——, *Foundations of Logic and Mathematics* (Chicago, 1939).

Frank, P., "Kausalgesetz und Erfahrung," *Annalen der Naturphilosophie*, 1907, reprinted in English translation in *Modern Science and Its Philosophy*.

——, *Modern Science and Its Philosophy* (Cambridge, Mass., 1949; New York, 1962, paperback).

Hempel, C. G., *Fundamentals of Concept Formation in Empirical Science* (Chicago, 1952).

Popper, K. R., *The Logic of Scientific Discovery* (London, 1958). Translation of *Logik der Forschung* (Vienna, 1935).

Reichenbach, H., *The Philosophy of Space and Time* (New York, 1957, paperback). Translation of *Philosophie der Raum-Zeit-Lehre* (Berlin and Leipzig, 1928).

——, *Experience and Prediction. An Analysis of the Foundations and the Structure of Knowledge* (Chicago, 1938).

——, *The Rise of Scientific Philosophy* (Berkeley and Los Angeles, 1951; 1958, paperback).

Schlick, M., *Space and Time in Contemporary Physics* (Oxford, 1920). Translation of *Raum und Zeit in der gegenwärtigen Physik* (Berlin, 1917).

——, *Gesammelte Aufsätze, 1926–1936* (Vienna, 1938).

——, *Problems of Ethics* (New York, 1939). Translation of *Fragen der Ethik* (Vienna, 1930).

——, *Philosophy of Nature* (New York, 1949). Translation of *Grundzüge der Naturphilosophie*, posthumous papers edited by W. Holitscher and J. Rauscher (Vienna, 1948).

Wittgenstein, L., *Tractatus Logico-Philosophicus* (London, 1922; new translation by Pears and McGuinness, 1961).

——, *Notebooks, 1914–1916* (Oxford, 1961). Contains material leading up to the *Tractatus*.

ANTHOLOGIES, GENERAL SURVEYS

Ayer, A. J., *Logical Positivism* (Glencoe, Ill., 1959). Selected papers with an introduction by Ayer.

Feigl, H., and Sellars, W., editors, *Readings in Philosophical Analysis* (New York, 1949). Selected papers by Carnap, Hempel, Quine, Reichenbach, and others.

Hanfling, O., *Logical Positivism* (Oxford, 1981).

Passmore, J., *A Hundred Years of Philosophy* (London, 1957). Chapter 16 discusses the Logical Positivists.

Urmson, J. O., *Philosophical Analysis* (Oxford, 1956). Part Two, "Logical Positivism and the Downfall of Logical Atomism," is especially relevant.

28. Existentialism *(pages 509–29)*

TEXTS

Kierkegaard, S., *Either/Or: A Fragment of Life*, 1843, two-volume translation by D. F. Swenson, L. M. Swenson, and W. Lowrie (Princeton, 1944; New York, 1959, paperback).

——, *Fear and Trembling*, 1843, trans. by W. Lowrie (Princeton, 1941; New York, 1954, paperback).

——, *Repetition: An Essay in Experimental Psychology*, 1843, trans. by W. Lowrie (Princeton, 1941).

——, *Philosophical Fragments: Or, A Fragment of Philosophy*, 1844, trans. by D. F. Swenson (Princeton, 1936).

——, *Stages on Life's Way*, 1845, trans. by W. Lowrie (Princeton, 1940).

——, *Concluding Unscientific Postscript*, 1846, trans. by D. F. Swenson and W. Lowrie (Princeton, 1941).

——, *The Sickness Unto Death*, 1849, trans. by W. Lowrie (Princeton, 1941; New York, 1954, paperback).

——, *Training in Christianity*, 1850, trans. by W. Lowrie (Princeton, 1944).

——, *The Attack upon "Christendom,"* 1854–55, trans. by W. Lowrie (Princeton, 1944; Boston, 1956, paperback).

——, *The Journals of Søren Kierkegaard: A Selection*, ed. and trans. by A. Dru (Oxford, 1938; New York, 1959, paperback).

——, *A Kierkegaard Anthology*, ed. by R. Bretall (Princeton, 1946).

Jaspers, K., *Philosophie*, three volumes (Berlin, 1932; second edition, 1948).

——, *Vernunft und Existenz* (Groningen, 1935). Translated by W. Earle as *Reason and Existenz* (New York, 1957, paperback).

——, *Der Philosophische Glaube* (Zurich, 1948). English translation by R. Mannheim, *The Perennial Scope of Philosophy* (New York, 1949).

——, *Einführung in die Philosophie* (Zurich, 1950). English translation, *Way to Wisdom, an Introduction to Philosophy* (New Haven, 1960, paperback).

Heidegger, M., *Sein und Zeit I* (Halle, 1972). English translation by J. Macquarrie and E. Robinson, *Being and Time* (New York, 1962).

——, *Einführung in die Metaphysik* (Tübingen, 1953). English translation, *Introduction to Metaphysics* by R. Mannheim (New York, 1959, paperback).

——, *Existence and Being* (Chicago, 1949). Translation by D. Scott, R. Hull, and A. Crick, of *Was Ist Metaphysik? Vom Wesen der Wahrheit, Hölderlin und das Wesen der Dichtung*, and *Andenken an den Dichter: "Heimkunft—An Die Verwandten."*

Sartre, J.-P., "La transcendence de L'Ego," *Recherches philosophiques* VI (1936–37). Translation by F. Williams and R. Kirkpatrick, *The Transcendence of the Ego* (New York, 1958, paperback).

——, *L'Etre et le néant, Essai d'ontologie phénoménologique* (Paris, 1943). English translation, *Being and Nothingness, an Essay on Phenomenological Ontology*, trans. by H. E. Barnes (New York, 1957).

——, *L'Existentialisme est un humanisme* (Paris, 1946). English translation by P. Mairet, *Existentialism and Humanism* (New York, 1948).

——, *Literary and Philosophical Essays*, trans. by A. Michelson (London, 1955; New York, 1962, paperback).

———, *The Wall and Other Stories*, trans. by L. Alexander (New York, 1948).

———, *No Exit* and *The Flies*, trans. by S. Gilbert (New York, 1952).

GENERAL SURVEYS

Ayer, A. J., "Some Aspects of Existentialism," *Rationalist Annual*, 1948.

Barrett, W., *Irrational Man* (New York, 1958; 1962, paperback).

Blackham, H. J., *Six Existential Thinkers: Kierkegaard, Nietzsche, Jaspers, Marcel, Heidegger, Sartre* (London, 1951; New York, 1952, paperback).

Collins, J., *The Existentialists: A Critical Study* (Chicago, 1952, paperback).

Grene, M., *Introduction to Existentialism* (Chicago, 1959, paperback). First published as *Dreadful Freedom*.

Kaufmann, W., editor, *Existentialism from Dostoevsky to Sartre* (New York, 1956, paperback). Selections in English, with an Introduction and Prefaces by the editor.

WORKS ON INDIVIDUAL PHILOSOPHERS

Cranston, M., *Jean-Paul Sartre* (Edinburgh and New York, 1962, paperback).

Danto, A. C., *Sartre* (London, 1975, paperback).

Grene, M., *Heidegger* (New York, 1957).

Hannay, A., *Kierkegaard* (London, 1982).

Murdoch, I., *Sartre, Romantic Rationalist* (Cambridge, 1953; New Haven, 1953, paperback).

Schilpp, P. A., editor, *The Philosophy of Karl Jaspers* (Evanston, Ill., 1958).

Warnock, M., *The Philosophy of Sartre* (London, 1975, paperback).

29. Contemporary British Philosophy *(pages 530–56)*

(See also the bibliographies to the chapters on Moore, Russell, and Logical Positivism.)

TEXTS

Austin, J. L., *Philosophical Papers* (Oxford, 1961), ed. by J. O. Urmson and G. J. Warnock.

———, *Sense and Sensibilia* (Oxford, 1962), reconstructed by G. J. Warnock from manuscript notes.

———, *How to Do Things with Words* (Oxford, 1962).

Hare, R. M., *The Language of Morals* (Oxford, 1952).

Hart, H. L. A., "The Ascription of Responsibility and Rights," *Aristotelian Society Proceedings*, 1948–49. Reprinted in *Logic and Language* (first series, Oxford, 1951), ed. by A. Flew.

———, "Are There Any Natural Rights?" *Philosophical Review*, 1955.

Ryle, G., *The Concept of Mind* (London, 1949; New York, 1960, paperback).

———, " 'If,' 'So' and 'Because'," in *Philosophical Analysis* (Ithaca, 1950), ed. by M. Black.

———, *Dilemmas* (Cambridge, 1954).

Strawson, P. F., *Introduction to Logical Theory* (London, 1952).

———, *Individuals* (London, 1959).

Wisdom, J., *Interpretation and Analysis* (London, 1931).

———, *Problems of Mind and Matter* (Cambridge, 1934).

———, *Other Minds* (Oxford, 1952).

———, *Philosophy and Psycho-Analysis* (Oxford, 1953).

Wittgenstein, L., *Philosophical Investigations* (New York and Oxford, 1953).

———, *Remarks on the Foundations of Mathematics* (Oxford, 1956).

———, *The Blue and Brown Books* (Oxford, 1958).

ANTHOLOGIES, GENERAL SURVEYS

Ackermann, R. J., *Philosophy of Karl Popper* (Amherst, Mass., 1976).

Flew, A., editor, *Logic and Language* (first and second series, Oxford, 1951, 1953).

———, editor, *Essays in Conceptual Analysis* (London, 1956).

Kenny, A., *Wittgenstein* (London, 1973).

O'Hear, A., *Karl Popper* (London, 1980).

Passmore, J., *A Hundred Years of Philosophy* (London, 1957).

Urmson, J. O., *Philosophical Analysis* (Oxford, 1956).

Warnock, G. J., *English Philosophy Since 1900* (Oxford, 1958).

Index

Pages in which the chief discussion of a given philosopher occurs are in **bold face.**